THE INTERNATIONAL BIBLIOGRAPHY OF SOCIOLOGY

This bibliography, with its sister publications, Anthropology, Economics, and Political Science (known together as the *International Bibliography of the Social Sciences (IBSS)*) is an essential tool for librarians, academics and researchers wishing to keep up to date with the published literature in the social sciences.

The *IBSS* offers a large scale database of journal articles and monographs from all over the world and in over 30 languages, all with English title translations where needed.

From 1991, users already familiar with the bibliography will notice major improvements in contents and currency. There is greater coverage of monographs as well as journals, with continued emphasis on international publications, especially those from the developing world and Eastern Europe. Indexing techniques have been refined: the *IBSS* now offers more specific subject and place indexes together with a name index. A subject index in French continues to be provided.

Prepared until 1989 at the *Fondation nationale des sciences politiques* in Paris, the *IBSS* is now compiled and edited by the *British Library of Political and Economic Science* at the *London School of Economics*. The UNESCO *International Committee for Social Science Information and Documentation* continues to support the publication. The new *International Bibliography* not only maintains its traditional extensive coverage of periodical literature, but considerably extends its coverage of monographic material by incorporating most of that which would previously have been included in the *London Bibliography of the Social Sciences*, publication of which has now been discontinued.

Also available from Routledge

Copies of the *International Bibliography of the Social Sciences* for previous years.

Thematic Lists of Descriptors. Four subject volumes published in 1989, following the classification and index terms of the relevant volume of the *IBSS*.

The *International Current Awareness Services (ICAS)* complement the *IBSS* with the same geographical sweep, but offering full contents information on current journals. These four new monthly sevices — Anthropology, Economics, Political Science and Sociology — provide coverage, with indexing by keyword, of items received during the previous month, including not only articles but also items such as book reviews, short articles, interviews, speeches, reports, editorials and letters.

Copies of the *London Bibliography of the Social Sciences* for previous years are available from Schmidt Periodicals, Dettendorf, D-8201 Bad Feilnbach 2, Germany.

INTERNATIONAL BIBLIOGRAPHY OF THE SOCIAL SCIENCES
BIBLIOGRAPHIE INTERNATIONALE DES SCIENCES SOCIALES

[published annually in four parts / paraissant chaque année en quatre parties: since 1961/ jusqu'en 1961: UNESCO, Paris]

International bibliography of sociology / Bibliographie internationale de sociologie [red cover / couverture rouge] Vol.1:1951 (publ. 1952)

International bibliography of political science/ Bibliographie internationale de science politique [grey cover / couverture grise] Vol.1: 1952 (publ. 1954)

International bibliography of economics / Bibliographie internationale de science economique [yellow cover / couverture jaune] Vol.1: 1952 (publ. 1955)

International bibliography of social and cultural anthropology / Bibliographie internationale d'anthropologie sociale et culturelle [green cover/ couverture vert] Vol.1: 1955 (publ. 1958)

Prepared by

THE BRITISH LIBRARY OF POLITICAL AND ECONOMIC SCIENCE

with the support of the International Committee for Social Science Information and Documentation
with the assistance of UNESCO

Editor

Lynne J. Brindley
Librarian, British Library of Political and Economic Science

Editorial Manager

Christopher C.P. Doutney

Assistant Manager

Caroline S. Shaw

Consultant/Technical Manager

N.S.M. Cox

Editorial Assistants

Imogen Daulby
Louise Hilditch
Miranda Hutt
Ricarda O'Driscoll

INTERNATIONAL BIBLIOGRAPHY OF THE SOCIAL SCIENCES

1991

INTERNATIONAL BIBLIOGRAPHY OF SOCIOLOGY

VOLUME XLI

BIBLIOGRAPHIE INTERNATIONALE DES SCIENCES SOCIALES

BIBLIOGRAPHIE INTERNATIONALE DE SOCIOLOGIE

Prepared with the support of the International Committee for Social Science Information and Documentation with the financial assistance of UNESCO

Établie avec le concours du Comité international pour l'information et la documentation en sciences sociales avec l'assistance financière de l'UNESCO

London and New York

First published in 1993 by
Routledge
(on behalf of The British Library of Political and Economic Science)
UNESCO subvention 1992-1993, SHS/IST/53

11 New Fetter Lane
London EC4P 4EE
&
29 West 35th Street
New York, NY 10001

© 1993, British Library of Political and Economic Science

Processed and composed in Great Britain by
Information Design & Delivery Limited, Newent, Gloucestershire

Typeset in Great Britain by
W.E. Baxter Limited, Lewes, East Sussex

Printed in Great Britain by
T.J. Press (Padstow), Padstow, Cornwall

All rights reserved. No part of this book may be reprinted or reproduced or utilized in any form or by any electronic, mechanical, or other means, now known or hereafter invented, including photocoping and recording, or in any information storage or retrieval system, without permission in writing from the publishers.

British Library Cataloguing in Publication Data

A CIP catalogue record for this book is available from the British Library.
ISBN 0–415–07463–0
ISSN 0085–2066

Editorial Correspondence should be sent to:

International Bibliography of the Social Sciences
British Library of Political and Economic Science
London School of Economics
10 Portugal Street
London WC2A 2HD
United Kingdom

Telephone: (U.K.) 071-955-7144

Fax: (U.K.) 071-242-5904

CONTENTS

International Committee for Social Science Information and Documentation	vii
Preface	viii
Selection criteria	xix
Correspondents	xx
List of periodicals consulted	xxi
List of abbreviations	lxviii
Classification scheme	lxxxvii
Bibliography for 1991	1
Author index	316
Placename index	421
Subject index	429
Index des matières	476

Immediate access to the world's journals

International Current Awareness Services

●Anthropology ●Economics ●Political Science ●Sociology

A major new bibliographic service providing rapid international coverage of the world's significant social science literature

Users of *IBSS* will be aware that the merger in 1990 of the *IBSS* and the *London Bibliography of the Social Sciences* databases, under the auspices of the British Library of Political and Economic Science at the London School of Economics, has brought a substantial improvement in the breadth of coverage of literature.

This merger has not only enriched *IBSS* contents but allowed the development of a new *International Current Awareness Service (ICAS)* in each of the four subjects covered by *IBSS*.

ICAS is published monthly as an immediate, comprehensive and easy-to-use tool for accessing the latest in the world's constantly expanding social science literature.

Special features of *ICAS* include:

- monthly publication for each subject, permitting users to scan the contents of journals often *before* they reach the library shelf

- unparalleled coverage of the world's journal literature through a service that scans at least 120,000 articles per year

- access to literature in 30 languages with each accompanied by English language title translation and identification of any summaries in English

- reports of book reviews, making rapidly available invaluable information on monographs

- indexing of important papers in monographic works of edited collections, a unique feature in a bibliographic service

- full contents listings of journal parts, enabling the user to scan contents of all current journals in a single source

- coverage of significant interviews, speeches, reports, editorials and letters

- in-depth subject keyword attribution, giving the user ease and precision of usage unprecedented in any other current awareness service

Printed in standardized formats with clear typeset listings of contents pages, *ICAS* is produced in a high quality, easy-to-read layout. Average extent 120pp per issue.

ICAS ISSNs   Anthropology 0960 1511   Economics 0960 152X
                    Political Science 0960 1538   Sociology 0960 1546

For further details, sample copies and annual subscription rates please contact:
Promotions Department, Routledge, 11 New Fetter Lane, London EC4P 4EE, Telephone: 071 583 9855

INTERNATIONAL COMMITTEE FOR SOCIAL SCIENCE INFORMATION AND DOCUMENTATION
LE COMITÉ INTERNATIONAL POUR L'INFORMATION ET LA DOCUMENTATION EN SCIENCES SOCIALES

Kyllikki Ruokonen, Helsinki School of Economics Library (Chair)
Jean Meyriat, Fondation nationale des sciences politiques, Paris (Secretary General)

MEMBERS

Dominique Babini, Consejo Latinoamericano de Ciencias Sociales, Buenos Aires
Jonathan Benthall, International Union of Anthropological and Ethnological Sciences
Raimondo Cagiano de Azevedo, Università di Roma
Christopher Hunt, John Rylands University Library of Manchester, University of Manchester
Serge Hurtig, Fondation nationale des sciences politiques, Paris
Yoshiro Matsuda, Hitotsubashi University, Tokyo
Lars-Goran Nilsson, University of Umea
Boris Polunin, USSR Academy of Sciences, Moscow
Mark Perlman, University of Pittsburgh
William A. Steiner, Squire Law Library, Cambridge
Ekkehart Seusing, International Federation of Library Associations
K.G. Tyagi, Asia-Pacific Information Network in Social Sciences

ASSOCIATES

Margarita Almada de Ascencio, Universidad Nacional Autónoma de México
Wilhelm Bartenbach, Foundation Center, New York
Mastini Hardjoprakoso, National Library of Indonesia
Paul Kaegbein, Lehrstuhl für Bibliothekswissenschaft der Universität zu Köln
J.M. Ng'ang'a, Kenyatta University, Nairobi
N.J. Sebastian, National Council of Applied Economic Research, New Delhi
Kirsti Thesen Saelen, University of Bergen
Libuše Švábová, Czechoslovakian Academy of Sciences, Prague
Wambui Wagacha, C.O.D.E.S.R.I.A.

PREFACE

Under the sponsorship of the International Committee for Social Science Information and Documentation, established by UNESCO in 1950, the four divisions of the *International Bibliography of the Social Sciences* (Anthropology: Economics: Political Science: Sociology) have been published from Paris since 1952. Together they form the most extensive bibliography of the social sciences in existence, with a world wide coverage achieved by no other bibliographical series. In 1990 the British Library of Political and Economic Science assumed responsibility for the compilation and editing of the *International Bibliography*.

The British Library of Political and Economic Science has published the *London Bibliography of the Social Sciences* since 1931. In 47 volumes it forms an unrivalled record of twentieth century monograph literature in social sciences. The volume covering 1989 was issued early in 1990 and it will be the last of the series. The bulk of the data which would previously have been published as the *London Bibliography* will, from 1990 onwards, appear within the structure of the *International Bibliography of the Social Sciences*.

The *International Bibliography of Sociology* has been compiled from two sources: analysis of the published literature (particularly as contained in periodicals) accessible to the editors; and contributions from correspondents throughout the world, reporting publications, details of which are not easily obtainable outside their countries of origin. These dual sources of data will continue to be the basis of the *Bibliography*. The *international* emphasis will be maintained, without bias towards the publications of any one country. Some 120,000 journal articles per year are scanned for indexing in the four divisions, and a selection is made from over 20,000 monograph titles. Material in over 25 languages is included, but all titles, in addition to being cited in their original form, also appear in English. The work is produced from a computer maintained data base. The long established subject classifications continue to be the basis for indexing, governing an alphabetical arrangement by keywords.

The annual volumes of the *International Bibliography* are complemented by the *International Current Awareness Services in the Social Sciences*, issued in the same four subject divisions as the annual volumes, but on a monthly basis. The *Current Awareness Services* include full contents listings (indexed by keyword) of all relevant periodicals received at the editorial office in London during the previous month. They index not only principal articles but also more ephemeral material such as short articles and book reviews, omitted in the annual volumes. Together, the two publication series provide immediate access to new publications and form a permanent record of printed material in the social sciences.

PRÉFACE

Paris est depuis 1952 siège de la publication des quatre sections de la *Bibliographie Internationale des Sciences Sociales* (Anthropologie: Sciences Economiques: Sciences Politiques: Sociologie.) sous le patronage du Comité International pour l'Information et la Documentation des Sciences Sociales créé par l'UNESCO en 1950. Dans l'ensemble, elles constituent la bibliographie la plus étendue des sciences sociales et jouit d'une portée mondiale unique dans le domaine. En 1990, la British Library of Political and Economic Science prit responsibilité de la composition et rédaction de la *Bibliographie Internationale*.

La British Library of Political and Economic Science a publié la *London Bibliography of the Social Sciences*, depuis 1931. Ses 47 volumes présentent des archives incomparables de la littérature monographique du vingtième siècle en ce qui concerne les sciences sociales. Le volume de 1989, paru en 1990, était le dernier de la série. La plupart des données figurant auparavant dans la *London Bibliography* se trouvent maintenant dans la *Bibliographie Internationale des Sciences Sociales*.

La *Bibliographie Internationale de Sociologie* recueille les informations à partir de deux sources: l'analyse par les rédacteurs de la littérature publiée (surtout des périodiques) et les contributions de correspondants dans le monde entier fournissant des comptes-rendus de publications dont on n'aurait guère connaissance hors de leurs pays d'origine. Cette dualité des sources continue à servir de base à la *Bibliographie*. Il est important de souligner la qualité véritablement internationale de cette *Bibliographie*. Chaque année une moyenne de 220,000 articles de périodiques sont analysés et indexés pour les quatre parties et les monographies sont sélectionnées parmi plus de 20,000 titres. La *Bibliographie* comprend des contributions en 25 langues: tous les titres paraissent en anglais ainsi que dans leur langue d'origine. La *Bibliographie* est produite à partir d'une base de données. Une classification établie de longue date sert de base à l'indexation et à la présentation des réferences par mots-clés.

Les volumes annuels de la *Bibliograhie Internationale* sont complétés par les *International Current Awareness Services in the Social Sciences*, publications mensuelles consacrées aux quatre mêmes disciplines des volumes annuels. Les *Current Awareness Services* comprennent les listes complètes des sujets (indexés par mots-clés) de tous les périodiques pertinents reçus à la rédaction au cours du mois précédent. Y sont indexés non seulement les articles standard, mais aussi les études plus éphémères comme de brefs articles et des comptes-rendus de livres dont les volumes annuels ne font pas mention. Ensemble, ces deux séries de publications offrent un accès immédiat aux nouvelles publications et constituent les archives permanentes des travaux publiés en sciences sociales.

PREFACIO

Las cuatro divisiones de la *Bibliografía Internacional de las Ciencias Sociales* (Antropología: Ciencias Económicas: Ciencias Políticas y Sociología) se han venido publicando en París desde el año 1952, por gentileza patrocinal del Comité Internacional de Información y Documentación de las Ciencias Sociales, establecido por UNESCO en el año 1950. En su conjunto, constituyen la bibliografía más extensa en materia de Ciencias Sociales, con alcance mundial, e inigualable en otras series bibliográficas. En 1990 la British Library of Political and Economic Science asumía la responsabilidad para la compilación y redacción de la *Bibliografía Internacional*.

La British Library of Political and Economic Science ya publicaba la *London Bibliography of the Social Sciences* a partir del año 1931. En sus 47 tomos, constituye un registro de literatura monográfica sin rival sobre temas sociocientíficos del siglo XX. El tomo que abarca el año 1989 se publicó a principios del 1990, siendo éste el último de aquella serie. La mayoría de los datos se habrían publicado en épocas anteriores bajo el título *London Bibliography*. A partir del año 1990, aparecerán dentro de la estructura de las *Bibliografía Internacional de las Ciencias Sociales*.

La *Bibliografía Internacional de Sociología* ha sido compilada con base en dos fuentes: el análisis de la literatura publicada (en particular, tal como contenidos en los periódicos) accesible a redactores, y las contribuciones de corresponsales de todas partes del mundo, publicaciones de tipo informe, detalles de los cuales no resultan ser fácilmente obtenibles fuera de sus países de orígen. Dichas fuentes duales de información seguirán siendo la base de la Bibliografía. Se mantendrá el énfasis internacional, sin tendencias hacia las publicaciones de un sólo país dado. Se exploran al año unos 120,000 artículos para pasar a índices en las cuatro divisiones, y se efectúa una selección de más de 20,000 títulos monográficos. Se incluyen temas en más de 25 idiomas, pero todos los antedichos títulos, además de ser citados en su forma original, también aparecen traducidos al idioma inglés. Se lleva a cabo el trabajo a partir de una base de datos mantenida en ordenadores. Siguen siendo la base de la tarea de la puesta en índices, las clasificaciones por materias como se establecieron antiguamente, las cuales controlan una esquematización alfabética por palabra clave.

Los tomos anuales de la *Bibliografía Internacional* se ven complementados mediante los *International Current Awareness Services in the Social Sciences*, con acuerdo a cada una de las mismas cuatro divisiones que se emplearon para los tomos anuales, pero sobre una base mensual. The *International Current Awareness Services in the Social Sciences* comprenden relaciones completas de materias, con puesta en índice por palabra clave, en relación con citas de todos los periódicos aplicaderos recibidos en la Casa Editorial de Londres durante el mes anterior. Abarcan índices no sólo de los artículos principales, sino también más materia efémera tal como sueltos cortos y críticas literarias que fueron omitidos de los tomos anuales. En conjunto, ambas series de publicaciones facilitan un acceso inmediato a las nuevas publicaciones, y constituyen un registro permanente de materias impresas comprendidas dentro del marco de las Ciencias Sociales.

ПРЕДИСЛОВИЕ

Под покровительством Международного Комитета Социологической Информации и Документации, основанной УНЕСКО в 1950 г., четыре части Международной Библиографии Общественных Наук/Антропология: Экономика: Политические Науки: Социология/издавались из Парижа с 1952 года. Вместе они составляют найболее обширную существующую библиографию общественных наук, с распространенным по всему свету обхватом не достигнутым никакой другой серийной библиографией. В 1990 Британская Библиотека Политических и Экономических Наук взяла на себя ответственность за составление и репактирование Международной Библиографии.

Британская Библиотека Политических и Экономических Наук издаёт Лондонскую Библиографию Общественных Наук с 1931-го года. В 47 томах это составляет непревзойдённую запись монографической литературы социологии двадцатого века. Том обхватывающий 1989-ый год был издан в начале 1990-ого года и это будет последнее издание этой серии. Большая часть данных, которая раньше должна издаваться как Лондонская Библиография с 1990-ого года будет появляться в структуре Международной Библиографии Общественных Наук.

Международная Библиография Социология была составлена из двух источников, анализ изданной литературы/ особенно тот в периодических изданиях/ доступный для редакторов; и вклад корреспондентов со всего мира, репортажные публикации, деталь которых трудно получить, кроме в странах их происхождения. Эти двойственного характера источники данных будут являться основой Библиографии. Будет продолжаться международное значение библиографии без оказывания предпочтения изданиям каких-либо стран.

Ежегодно просматривается некоторые 120000 журнальных статей с целью составления указателей в четырёх частях, и тогда составляется сборник из больше чем 20000 монографических титулов. Включаются материалы на больше чем 25-и языках, но все титулы, вдобавок цитируются и в оригинальной версии и по английски. Произведение издётся с помощью компьютерной базы данных. Долгосуществующая система классификации по предметам продолжается и употребляется в качестве основы для составления указателей, которые ведут алфавитный порядок ключевых слов.

Годовые тома Международной Библиографии дополняются Международными Текущими Осведомительными Услугами в Общественных Наук, изданными в тех же самых четырёх частях по предметам что и годовые тома, но их издаются ежемесячно. Текущие Осведомительные Услуги включают указатели полных содержаний/ индексираны по ключевым словам/ всех уместных периодических журналов полученных в редакции в Лондоне в течение прошлого месяца. Они указывают не только главные статьи но тоже более эфемерные/ скоропроходящие/ материалы такие как короткие статьи и рецензии книг, пропущены в годовых томах. Вместе, эти две серии изданий предоставляют прямой доступ к новым изданиям и являются постоянной записью напечатанных материалов общественных наук.

ببليوغرافية علم الاجتماع الدولية

المقدمة

قد نشرت الاجزاء الاربعة من الببليوغرافية الدولية للعلوم الاجتماعية (وهي اولاً دراسة المجتمعات البشرية وثانياً علم الاقتصاد وثالثاً علم السياسة ورابعاً علم الاجتماع) من باريس منذ سنة ١٩٥٢ تحت رعاية اللجنة الدولية لمعلومات وللتدوين المستند لعلم الاجتماع والتي اسستها اليونسكو عام ١٩٥٠ وتشكل معاً هذه الاجزاء ببليوغرافية لها اوسع نطاق في الوجود ويشمل مداها انحاء العالم بكامله الى حد لم يبلغه اية سلسلة ببليوغرافية اخرى. في عام ١٩٩٠ تولت المكتبة البريطانية لعلم السياسة والاقتصاد المسؤولية لصنف الببليوغرافية الدولية واعدادها للنشر.

لقد نشرت المكتبة البريطانية لعلم السياسة والاقتصاد، نشرت الببليوغرافية اللندنية للعلوم الاجتماعية منذ سنة ١٩٣١ وهي تتألف من ٤٧ جزء وتكوّن سجلاً للمؤلفات التي تبحث العلوم الاجتماعية في القرن العشرين لا يضاهيه ايّ آخر وقد نشر المجلد الذي يشمل سنة ١٩٨٩ في اوائل ١٩٩٠ ويكوّن الجزء الاخير في السلسلة. ستنشر بعد سنة ١٩٩٠ في مضمون اطار الببليوغرافية الدولية للعلوم الاجتماعية، ستنشر معظم تلك المعلومات التي كانت قد تنشر سابقاً تحت اسم الببليوغرافية اللندنية.

تم جمع وتدوين معلومات ببليوغرافية علم الاجتماع الدولية من مصدرين - الاول من تحليل المؤلفات وعلى وجه خاص ما احتوته المجلات الدورية التي هي في مدى تناول المحررين وثم ما قدّمه المراسلون في جميع انحاء العالم مع مطبوعات تقريرية يصعب الحصول على تفاصيلها خارج البلاد مصدر تلك الطبوعات. هذا وان مصدري المعلومات هذين سيبقيا اساس الببليوغرافية كما انه يتم الاستمرار في تولية الناحية الدولية اهمية خاصة، لكن دون اي ميول او انحياز نحو مطبوعات اي بلد. يتم تصفّح حوالي ١٢٠٠٠٠ من مقالات المجلات سنوياً للادراج في قوائم الاجزاء الاربعة، كما يتم الانتقاء من بين ما يزيد عن ٢٠٠٠٠ عنوان لمؤلفات تبحث العلوم، كل موضوع منفرداً. ثم ان ضمن المحتويات هناك مواد في ما يزيد عن ٢٥ لغة

، هذا كما ان العناوين مدرجة في لغتها الاصلية بالاضافة الى تدوينها بالانجليزية ، وهذا الشغل ينتج من خلال مستودع للمعلومات والحقائق العلمية يزقّه دماغ الكتروني . هذا وستبقى تبويبات الموضوعات الجارية من مدة طويلة ، تبقى هذه التبويبات الاساس للادراج في القائمة ، تضبط وترتَب هجائياً عن طريق كلمات مفتاح معيّنة .

المجلدات السنوية من الببليوغرافية الدولية ستستكملها مطبوعات خدمات الالمام الجاري الدولية للعلوم الاجتماعية وتصدر هذه المطبوعات في اجزاء الموضوعات الاربعة ذاتها ، لكنها تصدر على ترتيب شهري وتشمل مطبوعات خدمات الالمام الجاري قوائم محتويات كاملة (مدرجة عن طريق كلمات مفتاح معيّنة) لجميع المجلات الدورية التي وصلت مكتب التحرير في لندن خلال الشهر السالف ، حيث يدرجون ليس الموضوعات الرئيسية فقط ، بل كذلك مواد سريعة الزوال - كالمقالات القصيرة وعرض ونقد الكتب مثلاً وهذه مواد ليست من ضمن المجلدات السنوية . وهكذا توفر سلسلتا المؤلفات هاتان اتصالاً فورياً بالمؤلفات الجديدة وتشكلا سجلاً دائماً للمواد المطبوعة في ميادين العلوم الاجتماعية .

序文

　１９５０年にユネスコにより設立された社会科学情報・文書取扱国際委員会後援の下に<u>社会科学国際書誌</u>の４部（人類学：経済学：政治学：社会学）は、１９５２年からパリで発行されてきております。此の４部各書誌は、現存の最も広範囲に亙る社会科学の書誌を形成し、他の書誌シリーズによっては成就されなかった世界的取材を網羅するものであります。１９９０年に、英国政治・経済学図書館は<u>国際書誌</u>の整理編集の責任を負う事になりました。

　　英国政治・経済学図書館は１９３１年より、<u>社会科学ロンドン書誌</u>を発行して来ております。その４７巻は２０世紀に於ける比類のない社会科学の各専攻文献の記録を形成するものです。１９８９年を網羅する版は１９９０年初期に発行されましたが、これは此のシリーズの最後のものとなります。<u>ロンドン書誌</u>として前に発行されれる筈だった膨大な資料は、１９９０年以降、<u>国際社会科学書誌</u>の構築の中に包含されることになります。

　　<u>国際社会書誌</u>は、２つの出典から編纂されたものです。即ち、編集者が利用できる文献（特に期間誌に含まれているもの）の解析と全世界の報道員の寄稿、それは、該当各国以外では入手困難な刊行物の詳細な資料とから編纂されてきているものです。これらの資料の複式出典は継続して書誌の基礎になるものです。「国際性」の意味は、どの国の刊行物に対しても偏見無しに維持されている事を強調しています。毎年凡そ１２万のジャーナル記事が図書目録のために鑑査走査され、４部門に分けられ、その上、２万以上の専攻書名から選択が行われます。２５以上の各国語からの資料が包含されておりますが、すべての書名は該当国語によるものが列挙されており、それに加えて、英語でも表記されています。此の仕事はコンピュータによる維持されたデータ・ベースから作成されます。図書目録の基礎として長期に亙り定着している首題の分類法は、今迄と同様に行われ、ａｂｃ順の見出語によるように統制されています。

国際書誌年刊の各巻は、社会科学学に於ける国際現代意識サービスによって補足され、これは、各巻の年刊と同じ4部門の首題で発行されていますが、月刊を基礎にしております。現代意識サービスは、ロンドン編集事務所で受け取った前月間のすべての該当期間誌の全内容目録（見出語による目録）を含みます。これらの目録は主要記事ばかりでなく、年刊には省略される短い記事や書評などのような、その時だけの記事も含まれています。2つの刊行シリーズは共に、新刊行物への即時利用を提供し、社会科学の印刷資料の永久記録となります。

VORWORT

Die vier Teilbände der *Internationalen Bibliographie der Sozialwissenschaften* (Anthropologie: Politologie: Soziologie: Volkswirtschaft) wurden seit 1952 mit finanzieller Unterstützung des 1950 von der UNESCO eingesetzten Internationalen Komitees für Sozialwissenschaftliche Information und Dokumentation in Paris herausgegeben. Zusammen bilden sie die umfangreichste bestehende sozialwissenschaftliche Bibliographie mit einer weltweiten Reichweite in der Datenerfassung, wie sie keine andere bibliographische Reihe bietet. Im Jahr 1990 übernahm die British Library of Political and Economic Science die Verantwortung für die Erstellung und Redaktion der *Internationalen Bibliographie*.

Die British Library of Political and Economic Science veröffentlicht seit 1931 die *London Bibliography of the Social Sciences*. In 47 Bänden bildet sie ein unübertroffenes Verzeichnis der in Einzeldarstellungen erschienenen sozialwissenschaftlichen Literatur des 20. Jahrhunderts. Mit dem Band für 1989, der Anfang 1990 erschien, wurde diese Reihe eingestellt. Der Großteil der Daten, die vormals in der *London Bibliography* erschienen wären, wird von 1990 an im Rahmen der *Internationalen Bibliographie der Sozialwissenschaften* veröffentlicht werden.

Für die *Internationale Bibliographie der Soziologie* wurden zwei Arten von Quellen herangezogen: zum einen die (insbesondere in Fachzeitschriften) veröffentlichte Literatur, die der Redaktion im Original zugänglich war; zum andern Beiträge von Korrespondenten, die weltweit Publikationen erfassen, über die außerhalb ihrer Ursprungsländer nur schwer Einzelheiten in Erfahrung zu bringen sind. Diese beiden Datenquellen werden auch weiterhin die Grundlage für die *Bibliographie* bilden. Die *internationale* Ausrichtung wird erhalten bleiben, ohne Bevorzugung der Publikationen eines bestimmten Landes. Jährlich werden ca. 120.000 Zeitschriftenartikel auf eine Aufnahme in die vier Teilbände hin durchgesehen und eine Auswahl aus über 20.000 Monographien getroffen. Die *Internationale Bibliographie* enthält Material in mehr als 25 Sprachen; sämtliche Titel erscheinen außer in ihrer Originalsprache auch in englischer Übersetzung. Die vier Teilbände werden mit Hilfe einer computergestützten Datenbank erstellt. Die seit langem gebräuchliche Gliederung der Sachregister wurde beibehalten und liegt der alphabetischen Anordnung nach Schlagworten zugrunde.

Die jährlichen Bände der *Internationalen Bibliographie* werden ergänzt durch die *International Current Awareness Services in the Social Sciences*, die wie die Jahresbände in vier Teilen, jedoch monatlich erscheinen. Die *Current Awareness Services* enthalten vollständige Inhaltsverzeichnisse aller im vorausgegangenen Monat bei der Londoner Redaktion eingegangenen Zeitschriften, ergänzt um ein Schlagwortregister. Sie verzeichnen nicht nur Hauptartikel, sondern auch vergänglicheres Material wie Kurzbeiträge und Buchbesprechungen, die in den Jahresbänden unberücksichtigt bleiben. Beide Veröffentlichungen zusammen bieten direkten Zugriff auf neue Publikationen und ergeben ein dauerhaftes Verzeichnis von Druckschriften in den Sozialwissenschaften.

序文

　　<u>国际社会科学书志</u> (International Bibliography of the Social Sciences) 的四部分 (人类学:经济学:政治学:社会学) 由联合国教育科学及文化组织 (UNESCO) 1950 年成立的社会科学情报与文书国际委员会 (International Committee for Social Science Information and Documentation) 发起, 自从 1952 年由巴黎而初版。该四部分形成目前世界上最广泛的社会科学书志, 具有其他书志系列未达到的世界性范围。于1990 年英国政治、经济学图书馆负起国际书志汇编和编排的责任。

　　自 1931 年以来, 英国政治、经济学图书馆发行了<u>社会科学的伦敦书志</u> (London Bibliography of the Social Sciences)。他的四十七卷形成关于社会科学二十世纪专题文献的无比记录。涉及 1989 年的卷于 1990 年初发行了, 是上述系列的最后一卷。由 1990 年开始, 以前所发行为<u>伦敦书志</u> (London Bibliography) 的大部分资料将于<u>国际社会科学书志</u>的结构之内出版。

　　国际社会学书志由两种来源而编辑, 即受编者容易会见已出版文献(特别是杂志)的解析以及来自全世界通讯员系统的贡献。他们报道在产地外不容易得到出版的详细资料。书志将继续以该资料的两种来源为基础。<u>书志</u>也将维持国际性的观点, 不重视任何一个国家的出版物。为于上述四部分内的排列, 每年发表于杂志内的约十二万论文被审视, 由二万以上专题的书名做出选择。虽然资料原文的语言数二十五以上, 但所有书名, 除引用原文以外, 又附有英文翻译。<u>书志</u>是采用计算机化数据库产生的。长期确定的题目分类法继续作为资料排列的基础。关键词按照字母顺序而排列。

年度出版的国际书志为关于社会科学国际目前认识的服务 (International Current Awareness Services in the Social Sciences) 所补充，后者采用国际书志同样四个题目分类但是每月一次发行。不但主要的论文而且缩写论和书评等，以及年度出版各卷所略去的较为朝生暮死的资料均编入索引。该两个出版系列共同提供与新出版的资料的直接接口，成为关于社会科学出版资料的永久记录。

SELECTION CRITERIA

1. Subject

Documents relevent to sociology.

2. Nature and form

Publications of known authorship and lasting significance to sociology, whether in serial or monographic form, typically works with a theoretical component intending to communicate new knowledge, new ideas or making use of new materials.

Previously published materials in all formats are omitted, including most translations. Also excluded are textbooks, materials from newspapers or news magazines, popular or purely informative papers, presentations of predominantly primary data and legislative or judicial texts and items of parochial relevance only.

CORRESPONDENTS FOR SOCIOLOGY

This bibliography has been compiled by combining the work of the editorial office in London, which has established a large core of source publications, and the contributions of our foreign correspondents who provide first-hand knowledge of their countries' publications. We would like to to take this opportunity to thank our correspondents for their long-standing assistance and for adapting so helpfully to our new methods of working.

ARGENTINA — Fundación José María Aragón, Buenos Aires - Corina de Seoane

FRANCE — Bibliothèque de la Fondation nationale des sciences politiques, Paris - Professor Jean Meyriat

GERMANY — Akademie der Wissenschaften der DDR, Zentralinstitüt für Geschichte, Berlin - Dr. W. Wächter

INDIA — National Social Science Documentation Centre, Indian Council of Social Science Research, New Delhi - Dr. K.G. Tyagi and Dr. Savitri Devi

JAPAN — Japanese Sociological Association, Tokyo - Dr. Mamoru Yamada

POLAND — Polska Akademia Nauk, Ośrodek Informacji Naukowej, Warsaw - Dr. Janusz Sach

USSR — USSR Academy of Sciences
— Institute for Scientific Information in the Social Sciences, Moscow - Boris Polunin
— N.N. Miklukho-Maklay Institute of Ethnography, Leningrad - Alla V. Paneyakh and Tat'yana N. Sintsova

It should be noted that this list is not exhaustive, but consists only of those who contribute material in a systematic fashion on a regular basis.

LIST OF PERIODICALS CONSULTED
LISTE DES PERIODIQUES CONSULTÉS

Acadiensis.:*Journal of the history of the Atlantic Region* [*Acadiensis*] *ISSN: 0004-5851. University of New Brunswick, Department of History*: Fredericton, N.B. E3B 5A3, Canada

Acta asiatica. [*Acta Asia.*] *ISSN: 0567-7254. Institute of Eastern Culture*: 4- 1 Nishi-kanda 2 Chōme, Chiyoda, Tokyo, Japan

Acta politica. [*Acta Pol.*] *ISSN: 0001-6810. Boom*: Postbus 1058, 7940 KB Meppel, The Netherlands

Acta sociologica. [*Acta Sociol.*] *ISSN: 0001- 6993. Scandinavian Sociological Association*; **Publisher**: *Universitetsforlaget*: Journals Department, P.O.Box 2959 Tøyen, 0608-Oslo 6, Norway

Acta Universitatis Łódziensis.:*Folia sociologica* [*Acta Univ. Łódz. Folia Soc.*] *ISSN: 0208-600X. Wydawnictwo Uniwersytetu Łódzkiego*: ul. Jaracza 34, Łódz, Poland

Actualité économique. [*Act. Econ.*] *ISSN: 0001-771X. Ecole des Hautes Études Commerciales/ Société canadienne de science économique/ Association des économistes québécois*: 5255 avenue Decelles, Montréal, Québec, Canada H3T 1V6

Administration. [*Administration*] *ISSN: 0001-8325. Institute of Public Administration of Ireland*: 57-61 Lansdowne Road, Dublin 4, Ireland

Administration and society. [*Admin. Soc.*] *ISSN: 0095-3997. Sage Publications*: 2455 Teller Road, Newbury Park, CA. 91320, U.S.A.

Administration for development. [*Admin. Devel.*] *ISSN: 0311-4511. Administrative College of Papua New Guinea*: P.O. Box 1216, Boroko, Papua New Guinea

Administrative science quarterly. [*Adm. Sci. Qua.*] *ISSN: 0001-8392. Cornell University, Johnson Graduate School of Management*: Caldwell Hall, Cornell University, Ithaca, N.Y. 14853, U.S.A.

Adoption and fostering. [*Adopt. Fost.*] *ISSN: 0308-5759. British Agencies for Adoption and Fostering*: 11 Southwark Street, London SE1 1RQ, U.K.

Advances in public interest accounting. [*Ad. Pub. Inter. Acc.*]; *JAI Press*: 55 Old Post Road, No 2., Greenwich, CN. 06836, U.S.A.

Affari sociali internazionali. [*Aff. Soc. Int.*]; *Franco Angeli Editore*: viale Monza 106, 20127 Milan, Italy

Africa. [*Africa*] *ISSN: 0001-9720. International African Institute*: Connaught House, Aldwych, London, WC2A 2AE, U.K.; **Publisher**: *Manchester University Press*: Oxford Road, Manchester M13 9PL, U.K.

Africa insight. [*Afr. Insight*] *ISSN: 0256-2804. Africa Institute of South Africa*: P.O. Box 630, Pretoria 0001, South Africa

Africa today. [*Afr. Tod.*] *ISSN: 0001-9887. Africa Today Associates*: c/o Graduate School of International Studies, University of Denver, Denver, CO. 80208, U.S.A.

African affairs. [*Afr. Affairs*] *ISSN: 0001-9909. Royal African Society*: 18 Northumberland Avenue, London WC2N 5BJ, U.K.; **Publisher**: *Oxford University Press*: Pinkhill House, Southfield Road, Eynsham, Oxford OX8 1JJ, U.K.

African arts. [*Afr. Arts*] *ISSN: 0001-9933. University of California, James S. Coleman African Studies Center*: Los Angeles, CA.90024-1310, U.S.A.

African communist. [*Afr. Comm.*] *ISSN: 0001-9976. Inkululeko Publications*: P.O. Box 902, London N19 2YY, U.K.; **Subscriptions**: *idem*: P.O. Box 1027, Johannesburg 2000, South Africa

African notes. [*Afr. Not.*] *ISSN: 0002-0087. University of Ibadan, Institute of African Studies*: Ibadan, Nigeria

African review. [*Afr. R.*] *ISSN: 0856-0056. University of Dar es Salaam, Department of Political Science and Public Administration*: P.O. Box 35042, Dar es Salaam, Tanzania

African studies. [*Afr. Stud.*] *ISSN: 0002-0184. Witwatersrand University Press*: P.O. Wits, 2050 South Africa

African studies review. [*Afr. Stud. R.*] *ISSN: 0002-0206. African Studies Association*: Credit Union Building, Emory University, Atlanta, GA. 30322, U.S.A.

African study monographs. [*Afr. St. Mono.*] *ISSN: 0285- 1601. Kyoto University, Center for African Area Studies*: 46 Shimoadachi-cho, Yoshida, Sakyo-ku, Kyoto 606, Japan

Africana bulletin. [*Afr. Bul.*] *ISSN: 0002-029X. Uniwersytet Warszawski, Instytut Krajów Rozwijających Się*: Ul. Obozna 8, 00-032 Warsaw, Poland

Africana research bulletin. *[Afr. Res. Bul.]*; *University of Sierra Leone, Institute of African Studies*: Freetown, Sierra Leone

Afrika Spectrum. *[Af. Spec.] ISSN: 0002-0397. Institut für Afrika-Kunde*: Neuer Jungfernstieg 21, 2000 Hamburg 36, Germany

Afrique 2000. *[Afr. 2000] ISSN: 1017-0952. Institut panafricain de relations internationales*: Av. de Fré 265 - 1180, Brussels, Belgium

Afrique contemporaine. *[Afr. Cont.] ISSN: 0002-0478. Documentation française*: 29-31 Quai Voltaire, 75340 Paris Cedex 07, France

Afro-Asian solidarity. *[Af-As. Solid.]*; *Afro-Asian Peoples Solidarity Organisation (AAPSO)*: 89 Abdel Aziz Al-Seoud Street, 11451-61 Manial El-Roda, Cairo, Egypt

Ageing and society. *[Age. Soc.] ISSN: 0144-686X. Centre for Policy on Ageing/ British Society of Gerontology*; **Publisher**: *Cambridge University Press*: The Edinburgh Building, Shaftesbury Road, Cambridge CB2 2RU, U.K.

Agenda. *[Agenda] ISSN: 1013-0950. Agenda Collective*: P.O. Box 37432, Overport, 4067 Durban, South Africa

Agrekon. *[Agrekon] ISSN: 0303-1853. Landbou- Economievereniging van Suider-Afrika = Agricultural Economics Association of Southern Africa*: 210 Orion Avenue, Monument Park 0181, South Africa

Agricultura y sociedad. *[Agr. Soc.] ISSN: 0211-8394. Ministerio de Agricultura, Pesca y Alimentacion*: Centro de Publicaciones, Paseo de Infanta Isabel 1, 28071 Madrid, Spain

Ahfad journal. *[Ahfad J.]*; *Ahfad University for Women*: P.O. Box 167, Omdurman, Sudan

Akademika. *[Akademika] ISSN: 0126-5008. Penerbit Universiti Kebangsaan Malaysia, Faculty of Social Sciences and Humanities*: 43500 UKM Bangi, Selangor D.E., Malaysia

Al-Abhath. *[Al-Abhath]*; *American University of Beirut, Faculty of Arts and Sciences*: Beirut, Lebanon

Albania today. *[Alb. Today] ISSN: 0044-7072. Drejtoria Qendrore e Librit*: Pruga Konferenca e Pezec, Tirana, Albania

Allgemeines statistisches Archiv. *[All. Stat. A.] ISSN: 0002-6018. Deutsche Statistische Gesellschaft*; **Publisher**: *Vandenhoeck & Ruprecht*: Theaterstraße 13, 3400 Göttingen, Germany

Alternatives. *[Alternatives] ISSN: 0304-3754. Lynne Rienner Publishers*: 1800 30th Street, Boulder, CO.. 80301, U.S.A.

American anthropologist. *[Am. Anthrop.] ISSN: 0002-7294. American Anthropological Association*: 1703 New Hampshire Avenue, N.W. Washington, DC. 20009, U.S.A.

American behavioral scientist. *[Am. Behav. Sc.] ISSN: 0002- 7642. Sage Publications*: 2455 Teller Road, Newbury Park, CA. 91320, U.S.A.

American economic review. *[Am. Econ. Rev.] ISSN: 0002-8282. American Economic Association*: 2014 Broadway, Suite 305, Nashville, TN. 37203, U.S.A.

American ethnologist. *[Am. Ethn.] ISSN: 0094-0496. American Ethnological Society*: 1703 New Hampshire Avenue, N.W., Washington DC. 20009, U.S.A.

American historical review. *[Am. Hist. Rev.] ISSN: 0002-8702. American Historical Association*: 400 A Street S.E., Washington DC. 20003, U.S.A.

American Jewish history. *[Am. Jew. Hist.] ISSN: 0164-0178. American Jewish Historical Society*: 2 Thornton Road, Waltham, MA. 02154, U.S.A.

American journal of economics and sociology. *[Am. J. Econ. S.] ISSN: 0002-9246. American Journal of Economics and Sociology*: 42 East 72 Street, New York, NY. 10021, U.S.A.

American journal of Islamic social sciences. *[Am. J. Islam. Soc. Sci.] ISSN: 0742-6763. Association of Muslim Social Scientists/ International Institute of Islamic Thought*: P.O. Box 669, Herndon, VA 22070, U.S.A.

American journal of orthopsychiatry. *[Am. J. Orthopsy.] ISSN: 0002-9432. American Orthopsychiatric Association*: 19 W. 44th Street, New York, NY. 10036, U.S.A.; **Subscriptions**: *AOA Publications*: Sales Office, 49 Sheridan Avenue, Albany, NY. 12201-1413, U.S.A.

American journal of political science. *[Am. J. Pol. Sc.] ISSN: 0092-5853. Midwest Political Science Association*; **Publisher**: *University of Texas Press, Journals Department*: 2100 Comal, Austin TX. 78722, U.S.A.

American journal of sociology. *[A.J.S.] ISSN: 0024-9602. University of Chicago Press*: Journals Division, P.O. Box 37005, Chicago, IL. 60637, U.S.A.

American philosophical quarterly. *[Am. Phil. Q.] ISSN: 0003-0481. Philosophy Documentation Center*: Bowling Green State University, Bowling Green, OH. 43403-0189, U.S.A.

American political science review. *[Am. Poli. Sci.] ISSN: 0003-0554. American Political Science Association*: 1527 New Hampshire Avenue, N.W., Washington, DC. 20036, U.S.A.

American psychologist. *[Am. Psychol.] ISSN: 0003-066X. American Psychological Association*: 1400 North Uhle Street, Arlington, VA. 22201, U.S.A.

American review of Canadian studies. *[Am. R. Can. S.] ISSN: 0272-2011. Association for Canadian Studies in the United States*: One Dupont Circle, Suite 620, Washington DC. 20036, U.S.A.

American sociological review. *[Am. Sociol. R.] ISSN: 0003-1224. American Sociological Association*: 1722 N. Street, N.W. Washington, DC. 20036, U.S.A.

American sociologist. *[Am. Sociol.] ISSN: 0003-1232. Transaction Periodicals Consortium*: Rutgers University, New Brunswick, NJ. 08903, U.S.A.

Análise social. *[Anál. Soc.] ISSN: 0003-2573. Junta Nacional de Investigação Científica e Tecnológia/ Instituto Nacional de Investigação Científica*; **Publisher**: *Instituto de Ciências Sociais da Universidade de Lisboa*: Avenida das Forças Armadas, Edifício I.S.C.T.E., Ala Sul, 1° andar, 1600 Lisbon, Portugal

Analysis. *[Analysis] ISSN: 0003-2638. Basil Blackwell*: 108 Cowley Road, Oxford OX4 1JF, U.K.; **Subscriptions**: *Marston,Book Services*: P.O. Box 87, Oxford OX2 0DT, U.K.

Annales.:*Economies, sociétés, civilisations [Annales] ISSN: 0395-2649. C.N.R.S./ École des hautes études en sciences sociales*; **Publisher**: *Armand Colin*: 103 boulevard Saint-Michel, 75240 Paris Cedex 05, France; **Subscriptions**: *Armand Colin*: B.P.22, 41353 Vineuil, France

Annales de géographie. *[Ann. Géogr.] ISSN: 0003-4010. Armand Colin Éditeur*: 103, boulevard Saint-Michel, 75240 Paris Cedex 05, France; **Subscriptions**: *Armand Colin*: B.P. 22, 41353 Vineuil, France

Annales de l'IFORD. *[Ann. IFORD]*; *L'institut de formation et de recherche demographiques*: Section des Publications, B.P. 1556 Yaounde, Cameroon

Annales internationales de criminologie; International annals of criminology; Anales internacionales de criminologia. *[Ann. Inter. Crimin.] ISSN: 0003-4452. Société Internationale de Criminologie = International Society for Criminology = Sociedad Internacional de Criminologia*: 4 rue Mondavi, 75001 Paris, France

Annali della fondazione Luigi Micheletti. *[Ann. Fond. L. Mich.]*; *Fondazione Luigi Micheletti, Centro de ricerca sull'età contemporanea*: Via Cairoli 9, 15122 Brescia, Italy

Annali di ca'foscari. *[A. Ca'fos.]*; *Università degli Studi di Venezia*: San Polo 2035, 1- 30125 Venice, Italy

Annals of family studies. *[Ann. Fam. St.]*; *Council on family relations*: Tokyo, Japan

Annals of regional science. *[Ann. Reg. Sci.] ISSN: 0570-1864. Western Regional Science Association*; **Publisher**: *Springer-Verlag*: Heidelberger Platz 3, W-1000 Berlin 33, Germany

Annals of the American Academy of Political and Social Science. *[Ann. Am. Poli.] ISSN: 0002-7162. American Academy of Political and Social Science*: 3937 Chestnut Street, Philadelphia, PA. 19104, U.S.A.; **Publisher**: *Sage Publications*: 2455 Teller Road, Newbury Park, CA. 91320, U.S.A.

Annals of the Association of American Geographers. *[Ann. As. Am. G.] ISBN: 0004-5608. Association of American Geographers*: 1710 Sixteenth Street, N.W., Washington, DC. 20009, U.S.A.

Annals of the Institute of Social Science. *[Ann. Inst. Soc. Sci.] ISSN: 0563-8054. University of Tokyo, Institute of Social Science*: 7-3-1 Hongo, Bunkyo-ku, Tokyo 113, Japan

Année africaine. *[Ann. Afri.] ISSN: 0570-1937. Centre d'Etude d'Afique Noire/ Centre de Recherche et d'Étude sur les Pays d'Afrique Orientale*: Institut d'Etudes Politiques de Bordeaux, Domaine University, BP 101, 33405 Talence Cedex, France; **Publisher**: *Editions A. Pedone*: Paris, France

Année sociale. *[Ann. Soc.] ISSN: 0066-2380. Univeristé libre de Bruxelles, Institut de sociologie*: Avenue Jeanne, 44-1050 Brussels, Belgium

Année sociologique. *[Ann. Sociol.] ISSN: 0066-2399. Presses Universitaires de France*: 108 boulevard Saint- Germain, 75006 Paris, France; **Subscriptions**: *Presses Universitaires de France*: 14 avenue du Bois-de-l'Epine, BP 90, 91003 Evry Cedex, France

Annuaire de l'Afrique du Nord. *[Ann. Afr. Nord] ISSN: 0242- 7540. Editions du Centre national de la recherche scientifique*: 15 quai Anatole France, 75700 Paris, France

Annuaire des pays de l'Ocean indien. *[Ann. Pays Oc. Ind.] ISSN: 0247-400X. Université d'Aix-Marseille III, Centre d'études et de recherches sur les sociétés d l'Ocean indien*: 3 avenue Robert Schuman, 13628 Aix en Provence Cedex 1, France; **Publisher**: *Editions du Centre Nationale de la Recherche Scientifique*: 15 quai Anatole France, 75700 Paris, France

Annual report of University of Shizuoka, Hamamatsu College. *[Ann. Rep. Shiz., Hamam. Coll.]*; *Shizuoka University, Hamamatsu College*: Ohya 836, Shizuoka-shi 422, Japan

Annual review of anthropology. *[Ann. R. Anthr.] ISSN: 0084-6570. Annual Reviews*: 4139 El Camino Way, P.O. Box 10139, Palo Alto, CA. 94303-0897, U.S.A.

Annual review of information science and technology. *[Ann. R. Info. Sci. Tech.] ISSN: 0066-4200. American Society for Information Science*: 8720 Georgia Avenue, Suite 501, Silver Spring, MD. 20910-3602, U.S.A.; **Publisher**: *Elsevier Science Publishers (North-Holland)*: Sara Burgerhartstraat 25, P.O. Box 211, 1000 AE Amsterdam, The Netherlands

Annual review of psychology. *[Ann. R. Psych.] ISSN: 0066-4308. Annual Reviews*: 4139 El Camino Way, P.O. Box 10139, Palo Alto, CA. 94303-0897, U.S.A.

INTERNATIONAL BIBLIOGRAPHY OF SOCIOLOGY — 1991

Annual review of public health. *[Ann. R. Pub. H.] ISSN: 0163-7525. Annual Reviews*: 4139 El Camino Way, P.O. Box 10139, Palo Alto, CA. 94303 0897, U.S.A.

Annual review of sociology. *[Ann. R. Soc.] ISSN: 0360-0572. Annual Reviews*: 4139 El Camino Way, P.O. Box 10139, Palo Alto, CA. 94303-0899, U.S.A.

Anthropological linguistics. *[Anthrop. Ling.] ISSN: 0003-5483. University of Indiana, Department of Anthropology*: Rawles Hall 108, Bloomington, IN. 47405, U.S.A.

Anthropological quarterly. *[Anthr. Quart.] ISSN: 0003-5491. Catholic University of America, Department of Anthropology*: Washington, DC. 200064, U.S.A.; **Publisher**: *Catholic University of America Press*: 620 Michigan Avenue, N.E., Administration Building Room 303, Washington DC. 20064, U.S.A.

Antipode. *[Antipode] ISSN: 0066-4812. Basil Blackwell*: 108 Cowley Road, Oxford OX4 1JF, U.K.

Antiquity. *[Antiquity] ISSN: 0003-598X. Antiquity Publications*: c/o 85 Hills Road, Cambridge CB2 1PG, U.K.; **Publisher**: *Oxford University Press*: Pinkhill House, Southfield Road, Eynsham, Oxford OX8 1JJ, U.K.

Anuario de estudios centroamericanos. *[An. Est. Cent.Am.] ISSN: 0377-7316. Universidad de Costa Rica, Instituto de Investigaciones Sociales*: Apartado 75, 2060 Ciudad Universitaria, Rodrigo Facio, 2050 San Pedro de Montes de Oca, San Jose, Costa Rica

Applied community studies. *[App. Commun. Stud.] ISSN: 0954-4232. Manchester Polytechnic*: Department of Applied Community Studies, 799 Wilmslow Road, Didsbury, Manchester, M20 8RR, U.K., **Publisher**: *Whiting & Birch*: P.O. Box 872, Forest Hill, London SE23 3HL, U.K.

Applied economics. *[Appl. Econ.] ISSN: 0003 6846. Chapman and Hall*: 2-6 Boundary Row, London SE1 8HN, U.K.; **Subscriptions**: *International Thomson Publishing Services*: North Way, Andover, Hampshire SP10 5BE, U.K.

Apuntes. *[Apuntes] ISSN: 0252-1865. Revista Apuntes*: Apartado Postal 4683, Lima 1, Peru

Arab journal for the humanities. *[Arab J. Hum.]; Kuwait University*: P.O. Box 26585, Safat, 13126 Kuwait

Arab studies quarterly. *[Arab St. Q.] ISSN: 0271-3519. Institute of Arab Studies/ Association of Arab-American University Graduates*: 556 Trapelo Road, Belmont, MA. 02178, U.S.A.

Archiv für Kommunalwissenschaften. *[Arc. Kommunal.] ISSN: 0003- 9209. Deutsches Institut für Urbanistik*: Straße des 17. Juni 112, Postfach 12 62 24, 1000 Berlin 12, Germany; **Publisher**: *Verlag W. Kohlhammer*: Heßbrühlstraße 69, Postfach 80 04 30, 7000 Stuttgart 80 (Vaihingen), Germany

Archiv für Rechts- und Sozialphilosophie; Archives de philosophie du droit et de philosophie sociale; Archives for philosophy of law and social philosophy; Archivo de filosofía jurídica y social. *[Arc. Recht. Soz.] ISSN: 0001-2343. Internationale Vereinigung für Rechts- und Sozialphilosophie*; **Publisher**: *Franz Steiner Verlag*: Birkenwaldstraße 44, Postfach 10 15 26, D-7000 Stuttgart 1, Germany

Archív orientální. *[Arch. Orient.] ISSN: 0044-8699. Czechoslovak Academy of Sciences, Oriental Institute*; **Publisher**: *Academia Publishing House*: Vodičkova 40, 112 29 Prague 1, Czechoslovakia; **Subscriptions**: *John Benjamins*: Postbus 52519, 1007 HA Amsterdam, The Netherlands

Archives européennes de sociologie; European journal of sociology; Europäisches Archiv für Soziologie. *[Eur. J. Soc.] ISSN: 0003-9756. Cambridge University Press*: The Edinburgh Building, Shaftesbury Road, Cambridge CB2 2RU, U.K.

Archivio di studi urbani e regionali. *[Arch. St. Urb. Region.]; Franco Angeli editore*: Viale Monza 106, 20127 Milan, Italy

Area. *[Area] ISSN: 0004-0894. Institute of British Geographers*: 1 Kensington Gore, London SW7 2AR, U.K.

Argumentation. *[Argumentation] ISSN: 0920-427X. European Centre for the Study of Argumentation*: Unversité Libre de Bruxelles, Institut de Philosophie, 143 avenue A.-Buyl, C.P. 188, B-1050 Brussels, Belgium; **Publisher**: *Kluwer Academic Publishers*: P.O. Box 322, 3300 AH Dordrecht, The Netherlands

Armed forces and society. *[Arm. Forces Soc.] ISSN: 0095-327X. Inter-University Seminar on Armed Forces and Society*: Box 46, 1126 East 59th Street, Chicago, IL. 60637, U.S.A.; **Publisher**: *Transaction Periodicals Consortium*: Rutgers University, New Brunswick, NJ. 08903, U.S.A.; **Subscriptions**: *Swets Publishing Service*: Heereweg 347, 2161 CA. Lisse, The Netherlands

Artha vijñāna. *[Art. Vij.] ISSN: 0004- 3559. Gokhale Institute of Politics and Economics*: Pune 411004, India

Asia journal of theology. *[Asia J. Theol.] ISSN: 0218-0812. Asia Journal of Theology*: 324 Onan Road, Singapore 1542

Asian and African studies. *[Asian. Afr. Stud.] ISSN: 0066-8281. University of Haifa, Gustav Heinemann Institute of Middle Eastern Studies*: Haifa 31999, Israel

Asian culture (Asian-Pacific culture) quarterly. *[Asian Cult. (Asian-Pac. Cult.) Q.] ISSN: 0378-8911. Asian-Pacific Cultural Center*: Asian-Pacific Parliamentarians' Union, 6F, 66 Aikuo East Road, Taipei, Taiwan 10726

Asian journal of public administration. *[Asian J. Pub. Admin.] ISSN: 0259-8272. University of Hong Kong, Department of Political Science*: Pokfulam Road, Hong Kong

Asian profile. *[Asian Prof.] ISSN: 0304-8675. Asian Research Service*: Rm. 704, Federal Building, 369 Lockhart Road, Hong Kong; **Subscriptions**: *idem*: G.P.O. Box 2232, Hong Kong

Asian studies review. *[Asian Stud. R.] ISSN: 0314-7533. Asian Studies Association of Australia*: c/o Social and Policy Studies in Education, University of Sydney, N.S.W. 2006, Australia

Asian survey. *[Asian Sur.] ISSN: 0004-4687. University of California Press*: Berkeley, CA. 94720, U.S.A.

Asian thought and society. *[Asian Thoug. Soc.] ISSN: 0361-3968. State University of New York-Oneonta/Boston College, Center for East Europe, Russia, and Asia/University of Hong Kong*; **Publisher**: *East-West Publishing*: 1 Bugbee Road, Oneonta, NY. 13820, U.S.A.

Asian-Pacific economic literature. *[Asian-Pacific Ec. Lit.] ISSN: 0818-9935. Australian National University, National Centre for Development Studies*: G.P.O. Box 4, Canberra, ACT 2601, Australia; **Publisher**: *Beech Tree Publishing*: 10 Watford Close, Guildford, Surrey GU1 2EP, U.K.

Asien Afrika Lateinamerika. *[Asien. Af. Lat.am.] ISSN: 0323-3790. Akademie der Wissenschaften zu Berlin*; **Publisher**: *Akademie-Verlag*: Leipziger Straße 3-4, 01086 Berlin, Germany

Aussenpolitik. *[Aussenpolitik] ISSN: 0587-3835. Interpress Verlag*: Hartwicusstraße 3-4, D-2000 Hamburg 76, Germany

Australian Aboriginal studies. *[Aust. Abor. S.] ISSN: 0729-4352. Australian Institute of Aboriginal and Torres Strait Islander Studies*: G.P.O. Box 553, Canberra ACT 2601, Australia

Australian and New Zealand journal of sociology. *[Aust. N.Z. J. Soc.] ISSN: 0004-8690. Australian Sociological Association*: c/o Research School of Social Sciences, Australian National University, GPO Box 4, Canberra, ACT 2601, Australia; **Publisher**: *La Trobe University Press*: Bundoora, Victoria 3083, Australia

Australian cultural history. *[Aust. Cult. Hist.] ISSN: 0728- 8433. University of New South Wales, School of History*: P.O. Box 1, Kensington, N.S.W. 2033, Australia

Australian economic papers. *[Aust. Econ. P.] ISSN: 0004-900X. Flinders University of South Australia*: G.P.O. Box 2100, Adelaide, South Australia 5042, Australia; **Subscriptions**: *University of Adelaide*: G.P.O. Box 498, Adelaide, South Australia 5001, Australia

Australian economic review. *[Aust. Ec. Rev.] ISSN: 0004-9018. University of Melbourne, Institute of Applied Economic and Social Research*: Baldwin Spencer Building, University of Melbourne, Parkville, Victoria 3052, Australia

Australian geographer. *[Aust. Geogr.] ISSN: 0004-9182. Geographical Society of New South Wales*: P.O. Box 602, Gladesville, NSW 2111, Australia

Australian geographical studies. *[Aust. Geogr. Stud.] ISSN: 0004-9190. Institute of Australian Geographers*: Department of Geography and Oceanography, University College, University of New South Wales, Australian Defence Force Academy, Campbell, ACT 2600, Australia

Australian historical studies. *[Aust. Hist. St.] ISSN: 1031-461X. University of Melbourne*: Department of History, University of Melbourne, Parkville, Victoria 3052, Australia

Australian journal of Chinese affairs. *[Aust. J. Chin. Aff.] ISSN: 0156-7365. Australian National University, Contemporary China Centre*: G.P.O. Box 4, Canberra ACT 2601, Australia

Australian journal of linguistics. *[Aust. J. Ling.] ISSN: 0726-8602. Australian Linguistic Society*: Department of Linguistics, La Trobe University, Bundoora 3083, Victoria, Australia; **Publisher**: *Cambridge University Press*: The Edinburgh Building, Shaftesbury Road, Cambridge CB2 2RU, U.K.

Australian journal of politics and history. *[Aust. J. Poli.] ISSN: 0004-9522. University of Queensland Press*: P.O. Box 42, Queensland 4072, Australia

Australian journal of public administration. *[Aust. J. Publ.] ISSN: 0313-6647. Royal Australian Institute of Public Administration*: Box 904, GPO, Sydney, N.S.W. 2001, Australia

Australian journal of social issues. *[Aust. J. Soc. Iss.] ISSN: 0157-6321. Australian Council of Social Services*: Box 45, Railway Square, Sydney 2000, N.S.W., Australia

Australian journal of statistics. *[Aust. J. Statist.] ISSN: 0004-9581. Australian Statistical Publishing Association*: Treasurer, Statistical Society of Australia, G.P.O. Box 573, Canberra, ACT 2601, Australia

Australian quarterly. *[Aust. Q.] ISSN: 0005-0091. Australian Institute of Political Science*: P.O. Box 145, Balmain NSW 2041, Australia

Australian studies. *[Aust. Stud.] ISSN: 0954-0954. British Australian Studies Association*: Sir Robert Menzies Centre for Australian Studies, 27-28 Russell Square, London WC1B 5DS, U.K.; **Publisher**: *University of Stirling, Department of English Studies*: Stirling FK9 4LA, U.K.

AWR Bulletin. *[AWR B.] ISSN: 0014-2492. Association for the Study of the World Refugee Problem*: FL- 9490 Vaduz, P.O.B. 75, Liechtenstein; **Publisher**: *Wilhelm Braumueller, Universitäts-Verlagsbuchhandlung*: Servitengasse 5, A-1092, Vienna, Austria

Azania. *[Azania] ISSN: 0067-270X. British Institute in Eastern Africa*: P.O. Box 30710, Nairobi, Kenya/ 1 Kensington Gore, London SW7 2AR, U.K.

Banaras law journal. *[Banaras Law J.]*; *Banaras Hindu University, Law School*: Varanasi 221005, India

Bangladesh development studies. *[Bang. Dev. Stud.] ISSN: 0304-095X. Bangladesh Unnayan Gobeshona Protishthan = Bangladesh Institute of Development Studies*: G.P.O. Box No.3854, E-17 Agargaon, Sher-e-Bangla Nagar, Dhaka, Bangladesh

Bangladesh journal of political economy. *[Bang. J. Pol. Econ.]; Bangladesh Economic Association*: Department of Economics, University of Dhaka, Dhaka-1000, Bangladesh

Bangladesh journal of public administration. *[Bang. J. Pub. Admin.]; Bangladesh Public Administration Training Centre*: Savar, Dhaka 1343, Bangladesh

BC studies. *[BC. Stud.] ISSN: 0005-2949. University of British Columbia*: 2029 West Mall, University of British Columbia, Vancouver B.C. V6T 1W5, Canada

Behavior science research. *[Behav. Sc. Res.] ISSN: 0094-3673. Society for Cross-Cultural Research*; **Publisher**: *Human Relations Area Files*: Box 2015, Yale Sta., New Haven, CT. 06520, U.S.A.

Behavioral and brain sciences. *[Behav. Brain Sci.] ISSN: 0140-525X. Cambridge University Press*: 40 West 20 Street, New York, NY. 10011, U.S.A.

Behavioral science. *[Behav. Sci.] ISSN: 0005-7940. International Society for Systems Sciences/ Institute of Management Sciences*: P.O. Box 64025, Baltimore, Maryland 21264, U.S.A.

Beiträge zur Japanologie. *[Beit. Japan.] ISSN: 0522- 6759. Universität Wien, Institut für Japanologie*: Universitätsstraße 7/4, A-1010 Vienna, Austria

Belizean studies. *[Beliz. St.] ISSN: 0250-6831. St. John's College*: P.O. Box 548, Belize City, Belize, Central America

Benelux. *[Benelux]; Secretariaat-Generaal van de Benelux Economische unie = Secrétariat général de l'Union économique Benelux = Generalsekretariat der Benelux-Wirtschaftsunion*: Regentschapsstraat, 39 rue de la Régence, Brussels 1000, Belgium

Berkeley journal of sociology. *[Berkeley J. Soc.] ISSN: 0067-5830. Berkeley Journal of Sociology*: 458A Barrows Hall, Department of Sociology, University of California Berkeley, Berkeley, CA 94720, U.S.A.

Berliner journal für Soziologie. *[Berl. J. Soziol.] ISSN: 0863-1808. Institut für Soziologie der Humbodt-Universität zu Berlin*: Hans-Loch-Str. 349, O-1136 Berlin, Germany; **Publisher**: *Akademie-Verlag Berlin*: Leipziger Str. 3-4, Postfach 1233, O-1086 Berlin, Germany

Bevolking en gezin. *[Bevolk. Gez.]; Centrum voor Bevolkings- en Gezinsstudiën/Nederlands Interdisciplinair Demografisch Instituut*: Markiesstrart 1, 1000 Brussels, Belgium/Lange Houtstraat 19, 2511 CV 's- Gravenhage, Postbus 11650, 2502 AR 's-Gravenhage, The Netherlands; **Subscriptions**: *N.V. Uitgecerij Pelckmans*: Kapelsestraat 222, 2950 Kapellen, Belgium

Biblioteka etnografii polskiej. *[Bibl. Etnogr. Pol.] ISSN: 0067-7655. Polska Akademia Nauk, Instytut Historii Materialnej*: ul. Swierczewskiego 105, 00-140 Warsaw, Poland

Bioethics. *[Bioethics] ISSN: 0269- 9702. Basil Blackwell*: 108 Cowley Road, Oxford OX4 1JF, U.K.

Biography. *[Biography] ISSN: 0162-4962. Center for Biographical Research*: Varsity College, University of Hawaii, Honolulu, HI. 96822, U.S.A.; **Publisher**: *University of Hawaii Press*: 2840 Kolowalu Street, Honolulu, HI. 96822, U.S.A.

Boletim informativo e bibliográfico de ciências sociais. *[Bol. Inf. Bibl. Soc.]; Associação Nacional de Pós-Graduação e Pesquisa em Ciências Sociais*: Editoria do BIB, Rua da Matriz 82, Botafogo 22.260. Rio de Janeiro RJ., Brazil

Boletin de la Asociación española de orientalistas. *[B. Asoc. Españ. Orient.]; Universidad Autónoma*: Edificio Rectorado, Ciudad Universitaria de Canto Blanco, 28049 Madrid, Spain

Borneo review. *[Born. R.]; Institute for Development Studies (Sabah)*: Locked Bag 127, 88999 Kota Kinabalu, Sabah, Malaysia

Botswana notes and records. *[Bots. Not. Rec.] ISSN: 0525-5059. Botswana Society*: P.O. Box 71, Gaborone, Botswana

British journal of addiction. *[Br. J. Addict.] ISSN: 0952-0481. Society for the Study of Addiction to Alcohol and Other Drugs*: Addiction Reseach Unit, National Addiction Centre, 101 Denmark Hill, London SE5 8AF, U.K.; **Publisher**: *Carfax Publishing*: P.O. Box 25, Abingdon, Oxfordshire, OX14 3UE, U.K.

British journal of Canadian studies. *[Br. J. Can. Stud.] ISSN: 0269-9222. British Association for Canadian Studies*: Centre of Canadian Studies, 21 George Square, Edinburgh EH8, U.K.

British journal of clinical psychology. *[Br. J. Clin. Psycho.] ISSN: 0144-6657. British Psychological Society*: St. Andrews House, 48 Princess Road East, Leicester LE1 7DR, U.K.; **Subscriptions**: *The Distribution Centre*: Blackhorse Road, Letchworth, Herts. SG6 1HN, U.K.

British journal of criminology. *[Br. J. Crimin.] ISSN: 0007-0955. Institute for the Study and Treatment of Delinquency*; **Publisher**: *Oxford University Press*: Pinkhill House, Southfield Road, Eynsham, Oxford OX8 1JJ, U.K.

British journal of educational studies. *[Br. J. Educ. S.] ISSN: 0007-1005. Basil Blackwell*: 108 Cowley Road, Oxford OX4 1JF, U.K.; **Subscriptions**: *Marston Book Services*: P.O. Box 87, Oxford OX2 0DT, U.K.

British journal of industrial relations. *[Br. J. Ind. R.] ISSN: 0007-1080. London School of Economics*: Houghton Street, London WC2A 2AE, U.K.; **Publisher**: *Basil Blackwell*: 108 Cowley Road, Oxford, OX4 1JF, U.K.; **Subscriptions**: *Journals Subscriptions, Industrial Relations Department, Marston Book Services*: P.O. Box 87, Oxford OX2 0DT, U.K.

British journal of management. *[Br. J. Manag.] ISSN: 1045-3172. British Academy of Management;* **Publisher**: *John Wiley & Sons*: Baffins Lane, Chichester, West Sussex PO19 1UD, U.K.
British journal of political science. *[Br. J. Poli. S.] ISSN: 0007-1234. Cambridge University Press*: The Pitt Building, Trumpington Street, Cambridge CB2 1RP, U.K.
British journal of psychology. *[Br. J. Psy.] ISSN: 0007- 1269. British Psychological Society*: St. Andrews House, 48 Princess Road East, Leicester LE1 7DR, U.K.
British journal of social psychology. *[Br. J. Soc. P.] ISSN: 0144-6665. British Psychological Society*: St. Andrews House, 48 Princess Road East, Leicester LE1 7DR, U.K.; **Subscriptions**: *Distribution Centre*: Blackhorse Road, Letchworth, Herts SG6 1HN, U.K.
British journal of social work. *[Br. J. Soc. W.] ISSN: 0045-3102. British Association of Social Workers;* **Publisher**: *Oxford University Press*: Pinkhill House, Southfield Road, Eynsham, Oxford, OX8 1JJ, U.K.
British journal of sociology. *[Br. J. Soc.] ISSN: 0007-1315. London School of Economics and Political Science*: Houghton Street, Aldwych, London WC2A 2AE; **Publisher**: *Routledge*: 11 New Fetter Lane, London EC4P 4EE, U.K.
British review of New Zealand studies. *[Br. R. N.Z. Stud.] ISSN: 0951-6204. University of Edinburgh, New Zealand Studies Committee*: 21 George Square, Edinburgh EH8 9LD, U.K.
Bulletin de la Société des études océaniennes. *[Soc. Et. Océan.]*; *Société des études océaniennes*: B.P. 110 Papeete, French Polynesia
Bulletin des études africaines de l'INALCO. *[B. Et. Afr. INALCO]; Institut national des langues et civilisations orientales*: 2 rue de Lille, 75007 Paris, France
Bulletin of concerned Asian scholars. *[B. Concern. Asia. Schol.] ISSN: 0007-4810. Bulletin of Concerned Asian Scholars*: 3239 9th Street, Boulder, CO. 80304-2112, U.S.A.
Bulletin of Eastern Caribbean affairs. *[B. E.Carib. Aff.] ISSN: 0254-7406. Institute of Social and Economic Research (Eastern Caribbean)*: University of the West Indies, Cave Hill, Barbados
Bulletin of economic research. *[B. Econ. Res.] ISSN: 0307-3378. Basil Blackwell*: 108 Cowley Road, Oxford OX4 1JF, U.K.
Bulletin of Indonesian economic studies. *[B. Ind. Econ. St.] ISSN: 0007-4918. Australian National University*: Department of Economics, Research School of Pacific Studies, G.P.O. Box 4, Canberra, A.C.T. 2601, Australia
Bulletin of Latin American research. *[B. Lat. Am. Res.] ISSN: 0261-3050. Society for Latin American Studies;* **Publisher**: *Pergamon Press*: Headington Hill Hall, Oxford OX3 0BW, U.K.
Bulletin of Tanzanian affairs. *[B. Tanzan. Aff.] ISSN: 0952-2948. British Tanzania Society*: 14B Westbourne Grove Terrace, London W2 5SD, U.K.
Bulletin of the Faculty of School Education Hiroshima. *[B. Sch. Ed. Hiroshima]*
Bulletin of the Institute of Ethnology, Academia Sinica. *[B. Inst. Ethn. Ac. Sin.] ISSN: 0001-3935. Institute of Ethnology Academia Sinica*: Nankang, Taipei, Taiwan
Bulletin of the School of Oriental and African Studies. *[B. Sch. Orient. Afr. Stud.] ISSN: 0041- 977X. University of London, School of Oriental and African Studies*: Thornhough Street, London WC1 0XG, U.K.
Bulletin, Yokohama City University. *[B. Yoko. Univ.]*; *Yokohama City University*: 22-2 Seto, Kunazawa-Ku, Yokohama 236, Japan
Business economist. *[Bus. Econ.] ISSN: 0306-5049. Society of Business Economists*: Business Economist, 56 Malden Road, Watford, WD1 3EW, U.K.
Business history review. *[Bus. Hist. Rev.] ISSN: 0007-6805. Harvard Business School*: Baker Library 5A, Harvard Business School, Boston, MA. 02163, U.S.A.
Cahiers africains d'administration publique; African administrative studies. *[Cah. Afr. Admin. Pub.] ISSN: 0007-9588. Centre Africain de Formation et de Recherche Administratives pour le Développement (CAFRAD)*: P.O. Box 310, Tangiers, Morocco
Cahiers d'anthropologie et biométrie humaine. *[Cah. Anthr. Bio. Hum.] ISSN: 0758-2714. Société de Biometrie Humaine*: 41 rue Gay-Lussac, Paris, France; **Publisher**: *C.N.R.S.*: 45, rue des Saints-Pères, 75006 Paris, France
Cahiers de l'homme. *[Cah. Homme] ISSN: 0068-5046. Editions de l'Ecole des Hautes Etudes en Sciences Sociales*: 131 boulevard Saint-Michel, F-75005 Paris, France
Cahiers de linguistique asie orientale. *[Cah. Ling. Asie Orient.] ISSN: 0153-3320. École des Hautes Études en Sciences Sociales, Centre de Recherches Linguistiques sur l'Asie Orientale*: 54 boulevard Raspail, 75006 Paris, France
Cahiers de l'ISSP. *[Cah. ISSP]; Université de Neuchâtel, Institut de Sociologie et de Science Politique, Faculté de droit et des sciences économiques;* **Publisher**: *Editions EDES*: Neuchâtel, Switzerland
Cahiers de Tunisie. *[Cah. Tunis.] ISSN: 0008-0012. Faculté des Lettres et Sciences Humaines de Tunis*: boulevard du 9 Avril 1938, Tunis, Tunisia

Cahiers des Amériques latines. *[Cah. Amer. Lat.]* ISSN: 0008-0020. *Université de la Sorbonne Nouvelle (Paris III), Institut des Hautes Etudes de l'Amérique latine*: 28 rue Saint-Guillaume, 75007 Paris, France

Cahiers des sciences humaines. *[Cah. Sci. Hum.]* ISSN: 0768-9829. *Editions de l'ORSTOM, Institut français de recherche scientifique pour le developpement en cooperation*: Commission des Sciences Sociales, 213 rue la Fayette, 75480 Paris, France; **Subscriptions**: *Éditions de l'ORSTOM*: Librairie-Vente-Publicité, 70-74 Route d'Aulnay, 93143 Bondy Cedex, France

Cahiers d'études africaines. *[Cah. Et. Afr.]* ISSN: 0008-0055. *Éditions de l'École des Hautes Études en Sciences Sociales*: 131 boulevard Saint-Michel, 75005 Paris, France; **Subscriptions**: *Centrale des Revues*: 11 rue Gossin, 92543 Montrouge Cedex, France

Cahiers d'études sur la méditerranée orientale, et le monde turco-iranien. *[Cah. Ét. Méd. Ori. Tur-Iran.]* ISSN: 0764-9878. *Association Française pour l'Etude de la Méditerranée Orientale et le Monde Turco-Iranien*: 4 rue de Chevreuse, 75006 Paris, France

Cahiers d'histoire de l'institut de recherches Marxistes. *[Cah. Inst. Rech. Marx.]* ISSN: 0246-9731. *Société d'Édition des Publications de l'Institut des Recherches Marxistes*: 15 rue Montmartre, 75001 Paris, France; **Subscriptions**: *Institut de Recherches Marxistes*: 64 boulevard Auguste-Blanqui, 75013 Paris, France

Cahiers d'outre-mer. *[Cah. Outre-mer]* ISSN: 0373-5843. *Université de Bordeaux III, Institut de Géographie*: Domaine Universitaire, 33405 Talence, France

Cahiers du CEDAF/ ASDOC-studies. *[Cah. CEDAF]* ISSN: 0250-1619. *Centre d'étude et de documentation africaines = Afrika Studie-en Documentatiecentrum*: 7 Place Royale, B-1000 Brussels, Belgium

Cahiers internationaux de sociologie. *[Cah. Int. Soc.]* ISSN: 0008-0276. *Presses Universitaires de France*: 108 boulevard Saint-Germain, 75006 Paris, France

California management review. *[Calif. Manag. R.]* ISSN: 0008-1256. *University of California, Walter A. Haas School of Business*: 350 Barrows Hall. University of California, Berkeley, CA. 94720, U.S.A.

Cambridge anthropology. *[Cam. Anthrop.]*; *University of Cambridge, Department of Social Anthropology*: Free School Lane, Cambridge CB2 3RF, U.K.

Cambridge journal of economics. *[Camb. J. Econ.]* ISSN: 0309-166X. *University of Cambridge, Faculty of Economics and Politics*: Sidgwick Avenue, Cambridge CB3 9DD, U.K.; **Publisher**: *Academic Press*: 24-28 Oval Road, London NW1 7DX, U.K.; **Subscriptions**: *idem*: Foots Cray, Sidcup, Kent DA14 5HP, U.K.

Cambridge law journal. *[Camb. Law J.]* ISSN: 0008-1973. *University of Cambridge, Faculty of Law*; **Publisher**: *Cambridge University Press*: The Edinburgh Building, Shaftesbury Road, Cambridge CB2 2RU, U.K.

Canadian Association of African Studies newsletter; Association canadienne des études africaines bulletin. *[Can. Ass. Afr. S. News]* ISSN: 0228-8397. *Canadian Association of African Studies = Association canadienne des études africaines*: 308, 294 Albert Street, Ottawa, Ontario, K1P 6E6 Canada

Canadian historical review. *[Can. Hist. R.]* ISSN: 0008-3755. *University of Toronto Press*: 5201 Dufferin Street, Downsview, Ontario M3H 5T8, Canada

Canadian journal of African studies; Revue canadienne des études africaines. *[Can. J. Afr. St.]* ISSN: 0008-3968. *Canadian Association of African Studies = Association canadienne des études africaines*: Innis College, University of Toronto, 2 Sussex Avenue, Toronto, Ontario M5S IAI, Canada

Canadian journal of economics; Revue canadienne d'économique. *[Can. J. Econ.]* ISSN: 0008-4085. *Canadian Economics Association*; **Publisher**: *University of Toronto Press*: 5201 Dufferin Street, Downsview, Ontario M3H 5T8, Canada

Canadian journal of philosophy. *[Can. J. Phil.]* ISSN: 0045-5091. *University of Calgary Press*: Calgary, Alberta T2N 1N4, Canada

Canadian journal of political and social theory. *[Can. J. Pol. Soc. Theo.]* ISSN: 0380-9420. *A. and M. Kroker*: Concordia University, 1455 de Maisonneuve West, Montreal, Quebec H3G 1M8, Canada

Canadian journal of sociology; Cahiers canadiens de sociologie. *[Can. J. Soc.]* ISSN: 0318-6431. *University of Alberta, Department of Sociology*: Edmonton, Alberta T6G 2H4, Canada

Canadian public administration; Administration publique du Canada. *[Can. Publ. Ad.]* ISSN: 0008-4840. *Institute of Public Administration of Canada*: 897 Bay Street, Toronto, Ontario M5S 1Z7, Canada

Canadian review of sociology and anthropology; Revue canadienne de sociologie et d'anthropologie. *[Can. R. Soc. A.]* ISSN: 0008-4948. *Canadian Sociology and Anthropology Association*: Concordia University, 1455 boulevard de Maisonneuve W., Montreal, Quebec H3G 1M8, Canada

Canadian review of studies in nationalism; Revue canadienne des études sur le nationalisme. *[Can R. Stud. N.]* ISSN: 0317-7904. *CRSN/RCEN*: University of Prince Edward Island, Charlottetown, P.E.I. C1A 4P3, Canada

Canadian yearbook of international law; Annuaire canadien de droit international. *[Can. Yb. Int. Law]* ISSN: 0069-0058. *International Law Association, Canadian Branch*; **Publisher**: *University of British Columbia Press*: 303-6344 Memorial Road, Vancouver, B.C., V16 1WS Canada

Capital and class. *[Cap. Class]* ISSN: 0309-8786. *Conference of Socialist Economists*: Editorial Committee, Conference of Socialist Economists, 25 Horsell Road, London N5 1XL, U.K.

Caribbean quarterly. *[Car. Quart.]* ISSN: 0008-6495. *University of the West Indies, Department of Extra-Mural Studies*: Mona, Kingston 7, Jamaica

Caribbean studies; Estudios del Caribe; Études des Caraïbes. *[Carib. Stud.]* ISSN: 0008-6533. *Universidad de Puerto Rico, Facultad de Ciencias Sociales, Instituto de Estudios del Caribe*: P.O. Box 23361 University Station, Pío Piedras, Puerto Rico 00931

Central Asian survey. *[C.Asian Sur.]* ISSN: 0263-4937. *Society for Central Asian Studies*: Unit 8, 92 Lots Road, London SW10 4BQ, U.K.; **Publisher**: *Pergamon Press*: Headington Hill Hall, Oxford OX3 OBW, U.K.

Central Asiatic journal. *[Cent. Asia. J.]*; *Otto Harrassowitz*: Taunusstrasse 5, 6200 Wiesbaden, Germany

CEPAL review. *[CEPAL R.]* ISSN: 0251-2920. *United Nations Economic Commission for Latin America and the Caribbean*: Casilla 179-D, Santiago, Chile; **Subscriptions**: *United Nations Publications, Sales Section*: Palais des Nations, 1211 Geneva 10, Switzerland

Child development. *[Child. Devel.]* ISSN: 0009-3920. *Society for Research in Child Development*: 5720 South Woodlawn Avenue, Chicago, IL. 60637, U.S.A.; **Publisher**: *University of Chicago Press*: c/o 5720 South Woodlawn Avenue, Chicago, IL. 60637, U.S.A.; **Subscriptions**: *idem*: Journals Division, P.O. Box 37005, Chicago, IL. 60637, U.S.A.

Children and society. *[Child. Soc.]* ISSN: 0951-0605. *National Children's Bureau of the United Kingdom*; **Publisher**: *Whiting and Birch*: P.O. Box 872, Forest Hill, London SE23 3HZ, U.K.

China quarterly. *[China Quart.]* ISSN: 0009 4439. *University of London, School of Oriental and African Studies*: Thornhaugh Street, Russell Square, London WC1H 0XG, U.K.

Ching feng. *[Ch. Feng]*; *Christian Study Centre on Chinese Religion and Culture*: 6/F Kiu Kin Mansion, No.566 Nathan Road, Kowloon, Hong Kong

Ciências sociais hoje. *[Ciên. Soc. Hoje.]*; *Associção Nacional de Pós-Graduação e Pesquisa em Cięncias Sociais*; **Publisher**: *Edições Vértice*: Rua Conde do Pinhal 78, Caixa Postal 678, 01501 São Paulo, SP. Brazil

Cities. *[Cities]* ISSN: 0264-2751. *Butterworth-Heinemann*: 88 Kingsway, London WC2 6AB, U.K.; **Subscriptions**: *Turpin Transactions*: Distribution Centre, Blackhorse Road, Letchworth, Herts. SG6 1HN, U.K.

Civilisations. *[Civilisations]* ISSN: 0009-8140. *Université Libre de Bruxelles, Institut de Sociologie*: 44 avenue Jeanneaterloo, 1050 Brussels, Belgium

Civitas. *[Civitas]* ISSN: 0009-8191. *Edizioni Civitas*: Via Tirso 92, 00198 Rome, Italy

Coexistence. *[Coexistence]* ISSN: 0587-5994. *Martinus Nijhoff Publishers*: Postbus 17, 3300 AA Dordrecht, The Netherlands

Cognition. *[Cognition]* ISSN: 0010-0277. *Elsevier Science Publishers*: P.O. Box 211, 1000 AE Amsterdam, The Netherlands

Cognitive linguistics. *[Cogn. Ling.]* ISSN: 0936-5907. *Walter de Gruyter*: Postfach 110240, D-Berlin 11, Germany

Cognitive science. *[Cogn. Sci.]* ISSN: 0364-0213. *Cognitive Science Society*: Learning Research and Development Center, University of Pittsburgh, 3939 O'Hara Street, Pittsburgh, PA. 15260, U.S.A.; **Publisher**: *Ablex Publishing*: 355 Chestnut Street, Norwood, NJ. 07648, U.S.A.

Collegium antropologicum. *[Coll. Antrop.]* ISSN: 0350- 6134. *Croatian Anthropological Society*: 41000 Zagreb, Moše Pijade 158, P.O. Box 291, Yugoslavia

Columbia law review. *[Columb. Law.]* ISSN: 0010-1958. *Columbia Law Review Association*: 435 West 116th Street, New York, NY. 10027, U.S.A.

Commentary. *[Commentary]* ISSN: 0010- 2601. *American Jewish Committee*: 165 East 56th Street, New York, NY. 10022, U.S.A.

Communautés. *[Communautés]* ISSN: 0010-3462. *Université Coopérative Internationale*; **Publisher**: *Bureau d' École Coopératives et Communautaires*: 1 rue du 11 Novembre, 92129 Montrouge, France

Communication. *[Communication]* ISSN: 0305-4233. *Gordon and Breach Science Publishers*: 270 8th Avenue, New York, NY. 10011, U.S.A.

Communication theory. *[Commun. Theory]* ISSN: 1050-3293. *International Communication Association*: 8140 Burnet Road, P.O. Box 9589, Austin, TX. 78766-9589, U.S.A.; **Publisher**: *Guilford Publications*: 72 Spring Street, New York, NY. 10012, U.S.A.

Communisme. *[Communisme]* ISSN: 2209-7007. *Éditions L'Age d'Homme*: 5 rue Férou, 75006 Paris, France

Community development journal. *[Comm. Dev. J.]* ISSN: 0010-3802. *Oxford University Press*: Walton Street, Oxford OX2 6DP, U.K.; **Subscriptions**: *idem*: Journals Subscription Dept., Pinkhill House, Southfield Road, Eynsham, Oxon OX8 1JJ, U.K.

Comparative and international law journal of Southern Africa. *[Comp. Int. Law J. S.Afr.]* ISSN: 0010-4051. *University of South Africa, Institute of Foreign and Comparative Law*: P.O. Box 392, Pretoria, South Africa

INTERNATIONAL BIBLIOGRAPHY OF SOCIOLOGY — 1991

Comparative political studies. *[Comp. Poli. S.] ISSN: 0010- 4140. Sage Publications*: 2455 Teller Road, Newbury Park, CA 91320, U.S.A.; **Subscriptions**: *Sage Publications*: 6 Bonhill Street, London EC2A 4PU, U.K.

Comparative politics. *[Comp. Polit.] ISSN: 0010-4159. City University of New York*: 33 West 42nd Street, New York, NY. 10036, U.S.A.

Comparative social research. *[Comp. Soc. Res.] ISSN: 0195-6310. JAI Press*: 55 Old Post Road No. 2., Greenwich, CT. 06836, U.S.A.

Comparative studies in society and history. *[Comp. Stud. S.] ISSN: 0010- 4175. Society for the Comparative Study of Society and History*; **Publisher**: *Cambridge University Press*: 40 West 20th Street, New York, NY. 10011, U.S.A.

Comprehensive urban studies. *[Comp. Urban St.]*; *Tokyo Metropolitan University*: Tokyo, Japan

Contemporary Pacific. *[Cont. Pac.] ISSN: 1043-898X. Center for Pacific Islands Studies*: University of Hawaii at Manoa, 1890 East-West Road, 215 Moore Hall, Honolulu, Hawaii 96822, U.S.A.; **Publisher**: *University of Hawaii Press*: 2840 Kolowalu Street, Honolulu, Hawaii 96822-1888, U.S.A.

Contemporary policy issues. *[Cont. Policy] ISSN: 0735-0007. Western Economic Association International*: 7400 Center Avenue, Suite 109, Huntington Beach, CA. 92647-3039, U.S.A.

Contemporary sociology — a journal of reviews. *[Contemp. Sociol. — J. Rev.] ISSN: 0094-3061. American Sociological Association*: 1722 N Street, NW, Washington DC., 20036, U.S.A.

Continuity and change. *[Contin. Change] ISSN: 0268-4160. Cambridge University Press*: The Edinburgh Building, Shaftesbury Road, Cambridge CB2 2RU, U.K.

Contributions to Indian sociology. *[Contr. I. Soc.] ISSN: 0069-9667. Institute of Economic Growth*: University of Delhi, Delhi 110007, India; **Publisher**: *Sage Publications India*: 32 M-Block Market, Greater Kailash 1, New Delhi 110 048, India

Corruption and reform. *[Corr. Reform] ISSN: 0169-7528. Martinus Nijhoff Publishers*: P.O. Box 322, 3300 AH Dordrecht, The Netherlands

Crime and delinquency. *[Crime Delin.] ISSN: 0011-1287. Sage Publications*: 2455 Teller Road, Newbury Park, CA. 91320, U.S.A.

Crime and justice. *[Crime Just.] ISSN: 0192-3234. University of Chicago Press*: 5720 S. Woodlawn, Chicago, IL. 60637, U.S.A.

Crime, law and social change. *[Cr. Law Soc. Chan.] ISSN: 0925 4994. Kluwer Academic Publishers*: Spuiboulevard 50, P.O. Box 17, 3300 AA Dordrecht, The Netherlands

Criminal law review. *[Crim. Law Rev.] ISSN: 0011-135X. Sweet & Maxwell*: South Quay Plaza, 183 Marsh Wall, London E14 9FT, U.K.; **Subscriptions**: *idem*: Freepost, Andover, Hants, SP10 5BR, U.K.

Critica marxista. *[Crit. Marx.] ISSN: 0011-152X. Editori Riuniti Riviste*: via Serchio 9, 00198 Rome, Italy

Critica sociologica. *[Crit. Sociol.] ISSN: 0011 1546. S.I.A.R.E.S.*: Corso Vittorio Emanuele 24, 00186 Rome, Italy

Critical review. *[Crit. Rev.] ISSN: 0891-3811. Center for Independent Thought*: 942 Howard Street, Room 109, San Francisco, CA 94103, U.S.A.; **Publisher**: *Critical Review*: P.O. Box 14528, Chicago IL. 60614, U.S.A.

Critical sociology. *[Crit. Sociol.] ISSN: 0896- 9205. University of Oregon, Department of Sociology*: OR. 97403, U.S.A.

Crossroads. *[Crossroads] ISSN: 0741-2037. Northern Illinois University, Center for Southeast Asian Studies*: 140 Carroll Avenue, Northern Illinois University, DeKalb, IL. 60115, U.S.A.

Cuadernos americanos. *[Cuad. Am.] ISSN: 0185-156X. Universidad Nacional Autónoma de México*: Ciudad Universitaria, 04510 México, D.F., Apartado Postal 965, México 1.

Cuadernos de nuestra América. *[Cuad. Nues. Am.]*; *Centro de Estudios Sobre America*: Ave. 3ra no. 1805e/ 18 y 20, Playa Zona Postal 13, Havana, Cuba

Cultural anthropology. *[Cult. Anthro.] ISSN: 0886-7356. Society for Cultural Anthropology*; **Publisher**: *American Anthropological Association*: 1703 New Hampshire Avenue, N.W., Washington DC. 20009, U.S.A.

Cultural studies. *[Cult. St.] ISSN: 0950-2386. Routledge*: 11 New Fetter Lane, London, EC4P 4EE, U.K.; **Subscriptions**: *Routledge*: Cheriton House, North Way, Andover, Hants SP10 5BE, U.K.

Culture et société. *[Cult. Soc.]*; *Ministère de la Jeunesse des Sports et de la Culture, Centre de Civilisation Burundaise*: B.P. 1095, Bujumbura, Burundi

Culture, medicine and psychiatry. *[Cult. Medic. Psych.] ISSN: 0165-005X. Kluwer Academic Publishers*: P.O. Box 322, 3300 AH Dordrecht, The Netherlands

Current history. *[Curr. Hist.] ISSN: 0011-3530. Current History*: Publications Office, 4225 Main Street, Philadelphia, PA. 19127, U.S.A.

Current sociology. *[Curr. Sociol.] ISSN: 0011-3921. International Sociological Association*; **Publisher**: *Sage Publications*: 6 Bonhill Street, London EC2A 4PU, U.K.

Curriculum journal. *[Curric. J.] ISSN: 0958-5176. Routledge*: 11 New Fetter Lane, London, EC4P 4EE, U.K.; **Subscriptions**: *Routledge*: Cheriton House, North Way, Andover, Hants SP10 5BE, U.K.

INTERNATIONAL BIBLIOGRAPHY OF SOCIOLOGY — 1991

Cyprus review. *[Cyprus Rev.]* ISSN: 1015-2881. Intercollege/ University of Indianapolis: P.O. Box 4005, 17 Heroes Avenue, Ayios Andreas, Nicosia, Cyprus/ 1400 Hanna Avenue, Indianapolis, IN. 46227-3687, U.S.A.

Dædalus. *[Dædalus]* ISSN: 0011-5266. American Academy of Arts and Sciences: 136 Irving Street, Cambridge, MA. 02138, U.S.A.; **Subscriptions**: Dædalus Business Office: P.O. Box 515, Canton, MA. 02021, U.S.A.

Demográfia. *[Demográfia]* ISSN: 0011-8249. Magyar Tudomanyos Akademia, Demografiai Bizottsag; **Publisher**: Statisztikai Kiado Vallalat: Kaszasdulo u. 2, P.O. Box 99, 1300 Budapest 3, Hungary; **Subscriptions**: Kultura: Box 149, H-1389 Budapest 3, Hungary

Demografie. *[Demografie]* ISSN: 0011-8265. Federální Statistický Úřad; **Publisher**: Panorama: Hálkova 1, 120 72 Prague 2, Czechoslovakia

Demography. *[Demography]* ISSN: 0070-3370. Population Association of America: 1722 N. Street, N.W., Washington, DC. 20036, U.S.A.

Derechos humanos. *[Der. Human.]* ISSN: 0327-1846. Asamblea Permanente por los Derechos Humanos: Avenida Callao 569, Piso 1°, oficina 15, 1022 Buenos Aires, Argentina

Desarrollo económico. *[Desar. Econ.]* ISSN: 0046-001X. Instituto de Desarrollo Económico y Social: Aráoz 2838, 1425 Buenos Aires, Argentina

Deutschland Archiv.:Zeitschrift für das vereinigte Deutschland *[Deut. Arch.]* ISSN: 0012-1428. Verlag Wissenschaft und Politik: Salierring 14-16, 5000 Cologne, Germany

Developing economies. *[Develop. Eco.]* ISSN: 0012-1533. Institute of Developing Economies: 42 Ichigaya-Hommura-chō, Shinjuku-ku, Tokyo 162, Japan; **Subscriptions**: Maruzen: P.O. Box 5050, Tokyo 100-31, Japan

Development. *[Development]* ISSN: 1011-6370. Society for International Development: Palazzo della Civiltà del Lavoro, Rome 00144, Italy

Development & socio-economic progress. *[Devel. & Socio-eco. Pro.]*; Afro-Asian Peoples' Solidarity Organisation (AAPSO): 89 Abdel Aziz Al-Saoud Street, 11451- 61 Manial El-Roda, Cairo, Egypt

Development and change. *[Develop. Cha.]* ISSN: 0012-155X. Sage Publications: 6 Bonhill Street, London EC2A 4PU, U.K.

Development Southern Africa. *[Develop. S. Afr.]* ISSN: 0376-835X. Development Bank of Southern Africa: P.O. Box 1234, Halfway House, 1685 South Africa

Diachronica. *[Diachronica]* ISSN: 0176-4225. John Benjamins Publishing: Amsteldijk 44, P.O. Box 52519, NL-1007 HA Amsterdam, The Netherlands

Dirasat.:Series A — the humanities *[Dirasat Ser. A.]* ISSN: 0255-8033. Deanship of Academic Research: University of Jordan, Amman, Jordan

Disasters.:Journal of disaster studies and management *[Disasters]* ISSN: 0361-3666. Basil Blackwell: 108 Cowley Road, Oxford OX4 1JF, U.K.

Dissent. *[Dissent]* ISSN: 0012-3846. Foundation for the Study of Independent Social Ideas: 521 Fifth Avenue, New York, NY. 10017, U.S.A.

Documents. *[Documents]* ISSN: 0151- 0827. Documents: 50 rue de Laborde, 75008 Paris, France; **Subscriptions**: *idem*: 21 rue du Faubourg-Saint-Antoine, 75011 Paris, France

Dreaming.*[Journal of the Association for the Study of Dreams]— [Dreaming]* ISSN: 1053-0797. Human Sciences Press: 233 Spring Street, New York, NY., 10013-1578, U.S.A.

Droit social. *[Droit Soc.]* ISSN: 0012-6438. Editions Techniques et Économiques: 3, rue Soufflot, 75005 Paris, France

E & S.:Economie et statistique *[E & S]* ISSN: 0336-1451. Institut national de la statistique et des études économiques: 18 boulevard A. Pinard, 75675 Paris Cedex 14, France

East European Jewish affairs. *[E.Eur. Jew. Aff.]* ISSN: 0038- 545X. Institute of Jewish Affairs: 11 Hertford Street, London, W1Y 7DX, United Kingdom

East European politics and societies. *[E.Eur. Pol. Soc.]* ISSN: 0888-3254. University of California: Berkeley, CA. 94720, U.S.A.

East European quarterly. *[E. Eur. Quart.]* ISSN: 0012-8449. University of Colorado: 1200 University Avenue, Boulder, CO. 80309, U.S.A.

Eastern Africa economic review. *[E. Afr. Econ. Rev.]* ISSN: 0012-866X. Kenyan Economic Association: Economics Department, University of Nairobi, P.O. Box 30197, Nairobi, Kenya

Eastern Africa social science research review. *[E.Afr. Soc. Sci. Res. R.]*; Organization for Social Science Research in Eastern Africa - OSSREA: P.O. Box 31971, Addis Ababa, Ethiopia

Eastern anthropologist. *[East. Anthrop.]* ISSN: 0012-8686. Ethnographic and Folk Culture Society: Post Box No. 209, 7-A, Ram Krishna Marg, Faizabad Road, Lucknow, India

Eastern Buddhist. *[East. Bud.]*; Eastern Buddhist Society: Otani University, Koyama, Kita-ku, Kyoto 603, Japan

INTERNATIONAL BIBLIOGRAPHY OF SOCIOLOGY — 1991

Ecological economics. *[Ecol. Eco.]* ISSN: 0921-8009. *International Society for Ecological Economics*; **Publisher**: *Elsevier Science Publishers*: P.O. Box 211, 1000 AE Amsterdam, The Netherlands

Economia & lavoro. *[Ec. Lav.]* ISSN: 0012-978X. *Fondazione Giacomo Brodolini*: via Torino 122, 00184 Rome, Italy; **Publisher**: *Marsilio Editori*: Marittima — Fabbricato 205, 30135, Venice, Italy

Economia [Lisbon]. *[Economia [Lisbon]]* ISSN: 0870-3531. *Universidade Católica Portuguesa, Faculdade de Ciências Económicas e Empresariais*: Caminho da Palma de Cima, 1600 Lisbon, Portugal

Economia y desarrollo. *[Econ. Desar.]* ISSN: 0252- 8584. *Universidad de la Habana, Facultad de Economia*: Calle O No.262 e/ 25 y 27, Vedado, Havana 4, Cuba

Economic and industrial democracy. *[Econ. Ind. Dem.]* ISSN: 0143-831X. *Arbetslivscentrum (The Swedish Center for Working Life)*: Box 5606, S-114 86 Stockholm, Sweden; **Publisher**: *Sage Publications*: 6 Bonhill Street, London EC2A 4PU, U.K.

Economic and social history in the Netherlands. *[Econ. Soc. Hist. Nether.]* ISSN: 0925-1669. *Nederlandsch Economisch-Historisch Archief = Netherlands Economic History Archive*: Cruquiusweg 31, 1019 AT Amsterdam, The Netherlands

Economic and social review. *[Econ. Soc. R.]* ISSN: 0012-9984. *Economic and Social Studies*: 4 Burlington Road, Dublin 4, Ireland

Economic development and cultural change. *[Econ. Dev. Cult. Change]* ISSN: 0013 0079. *University of Chicago Press*: Journals Division, 5720 S. Woodlawn, Chicago, IL. 60637, U.S.A.

Economic development quarterly. *[Econ. Devel. Q.]* ISSN: 0891-2424. *Sage Publications*: 2455 Teller Road, Newbury Park, CA. 91320, U.S.A.

Economic geography. *[Econ. Geogr.]* ISSN: 0013-0095. *Clark University*: Worcester, MA. 01610, U.S.A.; **Publisher**: *Commonwealth Press*: 44 Portland Street, Worcester, MA., U.S.A.

Economic history review. *[Econ. Hist. R.]* ISSN: 0013-0117. *Economic History Society*: P.O. Box 190, 1 Greville Road, Cambridge CB1 3QG, U.K.; **Publisher**: *Basil Blackwell*: 108 Cowley Road, Oxford OX4 1JF, U.K.

Economic inquiry. *[Econ. Inq.]* ISSN: 0095-2583. *Western Economic Association International*: 7400 Center Avenue, Suite 109, Huntington Beach, CA. 92647-3039, U.S.A.; **Subscriptions**: *idem*: Subscription Services, P.O. Box 368, Lawrence, KS. 66044-0368, U.S.A.

Economic journal. *[Econ. J.]* ISSN: 0013-0133. *Royal Economic Society*: Imperial College of Science and Technology, London SW7 2AZ, U.K.; **Publisher**: *Basil Blackwell*: 108 Cowley Road, Oxford OX4 1JF, U.K.

Economica. *[Economica]* ISSN: 0013-0427. *London School of Economics and Political Science*: Houghton Street, London WC2A 2AE, U.K.; **Publisher**: *Basil Blackwell*: 108 Cowley Road, Oxford OX4 1JF, U.K.

Economics and philosophy. *[Econ. Philos.]* ISSN: 0266-2671. *Cambridge University Press*: 40 West 20th Street, New York, NY 10011, U.S.A.

Economie appliquée. *[Econ. App.]* ISSN: 0013-0494. *Institut de Sciences Mathematiques et Économiques Appliquées*: 11 rue Pierre et Marie Curie, 75005 Paris, France; **Publisher**: *Presses Universitaries de Grenoble*: B.P. 47 X, 38 040 Grenoble Cedex, France

Economie du centre-est. *[Econ. Cen.E.]* ISSN: 0153-4459. *Institut d'Economie Régionale Bourgogne-Franche-Comte*: 4 boulevard Gabriel, 21000 Dijon, France; **Publisher**: *Dijon Presses de l'Université de Bourgogne*

Economies et sociétés. *[Ec. Sociét.]* ISSN: 0013-0567. *I.S.M.E.A.*: 11, rue Pierre-et-Marie Curie, 75005 Paris, France; **Publisher**: *Presses Universitaires de Grenoble (PUG)*: B.P. 47 X, 38040 Grenoble Cedex, France

Economisch en sociaal tijdschrift. *[Econ. Soc. Tijd.]* ISSN: 0013-0575. *Universtaire Faculteiten Sint-Ignatius te Antwerpen*: Kipdorp 19, 2000 Antwerp, Belgium

Economist [Leiden]. *[Economist [Leiden]]* ISSN: 0013-063X. *Royal Netherlands Economic Association*; **Publisher**: *Stenfert Kroese Uitgevers*: P.O. Box 33, 2300 AA Leiden, The Netherlands

Economy and society. *[Econ. Soc.]* ISSN: 0308-5147. *Routledge*: 11 New Fetter Lane, London EC4P 4EE, U.K.

Education and urban society. *[Educ. Urban. Soc.]* ISSN: 0013- 1245. *Sage Publications*: 2455 Teller Road, Newbury Park, CA. 91320, U.S.A.

Educational research. *[Educat. Res.]* ISSN: 0013- 1881. *National Foundation for Educational Research*: The Mere, Upton Park, Slough, Berkshire SL1 2DQ, U.K.; **Publisher**: *Routledge*: 11 New Fetter Lane, London, EC4P 4EE, U.K.

Ekistics. *[Ekistics]* ISSN: 0013-2942. *Athens Technological Organization, Athens Center of Ekistics*: 24 Strat. Syndesmou St., 10673 Athens, Greece; **Subscriptions**: *idem*: P.O. Box 3471, 10210 Athens, Greece

Ekonomisk debatt. *[Ekon. Deb.]* ISSN: 0345-2646. *Nationalekonomiska föreningen*: Box 16408, 10327 Stockholm, Sweden

Ekonomski pregled. *[Ekon. Preg.]* ISSN: 0424-7558. *Savez Ekonimista Hrvatske*: Berislaviceva 6, Zagreb, Yugoslavia

Electoral studies. *[Elec. Stud.]* ISSN: 0261- 3794. *Butterworth-Heinemann*: Linacre House, Jordan Hill, Oxford OX2 8DP, U.K.

Employee relations. [*Employ. Relat.*] *ISSN: 0142-5455*. *MCB University Press*: 62 Toller Lane, Bradford, West Yorkshire, BD8 9BY, U.K.

English world-wide. [*Eng. Wor.-wide*] *ISSN: 0172-8865*. *John Benjamins Publishing*: P.O. Box 75577, Amstedldijk 44, 1007 AN Amsterdam, The Netherlands

Environment and behavior. [*Envir. Behav.*] *ISSN: 0013-9165*. *Environmental Design Research Association*; **Publisher**: *Sage Publications*: 2455 Teller Road, Newbury Park CA. 91320, U.S.A.

Environment and planning A.:*International journal of urban and regional research* [*Envir. Plan.A.*] *ISSN: 0308-518X*. *Pion*: 207 Brondesbury Park, London NW2 5JN, U.K.

Environment and planning B.:*Planning and design* [*Envir. Plan. B.*] *ISSN: 0265-8135*. *Pion*: 207 Brondesbury Park, London NW2 5JN, U.K.

Environment and planning C.:*Government and policy* [*Envir. Plan. C.*] *ISSN: 0263 774X*. *Pion*: 207 Brondesbury Park, London NW2 5JN, U.K.

Environment and planning D.:*Society and space* [*Envir. Plan. D*] *ISSN: 0263-7758*. *Pion*: 207 Brondesbury Park, London, NW2 5JN, U.K

Environment and urbanization. [*Environ. Urban.*] *ISSN: 0956-2478*. *International Insitute for Environment and Development*: 3 Endsleigh Street, London, WC1H 0DD, U.K.

Espace géographique. [*Espace Géogr.*] *ISSN: 0046- 2497*. *Doin editeurs*: 8 place de l'Odéon, 75006 Paris, France

Espace populations sociétés. [*Espace Pop. Soc.*] *ISSN: 0755-7809*. *Université des Sciences et Techniques de Lille-Flandres-Artois*: 59655 Villeneuve d'Ascq Cedex, France

Esprit. [*Esprit*] *ISSN: 0014-0759*. *Esprit*: 212 rue Saint-Martin, 75003 Paris, France

Estudios de Asia y Africa. [*Est. Asia Afr.*] *ISSN: 0185-0164*. *El Colegio de México*: Camino al Ajusco 20, Pedregal de Santa Teresa, 10740 México D.F., México

Estudios demográficos y urbanos. [*Est. Demog. Urb.*] *ISSN: 0186-7210*. *Colégio de México, Centro de Estudios Demográficos y de Desarrollo Urbano*: Departamento de Publicaciones, Camino al Ajusco 20, 10740 México D.F., México

Estudios internacionales. [*Est. Inter.*] *ISSN: 0716-0240*. *Universidad de Chile, Instituto de Estudios Internacionales*: Condell 249, Casilla 14187 Suc 21, Santiago 9, Chile

Estudios sociológicos. [*Est. Sociol.*] *ISSN: 0185-4186*. *Colegio de México*: Camino al Ajusco 20, Pedregal de Santa Teresa, 10740 Mexico, D.F., Mexico

Estudos jurídicos. [*Est. Juríd.*] *ISSN: 0100-2538*. *Universidade do Vale do Rio dos Sinos*: 93.000 São Leopoldo RS, Brazil

Estudos leopoldenses. [*Est. Leop.*] *ISSN: 0014-1607*. *Universidade do Vale do Rio dos Sinos*: 93.000 São Leopoldo RS, Brazil

Ethics. [*Ethics*] *ISSN: 0014-1704*. *University of Chicago Press*: Journals Division, 5720 S. Woodlawn Avenue, Chicago, IL. 60637, U.S.A.

Ethnic and racial studies. [*Ethn. Racial*] *ISSN: 0141-9870*. *Routledge*: 11 New Fetter Lane, London EC4P 4EE, U.K.; **Subscriptions**: *Routledge Journals*: Cheriton House, North Way, Andover, Hants. SP10 5BE, U.K.

Ethnic groups. [*Eth. Groups*] *ISSN: 0308-6860*. *Gordon and Breach Science Publishers*: 270 8th Avenue, New York, NY. 10011, U.S.A.

Ethnic studies report. [*Ethnic St. Rep.*] *ISSN: 1010-5832*. *International Centre for Ethnic Studies*: 554/1 Peradeniya Rpad, Kandy, Sri Lanka

Ethnologica Helvetica. [*Ethnol. Helvet.*]; *Schweizerische Ethnologische Gesellschaft = Société Suisse d'Ethnologie = Swiss Ethnological Society*: c/o Institut für Ethnologie, Schwanengasse 7, CH-3011 Bern, Switzerland; **Subscriptions**: *Dietrich Reimer Verlag*: Unter den Eichen 57, D-1000 Berlin 45, Germany

Ethnologie française. [*Ethn. Fr.*] *ISSN: 0046-2616*. *Armand Colin*: 103 boulevard Saint-Michel, 75420 Paris Cedex 05, France

Ethology & sociobiology. [*Ethol. Socio.*] *ISSN: 0162-3095*. *Elsevier Science Publishing (New York)*: 655 Avenue of the Americas, New York, NY. 10010, U.S.A.

Etnografija juznih Slavena u Madarskoj. [*Etnogr. Juz. Slav. Mad*]

Etudes canadiennes; Canadian studies. [*Etud. Can.*] *ISSN: 0153-1700*. *Association Française d'Études Canadiennes*: Maison des Sciences de l'Homme d'Aquitaine, Domaine Universitaire, 33405 Talence, France

Etudes rurales. [*Rural Stud.*] *ISSN: 0014-2182*. *Laboratoire d'Anthropologie Sociale*: Collège de France, 52 rue du Cardinal Lemoine, 75005 Paris, France; **Publisher**: *Editions de l'Ecole des Hautes Etudes en Sciences Sociales*: 131 boulevard Saint-Michel, 75005 Paris, France; **Subscriptions**: *Centrale des Revue*: 11 rue Gossin, 92543 Montrouge Cedex, France

Etudes rwandaises.:*Série lettres et sciences humaines* [*Ét. Rwand.*]; *Éditions de l'Université Nationale du Rwanda*: B.P. 56 Butare, Rwanda

Études sociales. [*Étud. Soc.*]; *Société d'Économie et de Science Sociales*: 80 rue Vaneau, 75007 Paris, France

Eure.:*Revista latinoamericana de estudios urbanos regionales* [*Eure*] ISSN: 0250-7161. *Pontificia Universidad Catolica de Chile, Facultad de Arquitectura y Bellas Artes, Instituto de Estudios Urbanos*: Los Navegantes 1919, Casilla 16.002, Correo 9, Santiago, Chile

Europa ethnica. [*Eur. Ethn.*] ISSN: 0014-2492. *Wilhelm Braumüller*: A-1092 Vienna, Servitengasse 5, Austria

European journal of operational research. [*Eur. J. Oper. Res.*] ISSN: 0377-2217. *Association of European Operational Research Societies*; **Publisher**: *Elsevier Science Publishers (North-Holland)*: P.O. Box 1991, 1000 BZ Amsterdam, The Netherlands

European journal of political economy. [*Eur. J. Pol. Ec.*] ISSN: 0176-2680. *Elsevier Science Publishers (North-Holland)*: P.O. Box 1991, 1000 BZ Amsterdam, The Netherlands

European journal of political research. [*Eur. J. Pol. R.*] ISSN: 0304-4130. *European Consortium for Political Research*: University of Essex, Wivenhoe Park, Colchester CO4 3SQ, U.K.; **Publisher**: *Kluwer Academic Publishers*: Spuiboulevard 50, P.O. Box 17, 3300 AA Dordrecht, The Netherlands; **Subscriptions**: *idem*: P.O. Box 322, 3300 AH Dordrecht, The Netherlands

European journal of population; Revue européenne de démographie. [*Eur. J. Pop.*] ISSN: 0168-6577. *Elsevier Science Publishers (North Holland)*: P.O. Box 1991, 1000 BZ Amsterdam, The Netherlands

European journal of social psychology. [*Eur. J. Soc. Psychol.*] ISSN: 0046-2772. *European Association of Experimental Social Psychology*; **Publisher**: *John Wiley & Sons*: Baffins Lane, Chichester, West Sussex PO19 1UD, U.K.

European review of Latin American and Caribbean studies; Revista europea de estudios latinoamericanos y del caribe. [*R. Eur. Lat.am. Caribe*] ISSN: 0924-0608. *CEDLA, Interuniversitair Centrum voor Studie en Documentatie van Latijns Amerika/ RILA, Royal Institute of Linguistics and Anthropology*: Keizersgracht 395-397, 1016 Amsterdam, The Netherlands; **Publisher**: *CEDLA Edita*: Keizersgracht 395-397, 1016 Amsterdam, The Netherlands

European sociological review. [*Eur. Sociol. R.*] ISSN: 0266-7215. *Oxford University Press*: Pinkhill House, Southfield Road, Eynsham, Oxford OX8 1JJ, U.K.

Europe-Asia studies. [*Eur.-Asia Stud.*] ISSN: 0038- 5859. *Carfax Publishing*: P.O. Box 25, Abingdon, Oxfordshire OX14 3UE, U.K.

Evaluation review. [*Eval. Rev.*] ISSN: 0193-841X. *Sage Publications*: 2455 Teller Road, Newbury Park, CA. 91320, U.S.A.

Families in society. [*Fam. Soc.*] ISSN: 1044-3894. *Family Service America*: 11700 West Lake Park Drive, Milwaukee, WI. 53224, U.S.A.; **Subscriptions**: *Families in Society*: Subscription Department, P.O. Box 6649, Syracuse, NY. 13217, U.S.A.

Federalist. [*Federalist*] ISSN: 0393-1358. *Fondazione Europea Luciano Bolis*; **Publisher**: *EDIF*: Via Porta Pertusi 6, 27100 Pavia, Italy

Feminist review. [*Feminist R.*] ISSN: 0141-7789. *Feminist Review*: 11 Carleton Gardens, Brecknock Road, London N19 5AQ, U.K.; **Publisher**: *Routledge*: 11 New Fetter Lane, London EC4P 4EE, U.K.

Folia linguistica. [*Folia Ling.*] ISSN: 0165-4004. *Societas Linguistica Europaea*: Olshausenstraße 40-60, DW 2300 Kiel, Germany; **Publisher**: *Mouton de Gruyter*: Postfach 110240, 1000 Berlin 11, Germany

Folia linguistica historica. [*Folia Ling. Hist.*]; *Societas Linguistica Europaea*; **Publisher**: *Mouton de Gruyter*: Postfach 110240, D-1000 Berlin 11, Germany

Food and foodways. [*Food Food.*] ISSN: 0740-9710. *Harwood Academic Publishers*: 270 Eighth Avenue, New York, NY.10011, U.S.A.; **Subscriptions**: *idem*: c/o STBS Limited, P.O. Box 90, Reading, Berks, RG1 8JL, U.K.

Formation emploi. [*Form. Emp.*] ISSN: 0759-6340. *Documentation Française*: 29-31 quai Voltaire, 75340 Paris Cedex 07, France; **Subscriptions**: *La Documentation Française*: 124 rue Henri Barbusse, 93308 Aubervilliers Cedex, France

Foro internacional. [*Foro Int.*] ISSN: 0185-013X. *El Colegio de México*: Departamento de Publicaciones, Camino al Ajusco 20, Pedregal de Santa Teresa, 10740 México D.F., Mexico

Forschungsjournal Neue Soziale Bewegungen. [*Fors.Jour. Soz. Beweg.*] ISSN: 0933-9361. *Forschungsgruppe Neue Soziale Bewegungen*; **Publisher**: *Schüren Presseverlag*: Deutschhausstr. 31, 3550 Marburg, Germany

Forum. [*Forum*]

Free associations. [*Free Assoc.*] ISSN: 0267-0887. *Free Association Books*: 26 Freegrove Road, London N7 9RQ, U.K.

Free China review. [*Free China R.*] ISSN: 0016- 030X. *Kwang Hwa Publishing*: 2 Tientsin Street, Taipei, Taiwan

Gendaishakaigaku kenkyu. [*Gend.shak. Kenk.*]

Gender and history. [*Gend. Hist.*] ISSN: 9053-5233. *Basil Blackwell*: 108 Cowley Road, Oxford OX4 1JF, U.K.; **Subscriptions**: *Marston Book Services*: P.O. Box 87, Oxford OX2 0DT, U.K.

Gender and society. [*Gender Soc.*] ISSN: 0891-2432. *Sociologists for Women in Society*; **Publisher**: *Sage Publications*: 2455 Teller Road, Newbury Park, CA. 91320, U.S.A.

Genèses. [*Genèses*] ISSN: 1135-3219. *Calman-Lévy*: 16, villa Saint- Jacques, 75014 Paris, France

INTERNATIONAL BIBLIOGRAPHY OF SOCIOLOGY — 1991

Genève-Afrique. *[Genève-Afrique] ISSN: 0016-6774. Institut Universitaire d'Études du Développement (IUED)*: Case postale 136, CH-1211 Geneva 21, Switzerland

Genus. *[Genus] ISSN: 0016-6987. Comitato Italiano per lo Studio dei Problemi della Popolazione*: Via Nomentana 41, 00161 Rome, Italy; **Subscriptions**: *Edizioni Scientifiche Inglesi Americane*: Via Palestro 30, 00185 Rome, Italy

Geoforum. *[Geoforum] ISSN: 0016-7185. Pergamon Press*: Headington Hill Hall, Oxford OX3 0BW, U.K.

Geografiska annaler.:*Series B — Human geography [Geog.ann. B.] ISSN: 0435-3676. Svenska Sällskapet för Antropologi och Geografi = Swedish Society for Anthropology and Geography*: University of Uppsala, Department of Physical Geography, Box 554, S-751 22 Uppsala, Sweden; **Subscriptions**: *Universitetsforlaget*: P.O. Box 2959, Tøyen, N-0608 Oslo 6, Norway

Geographia polonica. *[Geogr. Pol.] ISSN: 0016-7282. Polish Academy of Sciences, Institute of Geography and Spatial Organization*; **Publisher**: *Polish Scientific Publishers*: Krakowskie Przedmieście 7, 00-068 Warsaw, Poland

Geographical analysis. *[Geogr. Anal.] ISSN: 0016-7363. Ohio State University Press*: 1070 Carmack Road, Columbus, OH. 43210, U.S.A.

Geographical journal. *[Geogr. J.] ISSN: 0016-7398. Royal Geographical Society*: 1 Kensington Gore, London SW7 2AR, U.K.

Geographical review. *[Geogr. Rev.] ISSN: 0016-7428. American Geographical Society*: Suite 600, 156 Fifth Avenue, New York, N.Y. 10010, U.S.A.

Geographical review of India. *[Geogr. Rev. Ind.] ISSN: 0375-6386. Geographical Society of India*: Department of Geography, University of Calcutta, 35 Ballygunge Circular Road, Calcutta 700 019, India

Geographical review of Japan. *[Geogr. Rev. Jpn.] ISSN: 0016 7444. Association of Japanese Geographers*: Japan Academic Societies Center, 2-4-16 Yayoi, Bunkyo-ku, Tokyo 113, Japan

Geographische Rundschau. *[Geogr. Rund.] ISSN: 0016-7460. Westermann Schulbuchverlag*: Georg-Westermann-Allee 66, 3300 Braunschweig, Germany

Geography. *[Geography]; Geographical Association*: 343 Fulwood Road, Sheffield S10 3PB, U.K.

Geography research forum. *[Geogr. Res. For.] ISSN: 0333-5275. Ben-Gurion University of the Negev, Department of Geography*: Beer-Sheeva 84105, Israel

Geschichte und Gesellschaft. *[Gesch. Ges.] ISSN: 0340-613X. Vandenhoeck und Ruprecht*: Postfach 3753, D-3400 Göttingen, Germany

Gestion 2000.:*Management et prospective [Gestion] ISSN: 0773-0543. Université Catholique de Louvain, Institut d'administration et de gestion*: 16 avenue de l'Espinette, B-1348 Louvain-la- Neuve, Belgium

Gewerkschaftliche Monatshefte. *[Gewerk. Monat.] ISSN: 0016-9447. Bundesvorstand des DGB*: Hans-Böckler-Straße 39, 4000 Düsseldorf 30, Germany; **Publisher**: *Bund-Verlag*: Postfach 900840, 5000 Cologne 90, Germany

Göteborg studies in educational sciences. *[Göt. Stud. Ed. Sci.] ISSN: 0436-1121. Acta Universitatis Gothoburgensis*: Box 5096, S-402 22 Göteborg, Sweden

Government and opposition. *[Govt. Oppos.] ISSN: 0017-257X. Government and Opposition*: Houghton Street, London WC2A 2AE, U.K.

Group decision and negotiation. *[Group Decis. Negot.] ISSN: 0926-2644. Kluwer Academic Publishers*: P.O. Box 17, 3300 AA Dordrecht, The Netherlands

Groupwork. *[Groupwork] ISSN: 0951-824X. Whiting & Birch*: P.O. Box 872, Forest Hill, London SE23 3HL, U.K.

Hamburger Jahrbuch für Wirtschafts- und Gesellschaftspolitik. *[Ham. Jahrb. Wirt- Ges.pol.]; HWWA- Institut für Wirtschaftsforschung*; **Publisher**: *J.C.B. Mohr (Paul Siebeck)*: Postfach 2040, D-7400 Tubingen, Germany

Hanzai shakaigaku kenkyu. *[Han. Shak. Kenk.]*

Harvard business review. *[Harv. Bus. Re.] ISSN: 0017-8012. Harvard Business Review*: Harvard Business School, Publishing Division, Boston, MA 02163, U.S.A.; **Subscriptions**: *idem*: Subscriber Service, P.O. Box 52623, Boulder, CO 80322-2623, U.S.A.

Harvard law review. *[Harv. Law. Rev.] ISSN: 0017-811X. Harvard Law Review Association*: Gannett House, 1511 Massachusetts Avenue, Cambridge, MA. 02138, U.S.A.

Health policy and planning. *[Health Pol. Plan.] ISSN: 0268-1080. London School of Hygiene and Tropical Medicine*: Keppel (Gower) Street, London WC1E 7HT, U.K.; **Publisher**: *Oxford University Press*: Pinkhill House, Southfield Road, Eynsham, Oxford, OX8 1JJ, U.K.

Hemispheres. *[Hemispheres] ISSN: 0239-8818. Polish Academy of Sciences, Centre for Studies on non-European Countries*: Rynek 9, 50-106 Wroclaw, Poland

Heritage of Zimbabwe. *[Herit. Zimb.] ISSN: 0556-9605. History Society of Zimbabwe*: P.O. Box 8268, Causeway, Harare, Zimbabwe

Hessische Blätter für Volks- und Kulturforschung. *[Hess. Blät. Volk.Kultur.] ISSN: 1075-3479. Jonas Verlag für Kunst und Literatur*: Weidenhäuser Straße 88, D-3550 Marburg 1, Germany

High technology law journal. [*High Tech. Law J.*] *ISSN: 0885-2715. University of California Press*: 2120 Berkeley Way, Berkeley, CA. 94720, U.S.A.

Higher Education. [*High. Educ.*] *ISSN: 0018-1560. Kluwer Academic Publishers*: P.O. Box 17, 3300 AA Dordrecht, The Netherlands

Himal. [*Himal*] *ISSN: 1012-9804. Himal Associates*: P.O. Box 42, Lalitpur, Nepal

Hispanic American historical review.*[HAHR]*— [*Hisp. Am. Hist. Rev.*] *ISSN: 0018-2168. American Historical Association, Conference on Latin American History*; **Publisher**: *Duke University Press*: Box 6697 College Station, Durham, NC. 27708, U.S.A.

Historical journal. [*Hist. J.*] *ISSN: 0018-246X. Cambridge University Press*: The Edinburgh Building, Shaftesbury Road, Cambridge CB2 2RU, U.K.

Historical social research; Historische Sozialforschung. [*Hist. Soc. R.*] *ISSN: 0172-6404. Arbeitsgemeinschaft für Quantifizierung und Methoden in der historisch sozialwissenschaftlichen Forschung/ International Commission for the Application of Quantitative Methods in History/ Association for History and Computing*: Bachemerstr. 40, D-5000 Cologne 41, Germany/ University of London, Westfield College, Department of History, Kidderpore Avenue, London NW3 7ST, U.K.; **Publisher**: *Zentrum für Historische Sozialforschung*: Zentralarchiv für Empirische Sozialforschung, Universität zu Köln, Bachemerstr. 40, D-5000 Cologne, Germany

Historical studies. [*Hist. S.*] *ISSN: 0018-2559. University of Melbourne*; Parkville, Victoria 3052, Australia

History and technology. [*Hist. Technol.*] *ISSN: 0734-1512. Harwood Academic Publishers*: P.O. Box 90, Reading, Berkshire RG1 8JL, U.K.

History and theory. [*Hist. Theory*] *ISSN: 0018-2656. Wesleyan University*: 287 High Street, Middletown, CT. 06457, U.S.A.

History of political economy. [*Hist. Polit. Ec.*] *ISSN: 0018-2702. Duke University Press*: Crowell Hall, East Campus, Duke University, Durham, NC. 27708, U.S.A.; **Subscriptions**: *Duke University Press*: Box 6697 College Station, Durham, NC 27708, U.S.A.

History of political thought. [*Hist. Polit. Thou.*] *ISSN: 0143-781X. Imprint Academic*: 32 Haldon Road, Exeter, Devon, EX4 4DZ, U.K.

History of religions. [*Hist. Relig.*] *ISSN: 0018-2710. University of Chicago Press*: 5720 S. Woodlawn, Chicago, IL. 60637, U.S.A.

History of the human sciences. [*Hist. Human Sci.*] *ISSN: 0952-6951. Routledge*: 11 New Fetter Lane, London EC4P 4EE, U.K.

Hitotsubashi journal of social studies. [*Hito. J. Soc. Stud.*] *ISSN: 0073- 280X. Hitotsubashi University, Hitotsubashi Academy*: 2-1 Naka, Kunitachi, Tokyo 186, Japan

Hogaku kenyū. [*Hog. Ken*]; *Keio University*: Tokyo, Japan

Homines. [*Homines*] *ISSN: 0252-8908. Universidad Interamericana de Puerto Rico*: Recinto Metropolitano, División de Ciencias Sociales, Apartado 1293, Hato Rey 00919, Puerto Rico

Homme. [*Homme*] *ISSN: 0439-4216. Laboratoire d'anthropologie sociale*: Collège de France, 52 rue du Cardinal-Lemoine, 75005 Paris, France; **Publisher**: *Ecole des hautes études en science sociales*: 131 boulevard Saint-Michel, 75005 Paris, France

Homme et la société. [*Hom. Soc.*] *ISSN: 0018-4306. Centre National des Lettres/ Centre National de la Recherche Scientifique*; **Publisher**: *Editions l'Harmattan*: 5-7 rue de l'Ecole-Polytechnique, 75005 Paris, France

Hosogaku Kenkyu. [*Hosog. Kenk*]; *N.H .K*.: Tokyo, Japan

Housing policy debate. [*Hous. Pol. Deb.*] *ISSN: 1051-1482. Office of Housing Policy, Fannie Mae*: 3900 Wisconsin Avenue, NW Washington, DC 20016-2899, U.S.A.

Howard journal of criminal justice. [*Howard J. Crim. Just.*] *ISSN: 0265-5527. Howard League*: 708 Holloway Road, London N19 3NL, U.K.; **Publisher**: *Basil Blackwell*: 108 Cowley Road, Oxford OX4 1JF, U.K.

Human ethology newsletter. [*Human Eth. New.*] *ISSN: 0739-2036. International Society for Human Ethology*: Paedological Institute of the City of Amsterdam, Ijsbaanpad 9, 1076 CV Amsterdam, The Netherlands

Human nature. [*Hum. Nature*] *ISSN: 1045-6767. Aldine de Gruyter*: 200 Saw Mill River Road, Hawthorne, N.Y. 10532, U.S.A.

Human organization. [*Human. Org.*] *ISSN: 0018-7259. Society for Applied Anthropology*: 5205 E.Flowler Avenue, Suite 310, Temple Terrace, FL. 33617, U.S.A.

Human relations. [*Human Relat.*] *ISSN: 0018-7267. Plenum Press*: 233 Spring Street, New York, N.Y. 10013, U.S.A.

Human rights quarterly. [*Hum. Rights Q.*] *ISSN: 0275-0392. Johns Hopkins University Press*: Journals Publishing Division, 701 W. 40th Street, Suite 275, Baltimore, MD. 21211, U.S.A.

Human studies. [*Human St.*] *ISSN: 0163-8548. Kluwer Academic Publishers*: P.O. Box 322, 3300 AH Dordrecht, The Netherlands

Humor. *[Humor]* ISSN: 0933-1719. *Mouton de Gruyter*: Postfach 110240, D-1000 Berlin 11, Germany

IBLA. *[IBLA]* ISSN: 0018-862X. *Institut des Belles Lettres Arabes*: 12 rue Jamaâ El-Haoua, 1008 Tunis, Tunisia

ICSSR newsletter. *[ICSSR News.]* ISSN: 0018-9049. *Indian Council of Social Science Research*: 35 Ferozeshah Road, New Delhi-110 001, India

IDS bulletin. *[IDS Bull.]* ISSN: 0265-5012. *Institute of Development Studies*: University of Sussex, Brighton BN1 9RE, U.K.

Ilmu alam. *[Il. Alam]* ISSN: 0126-7000. *Universiti Kebangsaan Malaysia, Geography Department*: 43600 UKM Bangi, Selangor D.E., Malaysia; **Publisher**: *Universiti Kebangsaan Malaysia Press*: 43600 UKM Bang, Selangor D.E., Malaysia

Immigrants and minorities. *[Imm. Minor.]* ISSN: 0261-9288. *Frank Cass*: Gainsborough House, 11 Gainsborough Road, London E11 1RS, U.K.

Impact of science on society. *[Impact Sci.]* ISSN: 0019-2872. *UNESCO*: 7 place de Fontenoy, 75700 Paris, France; **Subscriptions**: *Taylor and Francis*: Rankine Road, Basingstoke, Hampshire RG24 0PR, U.K.

Index on censorship. *[Index Censor.]* ISSN: 0306-4220. *Writers and Scholars International*: 39c Highbury Place, London N5 1QP, U.K.

Indian economic and social history review. *[Indian Ec. Soc. His. R.]* ISSN: 0019- 4646. *Indian Economic and Social History Association*; **Publisher**: *Sage Publications*: 32 M- Block Market, Greater Kailash-I, New Delhi 110 048, India

Indian geographical journal. *[Ind. Geograph. J.]* ISSN: 0019-4824. *Indian Geographical Society*: c/o The editor, Indian Geographical Journal, Department of Geography, University of Madras, Madras 600 005, India

Indian journal of agricultural economics. *[Ind. J. Agri. Eco.]* ISSN: 0019-5014. *Indian Society of Agricultural Economics*: 46-48 Esplanade Mansions, Mahatma Gandhi Road, Fort, Bombay 400 001, India

Indian journal of industrial relations. *[Ind. J. Ind. Rel.]* ISSN: 0019-5286. *Shri Ram Centre for Industrial Relations and Human Resources*: 4E/16 Jhandewalan Extension, New Delhi- 110015, India

Indian journal of labour economics. *[Ind. J. Lab. Econ.]*; *Indian Society of Labour Economics*; **Publisher**: *Dr. R.C. Singh*: Department of Labour and Social Welfare, Patna University, Patna 800005, India

Indian journal of public administration. *[Indian J. Publ. Admin.]* ISSN: 0019-5561. *Indian Institute of Public Administration*: Indraprastha Estate, Ring Road East, New Delhi 110002, India

Indian journal of regional science. *[Ind. J. Reg. Sci.]* ISSN: 0046-9017. *Indian Institute of Technology, Regional Science Association*: Department of Architecture and Regional Planning, Kharagpur, West Bengal, India

Indian journal of social science. *[Ind. J. Soc. Sci.]*; *Indian Council of Social Science Research*; **Publisher**: *Sage Publications India*: 32 M-Block Market, Greater Kailash I, New Delhi 110 048, India

Indian journal of social work. *[Indian J. Soc. W.]* ISSN: 0019-5634. *Tata Institute of Social Sciences*: Deonar, Bombay 400 088, India

Indian labour journal. *[Indian. Lab. J.]* ISSN: 0019-5723. *Labour Bureau*: Cleremont Shimla - 171004, Uttar Pradesh, India; **Subscriptions**: *Controller of Publications*: Civil Lines, Delhi-110 054, India

Indo Asia. *[In. Asia]* ISSN: 0019-719X. *Burg-Verlag*: Untere Au 41, 7123 Sachsenheim- Hohenhaslach, Germany

Indogermanische Forschungen. *[Indoger. Fors.]* ISSN: 0019-7262. *Walter de Gruyter*: Postfach 110240, D-1000 Berlin 30, Germany

Indo-Iranian journal. *[Indo-Iran. J.]* ISSN: 0019-7246. *Kluwer Academic Publishers*: Spuiboulevard 50, P.O. Box 17, 3300 AA Dordrecht, The Netherlands; **Subscriptions**: *idem*: P.O. Box 322, 3300 AH Dordrecht, The Netherlands

Indonesia circle. *[Ind. Cir.]* ISSN: 0306-2848. *Indonesia Circle*: School of Oriental and African Studies, Thornhaugh Street, Russell Square, London WC1H 0XG, U.K.

Industria. *[Industria]*; *Società editrice il Mulino*: Strada Maggiore 37, 40125 Bologna, Italy

Industrial and labor relations review. *[Ind. Lab. Rel.]* ISSN: 0019-7939. *Cornell University, New York State School of Industrial and Labor Relations*: 207 ILR Research Building, Cornell University, Ithaca, New York 14851-0952, U.S.A.

Industrial archaeology review. *[Ind. Arch. Rev.]* ISSN: 0309- 0728. *Association for Industrial Archaeology*: The Wharfage, Ironbridge, Telford, Shropshire TF8 7AW, U.K.

Industrial crisis quarterly. *[Ind. Crisis Q.]* ISSN: 0921-8106. *Industrial Crisis Institute*: New York, U.S.A.; **Publisher**: *Elsevier Science Publishers (North-Holland)*: P.O. Box 1991, 1000 BZ Amsterdam, The Netherlands; **Subscriptions**: *idem*: Journal Department, Postbus 211, 1000 AE Amsterdam, The Netherlands

Industrial law journal. *[Ind. Law J.]* ISSN: 0395-9332. *Industrial Law Society*: 28 Boundary Road, Sidcup, Kent DA15 8ST, U.K.; **Publisher**: *Oxford University Press*: Pinkhill House, Southfield Road, Eynsham, Oxford OX8 1JJ, U.K.

Industrial relations. *[Ind. Relat.]* ISSN: 0019- 8676. *University of California, Berkeley, Institute of Industrial Relations*: Berkeley CA. 94720, U.S.A.; **Publisher**: *Basil Blackwell*: 108 Cowley Road, Oxford OX4 1JF, U.K.

Industrial relations journal. *[Ind. Relat. J.] ISSN: 0019-8692. Basil Blackwell*: 108 Cowley Road, Oxford OX4 1JF, U.K.

Industrial relations journal of South Africa. *[Ind. Rel. J. S.Afr.] ISSN: 0258-7181. University of Stellenbosch Business School*: P.O. Box 610, Bellville 7535, South Africa

Industry of free China. *[Ind. Free China] ISSN: 0019-946X. Council for Economic Planning and Development*: 9th Floor, 87 Nanking E. Road, Sec.2, Taipei, Taiwan

Informationen zur Raumentwicklung. *[Inf. Raum.] ISSN: 0303-2493. Bundesforschungsanstalt für Landeskunde und Raumordnung*: Am Michaelshof 8, Postfach 20 01 30, 5300 Bonn 2, Germany

Informations sociales. *[Inf. Soc.] ISSN: 0046-9459. Caisse Nationale des Allocations Familiales*: 23 rue Daviel, 75634 Paris Cedex 13, France

Inquiry. *[Inquiry] ISSN: 0020-174X. Universitetsforlaget (Norwegian University Press)*: P.O. Box 2959 Tøyen, N-0608 Oslo 6, Norway

Institut d'histoire du temps present bulletin. *[Inst. Hist. T. Pres.] ISSN: 0247-0101. Institut d'Histoire du Temps Present*: 44 rue de l'Amiral Mouchez, 75014 Paris, France

Interchange. *[Interchange] ISSN: 0826- 4805. Kluwer Academic Publishers*: P.O. Box 322, 3300 AH Dordrecht, The Netherlands

Intercultural communication studies. *[Intercult. Commun. St.] ISSN: 1057-7769. Institute for Cross-Cultural Research*: Box 418, Trinity University, 715 Stadium Drive, San Antonio, TX 78232, U.S.A.

Interfaces. *[Interfaces] ISSN: 0092-2102. Institute of Management Sciences and the Operations Research Society of America*: 290 Westminster Street, Providence, RI. 02903, U.S.A.

Internasjonal politikk. *[Int. Pol.] ISSN: 0020-577X. Norsk Utenrikspolitisk Institutt*: Postboks 8159 Dep., 0033 Oslo 1, Norway

International affairs [Moscow]. *[Int. Aff. Mos.] ISSN: 0130-9641. Progress Publishers*: 14 Gorokhovsky Pereulok, Moscow K-16, U.S.S.R.

International and comparative law quarterly. *[Int. Comp. L.] ISSN: 0020-5893. British Institute of International and Comparative Law*: 17 Russell Square, London WC1B 5DR, U.K.

International economic review. *[Int. Econ. R.] ISSN: 0020-6598. University of Pennsylvania, Department of Economics/Osaka University, Institute of Social and Economic Research Association*: 3718 Locust Walk, University of Pennsylvania, Philadelphia, PA. 19104-6297, U.S.A./ 6-1 Mihagaoka, Ibaraki, Osaka 567, Japan

International journal. *[Int. J.] ISSN: 0020-7020. Canadian Institute of International Affairs*: 15 Kings College Circle, Toronto, Ontario, Canada M5S 2V9

International journal for philosophy of religion. *[Int. J. Philos. Relig.] ISSN: 0020- 7047. Kluwer Academic Publishers*: P.O. Box 322, 3300 AH Dordrecht, The Netherlands

International journal for the advancement of counselling. *[Int. J. Advance. Counsel.] ISSN: 0165- 0653. Kluwer Academic Publishers*: P.O. Box 322, 3300 AH Dordrecht, The Netherlands

International journal of American linguistics. *[Int. J. Am. Ling.] ISSN: 0020-7071. University of Chicago Press*: 5720 S Woodlawn Avenue, Chicago, IL. 60637, U.S.A.

International journal of comparative sociology. *[Int. J. Comp. Soc] ISSN: 0020-7152. E.J. Brill*: P.O. Box 9000, 2300 PA Leiden, The Netherlands

International journal of conflict management. *[Int. J. Confl. Manag.] ISSN: 1044-4068. 3-R Executive Systems*: 3109 Copperfield Court, Bowling Green, KY. 42104, U.S.A.

International journal of health services. *[Int. J. Health. Ser.] ISSN: 0020-7314. Baywood Publishing*: 26 Austin Avenue, P.O. Box 337, Amityville, NY. 11701, U.S.A.

International journal of human resource management. *[Int. J. Hum. Res. Man.] ISSN: 0958-5192. Routledge*: 11 New Fetter Lane, London EC4P 4EE, U.K.; **Subscriptions**: *idem*: Subscriptions Department, Cheriton House, North Way, Andover, Hants SP10 5BE, U.K.

International journal of industrial organization. *[Int. J. Ind. O.] ISSN: 0167-7187. Elsevier Science Publishers (North-Holland)*: P.O. Box 1991, 1000 BZ Amsterdam, The Netherlands; **Subscriptions**: *idem*: Journal Department, P.O. Box 211, 1000 AE Amsterdam, The Netherlands

International journal of law and the family. *[Int. J. Law Fam.] ISSN: 0950- 4109. Oxford University Press*: Pinkhill House, Southfield Road, Eynsham, Oxford OX8 1JJ, U.K.

International journal of Middle East studies. *[Int. J. M.E. Stud.] ISSN: 0020-7438. Middle East Studies Association of North America*: University of Arizona, 1232 North Cherry, Tuscon, AZ. 85721, U.S.A.; **Publisher**: *Cambridge University Press*: 40 West Street 20th, New York, NY. 10011, U.S.A.

International journal of moral and social studies. *[Int. J. Moral Soc. S.] ISSN: 0267-9655. Journals*: 1 Harewood Row, London NW1 6SE, U.K.

International journal of offender therapy and comparative criminology. *[Int. J. Offen.]* ISSN: 0306-624X. *Guilford Press*: 72 Spring Street, New York, NY. 10012, U.S.A.

International journal of organization analysis. *[Intern. J. Organiz. Anal.]* ISSN: 1055-3185. *3-R Executive Systems*: 3109 Copperfield Court, Bowling Green, KY., 42104, U.S.A.

International journal of politics, culture and society. *[Int. J. Pol. C. S.]* ISSN: 0891-4486. *Human Sciences Press*: 233 Spring Street, New York, NY. 10013-1578, U.S.A.

International journal of psycho-analysis. *[Int. J.Psy.]* ISSN: 0020-7578. *Institute of Psychoanalysis*: 63 New Cavendish Street, London W1M 7RD, U.K.; **Publisher**: *Routledge*: 11 New Fetter Lane, London, EC4P 4EE, U.K.; **Subscriptions**: *Routledge*: Cheriton House, North Way, Andover, Hants SP10 5BE, U.K.

International journal of social economics. *[Int. J. Soc. E.]* ISSN: 0306-8293. *MCB University Press*: 62 Toller Lane, Bradford, West Yorkshire, BD8 9BY, U.K.

International journal of social psychiatry. *[Int. J. Soc. Psyc.]* ISSN: 0020-7640. *Avenue Publishing*: 55 Woodstock Avenue, London NW11 9RG, U.K.

International journal of the sociology of language. *[Int. J. S. Lang.]* ISSN: 0165-2516. *Mouton de Gruyter*: Postfach 110240, D-1000 Berlin 11, Germany

International journal of the sociology of law. *[Int. J. S. Law]* ISSN: 0194-6595. *Academic Press*: 24-28 Oval Road, London NW1 7DX, U.K.

International journal of therapeutic communities. *[Inter. J. Therap. Comm.]* ISSN: 0196-1365. *Association of Therapeutic Communities*: 14 Charterhouse Square, London, EC1M 6AX, U.K.; **Subscriptions**: *idem*: P.O. Box 109, Dorking Surrey, RH5 4FA, U.K.

International journal of urban and regional research. *[Int. J. Urban]* ISSN: 0309-1317. *Edward Arnold*: Mill Road, Dunton Green, Sevenoaks, Kent TN13 2YA, U.K.; **Subscriptions**: *Edward Arnold*: Subscriptions Department, 42 Bedford Square, London WC1B 3SL, U.K.

International labour review. *[Int. Lab. Rev.]* ISSN: 0020-7780. *International Labour Office (ILO)*: CH-1211 Geneva 22, Switzerland

International migration; Migrations internationales; Migraciones internacionales. *[Int. Migr.]* ISSN: 0020- 7985. *International Organization for Migration*: P.O. Box 71, 1211 Geneva 19, Switzerland

International migration review. *[Int. Migr. Rev.]* ISSN: 0197- 9183. *Center for Migration Studies*: 209 Flagg Place, Staten Island, NY. 10304-1199, U.S.A.

International minds. *[Inter. Minds]* ISSN: 0957-1299. *International Minds*: 19 Hugh Street, London SW1V 1QJ, U.K.

International public relations review. *[Int. Pub. Relat. R.]* ISSN: 0269-0357. *International Public Relations Association*: Case postale 126, CH-1211 Geneva 20, Switzerland; **Publisher**: *Whiting and Birch*: 90 Dartmouth Road, Forest Hill, London SE23 3HZ, U.K.

International regional science review. *[Int. Reg. Sci. R.]* ISSN: 0160-0176. *Regional Research Institute*: West Virginia University, Morgantown, WV. 26506, U.S.A.

International relations. *[Int. Rel.]* ISSN: 0047- 1178. *David Davies Memorial Institute of International Studies*: 2 Chadwick Street, London SW1P 2EP, U.K.

International review of administrative sciences. *[Int. Rev. Admin. Sci.]* ISSN: 0020-8523. *International Institute of Administrative Sciences, European Group of Public Administration*: rue Defacqz 1, Box 11, B-1050 Brussels, Belgium; **Publisher**: *Sage Publications*: 6 Bonhill Street, London EC2A 4PU, U.K.

International review of applied economics. *[Int. R. Applied Ec.]* ISSN: 0269-2171. *Edward Arnold*: Mill Road, Dunton Green, Sevenoaks, Kent TN13 2YA, U.K.; **Subscriptions**: *Edward Arnold, Subscription Department*: 42 Bedford Square, WC1I 3SL, U.K.

International review of education. *[Int. R. Educat.]* ISSN: 0020- 8566. *UNESCO Institute for Education*: Feldbrunnenstrasse 58, 2000 Hamburg 13, Germany

International review of mission. *[Inter. R. Miss.]* ISSN: 0020-8582. *World Council of Churches, Commission on World Mission and Evangelism*: 150 route de Ferney, 1211 Geneva 2, Switzerland

International review of psycho-analysis. *[Int. Rev. Psy.]* ISSN: 0306-2643. *Institute of Psychoanalysis*: 63 New Cavendish Street, London W1M 7RD, U.K.; **Publisher**: *Routledge*: 11 New Fetter Lane, London, EC4P 4EE, U.K.; **Subscriptions**: *idem*: Cheriton House, North Way, Andover, Hants SP10 5BE, U.K.

International review of retail, distribution and consumer research. *[Int. R. Ret. Dist. Res.]* ISSN: 0959-3969. *Routledge*: 11 New Fetter Lane, London EC4P 4EE, U.K.

International review of social history. *[Int. Rev. S. H.]* ISSN: 0020- 8590. *International Institute for Social History*: Cruquiusweg 31, 1019 AT Amsterdam, The Netherlands; **Publisher**: *Van Gorcum*: POB 43, 9400 AA Assen, The Netherlands

International review of strategic management. *[Inter. R. Strat. Manag.]* ISSN: 1047-7918. *John Wiley & Sons*: Baffins Lane, Chichester, West Sussex PO19 1UD, U.K.

INTERNATIONAL BIBLIOGRAPHY OF SOCIOLOGY — 1991

International social science journal. *[Int. Soc. Sci. J.]* *ISSN: 0020-8701. Basil Blackwell/ UNESCO*: 108 Cowley Road, Oxford OX4 1JF, U.K./ UNESCO Periodicals Division, 7 place de Fontenoy, 75700 Paris, France

International socialism. *[Int. Soc.]* *ISSN: 0020-8736. Socialist Workers Party*: PO Box 82, London E3, U.K.; **Subscriptions**: *Bookmarks*: 265 Seven Sisters Road, London N4 2DE, U.K.

International sociology. *[Int. Sociol.]* *ISSN: 0268-5809. International Sociological Association*: Consejo Superior de Investigaciones Cientificas. Pinar 25, 28006 Madrid, Spain; **Publisher**: *Sage Publications*: 6 Bonhill Street, London EC2A 4PU, U.K.

International studies. *[Int. Stud.]* *ISSN: 0020-8817. Sage Publications India*: 32 M-Block Market, Greater Kailash I, New Delhi 110 048, India

International studies in the philosophy of science. *[Inter. Phil. Sci.]* *ISSN: 0269-8595. Carfax Publishing*: P.O. Box 25, Abingdon, Oxfordshire, OX14 3UE, U.K.

International studies quarterly. *[Int. Stud. Q.]* *ISSN: 0020-8833. International Studies Association*: University of South Carolina, Columbia SC. 29208, U.S.A.; **Publisher**: *Butterworth-Heinemann*: 80 Montvale Avenue, Stoneham, MA. 02180, U.S.A.

Investigación y gerencia. *[Invest. Ger.]*; *PARAL*: Apartado 47066, Los Chaguaramos, Caracas 1041-A, Venezuela

IRAL. *[IRAL]* *ISSN: 0019-042X. Julius Groos Verlag*: P.O. Box 102423, Hertzstraße 6, D-6900 Heidelberg 1, Germany

Iran namch. *[Ir. Nam.]*; *Foundation for Iranian Studies*: 4343 Montgomery Avenue, Suite 200, Bethesda, MD. 20814, U.S.A.

Irish geography. *[Irish Geogr.]* *ISSN: 0075-0778. Geographical Society of Ireland*: University College Dublin, Department of Geography, Belfield, Dublin 4, Ireland

Islam et sociétés au sud du Sahara. *[Islam Soc. S.Sah.]* *ISSN: 0984-7685. Editions de la Maison des Sciences de l'Homme*: Secrétariat scientifique, 54 boulevard Raspail, 75270 Paris Cedex 06, France; **Subscriptions**: *C.I.D.*: 131 boulevard Saint- Michel, 75005 Paris, France

Islamic quarterly. *[Islam. Q.]* *ISSN: 0021-1842. Islamic Cultural Centre*: 146 Park Road, London NW8 7RG, U.K.

Israel law review. *[Isr. Law R.]* *ISSN: 0021-2237. Israel Law Review Association*: c/o Faculty of Law, Hebrew University, Mt. Scopus, P.O.B. 24100, Jerusalem 91240, Israel

Israel yearbook on human rights. *[Isr. Y.book. Hum. Rig.]* *ISSN: 0333-5925. Tel Aviv University, Faculty of Law*; **Publisher**: *Martinus Nijhoff Publishers*: Spuiboulevard 50, 3311 GR Dordrecht, The Netherlands; **Subscriptions**: *Kluwer Academic Publishers*: P.O. Box 322, 3300 AH Dordrecht, The Netherlands

Issue. *[Issue]* *ISSN: 0047-1607. African Studies Association*: Credit Union Building, Emory University, GA. 30322, U.S.A.

Issues in reproductive and genetic engineering. *[Iss. Repro. Gen. Engin.]* *ISSN: 0958- 6415. Pergamon Press*: Fairview Park, Elmsford, NY. 10523, U.S.A.

Jahrbuch.:Asien - Afrika - Lateinamerika *[Jahr. As. Afr. Lat.am.]*; *VEB Deutscher Verlag der Wissenschaften*: Postfach 1216, 1080 Berlin, Germany

Jahrbuch für christliche Sozialwissenschaften. *[Jahr. Christ. Sozialwiss.]* *ISSN: 0075-2584. Universität Münster, Institut für Christliche Sozialwissenschaften*; **Publisher**: *Verlag Regensberg*: Daimlerweg 58, Postfach 6748-6749, 4400 Münster, Germany

Jahrbuch für Geschichte von Staat, Wirtschaft und Gesellschaft Lateinamerikas. *[Jahrb. Ges. St. Wirt. Ges. Lat.am.]* *ISSN: 0075-2673. Böhlaü Verlag*: Niehler Straße 272-274, 5000 Cologne 60, Germany

Jahrbuch für Ostrecht. *[Jahrb. Ost.]* *ISSN: 0075-2746. Institut für Ostrecht München*: Kessenicher Straße 116, Postfach 120380, 5300 Bonn 1, Germany; **Publisher**: *Deutscher Bundes-Verlag*: 8000 München 2, Theresienstraße 40, Germany

Jahrbuch für Wirtschaftsgeschichte. *[Jahrb. Wirt. Gesch.]* *ISSN: 0075-2800. Akademie-Verlag Berlin*: Postfach 1233, Leipziger Straße 3-4 1086 Berlin, Germany

Jahrbücher für Geschichte Osteuropas. *[Jahrb. Gesch. O.eur.]* *ISSN: 0021-4019. Osteuropa Institut*: Scheinerstraße 11, D-8000 Munich 80, Germany; **Publisher**: *Franz Steiner Verlag*: Birkenwaldstraße 44, Postfach 10 15 26, D-7000 Stuttgart, Germany

Jahrbücher für Nationalökonomie und Statistik. *[Jahrb. N. St.]* *ISSN: 0021-4027. Gustav Fischer Verlag*: Wollgrasweg 49, 7000 Stuttgart 70, Germany

Japan Christian quarterly. *[Jpn. Christ. Q.]* *ISSN: 0021-4361. Japan Christian Quarterly*: Kyo Bun Kwan, 4-5-1 Ginza, Chou-ku, Tokyo 104, Japan

Japan digest. *[Jpn. Dig.]* *ISSN: 0960-1473. Japan Library*: Knoll House, 35 The Crescent, Sandgate, Folkestone, Kent CT20 3EE, U.K.

Japan forum. *[Jpn. Forum]* *ISSN: 0955-5803. British Association for Japanese Studies*; **Publisher**: *Oxford University Press*: Pinkhill House, Southfield Road, Eynsham, Oxford OX8 1JJ, U.K.

Japanese journal of religious studies. *[Jap. J. Relig. St.]* ISSN: 0304-1042. *Nanzan Institute for Religion and Culture*: 18 Yamazato-chō, Shōwa-ku, Nagoya 466, Japan

Japanese religions. *[Jpn. Relig.]* ISSN: 0448-8954. *NCC Center for the Study of Japanese Religions*: Karasuma-Shimotachiun, Kamikyo-ku, Kyoto-shi 602, Japan

Jewish journal of sociology. *[Jew. J. Socio.]* ISSN: 0021-6534. *Maurice Freedman Research Trust*: 187 Gloucester Place, London NW1 6BU, U.K.

Jewish quarterly review. *[Jew. Q. Rev.]* ISSN: 0021-6682. *Annenberg Research Institute*: 420 Walnut Street, Philadelphia, PA. 19106, U.S.A.

Jewish social studies. *[Jew. Soc. Stud.]* ISSN: 0021-6704. *Conference on Jewish Social Studies*: 2112 Broadway, New York, NY. 10023, U.S.A.

Journal de la Société de Statistique de Paris. *[J. Soc. Stat. Paris]* ISSN: 0037-914X. *Société de Statistique de France*: B-212, INSEE, 12 rue Boulitte, 75675 Paris Cedex 14, France; **Subscriptions**: *UAP International*: 9 Place Vendôme, 75001 Paris, France

Journal de la Société des océanistes. *[J. Soc. Océan.]* ISSN: 0300-953X. *Société des Oceanistes*: Musée de l'homme, 75116 Paris, France

Journal for Japanese studies. *[J. Jpn. Stud.]* ISSN: 0095-6848. *Society for Japanese Studies*: Thomson Hall DR-05, University of Washington, Seattle, Washington 98195, U.S.A.

Journal for the scientific study of religion. *[J. Sci. S. Relig.]* ISSN: 0021-8294. *Society for the Scientific Study of Religion*: Pierce Hall, Room 193, Purdue University, West Lafayette, IN. 47907, U.S.A.

Journal for the study of Judaism in the Persian, Hellenistic and Roman periods. *[J. S. Jud. Per. Hellen. Rom.]* ISSN: 0047-2212. *E.J. Brill*: P.O. Box 900, 2300 PA Leiden, The Netherlands

Journal for the theory of social behaviour. *[J. Theory Soc. Behav.]* ISSN: 0021-8308. *Basil Blackwell*: 108 Cowley Road, Oxford OX4 1JF, U.K.

Journal für Entwicklungspolitik. *[J. Entwick.pol.]* ISSN: 0258-2384. *Mattersburger Kreis für Entwicklungspolitik an den Österreichischen Universitäten*: Weyrgasse 5, A-1030 Vienna, Austria

Journal of accounting and public policy. *[J. Acc. Pub. Pol.]* ISSN: 0278-4254. *Elsevier Science Publishers (North-Holland)*: 655 Avenue of the Americas, New York, N.Y. 10010, U.S.A.; **Subscriptions**: *Elsevier Science Publishers*: Journals Department, P.O. Box 882, Madison Square Station, New York, NY. 10159, U.S.A.

Journal of African Marxists. *[J. Afr. Marx.]* ISSN: 0263-2268. *Journal of African Marxists*: 23 Bevenden Street, London N1 6BH, U.K.

Journal of American studies. *[J. Am. Stud.]* ISSN: 0021-8758. *Cambridge University Press*: The Edinburgh Building, Shaftesbury Road, Cambridge CB2 2RU, U.K.

Journal of analytical psychology. *[J. Analyt. Psychol.]* ISSN: 0021-8774. *Routledge*: 11 New Fetter Lane, London, EC4P 4EE, U.K.; **Subscriptions**: *Routledge*: Cheriton House, North Way, Andover, Hants SP10 5BE, U.K.

Journal of applied psychology. *[J. Appl. Psychol.]* ISSN: 0021-9010. *American Psychological Association*: 1400 North Uhle Street, Arlington, VA. 22201, U.S.A.

Journal of applied social psychology. *[J. Appl. Soc. Psychol.]* ISSN: 0021-9029. *V.H. Winston & Son*: 7961 Eastern Avenue, Silver Spring, MD. 20910, U.S.A.

Journal of architectural and planning research. *[J. Arch. Plan. Res.]*; *Locke Science Publishing*: P.O. Box 146413, Chicago, IL. 60614, U.S.A.

Journal of Asian and African affairs. *[J. Asian Afr. Aff.]* ISSN: 1044-2979. *Journal of Asian and African Affairs*: P.O. Box 23099, Washington, DC. 20026, U.S.A.

Journal of Asian and African studies [Leiden]. *[J. As. Afr. S.]* ISSN: 0021 9096. *E.J. Brill*: P.O. Box 9000, 2300 PA Leiden, The Netherlands

Journal of Asian studies. *[J. Asian St.]* ISSN: 0021-9118. *Association for Asian Studies*: 1 Lane Hall, University of Michigan, Ann Arbor, MI. 48109, U.S.A.; **Publisher**: *University of Wisconsin-Milwaukee*: Milwaukee, WI. 53201, U.S.A.

Journal of Australian political economy. *[J. Aust. Pol. Econ.]* ISSN: 0156-5826. *Australian Political Economy Movement*: P.O. Box 76, Wentworth Building, University of Sydney, NSW 2006, Australia

Journal of Australian studies. *[J. Aust. Stud.]*; *La Trobe University Press*: La Trobe University, Bundoora, Victoria, 3083 Australia

Journal of biogeography. *[J. Biogeogr.]* ISSN: 0305-0270. *Blackwell Scientific Publications*: Osney Mead, Oxford OX2, U.K.; **Subscriptions**: *idem*: P.O. Box 88, Oxford OX2 0EL, U.K.

Journal of biosocial science. *[J. Biosoc. Sc.]* ISSN: 0021-9320. *Biosocial Society*: Department of Biological Anthropology, Downing Street, Cambridge CB2 3DZ, U.K.; **Subscriptions**: *Portland Press*: P.O. Box 32, Commerce Way, Colchester CO2 8HP, U.K.

INTERNATIONAL BIBLIOGRAPHY OF SOCIOLOGY — 1991

Journal of British studies. [*J. Br. Stud.*] *ISSN: 0021- 9371. University of Chicago Press*: 5720 S. Woodlawn Avenue, Chicago, Illinois 60637, U.S.A.

Journal of business & economic statistics. [*J. Bus. Econ. Stat.*] *ISSN: 0735-0015. American Statistical Association*: 1429 Duke Street, Alexandria, VA. 22314, U.S.A.

Journal of business and society. [*J. Bus. Soc.*] *ISSN: 1012-2591. Cyprus College*: P.O. Box 2006, Corner Stasinos and Diogenes Streets, Nicosia, Cyprus

Journal of Canadian studies; Revue d'études canadiennes. [*J. Can. Stud.*] *ISSN: 0021-9495. Trent University*: Box 4800, Peterborough, Ontario, Canada K9J 7B8

Journal of child and adolescent group therapy. [*J. Child Adol. Gr. Ther.*] *ISSN: 1053-0800. Human Sciences Press*: 233 Spring Street, New York, NY., 10013-1578, U.S.A.

Journal of church and state. [*J. Chur. State*] *ISSN: 0021- 969X. Baylor University, J.M. Dawson Institute of Church-State Studies*: P.O. Box 97308, Waco, TX. 76798-7308, U.S.A.

Journal of Commonwealth & comparative politics. [*J. Comm. C. Pol.*] *ISSN: 03060-3631. Frank Cass*: Gainsborough House, 11 Gainsborough Road, London E11 1RS, U.K.

Journal of communication. [*J. Comm.*] *ISSN: 0021-9916. Oxford University Press*: 200 Madison Avenue, New York, NY. 10016, U.S.A.

Journal of communist studies. [*J. Commun. S.*] *ISSN: 0268-4535. Frank Cass*: Gainsborough House, 11 Gainsborough Road, London W11 1RS, U.K.

Journal of community and applied social psychology. [*J. Comm. App. Soc. Psychol.*] *ISSN: 1052-9284. John Wiley & Sons*: Baffins Lane, Chichester, West Sussex PO19 1UD, U.K.

Journal of comparative family studies. [*J. Comp. Fam. Stud.*] *ISSN: 0047-2328. University of Calgary, Department of Sociology*: 2500 University Drive, N.W., Calgary, Alberta T2N 1N4, Canada

Journal of conflict resolution. [*Confl. Resolut.*] *ISSN: 0022-0027. Peace Science Society (International)*; **Publisher**: *Sage Publications*: 2455 Teller Road, Newbury Park, CA. 91320, U.S.A.

Journal of contemporary African studies. [*J. Contemp. Afr. St.*] *ISSN: 0258-9001. Africa Institute of South Africa*: P.O. Box 630, Pretoria 0001, South Africa

Journal of contemporary Asia. [*J. Cont. Asia*] *ISSN: 0047-2336. Journal of Contemporary Asia Publishers*: P.O. Box 592, Manila, 1099 Philippines

Journal of criminal law. [*J. Crim. Law*] *ISSN: 0022- 0183. Pageant Publishing*: 5 Turners Wood, London NW11 6TD, U.K.; **Subscriptions**: *Bailey Management Services*: Warner House, Bowles Well Gardens, Folkestone, Kent CT19 6PH, U.K.

Journal of criminal law and criminology. [*J. Crim. Law*] *ISSN: 0091-4169. Northwestern University School of Law*: 357 East Chicago Avenue, Chicago, IL. 60611, U.S.A.

Journal of cross-cultural gerontology. [*J. Cr-cult. Gerontol.*] *ISSN: 0169-3816. Kluwer Academic Publishers*: P.O. Box 17, 3300 AA Dordrecht, The Netherlands; **Subscriptions**: *idem*: P.O. Box 322, 3300 AH Dordrecht, The Netherlands/P.O. Box 358, Accord Station, Hingham, MA 02018-0358, U.S.A.

Journal of developing areas. [*J. Dev. Areas*] *ISSN: 0022-037X. Western Illinois University*: 900 West Adams Street, Macomb, IL. 61455, U.S.A.

Journal of developing societies. [*J. Dev. Soc.*] *ISSN: 0169-796X. E.J. Brill*: P.O.B. 9000, 2300 PA Leiden, The Netherlands

Journal of development economics. [*J. Dev. Econ.*] *ISSN: 0304- 3878. Elsevier Science Publishers (North-Holland)*: P.O. Box 1991, 1000 BZ Amsterdam, The Netherlands

Journal of development studies. [*J. Dev. Stud.*] *ISSN: 0022-0388. Frank Cass*: Gainsborough House, 11 Gainsborough Road, London E11 1RS, U.K.

Journal of Eastern African research & development. [*J. E.Afr. Res. Devel.*] *ISSN: 0251-0405. Gideon S. Were*: P.O. Box 10622, Nairobi, Kenya

Journal of econometrics. [*J. Economet.*] *ISSN: 0304-4076. Elsevier Science Publishers (North-Holland)*: P.O. Box 1991, 1000 BZ Amsterdam, The Netherlands

Journal of economic and social measurement. [*J. Econ. Soc.*] *ISSN: 0747-9662. International Organisations Services*: Van Diemenstraat 94, 1013 CN Amsterdam, The Netherlands

Journal of economic history. [*J. Econ. Hist.*] *ISSN: 0022-0507. Economic History Association/ University of Kansas*: Department of History, George Washington University, Washington DC. 20052, U.S.A./ 211 Watkins Home, Hall Center for the Humanities, Lawrence, KS. 66045, U.S.A.; **Publisher**: *Cambridge University Press*: 40 West 20th Street, New York, N.Y. 10011, U.S.A.

Journal of economic issues. [*J. Econ. Iss.*] *ISSN: 0021-3624. Association for Evolutionary Economics*: Department of Economics, University of Nebraska-Lincoln, Lincoln, NE. 68588, U.S.A.

INTERNATIONAL BIBLIOGRAPHY OF SOCIOLOGY — 1991

Journal of economic literature. *[J. Econ. Lit.] ISSN: 0022-8515. American Economic Association*: 2014 Broadway, Suite 305, Nashville, TN. 37203, U.S.A.

Journal of economic perspectives. *[J. Econ. Pers.] ISSN: 0895-3309. American Economic Association*: 2014 Broadway, Suite 305, Nashville, TN. 37203, U.S.A.

Journal of economic psychology. *[J. Econ. Psyc.] ISSN: 0167-4870. International Association for Research in Economic Psychology*: Egmontstraat 13, 1050 Brussels, Belgium; **Publisher**: *Elsevier Science Publishers (North-Holland)*: P.O. Box 1991, 1000 BZ Amsterdam, The Netherlands; **Subscriptions**: *idem*: Journals Division, P.O. Box 211, 1000 AE Amsterdam, The Netherlands

Journal of economic studies. *[J. Econ. Stud.] ISSN: 0144-3585. MCB University Press*: 62 Toller Lane, Bradford, W. Yorkshire BD8 9BY, U.K.

Journal of educational sociology. *[J. Ed. Soc.]*; *Japan Society of Educational Sociology*: Tokyo, Japan

Journal of environmental management. *[J. Environ. Manag.] ISSN: 0301-4797. Academic Press*: 24-28 Oval Road, London NW1 7DX, U.K.; **Subscriptions**: *idem*: Foots Cray, Sidcup, Kent, DA14 5HP, U.K.

Journal of environmental planning and management. *[J. Environ. Plan. Manag.] ISSN: 0964-0568. Carfax Publishing*: P.O. Box 25, Abingdon, Oxfordshire, OX14 3UE, U.K.

Journal of experimental child psychology. *[J. Exper. Child Psychol.] ISSN: 0022-0965. Academic Press*: 1 East First Street, Duluth, MN. 55802, U.S.A.

Journal of experimental social psychology. *[J. Exp. S. Psychol.] ISSN: 0022-1031. Academic Press*: 1 East First Street, Duluth, MN. 55802, U.S.A.

Journal of Family Education Center. *[J. Fam. Ed. Cent.]*

Journal of family history. *[J. Fam. Hist.] ISSN: 0363-1990. National Council on Family Relations*; **Publisher**: *JAI Press*: 55 Old Post Road, No. 2, P.O. Box 1678, Greenwich, CT. 06836-1678, U.S.A.

Journal of family law. *[J. Fam. Law] ISSN: 0022- 1066. University of Louisville, School of Law*: 2301 South Third Street, Louisville, KY. 40292, U.S.A.

Journal of family therapy. *[J. Fam. Ther.] ISSN: 0163-4445. Association for Family Therapy*: 6 Ileol, Seddon, Danescourt, Llandaff, Cardiff CF5 2QX, U.K.; **Publisher**: *Basil Blackwell*: 108 Cowley Road, Oxford OX4 1JF, U.K.; **Subscriptions**: *Marston Book Services*: P.O. Box 87, Oxford OX2 0DT, U.K.

Journal of family violence. *[J. Fam. Viol.] ISSN: 0885-7482. Plenum Publishing Corporation*: 233 Spring Street, New York, NY. 10013, U.S.A.

Journal of folklore research. *[J. Folk. Res.] ISSN: 0737-7037. Indiana University Folklore Institute*: 504 North Fess, Bloomington, Indiana 47205, U.S.A.

Journal of forecasting. *[J. Forecast.] ISSN: 0277-6693. John Wiley & Sons*: Baffins Lane, Chichester, West Sussex PO19 1UD, U.K.

Journal of forensic psychiatry. *[J. For. Psy.] ISSN: 0958-5184. Routledge*: 11 New Fetter Lane, London, EC4P 4EE, U.K.; **Subscriptions**: *Routledge*: Cheriton House, North Way, Andover, Hants SP10 5BE, U.K.

Journal of health economics. *[J. Health Econ.] ISSN: 0167-6296. Elsevier Science Publishers (North-Holland)*: P.O. Box 1991, 1000 BZ Amsterdam, The Netherlands; **Subscriptions**: *idem*: P.O. Box 211, 1000 AE Amsterdam, The Netherlands

Journal of historical sociology. *[J. Hist. Soc.] ISSN: 0952-1909. Basil Blackwell*: 108 Cowley Road, Oxford OX4 1JF, U.K.

Journal of housing research. *[J. Hous. Res.] ISSN: 1052-7001. Office of Housing Policy, Fannie Mae*: 3900 Wisconsin Avenue, N.W., Washington, DC. 20016-2899, U.S.A.

Journal of human resources. *[J. Hum. Res.] ISSN: 0022-166X. University of Wisconsin Press*: 4315 Social Science Building, University of Wisconsin, 1180 Observatory Drive, Madison, WI. 53706, U.S.A.; **Subscriptions**: *University of Wisconsin Press*: 114 North Murray Street, Madison, WI. 53715, U.S.A.

Journal of Indian philosophy. *[J. Ind. Phil.] ISSN: 0022-1791. Kluwer Academic Publishers*: Spuiboulevard 50, P.O. Box 17, 3300 AA Dordrecht, The Netherlands; **Subscriptions**: *idem*: P.O. Box 322, 3300 AH Dordrecht, The Netherlands

Journal of industrial relations. *[J. Ind. Relat.] ISSN: 0022-1856. Journal of Industrial Relations*: GPO Box 4479, Sydney, NSW 2001, Australia

Journal of interdisciplinary economics. *[J. Interd. Ec.] ISSN: 0260-1079. A.B. Academic Publishers*: P.O. Box 42, Bicester, Oxon OX6 7NW, U.K.

Journal of interdisciplinary history. *[J. Interd. Hist.] ISSN: 0022-1953. Tufts University/ Lafayette College*: 26 Winthrop Street, Medford, MA. 02155, U.S.A.; **Publisher**: *MIT Press*: 55 Hayward Street, Cambridge, MA. 02142, U.S.A.

Journal of international business studies. *[J. Int. Bus. Stud.] ISSN: 0047-2506. Academy of International Business/ University of South Carolina, College of Business Administration*: Tulane University, A.B. Freeman School of Business, New Orleans, LA. 70118, U.S.A./ Columbia, SC. 29208, U.S.A.

INTERNATIONAL BIBLIOGRAPHY OF SOCIOLOGY — 1991

Journal of Jewish studies. *[J. Jew. Stud.]* ISSN: 0022-2097. *Oxford Centre for Postgraduate Hebrew Studies*: 45 St. Giles, Oxford OX1 2LP, U.K.

Journal of Jewish thought and philosophy. *[J. Jew. Thoug. Philos.]* ISSN: 1053-699X. *Harwood Academic Publishers*: 270 Eighth Avenue, New York, NY.10011, U.S.A.; **Subscriptions**: *idem:* c/o STBS Limited, P.O. Box 90, Reading, Berks, RG1 8JL, U.K.

Journal of labor economics. *[J. Labor Ec.]* ISSN: 0734-306X. *Economics Research Center/NORC*; **Publisher**: *University of Chicago Press*: Journals Division, P.O. Box 37005, Chicago, IL 60637, U.S.A.

Journal of labor research. *[J. Labor Res.]* ISSN: 0195-3613. *George Mason University, Department of Economics*: Fairfax, VA. 22030, U.S.A.

Journal of language and social psychology. *[J. Lang. Soc. Psychol.]* ISSN: 0261-927X. *Multilingual Matters*: Bank House, 8a Hill Road, Clevedon, Avon BS21 7HH, U.K.

Journal of Latin American studies. *[J. Lat. Am. St.]* ISSN: 0022- 216X. *Cambridge University Press*: The Edinburgh Building, Shaftesbury Road, Cambridge CB2 2RU, U.K.

Journal of law and society. *[J. Law Soc.]* ISSN: 0263-323X. *Basil Blackwell*: 108 Cowley Road, Oxford OX4 1JF , U.K.

Journal of law, economics, & organization. *[J. Law Ec. Organ.]* ISSN: 8756-6222. *Oxford University Press*: 2001 Evans Road, Cary, NC. 27513, U.S.A.

Journal of legal studies. *[J. Leg. Stud]* ISSN: 0047-2530. *University of Chicago Press*: 5720 S. Woodlawn Avenue, Chicago, IL. 60637, U.S.A.

Journal of leisure research. *[J. Leis. Res.]* ISSN: 0022-2216. *National Recreation and Park Association*: 3101 Park Center Drive, Alexandria VA. 22302, U.S.A.

Journal of libertarian studies. *[J. Libert. Stud.]* ISSN: 0363-2873. *Center for Libertarian Studies*: P.O. Box 4091, Burlingame, CA. 94011, U.S.A.

Journal of linguistics. *[J. Linguist.]* ISSN: 0022-2267. *Linguistics Association of Great Britain*: c/o Department of Linguistics, University College of North Wales, Bangor, Gwynedd LL57 2DG, U.K.; **Publisher**: *Cambridge University Press*: The Edinburgh Building, Shaftesbury Road, Cambridge CB2 2RU, U.K.

Journal of management studies. *[J. Manag. Stu.]* ISSN: 0022-2380. *Basil Blackwell*: 108 Cowley Road, Oxford OX4 1JF, U.K.; **Subscriptions**: *Marston Book Services*: P.O. Box 87, Oxford OX2 0DT, U.K.

Journal of marriage and the family. *[J. Marriage Fam.]* ISSN: 0022-2445. *National Council on Family Relations*: 3989 Central Avenue Northeast, Suite 550, Minneapolis, MN. 55421, U.S.A.

Journal of mathematical sociology. *[J. Math. Sociol.]* ISSN: 0022-250X. *Gordon & Breach Science Publishers*: P.O. Box 786, Cooper Station, New York, NY. 10276, U.S.A.

Journal of Mauritian studies. *[J. Maur. Stud.]*; *Mahatma Gandhi Institute*: Moka, Mauritius

Journal of medicine and philosophy. *[J. Medic. Philos.]* ISSN: 0360- 5310. *Kluwer Academic Publishers*: P.O. Box 322, 3300 AH Dordrecht, The Netherlands

Journal of Mediterranean studies. *[J. Mediter. St.]* ISSN: 1016-3476. *Mediterranean Institute*: University of Malta, Msida, Malta

Journal of modern African studies. *[J. Mod. Afr. S.]* ISSN: 0022-278X. *Cambridge University Press*: The Edinburgh Building, Shaftesbury Road, Cambridge CB2 2RU, U.K.

Journal of modern history. *[J. Mod. Hist.]* ISSN: 0022-2801. *American Historical Association, Modern European History Section*; **Publisher**: *University of Chicago Press*: 5720 S. Woodlawn, Chicago, IL. 60637, U.S.A.

Journal of modern Korean studies. *[J. Mod. Kor. S.]*; *Mary Washington College*: Monroe Hall, 209E, Fredericksburg, VI. 22401, U.S.A.

Journal of multilingual and multicultural development. *[J. Multiling.]* ISSN: 0143- 4632. *Multilingual Matters*: Bank House, 8a Hill Road, Clevedon, Avon BS21 7HH, U.K.

Journal of occupational psychology. *[J. Occup. Psychol.]* ISSN: 0305-8107. *British Psychological Society*: St. Andrews House, 48 Princess Road East, Leicester LE1 7DR, U.K.

Journal of oriental studies. *[J. Orient. Stud.]*

Journal of Pacific studies. *[J. Pac. Stud.]* ISSN: 1011-3029. *University of the South Pacific, School of Social and Economic Development*: Editorial Secretariat, P.O. Box 1168, Suva, Fiji

Journal of Palestine studies. *[J. Pal. Stud.]* ISSN: 0377-919X. *Institute for Palestine Studies*: 3501 M Street, N.W. Washington, DC. 20007, U.S.A.; **Publisher**: *University of California Press*: 2120 Berkeley Way, Berkeley, CA. 94720, U.S.A.

Journal of peasant studies. *[J. Peasant Stud.]* ISSN: 0306-6150. *Frank Cass*: Gainsborough House, 11 Gainsborough Road, London E11 1RS, U.K.

Journal of personality. *[J. Personal.]* ISSN: 0022-3506. *Duke University Press*: Box 6697, College Station, Durham, NC. 27708, U.S.A.

INTERNATIONAL BIBLIOGRAPHY OF SOCIOLOGY — 1991

Journal of personality and social psychology. *[J. Pers. Soc. Psychol.]* ISSN: 0022-3514. *American Psychological Association*: 1400 North Uhle Street, Arlington, VA. 22201, U.S.A.

Journal of philosophy. *[J. Phil.]* ISSN: 0022-362X. *Journal of Philosophy*: 709 Philosophy Hall, Columbia University, New York, NY. 10027, U.S.A.

Journal of phonetics. *[J. Phon.]* ISSN: 0095- 4470. *Academic Press*: 24-28 Oval Road, London NW1 7DX, U.K.

Journal of pidgin and creole languages. *[J. Pid. Creo. Lang.]* ISSN: 0920-9034. *John Benjamins Publishing*: Amsteldijk 44, P.O. Box 52519, 1007 HA Amsterdam, The Netherlands

Journal of planning literature. *[J. Plan. Lit.]* ISSN: 0885-4122. *Ohio State University Press*: 1070 Carmack Road, Columbus, OH. 43210-1002, U.S.A.

Journal of political economy. *[J. Polit. Ec.]* ISSN: 0022-3808. *University of Chicago Press*: 5720 S. Woodlawn Avenue, Chicago, IL. 60637, U.S.A.

Journal of politics. *[J. Polit.]* ISSN: 0022-3816. *University of Texas Press, Journals Department*: 2100 Comal, Austin TX. 78722, U.S.A.

Journal of popular culture. *[J. Pop. Cult.]* ISSN: 0022-3840. *Modern Language Association of America, Popular Literature Section/ Midwest Modern Language Association, Folklore Section*; **Publisher**: *Popular Press*: Bowling Green State University, Bowling Green OH 43402, U.S.A.

Journal of population economics. *[J. Pop. Ec.]* ISSN: 0933-1433. *Springer-Verlag*: Heidelberger Platz 3, D-1000 Berlin 33, Germany

Journal of post Keynesian economics. *[J. Post. Keyn. Ec.]* ISSN: 0160-3477. *M.E.Sharpe*: 80 Business Park Drive, Armonk N.Y. 10504, U.S.A.

Journal of pragmatics. *[J. Prag.]* ISSN: 0378-2166. *Elsevier Science Publishers (North-Holland)*: P.O. Box 1991, 1000 BZ Amsterdam, The Netherlands

Journal of psychology. *[J. Psychol.]* ISSN: 0022-3980. *Heldref Publications*: 4000 Albemarle Street, NW, Washington, DC. 20016, U.S.A.

Journal of public economics. *[J. Publ. Ec.]* ISSN: 0047-2727. *Elsevier Science Publishers (North-Holland)*: P.O. Box 1991, BZ Amsterdam, The Netherlands; **Subscriptions**: *Elsevier Sequoia*: P.O. Box 564, Lausanne, Switzerland

Journal of real estate research. *[J. Real Est. Res.]* ISSN: 0896-5803. *American Real Estate Society*: Box B, University Station, University of North Dakota, Grand Forks, ND. 58202, U.S.A.

Journal of refugee studies. *[J. Refug. S.]* ISSN: 0951-6328. *University of Oxford, Refugee Studies Programme*: Queen Elizabeth House, 21 St. Giles, Oxford OX1 3LA, U.K.; **Publisher**: *Oxford University Press*: Pinkhill House, Southfield Road, Eynsham, Oxford OX8 1JJ, U.K.

Journal of regional policy. *[J. Reg. Pol.]*; *Isveimer*: via S. Giacomo, 19 Naples, Italy

Journal of religion in Africa. *[J. Relig. Afr.]* ISSN: 0022-4200. *E.J. Brill*: Postbus 9000, 2300 PA Leiden, The Netherlands

Journal of research in crime and delinquency. *[J. Res. Crim. Delin.]* ISSN: 0022- 4278. *National Council on Crime and Delinquency*: 685 Market Street, Suite 620, San Francisco, CA. 94105, U.S.A.; **Publisher**: *Sage Publications*: 2455 Teller Road, Newbury Park, CA. 91320, U.S.A.

Journal of rural development and administration. *[J. Rural Devel. Admin.]* ISSN: 0047-2751. *Academy for Rural Development*: Academy Town, Peshawar, Pakistan

Journal of rural studies. *[J. Rural St.]* ISSN: 0743-0167. *Pergamon Press*: Headington Hill Hall, Oxford OX3 0BW, U.K.

Journal of semantics. *[J. Sem.]* ISSN: 0167-5133. *IBM Germany Scientific Center*: Postfach 800880, D-7000 Stuttgart 80, Germany; **Publisher**: *Oxford University Press*: Pinkhill House, Southfield Road, Eynsham, OX8 1JJ, Oxford, U.K.

Journal of social and biological structures. *[J. Soc. Biol. Struct.]* ISSN: 0140 1750. *JAI Press*: 55 Old Post Road No.2, P.O. Box 1678, Greenwich, CT. 06836-1678, U.S.A.

Journal of social and clinical psychology. *[J. Soc. Clin. Psychol.]* ISSN: 0736-7236. *Guilford Publications*: 72 Spring Street, New York, NY. 10012, U.S.A.

Journal of social and evolutionary systems. *[J. Soc. Evol. Sys.]* ISSN: 1061-7361. *JAI Press*: 55 Old Post Road — No.2, P.O. Box 1678, Greenwich, CT., 06836-1678, U.S.A.

Journal of social development in Africa. *[J. Soc. Devel. Afr.]* ISSN: 1012- 1080. *School of Social Work*: P/ Bag 66022 Kopje, Harare, Zimbabwe

Journal of social history. *[J. Soc. Hist]* ISSN: 0022-4529. *Carnegie Mellon University*: Pittsburgh, PA. 15213, U.S.A.

Journal of social issues. *[J. Soc. Issues]* ISSN: 0022-4537. *Society for the Psychological Study of Social Issues*; **Publisher**: *Plenum Publishing*: 233 Spring Street, NY. 10013, U.S.A.

Journal of social policy. *[J. Soc. Pol.]* ISSN: 0047-2794. *Social Policy Association*; **Publisher**: *Cambridge University Press*: The Edinburgh Building, Shaftesbury Road, Cambridge CB2 2RU, U.K.

INTERNATIONAL BIBLIOGRAPHY OF SOCIOLOGY — 1991

Journal of social psychology. *[J. Soc. Psychol.]* ISSN: 0022-4545. Heldref Publications: 4000 Albemarle St., N.W. Washington DC. 20016, U.S.A.

Journal of social science. *[J. Soc. Sci.]*; University of Malawi, Faculty of Social Science: Chancellor College, P.O. Box 280, Zomba, Malawi

Journal of social sciences and humanities. *[J. Soc. Sci. Human.]* ISSN: 0023-4044. Korean Research Center: 228 Pyong-dong, Chongno-ku, Seoul, Korea

Journal of social studies. *[J. Soc. Stud. Dhaka]*; Centre for Social Studies: Room no. 1107, Arts Building, University of Dhaka, Dhaka 1000, Bangladesh

Journal of social, political and economic studies. *[J. Soc. Pol. E.]* ISSN: 0193-5941. Council for Social and Economic Studies: Suite C-2, 1133 13th St. N.W., Washington, DC. 20005-4297, U.S.A.

Journal of South Asian literature. *[J. S.Asian Lit.]*; Asian Studies Center: Michigan State University, East Lansing, MI. 48824-1035, U.S.A.

Journal of Southeast Asian studies. *[J. SE. As. Stud.]* ISSN: 0022-4634. National University of Singapore, Department of History: 10 Kent Ridge Crescent, Singapore 0511; **Publisher**: Singapore University Press: Yusof Ishak House, 10 Kent Ridge Crescent, Singapore 0511

Journal of Southern African studies. *[J. S.Afr. Stud.]* ISSN: 0305- 7070. Oxford University Press: Pinkhill House, Southfield Road, Eynsham, Oxford OX8 1JJ, U.K.

Journal of structural learning. *[J. Struct. Learn.]* ISSN: 0022-4774. Gordon and Breach Science Publishers: 270 8th Avenue, New York, NY. 10011, U.S.A.; **Subscriptions**: *idem*: P.O. Box 90, Reading, Berkshire, RG1 8JL, U.K.

Journal of the American Planning Association. *[J. Am. Plann.]* ISSN: 0194-4363. American Planning Association: 1313 East 60th Street, Chicago, IL 60637-2891, U.S.A.

Journal of the American Statistical Association. *[J. Am. Stat. Ass.]* ISSN: 0162-1459. American Statistical Association: 1429 Duke Street, Alexandria, VA. 22314, U.S.A.

Journal of the Anthropological Society of Oxford. *[J. Anthrop. Soc. Oxford]* ISSN: 0044- 8370. Anthropology Society of Oxford: 51 Banbury Road, Oxford OX2 6PE, U.K.

Journal of the Australian Population Association. *[J. Aust. Pop. Ass.]* ISSN: 0814-5725. Australian Population Association: Division of Demography and Sociology, Research School of Social Sciences, The Australian National University, GPO Box 4, Canberra ACT 2601, Australia

Journal of the economic and social history of the orient. *[J. Ec. Soc. Hist. O.]* ISSN: 0022-4995. E.J. Brill: P.O. Box 9000, 2300 PA Leiden, The Netherlands

Journal of the Gypsy Lore Society. *[J. Gypsy Lore Soc.]* ISSN: 0017-6087. Gypsy Lore Society: 5607 Greenleaf Road, Cheverly, MD. 20785, U.S.A.

Journal of the history of ideas. *[J. Hist. Ideas.]* ISSN: 0022-5037. Journal of the History of Ideas: Temple University, Philadelphia, PA. 19122, U.S.A.

Journal of the history of philosophy. *[J. Hist. Philos.]* ISSN: 0022-5053. Journal of the History of Philosophy: Business Office, Department of Philosophy, Washington University, One Brookings Drive, St. Louis, MO. 63130-4899, U.S.A.

Journal of the history of sexuality. *[J. Hist. Sexual.]* ISSN: 1043-4070. University of Chicago Press: 5720 S. Woodlawn, Chicago, IL. 60637, U.S.A.

Journal of the history of the behavioral sciences. *[J. Hist. Beh. Sci.]* ISSN: 0022-5061. Clinical Psychology Publishing: 4 Conant Square, Brandon, VT. 05733, U.S.A.

Journal of the International Phonetic Association. *[J. Inter. Phon. Ass.]*; International Phonetic Association: Phonetics Laboratory, Department of Linguistics, UCLA, Los Angeles, CA. 90024-1543, U.S.A.

Journal of the Market Research Society. *[J. Market R.]* ISSN: 0025-3618. Market Research Society: 15 Northburgh Street, London EC1V 0AH, U.K.; **Subscriptions**: NTC Publications: P.O. Box 69, Henley-on-Thames, Oxon RG9 2BZ, U.K.

Journal of the Mysore University.:*Section A-Arts [J. Mysore Univ. Arts]*; K.T. Veerappa, M.A.: Prasaranga, Manasagangotri, Mysore-6, India

Journal of the Oriental Institute. *[J. Orient. Inst.]* ISSN: 0030-5324. Maharaja Sayairao University of Baroda, Oriental Institute: Baroda 390 002, Gujarat, India

Journal of the Pacific Society. *[J. Pacific Soc.]* ISSN: 0387-4745. Pacific Society: 4-1-6 Akasaka, Minato-ku, Tokyo, Japan

Journal of the Research Society of Pakistan. *[J. Res. Soc. Pakist.]*; University of the Punjab, Punjab University Library: Old Campus, Lahore, Pakistan

Journal of the Royal Statistical Society.:*Series A (statistics in society) [J. Roy. Stat. Soc. A.]* ISSN: 0035- 9238. Royal Statistical Society: 25 Enford Street, London W1H 2BH, U.K.

INTERNATIONAL BIBLIOGRAPHY OF SOCIOLOGY — 1991

Journal of theoretical politics. *[J. Theor. Pol.]* *ISSN: 0951-6928*. Sage Publications: 6 Bonhill Street, London EC2A 4PU, U.K.
Journal of urban economics. *[J. Urban Ec.]* *ISSN: 0094-1190*. Academic Press: 1 First East Street, Duluth, MN 55802, U.S.A.
Journal of urban history. *[J. Urban Hist.]* *ISSN: 0096-1442*. Sage Publications: 2455 Teller Road, Newbury Park, CA 91320, U.S.A.
Journal of West African languages. *[J. W.Afr. Lang.]* *ISSN: 0022-5401*. West African Linguistics Society: Summer Institute of Linguistics, 7500 W.Camp Wisdom Road, Dallas, TX. 75236, U.S.A.
Journal of world history. *[J. World. Hist.]* *ISSN: 1045-6007*. World History Association: Department of History and Politics, Drexel University, Philadephia, PA. 19104, U.S.A.; **Publisher**: University of Hawaii Press: 2840 Kolowalu Street, Honolulu, HI. 96822, U.S.A.
Journal. Institute of Muslim Minority Affairs. *[J. Inst. Muslim Minor. Aff.]* *ISSN: 0266-6952*. Institute of Muslim Minority Affairs: 46 Goodge Street, London W1P 1FJ, U.K.
Jurnal antropologi dan sosiologi. *[J. Antro. Sosiol.]* *ISSN: 0126-9518*. Universiti Kebangsaan Malaysia, Department of Anthropology and Sociology: 43600 UKM Bangi, Selangor D.E., Malaysia
Jurnal Pendidikan. *[J.Pendid.]* *ISSN: 0126-6020*. Universiti Kebangsaan Malaysia Press: 43600 UKM Bangi, Selangor Darul Ehsan, Malaysia
Jurnal psikologi malaysia. *[J. Psik. Mal.]* *ISSN: 0127-8029*. Universiti Kebangsaan Malaysia Press: 43600 UKM Bangi, Selangor D.E., Malaysia
Kabar seberang. *[Kab. Seber.]* *ISSN: 0314-5786*. Centre for Southeast Asia Studies, James Cook University of North Queensland: Townsville, Queensland 4811, Australia
Kansaneläkelaitoksen julkaisuja. *[Kansan. Julk.]* *ISSN: 0355-4821*. Kansaneläkelaitoksen: P.O. Box 78, SF- 00381, Helsinki 38, Finland
Kenkyu-kiyo. *[Kenk.-Kiyo]*; Nihon University: Tokyo, Japan
Kiswahili. *[Kiswahili]* *ISSN: 0856-048X*. University of Dar es Salaam, Institute of Kiswahili Research: P.O. Box 35110, Dar es Salaam, Tanzania
Kölner Zeitschrift für Soziologie und Sozialpsychologie. *[Kölner Z. Soz. Soz. psy.]* *ISSN: 0340-0425*. Westdeutscher Verlag: Postfach 5829, D-6200 Wiesbaden 1, Germany
Коммунист; Kommunist. *[Kommunist]* *ISSN: 0131-1212*. Kommunisticheskaya Partiia Sovetskogo Soiuza. Tsentral' nyi Komitet; **Publisher**: Izdatel'stvo Pravda: Ul. Pravdy 24, 125047, Moscow, U.S.S.R.
Konjunkturpolitik. *[Konjunkturpolitik]* *ISSN: 0023-3498*. Duncker und Humblot: Dietrich-Schäfer-Weg 9, 1000 Berlin 41, Germany
Korea journal. *[Korea J.]* *ISSN: 0023-3900*. Korean National Commission for Unesco: C.P.O. Box 64, Seoul, 100-022 Korea
Korea observer. *[Korea Obs.]* *ISSN: 0023-3919*. Institute of Korean Studies: C.P.O. Box 3410, Seoul 100-643, Korea
Korean social science journal. *[Korean Soc. Sci. J.]*; Korean Social Science Research Council/ Korean National Commission for UNESCO: Box Central 64, Seoul, Korea
Korean studies. *[Kor. Stud.]* *ISSN: 0145-840X*. University of Hawaii Press: 2840 Kolowalu Street, Honolulu, HI. 96822, U.S.A.
Kredit und Kapital. *[Kred. Kap.]* *ISSN: 0023-4591*. Gesellschaft zur Förderung der wissenschaftlichen Forschung über das Spar- und Girowesen: Sigrid Wehrmeister, Adenauerallee 110, 5300 Bonn 1, Germany; **Publisher**: Duncker & Humblot: Postfach 410329, Dietrich-Schäfer-Weg 9, 1000 Berlin 41, Germany
Kwansai Gakuin University Annual Studies. *[Kwan. Gak. Univ. Ann. St.]*; Kwansei Gakuin University: 155-1-1 Uegahara, Nishinomiya, Hyôgo, Japan
Kwartalnik historii kultury materialnej. *[Kwart. Hist. Kult. Mater.]* *ISSN: 0023-5881*. Polska Akademia Nauk, Instytut Historii Kultury Materialnej; **Publisher**: Państwowe Wydawnictwo Naukowe: ul. Swierczewskiego 105, 00-140 Warsaw, Poland
L.S.E. quarterly. *[L.S.E. Q.]* *ISSN: 0269 9710*. London School of Economics and Political Science: Houghton Street, London WC2A 2AE, U.K.; **Publisher**: Basil Blackwell: 108 Cowley Road, Oxford OX4 1JF, U.K.
Labor law journal. *[Lab. Law J.]* *ISSN: 0023-6586*. Commerce Clearing House: 4025 W. Peterson Avenue, Chicago, IL. 60646, U.S.A.
Labour [Canada]; Travail. *[Labour [Canada]]* *ISSN: 0700-3862*. Committee on Canadian Labour History = Comité de l'histoire du travail du Canada: Department of History, Memorial University of Newfoundland, St. John's, Newfoundland. A1C 5S7, Canada
Labour [Italy]. *[Labour [Italy]]*; Fondazione Giacomo Brodolini: Via Torino 122, 00184 Rome, Italy; **Subscriptions**: Libreria Commissionaria Sansoni: Via Benedetto Fortini 120/10, Casella Postale 552, 50125 Florence, Italy

INTERNATIONAL BIBLIOGRAPHY OF SOCIOLOGY — 1991

Labour, capital and society; Travail, capital et société. *[Labour Cap. Soc.]* ISSN: 0706- 1706. *McGill University, Centre for Developing Area Studies*: 3715 rue Peel, Montréal, Québec H31 1X1, Canada

Land economics. *[Land Econ.]* ISSN: 0023-7639. *University of Wisconsin Press*: 114 North Murray Street, Madison, WI. 53715, U.S.A.

Language. *[Language]* ISSN: 0097-8507. *Linguistic Society of America*: 428 East Preston Street, Baltimore, MD 21202, U.S.A.

Language in society. *[Lang. Soc.]* ISSN: 0047-4045. *Cambridge University Press*: 40 West 20th Street, New York, NY. 10011, U.S.A.

Language problems and language planning. *[Lang. Prob. Lang. Plan.]* ISSN: 0270- 2690. *John Benjamins Publishing*: P.O. Box 75577, Amstedldijk 44, 1007 AN Amsterdam, The Netherlands

Latin American perspectives. *[Lat. Am. Pers.]* ISSN: 0094-582X. *Sage Publishers*: 2455 Teller Road Newbury Park, CA. 91320, U.S.A.

Latin American research review. *[Lat. Am. Res. R.]* ISSN: 0023-8791. *Latin American Studies Association*: Latin American Institute, 801 Yale NE, University of New Mexico, Albuquerque, NM. 87131-1016, U.S.A.

Law and contemporary problems. *[Law Cont. Pr.]* ISSN: 0023-9186. *Duke University, School of Law*: Room 006, Durham, NC 27706, U.S.A.

Law and policy. *[Law Policy]* ISSN: 0265 8240. *Basil Blackwell*: 108 Cowley Road, Oxford OX4 1JF, U.K.; **Subscriptions**: *Marston Book Services*: P.O. Box 87, Oxford OX2 0DT, U.K.

Law and society review. *[Law Soc. Rev.]* ISSN: 0023-9216. *Law and Society Association*: Hampshire House, University of Massachusetts at Amherst, Amherst MA. 01003, U.S.A.

Leviatán. *[Leviatán]* ISSN: 0210-6337. *Fundación Pablo Iglesias*: Monte Esquinza 30, 28010 Madrid, Spain

Linguistic inquiry. *[Linguist. In.]* ISSN: 0024-3892. *MIT Press*: 55 Hayward Street, Cambridge, MA 02142, U.S.A.

Linguistics. *[Linguistics]* ISSN: 0024-3949. *Mouton de Gruyter*: Postfach 110240, D-1000 Berlin 11, Germany

Linguistics and philosophy. *[Ling. Philos.]* ISSN: 0165-0157. *Kluwer Academic Publishers*: Spuiboulevard 50, P.O. Box 17, 3300 AA Dordrecht, The Netherlands

Links. *[Links]* ISSN: 0024-404X. *Verlag 2000*: Bleichstraße 5/7, Postfach 10 20 62, 6050 Offenbach 1, Germany

Literary and linguistic computing. *[Lit. Ling. Comput.]*; *Association for Literary and Linguistic Computing*; **Publisher**: *Oxford University Press*: Pinkhill House, Southfield Road, Eynsham, Oxford OX8 1JJ, U.K.

Local economy. *[Local. Ec.]* ISSN: 0269-0942. *Local Economy Policy Unit*: Southbank Polytechnic, Borough Road, London SE1 0AA, U.K.; **Publisher**: *Longman Group*: 6th Floor, Westgate House, The High, Harlow, Essex CM20 1YR, U.K.

Local population studies. *[Local. Pop. S.]* ISSN: 0143-2974. *Local Population Studies Society*: Tawney House, Matlock, Derbyshire, DE4 3BT, U.K.; **Subscriptions**: *Subscriptions Secretary*: 27 St. Margarets Road, St. Marychurch, Torquay, Devon, TQ1 4NU, U.K.

Lokayan bulletin. *[Lokay. B.]* ISSN: 0970-5406. *Lokayan Bulletin*: 13 Alipur Road, New Delhi 110 054, India

Maandschrift economie. *[Maan. Econ.]* ISSN: 0013-0486. *Wolters-Noordhoff*: Postbus 58, 9700 MB Groningen, The Netherlands

Magyar Közigazgatás. *[Mag. Köz.]* ISSN: 0865-736X.

Magyar tudomány. *[Mag. Tud.]* ISSN: 0025-0325. *Magyar Tudományos Akadémia*: Roosevelt-tér 9, 1051 Budapest, Hungary; **Publisher**: *Akademiai Kiado, Publishing House of the Hungarian Academy of Sciences*: P.O. Box 24, H-1363 Budapest, Hungary

Majalah demografi Indonesia; Indonesian journal of demography. *[Maj. Dem. Indonesia]* ISSN: 0126-0251. *Indonesian Demographers Association*: Demographic Institute, Faculty of Economics, University of Indonesia, Jln. Salemba 4, Jakarta 10430, Indonesia

Malaysian journal of tropical geography. *[Malay. J. Trop. Geogr.]* ISSN: 0127-1474. *University of Malaya, Department of Geography*: Kuala Lumpur 59100, Malaysia

Man. *[Man]* ISSN: 0025-1496. *Royal Anthropological Institute*: 50 Fitzroy Street, London W1P 5HS, U.K.; **Subscriptions**: *Distribution Centre*: Blackhorse Road, Letchworth SG6 1HN, Herts, U.K.

Man in India. *[Man India]* ISSN: 0025-1569. *Sudarshan Press*: Church Road, Ranchi 834 001 Bihar, India

Manchester School of economic and social studies. *[Manch. Sch. E.]* ISSN: 0025-2034. *Basil Blackwell*: 108 Cowley Road, Oxford, OX4 1JF, U.K.

Mankind. *[Mankind]* ISSN: 0025-2328. *Anthropological Society of N.S.W.*: Department of Anthropology, University of Sydney, NSW 2006, Australia

Mankind quarterly. *[Mankind Q.]* ISSN: 0025-2344. *Cliveden Press*: Suite C-2, 1133 13th Street N.W., Washington, DC. 20005-4298, U.S.A.

INTERNATIONAL BIBLIOGRAPHY OF SOCIOLOGY — 1991

Marine policy. *[Mar. Pol.] ISSN: 0308-597X. Butterworth-Heinemann*: P.O. Box 63, Westbury House, Bury St. Guildford, Surrey GU2 5BH, U.K.; **Subscriptions**: *Turpin Transactions*: Distribution Centre, Blackhorse Road, Letchworth, Herts SG6 1HN, U.K.

Marketing letters. *[Market. Lett.] ISSN: 0923-0645. Kluwer Academic Publishers*: P.O. Box 322, 3300 AH Dordrecht, The Netherlands

Marxistische Blätter. *[Marx. Blät] ISSN: 0542-7770. Neue Impulse Verlag*: Hoffnungstraße 18, 4300 Essen 1, Germany

Mathematical social sciences. *[Math. Soc. Sc.] ISSN: 0165 4896. Elsevier Science Publishers (North-Holland)*: P.O. Box 1991, 1000 BZ Amsterdam, The Netherlands

Media culture and society. *[Media Cult. Soc.] ISSN: 0163-4437. Sage Publications*: 6 Bonhill Street, London EC2A 4PU, U.K.

Medical anthropology. *[Med. Anthrop.] ISSN: 0145- 9740. Gordon and Breach*: P.O. Box 90, Reading RG1 8JL, U.K.

Medical anthropology quarterly. *[Med. Anthr. Q.] ISSN: 0745-5194. Society for Medical Anthropology*; **Publisher**: *American Anthropological Association*: 1703 New Hampshire Avenue, N.W., Washington D.C. 20009, U.S.A.

Medizin Mensch Gesellschaft. *[Medi. Mensch Gesell.] ISSN: 0340-8183. Ferdinand Enke Verlag*: Postfach 10 12 54. D-7000 Stuttgart 10, Germany

Megamot. *[Megamot] ISSN: 0025-8679. National Institute for Research in the Behavioural Sciences, Henrietta Szold Institute*: 9 Colombia Street, Kiryat Menachem, Jerusalem 96583, Israel

Meiji gakuin ronso. *[Meiji. Gak. Ron.]*; *Meiji University*: 1- 1 Kanda, Surugadai, Chiyoda-Ku, Tokyo 101, Japan

Melanesian law journal. *[Melan. Law J.]*; *University of Papua New Guinea, Faculty of Law*: Box 317, University P.O., Papua New Guinea; **Subscriptions**: *W.M. Gaunt and Sons*: 3001 Gulf Drive, Holmes Beach, FL. 33510, U.S.A.

Melbourne historical journal. *[Mel. Hist. J.] ISSN: 0076-6232. University of Melbourne, Department of History*: Parkville, Victoria 3052, Australia

Melbourne journal of politics. *[Mel. J. Pol.] ISSN: 0085-3224. Political Science Society*: University of Melbourne, Parkville, Vic. 3052, Australia

Memoria. *[Memoria]*; *El Colegio Nacional*: Calle Luis González Obregón No. 23, Centro Histórico 06020, Mexico D.F., Mexico

Mens en maatschappij. *[Mens Maat.] ISSN: 0025-9454. Bohn Stafleu Van Loghum*: Postbus 246, 3990 GA Houten, The Netherlands; **Subscriptions**: *Intermedia*: Postbus 4, 2400 MA Alphen aan den Rijn, The Netherlands

Merhavim. *[Merhavim]*; *Tel Aviv University, Department of Geography*: Tel Aviv, Israel

Mesoamérica. *[Mesoamérica] ISSN: 0252-9963. Centro de Investigaciones Regionales de Mesoamérica*: Apartado Postal 336. Antigua, Guatemala

Michigan law review. *[MI. law. R.] ISSN: 0026-2234. Michigan Law Review*: Hutchins Hall, Ann Arbor, MI. 48109-1215, U.S.A.

Middle East journal. *[Middle E. J.] ISSN: 0026- 3141. Middle East Institute*: 1761 N. Street, N.W., Washington, DC. 20036, U.S.A.; **Publisher**: *Indiana University Press*: 10th and Morton, Bloomington, IN. 47405, U.S.A.

Middle Eastern studies. *[Middle E. Stud.] ISSN: 0026-3206. Frank Cass*: Gainsborough House, 11 Gainsborough Road, London E11 1RS, U.K.

Migracijske teme. *[Migrac. Teme] ISSN: 0352-5600. University of Zagreb, Institute for Migration and Nationalities Studies/ Yugoslav Sociological Association, Section for Migration*: 41001 Zagreb, Trnjanska bb, p.p. 88, Yugoslavia

Milbank quarterly. *[Milbank Q.] ISSN: 0887-378X. Milbank Memorial Fund*; **Publisher**: *Cambridge University Press*: 40 West 20th Street, New York, NY. 10011, U.S.A.

Millennium. *[Millennium] ISSN: 0305-8298. Millenium Publishing Group*: London School of Economics and Political Science, Houghton Street, London WC2A 2AE, U.K.

Mind. *[Mind] ISSN: 0026-4423. Oxford University Press*: Pinkhill House, Southfield Road, Eynsham, OX8 1JJ, U.K.

Mind and language. *[Mind Lang.] ISSN: 0268 1064. Basil Blackwell*: 108 Cowley Road, Oxford OX4 1JF, U.K.

Minerva. *[Minerva] ISSN: 0026-4695. International Council on the Future of the University*: 11 Dupont Circle, Suite 300, Washington DC. 20036-1257, U.S.A.; **Publisher**: *Minerva*: 19 Nottingham Road, London SW17 7EA, U.K.

Modern Asian studies. *[Mod. Asian S.] ISSN: 0026- 749X. Cambridge University Press*: The Edinburgh Building, Shaftesbury Road, Cambridge CB2 2RU, U.K.

Modern China. *[Mod. Chi.] ISSN: 0097-7004. Sage Publications*: 2455 Teller Road, Newbury Park, CA. 91320, U.S.A.

Modern law review. *[Mod. Law R.] ISSN: 0026-7961. Basil Blackwell*: 108 Cowley Road, Oxford OX4 1JF, U.K.

Mondes en développement. *[Mon. Dévelop.] ISSN: 0302-3052. CECOEDUC/I.S.M.E.A.*: Avenue des Naïades 11, B-1170 Brussels, Belgium/ Rue Pierre et Marie Curie 11, Institut Henri Poincaré, F-75005 Paris, France

Monthly review. *[Mon. Rev.] ISSN: 0027- 0520. Monthly Review Foundation*: 122 West 27th Street, New York, NY. 10001, U.S.A.

INTERNATIONAL BIBLIOGRAPHY OF SOCIOLOGY — 1991

Monumenta Nipponica. [*Monu. Nippon.*] *ISSN: 0027-0741*. *Sophia University*: 7-1 Kioi-chō, Chiyoda-ku, Tokyo 102, Japan

Mouvement social. [*Mouve. Soc.*] *ISSN: 0027-2671*. *Association «Le Mouvement Social»*: 9 rue Malher, 75004 Paris, France; **Publisher**: *Editions Ouvrières*: 47 rue Servan, 75011 Paris, France

Multilingua. [*Multilingua*] *ISSN: 0167-8507*. *Mouton de Gruyter*: Postfach 110240, D-1000 Berlin 30, Germany

Národní hospodářství. [*Nár. Hosp.*] *ISSN: 0032-0749*. *Panorama*: Hálkova 1, 12072 Prague, Czechoslovakia

National Museum papers. [*Nat. Mus. Pap.*]; *National Museum of the Philippines/ Concerned Citizens for the National Museum*: Executive House, P.Burgos Street, 1000 Malate, Metro-Manila, Philippines

Nationalities papers. [*Nat. Pap.*] *ISSN: 0090-5992*. *Association for the Study of Nationalities (U.S.S.R. and East Europe)*: Department of Sociology, University of Nebraska, Omaha, NE. 68182, U.S.A.

Natural resources forum. [*Nat. Res. For.*] *ISSN: 0165-0203*. *United Nations Department of Technical Cooperation for Development*: New York, NY. 10017, U.S.A.; **Publisher**: *Butterworth-Heinemann*: P.O. Box 63, Westbury House, Bury Street, Guildford, Surrey GU2 5BH, U.K.

Natural resources journal. [*Natur. Res. J.*] *ISSN: 0028-0739*. *University of New Mexico, School of Law*: Albuquerque, NM. 87131, U.S.A.

Negotiation journal. [*Negot. J.*] *ISSN: 0748-4526*. *Plenum Press*: 233 Spring Street, New York, N.Y. 10013, U.S.A.

NEHA-bulletin. [*NEHA-B.*] *ISSN: 0920-9875*. *Nederlandsch Economisch-Historisch Archief* = *Netherlands Economic History Archive*: Cruquiusweg 31, 1019 AT Amsterdam, The Netherlands

Nenpo Shakaigaku Ronsyu. [*Nen. Shak. Ron.*]

Néprajzi Ertesítő. [*Népray. Ertes*] *ISSN: 0077- 6599*. *Library of the Ethnographical Museum*: 1055 Budapest, Kossuth Lajos ter 12., Hungary

Netherlands' journal of social sciences/Sociologia Neerlandica. [*Neth. J. Soc. Sci.*] *ISSN: 0038-0172*. *Netherlands' Sociological and Anthropological Society*; **Publisher**: *Van Gorcum*: P.O. Box 43, 4900 AA Assen, The Netherlands

Neue Gesellschaft/ Frankfurter Hefte. [*Neue Ges. Frank.*] *ISSN: 0177-6738*. *Friedrich-Ebert-Stiftung*; **Publisher**: *Verlag J.H.W. Dietz Nachf.*: In der Raste 2, 5300 Bonn 1, Germany

Neue politische literatur. [*Neue Pol. Liter.*] *ISSN: 0028-3320*. *Verlag Peter Lang*: Eschborner Landstraße 42-50, Postfach 940225, 6000 Frankfurt 90, Germany; **Subscriptions**: *idem*: Jupiterstrasse 15, CH-3000 Bern 15, Switzerland

New community. [*New Comm.*] *ISSN: 0047-9586*. *Commission for Racial Equality*: London, U.K.; **Publisher**: *University of Warwick, Centre for Research in Ethnic Relations*: Coventry CV4 7AL, U.K.

New European. [*New Eur.*] *ISSN: 0953-1432*. *MCB University Press*: 60/62, Toller Lane, Bradford, West Yorkshire BD8 9BY, U.K.

New formations. [*New Form.*] *ISSN: 0950-2378*. *Routledge*: 11 New Fetter Lane, London EC4P 4EE, U.K.; **Subscriptions**: *idem*: House, North Way, Andover, Hants. SP10 5BE, U.K.

New ground. [*New Gro.*]; *Environmental and Development Agency (EDA)*: P.O. Box 322, Newtown, 2113 South Africa

New internationalist. [*N.I.*] *ISSN: 0305-9529*. *New Internationalist Publications*: 42 Hythe Bridge Street, Oxford OX1 2EP, U.K.; **Subscriptions**: *New Internationalist*: 120-126 Lavender Avenue, Mitcham, Surrey CR4 3HP, U.K.

New left review. [*New Left R.*] *ISSN: 0028- 6060*. *New Left Review*: 6 Meard Street, London W1V 3HR, U.K.

New perspectives on Turkey. [*New Persp. Turk.*] *ISSN: 0896-6346*. *Simon's Rock of Bard College*: Great Barrington, MA., U.S.A.

New politics. [*New Polit.*] *ISSN: 0028-6494*. *New Politics Associates*: P.O. Box 98, Brooklyn, NY. 11231, U.S.A.

New quest. [*New Que.*] *ISSN: 0258-0381*. *Indian Association for Cultural Freedom*: 850/8A Shivajinagar, Pune 411 004, India

New technology, work and employment. [*New Tech. Work. Empl.*] *ISSN: 0268-1072*. *Basil Blackwell*: 108 Cowley Road, Oxford OX4 1JF, U.K.

New Vico studies. [*New Vico S.*] *ISSN: 0733-9542*. *Institute for Vico Studies*: 69 Fifth Avenue, New York, NY. 10003, U.S.A.

New York University journal of international law and politics. [*N.Y.U. J. Int'l. L. & Pol.*] *ISSN: 0028-7873*. *New York University Law Publications*: 110 West Third Street, New York, NY. 10012, U.S.A.

New York University law review. [*NY. U. Law. Re.*] *ISSN: 0028-7881*. *New York University Law Review*: 110 W. Third Street, New York, NY. 10012, U.S.A.

New Zealand journal of history. [*N.Z. J. Hist.*] *ISSN: 0028-8322*. *University of Auckland, History Department*: Private Bag, Auckland, New Zealand

NIAS. [*NIAS*] *ISSN: 0904- 597X*. *Nordic Institute of Asian Studies*: 84 Njalsgade, DK-2300 Copenhagen S, Denmark

Nieuwe West-Indische gids; New West Indian guide. [*Nie. West-Ind. Gids*] *ISSN: 0028-9930*. *Stichting Nieuwe West-Indische Gids/ Johns Hopkins University, Program in Atlantic History, Culture and Society*: Utrecht, The Netherlands/ Baltimore, M.D., U.S.A.; **Publisher**: *Foris*: Box 509, 3300 AM Dordrecht, The Netherlands

INTERNATIONAL BIBLIOGRAPHY OF SOCIOLOGY — 1991

Nigerian field. *[Niger. F.] ISSN: 0029-0076. Nigerian Field Society*; **Subscriptions**: Mr. P.V. Hartley/ Mrs H. Fell: PMB 5320, Ibadan, Oyo State, Nigeria/ Limestone House, Alma Road, Tideswell, Buxton, Derbyshire SK17 8ND, U.K.

Nigerian forum. *[Nig. For.] ISSN: 0189-0816. Nigerian Institute of International Affairs*: Kofo Aboyomi Road, Victoria Island, G.P.O. Box 1727, Lagos, Nigeria

Nigerian journal of economic and social studies. *[Nig. J. Econ. Soc. Stud.] ISSN: 0029-0092. Nigerian Economic Society*: University of Ibadan, Department of Economics, Ibadan, Nigeria

Nonprofit and voluntary sector quarterly. *[Nonprof. Volun. Sec. Q.] ISSN: 0899-7640. Association for Research on Nonprofit Organizations and Voluntary Action*: Route 2, Box 696, Pullman, Washington 99163, U.S.A.; **Publisher**: *Jossey-Bass*: 350 Sansome Street, San Francisco, CA. 94104, U.S.A.

Nonprofit management and leadership. *[Non. Manag. Leader.] ISSN: 1048-6682. Jossey-Bass*: 350 Sansome Street, San Francisco, CA. 94104-1310, U.S.A.

Nord nytt. *[Nord. Ny.] ISSN: 0008-1345. Institute foe Europeaeisk Folkelivsforskning*: Brede Alle 69, DK-2800, Lyngby, Denmark; **Subscriptions**: *Nordisk Etnologisk Folkloristisk Arbejdsgruppe*

Nordic journal of linguistics. *[Nordic J. Linguist.] ISSN: 0332-5865. Nordic Association of Linguists*; **Publisher**: *Universitetsforlaget = Norwegian University Press*: Journals Department, P.O. Box 2959 Tøyen, 0608 Oslo 6, Norway

Notes and records of the Royal Society of London. *[Not. & Rec. Roy. Soc.] ISSN: 0035-9149. Royal Society of London*: 6 Carlton House Terrace, London SW1Y 5AG, U.K.

Nueva sociedad. *[Nueva Soc.]*; *Nueva Sociedad*: Apartado 61.712, Caracas 1060-A, Venezuela

Numen. *[Numen] ISSN: 0029-5973. International Association for the History of Religions*; **Publisher**: *E.J. Brill*: P.O. Box 9000, 2300 PA Leiden, The Netherlands

Общественные науки в Узбекисана; Obshchestnnnye nauki v Uzbekistane. *[Obshch. N. Usbek.]*

Oceania. *[Oceania] ISSN: 0029-8077. Oceania Publications, University of Sydney*: 116 Darlington Road, N.S.W. 2006, Australia

Oceanic linguistics. *[Oceanic Ling.] ISSN: 0029-8115. University of Hawaii Press*: 2840 Kolowalu Street, Honolulu, HI. 96822, U.S.A.

Odu. *[Odu] ISSN: 0029-8522. University of Ife Press*: Periodicals Department, University of Ife, Ile-Ife, Nigeria

Option = Избор. *[Option] ISSN: 0861-1667. Izbor*: 4 Alexander Battenberg str., Sofia 1000, Bulgaria

Oral history. *[Oral Hist.] ISSN: 0143-0955. Oral History Society*: University of Essex, Department of Sociology, Wivenhoe Park, Colchester, Essex CO4 3SQ, U.K.

Ordo. *[Ordo] ISSN: 0048- 2129. Gustav Fischer Verlag*: Wollgrasweg 49, D-7000 Stuttgart, Germany

Organization studies. *[Organ. Stud.] ISSN: 0170-8406. European Group for Organizational Studies*; **Publisher**: *Walter de Gruyter*: Genthiner Str. 13, D-1000 Berlin 30, Germany

Organizational behavior and human decision processes. *[Organ. Beh. Hum. Dec. Proces.] ISSN: 0749- 5978. Academic Press*: 1 East First Street, Duluth, MN. 55802, U.S.A.

Organizational science. *[Organ. Sc.]*

Orient. *[Orient] ISSN: 0030-5227. Deutsches Orient- Institut*: Mittelweg 150, 2000 Hamburg 13, Germany; **Publisher**: *Leske + Budrich*: Postfach 300551, 5090 Leverkusen 3, Germany

Orientalia lovaniensia periodica. *[Orient. Lovan. Period.]*; *Universitaire Stichting Van België*: Departement Oriëntalistiek, Blijde Inkomststraat 21, B-3000 Leuven, Belgium

Orita. *[Orita] ISSN: 0030-5596. University of Ibadan*: Department of Religious Studies, Ibadan, Nigeria

Österreichische Zeitschrift für öffentliches Recht und Völkerrechte. *[Öster. Z. Öffent. Völk.] ISSN: 0378-3073. Springer-Verlag*: Mölkerbastei 5, P.O. Box 367, A-1011 Vienna, Austria

Österreichische Zeitschrift für Politikwissenschaft. *[Öster. Z. Polit.]*; *Österreichische Gesellschaft für Politikwissenschaft*; **Publisher**: *Verlag für Gesellschaftskritik*: Kaiserstraße 91, A-1070 Vienna, Austria

Osteuropa. *[Osteuropa] ISSN: 0030-6428. Deutsche Gesellschaft für Osteuropakunde*: Schaperstraße 30, 1000 Berlin 15, Germany; **Publisher**: *Deutsche Verlags-Anstalt*: Neckarstraße 121, Postfach 1060 12, 7000 Stuttgart 10, Germany

Our generation. *[Our Gener.] ISSN: 0030-686X. Our Generation*: Suite 444, 3981 boulevard St-Laurent, Montréal, Québec H2W 1Y5, Canada

Oxford agrarian studies. *[Ox. Agrar. Stud.] ISSN: 0264-5491. Carfax Publishing*: P.O. Box 25, Abingdon, Oxfordshire OX14 3UE, U.K.

Oxford bulletin of economics and statistics. *[Ox. B. Econ. S.] ISSN: 0305-9049. Basil Blackwell*: 108 Cowley Road, Oxford OX4 1JF, U.K.; **Subscriptions**: *Marston Book Services, Journals Subscriptions Department*: PO Box 87, Oxford, OX23 0DT, U.K.

Oxford economic papers. *[Ox. Econ. Pap.] ISSN: 0030-7653. Oxford University Press*: Pinkhill House, Southfield Road, Eynsham, Oxford, OX8 1JJ, U.K.
Oxford review of economic policy. *[Ox. R. Econ. Pol.] ISSN: 0266-903X. Oxford University Press*: Pinkhill House, Southfield Road, Eynsham, Oxford OX8 1JJ, U.K.
Pacific affairs. *[Pac. Aff.] ISSN: 0030-851X. University of British Columbia*: Vancouver, BC., V6T 1W5 Canada
Pacific historical review. *[Pac. Hist. R.] ISSN: 0030-8684. American Historical Association, Pacific Coast Branch*: 6339 Bunche Hall, Los Angeles, CA. 90024, U.S.A.; **Publisher**: *University of California Press*: 2120 Berkeley Way, Berkeley, CA. 94720, U.S.A.
Pacific review. *[Pac. Rev.] ISSN: 0951-2748. Oxford University Press*: Pinkhill House, Southfield Road, Eynsham OX8 1JJ, U.K.
Pacific viewpoint. *[Pac. View.] ISSN: 0030-8978. Victoria University of Wellington, Department of Geography*: Private Bag, Wellington, New Zealand; **Publisher**: *Victoria University Press*: P.O. Box 600, Wellington, New Zealand
Pakistan development review. *[Pak. Dev. R.] ISSN: 0030-9729. Pakistan Institute of Development Economics*: P.O. Box 1091, Islamabad, Pakistan
Pakistan economic and social review. *[Pak. Ec. Soc. R.]; University of the Punjab, Department of Economics*: New Campus, Lahore, Pakistan
Pakistan journal of history and culture. *[Pak. J. Hist. Cult.] ISSN: 1012-7682. National Institute of Historical and Cultural Research*: Rauf Centre, 102 Blue Area, Islamabad, Pakistan
Państwo i prawo. *[Pań. Prawo] ISSN: 0031-0980. Polska Academia Nauk, Instytut Nauk Prawnych*: Ul. Wiejska 12, 00-490 Warsaw, Poland
Papers. *[Papers] ISSN: 0210-2862. Universitat Autònoma de Barcelona, Departament de Sociologia*: Servei de Publicacions, Edifici A, 08193 Barcelona, Spain
Papers in regional science. *[Pap. Reg. Sci.] ISSN: 0486-2902. Regional Science Association International*: University of Illinois at Urbana-Champaign, 1-3 Observatory, 901 South Mathews Avenue, Urbana, IL. 61801-3682, U.S.A.
Past and present. *[Past Pres.]; Oxford University Press*: Pinkhill House, Southfield Road, Eynsham, Oxford OX8 1JJ, U.K.
Peasant studies. *[Peasant Stud.]; University of Utah*: Department of History, University of Utah, Salt Lake City, UT. 84112, U.S.A.
Peninsule. *[Peninsule]; Cercle de Culture et de Recherches Laotiennes*: 14 rue Dame Genette, 57070 Metz, France
Pensamiento iberoamericano. *[Pen. Iber.] ISSN: 0212-2208. Sociedad Estatal Quinto Centenario*: c/ Serrano, 187-189.28002 Madrid, Spain; **Subscriptions**: *Instituto de Cooperación Iberoamericana*: Avenida de los Reyes Católicos, 4.28040 Madrid, Spain
Pensée. *[Pensée] ISSN: 0031-4773. Institut de recherches marxistes*: 64, Boulevard Auguste-Blanqui, 75013 Paris, France
Perception & psychophysics. *[Perc. Psych.] ISSN: 0031-5117. Psychonomic Society*: 1710 Fortview Road, Austin, TX. 78704, U.S.A.
Peripherie. *[Peripherie] ISSN: 0173-184X. Wissenschaftliche Vereinigung für Entwicklungstheorie und Entwicklungspolitik*: Institut für Soziologie, Scharnhorststraße 121, D-4400 Münster, Germany; **Publisher**: *Verlag Peripherie*: LN-Vertrieb, Gneisenaustraße 2, D-1000 Berlin 61, Germany
Pesquisa e planejamento econômico. *[Pesq. Plan. Ec.] ISSN: 0100-0551. Instituto de Planejamento Econômico e Social (IPEA)*: Av. Presidente Antônio Carlos 51, CEP 20 020, Rio de Janeiro, Brazil
Peuples méditerranéens; Mediterranean peoples. *[Peup. Médit.] ISSN: 0399-1253. Institut d'Études Méditerranéenes*: B.P. 188-07, 75326 Paris Cedex 07, France
Philippine quarterly of culture and society. *[Phil. Q. Cult. Soc.] ISSN: 0115-0243. University of San Carlos*: Publications Section, Cebu City 6000, Philippines
Philippine studies. *[Phil. Stud.] ISSN: 0031-7837. Ateneo de Manila University Press*: P.O. Box 154, Manila 1099, Philippines
Philosophy & public affairs. *[Philos. Pub.] ISSN: 0048-3915. Princeton University Press*: 41 William Street, Princeton, NJ. 08540, U.S.A.; **Subscriptions**: *Johns Hopkins University Press*: Journals Division, 701 West 40th Street, Suite 275, Baltimore, MD. 21211, U.S.A.
Philosophy east and west. *[Philos. E.W.] ISSN: 0031-8221. University of Hawaii Press*: 2840 Kolowalu Street, Honolulu, HI. 96822, U.S.A.
Philosophy of the social sciences. *[Philos. S. Sc.] ISSN: 0048-3931. Sage Publications*: 2455 Teller Road, Newbury Park, CA. 91320, U.S.A.
Planning and administration. *[Plan. Admin.] ISSN: 0304-117X. International Union of Local Authorities*: 41 Wassenaarseweg, 2596 CG The Hague, The Netherlands

Planning outlook. *[Plan. Out.] ISSN: 0032-0714. University of Newcastle-upon-Tyne, Department of Town and Country Planning*: Newcastle-upon-Tyne NE1 7RU, U.K.

Planning practice and research. *[Plan. Pract. Res.] ISSN: 0269-7459. Pion*: 207 Brondesbury Park, London NW2 5JN, U.K.

Плановое Хозяйство; Planovoe khoziaistvo. *[Plan. Khoz.] ISSN: 0370-0356. Gosplan, SSSR*; **Publisher**: *Izdatel'stvo Ekonomika*: Berezhkovskaia naberezhnaia 6, 121864 Moscow, U.S.S.R.

Policing and society. *[Poli. Soc.] ISSN: 1043-9463. Harwood Academic Publishers*: 270 8th Avenue, New York, NY.10011, U.S.A.

Policy and politics. *[Policy Pol.] ISSN: 0305-5736. University of Bristol, School for Advanced Urban Studies*: Rodney Lodge, Grange Road, Bristol BS8 4EA, U.K.

Polin. *[Polin] ISSN: 0268-1056; ISBN: 0 631 17624 1. Institute for Polish-Jewish Studies*: 45 St. Giles, Oxford OX1 3LP, U.K.; **Publisher**: *Basil Blackwell*: 108 Cowley Road, Oxford OX4 1JF, U.K.

Полис; Polis. *[Polis] ISSN: 0321-2017. Izdatel'stvo Progress Publishers*: Zuborsky bul'var 17, Moscow 119847, U.S.S.R.

Polish perspectives. *[Polish Persp.] ISSN: 0032-2962. Polska Instytut Spraw Miedzynasodowych*: ul. Warecka 1a, P.O. Box 159, 00-950 Warsaw, Poland; **Subscriptions**: *Ars Polona*: Krakowskie Przedmieście 7, 00-068 Warsaw, Poland

Political geography. *[Pol. Geogr.] ISSN: 0962-6298. Butterworth-Heinemann*: Linacre House, Jordan Hill, Oxford OX2 8DP, U.K.

Political geography quarterly. *[Polit. Geogr. Q.] ISSN: 0260-9827. Butterworth-Heinemann*: Westbury House, Bury Street, P.O. Box 63, Guildford, Surrey GU2 5BH, U.K.

Political psychology. *[Polit. Psych.] ISSN: 0162-895X. International Society of Political Psychology*; **Publisher**: *Plenum Publishing*: 233 Spring Street, New York, NY. 10013, U.S.A.

Political science quarterly. *[Pol. Sci. Q.] ISSN: 0032-3195. Academy of Political Science*: 475 Riverside Drive, Suite 1274, New York, NY. 10115-0012, U.S.A.

Political theory. *[Polit. Theory] ISSN: 0090-5917. Sage Publications*: 2111 West Hillcrest Drive, Newbury Park, CA. 91320, U.S.A.

Politička misao. *[Pol. Misao] ISSN: 0032-3241. Facultet Političkih Nauka u Zagrebu*: 41000 Zagreb, Lepušićeva 6, Yugoslavia

Politics and society. *[Polit. Soc.] ISSN: 0032-3292. Butterworth-Heinemann*: 80 Montvale Avenue, Stoneham, MA. 02180, U.S.A.

Politics and society in Germany, Austria and Switzerland. *[Pol. Soc. Ger. Aust. Swit.] ISSN: 0954-6030. University of Nottingham, Institute of German, Austrian and Swiss Affairs*: University Park, Nottingham NG7 2RD, U.K.

Politics and the life sciences. *[Polit. Life] ISSN: 0730-9384. Association for Politics and the Life Sciences*: Northern Illinois University, DeKalb, IL. 60115-2854, U.S.A.

Politique africaine. *[Pol. Afr.] ISSN: 0244-7827. Association des chercheurs de politique africaine*; **Publisher**: *Editions Karthala*: 22-24 boulevard Arago, 75013 Paris, France

Politique internationale. *[Polit. Int.] ISSN: 0221-2781. Politique Internationale*: 11 rue du Bois de Boulogne, 75116 Paris, France

Politische Vierteljahresschrift. *[Polit. Viertel.] ISSN: 0032-3470. Deutsche Vereinigung für Politische Wissenschaft*; **Publisher**: *Westdeutscher Verlag*: Postfach 5829 D-6200 Wiesbaden 1, Germany

Population. *[Population] ISSN: 0032-4663. Institut National d'Etudes Démographiques*: 27 rue du Commandeur, 75675 Paris Cedex 14, France; **Publisher**: *Editions de l'Institut National d'Etudes Démographiques*: 27 rue du Commandeur, 75675 Paris Cedex 14, France

Population and development review. *[Pop. Dev. Rev.] ISSN: 0098-7921. Population Council*: One Dag Hammarskjold Plaza, New York, N.Y. 10017, U.S.A.

Population and environment. *[Popul. Envir.] ISSN: 0199-0039. Human Sciences Press*: 233 Spring Street, New York, N.Y. 10013-1578, U.S.A.

Population research and policy review. *[Pop. Res. Pol. R.] ISSN: 0167-5923. Kluwer Academic Publishers*: P.O. Box 17, 3300 AH Dordrecht, The Netherlands; **Subscriptions**: *idem*: P.O. Box 322, 3300 AH Dordrecht, The Netherlands

Population review. *[Popul. R.] ISSN: 0032-471X. Indian Institute for Population Studies*: 8976 Cliffridge Avenue, La Jolla, CA. 92037, U.S.A.

Population studies. *[Pop. Stud.] ISSN: 0032-4728. London School of Economics, Population Investigation Committee*: Houghton Street, Aldwych, London WC2A 2AE, U.K.

Postmodern critical theorising. *[Postmod. Critic. Theor.]; University of Adelaide, Department of Anthropology*: G.P.O. Box 498, Adelaide, South Australia, 5001, Australia

Praca i zabezpieczenie społeczne. *[Pra. Zab. Społ.] ISSN: 0032-6186. Państwowe Wydawnictwo Ekonomiczne*: Ul. Niecała 4a, Warsaw, Poland

INTERNATIONAL BIBLIOGRAPHY OF SOCIOLOGY — 1991

Practice. *[Practice]* ISSN: 0950-3153. *British Association of Social Workers*: 16 Kent Street, Birmingham B5 6RD, U.K.; **Subscriptions**: *BASW-Practice*: c/o Whiting & Birch, P.O. Box 872, London SE23 3HL, U.K.

Praxis international. *[Prax. Int.]* ISSN: 0260-8448. *Basil Blackwell*: 108 Cowley Road, Oxford OX4 JJF, U.K.

Présence africaine. *[Prés. Afr.]* ISSN: 0032-7638. *Société Africaine de Culture*: 25 bis, rue des Ecoles, 75005 Paris, France

Природа; Priroda. *[Priroda]*

Problèmes politiques et sociaux. *[Prob. Pol. Soc.]* ISSN: 0015-9743. *Documentation Française*: 29 quai Voltaire, 75007 Paris, France

Problems of communism. *[Probl. Commu.]* ISSN: 0032-941X. *US Information Agency*: 301 4th Street SW Washington, DC. 20547, U.S.A.; **Subscriptions**: *Superintendent of Documents*: US Government Printing Office, Washington DC. 20402, U.S.A.

Proceedings of the Academy of Political Science. *[Proceed. Acad. Polit. Sci.]* ISSN: 0065-0684. *Academy of Political Science*: 475 Riverside Drive, Suite 1274, New York, NY. 10115- 0012, U.S.A.

Proceedings. American Statistical Association. *[Proc. Am. Stat. Ass.]*; *American Statistical Association*: 1429 Duke Street, Alexandria, VA. 22314, U.S.A.

Professional geographer. *[Prof. Geogr.]* ISSN: 0033-0124. *Association of American Geographers*: 1710 Sixteenth Street, N.W., Washington, DC. 20009-3198, U.S.A.

Progress in human geography. *[Prog. H. Geog.]* ISSN: 0309-1325. *Edward Arnold*: Mill Road, Dunton Green, Sevenoaks, Kent TN13 2YA, U.K.; **Subscriptions**: *Subscription Department, Edward Arnold Journals*: 42 Bedford Square, London WC1B 3SL, U.K.

Progress in planning. *[Prog. Plan.]* ISSN: 0305-9006. *Pergamon Press*: Headington Hill Hall, Oxford OX3 0BW, U.K.

Project appraisal. *[Proj. App.]* ISSN: 0268-8867. *Beech Tree Publishing*: 10 Watford Close, Guildford, Surrey GU1 2EP, U.K.

Prokla.:*Probleme des Klassenkampfs* **[Prokla]**; *Vereinigung zur Kritik der politischen Ökonomie*; **Publisher**: *Rotbuch Verlag*: Potsdamer Str. 98, 1000 Berlin 30, Germany

Przegląd polonijny. *[Prz. Pol.]* ISSN: 0137-303X. *Polska Akademia Nauk, Komitet Badania Polonii*; **Publisher**: *Ossolineum, Publishing House of the Polish Academy of Sciences*: Rynek 9, 50-106 Wroclaw, Poland

Przegląd socjologiczny. *[Prz. Soc.]* ISSN: 0033-2356. *Łódzkie towarzystwo naukowe*: ul Rewolucji 1905 roku 41/43, Łódź, Poland; **Publisher**: *Zakład Narodowy im. Ossolińskich, Wydawnictwo Polskiej Akademii Nauk*: Poland

Przegląd statystyczny. *[Prz. Staty.]* ISSN: 0033- 2372. *Polska Akademia nauk, Komitet Statystyki i Ekonometrii*: ul. Miodowa 10, Warsaw, Poland; **Subscriptions**: *ARS Polona*: Krakowskie Przedmieście 7, 00-068 Warsaw, Poland

Psychoanalytic review. *[Psychoanal. Rev.]* ISSN: 0033-2836. *Guilford Publications*: 72 Spring Street, New York, NY. 10012, U.S.A.

Psychological bulletin. *[Psychol .B.]* ISSN: 0033- 2909. *American Psychological Association*: 1400 North Uhle Street, Arlington, VA. 22201, U.S.A.

Psychological review. *[Psychol. Rev.]* ISSN: 0033-295X. *American Psychological Association*: 1400 North Uhle Street, Arlington, VA. 22201, U.S.A.

Psychology and developing societies. *[Psychol. Devel. Soc.]*; *Sage Publications India*: 32 M-Block Market, Greater Kailash I, New Delhi 110 048, India

Psychotherapy research. *[Psychoth. Res.]* ISSN: 0894-7597. *Society for Psychotherapy Research*; **Publisher**: *Guilford Publications*: 72 Spring Street, New York, NY. 10012, U.S.A.

Public administration. *[Publ. Admin.]* ISSN: 0033- 3298. *Royal Institute for Public Administration*: 3 Birdcage Walk, London SW1H 9JH, U.K.; **Publisher**: *Basil Blackwell*: 108 Cowley Road, Oxford OX4 1JF, U.K.

Public administration and development. *[Publ. Adm. D.]* ISSN: 0271-2075. *Royal Institute of Public Administration*: Regent's College, Inner Circle, Regent's Park, London NW1 4NS, U.K.; **Publisher**: *John Wiley & Sons*: Baffins Lane, Chichester, West Sussex PO19 1UD, U.K.

Public administration review. *[Publ. Adm. Re.]* ISSN: 0033-3352. *American Society for Public Administration*: 1120 G. Street, NW, Suite 500, Washington, DC. 20005, U.S.A.

Public affairs quarterly. *[Publ. Aff. Q.]* ISSN: 0887-0373. *Philosophy Documentation Center/ North American Philosophical Publications*: Bowling Green State University, Bowling Green, OH. 43403, U.S.A.

Public culture. *[Publ. Cult.]* ISSN: 0899-2363. *Center for Transnational Cultural Studies*: University Museum, University of Pennsylvania, 33rd and Spruce Streets, Pennsylvania, PA. 19104-6324, U.S.A.; **Publisher**: *University of Pennsylvania, University Museum*: University of Pennsylvania, 33rd and Spruce Streets, Pennsylvania, PA. 19104-6324, U.S.A.

Public interest. *[Publ. Inter.]* ISSN: 0033-3557. *National Affairs*: 1112 16th Street, N.W., Suite 530, Washington, D.C. 20036, U.S.A; **Subscriptions**: *Public Interest subscription office*: P.O. Box 3000, Denville, NJ. 07834, U.S.A.

Public law. *[Publ. Law] ISSN: 0033 3565. Sweet & Maxwell*: South Quay Plaza, 8th Floor, 183 Marsh Wall, London E14 9FT, U.K.

Public opinion quarterly. *[Publ. Opin. Q.] ISSN: 0033-362X. American Association for Public Opinion Research*: P.O. Box 17, Princeton, NJ. 08540, U.S.A.; **Publisher**: *University of Chicago Press*: Journals Division, 5720 S. Woodlawn Avenue, Chicago, IL. 60637, U.S.A.

Publizistik. *[Publizistik] ISSN: 0033-4006. Deutsche Gesellschaft für Publizistik- und Kommunikationswissenschaft/ Österreichische Gesellschaft für Publizistik- und Kommunikationswissenschaft/ Schweizerische Gesellschaft für Kommunikations- und Medienwissenschaft*: Martin-Legros-Straße 53, D-5300 Bonn 1, Germany; **Publisher**: *Universitätsverlag Konstanz*: Postfach 102051, D-7750 Konstanz, Germany

Quaderni di sociologia. *[Quad. Sociol.] ISSN: 0033- 4952. Edizioni di Comunità*: 20090 Segrate, Milan, Italy

Quadrant. *[Quadrant] ISSN: 0033-5002. Quadrant Magazine*: 46 George Street, Fitzroy, Melbourne, Victoria 3065, Australia

Quarterly journal of economics. *[Q. J. Econ.] ISSN: 0033-5533. Harvard University*: Cambridge, MA. 02138, U.S.A.; **Publisher**: *MIT Press*: 55 Hayward Street, Cambridge, MA. 02142, U.S.A.

Quest. *[Quest] ISSN: 1011-226X. University of Zambia, Department of Philosophy*: P.O. Box 32379, Lusaka, Zambia; **Subscriptions**: *Quest*: P.O. Box 9114, 9703 LC Groningen, The Netherlands

R&D management. *[R&D Manag.] ISSN: 0033-6807. Basil Blackwell*: 108 Cowley Road, Oxford OX4 1JF, U.K.

Race and class. *[Race Class] ISSN: 0306-3965. Institute of Race Relations*: 2-6 Leeke Street, King's Cross Road, London WC1X 9HS, U.K.

Радуга; Raduga. *[Raduga]; Izdatel'stvo "Periodika"*: 200001 Tallin, Piarnuskoe shosse 8

Rassegna italiana di sociologia. *[Rass. It. Soc.] ISSN: 0486 0349. Società Editrice il Mulino*: Strada Maggiore 37, 40125 Bologna, Italy

Raven. *[Raven] ISSN: 0951- 4066. Freedom Press*: 84b Whitechapel High Street, London E1 7QX, U.K.

Recherches sociographiques. *[Rech. Soc.graph] ISSN: 0034-1282. Université Laval, Département de Sociologie*: Québec G1K 7P4, Canada

Recht der internationalen Wirtschaft. *[Recht Int. Wirst.] ISSN: 0340-7926. Verlag Recht und Wirtschaft*: Häusserstraße 14, Postfach 10 59 60, 6900 Heidelberg, Germany

Regards sur l'actualité. *[Regar. Actual.] ISSN: 0337-7091. Documentation Française*: 29, Quai Voltaire, 75340 Paris Cedex 07, France

Regional science and urban economics. *[Reg. Sci. Urb. Econ.] ISSN: 0166- 0462. Elsevier Science Publishers (North-Holland)*: P.O. Box 1991, 1000 BZ Amsterdam, The Netherlands; **Subscriptions**: *idem*: Journals Division, P.O. Box 211, 1000 AE Amsterdam, The Netherlands

Regional studies. *[Reg. Stud.] ISSN: 0034-3404. Regional Studies Association*; **Publisher**: *Cambridge University Press*: The Edinburgh Building, Shaftesbury Road, Cambridge CB2 2RU, U.K.

Religion. *[Religion] ISSN: 0048-721X. Academic Press*: 24-28 Oval Road, London NW1 7DX, U.K.

Religion in communist lands. *[Relig. Comm. Lands] ISSN: 0307-5974. Keston College*: Heathfield Road, Keston, Kent BR2 6BA, U.K.

Religion, state and society. *[Relig. State Soc.] ISSN: 0963-7494. Keston College*: 33a Canal Street, Oxford OX2 6BQ, U.K.; **Publisher**: *Carfax Publishing Company*: P.O. Box 25, Abingdon, Oxfordshire OX14 3UE, U.K.

Research in Melanesia. *[R. Melan.] ISSN: 0254-0665. University of Papua New Guinea, Department of Anthropology and Sociology*: Box 320 University, Port Moresby, Papua New Guinea

Research in social movements, conflicts and change. *[R. Soc. Move. Con. Cha.] ISSN: 0163-786X. JAI Press*: 55 Old Post Road No.2, Greenwich, CT. 066830, U.S.A.

Research in social stratification and mobility. *[R. Soc. Strat. Mob.] ISSN: 0276-5624. JAI Press*: 55 Old Post Road No.2, Greenwich, CT. 066830, U.S.A.

Resources policy. *[Res. Pol.] ISSN: 0301-4207. Butterworth-Heinemann*: Linacre House, Jordan Hill, Oxford, OX2 8DP, U.K.

Response to the victimization of women and children. *[Resp. Victim. Women Child.] ISSN: 0894-7597. Center for Women Policy Studies*: Washington, DC., U.S.A.; **Publisher**: *Guilford Publications*: 72 Spring Street, New York, NY. 10012, U.S.A.

Rethinking Marxism. *[Rethink. Marx.] ISSN: 0893-5696. Association for Economic and Social Analysis*: University of Massachusetts-Amhurst, Amhurst, MA., U.S.A.; **Publisher**: *Guilford Publications*: 72 Spring Street, New York, NY. 10012, U.S.A.

Review of African political economy. *[Rev. Afr. Pol. Ec.] ISSN: 0305- 6244. ROAPE Publications*: Regency House, 75-77 St. Mary's Road, Sheffield S2 4AN, U.K.

Review of black political economy. *[Rev. Bl. Pol. Ec.] ISSN: 0034-6446. National Economic Association/ Clark Atlanta University, Southern Center for Studies in Public Policy*: 240 Brawley Drive, S.W. Atlanta, GA. 30314, U.S.A.; **Publisher**: *Transaction Publishers*: Rutgers University, New Brunswick, NJ. 08903, U.S.A.

INTERNATIONAL BIBLIOGRAPHY OF SOCIOLOGY — 1991

Review of economic conditions in Italy. *[Rev. Ec. Con. It.] ISSN: 0034-6799. Banco di Roma*: Viale U. Tupini 180, 00144 Rome, Italy

Review of economics and statistics. *[Rev. Econ. St.] ISSN: 0034-6535. Harvard University*; **Publisher**: *Elsevier Science Publishers (North-Holland)*: P.O. Box 1991, 1000 BZ Amsterdam, The Netherlands; **Subscriptions**: *idem*: Journal Department, P.O. Box 211, 1000 AE Amsterdam, The Netherlands

Review of income and wealth. *[R. In. Weal.] ISSN: 0034-6586. International Association for Research in Income and Wealth*: Dept. of Economics, 269 Mercer Street, Room 700, New York University, New York, NY. 10003, U.S.A.; **Subscriptions**: *The Review of Income and Wealth*: c/o J.W. Arrowsmith, Winterstoke Road, Bristol BS3 2NT, U.K.

Review of Indonesian and Malaysian affairs.*[RIMA]— [R. Ind. Malay. Aff.] ISSN: 0034- 6594. University of Sydney, Department of Indonesian and Malayan Studies*: Sydney, NSW 2001, Australia

Review of international co-operation. *[R. Int. Co-op.] ISSN: 0034-6608. International Co-operative Alliance*: Route des Morillons 15, CH-1218 Le Grand Saconnex, Geneva, Switzerland

Review of rural and urban planning in Southern and Eastern Africa. *[R. Rur. Urb. Plan. S.& E.Afr.]; University of Zimbabwe, Department of Rural and Urban Planning*: P.O. Box MP 167, Mount Pleasant, Harare, Zimbabwe

Review of social economy. *[R. Soc. Econ.] ISSN: 0034-6764. Association for Social Economics*: c/o Department of Economics, Northern Illinois University, DeKalb, IL. 60115, U.S.A.

Review of the economic situation of Mexico. *[Rev. Econ. Sit. Mex.] ISSN. 0187-3407. Banco Nacional de Mexico, Department of Economic Research*: Av. Madero 21, Mexico, D.F. 06000, Mexico

Review of urban and regional development studies. *[R. Urban. Region. Dev. S.]; Applied Regional Science Conference*; **Publisher**: *Tokyo International University, Urban Development Institute*: Nakanishi Building 6F, 8-4 Takadanobaba 4-chome, Shinjuku-Ku, Tokyo 169, Japan

Review. Fernand Braudel Center. *[Rev. F. Braudel. Ctr.] ISSN: 0147-9032. State University of New York, Fernand Braudel Center*: P.O. Box 6000, Binghamton, NY. 13902-6000, U.S.A.

Revista brasileira de ciências sociais. *[Rev. Bras. Ciên. Soc.] ISSN: 0102-6909. Associação Nacional de Pós-Graduação e Pesquisa em Ciências Sociais*: Largo de São Francisco, 01-4° andar, s/408 Centro, Rio de Janeiro RJ., Cep 20051, Brazil; **Publisher**: *Editora Revista dos Tribunais*: Rua Conde do Pinhal 78, 01501 São Paulo, SP. Brazil

Revista brasileira de estudos de população. *[Rev. Brasil. Est. Popul.] ISSN: 0102-3098. Associação Brasileira de Estudos Populacionais*: NEPO/UNICAMP- CP6166, CEP 13081-Campinas SP, Brazil

Revista de administración pública. *[Rev. Admin. Públ.] ISSN: 0034-7639. Centro de Estudios Constitucionales*: Fuencarral 45, 28004 Madrid, Spain

Revista de ciência política. *[Rev. Ciê. Pol.] ISSN: 0034-8023. Fundação Getulio Vargas*: Praia de Botafogo, 188-CEP 22.253 Caixa Postal 9.052, 20.000 Rio de Janeiro, Brazil

Revista de ciências sociais. *[Rev. Ciê. Soc.] ISSN: 0041-8862. Universidade Federal do Ceará, Centro de Humanidades, Departamento de Ciências Sociais e Filosofia*: Caixa Postal 3025, CEP 6000 Fortaleza, Ceará, Brazil

Revista de ciencias sociales. *[Rev. Cien. Soc.] ISSN: 0034-7817. Universidad de Puerto Rico, Facultad de Ciencias Sociales, Centro de Investigaciones Sociales*: Rio Piedras, Puerto Rico 00931

Revista de fomento social. *[Rev. Fom. Soc.] ISSN: 0015-6043. INSA-ETEA*: Escritor Castilla Aguayo 4, Apartado 439, 14004 Cordoba, Spain; **Publisher**: *CESI-JESPRE*: Pablo Aranda 3, 28006 Madrid, Spain

Revista interamericana de planificación. *[Rev. Int.Am. Plan.] ISSN: 0037-8593. Sociedad Interamericana de Planificación*: 3a Avenida Norte No.4, Antigua Guatemala, Guatemala

Revista mexicana de sociología. *[Rev. Mexicana Soc.] ISSN: 0035-0087. Universidad Nacional Autónoma de México*: Torre II de Humanidades 7° piso, Ciudad Universitaria, 04510 México D.F., Mexico

Revista occidental. *[Rev. Occid.]; Instituto de Investigaciones Culturales Latinoamericanas (IICLA)*: Apartado 38, Correo Central, 22000 Tijuana, Baja California, N., Mexico

Revista paraguaya de sociología. *[Rev. Parag. Sociol.]; Centro Paraguayo de Estudios Sociológicos*: Eligio Ayala 973, Casilla no.2.157, Asunción, Paraguay

Revue algérienne des sciences juridiques économiques et politiques. *[Rev. Algér.]; Université d'Alger, Institut de Droit et des Sciences Administratives*: 2 rue Didouche Mourad, Algiers, Algeria

Revue canadienne d'études de développement; Canadian journal of development studies. *[Rev. Can. Etud. Dével.] ISSN: 0225-5189. Université d'Ottawa, Institut de développement international et de coopération/ University of Ottawa, Institute for International Development and Co-operation*: 25 University Street, Ottawa, Ontario K1N 6N5, Canada

Revue de Corée. *[Rev. Cor.]; UNESCO*; **Publisher**: *Commission Nationale Coréene*: BP 64 Poste Centrale, Seoul, Korea

Revue de droit social = Tijdschrift voor sociaal recht. *[R. Droit. Soc.] ISSN: 0035-1113. Lacier*: rue des Minimes, 1000 Brussels, Belgium

INTERNATIONAL BIBLIOGRAPHY OF SOCIOLOGY — 1991

Revue de l'économie meridionale. *[R.E.M.] ISSN: 0987-3813. Université de Montpellier, Faculté de droit et des sciences économiques, Centre regional de la productivité et des études économiques*: 39 rue de l'Université, 34060 Montpellier Cedex, France; **Publisher**: *Centre national de la recherche scientifique*: 1 Place Aristide Briand, 92195 Meudon Cedex, France

Revue de l'histoire des religions. *[R. Hist. Relig.] ISSN: 0035-1423. Centre National de la Recherche Scientifique/ Centre National des Lettres*: 1 place Aristide Briand, 92195 Meuden Cedex, France; **Publisher**: *Presses Universitaires de France*: 108 boulevard Saint-Germain, 75006, Paris, France; **Subscriptions**: *idem*: Département des Revues, 14 avenue du Bois-de-l'Epine, B.P. 90, 91003 Evry Cedex, France

Revue de l'Institut de sociologie. *[R. Inst. Sociol.] ISSN: 0770-1055. Institut de Sociologie*: 44 avenue Jeanne, (CP 124) B-1050 Brussels, Belgium

Revue de science criminelle et de droit pénal comparé. *[Rev. Sci. Crim. D. P.] ISSN: 0035-1733. Université Panthéon-Assas (Paris 2), Institut de Droit Comparé, Section de Science Criminelle*; **Publisher**: *Editions Sirey*: 22 rue Soufflot, 75005 Paris Cedex 05, France; **Subscriptions**: *Dalloz*: 35 rue Tournefort, 75240 Paris Cedex 05, France

Revue d'économie régionale et urbaine. *[R. Ec. Reg. Urb.] ISSN: 0180-7307. ADICUEER (Association des Directeurs d'Instituts et des Centres Universitaires d'Etudes Economiques Régionales)*: 4 Rue Michelet, 75006 Paris, France

Revue des études coopératives mutualistes et associatives. *[R. Et. Coop. Mut. Ass.] ISSN: 0035-2020. Coopérative d'Information et d'Edition Mutualiste*: 255 rue de Vaugirard, 75719 Paris Cedex 15, France

Revue d'études comparatives est- ouest. *[Rev. Et. Comp.] ISSN: 0338-0599. Institut de recherches juridiques comparatives du C.N.R.S., Centre d'études des pays socialistes/ Economie et techniques de planification des pays de l'est*; **Publisher**: *Editions de Centre national de la recherche scientifique*: 1 Place Aristide Briand, 92195 Meudon Cedex, France; **Subscriptions**: *Service des Abonnements*: 26 rue Boyer, 75020 Paris, France

Revue d'études palestiniennes. *[R. Et. Palest.] ISSN: 0252-8290. Institut des Etudes Palestiniennes / Fondation Diana Tamari Sabbagh*; **Publisher**: *Editions de Minuit*: 7 rue Bernard- Palissy, 75006 Paris, France

Revue d'histoire moderne et contemporaine. *[R. Hist. Mod. Cont.] ISSN: 0048-8003. Société d'histoire moderne et contemporaine*: 47 boulevard Bessières, 75017 Paris, France

Revue du monde musulman et de la Méditerranée. *[R. Mon. Musul. Med.] ISSN: 0997-1327. Association pour l'étude des sciences humaines en Afrique du Nord et au Proche-Orient*; **Publisher**: *Editions EDISUD*: La Calade, 13090 Aix-en-Provence, France

Revue du travail. *[Rev. Trav.] ISSN: 0035-2705. Ministère de l'emploi et du travail*: Revue du Travail, rue Belliard 53, Brussels 1040, Belgium

Revue économique et sociale. *[R. Econ. Soc.] ISSN: 0035-2772. Société d'Etudes Economiques et Sociales*: Bâtiment des Facultés des Sciences Humaines (BFSH1), 1015 Lausanne-Dorigny, Switzerland

Revue européenne des sciences sociales.:*Cahiers Vilfredo Pareto* *[Rev. Eur. Sci. Soc.] ISSN: 0008- 0497. Librairie DROZ*: 11 rue Massot, CH-1211 Geneva, Switzerland

Revue française d'administration publique. *[R. Fr. Admin. Publ.] ISSN: 0152-7401. Institut International d'Administration Publique*: 2 avenue de l'Observatoire, 75006 Paris, France; **Subscriptions**: *La Documentation Française*: 29-31 quai Voltaire, 75340 Paris Cedex 07, France

Revue française de science politique. *[R. Fr. Sci. Pol.] ISSN: 0035-2950. Fondation nationale des sciences politiques/ Association française de science politique*: 27 rue Saint-Guillame, 75341 Paris, France

Revue française de sociologie. *[Rev. Fr. Soc.] ISSN: 0035-2969. Institut de recherche sur les sociétés contemporaines*: 59-61 rue Pouchet, 75017 Paris, France; **Publisher**: *Editions du Centre National de la Recherche Scientifique*: 20-22 rue Saint-Amand, 75015 Paris, France; **Subscriptions**: *Centrale des Revues/ CDR*: 11 rue Gossin, 92543 Montrouge Cedex, France

Revue française des affaires sociales. *[R. Fr. Aff. Soc.] ISSN: 0035-2985. Ministère des Affaires Sociales et de la Solidarité Nationale*: 1 place de Fontenoy, 75700 Paris, France; **Publisher**: *Masson*: 120 boulevard St. Germain, 75005 Paris Cedex 06, France

Revue générale de droit international public. *[R. Gén. Droit Inter.] ISSN: 0035-3094. Editions A. Pedone*: 13 rue Soufflot, Paris, France

Revue internationale de droit comparé. *[Rev. Int. D. C.] ISSN: 0035-3337. Société de Legislation Comparée*: 28 rue Saint-Guillaume, 75007 Paris, France

Revue roumaine des sciences sociales.:*Série des sciences juridiques* *[Rev. Roumaine Sci. Soc. Sér. Sci. Jurid.] ISSN: 0035-4023. Editura Academiei Române*: Calea Victoriei 125, 79717 Bucharest, Romania; **Subscriptions**: *Rompresfilatelia*: P.O. Box 12-201, Calea Grivitei 64-66, Bucharest, Romania

Revue roumaine d'études internationales. *[Rev. Roumaine Et. Int.] ISSN: 0048-8178. Editura Academiei Române*: Calea Victoriei 125, 79717 Bucharest, Romania; **Subscriptions**: *Rompresfilatelia*: P.O. Box 12-201, Calea Grivitei 64-66, 78104 Bucharest, Romania

Revue syndicale suisse. *[R. Synd. Suisse] ISSN: 0035-421X. Revue Syndicale Suisse*: Case Postale 64, 3000 Berne 23 , Switzerland

INTERNATIONAL BIBLIOGRAPHY OF SOCIOLOGY — 1991

Revue Tiers-Monde. [*R. T-Monde*] *ISSN: 0040-7356. Université de Paris, Institut d'étude du développement économique et social*: 58 boulevard Arago, 75013 Paris, France; **Publisher**: *Presses Universitaires de France*: 108 boulevard Saint-Germain, Paris, France

Revue tunisienne de sciences sociales. [***R. Tun. Sci. Soc.***] *ISSN: 0035-4333. Université de Tunis, Centre d'Études et de Recherches Economiques et Sociales*: 23 rue d'Espagne, 1000 Tunis, Tunisia

Rivista internazionale di scienze economiche e commerciali. [***Rev. Int. Sci. Ec. Com.***] *ISSN: 0035-6751. Università Commerciale Luigi Bocconi/ Università degli Studi di Milano*; **Publisher**: *Casa Editrice Dott. Antonio Milani*: Via Teuliè 1, 20136 Milan, Italy

Rivista internazionale di scienze sociali. [***Riv. Int. Sci. Soc.***] *ISSN: 0035-676X. Università Cattolica del Sacro Cuore*: Vita e Pensiero, Largo A. Gemelli, 1-1 20123 Milan, Italy

Rivista italiana di scienza politica. [***Riv. It. Sci. Pol.***] *ISSN: 0048-8402. Dipartimento di scienza politica e sociologia politica*: via S. Caterina d'Alessandria 3, 50129 Florence, Italy; **Publisher**: *Società Editrice il Mulino*: Strada Maggiore 37, 40125 Bologna, Italy

Rivista trimestrale di diritto pubblico. [***Riv. Trim. Pubbl.***] *ISSN: 0557-1464. A. Giuffrè Editore*: via Busto Arsizio 40, 20151 Milan, Italy

Roma. [*Roma*]; *Roma Publications*: 3290/15-D Chandigarh- 160015, India

Ronso. [*Ronso*]; *Chukyo Junior College*: Mizunami, Japan

Rural africana. [***Rur. Afr.***] *ISSN: 0085- 5839. Michigan State University African Studies Center*: 100 Center for International Programs, E.Lansing, MI. 48824-1035, U.S.A.

Rural history.:*Economy, society, culture* [***Rural Hist.***] *ISSN: 0956-7933. Cambridge University Press*: The Edinburgh Building, Shaftesbury Road, Cambridge CB2 2RU, U.K.

Rural sociology. [***Rural Sociol.***] *ISSN: 0036- 0112. Rural Sociological Society*: Texas A & M University, College Station, U.S.A.; **Publisher**: *idem*: Department of Sociology, Wilson Hall, Montana State University, Bozeman, MT. 59715, U.S.A.

Saeculum. [*Saeculum*] *ISSN: 0080-5319. Verlag Karl Alber*: Hermann-Herder-Straße 4, 7800 Freiburg im Breisgau, Germany

Sangeet natak. [***San. Nat.***]; *Sangeet Natak Akademi*: Rabindra Bhavan, Feroze Shah Road, New Delhi 110-001, India

Santé mentale au Québec. [***San. Ment. Qué***] *ISSN: 0383-6320. Revue Santé mentale au Québec*: C.P. 548, Succ. Places d'Armes, Montréal, Québec H2Y 3H3, Canada

Sarawak gazette. [***Sara. Gaz.***]; *Sarawak Museum*: Kuching, Sarawak

Sarjana. [***Sarjana***]; *University of Malaya, Faculty of Arts and Social Sciences*: Lembah Pantai, Kuala Lumpur 22-11, Malaysia

Savanna. [***Savanna***] *ISSN: 0331-0523. Ahmadu Bello University Press*: PMB 1094, Zaria, Kaduna State, Nigeria

Savings and development. [***Sav. Develop.***] *ISSN: 0393-4551. Centre for Financial Assistance to African Countries (Finafrica)*: Via S. Vigilio 10, 20142 Milan, Italy

Scandinavian economic history review. [***Sc. Ec. Hist. R.***] *ISSN: 0358-5522. Scandinavian Society for Economic and Social History*: Department of Economic History, Box 7083, S- 220 07 Lund, Sweden

Scandinavian housing and planning research. [***Scand. Hous. Plan. R.***] *ISSN: 0281-5737. Building Research Institute (Denmark)/ Ministry of Environment (Finland)/ Institute for Urban and Regional Research (Norway)/ Institute for Building Research (Sweden)*; **Publisher**: *Almqvist & Wiksell International*: P.O. Box 638, S-101 28 Stockholm, Sweden

Scandinavian journal of development alternatives. [***Scand. J. Devel. Altern.***] *ISSN: 0280-2791. Bethany Books*: P.O. Box 7444, S-103 91 Stockholm, Sweden

Scandinavian journal of the Old Testament. [***Scan. J. Old. Test.***] *ISSN: 0901-8328. University of Aarhus, Department of Old Testament Studies*: DK-8000 Aarhus C., Denmark; **Publisher**: *Aarhus University Press*

Science and society. [***Sci. Soc.***] *ISSN: 0036-8237. Guilford Publications*: 72 Spring Street, New York, NY. 10012, U.S.A.

Science as culture. [***Sci. Cult.***] *ISSN: 0959-5431. Free Association Books*: 26 Freegrove Road, London N7 9RQ, U.K.

Science, technology & development. [***Sc. Tech. Devel.***] *ISSN: 0950-0707. Frank Cass*: Gainsborough House, 11 Gainsborough Road, London E11 1RS, U.K.

Scientific American. [***Sci. Am.***] *ISSN: 0036-8733. Scientific American*: 415 Madison Avenue, New York, NY. 10017, U.S.A.

Scottish journal of political economy. [***Scot. J. Poli.***] *ISSN: 0036-9292. Scottish Economic Society*: Division of Economics, University of Stirling, Stirling FK9 4LA, U.K.; **Publisher**: *Basil Blackwell*: 108 Cowley Road, Oxford OX4 1JF, U.K.

INTERNATIONAL BIBLIOGRAPHY OF SOCIOLOGY — 1991

Security dialogue. *[Secur. Dial.] ISSN: 0967-0106. Sage Publications*: 6 Bonhill Street, London, EC2A 4PU, U.K.

Semiotica. *[Semiotica]; International Association for Semiotic Studies*; **Publisher**: *Walter de Gruyter*: Postfach 110240, D-1000 Berlin 11, Germany

Shakaigaku hyoron. *[Shak. Hyor.]; Nippon Shakai Gakkai = Japanese Sociological Society*: Department of Sociology, Faculty of Letters, University of Yokyo, Bunkyo-Ku, Tokyo 113, Japan

Shakaigaku kenkyu. *[Shak. Kenk.]; Tohoku Sociological Association*: Sendai, Japan

Shakaigaku nenpō. *[Shak. Nen.]; Tohoku Sociological Society*: Sendai, Japan

Shakaigaku ronso. *[Shak. Ron.]; Nihon University*: Tokyo, Japan

Shakaigaku-nenshi. *[Shak-nen.]; Waseda Sociological Society*: Tokyo, Japan

Shakai-rōdō Kenkyū. *[Shak.-rōd. Kenk.]*

Shinbungaku hyoron. *[Shin. Hy.]; Japan Society for Studies in Journalism and Mass Communication*: Japan

Shisō. *[Shisō]*

SIER Bulletin. *[SIER B.]; University of Swaziland, Faculty of Education*: P/Bag, Kwaluseni, Swaziland

Signs. *[Signs] ISSN: 0097-9740. University of Chicago Press*: 5720 S. Woodlawn, Chicago, IL. 60637, U.S.A.; **Subscriptions**: *idem*: Journals Division, P.O. Box 37005, Chicago, IL. 60637, U.S.A.

Sikh review. *[Sikh Rev.] ISSN: 0037-5123. Sikh Cultural Centre*: 116 Karnani Mansion, 25A Park Street, Calcutta 700 016, India

Simulation and gaming. *[Simulat. Gam.] ISSN: 0037-5500. Sage Publications*: 2455 Teller Road, Newbury Park, CA. 91320, U.S.A.

Singapore journal of tropical geography. *[Sing. J. Trop. Geogr.] ISSN: 0129-7619. National University of Singapore*: Department of Geography, Kent Ridge, Republic of Singapore 0511

Sistema. *[Sistema] ISSN: 0210-0223. Fundación Sistema*: Fuencarral 127, 1° 28010, Madrid, Spain

Slavic review. *[Slavic R.] ISSN: 0037-6779. American Association for the Advancement of Slavic Studies*: 128 Encina Commons, Stanford University, Stanford, CA. 94305, U.S.A.

Slavonic and East European review. *[Slav. E.Eur. Rev.] ISSN: 0037-6795. University of London, School of Slavonic and East European Studies*: Malet Street, London WC1E 7HU, U.K.; **Publisher**: *Modern Humanities Research Association*: King's College, Strand, London EC2R 2LS, U.K.

Slovo. *[Slovo] ISSN: 0954-6839. School of Slavonic and East European Studies*; **Publisher**: *University of London*: Malet Street, London WC1E 7HU, U.K.

Social action. *[Soc. Act.] ISSN: 0037-7627. Indian Social Institute, Social Action Trust*: Lodi Road, New Delhi 130003, India

Social analysis. *[Soc. Anal.] ISSN: 0155-977X. University of Adelaide, Department of Anthropology*: G.P.O. Box 498, Adelaide 5A 5001, Australia

Social and economic studies. *[Soc. Econ. S.] ISSN: 0037-7651. University of the West Indies, Institute of Social and Economic Research*: Mona, Kingston 7, Jamaica

Social and Economic Systems Studies. *[Soc. Econ. Sys. St.]*

Social attitudes in Northern Ireland. *[Soc. Attit. N.Ire.]; Blackstaff Press*: 3 Galway Park, Dundonald, Belfast BT16 0AN, Northern Ireland

Social behaviour. *[Soc. Behav.] ISSN: 0885-6249. John Wiley & Sons*: Baffins Lane, Chichester, West Sussex PO19 1UD, U.K.

Social biology. *[Soc. Biol.] ISSN: 0037-766X. Society for the Study of Social Biology*: c/o Population Council, One Dag Hammarskjold Place, New York, NY. 10017, U.S.A.

Social choice and welfare. *[Soc. Choice] ISSN: 0176-1714. Springer International*: Heidelberger Platz 3, W-1000 Berlin 33, Germany

Social cognition. *[Soc. Cogn.] ISSN: 0278-616X. Guilford Publications*: 72 Spring Street, New York, NY. 10012, U.S.A.

Social compass. *[Soc. Compass] ISSN: 0037-7686. International Federation of Institutes for Social and Socio-Religious Research (FERES)/ Centre de Recherches Socio-Religieuses*: Université Catholique de Louvain, Belgium; **Publisher**: *Sage Publications*: 6 Bonhill Street, London EC2A 4PU, U.K.

Social dynamics. *[Soc. Dyn.] ISSN: 0253-3952. Centre for African Studies, University of Cape Town*: Rondebosch 7700, South Africa

Social forces. *[Soc. Forc.] ISSN: 0037-7732. University of North Carolina, Department of Sociology*: 168 Hamilton Hall, University of North Carolina, Chapel Hill, NC. 27599-3210, U.S.A.; **Publisher**: *University of North Carolina Press*: P.O. Box 2288, Chapel Hill, NC. 27515, U.S.A.

Social history. *[Soc. Hist.] ISSN: 0307-1022. Routledge*: 11 New Fetter Lane, London EC4P 4EE, U.K.; **Subscriptions**: *idem*: Cheriton House, North Way, Andover, Hants SP10 5BE, U. K.

INTERNATIONAL BIBLIOGRAPHY OF SOCIOLOGY — 1991

Social indicators research. *[Soc. Ind.] ISSN: 0303-8300. Kluwer Academic Publishers*: Spuiboulevard 50, P.O. Box 17, 3300 AA Dordrecht, The Netherlands

Social justice. *[Soc. Just.] ISSN: 0094-7571. Global Options*: P.O. Box 40601, San Francisco, CA. 94140, U.S.A.

Social networks. *[Soc. Networks] ISSN: 0378-8733. International Network for Social Network Analysis (INSNA)*; **Publisher**: *Elsevier Science Publishers (North-Holland)*: P.O. Box 1991, 1000 BZ Amsterdam, The Netherlands; **Subscriptions**: *idem*: Journals Division, P.O. Box 211, 1000 BZ Amsterdam, The Netherlands

Social philosophy & policy. *[Soc. Philos. Pol.] ISSN: 0265-0525. Bowling Green State University, Social Philosophy and Policy Center*: Bowling Green, Ohio 43403, U.S.A.; **Publisher**: *Basil Blackwell*: 108 Cowley Road, Oxford OX4 1JF, U.K.

Social policy. *[Soc. Pol.] ISSN: 0037-7783. Social Policy Corporation*: 25 West 43rd Street, Room 620, New York, NY. 10036, U.S.A.

Social policy and administration. *[Soc. Pol. Admin.] ISSN: 0144-5596. Basil Blackwell*: 108 Cowley Road, Oxford OX4 1JF, U.K.

Social problems. *[Soc. Prob.] ISSN: 0037-7791. Society for the Study of Social Problems*: N631, University of San Francisco, CA. 94143-0612, U.S.A.; **Publisher**: *University of California Press*: 2120 Berkeley Way, Berkeley, CA. 94720, U.S.A.

Social research. *[Soc. Res.] ISSN: 0037-783X, New School for Social Research, Graduate Faculty of Political and Social Science*: 66 West 12th Street, New York, NY. 10011, U.S.A.

Social science & medicine. *[Soc. Sci. Med.] ISSN: 0277-9536. Pergamon Press*: Hennock Road, Marsh Barton, Exeter, Devon EX2 8NE, U.K.; **Subscriptions**: *idem*: Headington Hill Hall, Oxford OX3 0BW, U.K.

Social science history. *[Soc. Sci. Hist.] ISSN: 0145-5532. Social Science History Association*; **Publisher**: *Duke University Press*: Box 6697 College Station, Durham, NC. 27708, U.S.A.

Social science information. *[Soc. Sci. Info.] ISSN: 0539-0184. Maison des sciences de l'homme/ École des hautes études en science sociales*; **Publisher**: *Sage Publications*: 6 Bonhill Street, London EC2A 4PU, U.K.

Social science quarterly. *[Soc. Sci. Q.] ISSN: 0038-4941. Southwestern Social Science Association*: W.C. Hogg Building, The University of Texas at Austin, Austin, TX. 78713, U.S.A.; **Publisher**: *University of Texas Press*: P.O. Box 7819, Austin, TX. 78713, U.S.A.

Social science teacher. *[Soc. Sci. Teach.] ISSN: 0309- 7544. Association for the Teaching of the Social Sciences*: 6 Rosemont Road, Aigburth, Liverpool L17 6BZ, U.K.

Social sciences. *[Soc. Sci.] ISSN: 0134-5486. Nauka Moscow*: 33/12 Arbat, Moscow G-2. 121818, U.S.S.R.

Social sciences in China. *[Soc. Sci. China] ISSN: 0252-9203. Chinese Academy of Social Science*; **Publisher**: *China Social Sciences Publishing House*: Jia 158 Gulouxidajie, Beijing 100720, China

Social scientist. *[Soc. Scient.] ISSN: 0970-0293. Indian School of Social Sciences*: 424 Vithalbhai Patel House, Rafi Marg, New Delhi 110 001, India; **Subscriptions**: *idem*: 15/15 Sarvapriya Vihar, New Delhi 110 016, India

Social security journal. *[Soc. Sec. J.] ISSN: 0726-1195. Australian Government Publishing Service*: G.P.O. Box 84, Canberra, A.C.T. 2601, Australia

Social service review. *[Soc. Ser. R.] ISSN: 0037- 7961. University of Chicago Press*: 5720 S. Woodlawn, Chicago, IL. 60637, U.S.A.; **Subscriptions**: *University of Chicago Press*: P.O. Box 37005, Chicago IL. 60637, U.S.A.

Social services abstracts. *[Soc. Ser. Abstr.] ISSN: 0309- 4693. HMSO*: P.O. Box 276, London SW8 5DT, U.K.

Social work and social sciences review. *[Soc. Work Soc. Sci. R.] ISSN: 0953-5225. Whiting and Birch*: 90 Dartmouth Road, London SE23 3HZ, U.K.

Social work education. *[Soc. Work. Ed.] ISSN: 0261-5479. Whiting and Birch*: P.O. Box 872, Forest Hill, London SE23 3HZ, U.K.

Socialisme. *[Socialisme] ISSN: 0037-8127. Institut Emile Vandervelde*: 13 boulevard de l'Empereur, Brussels 1000, Belgium

Socialismo y participación. *[Soc. Part.]; CEDEP (Centro de Estudios para el Desarrollo y la Participación)*: Ediciones Socialismo y Participación, Av. José Faustino Sánchez Carrión 790, Lima 17, Peru

Socialistische standpunten. *[Social. Stand.]; Emile Vandervelde Instituut*: Grasmarkt 105/51, 1000 Brussels, Belgium

Sociétés contemporaines. *[Soc. Contemp.] ISSN: 1150-1944. Institut de Recherche sur les Sociétés Contemporaines (IRESCO), CNRS*: 59/61 rue Pouchet, 75849 Paris Cedex 17, France; **Publisher**: *L'Harmattan*: 16 rue des Ecoles, 75005 Paris, France

Society. *[Society] ISSN: 0147-2011. Transaction*: Rutgers — The State University, New Brunswick, NJ. 08903, U.S.A.

Socio-economic planning sciences. *[Socio. Econ.] ISSN: 0038- 0121. Pergamon Press*: Journals Production Unit, Hennock Road, Marsh Barton, Exeter EX2 8NE, U.K.; **Subscriptions**: *Pergamon Press*: Headington Hill Hall, Oxford OX3 0BW, U.K.

Sociolinguistics. *[Sociolinguistics] ISSN: 0257-7135. International Sociological Association, Research Committee on Sociolinguistics*; **Publisher**: *Foris Publications*: P.O. Box 509, 3300 AM Dordrecht, The Netherlands

INTERNATIONAL BIBLIOGRAPHY OF SOCIOLOGY — 1991

Sociologia [Bratislavia]; Sociology. *[Sociologia [Brat.]]* ISSN: 0049-1225. *Slovak Academy of Sciences, Institute of Sociology*; **Publisher**: *VEDA*: Klemensova 19, 814 30 Bratislava, Czechoslovakia

Sociologia del lavoro. *[Sociol. Lav.]*; *Università di Bologna, Centro Internazionale di Documentazione e Studi Sociologico Sui Problemi del Lavoro*: Casella postale 413, 40100 Bologna, Italy; **Publisher**: *Franco Angeli Editore*: Viale Monza 106, 20127 Milan, Italy

Sociologia della comunicazione. *[Sociol. Comun.]*; *Franco Angeli editore*: Viale Monza 106, 20127 Milan, Italy

Sociologia internationalis. *[Social. Int.]* ISSN: 0038-0164. *Verlag Duncker & Humblot*: Dietrich-Schäfer- Weg 9, 1000 Berlin 41, Germany

Sociologia [Rome]. *[Sociologia [Rome]]* ISSN: 0038-0156. *Istituto Luigi Sturzo*: Via delle Coppelle 35, 00186 Rome, Italy

Sociologia ruralis. *[Sociol. Rur.]* ISSN: 0038-0199. *European Society for Rural Sociology/Société Européenne de Sociologie Rurale/ Europäischen Gesellschaft für Land- und Agrarsoziologie*: c/o Pavel Uttitz (Secretary Treasurer), Forschungsgesellschaft für Agrarpolitik und Agrarsoziologie e.V., Meckenheimer Allee 125, 5300 Bonn 1, Germany; **Publisher**: *Van Gorcum*: P.O. Box 43, 9400 AA, Assen, The Netherlands

Sociologia urbana e rurale. *[Sociol. Urb. Rur.]*; *Università di Bologna, Dipartimento di Sociologia, Centro Studi sui problemi della Città e del Territorio (CE.P.CI.T.)*: via Strada Maggiore 45, 40125 Bologna, Italy; **Subscriptions**: *Franco Angeli*: Viale Monza, 126, Milan, Italy

Sociologica. *[Sociologica]*; *Soka University*: Tokyo, Japan

Sociological analysis. *[Sociol. Anal.]* ISSN: 0038-0210. *Association for the Sociology of Religion*: Marist Hall Room 108, CUA, Washington, DC. 20064, U.S.A.

Sociological bulletin. *[Sociol. Bul.]* ISSN: 0038-0229. *Indian Sociogical Society*: Institute of Social Sciences, B- 7/18 Safdarjung Enclave, New Delhi 110 029, India

Sociological forum. *[Sociol. For.]* ISSN: 0854-8971. *Plenum Publishing*: 233 Spring Street, New York, NY. 10013, U.S.A.

Sociological methodology. *[Soc. Method.]* ISSN: 0081-1750. *American Sociological Association*: 1722 N. Street, N.W., Washington, DC. 20036, U.S.A.; **Publisher**: *Basil Blackwell*: 108 Cowley Road, Oxford OX4 1JF, U.K.

Sociological methods and research. *[Sociol. Meth.]* ISSN: 0049 1241. *Sage Publications*: 2455 Teller Road, Newbury Park, CA. 91320, U.S.A.

Sociological perspectives. *[Sociol. Pers.]* ISSN: 0731-1214. *Pacific Sociological Association*: Department of Sociology, University of Nevada, Las Vegas, Nevada 89154, U.S.A.; **Publisher**: *JAI Press*: 55 Old Post Road, No.2, P.O. Box 1678, Greenwich, CT 06836-1678, U.S.A.

Sociological quarterly. *[Sociol. Q.]* ISSN: 0038-0253. *J.A.I. Press*: Old Post Road, No.2, P.O. Box 1678, Greenwich, CT. 06836-1678, U.S.A.

Sociological review. *[Sociol. Rev.]* ISSN: 0038-0261. *University of Keele*: Keele, Staffordshire ST5 5BG, U.K.; **Publisher**: *Routledge*: 11 New Fetter Lane, London EC4P 4EE, U.K.

Sociological theory. *[Sociol. Theory]* ISSN: 0735-2751. *American Sociological Association*: 1722 N. Street, N.W., Washington DC. 20036, U.S.A.; **Publisher**: *Basil Blackwell*: 3 Cambridge Center, Cambridge, MA. 02142, U.S.A.; **Subscriptions**: *Marston Book Services*: Journals Department, P.O. Box 87, Oxford OX2 0DT, U.K.

Sociologie du travail. *[Sociol. Trav.]* ISSN: 0038-0296. *Dunod*: 15 rue Gossin, 92543 Montrouge Cedex, France; **Subscriptions**: *CDR — Centrale des revues*: 11 rue Gossin, 92543 Montrouge Cedex, France

Sociologische gids. *[Sociol. Gids]* ISSN: 0038-0334. *Boom*: Postbus 1058, 7940 KB Meppel, The Netherlands

Sociologos. *[Sociologos]*; *Sociologos*: Tokyo, Japan

Sociologus. *[Sociologus]* ISSN: 0038-0377. *Duncker & Humblot*: Postfach 41 03 29, Dietrich-Schäfer- Weg 9, Berlin 41, Germany

Sociology. *[Sociology]* ISSN: 0038-0385. *British Sociological Association*: 351 Station Road, Dorridge, Solihull, W. Midlands B93 8EY, U.K.

Sociology and social research. *[Social Soc. Res.]* ISSN: 0038- 0393. *University of Southern California*: Social Science Building, Rooms 168-169, University Park, Los Angeles, CA. 90089-0032, U.S.A.

Sociology of health and illness. *[Sociol. Health Ill.]* ISBN: 0141-9889. *Basil Blackwell*: 108 Cowley Road, Oxford OX4 1JF, U.K.; **Subscriptions**: *Marston Book Services*: P.O. Box 87, Oxford OX2 0DT, U.K.

Sociology of the sciences. *[Sociol. Sci.]*; *Kluwer Academic Publishers*: P.O. Box 17, 3300 AA Dordrecht, The Netherlands

Sojourn. *[Sojourn]* ISSN: 0217-9520. *Institute of Southeast Asian Studies*: Heng Mui Keng Terrace, Pasir Panjang, Singapore 0511

Soshioroji. *[Soshioroji]*; *Shakaigaku Kenkyukai*: Kyoto, Japan

Социологические исследования (социс); Sotsiologicheskie issledovaniia (sotsis). *[Sot. Issle.]* ISSN: 0132-1625. *Akademii Nauk SSSR*; **Publisher**: *Izdatel'stvo Nauka*: Profsoiuznaja ul. 90, Moscow, U.S.S.R.

South African geographical journal; Suid-Afrikaanse geografiese tydskrif. *[S.Afr. Geogr. J.] ISSN: 0373-6245. South African Geographical Society = Suid-Afrikaanse Geografiese Vereniging*: Department of Geography and Environmental Studies, University of the Witwatersrand, P.O. Wits 2050, South Africa

South African historical journal; Suid-Afrikaanse historiese joernaal. *[S.Afr. Hist. J.] ISSN: 0258-2473. South African Historical Society*: Department of History, University of South Africa, P.O. Box 392, Pretoria 0001, South Africa

South African journal of African languages; Suid-Afrikaanse tydskrif vir Afrikatale. *[S.Afr. J. Afr. Lang.] ISSN: 0257-2117. African Languages Association of Southern Africa/ Afrikatale-Vereniging van Suider-Afrika*: Department of African Languages, University of South Africa, P.O. Box 392, Pretoria 0001, South Africa; **Publisher**: *Foundation for Education, Science and Technology, Bureau for Scientific Publications*: P.O. Box 1758, Pretoria 0001, South Africa

South African journal of economic history. *[S.Afr. J. Ec. Hist.]; Economic History Society of Southern Africa*: Department of History, Rand Afrikaans University, P.O. Box 524, Johannesburg 2000, South Africa

South African journal of ethnology; Suid-Afrikaanse tydskrif vir etnologie. *[S.Afr. J. Ethnol.]; Association of Afrikaans Ethnologists = Vereniging van Afrikaanse Volkekundiges*; **Publisher**: *Bureau for Scientific Publications*: P.O. Box 1758, Pretoria 0001, South Africa

South African journal of labour relations. *[S. Afr. J. Labour Relat.] ISSN: 0379-8410. University of South Africa, School of Business Leadership*: P.O. Box 392, Pretoria 0001, South Africa

South African journal of sociology; Suid-Afrikaanse tydskrif vir sosiologie. *[S.Afr. J. Sociol.]; South African Sociological Association = Suid-Afrikaanse Sosiologievereniging*: School of Business Leadership, University of South Africa, P.O. Box 392, Pretoria 001, South Africa; **Publisher**: *Bureau for Scientific Publications*: P.O. Box 1758, Pretoria 0001, South Africa

South African journal on human rights. *[S. Afr. J. Human Rights] ISSN: 0258-7203. Centre for Applied Legal Studies*: University of the Witwatersrand, Wits 2050, South Africa; **Publisher**: *Juta*: P.O. Box 14373, Kenwyn 7790, South Africa

South African labour bulletin. *[S.Afr. Lab. B.]; Umanyano Publications*: 700 Medical Arts Building 220 Jeppe St. (cnr. Troye Street), Johannesburg, 2001 South Africa

South African sociological review. *[S.Afr. Sociol. R.] ISSN: 1015-1370. Association for Sociology in South Africa*: Department of Sociology, University of Cape Town, 7700 Rondebosch, South Africa

South Asia. *[S. Asia] ISSN: 0085-6401. South Asian Studies Association of Australia*: c/o Department of History, University of New England, Armidale NSW 2351, Australia

South Asia bulletin. *[S.Asia B.] ISSN: 0732-3867. South Asia Bulletin*: c/o Department of History, State University of New York, Albany, NY. 12222, U.S.A.

South Asia journal. *[S.Asia. J.] ISSN: 0970-4868. Indian Council of South Asian Cooperation*; **Publisher**: *Sage Publications India*: 32 M-Block Market, Greater Kailash I, New Delhi 110 048, India

South Asia research. *[S.Asia R.] ISSN: 0262-7280. South Asia Research*: Room 472, School of Oriental and African Studies, Thornhaugh Street, Russell Square, London WC1H 0XG, U.K.

South Asian studies. *[S. Asian Stud.] ISSN: 0266-6030. Society for South Asian Studies*: c/o British Academy, 20- 21 Cornwall Terrace, London NW1 4QP, U.K.

Southeast Asian affairs. *[S.E.Asian Aff.]; Institute of Southeast Asian Studies*: Heng Mui Keng Terrace, Pasir Panjang, Singapore 0511

Southern economic journal. *[S. Econ. J.] ISSN: 0038-4038. Southern Economic Association/ University of North Carolina at Chapel Hill*: CB3540, UNC, Chapel Hill, NC 27599-3540, U.S.A.

Советская этнография; Sovetskaia etnografiia. *[Sovet. Etno.] ISSN: 0038-5050. Akademiya Nauk S.S.S.R., Institut Etnografii*; **Publisher**: *Izdatel' stvo Nauka*: 90 Profsouuznaya ul., 117864 Moscow, Russia

Советское государство и право; Sovetskoe gosudarstvo i pravo. *[Sovet. Gos. Pr.] ISSN: 0132-0769. Institut gosudarstva i prava*; **Publisher**: *Izdatel'stvo Nauka*: Profsoiuznaia ul. 90, V-485, Moscow, U.S.S.R.

Soviet Jewish affairs. *[Sov. Jew. Aff.] ISSN: 0038-545X. Institute of Jewish Affairs*: 11 Hertford Street, London W1Y 7DX, U.K.

Soziale Welt. *[Soz. Welt.] ISSN: 0038-6073. Arbeitsgemeinschaft sozialwissenschaftlicher Institute*: Universität Bamberg, Feldkirchenstraße 21, 8600 Bamberg, Germany; **Publisher**: *Verlag Otto Schwartz*: Annastraße 7, 3400 Göttingen, Germany

Soziologie. *[Soziologie] ISSN: 0340- 918X. Deutsche Gesellschaft für Soziologie*; **Publisher**: *Ferdinand Enke Verlag*: Postfach 10 12 54, D-7000 Stuttgart 10, Germany

Speaking of Japan. *[Speak. Jpn.] ISSN: 0389-3510. Keizai Koho Center, Japan Institute for Social and Economic Affairs*: 6-1 Otemachi 1-chome, Chiyoda-Ku, Tokyo 100, Japan

Sprawy międzynarodowe. *[Spr. Między.] ISSN: 0038-853X. Polski Instytut Spraw Międzynarodowych*: ul. Warecka 1a, Warsaw 00-950, Poland

INTERNATIONAL BIBLIOGRAPHY OF SOCIOLOGY — 1991

Sri Lanka journal of social sciences. *[Sri Lanka J. Soc. Sci.] ISSN: 0258-9710. Natural Resources, Energy & Science Authority of Sri Lanka*: 47/5 Maitland Place, Colombo 7, Sri Lanka

Sri Lanka journal of the humanities. *[Sri Lanka J. Human.]; University of Peradeniya*: Peradeniya, Sri Lanka

St. Andrew's University sociological review. *[St.And. Soc. Rev.]*

Staat und recht. *[Sta. Recht] ISSN: 0038-8858. Märkische Verlag- und Druck-Gesellschaft*: Friedrich-Engels- Straße 24, Postfach Postdam 1561, Germany

Statistica. *[Statistica] ISSN: 0039-0380. Cooperitiva Libraria Universitaria Editrice*: Piazza G. Verdi 2/a, 40126 Bologna, Italy

Statistician. *[Statistician] ISSN: 0039-0526. Institute of Statisticians*; **Publisher**: *Carfax Publishing Company*: P.O. Box 25, Abingdon, Oxfordshire OX14 3UE, U.K.

Stato e mercato. *[Sta. Mer.]; Società Editrice il Mulino*: Strada Maggiore 37, 40125 Bologna, Italy

Storia contemporanea. *[Stor. Contemp.] ISSN: 0039-1875. Società editrice il Mulino*: Strada Maggiore 37, Bologna, Italy

Studi storici. *[St. Stor.] ISSN: 0039-3037. Istituto Gramsci*; **Publisher**: *Editori Riuniti Riviste*: via Serchio 9, 00198 Rome, Italy

Studia demograficzne. *[Stud. Demogr.] ISSN: 0039-3134. Polska Akademia Nauk, Komitet Nauk Demograficznych*; **Publisher**: *Panstwowe Wydawnictwo Naukowe*: Miodowa 10, 00-251 Warsaw, Poland

Studies in comparative communism. *[Stud. Comp. Commun.] ISSN: 0039-3592. Butterworth-Heinemann*: Westbury House, Bury Street, P.O. Box 63, Guildford GU2 5BH, U.K.; **Subscriptions**: *Westbury Subscriptions Services*: P.O. Box 101, Sevenoaks, Kent TN15 8PL, U.K.

Studies in comparative international development. *[Stud. Comp. ID.] ISSN: 0039-3606. Transaction Periodicals Consortium*: Dept. 4010, Rutgers University, New Brunswick, NJ. 08903, U.S.A.; **Subscriptions**: *Swets-Zeitlinger Publishing Services*: Heereweg 347, 2161 CA Lisse, The Netherlands

Studies in family planning. *[Stud. Fam. Pl.] ISSN: 0039-3665. Population Council*: One Dag Hammarskjold Plaza, New York, NY. 10017, U.S.A.

Studies in history. *[Stud. Hist.] ISSN: 0257-6430. Sage Publications India*: 32 M-Block Market, Greater Kailash I, New Delhi 110 048, India; **Subscriptions**: *idem*: 6, Bonhill Street, London EC2A 4PU, U.K.

Studies in history and philosophy of science. *[Stud. Hist. Phil. Sci.] ISSN: 0039-3681. Pergamon Press*: Headington Hill Hall, Oxford OX3 0BW, U.K.

Studies in law, politics, and society. *[Stud. Law. Pol. Soc.]; JAI Press*: 118 Pentonville Road, London N1 9JN, U.K.

Studies in philosophy and education. *[St. Philos. Educ.] ISSN: 0039-3746. Kluwer Academic Publishers*: P.O. Box 322, 3300 AH Dordrecht, The Netherlands

Studies in political economy. *[Stud. Pol. Ec.] ISSN: 0707-8552. Studies in Political Economy*: P.O. Box 4729, Station E, Ottowa, Ontario, Canada K1S 5H9

Studies in Third World societies. *[St. Third Wor. Soc.]; College of William and Mary, Department of Anthropology*: Williamsburg, VA. 23185, U.S.A.

Studies in Western Australian history. *[Stud. W.Aust. Hist.]; University of Western Australia, Department of History*: Nedlands, W.A. 6009, Australia; **Publisher**: *University of Western Australia Press*

Studies of broadcasting. *[St. Broad.]; N.H.K.*: Tokyo, Japan

Study of sociology. *[Stud. Soc.]; Tohoku Sociological Association*: Sendai, Japan

Survey of Jewish affairs. *[Sur. Jew. Aff.] ISSN: 0741-6571. Institute of Jewish Affairs*; **Publisher**: *Basil Blackwell*: 108 Cowley Road, Oxford OX4 1JF, U.K.

Survival. *[Survival] ISSN: 0039-6338. International Institute for Strategic Studies*: 23 Tavistock Street, London WC2E 7NQ, U.K.; **Publisher**: *Brassey's*: Headington Hill Hall, Oxford OX3 0BW, U.K.

Свободная мысль: Svobodnaia Mysl'. *[Svobod. Mysl'] ISSN: 0131-1212. Izdatel'stvo Pravda*: Ul. Pravdy 24, 125047 Moscow, U.S.S.R.

Szociologia. *[Szociologia] ISSN: 0133-3461. Magyar Tudomanyos Akademia, Szociologiai Intezet*; **Publisher**: *Akademiai Kiado, Publishing House of the Hungarian Academy of Science*: P.O. Box 24, H-1363 Budapest, Hungary

Tafsut. *[Tafsut]; Mouvement Culturel Berbère*; **Publisher**: *Université de Provence*: 13 621 Aix-en-Provence Cedex, France

Tarsadalomkutatás. *[Tarsadalomkutatás] ISSN: 0580-4795. Magyar Tudomanyos Akademia*; **Publisher**: *Akademiai Kiado, Publishing House of the Hungarian Academy of Sciences*: P.O. Box 24, H-1363, Budapest, Hungary

Társadalomtudomanyi kozlemenyek. *[Tarsad. Kozl.] ISSN: 0133-0381. Magyar szocialista munkaspart (MSZMP), Tarsadalomtudomanyi Intezet*; **Publisher**: *Kossuth Konyvkiado*: Steindl Imre u. 6, 1366 Budapest 5, Hungary

Te reo. *[Te reo] ISSN: 0494-8440. Linguistic Society of New Zealand*: c/o University of Auckland, Private Bag, Auckland, New Zealand

INTERNATIONAL BIBLIOGRAPHY OF SOCIOLOGY — 1991

Technology and culture. *[Technol. Cul.] ISSN: 0040-165X. Society for the History of Technology*; **Publisher**: *University of Chicago Press*: 5720 South Woodlawn Avenue, Chicago, IL. 60637, U.S.A.

Technology and development. *[Tech. Devel.]*; *Institute for International Cooperation/ Japan International Cooperation Agency*: International Cooperation Center Building, 10-5 Ichigaya-Honmura-cho, Shinjuku-ku, Tokyo 162, Japan

Telos. *[Telos] ISSN: 0090-6514. Telos Press*: 431 E. 12th Street, New York, NY. 10009, U.S.A.

Temps modernes. *[Temps Mod.] ISSN: 0040-3075. Gallimard/ Les Temps Modernes*: 4, rue Férou, Paris 6e, France; **Subscriptions**: *B.S.I.*: 49, rue de la Vanne, 92120 Montrouge, France

Terrain. *[Terrain] ISSN: 0760-5668. Ministère de la Culture et de la Communication, Mission du Patrimoine ethnologique*: 65 rue de Richelieu, 75002 Paris, France

Terrorism. *[Terrorism] ISSN: 0149-0389. State University of New York, Institute for Studies in International Terrorism/ George Washington University, Elliot School of International Affairs*; **Publisher**: *Taylor & Francis*: 4 John Street, London WC1N 2ET, U.K.; **Subscriptions**: *idem*: Rankine Road, Basingstoke, Hampshire RG24 0PR, U.K.

Terrorism and political violence. *[Terror. Pol. Viol.] ISSN: 0954-6553. Frank Cass*: Gainsborough House, 11 Gainsborough Road, London E11 1RS, U.K.

Text. *[Text] ISSN: 0165-4888. Walter de Gruyter*: Postfach 110240, D-1000 Berlin 11, Germany

Theory and decision. *[Theory Decis.] ISSN: 0040-5833. Kluwer Academic Publishers*: P.O. Box 17, 3300 AA Dordrecht, The Netherlands; **Subscriptions**: *idem*: P.O. Box 322, 3300 AA Dordrecht, The Netherlands

Theory and society. *[Theory Soc.] ISSN: 0304-2421. Kluwer Academic Publishers*: Spuiboulevard 50, P.O. Box 17, 3300 AA Dordrecht, The Netherlands

Theory culture and society. *[Theory Cult. Soc.] ISSN: 0263-2764. Sage Publications*: 6 Bonhill Street, London EC2A 4PU, U.K.

Third World planning review. *[Third Wor. P.] ISSN: 0142-7849. Liverpool University Press*: P.O. Box 147, Liverpool L69 3BX, U.K.

Tibet journal. *[Tibet J.] ISSN: 0970-55368. Library of Tibetan Works and Archives (LTWA)*: Gangchen Kyishong, Dharamshala 176 215, India; **Subscriptions**: *Tibet Journal*: c/o 2/18 Ansari Road, New Delhi 110 002, India

Tidsskriftet antropologi. *[Tids. Antrop.] ISSN: 0109-1012. Stofskifte*: Frederiksholms Kanal 4, 1220 Copenhagen, Denmark

Tijdschrift voor economie en management. *[Tijds. Econ. Manag.] ISSN: 0772-7664. Katholieke Universiteit Te Leuven, Faculteit der Economische en Toegepaste Economische Wetenschappen*: Dekenstraat 2, 3000 Leuven, Belgium

Tijdschrift voor economische en sociale geografie; Journal of economic and social geography. *[J. Econ. Soc. Geogr.] ISSN: 0040- 747X. Royal Dutch Geographical Society = Koninklijk Nederlands Aardrijkskundig Genootschap*: Weteringschans 12, 1017 SG Amsterdam, The Netherlands

Tijdschrift voor sociale geschiedenis. *[Tijd. Soc. Gesch.] ISSN: 0303-9935. Nederlandse Vereniging tot beoefening van de Sociale Geschiedenis*: c/o R. de Peuter, Instituut voor Geschiedenis, Lucas Bolwerk 5, 3512 EG Utrecht, The Netherlands

Toshi mondai. *[Tos. Mon.]*; *Tokyo Institute for Municpal Research*: Tokyo, Japan

Town planning review. *[Town Plan. R.] ISSN: 0041-0020. University of Liverpool, Department of Civic Design (Town and Regional Planning)*; **Publisher**: *Liverpool University Press*: P.O. Box 147, Liverpool L69 3BX, U.K.

TRACE. *[TRACE] ISSN: 0185-6286. Centre d'Etudes Mexicaines et Centraméricaines*: Sierra Leona 330, 11000 Mexico D.F., Mexico

Transactions of the Institute of British Geographers.:*New series [Trans. Inst. Br. Geogr.]*; *Institute of British Geographers*: 1 Kensington Gore, London SW7 2AR, U.K.

Transactions of the Philological Society. *[Trans. Philolog. Soc.] ISSN: 0079-1636. Basil Blackwell*: 108 Cowley Road, Oxford OX4 1JF, U.K.

Transformation. *[Transformation] ISSN: 0258- 7696. Transformation*: Economic History Department, University of Natal, King George V Avenue, 4001 Durban, South Africa

Transit.:*Europäische Revue [Transit] ISSN: 0938- 2062. Institut für die Wissenschaften vom Menschen*: Spittelauer Lände 3, A-1090, Vienna, Austria; **Publisher**: *Verlag Neue Kritik*: Kettenhofweg 53, D-6000 Frankfurt am Main, Germany

Transition. *[Transition] ISSN: 1012-8263. University of Guyana, Faculty of Social Sciences and Institute of Development Studies*: P.O. Box 10110, Turkeyen, Georgetown, Guyana

Travail et emploi. *[Trav. Emp.] ISSN: 0224-4365. Ministère du Travail, de l'Emploi et de la Formation Professionnelle, Service des études et de la statistique*: Bureau 3205A, 1 place de Fontenoy, 75700 Paris, France; **Publisher**: *Documentation Fraçaise*: 29-31 quai Voltaire, 75340 Paris Cedex 07, France

Tribus. *[Tribus] ISSN: 0082-6413. Linden- Museum Stuttgart*: Linden-Museum Stuttgart/ Staatliches Museum für Völkerkunde, Hegelplatz 1 D-7000 Stuttgart 1, Germany

INTERNATIONAL BIBLIOGRAPHY OF SOCIOLOGY — 1991

Tricontinental. *[Tricontinental] ISSN: 0864-1595. Executive Secretariat of the Organization of Solidarity of the Peoples of Africa, Asia and Latin America (OSPAAAL)*: Apartado Postale 4224 y 6130, Calle C No. 668 e/27 y 29 Vedado, Havana, Cuba

Tuttogiovani notizie. *[Tutt. Not.]; Osservatorio della Gioventu*: Facoltà di Scienze dell'Educazione dell'Università, Pontificia Salesiano, Rome, Italy; **Publisher**: *Editrice LAS*: Piazza dell'Ateneo Salesiano 1, 00139 Rome, Italy

Twentieth century British history. *[Twent. Cent. Br. Hist.] ISSN: 0955-2359. Oxford University Press*: Pinkhill House, Southfield Road, Eynsham, Oxford OX8 1JJ, United Kingdom

Ufahamu. *[Ufahamu] ISSN: 0041-5715. African Activist Association*: James S. Coleman African Studies Centre, University of California, Los Angeles, CA. 90024-1130, U.S.A.

Unasylva. *[Unasylva] ISSN: 0041-6436. United Nations, Food and Agriculture Organization*: FAO, Via delle Terme di Caracalla, 00100 Rome, Italy

Unisa Latin American report. *[Unisa Lat.Am. Rep.] ISSN: 0256-6060. Unisa Centre for Latin American Studies*; **Publisher**: *University of South Africa*: P.O. Box 392, 0001 Pretoria, South Africa

Uniswa research journal. *[Uniswa Res. J.]; University of Swaziland*: P/ Bag, Kwaluseni, Swaziland

Universitas. *[Universitas] ISSN: 0049-5530. University of Ghana*: Department of English, P.O. Box 25, Legon, Ghana

Urban affairs annual reviews. *[Urb. Aff. Ann. R.] ISSN: 0083-4688. Sage Publications*: 2455 Teller Road, Newbury Park, CA. 91320, U.S.A.

Urban affairs quarterly. *[Urban Aff. Q.] ISSN: 0042-0816. Sage Publications*: 2455 Teller Road, Newbury Park, CA. 91320, U.S.A.

Urban anthropology. *[Urban Anthro.] ISSN: 0894-6019. The Institute*: 56 Centennial Avenue, Brockport, NY. 14420, U.S.A.

Urban forum. *[Urban For.] ISSN: 1015-3802. Witwatersrand University Press*: P.O. Wits, Johannesburg 2050, South Africa

Urban geography. *[Urban Geogr.] ISSN: 0272-3638. V.H. Winston & Son*: 7961 Eastern Avenue, Silver Spring, MD. 20910, U.S.A.

Urban law and policy. *[Urban Law P.] ISSN: 0165-0068. Elsevier Science Publishers (North-Holland)*: Journals Division, P.O. Box 211, 1000 AE Amsterdam, The Netherlands

Urban studies. *[Urban Stud.] ISSN: 0042 0980. University of Glasgow, Centre for Urban and Regional Research*: Adam Smith Building, University of Glasgow, Glasgow G12 8RT, U.K.; **Publisher**: *Carfax Publishing Company*: P.O.Box 25, Abingdon, Oxfordshire OX14 3UE, U.K.

Utafiti. *[Utafiti] ISSN: 0856-096X. University of Dar es Salaam, Faculty of Arts and Social Sciences*: P.O. Box 35151, Dar es Salaam, Tanzania

Verfassung und Recht in Übersee; Law and politics in Africa, Asia and Latin America. *[Verf. Rec. Über.] ISSN: 0506-7286. Hamburger Gesellschaft für Völkerrecht und Auswärtige Politik*: Rothenbaumchaussee 21-23, D-2000 Hamburg 13, Germany; **Publisher**: *Nomos Verlagsgesellschaft*: Postfach 610, D-7570 Baden-Baden, Germany

Вестник ленинградского университета; Vestnik Leningradskogo universiteta.:Серия 5 экономика, Seriia 5 ekonomika *[Ves. Lenin. Univ. Ser. 5] ISSN: 0132- 4624; ISSN: 0233-755X. Izdatel' stvo Leningradskogo Universiteta*: Universitetskaia Nab. 7/9, 199034 Leningrad, U.S.S.R.

Вестник ленинградского университета ; Vestnik Leningradskogo universiteta.:Серия 6 история кпсс, научный коммунизм, философия право; Seriia 6, istoriia KPSS nauchnyi kommunizm filosofiia pravo *[Vest. Lenin. Univ. 6] ISSN: 0132- 4624; ISSN: 0233-7541. Izdatel'stvo Leningradskogo Universiteta*: Universiteta Nab. 7/9, 199034 Leningrad, U.S.S.R.

Вестник Московского Университета ; Vestnik Moskovskogo Universiteta.:Серия 12 Социально политические исследования; Seriia 12 Sotsialno-politicheskie isseldovaniia *[Vest. Mosk. Univ. 12] ISSN: 0201-7385; ISSN: 0320 8087. Izdatel'stvo Moskovskogo Universiteta*: ul. Gertsena 5/7, 103009 Moscow, U.S.S.R.

Весці Акадэмii Навук БССР; Vestsi akademii navuk BSSR.:Сурыя грамадскiх навук; Seryia gramadskikh navuk *[V. Aka. BSSR] ISSN: 0321-1649. Akademii Navuk, BSSR*; **Publisher**: *Navuka i Tekhnika*: Zhodzinskaia 18, 220600 Minsk, Belorussia, U.S.S.R.

Vierteljahrshefte zur Wirtschaftsforschung. *[Vier. Wirt.schung] ISSN: 0340-1707. Deutsches Institut für Wirtschaftsforschung*: Königin-Luise-Straße 5, D- 1000 Berlin 33, Germany; **Publisher**: *Duncker & Humblot*: Dietrich- Schäfer-Weg 9, D-1000 Berlin 41, Germany

Viitorul social. *[Viit. Soc.]; Editura Academiei Române*: Calea Victoriei 125, 79717 Bucharest, Romania; **Subscriptions**: *Rompresfilatelia*: P.O. Box 12-201, Calea Grivitei 64- 66, 78104 Bucharest, Romania

Volkskundig bulletin. *[Volks. Bul.] ISSN: 0166-0667. Koninklijke Nederlandse Akademie van Wetenschappen, P.J. Meertens Instituut*: Keizersgracht 569-571, 1017 DR Amsterdam, The Netherlands.

INTERNATIONAL BIBLIOGRAPHY OF SOCIOLOGY — 1991

Volonta. [*Volonta*] *ISSN: 0392-5013. Editrice A*: via Rovetta 27, 20127 Milan, Italy

Вопросы философии; Voprosy filosofii. [*Vop. Filo.*] *ISSN: 0042-8744. Akademiia Nauk SSR, Institut filosofii*; **Publisher**: *Izdatel'stvo Pravda*: Ul. Pravdy 24, 125047 Moscow, U.S.S.R.

Вопросы истории; Voprosy istorii. [*Vop. Ist.*] *ISSN: 0042-8779. Izdatel'stvo Pravda*: Ul. Pravdy 24, 125865 Moscow, U.S.S.R.

Вопросы научного атеизма; Voprosy nauchnogo ateizma. [*Vop. Nau. At.*] *ISSN: 0321-0847. Akademiia Obshchestvennych Nauk, Institut Nauchnogo Ateizma*; **Publisher**: *Izdatel'stvo Mysl*: Leninsky Prospekt 15, Moscow V-17, U.S.S.R.

West European politics. [*W. Eur. Pol.*] *ISSN: 0140-2382. Frank Cass*: Gainsborough House, 11 Gainsborough Road, London E11 1RS, U.K.

Western political quarterly. [*West. Pol. Q.*] *ISSN: 0043-4078. Western Political Science Association/ Pacific Northwest Political Science Association/ Southern California Political Science Association/ Northern California Political Science Association*; **Publisher**: *University of Utah*: Salt Lake City, UT. 84112, U.S.A.

Wisconsin law review. [*Wiscon. Law R.*] *ISSN: 0043-650X. University of Wisconsin, Law School*: 975 Bascom Mall, Madison, WI. 53706-1399, U.S.A.

Wissenschaftliche Zeitschrift der Humboldt-Universität zu Berlin.:*Reihe Gesellschaftswissenschaften* [**Wissensch. Z. Humboldt-Univ.**] *ISSN: 0863-0623. Humboldt-Universität*: Mittelstraße 7/8, 1086 Berlin, Germany

Without prejudice. [*With. Prej.*] *ISSN: 1035-4220. Australian Institute of Jewish Affairs*: GPO Box 5402CC, Melbourne, Victoria 3001, Australia

Women's studies. [*Wom. Stud.*] *ISSN: 0049-7878. Gordon and Breach Science Publishers*: P.O. Box 90, Reading, Berkshire RG1 8JL, U.K.

Women's studies international forum. [*Wom. St. Inter. For.*] *ISSN: 0277-5395. Pergamon Press*: Fairview Park, Elmsford, NY. 10523, U.S.A.

Work and occupations. [*Work Occup.*] *ISSN: 0730-8884. Sage Publications*: 2455 Teller Road, Newbury Park CA. 91320, U.S.A.; **Subscriptions**: *Sage Publications*: 6 Bonhill Street, London EC2A 4PU, U.K.

Work, employment and society. [*Work Emp. Soc.*] *ISSN: 0950-0170. British Sociological Association*: 10 Portugal Street, London WC2A 2HU, U.K.; **Subscriptions**: *Business Manager*: Work, Employment and Society, 351 Station Road, Dorridge, Solihull, West Midlands B93 8EY, U.K.

Working papers in linguistics. [*Work. Pap. Ling.*]; *Ohio State University*: 204 Cunz Hall, 1841 Millikin Road, Columbus, OH. 43210-1229, U.S.A.

World Bank economic review. [*W.B. Econ. R.*] *ISSN: 0258-6770. International Bank for Reconstruction and Development*: World Bank, Washington, DC. 20433, U.S.A.; **Subscriptions**: *World Bank Publications*: Box 7247-8619, Philadelphia, PA. 19170-8619, U.S.A.

World development. [*World Dev.*] *ISSN: 0305-750X. Pergamon Press*: Headington Hill Hall, Oxford OX3 0BW, U.K.

World futures. [*Wor. Futur.*] *ISSN: 0260-4027. Gordon and Breach Science Publishers*: 270 8th Avenue, New York, NY. 10011, U.S.A.; **Subscriptions**: *idem*: P.O. Box 90, Reading, Berkshire, RG1 8JL, U.K.

World politics. [*World Polit.*] *ISSN: 0043-8871. Princeton University, Center of International Studies*: Bendheim Hall, Princeton, NJ. 08544, U.S.A.; **Publisher**: *Johns Hopkins University Press*: Journals Publishing Division, 701 W 40th Street, Suite 275, Baltimore, MD. 21211-2190, U.S.A.

World today. [*World Today*] *ISSN: 0043-9134. Royal Institute of International Affairs*: 10 St. James's Square, London SW1Y 4LE, U.K.

Wuqûf. [*Wuqûf*] *ISSN: 0930-9306. Hanspeter Mattes Verlag/ edition Wuqûf*: Postfach 13 22 42, 2000 Hamburg 13, Germany

XXI Secolo. [*XXI Secolo*]; *Fondazione Giovanni Agnelli*: via Giacosa 38, 10125 Turin, Italy

Yagl-Ambu. [*Yagl-Ambu*] *ISSN: 0254-0681. University of Papua New Guinea*: Box 320, University Post Office, Papua New Guinea

Yale law journal. [*Yale Law J.*] *ISSN: 0044-0094. Yale Law Journal Co.*: 401-A Yale Station, New Haven CT 06520, U.S.A.

York papers in linguistics. [*York Pap. Ling.*] *ISSN: 0307-3238. University of York, Department of Language and Linguistic Science*: Heslington, York YO1 5DD, U.K.

Zaïre-Afrique. [*Za-Afr.*] *ISSN: 0049-8513. Centre d'études pour l'action sociale (CEPAS)*: Avenue Père Boka no.9, B.P. 3375 Kinshasa/ Gombe, Zaire

Zambezia. [*Zambezia*] *ISSN: 0379-0622. University of Zimbabwe*: Publications Office, P.O. Box MP 45, Mount Pleasant, Harare, Zimbabwe

Zambia journal of history. [*Zamb. J. Hist.*]; *University of Zambia, Department of History*: P.O. Box 32379, Lusaka, Zambia

Zeitschrift für ausländisches öffentliches Recht und Völkerrecht. *[Z. Aus. Recht. Völk] ISSN: 0044-2348. Verlag W. Kohlhammer*: P.B. 800430, D-7000 Stuttgart 80, Germany

Zeitschrift für Ethnologie. *[Z. Ethn.] ISSN: 0044-2666. Deutsche Gesellschaft für Völkerkunde/ Berliner Gesellschaft für Anthropologie, Ethnologie und Urgeschichte*; **Publisher**: *Dietrich Reimer Verlag*: Unter den Eichen 57, 1000 Berlin 45, Federal Republic of Germany

Zeitschrift für Missionswissenschaft und Religionswissenschaft. *[Z. Mission. Religion.] ISSN: 0044-3123. Internationales Institut für missionswissenschaftliche Forschungen*: Albertus-Magnus-Staße 39, 5300 Bonn 2, Germany; **Publisher**: *Aschendorffsche Verlagsbuchhandlung*: Postfach 1124, 4400 Münster, Germany

Zeitschrift für Politik. *[Z. Polit.] ISSN: 0044- 3360. Hochschule für Politik München*: Ludwigstraße 8, 8000 Munchen, Germany; **Publisher**: *Carl Heymanns Verlag*: Luxemburger Straße 449, 5000 Cologne 41, Germany

Zeitschrift für Sexualforschung. *[Z. Sexual.] ISSN: 0932-8114. Ferdinand Enke Verlag*: Postfach 10 12 54, D-7000 Stuttgart 10, Germany

Zeitschrift für Soziologie. *[Z. Soziol.] ISSN: 0340-1804. Ferdinand Enke Verlag*: Postfach 10 12 54, D-7000 Stuttgart 10, Germany

Zeitschrift für Unternehmensgeschichte. *[Z. Unter.gesch.] ISSN: 0342-2852. Gesellschaft für Unternehmensgeschichte*: Bonner Straße 211, 9. Etage, D-5000 Cologne 51, Germany; **Publisher**: *Franz Steiner Verlag*: Birkenwaldstraße 44, Postfach 10 15 26, D-7000 Stuttgart 1, Germany

Zeitschrift für Verkehrswissenschaft. *[Z. Verkehr.] ISSN: 0044-3670. Verkehrs-Verlag J. Fischer*: Paulusstraße 1, 4000 Düsseldorf 1, Germany

Zeitschrift für Wirtschafts- und Sozialwissenschaften. *[Z. Wirt. Soz.] ISSN: 0342-1783. Gesellschaft für Wirtschafts- und Sozialwissenschafen — Verein für Sozialpolitik*; **Publisher**: *Duncker and Humblot*: Dietrich-Schäfer-Weg 9, 1000 Berlin 41, Germany

Zeitschrift für Wirtschaftspolitik. *[Z. Wirt.pol.] ISSN: 0721-3808. Universität zu Köln, Institut für Wirtschaftspolitik*: Postfach 41 05 29, Lindenburger Allee 32, 5000 Cologne 41, Germany

LIST OF ABBREVIATIONS USED
LISTE DES ABBREVIATIONS UTILISÉS

A.J.S. — American journal of sociology. — Chicago, IL.: *University of Chicago Press*
Act. Econ. — Actualité économique. — Montreal: *Ecole des Hautes Etudes Commerciales/ Société canadienne de science économique/ Association des économistes québécois*
Acta Asia. — Acta asiatica. — Tokyo: *Institute of Eastern Culture*
Acta Pol. — Acta politica. — Meppel: *Boom*
Acta Sociol. — Acta sociologica. — Oslo: *Scandinavian Sociological Association*
Acta Univ. Łódz. Folia Soc. — Acta Universitatis Łódziensis.: *Folia sociologica* — Łódz: *Wydawnictwo Uniwersytetu Łódzkiego*
Adm. Sci. Qua. — Administrative science quarterly. — Ithaca, NY.: *Cornell University, Johnson Graduate School of Management*
Admin. Soc. — Administration and society. — Newbury Park, CA.: *Sage Publications*
Administration — Administration. — Dublin: *Institute of Public Administration of Ireland*
Adopt. Fost. — Adoption and fostering. — London: *British Agencies for Adoption and Fostering*
Aff. Soc. Int. — Affari sociali internazionali. — Milan: *Franco Angeli Editore*
Afr. Affairs — African affairs. — Oxford: *Royal African Society*
Afr. Arts — African arts. — Los Angeles, CA.: *University of California, James S. Coleman African Studies Center*
Afr. Cont. — Afrique contemporaine. — Paris: *Documentation française*
Afr. St. Mono. — African study monographs. — Kyoto: *Kyoto University, Center for African Area Studies*
Afr. Stud. R. — African studies review. — Atlanta, GA.: *African Studies Association*
Age. Soc. — Ageing and society. — Cambridge: *Centre for Policy on Ageing/ British Society of Gerontology*
Agenda — Agenda. — Durban: *Agenda Collective*
Agr. Soc. — Agricultura y sociedad. — Madrid: *Ministerio de Agricultura, Pesca y Alimentacion*
Agrekon — Agrekon. — Monument Park: *Landbou- Economievereniging van Suider-Afrika = Agricultural Economics Association of Southern Africa*
Ahfad J. — Ahfad journal. — Omdurman: *Ahfad University for Women*
Am. Anthrop. — American anthropologist. — Washington, DC.: *American Anthropological Association*
Am. Behav. Sc. — American behavioral scientist. — Newbury Park, CA.: *Sage Publications*
Am. Econ. Rev. — American economic review. — Nashville, TN: *American Economic Association*
Am. Ethn. — American ethnologist. — Washington, DC.: *American Ethnological Society*
Am. Hist. Rev. — American historical review. — Washington, DC.: *American Historical Association*
Am. J. Econ. S. — American journal of economics and sociology. — New York, NY.: *American Journal of Economics and Sociology*
Am. J. Islam. Soc. Sci. — American journal of Islamic social sciences. — Herndon, VA.: *Association of Muslim Social Scientists/ International Institute of Islamic Thought*
Am. J. Orthopsy. — American journal of orthopsychiatry. — New York, NY.: *American Orthopsychiatric Association*
Am. J. Pol. Sc. — American journal of political science. — Austin, TX: *Midwest Political Science Association*
Am. Phil. Q. — American philosophical quarterly. — Bowling Green, OH.: *Philosophy Documentation Center*
Am. Poli. Sci. — American political science review. — Washington, DC.: *American Political Science Association*
Am. Psychol. — American psychologist. — Arlington, VA: *American Psychological Association*
Am. Sociol. — American sociologist. — New Brunswick, NJ.: *Transaction Periodicals Consortium*
Am. Sociol. R. — American sociological review. — Washington, D.C.: *American Sociological Association*

INTERNATIONAL BIBLIOGRAPHY OF SOCIOLOGY — 1991

An. Est. Cent.Am. — Anuario de estudios centroamericanos. — San Jose: *Universidad de Costa Rica, Instituto de Investigaciones Sociales*
Ann. Afr. Nord — Annuaire de l'Afrique du Nord. — Paris: *Editions du Centre national de la recherche scientifique*
Ann. Am. Poli. — Annals of the American Academy of Political and Social Science. — Newbury Park, CA.: *American Academy of Political and Social Science*
Ann. As. Am. G. — Annals of the Association of American Geographers. — Washington, DC.: *Association of American Geographers*
Ann. Géogr. — Annales de géographie. — Paris: *Armand Colin Éditeur*
Ann. Inst. Soc. Sci. — Annals of the Institute of Social Science. — Tokyo: *University of Tokyo, Institute of Social Science*
Ann. Inter. Crimin. — Annales internationales de criminologie; International annals of criminology; Anales internacionales de criminologia. — Paris: *Société Internationale de Criminologie = International Society for Criminology = Sociedad Internacional de Criminologia*
Ann. R. Anthr. — Annual review of anthropology. — Palo Alto, CA.: *Annual Reviews*
Ann. R. Pub. H. — Annual review of public health. — Palo Alto, CA.: *Annual Reviews*
Ann. Reg. Sci. — Annals of regional science. — Berlin: *Western Regional Science Association*
Ann. Rep. Shiz., Hamam. Coll. — Annual report of University of Shizuoka, Hamamatsu College. — Shizuoka: *Shizuoka University, Hamamatsu College*
Annales — Annales.: *Economies, sociétés, civilisations* — Paris: *C.N.R.S./ École des hautes études en sciences sociales*
Anthr. Quart. — Anthropological quarterly. — Washington, DC.: *Catholic University of America, Department of Anthropology*
Anthrop. Ling. — Anthropological linguistics. — Bloomington, IN.: *University of Indiana, Department of Anthropology*
Antipode — Antipode. — Oxford: *Basil Blackwell*
Antiquity — Antiquity. — Oxford: *Antiquity Publications*
App. Commun. Stud. — Applied community studies. — London: *Manchester Polytechnic*
Appl. Econ. — Applied economics. — London: *Chapman and Hall*
Apuntes — Apuntes. — Lima: *Revista Apuntes*
Arc. Kommunal. — Archiv für Kommunalwissenschaften. — Stuttgart: *Deutsches Institut für Urbanistik*
Arc. Recht. Soz. — Archiv für Rechts- und Sozialphilosophie; Archives de philosophie du droit et de philosophie sociale; Archives for philosophy of law and social philosophy; Archivo de filosofía jurídica y social. — Stuttgart: *Internationale Vereinigung für Rechts- und Sozialphilosophie*
Arch. Orient. — Archív orientální. — Prague: *Czechoslovak Academy of Sciences, Oriental Institute*
Area — Area. — London: *Institute of British Geographers*
Arm. Forces Soc. — Armed forces and society. — New Brunswick, NJ.: *Inter-University Seminar on Armed Forces and Society*
Art. Vij. — Artha vijñāna. — Pune: *Gokhale Institute of Politics and Economics*
Asia J. Theol. — Asia journal of theology. — Singapore: *Asia Journal of Theology*
Asian Cult. (Asian-Pac. Cult.) Q. — Asian culture (Asian-Pacific culture) quarterly. — Taipei: *Asian-Pacific Cultural Center*
Asian J. Pub. Admin. — Asian journal of public administration. — Hong Kong: *University of Hong Kong, Department of Political Science*
Asian Prof. — Asian profile. — Hong Kong: *Asian Research Service*
Asian Stud. R. — Asian studies review. — Sydney: *Asian Studies Association of Australia*
Asian Sur. — Asian survey. — Berkeley, CA: *University of California Press*
Asian-Pacific Ec. Lit. — Asian-Pacific economic literature. — Guildford: *Australian National University, National Centre for Development Studies*
Asien. Af. Lat.am. — Asien Afrika Lateinamerika. — Berlin: *Akademie der Wissenschaften zu Berlin*
Aussenpolitik — Aussenpolitik. — Hamburg: *Interpress Verlag*
Aust. Abor. S. — Australian Aboriginal studies. — Canberra: *Australian Institute of Aboriginal and Torres Strait Islander Studies*
Aust. Ec. Rev. — Australian economic review. — Melbourne: *University of Melbourne, Institute of Applied Economic and Social Research*
Aust. Econ. P. — Australian economic papers. — Adelaide: *Flinders University of South Australia*

Aust. Geogr. — Australian geographer. — Gladesville, NSW: *Geographical Society of New South Wales*
Aust. Geogr. Stud. — Australian geographical studies. — Campbell: *Institute of Australian Geographers*
Aust. J. Chin. Aff. — Australian journal of Chinese affairs. — Canberra: *Australian National University, Contemporary China Centre*
Aust. J. Poli. — Australian journal of politics and history. — Queensland: *University of Queensland Press*
Aust. J. Publ. — Australian journal of public administration. — Sydney: *Royal Australian Institute of Public Administration*
Aust. J. Soc. Iss. — Australian journal of social issues. — Sydney: *Australian Council of Social Services*
Aust. J. Statist. — Australian journal of statistics. — Canberra: *Australian Statistical Publishing Association*
Aust. N.Z. J. Soc. — Australian and New Zealand journal of sociology. — Bundoora: *Australian Sociological Association*
Aust. Stud. — Australian studies. — Stirling: *British Australian Studies Association*
AWR B. — AWR Bulletin — Vienna: *Association for the Study of the World Refugee Problem*
B. Concern. Asia. Schol. — Bulletin of concerned Asian scholars. — Boulder, CO.: *Bulletin of Concerned Asian Scholars*
B. Ind. Econ. St. — Bulletin of Indonesian economic studies. — Canberra: *Australian National University*
B. Inst. Ethn. Ac. Sin. — Bulletin of the Institute of Ethnology, Academia Sinica. — Taipei: *Institute of Ethnology Academia Sinica*
B. Sch. Ed. Hiroshima — Bulletin of the Faculty of School Education Hiroshima.
B. Sch. Orient. Afr. Stud. — Bulletin of the School of Oriental and African Studies. — London: *University of London, School of Oriental and African Studies*
B. Yoko. Univ. — Bulletin, Yokohama City University. — Yokohama: *Yokohama City University*
Bang. Dev. Stud. — Bangladesh development studies. — Dhaka: *Bangladesh Unnayan Gobeshona Protishthan = Bangladesh Institute of Development Studies*
Bang. J. Pol. Econ. — Bangladesh journal of political economy. — Dhaka: *Bangladesh Economic Association*
Behav. Brain Sci. — Behavioral and brain sciences. — New York, NY.: *Cambridge University Press*
Behav. Sci. — Behavioral science. — Baltimore, MD: *International Society for Systems Sciences/Institute of Management Sciences*
Beit. Japan. — Beiträge zur Japanologie. — Vienna: *Universität Wien, Institut für Japanologie*
Beliz. St. — Belizean studies. — Belize City: *St. John's College*
Berkeley J. Soc. — Berkeley journal of sociology. — Berkeley, CA.: *Berkeley Journal of Sociology*
Berl. J. Soziol. — Berliner journal für Soziologie. — Berlin: *Institut für Soziologie der Humbodt-Universität zu Berlin*
Bevolk. Gez. — Bevolking en gezin. — Brussels/'s-Gravenhage: *Centrum voor Bevolkings- en Gezinsstudiën/Nederlands Interdisciplinair Demografisch Instituut*
Bibl. Etnogr. Pol. — Biblioteka etnografii polskiej. — Warsaw: *Polska Akademia Nauk, Instytut Historii Materialnej*
Bioethics — Bioethics. — Oxford: *Basil Blackwell*
Biography — Biography. — Honolulu, HI.: *Center for Biographical Research*
Bol. Inf. Bibl. Soc. — Boletim informativo e bibliográfico de ciências sociais. — Rio de Janeiro: *Associação Nacional de Pós-Graduação e Pesquisa em Ciências Sociais*
Br. J. Addict. — British journal of addiction. — Abingdon: *Society for the Study of Addiction to Alcohol and Other Drugs*
Br. J. Clin. Psycho. — British journal of clinical psychology. — Leicester: *British Psychological Society*
Br. J. Crimin. — British journal of criminology. — London: *Institute for the Study and Treatment of Delinquency*
Br. J. Ind. R. — British journal of industrial relations. — Oxford: *London School of Economics*
Br. J. Manag. — British journal of management. — Chichester: *British Academy of Management*
Br. J. Poli. S. — British journal of political science. — Cambridge: *Cambridge University Press*
Br. J. Psy. — British journal of psychology. — Leicester: *British Psychological Society*

Br. J. Soc. — British journal of sociology. — London: *London School of Economics and Political Science*
Br. J. Soc. P. — British journal of social psychology. — Leicester: *British Psychological Society*
Br. J. Soc. W. — British journal of social work. — Oxford: *British Association of Social Workers*
Bus. Econ. — Business economist. — Watford: *Society of Business Economists*
C.Asian Sur. — Central Asian survey. — Oxford: *Society for Central Asian Studies*
Cah. Afr. Admin. Pub. — Cahiers africains d'administration publique; African administrative studies. — Tangiers: *Centre Africain de Formation et de Recherche Administratives pour le Développement (CAFRAD)*
Cah. Amer. Lat. — Cahiers des Amériques latines. — Paris: *Université de la Sorbonne Nouvelle (Paris III), Institut des Hautes Etudes de l'Amérique latine*
Cah. Anthr. Bio. Hum. — Cahiers d'anthropologie et biométrie humaine. — Paris: *Société de Biometrie Humaine*
Cah. Et. Afr. — Cahiers d'études africaines. — Paris: *Éditions de l'École des Hautes Études en Sciences Sociales*
Cah. Et. Méd. Ori. Tur-Iran. — Cahiers d'études sur la méditerranée orientale et le monde turco-iranien. — Paris: *Association Française pour l'Etude de la Méditerranée Orientale et le Monde Turco-Iranien*
Cah. Int. Soc. — Cahiers internationaux de sociologie. — Paris: *Presses Universitaires de France*
Cah. Outre-mer — Cahiers d'outre-mer. — Bordeaux: *Université de Bordeaux III, Institut de Géographie*
Calif. Manag. R. — California management review. — Berkeley, CA.: *University of California, Walter A. Haas School of Business*
Cam. Anthrop. — Cambridge anthropology. — Cambridge: *University of Cambridge, Department of Social Anthropology*
Camb. J. Econ. — Cambridge journal of economics. — London: *University of Cambridge, Faculty of Economics and Politics*
Can R. Stud. N. — Canadian review of studies in nationalism; Revue canadienne des études sur le nationalisme. — Charlottetown: *CRSN/RCEN*
Can. J. Afr. St. — Canadian journal of African studies; Revue canadienne des études africaines. — Ottawa: *Canadian Association of African Studies = Association canadienne des études africaines*
Can. J. Econ. — Canadian journal of economics; Revue canadienne d'économique. — Downsview: *Canadian Economics Association*
Can. J. Soc. — Canadian journal of sociology; Cahiers canadiens de sociologie. — Edmonton: *University of Alberta, Department of Sociology*
Can. Publ. Ad. — Canadian public administration; Administration publique du Canada. — Toronto: *Institute of Public Administration of Canada*
Can. R. Soc. A. — Canadian review of sociology and anthropology; Revue canadienne de sociologie et d'anthropologie. — Montreal: *Canadian Sociology and Anthropology Association*
Cap. Class — Capital and class. — London: *Conference of Socialist Economists*
Cent. Asia. J. — Central Asiatic journal. — Wiesbaden: *Otto Harrassowitz*
CEPAL R. — CEPAL review. — Santiago, Chile: *United Nations Economic Commission for Latin America and the Caribbean*
Ch. Feng — Ching feng. — Hong Kong: *Christian Study Centre on Chinese Religion and Culture*
Child. Devel. — Child development. — Chicago, IL.: *Society for Research in Child Development*
Child. Soc. — Children and society. — London: *National Children's Bureau of the United Kingdom*
China Quart. — China quarterly. — London: *University of London, School of Oriental and African Studies*
Cities — Cities. — London: *Butterworth-Heinemann*
Civitas — Civitas. — Rome: *Edizioni Civitas*
Coexistence — Coexistence. — Dordrecht: *Martinus Nijhoff Publishers*
Cognition — Cognition. — Amsterdam: *Elsevier Science Publishers*
Coll. Antrop. — Collegium antropologicum. — Zagreb: *Croatian Anthropological Society*
Comm. Dev. J. — Community development journal. — Oxford: *Oxford University Press*
Commun. Theory — Communication theory. — New York, NY.: *International Communication Association*
Communication — Communication. — New York, NY.: *Gordon and Breach Science Publishers*

Comp. Poli. S. — Comparative political studies. — Newbury Park, CA.: *Sage Publications*
Comp. Polit. — Comparative politics. — New York, NY.: *City University of New York*
Comp. Soc. Res. — Comparative social research. — Greenwich, CT.: *JAI Press*
Comp. Stud. S. — Comparative studies in society and history. — New York, NY.: *Society for the Comparative Study of Society and History*
Confl. Resolut. — Journal of conflict resolution. — Newbury Park, CA.: *Peace Science Society (International)*
Cont. Policy — Contemporary policy issues. — Huntington Beach, CA.: *Western Economic Association International*
Contin. Change — Continuity and change. — Cambridge: *Cambridge University Press*
Contr. I. Soc. — Contributions to Indian sociology. — New Delhi: *Institute of Economic Growth*
Cr. Law Soc. Chan. — Crime, law and social change. — Dordrecht: *Kluwer Academic Publishers*
Crime Delin. — Crime and delinquency. — Newbury Park, CA.: *Sage Publications*
Crime Just. — Crime and justice. — Chicago, IL.: *University of Chicago Press*
Crit. Marx. — Critica marxista. — Rome: *Editori Riuniti Riviste*
Crit. Rev. — Critical review. — Chicago: *Center for Independent Thought*
Crit. Sociol. — Critical sociology. — Eugene, OR.: *University of Oregon, Department of Sociology*
Crossroads — Crossroads. — DeKalb, IL.: *Northern Illinois University, Center for Southeast Asian Studies*
Cuad. Am. — Cuadernos americanos. — Mexico City: *Universidad Nacional Autónoma de México*
Cult. Anthro. — Cultural anthropology. — Washington, DC.: *Society for Cultural Anthropology*
Cult. Medic. Psych. — Culture, medicine and psychiatry. — Dordrecht: *Kluwer Academic Publishers*
Cult. St. — Cultural studies. — London: *Routledge*
Curr. Sociol. — Current sociology. — London: *International Sociological Association*
Curric. J. — Curriculum journal. — London: *Routledge*
Cyprus Rev. — Cyprus review. — Nicosia and Indianapolis: *Intercollege/ University of Indianapolis*
Dædalus — Dædalus. — Cambridge, MA.: *American Academy of Arts and Sciences*
Demográfia — Demográfia. — Budapest: *Magyar Tudomanyos Akademia, Demografiai Bizottsag*
Demografie — Demografie. — Prague: *Federální Statistický Uřad*
Demography — Demography. — Washington, DC.: *Population Association of America*
Desar. Econ. — Desarrollo económico. — Buenos Aires: *Instituto de Desarrollo Económico y Social*
Deut. Arch. — Deutschland Archiv.: *Zeitschrift für das vereinigte Deutschland* — Cologne: *Verlag Wissenschaft und Politik*
Develop. Cha. — Development and change. — London: *Sage Publications*
Develop. Eco. — Developing economies. — Tokyo: *Institute of Developing Economies*
Develop. S. Afr. — Development Southern Africa. — Halfway House: *Development Bank of Southern Africa*
Dirasat Ser. A. — Dirasat.: *Series A — the humanities* — Amman: *Deanship of Academic Research*
Disasters — Disasters.: *Journal of disaster studies and management* — Oxford: *Basil Blackwell*
Dissent — Dissent. — New York, NY.: *Foundation for the Study of Independent Social Ideas*
Droit Soc. — Droit social. — Paris: *Editions Techniques et Economiques*
E & S — E & S.: *Economie et statistique* — Paris: *Institut national de la statistique et des études économiques*
E. Afr. Econ. Rev. — Eastern Africa economic review. — Nairobi: *Kenyan Economic Association*
E. Eur. Quart. — East European quarterly. — Boulder, CO.: *University of Colorado*
E.Eur. Pol. Soc. — East European politics and societies. — Berkeley: *University of California*
East. Anthrop. — Eastern anthropologist. — Lucknow: *Ethnographic and Folk Culture Society*
Ec. Lav. — Economia & lavoro. — Rome: *Fondazione Giacomo Brodolini*
Ec. Sociét. — Economies et sociétés. — Grenoble: *I.S.M.E.A.*
Econ. Dev. Cult. Change — Economic development and cultural change. — Chicago, IL.: *University of Chicago Press*
Econ. Devel. Q. — Economic development quarterly. — Newbury Park, CA.: *Sage Publications*
Econ. Geogr. — Economic geography. — Worcester, MA.: *Clark University*
Econ. Ind. Dem. — Economic and industrial democracy. — London: *Arbetslivscentrum (The Swedish Center for Working Life)*
Econ. Inq. — Economic inquiry. — Huntington Beach, CA.: *Western Economic Association International*

INTERNATIONAL BIBLIOGRAPHY OF SOCIOLOGY — 1991

Econ. J. — Economic journal. — Oxford: *Royal Economic Society*
Econ. Philos. — Economics and philosophy. — New York, NY.: *Cambridge University Press*
Econ. Soc. — Economy and society. — London: *Routledge*
Econ. Soc. R. — Economic and social review. — Dublin: *Economic and Social Studies*
Economia [Lisbon] — Economia [Lisbon]. — Lisbon: *Universidade Católica Portuguesa, Faculdade de Ciências Económicas e Empresariais*
Economica — Economica. — London: *London School of Economics and Political Science*
Economist [Leiden] — Economist [Leiden]. — Leiden: *Royal Netherlands Economic Association*
Educ. Urban. Soc. — Education and urban society. — Newbury Park, CA.: *Sage Publications*
Ekistics — Ekistics. — Athens: *Athens Technological Organization, Athens Center of Ekistics*
Ekon. Deb. — Ekonomisk debatt. — Stockholm: *Nationalekonomiska föreningen*
Ekon. Preg. — Ekonomski pregled. — Zagreb: *Savez Ekonimista Hrvatske*
Employ. Relat. — Employee relations. — Bradford: *MCB University Press*
Envir. Behav. — Environment and behavior. — Newbury Park, CA.: *Environmental Design Research Association*
Envir. Plan. B. — Environment and planning B.: *Planning and design* — London: *Pion*
Envir. Plan. C. — Environment and planning C.: *Government and policy* — London: *Pion*
Envir. Plan. D — Environment and planning D.: *Society and space* — London: *Pion*
Envir. Plan.A. — Environment and planning A.: *International journal of urban and regional research* — London: *Pion*
Environ. Urban. — Environment and urbanization. — London: *International Insitute for Environment and Development*
Espace Pop. Soc. — Espace populations sociétés. — Villeneuve d'Ascq: *Université des Sciences et Techniques de Lille-Flandres-Artois*
Esprit — Esprit. — Paris: *Esprit*
Est. Demog. Urb. — Estudios demográficos y urbanos. — Mexico City: *Colégio de México, Centro de Estudios Demográficos y de Desarrollo Urbano*
Est. Inter. — Estudios internacionales. — Santiago: *Universidad de Chile, Instituto de Estudios Internacionales*
Est. Juríd. — Estudos jurídicos. — São Leopoldo: *Universidade do Vale do Rio dos Sinos*
Est. Leop. — Estudos leopoldenses. — São Leopoldo: *Universidade do Vale do Rio dos Sinos*
Est. Sociol. — Estudios sociológicos. — Pedregal de Santa Teresa: *Colegio de México*
Eth. Groups — Ethnic groups. — New York, NY.: *Gordon and Breach Science Publishers*
Ethics — Ethics. — Chicago, IL.: *University of Chicago Press*
Ethn. Fr. — Ethnologie française. — Paris: *Armand Colin*
Ethn. Racial — Ethnic and racial studies. — London: *Routledge*
Ethol. Socio. — Ethology & sociobiology. — New York, NY.: *Elsevier Science Publishing (New York)*
Eur. J. Pol. Ec. — European journal of political economy. — Amsterdam: *Elsevier Science Publishers (North-Holland)*
Eur. J. Pol. R. — European journal of political research. — Dordrecht: *European Consortium for Political Research*
Eur. J. Pop. — European journal of population; Revue européenne de démographie. — Amsterdam: *Elsevier Science Publishers (North Holland)*
Eur. J. Soc. — Archives européennes de sociologie; European journal of sociology; Europäisches Archiv für Soziologie. — Cambridge: *Cambridge University Press*
Eur. J. Soc. Psychol. — European journal of social psychology. — Chichester: *European Association of Experimental Social Psychology*
Eur. Sociol. R. — European sociological review. — Oxford: *Oxford University Press*
Eur.-Asia Stud. — Europe-Asia studies. — Abingdon: *Carfax Publishing*
Eval. Rev. — Evaluation review. — Newbury Park, CA.: *Sage Publications*
Federalist — Federalist. — Pavia: *Fondazione Europea Luciano Bolis*
Feminist R. — Feminist review. — London: *Feminist Review*
Form. Emp. — Formation emploi. — Paris: *Documentation Française*
Foro Int. — Foro internacional. — Mexico City: *El Colegio de México*
Free Assoc. — Free associations. — London: *Free Association Books*
Gend. Hist. — Gender and history. — Oxford: *Basil Blackwell*
Gender Soc. — Gender and society. — Newbury Park, CA.: *Sociologists for Women in Society*
Genève-Afrique — Genève-Afrique. — Geneva: *Institut Universitaire d'Etudes du Développement (IUED)*

INTERNATIONAL BIBLIOGRAPHY OF SOCIOLOGY — 1991

Genus — Genus. — Rome: *Comitato Italiano per lo Studio dei Problemi della Popolazione*
Geoforum — Geoforum. — Oxford: *Pergamon Press*
Geog. ann. B. — Geografiska annaler.: *Series B — Human geography* — Uppsala: *Svenska Sällskapet för Antropologi och Geografi = Swedish Society for Anthropology and Geography*
Geogr. Anal. — Geographical analysis. — Columbus, OH.: *Ohio State University Press*
Geogr. J. — Geographical journal. — London: *Royal Geographical Society*
Geogr. Res. For. — Geography research forum. — Beer- Sheva: *Ben-Gurion University of the Negev, Department of Geography*
Geogr. Rev. — Geographical review. — New York, N.Y.: *American Geographical Society*
Geogr. Rund. — Geographische Rundschau. — Braunschweig: *Westermann Schulbuchverlag*
Geography — Geography. — Sheffield: *Geographical Association*
Gestion — Gestion 2000.: *Management et prospective* — Louvain: *Université Catholique de Louvain, Institut d'administration et de gestion*
Gewerk. Monat. — Gewerkschaftliche Monatshefte. — Düsseldorf: *Bundesvorstand des DGB*
Govt. Oppos. — Government and opposition. — London: *Government and Opposition*
Han. Shak. Kenk. — Hanzai shakaigaku kenkyu.
Harv. Bus. Re. — Harvard business review. — Boston, MA: *Harvard Business Review*
Harv. Law. Rev. — Harvard law review. — Cambridge, MA.: *Harvard Law Review Association*
Health Pol. Plan. — Health policy and planning. — Oxford: *London School of Hygiene and Tropical Medicine*
Hisp. Am. Hist. Rev. — *[HAHR]* — Hispanic American historical review. — Durham, NC.: *American Historical Association, Conference on Latin American History*
Hist. Human Sci. — History of the human sciences. — London: *Routledge*
Hist. Polit. Ec. — History of political economy. — Durham, NC.: *Duke University Press*
Hist. Polit. Thou. — History of political thought. — Exeter: *Imprint Academic*
Hist. Relig. — History of religions. — Chicago, IL.: *University of Chicago Press*
Hist. Soc. R. — Historical social research; Historische Sozialforschung. — Cologne: *Arbeitsgemeinschaft für Quantifizierung und Methoden in der historisch sozialwissenschaftlichen Forschung/ International Commission for the Application of Quantitative Methods in History/ Association for History and Computing*
Hist. Theory — History and theory. — Middletown, CT.: *Wesleyan University*
Hom. Soc. — Homme et la société. — Paris: *Centre National des Lettres/ Centre National de la Recherche Scientifique*
Homines — Homines. — Hato Rey (Puerto Rico): *Universidad Interamericana de Puerto Rico*
Homme — Homme. — Paris: *Laboratoire d'anthropologie sociale*
Hous. Pol. Deb. — Housing policy debate. — Washington, D.C.: *Office of Housing Policy, Fannie Mae*
Howard J. Crim. Just. — Howard journal of criminal justice. — Oxford: *Howard League*
Hum. Nature — Human nature. — Hawthorne, NY.: *Aldine de Gruyter*
Human Relat. — Human relations. — New York, N.Y.: *Plenum Press*
Human. Org. — Human organization. — Temple Terrace, FL.: *Society for Applied Anthropology*
IBLA — IBLA. — Tunisia: *Institut des Belles Lettres Arabes*
IDS Bull. — IDS bulletin. — Brighton: *Institute of Development Studies*
Imm. Minor. — Immigrants and minorities. — London: *Frank Cass*
Impact Sci. — Impact of science on society. — Paris: *UNESCO*
Ind. Cir. — Indonesia circle. — London: *Indonesia Circle*
Ind. Crisis Q. — Industrial crisis quarterly. — Amsterdam: *Industrial Crisis Institute*
Ind. Free China — Industry of free China. — Taipei: *Council for Economic Planning and Development*
Ind. J. Agri. Eco. — Indian journal of agricultural economics. — Bombay: *Indian Society of Agricultural Economics*
Ind. J. Ind. Rel. — Indian journal of industrial relations. — New Delhi: *Shri Ram Centre for Industrial Relations and Human Resources*
Ind. J. Reg. Sci. — Indian journal of regional science. — Kharagpur: *Indian Institute of Technology, Regional Science Association*
Ind. J. Soc. Sci. — Indian journal of social science. — New Delhi: *Indian Council of Social Science Research*
Ind. Lab. Rel. — Industrial and labor relations review. — Ithaca, N.Y.: *Cornell University, New York State School of Industrial and Labor Relations*
Ind. Law J. — Industrial law journal. — Oxford: *Industrial Law Society*

Ind. Rel. J. S.Afr. — Industrial relations journal of South Africa. — Bellville: *University of Stellenbosch Business School*
Ind. Relat. — Industrial relations. — Oxford: *University of California, Berkeley, Institute of Industrial Relations*
Ind. Relat. J. — Industrial relations journal. — Oxford: *Basil Blackwell*
Indian J. Soc. W. — Indian journal of social work. — Bombay: *Tata Institute of Social Sciences*
Indian. Lab. J. — Indian labour journal. — Shimla: *Labour Bureau*
Indo-Iran. J. — Indo-lranian journal. — Dordrecht: *Kluwer Academic Publishers*
Industria — Industria. — Bologna: *Società editrice il Mulino*
Inf. Raum. — Informationen zur Raumentwicklung. — Bonn: *Bundesforschungsanstalt für Landeskunde und Raumordnung*
Inf. Soc. — Informations sociales. — Paris: *Caisse Nationale des Allocations Familiales*
Inquiry — Inquiry. — Oslo: *Universitetsforlaget (Norwegian University Press)*
Int. Aff. Mos. — International affairs [Moscow]. — Moscow: *Progress Publishers*
Int. Econ. R. — International economic review. — Philadelphia, PA. and Osaka: *University of Pennsylvania, Department of Economics/Osaka University, Institute of Social and Economic Research Association*
Int. J. Comp. Soc — International journal of comparative sociology. — Leiden: *E.J. Brill*
Int. J. Confl. Manag. — International journal of conflict management. — Bowling Green, KY.: *3-R Executive Systems*
Int. J. Health. Ser. — International journal of health services. — Amityville, NY.: *Baywood Publishing*
Int. J. Hum. Res. Man. — International journal of human resource management. — London: *Routledge*
Int. J. Law Fam. — International journal of law and the family. — Oxford: *Oxford University Press*
Int. J. M.E. Stud. — International journal of Middle East studies. — New York, N.Y.: *Middle East Studies Association of North America*
Int. J. Moral Soc. S. — International journal of moral and social studies. — London: *Journals*
Int. J. Offen. — International journal of offender therapy and comparative criminology. — New York, NY.: *Guilford Press*
Int. J. Pol. C. S. — International journal of politics, culture and society. — New York, NY.: *Human Sciences Press*
Int. J. S. Lang. — International journal of the sociology of language. — Berlin: *Mouton de Gruyter*
Int. J. S. Law — International journal of the sociology of law. — London: *Academic Press*
Int. J. Soc. E. — International journal of social economics. — Bradford: *MCB University Press*
Int. J. Soc. Psyc. — International journal of social psychiatry. — London: *Avenue Publishing*
Int. J. Urban — International journal of urban and regional research. — Sevenoaks: *Edward Arnold*
Int. J.Psy. — International journal of psycho-analysis. — London: *Institute of Psychoanalysis*
Int. Lab. Rev. — International labour review. — Geneva: *International Labour Office (ILO)*
Int. Migr. — International migration; Migrations internationales; Migraciones internacionales. — Geneva: *International Organization for Migration*
Int. Migr. Rev. — International migration review. — New York, NY.: *Center for Migration Studies*
Int. Pol. — Internasjonal politikk. — Oslo: *Norsk Utenrikspolitisk Institutt*
Int. R. Ret. Dist. Res. — International review of retail, distribution and consumer research. — London: *Routledge*
Int. Reg. Sci. R. — International regional science review. — Morgantown, WV.: *Regional Research Institute*
Int. Rel. — International relations. — London: *David Davies Memorial Institute of International Studies*
Int. Rev. Psy. — International review of psycho-analysis. — London: *Institute of Psychoanalysis*
Int. Soc. — International socialism. — London: *Socialist Workers Party*
Int. Sociol. — International sociology. — London: *International Sociological Association*
Int. Stud. — International studies. — New Delhi: *Sage Publications India*
Inter. J. Therap. Comm. — International journal of therapeutic communities. — London: *Association of Therapeutic Communities*
Inter. Phil. Sci. — International studies in the philosophy of science. — Abingdon: *Carfax Publishing*

Inter. R. Strat. Manag. — International review of strategic management. — Chichester: *John Wiley & Sons*
Intercult. Commun. St. — Intercultural communication studies. — San Antonio, TX.: *Institute for Cross-Cultural Research*
Interfaces — Interfaces. — Providence, RI.: *Institute of Management Sciences and the Operations Research Society of America*
Invest. Ger. — Investigación y gerencia. — Caracas: *PARAL*
Ir. Nam. — Iran nameh. — Bethesda, MD.: *Foundation for Iranian Studies*
IRAL — IRAL. — Heidelberg: *Julius Groos Verlag*
Irish Geogr. — Irish geography. — Dublin: *Geographical Society of Ireland*
Islam Soc. S.Sah. — Islam et sociétés au sud du Sahara. — Paris: *Editions de la Maison des Sciences de l'Homme*
Iss. Repro. Gen. Engin. — Issues in reproductive and genetic engineering. — Elmsford, NY.: *Pergamon Press*
J. Acc. Pub. Pol. — Journal of accounting and public policy. — New York, NY.: *Elsevier Science Publishers (North-Holland)*
J. Am. Plann. — Journal of the American Planning Association. — Chicago, IL.: *American Planning Association*
J. Am. Stat. Ass. — Journal of the American Statistical Association. — Alexandria, VA: *American Statistical Association*
J. Am. Stud. — Journal of American studies. — Cambridge: *Cambridge University Press*
J. Analyt. Psychol. — Journal of analytical psychology. — London: *Routledge*
J. Anthrop. Soc. Oxford — Journal of the Anthropological Society of Oxford. — Oxford: *Anthropology Society of Oxford*
J. Appl. Psychol. — Journal of applied psychology. — Arlington, VA.: *American Psychological Association*
J. Appl. Soc. Psychol. — Journal of applied social psychology. — Silver Spring, MD.: *V.H. Winston & Son*
J. Arch. Plan. Res. — Journal of architectural and planning research. — Chicago, IL.: *Locke Science Publishing*
J. As. Afr. S. — Journal of Asian and African studies [Leiden]. — Leiden: *E.J. Brill*
J. Asian Afr. Aff. — Journal of Asian and African affairs. — Washington, DC.: *Journal of Asian and African Affairs*
J. Asian St. — Journal of Asian studies. — Ann Arbor, MI.: *Association for Asian Studies*
J. Aust. Pop. Ass. — Journal of the Australian Population Association. — Canberra: *Australian Population Association*
J. Aust. Stud. — Journal of Australian studies. — Bundoora: *La Trobe University Press*
J. Biogeogr. — Journal of biogeography. — Oxford: *Blackwell Scientific Publications*
J. Biosoc. Sc. — Journal of biosocial science. — Cambridge: *Biosocial Society*
J. Comm. — Journal of communication. — New York, N.Y.: *Oxford University Press*
J. Comm. App. Soc. Psychol. — Journal of community and applied social psychology. — Chichester: *John Wiley & Sons*
J. Comm. C. Pol. — Journal of Commonwealth & comparative politics. — London: *Frank Cass*
J. Commun. S. — Journal of communist studies. — London: *Frank Cass*
J. Comp. Fam. Stud. — Journal of comparative family studies. — Calgary: *University of Calgary, Department of Sociology*
J. Cont. Asia — Journal of contemporary Asia. — Manila: *Journal of Contemporary Asia Publishers*
J. Crim. Law — Journal of criminal law and criminology. — Chicago, IL.: *Northwestern University School of Law*
J. Dev. Areas — Journal of developing areas. — Macomb, IL.: *Western Illinois University*
J. Dev. Econ. — Journal of development economics. — Amsterdam: *Elsevier Science Publishers (North-Holland)*
J. Dev. Soc. — Journal of developing societies. — Leiden: *E.J. Brill*
J. Dev. Stud. — Journal of development studies. — London: *Frank Cass*
J. Econ. Iss. — Journal of economic issues. — Lincoln, NE.: *Association for Evolutionary Economics*
J. Econ. Lit. — Journal of economic literature. — Nashville, TN.: *American Economic Association*
J. Econ. Pers. — Journal of economic perspectives. — Nashville, TN.: *American Economic Association*

INTERNATIONAL BIBLIOGRAPHY OF SOCIOLOGY — 1991

J. Econ. Psyc. — Journal of economic psychology. — Amsterdam: *International Association for Research in Economic Psychology*
J. Econ. Soc. — Journal of economic and social measurement. — Amsterdam: *International Organisations Services*
J. Econ. Soc. Geogr. — Tijdschrift voor economische en sociale geografie; Journal of economic and social geography. — Amsterdam: *Royal Dutch Geographical Society = Koninklijk Nederlands Aardrijkskundig Genootschap*
J. Econ. Stud. — Journal of economic studies. — Bradford: *MCB University Press*
J. Economet. — Journal of econometrics. — Amsterdam: *Elsevier Science Publishers (North-Holland)*
J. Ed. Soc. — Journal of educational sociology.
J. Entwick.pol. — Journal für Entwicklungspolitik. — Vienna: *Mattersburger Kreis für Entwicklungspolitik an den Österreichischen Universitäten*
J. Environ. Manag. — Journal of environmental management. — London: *Academic Press*
J. Exp. S. Psychol. — Journal of experimental social psychology. — Duluth, MN.: *Academic Press*
J. Exper. Child Psychol. — Journal of experimental child psychology. — Duluth, MN.: *Academic Press*
J. Fam. Hist. — Journal of family history. — Greenwich, CT.: *National Council on Family Relations*
J. Fam. Law — Journal of family law. — Louisville, KY.: *University of Louisville, School of Law*
J. Fam. Ther. — Journal of family therapy. — Oxford: *Association for Family Therapy*
J. Fam. Viol. — Journal of family violence. — New York, N.Y.: *Plenum Publishing Corporation*
J. Folk. Res. — Journal of folklore research. — Bloomington, IN.: *Indiana University Folklore Institute*
J. For. Psy. — Journal of forensic psychiatry. — London: *Routledge*
J. Forecast. — Journal of forecasting. — Chichester: *John Wiley & Sons*
J. Gypsy Lore Soc. — Journal of the Gypsy Lore Society. — Cheverly, MD.: *Gypsy Lore Society*
J. Hist. Beh. Sci. — Journal of the history of the behavioral sciences. — Brandon, VT.: *Clinical Psychology Publishing*
J. Hist. Philos. — Journal of the history of philosophy. — St. Louis, MO.: *Journal of the History of Philosophy*
J. Hist. Soc. — Journal of historical sociology. — Oxford: *Basil Blackwell*
J. Hous. Res. — Journal of housing research. — Washington, D.C.: *Office of Housing Policy, Fannie Mae*
J. Hum. Res. — Journal of human resources. — Madison, WI.: *University of Wisconsin Press*
J. Ind. Phil. — Journal of Indian philosophy. — Dordrecht: *Kluwer Academic Publishers*
J. Ind. Relat. — Journal of industrial relations. — Sydney: *Journal of Industrial Relations*
J. Int. Bus. Stud. — Journal of international business studies. — New Orleans, LA.: *Academy of International Business/ University of South Carolina, College of Business Administration*
J. Interd. Ec. — Journal of interdisciplinary economics. — Bicester: *A.B. Academic Publishers*
J. Jpn. Stud. — Journal for Japanese studies. — Seattle, WA.: *Society for Japanese Studies*
J. Labor Ec. — Journal of labor economics. — Chicago, IL.: *Economics Research Center/NORC*
J. Labor Res. — Journal of labor research. — Fairfax, VA: *George Mason University, Department of Economics*
J. Lang. Soc. Psychol. — Journal of language and social psychology. — Clevedon: *Multilingual Matters*
J. Lat. Am. St. — Journal of Latin American studies. — Cambridge: *Cambridge University Press*
J. Law Soc. — Journal of law and society. — Oxford: *Basil Blackwell*
J. Leis. Res. — Journal of leisure research. — Alexandria, VA.: *National Recreation and Park Association*
J. Manag. Stu. — Journal of management studies. — Oxford: *Basil Blackwell*
J. Market R. — Journal of the Market Research Society. — London: *Market Research Society*
J. Marriage Fam. — Journal of marriage and the family. — Minneapolis, MN.: *National Council on Family Relations*
J. Math. Sociol. — Journal of mathematical sociology. — New York: *Gordon & Breach Science Publishers*
J. Mediter. St. — Journal of Mediterranean studies. — Msida: *Mediterranean Institute*
J. Mod. Hist. — Journal of modern history. — Chicago IL.: *American Historical Association, Modern European History Section*

J. Multiling. — Journal of multilingual and multicultural development. — Clevedon: *Multilingual Matters*
J. Occup. Psychol. — Journal of occupational psychology. — Leicester: *British Psychological Society*
J. Orient. Stud. — Journal of oriental studies.
J. Pacific Soc. — Journal of the Pacific Society. — Tokyo: *Pacific Society*
J. Pal. Stud. — Journal of Palestine studies. — Berkeley, CA.: *Institute for Palestine Studies*
J. Peasant Stud. — Journal of peasant studies. — London: *Frank Cass*
J. Pers. Soc. Psychol. — Journal of personality and social psychology. — Arlington, VA: *American Psychological Association*
J. Personal. — Journal of personality. — Durham, NC.: *Duke University Press*
J. Phil. — Journal of philosophy. — New York, NY.: *Journal of Philosophy*
J. Phon. — Journal of phonetics. — London: *Academic Press*
J. Plan. Lit. — Journal of planning literature. — Columbus: *Ohio State University Press*
J. Polit. — Journal of politics. — Austin, TX.: *University of Texas Press, Journals Department*
J. Polit. Ec. — Journal of political economy. — Chicago: *University of Chicago Press*
J. Pop. Cult. — Journal of popular culture. — Bowling Green, OH: *Modern Language Association of America, Popular Literature Section/ Midwest Modern Language Association, Folklore Section*
J. Pop. Ec. — Journal of population economics. — Berlin: *Springer-Verlag*
J. Post. Keyn. Ec. — Journal of post Keynesian economics. — Armonk, NY.: *M.E.Sharpe*
J. Prag. — Journal of pragmatics. — Amsterdam: *Elsevier Science Publishers (North-Holland)*
J. Psychol. — Journal of psychology. — Washington, DC: *Heldref Publications*
J. Publ. Ec. — Journal of public economics. — Amsterdam: *Elsevier Science Publishers (North-Holland)*
J. Real Est. Res. — Journal of real estate research. — Grand Forks: *American Real Estate Society*
J. Reg. Pol. — Journal of regional policy. — Naples: *Isveimer*
J. Res. Crim. Delin. — Journal of research in crime and delinquency. — Newbury Park, CA.: *National Council on Crime and Delinquency*
J. Res. Soc. Pakist. — Journal of the Research Society of Pakistan. — Lahore: *University of the Punjab, Punjab University Library*
J. Roy. Stat. Soc. A. — Journal of the Royal Statistical Society.: *Series A (statistics in society)* — London: *Royal Statistical Society*
J. Rural St. — Journal of rural studies. — Oxford: *Pergamon Press*
J. S.Afr. Stud. — Journal of Southern African studies. — Oxford: *Oxford University Press*
J. Sci. S. Relig. — Journal for the scientific study of religion. — West Lafayette, IN.: *Society for the Scientific Study of Religion*
J. SE. As. Stud. — Journal of Southeast Asian studies. — Singapore: *National University of Singapore, Department of History*
J. Soc. Biol. Struct. — Journal of social and biological structures. — Greenwich, CT.: *JAI Press*
J. Soc. Clin. Psychol. — Journal of social and clinical psychology. — New York, NY.: *Guilford Publications*
J. Soc. Devel. Afr. — Journal of social development in Africa. — Harare: *School of Social Work*
J. Soc. Hist — Journal of social history. — Pittsburgh, PA.: *Carnegie Mellon University*
J. Soc. Issues — Journal of social issues. — New York, NY.: *Society for the Psychological Study of Social Issues*
J. Soc. Océan. — Journal de la Société des océanistes. — Paris: *Société des Oceanistes*
J. Soc. Pol. — Journal of social policy. — Cambridge: *Social Policy Association*
J. Soc. Pol. E. — Journal of social, political and economic studies. — Washington, D.C.: *Council for Social and Economic Studies*
J. Soc. Psychol. — Journal of social psychology. — Washington, DC.: *Heldref Publications*
J. Soc. Stud. Dhaka — Journal of social studies. — Dhaka: *Centre for Social Studies*
J. Theory Soc. Behav. — Journal for the theory of social behaviour. — Oxford: *Basil Blackwell*
J. Urban Ec. — Journal of urban economics. — Duluth, MN.: *Academic Press*
J. Urban Hist. — Journal of urban history. — Newbury Park, CA.: *Sage Publications*
J. World. Hist. — Journal of world history. — Honolulu, HI.: *World History Association*
Jahr. Christ. Sozialwiss. — Jahrbuch für christliche Sozialwissenschaften. — Münster: *Universität Münster, Institut für Christliche Sozialwissenschaften*
Jahrb. N. St. — Jahrbücher für Nationalökonomie und Statistik. — Stuttgart: *Gustav Fischer Verlag*

Jap. J. Relig. St. — Japanese journal of religious studies. — Nagoya: *Nanzan Institute for Religion and Culture*
Jew. J. Socio. — Jewish journal of sociology. — London: *Maurice Freedman Research Trust*
Jew. Soc. Stud. — Jewish social studies. — New York, NY.: *Conference on Jewish Social Studies*
Jpn. Christ. Q. — Japan Christian quarterly. — Tokyo: *Japan Christian Quarterly*
Kansan. Julk. — Kansaneläkelaitoksen julkaisuja. — Helsinki: *Kansaneläkelaitoksen*
Kölner Z. Soz. Soz. psy. — Kölner Zeitschrift für Soziologie und Sozialpsychologie. — Wiesbaden: *Westdeutscher Verlag*
Kommunist — Коммунист; Kommunist. — Moscow: *Kommunisticheskaya Partiia Sovetskogo Soiuza. Tsentral'nyi Komitet*
Konjunkturpolitik — Konjunkturpolitik. — Berlin: *Duncker und Humblot*
Kor. Stud. — Korean studies. — Honolulu, HI.: *University of Hawaii Press*
Korea J. — Korea journal. — Seoul: *Korean National Commission for Unesco*
Korea Obs. — Korea observer. — Seoul: *Institute of Korean Studies*
Kwan. Gak. Univ. Ann. St. — Kwansai Gakuin University Annual Studies. — Hyôgo: *Kwansei Gakuin University*
Lab. Law J. — Labor law journal. — Chicago, IL.: *Commerce Clearing House*
Labour Cap. Soc. — Labour, capital and society; Travail, capital et société. — Montreal: *McGill University, Centre for Developing Area Studies*
Labour [Italy] — Labour [Italy]. — Rome: *Fondazione Giacomo Brodolini*
Land Econ. — Land economics. — Madison, WI.: *University of Wisconsin Press*
Lang. Prob. Lang. Plan. — Language problems and language planning. — Amsterdam: *John Benjamins Publishing*
Lang. Soc. — Language in society. — New York, NY.: *Cambridge University Press*
Language — Language. — Baltimore, MD.: *Linguistic Society of America*
Lat. Am. Pers. — Latin American perspectives. — Newbury Park, CA.: *Sage Publishers*
Lat. Am. Res. R. — Latin American research review. — Albuquerque, NM.: *Latin American Studies Association*
Law Soc. Rev. — Law and society review. — Amherst, MA.: *Law and Society Association*
Leviatán — Leviatán. — Madrid: *Fundación Pablo Iglesias*
Ling. Philos. — Linguistics and philosophy. — Dordrecht: *Kluwer Academic Publishers*
Linguist. In. — Linguistic inquiry. — Cambridge, MA: *MIT Press*
Local. Ec. — Local economy. — Harlow: *Local Economy Policy Unit*
Maan. Econ. — Maandschrift economie. — Groningen: *Wolters-Noordhoff*
Mag. Köz. — Magyar Közigazgatás. — Budapest:
Mag. Tud. — Magyar tudomány. — Budapest: *Magyar Tudományos Akadémia*
Man — Man. — London: *Royal Anthropological Institute*
Man India — Man in India. — Ranchi: *Sudarshan Press*
Manch. Sch. E. — Manchester School of economic and social studies. — Oxford: *Basil Blackwell*
Mankind — Mankind. — Sydney: *Anthropological Society of N.S.W.*
Mankind Q. — Mankind quarterly. — Washington, DC.: *Cliveden Press*
Mar. Pol. — Marine policy. — Guildford: *Butterworth-Heinemann*
Market. Lett. — Marketing letters. — Dordrecht: *Kluwer Academic Publishers*
Math. Soc. Sc. — Mathematical social sciences. — Amsterdam: *Elsevier Science Publishers (North-Holland)*
Med. Anthr. Q. — Medical anthropology quarterly. — Washington, D.C.: *Society for Medical Anthropology*
Med. Anthrop. — Medical anthropology. — Reading: *Gordon and Breach*
Medi. Mensch Gesell. — Medizin Mensch Gesellschaft. — Stuttgart: *Ferdinand Enke Verlag*
Media Cult. Soc. — Media culture and society. — London: *Sage Publications*
Meiji. Gak. Ron. — Meiji gakuin ronso. — Tokyo: *Meiji University*
Mel. J. Pol. — Melbourne journal of politics. — Melbourne: *Political Science Society*
Melan. Law J. — Melanesian law journal. — Papua New Guinea: *University of Papua New Guinea, Faculty of Law*
Mens Maat. — Mens en maatschappij. — Houten: *Bohn Stafleu Van Loghum*
MI. law. R. — Michigan law review. — Ann Arbor, MI.: *Michigan Law Review*
Middle E. Stud. — Middle Eastern studies. — London: *Frank Cass*
Migrac. Teme — Migracijske teme. — Zagreb: *University of Zagreb, Institute for Migration and Nationalities Studies/ Yugoslav Sociological Association, Section for Migration*

INTERNATIONAL BIBLIOGRAPHY OF SOCIOLOGY — 1991

Milbank Q. — Milbank quarterly. — New York, NY.: *Milbank Memorial Fund*
Millennium — Millennium. — London: *Millenium Publishing Group*
Mind — Mind. — Oxford: *Oxford University Press*
Mod. Asian S. — Modern Asian studies. — Cambridge: *Cambridge University Press*
Mod. Chi. — Modern China. — Newbury Park, CA.: *Sage Publications*
Mod. Law R. — Modern law review. — Oxford: *Basil Blackwell*
Mon. Rev. — Monthly review. — New York, NY.: *Monthly Review Foundation*
Multilingua — Multilingua. — Berlin: *Mouton de Gruyter*
Negot. J. — Negotiation journal. — New York, NY.: *Plenum Press*
Nen. Shak. Ron. — Nenpo Shakaigaku Ronsyu. — Tokyo:
Neth. J. Soc. Sci. — Netherlands' journal of social sciences/Sociologia Neerlandica. — Assen: *Netherlands' Sociological and Anthropological Society*
New Comm. — New community. — Coventry: *Commission for Racial Equality*
New Form. — New formations. — London: *Routledge*
New Left R. — New left review. — London: *New Left Review*
New Polit. — New politics. — Brooklyn, NY.: *New Politics Associates*
New Que. — New quest. — Pune: *Indian Association for Cultural Freedom*
New Tech. Work. Empl. — New technology, work and employment. — Oxford: *Basil Blackwell*
Non. Manag. Leader. — Nonprofit management and leadership. — San Francisco, CA.: *Jossey-Bass*
Nueva Soc. — Nueva sociedad. — Caracas: *Nueva Sociedad*
Numen — Numen. — Leiden: *International Association for the History of Religions*
Obshch. N. Usbek. — Общественные науки в Узбекисана; Obshchestrennye nauki v Uzbekistane. — Tashkent:
Oceania — Oceania. — Sydney: *Oceania Publications, University of Sydney*
Oral Hist. — Oral history. — Colchester: *Oral History Society*
Organ. Beh. Hum. Dec. Proces. — Organizational behavior and human decision processes. — Duluth, MN.: *Academic Press*
Organ. Sc. — Organizational science.
Organ. Stud. — Organization studies. — Berlin: *European Group for Organizational Studies*
Orient — Orient. — Leverkusen: *Deutsches Orient- Institut*
Öster. Z. Polit. — Österreichische Zeitschrift für Politikwissenschaft. — Vienna: *Österreichische Gesellschaft für Politikwissenschaft*
Osteuropa — Osteuropa. — Stuttgart: *Deutsche Gesellschaft für Osteuropakunde*
Ox. B. Econ. S. — Oxford bulletin of economics and statistics. — Oxford: *Basil Blackwell*
Ox. Econ. Pap. — Oxford economic papers. — Oxford: *Oxford University Press*
Ox. R. Econ. Pol. — Oxford review of economic policy. — Oxford: *Oxford University Press*
Pak. Dev. R. — Pakistan development review. — Islamabad: *Pakistan Institute of Development Economics*
Pań. Prawo — Państwo i prawo. — Warsaw: *Polska Academia Nauk, Instytut Nauk Prawnych*
Pap. Reg. Sci. — Papers in regional science. — Urbana, IL.: *Regional Science Association International*
Papers — Papers. — Barcelona: *Universitat Autònoma de Barcelona, Departament de Sociologia*
Peasant Stud. — Peasant studies. — Salt Lake City, UT: *University of Utah*
Pen. Iber. — Pensamiento iberoamericano. — Madrid: *Sociedad Estatal Quinto Centenario*
Pensée — Pensée. — Paris: *Institut de recherches marxistes*
Perc. Psych. — Perception & psychophysics. — Austin, TX.: *Psychonomic Society*
Peripherie — Peripherie. — Berlin: *Wissenschaftliche Vereinigung für Entwicklungstheorie und Entwicklungspolitik*
Phil. Stud. — Philippine studies. — Quezon City: *Ateneo de Manila University Press*
Philos. E.W. — Philosophy east and west. — Honolulu, Hl.: *University of Hawaii Press*
Philos. Pub. — Philosophy & public affairs. — Princeton, N.J.: *Princeton University Press*
Philos. S. Sc. — Philosophy of the social sciences. — Newbury Park, CA.: *Sage Publications*
Plan. Khoz. — Плановое Хозяйство; Planovoe khoziaistvo. — Moscow: *Gosplan, SSSR*
Plan. Out. — Planning outlook. — Newcastle-upon-Tyne: *University of Newcastle-upon-Tyne, Department of Town and Country Planning*
Plan. Pract. Res. — Planning practice and research. — London: *Pion*
Pol. Misao — Politička misao. — Zagreb: *Faculet Političkih Nauka u Zagrebu*
Pol. Sci. Q. — Political science quarterly. — New York, NY.: *Academy of Political Science*
Pol. Soc. Ger. Aust. Swit. — Politics and society in Germany, Austria and Switzerland. — Nottingham: *University of Nottingham, Institute of German, Austrian and Swiss Affairs*

INTERNATIONAL BIBLIOGRAPHY OF SOCIOLOGY — 1991

Poli. Soc. — Policing and society. — New York, N.Y.: *Harwood Academic Publishers*
Policy Pol. — Policy and politics. — Bristol: *University of Bristol, School for Advanced Urban Studies*
Polis — Полис; Polis. — Moscow: *Izdatel' stvo Progress Publishers*
Polit. Geogr. Q. — Political geography quarterly. — Guildford: *Butterworth-Heinemann*
Polit. Life — Politics and the life sciences. — Dekalb, IL: *Association for Politics and the Life Sciences*
Polit. Psych. — Political psychology. — New York, NY.: *International Society of Political Psychology*
Polit. Soc. — Politics and society. — Stoneham, MA.: *Butterworth-Heinemann*
Polit. Theory — Political theory. — Newbury Park, CA.: *Sage Publications*
Pop. Dev. Rev. — Population and development review. — New York, N.Y.: *Population Council*
Pop. Res. Pol. R. — Population research and policy review. — Dordrecht: *Kluwer Academic Publishers*
Pop. Stud. — Population studies. — London: *London School of Economics, Population Investigation Committee*
Pop. Stud. Egy. — Population studies. — New York, NY.: *United Nations Publications*
Popul. Envir. — Population and environment. — New York, N.Y.: *Human Sciences Press*
Popul. R. — Population review. — La Jolla, CA.: *Indian Institute for Population Studies*
Population — Population. — Paris: *Institut National d'Etudes Démographiques*
Pra. Zab. Społ. — Praca i zabezpieczenie społeczne. — Warsaw: *Państwowe Wydawnictwo Ekonomiczne*
Practice — Practice. — Birmingham: *British Association of Social Workers*
Prax. Int. — Praxis international. — Oxford: *Basil Blackwell*
Priroda — Природа; Priroda. — Moscow:
Prob. Pol. Soc. — Problèmes politiques et sociaux. — Paris: *Documentation Française*
Probl. Commu. — Problems of communism. — Washington, D.C.: *US Information Agency*
Proceed. Acad. Polit. Sci. — Proceedings of the Academy of Political Science. — New York, NY.: *Academy of Political Science*
Prof. Geogr. — Professional geographer. — Washington, D.C.: *Association of American Geographers*
Prog. H. Geog. — Progress in human geography. — Sevenoaks: *Edward Arnold*
Proj. App. — Project appraisal. — Guildford: *Beech Tree Publishing*
Prokla — Prokla.: *Probleme des Klassenkampfs* — Berlin: *Vereinigung zur Kritik der politischen Ökonomie*
Prz. Pol. — Przegląd polonijny. — Wroclaw: *Polska Akademia Nauk, Komitet Badania Polonii*
Prz. Soc. — Przegląd socjologiczny. — Łódź: *Łódzkie towarzystwo naukowe*
Psychol .B. — Psychological bulletin. — Arlington, VA.: *American Psychological Association*
Psychol. Devel. Soc. — Psychology and developing societies. — New Delhi: *Sage Publications India*
Psychol. Rev. — Psychological review. — Arlington, VA.: *American Psychological Association*
Publ. Adm. D. — Public administration and development. — Chichester: *Royal Institute of Public Administration*
Publ. Adm. Re. — Public administration review. — Washington, DC.: *American Society for Public Administration*
Publ. Admin. — Public administration. — Oxford: *Royal Institute for Public Administration*
Publ. Aff. Q. — Public affairs quarterly. — Bowling Green, OH.: *Philosophy Documentation Center/ North American Philosophical Publications*
Publ. Cult. — Public culture. — Philadelphia, PA.: *Center for Transnational Cultural Studies*
Publ. Inter. — Public interest. — Washington, DC.: *National Affairs*
Publ. Law — Public law. — London: *Sweet & Maxwell*
Publ. Opin. Q. — Public opinion quarterly. — Chicago, IL.: *American Association for Public Opinion Research*
Publizistik — Publizistik. — Konstanz: *Deutsche Gesellschaft für Publizistik- und Kommunikationswissenschaft/ Österreichische Gesellschaft für Publizistik- und Kommunikationswissenschaft/ Schweizerische Gesellschaft für Kommunikations- und Medienwissenschaft*
Q. J. Econ. — Quarterly journal of economics. — Cambridge, MA.: *Harvard University*
Quest — Quest. — Lusaka: *University of Zambia, Department of Philosophy*
R&D Manag. — R&D management. — Oxford: *Basil Blackwell*

INTERNATIONAL BIBLIOGRAPHY OF SOCIOLOGY — 1991

R. Ec. Reg. Urb. — Revue d'économie régionale et urbaine. — Paris: *ADICUEER (Association des Directeurs d'Instituts et des Centres Universitaires d'Etudes Economiques Régionales)*

R. Et. Coop. Mut. Ass. — Revue des études coopératives mutualistes et associatives. — Paris: *Coopérative d'Information et d'Edition Mutualiste*

R. Et. Palest. — Revue d'études palestiniennes. — Paris: *Institut des Études Palestiniennes / Fondation Diana Tamari Sabbagh*

R. Eur. Lat.am. Caribe — European review of Latin American and Caribbean studies; Revista europea de estudios latinoamericanos y del caribe. — Amsterdam: *CEDLA, Interuniversitair Centrum voor Studie en Documentatie van Latijns Amerika/ RILA, Royal Institute of Linguistics and Anthropology*

R. Fr. Admin. Publ. — Revue française d'administration publique. — Paris: *Institut International d'Administration Publique*

R. Fr. Sci. Pol. — Revue française de science politique. — Paris: *Fondation nationale des sciences politiques/ Association française de science politique*

R. Gén. Droit Inter. — Revue générale de droit international public. — Paris: *Editions A. Pedone*

R. In. Weal. — Review of income and wealth. — New York, NY.: *International Association for Research in Income and Wealth*

R. Ind. Malay. Aff. — [RIMA] — Review of Indonesian and Malaysian affairs. — Sydney: *University of Sydney, Department of Indonesian and Malayan Studies*

R. Mon. Musul. Med. — Revue du monde musulman et de la Méditerranée. — Aix-en-Provence: *Association pour l'étude des sciences humaines en Afrique du Nord et au Proche-Orient*

R. Rur. Urb. Plan. S.& E.Afr. — Review of rural and urban planning in Southern and Eastern Africa. — Harare: *University of Zimbabwe, Department of Rural and Urban Planning*

R. Soc. Econ. — Review of social economy. — DeKalb, IL.: *Association for Social Economics*

R. T-Monde — Revue Tiers-Monde. — Paris: *Université de Paris, Institut d'étude du développement économique et social*

R.E.M. — Revue de l'économie meridionale. — Montpellier: *Université de Montpellier, Faculté de droit et des sciences économiques, Centre regional de la productivité et des études économiques*

Race Class — Race and class. — London: *Institute of Race Relations*

Raduga — Радуга; Raduga. — Tallin: *Izdatel'stvo "Periodika"*

Rass. It. Soc. — Rassegna italiana di sociologia. — Bologna: *Societá Editrice il Mulino*

Rech. Soc.graph — Recherches sociographiques. — Québec: *Université Laval, Département de Sociologie*

Recht Int. Wirst. — Recht der internationalen Wirtschaft. — Heidelberg: *Verlag Recht und Wirtschaft*

Reg. Sci. Urb. Econ. — Regional science and urban economics. — Amsterdam: *Elsevier Science Publishers (North-Holland)*

Reg. Stud. — Regional studies. — Cambridge: *Regional Studies Association*

Regar. Actual. — Regards sur l'actualité. — Paris: *Documentation Française*

Relig. Comm. Lands — Religion in communist lands. — Keston: *Keston College*

Religion — Religion. — London: *Academic Press*

Resp. Victim. Women Child. — Response to the victimization of women and children. — New York, NY.: *Center for Women Policy Studies*

Rethink. Marx. — Rethinking Marxism. — New York, NY.: *Association for Economic and Social Analysis*

Rev. Algér. — Revue algérienne des sciences juridiques économiques et politiques. — Algiers: *Université d'Alger, Institut de Droit et des Sciences Administratives*

Rev. Bl. Pol. Ec. — Review of black political economy. — New Brunswick, NJ.: *National Economic Association/ Clark Atlanta University, Southern Center for Studies in Public Policy*

Rev. Bras. Ciên. Soc. — Revista brasileira de ciências sociais. — São Paulo: *Associação Nacional de Pós-Graduação e Pesquisa em Ciências Sociais*

Rev. Brasil. Est. Popul. — Revista brasileira de estudos de população. — Brazil: *Associação Brasileira de Estudos Populacionais*

Rev. Ec. Con. It. — Review of economic conditions in Italy. — Rome: *Banco di Roma*

Rev. Econ. St. — Review of economics and statistics. — Amsterdam: *Harvard University*

Rev. Et. Comp. — Revue d'études comparatives est- ouest. — Paris: *Institut de recherches juridiques comparatives du C.N.R.S., Centre d'études des pays socialistes/ Economie et techniques de planification des pays de l'est*

Rev. F. Braudel. Ctr. — Review. Fernand Braudel Center. — Binghamton, NY.: *State University of New York, Fernand Braudel Center*
Rev. Fom. Soc. — Revista de fomento social. — Madrid: *INSA-ETEA*
Rev. Fr. Soc. — Revue française de sociologie. — Paris: *Institut de recherche sur les sociétés contemporaines*
Rev. Int. D. C. — Revue internationale de droit comparé. — Paris: *Société de Legislation Comparée*
Rev. Int. Sci. Ec. Com. — Rivista internazionale di scienze economiche e commerciali. — Milan: *Università Commerciale Luigi Bocconi/ Università degli Studi di Milano*
Rev. Int.Am. Plan. — Revista interamericana de planificación. — Guatemala: *Sociedad Interamericana de Planificación*
Rev. Parag. Sociol. — Revista paraguaya de sociología. — Asunción: *Centro Paraguayo de Estudios Sociológicos*
Rev. Roumaine Et. Int. — Revue roumaine d'études internationales. — Bucharest: *Editura Academiei Române*
Roma — Roma. — Chandigarh: *Roma Publications*
Rural Sociol. — Rural sociology. — College Station, TX.: *Rural Sociological Society*
S. Afr. J. Labour Relat. — South African journal of labour relations. — Pretoria: *University of South Africa, School of Business Leadership*
S. Asia — South Asia. — Armidale: *South Asian Studies Association of Australia*
S. Econ. J. — Southern economic journal. — Chapel Hill, NC: *Southern Economic Association/ University of North Carolina at Chapel Hill*
S.Afr. J. Afr. Lang. — South African journal of African languages; Suid-Afrikaanse tydskrif vir Afrikatale. — Pretoria: *African Languages Association of Southern Africa/ Afrikatale-Vereniging van Suider-Afrika*
S.Afr. J. Sociol. — South African journal of sociology; Suid- Afrikaanse tydskrif vir sosiologie. — Pretoria: *South African Sociological Association = Suid-Afrikaanse Sosiologievereniging*
S.Afr. Lab. B. — South African labour bulletin. — Johannesburg: *Umanyano Publications*
S.Afr. Sociol. R. — South African sociological review. — Rondebosch: *Association for Sociology in South Africa*
S.Asia. J. — South Asia journal. — New Delhi: *Indian Council of South Asian Cooperation*
San. Ment. Qué — Santé mentale au Québec. — Montréal: *Revue Santé mentale au Québec*
San. Nat. — Sangeet natak. — New Delhi: *Sangeet Natak Akademi*
Sav. Develop. — Savings and development. — Milan: *Centre for Financial Assistance to African Countries (Finafrica)*
Scand. Hous. Plan. R. — Scandinavian housing and planning research. — Stockholm: *Building Research Institute (Denmark)/ Ministry of Environment (Finland)/ Institute for Urban and Regional Research (Norway)/ Institute for Building Research (Sweden)*
Scand. J. Devel. Altern. — Scandinavian journal of development alternatives. — Stockholm: *Bethany Books*
Sci. Am. — Scientific American. — New York, NY.: *Scientific American*
Sci. Cult. — Science as culture. — London: *Free Association Books*
Sci. Soc. — Science and society. — New York, NY.: *Guilford Publications*
Scot. J. Poli. — Scottish journal of political economy. — Oxford: *Scottish Economic Society*
Secur. Dial. — Security dialogue. — London: *Sage Publications*
Semiotica — Semiotica. — Berlin: *International Association for Semiotic Studies*
Shak-nen. — Shakaigaku-nenshi. — Tokyo: *Waseda Sociological Society*
Shak. Hyor. — Shakaigaku hyoron. — Tokyo: *Nippon Shakai Gakkai = Japanese Sociological Society*
Shak. Kenk. — Shakaigaku kenkyu. — Sendai: *Tohoku Sociological Association*
Shak. Ron. — Shakaigaku ronso. — Tokyo: *Nihon University*
Shak.-rōd. Kenk. — Shakai-rōdō Kenkyū.
Shin. Hy. — Shinbungaku hyoron. — Japan: *Japan Society for Studies in Journalism and Mass Communication*
Shisō — Shisō.
Signs — Signs. — Chicago, IL.: *University of Chicago Press*
Simulat. Gam. — Simulation and gaming. — Newbury Park, CA.: *Sage Publications*
Slav. E.Eur. Rev. — Slavonic and East European review. — London: *University of London, School of Slavonic and East European Studies*
Slovo — Slovo. — London: *School of Slavonic and East European Studies*

INTERNATIONAL BIBLIOGRAPHY OF SOCIOLOGY — 1991

Soc. Act. — Social action. — New Delhi: *Indian Social Institute, Social Action Trust*
Soc. Anal. — Social analysis. — Adelaide: *University of Adelaide, Department of Anthropology*
Soc. Attit. N.Ire. — Social attitudes in Northern Ireland. — Belfast: *Blackstaff Press*
Soc. Biol. — Social biology. — New York, NY.: *Society for the Study of Social Biology*
Soc. Choice — Social choice and welfare. — Berlin: *Springer International*
Soc. Cogn. — Social cognition. — New York, NY.: *Guilford Publications*
Soc. Compass — Social compass. — London: *International Federation of Institutes for Social and Socio-Religious Research (FERES)/ Centre de Recherches Socio-Religieuses*
Soc. Contemp. — Sociétés contemporaines. — Paris: *Institut de Recherche sur les Sociétés Contemporaines (IRESCO), CNRS*
Soc. Dyn. — Social dynamics. — Rondebosch: *Centre for African Studies, University of Cape Town*
Soc. Econ. S. — Social and economic studies. — Kingston: *University of the West Indies, Institute of Social and Economic Research*
Soc. Econ. Sys. St. — Social and Economic Systems Studies.
Soc. Et. Océan. — Bulletin de la Société des études océaniennes. — Papeete: *Société des études océaniennes*
Soc. Forc. — Social forces. — Chapel Hill, NC.: *University of North Carolina, Department of Sociology*
Soc. Ind. — Social indicators research. — Dordrecht: *Kluwer Academic Publishers*
Soc. Just. — Social justice. — San Francisco, CA.: *Global Options*
Soc. Method. — Sociological methodology. — Oxford: *American Sociological Association*
Soc. Networks — Social networks. — Amsterdam: *International Network for Social Network Analysis (INSNA)*
Soc. Part. — Socialismo y participación. — Lima: *CEDEP (Centro de Estudios para el Desarrollo y la Participación)*
Soc. Pol. — Social policy. — New York, NY.: *Social Policy Corporation*
Soc. Pol. Admin. — Social policy and administration. — Oxford: *Basil Blackwell*
Soc. Prob. — Social problems. — Berkeley, CA.: *Society for the Study of Social Problems*
Soc. Res. — Social research. — New York, NY: *New School for Social Research, Graduate Faculty of Political and Social Science*
Soc. Sci. — Social sciences. — Moscow: *Nauka Moscow*
Soc. Sci. China — Social sciences in China. — Beijing: *Chinese Academy of Social Science*
Soc. Sci. Hist. — Social science history. — Durham, NC.: *Social Science History Association*
Soc. Sci. Info. — Social science information. — London: *Maison des sciences de l'homme/ Ecole des hautes études en science sociales*
Soc. Sci. Med. — Social science & medicine. — Exeter: *Pergamon Press*
Soc. Sci. Q. — Social science quarterly. — Austin, TX.: *Southwestern Social Science Association*
Soc. Scient. — Social scientist. — New Delhi: *Indian School of Social Sciences*
Soc. Ser. R. — Social service review. — Chicago, IL.: *University of Chicago Press*
Soc. Work. Ed. — Social work education. — London: *Whiting and Birch*
Social Soc. Res. — Sociology and social research. — Los Angeles, CA.: *University of Southern California*
Social. Int. — Sociologia internationalis. — Berlin: *Verlag Duncker & Humblot*
Socialisme — Socialisme. — Brussels: *Institut Emile Vandervelde*
Society — Society. — New Brunswick, NJ.: *Transaction*
Socio. Econ. — Socio-economic planning sciences. — Exeter: *Pergamon Press*
Sociol. Anal. — Sociological analysis. — Washington, DC: *Association for the Sociology of Religion*
Sociol. Bul. — Sociological bulletin. — New Delhi: *Indian Sociogical Society*
Sociol. For. — Sociological forum. — New York, NY.: *Plenum Publishing*
Sociol. Gids — Sociologische gids. — Meppel: *Boom*
Sociol. Health Ill. — Sociology of health and illness. — Oxford: *Basil Blackwell*
Sociol. Meth. — Sociological methods and research. — Newbury Park, CA.: *Sage Publications*
Sociol. Q. — Sociological quarterly. — Greenwich, CT.: *J.A.I. Press*
Sociol. Rev. — Sociological review. — London: *University of Keele*
Sociol. Rur. — Sociologia ruralis. — Assen: *European Society for Rural Sociology/Société Européenne de Sociologie Rurale/ Europäischen Gesellschaft für Land- und Agrarsoziologie*
Sociol. Theory — Sociological theory. — Cambridge, MA.: *American Sociological Association*
Sociol. Trav. — Sociologie du travail. — Paris: *Dunod*

Sociologia [Rome] — Sociologia [Rome]. — Rome: *Istituto Luigi Sturzo*
Sociologica — Sociologica. — Tokyo: *Soka University*
Sociologos — Sociologos. — Tokyo: *Sociologos*
Sociologus — Sociologus. — Berlin: *Duncker & Humblot*
Sociology — Sociology. — Solihull: *British Sociological Association*
Soshioroji — Soshioroji. — Kyoto: *Shakaigaku Kenkyukai*
Sot. Issle. — Социологические исследования (социс); Sotsiologicheskie issledovaniia (sotsis). — Moscow: *Akademii Nauk SSSR*
Sov. Jew. Aff. — Soviet Jewish affairs. — London: *Institute of Jewish Affairs*
Sovet. Etno. — Советская этнография; Sovetskaia etnografiia. — Moscow: *Akademiya Nauk S.S.S.R., Institut Etnografii*
Sovet. Gos. Pr. — Советское государство и право; Sovetskoe gosudarstvo i pravo. — Moscow: *Institut gosudarstva i prava*
Soz. Welt. — Soziale Welt. — Göttingen: *Arbeitsgemeinschaft sozialwissenschaftlicher Institute*
Spr. Między. — Sprawy międzynarodowe. — Warsaw: *Polski Instytut Spraw Międzynarodowych*
St. Philos. Educ. — Studies in philosophy and education. — Dordrecht: *Kluwer Academic Publishers*
Statistica — Statistica. — Bologna: *Cooperitiva Libraria Universitaria Editrice*
Statistician — Statistician. — Abingdon: *Institute of Statisticians*
Stud. Comp. Commun. — Studies in comparative communism. — Guildford: *Butterworth-Heinemann*
Stud. Comp. ID. — Studies in comparative international development. — New Brunswick, NJ: *Transaction Periodicals Consortium*
Stud. Hist. — Studies in history. — New Delhi: *Sage Publications India*
Stud. Hist. Phil. Sci. — Studies in history and philosophy of science. — Oxford: *Pergamon Press*
Stud. Pol. Ec. — Studies in political economy. — Ottawa: *Studies in Political Economy*
Stud. W.Aust. Hist. — Studies in Western Australian history. — Nedlands: *University of Western Australia, Department of History*
Survival — Survival. — Oxford: *International Institute for Strategic Studies*
Svobod. Mysl' — Свободная мысль; Svobodnaia Mysl'. — Moscow: *Izdatel'stvo Pravda*
Szociologia — Szociologia. — Budapest: *Magyar Tudomanyos Akademia, Szociologiai Intezet*
Tarsad. Kozl. — Társadalomtudomanyi kozlemenyek. — Budapest: *Magyar szocialista munkaspart (MSZMP), Tarsadalomtudomanyi Intezet*
Tarsadalomkutatás — Tarsadalomkutatás. — Budapest: *Magyar Tudomanyos Akademia*
Tech. Devel. — Technology and development. — Tokyo: *Institute for International Cooperation/ Japan International Cooperation Agency*
Telos — Telos. — New York, NY.: *Telos Press*
Temps Mod. — Temps modernes. — Paris: *Gallimard/ Les Temps Modernes*
Terror. Pol. Viol. — Terrorism and political violence. — London: *Frank Cass*
Text — Text. — Berlin: *Walter de Gruyter*
Theory Cult. Soc. — Theory culture and society. — London: *Sage Publications*
Theory Decis. — Theory and decision. — Dordrecht: *Kluwer Academic Publishers*
Theory Soc. — Theory and society. — Dordrecht: *Kluwer Academic Publishers*
Third Wor. P. — Third World planning review. — Liverpool: *Liverpool University Press*
Tibet J. — Tibet journal. — Dharamshala: *Library of Tibetan Works and Archives (LTWA)*
Tids. Antrop. — Tidsskriftet antropologi. — Copenhagen: *Stofskifte*
Tijds. Econ. Manag. — Tijdschrift voor economie en management. — Louvain: *Katholieke Universiteit Te Leuven, Faculteit der Economische en Toegepaste Economische Wetenschappen*
Tos. Mon. — Toshi mondai. — Tokyo: *Tokyo Institute for Municpal Research*
Town Plan. R. — Town planning review. — Liverpool: *University of Liverpool, Department of Civic Design (Town and Regional Planning)*
Trans. Inst. Br. Geogr. — Transactions of the Institute of British Geographers.: *New series* — London: *Institute of British Geographers*
Transformation — Transformation. — Durban: *Transformation*
Transition — Transition. — Georgetown: *University of Guyana, Faculty of Social Sciences and Institute of Development Studies*
Unisa Lat.Am. Rep. — Unisa Latin American report. — Pretoria: *Unisa Centre for Latin American Studies*
Urban Aff. Q. — Urban affairs quarterly. — Newbury Park, CA.: *Sage Publications*

Urban Anthro. — Urban anthropology. — Brockport, NY.: *The Institute*
Urban Geogr. — Urban geography. — Silver Spring, MD.: *V.H. Winston & Son*
Urban Stud. — Urban studies. — Abingdon: *University of Glasgow, Centre for Urban and Regional Research*
V. Aka. BSSR — Весці Акадэміі Навук БССР; Vestsi akademii navuk BSSR.: Сурыя грамадскіх навук; Seryia gramadskikh navuk — Minsk: *Akademii Navuk, BSSR*
Ves. Lenin. Univ. Ser. 5 — Вестник ленинградского университета; Vestnik Leningradskogo universiteta.: Серия 5 экономика, Seriia 5 ekonomika — Leningrad: *Izdatel'stvo Leningradskogo Universiteta*
Vest. Lenin. Univ. 6 — Вестник ленинградского университета ; Vestnik Leningradskogo universiteta.: Серия 6 история кпсс, научный коммунизм, философия право; Seriia 6, istoriia KPSS nauchnyi kommunizm filosofiia pravo — Leningrad: *Izdatel'stvo Leningradskogo Universiteta*
Vest. Mosk. Univ. 12 — Вестник Московского Университета ; Vestnik Moskovskogo Universiteta.: Серия 12 Социально политические исследования; Seriia 12 Sotsialno-politicheskie isseldovaniia — Moscow: *Izdatel'stvo Moskovskogo Universiteta*
Volks. Bul. — Volkskundig bulletin. — Amsterdam: *Koninklijke Nederlandse Akademie van Wetenschappen, P.J. Meertens Instituut*
Volonta — Volonta. — Milan: *Editrice A*
W. Eur. Pol. — West European politics. — London: *Frank Cass*
W.B. Econ. R. — World Bank economic review. — Washington, DC.: *International Bank for Reconstruction and Development*
West. Pol. Q. — Western political quarterly. — Salt Lake City, UT.: *Western Political Science Association/ Pacific Northwest Political Science Association/ Southern California Political Science Association/ Northern California Political Science Association*
Wom. St. Inter. For. — Women's studies international forum. — Elmsford, NY.: *Pergamon Press*
Work Emp. Soc. — Work, employment and society. — London: *British Sociological Association*
Work Occup. — Work and occupations. — Newbury Park, CA.: *Sage Publications*
World Dev. — World development. — Oxford: *Pergamon Press*
World Polit. — World politics. — Baltimore, MD.: *Princeton University, Center of International Studies*
Yale Law J. — Yale law journal. — New Haven, CT: *Yale Law Journal Co.*
Z. Ethn. — Zeitschrift für Ethnologie. — Berlin: *Deutsche Gesellschaft für Völkerkunde/ Berliner Gesellschaft für Anthropologie, Ethnologie und Urgeschichte*
Z. Sexual. — Zeitschrift für Sexualforschung. — Stuttgart: *Ferdinand Enke Verlag*
Z. Soziol. — Zeitschrift für Soziologie. — Stuttgart: *Ferdinand Enke Verlag*
Z. Verkehr. — Zeitschrift für Verkehrswissenschaft. — Düsseldorf: *Verkehrs-Verlag J. Fischer*
Za-Afr. — Zaïre-Afrique. — Kinshasa: *Centre d'études pour l'action sociale (CEPAS)*

INTERNATIONAL BIBLIOGRAPHY OF SOCIOLOGY — 1991

CLASSIFICATION SCHEME
PLAN DE CLASSIFICATION

A: General studies — *Études générales*

A.1: Sociology and the social sciences — *Sociologie et sciences sociales*

A.2: Sociological research — *Recherche sociologique*

A.3: Reference works, information services and documents — *Ouvrages de référence, services d'information et documents*

B: Theory and methodology — *Théorie et méthodologie*

B.1: Theory — *Théorie*

> Epistemology *[Epistémologie]*; Philosophy *[Philosophie]*; Sociological theory *[Théorie sociologique]*

B.2: Research methods — *Méthodes de recherche*

> Data analysis *[Analyse des données]*; Data collection *[Rassemblement des données]*

C: Individuals. Groups. Organizations — *Individus. Groupes. Organisations*

C.1: Psychology and social psychology — *Psychologie et psychologie sociale*

> Psychiatry *[Psychiatrie]*; Psychology *[Psychologie]*; Social psychology *[Psychologie sociale]*

C.2: Individuals — *Individus*

> Cognition *[Cognition]*; Decision making *[Prise de décision]*; Memory *[Mémoire]*; Motivation *[Motivation]*; Personality *[Personnalité]*; Self-concept *[Conception de soi]*

C.3: Interpersonal relations — *Relations interpersonnelles*

> Altruism *[Altruisme]*; Conflict *[Conflit]*; Emotions *[Emotions]*; Partners *[Partenaires]*; Social perception *[Perception sociale]*

C.4: Groups — *Groupes*

INTERNATIONAL BIBLIOGRAPHY OF SOCIOLOGY — 1991

C.5: Organizations — *Organisations*

C.6: Power, leadership and social roles — *Pouvoir, leadership et rôles sociaux*

C.7: Opinions and attitudes — *Opinions et attitudes*

D: Culture. Socialization. Social life — *Culture. Socialisation. Vie sociale*

D.1: Culture — *Culture*

> Culture and cultural relations *[Culture et relations culturelles]*; Social norms, social control and value systems *[Normes sociales, régulation sociale et systèmes de valeur]*; Socialization and alienation *[Socialisation et aliénation]*

D.2: Everyday culture — *Culture quotidienne*

D.3: Ethics and morals — *Ethique et morale*

> Ethics *[Ethique]*; Morality *[Moralité]*

D.4: Law — *Loi*

D.5: Magic, mythology and religion — *Magie, mythologie et religion*

> Buddhism *[Bouddhisme]*; Christianity *[Christianisme]*; Hinduism *[Hindouisme]*; Islam *[Islam]*; Judaism *[Judaïsme]*; Magic and witchcraft *[Magie et sorcellerie]*

D.6: Science and knowledge — *Science et connaissance*

D.7: Language, communication and media — *Langage, communication et moyens de communication*

> Advertising *[Publicité]*; Communication *[Communication]*; Linguistics *[Linguistique]*; Media *[Moyens de communication]*; Multilingualism and language policy *[Multilinguisme et politique linguistique]*; Television *[Télévision]*

D.8: Art — *Art*

D.9: Education — *Education*

> Education policy *[Politique de l'éducation]*; Education systems *[Systèmes d'enseignement]*; Educational sociology *[Sociologie de l'éducation]*; Primary education *[Enseignement primaire]*; Secondary education *[Enseignement secondaire]*; Tertiary education *[Enseignement post-scolaire]*

E: Social structure — *Structure sociale*

E.1: Social system — *Système social*

E.2: Social stratification — *Stratification sociale*

    Class *[Classe]*

E.3: Social change — *Changement social*

F: Population. Family. Gender. Ethnic group — *Population. Famille. Sexe. Groupe ethnique*

F.1: Demography — *Démographie*

F.2: Age groups — *Groupes d'âges*

    Ageing *[Vieillissement]*; Childhood *[Enfance]*; Youth *[Jeunesse]*

F.3: Demographic trends and population policy — *Tendances démographiques et politique démographique*

    Family planning *[Planification de la famille]*; Fertility *[Fécondité]*; Morbidity *[Morbidité]*; Mortality *[Mortalité]*; Population growth *[Croissance démographique]*

F.4: Marriage and family — *Mariage et famille*

    Divorce *[Divorce]*; Domestic violence and child abuse *[Violence domestique et enfants martyrs]*; Family law *[Droit de la famille]*; Marriage and cohabitation *[Mariage et cohabitation]*; Parenthood and parent-child relations *[Paternité-maternité et relations parents-enfants]*; Siblings and family structure *[Fratrie et structure de la famille]*

F.5: Gender — *Sexe*

    Feminism *[Féminisme]*; Gender differentiation *[Différenciation sexuelle]*; Gender roles *[Rôles de sexe]*

F.6: Sexual behaviour — *Comportement sexuelle*

F.7: Ethnic groups — *Groupes ethniques*

    Ethnicity *[Ethnicité]*; Race relations *[Relations raciales]*; Racial discrimination *[Discrimination raciale]*

F.8: Migration — *Migration*

    Immigrant adaptation *[Adaptation des immigrants]*; Internal migration *[Migration interne]*; International migration *[Migration internationale]*

G: Environment. Community. Rural. Urban — *Environment. Communauté. Rural. Urbain*

G.1: Ecology. Geography. Human settlements — *Ecologie. Géographie. Etablissements humains*

> Geography *[Géographie]*

G.2: Community — *Communauté*

G.3: Rural and urban sociology — *Sociologie rurale et urbaine*

G.3.1: Rural sociology — *Sociologie rurale*

> Peasant studies *[Etudes paysannes]*; Rural development *[Développement rurale]*

G.3.2: Urban sociology — *Sociologie urbaine*

> Housing *[Logement]*; Spatial and social differentiation *[Différenciation spatio-sociale]*; Urban planning and development *[Aménagement et développement urbain]*; Urbanization *[Urbanisation]*

H: Economic life — *Vie économique*

H.1: Economic sociology — *Sociologie économique*

H.2: Economic systems — *Systèmes économiques*

H.3: Economic conditions and living standards — *Conditions économiques et niveau de vie*

> Income *[Revenu]*

H.4: Enterprises and production systems — *Entreprises et systèmes de production*

> Enterprises *[Entreprises]*; Technology *[Technologie]*

H.5: Markets and consumption — *Marchés et consommation*

H.6: Finance — *Finance*

H.7: Economic policy and planning — *Politique économique et planification*

I: Labour — *Travail*

I.1: Sociology of industry and work — *Sociologie de l'industrie et du travail*

I.2: Employment and labour market — *Emploi et marché du travail*

> Gender issues *[Questions de sexe]*; Labour force *[Main d'oeuvre]*; Labour policy and employment policy; *[Politique du travail et politique de l'emploi]*; Unemployment *[Chômage]*

I.3: Personnel management and working conditions — *Administration du personnel et conditions de travail*

> Job satisfaction *[Satisfaction au travail]*; Occupational safety *[Sécurité du travail]*; Personnel management *[Gestion du personnel]*

I.4: Vocational training, occupations and careers — *Formation professionnelle, professions et carrières*

> Career development *[Déroulement de carrière]*; Managers *[Cadres]*; Professional workers *[Travailleurs professionnels]*; Vocational training *[Formation professionnelle]*

I.5: Labour relations — *Relations du travail*

> Collective bargaining *[Négociation collective]*; Labour disputes *[Conflits du travail]*; Labour law *[Droit du travail]*; Trade unions *[Syndicats]*; Workers' participation *[Participation des travailleurs]*

I.6: Leisure — *Loisir*

J: Politics. State. International relations — *Politique. Etat. Relations internationales*

J.1: Political sociology — *Sociologie politique*

J.2: Political thought — *Pensée politique*

J.3: Political systems — *Systèmes politiques*

> Police *[Police]*

J.4: Public administration — *Administration publique*

J.5: Political parties, pressure groups and political movements — *Partis politiques, groupes de pression et mouvements politiques*

J.6: Political behaviour and elections — *Comportement politique et élections*

> Elections *[Elections]*

J.7: Armed forces — *Forces armées*

J.8: International relations — *Relations internationales*

K: Social problems. Social services. Social work — *Problèmes sociaux. Services sociaux. Travail social*

K.1: Social problems — *Problèmes sociaux*

> Child neglect and abuse *[Enfants martyrs et abandon d'enfant]*; Crime *[Délits]*; Criminal justice *[Justice criminelle]*; Poverty *[Pauvreté]*; Substance abuse *[Usage des stupéfiants]*; Suicide *[Suicide]*; Violence *[Violence]*

K.2: Social security — *Sécurité sociale*

> Child care *[Aide à l'enfance]*; Welfare services *[Services de bien-être]*

K.3: Social work — *Travail social*

K.4: Health care — *Soins médicaux*

> Community care *[Garde communitaire]*; Geriatrics *[Gériatrie]*; Health economics *[Economie de la santé]*; Health policy *[Politique sanitaire]*; Medical ethics *[Code déontologique médical]*

BIBLIOGRAPHY FOR 1991
BIBLIOGRAPHIE POUR 1991

A: General studies — *Études générales*

A.1: Sociology and the social sciences — *Sociologie et sciences sociales*

1 Am Ende der kritischen Soziologie *[In German]*; At the end of critical sociology *[Summary]*. Niklas Luhmann. *Z. Soziol.* **20:2** 4:1991 pp. 147 – 152
2 American sociology and political science today. V. Zubok; A. Kokoshin. *Soc. Sci.* **XXII:3** 1991 pp. 21 – 36
3 As ciências sociais nos anos 90 *[In Portuguese]*; The social sciences in the nineties *[Summary]*; Les sciences sociales des années 90 *[French summary]*. Simon Schwartzman. *Rev. Bras. Ciên. Soc.* **6:16** 7:1991 pp. 51 – 60
4 Biology and social science — why the return of the repressed should be given a (cautious) welcome. Ted Benton. *Sociology* **25:1** 2:1991 pp. 1 – 29
5 *[In Japanese]*; [Contemporary sociology]. Juichi Aiba; et al. Kyoto: Mineruba Shobo, 1991: 224 p.
6 Declining enrollments of sociology majors — department responses. David Fabianic. *Am. Sociol.* **22:1** Spring:1991 pp. 25 – 36
7 Découverte de la sociologie *[In French]*; [Discovery of sociology]. Yves Léonard *[Ed.]*. Paris: La Documentation française, 1991: 95 p. [Cahiers français. : No. 247]
8 Disparate voices — the magic show of sociology. Barbara J. Peter. *Am. Sociol.* **22:3 and 4** Fall/Winter:1991 pp. 246 – 260
9 È davvero in-sostenibile la leggerezza delle scienze sociali? *[In Italian]*; Is the lightness of the social sciences really unbearable? *[Summary]*. Franco Sarcinelli. *Rass. It. Soc.* **32:1** 1-3:1991 pp. 95 – 101
10 Economics as universal science. Robert Heilbroner. *Soc. Res.* **58:2** Summer:1991 pp. 457 – 474
11 The estate of social knowledge. JoAnne Brown *[Ed.]*; David Keith van Keuren *[Ed.]*. Baltimore: Johns Hopkins University Press, c1991: xxvi, 266 p. (ill) *ISBN: 0801840600; LofC: 90039696. Includes bibliographical references and index.* [Johns Hopkins symposia in comparative history.]
12 Forging new syntheses — theories and theorists. Reba Rowe Lewis. *Am. Sociol.* **22:3 and 4** Fall/Winter:1991 pp. 221 – 231
13 *[In Japanese]*; [The foundations of sociology]. Takatoshi Imada *[Ed.]*; et al. Tokyo: Yuhikaku, 1991: 326 p.
14 History and sociology — the lost synthesis. Andrew Abbott. *Soc. Sci. Hist.* **15:2** Summer:1991 pp. 201 – 238
15 The honey bee dance language controversy. Subhash C. Kak. *Mankind Q.* **XXXI:4** Summer:1991 pp. 357 – 366
16 Hungarian sociology in the face of the political, economic and social transition. Rudolf Andorka. *Int. Sociol.* **6:4** 12:1991 pp. 465 – 470
17 Историческое знание и современность: Сб.науч.тр *[In Russian]*; [Historical knowledge and contemporaneity — collection of scientific treatise]. V.D. Viktorova *[Ed.]*; V.E. Kemerov *[Ed.]*. Sverdlovsk: , 1987: 152 p.

INTERNATIONAL BIBLIOGRAPHY OF SOCIOLOGY — 1991

A.1: Sociology and the social sciences [Sociologie et sciences sociales]

18 Macro-micro linkages in sociology. Joan Huber [Ed.]. Newbury Park, Calif: Sage, c1991: 298 p. ISBN: oc22766867; LofC: 90024238. Includes bibliographical references and index. [American Sociological Association presidential series.]

19 Много социологий для одного мира [In Russian]; (Many sociologies for a single world). P. Stompka. Sot. Issle. :2 1991 pp. 13 – 23

20 Modernisation — exhumetur in pace (rethinking macrosociology in the 1990s); [French summary]. Edward A. Tiryakian. Int. Sociol. 6:2 6:1991 pp. 165 – 180

21 Новое политическое мышление и общественные науки [In Russian]; [The new political thinking and the social science]. S. Shermukhamedova. Obshch. N. Usbek. :3 1991 pp. 15 – 19

22 O tabelão e a lupa — teoria, método generalizante e idiografia no contexto brasileiro [In Portuguese]; The table and the magnifying glass [Summary]; Le tableau immense et la loupe [French summary]. Fabio Wanderley Reis. Rev. Bras. Ciên. Soc. 6:16 7:1991 pp. 27 – 42

23 Обоснование научного вывода в прикладной социологии [In Russian]; [The basis of scientific deduction in applied sociology]. G.V. Osipov [Ed.]; G.S. Batygin. Moscow: Nauka, 1986: 271 p.

24 On the macrofoundations of microsociology — constraint and the exterior reality of structure. Gary Alan Fine. Sociol. Q. 32:2 Summer:1991 pp. 161 – 177

25 От «1968» к «1989»: социология и "annus mirabilis" [In Russian]; (From "1968" to "1989" — sociology and "annus mirabilis"). E.A. Tiryakian. Sot. Issle. :5 1991 pp. 26 – 34

26 Paradigms gained, paradigms lost. Die Entwicklung der Nachkriegssoziologie im Spiegel der Fachzeitschriften — mit besonderer Berücksichtigung der SOZIALEN WELT [In German]; [Paradigms gained, paradigms lost. The development of post-war sociology as reflected in specialist journals — with special reference to Soziale Welt]. Heinz Sahner. Soz. Welt. **Supplement** 1991 pp. 5 – 26

27 Passé d'ici, présent d'ailleurs — une gageure pour les sciences humaines? [In French]; [Past here, present elsewhere — a challenge for the social sciences]. Jean-Michel Chazine. Soc. Ét. Océan. **XXI:253** 3:1991 pp. 49 – 58

28 Post-war philosophy and empirical sociology in France — the connection of the sixties and after. Henri Peretz. Int. J. Pol. C. S. **4:4** Summer:1991 pp. 549 – 572

29 The prospects for sociology into the twenty-first century. D. Stanley Eitzen. Am. Sociol. **22:2** Summer:1991 pp. 109 – 116

30 Putting social science to work. Lisl Klein; Ken Eason [Ed.]. Cambridge: Cambridge University Press, 1991: 266 p. ISBN: 0521372429.

31 A quoi servait la sociologie en RDA [In French]; The purpose of sociology in GDR (German Democratic Republic) [Summary]; Wozu diente die Soziologie in der DDR [German summary]; ¿A qué servía la sociología en la RDA? [Spanish summary]. François Bafoil. Rev. Fr. Soc. **XXXII:2** 4-6:1991 pp. 263 – 284

32 Sciences du centre et sciences de la périphérie — la représentation sociale de la hiérarchisation des champs disciplinaires [In French]; [Central sciences and peripheral sciences — social representation and the creation of a hierarchy of disciplines] [Summary]. Béatrice Bonfils. Cah. Int. Soc. **XCI:** 7-12:1991 pp. 371 – 384

33 Sciences sociales sociétés arabes [In French]; [Social sciences in the Arab world]. Roland Lardinois [Contrib.]; Mustapha Al-Ahnaf [Contrib.]; François Ireton [Contrib.]; Kamal Boullata [Contrib.]; Alain Roussillon [Contrib.]; Aïssa Kadri [Contrib.]; Robert Santo-Martino [Contrib.]; Mohamed Ennaji [Contrib.]; Lahourai Addi [Contrib.]; Jean-Noël Ferrié [Contrib.] and others. Collection of 12 articles. **Peup. Médit.** , :54-55, 1-6:1991 pp. 15 – 273

34 Social science, communism, and the dynamics of political change. Andrew C. Janos. World Polit. **44:1** 10:1991 pp. 81 – 112

35 The social sciences and humanities and the renewal of Soviet society. V. Kudryavtsev. Soc. Sci. **XXII:1** :1991 pp. 8 – 16

36 Sociology and value neutrality — limiting sociology to the empirical level. Virginia R. Seubert. Am. Sociol. **22:3 and 4** Fall/Winter:1991 pp. 210 – 220

37 Sociology as a discipline — quasi-science and quasi-humanities. Mayer N. Zald. Am. Sociol. **22:3 and 4** Fall/Winter:1991 pp. 165 – 187

38 Sociology for one world — unity and diversity; [French summary]. Margaret Archer. Int. Sociol. **6:2** 6:1991 p. 131

39 Социальная философия в XX веке. Социология в меняющемся мире. Съезд молодых социологов [In Russian]; (Social philosophy of twentieth century — sociology in a changing world. Congress of young socialists). Sot. Issle. **:5** 1991

A.1: Sociology and the social sciences [Sociologie et sciences sociales]
pp. 151 – 155

40 Социальная трансформация научного знания: (Филос.аспект) *[In Russian]*; [Social transformation of scientific knowledge — (philosophical aspect)]. N.V. Karamysheva. L'vov: Vishcha shk. Izd-vo pri L'v.gos.un-te, 1987: 126 p. *Bibliogr..*
41 Социология *[In Russian]*; (Sociology). N.J. Smelser. *Sot. Issle.* **:5** 1991 pp. 109 – 116
42 *[In Japanese]*; [Thinking sociology]. Kunihiro Kimura; et al. Kyoto: Mineruba Shobo, 1991: 298 p.
43 The trends, development and future of the social sciences in Asia. Julia W. Sze. *Ind. J. Soc. Sci.* **4:4** 10-12:1991 pp. 475 – 502

A.2: Sociological research — *Recherche sociologique*

1 Are you now or have you ever been a sociologist? Barry Krisberg. *J. Crim. Law* **82:1** Spring:1991 pp. 141 – 155
2 Le chercheur et son objet — implications, pratiques, rôle et représentations du chercheur latino-américaniste en sciences sociales *[In French]*; [The research and the object — implications, practices, role and representations of the Latin American social science researcher]. Valérie de Campos Mello; Valérie Philippe; Eric Calcagno; Pablo Martin. *Cah. Amer. Lat.* **:11** 1991 pp. 109 – 114
3 Les comités d'éthique pour la recherche comme entreprise d'interprétation *[In French]*; [Research ethics committees as interpretative enterprises] *[Summary]*. Éric Gagnon. *Rech. Soc.graph* **XXXII:2** 5-8: 1991 pp. 221 – 236
4 Doctoral social scientists and the labour market. Richard Pearson; et al. Falmer: University of Sussex Institute of Manpower Studies, 1991: 215 p. *Report for the Economic and Social Research Council.* [IMS report. : No. 217]
5 *[In Japanese]*; [The history of social research in modern Japan — vol 2]. Takao Kawai *[Ed.]*. Tokyo: Keio Tsushin, 1991: 326 p.
6 Indians in the halls of academe — rural Andean peoples confront social science. Barbara Schroder. *Peasant Stud.* **XVIII:2** Winter:1991 pp. 97 – 116
7 Internationalization of social science knowledge. Neil J. Smelser. *Am. Behav. Sc.* **35:1** 9-10:1991 pp. 65 – 91
8 Issues and alternatives in comparative social research. Charles C. Ragin *[Contrib.]*; Dietrich Rueschemeyer *[Contrib.]*; David A. Smith *[Contrib.]*; Thomas Janoski *[Contrib.]*; Timothy P. Wickham-Crowley *[Contrib.]*; Larry J. Griffin *[Contrib.]*; Christopher Botsko *[Contrib.]*; Ana-Maria Wahl *[Contrib.]*; Larry W. Isaac *[Contrib.]*; John Bynner *[Contrib.] and others.* Collection of 10 articles. **Int. J. Comp. Soc** , *XXXII: 1-2*, 1-4:1991 pp. 1 – 216
9 Jean Piaget — the unknown sociologist? Richard F. Kitchener. *Br. J. Soc.* **42:3** 9:1991 pp. 421 – 442
10 Jessie Bernard — the making of a feminist. Robert C. Bannister. New Brunswick: Rutgers University Press, c1991: xii, 276 p., 8 p. of plates (ill) *ISBN: 0813516145; LofC: 90034390. Includes bibliographical references (p. [255]-270) and index.*
11 Michel de Certeau and the practice of representation. John Frow. *Cult. St.* **5:1** 1:1991 pp. 52 – 66
12 Mutual manipulations in the relationship-research dance. N.P. Greenman. *Int. J. Moral Soc. S.* **6:3** Autumn:1991 pp. 257 – 268
13 Norbert Elias — un sociologo europeo des XXI secolo *[In Italian]*; Norbert Elias — European sociologist for the 21st century *[Summary]*. Dirk Käsler. *Rass. It. Soc.* **32:4** 12:1991 pp. 465 – 476
14 On the uses and abuses of psychoanalysis in cultural research. Eugene Victor Wolfenstein. *Free Assoc.* **2:4(24)** 1991 pp. 515 – 547
15 Osservazioni coinvolte e distaccate su un sociologo europeo *[In Italian]*; Involved and detached insights on an European sociologist *[Summary]*. Peter R. Gleichmann. *Rass. It. Soc.* **32:4** 12:1991 pp. 401 – 426
16 Pesquisa rica em países pobres? *[In Portuguese]*; Rich research in poor nations? *[Summary]*; Recherche riche en pays pauvres? *[French summary]*. Gláucio Ary Dillon Soares. *Rev. Bras. Ciên. Soc.* **6:16** 7:1991 pp. 66 – 79
17 Практикум по прикладной социологии *[In Russian]*; [A practical course in applied sociology]. B.V. Kniazeva *[Ed.]*; M.V. Lomonosova. Moscow: Izd-vo. Moskva Universitet, 1987: 261 p. *Bibliogr. at the end of the section.*

A.2: Sociological research *[Recherche sociologique]*

18 The predicament of sincerity — from distance to connection in long-term fieldwork. S.-E. Jacobs. *Int. J. Moral Soc. S.* **6**:3 Autumn:1991 pp. 237 – 245
19 *[In Japanese]*; [The public opinion survey and informalization — the new obligation of 1990 pollster to the 2000 historian]. Kazuto Kojima. **Bulletin of the Institute of Journalism and Communication Studies, University of Tokyo** No.(44) - *1991*. pp. 43 – 72
20 Public utilities — an annotated guide to information sources. Anne C Roess. Metuchen, N.J: Scarecrow Press, 1991: viii, 398 p. *ISBN: 0810824434; LofC: 91022954. Includes index.*
21 Simmel and Parsons reconsidered. Donald N. Levine. *A.J.S.* **96**:5 3:1991 pp. 1097 – 1116
22 Il sociologo e le sue muse. Qualità e quantità nella ricerca sociologica *[In Italian]*; The sociologist and his muses — quality and quantity in sociological research *[Summary]*. Mario Cardano. *Rass. It. Soc.* **XXXII:2** 4-6:1991 p. 181
23 Survival and sociology — vindicating the human subject. Kurt H. Wolff. New Brunswick, U.S.A: Transaction Publishers, c1991: 119 p. *ISBN: 0887383572; LofC: 90010802. Includes bibliographical references (p. 113) and index.*
24 Von der Revolution zur Demokratie. Zum Paradigmenwechsel in den lateinamerikanischen Sozialwissenschaften *[In German]*; [From revolution to democracy. On the paradigm shift in Latin America social sciences] *[Summary]*, Norbert Lechner. *J. Entwick.pol.* **VII:4** 1991 pp. 7 – 20

A.3: Reference works, information services and documents — *Ouvrages de référence, services d'information et documents*

1 Building a city advisor in a "hypermedia" environment; *[French summary]*. P. Christiansson. *Envir. Plan. B.* **18:1** 1:1991 pp. 39 – 50
2 Conducting descriptive and analytical research with the Immigration and Naturalization Service public use tapes. M.J. Greenwood; J.M. McDowell; E. Trabka. *J. Econ. Soc.* **17:3-4** 1991 pp. 131 – 154
3 Handbook of clinical sociology. Howard M. Rebach *[Ed.]*; John G. Bruhn *[Ed.]*. New York: Plenum Press, c1991: xxiv, 410 p. (ill) *ISBN: 0306435594; LofC: 90007998. Includes bibliographical references and index.*
4 Organizational analysis of information processing using living systems theory. Robert J. Taormina. *Behav. Sci.* **36:3** 07:1991 pp. 196 – 223
5 Perspectives on literacy — a selected world bibliography. Shapour Rassekh *[Ed.]*. Librairie du Liban, Lebanon: UNESCO, 1991: 300 p. *ISBN: 9231027050. prepared for the International Bureau of Education.* [Ibedata.]
6 Sharing social science data — advantages and challenges. Joan E. Sieber *[Ed.]*. Newbury Park, Calif: Sage Publications, c1991: 168 p. *ISBN: 0803940823; LofC: 90021958. Includes bibliographical references and indexes.* [Sage focus editions.]
7 Sociological computing — an opportunity missed? Ronald E. Anderson; Edward E. Brent. *Am. Sociol.* **22:1** Spring:1991 pp. 65 – 76
8 Three underlying messages and their instructional implications. Norman L. Friedman. *Am. Sociol.* **22:2** Summer:1991 pp. 137 – 146

B: Theory and methodology — *Théorie et méthodologie*

B.1: Theory — *Théorie*

Sub-divisions: Epistemology *[Epistémologie]*; Philosophy *[Philosophie]*; Sociological theory *[Théorie sociologique]*

1 Can any final ends be rational? Alan Gewirth. *Ethics* **102:1** 10:1991 pp. 66 – 95
2 Concepts of process in social science explanations. Andrew P. Vayda; Bonnie J. McCay; Christina Eghenter. *Philos. S. Sc.* **21:3** 9:1991 pp. 318 – 331
3 Contingent foundations — feminism and the question of "postmodernism". Judith Butler. *Prax. Int.* **11:2** 7:1991 pp. 150 – 165
4 Does critical theory need saints or foundations? Paul Piccone. *Telos* **:87** Spring:1991 pp. 146 – 157
5 Embarrassment and civilization — on some similarities and differences in the work of Goffman and Elias. Helmut Kuzmics. *Theory Cult. Soc.* **8:2** 5:1991 pp. 1 – 30
6 Explanation and social theory. John Holmwood; Alexander Stewart. London: Macmillan, 1991: 244 p. *ISBN: 0333545451. Includes bibliography and index.*
7 Fare il tempo. Sulla sociologia del tempo di Norbert Elias *[In Italian]*; On Norbert Elias' sociology of time *[Summary]*. Helga Nowotny. *Rass. It. Soc.* **32:4** 12:1991 pp. 495 – 506
8 The function of new theory — what does it mean to talk about post-modernism in China. Xiaobing Tang. *Publ. Cult.* **4:1** Fall:1991 pp. 89 – 108
9 The ideal society. Ann Swidler. *Am. Behav. Sc.* **34:5** 5/6:1991 pp. 563 – 580
10 Intentionalistic explanations in the social sciences. John R. Searle. *Philos. S. Sc.* **21:3** 9:1991 pp. 332 – 344
11 The methodologies of social history — a critical survey and defence of structuralism. Christopher Lloyd. *Hist. Theory* **XXX:2** 1991 pp. 180 – 218
12 Modern conditions — postmodern controversies. Barry Smart. London: Routledge, 1991: 241 p. *ISBN: 0415029023; LofC: 91012946. Includes bibliographical references and index.* [Social futures.]
13 Modernity and ambivalence. Zygmunt Bauman. Oxford: Polity, 1991: 285 p. *ISBN: 0745605737. Includes bibliography and index.*
14 The new constellation — the ethical-political horizons of modernity/postmodernity. Richard J. Bernstein. Cambridge: Polity press in association with Basil Blackwell Ltd., 1991: 358 p. *ISBN: 0745609201.*
15 *[In Japanese]*; [On the Schutz-Parsons' dispute]. Hisashi Nasu. **Shak-nen.** *No.(32) - 1991.* pp. 17 – 43
16 Penser l'anti-économisme *[In French]*; ["Anti-economic" thinking]. Jean Jacob. *Temps Mod.* **45:526** 5:1990 pp. 118 – 138
17 *[In Japanese]*; [The possibility of postmodernism]. Noriyuki Imaeda. **Shak. Hyor.** *No.42(2) - 1991.* pp. 18 – 31
18 Postmodern theory — critical interrogations. Steven Best; Douglas Kellner. London: Macmillan, 1991: 324 p. *ISBN: 033348844x. Sociological theory.*
19 Rawls, Sandel and the self. S. Caney. *Int. J. Moral Soc. S.* **6:2** Summer:1991 pp. 161 – 171
20 Le secret de Polichinelle de la sociologie *[In French]*; Sociology's open secret *[Summary]*. Pierre-Jean Simon. *Hom. Soc.* **XXV:4(102)** 1991 pp. 65 – 74
21 *[In Japanese]*; [Sociology of selection and habitus]. Takashi Miyajima. **Shisō** *No.(804) - 1991.* pp. 50 – 64
22 Symposium on postmodernism. Steven Seidman *[Contrib.]*; Jeffrey C. Alexander *[Contrib.]*; Robert J. Antonio *[Contrib.]*; Charles Lemert *[Contrib.]*; Laurel Richardson *[Contrib.]*. Collection of 6 articles. **Sociol. Theory** , *9:2*, Fall:1991 pp. 131 – 190
23 Unintended consequences — a typology and examples; *[French summary]*. Patrick Baert. *Int. Sociol.* **6:2** 6:1991 pp. 201 – 210
24 Utopie et sociologie. Les questions de la perspective habermasienne à la sociologie *[In French]*; Utopia and Habermasian sociology, questions in sociology *[Summary]*. Pierre Achard; Ulysses Santamaria. *Hom. Soc.* **XXV:4(102)** 1991 pp. 39 – 50
25 Verstehen des Verstehens — eine systemtheoretische Revision der Hermeneutik *[In German]*; To understand understanding — a systems theoretical review of hermeneutics *[Summary]*. Georg Kneer; Armin Nassehi. *Z. Soziol.* **20:5** 10:1991 pp. 341 – 356

B.1: Theory *[Théorie]*
26 Viewpoint — power/difference. Philip Corrigan. *Sociol. Rev.* **39:2** 5:1991 pp. 309 – 334
27 What is the problem concerning social entities? J.L. Thompson. *Int. J. Moral Soc. S.* **6:1** Spring:1991 pp. 77 – 90

Epistemology *[Epistémologie]*

28 Constructing knowledge — authority and critique in social science. Lorraine Nencel *[Ed.]*; Peter Pels *[Ed.]*. London: Sage Publications, 1991: 256 p. *ISBN: 0803984014*. [Inquiries in social construction.]
29 A critical theory of public life — knowledge, discourse, and politics in an age of decline. Ben Agger. London: Falmer Press, 1991: xii, 229 p. *ISBN: 185000966x; LofC: 91028492. Includes bibliographical references and index.* [Critical perspectives on literacy and education.]
30 Décadence de l'analyse épistémologique *[In French]*; [The decadence of epistemological analysis]. Henri Leridon. *Temps Mod.* **46:534** 1:1991 pp. 137 – 148
31 The dogma that didn't bark (a fragment of a naturalized epistemology). Jerry A. Fodor. *Mind* **100 (2):398** 4:1991 pp. 201 – 220
32 Empathy and evaluation — understanding the private meanings of behavior. H.A. Alexander. *St. Philos. Educ.* **11:2** 1991 pp. 123 – 134
33 *[In Japanese]*; [Epistemological problems in sociology — arrangement and examination]. Kouji Miyamoto. ***Momoyama Gakuin Daigaku Shakaigaku Ronshu*** *No.25(1) - 1991.* pp. 43 – 65
34 Ethnologie des sciences et logiques de la science *[In French]*; Ethnology of the sciences and logics of science *[Summary]*; Ethnologie der Wissenschaften und Wissenschaftslogik *[German summary]*; Etnología de las ciencias y logicas de la ciencia *[Spanish summary]*. Georges Guille-Escuret. *Homme* **XXXI:119** 7-9:1991 pp. 81 – 112
35 Fallibilism, naturalism and the traditional requirements for knowledge. David Stump. *Stud. Hist. Phil. Sci.* **22:3** 9:1991 pp. 451 – 470
36 Geometrical and physical conventionalism of Henri Poincaré in epistemological formulation. Jerzy Giedymin. *Stud. Hist. Phil. Sci.* **22:1** 3:1991 pp. 1 – 2
37 Is epistemology enough? An existential consideration of development. Brian Vandenberg. *Am. Psychol.* **46:12** 12:1991 pp. 1278 – 1286
38 Making knowledge count — advocacy and social science. Peter Harries-Jones *[Ed.]*. Montréal: McGill-Queen's University Press, 1991: 250 p. *ISBN: 0773508198; LofC: cn 91090070. Includes bibliographical references and index.*
39 *[In Japanese]*; [Meaning, typification and reification — on the phenomenological sociology of knowledge]. Kazuhisa Nishihara. ***Gendai Shakai-Riron Kenkyu*** *No.(1) - 1991.* pp. 1 – 16
40 Методологические проблемы социального познанияа: Сб.науч.тр *[In Russian]*; [Methodological problems of social knowledge — collected academic articles]. V.I. Kutsenko *[Ed.]*. Kiev: Nauka Dumka, 1987: 216 p. *Bibliogr..*
41 Социальное знание: логико-методологический анализ Межвуз.сбнауч.сб *[In Russian]*; [Social knowledge — logical methodological analysis. Inter-college symposium of collected articles]. T.V. Nikol'skaia *[Ed.]*. Saratov: Saratov University Publishers, 1987: 142 p.
42 Toward a feminist epistemology. Jane Duran. Savage, Md: Rowman & Littlefield, c1991: xiii, 275 p. *ISBN: 0847676358; LofC: 90046615 //r91. Includes bibliographical references (p. 263-270) and index.* [New feminist perspectives series.]

Philosophy *[Philosophie]*

43 Analytical Marxism — a critical overview. Jack Amariglio; Antonio Callari; Stephen Cullenberg. *Soc. Scient.* **19:1-2** 1-2:1991 pp. 3 – 17
44 Arational actions. Rosalind Hursthouse. *J. Phil.* **LXXXVIII:2** 2:1991 pp. 57 – 68
45 Beyond ethnocentrism — a reconstruction of Marx's concept of science. Charles McKelvey. New York: Greenwood Press, 1991: x, 220 p. *ISBN: 0313274207; LofC: 90045602. Philosophy; Includes bibliographical references (p. [207]-216) and index.* [Contributions in sociology.]
46 British cultural Marxism. Ioan Davies. *Int. J. Pol. C. S.* **4:3** Spring:1991 pp. 323 – 344
47 *[In Japanese]*; [Capitalist society and the logic of "life"]. Yoshio Fujiyama. *B. Yoko. Univ.* *No.41(2) - 1991.* pp. 57 – 90
48 The correlation coefficient and models of subjective well-being. M.J. Stones; A. Kozma; T.E. Hannah; W.A. Mckim. *Soc. Ind.* **24:4** 6:1991 pp. 317 – 327

INTERNATIONAL BIBLIOGRAPHY OF SOCIOLOGY — 1991

B.1: Theory *[Théorie]* — *Philosophy [Philosophie]*
49 Deconstruction versus postmodernism — critical theory and the "nuclear sublime". Christopher Norris. *New Form.* **:15** Winter:1991 pp. 83 – 99
50 Dialectic and diagonalization. John Kadvany. *Inquiry* **34:1** 3:1991 pp. 3 – 25
51 Feminism and postmodernism — an uneasy alliance. Seyla Benhabib. *Prax. Int.* **11:2** 7:1991 pp. 137 – 149
52 Foucault's dialogical artistic ethos. Romand Coles. *Theory Cult. Soc.* **8:2** 5:1991 pp. 99 – 120
53 Free will and being a victim. S. Smilanskey. *Int. J. Moral Soc. S.* **6:1** Spring:1991 pp. 19 – 32
54 Gadamer's conception of hermeneutic understanding; *[Arabic summary]*. Walid A. Atari. *Dirasat Ser. A.* **18A:2** 1991 pp. 25 – 50
55 Have incommensurability and causal theory of reference anything to do with actual science? Incommensurability, no — causal theory, yes. Arthur I. Miller. *Inter. Phil. Sci.* **5:2** 1991 pp. 97 – 108
56 Hume's "Of miracles," Pierce, and the balancing of likelihoods. Kenneth R. Merrill. *J. Hist. Philos.* **XXIX:1** 1:1991 pp. 85 – 113
57 In defence of human individuality. H. Diligensky. *Soc. Sci.* **XXII:4** 1991 pp. 103 – 122
58 John Stuart Mill on induction and hypothesis. Struan Jacobs. *J. Hist. Philos.* **XXIX:1** 1:1991 pp. 69 – 83
59 Jurgen Habermas — critic in the public sphere. Robert C. Holub. London: Routledge, 1991: 210 p. *ISBN: 0415022088. Includes bibliography and index.* [Critics of the twentieth century.]
60 Locke and the right to punish. A. John Simmons. *Philos. Pub.* **20:4** Fall:1991 pp. 311 – 349
61 The merchant of Venice, or Marxism in the mathematical mode. David F. Ruccio. *Soc. Scient.* **19:1-2** 1-2:1991 pp. 18 – 46
62 Методологические проблемы социального познанияа: Сб.науч.тр *[In Russian]*; [Methodological problems of social knowledge — collected academic articles]. V.I. Kutsenko *[Ed.]*. Kiev: Nauka Dumka, 1987: 216 p. *Bibliogr..*
63 Mill and Comte on the method of introspection. Fred Wilson. *J. Hist. Beh. Sci.* **XXVII:2** 4:1991 pp. 107 – 129
64 Morality and modernity. Ross Poole. London: Routledge, 1991: 196 p. *ISBN: 0415036003. Includes bibliography and index.* [Ideas.]
65 New philosophy of social science — problems of indeterminacy. James Bohman. Oxford: Polity Press, 1991: 273 p. *ISBN: 0745606326; LofC: gb 91003329.*
66 "Personality" and "inner distance" — the conception of the individual in Max Weber's sociology. Ralph Schroeder. *Hist. Human Sci.* **4:1** 2:1991 pp. 61 – 78
67 Philosophy, social theory, and the thought of George Herbert Mead. Mitchell Aboulafia *[Ed.]*. Albany: State University of New York Press, c1991: xx, 319 p. *ISBN: 0791403599; LofC: 90030134. Includes bibliographical references (p. [295]-305) and index.* [SUNY series in the philosophy of the social sciences.]
68 Pluralism and rationality in the social sciences. Ingvar Johansson. *Philos. S. Sc.* **21:4** 12:1991 pp. 427 – 443
69 The problem of other cultures and other periods in action explanations. Rex Martin. *Philos. S. Sc.* **21:3** 9:1991 pp. 345 – 366
70 Психолого-педагогические интенции философского учения Гегеля *[In Russian]*; (Psychological and pedagogical intentions of Hegel's philosophical teaching). V.I. Ginetsinsky. *Vest. Lenin. Univ. 6* **6:3** 9:1991 pp. 73 – 81
71 Rational choice theory considered as psychology and moral philosophy. Philippe Mongin. *Philos. S. Sc.* **21:1** 3:1991 pp. 5 – 37
72 A reconsideration of the question of "the true, the good and the beautiful" in traditional Chinese philosophy. Yijie Tang. *Soc. Sci. China* **XII:1** 3:1991 pp. 222 – 237
73 Scheler. Francis Dunlop. London: Claridge Press, 1991: 97 p. *ISBN: 1870626710.*
74 The slippery slope argument. Wibren van der Burg. *Ethics* **102:1** 10:1991 pp. 42 – 65
75 Spontaneity and the generation of rational beings in Leibniz's theory of biological reproduction. Daniel C. Fouke. *J. Hist. Philos.* **XXIX:1** 1:1991 pp. 33 – 45
76 Тэарэтыка-метадалагічны сінкрэтызм «крытычнай тэорыі» франкфурцкай школы *[In Belorussian]*; *[Russian summary]*; [The theoretical-methodological syncretism of the "critical theory" of the Frankfurt school] *[Summary]*. A.P. Punchanka. *V. Aka. BSSR* **:4** :1991 pp. 10 – 15
77 Textual deference. Barry Smith. *Am. Phil. Q.* **28:1** 1:1991 pp. 1 – 12
78 Unity in multiformity. E. Batalov. *Soc. Sci.* **XXII:4** 1991 pp. 91 – 102

B.1: Theory [Théorie] — Philosophy [Philosophie]

79 Value-free science? — purity and power in modern knowledge. Robert Proctor. Cambridge, Mass: Harvard University Press, 1991: xi, 331 p. *ISBN: 067493170x; LofC: 90028895. Includes bibliographical references (p. [311]-320) and index.*

80 *[In Japanese]*; [What should we think in modern thoughts?]. Daisaburo Hashizume. Tokyo: Keiso Shobo, 1991: 265 p.

81 Здоровье и экология человека: филос.и методол.аспекты. Препр.докл.к методол. семинару сектора филос. исслед.коиплекс. пробд.соврем.науки *[In Russian]*; [Philosophical and methodological aspects. Forwarding report towards methodological seminar of sector philosophical research of complex problems of current science]. I.N. Smirnov *[Ed.]*. Moscow: , 1986: 63 p.

Sociological theory [Théorie sociologique]

82 *[In Japanese]*; [Action as differentiating power — an interpretation of Giddens' action theory]. Kiyonori Wakasa. **Shak-nen.** *No.(32) - 1991.* pp. 167 – 180

83 Action, movement, and intervention — reflections on the sociology of Alain Touraine; *[French summary]*. Alan Scott. *Can. R. Soc. A.* **28:1** 2:1991 pp. 30 – 45

84 Analogy and argumentation in an interdisciplinary context — Durkheim's "individual and collective representations". John I. Brooks. *Hist. Human Sci.* **4:2** 6:1991 pp. 223 – 259

85 *[In Japanese]*; ["Aspiration" — the conception of Durkheim]. Mahito Tsuda. **Shak. Hyor.** *No.41(4) - 1991.* pp. 62 – 76

86 Autonomy and "inner distance" — a trace of Nietzsche in Weber. David Owen. *Hist. Human Sci.* **4:1** 2:1991 pp. 79 – 91

87 Back to sociological theory — the construction of social orders. Nicos P. Mouzelis. London: Macmillan, 1991: 214 p. *ISBN: 0333531558.*

88 Baudrillard — critical and fatal theory. Mike Gane. London: Routledge, 1991: 243 p. *ISBN: 0415037743; LofC: 90049946. Includes bibliographical references and index.*

89 Baudrillard's bestiary — Baudrillard and culture. Mike Gane. New York, NY: Routledge, 1991: 184 p. *ISBN: 041506306x; LofC: 90023427. Includes bibliographical references.*

90 A case for the case study. Joe R Feagin *[Ed.]*; Anthony M Orum *[Ed.]*; Gideon Sjoberg *[Ed.]*. Chapel Hill: University of North Carolina Press, c1991: viii, 290 p. *ISBN: 0807819735; LofC: 90027036. Includes bibliographical references and index.*

91 Communicative action — essays on Jürgen Habermas's The Theory of Communicative Action. Jürgen Habermas *[Ed.]*; Axel Honneth *[Ed.]*; Hans Joas *[Ed.]*. Cambridge: Polity, 1991: 301 p. *ISBN: 0745605540.*

92 Complicity and struggle — theory and society. Upendra Baxi. *Soc. Scient.* **19:221-222** 10-11:1991 pp. 19 – 26

93 The conditions of fruitfulness of theorizing about mechanisms in social science. Arthur L. Stinchcombe. *Philos. S. Sc.* **21:3** 9:1991 pp. 367 – 388

94 Critical issues in social theory. John K. Rhoads. University Park, Pa: Pennsylvania State University Press, c1991: x, 374 p. *ISBN: 0271007095; LofC: 90006873. Includes bibliographical references (p. [323]-366) and index.*

95 *[In Japanese]*; [Domination on the basis of "Einverstandis" in the work of Weber]. Katsuhiro Matsui. **Bulletin of the College of General Education, Niigata University** *No.(22) - 1991.* pp. 77 – 88

96 The early essays. Talcott Parsons. Chicago: University of Chicago Press, 1991: lxix, 299 p. *ISBN: 0226092364; LofC: 90019213. Philosophy; Includes bibliographical references and index.* [The heritage of sociology.]

97 Erving Goffman. Tom Burns. New York: Routledge, c1991: 386 p. *ISBN: 0415064929; LofC: 90028958. Sociological theory; Includes bibliographical references and index.*

98 *[In Japanese]*; [An essay on revitalization of case study method]. Sadao Murata. **Communication and Society** *No.(1) - 1991.* pp. 31 – 40

99 *[In Japanese]*; [An essay on the problem of Aron Gurvitsch's theory of perception]. Bunya Nakamura. **Ritsumeikan Social Science Review** *No.26(4) - 1991.* pp. 125 – 154

100 Estatísticas, teoria social e planejamento *[In Portuguese]*; Statistics, social theory, and planning *[Summary]*; Statistiques, théorie sociale et planification *[French summary]*. Isaac Kerstenetzky. *Rev. Bras. Ciên. Soc.* **6:17** 10:1991 pp. 15 – 27

101 *[In Japanese]*; [The examination of Bendix's theory of comparative modernization]. Kiyotake Ohkawa. **Soshioroji** *No.35(3) - 1991.* pp. 37 – 51

102 Feminism without illusions — a critique of individualism. Elizabeth Fox-Genovese. Chapel Hill: University of North Carolina Press, c1991: xiii, 347 p. *ISBN: 0807819409; LofC: 90041044. Includes bibliographical references (p. 289-326) and index.*

B.1: Theory [Théorie] — Sociological theory [Théorie sociologique]

103 Formale Rekonstruktion und vergleichende Rahmung soziologischer Theorien *[In German]*; The formal reconstruction and the structural comparison of sociological theories *[Summary]*. Jürgen Klüver. *Z. Soziol.* **20:3** 6:1991 pp. 209 – 222

104 From expectations to behavior — an improved postulate for expectation states theory. James W. Balkwell. *Am. Sociol. R.* **56:3** 6:1991 pp. 355 – 369

105 *[In Japanese]*; [Functionalism and structuralism (3) — on Parsons' grasp of Durkheim's theory]. Kazuyoshi Matsumoto. **Ginbunkagakukenkyu** *No.(79) - 1991.* pp. 31 – 63

106 *[In Japanese]*; [G. Davy in Durkheimian sociology]. Meikun Nakajima. **Bulletin of Nagoya Institute of Technology** *No.(42) - 1991.* pp. 21 – 30

107 Habermas's critical theory of society. Jane Braaten. Albany, N.Y: State University of New York Press, c1991: x, 191 p. *ISBN: 0791407594; LofC: 90047708. Includes bibliographical references (p. 157-183) and index.* [SUNY series in the philosophy of the social sciences.]

108 *[In Japanese]*; [The historical view of Parsons' social evolutionism]. Motohiro Matsuoka. **Studies, The Institute of Humanities and Social Sciences, Nihon University** *No.(41) - 1991.* pp. 51 – 66

109 The integrity of cultures. Lawrence Rosen. *Am. Behav. Sc.* **34:5** 5/6:1991 pp. 594 – 617

110 Intersubjectivity and critical consciousness — remarks on Habermas's theory of communicative action. Gerhard Wagner; Heinz Zipprian. *Inquiry* **34:1** 3:1991 pp. 49 – 62

111 Istoria i ratsional´nost´ — sotsiologiia Maksa Vebera i veberovskii renessans *[In Russian]*; [History and rationality — the sociology of Max Weber and the Weberian renaissance]. P.P. Gaidenko; Iu.N. Davydov. Moskva: Politizdat, 1991: 366 p. *ISBN: 5250007570. Bibliography — p356-364.*

112 *[In Japanese]*; [J. Habermas and modern Europe]. Shoji Ishitsuka. **Journal for History of Social Thought** *No.(15) - 1991.* pp. 105 – 110

113 *[In Japanese]*; [J.S. Mill's thought of social harmony]. Hiroshi Fukada. **Journal of Sociology, the Sociological Society of Nihon University** *No.(112) - 1991.* pp. 79 – 92

114 The legacy of the enlightenment — Foucault and Lacan. Mladen Dolar. *New Form.* **:14** Summer:1991 pp. 43 – 56

115 Lessons from the nonlinear paradigm — applications of the theory of dissipative structures in the social sciences. L. Douglas Kiel. *Soc. Sci. Q.* **72:3** 9:1991 pp. 431 – 442

116 The limits of synthesis — some comments on Habermas' recent sociological writings. David L. Harvey; Mike Reed. *Int. J. Pol. C. S.* **4:3** Spring:1991 pp. 345 – 370

117 Max Weber as "Christian sociologist". William H. Swatos; Peter Kivisto. *J. Sci. S. Relig.* **30:4** 12:1991 pp. 347 – 362

118 Max Weber, critical assessments 2. Peter Hamilton *[Ed.]*. London: Routledge, 1991: 4 v (ill) *ISBN: 041506211x. Includes bibliographical references.*

119 Mead's multiple conceptions of time and evolution — their contexts and their consequences for theory; Les diverses approches de Mead sur le temps et l'évolution — leurs contextes et leurs implications théoriques *[French summary]*. Anselm Strauss. *Int. Sociol.* **6:4** 12:1991 pp. 411 – 426

120 Metatheorizing in sociology. George Ritzer. Lexington, Mass: Lexington Books, c1991: xi, 362 p. *ISBN: 0669250082; LofC: 90047068. Includes bibliographical references (p. [323]-350) and indexes.*

121 Modernist radicalism and its aftermath — foundationalism and anti-foundationalism in radical social theory. Stephen Crook. London: Routledge, 1991: 261 p. *ISBN: 0415028604. Includes bibliography.*

122 On the materialist appropriation of Hegel's dialectical method. George Boger. *Sci. Soc.* **55:1** Spring:1991 pp. 26 – 59

123 Oppositional poverty — the quantitative/qualitative divide and other dichotomies. Eithne McLaughlin. *Sociol. Rev.* **39:2** 5:1991 pp. 292 – 308

124 Die Ordnung des Handelns — Talcott Parsons' Theorie des allgemeinen Handlungssystems *[In German]*; [The behavioural order — Talcott Parsons theory of a general behavioural system]. Harald Wenzel. Frankfurt am Main: Suhrkamp, 1990: 535 p. *ISBN: 351858071x. Includes bibliographical references (p. 479-514).*

125 Ordnung und Handeln — die kultursoziologische und anthropologische Fragestellung in Max Webers Religionssoziologie *[In German]*; [Order and behaviour — the cultural, sociological and anthropological questions posed in Max Weber's sociology of religion]. Seong-hwan Park. Bern: Lang, 1990: 243 p. *ISBN: 3631431201.* [Europäische Hochschulschriften.]

B.1: Theory *[Théorie]* — Sociological theory *[Théorie sociologique]*

126 Political connections, professional advancement, and moral education in Durkheimian sociology. W. Paul Vogt. *J. Hist. Beh. Sci.* **XXVII:1** 1:1991 pp. 56 – 75

127 Positivism's future — and sociology's. Gerhard Lenski. *Can. J. Soc.* **16:2** Spring:1991 pp. 187 – 194

128 Race and gender aspects of Marxian macromodels — the case of the social structure of accumulation school, 1948-68. Robert Cherry. *Sci. Soc.* **55:1** Spring:1991 pp. 60 – 78

129 Die Rationalität des Alltagshandelns — Eine Rekonstruktion der Handlungstheorie von Alfred Schütz *[In German]*; The rationality of every-day action. A reconstruction of the action theory of Alfred Schultz *[Summary]*. Hartmut Esser. *Z. Soziol.* **20:6** 12:1991 pp. 430 – 445

130 Rationality, human nature, and society in Weber's theory. Walter L. Wallace. *Theory Soc.* **19:2** 4:1990 pp. 199 – 223

131 The recent history and the emerging reality of American sociological theory — a metatheoretical interpretation. George Ritzer. *Sociol. For.* **6:2** 6:1991 pp. 269 – 288

132 Re-examining Mills on motive — a character vocabulary approach. Colin Campbell. *Sociol. Anal.* **52:1** Spring: 1991 pp. 89 – 97

133 Regelmäßigkeiten und Typen — Das Durchschnittshandeln in Max Webers Methodologie *[In German]*; Regularities and types — average social action in Max Weber's methodology *[Summary]*. Wulf Hopf. *Z. Soziol.* **20:2** 4:1991 pp. 124 – 137

134 The role of general theory in comparative-historical sociology. Edgar Kiser; Michael Hechter. *A.J.S.* **97:1** 7:1991 pp. 1 – 30

135 Selecting social goals — alternative concepts of rationality. L.E. Johnson; R.D. Ley. *Am. J. Econ. S.* **49:4** 10:1990 pp. 469 – 482

136 *[In Japanese]*; [Significance of phenomenology in Weber's sociology and it's influence]. Kyoko Utsunomiya. *Shak. Hyor.* *No.42(3) - 1991.* pp. 293 – 306

137 Social theory and the substantive problems of sociology. Arthur J. Vidich. *Int. J. Pol. C. S.* **4:4** Summer:1991 pp. 517 – 534

138 Las sociedades como hechos construidos — el enfoque de Weber de la realidad social *[In Spanish]*; [Societies as constructed realities — Weber's focus on social facts]. Martin Albrow. *Est. Sociol.* **IX:26** 5-8:1991 pp. 339 – 356

139 Society in action — the theory of social becoming. Piotr Sztompka. Cambridge: Polity, 1991: 211 p. *ISBN: 0745606385. Includes bibliography and index.*

140 Sociological realism — an Islamic paradigm. Ilyas Ba-Yunus. *Am. J. Islam. Soc. Sci.* **8:1** 3:1991 pp. 43 – 66

141 Strategic context analysis — a new research strategy for structuration theory. Rob Stones. *Sociology* **25:4** 11:1991 pp. 673 – 695

142 Substance — prolegomena to a realist theory of identity. Michael Ayres. *J. Phil.* **LXXXVIII:2** 2:1991 pp. 69 – 90

143 The symbol theory. Norbert Elias; Richard Kilminster *[Ed.]*. London: Sage Publications, 1991: 147 p. *ISBN: 0803984189.*

144 Synthetic strategies in comparative sociological research — methods and problems of internal and external analysis. Thomas Janoski. *Int. J. Comp. Soc* **XXXII: 1-2** 1-4:1991 pp. 59 – 81

145 Talcott Parsons — theorist of modernity. Roland Robertson *[Ed.]*; Bryan S. Turner *[Ed.]*. London: Sage Publications, 1991: 264 p. (ill) *ISBN: 0803985134. Includes bibliographical references and index.* [Theory, culture & society.]

146 La teoría sociológica — un marco de referencia analítico de la modernidad *[In Spanish]*; [Sociological theory — an analytic reference point on modernity]. Juan del Pino Artacho. Madrid: Editorial Tecnos, 1990: 234p. *ISBN: 8430918159.*

147 *[In Japanese]*; [A turning of society and sociological theory]. Hiroshi Taniguchi *[Ed.]*; et al. Kyoto: Horitsubunkasha, 1991: 290 p.

148 Undoing the social — towards a deconstructive sociology. Ann Game. Milton Keynes: Open University Press, 1991: 210 p. *ISBN: 0335093841. Includes index.*

149 Уччение Э.Берка о человеке и обществе. Идейные истоки неоконсерватизма *[In Russian]*; (Burke's doctrine on the man and society — origins of neoconservatism). V.I. Shamshurin. *Sot. Issle.* **:6** 1991 pp. 100 – 113

150 *[In Japanese]*; [The Weber thesis (3) — protestantism and capitalism]. Takao Yamada. *Chukyo University Bulletin of the Faculty of Liberal Arts No.32(1) - 1991.* pp. 201 – 220

151 Western evolutionism in the Muslim world. Victor Danner. *Am. J. Islam. Soc. Sci.* **8:1** 3:1991 pp. 67 – 82

152 Wittgenstein versus Hart — two models of rules for social and legal theory. John Hund. *Philos. S. Sc.* **21:1** 3:1991 pp. 72 – 85

B.2: Research methods — *Méthodes de recherche*

Sub-divisions: Data analysis *[Analyse des données]*; Data collection *[Rassemblement des données]*

1. Action and knowledge — breaking the monopoly with participatory action-research. Muhammad Anisur Rahman *[Ed.]*; Orlando Fals-Borda *[Ed.]*. London: Intermediate Technology Publications, 1991: 182 p. *ISBN: 1853390984. Data collection.*
2. Advanced research methodology — an annotated guide to sources. R. Barker Bausell. Metuchen, N.J: Scarecrow Press, 1991: viii, 903 p. *ISBN: 0810823551; LofC: 91016135. by R. Barker Bausell; Includes indexes.*
3. Computer simulation applications — an introduction. Marcia Lynn Whicker; Lee Sigelman *[Ed.]*. Newbury Park: Sage Publications, c1991: 152 p. (ill) *ISBN: 0803932456; LofC: 90025980. Includes bibliographical references (p. 138-151).* [Applied social research methods series. : Vol. 25]
4. Different methods — contradictory results? Research on development and democracy. Dietrich Rueschemeyer. *Int. J. Comp. Soc* **XXXII: 1-2** 1-4:1991 pp. 9 – 38
5. Estimating point centrality using different network sampling techniques. Joseph Galaskiewicz. *Soc. Networks* **13:4** 12:1991 pp. 347 – 386
6. The ethics of social research. Roger Homan. London: Longman, 1991: ix, 197 p. *ISBN: 0582058791; LofC: 90-6651. Bibliography — p184-194. -Includes index.* [Aspects of modern sociology.]
7. Evaluating and rethinking the case study. Randy Stoecker. *Sociol. Rev.* **39:1** 2:1991 pp. 88 – 112
8. Expert systems. Robert Alfred Benfer; Edward E. Brent *[Ed.]*; Louanna Furbee-Losee *[Ed.]*. Newbury Park, Calif: Sage Publications, c1991: 92 p. (ill) *ISBN: 080394036x; LofC: 90020105. Includes bibliographical references (p. 85-91).* [Sage university papers series.]
9. Foundations of program evaluation — theories of practice. William R. Shadish; Thomas D. Cook; Laura C. Leviton. Newbury Park, Calif: Sage Publications, c1991: 529 p. *ISBN: 0080393551; LofC: 90043944. Includes bibliographical references (p. 486-511) and indexes.*
10. Generalizability theory — a primer. Richard J. Shavelson; Noreen M. Webb *[Ed.]*. Newbury Park, Calif: Sage Publications, c1991: xiii, 137 p. (ill) *ISBN: 080393744x; LofC: 91022006. Includes bibliographical references (p. 131-132) and index.* [Measurement methods for the social sciences series. : No. 1]
11. A handbook of qualitative methodologies for mass communication research. Klaus Bruhn Jensen *[Ed.]*; Nick Jankowski *[Ed.]*. London: Routledge, 1991: 272 p. *ISBN: 0415054044; LofC: 91003686. Includes bibliographical references and index.*
12. Ижтимоий билишнинг эмпирик ва назарий муаммолари *[In Uzbek]*; Проблема эмпирического и теоретического в социальном познании *[In Russian]*; [The problem of the empirical and the theoretical in social cognition]. B.D. Babaev. *Obshch. N. Usbek.* **:5** 1991 pp. 7 – 12
13. A methodology for twenty-first century sociology. Joel Smith. *Soc. Forc.* **70:1** 9:1991 pp. 1 – 18
14. Multilevel modelling of survey data. Harvey Goldstein. *Statistician* **40:2** 1991 pp. 235 – 244
15. Multiple comparisons for researchers. Larry E. Toothaker. Newbury Park, Calif: Sage Publications, c1991: viii, 168 p. (ill) *ISBN: 0803941765; LofC: 91022011. Includes bibliographical references (p. 160-163) and index.*
16. The oral biography. David King Dunaway. *Biography* **14:3** Summer:1991 pp. 256 – 266
17. Photo-interviewing — a tool for evaluating technological innovations. Susan A. Tucker; John V. Dempsey. *Eval. Rev.* **15:5** 10:1991 pp. 639 – 654
18. Random measurement error does not bias the treatment effect estimate in the regression-discontinuity design — I. The case of no interaction. Joseph C. Cappelleri; William M.K. Trochim; T.D. Stanley; Charles S. Reichardt. *Eval. Rev.* **15:4** 8:1991 pp. 395 – 419
19. Reliability of attitude scores based on a latent trait model. David J. Bartholomew; Karl F. Schuessler. *Soc. Method.* **21** 1991 pp. 97 – 124
20. The reliability of survey attitude measurement — the influence of question and respondent attributes. Duane F. Alwin; Jon A. Krosnick. *Sociol. Meth.* **210:1** 8:1991 pp. 139 – 181

B.2: Research methods [Méthodes de recherche]

21 Research on survey quality. Duane F. Alwin [Contrib.]; Nora Cate Schaeffer [Contrib.]; Judith A. Seltzer [Contrib.]; Marieka Klawitter [Contrib.]; McKee J. McClendon [Contrib.]; U.N. Umesh [Contrib.]; Robert A. Peterson [Contrib.]; Jon A. Krosnick [Contrib.]. Collection of 5 articles. **Sociol. Meth.**, *210:1*, 8:1991 pp. 3 – 181
22 Research with Hispanic populations. Gerardo Marín; Barbara VanOss Marín [Ed.]. Newbury Park: Sage Publications, c1991: ix, 130 p. *ISBN: 0803937202; LofC: 90026197. Includes bibliographical references (p. 113-123) and index.* [Applied social research methods series. : Vol. 23]
23 Spotting the invisible man — the influence of male gender on fieldwork relations. Neil McKeganey; Michael Bloor. *Br. J. Soc.* **42:2** 6:1991 pp. 195 – 210
24 Students as arbitrators — an empirical investigation. Sharon L. Oswald. *Ind. Relat.* **30:2** Spring:1991 pp. 286 – 293
25 Task conditions, response formulation processes, and response accuracy for behavioral frequency questions in surveys. Scot Burton; Edward Blair. *Publ. Opin. Q.* **55:1** Spring:1991 pp. 50 – 79
26 Who is the other? An anthropological itinerary. Marc Auge. *J. Soc. Stud. Dhaka* **:54** 10:1991 pp. 1 – 27

Data analysis [Analyse des données]

27 Adding social structure to diffusion models — an event history framework. David Strang. *Sociol. Meth.* **19:3** 2:1991 pp. 324 – 353
28 Adjustment for non-response in two-year panel data — applications to problems of household income distribution. S.S. Laaksonen. *Statistician* **40:2** 1991 pp. 153 – 168
29 L'análisi multivariable de dades [In Spanish]; [Multivariate analysis of data]. Carlos Lozares Colina [Contrib.]; Pedro López Roldán [Contrib.]; Óscar Fernández Santana [Contrib.]; Margarita Latiesa [Contrib.]; Mónica Bécue Bertaut [Contrib.]. Collection of 6 articles. **Papers**, :*37*, 1991 pp. 9 – 142
30 Analiza trafności zewnętrznej skali PIL (Crumbaugh, Macholick) jako zmiennej różnicującej wyniki babania socjologicznego [In Polish]; Analysis of external relevance of PIL scale (Crumbaugh, Macholick) as a variable differentiating the results of sociological study [Summary]. Wojciech Konopacki. *Acta Univ. Łódz. Folia Soc.* **20** 1991 pp. 137 – 152
31 The analysis of factorial surveys. Joop J. Hox; Ita G.G. Kreft; Piet L.J. Hermkens. *Sociol. Meth.* **19:4** 5:1991 pp. 493 – 510
32 The analysis of mobility regimes — implementation using SAS procedures and an Australian case study. David Chant; Mark Western. *Sociol. Meth.* **20:2** 11:1991 pp. 256 – 286
33 Approche biographique et approche structurelle — quelques remarques sur le "retour du biographique" en sociologie [In French]; Biographical approach and structural approach — some remarks on the "return to biography" in sociology [Summary]. Jean-René Pendaries. *Hom. Soc.* **XXV:4(102)** 1991 pp. 51 – 64
34 Assessing bias and fit of global and local hazard models. Lawrence L. Wu; Nancy Brandon Tuma. *Sociol. Meth.* **19:3** 2:1991 pp. 354 – 387
35 The case for samples of anonymized records from the 1991 census (with comments). C. Marsh; C. Skinner; S. Arber; B. Penhale; S. Openshaw; J. Hobcraft; D. Lievesley; N. Walford. *J. Roy. Stat. Soc. A.* **154:2** :1991 pp. 305 – 339
36 Combining qualitative and quantitative data in the longitudinal study of household allocations. Heather Laurie; Oriel Sullivan. *Sociol. Rev.* **39:1** 2:1991 pp. 113 – 130
37 A comparison of Lambda-transfer and core solutions in constant-sum non-sidepayment games. H. Andrew Michener; Mark S. Salzer; Mark S. Reimer; Joohee Lee. *Behav. Sci.* **36:2** 4:1991 pp. 115 – 132
38 Cooperating when you know your outcomes will differ. J. Keith Murnighan. *Simulat. Gam.* **22:4** 12:1991 pp. 463 – 475
39 Criterion-referenced judgemental forecasting models. W.E. Remus. *J. Forecast.* **10:4** 7:1991 pp. 415 – 424
40 A critical evaluation of the randomized response method — applications, validation, and research agenda. U.N. Umesh; Robert A. Peterson. *Sociol. Meth.* **210:1** 8:1991 pp. 104 – 138
41 Data theory and dimensional analysis. William G. Jacoby. Newbury Park, Calif: Sage Publications, c1991: 89 p. *ISBN: 0803941781; LofC: 90026165. Includes bibliographical references.* [Quantitative applications in the social sciences.]
42 Dimensional variation estimation — a methodological comparison. David B. MacKay. *Geogr. Anal.* **23:1** 1:1991 pp. 39 – 55

B.2: Research methods [Méthodes de recherche] — Data analysis [Analyse des données]

43 An empirical investigation of human dyadic systems in the time and frequency domains. Anthony F. Badalamenti; Robert J. Langs. *Behav. Sci.* **36:2** 4:1991 pp. 100 – 114

44 Errors caused by rounded data in two simple facility location problems. Yoshiaki Ohsawa; Takeshi Koshizuka; Osamu Kurita. *Geogr. Anal.* **23:1** 1:1991 pp. 56 – 73

45 Estimating individual developmental functions — methods and their assumptions. Margaret Burchinal; Mark I. Appelbaum. *Child. Devel.* **62:1** 2:1991 pp. 23 – 43

46 Estimating multiplicative regression terms in the presence of measurement error. Thomas E. Feucht. *Sociol. Meth.* **17:3** 2:1989 pp. 257 – 282

47 Evaluating the use of entropy-maximising procedures in the study of voting patterns — 1. Sampling and measurement error in the flow-of-the-vote matrix and the robustness of estimates. R.J. Johnston; C.J. Pattie. *Envir. Plan.A.* **23:3** 3:1991 pp. 411 – 420

48 Event history analysis. Trond Petersen *[Ed.]*; David Strang *[Contrib.]*; Lawrence L. Wu *[Contrib.]*; Nancy Brandon Tuma *[Contrib.]*; Alfred Hamerle *[Contrib.]*. *Collection of 4 articles*. **Sociol. Meth.**, *19:3*, 2:1991 pp. 270 – 414

49 The exploratory analysis of survey data using log-linear models. Graham J.G. Upton. *Statistician* **40:2** 1991 pp. 169 – 182

50 Flatness and continuity in the percentile clustering model. R. Powers. *Math. Soc. Sc.* **21:1** 2:1991 pp. 53 – 66

51 Geographic information abstractions — conceptual clarity for geographic modeling. T.L. Nyerges. *Envir. Plan.A.* **23:10** 10:1991 pp. 1483 – 1500

52 A hierarchy for some latent structure models. Mark Reiser; Karl F. Schuessler. *Sociol. Meth.* **19:4** 5:1991 pp. 419 – 464

53 Improving information for social policy decisions — the uses of microsimulation modeling. Constance F Citro *[Ed.]*; Eric Alan Hanushek *[Ed.]*. Washington, DC: National Academy Press, 1991: 3 vols *BNB: 91062261; LofC: 91062261; ISBN: 030904541X. Panel to Evaluate Microsimulation Models for Social Welfare Programs, Committee on National Statistics, Commission on Behavioral and Social Sciences and Education, National Research Council; Includes bibliographical references and index.*

54 Latent variable models for dichotomous outcomes. William W. Eaton *[Contrib.]*; George Bohrnstedt *[Contrib.]*; Bengt O. Muthén *[Contrib.]*; Mark Reiser *[Contrib.]*; Allan McCutcheon *[Contrib.]*; Amy Dryman *[Contrib.]*; Ann Sorenson *[Contrib.]*; Max A. Woodbury *[Contrib.]*; Kenneth G. Manton *[Contrib.]*; Ronald Schoenberg *[Contrib.]* and others. *Collection of 6 articles.* **Sociol. Meth.**, *18:1*, 8:1989 pp. 4 – 182

55 Legal and statistical aspects of some mysterious clusters. S.E. Feinberg; D.H. Kaye. *J. Roy. Stat. Soc. A.* **154:1** :1991 pp. 61 – 74

56 Life and work history analyses — qualitative and quantitative developments. Shirley Dex *[Ed.]*. London: Routledge, 1991: 244 p. *ISBN: 0415053382.* [Sociological review monograph.]

57 Longitudinal research. Scott Menard. Newbury Park, Calif: Sage Publications, c1991: 81 p. (ill) *ISBN: oc22597078; LofC: 90020103. Includes bibliographical references (p. 73-80).* [Sage university papers series.]

58 Magnitude estimation of the utility of public goods. Simon Kemp. *J. Appl. Psychol.* **76:4** 8:1991 pp. 533 – 540

59 Model estimation when observations are not independent — application of Liang and Zeger's methodology to linear and logistic regression analysis. Barry V. Bye; Gerald F. Riley. *Sociol. Meth.* **17:4** 5:1989 pp. 353 – 375

60 Models for the assessment of the value of forecast information. D.B. Lawrence. *J. Forecast.* **10:4** 7:1991 pp. 425 – 443

61 A new incremental fit index for general structural equation models. Kenneth A. Bollen. *Sociol. Meth.* **17:3** 2:1989 pp. 303 – 316

62 Noninferior bandwidth line simplification — algorithm and structural analysis. Robert G. Cromley; Gerard M. Campbell. *Geogr. Anal.* **23:1** 1:1991 pp. 25 – 38

63 On the treatment of interrupted spells and initial conditions in event history analysis. Alfred Hamerle. *Sociol. Meth.* **19:3** 2:1991 pp. 388 – 414

64 Partialling and purging — equivalencies between log-linear analysis and the purging method of rate adjustment. Lawrence L. Santi. *Sociol. Meth.* **17:4** 5:1989 pp. 376 – 397

65 The perils of provocative statistics. James P. Scanlan. *Publ. Inter.* **:102** Winter:1991 pp. 3 – 14

66 Practical and innovative uses of correspondence analysis. N.T. Higgs. *Statistician* **40:2** 1991 pp. 183 – 194

INTERNATIONAL BIBLIOGRAPHY OF SOCIOLOGY — 1991

B.2: Research methods [Méthodes de recherche] — Data analysis [Analyse des données]

67 Reach and selectivity as strategies of recruitment for collective action — a theory of the critical mass, V. Ralph Prahl; Gerald Marwell; Pamela E. Oliver. *J. Math. Sociol.* **16:2** 1991 pp. 137 – 164

68 Reducing bias in estimates of linear models by remeasurement of a random subsample. Paul D. Allison; Robert M. Hauser. *Sociol. Meth.* **19:4** 5:1991 pp. 466 – 491

69 The role of geographic information systems in survey analysis. Derek Bond; Paula Devine. *Statistician* **40:2** 1991 pp. 209 – 216

70 Scale development — theory and applications. Robert F. DeVellis. Newbury Park, Calif: Sage, c1991: 120 p. (ill) *ISBN:* 080393775x; *LofC:* 91010257. *Includes bibliographical references (p. 115-118) and index.* [Applied social research methods series. : Vol. 26]

71 A seemingly unrelated Poisson regression model. Gary King. *Sociol. Meth.* **17:3** 2:1989 pp. 235 – 255

72 Shift-share analysis as a linear model. D.C. Knudsen; R. Barff. *Envir. Plan.A.* **23:3** 3:1991 pp. 421 – 431

73 Simulation of global and local intransitivities in a simple voting game under majority rule. Eric C. Browne; Peggy A. James; Martin A. Miller *Behav. Sci.* **36:2** 4:1991 pp. 148 – 156

74 Small N's and big conclusions — an examination of the reasoning in comparative studies based on a small number of cases. Stanley Lieberson. *Soc. Forc.* **70:2** 12:1991 pp. 307 – 320

75 Social network analysis — a handbook. John Scott. London: Sage Publications, 1991: 210 p. *ISBN:* 0803984804.

76 Some problems in the use of network analysis for comparative enquiry. Pempelani Mufune. *Int. Sociol.* **6:1** 3:1991 pp. 97 – 110

77 Spatial interaction modelling in retail planning practice — the need for robust statistical methods. C.M. Guy. *Envir. Plan. B.* **18:(2)** 4:1991 pp. 191 – 203

78 Standard, meta-standard — a framework for coding occupational data. Daniel I. Greenstein. *Hist. Soc. R.* **16:57** 1:1991 pp. 3 – 22

79 The static and dynamic analysis of network data using information theory. Loet Leydesdorff. *Soc. Networks* **13:4** 12:1991 pp. 301 – 345

80 The statistical analysis of event histories. Trond Petersen. *Sociol. Meth.* **19:3** 2:1991 pp. 270 – 323

81 Structural equations modeling test of a turnover theory — cross-sectional and longitudinal analyses. Peter W. Hom; Rodger W. Griffeth. *J. Appl. Psychol.* **76:3** 6:1991 pp. 350 – 366

82 Subjective probability, decision analysis and their legal consequences. D.V. Lindley. *J. Roy. Stat. Soc. A.* **154:1** :1991 pp. 83 – 92

83 Suppression situations in psychological research — definitions, implications, and applications. Joseph Tzelgov; Avishai Henik. *Psychol .B.* **109:3** 5:1991 pp. 524 – 536

84 Techniques and software for the processing of a large postal survey. Joanne Lamb; Lyn Middleton. *Statistician* **40:2** 1991 pp. 139 – 144

85 Testing regression residuals for spatial autocorrelation using SAS — a technical note. John Paul Jones; Stuart A. Foster. *Geogr. Res. For.* **11:** 1991 pp. 78 – 83

86 Triadic comparison judgements and place significance. Boyowa A. Chokor. *Area* **23:2** 6:1991 pp. 136 – 149

87 The tricky nature of skewed frequency tables — an information loss account of distinctiveness-based illusory correlations. Klaus Fiedler. *J. Pers. Soc. Psychol.* **60:1** 1:1991 pp. 24 – 36

88 Using Cox models to study multiepisode processes. Hans-Peter Blossfeld; Alfred Hamerle. *Sociol. Meth.* **17:4** 5:1989 pp. 432 – 448

89 Weryfikacja wyników badania budżetów czasu *[In Polish]*; Verification of results of time-budgets survey *[Summary]*. Marek Żelazo. *Acta Univ. Łódz. Folia Soc.* **20** 1991 pp. 117 – 135

90 Zastosowanie nagrania magnetofonowego i wywiadu o wywiadzie w analizie wywiadu kwestionariuszowego *[In Polish]*; Tape recording and interview about interview in analysis of questionnaire interview *[Summary]*. Jolanta Lisek-Michalska. *Acta Univ. Łódz. Folia Soc.* **20** 1991 pp. 87 – 115

INTERNATIONAL BIBLIOGRAPHY OF SOCIOLOGY — 1991

B.2: Research methods *[Méthodes de recherche]* —

Data collection *[Rassemblement des données]*

91 Acquiescence and regency response-order effects in interview surveys. McKee J. McClendon. *Sociol. Meth.* **210:1** 8:1991 pp. 60 – 103
92 The answering machine poses many questions for telephone survey researchers. Peter S. Tuckel; Barry M. Feinberg. *Publ. Opin. Q.* **55:2** Summer:1991 pp. 200 – 217
93 Applications for the modified scree test revisited. Keith Zoski; Stephen Jurs. *Eval. Rev.* **15:2** 4:1991 pp. 189 – 190
94 Асимметрия приписывания в социологических опросах *[In Russian]*; (Ascribition asymmetry in surveys). V.B. Moin. *Sot. Issle.* **:5** 1991 pp. 40 – 52
95 Asking threatening questions and situational framing — the effects of decomposing survey items. Linda Mooney; Robert B. Gramling. *Sociol. Q.* **32:2** Summer:1991 pp. 289 – 300
96 The cognitive interview — its origins, empirical support, evaluation and practical implications. A. Memon; R. Bull. *J. Comm. App. Soc. Psychol.* **1:4** 11:1991 pp. 291 – 307
97 Considerations in the application of a modified scree test for Delphi survey data. James W. Altschuld; Phyllis M. Thomas. *Eval. Rev.* **15:2** 4:1991 pp. 179 – 188
98 The corporative interview as a research method in economic geography. Erica Schoenberger. *Prof. Geogr.* **43:2** 5:1991 pp. 180 – 189
99 The data game — controversies in social science statistics. Mark Maier. Armonk, N.Y: M.E. Sharpe, c1991: xv, 245 p. *ISBN: 0873353885; LofC: 90039658. Includes bibliographical references (p. 201-234) and index.*
100 Doing educational research. Geoffrey Walford *[Ed.]*. London: Routledge, 1991: 237 p. *ISBN: 0415052890. Includes index.*
101 The effects of monetary incentives on the response rate and cost-effectiveness of a mail survey. Mike Brennan; Janet Hoek; Craig Astridge. *J. Market R.* **33:3** 7:1991 pp. 229 – 242
102 Der Einfluß gefälschter Interviews auf Survey-Ergebnisse *[In German]*; The effect of interviewer cheating on survey results *[Summary]*. Rainer Schnell. *Z. Soziol.* **20:1** 2:1991 pp. 25 – 35
103 Experiencing fieldwork — an inside view of qualitative research. William Shaffir *[Ed.]*; Robert A. Stebbins *[Ed.]*. Newbury Park, [Calif.]: Sage, 1991: 274 p. *ISBN: 0803936443. Includes bibliographical references and index.* [Sage focus editions.]
104 Going up the ladder — multiplicity sampling to create linked macro-to-micro organizational samples. Toby L. Parcel; Robert L. Kaufman; Leeann Jolly. *Soc. Method.* **21** 1991 pp. 43 – 80
105 Informing generality and explaining uniqueness — the place of case studies in comparative research. York Bradshaw; Michael Wallace. *Int. J. Comp. Soc* **XXXII: 1-2** 1-4:1991 pp. 154 – 171
106 Institutions statistiques et nomenclatures socio-professionnelles. Essai comparatif — Royaume-Uni, Espagne, France *[In French]*; Institutions for socio-professional statistics and nomenclatures. Comparative essay — United Kingdom, Spain, France *[Summary]*; Statistische Institutionen und sozioprofessionelle Nomenklaturen. Versuch eines Vergleichs — Grossbritannien, Spanien, Frankreich *[German summary]*; Instituciones estadísticas y nomenclaturas socio-profesionales. Ensayo comparativo — Inglaterra, España y Francia *[Spanish summary]*. B. Duriez; J. Ion; M. Pinçon; M. Pinçon-Charlot. *Rev. Fr. Soc.* **XXXII:1** 1-3:1991 pp. 29 – 59
107 Как помочь интервьюеру (из опыта методических исследований) *[In Russian]*; (How to help the interviewer (an experience of methodical research)). S.R. Khaykin; E.P. Pavlov. *Sot. Issle.* **:4** 1991 pp. 58 – 65
108 Ein konzeptuelles Schema für Familiendaten *[In German]*; A conceptual scheme for data on families *[Summary]*. Karl Pierau. *Hist. Soc. R.* **16:57** 1:1991 pp. 48 – 59
109 The logit model and response- based samples. Yu Xie; Charles F. Manski. *Sociol. Meth.* **17:3** 2:1989 pp. 283 – 302
110 The measurement of parental influence — assessing the relative effects of father and mother. Ann Marie Sorenson; David Brownfield. *Sociol. Meth.* **19:4** 5:1991 pp. 511 – 535
111 Open survey questions as measures of personal concern with issues — a reanalysis of Stouffer's Communism, Conformity, and Civil Liberties. Emily W. Kane; Howard Schuman. *Soc. Method.* **21** 1991 pp. 81 – 96
112 Организационно-методические проблемы социологическго опроса: Сборник *[In*

INTERNATIONAL BIBLIOGRAPHY OF SOCIOLOGY — 1991

B.2: Research methods *[Méthodes de recherche]* — *Data collection [Rassemblement des données]*

Russian]; [Organizational and methodological problems of the sociological questionnaire — collected artifacts]. V.N. Ivanov *[Ed.]*. Moscow: AN USSR. Institute социол.исслед., Сов.социол.ассоц, 1986: 194 p.

113 The potential of mail surveys in geography — some empirical evidence. Eran Feitelson. *Prof. Geogr.* **43:2** 5:1991 pp. 190 – 205

114 Precision of net change in a rotating panel survey. N.J. Nieuwenbroek. *Statistician* **40:2** 1991 pp. 195 – 201

115 Процесс обработки данных анкетных опросов на ЭВМ: Метод.рекомендации *[In Russian]*; [Data-processing of questionnaires on computer — methodological recommendations]. V.N. Ivanov *[Ed.]*; V.G. Andreenkov; A.O. Kryshtanovskii. Moscow: , 1985: 115 p.

116 Research on survey quality. Duane F. Alwin. *Sociol. Meth.* **210:1** 8:1991 pp. 3 – 29

117 Response effects over time — two experiments. Howard Schuman; Jacqueline Scott. *Sociol. Meth.* **17:4** 5:1989 pp. 398 – 408

118 Response to mail questionnaires by health professionals. B.T. Maguire. *J. Econ. Soc.* **17:2** 1991 pp. 87 – 100

119 Sampling establishments for social survey research. Neil Millward. *Statistician* **40:2** 1991 pp. 145 – 152

120 Self-report, situation-specific coping questionnaires — what are they measuring? Arthur A. Stone; Melanie A. Greenberg; Eileen Kennedy-Moore; Michelle G. Newman. *J. Pers. Soc. Psychol.* **61:4** 10:1991 pp. 648 – 658

121 A split-run experiment in a postal survey. Peter Lynn. *Statistician* **40:1** :1991 pp. 61 – 66

122 Status metodologiczny dyrektyw dotyczących konstrukcji pytań kwestionariusza wywiadu socjologicznego *[In Polish]*; Methodological status of directives for constructing questions for the questionnaire of sociological interview *[Summary]*. Włodzimierz Andrzej Rostocki. *Acta Univ. Łódz. Folia Soc.* **20** 1991 pp. 65 – 86

123 Studia metodologiczne prowadzone e łódzkim ośrodku socjologicznym. Ich ogólna charakterystyka i ocena *[In Polish]*; Methodological studies carried out in Lódź Sociological Centre. General characteristics and evaluation *[Summary]*. Jan Lutyński. *Acta Univ. Łódz. Folia Soc.* **20** 1991 pp. 7 – 41

124 Survey design, methodology and analysis (1). W.F. de Heer *[Contrib.]*; Joanne Lamb *[Contrib.]*; Lyn Middleton *[Contrib.]*; Neil Millward *[Contrib.]*; S.S. Laaksonen *[Contrib.]*; Graham J.G. Upton *[Contrib.]*; N.T. Higgs *[Contrib.]*; N.J. Nieuwenbroek *[Contrib.]*; Ken Baker *[Contrib.]*; Derek Bond *[Contrib.]* and others. Collection of 12 articles. **Statistician**, *40:2*, 1991 pp. 123 – 244

125 Survey design, methodology and analysis (2). P.C. Campanelli *[Contrib.]*; E.A. Martin *[Contrib.]*; J.M. Rothgeb *[Contrib.]*; R.E. Fay *[Contrib.]*; R. Bolstein *[Contrib.]*; K. Rennolls *[Contrib.]*; J.F. Bell *[Contrib.]*; M.J. Heerschop *[Contrib.]*; C.A.J. Liefstinck-Koeijers *[Contrib.]*; T.M.F. Smith *[Contrib.]* and others. Collection of 9 articles. **Statistician**, *40:3*, :1991 pp. 251 – 342

126 Taking society's measure — a personal history of survey research. Herbert Hiram Hyman; Hubert J O'Gorman *[Ed.]*; Eleanor Singer *[Ed.]*. New York: Russell Sage Foundation, c1991: xxiv, 257 p. *ISBN: 0871543958; LofC: 90046449.* Includes bibliographical references (p. 223-236) and index.

127 Understanding mail survey response behavior — a meta-analysis. Francis J. Yammarino; Steven J. Skinner; Terry L. Childers. *Publ. Opin. Q.* **55:4** Winter:1991 pp. 613 – 639

128 The use of handheld computers in social surveys of the Netherlands Central Bureau of Statistics. W.F. de Heer. *Statistician* **40:2** 1991 pp. 125 – 138

129 Using geodemographics in market research surveys. Ken Baker. *Statistician* **40:2** 1991 pp. 203 – 208

130 Wartość danych a cechy badań kwestionariuszowych *[In Polish]*; Quality of data and features of questionnaire surveys *[Summary]*. Anna Kubiak. *Acta Univ. Łódz. Folia Soc.* **20** 1991 pp. 43 – 63

131 Wer ist das Volk? Zur faktischen Grundgesamtheit bei „allgemeinen Bevölkerungsumfragen" — Undercoverage, Schwererreichbare und Nichtbefragbare *[In German]*; Who is the people? The factual population of general population surveys — undercoverage, not-at-homes, unable-to-answer *[Summary]*. Rainer Schnell. *Kölner Z. Soz. Soz. psy.* **43:1** 1991 pp. 106 – 137

C: Individuals. Groups. Organizations — *Individus. Groupes. Organisations*

C.1: Psychology and social psychology — *Psychologie et psychologie sociale*

Sub-divisions: Psychiatry *[Psychiatrie]*; Psychology *[Psychologie]*; Social psychology *[Psychologie sociale]*

1 Un altre Freud, si us plau — sobre les relacions entre psicoanàlisi i sociologia *[In Catalan]*; *[Spanish summary]*; [Another Freud, please — on the relations between psychoanalysis and sociology] *[Summary]*. Joan Estruch. *Papers* :36 1991 pp. 117 – 134
2 The analysis of an elderly patient; *[German summary]*; *[French summary]*; *[Spanish summary]*. Nina E.C. Coltart. *Int. J.Psy.* **72:2** 1991 pp. 209 – 220
3 An approach to conceptual research in psychoanalysis illustrated by a consideration of psychic trauma; *[French summary]*; *[German summary]*; *[Spanish summary]*. Joseph Sandler; Anna Ursula Dreher; Sibylle Drews. *Int. Rev. Psy.* **18:2** 1991 pp. 133 – 141
4 Archetypes — the strange attractors of the psyche. J.R. Van Eenwyk. *J. Analyt. Psychol.* **36:1** 1:1991 pp. 1 – 25
5 Aspects of the analytic relationship; *[French summary]*; *[German summary]*; *[Spanish summary]*. F. de Jonghe; P. Rijnierse; R. Janssen. *Int. J.Psy.* **72:4** 1991 pp. 693 – 707
6 Beyond the archaic maternal background. V. Marc. *J. Analyt. Psychol.* **36:2** 4:1991 pp. 231 – 240
7 Body image, sexuality and the psychotic core; *[French summary]*; *[German summary]*; *[Spanish summary]*. Eglé Laufer. *Int. J.Psy.* **72:1** 1991 pp. 63 – 72
8 Chaos theory and psychoanalysis; *[French summary]*; *[German summary]*; *[Spanish summary]*. Michael G. Moran. *Int. Rev. Psy.* **18:2** 1991 pp. 211 – 221
9 Characteristics of men and women completing cognitive/behavioral spouse abuse treatment. Kim K. Faulkner; Rosemary Cogan; Mark Nolder; Gene Shooter. *J. Fam. Viol.* **6:3** 9:1991 pp. 243 – 254
10 Classical intuitive thinking in China. Ma Wenfeng; Shan Shaojie. *Soc. Sci. China* **XII:1** 3:1991 pp. 142 – 164
11 Client-centered and experiential psychotherapy in the nineties. G. Lietaer *[Ed.]*; J. Rombauts *[Ed.]*; R. van Balen *[Ed.]*. Leuven, Belgium: Leuven University Press, 1990: 863 p. ISBN: 9061863643; LofC: 91207961. Chiefly rev. papers presented at the First International Conference on Client-Centered and Experiential Psychotherapy held Sept. 1988 at the Catholic University of Leuven; Includes bibliographical references. [Studia psychologica.]
12 Le concept de crise psychotique et son traitement psychanalytique *[In French]*; The notion of psychotic crisis and its psychoanalytic treatment *[Summary]*. France Turmel. *San. Ment. Qué* **XVI:2** Automne:1991 pp. 195 – 217
13 The consequences of an instance of acting out in the transference. Annette Watillon. *Int. J.Psy.* **72:3** :1991 pp. 553 – 572
14 Crowding, perceived control, and relative power — an analysis of households in India. R. Barry Ruback; Janak Pandey. *J. Appl. Soc. Psychol.* **21:4** 2:1991 pp. 315 – 344
15 Developmental antecedents of masochism — vignettes from the analysis of a 3-year-old girl; *[French summary]*; *[German summary]*; *[Spanish summary]*. Alan Sugarman. *Int. J.Psy.* **72:1** 1991 pp. 107 – 116
16 A dream of the red shoes — separation conflict in the phallic-narcissistic phase; *[German summary]*; *[French summary]*; *[Spanish summary]*. Leon E.A. Berman. *Int. J.Psy.* **72:2** 1991 pp. 233 – 242
17 Extra-analytic contacts — fantasy and reality; *[French summary]*; *[German summary]*; *[Spanish summary]*. Ramon Ganzarain. *Int. J.Psy.* **72:1** 1991 pp. 131 – 140
18 Freud's Irma dream — a psychoanalytic interpretation; *[German summary]*; *[French summary]*; *[Spanish summary]*. Barbara Mautner. *Int. J.Psy.* **72:2** 1991 pp. 275 – 286

C.1: Psychology and social psychology [Psychologie et psychologie sociale]

19 Freud's pessimism, the death instinct, and the theme of disintegration in "Analysis terminable and interminable"; [French summary]; [German summary]; [Spanish summary]. Anne E. Thompson. *Int. Rev. Psy.* **18:2** 1991 pp. 165 – 179
20 The genetic mechanism of thinking integration. Xiaoming Li. *Soc. Sci. China* **XII:1** 3:1991 pp. 183 – 207
21 The good society and the inner world — psychoanalysis, politics and culture. Michael Rustin. London: Verso, 1991: 270 p. *ISBN: 0860913287; LofC: 91011764. Includes bibliographical references and index.*
22 Infant observation re-viewed. C. Covington. *J. Analyt. Psychol.* **36:1** 1:1991 pp. 63 – 76
23 The influence of theory on the psychoanalyst's countertransference; [German summary]; [French summary]; [Spanish summary]. Samuel Stein. *Int. J.Psy.* **72:2** 1991 pp. 325 – 334
24 Internalization of the absent father; [German summary]; [French summary]; [Spanish summary]. Harwant S. Gill. *Int. J.Psy.* **72:2** 1991 pp. 243 – 252
25 Into the wild blue yonder — on the emergence of the ethnoneurologies — the social science-based neurologies and the philosophy-based neurologies. Warren TenHouten. *J. Soc. Biol. Struct.* **14:4** 1991 pp. 381 – 408
26 Критерии невменяемости и пределы компетенции психиатра-эксперта *[In Russian]*; Criteria for insanity and limits of psychoanalysis *[Summary]*; (Les critères de la non-imputabilité et les limites de la compétence du psychiatre-expert: *Title only in French*). V.B. Pervomajskii. *Sovet. Gos. Pr.* **5** 1991 pp. 68 – 76
27 Lacan and the human sciences. Alexandre Leupin *[Ed.]*. Lincoln: University of Nebraska Press, c1991: 191 p. *ISBN: 0803228945; LofC: 90039325. Includes index.*
28 Lay theories of psychotherapy II — the efficacy of different therapies and prognosis for different problems. Adrian Furnham; Zoe Wardey. *Human Relat.* **44:11** 11:1991 pp. 1197 – 1211
29 The legacy of Erich Fromm. Daniel Burston. Cambridge, Mass: Harvard University Press, 1991: 260 p. *ISBN: 0674521684; LofC: 90005348. Includes bibliographical references (p.) and index.*
30 A living systems approach to understanding the concept of stress. Alan Steinberg; Ron F. Ritzmann. *Behav. Sci.* **35:2** 4:1990 pp. 138 – 146
31 Locus of control as moderator — an explanation for additive versus interactive findings in the demand-discretion model of work stress? Katharine R. Parkes. *Br. J. Psy.* **82:3** 8:1991 pp. 291 – 312
32 Locus of control of behaviour — is high externality associated with substance misuse?; Le locus du contrôle du comportement — la grande superficialité est-elle associée à l'abus de substances? *[French summary]*; Locus de control de la conducta — ¿Esta asociada una elevada exteriorizacion con el mal uso de sustancias psicoactivas? *[Spanish summary]*. Philip Haynes; Glenda Ayliffe. *Br. J. Addict.* **86:9** 9:1991 pp. 1111 – 1117
33 The maternal erotic transference; *[French summary]*; *[German summary]*; *[Spanish summary]*. Judith K. Welles; Harriet Kimble Wrye. *Int. J.Psy.* **72:1** 1991 pp. 93 – 106
34 The mind of the political terrorist. Richard M. Pearlstein. Wilmington, Del: SR Books, 1991: xii, 237 p. *ISBN: 0842023453; LofC: 90009134. Includes bibliographical references (p. 183-225) and index.*
35 Mind, body and behaviour — theorisations of madness and the organisation of therapy. Lindsay Prior. *Sociology* **25:3** 8:1991 pp. 403 – 421
36 Modeling the days of our lives — using survival analysis when designing and analyzing longitudinal studies of duration and the timing of events. Judith D. Singer; John B. Willett. *Psychol .B.* **110:2** 9:1991 pp. 268 – 290
37 Negative affectivity as the underlying cause of correlations between stressors and strains. Peter Y. Chen; Paul E. Spector. *J. Appl. Psychol.* **76:3** 6:1991 pp. 398 – 407
38 On being a psychoanalyst in Brazil — pressures, pitfalls and perspectives. Sérvulo Augusto Figueira. *Free Assoc.* **2:3(23)** 1991 pp. 423 – 445
39 On some relationships of fantasies of perfection to the calamities of childhood; *[German summary]*; *[French summary]*; *[Spanish summary]*. Arnold Rothstein. *Int. J.Psy.* **72:2** 1991 pp. 313 – 324
40 The ontogeny of silence in an analytic case; *[French summary]*; *[German summary]*; *[Spanish summary]*. Janet Hadda. *Int. J.Psy.* **72:1** 1991 pp. 117 – 130
41 Ontological categories guide young children's inductions of word meaning — object terms and substance terms. Nancy N. Soja; Susan Carey; Elizabeth S. Spelke. *Cognition* **38:2** 2:1991 pp. 179 – 211

C.1: Psychology and social psychology *[Psychologie et psychologie sociale]*

42 Otto Fenichel and the left opposition in psychoanalysis. Benjamin Harris; Adrian Brock. *J. Hist. Beh. Sci.* **XXVII:2** 4:1991 pp. 157 – 165

43 La place du djinn dans les psycho-thérapies traditionnelles — approche psychanalytique *[In French]*; [The role of the djinn in traditional psychotherapy — a psychoanalytical approach]. Riadh Ben Rejeb. *IBLA* **54:168** 1991 pp. 215 – 221

44 The practice of behavioural and cognitive psychotherapy. Richard Stern; Lynne M. Drummond *[Ed.]*; Mandy Assin *[Intro.]*. Cambridge: Cambridge University Press, 1991: xvi, 248 p. *ISBN: 0521387426; LofC: 91-8015. illustrations by Mandy Assin.*

45 Projective identification — mechanism or mystery? N. Field. *J. Analyt. Psychol.* **36:1** 1:1991 pp. 93 – 109

46 Psychoanalysis and ethics. Ernest Wallwork. New Haven: Yale University Press, c1991: xiii, 344 p. *ISBN: 0300048785; LofC: 91015276. Includes bibliographical references and index.*

47 Psychoanalysis, psychosis, and postmodernism. Stephen Frosh. *Human Relat.* **44:1** 1:1991 pp. 93 – 104

48 The psychoanalyst in the mirror — doubts galore but few certainties; *[German summary]*; *[French summary]*; *[Spanish summary]*. Luciana Nissim Momigliano. *Int. J.Psy.* **72:2** 1991 pp. 287 – 296

49 The psychoanalytic semiosis of absence or, the semiotic murder of the mother; *[French summary]*; *[German summary]*; *[Spanish summary]*. Jane van Buren. *Int. Rev. Psy.* **18:2** 1991 pp. 249 – 263

50 Reality monitoring and psychotic hallucinations. Richard P. Bentall; Guy A. Baker; Sue Havers. *Br. J. Clin. Psycho.* **30:3** 9:1991 pp. 213 – 222

51 Reflections on perverse states of mind. Margot Waddell; Gianna Williams. *Free Assoc.* **2:22** 1991 pp. 203 – 213

52 The search for common ground — clinical aims and processes; *[French summary]*; *[German summary]*; *[Spanish summary]*. Arnold B. Richards. *Int. J.Psy.* **72:1** 1991 pp. 45 – 56

53 The self in social theory — a psychoanalytic account of its construction in Plato, Hobbes, Locke, Rawls, and Rousseau. C. Fred Alford. New Haven: Yale University Press, c1991: viii, 229 p. *ISBN: 0300049226; LofC: 90039887. Includes bibliographical references (p. 211-219) and index.*

54 Shame in psychoanalysis — the function of unconscious fantasies; *[German summary]*; *[French summary]*; *[Spanish summary]*. Ana-Maria Rizzuto. *Int. J.Psy.* **72:2** 1991 pp. 297 – 312

55 Sigmund Freud — the secrets of nature and the nature of secrets; *[French summary]*; *[German summary]*; *[Spanish summary]*. Ana-Maria Rizzuto; et al. *Int. Rev. Psy.* **18:2** 1991 pp. 143 – 163

56 Social influences on remembering — intellectual, interpersonal and intergroup components. G.M. Stephenson; B.H. Kniveton; W. Wagner. *Eur. J. Soc. Psychol.* **21:6** 11-12:1991 pp. 463 – 475

57 The subject of mind; *[French summary]*; *[German summary]*; *[Spanish summary]*. Marcia Cavell. *Int. J.Psy.* **72:1** 1991 pp. 141 – 154

58 The subject of the father — from ethics to love. Lyndsey Stonebridge. *New Form.* **:13** Spring:1991 pp. 91 – 101

59 Le thérapeute conjugal est un cheval de Troie — réflexions inspirées des résultats de recherches sur l'intervention auprés des couples *[In French]*; [The therapist in marital relations is a Trojan horse — notions drawn from research on the practice of therapy with couples] *[Summary]*. Jean-Marie Boisvert; Madelaine Beaudry. *San. Ment. Qué* **XVI:1** 6:1991 pp. 269 – 286

60 "To be or not to be, that is the question". On enactment, play and acting out. Adeline van Waning. *Int. J.Psy.* **72:3** :1991 pp. 539 – 552

61 Transference regression and psychoanalytic technique with infantile personalities; *[German summary]*; *[French summary]*; *[Spanish summary]*. Otto Kernberg. *Int. J.Psy.* **72:2** 1991 pp. 189 – 200

62 Truth in interpretation — the case of psychoanalysis. Paul A. Roth. *Philos. S. Sc.* **21:2** 6:1991 pp. 175 – 195

63 Value conflict and thought-induced attitude change. Akiva Liberman; Shelly Chaiken. *J. Exp. S. Psychol.* **27:3** 5:1991 pp. 203 – 216

64 When self-interest makes a difference — the role of construct accessibility in political reasoning. Jason Young; Cynthia J. Thomsen; Eugene Borgida; John L. Sullivan; John H. Aldrich. *J. Exp. S. Psychol.* **27:3** 5:1991 pp. 271 – 296

C.1: Psychology and social psychology [Psychologie et psychologie sociale]
65 The wish for a sex change — a challenge to psychoanalysis?; [German summary]; [French summary]; [Spanish summary]. Agnes Oppenheimer. Int. J.Psy. **72:2** 1991 pp. 221 – 232

Psychiatry [Psychiatrie]

66 A cross-cultural adaptation of a psychiatric epidemiologic instrument — the diagnostic interview schedule's adaptation in Puerto Rico. Milagros Bravo; Glorisa J. Canino; Maritza Rubiostipec; Michel Woodbury-Fariña. Cult. Medic. Psych. **15:1** 3:1991 pp. 1 – 18
67 Innovation without change? — consumer power in psychiatric services. David Brandon. Basingstoke: Macmillan Education, 1991: 184 p. ISBN: 0333488237; LofC: gb 91002767. Includes index.
68 The loony bin trip. Kate Millett. London: Virago, 1991: 316 p. ISBN: 1853813265.
69 Mental health, race and culture. Suman Fernando. Basingstoke: Macmillan in association with MIND, 1991: ix, 243 p. ISBN: 0333474759. Bibliography — p.214-235.Includes index. [Issues in mental health.]
70 Out of harm's way — MIND's research into police and psychiatric action under section 136 of the Mental Health Act. Philip Bean [Ed.]. London: MIND Publications, 1991: 199 p. ISBN: 0900557885.
71 Psychiatriereform und Sozialwissenschaften — Erfahrungsberichte aus Österreich [In German]; [Psychiatry reform and the social sciences — reports from Austria]. Rudolf Forster [Ed.]; Jürgen M. Pelikan [Ed.]. Wien: Facultas, Univ.-Verl., 1990 ISBN: 3850762793. [Schriften zur Medizinsoziologie. : No. 4]
72 Le rôle de la culture en épidémiologie psychiatrique — examen de la recherche sur la santé mentale des Latino-Américains [In French]; [The role of culture in psychiatric epidemiology — an examination of research on Latino mental health] [Summary]. Peter J. Guarnaccia. San. Ment. Qué **XVI:1** 6:1991 pp. 27 – 44
73 Some old questions for the new cross-cultural psychiatry. Kim Hopper. Med. Anthr. Q. **5:4** 12:1991 pp. 299 – 330
74 The state, violence and race in psychiatry. Janis Hunter Jenkins [Contrib.]; Pablo J. Farias [Contrib.]; Josep M. Comelles [Contrib.]; Leslie Swartz [Contrib.]; Kathryn Hopkins Kavanagh [Contrib.]. Collection of 5 articles. Cult. Medic. Psych. , 15:2, 6:1991 pp. 139 – 274

Psychology [Psychologie]

75 Acculturation and mental health status among Hispanics — convergence and new directions for research. Lloyd H. Rogler; Dharma E. Cortes; Robert G. Malgady. Am. Psychol. **46:6** 6:1991 pp. 585 – 597
76 Adolescence and the repetition compulsion; [German summary]; [French summary]; [Spanish summary]. François Ladame. Int. J.Psy. **72:2** 1991 pp. 253 – 274
77 Adult play — a reversal theory approach. John H. Kerr [Ed.]; Michael J. Apter [Ed.]. Amsterdam: Swets & Zeitlinger, 1991: 192 p. ISBN: 9026510144.
78 Alternative to psychological testing. Anima Sen. Psychol. Devel. Soc. **3:2** 7-12:1991 pp. 203 – 220
79 The analysis of defences. J.R. van Eenwyk. J. Analyt. Psychol. **36:2** 4:1991 pp. 141 – 163
80 The art and science of family psychology — retrospective and perspective. Florence W. Kaslow. Am. Psychol. **46:6** 6:1991 pp. 621 – 626
81 Asymmetry of doubt in medical self-diagnosis — the ambiguity of "uncertain wellness". Delia Cioffi. J. Pers. Soc. Psychol. **61:6** 12:1991 pp. 969 – 980
82 Auditory attention switching — a developmental study. Deborah A. Pearson; David M. Lane. J. Exper. Child Psychol. **51:2** 4:1991 pp. 320 – 334
83 Avoiding heterosexist bias in psychological research. Gregory M. Herek; Douglas C. Kimmel; Hortensia Amaro; Gary B. Melton. Am. Psychol. **46:9** 9:1991 pp. 957 – 963
84 Blowing the whistle on data fudging — a controlled field experiment. Marcia P. Miceli; Janelle B. Dozier; Janet P. Near. J. Appl. Soc. Psychol. **21:4** 2:1991 pp. 271 – 295
85 Cognitive and emotional change in written essays and therapy interviews. Daniel A. Donnelly; Edward J. Murray. J. Soc. Clin. Psychol. **10:3** Fall:1991 pp. 334 – 350
86 Concepts, constructs, cognitive psychology, and personal construct theory. Bill Warren. J. Psychol. **125:5** 9:1991 pp. 525 – 536
87 Concerning psychology — psychology applied to social issues. Dennis Howitt. Milton Keynes: Open University Press, 1991: 188 p. ISBN: 0335093736; LofC: 91003309. Includes bibliographical references (p.[167]-180) and indexes.

INTERNATIONAL BIBLIOGRAPHY OF SOCIOLOGY — 1991

C.1: Psychology and social psychology *[Psychologie et psychologie sociale]* —
Psychology *[Psychologie]*

88 Conflict under the microscope. Roderick Ogley. Aldershot: Avebury, 1991: 259 p. (ill) *ISBN: 1856280233. Includes bibliogrpahy and index.*
89 Connection and disconnection of research and practice in the education of professional psychologists. Donald R. Peterson. *Am. Psychol.* **46:4** 4:1991 pp. 422 – 429
90 Connectionism and psychology — a psychological perspective on new connectionist research. Philip T. Quinlan. Hemel Hempstead: Harvester Wheatsheaf, 1991: 293 p. *ISBN: 0745008348.*
91 A controllability attributional model of problems in living — dimensional and situational interactions in the prediction of depression and loneliness. Craig A. Anderson; Alice L. Riger. *Soc. Cogn.* **9:2** Summer:1991 pp. 149 – 181
92 Coping success and its relationship to psychological distress for older adults. Alex J. Zautra; Amy B. Wrabetz. *J. Pers. Soc. Psychol.* **61:5** 11:1991 pp. 801 – 810
93 The culture of pain. David B. Morris. Berkeley: University of California Press, c1991: xii, 342 p. (ill) *ISBN: 0520072669; LofC: 90011305. Includes bibliographical references (p. 291-336) and index.*
94 Culture tales — a narrative approach to thinking, cross-cultural psychology, and psychotherapy. George S. Howard. *Am. Psychol.* **46:3** 3:1991 pp. 187 – 197
95 La dépression post-natale — les facteurs socio-environnementaux *[In French]*; [Post-natal depression — the socio-environmental factors] *[Summary]*. Louise Séguin; Louise Cossette. *San. Ment. Qué* **XVI:1** 6:1991 pp. 149 – 164
96 Do students with different characteristics take part in psychology experiments at different times of the semester? Harris Cooper; Ann H. Baumgardner; Alan Strathman. *J. Personal.* **59:1** 3:1991 pp. 109 – 128
97 Effect of client race and depression on evaluations by white therapists. K. Jenkins-Hall; William P. Sacco. *J. Soc. Clin. Psychol.* **10:3** Fall:1991 pp. 322 – 333
98 Empirical study of associations between symbols and their meanings — evidence of collective unconscious (archetypal) memory. D.H. Rosen; S.M. Smith; H.L. Huston; G. Gonzalez. *J. Analyt. Psychol.* **36:2** 4:1991 pp. 211 – 228
99 From Freud to cognitive science — a contemporary account of the unconscious. Mick Power; Chris R. Brewin. *Br. J. Clin. Psycho.* **30:4** 11:1991 pp. 289 – 310
100 Gas station psychology — the case for specialization in ecological psychology. Robert Sommer; Allan W. Wicker. *Envir. Behav.* **23:2** 3:1991 pp. 131 – 149
101 Global report on student well-being. Alex C. Michalos. New York: Springer-Verlag, -: 253 p. *ISBN: 0387974601; LofC: cn 91007249. Includes bibliographical references.* [Recent research in psychology.]
102 Human nature as social order — a hundred years of psychometrics. José A. López Cerezo. *J. Soc. Biol. Struct.* **14:4** 1991 pp. 409 – 434
103 In defense of modernity — role complexity and individual autonomy. Rose Laub Coser. Stanford, Calif: Stanford University Press, 1991: ix, 199 p. *ISBN: 0804718717; LofC: 91006374. Includes bibliographical references (p. 173-187) and indexes.*
104 Inductive measures of psychological climate. Daniel J. Koys; Thomas A. DeCotiis. *Human Relat.* **44:3** 3:1991 pp. 265 – 285
105 Is psychopathic disorder a useful clinical concept? A perspective from England and Wales. Herschel Prins. *Int. J. Offen.* **35:2** Summer:1991 pp. 119 – 125
106 Issues in evolutionary psychology. Linnda R. Caporael *[Contrib.]*; Marilynn B. Brewer *[Contrib.]*; John Archer *[Contrib.]*; Susan Oyama *[Contrib.]*; Stephen Jay Gould *[Contrib.]*; Nikolai L. Krementsov *[Contrib.]*; Daniel P. Todes *[Contrib.]*; Anatol Rapoport *[Contrib.]*; Halford H. Fairchild *[Contrib.]*; Cheryl Brown Travis *[Contrib.]* and others. Collection of 12 articles. **J. Soc. Issues**, *47:3*, 1991 pp. 1 – 195
107 Issues in psychotherapy with lesbians and gay men — a survey of psychologists. Linda Garnets; Kristin A. Hancock; Susan D. Cochran; Jacqueline Goodchilds; Letitia Anne Peplau. *Am. Psychol.* **46:9** 9:1991 pp. 964 – 972
108 Историческая психология как самостоятельная научная дисциплина *[In Russian]*; Historical psychology as a separate scientific discipline *[Summary]*. V.V. Nukandrov. *Vest. Lenin. Univ. 6* **L:6** 5:1991 pp. 55 – 64
109 The Klein connection in the London school — the search for origins. L. Zinkin. *J. Analyt. Psychol.* **36:1** 1:1991 pp. 37 – 61
110 Liberal education, study in depth, and the arts and sciences major — psychology. Thomas V. McGovern; Laurel Furumoto; Diane F. Halpern; Gregory A. Kimble; Wilbert J. McKeachie. *Am. Psychol.* **46:6** 6:1991 pp. 598 – 605

C.1: Psychology and social psychology [Psychologie et psychologie sociale] — Psychology [Psychologie]

111 Modern psychology. Hans H. Gerth. *Int. J. Pol. C. S.* **5:2** Winter:1991 pp. 273 – 318
112 Nature-nurture issues in Freud's writings — "the complemental series"; *[French summary]*; *[German summary]*; *[Spanish summary]*. Ehud Koch. *Int. Rev. Psy.* **18:4** 1991 pp. 473 – 487
113 The need for organismic psychology in psychotherapy. Joseph S. Jacob. *Mankind Q.* **XXXI:4** Summer:1991 pp. 367 – 413
114 New developments in the history of psychology. Kurt Danziger *[Ed.]*; Trudy Dehue *[Contrib.]*; Pieter J. Van Strien *[Contrib.]*; Richard T. Von Mayrhauser *[Contrib.]*; Mitchell G. Ash *[Contrib.]*; Irmingard Staeuble *[Contrib.]*. Collection of 6 articles. **Hist. Human Sci.**, *4:3*, 10:1991 pp. 327 – 432
115 The Oedipal complex in adolescence. H. Gee. *J. Analyt. Psychol.* **36:2** 4:1991 pp. 193 – 210
116 Of mice and men — the comparative assumption in psychology. K.V. Wilkes. *Inter. Phil. Sci.* **5:1** 1991 pp. 3 – 20
117 Penis envy — libidinal metaphor and experiential metonym; *[German summary]*; *[French summary]*; *[Spanish summary]*. Sallye M. Wilkinson. *Int. J.Psy.* **72:2** 1991 pp. 335 – 346
118 Persuasion in practice. Kathleen Kelley Reardon. London: Sage, 1991: viii, 232 p. *ISBN: 0803933169; LofC: 90-23689. Bibliography — p211-230. - Includes index.*
119 Polar psychology. Peter Suedfeld *[Contrib.]*; Brian Goehring *[Contrib.]*; John K. Stager *[Contrib.]*; Joanna Burger *[Contrib.]*; Michael Gochfeld *[Contrib.]*; Jane S.P. Mocellin *[Contrib.]*; Gloria R. Leon *[Contrib.]*; Gary Daniel Steel *[Contrib.]*; H. Ursin *[Contrib.]*; T. Bergan *[Contrib.] and others*. Collection of 8 articles. **Envir. Behav.**, *23:6*, 11:1991 pp. 653 – 781
120 Pourquoi la psychologie cognitive? *[In French]*; Cognitive psychology, why? *[Summary]*. Gérard Vergnaud. *Pensée* **:282** 7-8:1991 pp. 9 – 19
121 The problem of analyzing multiplicative composites — interactions revisited. Martin G. Evans. *Am. Psychol.* **46:1** 1:1991 pp. 6 – 15
122 Психология здоровья *[In Russian]*; (The psychology of health). N.E. Vodopjanova; N.V. Hodyreva. *Vest. Lenin. Univ.* 6 **:4** 1991 pp. 50 – 57
123 "Psychobiology". Donald A. Dewsbury. *Am. Psychol.* **46:3** 3:1991 pp. 198 – 205
124 Psychological counseling over the radio — listening motivations and the threat to self-esteem. Amiram Raviv; Alona Raviv; Gilad Arnon. *J. Appl. Soc. Psychol.* **21:4** 2:1991 pp. 253 – 270
125 Psychology in economics and business — an introduction to economic psychology. Gerrit Antonides. Dordrecht, The Netherlands: Kluwer Academic Publishers, c1991: x, 354 p. (ill) *ISBN: 0792313755; LofC: 91031223. Includes bibliographical references (p. 325-342) and indexes.*
126 The psychology of moderate prediction. II. Leniency and uncertainty. Yoav Ganzach; David H. Krantz. *Organ. Beh. Hum. Dec. Proces.* **48:2** 4:1991 pp. 169 – 192
127 Rational chocolate addiction or how chocolate cures irrationality. C.S. Elliott. *Int. J. Moral Soc. S.* **6:2** Summer:1991 pp. 172 – 184
128 Reliability and validity of a psychotic traits questionnaire (STQ). Michael Jackson; Gordon Claridge. *Br. J. Clin. Psycho.* **30:4** 11:1991 pp. 311 – 332
129 The role of psychology in the analysis of poverty — some suggestions. David Harper. *Psychol. Devel. Soc.* **3:2** 7-12:1991 pp. 193 – 202
130 Rule structure in the psychological representation of physical settings. W. Jeffrey Burroughs; David R. Drews. *J. Exp. S. Psychol.* **27:3** 5:1991 pp. 217 – 238
131 Self-regulatory mechanisms governing the impact of social comparison on complex decision making. Albert Bandura; Forest J. Jourden. *J. Pers. Soc. Psychol.* **60:6** 6:1991 pp. 941 – 951
132 Систематика психических состояний человека *[In Russian]*; The classification of psychical states of a person *[Summary]*. V.A. Ganzen; V.N. Jurchenko. *Vest. Lenin. Univ.* 6 **L:6** 5:1991 pp. 47 – 55
133 The social and cognitive determinants of aberrant driving behaviour. J.T. Reason; et al. Crowthorne: Transport and Road Research Laboratory, 1991: 75 p.
134 Social comparison and smoking cessation — the role of the "typical smoker". Frederick X. Gibbons; Meg Gerrard; Harry A. Lando; Paul G. McGovern. *J. Exp. S. Psychol.* **27:3** 5:1991 pp. 239 – 258
135 Social comparisons and their affective consequences — the importance of comparison dimension and individual difference variables. Kenneth J. Hemphill; Darrin R. Lehman. *J. Soc. Clin. Psychol.* **10:4** Winter:1991 pp. 372 – 394

C.1: Psychology and social psychology [Psychologie et psychologie sociale] — Psychology [Psychologie]

136 Statistical models in behavioral research. William K Estes. Hillsdale, N.J: L. Erlbaum Associates, 1991: ix, 159 p. (ill) *ISBN: 0805806865; LofC: 90043392 //r91. Includes bibliographical references (p. 149-150) and indexes.*

137 Supervision, training, and the institution as an internal pressure. J. Astor. *J. Analyt. Psychol.* **36:2** 4:1991 pp. 177 – 191

138 The supposed limits of interpretation. M. Fordham. *J. Analyt. Psychol.* **36:2** 4:1991 pp. 165 – 175

139 Unified positivism and unification psychology — fad or new field? Arthur W. Staats. *Am. Psychol.* **46:9** 9:1991 pp. 899 – 912

140 Values and religious issues in psychotherapy and mental health. Allen E. Bergin. *Am. Psychol.* **46:4** 4:1991 pp. 394 – 403

141 What can specificity designs say about causality in psychopathology research. Judy Garber; Steven D. Hollon. *Psychol .B.* **110:1** 7:1991 pp. 129 – 136

Social psychology [Psychologie sociale]

142 Актуальные проблемы социалистической педагогики: Сб. науч. тр. *[In Russian]*; [Current problems in social psychology — a paper to a meeting of an All-Union symposium on social psychology]. N.D. Nikandrov *[Ed.]*. Moscow: , 1987: 129 p.

143 Alienation, community, and work. Andrew Oldenquist *[Ed.]*; Menahem Rosner *[Ed.]*. New York: Greenwood Press, 1991: viii, 211 p. (ill) *ISBN: 0313275416; LofC: 91006282. Includes bibliographical references (p. [199]-201) and index.* [Contributions in sociology.]

144 Ambiguity in the internal/external distinction in causal attribution. Peter A. White. *J. Exp. S. Psychol.* **27:3** 5:1991 pp. 259 – 270

145 Behavioral analysis of societies and cultural practices. Peter A. Lamal *[Ed.]*. New York: Hemisphere Pub. Corp, c1991: xiv, 257 p. *ISBN: 1560321237; LofC: 91013232. Includes bibliographical references and index.* [The series in health psychology and behavioral medicine.]

146 The body and social psychology. Alan Radley. New York: Springer-Verlag, c1991: xi, 213 p. *ISBN: 0387975845; LofC: 91004196. Includes bibliographical references and index.* [Springer series in social psychology.]

147 Currents of thought in American social psychology. Gary Collier; Henry L Minton *[Ed.]*; Graham Reynolds *[Ed.]*. New York: Oxford University Press, 1991: xi, 335 p. *ISBN: 0195061292; LofC: 90026340. Includes bibliographical references (p. 299-323) and indexes.*

148 Dynamic role of social support in the link between chronic stress and psychological distress. Stephen J. Lepore; Gary W. Evans; Margaret L. Schneider. *J. Pers. Soc. Psychol.* **61:6** 12:1991 pp. 899 – 909

149 Eros and evolution — prospects for PASO. Robert Endleman. New York: Psyche Press, 1991: 218 p. *ISBN: 0962288527.*

150 The fashioned self. Joanne Finkelstein. Oxford: Polity, 1991: 213 p. *ISBN: 0745606873. Includes index.*

151 From Brahma to a blade of grass. Alfred Collins. *J. Ind. Phil.* **19:2** 6:1991 pp. 143 – 189

152 General and relationship-based perceptions of social support — are two constructs better than one? Gregory R. Pierce; Irwin G. Sarason; Barbara R. Sarason. *J. Pers. Soc. Psychol.* **61:6** 12:1991 pp. 1028 – 1039

153 L'homme et la société dix ans après Piaget *[In French]*; [Man and society ten years after Piaget]. W. Doise *[Contrib.]*; E. Ascher *[Contrib.]*; A. Renaut *[Contrib.]*; R. Droz *[Contrib.]*; H. Volken *[Contrib.]*; E. Enriquez *[Contrib.]*; J.-Cl. Gardin *[Contrib.]*; A. Delessert *[Contrib.]*; R. Boudon *[Contrib.]*; C. Lefort *[Contrib.] and others. Collection of 15 articles.* **Rev. Eur. Sci. Soc.**, *XXIX:89*, 1991 pp. 5 – 251

154 Human behavior in the social environment — an ecological view. Carel B Germain. New York: Columbia University Press, c1991: xiv, 543 p. (ill) *ISBN: 0231054041; LofC: 90047014. Includes bibliographical references (p. 471-514) and indexes.*

155 In social relationships — an introduction to the social psychology of membership and intimacy. Alan Radley. Milton Keynes: Open University Press, 1991: 142 p. *ISBN: 0335151965; LofC: gb 91002951.*

156 Language — contexts and consequences. Howard Giles; Nikolas Coupland. Milton Keynes: Open University Press, 1991: 244 p. *ISBN: 0335098738. Includes bibliography and index.* [Mapping social psychology.]

C.1: Psychology and social psychology [Psychologie et psychologie sociale] — Social psychology [Psychologie sociale]

157 The long past and the short history of social psychology. R.M. Farr. *Eur. J. Soc. Psychol.* **21:5** 9-10:1991 pp. 371 – 380

158 Lost in familiar places — creating new connections between the individual and society. Edward R. Shapiro; A. Wesley Carr. New Haven: Yale University Press, c1991: 193 p. *ISBN: 0300049471; LofC: 90019662. Includes bibliographical references and index.*

159 Lying — thoughts of an applied social psychologist. Leonard Saxe. *Am. Psychol.* **46:4** 4:1991 pp. 409 – 415

160 Mixed emotions — certain steps toward understanding ambivalence. Andrew J. Weigert. Albany: State University of New York Press, c1991: xv, 197 p. *ISBN: 0791406008; LofC: 90009888. Includes bibliographical references (p. 181-194) and index.* [SUNY series in the sociology of emotions.]

161 The other half — wives of alcoholics and their social-psychological situation. Jacqueline P. Wiseman; Robin Room [Foreword]. New York: A. de Gruyter, c1991: xx, 297 p. *ISBN: 0202303829; LofC: 91011740. Includes bibliographical references (p. 269-290) and index.* [Communication and social order.]

162 The person and the situation — perspectives of social psychology. Lee Ross; Richard Nisbett. Philadelphia: Temple University Press, 1991: xvi, 286 p. (ill) *ISBN: 0877228515; LofC: 91006602. Includes bibliographical references (p. 247-272) and indexes.*

163 Psychosocial competence in developing countries. Forrest B. Tyler. *Psychol. Devel. Soc.* **3:2** 7-12:1991 pp. 171 – 192

164 Relations and representations — an introduction to the philosophy of social psychological science. John D. Greenwood. London: Routledge, 1991: 179 p. *ISBN: 0415055148. Includes bibliography and index.*

165 Self-recording of everyday life events — origins, types, and uses. Ladd Wheeler; Harry T. Reis. *J. Personal.* **59:3** 9:1991 pp. 339 – 354

166 Social influence. John C. Turner. Milton Keynes: Open University Press, 1991: 206 p. *ISBN: 0335153410. Includes bibliography.* [Mapping social psychology.]

167 Social psychology in a postmodern age — a discipline without a subject. James J. Dowd. *Am. Sociol.* **22:3 and 4** Fall/Winter:1991 pp. 188 – 209

168 A social psychology of organizing — people, processes and contexts. Dian-Marie Hosking; Ian E. Morley [Ed.]. New York: Harvester, 1991: 289 p. *ISBN: 0745010539.*

169 Social psychology of political and economic cognition. Glynis M. Breakwell [Ed.]. London: Academic Press, 1991: 189 p. *ISBN: 0121286800.* [Surrey seminars in social psychology.]

170 Social selves — theories of the social formation of personality. Ian Burkitt. London: Sage Publications, 1991: 240 p. *ISBN: 0803983840.*

171 Social worlds, personal lives — an introduction to social psychology. Edward E. Sampson. San Diego: Harcourt Brace Jovanovich, c1991: xi, 369 p. *ISBN: 0155818058; LofC: 90084204. Includes index; Includes bibliographical references (p. 329-357).*

172 Социальная психология научного коллектива *[In Russian]*; [Social psychology of the scientific team]. M.G. Iaroshevskii [Ed.]; P.G. Belkin; E.N. Emekianov; M.A. Ivanov. Moscow: Nauka, 1987: 214 p. *Bibliogr. pp.197-205.*

173 Time structure and purpose as a mediator of work-life linkages. Jennifer M. George. *J. Appl. Soc. Psychol.* **21:4** 2:1991 pp. 296 – 314

174 В ответе за каждого: Социал.-психол.аспекты борьбы с пьянством и алкоголизмом *[In Russian]*; [Responsible for everyone — social-psychological aspects of the struggle against drunkenness and alcoholism]. V.V. Boiko. Leningrad: Lenizdat, 1986: 160 p.

C.2: Individuals — *Individus*

Sub-divisions: Cognition *[Cognition]*; Decision making *[Prise de décision]*; Memory *[Mémoire]*; Motivation *[Motivation]*; Personality *[Personnalité]*; Self-concept *[Conception de soi]*

1 Absorption, openness to experience, and hypnotizability. Martha L. Glisky; Douglas J. Tataryn; Betsy A. Tobias; John F. Kihlstrom; Kevin M. McConkey. *J. Pers. Soc. Psychol.* **60:2** 2:1991 pp. 263 – 272
2 Accuracy and bias in estimates of others' knowledge. S.R. Fussell; R.M. Krauss. *Eur. J. Soc. Psychol.* **21:5** 9-10:1991 pp. 445 – 454
3 Adaptation to divorce and ego development in adult women. Krisanne Bursik. *J. Pers. Soc. Psychol.* **60:2** 2:1991 pp. 300 – 306
4 Anger and the use of defense mechanisms in college students. Phebe Cramer. *J. Personal.* **59:1** 3:1991 pp. 39 – 56
5 Anxiety disorders research with African Americans — current status. Angela M. Neal; Samuel M. Turner. *Psychol .B.* **109:3** 5:1991 pp. 400 – 410
6 Authors in search of a character — personhood, agency and identity in the Mediterranean. Paul Sant Cassia. *J. Mediter. St.* **1:1** 1991 pp. 1 – 17
7 Behavioral other-enhancement — strategically obscuring the link between performance and evaluation. James A. Shepperd; Robert M. Arkin. *J. Pers. Soc. Psychol.* **60:1** 1:1991 pp. 79 – 88
8 A catastrophe model of anxiety and performance. Lew Hardy; Gaynor Parfitt. *Br. J. Psy.* **82:2** 5:1991 pp. 163 – 178
9 The celebration of emotion — Vallabha's ontology of affective experience. Jeffrey R. Timm. *Philos. E.W.* **41:1** 1:1991 pp. 59 – 76
10 Changements sociaux et psychopathologie individuelle — le cas des Peuls du Nord-Cameroun *[In French]*; Social changes and individual psychopathology — the Peuls of North-Cameroon *[Summary]*. J.C. Lambret. *Cah. Anthr. Bio. Hum.* **VVI:3-4** 1989 pp. 181 – 196
11 Children's early understanding of false belief. Peter Mitchell; Hazel Lacohée. *Cognition* **39:2** 5:1991 pp. 107 – 127
12 Children's perception of safety and danger on the road. Kwame Ampofo-Boateng; James A. Thomson. *Br. J. Psy.* **82:4** 11:1991 pp. 487 – 506
13 The concept of consciousness$_2$ — the personal meaning. Thomas Natsoulas. *J. Theory Soc. Behav.* **21:3** 9:1991 pp. 339 – 368
14 Conscience, sympathy and the foundation of morality. Jiwei Ci. *Am. Phil. Q.* **28:1** 1:1991 pp. 49 – 60
15 Consciousness naturalized — supervenience without physical determinism. Dennis M. Senchuk. *Am. Phil. Q.* **28:1** 1:1991 pp. 37 – 48
16 Conservatism and the comprehension of implausible text. A. Anderson; P.O. McAllister. *Eur. J. Soc. Psychol.* **21:2** 3-4:1991 pp. 147 – 164
17 Construct differentiation and person-centred regulative messages. S.L. Kline. *J. Lang. Soc. Psychol.* **10:1** 1991 pp. 1 – 28
18 Control versus autonomy during early adolescence. Jacquelynne S. Eccles; Christy Miller Buchanan; Constance Flanagan; Andrew Fuligni; Carol Midgley; Doris Yee. *J. Soc. Issues* **47:4** 1991 pp. 53 – 68
19 The creative edge — emerging individualism in Japan. Kuniko Miyanaga. New Brunswick (U.S.A.): Transaction Publishers, c1991: xx, 137 p. *ISBN: 0887384072; LofC: 90049774. Includes bibliographical references (p. 131-133) and index.*
20 Daily hassles and mental health — a longitudinal study. Luo Lu. *Br. J. Psy.* **82:4** 11:1991 pp. 441 – 448
21 David Wong on emotions in Mencius. Craig K. Ihara. *Philos. E.W.* **41:1** 1:1991 pp. 45 – 54
22 Day-to-day physical symptoms — individual differences in the occurrence, duration, and emotional concomitants of minor daily illnesses. Randy J. Larsen; Margaret Kasimatis. *J. Personal.* **59:3** 9:1991 pp. 387 – 423
23 The effect of dimension content on observation and ratings of job performance. Tracy McDonald. *Organ. Beh. Hum. Dec. Proces.* **48:2** 4:1991 pp. 252 – 271
24 The effects of attractiveness, dominance, and attribute differences on information acquisition in multiattribute binary choice. Ulf Bockenhelt; Dietrich Albert; Michael Aschenbrenner; Franz Schmalhofer. *Organ. Beh. Hum. Dec. Proces.* **49:2** 8:1991 pp. 258 – 281

C.2: Individuals *[Individus]*

25 The effects of codability and discriminability of the referents on the collaborative referring procedure. Michel Hupet; Xavier Seron; Yves Chantraine. *Br. J. Psy.* **82:4** 11:1991 pp. 449 – 462
26 The effects of feature necessity and extrinsicity on gradedness of category membership and class inclusion relations. Leslie J. Caplan; Robin A. Barr. *Br. J. Psy.* **82:4** 11:1991 pp. 427 – 440
27 Emergence and realization of genius — the lives and works of 120 classical composers. Dean Keith Simonton. *J. Pers. Soc. Psychol.* **61:5** 11:1991 pp. 829 – 840
28 Emotional distress and its socio-political correlates in Salvadoran refugees — analysis of a clinical sample. Pablo J. Farias. *Cult. Medic. Psych.* **15:2** 6:1991 pp. 167 – 192
29 Everyday explanations for personal debt — a network approach. Peter K. Lunt; Sonia M. Livingstone. *Br. J. Soc. P.* **30:4** 12:1991 pp. 309 – 324
30 Expressed emotion and panic-fear in the prediction of diet treatment compliance. Desmond A.J. Flanagan; Hugh L. Wagner. *Br. J. Clin. Psycho.* **30:3** 9:1991 pp. 231 – 240
31 Facial asymmetry in emotional expression — a meta-analysis of research. Martin Skinner; Brian Mullen. *Br. J. Soc. P.* **30:2** 6:1991 pp. 113 – 124
32 Feature matching, unique features, and the dynamics of the choice process — predecision conflict and postdecision satisfaction. David A. Houston; Steven J. Sherman; Sara M. Baker. *J. Exp. S. Psychol.* **27:5** 9:1991 pp. 411 – 430
33 Filipino conceptualizations of creativity. Claribel D. Bartolome. *Phil. Stud.* **39:2** Second Quarter:1991 pp. 212 – 220
34 Die Form „Person" *[In German]*; The form "Person" *[Summary]*. Niklas Luhmann. *Soz. Welt.* **42:2** 1991 pp. 166 – 175
35 Further evidence on the relationship between goal setting and expectancy theories. Howard J. Klein. *Organ. Beh. Hum. Dec. Proces.* **49:2** 8:1991 pp. 230 – 257
36 Gender differences in negative affect and well-being — the case for emotional intensity. Frank Fujita; Ed Diener; Ed Sandvik. *J. Pers. Soc. Psychol.* **61:3** 9:1991 pp. 427 – 434
37 Genetyczne i środowiskowe źródła zróżnicowania w poziomie umysłowym *[In Polish]*; Genetic and environmental sources of differentiation in intellectual levels *[Summary]*. Anna Firkowska-Mankiewicz. *Prz. Soc.* **39** 1991 pp. 33 – 44
38 Geography of well-being in the Soviet Union — an automated data base approach. Olga L. Medvedkov. *J. Econ. Soc. Geogr.* **82:2** 1991 pp. 82 – 93
39 Grief and the search for meaning — exploring the assumptive worlds of bereaved college students. Steven S. Schwartzberg; Ronnie Janoff-Bulman. *J. Soc. Clin. Psychol.* **10:3** Fall:1991 pp. 270 – 288
40 Home sweet home! Dimensions and determinants of life satisfaction in an underdeveloped region; *[French summary]*. Lawrence F. Felt; Peter R. Sinclair. *Can. J. Soc.* **16:7** Winter:1991 pp. 1 – 21
41 How neuroticism, long-term difficulties, and life situation change influence psychological distress — a longitudinal model. Johan Ormel; Tamar Wohlfarth. *J. Pers. Soc. Psychol.* **60:5** 5:1991 pp. 744 – 755
42 Human development and criminal behavior — new ways of advancing knowledge. Michael H. Tonry; Lloyd E. Ohlin; D. P. Farrington. New York: Springer-Verlag, c1991: x, 223 p. (ill) *ISBN: 0387973605; LofC: 90039022. Includes bibliographical references (p. 211-223).* [Research in criminology.]
43 Human suggestibility — advances in theory, research, and application. John F Schumaker *[Ed.]*. New York: Routledge, 1991: 372 p. *ISBN: 0415902150; LofC: 90042174. Includes bibliographical references and index.*
44 Humor — the beauty and the beast. Glenn A. Hartz; Ralph Hunt. *Am. Phil. Q.* **28:4** 10:1991 pp. 299 – 309
45 Hypnosis and pseudomemories — the effects of prehypnotic expectancies. Steven Jay Lynn; Matthew Milano; John R. Weekes. *J. Pers. Soc. Psychol.* **60:2** 2:1991 pp. 318 – 326
46 Identity processes and social stress. Peter J. Burke. *Am. Sociol. R.* **56:6** 12:1991 pp. 836 – 849
47 Idioms of distress — somatic responses to distress in everyday life. Claire D.F. Parsons; Pat Wakeley. *Cult. Medic. Psych.* **15:1** 3:1991 pp. 111 – 132
48 An implicit theory of intelligence-related mental activities. Machteld Hoskens; Paul De Boeck. *J. Personal.* **59:4** 12:1991 pp. 793 – 814
49 Individual and group differences in adoption studies of IQ. Eric Turkheimer. *Psychol .B.* **110:3** 11:1991 pp. 392 – 405

C.2: Individuals [Individus]

50 Individualism and solidarity today — twelve theses. Christian Lalive d' Epinay. *Theory Cult. Soc.* **8:2** 5:1991 pp. 57 – 74
51 The influence of the causal background on the selection of causal explanations. Ann L. McGill. *Br. J. Soc. P.* **30:1** 3:1991 pp. 79 – 87
52 The influencing machine and the mad scientist — the influence of contemporary culture on the evolution of a basic delusion; *[French summary]*; *[German summary]*; *[Spanish summary]*. Stuart S. Asch. *Int. Rev. Psy.* **18:2** 1991 pp. 185 – 193
53 Ingestion and emotional health. Nancy K. Dess. *Hum. Nature* **2:3** 1991 pp. 235 – 270
54 Inhibitory mechanisms of attention — locus, stability, and relationship with distractor interference effects. Steven P. Tipper; Bruce Weaver; John Kirkpatrick; Stevan Lewis. *Br. J. Psy.* **82:4** 11:1991 pp. 507 – 520
55 Insides and essences — early understandings of the non-obvious. Susan A. Gelman; Henry M. Wellman. *Cognition* **38:3** 3:1991 pp. 213 – 244
56 Is happiness relative? Ruut Veenhoven. *Soc. Ind.* **24:1** 2:1991 pp. 1 – 34
57 Is there a distinction between reason and emotion in Mencius? David B. Wong. *Philos. E.W.* **41:1** 1:1991 pp. 31 – 45
58 Lebenszufriedenheit und Lebenserfolg im Übergang vom Jugendlichen zum Erwachsenen. Ein Längsschnitt ehemaliger Gymnasiasten vom 15. bis zum 30. Lebensjahr *[In German]*; Well-being and career success during the transition from adolescence to adult status *[Summary]*. Heiner Meulemann. *Kölner Z. Soz. Soz. psy.* **43:3** 1991 pp. 476 – 501
59 Life tasks and daily life experience. Nancy Cantor; Julie Norem; Christopher Langston; Sabrina Zirkel; William Fleeson; Carol Cook-Flannagan. *J. Personal.* **59:3** 9:1991 pp. 425 – 451
60 A magical model of happiness. M.J. Stones; A. Kozma. *Soc. Ind.* **25:1** 8:1991 pp. 31 – 50
61 *[In Japanese]*; [Man in the historical crisis — from the point of view on self-absorption and self-alienation]. Takashi Hasegawa. ***Himeji Gakuin Women's Junior College Review*** *No.(18) - 1991.* pp. 55 – 82
62 Measuring happiness in surveys — a test of the subtraction hypothesis. Roger Tourangeau; Kenneth A. Rasinski; Norman Bradburn. *Publ. Opin. Q.* **55:2** Summer:1991 pp. 255 – 266
63 Mental causes. John Heil; Alfred Mele. *Am. Phil. Q.* **28:1** 1:1991 pp. 61 – 71
64 Mind, self, society, and computer — artificial intelligence and the sociology of mind. Alan Wolfe. *A.J.S.* **96:5** 3:1991 pp. 1073 – 1096
65 Morality, identity, and historical explanation — Charles Taylor on the sources of the self. Graig Calhoun. *Sociol. Theory* **9:2** Fall:1991 pp. 232 – 263
66 Narcissistic acts in everyday life. David M. Buss; Lisa Mancinelli Chiodo. *J. Personal.* **59:2** 6:1991 pp. 179 – 215
67 Noise and aspects of attention. Andrew P. Smith. *Br. J. Psy.* **82:3** 8:1991 pp. 313 – 324
68 On the "absoluteness" of category and magnitude scales of pain. Wolfgang Ellermeier; Wolfgang Westphal; Martina Heidenfelder. *Perc. Psych.* **49:2** 2:1991 pp. 159 – 166
69 On the origins of dynamical awareness. David L. Gilden. *Psychol. Rev.* **98:4** 10:1991 pp. 554 – 568
70 Organisation de identités de soi et d'autrui dans une situation de choix électoral — une approche de psychologie sociale *[In French]*; [Organization of identities of self and others in an electoral choice situation — a social psychology approach]. Jean-Louis Nakhi; Joëlle Lebreuilly. *R. Fr. Sci. Pol.* **41:4** 8:1991 pp. 560 – 577
71 Overconfidence in estimation — testing the anchoring-and-adjustment hypothesis. Richard A. Block; David R. Harper. *Organ. Beh. Hum. Dec. Proces.* **49:2** 8:1991 pp. 188 – 207
72 Per una concezione non individualistica dell'autonomia individuale *[In Italian]*; For a non-individualistic conception of individual autonomy *[Summary]*. Emilio Santoro. *Rass. It. Soc.* **32:3** 9:1991 pp. 267 – 312
73 Perceived control and coping with stress — a development perspective. Bruce E. Compas; Gerard A. Banez; Vanessa Malcarne; Nancy Worsham. *J. Soc. Issues* **47:4** 1991 pp. 23 – 34
74 Perceived control, drive for thinness, and food consumption — anorexic tendencies as displaced reactance. Pamela J. Rezek; Mark R. Leary. *J. Personal.* **59:1** 3:1991 pp. 129 – 142
75 Performance and state changes during the menstrual cycle, conceptualised within a broad band testing framework. J.M. Ussher; J.M. Wilding. *Soc. Sci. Med.* **32:5** 1991 pp. 525 – 534
76 Personal strivings, daily life events, and psychological and physical well-being. Robert A. Emmons. *J. Personal.* **59:3** 9:1991 pp. 453 – 472

C.2: Individuals *[Individus]*

77 The physiology of perception. Walter J. Freeman. *Sci. Am.* **264:2** 2:1991 pp. 34 – 41
78 Primary prevention of acculturative stress among refugees — application of psychological theory and practice. Carolyn L. Williams; J.W. Berry. *Am. Psychol.* **46:6** 6:1991 pp. 632 – 641
79 Profile analysis of the Wechsler intelligence scales — a new index of subtest scatter. Adrian Burgess. *Br. J. Clin. Psycho.* **30:3** 9:1991 pp. 257 – 263
80 A prospective study of depression and posttraumatic stress symptoms after a natural disaster — the 1989 Loma Prieta earthquake. Susan Nolen-Hoeksema; Jannay Morrow. *J. Pers. Soc. Psychol.* **61:1** 7:1991 pp. 115 – 121
81 Pseudomemory effects and their relationship to level of susceptibility to hypnosis and state instruction. Peter W. Sheehan; Dixie Statham; Graham A. Jamieson. *J. Pers. Soc. Psychol.* **60:1** 1:1991 pp. 130 – 137
82 The psychic costs of intense positive affect. Ed Diener; C. Randall Colvin; William G. Pavot; Amanda Allman. *J. Pers. Soc. Psychol.* **61:3** 9:1991 pp. 492 – 503
83 The psychological impact of unemployment and unsatisfactory employment in young men and women — longitudinal and cross-sectional data. Anthony H. Winefield; Marika Tiggemann; Helen R. Winefield. *Br. J. Psy.* **82:4** 11:1991 pp. 473 – 486
84 Related measures of constructive and rational thinking. John R. Hurley. *J. Psychol.* **125:2** 3:1991 pp. 229 – 236
85 The relative utility of complementary disparate views on voluntarism and determinism. E. Rae Harcum. *J. Psychol.* **125:2** 3:1991 pp. 217 – 228
86 Relégation territoriale et aspiration à la mobilité résidentielle *[In French]*; Territorial assignment and desire for residential mobility *[Summary]*. Monique Vervaeke. *Soc. Contemp.* **:5** 3:1991 pp. 117 – 134
87 *[In Japanese]*; [Reorganization of behavioral theorics — beyond mentalism and objectivism]. Takao Mamada. Tokyo: Fukumura Publishing, 1991: 274 p.
88 Research and reflexivity. Frederick Steier *[Ed.]*. London: Sage Publications, 1991: 257 p. *ISBN: 0803982380.* [Inquiries in social construction.]
89 Response artifacts in the measurement of subjective well-being. Ed Diener; Ed Sandvik; William Pavot; Dennis Gallagher. *Soc. Ind.* **24:1** 2:1991 pp. 35 – 56
90 Restorative effects of natural environment experiences. Terry Hartig; Marlis Mang; Gary W. Evans. *Envir. Behav.* **23:1** 1:1991 pp. 3 – 26
91 Reversal of the preference reversal phenomenon. Jeff T. Casey. *Organ. Beh. Hum. Dec. Proces.* **48:2** 4:1991 pp. 224 – 251
92 Self-constraint versus self-liberation. Tyler Cowen. *Ethics* **101:2** 1:1991 pp. 360 – 373
93 The short NART — cross-validation, relationship to IQ and some practical considerations. J.R. Crawford; D.M. Parker; K.M. Allan; A.M. Jack; F.M. Morrison. *Br. J. Clin. Psycho.* **30:3** 9:1991 pp. 223 – 230
94 Social choice — a framework for collective decisions and individual judgements. John Craven. Cambridge [England]: Cambridge University Press, 1991: 152 p. *ISBN: oc22811716; LofC: 90024763.* Includes bibliographical references and index.
95 Совесть как этическая категория *[In Russian]*; [The conscience as an ethical category]. Z.A. Berbeshkina. Moscow: Vyssh.shk., 1986: 103 p. *Bibliogr. pp.97-102.*
96 Stability and change in levels and structure of subjective well-being — USA 1972 and 1988. Frank M. Andrews. *Soc. Ind.* **25:1** 8:1991 pp. 1 – 30
97 The stability of attributional style and its relation to psychological distress. M. Tiggemann; Anthony H. Winefield; Helen R. Winefield; Robert D. Goldney. *Br. J. Clin. Psycho.* **30:3** 9:1991 pp. 247 – 256
98 The stability of work, self and interpersonal goals in young women and men. J. Langan-Fox. *Eur. J. Soc. Psychol.* **21:5** 9-10:1991 pp. 419 – 428
99 Stress specificities — differential effects of coping style, gender, and type of stressor on autonomic arousal, facial expression, and subjective feeling. Harald G. Wallbott; Klaus R. Scherer. *J. Pers. Soc. Psychol.* **61:1** 7:1991 pp. 147 – 156
100 Testing judgments about attribution-emotion-action linkages — a lifespan approach. Sandra Graham; Bernard Weiner. *Soc. Cogn.* **9:3** Fall:1991 pp. 254 – 276
101 The theoretical and empirical structure of general well-being. Robert J. Wheeler. *Soc. Ind.* **24:1** 2:1991 pp. 71 – 79
102 The theoretical foundations of incorporating Islamic beliefs in a stress inoculation program for Muslims. Ola Abdel-Kawi. *Am. J. Islam. Soc. Sci.* **8:2** 9:1991 pp. 275 – 288
103 This reminds me of the time when — expectation failures in reminding and explanation. Stephen J. Read; Ian L. Cesa. *J. Exp. S. Psychol.* **27:1** 1:1991 pp. 1 – 25

C.2: Individuals [Individus]

104 Top-down versus bottom-up theories of subjective well-being. Bruce Headey; Ruut Veenhoven; Alex Wearing. *Soc. Ind.* **24:1** 2:1991 pp. 81 – 100

105 Understanding the mind as an active information processor — do young children have a "copy theory of mind"? Josef Perner; Graham Davies. *Cognition* **39:1** 4:1991 pp. 51 – 70

106 Unity of perception. Bruce M. Bennett; Donald D. Hoffman; Chetan Prakash. *Cognition* **38:3** 3:1991 pp. 295 – 334

107 The universal applicability of the theory of neutralization — German youth coming to terms with the Holocaust. An empirical study with theoretical implications. M. Hazani. *Cr. Law Soc. Chan.* **15:2** 3:1991 pp. 135 – 149

108 What children can tell us about living in danger. James Garbarino; Kathleen Kostelny; Nancy Dubrow. *Am. Psychol.* **46:4** 4:1991 pp. 376 – 383

109 What is wrong with wicked feelings? Robert C. Roberts. *Am. Phil. Q.* **28:1** 1:1991 pp. 13 – 24

110 The wounded caretaker and guilt; *[French summary]*; *[German summary]*; *[Spanish summary]*. O. Kitayama. *Int. Rev. Psy.* **18:2** 1991 pp. 229 – 240

Cognition [Cognition]

111 Administrative and organization behavior — some insights from cognitive psychology. Richard L. Schott. *Admin. Soc.* **23:1** 5:1991 pp. 54 – 73

112 Analogical reasoning — what develops? A review of research and theory. Usha Goswami. *Child. Devel.* **62:1** 2:1991 pp. 1 – 22

113 Can valid inferences be suppressed? Ruth M.J. Byrne. *Cognition* **39:1** 4:1991 pp. 71 – 78

114 Cognition and rationality in negotiation. Margaret Ann Neale; Max H. Bazerman. New York: Free Press, c1991: xi, 211 p. (ill) ISBN: 0029225159; LofC: 90021585. Includes bibliographical references (p. 173-197) and index.

115 La cognition des systèmes d'intelligence artificielle *[In French]*; Cognition of systems of artificial intelligence *[Summary]*. Jacques Pitrat. *Pensée* **:282** 7-8:1991 pp. 20 – 30

116 Cognitive ability and career attainment — moderating effects of early career success. George F. Dreher; Robert D. Brets. *J. Appl. Psychol.* **76:3** 6:1991 pp. 392 – 397

117 Cognitive and emotional reactions to daily events — the effects of self-esteem and self-complexity. Jennifer D. Campbell; Barry Chew; Linda S. Scratchley. *J. Personal.* **59:3** 9:1991 pp. 473 – 505

118 Cognitive effects of LOGO and computer-aided instruction among black and white Zimbabwean primary school girls. David Wilson; Alistair Mundy-Castle; Pauline Sibanda. *J. Soc. Psychol.* **131:1** 2:1991 pp. 107 – 116

119 Cognitive therapy — a 30-year retrospective. Aaron T. Beck. *Am. Psychol.* **46:4** 4:1991 pp. 368 – 375

120 Computer games and cognitive processes — two tasks, two modes, too much? David B. Porter. *Br. J. Psy.* **82:3** 8:1991 pp. 343 – 358

121 Constructive thinking and coping with laboratory-induced stress. Lori Katz; Seymour Epstein. *J. Pers. Soc. Psychol.* **61:5** 11:1991 pp. 789 – 800

122 Emotions and politics — hot cognitions and the rediscovery of passion. George E. Marcus. *Soc. Sci. Info.* **30:2** 1991 pp. 195 – 232

123 Fledgling theories of mind — deception as a marker of three-year olds' understanding of false belief. Suzanne Hala; Michael Chandler; Anna S. Fritz. *Child. Devel.* **62:1** 2:1991 pp. 83 – 97

124 How mental systems believe. Daniel T. Gilbert. *Am. Psychol.* **46:2** 2:1991 pp. 107 – 119

125 Individual differences in cognitive processes — towards an explanation of schizophrenic symptomatology. Anthony Beech; Denis McManus; Gordon Baylis; Steven Tipper; Kirsten Agar. *Br. J. Psy.* **82:4** 11:1991 pp. 417 – 426

126 Is human information processing conscious? M. Velmans. *Behav. Brain Sci.* **14:4** 12:1991 pp. 651 – 726

127 The microgenetic method — a direct means for studying cognitive development. Robert S. Siegler; Kevin Crowley. *Am. Psychol.* **46:6** 6:1991 pp. 606 – 620

128 La pensée... artificielle? *[In French]*; Artificial thought? *[Summary]*. Ivan Lavallée. *Pensée* **:282** 7-8:1991 pp. 31 – 44

129 Progress on a cognitive-motivational-relational theory of emotion. Richard S. Lazarus. *Am. Psychol.* **46:8** 8:1991 pp. 819 – 834

130 Promoting cognitive competence in children at risk. Susan C. Hupp. *Am. Behav. Sc.* **34:4** 3/4:1991 pp. 454 – 467

131 The representation of self in multidimensional cognitive space. Stephen J. Breckler; Anthony R. Pratkanis; C. Douglas McCann. *Br. J. Soc. P.* **30:2** 6:1991 pp. 97 – 112

C.2: Individuals *[Individus]* — Cognition *[Cognition]*

132 Self-serving prototypes of social categories. David Dunning; Marianne Perie; Amber L. Story. *J. Pers. Soc. Psychol.* **61:6** 12:1991 pp. 957 – 968

133 Settled objectives and rational constraints. Hugh J. McCann. *Am. Phil. Q.* **28:1** 1:1991 pp. 25 – 36

134 Social and cognitive motivations of change — measuring variability in color semantics. Robert E. MacLaury. *Language* **67:1** 3:1991 pp. 34 – 62

135 Social cognition and object relations. Drew Westen. *Psychol .B.* **109:3** 5:1991 pp. 429 – 455

136 Social regulation and individual cognitive function — effects of individuation on cognitive performance. J.-M. Monteil. *Eur. J. Soc. Psychol.* **21:3** 5-6:1991 pp. 225 – 237

137 The social-cognitive construction of therapeutic change — a dual coding analysis. Jack Martin. *J. Soc. Clin. Psychol.* **10:3** Fall:1991 pp. 305 – 321

138 Spatial representation of objects in the young blind child. Barbara Landau. *Cognition* **38:2** 2:1991 pp. 145 – 178

139 Switching cognitive gears — from habits of mind to active thinking. Meryl Reis Louis; Robert I. Sutton. *Human Relat.* **44:1** 1:1991 pp. 55 – 76

140 Understanding children — essays in honor of Margaret Donaldson. Robert B. Grieve *[Ed.]*; Martin Hughes *[Ed.]*. Oxford, UK; Blackwell, c1991: 243 p. *ISBN: 063115538/x; LofC: 90086327. Bibliographical references and index.*

141 Understanding covert recognition. A. Mike Burton; Andrew W. Young; Vicki Bruce; Robert A. Johnston. *Cognition* **39:2** 5:1991 pp. 129 – 165

142 The Whorfian hypothesis — a cognitive psychology perspective. Earl Hunt; Franca Agnoli. *Psychol. Rev.* **98:3** 7:1991 pp. 377 – 389

Decision making *[Prise de décision]*

143 Cognition and rationality in negotiation. Margaret Ann Neale; Max H. Bazerman. New York: Free Press, c1991: xi, 211 p. (ill) *ISBN: 0029225159; LofC: 90021585. Includes bibliographical references (p. 173-197) and index.*

144 Computer-assisted, outcomes-based evaluation for school programs. Tim L. Wentling; Chris A. Roegge. *Eval. Rev.* **15:3** 6:1991 pp. 378 – 392

145 Decision making in the graduate selection interview — an experimental investigation. Neil R. Anderson. *Human Relat.* **44:4** 4:1991 pp. 403 – 417

146 Disasters and dilemmas — strategies for real-life decision making. Adam Morton. Oxford: Basil Blackwell, 1991: 209 p *ISBN: 063116216x. Includes bibliography and index.*

147 Exploring connectionist approaches to legal decision making. Wullianallur Raghupathi; Lawrence E. Schkade; Raju S. Bapi; Daniel S. Levine. *Behav. Sci.* **36:2** 4:1991 pp. 133 – 139

148 The fine line — making distinctions in everyday life. Eviatar Zerubavel. New York: Free Press, c1991: xii, 205 p. (ill) *ISBN: 0029344204; LofC: 91021867. Includes bibliographical references (p. 123-189) and indexes.*

149 Intuition — a human tool for generalizing. Donald B. Straus. *J. Soc. Biol. Struct.* **14:3** 1991 pp. 333 – 352

150 Measuring daily events and experiences — decisions for the researcher. Arthur A. Stone; Ronald C. Kessler; Jennifer A. Haythornthwaite. *J. Personal.* **59:3** 9:1991 pp. 575 – 607

151 Personnel decision making — the impact of missing information. Carolyn M. Jagacinski. *J. Appl. Psychol.* **76:1** 2:1991 pp. 19 – 30

152 The role of contextual variables in evaluation decision making — perceptions of potential loss, time, and self-efficacy on nurse managers' need for information. Linnea L. Jatulis; Dianna L. Newman. *Eval. Rev.* **15:3** 6:1991 pp. 364 – 377

153 Strategy and choice. Richard J. Zeckhauser *[Ed.]*. Cambridge, Mass: MIT Press, c1991: viii, 402 p. (ill) *ISBN: 0262240335; LofC: 91015837. Includes bibliographical references and index.*

Memory *[Mémoire]*

154 Ageing memory — use versus impairment. Carol A. Holland; Patrick M.A. Rabbitt. *Br. J. Psy.* **82:1** 2:1991 pp. 29 – 38

155 The development of children's memory for the time of past events. William J. Friedman. *Child. Devel.* **62:1** 2:1991 pp. 139 – 155

156 Differentiating phonological memory and awareness of rhyme — reading and vocabulary development in children. Susan E. Gathercole; Catherine Willis; Alan D. Baddeley. *Br. J. Psy.* **82:3** 8:1991 pp. 387 – 406

C.2: Individuals [Individus] — Memory [Mémoire]

157 Evidence of a negative environmental reinstatement effect. Stephen C. Wilhite. *Br. J. Psy.* **82:3** 8:1991 pp. 325 – 342
158 Eyewitness memory for a touching experience — accuracy differences between child and adult witnesses. Michael R. Leippe; Ann Romanczyk; Andrew P. Manion. *J. Appl. Psychol.* **76:3** 6:1991 pp. 367 – 379
159 In defense of everday memory. Martin A. Conway. *Am. Psychol.* **46:1** 1:1991 pp. 19 – 26
160 Perceived control over memory aging — developmental and intervention perspectives. Margie E. Lachman. *J. Soc. Issues* **47:4** 1991 pp. 159 – 176
161 Rater information acquisition processes — tracing the effects of prior knowledge, performance level, search constraint, and memory demand. Steve W.J. Kozlowski; J. Kevin Ford. *Organ. Beh. Hum. Dec. Proces.* **49:2** 8:1991 pp. 282 – 301
162 Recognition failure and the composite memory trace in CHARM. Janet Metcalfe. *Psychol. Rev.* **98:4** 10:1991 pp. 529 – 553
163 The relationship between implicit memory and implicit learning. Dianne C. Berry; Zoltan Dienes. *Br. J. Psy.* **82:3** 8:1991 pp. 359 – 374
164 Social memory in everyday life — recall of self-events and other-events. John J. Skowronski; Andrew L. Betz; Charles P. Thompson; Laura Shannon. *J. Pers. Soc. Psychol.* **60:6** 6:1991 pp. 831 – 843
165 Speech, "inner speech", and the development of short-term memory — effects of picture-labeling on recall. Graham J. Hitch; M. Sebastian Halliday; Alma M. Schaafstal; Thomas M. Heffernan. *J. Exper. Child Psychol.* **51:2** 4:1991 pp. 220 – 234
166 Working memory in children with specific arithmetical learning difficulties. Graham J. Hitch; Ellika McAuley. *Br. J. Psy.* **82:3** 8:1991 pp. 375 – 386

Motivation [Motivation]

167 Conditional probability judgments — effects of imagining vs experiencing the conditioning event. William S. Waller; Terence R. Mitchell. *Organ. Beh. Hum. Dec. Proces.* **49:2** 8:1991 pp. 302 – 324
168 Difficulty and instrumentality of imminent behavior as determinants of goal attractiveness. R.A. Wright; S.E. Gregorich. *Eur. J. Soc. Psychol.* **21:1** 1-2: 1991 pp. 75 – 88
169 Judgment processes in motivation — anchoring and adjustment effects on judgment and behavior. Fred S. Switzer; Janet A. Sniezek. *Organ. Beh. Hum. Dec. Proces.* **49:2** 8:1991 pp. 208 – 229
170 Metaphors in motivation and attribution. Bernard Weiner. *Am. Psychol.* **46:9** 9:1991 pp. 921 – 930
171 Moderating influence of self-motivating and gender on responses to humorous advertising. H. Bruce Lammers. *J. Soc. Psychol.* **131:1** 2:1991 pp. 57 – 70
172 Motivation and academic achievement — the effects of personality traits and the quality of experiences. Maria Mei-ha Wong; Mihaly Csikszentmihalyi. *J. Personal.* **59:3** 9:1991 pp. 539 – 574
173 The motivation for change from problem alcohol and heroin use; La motivation au changement par les problèmes de consommation d'alcool et d'héroïne *[French summary]*; La motivacion para el cambio en los problemas alcoholicos y de consumo de heroina *[Spanish summary]*. Harald K.-H. Klingemann. *Br. J. Addict.* **86:6** 6:1991 pp. 727 – 744
174 Motivation needs and their relationship to life success. Barbara Parker; Leonard H. Chusmir. *Human Relat.* **44:12** 12:1991 pp. 1301 – 1312
175 A perversion named desire; *[French summary]*; *[German summary]*; *[Spanish summary]*. Enrique R. Torres. *Int. J.Psy.* **72:1** 1991 pp. 73 – 92
176 Self- versus other-reward administration and intrinsic motivation. Michael E. Enzle; John P. Roggeveen; Sharon C. Look. *J. Exp. S. Psychol.* **27:5** 9:1991 pp. 468 – 479
177 Social and cognitive motivations of change — measuring variability in color semantics. Robert E. MacLaury. *Language* **67:1** 3:1991 pp. 34 – 62
178 Task-intrinsic and social-extrinsic sources of arousal for motives assessed in fantasy and self-report. Richard Koestner; Joel Weinberger; David C. McClelland. *J. Personal.* **59:1** 3:1991 pp. 57 – 82
179 Theory testing under adverse conditions — motivation to manage in the People's Republic of China. John B. Miner; Chao-Chuan Chen; K.C. Yu. *J. Appl. Psychol.* **76:3** 6:1991 pp. 343 – 349

C.2: Individuals [Individus] —

Personality [Personnalité]

180 Affective and semantic priming — effects of mood on category accessibility and inference. Ralph Erber. *J. Exp. S. Psychol.* **27:5** 9:1991 pp. 480–498

181 The altruistic personality — in what contexts is it apparent? Gustavo Carlo; Nancy Eisenberg; Debra Troyer; Galen Switzer; Anna L. Speer. *J. Pers. Soc. Psychol.* **61:3** 9:1991 pp. 450–458

182 Correlates of the temporal consistency of personality patterns in childhood. Jens B. Asendorpf; Marcel A.G. van Aken. *J. Personal.* **59:4** 12:1991 pp. 689–703

183 An ethological approach to personality development. Mary D. Salter Ainsworth; John Bowlby. *Am. Psychol.* **46:4** 4:1991 pp. 333–341

184 Evidence for the altruistic personality from data on accident research. Hans Werner Bierhoff; Renate Klein; Peter Kramp. *J. Personal.* **59:2** 6:1991 pp. 263–280

185 Family relationships and children's personality — a cross-cultural, cross-source comparison. William A. Scott; Ruth Scott; Morag McCabe. *Br. J. Soc. P.* **30:1** 3:1991 pp. 1–20

186 Handbook of personality — theory and research. Lawrence A. Pervin *[Ed.]*. New York: Guilford Press, c1990· 738 p. (ill) *ISBN: 0898624304.*

187 Individual differences are accentuated during periods of social change — the sample case of girls at puberty. Avshalom Caspi; Terrie E. Moffitt. *J. Pers. Soc. Psychol.* **61:1** 7:1991 pp. 157–168

188 Историческое развитие человека: филос. основу «фазовой» концепции развития соц.личности *[In Russian]*; [Historical development of man — philosophical basis "phase" concept of development of socialist personality]. V.P. Iarushkin. Saratov: Saratov University Publishers, 1987: 160 p.

189 Measures of personality and social psychological attitudes. John P. Robinson *[Ed.]*; Phillip R. Shaver *[Ed.]*; Lawrence S. Wrightsman *[Ed.]*; Frank M. Andrews *[Ed.]*. San Diego: Academic Press, c1991: xiv, 753 p. *ISBN: 0125902417; LofC: 90000091.* Includes bibliographical references. [Measures of social psychological attitudes. : Vol. 1]

190 Moral affect — the good, the bad, and the ugly. June Price Tangney. *J. Pers. Soc. Psychol.* **61:4** 10:1991 pp. 598–607

191 Multidimensionality of state and trait anxiety — factor structure of the Endler multidimensional anxiety scales. Norman S. Endler; James D.A. Parker; R. Michael Bagby; Brian J. Cox. *J. Pers. Soc. Psychol.* **60:6** 6:1991 pp. 919–926

192 Narcissistic self-esteem management. Robert Raskin; Jill Novacek; Robert Hogan. *J. Pers. Soc. Psychol.* **60:6** 6:1991 pp. 911–918

193 Научно-техническая революция и духовное развитие лиуности *[In Russian]*; [The scientific and technical revolution and the inner development of personality]. V.I. Kas'iana *[Ed.]*; O.V. Gaman; A.N. Goncharenko; P.A. Dovbush. Kiev: Vishcha shk., 1986: 215 p.

194 The next generation of moderator research in personality psychology. William F. Chaplin. *J. Personal.* **59:2** 6:1991 pp. 143–177

195 The nomological validity of the Type A personality among employed adults. Daniel C. Ganster; John Schaubroeck; Wesley E. Sime; Bronston T. Mayes. *J. Appl. Psychol.* **76:1** 2:1991 pp. 143–168

196 Nonverbal display of emotion in public and in private — self-monitoring, personality, and expressive cues. Howard S. Friedman; Terry Miller-Herringer. *J. Pers. Soc. Psychol.* **61:5** 11:1991 pp. 766–775

197 Нравств нность внутри нас. Структура индивидуал.нравств.сознания *[In Russian]*; [Morality within us. The structure of individual moral conscience]. V.A. Iakubanets. Riga: Avots, 1986: 293 p.

198 On confidence and consequence — the certainty and importance of self-knowledge. Brett W. Pelham. *J. Pers. Soc. Psychol.* **60:4** 4:1991 pp. 518–530

199 Personality and campus controversies — preferred boundaries as a function of openness to experience. Stephen J. Dollinger; Lisa A. Orf; Ann E. Robinson. *J. Psychol.* **125:4** 7:1991 pp. 399–406

200 Personality and daily experience. Howard Tennen *[Contrib.]*; Jerry Suls *[Contrib.]*; Glenn Affleck *[Contrib.]*; Ladd Wheeler *[Contrib.]*; Harry T. Reis *[Contrib.]*; Niall Bolger *[Contrib.]*; Elizabeth A. Schilling *[Contrib.]*; Randy J. Larsen *[Contrib.]*; Margaret Kasimatis *[Contrib.]*; Nancy Cantor *[Contrib.]* and others. Collection of 11 articles. **J. Personal.**, *59:3*, 9:1991 pp. 313–662

201 Personality and daily experience — the promise and the challenge. Howard Tennen; Jerry Suls; Glenn Affleck. *J. Personal.* **59:3** 9:1991 pp. 313–337

C.2: Individuals [Individus] — Personality [Personnalité]

202 Personality and susceptibility to positive and negative emotional states. Randy J. Larsen; Timothy Ketelaar. *J. Pers. Soc. Psychol.* **61:1** 7:1991 pp. 132 – 140

203 Personality and the problems of everyday life — the role of neuroticism in exposure and reactivity to daily stressors. Niall Bolger; Elizabeth A. Schilling. *J. Personal.* **59:3** 9:1991 pp. 355 – 386

204 Personality antecedents of depressive tendencies in 18-year-olds — a prospective study. Jack H. Block; Per F. Gjerde; Jeanne H. Block. *J. Pers. Soc. Psychol.* **60:5** 5:1991 pp. 726 – 738

205 Personality correlates of men who batter and nonviolent men — some continuities and discontinuities. L. Kevin Hamberger; James E. Hastings. *J. Fam. Viol.* **6:2** 6:1991 pp. 131 – 148

206 Personality, problem drinking, and drunk driving — mediating, moderating, and direct-effect models. Alan W. Stacy; Michael D. Newcomb; Peter M. Bentler. *J. Pers. Soc. Psychol.* **60:5** 5:1991 pp. 795 – 811

207 Predicting personality and behavior — a boundary on the acquaintanceship effect. C. Randall Colvin; David C. Funder. *J. Pers. Soc. Psychol.* **60:6** 6:1991 pp. 884 – 894

208 Probabilistic mental models — a Brunswikian theory of confidence. Gerd Gigerenzer; Ulrich Hoffrage; Heinz Kleinbölting. *Psychol. Rev.* **98:4** 10:1991 pp. 506 – 528

209 Psychological determinants of health and performance — the tangled web of desirable and undesirable characteristics. Ann S. Robbins; Janet T. Spence; Heather Clark. *J. Pers. Soc. Psychol.* **61:5** 11:1991 pp. 755 – 765

210 A psychotic organization of the personality; *[German summary]*; *[French summary]*; *[Spanish summary]*. John Steiner. *Int. J.Psy.* **72:2** 1991 pp. 201 – 208

211 The relationship between mood and subjective well-being. John K. Yardley; Robert W. Rice. *Soc. Ind.* **24:1** 2:1991 pp. 101 – 111

212 Self-congruence and the experience of happiness. Mario Mikulincer; Ilana Peer-Goldin. *Br. J. Soc. P.* **30:1** 3:1991 pp. 21 – 35

213 Situation cognition and coherence in personality — an individual-centred approach. Barbara Krahé. Cambridge: Cambridge University Press, 1991: 207 p. *ISBN: 0521352959. Includes index.* [European monographs in social psychology.]

214 Social selves — theories of the social formation of personality. Ian Burkitt *[Contrib.]*. Collection of 10 articles. **Curr. Sociol.**, *39:3*, Winter:1991 pp. 1 – 215

215 Stability and change in psychological distress and their relationship with self-esteem and locus of control — a dynamic equilibrium model. Johan Ormel; Wilmar B. Schaufeli. *J. Pers. Soc. Psychol.* **60:2** 2:1991 pp. 288 – 299

216 Структура и развития лиуности *[In Russian]*; [Structure and development of personality]. K.K. Platonov. Moscow: Nauka, 1986: 255 p. [An USSR. Institute of Psychology.]

217 Традиции, обряды в системе формирования идеалов личности *[In Russian]*; [Traditions, ceremonies in the system of forming of ideals of personality]. V.S. Chernyshev. Kiev: Vishcha shk. Kiev University Publishers, 1986: 143 p. *Bibliogr. pp.136-142.*

218 Type A behavior, its prevalence and consequences among women nurses — an empirical examination. Muhammad Jamal; Vishwanath V. Baba. *Human Relat.* **44:11** 11:1991 pp. 1213 – 1228

219 Understanding behavior in the Milgram obedience experiment — the role of personality, situations, and their interactions. Thomas Blass. *J. Pers. Soc. Psychol.* **60:3** 3:1991 pp. 398 – 413

220 Varieties of moral personality — ethics and psychological realism. Owen J. Flanagan. Cambridge, Mass.: Harvard University Press, 1991: 393 p. *ISBN: 0674932188.*

Self-concept [Conception de soi]

221 Alterity, identity, image — selves and others in society and scholarship. Raymond Corbey *[Ed.]*; Joep Leerssen *[Ed.]*. Amsterdam: Rodopi, 1991: xviii, 252 p. (ill) *ISBN: 9051832524. eng, fre; Text in English or French; Includes bibliographical references.* [Amsterdam studies on cultural identity. : No. 1]

222 The autogenesis of self. Michael L. Schwalbe. *J. Theory Soc. Behav.* **21:3** 9:1991 pp. 269 – 296

223 Binge eating as escape from self-awareness. Todd F. Heatherton; Roy F. Baumeister. *Psychol. B.* **110:1** 7:1991 pp. 86 – 108

C.2: Individuals [Individus] — Self-concept [Conception de soi]

224 Development and validation of a scale for measuring state self-esteem. Todd F. Heatherton; Janet Polivy. *J. Pers. Soc. Psychol.* **60:6** 6:1991 pp. 895 – 910

225 The development of the sense of self in adolescence. Augusto Blasi; Kathy Milton. *J. Personal.* **59:2** 6:1991 pp. 217 – 241

226 Differentiated additive androgyny model — relations between masculinity, femininity, and multiple dimensions of self-concept. Herbert W. Marsh; Barbara M. Byrne. *J. Pers. Soc. Psychol.* **61:5** 11:1991 pp. 811 – 828

227 Esteem protection or enhancement? Self-handicapping motives and attributions differ by trait self-esteem. Dianne M. Tice. *J. Pers. Soc. Psychol.* **60:5** 5:1991 pp. 711 – 725

228 Everybody's got a little mental illness — accounts of illness and self among people with severe, persistent mental illness. Sue Estroff; William S. Lachicotte; Linda C. Illingworth; Anna Johnston. *Med. Anthr. Q.* **5:4** 12:1991 pp. 331 – 369

229 From high school to college — changes in women's self concept and its relationship to eating problems. Sharlene Hesse-Biber; Margaret Marino. *J. Psychol.* **125:2** 3:1991 pp. 199 – 216

230 Ideology obscured — political uses of the self in Daniel Stern's infant. Philip Cushman. *Am. Psychol.* **46:3** 3:1991 pp. 206 – 219

231 Narcissism, self-esteem, and defensive self-enhancement. Robert Raskin; Jill Novacek, Robert Hogan. *J. Personal.* **59:1** 3:1991 pp. 19 – 38

232 On the confluence of self processes. Abraham Tesser; David P. Cornell. *J. Exp. S. Psychol.* **27:6** 11:1991 pp. 501 – 526

233 Provoking jealousy and envy — domain relevance and self-esteem threat. Peter Salovey; Judith Rodin. *J. Soc. Clin. Psychol.* **10:4** Winter:1991 pp. 395 – 413

234 Self- and object-directedness in adult women. Paul Wink. *J. Personal.* **59:4** 12:1991 pp. 769 – 791

235 Self-consciousness and strategic self-presentation. Kevin Doherty; Barry R. Schlenker. *J. Personal.* **59:1** 3:1991 pp. 1 – 18

236 Self-discrepancies and vulnerability to body dissatisfaction and disordered eating. Timothy J. Strauman; Jennifer Vookles; Veronica Berenstein; Shelly Chaiken; E. Tory Higgins. *J. Pers. Soc. Psychol.* **61:6** 12:1991 pp. 946 – 956

237 Self-handicapping — the role of discounting and augmentation in the preservation of self-esteem. Frederick Rhodewalt; Carolyn Morf; Susan Hazlett; Marita Fairfield. *J. Pers. Soc. Psychol.* **61:1** 7:1991 pp. 122 – 131

238 Self-image and guilt — a further test of the cognitive-developmental formulation. Jane A. Bybee; Edward Zigler. *J. Personal.* **59:4** 12:1991 pp. 733 – 745

239 Self-stereotyping and self-enhancement in gender groups. F. Lorenzi-Cioldi. *Eur. J. Soc. Psychol.* **21:5** 9-10:1991 pp. 403 – 418

240 Solitude, concept de soi et anxiété sociale *[In French]*; Loneliness, self-concept and social anxiety *[Summary]*. F. Neto. *Cah. Anthr. Bio. Hum.* **VVI:3-4** 1989 pp. 173 – 180

241 Социальная природа самосознания *[In Russian]*; [Social nature of self-consciousness]. E.F. Zvezdkina. Krasnoiarsk: Krasnoiarsk University Publishers, 1986: 196 p. *Bibliogr.* pp.183-195.

C.3: Interpersonal relations — *Relations interpersonnelles*

Sub-divisions: Altruism *[Altruisme]*; Conflict *[Conflit]*; Emotions *[Emotions]*; Partners *[Partenaires]*; Social perception *[Perception sociale]*

1 Accommodation processes in close relationships — theory and preliminary empirical evidence. Caryl E. Rusbult; Julie Verette; Gregory A. Whitney; Linda F. Slovik; Isaac Lipkus. *J. Pers. Soc. Psychol.* **60:1** 1:1991 pp. 53 – 78

2 Adjustment, depression, and minimal goal setting — the moderating effect of performance feedback. Salvatore J. Catanzaro. *J. Personal.* **59:2** 6:1991 pp. 243 – 261

3 Adolescent functioning — communication and the buffering of parental anger. Abraham Tesser; Rex Forehand. *J. Soc. Clin. Psychol.* **10:2** Summer:1991 pp. 152 – 175

4 ADR and life in Israel. David Matz. *Negot. J.* **7:1** 1: 1991 pp. 11 – 16

5 Affective influences on partner choice — role of mood in social decisions. Joseph P. Forgas. *J. Pers. Soc. Psychol.* **61:5** 11:1991 pp. 708 – 720

6 Affiliation motivation and daily experience — some issues on gender differences. Maria Mei-ha Wong; Mihaly Csikszentmihalyi. *J. Pers. Soc. Psychol.* **60:1** 1:1991 pp. 154 – 164

C.3: Interpersonal relations [Relations interpersonnelles]

7 L'amitié, les amis, leur histoire [In French]; Friendship, friends, their story [Summary]. Claire Bidart. *Soc. Contemp.* :**5** 3:1991 pp. 21 – 42
8 Attachment style and the structure of romantic love. Mario Mikulincer; Irit Erev. *Br. J. Soc. P.* **30:4** 12:1991 pp. 273 – 292
9 Attachment styles among young adults — a test of a four-category model. Kim Bartholomew; Leonard M. Horowitz. *J. Pers. Soc. Psychol.* **61:2** 8:1991 pp. 226 – 244
10 Attachment styles and patterns of self-disclosure. Mario Mikulincer; Orna Nachshon. *J. Pers. Soc. Psychol.* **61:2** 8:1991 pp. 321 – 331
11 Attributions as moderators of reactions to computer-simulated responsive and unresponsive children. Jeffrey Clayton Lewis; Daphne Blunt Bugental; Karen Fleck. *Soc. Cogn.* **9:3** Fall:1991 pp. 277 – 293
12 Beliefs about conversation abandonment — I do — you don't — but we will. R.A. Reynolds. *J. Lang. Soc. Psychol.* **10:1** 1991 pp. 61 – 70
13 Betrayal and betrayers — the sociology of treachery. Malin Akerström. New Brunswick (U.S.A.): Transaction Publishers, c1991: xiii, 152 p. (ill) *ISBN: 0887383580; LofC: 90010800. Includes bibliographical references (p. 141-148) and index.*
14 Children's interpersonal trust — sensitivity to lying, deception, and promise violations. Ken J. Rotenberg [Ed.]. New York: Springer-Verlag, c1991: viii, 172 p. (ill) *ISBN: 038797511x; LofC: 90025448. Includes bibliographical references.*
15 Close relationships as including other in the self. Arthur Aron; Elaine N. Aron; Michael Tudor; Greg Nelson. *J. Pers. Soc. Psychol.* **60:2** 2:1991 pp. 241 – 253
16 Communication network influences on information diffusion and persuasion. Mieneke W.H. Weenig; Cees J.H. Midden. *J. Pers. Soc. Psychol.* **61:5** 11:1991 pp. 734 – 742
17 The concept of consciousness — the interpersonal meaning. Thomas Natsoulas. *J. Theory Soc. Behav.* **21:1** 3:1991 pp. 63 – 89
18 La confidence — des relations au réseau [In French]; Confidence — from relations to network [Summary]. Alexis Ferrand. *Soc. Contemp.* :**5** 3:1991 pp. 7 – 20
19 Confusing one person with another — what errors reveal about the elementary forms of social relations. Alan Page Fiske; Nick Haslam; Susan T. Fiske. *J. Pers. Soc. Psychol.* **60:5** 5:1991 pp. 656 – 674
20 Controlling the ramifications of disclosure — "don't tell anybody but....". S. Petronio; C. Bantz. *J. Lang. Soc. Psychol.* **10:4** 1991 pp. 263 – 269
21 Cooperation and prosocial behaviour. Jo Groebel [Ed.]; Robert A. Hinde [Ed.]. Cambridge [England]: Cambridge University Press, 1991: 365 p. *ISBN: 0521391105; LofC: 91009981.*

22 Coordinated interpersonal timing of vision and voice as a function of interpersonal attraction. C.L. Crown. *J. Lang. Soc. Psychol.* **10:1** 1991 pp. 29 – 46
23 Coping with a breakup — negative mood regulation expectancies and depression following the end of a romantic relationship. Jack Mearns. *J. Pers. Soc. Psychol.* **60:2** 2:1991 pp. 327 – 334
24 Counterfactual reasoning as a framework for attribution theories. Marlys Gascho Lipe. *Psychol .B.* **109:3** 5:1991 pp. 456 – 471
25 Courtesy stigma — the social implications of associating with a gay person. Carol K. Sigelman; Jennifer L. Howell; David P. Cornell; John D. Cutright; Janine C. Dewey. *J. Soc. Psychol.* **131:1** 2:1991 pp. 45 – 56
26 Crisis bargaining — tracking relational paradox in hostage negotiation. William A. Donohue; Closepet Ramesh; Carl Borchgrevink. *Int. J. Confl. Manag.* **2:4** 10:1991 pp. 257 – 274
27 Crisis management — the psychological dimension. D.G. Doepel. *Ind. Crisis Q.* **5:3** :1991 pp. 177 – 188
28 Determinants of readiness for contact with Jewish children among young Arab students in Israel. Abraham Yogev; Naama Sabar Ben-Yehoshua; Yael Alper. *Confl. Resolut.* **35:3** 9:1991 pp. 547 – 562
29 Differential effects of identification with family and peers on coping with developmental tasks in adolescence. A. Palmonari; E. Kirchler; M.L. Pombeni. *Eur. J. Soc. Psychol.* **21:5** 9-10:1991 pp. 381 – 402
30 Do conversational hand gestures communicate? Robert M. Krauss; Palmer Morrel-Samuels; Christina Colasante. *J. Pers. Soc. Psychol.* **61:5** 11:1991 pp. 743 – 754
31 The effects of agreement, disagreement, gender and familiarity on patterns of dyadic interaction. A. McLachlan. *J. Lang. Soc. Psychol.* **10:3** 1991 pp. 205 – 212
32 Enhancement and denial in socially desirable responding. Delroy L. Paulhus; Douglas B. Reid. *J. Pers. Soc. Psychol.* **60:2** 2:1991 pp. 307 – 317

C.3: Interpersonal relations *[Relations interpersonnelles]*

33 Equity theory and exchange and communal orientation from a cross-national perspective. Nico W. VanYperen; Bram P. Buunk. *J. Soc. Psychol.* **131:1** 2:1991 pp. 5 – 20

34 An examination of how far close relationships are essential for our mental health. Rod Taylor. *App. Commun. Stud.* **1:1** 1991 pp. 5 – 15

35 Friendship patterns and culture — the control of organizational diversity. David Krackhardt; Martin Kilduff. *Am. Anthrop.* **92:1** 3:1990 pp. 142 – 154

36 From "normal appearances" to "simulation" in interaction. Andrew Travers. *J. Theory Soc. Behav.* **21:3** 9:1991 pp. 297 – 338

37 Homelessness and affiliation. Mark la Gory; Ferris J. Ritchey; Kevin M. Fitzpatrick. *Sociol. Q.* **32:2** Summer:1991 pp. 201 – 218

38 Human relationships — a philosophical introduction. Paul Gilbert. Oxford, UK: B. Blackwell, 1991: 164 p. *ISBN: 0631171576; LofC: 91012475. Includes bibliographical references and index.* [Philosophical introductions.]

39 The impact of an unpleasant and demeaning social interaction. Amerigo Farina; David S. Wheeler; Sheila Mehta. *J. Soc. Clin. Psychol.* **10:4** Winter:1991 pp. 351 – 371

40 The impact of stress on cognitive components of child abuse potential. Cynthia J. Schellenbach; Linda D. Monroe; Thomas V. Merluzzi. *J. Fam. Viol.* **6:1** 3:1991 pp. 61 – 79

41 Increasing consensus in trait judgments through outcome dependency. Cheryl Flink; Bernadette Park. *J. Exp. S. Psychol.* **27:5** 9:1991 pp. 453 – 467

42 Indirect majority and minority influence — an exploratory study. V. Brandstätter; N. Ellemers; E. Gaviria; F. Giosue; P. Huguet; M. Kroon; P. Morchain; M. Pujal; M. Rubini; G. Mugny and others.*Eur. J. Soc. Psychol.* **21:3** 5-6:1991 pp. 199 – 211

43 The influence of peers and parents on youth life satisfaction in Hong Kong. Peter Man. *Soc. Ind.* **24:4** 6:1991 pp. 347 – 365

44 Information exchange in negotiation. Leigh L. Thompson. *J. Exp. S. Psychol.* **27:2** 3:1991 pp. 161 – 179

45 Integrating speech information across talkers, gender, and sensory modality — female faces and male voices in the McGurk effect. Kerry P. Green; Patricia K. Kuhl; Andrew N. Meltzoff; Erica B. Stevens. *Perc. Psych.* **50:6** 12:1991 pp. 524 – 536

46 Interactive effects of need for closure and initial confidence on social information seeking. Arie W. Kruglanski; Nathaniel Peri; Dan Zakai. *Soc. Cogn.* **9:2** Summer:1991 pp. 127 – 148

47 Interpersonal choice and networks in China. Peter M. Blau; Danching Ruan; Monika Ardelt. *Soc. Forc.* **69:4** 6:1991 pp. 1037 – 1062

48 Interpersonal communication research as ideological practice. John W. Lannamann. *Commun. Theory* **1:3** 8:1991 pp. 179 – 203

49 Interpersonal comparisons of well-being. Jon Elster *[Ed.]*; John E. Roemer *[Ed.]*. Cambridge: Cambridge University Press, 1991: - *ISBN: 0521392748. Conference proceedings; Includes index.* [Studies in rationality and social change.]

50 Interpersonal expectancies and social anxiety in anticipating interaction. Miles L. Patterson; Mary E. Churchill; Jack L. Powell. *J. Soc. Clin. Psychol.* **10:4** Winter:1991 pp. 414 – 423

51 Jewish humour on psychoanalysis; *[French summary]; [German summary]; [Spanish summary]*. David Meghnagi. *Int. Rev. Psy.* **18:2** 1991 pp. 223 – 228

52 Kuan-hsi and network building — a sociological interpretation. Ambrose Yeo-chi King. *Dædalus* **120:2** Spring:1991 pp. 63 – 84

53 "A language with taste" — uses of proverbial sayings in intercultural communication. Susanne Günthner. *Text* **11:3** 1991 pp. 399 – 418

54 Learning to cooperate — stochastic and tacit collusion in social exchange. Michael W. Macy. *A.J.S.* **97:3** 11:1991 pp. 808 – 842

55 The low robustness of the low gain effect of interpersonal attraction — some empirical and theoretical considerations. M. Koller. *Eur. J. Soc. Psychol.* **21:3** 5-6:1991 pp. 239 – 248

56 Отчуждение в советском обществе: методологический аспект проблемы *[In Russian]*; (Alienation in Soviet society — methodological aspect of the problem). I.I. Kalnoy; M.B. Sapunov; E.N. Fetison. *Sot. Issle.* **:5** 1991 pp. 18 – 25

57 The other half of the picture — antecedents of spouse cross-cultural adjustment. J. Stewart Black; Hal B. Gregersen. *J. Int. Bus. Stud.* **22:3** Third quarter:1991 pp. 461 – 477

58 Partner preferences in middle school children's playful fighting and chasing — a test of some competing functional hypotheses. Michael J. Boulton. *Ethol. Socio.* **12:3** 1991 pp. 177 – 194

C.3: Interpersonal relations [Relations interpersonnelles]

59 Patterns of dominance and imitation in an infant peer group. A.E. Russon; B.E. Waite. *Ethol. Socio.* **12:1** 1991 pp. 55 – 73
60 The perceived causal structure of loneliness. Peter K. Lunt. *J. Pers. Soc. Psychol.* **61:1** 7:1991 pp. 26 – 34
61 *[In Japanese]*; [Personal relations in an age of information overload]. Keiko Hosotsuji. *Shakai Kagaku No.(47) - 1991.* pp. 337 – 350
62 Politeness and forms of address. L.S. Wood; R.O. Kroger. *J. Lang. Soc. Psychol.* **10:3** 1991 pp. 145 – 168
63 Potere e controllo in Norbert Elias *[In Italian]*; Power and control in Norbert Elias *[Summary].* Franco Crespi. *Rass. It. Soc.* **32:1** 1-3:1991 pp. 81 – 93
64 Predictors, elicitors, and concomitants of social blushing. Mark R. Leary; Sarah Meadows. *J. Pers. Soc. Psychol.* **60:2** 2:1991 pp. 254 – 262
65 Public confession and forgiveness. Bernard Weiner; Sandra Graham; Orli Peter; Mary Zmuidinas. *J. Personal.* **59:2** 6:1991 pp. 281 – 312
66 Братство *[In Russian]*; (Fraternity). E.I. Rerih. *Sot. Issle.* **:5** 1991 pp. 133 – 145
67 Reciprocity and cooperation in social dilemmas. S.S. Komorita; J.A. Hilty; C.D. Parks. *Confl. Resolut.* **35:3** 9:1991 pp. 494 – 518
68 Remembering facial configurations. Vicki Bruce; Tony Doyle; Neal Dench; Mike Burton. *Cognition* **38:2** 2:1991 pp. 109 – 144
69 Role relationships and their realization in mood and modality. Zhang Delu. *Text* **11:2** :1991 pp. 289 – 317
70 The self and social conduct — linking self-representations to prosocial behavior. Jonathon D. Brown; S. April Smart. *J. Pers. Soc. Psychol.* **60:3** 3:1991 pp. 368 – 375
71 Self-derogations and the interpersonal theory. Leonard M. Horowitz; Kenneth D. Locke; Marjorie B. Morse; Sachin V. Waikar; D. Christopher Dryer; Eugen Tarnow; Jess Ghannam. *J. Pers. Soc. Psychol.* **61:1** 7:1991 pp. 68 – 75
72 Self-esteem, similarity, and reactions to active versus passive downward comparison. Frederick X. Gibbons; Sue Boney McCoy. *J. Pers. Soc. Psychol.* **60:3** 3:1991 pp. 414 – 424
73 The self-society dynamic — cognition, emotion, and action. Judith A. Howard *[Ed.]*; Peter L. Callero *[Ed.].* Cambridge: Cambridge University Press, 1991: 337 p. *ISBN: 0521384338.*
74 Social communication and self identification — participatory behavior on the freeway. Adalberto Aguirre. *J. Pop. Cult.* **24:2** Fall:1990 pp. 91 – 102
75 Social comparisons with siblings made by adolescents with a learning difficulty. S.E. Szivos. *J. Comm. App. Soc. Psychol.* **1:3** 9:1991 pp. 201 – 212
76 Social influence processes affecting adolescent substance use. John W. Graham; Gary Marks; William B. Hansen. *J. Appl. Psychol.* **76:2** 4:1991 pp. 291 – 298
77 Social influence — the role of originality. A. Mucchi-Faina; A. Maass; C. Volpato. *Eur. J. Soc. Psychol.* **21:3** 5-6:1991 pp. 183 – 197
78 Social judgements of sex and blame in the context of AIDS — gender and linguistic frame. R. Spears; D. Abrams; P. Sheeran; S.C.S. Abraham; D. Marks. *Br. J. Soc. P.* **30:1** 3:1991 pp. 37 – 49
79 Social relationships and vulnerability to becoming homeless among poor families. Marybeth Shinn; James R. Knickman; Beth C. Weitzman. *Am. Psychol.* **46:11** 11:1991 pp. 1180 – 1187
80 Social stigma — the affective consequences of attributional ambiguity. Jennifer Crocker; Kristin Voelkl; Maria Testa; Brenda Major. *J. Pers. Soc. Psychol.* **60:2** 2:1991 pp. 218 – 228
81 Sociality of solitary smiling — potentiation by an implicit audience. Alan J. Fridlund. *J. Pers. Soc. Psychol.* **60:2** 2:1991 pp. 229 – 240
82 A sociology of smell; *[French summary].* Anthony Synnott. *Can. R. Soc. A.* **28:4** 11:1991 pp. 437 – 459
83 Some consequences of deep interruption in task-oriented communication. K. Hawkins. *J. Lang. Soc. Psychol.* **10:3** 1991 pp. 185 – 204
84 Spiritual well-being, social desirability and reasons for living — is there a connection? Jon. B. Ellis; Peggy C. Smith. *Int. J. Soc. Psyc.* **37:1** Spring: 1991 pp. 57 – 63
85 Status processes in enduring work groups. Bernard P. Cohen; Xueguang Zhou. *Am. Sociol. R.* **56:2** 4:1991 pp. 179 – 188
86 The storytelling organization — a study of story performance in an office-supply firm. David M. Boje. *Adm. Sci. Qua.* **36:1** 3:1991 p. 106

C.3: Interpersonal relations [Relations interpersonnelles]

87 Stranger intervention into child punishment in public places. Phillip W. Davis. *Soc. Prob.* **38:2** 5:1991 pp. 227 – 246
88 *[In Japanese]*; [A study of "iiwake (excuse)" in social interaction — introduction]. Tomihide Kashioka. *Nihon Kenkyu No.(4) - 1991.* pp. 113 – 121
89 Transactive memory in close relationships. Daniel M. Wegner; Ralph Erber; Paula Raymond. *J. Pers. Soc. Psychol.* **61:6** 12:1991 pp. 923 – 929
90 Turning points in the INF negotiations. Daniel Druckman; Jo L. Husbands; Karin Johnston. *Negot. J.* **7:1** 1: 1991 pp. 55 – 68
91 Value congruence and satisfaction with a leader — an examination of the role of interaction. Bruce M. Meglino; Elizabeth C. Ravlin; Cheryl L. Adkins. *Human Relat.* **44:5** 5:1991 pp. 481 – 495
92 What is beautiful is good, but... — a meta-analytic review of research on the physical attractiveness stereotype. Alice H. Eagly; Richard D. Ashmore; Mona G. Makhijani; Laura C. Longo. *Psychol .B.* **110:1** 7:1991 pp. 109 – 128
93 When in doubt... — cooperation in a noisy prisoner's dilemma. Jonathon Bendor; Roderick M. Kramer; Suzanne Stout. *Confl. Resolut.* **35:4** 12:1991 pp. 691 – 719
94 A willingness to talk — conciliatory gestures and de-escalation. C.R. Mitchell. *Negot. J.* **7:4** 10.1991 pp. 405 – 430

Altruism [Altruisme]

95 Acts of compassion — caring for others and helping ourselves. Robert Wuthnow. Princeton, N.J: Princeton University Press, c1991: viii, 334 p. *ISBN: 0691073902; LofC: 91002128. Includes bibliographical references (p. 311-330) and index.*
96 Altruism and sociology. Roberta G. Simmons. *Sociol. Q.* **32:1** Spring:1991 pp. 1 – 22
97 Altruism as a motivation to volunteer. L.S. Unger. *J. Econ. Psyc.* **12:1** 3:1991 pp. 71 – 100
98 The altruism question — toward a social psychological answer. C. Daniel Batson. Hillsdale, N.J: L. Erlbaum, 1991: ix, 257 p. *ISBN: 0805802452; LofC: 91006758. Includes bibliographical references and index.*
99 Compassion. Nancy E. Snow. *Am. Phil. Q.* **28:3** 7:1991 pp. 195 – 206
100 Empathic joy and the empathy-altruism hypothesis. C. Daniel Batson; Judy G. Batson; Jacqueline K. Slingsby; Kevin L. Harrell; Heli M. Peekna; R. Matthew Todd. *J. Pers. Soc. Psychol.* **61:3** 9:1991 pp. 413 – 426
101 Empathy, effectiveness and donations to charity — social psychology's contribution. Peter E. Warren; Iain Walker. *Br. J. Soc. P.* **30:4** 12:1991 pp. 325 – 338
102 Might versus morality explored — motivational and cognitive bases for social motives. David N. Sattler; Norbert L. Kerr. *J. Pers. Soc. Psychol.* **60:5** 5:1991 pp. 756 – 765
103 On promoting altruistic behavior. Vivek Patkar. *J. Soc. Biol. Struct.* **14:1** :1991 pp. 67 – 72

Conflict [Conflit]

104 The arbitration of fighting cases. Donald J. Peterson. *Int. J. Confl. Manag.* **2:3** 7:1991 pp. 201 – 216
105 Barriers to conflict resolution. Lee Ross; Constance Stillinger. *Negot. J.* **7:4** 10:1991 pp. 389 – 404
106 Chinese conflict preferences and negotiating behaviour — cultural and psychological influences. Paul S. Kirkbride; Sara F.Y. Tang; Robert I. Westwood. *Organ. Stud.* **12:3** 1991 pp. 365 – 385
107 Communication within a dispute mediation — interactants' perceptions of the process. Claudia L. Hale; Cathy Bast; Betsy Gordon. *Int. J. Confl. Manag.* **2:2** 4:1991 pp. 139 – 157
108 Community mediation in the People's Republic of China. James A. Wall; Michael Blum. *Confl. Resolut.* **35:1** 3:1991 pp. 3 – 20
109 Conflict resolution — cross-cultural perspectives. Kevin Avruch *[Ed.]*; Peter W. Black *[Ed.]*; Joseph A. Scimecca *[Ed.]*. New York: Greenwood Press, 1991: x, 244 p. (ill) *ISBN: 0313257965; LofC: 91015991. Conflict; Includes bibliographical references and index.* [Contributions in ethnic studies.]
110 Conflict strategies adolescents use with their parents — testing the cognitive communicator characteristics model. J. Comstock; D.B. Buller. *J. Lang. Soc. Psychol.* **10:1** 1991 pp. 47 – 60
111 A cross-cultural comparison of organizational conflict management behaviors. Hyun O. Lee; Randall G. Rogan. *Int. J. Confl. Manag.* **2:3** 7:1991 pp. 181 – 199

C.3: Interpersonal relations [Relations interpersonnelles] — Conflict [Conflit]

112 Culture, face maintenance, and styles of handling interpersonal conflict — a study in five cultures. Stella Ting-Toomey; Ge Gao; Paula Trubisky; Zhizhong Yang; Hak Soo Kim; Sung-Ling Lin; Tsukasa Nishida. *Int. J. Confl. Manag.* **2:4** 10:1991 pp. 275 – 296

113 Dispute resolution without disputing — how the interactional organization of mediation hearings minimizes argument. Angela Garcia. *Am. Sociol. R.* **56:6** 12:1991 pp. 818 – 835

114 General alignment and over support in biased mediation. Jerry M. Wittmer; Peter Carnevale; Michael E. Walker. *Confl. Resolut.* **35:4** 12:1991 pp. 594 – 610

115 Getting, spending — and losing — power in dispute systems design. Stephen B. Goldberg; Jeanne M. Brett. *Negot. J.* **7:2** 4:1991 pp. 119 – 129

116 Injustice and organizational conflict — the moderating effects of power restoration. Russell Cropanzano; Robert A. Baron. *Int. J. Confl. Manag.* **2:1** 1:1991 pp. 5 – 26

117 International mediation and dispute settlement — evaluating the conditions for successful mediation. Jacob Bercovitch. *Negot. J.* **7:1** 1: 1991 pp. 17 – 30

118 Mea culpa — a sociology of apology and reconciliation. Nicholas Tavuchis. Stanford, Calif: Stanford University Press, 1991: ix, 165 p. *ISBN: 0804719365; LofC: 91016463. Includes bibliographical references (p. [161]-165).*

119 Shame, anger, and conflict — case study of emotional violence. Suzanne M. Retzinger. *J. Fam. Viol.* **6:1** 3:1991 pp. 37 – 60

120 Value differences and conflict resolution — familiarity or liking? Daniel Druckman; Benjamin J. Broome. *Confl. Resolut.* **35:4** 12:1991 pp. 571 – 593

121 When negotiations fail — causes of breakdown and tactics for breaking the stalemate. Bryan M. Downie. *Negot. J.* **7:2** 4:1991 pp. 175 – 185

Emotions [Emotions]

122 Dangerous situations — social context and fear of victimization. Mark Warr. *Soc. Forc.* **68:3** 3:1990 pp. 891 – 907

123 Dimensions of love — a sociobiological interpretation. Clyde Hendrick; Susan S. Hendrick. *J. Soc. Clin. Psychol.* **10:2** Summer:1991 pp. 206 – 230

124 The effects of anger on negotiations over mergers and acquisitions. Joseph P. Daly. *Negot. J.* **7:1** 1: 1991 pp. 31 – 40

125 Emotions and rationality. F.M. Berenson. *Int. J. Moral Soc. S.* **6:1** Spring:1991 pp. 33 – 46

126 Experience and expression — the moral linguistic constitution of emotions. George Turski. *J. Theory Soc. Behav.* **21:4** 12:1991 pp. 373 – 392

127 Grief reactions and effective negotiation. Nancy Lewis Buck. *Negot. J.* **7:1** 1: 1991 pp. 69 – 86

128 In defense of a prototype approach to emotion concepts. James A. Russell. *J. Pers. Soc. Psychol.* **60:1** 1:1991 pp. 37 – 47

129 Love, friendship, and the aesthetics of character. David Novitz. *Am. Phil. Q.* **28:3** 7:1991 pp. 207 – 216

130 Maintaining organizational norms about expressed emotions — the case of bill collectors. Robert I. Sutton. *Adm. Sci. Qua.* **36:2** 6:1991 pp. 245 – 268

131 On status competition and emotion management. Cas Wouters. *J. Soc. Hist* **24:4** Summer:1991 pp. 699 – 718

132 Personality and socialization correlates of vicarious emotional responding. Nancy Eisenberg; Richard A. Fabes; Mark Schaller; Paul Miller; Gustavo Carlo; Rick Poulin; Cindy Shea; Rita Shell. *J. Pers. Soc. Psychol.* **61:3** 9:1991 pp. 459 – 470

133 Reactions to and willingness to express emotion in communal and exchange relationships. Margaret S. Clark; Carolyn Taraban. *J. Exp. S. Psychol.* **27:4** 7:1991 pp. 324 – 336

134 Recognition of emotion from facial expression via imitation? Some indirect evidence for an old theory. Harold G. Wallbott. *Br. J. Soc. P.* **30:3** 9:1991 pp. 207 – 219

135 The robustness of communication of emotion via facial expression — emotion recognition from photographs with deteriorated pictorial quality. H.G. Wallbott. *Eur. J. Soc. Psychol.* **21:1** 1-2: 1991 pp. 89 – 98

136 Seeking emotional support — the influence of affiliative need and partner warmth. Craig A. Hill. *J. Pers. Soc. Psychol.* **60:1** 1:1991 pp. 112 – 121

137 Self- versus peer ratings of specific emotional traits — evidence of convergent and discriminant validity. David Watson; Lee Anna Clark. *J. Pers. Soc. Psychol.* **60:6** 6:1991 pp. 927 – 940

138 *[In Japanese]*; [Shame and shame-related emotions — a sociological study]. Yoshinori Takahashi. ***Jinbun*** *No.(37) - 1991.* pp. 32 – 73

C.3: Interpersonal relations *[Relations interpersonnelles]* — **Emotions** *[Emotions]*

139 Shame, anger, and conflict — case study of emotional violence. Suzanne M. Retzinger. *J. Fam. Viol.* **6:1** 3:1991 pp. 37 – 60

140 Socioemotional behaviour and satisfaction in marital relationships — a longitudinal study. Ted L. Huston; Anita L. Vangelisti. *J. Pers. Soc. Psychol.* **61:5** 11:1991 pp. 721 – 733

Partners *[Partenaires]*

141 Correlates of relationship satisfaction in cohabiting gay and lesbian couples — integration of contextual, investment, and problem-solving models. Lawrence A. Kurdek. *J. Pers. Soc. Psychol.* **61:6** 12:1991 pp. 910 – 922

142 Moral reasoning and marital exchange relationship. Gary L. Hansen. *J. Soc. Psychol.* **131:1** 2:1991 pp. 71 – 81

143 Psychological aggression in dating relationships — the role of interpersonal control. Jan E. Stets. *J. Fam. Viol.* **6:1** 3:1991 pp. 97 – 114

144 Role of femininity and masculinity in distressed couples' communication. Steven L. Sayers; Donald H. Baucom. *J. Pers. Soc. Psychol.* **61:4** 10:1991 pp. 641 – 647

145 Seeking emotional support — the influence of affiliative need and partner warmth. Craig A. Hill. *J. Pers. Soc. Psychol.* **60:1** 1.1991 pp. 112 – 121

146 Shyness and physical attractiveness in mixed-sex dyads. Stella Garcia; Linda Stinson; William Ickes; Victor Bissonnette; Stephen R. Briggs. *J. Pers. Soc. Psychol.* **61:1** 7:1991 pp. 35 – 49

Social perception *[Perception sociale]*

147 Accuracy in social perception — contributions of facial and vocal information. Diane S. Berry. *J. Pers. Soc. Psychol.* **61:2** 8:1991 pp. 298 – 307

148 Automatic vigilance — the attention-grabbing power of negative social information. Felicia Pratto; Oliver P. John. *J. Pers. Soc. Psychol.* **61:3** 9:1991 pp. 380 – 391

149 Categorical effects on attributional inferences — a response-time analysis. C. Neil Macrae; John W. Shepherd. *Br. J. Soc. P.* **30:3** 9:1991 pp. 235 – 245

150 Dysphoria and social comparison — combining information regarding others' performances. Anthony H. Ahrens. *J. Soc. Clin. Psychol.* **10:2** Summer:1991 pp. 190 – 205

151 Mission destination, mission duration, gender, and student perceptions of space habitat acceptibility. Albert A. Harrison; Nancy J. Struthers; Bernard J. Putz. *Envir. Behav.* **23:2** 3:1991 pp. 221 – 232

152 On the accuracy of ratings of personality by strangers. Sampo V. Paunonen. *J. Pers. Soc. Psychol.* **61:3** 9:1991 pp. 471 – 478

153 Perceived social support and working models of self and actual others. Barbara R. Sarason; Gregory R. Pierce; Edward N. Shearin; Irwin G. Sarason; Jennifer A. Waltz; Leslie Poppe. *J. Pers. Soc. Psychol.* **60:2** 2:1991 pp. 273 – 267

154 Perceiving people as group members — the role of fit in the salience of social categorizations. Penelope J. Oakes; John C. Turner; S. Alexander Haslam. *Br. J. Soc. P.* **30:2** 6:1991 pp. 125 – 144

155 Perception of epistemic authority and attribution for its choice as a function of knowledge area and age. D. Bar-Tal; A. Raviv; A. Raviv; M.E. Brosh. *Eur. J. Soc. Psychol.* **21:6** 11-12:1991 pp. 477 – 492

156 Perceptions of control in vulnerable populations. Suzanne C. Thompson; Shirlynn Spacapan. *J. Soc. Issues* **47:4** 1991 pp. 1 – 22

157 Representing fundamentalism — the problem of the repugnant cultural other. Susan Harding. *Soc. Res.* **58:2** Summer:1991 pp. 373 – 394

158 The self and social judgment — effects of affective reaction and "own position" on judgments of unambiguous and ambiguous information about others. Alan J. Lambert; Douglas H. Wedell. *J. Pers. Soc. Psychol.* **61:6** 12:1991 pp. 884 – 897

159 Social relationships, personality, and anxiety during a major stressful event. Niall Bolger; John Eckenrode. *J. Pers. Soc. Psychol.* **61:3** 9:1991 pp. 440 – 449

160 Thinking about people — contributions of a typological alternative to associationistic and dimensional models of person perception. Craig A. Anderson; Constantine Sedikides. *J. Pers. Soc. Psychol.* **60:2** 2:1991 pp. 203 – 217

161 Who can catch a liar? Paul Ekman; Maureen O'Sullivan. *Am. Psychol.* **46:9** 9:1991 pp. 913 – 920

162 Why are traits inferred spontaneously? A developmental approach. Leonard S. Newman. *Soc. Cogn.* **9:3** Fall:1991 pp. 221 – 253

C.4: Groups — *Groupes*

1 Accuracy in the judgment of in-group and out-group variability. Charles M. Judd; Carey S. Ryan; Bernadette Park. *J. Pers. Soc. Psychol.* **61:3** 9:1991 pp. 366 – 379
2 Associations-réseaux et réseaux d'associations — une approche formelle de l'organisation réticulée *[In French]*; Association-networks and networks of associations — a formal approach to the study of network organisations *[Summary]*. Catherine Flament. *Soc. Contemp.* **:5** 3:1991 pp. 67 – 74
3 Beyond formalism — group theory in the symmetries of culture. Peter Lucich. *J. Math. Sociol.* **16:3** 1991 pp. 221 – 264
4 Beyond the call of duty — a field study of extra-role behavior in voluntary organizations. John Schaubroeck; Daniel C. Ganster. *Human Relat.* **44:6** 6:1991 pp. 569 – 582
5 Blame analysis — accounting for the behavior of protected groups. Richard E. Felson. *Am. Sociol.* **22:1** Spring:1991 pp. 5 – 24
6 Change in the small group — a dissipative structure perspective. Charles Smith; Gary Gemmill. *Human Relat.* **44:7** 7:1991 pp. 697 – 716
7 Closeness and peer group influence. Mark Morgan; Joel W. Grube. *Br. J. Soc. P.* **30:2** 6:1991 pp. 159 – 170
8 A comparison of structural and contextual features of middle school children's playful and aggresive fighting. Michael J. Boulton. *Ethol. Socio.* **12:2** 1991 pp. 119 – 145
9 Contextual analysis. Gudmund R. Iversen. Newbury Park, Calif: Sage Publications, c1991: 84 p. (ill) *ISBN: 0803942729; LofC: 91022014. Includes bibliographical references.* [Sage university papers series.]
10 Contribution à une morphologie des rôles réticulaires *[In French]*; Contribution to a morphology of roles in social networks *[Summary]*. Michel Forsé. *Soc. Contemp.* **:5** 3:1991 pp. 43 – 54
11 The development of an intragroup norm and the effects of interpersonal and structural challenges. Kenneth L. Bettenhausen; J. Keith Murnighan. *Adm. Sci. Qua.* **36:1** 3:1991 pp. 20 – 35
12 The dynamics of intense work groups — a study of British string quartets. J. Keith Murnighan; Donald Conlon. *Adm. Sci. Qua.* **36:2** 6:1991 pp. 165 – 186
13 The effect of multiple category membership on intergroup evaluations in a north Indian context — class, caste and religion. Louk Hagendoorn; Roger Henke. *Br. J. Soc. P.* **30:3** 9:1991 pp. 247 – 260
14 Effects of multiple task demands upon memory for information about social groups. Charles Stangor; Changming Duan. *J. Exp. S. Psychol.* **27:4** 7:1991 pp. 357 – 378
15 Ethnocentrism between groups of unequal power under threat in intergroup competition. Peter R. Grant. *J. Soc. Psychol.* **131:1** 2:1991 pp. 21 – 28
16 Facilitation of outgroup stereotypes by enhanced ingroup identity. David A. Wilder; Peter Shapiro. *J. Exp. S. Psychol.* **27:5** 9:1991 pp. 431 – 452
17 Familiarity and group productivity. Paul S. Goodman; Dennis Patrick Leyden. *J. Appl. Psychol.* **76:4** 8:1991 pp. 478 – 585
18 A field methodology for participatory self-evaluation. Norman Uphoff. *Comm. Dev. J.* **26:4** 10:1991 pp. 271 – 285
19 The frequency of self-limiting behavior in groups — a measure and an explanation. John F. Veiga. *Human Relat.* **44:8** 8:1991 pp. 877 – 895
20 From device to vice — social control and intergroup conflict at Rajneeshpuram. Carl Latkin. *Sociol. Anal.* **52:4** Winter:1991 pp. 363 – 378
21 The group and the shadow — explorations and echoes of relatedness in a small study group setting. Russell Forrest. *Human Relat.* **44:5** 5:1991 pp. 459 – 480
22 The group and what happens on the way to "yes". Deborah G. Ancona; Raymond A. Friedman; Deborah M. Kolb. *Negot. J.* **7:2** 4:1991 pp. 155 – 173
23 Group composition, salience, and cognitive representations — the phenomenology of being in a group. Brian Mullen. *J. Exp. S. Psychol.* **27:4** 7:1991 pp. 297 – 323
24 Group decision fiascoes continue — space shuttle Challenger and a revised groupthink framework. Gregory Moorhead; Richard Ference; Chris P. Neck. *Human Relat.* **44:6** 6:1991 pp. 539 – 549
25 Group decision making under stress. James E. Driskell; Eduardo Salas. *J. Appl. Psychol.* **76:3** 6:1991 pp. 473 – 478

C.4: Groups [Groupes]
26 Group decision making — suppositions and practice. Gerd Islei; Geoff Lockett. *Socio. Econ.* **25:1** 1991 pp. 67 – 81
27 Group development in the natural environment — expectations, outcomes, and techniques. Alan Ewert; John Heywood. *Envir. Behav.* **23:5** 9:1991 pp. 592 – 615
28 Group members' reactions to opinion deviates and conformists at varying degrees of proximity to decision deadline and of environmental noise. Arie W. Kruglanski; Donna M. Webster. *J. Pers. Soc. Psychol.* **61:2** 8:1991 pp. 212 – 225
29 Hindu-Muslim intergroup relations in India — applying socio-psychological perspectives. Emmanuel S.K. Ghosh; Rashmi Kumar. *Psychol. Devel. Soc.* **3:1** 1-6:1991 pp. 93 – 112
30 Les hommes sont des réseaux pensants *[In French]*; Men are thinking networks *[Summary]*. Jean-Pierre Darré. *Soc. Contemp.* **:5** 3:1991 pp. 55 – 66
31 Independence and interdependence of group judgments — xenophobia and minority influence. G. Mugny; M. Sanchez-Mazas; P. Roux; J.A. Pérez. *Eur. J. Soc. Psychol.* **21:3** 5-6:1991 pp. 213 – 223
32 Instinctual foundations of group analysis. A.P. Ormay. *Free Assoc.* **2:4(24)** 1991 pp. 569 – 587
33 Kamikaze biker — parody and anomy in affluent Japan. Ikuya Satō; Gerald D. Suttles *[Foreword]*. Chicago: University of Chicago Press, 1991: 277 p. *ISBN: 0226735257; LofC: 90048610.* Includes bibliographical references and index.
34 Kin-selection, reciprocal altruism, and information sharing among Maine lobstermen. Craig T. Palmer. *Ethol. Socio.* **12:3** 1991 pp. 221 – 236
35 Kollektív traumák, mint patogén társadalmi folyamatok gyökerei *[In Hungarian]*; [Collective traumas as roots of pathogen social processes]. Erika Varsányi. *Szociologia Vol.16; No.2 - 1987.* pp. 277 – 297
36 Managing group decision making processes — individual versus collective accountability and groupthink. Marceline B.R. Kroon; Paul't Hart; Dik van Kreveld. *Int. J. Confl. Manag.* **2:2** 4:1991 pp. 91 – 116
37 Member competence, group interaction, and group decision making — a longitudinal study. Warren Watson; Larry K. Michaelsen; Walt Sharp. *J. Appl. Psychol.* **76:6** 12:1991 pp. 803 – 809
38 Methods for estimating individual- and group-level correlations. Harry F. Gollob. *J. Pers. Soc. Psychol.* **60:3** 3:1991 pp. 376 – 381
39 Name generators in surveys of personal networks. Karen E. Campbell; Barrett A. Lee. *Soc. Networks* **13:3** 9:1991 pp. 203 – 222
40 Negotiating group decisions. Jeanne M. Brett. *Negot. J.* **7:3** 7:1991 pp. 291 – 310
41 Normative theory in intergroup relations — explaining both harmony and conflict. Thomas F. Pettigrew. *Psychol. Devel. Soc.* **3:1** 1-6:1991 pp. 3 – 16
42 Participation in heterogeneous and homogeneous groups — a theoretical integration. M. Hamit Fişek; Joseph Berger; Robert Z. Norman. *A.J.S.* **97:1** 7:1991 pp. 114 – 142
43 Police intervention in riots — the role of accountability and group norms — a field experiment. M.B.R. Kroon; D. van Kreveld; J.M. Rabbie. *J. Comm. App. Soc. Psychol.* **1:4** 11:1991 pp. 249 – 267
44 Power and status differentials in minority and majority group relations. I. Sachdev; R.Y. Bourhis. *Eur. J. Soc. Psychol.* **21:1** 1-2: 1991 pp. 1 – 24
45 Procedural influence in small-group decision making — deliberation style and assigned decision rule. Tatsuya Kameda. *J. Pers. Soc. Psychol.* **61:2** 8:1991 pp. 245 – 256
46 Processes that mediate the relationship between a group goal and improved group performance. Elizabeth Weldon; Karen A. Jehn; Priti Pradhan. *J. Pers. Soc. Psychol.* **61:4** 10:1991 pp. 555 – 569
47 Productivity loss in idea-generating groups — tracking down the blocking effect. Michael Diehl; Wolfgang Stroebe. *J. Pers. Soc. Psychol.* **61:3** 9:1991 pp. 392 – 403
48 Les relations au coeur du marché du travail *[In French]*; Social networks at the core of the labor-market *[Summary]*. Alain Degenne; Irène Fournier; Catherine Marry; Lise Mounier. *Soc. Contemp.* **:5** 3:1991 pp. 75 – 98
49 Réseaux sociaux *[In French]*; Social networks *[Summary]*. Alexis Ferrand *[Contrib.]*; Claire Bidart *[Contrib.]*; Michel Forsé *[Contrib.]*; Jean-Pierre Darré *[Contrib.]*; Catherine Flament *[Contrib.]*; Alain Degenne *[Contrib.]*; Irène Fournier *[Contrib.]*; Catherine Marry *[Contrib.]*; Lise Mounier *[Ed.]*; Sébastien Reichmann *[Contrib.]* and others. Collection of 8 articles. **Soc. Contemp.**, *:5*, 3:1991 pp. 7 – 134
50 Resource dilemmas and discount rates in decision making groups. Elizabeth A. Mannix. *J. Exp. S. Psychol.* **27:4** 7:1991 pp. 379 – 391

C.4: Groups [Groupes]

51 Self-directed groupwork — users taking action for empowerment. Audrey Mullender; David A. Ward. London: Whiting & Birch, 1991: 194 p. *ISBN: 187117709x*. [Groupwork series.]
52 Self-esteem and intergroup discrimination in the minimal group paradigm. Michael A. Hogg; Jane Sunderland. *Br. J. Soc. P.* **30:1** 3:1991 pp. 51 – 62
53 The signifier and the group. Susan Long. *Human Relat.* **44:4** 4:1991 pp. 389 – 401
54 Simultaneous group and individual centralities. Phillip Bonacich. *Soc. Networks* **13:2** 6:1991 pp. 155 – 168
55 Social categorization and the formation of group stereotypes — further evidence for biased information processing in the perception of group-behaviour correlations. M. Schaller. *Eur. J. Soc. Psychol.* **21:1** 1-2: 1991 pp. 25 – 35
56 Strategic decision-making tasks and group effectiveness — insights from theory and research on small group performance. Frances J. Milliken; David A. Vollrath. *Human Relat.* **44:12** 12:1991 pp. 1229 – 1253
57 A structural analysis of small groups. Susan Long. London: Routledge, 1991: 206 p. *ISBN: 0415065011; LofC: 91014208. Includes bibliographical references and index.*
58 Theoretical and methodological models of networks and relations. John Skvoretz. *Soc. Networks* **13:3** 9:1991 pp. 275 – 300
59 A theory of group stability. Kathleen Carley. *Am. Sociol. R.* **56:3** 6:1991 pp. 331 – 354
60 Toward an assessment of social identity — the structure of group identification and its effects on in-group evaluations. Minoru Karasawa. *Br. J. Soc. P.* **30:4** 12:1991 pp. 293 – 308
61 Towards a theory of collective phenomena — consensus and attitude changes in groups. S. Galam; S. Moscovici. *Eur. J. Soc. Psychol.* **21:1** 1-2: 1991 pp. 49 – 74
62 When anyone can veto — a laboratory study of committees governed by unanimous rule. James D. Laing; Benjamin Slotnik. *Behav. Sci.* **36:3** 07:1991 pp. 179 – 195
63 Women, men, and dominance in small groups — a social roles assessment. Aysan Sev'er. *Can. J. Soc.* **16:3** Summer:1991 pp. 265 – 280
64 Won from the void and formless infinite — experiences of social dreaming. W. Gordon Lawrence. *Free Assoc.* **2:22** 1991 pp. 259 – 294

C.5: Organizations — *Organisations*

1 Analysing organisational behaviour. Mike Smith [Ed.]. Basingstoke: Macmillan Education, 1991: 284 p. *ISBN: 0333517032. Includes index.*
2 Assessing construct validity in organizational research. Richard P. Bagozzi; Youjae Yi; Lynn W. Phillips. *Adm. Sci. Qua.* **36:3** 9:1991 pp. 421 – 458
3 Autocorrelation and density dependence in organizational founding rates. David N. Barron; Michael T. Hannan. *Sociol. Meth.* **20:2** 11:1991 pp. 218 – 241
4 Career professionals who volunteer — should their motives be accepted or managed? Sheila M. Puffer. *Non. Manag. Leader.* **2:2** Winter:1991 pp. 107 – 123
5 Champions of change and strategic shifts — the role of internal and external change advocates. Ari Ginsberg; Eric Abrahamson. *J. Manag. Stu.* **28:2** 3:1991 pp. 173 – 190
6 Combining head and heart in complex organizations — a test of Etzioni's dual compliance structure hypothesis. George P. Johnston; William E. Snizek. *Human Relat.* **44:12** 12:1991 pp. 1255 – 1271
7 Coming to terms with the field — understanding and doing organizational ethnography. Michael Rosen. *J. Manag. Stu.* **28:1** 1:1991 pp. 1 – 24
8 Communities of fate — readings in the social organization of risk. Charles E Marske [Ed.]. Lanham, Md: University Press of America, c1991: xii, 234 p. *ISBN: 0819183105; LofC: 91016230. Includes bibliographical references (p. 213-221) and index.*
9 Community context and complexity of organizational structure in neighborhood associations. D. Mark Austin. *Admin. Soc.* **22:4** 2:1991 pp. 516 – 531
10 [In Japanese]; [Company society and life value]. Kunio Motojima. *Nihonroudoushakaigakkai Nenpou* No.(2) - 1991. pp. 1 – 26
11 A comparative study of Beer's and Miller's systems designs as tools when analyzing the structure of a municipal organization. Sven Rasegård. *Behav. Sci.* **36:2** 4:1991 pp. 83 – 99
12 [In Japanese]; [Comparisons of organizational structure in Japanese and French firms]. Hiroshi Mannari. *Journal of Kibi International University* No.(1) - 1991. pp. 177 – 185
13 Conflict management, honor, and organizational change. Calvin Morrill. *A.J.S.* **97:3** 11:1991 pp. 585 – 621

C.5: Organizations [Organisations]

14 A construct validity study of the survey of perceived organizational support. Lynn McFarlane Shore; Lois E. Tetrick. *J. Appl. Psychol.* **76:5** 10:1991 pp. 637 – 643
15 Corporations, culture, and commitment — motivation and social control in organizations. Charles O'Reilly. *Calif. Manag. R.* **31:4** Summer:1989 pp. 9 – 25
16 Cosmetic, speculative, and adaptive organizational change in the wine industry — a longitudinal study. Jacques Delacroix; Anand Swaminathan. *Adm. Sci. Qua.* **36:4** 12:1991 pp. 631 – 661
17 Cultural knowledge in organizations — exploring the collective mind. Sonja Sackmann. Newbury Park, CA: Sage Club, c1991: x, 221 p. (ill) *ISBN: 0803942923; LofC: 91014913. Includes bibliographical references (p. 206-213) and index.*
18 Cultures and organizations — software of the mind. Geert Hofstede. London: McGraw-Hill, c1991: 279 p. *ISBN: 0077074742; LofC: 91000205. Includes bibliographical references and index.*
19 The customs of conflict management among corporate executives. Calvin Morrill. *Am. Anthrop.* **93:4** 12:1991 pp. 871 – 893
20 Designing organizational structures to cope with communication breakdowns — a simulation model. K M. Carley. *Ind. Crisis Q.* **5:1** 3:1991 pp. 19 – 57
21 Designing organizations — a decision making perspective. Richard Butler. London: Routledge, 1991: 281 p. *ISBN: 0415053315.*
22 Determinants of strategic planning systems in large organizations — a contingency approach. Sal Kukalis. *J. Manag. Stu.* **28:2** 3:1991 pp. 143 – 160
23 Dilemma organizzativo, lavoro, attore sociale *[In Italian]*; [Organizational dilemma, work, social participants]. Fedele Ruggeri. *Sociologia [Rome]* **XXV:1** :1991 pp. 153 – 175
24 Everyday methods for assessing organizational effectiveness. Renee R. Anspach. *Soc. Prob.* **38:1** 2:1991 pp. 1 – 19
25 Evolution on a dancing landscape — organizations and networks in dynamic blau space. J. Miller McPherson; James R. Ranger-Moore. *Soc. Forc.* **70:1** 9:1991 pp. 19 – 42
26 The evolutionary psychology of sexual harassment in organizations. Michael V. Studd; Urs E. Gattiker. *Ethol. Socio.* **12:4** 1991 pp. 249 – 290
27 Explaining decision processes. David Cray; Geoffrey R. Mallory; Richard J. Butler; David J. Hickson; David C. Wilson. *J. Manag. Stu.* **28:3** 5:1991 pp. 227 – 251
28 Further analyses of the dispositional argument in organizational behavior. Tim Newton; Tony Keenan. *J. Appl. Psychol.* **76:6** 12:1991 pp. 781 – 787
29 Heroic bureaucracies. Richard A. Couto. *Admin. Soc.* **23:1** 5:1991 pp. 123 – 147
30 History as a mode of inquiry in organizational life — a role for human cosmogony. Frank J. Barrett; Suresh Srivastva. *Human Relat.* **44:3** 3:1991 pp. 231 – 254
31 How nonprofit human service organizations manage their funding sources — key findings and policy implications. Kirsten A. Gronbjerg. *Non. Manag. Leader.* **2:2** Winter:1991 pp. 159 – 175
32 Humor, power and change in organizations. Tom Dwyer. *Human Relat.* **44:1** 1:1991 pp. 1 – 19
33 Institutional linkages and organizational mortality. Joel A.C. Baum; Christine Oliver. *Adm. Sci. Qua.* **36:2** 6:1991 pp. 187 – 218
34 Integration of information from multiple element displays. Robert D. Sorkin; Thomas R. Mabry; Mary Susan Weldon; Greg Elvers. *Organ. Beh. Hum. Dec. Proces.* **49:2** 8:1991 pp. 167 – 187
35 Investigating organisations — a feminist approach. Gill Coleman. Bristol: School for Advanced Urban Studies, 1991: iv, 75 p. *ISBN: 1873575114. Bibliography — p.71-75.* [Occasional paper.]
36 Irrationality and contradiction in organizational change — transformations in the corporate form of a U.S. steel corporation, 1930-1987. Harland Prechel. *Sociol. Q.* **32:3** Fall:1991 pp. 423 – 445
37 *[In Japanese]*; [The Japanese property of organizational communication]. Naoki Wakabayashi. *Keizaishakaigaku Nenpo No.(8) - 1991.* pp. 141 – 150
38 Keeping the faith — a model of cultural transmission in formal organizations. J. Richard Harrison; Glenn R. Carroll. *Adm. Sci. Qua.* **36:4** 12:1991 pp. 552 – 582
39 Классовая сущность «симбиоза» (теневая экономика в административно-командной системе) *[In Russian]*; (Class nature of "symbiosis". (Shadow economics in command-administrative system of management)). I.A. Goldenberg. *Sot. Issle.* **:1** 1991 pp. 39 – 49

C.5: Organizations [Organisations]

40 Labor economics and the psychology of organizations. Edward P. Lazear. *J. Econ. Pers.* **5:2** Spring:1991 pp. 89 – 110
41 A living systems analysis of organizational pathology. James Grier Miller; Jessie L. Miller. *Behav. Sci.* **36:4** 10:1991 pp. 239 – 252
42 Management as a cultural artefact; La gestion en tant qu'artefact culturel *[French summary]*. Nick Woodward. *Gestion* **7:2/3** 4-5/7:1991 pp. 49 – 68
43 Meaning, self and motivation in organizations. Boas Shamir. *Organ. Stud.* **12:3** 1991 pp. 405 – 424
44 The mentor/protege relationship — a biological perspective. Stephen C. Bushardt; Cherie Fretwell; B.J. Holdnak. *Human Relat.* **44:6** 6:1991 pp. 619 – 639
45 Muddling through a nuclear-political emergency — multilevel crisis management in West Germany after radioactive fallout from Chernobyl. R.M. Czada. *Ind. Crisis Q.* **5:4** :1991 pp. 293 – 322
46 National culture and police organization in Germany and the United States. Erika S. Fairchild. *Publ. Adm. Re.* **49:5** 9-10:1989 pp. 454 – 462
47 The new institutionalism in organizational analysis. Walter W Powell *[Ed.]*; Paul DiMaggio *[Ed.]*. Chicago: University of Chicago Press, c1991: vii, 478 p. *ISBN: 0226677087; LofC: 91009999. Includes bibliographical references (p. 423-463) and index.*
48 On organisational stories and myths — why it is easier to slay a dragon than to kill a myth; A propos d'histoires et de mythes dans les organisations — pourquoi il est plus facile de faire mourir un dragon que de tuer un mythe *[French summary]*. Yiannis Gabriel. *Int. Sociol.* **6:4** 12:1991 pp. 427 – 442
49 One good turn deserves another — exchange of favors within organizations. K.K. Fung. *Soc. Sci. Q.* **72:3** 9:1991 pp. 443 – 463
50 Organisational culture and organisational effectiveness. N.A. Jans; J.M. Frazer-Jans. *Aust. J. Publ.* **50:3** 9:1991 pp. 333 – 346
51 The organization dimension of global change. David L. Cooperrider; William A. Pasmore. *Human Relat.* **44:8** 8:1991 pp. 763 – 788
52 The organization shadow. Martin L. Bowles. *Organ. Stud.* **12:3** 1991 pp. 387 – 403
53 The organizational context of tracking in schools. Sally B. Kilgore. *Am. Sociol. R.* **56:2** 4:1991 pp. 189 – 203
54 Organizational determinants of managerial pay allocation decisions. Wanda A. Trahan; Irving M. Lane; Gregory H. Dobbins. *J. Soc. Psychol.* **131:1** 2:1991 pp. 93 – 106
55 Organizational environment in Africa — a factor analysis of critical incidents. J.C. Munene. *Human Relat.* **44:5** 5:1991 pp. 439 – 458
56 Organizational evolution and the social ecology of jobs. Anne S. Miner. *Am. Sociol. R.* **56:6** 12:1991 pp. 772 – 785
57 Organizational factors and technology-intensive industry — the US and Japan; *[French summary]*. Richard Florida; Martin Kenney. *New Tech. Work. Empl.* **6:1** Spring:1991 pp. 28 – 42
58 *[In Japanese]*; [Organizational learning and organizational ecology]. Takenori Takase. *Organ. Sc.* No.25(1) - 1991. pp. 58 – 66
59 Organizational mortality in the anti-drunk driving movement — failure among local MADD chapters. Frank J. Weed. *Soc. Forc.* **69:3** 3:1991 pp. 851 – 868
60 Organizational symbolism and ideology. Mats Alvesson. *J. Manag. Stu.* **28:3** 5:1991 pp. 207 – 225
61 Overt funding, buried goals, and moral turnover — the organizational transformation of radical experiments. Len Holmes; Margaret Grieco. *Human Relat.* **44:7** 7:1991 pp. 643 – 664
62 Pôles de croissance et technopoles — une lecture en termes d'organisation industrielle *[In French]*; Growth poles and technopolises — an interpretation in terms of industrial organization *[Summary]*. J.-L. Ravix; A. Torre. *Ec. Sociét.* **25:8** 8:1991 pp. 65 – 81
63 Problems of generalisation in cross- national studies of organisations; *[French summary]*. Martin Heidenreich. *Int. Sociol.* **6:2** 6:1991 pp. 181 – 200
64 Processi di integrazione nelle organizzazioni *[In Italian]*; [Processes of integration in organizations]. Alessandro Gobbicchi. *Sociologia [Rome]* **XXV:1** :1991 pp. 177 – 189
65 Proxy power and corporate democracy. F.P. Zampa; A.E. McCormick. *Am. J. Econ. S.* **50:1** 1:1991 pp. 1 – 15
66 Random walks and organizational mortality. Daniel Levinthal. *Adm. Sci. Qua.* **36:3** 9:1991 pp. 397 – 420

C.5: Organizations [Organisations]

67 Reframing organizational culture. Peter J. Frost *[Ed.]*; et al. Newbury Park, Calif: Sage Publications, c1991: x, 400 p. *ISBN: 0803936508; LofC: 91022013.*

68 Relationship between organizational justice and organizational citizenship behaviors — do fairness perceptions influence employee citizenship? Robert H. Moorman. *J. Appl. Psychol.* **76:6** 12:1991 pp. 845 – 855

69 The replicative model of the evolution of the business organization. Mika Pantzar; Vilmos Csányi. *J. Soc. Biol. Struct.* **14:2** 1991 pp. 149 – 163

70 Rethinking organization — new directions in organization theory and analysis. Michael Reed *[Ed.]*; Michael Hughes *[Ed.]*. London: Sage Publications, 1991: 309 p. *ISBN: 0803982879.*

71 Rigidity and fragility of large sociotechnical systems — advanced information technology, the dominant coalition and paradigm shift at the end of the 20th century. Kenyon B. de Greene. *Behav. Sci.* **36:1** 1:1991 pp. 64 – 79

72 Shaken, but alive — organizational behavior in the wake of catastrophic events. T.C. Powell. *Ind. Crisis Q.* **5:4** :1991 pp. 271 – 291

73 A society of organizations. Charles Perrow. *Theory Soc.* **20/6** 12:1991 pp. 725 – 762

74 Strategic flexibility for high technology manoeuvres — a conceptual framework. J. Stuart Evans. *J. Manag. Stu.* **28:1** 1:1991 pp. 69 – 89

75 A study of organizational "framework" and "process" modalities for the implementation of business-level strategic decisions. James Skivington; Richard L. Daft. *J. Manag. Stu.* **28:1** 1:1991 pp. 45 – 68

76 Swimming in newstreams — mastering innovation dilemmas. Rosabeth Moss Kanter. *Calif. Manag. R.* **31:4** Summer:1989 pp. 45 – 69

77 Targets of mergers — applying a negotiations perspective to predict degree of resistance. Anurag Sharma; Debra L. Shapiro; Idalene F. Kesner. *Int. J. Confl. Manag.* **2:2** 4:1991 pp. 117 – 138

78 Technology, organisations and innovation. Michael L. Tushman *[Ed.]*; Richard R. Nelson *[Ed.]*; Rebecca M. Henderson *[Contrib.]*; Kim B. Clark *[Contrib.]*; William P. Barnett *[Contrib.]*; Stephen R. Barley *[Contrib.]*; Marlene E. Burkhardt *[Contrib.]*; Daniel J. Brass *[Contrib.]*; Wesley M. Cohen *[Contrib.]*; Daniel A. Levinthal *[Contrib.]* and others. Collection of 8 articles. **Int. J. Ind. O.** , *35:1*, 3:1990 pp. 1 – 207

79 Theoretical and methodological issues in analysis of density-dependent legitimation in organizational evolution. Michael T. Hannan. *Soc. Method.* **21** 1991 pp. 1 – 42

80 A theory of partial systems — implications for organizational effectiveness. Jonathan I. Klein. *Behav. Sci.* **36:3** 07:1991 pp. 224 – 240

81 Toward the study of organizational coalitions — participant concerns and activities in a simulated organizational setting. Anthony T. Cobb. *Human Relat.* **44:10** 10:1991 pp. 1057 – 1080

82 La transformation du sens des règles selon les niveaux — le cas des classifications professionnelles *[In French]*; [The transformation of the meaning of rules according to rank — the case of professional classifications]. Annette Jobert. *Sociol. Trav.* **:3** 1991 pp. 429 – 439

83 Trust dynamics and organizational integration — the microsociology of Alan Fox. William K. Roche. *Br. J. Soc.* **42:1** 3:1991 pp. 95 – 113

84 Turning facts into stories and stories into facts — a hermeneutic exploration of organizational folklore. Yiannis Gabriel. *Human Relat.* **44:8** 8:1991 pp. 857 – 876

85 A typology of social partnership organizations. Sandra A. Waddock. *Admin. Soc.* **22:4** 2:1991 pp. 480 – 515

86 The use of dyadic alliances in informal organization — an ethnographic study. Nancy C. Morey; Fred Luthans. *Human Relat.* **44:6** 6:1991 pp. 597 – 618

87 Who do you know in the group? Location of organizations in interpersonal networks. Raymond V. Liedka. *Soc. Forc.* **70:2** 12:1991 pp. 455 – 474

C.6: Power, leadership and social roles — *Pouvoir, leadership et rôles sociaux*

1 The construction of leadership images in the popular press — the case of Donald Burr and People Express. Chao C. Chen; James R. Meindl. *Adm. Sci. Qua.* **36**:4 12:1991 pp. 521 – 551
2 Dilemmas and controversies concerning the leadership recruitment in Eastern Europe. Jacek Wasilewski. *Prax. Int.* **11**:2 7:1991 pp. 240 – 250
3 Gender and the emergence of leaders — a meta-analysis. Alice H. Eagly; Steven J. Karau. *J. Pers. Soc. Psychol.* **60**:5 5:1991 pp. 685 – 710
4 Hierarchisation and dominance assessment at first glance. A. Kalma. *Eur. J. Soc. Psychol.* **21**:2 3-4:1991 pp. 165 – 181
5 Individual and cultural differences in response to leaders' nonverbal displays. Roger D. Masters. *J. Soc. Issues* **47**:3 1991 pp. 151 – 166
6 The influentials — back to the concept of opinion leaders? Gabriel Weimann. *Publ. Opin. Q.* **55**:2 Summer:1991 pp. 267 – 279
7 The leader as a broker of dreams. Lessey Sooklal. *Human Relat.* **44**:8 8:1991 pp. 833 – 856
8 Leadership and information processing — linking perceptions and performance. Robert G. Lord; Karen J. Maher. London: Unwin Hyman, 1991: xi,340 p. *ISBN: 0044451520; LofC: 90-39001.* [People and organizations. : No. 1]
9 Leadership — toward paradigm expansion. James G. Hunt. Newbury Park, Calif: Sage Publications, c1991: 358 p. *ISBN: 0803937679; LofC: 91009342. Includes bibliographical references and index.*
10 Multiple role juggling and daily mood states in working mothers — an experience sampling study. Kevin J. Williams; Jerry Suls; George M. Alliger; Susan M. Learner; Choi K. Wan. *J. Appl. Psychol.* **76**:5 10:1991 pp. 664 – 674
11 Role-taking ability and Gough's theory of psychopathy. Paul D. O'Mahony; Paul G. Murphy. *Int. J. Offen.* **35**:2 Summer:1991 pp. 107 – 118
12 Social roles and social institutions — essays in honor of Rose Laub Coser. Judith R. Blau *[Ed.]*; Norman Goodman *[Ed.]*. Boulder: Westview Press, 1991: xxix, 288 p. *ISBN: 081338320x; LofC: 91013122. Includes bibliographical references; "Selected bibliography of Rose Laub Coser" (p. [277]-283).*
13 Social roles and utilities in reasoning with deontic conditionals. K.I. Manktelow; D.E. Over. *Cognition* **39**:2 5:1991 pp. 85 – 105
14 Tracing leadership in gifted children. Erika Landau; Kineret Weissler. *J. Psychol.* **125**:6 11:1991 pp. 681 – 688
15 Understanding group life — sociology's ten contributions to help people comprehend social roles. D.H. Bouma. *Am. J. Econ. S.* **50**:2 4:1991 pp. 157 – 167
16 Values leadership — toward a new philosophy of leadership. Gilbert W. Fairholm. New York: Praeger, 1991: xvi, 243 p. *ISBN: 0275939979; LofC: 91010664. Includes bibliographical references (p. [229]-238) and index.*
17 Varieties of positioning. Rom Harré; Luk van Langenhove. *J. Theory Soc. Behav.* **21**:4 12:1991 pp. 393 – 407
18 Whatever happened to the philosopher-king? The leader's addiction to power. Manfred F.R. de Vries. *J. Manag. Stu.* **28**:4 7:1991 pp. 339 – 352

C.7: Opinions and attitudes — *Opinions et attitudes*

1 Accentuation effects and illusory change in exemplar-based category learning. J. Krueger. *Eur. J. Soc. Psychol.* **21:1** 1-2:1991 pp. 37 – 48
2 Actitudes en las políticas económicas (1952-1989) *[In Spanish]*; [Public opinion and economic policy (1952-1989)]. Flavio Machicado Saravia. [La Paz, Bolivia?]: ILDIS, [1990]: 170 p. *BNB: 90199233; LofC: 90199233. Includes bibliographical references (p. 165-167).*
3 Adolescents' perceptions of friends' and parents' attitudes to sex and sexual risk-taking. S. Moore; D. Rosenthal. *J. Comm. App. Soc. Psychol.* **1:3** 9:1991 pp. 189 – 200
4 Affective and cognitive determinants of prejudice. Charles Stangor; Linda A. Sullivan; Thomas E. Ford. *Soc. Cogn.* **9:4** Winter:1991 pp. 359 – 380
5 Analogical transfer and expertise in legal reasoning. Garry Marchant; John Robinson; Urton Anderson; Michael Schadewald. *Organ. Beh. Hum. Dec. Proces.* **48:2** 4:1991 pp. 272 – 290
6 Applying cognitive decision theory to the study of regional patterns of illness treatment choice. Holly F. Mathews; Carole E. Hill. *Am. Anthrop.* **92:1** 3:1990 pp. 155 – 170
7 Are there any irrational beliefs? W.G. Runciman. *Eur. J. Soc.* **XXXII:2** 1991 pp. 215 – 228
8 Attitude structure and belief accessibility. Roger Tourangeau; Kenneth A. Rasinski; Roy D' Andrade. *J. Exp. S. Psychol.* **27:1** 1:1991 pp. 48 – 75
9 Attitudinal indexes on the "preparedness to help non-familial others in need" in the states of Uttar Pradesh, West Bengal and Karnataka, India. M. Radh Achuthan; Philip Leonhard. *Ind. J. Soc. Sci.* **4:2** 4-6:1991 pp. 223 – 240
10 The attribution of aggression and grief to body movements — the effect of sex-stereotypes. M. de Meijer. *Eur. J. Soc. Psychol.* **21:3** 5-6:1991 pp. 249 – 259
11 Availability of alternative positions and estimates of consensus. Gary Marks; Shelley Duval. *Br. J. Soc. P.* **30:2** 6:1991 pp. 179 – 184
12 Belief, knowledge, and uncertainty — a cognitive perspective on subjective probability. Gerald F. Smith; P. George Benson; Shawn P. Curley. *Organ. Beh. Hum. Dec. Proces.* **48:2** 4:1991 pp. 291 – 321
13 Biochemistry and power-seeking. Richard E. Vatz; Lee S. Weinberg. *Polit. Life* **10:1** 8:1991 pp. 69 – 75
14 Can modern physics provide a scientific basis for the "theory of cognitive subjectivity"? Zuoxiu He. *Soc. Sci. China* **XII:1** 3:1991 pp. 165 – 182
15 Categorization and interclass assimilation in social judgement. C. Martijn; E. Van Schie. *Eur. J. Soc. Psychol.* **21:6** 11-12:1991 pp. 493 – 505
16 Chains of cooperation — threshold effects in collective action. Michael W. Macy. *Am. Sociol. R.* **56:6** 12:1991 pp. 730 – 742
17 Changes in attributions over time — the ephemeral fundamental attribution error. Jerry M. Burger. *Soc. Cogn.* **9:2** Summer:1991 pp. 182 – 193
18 Children's social constructs — nature, assessment, and association with adaptive versus maladaptive behavior. Valerie J. Stromquist; Timothy J. Strauman. *Soc. Cogn.* **9:4** Winter:1991 pp. 330 – 358
19 The concept of development — its implications for self and society. Ramashray Roy. *Psychol. Devel. Soc.* **3:2** 7-12:1991 pp. 133 – 156
20 Consensual representations of social structure in different age groups. Martha Augoustinos. *Br. J. Soc. P.* **30:3** 9:1991 pp. 193 – 205
21 The contribution of domain-specific stereotypes to ethnic social distance. Louk Hagendoorn; Gerard Kleinpenning. *Br. J. Soc. P.* **30:1** 3:1991 pp. 63 – 78
22 Coping with "natural" hazards as stressors — the predictors of activism in a flood disaster. E. Burke Rochford; T. Jean Blocker. *Envir. Behav.* **23:2** 3:1991 pp. 171 – 194
23 Cultural differences in reward allocation — is collectivism the explanation? C. Harry Hui; Harry C. Triandis; Candice Yee. *Br. J. Soc. P.* **30:2** 6:1991 pp. 145 – 157
24 Effects of structured cooperative contact on changing negative attitudes toward stigmatized social groups. Donna M. Desforges; Charles G. Lord; Shawna L. Ramsey; Julie A. Mason; Marilyn D. Van Leeuwen; Sylvia C. West; Mark R. Lepper. *J. Pers. Soc. Psychol.* **60:4** 4:1991 pp. 531 – 544
25 The effects upon helping behaviour of pro-gay identification. Colin Gray; Phil Russell; Stephanie Blockley. *Br. J. Soc. P.* **30:2** 6:1991 pp. 171 – 178

C.7: Opinions and attitudes [Opinions et attitudes]

26 Eurobarometer — the dynamics of European public opinion. Karlheinz Reif [Ed.]; Ronald Inglehart [Ed.]; Jacques-René Rabier [Ed.]. London: Macmillan, 1991: 392 p. ISBN: 0333527542. Includes bibliography.
27 Evolutionary limits to self-preservation. Denys de Catanzaro. Ethol. Socio. 12:1 1991 pp. 13 – 28
28 Expectancy-value models of attitudes — a note on the relationship between theory and methodology. P. Sparks; D. Hedderley; R. Shepherd. Eur. J. Soc. Psychol. 21:3 5-6:1991 pp. 261 – 271
29 Explorations in behavioral consistency — properties of persons, situations, and behaviors. David C. Funder; C. Randall Colvin. J. Pers. Soc. Psychol. 60:5 5:1991 pp. 733 – 794
30 Hedging the bets — risk reduction among the Rom Gypsies. Rena C. Gropper. J. Gypsy Lore Soc. 1:1(5) 2:1991 pp. 45 – 60
31 Hindu-Muslim mutual stereotypes in South Asia. Theodore P. Wright. J. Asian Afr. Aff. III:1 7:1991 pp. 7 – 16
32 How objective interests explain actions. C. Behan McCullagh. Soc. Sci. Info. 30:1 :1991 pp. 29 – 54
33 How people think about causes — examination of the typical phenomenal organization of attributions for success and failure. Craig A. Anderson. Soc. Cogn. 9:4 Winter:1991 pp. 295 – 329
34 Human values, global self-esteem, and belief in a just world. N.T. Feather. J. Personal. 59:1 3:1991 pp. 83 – 108
35 Ideologia e sujeito [In Portuguese]; [Ideology and subject] [Summary]. Flávio Eduardo Silveira. Est. Leop. 27:124 9-10:1991 pp. 87 – 104
36 Idéologies et représentations sociales [In French]; [Ideologies and social representation]. Jean-Pierre Deconchy [Ed.]; E. Marc Lipiansky [Ed.]; Verena Aebischer [Ed.]. Cousset (Fribourg), Switzerland: Delval, 1991: 323 p.
37 Independence of irrelevant interpersonal comparisons. P.J. Hammond. Soc. Choice 8:1 1991 pp. 1 – 19
38 Investigating models of human performance. P.M.A. Rabbitt; E.A. Maylor. Br. J. Psy. 82:3 8:1991 pp. 259 – 290
39 Is human cognition adaptive? J.R. Anderson. Behav. Brain Sci. 14:3 9:1991 pp. 471 – 508
40 Измерение установки: становление социологической парадигмы [In Russian]; (Measurement of attitude — development of the sociological paradigm). I.F. Devyatko. Sot. Issle. :6 1991 pp. 49 – 59
41 De keuze van rechtvaardigheidsbeginselen — consensus of dissensus? [In Dutch]; The choice of justice principles — either consent or dissent? [Summary]. Wil Arts; Peter van Wijck. Mens Maat. 66:1 2:1991 pp. 65 – 84
42 Measures of national stereotypes as predictors of the latencies of inductive versus deductive stereotypic judgements. M. Diehl; K. Jonas. Eur. J. Soc. Psychol. 21:4 7-8:1991 pp. 317 – 330
43 Mixed effectivity and the essence of stability. V. Kolpin. Soc. Choice 8:1 1991 pp. 51 – 63
44 Общественное мнение в социальном управлении [In Russian]; [Social opinion in social management]. V.I. Boiko [Ed.]; V.B. Zhitenev. Novosibirsk: Nauka. Sib.otd-nie, 1987: 167 p. pp.165-166.
45 Omission and commission in judgment and choice. Mark Spranca; Elisa Minsk; Jonathan Baron. J. Exp. S. Psychol. 27:1 1:1991 pp. 76 – 105
46 L'opinion des Japonais — comparaison internationale [In French]; [The Japanese opinion — international comparison]. Shigeki Nishihira; et al. Paris: Sudestasie, 1991: 206 p.
47 Parental bonding in the treatment of autistic behaviour. Michele Zappella; Patrizia Chiarucci; Daniela Pinassi; Paolo Fidanzi; Patrizia Messeri. Ethol. Socio. 12:1 1991 pp. 1 – 11
48 Polling on the issues — public opinion and the nuclear freeze. J. Michael Hogan; Ted J. Smith. Publ. Opin. Q. 55:4 Winter:1991 pp. 534 – 569
49 Practicing and arguing for abstinence from smoking — a test of the double forced compliance paradigm. R.-V. Joule. Eur. J. Soc. Psychol. 21:2 3-4:1991 pp. 119 – 129
50 Procrastination and obedience. George A. Akerlof. Am. Econ. Rev. 81:2 5:1991 pp. 1 – 19
51 The Protestant work ethic in Barbados. Adrian Furnham. J. Soc. Psychol. 131:1 2:1991 pp. 29 – 44
52 Psychometric equivalence of a translated circadian rhythm questionnaire — implications for between-and within-population assessments. Carlla S. Smith; John Tisak; Todd Bauman; Elizabeth Green. J. Appl. Psychol. 76:5 10:1991 pp. 628 – 636

C.7: Opinions and attitudes *[Opinions et attitudes]*

53 Public reactions to the Chernobyl accident — a case of rationality? B. Verplanken. *Ind. Crisis Q.* **5:4** :1991 pp. 253 – 269
54 Reach and selectivity as strategies of recruitment for collective action — a theory of the critical mass, V. Ralph Prahl; Gerald Marwell; Pamela E. Oliver. *J. Math. Sociol.* **16:2** 1991 pp. 137 – 164
55 Reading restaurant facades — environmental inference in finding the right place to eat. Paul D. Cherulnik. *Envir. Behav.* **23:2** 3:1991 pp. 150 – 170
56 Relationship admitting families of candidates. D.G. Saari. *Soc. Choice* **8:1** 1991 pp. 21 – 50
57 Requesting information to form an impression — the influence of valence and confirmatory status. Vincent Y. Yzerbyt; Jacques-Philippe Leyens. *J. Exp. S. Psychol.* **27:4** 7:1991 pp. 337 – 356
58 Shadows of the past — the rise and fall of prejudice in an American city. D.J. Gray. *Am. J. Econ. S.* **50:1** 1:1991 pp. 33 – 43
59 Shame and embarassment as deterrents to noncompliance with the law — the case of an antilittering campaign. Harold G. Grasmick; Robert J. Bursik; Karyl A. Kinsey. *Envir. Behav.* **23:2** 3:1991 pp. 233 – 251
60 Should we be very cautious or extremely cautious on measures that may involve our destruction? On the finiteness of our expected welfare. Y.-K. Ng. *Soc. Choice* **8:1** 1991 pp. 79 – 88
61 Social choice in an Islamic economic framework. Masudul A. Choudhury. *Am. J. Islam. Soc. Sci.* **8:2** 9:1991 pp. 259 – 274
62 Social choice problems with fixed sets of alternatives. Ye Yanovskaya. *Math. Soc. Sc.* **21:2** 1991 pp. 129 – 152
63 Social context and modern attitudes — surveys in two colonias in Chihuahua, Chih; Sozialer Kontext und moderne Einstellungen — Umfrage in zwei Siedlungen in Chihuahua, Chih *[German summary]*. Gene N. Levine; Fernando Parra; Frank Malgesini; Emma Escobedo. *Sociologus* **41:2** 1991 pp. 139 – 149
64 Some dynamic properties of attitude structures — context-induced response facilitation and polarization. Charles M. Judd; Roger A. Drake; James W. Downing; Jon A. Krosnick. *J. Pers. Soc. Psychol.* **60:2** 2:1991 pp. 193 – 202
65 The stability and sensitivity of subjective well-being measures. James Horley; J. John Lavery. *Soc. Ind.* **24:2** 3:1991 pp. 113 – 122
66 Stereotypes and standards of judgment. Monica Biernat; Melvin Manis; Thomas E. Nelson. *J. Pers. Soc. Psychol.* **60:4** 4:1991 pp. 485 – 499
67 Stereotyping based on apparently individuating information — trait and global components of sex stereotypes under attention overload. Felicia Pratto; John A. Bargh. *J. Exp. S. Psychol.* **27:1** 1:1991 pp. 26 – 47
68 Stuart Hall and the Marxist concept of ideology. Jorge Larrain. *Theory Cult. Soc.* **8:4** 11:1991 pp. 1 – 28
69 Talking of the royal family. Michael Billig. London: Routledge, 1991: 244 p. ISBN: 0415067456; LofC: 91012628. Includes bibliographical references and index.
70 Les théories de la dissonance cognitive *[In French]*; [Theories of cognitive dissonance]. Alain Clémence. *Soc. Sci. Info.* **30:1** :1991 pp. 55 – 79
71 The Third World's illusions and realities. Alexei Kiva. *Int. Aff. Mos.* **:10** 10:1991 pp. 30 – 39
72 Towards psychological conceptualisation of fundamentalism. Janak Pandey; Yoganand Sinha. *Ind. J. Soc. Sci.* **4:3** 7-9:1991 pp. 347 – 358
73 *[In Japanese]*; [Trend and cross-national study of general social attitudes]. Masamichi Sasaki; et al. *Int. J. Comp. Soc No.(31) - 1991.* pp. 193 – 205
74 The trouble of thinking — activation and application of stereotypic beliefs. Daniel T. Gilbert; J. Gregory Hixon. *J. Pers. Soc. Psychol.* **60:4** 4:1991 pp. 509 – 517
75 Typicality effects in attitude/behavior consistency — effects of category discrimination and category knowledge. Charles G. Lord; Donna M. Desforges; Shawna L. Ramsey; Glenn R. Trezza; Mark R. Lepper. *J. Exp. S. Psychol.* **27:6** 11:1991 pp. 550 – 575
76 Undominated strategies and coordination in normalform games. T. Börgers. *Soc. Choice* **8:1** 1991 pp. 65 – 78
77 "Uneasy lies the head" — politics, economics, and the continuity of belief among Yoruba of Nigeria. P.J. Dixon. *Comp. Stud. S.* **33:1** 1:1991 pp. 56 – 85
78 The use and misuse of rational models in collective behavior and social psychology. Ralph H. Turner. *Eur. J. Soc.* **XXXII:1** 1991 pp. 84 – 108

C.7: Opinions and attitudes *[Opinions et attitudes]*
79 Where to look first for children's knowledge of false beliefs. Michael Siegal; Karen Beattie. *Cognition* **38**:1 1:1991 pp. 1 – 12
80 Who's to blame? Action identification in allocating responsibility for alleged rape. Robin R. Vallacher; Karen Selz. *Soc. Cogn.* **9**:2 Summer:1991 pp. 194 – 219

D.1: Culture — *Culture*

Sub-divisions: Culture and cultural relations *[Culture et relations culturelles]*; Social norms, social control and value systems *[Normes sociales, régulation sociale et systèmes de valeur]*; Socialization and alienation *[Socialisation et aliénation]*

1 Abus de société civile — étatisation de la société ou socialisation de l'Etat *[In French]*; [The civil society abused — etatization of society or socialization of the state] *[Summary]*. René Gallissot. *Hom. Soc.* **XXV:4(102)** 1991 pp. 3 – 10
2 The analysis of "culture". John Corner *[Ed.]*; Richard Hoggart *[Contrib.]*; Stuart Laing *[Contrib.]*; Sarah Franklin *[Contrib.]*; Celia Lury *[Contrib.]*; Jackie Stacey *[Contrib.]*; Thomas K. Fitzgerald *[Contrib.]*; James Curran *[Contrib.]*; Colin Sparks *[Contrib.]*. *Collection of 5 articles.* **Media Cult. Soc.**, *13:2*, 4:1991 pp. 131 – 237
3 Backward countryside, troubled city — French teachers' images of rural and working-class families. D. Reed-Danahay; K. Anderson-Levitt. *Am. Ethn.* **18**:3 8:1991 pp. 546 – 564
4 Being Chinese — the peripheralization of traditional identity. Myron L. Cohen. *Dædalus* **120:2** Spring:1991 pp. 113 – 134
5 Communication/social difficulties of Thai students in the process of social adaptation. Paul N. Lakey; L. Brooks Hill. *Intercult. Commun. St.* **1:1** Spring:1991 pp. 105 – 130
6 Community, commitment, and conservatism. Rob Eisinga; Jan Lammers; Jan Peters. *Eur. Sociol. R.* **7**:2 9:1991 pp. 123 – 134
7 Comparative American identities — race, sex and nationality in the modern text. Hortense Spillers *[Ed.]*. London: Routledge, 1991: 198 p. *ISBN: 0415903491. Includes bibliography and index.* [The English Institute.]
8 Comparative versus evolutionary approaches to European society. Bernd Hamm. *Int. Sociol.* **6:1** 3:1991 pp. 111 – 116
9 The construction of Chinese and non-Chinese identities. David Yen-ho Wu. *Dædalus* **120:2** Spring:1991 pp. 159 – 179
10 Contemporary Chinese culture — structure and emotionality. Lung-kee Sun. *Aust. J. Chin. Aff.* **:26** 7:1991 pp. 1 – 42
11 Contemporary urban Buddhist "cults" and the socio-political order in Thailand. J.L. Taylor. *Mankind* **19**:2 8:1989 pp. 112 – 125
12 *[In Japanese]*; [Culture and modern world — from the viewpoint of cultural anthropology]. Iwayumi Suzuki; et al. Kyoto: Sagano-shoin, 1991: 229 p.
13 Culture and society — a sociology of culture. Rosamund Billington; et al. London: Macmillan Education, 1991: x, 221 p. *ISBN: 0333460383; LofC: gb 91004152. Sociological theory; Includes bibliography and index.* [Sociology for a changing world.]
14 Culture as class symbolization or mass reification? A critique of Bourdieu's <u>Distinction</u>. David Gartman. *A.J.S.* **97**:2 9:1991 pp. 421 – 447
15 Culture as figurative action. Clifford D. Shearing; Richard V. Ericson. *Br. J. Soc.* **42:4** 12:1991 pp. 481 – 506
16 Le domicile — sphère privée et sphère publique *[In French]*; [The home — private and public domain] *[Summary]*. Jacques Coenen-Huther. *Cah. Int. Soc.* **XCI:** 7-12:1991 pp. 301 – 314
17 Enterprise culture and the ideology of excellence. Paul du Gay. *New Form.* **:13** Spring:1991 pp. 45 – 62
18 Etat et société civile *[In French]*; [State and civil society]. René Gallissot *[Contrib.]*; Christiane Veauvy *[Contrib.]*; Pierre Lantz *[Contrib.]*; Michel Trebitsch *[Contrib.]*; Roland Lew *[Contrib.]*; Pierre Achard *[Contrib.]*; Ulysses Santamaria *[Contrib.]*; Jean-René Pendaries *[Contrib.]*; Pierre- Jean Simon *[Contrib.]*; Véronique De Rudder *[Contrib.] and others. Collection of 10 articles.* **Hom. Soc.**, *XXV:4(102)*, 1991 pp. 3 – 112
19 Evaluative inference in social cognition — the roles of direct versus indirect evaluation and positive-negative asymmetry. G. Peeters. *Eur. J. Soc. Psychol.* **21**:2 3-4:1991 pp. 131 – 146

D.1: Culture *[Culture]*

20 Fashion, gender and the Bengali middle class. Dulali Nag. *Publ. Cult.* **3**:2 Spring:1991 pp. 93 – 112
21 Философия культуры: проблемы и перспективы *[In Russian]*; (The philosophy of culture — problems and prospects). M.S. Kagan *[Contrib.]*; G.A. Brandt *[Contrib.]*; Yu. N. Solonin *[Contrib.]*; N.V. Golik *[Contrib.]*; E.P. Yurovskaya *[Contrib.]*; E.N. Ustjugova *[Contrib.]*; V.G. Ivanov *[Contrib.]*; A.V. Zdor *[Contrib.]*; A.M. Sergeyev *[Contrib.]*; E.K. Lugovaya *[Contrib.] and others. Collection of 12 articles.* **Vest. Lenin. Univ. 6** , *6:3,* 9:1991 pp. 4 – 72
22 Le fondementalisme, le multiculturalisme et les femmes *[In French]*; [Fundamentalism, multiculturalism and women]. Gita Saghal; Nira Davis. *Temps Mod.* **46**:540-541 7-8:1991 pp. 258 – 270
23 Идеалистическая диалектика в XX столетии: (Критика мировоззренч.основ немарксистской диалектики) *[In Russian]*; [Idealistic dialectics in the twentieth century — (criticism of world view on basis on non-Marxist dialectics]. Iu.N. Davydov *[Ed.]*; A.S. Bogomolov; P.P. Gaidenko. Moscow: Politizdat, 1987: 333 p.
24 Ideology, cultural frameworks, and the process of revolution. Jack A. Goldstone, *Theory Soc.* **20**:4 8:1991 pp. 405 – 453
25 The imaginary life — landscape and culture in Australia. E.R. Hills. *J. Aust. Stud.* :**29** 6:1991 pp. 12 – 27
26 Intimations of postmodernity. Zygmunt Bauman. New York: Routledge, 1991: 232 p. *ISBN: 0415067499; LofC: 91003115. Sociological theory; Includes bibliographical references and index.*
27 Культура, философия и духовный мир человека: Теорет.-метод.аспект *[In Russian]*; [Culture, philosophy and the spiritual world of man — theoretical-methodological aspect]. T.I. Adulo. Minsk: Nauka i tekhnika, 1986: 149 p. *Bibliogr. pp.144-148.* [АН БССР.Ин-т философии и права; [AN Belorussian SSR Institute of Philosophy and Law].]
28 Kulturális-kommunikációs rétegződés (kutatási tervezet) *[In Hungarian]*; [Cultural and communicational stratification (a framework for research)]. Róbert Agelusz; Róbert Tardos. *Szociologia* Vol.16; No.2 - 1987. pp. 209 – 231
29 Left of ethnomethodology — the rise and decline of radical reflexivity. Melvin Pollner. *Am. Sociol. R.* **56**:3 6:1991 pp. 370 – 380
30 Let us learn our inheritance — get to know yourself. H.B. Paksoy. *Cah. Ét. Méd. Ori. Tur-Iran.* **11** 1991 pp. 141 – 158
31 Mass culture and perestroika in the Soviet Union. Marsha Siefert *[Ed.]*. New York: Oxford University Press, 1991: 200 p. *ISBN: 0195073657; LofC: 91018948. Includes bibliographical references.*
32 New Times in cultural studies. Angela McRobbie. *New Form.* :**13** Spring:1991 pp. 1 – 18
33 *[In Japanese]*; [Nihonjinron — the discursive manifestation of cultural nationalism]. Kazufumi Manabe; et al. ***Kwan. Gak. Univ. Ann. St.*** *No.(40) - 1991.*
34 On the politics of cultural theory — a case for "contaminated" cultural critque. Kathleen Stewart. *Soc. Res.* **58**:2 Summer:1991 pp. 395 – 412
35 Rethinking popular culture — contemporary perspectives in cultural studies. Chandra Mukerji *[Ed.]*; Michael Schudson *[Ed.]*. Berkeley: University of California Press, c1991: vii, 501 p. (ill) *ISBN: 0520068920; LofC: 90039009. Includes bibliographical references and index.*
36 Die Risikogesellschaft und das Risiko soziologischer Zuspitzung *[In German]*; Risk society and the risk of pointed sociological thinking *[Summary]*. Ditmar Brock. *Z. Soziol.* **20**:1 2:1991 pp. 12 – 24
37 The role of the intelligentsia in developing national consciousness among the peoples of the USSR under perestroika. L.M. Drobizheva. *Ethn. Racial* **14**:1 1:1991 pp. 87 – 99
38 Сацыяльныя ўмовы ажыццяўлення патрэбнасцей *[In Belorussian]*; [Russian summary]; [The social conditions of realising needs] *[Summary]*. A.A. Dmozna. *V. Aka. BSSR* :**4** :1991 pp. 3 – 9
39 The search for social cohesion — from Durkheim to the European Commission. Ray E. Pahl. *Eur. J. Soc.* **XXXII**:2 1991 pp. 345 – 360
40 The semantics of pain in Indian culture and medicine. Judy F. Pugh. *Cult. Medic. Psych.* **15**:1 3:1991 pp. 19 – 44
41 Shopping for identities — "a nation of nations" and the weak ethnicity of objects. Susan Hegeman. *Publ. Cult.* **3**:2 Spring:1991 pp. 71 – 92
42 Staat und Gesellschaft im Irak unter der Baath-Partei *[In German]*; State and society in Baath-dominated Iraq *[Summary]*. Ferhad Ibrahim. *Peripherie* **11**:42 8:1991 pp. 18 – 42

D.1: Culture [Culture]

43 Studies in social influence VI — is Lenin orange or red? Imagery and social influence. S Moscovici; B. Personnaz. *Eur. J. Soc. Psychol.* **21:2** 3-4:1991 pp. 101 – 118

44 Syria — society, culture, and polity. Richard T. Antoun *[Ed.]*; Donald Quataert *[Ed.]*. Albany (NY): SUNY Press, 1991: xxi, 165 p. *ISBN: 0791407144*. [SUNY series in Middle Eastern studies.]

45 Terrorism and argument from analogy. G. Wallace. *Int. J. Moral Soc. S.* **6:2** Summer:1991 pp. 149 – 160

46 Tre problemi della cultura — individualizzazione, esasperazione e paralisi *[In Italian]*; Three problems of culture — individualization, exaggeration and paralysation *[Summary]*. Birgitta Nedelmann. *Rass. It. Soc.* **XXXII:2** 4-6:1991 pp. 127 – 154

47 The virtue of civil society. Edward Shils *[Speech by]*. *Govt. Oppos.* **26:1** Winter:1991 pp. 3 – 20

48 Water, spirits, and plain white cloth — the ambiguity of things in Bunu social life. Elisha P. Renne. *Man* **26:4** 12:1991 pp. 709 – 721

49 The way the world is — cultural processes and social relations among the Mombasa Swahili. Marc J. Swartz. Berkeley: University of California Press, 1991: xiii, 350 p. (ill) *ISBN: 0520071379. Bibliography — pp.331-341.*

50 We through the eyes of tradition. M. Petrov. *Soc. Sci.* **XXII:1** :1991 pp. 242 – 253

51 Why people vote — free riding and the production and consumption of social pressure. A. Schram; F. van Winden. *J. Econ. Psyc.* **12:4** 12:1991 pp. 575 – 620

Culture and cultural relations [*Culture et relations culturelles*]

52 Antecedents to cross- cultural adjustment for expatriates in Pacific Rim assignments. Stewart J Black; Hal B. Gregersen. *Human Relat.* **44:5** 5:1991 pp. 497 – 515

53 *[In Japanese]*; [Bond between reason and humanity — a sociological study of the intellectual cultures of the East and West]. Hideaki Hirano. *Shak.-rōd. Kenk.* *No.38(1) - 1991.* pp. 1 – 96

54 *[In Japanese]*; [Can Japan be internationalized?]. Fumie Kumagai. *Kyorin University Review of the Faculty of Foreign Languages No.(3) - 1991.* pp. 134 – 168

55 Comment l'Europe s'est divisée entre l'Est et l'Ouest *[In French]*; How Europe was divided into East and West. Alain Monnier; Jitka Rychtarikova. *Population* **46:6** 11-12:1991 pp. 1617 – 1650

56 La comparazione inter-culturale. Problemi di identità antropologica *[In Italian]*; Intercultural comparison. Problems of anthropological identity *[Summary]*. Francesco Remotti. *Rass. It. Soc.* **32:1** 1-3:1991 pp. 25 – 46

57 Comparing Muslim societies — knowledge and the state in a world civilization. Juan R.I. Cole *[Ed.]*. Ann Arbor: University of Michigan, 1991: 328 p. *ISBN: 0472094491*. [Comparative studies in society and book series.]

58 Competing patterns of national identity in post-communist Hungary. György Csepeli. *Media Cult. Soc.* **13:3** 7:1991 pp. 325 – 340

59 Consumer poetics — a French episode. Peter Nicholls. *New Form.* :**13** Spring:1991 pp. 75 – 90

60 Csoporttudat — nemzettudat. Esszék, tanulmányok *[In Hungarian]*; [Group consciousness — national consciousness — essays and studies]. György Csepeli. Budapest: Magvető, 1987: 388 p.

61 Culture et «effet sociétal» *[In French]*; Culture and the "societal effect" *[Summary]*; Kultur und "Sozietaleffekt" *[German summary]*; Cultura y "efecto societal" *[Spanish summary]*. Philippe D' Iribarne. *Rev. Fr. Soc.* **XXXII:4** 10-12:1991 pp. 599 – 614

62 Culture in Britain since 1945. Arthur Marwick. Oxford: Basil Blackwell, 1991: xiv, 206 p. (ill) *ISBN: 0631171894. Includes index.* [Making contemporary Britain.]

63 Culture, globalisation and the world system. Anthony D. King *[Ed.]*. Basingstoke: Macmillan Education, 1991: 186 p. *ISBN: 033353560x; LofC: gb 91000704.*

64 Culture, politics, and national identity in Côte d'Ivoire. Jerome Vogel. *Soc. Res.* **58:2** Summer:1991 pp. 439 – 455

65 The cynical society — the culture of politics and the politics of culture in American life. Jeffrey C Goldfarb. Chicago: University of Chicago Press, 1991: xi, 200 p. *ISBN: 0226301060; LofC: 90011187. Includes bibliographical references (p. [183]-194) and index.*

66 Le deuil de l'ethnologue — l'adieu au terrain *[In French]*; [The mourning of the ethnologist — goodbye to the field]. La de Soudière. *Soc. Sci. Info.* **30:2** 1991 pp. 269 – 278

D.1: Culture *[Culture]* — *Culture and cultural relations [Culture et relations culturelles]*

67 The end of Anglo-America — historical essays in the study of cultural divergence. Robert Arthur Burchell *[Ed.]*. Manchester: Manchester University Press, 1991: 214p. *ISBN: 0719030773.*

68 The enlightenment redefined — the formation of modern civil society. Margaret C. Jacob. *Soc. Res.* **58:2** Summer:1991 pp. 475 – 495

69 Les expériences historiques du Japon pour une théorie de la modernisation des sociétés non occidentales *[In French]*; The historical stages of the development of Japan — towards a theory of modernisation of non-Western countries *[Summary]*. Ken'ichi Tominaga. *Sociol. Trav.* **XXXIII:1** 1991 pp. 189 – 206

70 Une exploration sociologique dans la personnalité tunisienne *[In French]*; [A sociological exploration of the Tunisian personality]. Mohamed Dhaouadi. *IBLA* **54:168** 1991 pp. 203 – 213

71 Filosofia y identidad latinoamericana — historia y perspectivas de una problemática *[In Spanish]*; [Philosophy and Latin American identity — history and perspectives on a problem] *[Summary]*. Santiago Castro-Gómez. *Est. Leop.* **27:124** 9-10:1991 pp. 37 – 64

72 *[In Japanese]*; [The foreign culture in parallel]. Satoshi Takeyama. *Journal of the Institute of Cultural Science* No.(12) - 1991. pp. 37 – 72

73 Gilding the smokestacks — the new symbolic representations of deindustrialised regions. S. Watson. *Envir. Plan. D* **9:1** 3:1991 pp. 59 – 70

74 Hayek's theory of cultural evolution — an evaluation in the light of Vanberg's critique. Geoffrey M. Hodgson. *Econ. Philos.* **7:1** 4:1991 pp. 67 – 82

75 Heimat in Osteuropa. Das Problem territorialer Bindung am Beispiel deutscher Aussiedler *[In German]*; Homeland in Eastern Europe *[Summary]*; Le «Heimat» en Europe de l'Est *[French summary]*. Joachim Stark. *Arc. Kommunal.* **30:2** 1991 pp. 273 – 286

76 Heimat in Osteuropa. Das Problem territorialer Bindung am Beispiel deutscher Aussiedler *[In German]*; Homeland in Eastern Europe *[Summary]*; Le «Heimat» en Europe de l'Est *[French summary]*. Joachim Stark. *Arc. Kommunal.* **30:2** 1991 pp. 273 – 286

77 Hot literacy in cold societies — a comparative study of the sacred value of writing. R.W. Niezen. *Comp. Stud. S.* **33:2** 4:1991 pp. 225 – 254

78 Human universals. Donald E. Brown. Philadelphia: Temple University Press, c1991: x, 220 p. *ISBN: 0877228418; LofC: 90024694. Includes bibliographical references (p. 157-201) and index.*

79 Les inventeurs de rythmes sociaux *[In French]*; [The inventors of social rhythms] *[Summary]*. Pierre Ansart. *Cah. Int. Soc.* **XCI:** 7-12:1991 pp. 229 – 240

80 Массовая мистификация: поп-культура и суеверие *[In Russian]*; [Mass mystification — pop culture and superstition]. V.V. Molchanov. Leningrad: Lenizdat, 1987: 111 p. *Bibliogr. p.110.* [(Мифы и реальность: на фронтах идеол.борьбы) [Myths and reality — at the front-line of the ideological struggle].]

81 Modernism as a philosophical problem — on the dissatisfactions of European high culture. Robert B. Pippin. Cambridge, Mass., USA: B. Blackwell, c1991: 218 p. *ISBN: 0631172580; LofC: 90038302. Includes bibliographical references and index.*

82 Modernity and identity. Scott Lash *[Ed.]*; Jonathan Friedman *[Ed.]*. Oxford: Blackwell, 1991: 379 p. *ISBN: 0631175857; LofC: 90027629. Includes index.*

83 National identity. Anthony D. Smith. London: Penguin Books, 1991: 256p. *ISBN: 0140125655.*

84 National identity in Eastern Europe and the Soviet Union. George Schöpflin *[Contrib.]*; George Liber *[Contrib.]*; Zvi Gitelman *[Contrib.]*; Tadeusz Swietochowski *[Contrib.]*; Dennis Deletant *[Contrib.]*; L.M. Drobizheva *[Contrib.]*; Rudolf Joó *[Contrib.]*. Collection of 6 articles. **Ethn. Racial**, *14:1*, 1:1991 pp. 3 – 106

85 Natural law and civilizations — images of "nature," intracivilizational polarities, and the emergence of heterodox ideals. Donald A. Nielsen. *Sociol. Anal.* **52:1** Spring: 1991 pp. 55 – 76

86 New times and old enemies — essays in cultural studies and America. John Clarke. London: HarperCollins Academic, 1991: 160 p. *ISBN: 0044454740.*

87 On German identity. Harry Pross. *Media Cult. Soc.* **13:3** 7:1991 pp. 341 – 356

88 On the rocky road to the first global civilization. Howard V. Perlmutter. *Human Relat.* **44:9** 9:1991 pp. 897 – 920

89 Othering the academy — professionalism and multiculturalism. Bruce Robbins. *Soc. Res.* **58:2** Summer:1991 pp. 355 – 372

D.1: Culture *[Culture]* — **Culture and cultural relations *[Culture et relations culturelles]***

90 Pakeha — the quest for identity in New Zealand. Michael King *[Ed.]*. Auckland: Penguin, 1991: 199 p. *ISBN: 0140158685.*

91 Partial visions — culture and politics in Britain, Canada, and the United States. Richard M. Merelman. Madison, Wis: University of Wisconsin Press, c1991: xii, 287 p. *ISBN: 029912990x; LofC: 91009089. Includes bibliographical references (p. 253-275) and index.*

92 Post-Marxism — between/beyond critical postmodernism and cultural studies. Kuan-Hsing Chen. *Media Cult. Soc.* **13:1** 1:1991 pp. 35 – 51

93 Postmodernism, or, the cultural logic of late capitalism. Fredric Jameson. London: Verso, 1991: 438 p. *ISBN: 0860913147. Includes index.*

94 La primitivisme, le post-colonialisme, les antiquités «nègres» et la question nationale *[In French]*; Primitivism, postcolonialism, Negro antiques and the national issue *[Summary]*. Bogumil Jewsiewicki. *Cah. Ét. Afr.* **XXXI:1-2(121-122)** 1991 pp. 191 – 213

95 The prospects of human civilization. V. Stepin. *Soc. Sci.* **XXII:4** 1991 pp. 18 – 34

96 La reversibilità della civilizzazione. Note di lettura su Elias e la questione tedesca *[In Italian]*; On the reversibility of civilization *[Summary]*. Alessandro Cavalli. *Rass. It. Soc.* **32:4** 12:1991 pp. 507 – 518

97 Russia and Japan — points of contact. V. Toporov. *Soc. Sci.* **XXII:1** :1991 pp. 220 – 232

98 The state construction of affect — political ethos and mental health among Salvadoran refugees. Janis Hunter Jenkins. *Cult. Medic. Psych.* **15:2** 6:1991 pp. 139 – 165

99 Struktur und Dynamik sozialer Prozesse — makrosoziologische Aspekte der Kulturentwicklung bei Georg Simmel *[In German]*; [Structure and dynamics of social processes — macrosociological aspects of cultural development according to Georg Simmel]. Manfred Kauffmann. München: Profil, 1990: 256 p. *ISBN: 3890192467; LofC: 91122420. Includes bibliographical references (p. 244-256).* [Reihe Wissenschaft.]

100 Структура культуры и человек в современном обществе *[In Russian]*; [Structure of culture and man in contemporary society]. A.S. Akhiezer; V.L. Glazychev; E.A. Orlova *[Ed.]*. Moscow: , 1987: 184 p.

101 Those horrific Ik — the testing point for a still-emerging Confucian anthropology. Wallace Gray. *Asian Prof.* **19:4** 8:1991 pp. 303 – 322

102 Unsicherheit und Gesellschaft — Argumente für eine soziologische Risikoanalyse *[In German]*; Uncertainty and society — arguments for sociological risk analysis *[Summary]*. Wolfgang Bonß. *Soz. Welt.* **42:2** 1991 pp. 258 – 277

103 Das „Volk" — zur ideologischen Struktur eines unvermeidbaren Begriffs *[In German]*; The "people" — on the ideological structure of an inevitable term *[Summary]*. Lutz Hoffmann. *Z. Soziol.* **20:3** 6:1991 pp. 191 – 208

104 When in Rome? The effects of cultural adaptation on intercultural business negotiations. June N.P. Francis. *J. Int. Bus. Stud.* **22:3** Third quarter:1991 pp. 403 – 428

105 The world civilizational process. G. Arbatov; et al. *Soc. Sci.* **XXII:4** 1991 pp. 35 – 62

106 Worldly discourses — reflections on pragmatic utterances and on the culture of capital. Dan Rose. *Publ. Cult.* **4:1** Fall:1991 pp. 109 – 130

Social norms, social control and value systems *[Normes sociales, régulation sociale et systèmes de valeur]*

107 Are there limits to rationality? Margaret Levi. *Eur. J. Soc.* **XXXII:1** 1991 pp. 130 – 141

108 Changes in ideological models. Nurith Gertz. *Semiotica* **86:3-4** 1991 pp. 247 – 275

109 Computerization and controversy — value conflicts and social choices. Charles Dunlop *[Ed.]*; Rob Kling *[Ed.]*. Boston: Academic Press, c1991: xviii, 758 p. (ill) *ISBN: 0122243560; LofC: 90019415. Includes bibliographical references and index.*

110 Cultural relativism and the theory of value. G.P. Foster. *Am. J. Econ. S.* **50:3** 7:1991 pp. 257 – 268

111 Divide and conquer — popular culture and social control in late capitalism. David Tetzlaff. *Media Cult. Soc.* **13:1** 1:1991 pp. 9 – 33

112 Estimating community standards — the use of social science evidence in an obscenity prosecution. Daniel Linz; Edward Donnerstein; Kenneth C. Land; Patricia L. McCall; Joseph Scott; Bradley J. Shafer; Lee J. Klein; Larry Lance. *Publ. Opin. Q.* **55:1** Spring:1991 pp. 80 – 112

113 An exchange of views about basic Chinese social organization — transfigured community — neo-traditionalism and work unit socialism in China. Brantly Womack. *China Quart.* **:126** 6:1991 pp. 313 – 332

D.1: Culture *[Culture]* — **Social norms, social control and value systems** *[Normes sociales, régulation sociale et systèmes de valeur]*

114 German war memories — narrability and the biographical and social functions of remembering. Gabriele Rosenthal. *Oral Hist.* **19:**2 Autumn:1991 pp. 34 – 41

115 Goals in space — American values and the future of technology. William Sims Bainbridge. Albany: State University of New York Press, c1991: 268 p. *ISBN: 0791406148; LofC: 90009901. Includes bibliographical references (p. [247]-258) and index.*

116 Inflation of symbols — loss of values in American culture. Orrin Edgar Klapp. New Brunswick, N.J: Transaction Publishers, c1991: 199 p. *ISBN: 0887383858; LofC: 90020349. Includes bibliographical references and index.*

117 Lettre ouverte aux Suisses, si bons, si gros, si tristes *[In French]*; [An open letter to the Swiss, so good, so far, so sad]. Jean-Luc Hennig. Paris: Albin Michel, 1991: 198p. *ISBN: 2226052941.*

118 Mapping meanings — a cultural critique of locality studies. P. Jackson. *Envir. Plan.A.* **23:**2 2:1991 pp. 215 – 228

119 Le modèle suisse *[In French]*; [The Swiss model]. Fabien Dunand. Paris: Payot, 1991: 311 p. *ISBN: 2228883549.* [Documents.]

120 Обыденное и массовое сознание (опыт социологического анализа) *[In Russian]*; (Usual and mass consciousness (an experience of sociological analysis)). E.I. Kukushkina; L.I. Nasonova. *Vest. Mosk. Univ. 12* **:1** 1-2:1991 pp. 22 – 33

121 *[In Japanese]*; [On the meaning of social norm]. Hisataka Kobayashi. ***Shak. Hyor.*** *No.42(1) - 1991.* pp. 32 – 46

122 The post-modern and the post-industrial — a critical analysis. Margaret A. Rose. Cambridge [England]: Cambridge University Press, 1991: 317 p. *ISBN: 0521401313; LofC: 90039993. Includes bibliographical references and index.*

123 The poverty of social control — explaining power in the historical sociology of the welfare state. Robert van Krieken. *Sociol. Rev.* **39:**1 2:1991 pp. 1 – 25

124 Rationality and social norms. Jon Elster. *Eur. J. Soc.* **XXXII:**1 1991 pp. 109 – 129

125 The rationality of norms. Steven Lukes. *Eur. J. Soc.* **XXXII:**1 1991 pp. 142 – 149

126 Social bonds in traditional East. G. Kiselev. *Soc. Sci.* **XXII:**1 :1991 pp. 28 – 39

127 The social construction of status value — gender and other nominal characteristics. Cecilia Ridgeway. *Soc. Forc.* **70:**2 12:1991 pp. 367 – 386

128 Social value orientation and intelligence — a test of the goal prescribes rationality principle. P.A.M. van Lange; W.B.G. Liebrand. *Eur. J. Soc. Psychol.* **21:**4 7-8:1991 pp. 273 – 292

129 Társadalmi értékek és szociálpolitika *[In Hungarian]*; [Social values and social policy]. Zsuzsa Ferge. ***Tarsad. Kozl.*** *Vol.17; No.2 - 1987.* pp. 179 – 190

130 Value elicitation — is there anything in there? Baruch Fischoff. *Am. Psychol.* **46:**8 8:1991 pp. 835 – 847

131 The values of Canadians and Americans — a critical analysis and reassessment. Doug Baer; Edward Grabb; William A. Johnston. *Soc. Forc.* **68:**3 3:1990 pp. 693 – 713

132 Values, self, and society — toward a humanist social psychology. M. Brewster Smith. New Brunswick, N.J: Transaction Publishers, c1991: xx, 289 p. *ISBN: 0887383734; LofC: 90040000. Includes bibliographical references (p. 155-277) and index.*

133 Why is being valuable? Branimir Luksic. *Arc. Recht. Soz.* **LXXVII:**2 1991 pp. 214 – 219

134 Why punish? Nigel Walker. Oxford: Oxford University Press, 1991: 168 p. *ISBN: 019219240x; LofC: 90025919. Includes bibliographical references and index.*

Socialization and alienation *[Socialisation et aliénation]*

135 Łapownictwo w społecznej świadomości. Wstępne ustalenia badawcze *[In Polish]*; Corruption in the social consciousness, introductory assumptions *[Summary]*. Jan Lutyński; Anna Kubiak. *Acta Univ. Łódz. Folia Soc.* **20** 1991 pp. 153 – 167

136 Értéválság vagy értékváltás? A fiatalok politikai szocializációjának néhány problémájáról *[In Hungarian]*; [Crisis or change of values? Some problems of the political socialization among young people]. Ildikó Szabó. ***Szociologia*** *Vol.16; No.1 - 1987.* pp. 101 – 128

137 Explanations, accounts, and illusions — a critical analysis. John McClure. Cambridge: Cambridge University Press, 1991 *ISBN: 0521385326. Includes index.* [European monographs in social psychology.]

138 Fashioning the future — fashion, clothing, and the manufacturing of post-Fordist culture. McKenzie Wark. *Cult. St.* **5:**1 1:1991 pp. 67 – 76

139 Les Japonais sont-ils des occidentaux? — sociologie d'une acculturation volontaire *[In French]*; [Are the Japanese Westerners? The sociology of voluntary acculturation]. Toshiaki Kozakaï. Paris: L'Harmattan, 1991: 224 p. *ISBN: 2738410308.*

D.1: Culture *[Culture]* — *Socialization and alienation [Socialisation et aliénation]*

140 Die modernisierte Hacienda — zum Vergesellschaftungsprozess Chiles im 20. Jahrhundert *[In German]*; [The modernised Hacienda — on Chile's socialization process in the 20th century]. Stephan Heieck. München: Eberhard, 1990: 290 p. *ISBN: 3926777206; LofC: 91108960. Includes bibliographical references (p. 271-289).* [Schriften zu Lateinamerika. : No. 2]

141 Reweaving the fringe — localism, tradition, and representation in British ethnography. J. Nadel-Klein. *Am. Ethn.* **18:3** 8:1991 pp. 500 – 517

142 Witchcraft and leprosy — two strategies of exclusion. Mary Douglas. *Man* **26:4** 12:1991 pp. 723 – 735

D.2: Everyday culture — *Culture quotidienne*

1 Communal webs — communication and culture in contemporary Israel. Tamar Katriel. Albany: State University of New York Press, c1991: 226 p. (ill) *ISBN: 0791406458; LofC: 90010057. Includes bibliographical references (p. 201-216) and index.* [SUNY series, anthropology and Judaic studies; SUNY series, human communication processes.]

2 Controlling motherhood — observations on the culture of the La Leche League; *[French summary]*. Florence Kellner Andrews. *Can. R. Soc. A.* **28:1** 2:1991 pp. 84 – 98

3 Days of honey, days of onion — the story of a Palestinian family in Israel. Michael Gorkin. Boston: Beacon Press, c1991: viii, 286 p. (map) *ISBN: 0807069027; LofC: 91009849. Includes bibliographical references.*

4 *[In Japanese]*; [Determinant of fashion acceptance]. Masako Nakamura. **Yokohama Shodai Ronshu** *No.24(2) - 1991.* pp. 85 – 99

5 Dress and popular culture. Patricia Anne Cunningham *[Ed.]*; Susan Voso Lab *[Ed.]*. Bowling Green, Ohio: Bowling Green State University Popular Press, c1991: 165 p. (ill) *ISBN: 0879725079; LofC: 90086155. Includes bibliographical references.*

6 Electronic hearth — creating an American television culture. Cecelia Tichi. New York: Oxford University Press, 1991: x, 249 p. (ill) *ISBN: 0195065492; LofC: 91010640. Includes bibliographical references (p. 233-245) and index.*

7 Los españoles — sociología de la vida cotidiana *[In Spanish]*; [The Spanish — a sociology of daily life]. Amando de Miguel. Madrid: Ediciones Temas de Hoy, 1990: 277 p. *ISBN: 8478800514; LofC: 91132683. Includes bibliographical references (p. 269-274) and index.* [Colección España hoy. : No. 9]

8 Etiquette in intercultural situations — a Japanese business luncheon. Helen E. Marriott. *Intercult. Commun. St.* **1:1** Spring:1991 pp. 69 – 94

9 Evolution of lifestyles and dwelling practices in France. Yvonne Bernard. *J. Arch. Plan. Res.* **8:3** Autumn:1991 pp. 192 – 202

10 Fashion, representation, femininity. Caroline Evans; Minna Thornton. *Feminist R.* **:38** Summer:1991 pp. 48 – 66

11 From tachi soba to naorai — cultural implications of the Japanese meal. Michael Ashkenazi. *Soc. Sci. Info.* **30:2** 1991 pp. 287 – 304

12 Italian family matters — women, politics and legal reform. Lesley Caldwell. London: Macmillan, 1991: 163 p. *ISBN: 0333426770. Includes bibliography and index.* [Language, discourse, society series.]

13 Javanese lives — women and men in modern Indonesian society. Walter L. Williams; Claire Siverson; et al. New Brunswick: Rutgers University Press, c1991: xxii, 238 p. (ill) *ISBN: 081351648x; LofC: 90045113. Includes bibliographical references (p. 225-231) and index.*

14 The last word — women, death, and divination in Inner Mani. C. Nadia Seremetakis. Chicago: University of Chicago Press, 1991: ix, 275 p., 36 p. of plates (ill., 2 maps) *ISBN: 0226748758; LofC: 90040640. Includes bibliographical references (p. 247-264) and indexes.*

15 Making food fast — from the frying pan into the fryer. Ester Reiter. Montréal: McGill-Queen's University Press, 1991: - *ISBN: 0773508430; LofC: cn 91090225. Includes bibliographical references and index.*

16 Il mito dell'URSS — la cultura occidentale e l'Unione Sovietica *[In Italian]*; [The power of the USSR — Western culture and the Soviet Union]. Marcello Flores *[Ed.]*; Francesca Gori *[Ed.]*; Ewa Bérard *[Ed.]*. Milan: Franco Angeli, 1990: 446 p. *Atti del convegno internazionale ...Cortona...1989.*

D.2: Everyday culture *[Culture quotidienne]*

17 Mudança cultural no Brasil *[In Portuguese]*; [Cultural change in Brazil]. Luís Forjaz Trigueiros *[Ed.]*. Lisboa: Instituto de Relações Internacionais, Instituto Superior de Ciências Sociais e Políticas, Universidade Técnica de Lisboa, 1990: 424 p. *BNB: 92105735; LofC: 92105735. Includes Bibliographical references.*
18 Neverending stories — the problem of reading in cultural studies. Colin Mercer. *New Form.* :13 Spring:1991 pp. 63 – 74
19 *[In Japanese]*; [On everyday activities and their relevence]. Chie Imai. ***Shak-nen.*** *No.(32)* - *1991.* pp. 91 – 105
20 A primer for daily life. Susan Willis. London: Routledge, 1991: 185 p. (ill) *ISBN: 0415041805. Includes bibliography and index.* [Studies in culture and communication.]
21 Refashioning nature — food, ecology, and culture. David Goodman; Michael Redclift *[Ed.]*. London: Routledge, 1991: 279 p. *ISBN: 0415067022; LofC: 90027217. Includes bibliographical references and index.*
22 Les représentations de la régulation normative de la vie quotidienne *[In French]*; (Views of the normative ordering of everyday life). Grazyna Skapska. *Rev. Ét. Comp.* **XXII:4** 12:1991 pp. 103 – 119
23 The social psychology of everyday life. Michael Argyle. New York: Routledge, 1991: 319 p. *ISBN: 0415010713; LofC: 91017444. Includes bibliographical references and indexes.*
24 Society, culture, and drinking patterns reexamined. David Joshua Pittman *[Ed.]*; Helene Raskin White *[Ed.]*. New Brunswick, N.J., USA: Publications Division, Rutgers Center of Alcohol Studies, 1991: xviii, 805 p. *ISBN: 0911290214; LofC: 91061680. Includes bibliographical references and index.*
25 La sociología de lo cotidiano dentro del marco de las sociologís francesas *[In Spanish]*; [The sociology of the everyday within the framework of French sociology]. Michel Maffessoli. *Est. Sociol.* **IX:27** 9-12:1991 pp. 623 – 632
26 Southern culture and firearms ownership. G. Ellison. *Soc. Sci. Q.* **72:2** 6:1991 pp. 267 – 283
27 Советские традиции, праздники и обряды: Опыт, проблемы, рекомендации *[In Russian]*; [Soviet traditions, holidays and ceremonies — experience, problems, recommendations]. V.I. Volovik; V.V. Dankov; M.A. Orlik *[Ed.]*; M.D. Dovbush *[Contrib.]*. Moscow: Profizdat, 1986: 334 p.
28 Svakodnevnica u obzoru post moderne *[In Serbo-Croatian]*; The quotidian within the postmodern horizon *[Summary]*. Tena Martinić. *Pol. Misao* **XXVIII:4** 1991 pp. 115 – 124
29 The transformation of the Norwegian notion of everyday life. M. Gullestad. *Am. Ethn.* **18:3** 8:1991 pp. 480 – 499

D.3: Ethics and morals — *Éthique et morale*

Sub-divisions: Ethics *[Éthique]*; Morality *[Moralité]*

1 Act as the limit of distributive justice. Slavoj Žižek. *New Form.* :14 Summer:1991 pp. 69 – 86
2 Agency, attachment, and difference. Barbara Herman. *Ethics* **101:4** 7:1991 pp. 775 – 797
3 Between states and markets — the voluntary sector in comparative perspective. Robert Wuthnow *[Ed.]*. Princeton: Princeton University Press, 1991: 318 p. *ISBN: 0691028613.*
4 Concepts of equity, fairness, and justice expressed by local transport policymakers. A. Hay; E. Trinder. *Envir. Plan. C.* **9:4** 11:1991 pp. 453 – 465
5 Decision-theoretic consequentialism and the nearest and dearest objection. Frank Jackson. *Ethics* **101:3** 4:1991 pp. 461 – 482
6 The effects of explanations on negative reactions to deceit. Debra L. Shapiro. *Adm. Sci. Qua.* **36:4** 12:1991 pp. 614 – 630
7 Ethics in human resource management — basic bargains and basic values. Ian Clark. *Can. Publ. Ad.* **34:1** Spring:1991 pp. 37 – 43
8 The ethics of self-concern. John Cottingham. *Ethics* **101:4** 7:1991 pp. 798 – 817
9 Ethics revisited. Robert Hyslop. *Aust. J. Publ.* **50:4** 12:1991 pp. 467 – 476
10 Gehorsam, Gehorsamsverweigerung und ziviler Ungehorsam gegenüber der staatlichen Autorität *[In German]*; [Obedience, insubordination and civil disobedience]. Kurt Remele. *Jahr. Christ. Sozialwiss.* **32** 1991 pp. 277 – 301
11 Haben Föten ein Lebensinteresse? *[In German]*; [Is it in the interest of a fetus to live?]. Norbert Hoerster. *Arc. Recht. Soz.* **LXXVII:3** :1991 p.385-395

D.3: Ethics and morals [Éthique et morale]

12 Impartiality and friendship. Marcia Baron. *Ethics* **101:4** 7:1991 pp. 836 – 857
13 Indivisible selves and moral practice. Vinit Haksar. Edinburgh: Edinburgh University Press, 1991: 250 p. *ISBN: 0748602496.*
14 The nature of responsibility — children's understanding of "your job". Pamela M. Warton; Jacqueline J. Goodnow. *Child. Devel.* **62:1** 2:1991 pp. 156 – 165
15 The paradox of deontology. Christopher McMahon. *Philos. Pub.* **20:4** Fall:1991 p. 350
16 Partial consideration. Margaret Urban Walker. *Ethics* **101:4** 7:1991 pp. 758 – 776
17 The practice of partiality. Marilyn Friedman. *Ethics* **101:4** 7:1991 pp. 818 – 835
18 Respect du patrimoine génétique et respect de la personne *[In French]*; [Respect for genetic inheritance and the person]. Anne Fagot-Largeault. *Esprit* **:171** 5:1991 pp. 40 – 53
19 Responsibility and inevitability. John Martin Fischer; Mark Ravizza. *Ethics* **101:2** 1:1991 pp. 258 – 278
20 Responsibility, agent-causation, and freedom — an eighteenth-century view. William L. Rowe. *Ethics* **101:2** 1:1991 pp. 237 – 257
21 Responsible action and virtuous character. Robert Audi. *Ethics* **101:2** 1:1991 pp. 304 – 321
22 Taking "free action" too seriously. W.J. Norman. *Ethics* **101:3** 4:1991 pp. 505 – 520
23 Theologie der Versöhnung und Katholische Soziallehre *[In German]*; [Reconciliation theology and Catholic social doctrine]. Theodor Herr. *Jahr. Christ. Sozialwiss.* **32** 1991 pp. 203 – 225
24 Value-based management for the information society — some new perspectives. Yassin Sankar. Toronto: Canadian Scholars' Press, 1991: 299 p. *ISBN: 0921627793; LofC: cn 91095300. Includes bibliographical references.*
25 Why it is wrong to be always guided by the best — consequentialism and friendship. Neera Badhwar Kapur. *Ethics* **101:3** 4:1991 pp. 483 – 504

Ethics [Éthique]

26 Accessing Canadian ethics research. Michael McDonald. *Can. Publ. Ad.* **34:1** Spring:1991 pp. 196 – 202
27 AIDS and ethics. Frederic G. Reamer *[Ed.]*. New York: Columbia University Press, c1991: xviii, 317 p. *ISBN: 0231073585; LofC: 91021477 //r92. Includes bibliographical references and index.*
28 Animal experimentation — the moral issues. Robert M. Baird *[Ed.]*; Stuart E. Rosenbaum *[Ed.]*. Buffalo: Prometheus Books, 1991: 182 p. *ISBN: 0879756675.* [Contemporary issues.]
29 Approaches to ethics education. Kenneth Kernaghan; Shirley Mancino. *Can. Publ. Ad.* **34:1** Spring:1991 pp. 184 – 191
30 *[In Japanese]*; [Belief types and economic ethics]. Mamoru Yamada. ***Annual of the Society of Economic Sociology** No.(13) - 1991.* pp. 184 – 194
31 Business and accounting ethics in Islam. Trevor Gambling; Rifaat Ahmed Abdel Karim. London: Mansell, 1991: 152 p. *ISBN: 0720120748; LofC: 90013366. Includes bibliographical references and index.* [Islamic futures and policy studies.]
32 Business ethics past and present. David Vogel. *Publ. Inter.* **:102** Winter:1991 pp. 49 – 64
33 Collective responsibility — five decades of debate in theoretical and applied ethics. Larry May *[Ed.]*; Stacey Hoffmann *[Ed.]*. Savage, Md: Rowman & Littlefield, c1991: viii, 292 p. *ISBN: 0847676919; LofC: 91016441. Includes bibliographical references.* [Studies in social & political philosophy.]
34 Economic development, ethics and civil development. Paolo Sylos Labini. *J. Reg. Pol.* **11:3-4** 7-12:1991 pp. 475 – 482
35 Ethics and agriculture — an anthology on current issues in world context. Charles V. Blatz. Moscow, Idaho: University of Idaho Press, 1991: x, 674 p. (ill) *ISBN: 0893011339; LofC: 91011713. Includes bibliographical references (p. 663-674).*
36 Ethics and economics — some considerations. Domenicantonio Fausto. *J. Reg. Pol.* **11:3-4** 7-12:1991 pp. 483 – 499
37 Ethics and increasing international income inequalities. Dominick Salvatore. *J. Reg. Pol.* **11:3-4** 7-12:1991 pp. 519 – 541
38 Ethics and the environment — a business perspective. Weldon Thoburn. *Can. Publ. Ad.* **34:1** Spring:1991 pp. 117 – 120
39 Ethics and the environment — beyond self-interest. Dorothy Richardson. *Can. Publ. Ad.* **34:1** Spring:1991 pp. 111 – 116
40 The ethics of information management. John Grace. *Can. Publ. Ad.* **34:1** Spring:1991 pp. 95 – 100

D.3: Ethics and morals *[Éthique et morale]* — Ethics *[Éthique]*

41 Ethics of teaching — beliefs and behaviors of psychologists as educators. Barbara G. Tabachnick; Patricia Keith-Spiegel; Kenneth S. Pope. *Am. Psychol.* **46:5** 5:1991 pp. 506 – 515
42 Ethics — informed consent or misinformed compliance? Sue Robson. *J. Market R.* **33:1** 1:1991 pp. 19 – 28
43 Ethics, development and the need for a new «paradigm». Amitai Etzioni. *J. Reg. Pol.* **11:3-4** 7-12:1991 pp. 587 – 599
44 Ethics, trust, and the professions — philosophical and cultural aspects. Edmund D. Pellegrino *[Ed.]*; Robert M. Veatch *[Ed.]*; John Langan *[Ed.]*. Washington, D.C: Georgetown University Press, c1991: xiv, 284 p. *ISBN: 0878405127; LofC: 90046368.* "This volume is part of a series of publications resulting from the bicentennial celebration of Georgetown University (1789-1989)." ; Includes bibliographical references.
45 Éthique et droit dans l'exercise de la fonction de justice *[In French]*; Ethic and law in the exercice of justice. Jacques Commaille. *Soc. Contemp.* **:7** 9:1991 pp. 87 – 102
46 Faut-il avoir peur de la bioéthique? *[In French]*; [Should we fear bioethics?]. Dominique Bourg. *Esprit* **:171** 5:1991 pp. 22 – 39
47 Government ethics commissioners — the way of the future? Ian Greene. *Can. Publ. Ad.* **34:1** Spring:1991 pp. 165 – 170
48 Governmental ethics and ethics agencies. Warren Bailie; David Johnson. *Can. Publ. Ad.* **34:1** Spring:1991 pp. 158 – 164
49 Биоэтика *[In Russian]*; (Bioethics). Iu.M. Lopukhin. *Priroda* **:10(914)** 10:1991 pp. 3 – 7
50 Jacques Derrida's response to the call for ethics. R.A. Champagne. *Int. J. Moral Soc. S.* **6:1** Spring:1991 pp. 3 – 18
51 Managing ethics — complementary approaches. Kenneth Kernaghan. *Can. Publ. Ad.* **34:1** Spring:1991 pp. 132 – 145
52 Market morality and company size. Brian Harvey *[Ed.]*; Henk van Luijk *[Ed.]*; Guido Corbetta *[Ed.]*. Dordrecht: Kluwer Academic Publishers in cooperation with the European Business Ethics Network, c1991: vii, 229 p. *ISBN: 0792313429; LofC: 91023946.* "Originally presented at the Third European Conference on Business Ethics, organized by EBEN, the European Business Ethics Network ...and held in September 1990 in Milan, Italy"--Introd; Includes bibliographical references and index. [Issues in business ethics. : Vol. 2]
53 Moral issues and multinational corporations. Gerard Elfstrom. London: Macmillan, 1991: 144 p. *ISBN: 0333526902. Includes bibliography and index.*
54 Perfect markets and easy virtue — business ethics and the invisible hand. William J. Baumol; Sue Anne Batey Blackman. Oxford: Blackwell, 1991: 134 p. *ISBN: 1557862486; LofC: 91016775. Includes bibliographical references and index.* [Mitsui lectures in economics.]
55 Physical possibility and potentiality in ethics. Edward Covey. *Am. Phil. Q.* **28:3** 7:1991 pp. 237 – 244
56 Promoting ethical behaviour for municipal councils. Marcia Sypnowich. *Can. Publ. Ad.* **34:1** Spring:1991 pp. 146 – 152
57 Rights of anonymity and rights of solitude — ethical information management in the private sector. Brian R. Bawden. *Can. Publ. Ad.* **34:1** Spring:1991 pp. 101 – 110
58 The role of ethics in social theory — essays from a Habermasian perspective. Tony Smith. Albany: State University of New York Press, c1991: xiii, 246 p. *ISBN: 0791406520; LofC: 90040194. Includes bibliographical references (p. 231-240) and index.* [Ethical theory.]
59 A time to be born and a time to die — the ethics of choice. Barry S Kogan *[Ed.]*. Hawthorne, N.Y: Aldine De Gruyter, c1991: x, 267 p. *ISBN: 0202303888; LofC: 91006504. Ethics; Revised versions of papers presented at a conference on ethics, held on Oct. 15-17, 1989 in Cincinnati, Ohio, sponsored by the Hebrew Union College-Jewish Institute of Religion through its Starkoff Institute of Ethics and Contemporary Moral Problems; Includes bibliographical references and index.* [Starkoff Institute studies in ethics and contemporary moral problems.]
60 Underdevelopment, economic development and ethics. Ferruccio Marzano. *J. Reg. Pol.* **11:3-4** 7-12:1991 pp. 507 – 518
61 Vulgar ethics for public administration. Lewis C. Mainzer. *Admin. Soc.* **23:1** 5:1991 pp. 3 – 28
62 Whose side are we on now? Ethical issues in social research and medical practice. Annette Lawson. *Soc. Sci. Med.* **32:5** 1991 pp. 591 – 599

D.3: Ethics and morals [Éthique et morale] —

Morality [Moralité]

63 Animal experimentation — the moral issues. Robert M. Baird [Ed.]; Stuart E. Rosenbaum [Ed.]. Buffalo: Prometheus Books, 1991: 182 p. ISBN: 0879756675. [Contemporary issues.]

64 [In Japanese]; [Beyond relativistic morality — on Kohlberg's contribution to "moral socialization"]. Masahito Takahashi. *Shak. Kenk. No.(57) - 1991.* pp. 159 – 181

65 Contractualism, moral motivation, and practical reason. Samuel Freeman. *J. Phil.* **LXXXVIII:6** 6:1991 pp. 281 – 303

66 Critical interaction — judgment, decision, and the social testing of moral hypotheses. A.P. Iannone. *Int. J. Moral Soc. S.* **6:2** Summer:1991 pp. 135 – 148

67 The development of the sense of justice — moral development, resources, and emotions. William R. Charlesworth. *Am. Behav. Sc.* **34:3** 1-2:1991 pp. 350 – 370

68 Discourse and the moral point of view — deriving a dialogical principle of universalization. William Rehg. *Inquiry* **34:1** 3:1991 p. 27

69 Ethics consultation as moral engagement. Jonathan D. Moreno. *Bioethics* **5:1** 1991 pp. 44 – 56

70 Фарміраванне маральнай свядомасці як дынамічны працэс [In Belorussian]; [Russian summary]; [The formation of moral consciousness as a dynamic process] [Summary]. A.R. Mkrtchan. *V. Aka. BSSR* **2** 1991 pp. 18 – 24

71 Impartiality, compassion, and modal imagination. Adrian M.S. Piper. *Ethics* **101:4** 7:1991 pp. 726 – 757

72 King Soloman and everyman — a problem in coordinating conflicting moral intuitions. Amelie Oksenberg Rorty. *Am. Phil. Q.* **28:3** 7:1991 pp. 181 – 194

73 Moral maturity — measuring the development of sociomoral reflection. John C Gibbs; Karen S Basinger [Ed.]; Dick Fuller [Ed.]. Hillsdale, N.J: L. Erlbaum Associates, 1991: xii, 218 p. *ISBN: 0805804250; LofC: 91006552. Includes bibliographical references and index.*

74 Moral perception and particularity. Lawrence Blum. *Ethics* **101:4** 7:1991 pp. 701 – 725

75 Moral values and higher education — a notion at risk. Dennis L. Thompson [Ed.]. [Provo, Utah]: Brigham Young University, c1991: vii, 179 p. *ISBN: 0791407934; LofC: 90019857. Includes bibliographical references and index.*

76 Moralistic aggression and the sense of justice. Michael T. McGuire. *Am. Behav. Sc.* **34:3** 1-2:1991 pp. 371 – 385

77 Objective morality. Robin Allott. *J. Soc. Biol. Struct.* **14:4** 1991 pp. 455 – 471

78 Perestroika and morality.*Soc. Sci.* **XXII:4** 1991 pp. 170 – 197

79 Permission and regulation — law and morals in post-war Britain. Tim Newburn. New York: Routledge, 1991: 227 p. *ISBN: 0415046394; LofC: 91010288. Includes bibliographical references and index.*

80 Personal morality in a professional context. George Thomson. *Can. Publ. Ad.* **34:1** Spring:1991 pp. 21 – 29

81 The revival of the moral base in the Soviet Union. Louis Baeck. *J. Reg. Pol.* **11:3-4** 7-12:1991 pp. 609 – 627

82 Role morality as a complex instance of ordinary morality. Judith Andre. *Am. Phil. Q.* **28:1** 1:1991 pp. 73 – 80

83 Сацыялагічны падыход да вымярэння ўзроўню маральнай свядомасці [In Belorussian]; [A sociological approach to the measurement of the level of moral consciousness] [Summary]; [Russian summary]. A.R. Mkrtchan; V.V. Tsiareshchanka. *V. Aka. BSSR* **:3** 1991 pp. 17 – 22

84 Self-defense. Judith Jarvis Thomson. *Philos. Pub.* **20:4** Fall:1991 pp. 283 – 310

85 Socio-cultural influences on moral behaviour. Girishwar Misra. *Indian J. Soc. W.* **LII:2** 4:1991 pp. 179 – 194

86 Structural flexibility of moral judgment. Dennis L. Krebs; Kathy L. Denton; Sandra C. Vermeulen; Jeremy I. Carpendale; Alice Bush. *J. Pers. Soc. Psychol.* **61:6** 12:1991 pp. 1012 – 1023

87 Symposium on moral responsibility. William L. Rowe [Contrib.]; John Martin Fischer [Contrib.]; Mark Ravizza [Contrib.]; Holly M. Smith [Contrib.]; Robert Audi [Contrib.]. Collection of 4 articles. *Ethics*, *101:2*, 1:1991 pp. 237 – 321

88 Varieties of moral worth and moral credit. Holly M. Smith. *Ethics* **101:2** 1:1991 pp. 279 – 303

89 The Vatican's dilemma — on the morality of IVF and the incarnation. Howard Ducharme. *Bioethics* **5:1** 1991 pp. 57 – 66

D.3: Ethics and morals [Éthique et morale] — Morality [Moralité]

90 Wybrane aspekty poczucia moralnego młodych nauczycieli łódzkich [In Polish]; Chosen aspects of moral attitudes of young teachers — the case of Łódź [Summary]. Zdzisława Kawka. Acta Univ. Łódz. Folia Soc. **21** 1991 pp. 143 – 158

D.4: Law — Loi

1 Appeals to civic virtue versus attention to self-interest — effects on tax compliance. Kathleen M. McGraw; John T. Scholz. Law Soc. Rev. **25**:3 1991 pp. 471 – 498
2 Automatism, insanity, and the psychology of criminal responsibility — a philosophical inquiry. Robert F. Schopp. Cambridge: Cambridge University Press, 1991: xi, 277 p. ISBN: 052140150x; LofC: 90027604. Includes bibliographical references and index. [Cambridge studies in philosophy and law.]
3 Behavior, evolution, and the sense of justice. Margaret Gruter [Ed.]; Roger D. Masters [Contrib.]; Wolfgang Fikentscher [Contrib.]; Frans B.M. de Waal [Contrib.]; William R. Charlesworth [Contrib.]; Michael T. McGuire [Contrib.]; William H. Rodgers [Contrib.]. Collection of 6 articles. Am. Behav. Sc , 34:3, 1-2:1991 pp. 289 – 406
4 The case for the prosecution. Michael McConville; Andrew Sanders [Ed.]; Roger Leng [Ed.]. London: Routledge, 1991: 227 p. ISBN: 0415055776. Includes bibliography and index.
5 The child witness — legal issues and dilemmas. Nancy W. Perry; Lawrence S. Wrightsman [Ed.]. Newbury Park, Calif: Sage Publications, c1991: 289 p. ISBN: 0803937717; LofC: 91000331. Includes bibliographical references and indexes.
6 Citizenship, colonisation and criminal justice. J. Pratt. Int. J. S. Law **19**:3 8:1991 pp. 293 – 320
7 Clement Haynsworth, the Senate, and the Supreme Court. John Paul Frank. Charlottesville: University Press of Virginia, 1991: xvi, 158 p. (ill) ISBN: 0813912911; LofC: 90040349. Includes bibliographical references (p. 137-151) and index.
8 The content, method, and epistemology of gender in sociolegal studies. Carrie Menkel-Meadow; Shari Seidman Diamond. Law Soc. Rev. **25**:2 1991 pp. 221 – 238
9 Cultural capital, gender, and the structural transformation of legal practice. John Hagan; Marjorie Zatz; Bruce Arnold; Fiona Kay. Law Soc. Rev. **25**:2 1991 pp. 239 – 262
10 Dealing with inequities in customary law — action, reaction and social change in Zimbabwe. Welshman Ncube. Int. J. Law Fam. **5**:1 4:1991 pp. 58 – 79
11 Defences for battered women who kill. Katherine O'Donovan. J. Law Soc. **18**:2 Summer:1991 pp. 219 – 240
12 The definition of sexual harassment. Edmund Wall. Publ. Aff. Q. **5**:4 10:1991 pp. 371 – 385
13 The demise of the reasonable man — a cross-cultural study of a legal concept. Michael Saltman. New Brunswick, N.J., U.S.A: Transaction Publishers, c1991: vii, 168 p. ISBN: 0887383882; LofC: 90011234. Includes bibliographical references (p. 153-158) and index.
14 Determinate sentencing — the promise and the reality of retributive justice. Pamala L. Griset. Albany: State University of New York Press, c1991: 237 p. ISBN: 0791405346; LofC: 90035293. Includes bibliographical references (p. 195-201) and index. [SUNY series in critical issues in criminal justice.]
15 Doing business — the management of uncertainty in lawyers' work. John Flood. Law Soc. Rev. **25**:1 1991 pp. 41 – 72
16 Droit public et droit social — Colloque organisé par la faculté de droit et des sciences économiques de Montpellier 14 décembre 1990 [In French]; [Public law and social law — colloquium organized by the Montpellier faculty of law and economic sciences, 14th December 1990]. Xavier Prétot [Contrib.]; Loïc Cadiet [Contrib.]; Dominique Chelle [Contrib.]; Jean-Emmanuel Ray [Contrib.]; Robert Donnadieu [Contrib.]. Collection of 5 articles. **Droit Soc.** , 3, 3:1991 pp. 187 – 240
17 The effects of interest group pressure on coal strip-mining legislation. Garey C. Durden; Jason F. Shogren; Jonathan I. Silberman. Soc. Sci. Q. **72**:2 6:1991 pp. 239 – 250
18 The geometry of legal principles. Rolando Chuaqui; Jerome Malitz. Theory Decis. **30**:1 1:1991 pp. 27 – 49
19 La gestion du contentieux social [In French]; Managing cases involving social disputes [Summary]. Philippe Waquet. R. Fr. Admin. Publ. :57 1-3:1991 pp. 35 – 43
20 The impact of gender-based family roles in criminal sentencing. Gayle S. Bickle; Ruth D. Peterson. Soc. Prob. **38**:3 8:1991 pp. 372 – 394

INTERNATIONAL BIBLIOGRAPHY OF SOCIOLOGY — 1991

D.4: Law *[Loi]*

21 Impact of pretrial instruction on jurors' information processing and decision making. Vicki L. Smith. *J. Appl. Psychol.* **76:2** 4:1991 pp. 220 – 227
22 An integrative conflict model of the criminal law formation process. Edmund F. McGarrell; Thomas C. Castellano. *J. Res. Crim. Delin.* **28:2** 5:1991 pp. 174 – 196
23 Intuition, altruism, and spite — justice as justification. William H. Rodgers. *Am. Behav. Sc.* **34:3** 1-2:1991 pp. 386 – 406
24 The judge as a mediator. James A. Wall; Dale E. Rude. *J. Appl. Psychol.* **76:1** 2:1991 pp. 54 – 59
25 Қонун тузиш жараёнида жамиятшунослик методининг қўлланиши *[In Uzbek]*; Использование социологического метода в законотворческом процессе *[In Russian]*; [Using sociological methods in lawmaking]. Kh.T. Adilkariev; M.G. Esanov. *Obshch. N. Usbek.* **:8** 1991 pp. 8 – 14
26 Ku adekwatnej teorii w socjologii prawa (prawo jako czynnik integralności systemu społecznego) *[In Polish]*; (Towards an adequate theory of the sociology of law (the law as an integration factor of the social system)); (Vers une théorie adéquate dans la sociologie du droit (le droit en tant que facteur d'intégralité du système social): *Title only in French)*; (К адекватной теории в социологии права (право ыкак показатель интегральности общественной системы): *Title only in Russian)*. Adam Podgórecki. *Pań. Prawo* **XLVI(541)** 3:1991 pp. 15 – 25
27 Law and the mind — biological origins of human behavior. Margaret Gruter. Newbury Park, Calif.: Sage, c1991.: xxv, 156 p. *ISBN: 0803940459. Bibliography — p151-156.* [Sage library of social research. : Vol. 184]
28 Magistrates at work — sentencing and social structure. Sheila Brown. Buckingham: Open University Press, 1991: 147 p. *ISBN: 0335096514. Includes bibliography and index.*
29 Naturalistic approaches to the concept of justice — perspectives from political philosophy and biology. Roger D. Masters. *Am. Behav. Sc.* **34:3** 1-2:1991 pp. 289 – 313
30 The oldest social science? The epistemic properties of the common law tradition. W.T. Murphy. *Mod. Law R.* **54:2** 3:1991 pp. 182 – 215
31 Order without law — how neighbors settle disputes. Robert C. Ellickson. London: Harvard University Press, 1991: ix, 302 p. (maps) *ISBN: 067464168x; LofC: 90025710. Includes bibliographical references and index.*
32 La perception du droit dans la vie quotidienne — les représentations des concepts de droit privé chez les 11-17 ans *[In French]*; (Perceptions of the law in the context of daily life — images of private law as seen by 11-17 year olds). Chantal Kourilsky. *Rev. Ét. Comp.* **XXII:4** 12:1991 pp. 77 – 101
33 Prototypes in the courtroom — lay representations of legal concepts. Vicki L. Smith. *J. Pers. Soc. Psychol.* **61:6** 12:1991 pp. 857 – 872
34 Public personnel administration by lawsuit — the impact of Supreme Court decisions on public employee litigiousness. Don Jaegel; N. Joseph Cayer. *Publ. Adm. Re.* **51:3** 5/6:1991 pp. 211 – 221
35 Rechtsethologie. Selbstverständnis — Erträge — Perspektiven *[In German]*; [Ethology of law. Self-perception — results — outlook]. Hagen Hof. *Arc. Recht. Soz.* **LXXVII:1** 1991 pp. 69 – 83
36 The sense of justice and the concept of cultural justice — views from law and anthropology. Wolfgang Fikentscher. *Am. Behav. Sc.* **34:3** 1-2:1991 pp. 314 – 334
37 Shame, culture, and American criminal law. Toni M. Massaro. *MI. law. R.* **89:7** 6:1991 pp. 1880 – 1943
38 The social and cognitive structure of legal decision-making. Ronald A. Farrell; Malcolm D. Holmes. *Sociol. Q.* **32:4** Winter:1991 pp. 529 – 542
39 The social and political context of rape law reform — an aggregate analysis. Ronald J. Berger; W. Lawrence Neuman; Patricia Searles. *Soc. Sci. Q.* **72:2** 6:1991 pp. 221 – 238
40 Social justice in human relations. Herman Steensma *[Ed.]*; Riël Vermunt *[Ed.]*. New York: Plenum Press, c1991: 2 vols. (ill) *ISBN: 0306436256; LofC: 90025382. Includes bibliographical references and indexes; Contents — v. 1. Societal and psychological origins of justice -- v. 2. Societal and psychological consequences of justice and injustice.* [The language of science; Critical issues in social justice.]
41 Social theory and legal argument — Catherine MacKinnon on sexual harassment. J.P. Minson. *Int. J. S. Law* **19:3** 8:1991 pp. 355 – 378
42 A tradition of women in the law. Sandra Day O'Connor *[Contrib.]*; Joan Williams *[Contrib.]*; Peggy C. Davis *[Contrib.]*; Judith Resnik *[Contrib.]*; Samuel W. Buell *[Contrib.]*; Megan

D.4: Law *[Loi]*
Golden *[Contrib.]*; Lisa Simotas *[Contrib.]*; Judith S. Kaye *[Contrib.]*; Nadine Strossen *[Contrib.]*; Sylvia A. Law *[Contrib.]* and others. Collection of 12 articles. **NY. U. Law. Re.**, *66:6*, 12:1991 pp. 1545 – 2017

43 Validity of the control question polygraph test — the problem of sampling bias. Christopher J. Patrick; William G. Iacono. *J. Appl. Psychol.* **76:2** 4:1991 pp. 229 – 238

44 The word of the law — approaches to legal discourse. Dennis R Klinck. Ottawa: Carleton University Press, 1991: 458p. *ISBN: 0886291585; LofC: cn 91090357.*

D.5: Magic, mythology and religion — *Magie, mythologie et religion*

Sub-divisions: Buddhism *[Bouddhisme]*; Christianity *[Christianisme]*; Hinduism *[Hindouisme]*; Islam *[Islam]*; Judaism *[Judaïsme]*; Magic and witchcraft *[Magie et sorcellerie]*

1 Beneath the status characteristic — gender variations in religiousness. Edward H. Thompson. *J. Sci. S. Relig.* **30:4** 12:1991 pp. 381 – 394

2 The case against secularization — a rebuttal. Frank J. Lechner. *Soc. Forc.* **69:4** 6:1991 pp. 1103 – 1120

3 "Civil religion" and "secularization" in Confucianism — Han Yü and Liu Chung-yüan. Implications for theological critique in Asia today. Peter K.H. Lee. *Ch. Feng* **XXXIV:1** 1:1991 pp. 28 – 50

4 Commentary on the new Soviet law on freedom of conscience and religious organisations. Giovanni Codevilla. *Relig. Comm. Lands* **19:1-2** Summer:1991 pp. 119 – 145

5 The concept of religion. H. Scott Hestevold. *Publ. Aff. Q.* **5:2** 4:1991 pp. 149 – 162

6 Conformity to religious norms of opposing abortion. Donald Granberg. *Sociol. Q.* **32:2** Summer:1991 pp. 267 – 275

7 Confucian-Protestant encounter in Korea — two cases of westernization and de-westernization. Chai-sik Chung. *Ch. Feng* **XXXIV:1** 1:1991 pp. 51 – 81

8 Cultism, insurgency, and vigilantism in the Philippines. David Kowalewski. *Sociol. Anal.* **52:3** Fall:1991 pp. 241 – 253

9 Denomination, religiosity, and compliance with the law — a study of adults. Harold G. Grasmick; Karyl Kinsey; John K. Cochran. *J. Sci. S. Relig.* **30:1** 3:1991 pp. 99 – 105

10 Denominational affiliation in Yugoslavia, 1931- 1987. Sergej Flere. *E. Eur. Quart.* **XXV:2** Summer:1991 pp. 145 – 165

11 The discomfiture of religious experience. Felicitas D. Goodman. *Religion* **21:4** 10:1991 pp. 339 – 344

12 Does religion influence adult health? Kenneth F. Ferraro; Cynthia M. Albrecht-Jensen. *J. Sci. S. Relig.* **30:2** 2-6:1991 pp. 193 – 202

13 Effects of gender inclusive/exclusive language in religious discourse. K. Greene; D.L. Rubin. *J. Lang. Soc. Psychol.* **10:2** 1991 pp. 81 – 98

14 The evolution of the Kami cult. Iwata Keiji. *Acta Asia.* **:61** 1991 pp. 47 – 67

15 Experiencing religious rituals — a Schutzian analysis of Navajo ceremonies. James V. Spickard. *Sociol. Anal.* **52:2** Summer:1991 pp. 191 – 203

16 Gender and God's word — another look at religious fundamentalism and sexism. Charles W. Peek; George D. Lowe; L. Susan Williams. *Soc. Forc.* **69:4** 6:1991 pp. 1205 – 1222

17 Gender and power in new religious movements. A feminist discourse on the scientific study of religion. Janet L. Jacobs. *Religion* **21:4** 10:1991 pp. 345 – 355

18 Health outcomes and a new index of spiritual experience. Jared D. Kass; Richard Friedman; Jane Leserman; Patricia C. Zuttermeister; Herbert Benson. *J. Sci. S. Relig.* **30:2** 2-6:1991 pp. 203 – 211

19 Hermeneutical — phenomenological study of the Aladura spirituality in Ijesa social history. David O. Olayiwola. *Asia J. Theol.* **5:2** 1991 pp. 253 – 263

20 The imperial metaphor — popular religion in China. Stephan Feuchtwang. London: Routledge, 1991: 214 p. *ISBN: 0415021464; LofC: 91010825.* Includes bibliographical references and index.

21 Individualisme, protestation holiste et hétéronomie dans les mouvances mystiques et

D.5: Magic, mythology and religion [Magie, mythologie et religion]

ésotériques contemporaines [In French]; [Individualism, holistic protest and heteronomy in mystic domains and contemporary esoterics] [Summary]. Françoise Champion. *Soc. Compass* **38:1** 1991 pp. 33 – 42

22 Japanese new religions abroad. Mark Mullins [Contrib.]; Richard F. Young [Contrib.]; Shimazono Susumu [Contrib.]; Inoue Nobutaka [Contrib.]; Yutaka Tisdall-Yamada [Contrib.]; Elizabeth Richards [Contrib.]; Ōkubo Masayuki [Contrib.]; Nakamaki Hirochika [Contrib.]; Laënnec Hurbon [Contrib.]; Catherine Cornille [Contrib.] and others. Collection of 8 articles. **Jap. J. Relig. St.**, *18:2-3*, 6-9:1991 pp. 105 – 285

23 Japan's fastest-growing new religions. Leroy Seat. *Jpn. Christ. Q.* **57:1** Winter:1991 pp. 12 – 17

24 Law and religion in the development of a world order. Harold J. Berman. *Sociol. Anal.* **52:1** Spring: 1991 pp. 27 – 36

25 Local Japanese responses to missionary activities; [French summary]. Michael Ashkenazi. *Soc. Compass* **38:2** 1991 pp. 141 – 154

26 Наука. Религия. Общество [In Russian]; [Science. Religion. Society]. К.К. Zhol'; Е.Iu. Merezhinskaia. Kiev: Politizdat, 1986: 159 p. *Bibliogr.pp.152-158.*

27 On secularism and its critics — notes on Turkey, India and Iran. Nur Yalman. *Contr. I. Soc.* **25:2** 7-12:1991 pp. 233 – 266

28 On stability and change in religious beliefs, practice, and attitudes — a Swedish panel study. Eva M. Hamberg. *J. Sci. S. Relig.* **30:1** 3:1991 pp. 63 – 80

29 The opportunity cost of discipleship — ethical mutual funds and their returns. Samuel A. Mueller. *Sociol. Anal.* **52:1** Spring: 1991 pp. 111 – 124

30 The persistence of faith — religion, morality and society in a secular age. Jonathan Sacks. London: Weidenfeld & Nicolson, 1991: 118 p. *ISBN: 0297820850.*

31 The politics of black religious change — disaffiliation from black mainline denominations. Darren E. Sherkat; Christopher G. Ellison. *Soc. Forc.* **70:2** 12:1991 pp. 431 – 454

32 [In Japanese]; [The problems and perspective of religious syncretism]. Yasuhisa Motobayashi. **Studies of Religious Folklore** *No.(1) - 1991.* pp. 137 – 147

33 Psychological adjustment and religiousness — the multivariate belief-motivation theory of religiousness. Charles A. Schaefer; Richard L. Gorsuch. *J. Sci. S. Relig.* **30:4** 12:1991 pp. 448 – 461

34 Reconceptualizing cult coercion and withdrawal — a comparative analysis of divorce and apostasy. Stuart A. Wright. *Soc. Forc.* **70:1** 9:1991 pp. 125 – 146

35 Reflexivity and objectivity in the study of controversial new religions. James T. Richardson. *Religion* **21:4** 10:1991 pp. 305 – 318

36 Relativizing the patriarchy — the sacred history of the feminist spirituality movement. Cynthia Eller. *Hist. Relig.* **30:3** 2:1991 pp. 279 – 295

37 Religijność a życie intymne studentów [In Polish]; Religiousness and students' intimate life [Summary]. Edmund Lewandowski. *Acta Univ. Łódz. Folia Soc.* **21** 1991 pp. 107 – 123

38 Religion and attitudes towards AIDS policy. Andrew M. Greeley. *Social Soc. Res.* **75:3** 4:1991 pp. 126 – 132

39 Religion and identity — concepts, data, questions. Benjamin Beit-Hallahmi. *Soc. Sci. Info.* **30:1** :1991 pp. 81 – 95

40 Religion and politics in Nigeria — the perspective of the indigenous religion. Christopher I. Ejizu. *Asia J. Theol.* **5:2** 1991 pp. 241 – 252

41 Religion and power decline and growth — sociological analyses of religion in Britain, Poland and the Americas. Peter Gee [Ed.]; John Fulton [Ed.]. London: British Sociological Association Sociology of Religion Study Group, 1991: 141 p. *ISBN: 0951722409.*

42 Religion and religiosity — ideas and their use. F.G. Bailey. *Contr. I. Soc.* **25:2** 7-12:1991 pp. 211 – 231

43 [In Japanese]; [Religion and social networks]. Akira Kawabata. **Bulletin of the Faculty of Human Sciences, Osaka University** *No.(17) - 1991.* pp. 149 – 166

44 Religion in Finland and the Scandinavian model; [French summary]. Nils G. Holm. *Soc. Compass* **38:1** 1991 pp. 9 – 16

45 Religion in India. T. N. Madan [Ed.]. New Delhi: Oxford University Press, 1991: xv,448 p. *ISBN: 0195628349.* [Oxford in India readings in sociology and social and cultural anthropology.]

46 Religion in the United States. Mark Chaves [Contrib.]; Mark A. Shibley [Contrib.]; Echo E. Fields [Contrib.]; James V. Spickard [Contrib.]. Collection of 4 articles. **Sociol. Anal.**, *52:2*, Summer:1991 pp. 143 – 203

D.5: Magic, mythology and religion *[Magie, mythologie et religion]*

47 Religion und Gesellschaft *[In German]*; [Religion and society] *[Summary]*. Niklas Luhmann. *Social. Int.* **29:2** 1991 pp. 133 – 139

48 Religion, laughter and the ludicrous. Ingvild Saelid Gilhus. *Religion* **21:3** 8:1991 pp. 257 – 278

49 Religions of South Africa. David Chidester. London: Routledge, 1991: 286 p. *ISBN: 041504779x; LofC: 91003329. Incudes bibliographical references and index.* [The library of religious beliefs and practices.]

50 Religious affiliation and the family. John Wilson; Sharon Sandomirsky. *Sociol. For.* **6:2** 6:1991 pp. 289 – 310

51 Religious conversion of adolescents — testing the Lofland and Stark model of religious conversion. Willem Kox; Wim Meeus; Harm' T. Hart. *Sociol. Anal.* **52:3** Fall:1991 pp. 227 – 240

52 *[In Japanese]*; [Religious education and religious liberty in the postwar reform (2)]. Minako Suzuki. *Ferris Studies Vol.(26). 1991.* pp. 1 – 22

53 Religious movements and social movements. John A. Hannigan *[Contrib.]*; Scott Thumma *[Contrib.]*; Nancy J. Finley *[Contrib.]*; Carl Latkin *[Contrib.]*; Henry C. Finney *[Contrib.]*; Armand L. Mauss *[Contrib.]*; Philip L, Barlow *[Contrib.]*. Collection of 6 articles. **Sociol. Anal.**, *52:4*, Winter:1991 pp. 311 – 413

54 Religious movements and the status of women in India; *[French summary]*. Helen Ralston. *Soc. Compass* **38:1** 1991 pp. 43 – 54

55 Religious transformation in Western society — the end of happiness. Harvie Ferguson. London: Routledge, 1991: 269 p. *ISBN: 0415025745; LofC: gb 91012511.*

56 Религиозный экстремизм: Содерж., причины и формы проявления, пути преодоления *[In Russian]*; [Religious extremism — its nature, causes and manifestations, and ways of combatting it]. V.N. Arestov. Kharkov: Vishcha shk. Izd-vo pri Khark. un-te, 1987: 149 p. *Bibliogr. pp.145-147.*

57 "Render unto Caesar what is Caesar's" — religiosity and taxpayers' inclinations to cheat. Harold G. Grasmick; Robert J. Bursik; John K. Cochran. *Sociol. Q.* **32:2** Summer:1991 pp. 251 – 266

58 Repensando la secularización — ¿desaparición o transformación de la religión? *[In Spanish]*; [Rethinking secularization — disappearance or transformation of religion?]. Juan Carlos Cortázar. *Soc. Part.* **:56** 12:1991 pp. 35 – 46

59 Rudolf Otto and the politics of Utopia. Gregory D. Alles. *Religion* **21:3** 8:1991 pp. 235 – 256

60 Sacrifice and cosmic war. Mark Juergensmeyer. *Terror. Pol. Viol.* **3:3** Autumn:1991 pp. 101 – 117

61 The Satanic cult scare. David G. Bromley. *Society* **28:4(192)** 5-6:1991 pp. 55 – 66

62 The secularization issue — prospect and retrospect. David Martin. *Br. J. Soc.* **42:3** 9:1991 pp. 465 – 474

63 Secularization or anomy? Interpreting religious change in communist societies; *[French summary]*. Miklós Tomka. *Soc. Compass* **38:1** 1991 pp. 93 – 102

64 Segmentation in a religious labor market. Mark Chaves. *Sociol. Anal.* **52:2** Summer:1991 pp. 143 – 158

65 Shots in the streets — violence and religion in South Africa. David Chidester. Boston: Beacon Press, c1991: xix, 220 p. *ISBN: 0807002186; LofC: 91012834. Includes bibliographical references (p. 173-199) and index.*

66 Social movement theory and the sociology of religion — toward a new synthesis. John A. Hannigan. *Sociol. Anal.* **52:4** Winter:1991 pp. 311 – 331

67 Socio-religious change in South Africa. Bernard Latagan. *S.Afr. J. Sociol.* **22:1** 3:1991 pp. 10 – 16

68 Some general observations on religion and violence. David C. Rapoport. *Terror. Pol. Viol.* **3:3** Autumn:1991 pp. 118 – 140

69 Spiritual resistance in Eastern Europe. John A. Coleman. *Proceed. Acad. Polit. Sci.* **38:1** 1991 pp. 113 – 128

70 The spread of religions and macrosocial relations. Robert L. Montgomery. *Sociol. Anal.* **52:1** Spring: 1991 pp. 37 – 53

71 State and religion in South Asia — some reflections. Surjit Mansingh. *S.Asia. J.* **4:3** 1-3:1991 pp. 293 – 312

72 Studies in the prevalence of religious beliefs and religious practice in contemporary Sweden. Eva M. Hamberg. Uppsala: Distributed by Almqvist and Wiksell, 1990: 62 p. *ISBN: 915542564x.* [Acta Universitatis Upsaliensis.]

D.5: Magic, mythology and religion *[Magie, mythologie et religion]*

73 Studying religion today. Controversiality and "objectivity" in the sociology of religion. Thomas Robbins; Roland Robertson. *Religion* **21:4** 10:1991 pp. 319 – 338

74 The Svetāmbar Mūrtipūjak Jain mendicant. John E. Cort. *Man* **26:4** 12:1991 pp. 651 – 671

75 *[In Arabic]*; Thoughts on Zoroaster *[Summary]*. J. Duchesne-Guillemin. *Ir. Nam.* **IX:1** Winter: 1991 pp. 1 – 20

76 A time of change — fundamental options in the present dialogue between believers and society. Constantin Galeriu. *Relig. Comm. Lands* **19:1-2** Summer:1991 pp. 66 – 74

77 La "tour de Babel" des définitions de la religion *[In French]*; [The "Tower of Babel" of definitions of religion] *[Summary]*. Yves Lambert. *Soc. Compass* **38:1** 1991 pp. 73 – 86

78 Understanding activist fundamentalism — capitalist crisis and the "colonization of the lifeworld". Echo E. Fields. *Sociol. Anal.* **52:2** Summer:1991 pp. 175 – 190

79 With justice and mercy — instrumental-masculine and expressive-feminine elements in religion. Eugen Schoenfeld; Stjepan Mestrovic. *J. Sci. S. Relig.* **30:4** 12:1991 pp. 363 – 380

80 Zoroastrianism in contemporary Iran. S. Bekhradnia. *Int. J. Moral Soc. S.* **6:2** Summer:1991 pp. 117 – 134

Buddhism *[Bouddhisme]*

81 American Zen's "Japan connection" — a critical case study of Zen Buddhism's diffusion to the West. Henry C. Finney. *Sociol. Anal.* **52:4** Winter:1991 pp. 379 – 396

82 A Buddhist economic system in practice. F.L. Pryor. *Am. J. Econ. S.* **50:1** 1:1991 pp. 17 – 32

83 Christianity and Buddhism in Thailand — the "battle of the axes" and the "contest of power"; *[French summary]*. Erik Cohen. *Soc. Compass* **38:2** 1991 pp. 115 – 140

84 The institution of the Dalai Lama as a symbolic matrix. P. Christiaan Klieger. *Tibet J.* **XVI:1** Spring:1991 pp. 96 – 107

85 The rise and fall of Buddhism in India — two perspectives. M.S. Gore. *Ind. J. Soc. Sci.* **4:2** 4-6:1991 pp. 175 – 198

86 Ritualized devotion, altruism, and meditation — the offering of the Guru Maṇḍala in Newar Buddhism. David N. Gellner. *Indo-Iran. J.* **34:3** 7:1991 pp. 161 – 198

87 Zhuangzi thought and the spread of Buddhism. Cui Dahua. *Soc. Sci. China* **XII:4** 11:1991 pp. 85 – 107

Christianity *[Christianisme]*

88 Antisémitisme et théologie chrétienne *[In French]*; [Antisemitism and Christian theology] *[Summary]*. Rosemary Radford Ruether. *Temps Mod.* **47:543** 10:1991 pp. 88 – 107

89 Асаблівасці выхавання дзяцей у сем′ях адвентыстаў сёмага дня *[In Belorussian]*; *[Russian summary]*; [Peculiarities in the upbringing of children of Seventh Day Adventist families] *[Summary]*. S.A. Myshapud. *V. Aka. BSSR* **2** 1991 pp. 113 – 118

90 Belief in "Armageddon theology" and willingness to risk nuclear war. Stephen Kierulff. *J. Sci. S. Relig.* **30:1** 3:1991 pp. 81 – 93

91 Belief in Central and Eastern Europe today. Archbishop Šuštar. *Relig. Comm. Lands* **19:1-2** Summer:1991 pp. 20 – 29

92 Born-again moon — fundamentalism in Christianity and the feminist spirituality movement. Janet E. McCrickard. *Feminist R.* **37** Spring:1991 pp. 59 – 67

93 Can the African independent churches of Southern Africa be interpreted with Max Weber's conceptual apparatus?; Können die Afrikanischen Unabhängigen Kirchen in Südafrika mit Max Webers Begriffsapparat interpretiert werden? *[German summary]*. Otto F. Raum. *Sociologus* **41:2** 1991 pp. 97 – 117

94 Christian faith and the Janus-headed European — observations on modern trends in East and West. Peter Hünermann. *Relig. Comm. Lands* **19:1-2** Summer:1991 pp. 95 – 111

95 Christianisme et politique en Asie orientale *[In French]*; [Christianity and politics in East Asia]. Guillaume Arotçarena *[Ed.]*; Jean Maïs *[Ed.]*. *Prob. Pol. Soc.* **:656** 5:1991 pp. 2 – 61

96 Christianity as indigenous religion in Southeast Asia. Charles F. Keyes. *Soc. Compass* **38:2** 1991 pp. 177 – 186

97 Christianity, Islam and Judaism (Eastern Europe and the Caucasus). A. Novoseltsev. *Soc. Sci.* **XXII:1** :1991 pp. 103 – 119

98 Christianity's answer to nationalism. Géza Németh. *Relig. Comm. Lands* **19:1-2** Summer:1991 pp. 82 – 87

D.5: Magic, mythology and religion *[Magie, mythologie et religion]* — **Christianity** *[Christianisme]*

99 Christianizing the urban empire — an analysis based on 22 Greco-Roman cities. Rodney Stark. *Sociol. Anal.* **52:1** Spring: 1991 pp. 77 – 88

100 Church ministry and the free rider problem — religious liberty and disestablishment. J.L. Wallis. *Am. J. Econ. S.* **50:2** 4:1991 pp. 183 – 196

101 The Church Urban Fund — a religio-geographical perspective. Michael Pacione. *Area* **23:2** 6:1991 pp. 101 – 110

102 Cloister and society — analyzing the public benefit of monastic and mendicant institutions. Guillermina Jasso. *J. Math. Sociol.* **16:2** 1991 pp. 109 – 136

103 Contemporary reactions to Mormonism — a case study from rural Alberta. Merlin B. Brinkerhoff; Elaine Grandin. *Can. J. Soc.* **16:2** Spring:1991 pp. 165 – 186

104 The contribution of Catholic Christians to social renewal in East Germany. Hans Joachim Meyer. *Relig. Comm. Lands* **19:1-2** Summer:1991 pp. 88 – 94

105 Dissonant voices — religious pluralism and the question of truth. Harold A. Netland. Grand Rapids, Michigan: W. B. Eerdmans, 1991: xii, 323 p. *ISBN: 0802806023; LofC: 91013553. Includes bibliographical references (p. 315-318) and index.*

106 Les eglises africaines face aux mutations actuelles de l'Afrique une analyse des prises de positions récentes des Eglises protestantes et catholiques du continent africain *[In French]*; [African churches facing current change in Africa — an analysis of recent stances taken by Protestant and Catholic churches in the African continent]. Kä Mana. *Za-Afr.* **31:257** 8-9:1991 pp. 349 – 366

107 The emergence of liberation theology — radical religion and social movement theory. Christian Smith. Chicago: University of Chicago Press, c1991: xiv, 300 p. (ill) *ISBN: 0226764095; LofC: 90026575. Includes bibliographical references (p. 269-291) and index.*

108 The Evangelical-Lutheran Church and state in Finland; *[French summary]*. Jouko Sihvo. *Soc. Compass* **38:1** 1991 pp. 17 – 24

109 Evangelicals and party realignment, 1976-1988. K. Jill Kiecolt; Hart M. Nelsen. *Soc. Sci. Q.* **72:3** 9:1991 pp. 552 – 569

110 Evangelization in context — human promotion and liberation. Elochukwu E. Uzukwu. *Asia J. Theol.* **5:2** 1991 pp. 274 – 285

111 Faith and lack of faith in Russia. Vladimir Poresh. *Relig. Comm. Lands* **19:1-2** Summer:1991 pp. 75 – 81

112 First conversion and second conversion in Nigeria. Dean S. Gilliland. *J. As. Afr. S.* **XXVI:3-4** 7-10:1991 pp. 237 – 252

113 From stability to growth — a study of factors related to the statistical revitalization of southern Baptist congregations. C. Kirk Hadaway. *J. Sci. S. Relig.* **30:2** 2-6:1991 pp. 181 – 192

114 La herencia iberocatólica y la esfera políticoinstitucional en América Latina *[In Spanish]*; The Iberian-Catholic heritage and the political-institutional sphere in Latin America *[Summary]*. H.C.F. Mansilla. *Soc. Part.* **:54** 6:1991 pp. 45 – 70

115 L'identité protestante — étude de la minorité protestante de France *[In French]*; [Protestant identity — a study of the protestant minority in France]. Yves Bizeul. Paris: Méridiens-Klincksieck, 1991: 278 p. *ISBN: 2865632849.* [Réponses sociologiques.]

116 La Iglesia mexicana y las relaciones internacionales del Vaticano *[In Spanish]*; [The Mexican Church and the international relations of the Vatican]. Soledad Loaeza. *Foro Int.* **XXXII:2** 10-12:1991 pp. 199 – 221

117 The influence of Nigerian music and dance on Christianity. Gabriel Oyedele Abe. *Asia J. Theol.* **5:2** 1991 pp. 296 – 310

118 Is America experiencing another religious revival — what would Tocqueville say?; *[French summary]*. Phillip E. Hammond. *Soc. Compass* **38:3** 1991 pp. 239 – 256

119 Islamic resurgence in Indonesia and Christian response. Victor Tanja. *Asia J. Theol.* **5:2** 1991 pp. 359 – 365

120 Jehovah's Witnesses, Mormons, and Moonies — a critical look at Christian heterodoxy in Japan. Timothy D. Boyle. *Jpn. Christ. Q.* **57:1** Winter:1991 pp. 29 – 35

121 Merit, man and ministry — traditional Thai hierarchies in a contemporary church; *[French summary]*. Edwin Zehner. *Soc. Compass* **38:2** 1991 pp. 155 – 175

122 Minorites chretiennes en Asie *[In French]*; Christian minorites in Asia. Erik Cohen *[Contrib.]*; Michael Ashkenazi *[Contrib.]*; Edwin Zehner *[Contrib.]*; Charles F. Keyes *[Contrib.]*. Collection of 4 articles. **Soc. Compass**, *38:2*, 1991 pp. 115 – 186

D.5: Magic, mythology and religion [Magie, mythologie et religion] — Christianity [Christianisme]

123 "Mundo Social", paradigma del proceso de secularización de la sociedad española [In Spanish]; ["Mundo Social", a paradigm of the secularization process in Spanish society]. Carlos Giner de Grado. *Rev. Fom. Soc.* **46:183** 7-9:1991 pp. 333 – 346

124 Muslim-Christian encounters — perceptions and misperceptions. W. Montgomery Watt. London: Routledge, 1991: 164 p. *ISBN: 0415054109; LofC: 90045261. Includes bibliographical references and index.*

125 Negotiating a religious identity — the case of the gay evangelical. Scott Thumma. *Sociol. Anal.* **52:4** Winter:1991 pp. 333 – 348

126 Never the same again — post-Vatican II Catholic-Protestant interactions. Martin E. Marty. *Sociol. Anal.* **52:1** Spring: 1991 pp. 13 – 26

127 "Of whole nations being born in one day" — marriage, money and magic in the Mormon cosmos, 1830-46. John L. Brooke. *Soc. Sci. Info.* **30:1** :1991 pp. 107 – 132

128 Opportunities for the church in the "quiet revolution" in Hungary. László Lukács. *Relig. Comm. Lands* **19:1-2** Summer:1991 pp. 58 – 65

129 Orthodox-Lutheran intermarriage in Finland; [French summary]. Voitto Huotari. *Soc. Compass* **38:1** 1991 pp. 25 – 32

130 Il «paradosso» dei cristiani [In Italian]; (The "paradox" of the Christians). Maria Eletta Martini. *Crit. Marx.* **29:3** 5-6:1991 pp. 71 – 78

131 Piety and politics — recent work on German Catholicism. Margaret Lavinia Anderson. *J. Mod. Hist.* **63:4** 12:1991 pp. 681 – 715

132 Понятие и виды религиозных организаций в СССР [In Russian]; (Notion and type of religious organizations in the USSR). G.P. Luparev. *Sovet. Gos. Pr.* **5** 1991 pp. 35 – 42

133 The problem of the Achsenzeit — a supraconfessional and Christocentric interpretation. A. Men. *Soc. Sci.* **XXII:1** :1991 pp. 40 – 54

134 The problems and tasks confronting the Church in Central and Eastern Europe today. Stefan Wilkanowicz. *Relig. Comm. Lands* **19:1-2** Summer:1991 pp. 30 – 36

135 Prophecy and propaganda in the Romanian orthodox patriarchate. Alexander F.C. Webster. *E. Eur. Quart.* **XXV:4** Winter:1991 p. 519

136 Protestantism and Catholicism. Francesco Paolo Casavola. *J. Reg. Pol.* **11:3-4** 7-12:1991 pp. 557 – 568

137 Religion and deviance among adult Catholics — a test of the "moral communities" hypothesis. Michael R. Welch; Charles R. Tittle; Thomas Petee. *J. Sci. S. Relig.* **30:2** 2-6:1991 pp. 159 – 172

138 Religious institutions. Craig Calhoun [Contrib.]; Pierre Bourdieu [Contrib.]; Shmuel N. Eisenstadt [Contrib.]; Adam B. Seligman [Contrib.]; Richard L. Rogers [Contrib.]; Ewa Morawska [Contrib.]; Deborah Podus [Contrib.]; Michael Lienesch [Contrib.]; James D. Faubion [Contrib.]. *Collection of 9 articles.* **Comp. Soc. Res.** *, 13,* 1991 pp. 9 – 248

139 Religious pluralism and church membership — a spatial diffusion model. Kenneth C. Land; Glenn Deane; Judith R. Blau. *Am. Sociol. R.* **56:2** 4:1991 pp. 237 – 249

140 The revitalization movement in the Catholic Church — the institutional dilemma of power. Helen Rose Ebaugh. *Sociol. Anal.* **52:1** Spring: 1991 pp. 1 – 12

141 Roman Catholic beliefs in England — customary Catholicism and transformations of religious authority. Michael P. Hornsby-Smith. Cambridge: Cambridge University Press, 1991: xvii, 265 p. *ISBN: 0521363276; LofC: 90-34003.*

142 Roman Catholicism and social justice in Canada — a comparative case study; [French summary]. W.E. Hewitt. *Can. R. Soc. A.* **28:3** 8:1991 pp. 299 – 323

143 Las sectas en Costa Rica — pentecostalismo y conflicto social [In Spanish]; [Sects in Costa Rica — pentecostalism and social conflict]. Jaime Valverde. San Jose, Costa Rica: D.E.I, c1990: 95 p. *ISBN: 9977830185. "Centro de Coordinación de Evangelización y Realidad Social (CECODERS), ...Consejo Superior Universitario Centroamericano (CSUCA)"--T.p. verso; Bibliography — p. 93-95.* [Colección sociología de la religión.]

144 The situation of Protestants in today's Poland. Bogdan Tranda. *Relig. Comm. Lands* **19:1-2** Summer:1991 pp. 37 – 44

145 Smashing idols and the state — the Protestant ethic and Egyptian Sunni radicalism. Ellis Goldberg. *Comp. Stud. S.* **33:1** 1:1991 pp. 3 – 35

146 The social characteristics of black Catholics. William Feigelman; Bernard S. Gorman; Joseph A. Varacalli. *Social Soc. Res.* **75:3** 4:1991 pp. 133 – 145

147 The social justice agenda — justice, ecology, power and the church. Donal Dorr. Dublin: Gill and Macmillan, 1991: 201 p. *ISBN: 0717118290. Includes index.*

D.5: Magic, mythology and religion *[Magie, mythologie et religion]* — **Christianity** *[Christianisme]*

148 Sociology and liturgy — re-presentations of the holy. Kieran Flanagan. London: Macmillan, 1991: 411 p. *ISBN: 033355079x. Includes bibliography and index.*

149 The sociology of Mennonites, Hutterites & Amish — a bibliography with annotations, volume II, 1977-1990. Donovan E. Smucker. Waterloo, Ont: Wilfrid Laurier University Press, c1991: xix, 194 p. *ISBN: 0889209995; LofC: cn 90095531. Includes indexes; Vol. 1, 1977 published under title — The sociology of Canadian Mennonites, Hutterites and Amish.*

150 The southernization of American religion — testing a hypothesis. Mark A. Shibley. *Sociol. Anal.* **52:2** Summer:1991 pp. 159 – 174

151 The struggle of the Czech church — what we can learn from a theological analysis. Oto Mádr. *Relig. Comm. Lands* **19:1-2** Summer:1991 pp. 45 – 53

152 Televangelism and American culture — the business of popular religion. Quentin J. Schultze. Grand Rapids, Mich: Baker Book House, c1991: 264 p. *ISBN: 0801083192; LofC: 90049378. Includes bibliographical references (p. 249-259) and index.*

153 "To suffer and never to die" — the concept of suffering in the cult of Padre Pio da Pietrelcina. Christopher McKevitt. *J. Mediter. St.* **1:1** 1991 pp. 54 – 67

Hinduism *[Hindouisme]*

154 Ayodhyā — a Hindu Jerusalem. An investigation of "holy war" as a religious idea in the light of communal unrest in India. Hans Bakker. *Numen* **XXXVIII:1** 6:1991 pp. 80 – 109

155 Dharma's daughters — contemporary Indian women and Hindu culture. Sara S. Mitter. New Brunswick, NJ.: Rutgers University Press, c1991: xi, 198 p. *ISBN: 0813516773; LofC: 90019387. Includes bibliographical references (p. [187]-190) and index.*

156 Karma und Caritas — soziale Arbeit im Kontext des Hinduismus *[In German]*; [Karma and charity — social work in the context of Hinduism]. Dorothea Kuhrau-Neumärker. Münster: Lit, 1990: 245 p. *ISBN: 3886606074.* [Schriftenreihe "Praxis und Forschung" des Fachbereichs Sozialwesen der Fachhochschule Münster. : No. 2/3]

157 Mountain goddess — gender and politics in a Himalayan pilgrimage. William Sturman Sax. New York: Oxford University Press, 1991: x, 235 p. (map) *ISBN: 0195064321; LofC: 90038030. Includes bibliographical references (p. 213-225) and index.*

158 Semitising Hinduism — changing paradigms of Brahmanical integration. Suvira Jaiswal. *Soc. Scient.* **19:12** 12:1991 pp. 20 – 32

Islam *[Islam]*

159 Ayatollah Khomeini's pantheism and the guardianship of the jurist as self-knowledge; *[Arabic summary]*. Salman Al-Bdour. *Dirasat Ser. A.* **18A:2** 1991 pp. 51 – 63

160 Christianity, Islam and Judaism (Eastern Europe and the Caucasus). A. Novoseltsev. *Soc. Sci.* **XXII:1** :1991 pp. 103 – 119

161 Entertainment video and the process of Islamization in Pakistan — theoretical perspectives on a policy imperative. Fazal R. Khan. *Am. J. Islam. Soc. Sci.* **8:2** 9:1991 pp. 289 – 306

162 The interaction between the Muslims and the African traditional society — the Akoko Yoruba as a case study. E.O. Babalola. *Asia J. Theol.* **5:2** 1991 pp. 264 – 273

163 Islam and science — religious orthodoxy and the battle for rationality. Pervez Hoodbhoy. London: Zed Books, c1991: 157 p. *ISBN: 1856490246; LofC: 91022885. Includes bibliographical references and index.*

164 Islam in Bangladesh. U.A.B. Razia Akter Banu. Leiden: Brill, 1991: 194 p. *ISBN: 9004094970; LofC: 91019061. Includes bibliographical references and index.* [International studies in sociology and social anthropology.]

165 Islam in Britain — past, present and the future. Mohammad Shahid Raza. Leicester: Volcano, 1991: 120 p. *ISBN: 1810128358.*

166 The Islamic idiom of violence — a view from Indonesia. Bruce B. Lawrence. *Terror. Pol. Viol.* **3:3** Autumn:1991 pp. 82 – 100

167 Islamic resurgence in Indonesia and Christian response. Victor Tanja. *Asia J. Theol.* **5:2** 1991 pp. 359 – 365

168 Muslim families in North America. Earle H. Waugh *[Ed.]*; Regula Burckhardt Qureshi *[Ed.]*; Sharon McIrvin Abu-Laban *[Ed.]*. Edmonton: University of Alberta Press, 1991: 369 p. *ISBN: 0888642253.*

169 Muslim identity and separatism in India — the significance of M.A. Ansari. P.G. Robb. *B. Sch. Orient. Afr. Stud.* **LIV:I** 1991 pp. 104 – 125

D.5: Magic, mythology and religion [Magie, mythologie et religion] — Islam [Islam]

170 Muslim-Christian encounters — perceptions and misperceptions. W. Montgomery Watt. London: Routledge, 1991: 164 p. *ISBN: 0415054109; LofC: 90045261.* Includes bibliographical references and index.
171 The Muslims of America. Yvonne Yazbeck Haddad *[Ed.]*. New York: Oxford University Press, 1991: x, 249 p. (ill) *ISBN: 0195067282; LofC: 90044510.* Includes bibliographical references. [Religion in America series.]
172 The mythologies of religious radicalism — Judaism and Islam. Emmanuel Sivan. *Terror. Pol. Viol.* **3:3** Autumn:1991 pp. 71 – 81
173 Le renouveau islamique en URSS *[In French]*; [The Islamic revival in U.S.S.R.]. O. Roy. *R. Mon. Musul. Med.* **59-60** 1-2:1991 p.133-144
174 Sacrifice and fratricide in Shiite Lebanon. Martin Kramer. *Terror. Pol. Viol.* **3:3** Autumn:1991 pp. 30 – 47
175 Sacrilege versus civility — the Muslim perspective on the Satanic Verses affair. M. M. Ahsan *[Ed.]*; A. R. Kidwai *[Ed.]*. Leicester: The Islamic Foundation, 1991: 383 p. *ISBN: 0860372111.*
176 Science and Muslim societies. Nasim Butt. London: Grey Seal, 1991: 135 p. *ISBN: 1856400239.* [Contemporary Islam.]
177 State-religion in Bangladesh — a critique of the eighth amendment to the constitution. Shah Alam. *S.Asia. J.* **4:3** 1-3:1991 pp. 313 – 333
178 Violence against violence — Islam in comparative context. Mark R. Anspach. *Terror. Pol. Viol.* **3:3** Autumn:1991 pp. 9 – 29
179 The work of the Imam, servant of the community and precarious worker in Bangladesh. Bernerd Hours. *J. Soc. Stud. Dhaka* **:54** 10:1991 pp. 142 – 154

Judaism [Judaïsme]

180 Antisémitisme et théologie chrétienne *[In French]*; [Antisemitism and Christian theology] *[Summary]*. Rosemary Radford Ruether. *Temps Mod.* **47:543** 10:1991 pp. 88 – 107
181 Christianity, Islam and Judaism (Eastern Europe and the Caucasus). A. Novoseltsev. *Soc. Sci.* **XXII:1** :1991 pp. 103 – 119
182 In partnership with God — contemporary Jewish law and ethics. Byron L. Sherwin. Syracuse: Syracuse University Press, 1991: 290p. *ISBN: 0815624905.*
183 Judaism and the secularization debate. Stephen Sharot. *Sociol. Anal.* **52:3** Fall:1991 pp. 255 – 275
184 The mythologies of religious radicalism — Judaism and Islam. Emmanuel Sivan. *Terror. Pol. Viol.* **3:3** Autumn:1991 pp. 71 – 81
185 Religious community, individual religiosity and health — a tale of two kibbutzim. Ofra Anson; Arieh Levenson; Benyamin Maoz; Dan Y. Bonneh. *Sociology* **25:1** 2:1991 pp. 119 – 132
186 Religious renewal in Orthodox Judaism in Israel — an interpretation; *[French summary]*. Margit Warburg. *Soc. Compass* **38:1** 1991 pp. 63 – 72

Magic and witchcraft [Magie et sorcellerie]

187 La cuisine des sorcières *[In French]*; Witches brew *[Summary]*. Claudine Fabre-Vassas. *Ethn. Fr.* **21:4** 10-12:1991 pp. 423 – 437
188 Mama Lola — a Vodou priestess in Brooklyn. Karen McCarthy Brown. Berkeley: University of California Press, c1991: x, 405 p. (ill) *ISBN: 0520070739; LofC: 90040070.* Includes bibliographical references (pp. 387-390) and index. [Comparative studies in religion and society. : No. 4]

D.6: Science and knowledge — *Science et connaissance*

1 The activation of schemata in relation to background knowledge and markedness. Abdullah Shakir; Mohammed Farghal. *Text* **11:2** :1991 pp. 201 – 222
2 Antiscience trends in the U.S.S.R. Sergei Kapitza. *Sci. Am.* **265:2** 8:1991 pp. 18 – 25
3 Bioscience and society. David J. Roy *[Ed.]*; R. W. Old *[Ed.]*; B. E. Wynne *[Ed.]*. Chichester: John Wiley and Sons, 1991: 424 p. *ISBN: 0471931527*. [Schering Foundation workshop.]
4 Le calcul et la raison — essais sur la formalisation du discours savant *[In French]*; [Calculation and reason — essays on the formalization of a knowledgeable discourse]. Jean-Claude Gardin. Paris: Ed. de l'Ecole des hautes études en sciences sociales, 1991: 296 p. (ill) *ISBN: 2713209560. Bibliogr. pp. 265-281. Index.* [Recherches d'histoire et de sciences sociales.]
5 Chaos and entropy. Metaphors in postmodern science and social theory. Steven Best. *Sci. Cult.* **2(2):11** :1991 pp. 188 – 226
6 The computerization of human service agencies — a critical appraisal. John W. Murphy; John T. Pardeck *[Ed.]*. New York: Auburn House, 1991: viii, 180 p. *ISBN: 0865690235; LofC: 90022750. Includes bibliographical references (p. [169]-172) and index.*
7 "Depth hermeneutics" — some problems in application to the public understanding of science. Simon Locke. *Sociology* **25:3** 8:1991 pp. 375 – 394
8 The egg and the sperm — how science has constructed a romance based on stereotypical male-female roles. Emily Martin. *Signs* **16:3** Spring:1991 pp. 485 – 500
9 F.H. Bradley and the philosophy of science. W.J. Mander. *Inter. Phil. Sci.* **5:1** 1991 pp. 65 – 78
10 The fail-safe society — community defiance and the end of American technological optimism. Charles Piller. [New York]: BasicBooks, c1991: xii, 240 p. *ISBN: 046502274x; LofC: 91070066. Includes bibliographical references (p. 206-227) and index.*
11 The Fleck affair — fashions v. heritage. John Wettersten. *Inquiry* **34:4** 12:1991 pp. 475 – 498
12 A history of consciousness — from Kant and Hegel to Derrida and Foucault. David Couzens Hoy. *Hist. Human Sci.* **4:2** 6:1991 pp. 261 – 281
13 Imagery and meaning, the cognitive science connection. Arthur I. Miller. *Inter. Phil. Sci.* **5:1** 1991 pp. 35 – 48
14 Is history and philosophy of science withering on the vine? Steve Fuller. *Philos. S. Sc.* **21:2** 6:1991 pp. 149 – 174
15 Knowledge, ideology & discourse — a sociological perspective. Tim Dant. London: Routledge, 1991: 253 p. *ISBN: 0415047862. Includes bibliography and index.*
16 The logic of impossible quantities. David Sherry. *Stud. Hist. Phil. Sci.* **22:1** 3:1991 pp. 37 – 62
17 Mathematical expressibility, perceptual relativity, and secondary qualities. Derk Pereboom. *Stud. Hist. Phil. Sci.* **22:1** 3:1991 pp. 63 – 88
18 Навука ў кантэксце культуры: філасофска-метадалагічны аспект *[In Belorussian]*; *[Russian summary]*; [Science in the context of culture — the philosophical-methodological aspect] *[Summary]*. V.K. Ban'ko; U.I. Mis'kevich. *V. Aka. BSSR* **2** 1991 pp. 3 – 11
19 On the aim model of scientific progress. Lin Dingyi. *Soc. Sci. China* **XII:4** 11:1991 pp. 132 – 148
20 Philosophy of science and the persistent narratives of modernity. Joseph Rouse. *Stud. Hist. Phil. Sci.* **22:1** 3:1991 pp. 141 – 161
21 The power of scientific knowledge — and its limits; *[French summary]*. Nico Stehr. *Can. R. Soc. A.* **28:4** 11:1991 pp. 460 – 482
22 Progress and rationality — Laudan's attempt to divorce a happy couple. Matthias Kaiser. *Inquiry* **34:4** 12:1991 pp. 433 – 455
23 Science, technology, and society in postwar Japan. Shigeru Nakayama. London: Kegan Paul International, 1991: 259 p. *ISBN: 0710304285; LofC: 91007998. Includes index.* [Japanese studies series.]
24 Штучны інтэлект і натуральная мова *[In Belorussian]*; [Artificial intelligence and the natural world] *[Summary]*; *[Russian summary]*. L.V. Uvarai; V.V. Gryb. *V. Aka. BSSR* **:3** 1991 pp. 10 – 17
25 The social horizon of knowledge. Piotr Buczkowski *[Ed.]*. Amsterdam: Rodopi, 1991: 195 p. *ISBN: 9051832702. eng, ger; One contribution in German; Includes bibliographical references.* [Poznań studies in the philosophy of the sciences and the humanities. : Vol. 22]

D.6: Science and knowledge *[Science et connaissance]*

26 A sociology of monsters — essays on power, technology and domination. John Law *[Ed.]*. London: Routledge, 1991: 273 p. *ISBN: 0415071399*.
27 Some reflections on the individuation of events. Rom Harré. *Inter. Phil. Sci.* **5:1** 1991 pp. 49 – 64
28 Strange weather — culture, science, and technology in the age of limits. Andrew Ross. London: Verso, 1991: 275 p. *ISBN: 0860913546; LofC: 91022782. Includes bibliographical references and index.*
29 Die Transformation sozialer Realität. Ein Beitrag zur empirischen Wissenssoziologie *[In German]*; The transformation of social reality. A contribution to an empirical sociology of knowledge *[Summary]*. Horst Stenger; Hans Geißlinger. *Kölner Z. Soz. Soz. psy.* **43:2** 1991 pp. 247 – 270
30 A tudás mint társadalmi konstrukció *[In Hungarian]*; [Knowledge as a social construction]. János Farkas. *Mag. Tud. Vol.32; No.10 - 1987.* pp. 759 – 769
31 Van Fraassen's metaphysical move. Adam Grobler. *Inter. Phil. Sci.* **5:1** 1991 pp. 21 – 34
32 What is wrong with the miracle argument? Martin Carrier. *Stud. Hist. Phil. Sci.* **22:1** 3:1991 pp. 23 – 36

D.7: Language, communication and media — *Langage, communication et moyens de communication*

Sub-divisions: Advertising *[Publicité]*; Communication *[Communication]*; Linguistics *[Linguistique]*; Media *[Moyens de communication]*; Multilingualism and language policy *[Multilinguisme et politique linguistique]*; Television *[Télévision]*

1 Affective cues in persuasion — an assessment of causal mediation. Thomas J. Madden; Icek Ajzen. *Market. Lett.* **2:4** 11:1991 pp. 359 – 366
2 Argumentation and the Arab voice in Western bestsellers. Toine van Teeffelen. *Text* **11:2** :1991 pp. 241 – 266
3 Art as information — the African portfolios of Charles Sheeler and Walker Evans. Virginia-Lee Webb. *Afr. Arts* **XXIV : 1** 1:1991 pp. 56 – 63
4 Basic aspects of language in human relations — toward a general theoretical framework. Harald Haarmann. Berlin: Mouton de Gruyter, 1991: x, 312 p. (ill) *ISBN: 3110126850; LofC: 91030526. Includes bibliographical references (p. [292]-304) and indexes.* [Contributions to the sociology of language. : No. 59]
5 Black and white at Stanford. John H. Bunzel. *Publ. Inter.* **:105** Fall:1991 pp. 61 – 77
6 Les cérémonies royales françaises entre performance juridique et compétence liturgique *[In French]*; The French royal ceremonies — juridicial performance and liturgical competence *[Summary]*. Alain Boureau. *Annales* **46:6** 11-12:1991 pp. 1253 – 1264
7 Chinese or English? Language choice amongst Chinese students in Newcastle upon Tyne. G. McGregor; Wei Li. *J. Multiling.* **12:6** 1991 pp. 493 – 509
8 Code-switching studies in the Philippines. Maria Lourdes S. Bautista. *Int. J. S. Lang.* **:88** 1991 pp. 19 – 32
9 Community languages — a handbook. Barbara M. Horvath; Paul Vaughan. Clevedon, England: Multilingual Matters, c1991: x, 276 p. *ISBN: 1853590916; LofC: 90006276. Includes bibliographical references.* [Multilingual matters. : No. 67]
10 Computers, networks and the corporation. Thomas W. Malone; John F. Rockart. *Sci. Am.* **265:3** 9:1991 pp. 92 – 99
11 Computers, networks and work. Lee Sproull; Sara Kiesler. *Sci. Am.* **265:3** 9:1991 pp. 84 – 91
12 Conversational implicature, conscious representation, and the conjunction fallacy. Don E. Dulany; Denis J. Hilton. *Soc. Cogn.* **9:1** Spring:1991 pp. 85 – 110
13 Culture and the categorization of emotions. James A. Russell. *Psychol .B.* **110:3** 11:1991 pp. 426 – 450
14 Diffusion and focusing — phonological variation and social networks in Ile-Ife, Nigeria. L.O. Salami. *Lang. Soc.* **20:2** 6:1991 pp. 217 – 246
15 Disarming images. *Publ. Cult.* **3:2** Spring:1991 pp. 113 – 118
16 The economics of language in the Asian Pacific. Florian Coulmas *[Ed.]*; François Vaillancourt *[Contrib.]*; Herbert W. Hildebrandt *[Contrib.]*; Jinyun Liu *[Contrib.]*; Anna Kwan-Terry *[Contrib.]*; Wanjin Zhu *[Contrib.]*; Jianmin Chen *[Contrib.]*; Rolf D. Cremer *[Contrib.]*; Mary J. Willes *[Contrib.]*; Alan Hirvela *[Contrib.]* <u>and others</u>. *Collection of 11 articles*. **Asian Pacif. Commun.** , *2:1*, 1991 pp. 1 – 189

D.7: Language, communication and media [Langage, communication et moyens de communication]

17 L'écrit, le document et les réseaux [In French]; The writing, the document and the networks [Summary]. Guy Pelachaud. Pensée :281 5-6:1991 pp. 5 – 20
18 English in a multicultural America. Dennis Baron. Soc. Pol. 21:4 Spring:1991 pp. 5 – 14
19 The English-only movement — myths, reality, and implications for psychology. Amado M. Padilla; Kathryn J. Lindholm; Andrew Chen; Richard Durán; Kenji Hakuta; Wallace Lambert; G. Richard Tucker. Am. Psychol. 46:2 2:1991 pp. 120 – 130
20 Error and the very advanced learner; [German summary]; [French summary]. Paul Lenon. IRAL XXIX:1 1991 pp. 31 – 44
21 Ethnic minority languages within the wider Philippine social context. William C. Hall. Int. J. S. Lang. :88 1991 pp. 59 – 68
22 Europe 1992 — a language perspective; Europa 1992 — eine sprachliche Perspektive [German summary]; Eŭropo 1992 — lingva perspektivo [Esperanto summary]. Gerhard Leitner. Lang. Prob. Lang. Plan. 15:3 Fall:1991 pp. 282 – 295
23 The evolution of the critical period for language acquisition. James R. Hurford. Cognition 40:3 9:1991 pp. 159 – 202
24 Familial aggregation of a developmental language disorder. M. Gopnik; Martha B. Crago. Cognition 39:1 4:1991 pp. 1 – 49
25 From calculus to language — the case of circus equine displays. Paul Bouissac. Semiotica 85:3-4 1991 pp. 291 – 318
26 Haiku as a discourse regulation device — a stanza analysis of Japanese children's personal narratives. M. Minami; A. McCabe. Lang. Soc. 20:4 12:1991 pp. 577 – 600
27 Hegemonic images — language and silence in the Royal Thai polity. Christine E. Gray. Man 26:1 3:1991 pp. 43 – 65
28 Holy land, holy language — a study of an ultraorthodox Jewish ideology. L. Glinert; Y. Shilhav. Lang. Soc. 20:1 3:1991 pp. 59 – 86
29 How valuable is the Awareness Index? Paul Feldwick; Sarah Carter; Louise Cook. J. Market R. 33:3 7:1991 pp. 179 – 196
30 How violence is justified — Sinn Fein's an phoblacht. Robert G. Picard. J. Comm. 41:4 Autumn:1991 pp. 90 – 103
31 Identitásproblémák rétegszéli helyzetben [In Hungarian]; [Problems of identity in marginal situations]. József Tarjányi. Budapest: Tömegkommunikációs Kutatóközpont, 1987: 64 p.
32 Ideological language in the transformation of identity. Peter G. Stromberg. Am. Anthrop. 92:1 3:1990 pp. 42 – 56
33 "Illegal aliens" and "opportunity" — myth-making in congressional testimony. P. Chock. Am. Ethn. 18:2 5:1991 pp. 279 – 294
34 L'image-son vidéo, une nouvelle source pour l'étude des problèmes socio-politiques dans les républiques asiatiques de l'URSS [In French]; [Video — a new source for the study of socio-political problems in the Asiatic republics in the U.S.S.R.]. S.A. Dudoignon. R. Mon. Musul. Med. 59-60 1-2:1991 pp. 145 – 155
35 The impact of church affiliation on language use in Kwara'ae (Solomon Islands). K.A. Watson-Gegeo; D.W. Gegeo. Lang. Soc. 20:4 12:1991 pp. 533 – 556
36 Individual style in an American public opinion survey — personal performance and the ideology of referentiality. B. Johnstone. Lang. Soc. 20:4 12:1991 pp. 557 – 576
37 The information crisis in Sweden after Chernobyl. Stig Arne Nohrstedt. Media Cult. Soc. 13:4 10:1991 pp. 477 – 498
38 The intellectualization of Filipino. Bonifacio P. Sibayan. Int. J. S. Lang. :88 1991 pp. 69 – 81
39 Języki etniczne w Australii — kierunki badań [In Polish]; Community languages in Australia — trends in research [Summary]. Camilla Bettoni. Prz. Pol. XVII:2 1991 pp. 5 – 24
40 Language acquisition in the absence of experience. S. Crain. Behav. Brain Sci. 14:4 12:1991 pp. 597 – 650
41 Language loss, language gain — cultural camouflage and social change among the Sekani of Northern British Columbia. G. Lanoue. Lang. Soc. 20:1 3:1991 pp. 87 – 115
42 Language maintenance and language shift in the speech behaviour of German-Australian migrants in Canberra. M. Pütz. J. Multiling. 12:6 1991 pp. 477 – 492
43 The language of the Greek Cypriots today. Dimitra Karoulla-Vrikkis. Cyprus Rev. 3:1 Spring:1991 pp. 42 – 58
44 Language, society, and the elderly — discourse, identity, and ageing. Nikolas Coupland; Justine Coupland [Ed.]; Howard Giles [Ed.]. Oxford, UK: B. Blackwell, 1991: 220 p. ISBN: 0631180044; LofC: 91010514. Includes bibliographical references and index. [Language and society.]

D.7: Language, communication and media *[Langage, communication et moyens de communication]*

45 Linguistic change among bilingual speakers of Finnish and American English in Sweden — background and some tentative findings. Sally Boyd; Paula Andersson. *Int. J. S. Lang.* **:90** 1991 pp. 13 – 36

46 Literacy as praxis — culture, language, and pedagogy. Catherine E. Walsh *[Ed.]*. Norwood, N.J: Ablex Pub, 1991: ix, 229 p. (ill) *ISBN: 089391648x; LofC: 90038886. Includes bibliographical references and indexes.*

47 Marshall McLuhan revisited — 1960s zeitgeist victim or pioneer postmodernist? Marjorie Ferguson. *Media Cult. Soc.* **13:1** 1:1991 pp. 71 – 90

48 The mastering of a non-native language as the study of sign operations. R. Frumkina; A. Mostovaya. *Soc. Sci.* **XXII:4** 1991 pp. 156 – 169

49 The national language question in Nigeria — is there an answer?; La demando pri nacia lingvo en Niĝerio — ĉu ekzistas respondo? *[Esperanto summary]*. James Oladejo. *Lang. Prob. Lang. Plan.* **15:3** Fall:1991 pp. 255 – 267

50 Networked computing in the 1990s. Lawrence G. Tesler. *Sci. Am.* **265:3** 9:1991 pp. 54 – 64

51 New Zealanders' attitudes to the revitalisation of the Maori language. R. Nicholson; R. Garland. *J. Multiling.* **12:5** 1991 pp. 393 – 410

52 Notes on the emerging global language system — regional, national and supranational. Abram de Swaan. *Media Cult. Soc.* **13:3** 7:1991 pp. 309 – 324

53 Out of the hands of babes — on a possible sign advantage in language acquisition. Richard P. Meier; Elissa L. Newport. *Language* **66:1** 3:1990 pp. 1 – 23

54 Paul Otlet, André Canonne — textes sur l'écrit et le document *[In French]*; P. Otlet and A. Canonne — texts about the writing and the document *[Summary]*. Guy Pelachaud. *Pensée* **:281** 5-6:1991 pp. 53 – 83

55 Perceived change in ethnolinguistic vitality by dominant and minority subgroups. J. Pittam; C. Gallois; M. Willemyns. *J. Multiling.* **12:6** 1991 pp. 449 – 457

56 Phonological abilities and reading disabilities. D.V.M. Bishop *[Contrib.]*; P.E. Bryant *[Contrib.]*; Ruth Campbell *[Contrib.]*; Alain Content *[Contrib.]*; Beatrice de Gelder *[Contrib.]*; Jean Vroomen *[Contrib.]*; Charles Hulme *[Contrib.]*; Margaret Snowling *[Contrib.]*; John C. Marshall *[Contrib.]*; Giuseppe Cossu *[Contrib.] and others. Collection of 10 articles.* **Mind Lang.** , *6:2,* Summer:1991 pp. 97 – 159

57 Plato's cave — desire, power, and the specular functions of the media. John O'Neill. Norwood, N.J: Ablex Pub. Corp, c1991: xi, 206 p. (ill) *ISBN: 0893917222; LofC: 90023352. Includes bibliographical references and indexes.* [Communication and information science.]

58 Politeness phenomena in Korean and American church business meetings. Bethyl A. Pearson; K. Samuel Lee. *Intercult. Commun. St.* **1:2** Fall:1991 pp. 149 – 163

59 The political topography of Spanish and English — the view from a New York Puerto Rican neighborhood. B. Urciuoli. *Am. Ethn.* **18:2** 5:1991 pp. 295 – 310

60 The politics of language in the Third World — toward theory building. Wilfrido V. Villacorta. *Int. J. S. Lang.* **:88** 1991 pp. 33 – 44

61 Powerful versus powerless language — consequences for persuasion, impression formation, and cognitive response. P. Gibbons; J. Busch; J.J. Bradac. *J. Lang. Soc. Psychol.* **10:2** 1991 pp. 115 – 134

62 The pragmatics of argumentation in Arabic — the rise and fall of a text type. Basil Hatim. *Text* **11:2** :1991 pp. 189 – 200

63 Problems of Cypriot language and identity. Yiannis E. Ioannou *[Contrib.]*; Dimitra Karoulla-Vrikkis *[Contrib.]*; Nikos A. Stamatakis *[Contrib.]*; Maria Roussou *[Contrib.]*. *Collection of 4 articles.* **Cyprus Rev.** , *3:1,* Spring:1991 pp. 15 – 106

64 Production and perception of stress-related durational patterns in Japanese learners of English. M. Mochizuki-Sudo; S. Kiritani. *J. Phon.* **19:2** 4:1991 pp. 231 – 248

65 Products and services for computer networks. Nicholas P. Negroponte. *Sci. Am.* **265:3** 9:1991 pp. 76 – 83

66 Promise and the theory of control. Richard K. Larson. *Linguist. In.* **22:1** winter:1991 pp. 103 – 139

67 Rapping — a sociolinguistic study of oral tradition in black urban communities in the United States. Pieter Remes. *J. Anthrop. Soc. Oxford* **XXII:2** 1991 pp. 129 – 149

68 A reexamination of the stress erasure convention and Spanish stress. Morris Halle; James W. Harris; Jean-Roger Vergnaud. *Linguist. In.* **22:1** winter:1991 pp. 141 – 159

69 Remembered passion — the implicate order in perception, language, and physics. Patricia A. Mutch. *Semiotica* **87:1-2** 1991 pp. 59 – 81

D.7: Language, communication and media *[Langage, communication et moyens de communication]*

70 Romāni child-directed speech and children's language among Gypsies in Hungary. Z. Réger; J.B. Gleason. *Lang. Soc.* **20**:4 12:1991 pp. 601 – 618

71 Schema-Theorie — ein brauchbarer Ansatz in der Wirkungsforschung? *[In German]*; Schema theory — a useful approach for effects research? *[Summary]*; La théorie des schémas — un modèle utilisable pour la recherche sur les effets? *[French summary]*; Teoría del esquema. ¿Un aproche útil para la investigación de efectos? *[Spanish summary]*. Hans-Bernd Brosius. *Publizistik* **36**:3 7-9:1991 pp. 285 – 297

72 Semiotics of the circus. Paul Bouissac *[Ed.]*; Mary Douglas *[Contrib.]*; Don Handelman *[Contrib.]*; W. Kenneth Little *[Contrib.]*; Yoram Carmeli *[Contrib.]*; Andréa Semprini *[Contrib.]*. Collection of 7 articles. **Semiotica** , *85:3-4*, 1991 pp. 189 – 333

73 .Kim Plunkett; Virginia Marchman. *Cognition* **38**:1 1:1991 pp. 43 – 102

74 Signs as information. Jeremy H. Peirce. *Semiotica* **87:1-2** 1991 pp. 83 – 94

75 Social determinants of language shift by Italians in the Netherlands and Flanders. Koen Jaspaert; Sjaak Kroon. *Int. J. S. Lang.* **:90** 1991 pp. 77 – 96

76 *[In Japanese]*; [Social role and language (2)]. Masatoshi Ikemiya. ***Journal of Language and Culture*** *No.(2) - 1991* pp. 87 – 98

77 Sociolinguistic issues in ageing. Nikolas Coupland *[Ed.]*; Angela Williams *[Contrib.]*; Howard Giles *[Ed.]*; Ronald Adelman *[Contrib.]*; Michele Greene *[Contrib.]*; Rita Charon *[Contrib.]*; Jon Nussbaum *[Contrib.]*; Linda Wood *[Contrib.]*; Ellen Ryan *[Contrib.]*; Justine Coupland *[Ed.] and others. Collection of 5 articles.* **Age. Soc.** , *11:2*, 6:1991 pp. 99 – 208

78 Sociolinguistic notes on the turcification of the Sogdians. K. Krippes. *Cent. Asia. J.* **35**:1-2 1991 pp. 67 – 80

79 Sociolinguistic studies in the Philippines. Andrew B. Gonzalez *[Contrib.]*; Maria Lourdes S. Bautista *[Contrib.]*; Wilfrido V. Villacorta *[Contrib.]*; Leonard E. Newell *[Contrib.]*; William C. Hall *[Contrib.]*; Bonifacio P. Sibayan *[Contrib.]*; Emma J. Fonacier Bernabe *[Contrib.]. Collection of 8 articles.* **Int. J. S. Lang.** , *:88*, 1991 pp. 5 – 119

80 Sociolinguistics in Brazil. Fernando Tarallo *[Contrib.]*; Stella Maris Bortoni *[Contrib.]*; Maria Isabel S. Magalhães *[Contrib.]*; Euzi Rodrigues Moraes *[Contrib.]*; Marco Antônio de Oliveira *[Contrib.]*; Leda Bisol *[Contrib.]*; Ulf Gregor Baranow *[Contrib.]. Collection of 8 articles.* **Int. J. S. Lang.** , *:89*, 1991 pp. 9 – 147

81 Sociolinguistics today — international perspectives. Kingsley Bolton *[Ed.]*; Helen Kwok *[Ed.]*. London: Routledge, 1991: 383 p. (ill) *ISBN: 0415064104. Includes bibliography and index.*

82 Some problems in the reconstruction of Old Korean. An Binghao. *Kor. Stud.* **15** 1991 pp. 99 – 112

83 Социопсихолингвистическое исследование текстов радио, телевидения, газеты *[In Russian]*; [Socio-psycholinguistic research of texts of radio, television and newspaper]. V.G. Kostomarova *[Ed.]*; B.A. Zil'bert. Saratov: Saratov University Publishers, 1986: 211 p. *Bibliogr. pp.166-178.*

84 *[In Japanese]*; [The "state language" as an assimilation apparatus — the change of reference group, intellectuals and educational system in penetration of the standard language into the Ryukyu cultural zone]. Hidenori Mashiko. ***Kyoikushakaigaku Kenkyu*** *No.(48) - 1991.* pp. 146 – 165

85 The state of the language; *1990's ed.* Christopher Ricks *[Ed.]*; Leonard Michaels *[Ed.]*. London: Faber & Faber, 1991 c1990: xiii, 530 p. *ISBN: 0571161324.*

86 The status of the Spanish language in the United States at the beginning of the 21st century. Calvin Veltman. *Int. Migr. Rev.* **XXIV:1** Spring:1990 pp. 108 – 123

87 Studies on language and society in the Philippines — state of the art. Andrew B. Gonzalez. *Int. J. S. Lang.* **:88** 1991 pp. 5 – 18

88 Talking Yiddish at the boundaries. Maria Damon. *Cult. St.* **5:1** 1:1991 pp. 14 – 29

89 Tense coherence and grounding in children's narrative. Carla Bazzanella; Daniela Calleri. *Text* **11:2** :1991 pp. 175 – 188

90 Thought-signs, sign-events. Floyd Merrell. *Semiotica* **87:1-2** 1991 pp. 1 – 58

91 Transport in the information age — wheels and wires. M. E. Hepworth; Ken Ducatel. London: Belhaven Press, 1991: 217 p. *ISBN: 1852932201.*

92 Transportation and telecommunications costs. Some implications of geographical scale. Salomon J. Schofer. *Ann. Reg. Sci.* **25:1** :1991 pp. 19 – 39

93 Turkish in contact with German — language maintenance and loss among immigrant children in Berlin (West). Carol W. Pffaf. *Int. J. S. Lang.* **:90** 1991 pp. 97 – 130

D.7: Language, communication and media *[Langage, communication et moyens de communication]*

94 *[In Japanese]*; [Urban legend — a theoretical approach to the phenomenon of rumor]. Joji Misumi. *Shak. Hyor. No.42(1) - 1991*. pp. 17 – 31

95 'I was just doing X...when Y' — some inferential properties of a device in accounts of paranormal experience. Robin Wooffitt. *Text* **11:2** :1991 pp. 267 – 288

96 When a response is not an answer — understanding conflict in non-native legal testimony. Mary I. Bresnahan. *Multilingua* **10:3** 1991 pp. 275 – 294

97 Wir sind das Volk — zur Rolle der Sprache bei den Revolutionen in der DDR, Tschechoslowakei, Rumänien und Bulgarien *[In German]*; [We are the people — on the role of language in the revolutions of the GDR, Czechoslavakia, Romania and Bulgaria]. Wolf Oschlies. Köln: Böhlau, 1990: 82 p. (ill) *ISBN: 3412044903; LofC: 91136882 //r91*. Includes bibliographical references.

98 Word-finding ability and design fluency in developmental dyslexia. Peter Griffiths. *Br. J. Clin. Psycho.* **30:1** 2:1991 pp. 47 – 60

99 Yiddish — the fifteenth Slavic language. A study of partial language shift from Judeo-Sorbian to German. Paul Wexler. *Int. J. S. Lang.* :91 1991 pp. 9 – 150

Advertising *[Publicité]*

100 Advertising and cultural politics. Svetlana Kolesnik. *J. Comm.* **41:2** Spring:1991 pp. 46 – 54

101 Advertising in Europe — promises, pressures and pitfalls. Armand Mattelart; Michael Palmer. *Media Cult. Soc.* **13:4** 10:1991 pp. 535 – 556

102 American media and commercial culture. Leo Bogart. *Society* **28:6** 9/10:1991 pp. 62 – 73

103 Cigarette advertising and adolescent experimentation with smoking. Michael Klitzner; Paul J. Gruenewald; Elizabeth Bamberger. *Br. J. Addict.* **86:3** 3:1991 pp. 287 – 298

104 Evaluative and factual ad claims, knowledge level, and making inferences. Sarah Gardial; Gabriel Biehal. *Market. Lett.* **2:4** 11:1991 pp. 349 – 358

105 Japan und die Werbung in den deutschen Printmedien *[In German]*; [Japan and advertising in German print media]. Matthias Scheer. *Beit. Japan.* **29** 1991 pp. 426 – 458

106 Język reklamy w prasie polonijnej USA (na przykładzie Dziennika Związkowego). Część II *[In Polish]*; The language of advertisements in the Polonia press in the USA (on the example of Dziennik Związkowy). Part II *[Summary]*. Jacek Serwański. *Prz. Pol.* **XVII:2** 1991 pp. 59 – 72

107 Looking at film hoardings — labour, gender, subjectivity and everyday life in India. R. Srivatsan. *Publ. Cult.* **4:1** Fall:1991 pp. 1 – 24

108 Memorability and persuasiveness of organ donation message strategies. Leigh Arden Ford; Sandi W. Smith. *Am. Behav. Sc.* **34:6** 7-8:1991 pp. 695 – 711

109 Memory in a jingle jungle — music as a mnemonic device in communicating advertising slogans. Richard F. Yalch. *J. Appl. Psychol.* **76:2** 4:1991 pp. 268 – 275

110 Negative versus positive television advertising in U.S. presidential campaigns, 1960-1988. Lynda Lee Kaid; Anne Johnston. *J. Comm.* **41:3** Summer:1991 pp. 53 – 64

111 Place in advertising. Douglas K. Fleming; Richard Roth. *Geogr. Rev.* **81:3** 7:1991 pp. 281 – 291

112 La politique s'affiche — les affiches de la politique *[In French]*; [Politics flaunts itself — political advertising]. Alain Guillemin. Paris: Didier Erudition, 1991: 211 p. (photograph) *ISBN: 2864601702. Biblogr. — p. 203-207*. [Collection langages, discours et sociétés.]

113 Promotional culture — advertising, ideology and symbolic expression. Andrew Wernick. London: Sage Publications, 1991: 208p. *ISBN: 0803983905; LofC: gb 91096743*. [Theory, culture and society.]

114 Regulating green advertising in the motor car industry. Jane Holder. *J. Law Soc.* **18:3** Autumn:1991 pp. 323 – 346

115 Taal en reklame *[In Dutch]*; [Language and advertising]. A. Dewaet; P. Vanden Abeele. *Tijds. Econ. Manag.* **XXXVI:4** 12:1991 pp. 433 – 450

116 Tobacco advertising restrictions, price, income and tobacco consumption in OECD countries, 1960-1986; Restrictions sur les publicités pour le tabac, les prix et la consommation de tabac dans les pays de l'OCDE, 1960-1986 *[French summary]*; Restricciones en la propaganda de tabaco, precio ingresos y consumo de tabaco en los paises de la OCDE *[Spanish summary]*. Murray Laugesen; Chris Meads. *Br. J. Addict.* **86:10** 10:1991 pp. 1343 – 1354

117 The voices of Swiss television commercials. David Lee. *Multilingua* **10:3** 1991 pp. 295 – 324

D.7: Language, communication and media *[Langage, communication et moyens de communication]* —

Communication *[Communication]*

118 An analysis of artificial intelligence based models for describing communicative choice. Charles Pavitt. *Commun. Theory* **1**:3 8:1991 pp. 204 – 224

119 Assimilation and contrast effects in part-whole question sequences — a conversational logic analysis. Norbert Schwarz; Fritz Strack; Hans-Peter Mai. *Publ. Opin. Q.* **55**:1 Spring:1991 pp. 3 – 23

120 Base rates, representativeness, and the logic of conversation — the contextual relevance of "irrelevant" information. Norbert Schwarz; Fritz Strack; Denis Hilton; Gabi Naderer. *Soc. Cogn.* **9**:1 Spring:1991 pp. 67 – 84

121 *[In Japanese]*; [Children's linguistic refusal of mother's request — development of recognition of communicative risk]. Akiko Kojima. ***Meiji. Gak. Ron.*** *No.(482) - 1991.* pp. 109 – 133

122 Common-sense in clinical discourse. A.J. Soyland. *Text* **11**:2 :1991 pp. 223 – 240

123 Communication and assimilation patterns of two generations of Thai immigrants. Kandawadee Sakdisubha; L. Brooks Hill; James F. Hottel. *Intercult. Commun. St.* **1**:2 Fall:1991 pp. 1 – 35

124 Communication and social change. P.C. Joshi *[Contrib.]*; Paul Gueriviere *[Contrib.]*; Pradip Chakravarty *[Contrib.]*; Sunita Vasudeva *[Contrib.]*; Sanjay Kumar *[Contrib.]*; T. Chandramohan Reddy *[Contrib.]*; S.V. Udayakumar *[Contrib.]*; R. Tamilselvi *[Contrib.]*. *Collection of 5 articles.* **Soc. Act.**, *41:2*, 4-6:1991 pp. 121 – 212

125 Communication and strategic inference. Prashant Parikh. *Ling. Philos.* **14**:5 10:1991 pp. 473 – 514

126 Communication in history — technology, culture, society. D. J Crowley *[Ed.]*; Paul Heyer *[Ed.]*. New York, N.Y: Longman, c1991: xiv, 290 p. (ill) *ISBN: 0801305985; LofC: 90033631. Includes bibliographical references and index.*

127 Communications in Canadian society. Benjamin D Singer *[Ed.]*. Scarborough, Ontario: Nelson Canada, c1991: ix, 454 p. (ill) *ISBN: 0176035249; LofC: cn 91093828. Includes bibliographical references and index.*

128 Communications research — one paradigm or plurality of views? Taking stock of a discipline. Pradip Chakravarty; Sunita Vasudeva. *Soc. Act.* **41**:2 4-6:1991 pp. 176 – 195

129 Communications, computers and networks. Michael L. Dertouzos. *Sci. Am.* **265**:3 9:1991 pp. 30 – 37

130 Competing discourses — language and ideology. David Lee. Essex, England: Longman, 1991: 210 p. *ISBN: 0582078490; LofC: 91012999. Includes bibliographical references and index.* [Real language series.]

131 *[In Japanese]*; [The contemporary development and problems in mass communication theory — from standpoint of "encoding/decoding model"]. Mamoru Ito. ***Journal of Japanese Scientists*** *No.26(10) - 1991.* pp. 22 – 27

132 Cross-cultural interpersonal communication. Felipe Korzenny *[Ed.]*; Stella Ting-Toomey *[Ed.]*. Newbury Park, Calif: SAGE Publications, c1991: viii, 283 p. (ill) *ISBN: 0803940475. Includes bibliographical references and index.* [International and intercultural communication annual. : Vol. 15]

133 Cross-cultural pragmatics — the semantics of human interaction. Anna Wierzbicka. Berlin: Mouton de Gruyter, 1991: xiii, 502 p. *ISBN: 0899256996; LofC: 90022563. Includes bibliographical references (p. [461]-485) and indexes.* [Trends in linguistics.]

134 *[In Japanese]*; [The development in information society and the change of communication structure (4) — youth communication and the changes of media environments]. Bun'ya Ogawa. ***Tokyo Kokusai Daigaku Ronso*** *No.(43) - 1991.* pp. 61 – 80

135 Discourse as space/discourse as time — reflections on the metalanguage of spoken and written discourse. S. Fleischman. *J. Prag.* **16**:4 1991 pp. 291 – 306

136 Discourse dynamics. Ian Parker. New York: Routledge, 1991: 169 p. *ISBN: 0415050170; LofC: 90028866. Includes bibliographical references and index.*

137 Discursive acts. R. S Perinbanayagam. New York: Aldine de Gruyter, c1991: xii, 211 p. *ISBN: 0202303675; LofC: 90047962. Communication; Includes bibliographical references (p. 199-207) and index.* [Communication and social order.]

138 Effective communication between the scientific community and the media. Bruna de Marchi. *Disasters* **15**:3 9:1991 pp. 237 – 243

139 Effects of communication network structure — components of positional centrality. Brian Mullen; Craig Johnson; Eduardo Salas. *Soc. Networks* **13**:2 6:1991 pp. 169 – 185

D.7: Language, communication and media *[Langage, communication et moyens de communication]* — Communication *[Communication]*

140 Envisioning information. Edward R. Tufte. Cheshire, Conn. (P.O. Box 430, Cheshire 06410): Graphics Press, c1990: 126 p. (ill. (some col.)) *ISBN: oc21270160; LofC: 90166920. Includes bibliographical references and index.*

141 The ethoglossic power dynamics of interaction — English across cultures and races. P.B. Nayar. *Intercult. Commun. St.* **1:2** Fall:1991 pp. 237 – 250

142 Everyday conversation. Robert E. Nofsinger. Newbury Park, Calif: Sage, c1991: xi, 180 p. (ill) *ISBN: 0803933096; LofC: 90020314. Includes bibliographical references (p. 170-176) and index.* [Interpersonal commtexts. : No. 1]

143 Extenuatory sociolinguistics — diverting attention from issues to symptoms in cross-cultural communication studies. Thiru Kandiah. *Multilingua* **10:4** :1991 pp. 345 – 380

144 Family of origin and cohort differences in verbal ability. Duane F. Alwin. *Am. Sociol. R.* **56:5** 10:1991 pp. 625 – 638

145 Focus on silences across cultures. Werner Enninger. *Intercult. Commun. St.* **1:1** Spring:1991 pp. 1 – 38

146 From the motor-car to television — cultural-historical arguments on the meaning of mobility for communication. Ben Bachmair. *Media Cult. Soc.* **13:4** 10:1991 pp. 521 – 534

147 Fundamentals of nonverbal behavior. Robert S. Feldman *[Ed.]*; Bernard Rimé *[Ed.]*. Cambridge: Cambridge University Press, 1991: - *ISBN: 0521363888.* [Studies in emotion and social interaction.]

148 Gestures and speech — psychological investigations. Pierre Feyereisen; Jacques-Dominique de Lannoy *[Ed.]*. Cambridge: Cambridge University Press, 1991: 210 p. *ISBN: 0521373956.* [Studies in emotion and social interaction.]

149 Handeln in Kommunikationssituationen. Versuch einer induktiven Modellbildung *[In German]*; Acting in communication situations — towards the inductive building of a model *[Summary]*; Agir dans des situations de communication. Essai de construction inductive de modèles *[French summary]*; Actuar en sitaciones de communicación. Hacia una inductiva formación de un modelo *[Spanish summary]*. Angela Fritz. *Publizistik* **36:1** 1-3:1991 pp. 5 – 21

150 "Hello Central?" — gender, technology, and culture in the formation of telephone systems. Michèle Martin. Montréal: McGill-Queen's University Press, c1991: 219 p. (ill) *ISBN: 0773508309; LofC: cn 91090009. Includes bibliographical references and index.*

151 The indeterminacy thesis reformulated. Ken Gemes. *J. Phil.* **LXXXVIII:2** 2:1991 pp. 91 – 108

152 Information. L. David Ritchie. Newbury Park, Calif: Sage Publications, c1991: viii, 75 p. (ill) *ISBN: 0803939043; LofC: 91028881. Includes bibliographical references (p. 68-72) and index.* [Communication concepts.]

153 Inside rumor — a personal journey. Ralph L. Rosnow. *Am. Psychol.* **46:5** 5:1991 pp. 484 – 496

154 Interaction and asymmetry in clinical discourse. Douglas W. Maynard. *A.J.S.* **97:2** 9:1991 pp. 448 – 495

155 Intercultural communication at work in Australia — complaints and apologies in turns. Michael Clyne; Martin Ball; Deborah Neil. *Multilingua* **10:3** 1991 pp. 251 – 274

156 Kommunikation im Kontext — J. Gumperz und die interaktionale Soziolinguistik *[In German]*; Communication in context — John J. Gumperz and the interactional sociolinguistics *[Summary]*. Hubert Knoblauch. *Z. Soziol.* **20:6** 12:1991 pp. 446 – 462

157 Kulturális-kommunikációs rétegződés (kutatási tervezet) *[In Hungarian]*; [Cultural and communicational stratification (a framework for research)]. Róbert Agelusz; Róbert Tardos. *Szociologia* Vol.16; No.2 - 1987. pp. 209 – 231

158 Literacy and orality. David R. Olson *[Ed.]*; Nancy Torrance *[Ed.]*. Cambridge: Cambridge University Press, 1991: xii, 288 p. (ill) *ISBN: 0521392179. Includes bibliographies and index.*

159 Mapping nonverbal behavior on the interpersonal circle. Robert Gifford. *J. Pers. Soc. Psychol.* **61:2** 8:1991 pp. 279 – 288

160 "Miscommunication" and problematic talk. Nikolas Coupland *[Ed.]*; John M. Wiemann *[Ed.]*; Howard Giles *[Ed.]*. Newbury Park, CA: Sage Publications, c1991: p. cm *ISBN: 0803940327; LofC: 90022484. Includes bibliographical references.*

161 Mixed messages — the multiple audience problem and strategic communication. John H. Fleming; John M. Darley. *Soc. Cogn.* **9:1** Spring:1991 pp. 25 – 46

162 A new stochastic path-length tree methodology for constructing communication networks. Jaewun Cho; Wayne S. DeSarbo. *Soc. Networks* **13:2** 6:1991 pp. 105 – 140

D.7: Language, communication and media *[Langage, communication et moyens de communication]* — Communication *[Communication]*

163 Nietzsche and autonomy in communication ethics. Daniel W. Conway. *Communication* **12:3** :1991 pp. 217 – 230

164 *[In Japanese]*; [On the concept of communicative productive powers]. Masumi Takeuchi. *Johomondai Kenkyu No.(4) - 1991.* pp. 8 – 13

165 On the organization of corrective exchanges in conversation. N.R. Norrick. *J. Prag.* **16:1** 7:1991 pp. 59 – 83

166 Perspective-taking in communication — representations of others' knowledge in reference. Robert M. Krauss; Susan R. Fussell. *Soc. Cogn.* **9:1** Spring:1991 pp. 2 – 24

167 Planning in ordinary conversation. A. Scholtens. *J. Prag.* **16:1** 7:1991 pp. 31 – 58

168 Power and the circuit of formal talk. Kwesi Yankah. *J. Folk. Res.* **28:1** 1-4:1991 pp. 1 – 22

169 The power of communication and the communication of power — toward an emancipatory theory of communication. Klaus Krippendorff. *Communication* **12:3** :1991 pp. 175 – 196

170 Primacy and recency in communication and self-persuasion — how successive audiences and multiple encodings influence subsequent evaluative judgments. C. Douglas McCann; E. Tory Higgins; Rocco A. Fondacaro. *Soc. Cogn.* **9:1** Spring:1991 pp. 47 – 66

171 Raum und Kommunikation. Impulse für die Forschung *[In German]*; Space and communication — Incentives for research *[Summary]*; Espace et communication. Stimulants pour la recherche *[French summary]*; Espacio y comunicación. Incentivos para la investigación *[Spanish summary]*. Ursula Maier-Rabler. *Publizistik* **36:1** 1-3:1991 pp. 22 – 35

172 Reductive and nonreductive simile theories of metaphor. Lynne Tirrell. *J. Phil.* **LXXXVIII:7** 7:1991 pp. 337 – 358

173 Reinterpreting speech-exchange systems — communication formats in Aids counselling. Anssi Peräkylä; David Silverman. *Sociology* **25:4** 11:1991 pp. 627 – 651

174 Représentation — le mot, l'idée, la chose *[In French]*; Representation — the word, the thought, the thing *[Summary]*. Carlo Ginsburg. *Annales* **46:6** 11-12:1991 pp. 1219 – 1234

175 Selection of verbal probabilities — a solution for some problems of verbal probability expression. Robert M. Hamm. *Organ. Beh. Hum. Dec. Proces.* **48:2** 4:1991 pp. 193 – 223

176 Social cognition and communication — human judgment in its social context. Robert M. Krauss *[Contrib.]*; Susan R. Fussell *[Contrib.]*; John H. Fleming *[Contrib.]*; John M. Darley *[Contrib.]*; C. Douglas McCann *[Contrib.]*; E. Tory Higgins *[Contrib.]*; Rocco A. Fondacaro *[Contrib.]*; Norbert Schwarz *[Contrib.]*; Fritz Strack *[Contrib.]*; Denis Hilton *[Contrib.]* and others. Collection of 6 articles. **Soc. Cogn.** , *9:1*, Spring:1991 pp. 2 – 125

177 Sociologie de la communication de masse *[In French]*; [The sociology of mass communication]. Judith Lazar. Paris: Armand Colin, 1991: 240 p. *ISBN: 2200312881.*

178 Source strategies and the communication of environmental affairs. Alison Anderson. *Media Cult. Soc.* **13:4** 10:1991 pp. 459 – 476

179 Speaking turns in face-to-face discussions. Garold Stasser; Laurie A. Taylor. *J. Pers. Soc. Psychol.* **60:5** 5:1991 pp. 675 – 684

180 Studying interpersonal communication — the research experience. Ruth Anne Clark. Newbury Park, Calif: Sage Publications, c1991: xiii, 166 p. (ill) *ISBN: 0803933053; LofC: 90024233. Includes bibliographical references (p. 159-161) and index.* [Interpersonal commtexts. : No. 2]

181 Teenage Samizdat — song-album scrapbooks as mass communication. Alexei Khaniutin. *J. Comm.* **41:2** Spring:1991 pp. 55 – 65

182 Les termes d'adresse dans un bureau parisien *[In French]*; How colleagues address each other in a Parisian office *[Summary]*; Anredeformen in einem Pariser Büro *[German summary]*; Términos de apelación en una oficina parisina *[Spanish summary]*. Denis Guigo. *Homme* **XXXI:119** 7-9:1991 pp. 41 – 60

183 Terms of address in Korean and American cultures. Shin Ja J. Hwang. *Intercult. Commun. St.* **1:2** Fall:1991 pp. 117 – 136

184 Transnational communications — wiring the Third World. John A. Lent *[Ed.]*; Gerald Sussman *[Ed.]*. Newbury Park, Calif: Sage Publications, 1991: 327 p. *ISBN: 0803937652; LofC: 90025943. Includes bibliographical references and index.* [Communication and human values.]

185 Understanding Mexicans and Americans — cultural perspectives in conflict. Rogelio Díaz-Guerrero; Lorand B. Szalay. New York: Plenum Press, c1991: x, 297 p. (ill) *ISBN: 0306438178; LofC: 90022262. Includes bibliographical references (p. 207-215).* [Cognition and language.]

D.7: Language, communication and media [Langage, communication et moyens de communication] — Communication [Communication]

186 Urban and rural sign language in India. J. Jepson. *Lang. Soc.* **20:1** 3:1991 pp. 37 – 58
187 Using communication theory — an introduction to planned communication. Sven Windahl; Benno Signitzer *[Ed.]*; Jean Olson *[Ed.]*. London: Sage Publications, 1991: 248 p. *ISBN: 0803984316*.
188 Verständigungsorientierte Öffentlichkeitsarbeit — eine kommunikationstheoretisch begründete Perspektive *[In German]*; Understanding-oriented public relations — a perspective based on communication theory *[Summary]*; Relations publiques orientes vers l'entente — une perspective fondée en ce qui concerne la théorie de la communication *[French summary]*; Trabajo de relaciones públicas orientado verso entendimiento — una perspectiva teórica-comunicativa *[Spanish summary]*. Roland Burkart; Sabine Probst. *Publizistik* **36:1** 1-3:1991 pp. 56 – 76
189 What causes communication problems between English speakers and Korean speakers. Kun-Ok Kim. *Intercult. Commun. St.* **1:2** Fall:1991 pp. 103 – 116
190 Writing in the community. David Barton *[Ed.]*; Roz Ivanic *[Ed.]*. Newbury Park: Sage Publications, 1991: x, 226 p. (ill) *ISBN: 080393632x*. Includes bibliographical references. [Written communication annual. : Vol. 6]
191 Zur Fruchtbarkeit der Konversationsanalyse für die Untersuchung schriftlicher Texte — dargestellt am Fall der Präferenzorganisation in psychiatrischen „Obergutachten" *[In German]*; On the fruitfulness of conversational analysis for the investigation of written texts *[Summary]*. Bettina Knauth; Stephan Wolff. *Z. Soziol.* **20:1** 2:1991 pp. 36 – 49
192 ¿Sistemas o modelos culturales? A propósito de la palabra hablada, de la escrita y de la electrónica *[In Spanish]*; [Cultural systems of models? On the spoken, written and electronic word]. Eduardo Zapata Saldaña. *Soc. Part.* **:56** 12:1991 pp. 27 – 34

Linguistics [Linguistique]

193 Bulgarian Turkish — the linguistic effects of recent nationality policy. Catherine Rudin; Ali Eminov. *Anthrop. Ling.* **32:1-2** Spring-Summer:1990 pp. 149 – 162
194 Contexts of accommodation — developments in applied sociolinguistics. Howard Giles *[Ed.]*; Justine Coupland *[Ed.]*; Nikolas Coupland *[Ed.]*. Cambridge: Cambridge University Press, 1991: viii, 321 p. (ill) *ISBN: 0521361516; LofC: 91024695*. Includes bibliographical references and index. [Studies in emotion and social interaction.]
195 Déclarer sa profession *[In French]*; Stating one's profession *[Summary]*; Seinen Beruf angeben *[German summary]*; Declarar su profesión *[Spanish summary]*. Francis Kramarz. *Rev. Fr. Soc.* **XXXII:1** 1-3:1991 pp. 3 – 27
196 Dialectics and the macrostructure of arguments — a theory of argument structure. James B. Freeman. Berlin ; New York: Foris Publications, 1991: xiv, 273 p. (ill) *ISBN: 3110133903; LofC: 91034309*. Includes bibliographical references (p. [263]-267) and index. [Studies of argumentation in pragmatics and discourse analysis. : No. 10]
197 Dynamic predicate logic. Jeroen Groenendijk; Martin Stokhof. *Ling. Philos.* **14:1** 2:1991 pp. 39 – 100
198 English around the world — sociolinguistic perspectives. Jenny Cheshire *[Ed.]*. Cambridge: Cambridge University Press, 1991: - *ISBN: 0521330807*. Includes index.
199 Ethnolinguistic vitality in "the Danish capital of America". T. Kristiansen; J. Harwood; H. Giles. *J. Multiling.* **12:6** 1991 pp. 421 – 448
200 Even, still and counterfactuals. Stephen Barker. *Ling. Philos.* **14:1** 2:1991 pp. 1 – 38
201 Evidence for foot structure in Japanese. William J. Poser. *Language* **66:1** 3:1990 pp. 78 – 105
202 The exponence of gender in Spanish. James W. Harris. *Linguist. In.* **22:1** winter:1991 pp. 27 – 62
203 Extraposition and focus. Geoffrey J. Huck; Younghee Na. *Language* **66:1** 3:1990 pp. 51 – 77
204 Floor structure of English and Japanese conversation. R. Hayashi. *J. Prag.* **16:1** 7:1991 pp. 1 – 30
205 Focus in phonetics, syntax, semantics and pragmatics. Joachim Jacobs *[Contrib.]*; Petr Sgall *[Contrib.]*; Jack Hoeksema *[Contrib.]*; Frans Zwarts *[Contrib.]*; Ulrich F.G. Klein *[Contrib.]*; Sjaak de Mey *[Contrib.]*; Rob T.P. Wiche *[Contrib.]*; Jay David Atlas *[Contrib.]*; Peter I. Blok *[Contrib.]*. Collection of 8 articles. **J. Sem.** , *8:1&2*, 1991 pp. 1 – 165
206 An integrated theory of complement control. Ivan A. Sag; Carl Pollard. *Language* **67:1** 3:1991 pp. 63 – 113
207 Interpersonal verbs — implicit causality of action verbs and contextual factors. L. Mannetti; E. de Grada. *Eur. J. Soc. Psychol.* **21:5** 9-10:1991 pp. 429 – 444

D.7: Language, communication and media *[Langage, communication et moyens de communication]* — **Linguistics** *[Linguistique]*

208 Issues in transnational financial reporting — a linguistic analysis. S. Archer; S. McLeay. *J. Multiling.* **12:5** 1991 pp. 347 – 361
209 Language, history and class. P. J. Corfield *[Ed.]*. Oxford: Basil Blackwell, 1991: 320 p. *ISBN: 0631167323. Includes bibliography and index.*
210 Lexical and conceptual semantics. Beth Levin *[Contrib.]*; Steven Pinker *[Contrib.]*; Ray Jackendoff *[Contrib.]*; James Pustejovsky *[Contrib.]*; Soonja Choi *[Contrib.]*; Melissa Bowerman *[Contrib.]*; Malka Rappaport Hovav *[Contrib.]*; Jess Gropen *[Contrib.]*; Michelle Hollander *[Contrib.]*; Richard Goldberg *[Contrib.] and others.* Collection of 7 articles. **Cognition**, *41:1-3*, 12:1991 pp. 1 – 230
211 Linguistic forms and social obligations — a critique of the doctrine of literal expression in Searle. David Bogen. *J. Theory Soc. Behav.* **21:1** 3:1991 pp. 31 – 62
212 Linguistic minority children's comprehension of language in the classroom and teachers' adjustment to their pupils' performance. S. Lie; A.H. Wold. *J. Multiling.* **12:5** 1991 pp. 363 – 381
213 The mental representation of lexical form — a phonological approach to the recognition lexicon. Aditi Lahiri; William Marslen Wilson. *Cognition* **38:3** 3:1991 pp. 245 – 294
214 The metaphors of radiation — or, why a beautiful woman is like a nuclear power plant. Jane Caputi. *Wom. St. Inter. For.* **14:5** :1991 pp. 423 – 442
215 The nature of tenses in African languages. A case study of the morphemes and their variants. O.E. Essien. *Arch. Orient.* **59:1** 1991 pp. 1 – 11
216 On diachronic sources and synchronic pattern — an investigation into the origin of linguistic universals. Anthony Rodrigues Aristar. *Language* **67:1** 3:1991 pp. 1 – 33
217 On "reciprocal scope". Irene Heim; Howard Lasnik; Robert May. *Linguist. In.* **22:1** winter:1991 pp. 173 – 192
218 On some (socio) linguistic properties of Italian foreign workers' children in contact with German. Aldo di Luzio. *Int. J. S. Lang.* **:90** 1991 pp. 131 – 158
219 Plain language — principles and practice. Erwin Ray Steinberg *[Ed.]*. Detroit: Wayne State University Press, c1991: 258 p. (ill) *ISBN: 0814320201; LofC: 90038008. Includes bibliographical references and index.*
220 Prototypes revisited. Robert E. MacLaury. *Ann. R. Anthr.* **20:** 1991 pp. 55 – 74
221 Reciprocal scope. Edwin Williams. *Linguist. In.* **22:1** winter:1991 pp. 159 – 173
222 Reciprocity and plurality. Irene Heim; Howard Lasnik; Robert May. *Linguist. In.* **22:1** winter:1991 pp. 63 – 101
223 Scandinavian extraction phenomena revisited — weak and strong generative capacity. Philip H. Miller. *Ling. Philos.* **14:1** 2:1991 pp. 101 – 113
224 The semantics of specificity. Mürvet Enç. *Linguist. In.* **22:1** winter:1991 pp. 1 – 25
225 Several theoretical problems in sociolinguistics. Cai Fuyou. *Soc. Sci. China* **XII:3** 9:1991 pp. 188 – 204
226 Sobre semántica social — conceptos y estratos en el español de México *[In Spanish]*; [On social semantics — concepts and strata in Mexican Spanish]. Raúl Ávila. *Est. Sociol.* **IX:26** 5-8:1991 pp. 279 – 314
227 Social linguistics and literacies — ideology in discourses. James Paul Gee. London: Falmer, 1991: 203p. *ISBN: 1850008299.* [Critical perspectives on literacy and education.]
228 Vowel context, rate and loudness effects on linguopalatal contact patterns in Hindi retroflex/t. R.P. Dixit; J.E. Flege. *J. Phon.* **19:2** 4:1991 pp. 213 – 229

Media *[Moyens de communication]*

229 Abgeordnete und Journalisten *[In German]*; Members of parliament and journalists *[Summary]*; Députés et journalistes *[French summary]*; Diputados y periodístas *[Spanish summary]*. Werner J. Patzelt. *Publizistik* **36:3** 7-9:1991 pp. 315 – 329
230 The adoring audience — fan culture and popular media. Lisa A Lewis *[Ed.]*. London: Routledge, 1991: 245 p. *ISBN: 0415078202; LofC: 91037332. Includes bibliographical references and index.*
231 Les agences de presse africaines *[In French]*; [African press agencies]. Claude Wauthier. *Afr. Cont.* **:157(1)** 1-3:1991 pp. 39 – 49
232 American media and commercial culture. Leo Bogart. *Society* **28:6** 9/10:1991 pp. 62 – 73
233 Artefakte der Medienwirkungsforschung — Kritik klassischer Annahmen *[In German]*; Artifacts of media-effects research — a critique of classic hypotheses *[Summary]*; Artefacts de la recherche sur les effets de media. Critique d'hypothèses classiques *[French*

D.7: Language, communication and media *[Langage, communication et moyens de communication]* — Media *[Moyens de communication]*

summary]; Artefactos de la investigación del efecto de los medios de comunicación. Una crítica de las hipótesis clasicas *[Spanish summary]*. Klaus Merten. **Publizistik 36:1** 1-3:1991 pp. 36 – 55

234 *[In Japanese]*; [The body and the media — on the paradox of the body]. Akeshi Watari. *Soshioroji No.36(1) - 1991.* pp. 41 – 51

235 Breaking the cocoon — cultural journalism in a global community. Kathryn J. Olmstead. *J. Pop. Cult.* **25:2** Fall:1991 pp. 153 – 166

236 The British press and broadcasting since 1945. Colin Seymour-Ure. Oxford: Blackwell, 1991: 269 p. *ISBN: 063116443x. Includes bibliography and index.* [Making contemporary Britain.]

237 Broadcasting — national cultures/international business. Geoffrey Nowell-Smith. *New Form.* **:13** Spring:1991 pp. 39 – 44

238 *[In Japanese]*; [The change of mass communication theory — the legacy of mass society theory and powerful media theory]. Yutaka Oishi. ***Bulletin of the Faculty of Sociology, Kansas University*** *No.23(1) - 1991.* pp.217-247.

239 Children and the commercial exploitation of violence in Sweden — public measures for mitigating commercially motivated violence and its social effects on children and young people. Nic Nilsson. Stockholm: Swedish Institute, 1991: 8 p. [Current Sweden. : No. 384]

240 The chosen few — Nightline and the politics of public affairs television. William Hoynes; David Croteau. *Crit. Sociol.* **18:1** Spring:1991 pp. 19 – 36

241 Communication and citizenship — journalism and the public sphere in the new media age. Peter Dahlgren *[Ed.]*; Colin Sparks *[Ed.]*. London: Routledge, 1991: 266 p. *ISBN: 0415057795. Conference proceedings; Includes index.* [Communication and society.]

242 Communications in Canadian society. Benjamin D Singer *[Ed.]*. Scarborough, Ontario: Nelson Canada, c1991: ix, 454 p. (ill) *ISBN: 0176035249; LofC: cn 91093828. Includes bibliographical references and index.*

243 Constructing race and violence — U.S. news coverage and the signifying practices of apartheid. Jo Ellen Fair; Roberta J. Astroff. *J. Comm.* **41:4** Autumn:1991 pp. 58 – 74

244 Contemporary terrorism in Peru — Sendero Luminoso and the media. Kevin G. Barnhurst. *J. Comm.* **41:4** Autumn:1991 pp. 75 – 89

245 Contested meanings — the consumption of news about nature conservation. Jacquelin Burgess; Carolyn Harrison; Paul Maiteny. *Media Cult. Soc.* **13:4** 10:1991 pp. 499 – 520

246 Dynamics of media politics — broadcast and electronic media in Western Europe. Karen Siune *[Ed.]*; Wolgang Truetzschler *[Ed.]*. London: Sage Publications, 1991: 206 p. *ISBN: 0803985738; LofC: gb 91086074.* [Communications in society.]

247 L'écran des titres de presse *[In French]*; The screen of the headlines — reflections about the staging of current events *[Summary]*. Francis Dard. *Pensée* **:281** 5-6:1991 pp. 33 – 52

248 Effective communication between the scientific community and the media. Bruna de Marchi. *Disasters* **15:3** 9:1991 pp. 237 – 243

249 Effects of media violence on viewers' aggression in unconstrained social interaction. Wendy Wood; Frank Y. Wong; J.Gregory Chachere. *Psychol .B.* **109:3** 5:1991 pp. 371 – 383

250 Environmental degradation in Brazilian Amazonia — perspectives in US news media. Jacob Bendix; Carol M. Liebler. *Prof. Geogr.* **43:4** 11:1991 pp. 474 – 485

251 European press coverage of the Grenada crisis. Jan Servaes. *J. Comm.* **41:4** Autumn:1991 pp. 28 – 41

252 L'évolution de la presse écrite turque au cours de la décennie 1980 *[In French]*; [The evolution of the written press in Turkey during the 1980s]. Gérard Groc. *Cah. Ét. Méd. Ori. Tur-Iran.* **11** 1991 pp. 89 – 118

253 The first amendment meets some new technologies — broadcasting, common carriers, and free speech in the 1990s. Robert B. Horwitz. *Theory Soc.* **20/1** 2:1991 pp. 21 – 72

254 Foreign voices as people's choices — BBC popularity in the Arab world. Muhammad I. Ayish. *Middle E. Stud.* **27:3** 7:1991 pp. 374 – 389

255 The fourth estate and the Constitution — freedom of the press in America. L. A. Scot Powe. Berkeley: University of California Press, c1991: xii, 357 p. *ISBN: 0520072901; LofC: 90045465. Includes bibliographical references (pp. 299-343) and index.*

256 Framing U.S. coverage of international news — contrasts in narratives of the KAL and Iran Air incidents. Robert M. Entman. *J. Comm.* **41:4** Autumn:1991 pp. 6 – 27

D.7: Language, communication and media *[Langage, communication et moyens de communication]* — **Media** *[Moyens de communication]*

257 The future of the mass audience. W. Russell Neuman. Cambridge: Cambridge University Press, 1991: xiv, 202 p. (ill) *ISBN: 0521413478; LofC: 91015353 //r91.* Includes bibliographical references (p. 179-193) and index.

258 Glasnost and the transformation of Moscow News. Elisabeth Schillinger; Catherine Porter. *J. Comm.* **41:2** Spring:1991 pp. 125 – 149

259 Glasnost, perestroika and the Soviet media. Brian McNair. London: Routledge, 1991: 231 p. (ill) *ISBN: 0415035511.* Includes bibliography and index. [Communication and society.]

260 La guerre dans les médias américains *[In French]*; [The war in the American media]. Serge Halimi. *R. Et. Palest.* **:41** Autumn:1991 pp. 59 – 77

261 The ideological octopus — an exploration of television and its audience. Justin Lewis. New York: Routledge, 1991: x, 218 p. *ISBN: 0415902878; LofC: 91029957.* Includes bibliographical references (p. 207-215) and index. [Studies in culture and communication.]

262 Images of a free press. Lee C Bollinger. Chicago: University of Chicago Press, 1991: xii, 209 p. *ISBN: 0226063488; LofC: 90027740.* Includes bibliographical references and index.

263 The influence of western radio on the democratization of Soviet youth. Oleg Manaev. *J. Comm.* **41:2** Spring:1991 pp. 72 – 89

264 The information industry — political economy of media. Paul Gueriviere. *Soc. Act.* **41:2** 4-6:1991 pp. 156 – 175

265 The Jewish press in the USSR today. Viktor Kelner. *Sov. Jew. Aff.* **21:2** Winter:1991 pp. 23 – 30

266 Journalism in an Islamic perspective. Inamul Haq. *J. Res. Soc. Pakist.* **XXVIII:2** 4:1991 pp. 1 – 8

267 Курьеры муз: Диалектика продуктив. и репродуктив. в творчестве радио и телевидения *[In Russian]*; [Messengers of muses — dialectics of productivity and reproductivity in the creative power of radio and television]. Y.A. Bogomolov. Moscow: Iskusstvo, 1986: 191 p. [ВНИИ исусствознания М-ва культуры СССР.]

268 Language in the news — discourse and ideology in the British press. Roger Fowler. London: Routledge, 1991: 254 p. *ISBN: 0415014182; LofC: 90040794.*

269 The language of news media. Allan Bell. Oxford: Basil Blackwell, 1991: 277 p. (ill) *ISBN: 0631164340.* [Language in society. : No. 15]

270 Latin and North American media. Joseph D. Straubhaar *[Contrib.]*; Gloria M. Viscasillas *[Contrib.]*; Conrad P. Kottak *[Contrib.]*; Michael Morgan *[Contrib.]*; James Shanahan *[Contrib.]*; Peter Manuel *[Contrib.]*; Leslie Snyder *[Contrib.]*; Connie Roser *[Contrib.]*; Steven Chaffee *[Contrib.]*. Collection of 5 articles. **J. Comm.** , *41:1,* Winter:1991 pp. 53 – 132

271 Literarischer Journalismus oder journalistische Literatur? Ein Beitrag zu Konzept, Vertretern und Philosophie des »new journalism« *[In German]*; Literary journalism or journalistic literature? A contribution to the concept, the representatives and the philosophy of «new journalism» *[Summary]*; Journalisme littéraire ou littérature journalistique? Une contribution sur le concept, les représentants et la philosophie du «new journalism» *[French summary]*; ¿Periodismo literario o literatura periodística? Una contribución al concepto, a los representantes y a la filosofía del «new journalism» *[Spanish summary]*. Hannes Haas; Gian-Luca Wallisch. *Publizistik* **36:3** 7-9:1991 pp. 298 – 314

272 Making local news. Phyllis C Kaniss. Chicago: University of Chicago Press, 1991: x, 260 p. (ill., maps) *ISBN: 0226423476; LofC: 90021587.* Includes bibliographical references (p. 235-253) and index.

273 Mass media, crime, law, and justice — an institutional approach. Richard V. Ericson. *Br. J. Crimin.* **31:3** Summer:1991 pp. 219 – 249

274 A matter of manners? — the limits of broadcast language. Andrea Millwood Hargrave *[Ed.]*. London: Libbey, 1991: 105 p. *ISBN: 0861963377.*

275 The media and the social construction of the environment. Anders Hansen. *Media Cult. Soc.* **13:4** 10:1991 pp. 443 – 458

276 Media battlefronts — political action and coverage in the press. Charlotte Ryan. *Soc. Pol.* **22:2** Fall:1991 pp. 8 – 16

277 Media debates — issues in mass communication. Everette E. Dennis; John Calhoun Merrill *[Ed.]*. New York: Longman, c1991: xi, 228 p. *ISBN: 0801304369; LofC: 90005748.* Includes bibliographical references and index.

278 *[In Japanese]*; [Media development and humanity]. Shinji Miyadai. **Journal of the Institute of Electronics and Communication Engineers** *No.74(9) - 1991.* pp. 980 – 984

D.7: Language, communication and media *[Langage, communication et moyens de communication]* — Media *[Moyens de communication]*

279 Media ethics and the public sphere. John Durham Peters; Kenneth Cmiel. *Communication* **12:3** :1991 pp. 197 – 216

280 The media in the 1984 and 1988 presidential campaigns. Guido Hermann Stempel *[Ed.]*; John W. Windhauser *[Ed.]*. New York: Greenwood Press, 1991: xi, 220 p. *ISBN: 0313265275; LofC: 90002920. Media; Includes bibliographical references (p. [211]-215) and index.* [Contributions to the study of mass media and communications.]

281 Media moguls. Jeremy Tunstall; Michael B. Palmer *[Ed.]*. London: Routledge, 1991: 258 p. *ISBN: 0415054672; LofC: 91016744. Includes bibliographical references and index.* [Communication and society.]

282 Media research techniques. Arthur Asa Berger. Newbury Park, Calif: Sage Publications, c1991: vii, 148 p. (ill) *ISBN: 080394179x; LofC: 90025948. Includes bibliographical references (p. 142-143) and indexes.*

283 Media worlds in the postjournalism era. David L Altheide; Robert P Snow *[Ed.]*. New York: Aldine de Gruyter, c1991: xiii, 274 p. *ISBN: 0202303764; LofC: 90048033. Media; Includes bibliographical references (p. 255-267) and indexes.* [Communication and social order.]

284 Media, consciousness, and culture — explorations of Walter Ong's thought. Bruce E. Gronbeck *[Ed.]*; Thomas J. Farrell *[Ed.]*; Paul A. Soukup *[Ed.]*. Newbury Park, Calif: Sage Publications, c1991: xviii, 272 p. *ISBN: 0803940254; LofC: 90027759. Includes bibliographical references (p. 237-252) and index.* [Communication and human values.]

285 Media, state and nation — political violence and collective identities. Philip Schlesinger. London: Sage Publications, 1991: 240 p. *ISBN: 0803985037.* [Media, culture and society series.]

286 Media, the political order and national identity. Philip Schlesinger. *Media Cult. Soc.* **13:3** 7:1991 pp. 297 – 308

287 The medium must not deconstruct — a postmodern ethnography of USA Today television show. Barry Glassner. *Media Cult. Soc.* **13:1** 1:1991 pp. 53 – 70

288 The mindscape of the presidency — Time magazine, 1945-1985. Roderick P. Hart; Deborah Smith-Howell; John Llewellyn. *J. Comm.* **41:3** Summer:1991 pp. 6 – 25

289 El mundo en una página — un análisis de la primera plana de tres periódicos costarricenses 1950- 1970 *[In Spanish]*; [The world on a page — an analysis of the front page of three Costa Rican daily newspapers, 1950-1970]. P. Vega J.. *An. Est. Cent.Am.* **16:2/17:1** 1990/1991 pp. 139 – 153

290 Musicians' magazines in the 1980s — the creation of a community and a consumer market. Paul Théberge. *Cult. St.* **5:3** 10:1991 pp. 270 – 293

291 Negativität als Nachrichtenideologie *[In German]*; Negativity as news ideology *[Summary]*; Négativité comme idéologie de l'information *[French summary]*; Negativismo como ideología de noticias *[Spanish summary]*. Hans Mathias Kepplinger; Helga Weißbecker. *Publizistik* **36:3** 7-9:1991 pp. 330 – 342

292 New technology and changes in the mass media — considerations for political scientists. Miquel de Morgas Spà. Barcelona: Institut de Ciències Polítiques i Socials, 1990: 31 p.

293 Old media on new media — national popular press reaction to mechanical television. James R. Walker. *J. Pop. Cult.* **25:1** Summer:1991 pp. 21 – 30

294 Out of focus — old age, the press and broadcasting. Eric Midwinter. London: Centre for Policy on Ageing, 1991: 64 p. *ISBN: 0904139816.*

295 Parteilichkeit oder Politikverdrossenheit? Die Darstellung von Motiven und Emotionen deutscher Politiker im »Spiegel« *[In German]*; Partiality of political malaise? The presentation of motives and emotions of German politicians in "Der Speigel" *[Summary]*; Partialité ou lassitude de la politique? La présentation de motifs et émotions de politiciens allemands dans le »Spiegel« *[French summary]*; Parcialidad ó tedio de la política? La presentación de motivos y emociones de políticos alemanes en la revista semanal »Der Speigel« *[Spanish summary]*. Simone Christine Ehmig. *Publizistik* **36:2** 4-6:1991 pp. 183 – 200

296 Patrolling the border — British broadcasting and the Irish question in the 1980s. Graham Murdock. *J. Comm.* **41:4** Autumn:1991 pp. 104 – 115

297 The people's voice — local radio and television in Europe. Nick Jankowski *[Ed.]*; Ole Prehn *[Ed.]*; James Stappers *[Ed.]*. London: John Libbey, 1991: 274 p. *ISBN: 0861963229.* [Acamedia research monograph. : No. 6]

298 Perestroika and media in deconstructivist perspective, part I. Helena Gourko. *J. Soc. Biol. Struct.* **14:3** 1991 pp. 241 – 253

D.7: Language, communication and media [Langage, communication et moyens de communication] — Media [Moyens de communication]

299 Perestroika and media in deconstructivist perspective, part II. Helena Gourko. *J. Soc. Biol. Struct.* **14:4** 1991 pp. 367 – 380

300 Pluralism, politics, and the marketplace — the regulation of German broadcasting. Vincent Porter; Suzanne Hasselbach *[Ed.]*. London: Routledge, 1991: 248 p. *ISBN: 0415053943; LofC: 91014012. Includes bibliographical references and index.* [Communication and society.]

301 The politics and coverage of terrorism — from media images to public consciousness. James H. Wittebols. *Commun. Theory* **1:3** 8:1991 pp. 253 – 266

302 Politische Kommunikation im Umbruch. Zur Rolle der Zeitungen im ersten freien Kommunalwahlkampf in Leipzig *[In German]*; Political communication in transition. On the role of newspapers during the first free local elections in Leipzig *[Summary]*; Communication politique en transition. Sur le rôle des journaux lors des premières élections communales libres à Leipzig *[French summary]*; Comunicación política en cambio. Sobre el papel de los periódicos durante las primeras elecciones comunales libres en Leipzig *[Spanish summary]*. Brigitta Lutz; Helmut Scherer; Winfried Schulz; Anita Kecke; Helga Wagner. *Publizistik* **36:4** 10-12:1991 pp. 428 – 445

303 Popular fiction as journalism. Elizaveta Pulkhritudova. *J. Comm.* **41:2** Spring:1991 pp. 92 – 101

304 The portable radio in American life. Michael B. Schiffer. Tucson: University of Arizona Press, c1991: xvii, 259 p. (ill) *ISBN: 0816512590; LofC: 91011749. Includes bibliographical references (p. [233]-239) and indexes.* [Culture and technology.]

305 Power change, co-optation, accommodation — Xinhua and the press in transitional Hong Kong. Joseph Man Chan; Chin-Chuan Lee. *China Quart.* **:126** 6:1991 pp. 290 – 312

306 Pray TV — televangelism in America. Steve Bruce. London: Routledge, 1990: 272 p. *ISBN: 0415030978. Includes bibliography and index.*

307 Press and popular culture. James Curran; Colin Sparks. *Media Cult. Soc.* **13:2** 4:1991 pp. 215 – 238

308 Press participation as a civil liberty — the model of academic freedom. Beverly James. *J. Comm.* **41:1** Winter:1991 pp. 31 – 52

309 La presse en France — de 1945 à nos jours *[In French]*; [The press in France — from 1945 to present day]. Jean-Marie Charon. Paris: Seuil, 1991: 423 p. *ISBN: 2020128705.*

310 Racism and the press. Teun A. van Dijk. London: Routledge, 1991: 276 p. *ISBN: 0415047331; LofC: gb 90029597. Includes bibliography.*

311 Radio drama with critical reference to three broadcasts by Radio Sesotho; *[Afrikaans summary]*. Rosemary H. Moeketsi. *S.Afr. J. Afr. Lang.* **11:1** 2:1991 pp. 25 – 35

312 Redefining glasnost in the Soviet media — the recontextualization of Chernobyl. Marilyn J. Young; Michael K. Launer. *J. Comm.* **41:2** Spring:1991 pp. 102 – 124

313 Reporting the Rushdie affair — a case study in the orchestration of public opinion. Simon Cottle. *Race Class* **32:4** 4-6:1991 pp. 45 – 64

314 Die Rolle des Fernsehens bei der revolutionären Wende in der DDR *[In German]*; The role of television in the revolutionary change of the GDR *[Summary]*; Le rôle de la télévision dans le changement révolutionnaire en RDA *[French summary]*; El papel de la televisión en el cambio revolucionario de la RDA *[Spanish summary]*. Peter Ludes. *Publizistik* **36:2** 4-6:1991 pp. 201 – 216

315 "Sad is too mild a word" — press coverage of the Exxon Valdez oil spill. Patrick Daley; Dan O'Neill. *J. Comm.* **41:4** Autumn:1991 pp. 42 – 57

316 The seamless web — media and power in the post-modern global village. J.R. McLeod. *J. Pop. Cult.* **25:2** Fall:1991 pp. 69 – 76

317 The shadow world — life between the news media and reality. William James Willis. New York: Praeger, 1991: 260 p. *ISBN: 0275934241; LofC: 90040802. Includes bibliographical references (p. [251]-253) and index.*

318 Singapore's joust with journalism. Michael Antolik. *Asian Prof.* **19:6** 12:1991 pp. 529 – 539

319 Struktur eines publizistischen Konflikts. Die Berichterstattung über das „Soldatenurteil" in der überregionalen Tagespresse der Bundesrepublik Deutschland *[In German]*; The structure of a mediated conflict. A content analysis of the coverage of the "soldier verdict" in West German prestige newspapers *[Summary]*. Joachim Friedrich Staab; Guido Augustin *[Comp.]*; Christof Ress *[Comp.]*; Hendrik Schmidt *[Comp.]*; Claudia Schunicht *[Comp.]*; Regina Vollmeyer *[Comp.]*. *Kölner Z. Soz. Soz. psy.* **43:1** 1991 pp. 70 – 85

320 *[In Japanese]*; [A study on media theory in Luhmann and Parsons]. Naoko Egawa. *Bulletin of Graduate Studies, Chuo University* No.(20) - 1991. pp. 151 – 160

D.7: Language, communication and media *[Langage, communication et moyens de communication]* — **Media** *[Moyens de communication]*

321 De Superman a superbarrios — comunicación masiva y cultura popular en los procesos sociales de América Latina — un libro de lectura sobre el Encuentro Latinoamericano de Cultura y Comunicación Popular, Panama, 1989 *[In Spanish]*; [From superman to superslum — mass communication and popular culture in Latin American society]. Hans Roeder *[Ed.]*. Santiago: Consejos de Educación de Adultos de América Latina con el apoyo del Centro de Estudios y Acción Social Panameño, 1990: 215 p.

322 Television and the cultivation of political attitudes in Argentina. Michael Morgan; James Shanahan. *J. Comm.* **41:1** Winter:1991 pp. 88 – 103

323 Television and the public interest — vulnerable values in Western European broadcasting. Jay G. Blumler *[Ed.]*. London: Sage Publications, 1991: 242 p. *ISBN: 0803986491; LofC: gb 91086006.*

324 "That misery of stringer's clichés" — sports writing. David Rowe. *Cult. St.* **5:1** 1:1991 pp. 77 – 90

325 To control our image — photojournalists and new technology. Karin E. Becker. *Media Cult. Soc.* **13:3** 7:1991 pp. 381 – 398

326 Understanding media — new behavioural science approaches. George Comstock *[Ed.]*; Stuart Fischoff *[Ed.]*; Robert McIlwraith *[Contrib.]*; Robin Smith Jacobvitz *[Contrib.]*; Robert Kubey *[Contrib.]*; Alison Alexander *[Contrib.]*; Michael Morgan *[Contrib.]*; James Shanahan *[Contrib.]*; Valerie P. Hans *[Contrib.]*; Juliet L. Dee *[Contrib.]* *and others*. Collection of 7 articles. **Am. Behav. Sc.** , *35:2*, 11-12:1991 pp. 101 – 202

327 Women watching television — gender, class, and generation in the American television experience. Andrea Lee Press. Philadelphia: University of Pennsylvania Press, c1991: x, 238 p. *ISBN: 081221286x; LofC: 90021274. Includes bibliographical references (p. [213]-232) and index.*

328 Журналистика и политика *[In Russian]*; [Journalism and politics]. Ia. N. Zasurskogo *[Ed.]*; E.A. Blaznhov; M.V. Shkondin. Moscow: Moscow University Publishers, 1987: 176 p.

329 Журнолистика и пропаганда *[In Russian]*; [Journalism and propaganda]. M.I. Skulenko. Kiev: Vishcha shk. Kiev University publishers, 1987: 160 p. pp.157-159 Bibliogr.

330 Zur Kritik der Wirtschaftsberichterstattung. Ursachen und Konsequenzen *[In German]*; A criticism of economic news coverage — causes and consequences *[Summary]*; Sur la critique de l'information économique — raisons et conséquences *[French summary]*; Una crítica del reportaje económico. Causas y consecuencias *[Spanish summary]*. Jürgen Heinrich. *Publizistik* **36:2** 4-6:1991 pp. 217 – 226

Multilingualism and language policy *[Multilinguisme et politique linguistique]*

331 The biculture in bilingual. M. Agar. *Lang. Soc.* **20:2** 6:1991 pp. 167 – 182

332 Le clivage linguistique au Canada *[In French]*; [The linguistic division in Canada] *[Summary]*. André Blais. *Rech. Soc.graph* **XXXII:1** 1-4:1991 pp. 43 – 54

333 Drunken speech and the construction of meaning — bilingual competence in the southern Peruvian Andes. P.M. Harvey. *Lang. Soc.* **20:1** 3:1991 pp. 1 – 36

334 Federalism and the development of language policy — preliminary investigations; Federalismo y el desarrollo de una política de idioma extranjero — investigaciones preliminares *[Spanish summary]*; Federaciismo kaj la evoluigo de lingvopolitiko — provizoraj esploroj *[Esperanto summary]*. Jeanne Denise Cloonan; James Michael Strine. *Lang. Prob. Lang. Plan.* **15:3** Fall:1991 pp. 268 – 281

335 Internationalisation and reform in foreign language education — the Japan Exchange and Teaching (JET) programme. Antony Cominos. *Asian Stud. R.* **15:1** 7:1991 pp. 114 – 124

336 Language and culture in Australian public policy — some critical reflections. Laksiri Jayasuriya. *Int. Migr. Rev.* **XXIV:1** Spring:1990 pp. 124 – 148

337 Language and the nation — the language question in sub-Saharan Africa. Ayo Bamgbose. Edinburgh: Edinburgh University Press, 1991: 192 p. *ISBN: 0748603069.*

338 Language planning. David F. Marshall *[Ed.]*; Joshua A. Fishman *[Ed.]*. Amsterdam: J. Benjamins Pub. Co, 1991: 360 p. (ill) *ISBN: 9027220824; LofC: 91000698. Includes bibliographical references (p. [311]-341) and index.* [Focusschrift in honor of Joshua A. Fishman on the occasion of his 65th birthday. : Vol. 3]

339 Language planning and national development — the Uzbek experience. William Fierman.

D.7: Language, communication and media *[Langage, communication et moyens de communication]* — **Multilingualism and language policy** *[Multilinguisme et politique linguistique]*
Berlin: Mouton de Gruyter, 1991: xiii, 358 p. *ISBN: 3110124548; LofC: 91019848. Includes bibliographical references (p. [313]-345) and index.* [Contributions to the sociology of language. : No. 60]

340 Language policy and language education in North Korea. Youngsoon Park. *Korea J.* **31:1** Spring:1991 pp. 28 – 40

341 Linguistic minorities, society, and territory. Colin H. Williams *[Ed.]*. Clevedon, Avon, England: Multilingual Matters, c1991: vi, 330 p. (ill., maps) *ISBN: 1853591327; LofC: 91016627. Contains rev. papers from a seminar held in May 1987 at the Dept. of Geography and Recreation Studies, North Staffordshire Polytechnic; Includes bibliographical references and index.* [Multilingual matters. : No. 78]

342 Linguistic policy in the Soviet Union. Mart Rannut. *Multilingua* **10:3** 1991 pp. 241 – 250

343 Parental attitudes to Gaelic-medium education in the Western Isles of Scotland. A. Roberts. *J. Multiling.* **12:4** 1991 pp. 253 – 270

344 Parental attitudes towards the Welsh language. J. Lyon; N Ellis. *J. Multiling.* **12:4** 1991 pp. 239 – 252

345 Planning language, planning inequality — language policy in the community. James W. Tollefson. London: Longman, 1991: xi, 234 p. *ISBN: 0582074541; LofC: 90-6101. Bibliography — pp.213-228. Includes index.* [Language in social life series.]

346 Le plurilinguisme au quotidien — Ziguinchor au Sénégal *[In French]*; Daily multilingual practices — Ziguinchor in Senegal *[Summary]*. Caroline Juillard. *Afr. Cont.* **:158(2)** 1991 pp. 31 – 52

347 Reversing language shift — theoretical and empirical foundations of assistance to threatened languages. Joshua A. Fishman. Clevedon: Multilingual Matters, 1991: 431 p. *ISBN: 185359122x; LofC: 91016626. Includes bibliographical references and indexes.* [Multilingual matters.]

348 Second-language fluency and person perception in China and the United States. M.J. White; Yan Li. *J. Lang. Soc. Psychol.* **10:2** 1991 pp. 99 – 114

349 Sociolinguistic surveys as a source of evidence in the study of bilingualism — a critical assessment of survey work conducted among linguistic minorities in three British cities. Marilyn Martin-Jones. *Int. J. S. Lang.* **:90** 1991 pp. 37 – 56

350 L'utilisation des codes linguistiques portugais et français par les migrants portugais en France *[In French]*; Utilisation of Portuguese and French linguistic codes by Portuguese migrants in France *[Summary]*. J.D. Gomes Sanches. *Cah. Anthr. Bio. Hum.* **VVI:3-4** 1989 pp. 269 – 290

Television *[Télévision]*

351 The adventures of Amos 'n' Andy — a social history of an American phenomenon. Melvin Patrick Ely. New York: Free Press, c1991: xiii, 322 p. (ill) *ISBN: 0029095026; LofC: 91007837. Includes bibliographical references (p. 301-309) and index.*

352 *[In Japanese]*; [Cable television in America]. Hiroshi Inoue. **Bulletin of the Faculty of Sociology, Kansas University** No.22(2) - 1991. pp. 23 – 234

353 Children's views about television. Barrie Gunter; Jill McAleer; Brian Clifford. Aldershot: Avebury, 1991: 192 p. *ISBN: 1856280691.*

354 China turned on — television, reform, and resistance. James Lull. London: Routledge, 1991: 230 p. *ISBN: 0415052157; LofC: 91002439. Includes bibliographical references and index.*

355 The Chinese television system and television. Xiaoping Li. *China Quart.* **:126** 6:1991 pp. 340 – 355

356 The chosen few — Nightline and the politics of public affairs television. William Hoynes; David Croteau. *Crit. Sociol.* **18:1** Spring:1991 pp. 19 – 36

357 Class, genre, and the regionalization of television programming in the Dominican Republic. Joseph D. Straubhaar; Gloria M. Viscasillas. *J. Comm.* **41:1** Winter:1991 pp. 53 – 69

358 Distant neighbours — notes on some Australian soap operas. Ian Craven. *Aust. Stud.* **3** 1989 pp. 1 – 35

359 Drinking on television — a content analysis of recent alcohol portrayal; L'alcool à la télévision — une analyse de contenu d'une représentation récente de l'alcool *[French summary]*; El consumo de alcohol en la televisión — un analisis del contenido de la imagen actual del alcohol *[Spanish summary]*. Laura L. Pendleton; Christopher Smith; John L. Roberts. *Br. J. Addict.* **86:6** 6:1991 pp. 769 – 774

D.7: Language, communication and media *[Langage, communication et moyens de communication]* — Television *[Télévision]*

360 Ethnicity and Soviet television news. Ellen Mickiewicz; Dawn Plumb Jamison. *J. Comm.* **41**:2 Spring:1991 pp. 150 – 161

361 The home ecology of children's television viewing — parental mediation and the new video environment. David J. Atkin; Bradley S. Greenberg; Thomas F. Baldwin. *J. Comm.* **41**:3 Summer:1991 pp. 40 – 52

362 The ideological octopus — an exploration of television and its audience. Justin Lewis. New York: Routledge, 1991: x, 218 p. *ISBN: 0415902878; LofC: 91029957. Includes bibliographical references (p. 207-215) and index.* [Studies in culture and communication.]

363 Images of disability on television. Guy Cumberbatch *[Ed.]*; Ralph M. Negrine *[Ed.]*. London: Routledge, 1991: 180 p. *ISBN: 0415063450; LofC: 91011154. Includes bibliographical references (p.) and index.*

364 The Intifada as a meta-televisual dialogue. Yosefa Loshitzky. *Media Cult. Soc.* **13**:4 10:1991 pp. 557 – 572

365 Курьеры муз: Диалектика продуктив. и репродуктив. в творчестве радио и телевидения *[In Russian]*; [Messengers of muses — dialectics of productivity and reproductivity in the creative power of radio and television]. Y.A. Bogomolov. Moscow: Iskusstvo, 1986: 191 p. [ВНИИ исусствознания М-ва культуры СССР.]

366 Literacy in the television age — the myth of the TV effect. Susan B. Neuman. Norwood, N.J: Ablex, c1991: xiv, 230 p. (ill) *ISBN: 0893914851; LofC: 90026123. Includes bibliographical references (p. 203-217) and indexes.* [Communication and information science.]

367 Mapping hegemony — television news coverage of industrial conflict. Robert Goldman; Arvind Rajagopal. Norwood: Albex, 1991: 258 p. *ISBN: 0893916978.* [Communication and information science.]

368 The medium must not deconstruct — a postmodern ethnography of USA Today television show. Barry Glassner. *Media Cult. Soc.* **13**:1 1:1991 pp. 53 – 70

369 Negative and positive television messages — effects of message type and context on attention and memory. Byron R. Reeves; John Newhagen; Edward Maibach; Michael Basil; Kathleen Kurz. *Am. Behav. Sc.* **34**:6 7-8:1991 pp. 679 – 694

370 Negative versus positive television advertising in U.S. presidential campaigns, 1960-1988. Lynda Lee Kaid; Anne Johnston. *J. Comm.* **41**:3 Summer:1991 pp. 53 – 64

371 Old media on new media — national popular press reaction to mechanical television. James R. Walker. *J. Pop. Cult.* **25**:1 Summer:1991 pp. 21 – 30

372 Overcoming language barriers in television — dubbing and subtitling for the European audience. Georg-Michael Luyken; et al. Manchester: European Institute for the Media, 1991: - *ISBN: 0948195193.* [Media monograph. : No. 13]

373 The people's voice — local radio and television in Europe. Nick Jankowski *[Ed.]*; Ole Prehn *[Ed.]*; James Stappers *[Ed.]*. London: John Libbey, 1991: 274 p. *ISBN: 0861963229.* [Acamedia research monograph. : No. 6]

374 Pluralism, politics, and the marketplace — the regulation of German broadcasting. Vincent Porter; Suzanne Hasselbach *[Ed.]*. London: Routledge, 1991: 248 p. *ISBN: 0415053943; LofC: 91014012. Includes bibliographical references and index.* [Communication and society.]

375 Pray TV — televangelism in America. Steve Bruce. London: Routledge, 1990: 272 p. *ISBN: 0415030978. Includes bibliography and index.*

376 Raymond Williams and the cultural analysis of television. Stuart Laing. *Media Cult. Soc.* **13**:2 4:1991 pp. 153 – 170

377 Die Rolle des Fernsehens bei der revolutionären Wende in der DDR *[In German]*; The role of television in the revolutionary change of the GDR *[Summary]*; Le rôle de la télévision dans le changement révolutionnaire en RDA *[French summary]*; El papel de la televisión en el cambio revolucionario de la RDA *[Spanish summary]*. Peter Ludes. *Publizistik* **36**:2 4-6:1991 pp. 201 – 216

378 Soviet television and the structure of broadcasting authority. Sergei Aleksandrovich Muratov. *J. Comm.* **41**:2 Spring:1991 pp. 172 – 184

379 The struggle for control over Soviet television. Elena Androunas. *J. Comm.* **41**:2 Spring:1991 pp. 185 – 200

380 Subscription television in the Third World — the Moroccan experience. Mark Poindexter. *J. Comm.* **41**:3 Summer:1991 pp. 26 – 39

381 Television and the American child. George Comstock; Hae-Jung Paik *[Ed.]*. San Diego: Academic Press, c1991: xiv, 386 p. (ill) *ISBN: 0121835758; LofC: 90027707. Includes bibliographical references (p. 313-355) and indexes.*

D.7: Language, communication and media *[Langage, communication et moyens de communication]* — *Television [Télévision]*

382 Television and the cultivation of political attitudes in Argentina. Michael Morgan; James Shanahan. *J. Comm.* **41:1** Winter:1991 pp. 88 – 103
383 Television and the public interest — vulnerable values in Western European broadcasting. Jay G. Blumler *[Ed.].* London: Sage Publications, 1991: 242 p. *ISBN: 0803986491; LofC: gb 91086006.*
384 Television as spectacle and myth. Anri Vartanov. *J. Comm.* **41:2** Spring:1991 pp. 162 – 171
385 Television in Europe. Eli M. Noam. New York: Oxford University Press, 1991: xii, 395 p. *ISBN: 0195069420; LofC: 90023042. Includes bibliographical references (p. 353-378) and index.* [Communication and society.]
386 Television viewing habits of Barbadian adolescents — a preliminary study; Les habitudes de regarder la télévision des adolescents barbadiens — une étude preliminaire *[French summary]*; Estudio preliminar de las costumbres de los televidentes jóvenes barbadienses *[Spanish summary].* Monica A. Payne. *Soc. Econ. S.* **40:3** 9:1991 pp. 91 – 113
387 Télévision — deuxième dynastie *[In French]*; [Television — the second dynasty]. Gaëtan Tremblay; Jean-Guy Lacroix *[Ed.].* Sillery: Quebec University Press, 1991: 163 p. *ISBN: 2760506444.*
388 Television's impact on values and local life in Brazil. Conrad P. Kottak. *J. Comm.* **41:1** Winter:1991 pp. 70 – 87
389 Transnationalization of television in Western Europe. Preben Sepstrup. London: John Libbey, 1991: 132 p. *ISBN: 0961962801.* [Acamedia research monograph. : No. 5]
390 Using entertainment television to educate — a case study. Lynn Hinds. *J. Pop. Cult.* **25:2** Fall:1991 pp. 117 – 126
391 The voices of Swiss television commercials. David Lee. *Multilingua* **10:3** 1991 pp. 295 – 324
392 What are words worth? Interpreting children's talk about television. David Buckingham. *Cult. St.* **5:2** 5:1991 pp. 228 – 245
393 When art becomes news — portrayals of art and artists on network television news. John Ryan; Deborah A. Sim. *Soc. Forc.* **68:3** 3:1990 pp. 869 – 889
394 Woman as sign in television news. Lana F. Rakow; Kimberlie Kranich. *J. Comm.* **41:1** Winter:1991 pp. 8 – 23
395 Women watching television — gender, class, and generation in the American television experience. Andrea Lee Press. Philadelphia: University of Pennsylvania Press, c1991: x, 238 p. *ISBN: 081221286x; LofC: 90021274. Includes bibliographical references (p. [213]-232) and index.*

D.8: Art — *Art*

1 Adorno and jazz — reflections on a failed encounter. Ulrich Schönherr. *Telos* **:87** Spring:1991 pp. 85 – 96
2 Africa's culture producers. Wole Soyinka. *Society* **28:2** 1-2:1991 pp. 32 – 40
3 Art at risk in the hands of the museum — from the museum to the private collection?; L'art au risque du musée — du musée à la collection? *[French summary].* Daniel Vander Gucht. *Int. Sociol.* **6:3** 9:1991 pp. 361 – 372
4 The art of growth — ties between development organizations and the performing arts. J. Allen Whitt; John C. Lammers. *Urban Aff. Q.* **26:3** 3:1991 pp. 376 – 393
5 Die ästhetische Dimension des Parsonsschen Voluntarismus *[In German]*; The aesthetic dimension of Parsons' voluntarism *[Summary].* Ronald Kurt. *Z. Soziol.* **20:1** 2:1991 pp. 64 – 76
6 The averted gaze in Iranian postrevolutionary cinema. Hamid Naficy. *Publ. Cult.* **3:2** Spring:1991 pp. 29 – 40
7 The body as art — still photographs of Marilyn Monroe. Kathryn N. Benzel. *J. Pop. Cult.* **25:2** Fall:1991 pp. 1 – 30
8 Contre-révolution ou modernité culturelles? *[In French]*; Cultural counter-revolution or modernity? *[Summary].* Jacques Chambaz. *Pensée* **:283** 9-10:1991 pp. 5 – 20
9 Critics and publics — cultural mediation in highbrow and popular performing arts. Wesley Shrum. *A.J.S.* **97:2** 9:1991 pp. 347 – 375
10 Curricula, credits and certificates — formalizing expressive skill training in performing arts. Kees P. Epskamp. *J. Dev. Soc.* **VII:2** 7-9:1991 pp. 238 – 255
11 Ecrivains, critiques et «tueurs» *[In French]*; Writers, critics and killers *[Summary].* Claude Prévost; Jean-Claude Lebrun. *Pensée* **:283** 9-10:1991 pp. 21 – 32

D.8: Art [Art]

12 European cinemas, European societies, 1939-1990. Pierre Sorlin. New York: Routledge, 1991: viii, 247 p. (ill) *ISBN: 0415047870; LofC: 90035003. Includes bibliographical references (p. 231-240) and index.* [Studies in film, television, and the media.]

13 Experimentation and innovation — possible directions. Mohan Maharishi. *San. Nat.* :**99** 1-3:1991 pp. 29 – 34

14 Francis Bacon, William Golding ou l'art défiguré *[In French]*; [Francis Bacon, William Golding or disfigured art]. François Regard. *Esprit* :**174** 9:1991 pp. 91 – 99

15 Frank Lloyd Wright and the passage to Fordism. Philip Gunn. *Cap. Class* :**44** Summer:1991 pp. 73 – 92

16 'Gimme shelter' — observations on cultural protectionism and the recording industry in Canada. Robert Wright. *Cult. St.* **5:3** 10:1991 pp. 306 – 316

17 Heritage without history — the open-air museums of Austria in comparative perspective; *[French summary]*. Adolf W. Ehrentraut. *Can. R. Soc. A.* **28:1** 2:1991 pp. 46 – 66

18 Icônes et iconoclasme en Afrique *[In French]*; Icons and iconoclasm in Africa *[Summary]*. Jack Goody. *Annales* **46:6** 11-12:1991 pp. 1235 – 1252

19 The Igbo novel and the literary communication of Igbo culture. Iheanyichukwu Duruoha. *Afr. St. Mono.* **12:4** 1991 pp. 185 – 200

20 Images of postmodern society — social theory and contemporary cinema. Norman K. Denzin. London: Sage Publications, 1991: 179 p. *ISBN: 0803985150.*

21 The impossibility of music — Adorno, popular and other music. Robert Hullot-Kentor. *Telos* :**87** Spring:1991 pp. 97 – 117

22 Innovation and experimentation in theatre. Utpal Dutt. *San. Nat.* :**99** 1-3:1991 pp. 17 – 23

23 Искусство и социокультуреый кониекст: Сб.науч.тр *[In Russian]*; [Art and socio-cultural context. Collection of scientific treatise]. Ia B. Ioskebich *[Ed.]*. Leningrad: , 1986: 161 p. *Bibliogr..*

24 Искусство в системе культуры. Сборник *[In Russian]*; [Art in the system of culture. Collected volume]. M.S. Kagan *[Ed.]*. Leningrad: Nauka, 1987: 267 p. *Bibliogr..*

25 It's sooner than you think, or where are we in the history of rock music? Terry Bloomfield. *New Left R.* :**190** 11/12:1991 pp. 59 – 81

26 Художественная культура: проблемы изучения и управления *[In Russian]*; [Artistic culture — problems of study and management]. A.Ia. Zis' *[Ed.]*; Iu.U. Fokht-Babushkin. Moscow: Nauka, 1986: 237 p.

27 Knocking at the doors of public culture — India's parallel cinema. Pradip Krishen. *Publ. Cult.* **4:1** Fall:1991 pp. 25 – 42

28 Kutiyattam and Noh — commonalities and divergences. Sudha Gopalakrishnan. *San. Nat.* :**99** 1-3:1991 pp. 35 – 42

29 Latin music in the United States — Salsa and the mass media. Peter Manuel. *J. Comm.* **41:1** Winter:1991 pp. 104 – 115

30 Literary myths and social structure. Helmut K. Anheier; Jürgen Gerhards. *Soc. Forc.* **69:3** 3:1991 pp. 811 – 830

31 Local popular music on the national and international markets. Paul Rutten. *Cult. St.* **5:3** 10:1991 pp. 294 – 305

32 Mass-produced art — towards a popular aesthetics. Martin S. Lindauer. *J. Pop. Cult.* **25:2** Fall:1991 pp. 57 – 68

33 Мир художественной культуры *[In Russian]*; [The world of artistic culture]. V.V. Zhuravlev. Moscow: Mysl', 1987: 239 p.

34 The monument — art, vulgarity and responsibility in Iraq. Samir al-Khalil. London: Deutsch, 1991: 153 p. (ill) *ISBN: 0233986561.*

35 Les musées de l'éducation nationale — mission d'étude et de réflexion *[In French]*; [The museums of national education — study and reflection]. Françoise Héritier-Augé; et al. Paris: La Documentation française, 1991: 176 p. (ill) *ISBN: 2110026189. Bibliography — p.169-170.* [Collection des rapports officiels.]

36 Music at the margins — popular music and global cultural diversity. Deanna Campbell Robinson *[Ed.]*; et al. Newbury Park, CA: Sage Publications, 1991: xiv, 312 p. *ISBN: 0803931921; LofC: 90026179 /MN. Includes bibliographical references and index.* [Communication and human values.]

37 Music videos, performance and resistance — feminist rappers. Robin Roberts. *J. Pop. Cult.* **25:2** Fall:1991 pp. 141 – 152

38 Musiques — le sémiologue est dans l'escalier *[In French]*; The semiologist is in the stairs *[Summary]*. Michel Thion. *Pensée* :**283** 9-10:1991 pp. 43 – 56

D.8: Art [Art]

39 The neglect of industrial design. D.O. Ughanwa. *R&D Manag.* **21:3** 7:1991 pp. 187 – 206
40 Notes from the underground — the emergence of rock music. Irina Orlova. *J. Comm.* **41:2** Spring:1991 pp. 66 – 71
41 The open-air market for art — the commercial expression of creativity. Kseniia Bogemskaya. *J. Comm.* **41:2** Spring:1991 pp. 19 – 30
42 Participation in the arts by black and white Americans. Paul Dimaggio; Francie Ostrower. *Soc. Forc.* **68:3** 3:1990 pp. 753 – 778
43 A phantasmagoria of the female body — the work of Cindy Sherman. Laura Mulvey. *Rev. F. Braudel. Ctr.* **:188** 7/8:1991 pp. 136 – 150
44 Politics and painting — murals and conflict in Northern Ireland. Bill Rolston. Rutherford: Fairleigh Dickinson University Press, 1991: 140 p. (ill. (some col.)) *ISBN: 0838633862; LofC: 89045981. Includes bibliographical references (p. 128-131) and indexes.*
45 Politics as art — Italian futurism and fascism. Anne Bowler. *Theory Soc.* **20/6** 12:1991 pp. 763 – 794
46 Popular culture and populist culture. Russell A. Berman. *Telos* **:87** Spring:1991 pp. 59 – 70
47 Popular music and postmodern theory. Andrew Goodwin. *Cult. St.* **5:2** 5:1991 pp. 174 – 190
48 Popular music and urban regeneration — the music industries of Merseyside. Sara Cohen. *Cult. St.* **5:3** 10:1991 pp. 332 – 346
49 Popular music from Adorno to Zappa. Russell A. Berman; Robert Amico. d'. *Telos* **:87** Spring:1991 pp. 71 – 78
50 Possession and commoditization in Fatal Attraction, Blue Velvet and Nine and 1/2 Weeks. Elizabeth C. Hirschman. *Semiotica* **86:1-2** 1991 pp. 1 – 42
51 Potboilers — methods, concepts and case studies in popular fiction. Jerry Palmer. London: Routledge, 1991: 219 p. *ISBN: 0415009774; LofC: 91014013. Includes bibliographical references.* [Communication and society.]
52 Pour une histoire de la lecture *[In French]*; For a history of reading *[Summary]*. Pierre Boutan. *Pensée* **:281** 5-6:1991 pp. 21 – 32
53 The presumption of influence — recent responses to popular music subcultures. Jill Leslie Rosenbaum; Lorraine Prinsky. *Crime Delin.* **37:4** 10:1991 pp. 528 – 535
54 Les publics de la danse *[In French]*; [Dance]. Jean-Michel Guy. Paris: La Documentation française, c1991: 479 p. (ill) *ISBN: 2110024666. Includes bibliographical references (p. 471-477).*
55 Reflections of change — sociopolitical commentary and criticism in Malaysian popular music since 1950. Craig A. Lockard. *Crossroads* **6:1** 1991 pp. 1 – 106
56 Reimaging America — the arts of social change. Mark O'Brien; Craig B. Little *[Ed.]*. Santa Cruz: New Society Publishers, 1990: 364 p. *ISBN: 0865711682.*
57 Representing culture — the production of discourse(s) for Aboriginal acrylic paintings. Fred Myers. *Cult. Anthro.* **6:1** 2:1991 pp. 26 – 62
58 The revisionist cinema of the 1980s — images of America. Albert Paolini. *Mel. J. Pol.* **20** 1991 pp. 122 – 147
59 The revitalization of the Soviet film industry. Yuri Bogomolov. *J. Comm.* **41:2** Spring:1991 pp. 39 – 45
60 Rock culture in Liverpool — popular music in the making. Sara Cohe. Oxford: Clarendon Press, 1991: 246 p. (ill) *ISBN: 0198161786; LofC: 90042402 /MN. Discography — p.[238]; Includes bibliographical references (p.[239]-242) and index.*
61 Rocking the state — youth and rock music culture in Hungary, 1976-1990. László Kűrti. *E.Eur. Pol. Soc.* **5:3** Fall:1991 pp. 483 – 513
62 Role as resource in the Hollywood film industry. Wayne E. Baker; Robert R. Faulkner. *A.J.S.* **97:2** 9:1991 pp. 279 – 309
63 Rythme et révolution *[In French]*; [Rythmn and revolution] *[Summary]*. Pierre Lantz. *Cah. Int. Soc.* **XCI:** 7-12:1991 pp. 241 – 258
64 La satira politica in Italia *[In Italian]*; [Political satire in Italy]. Adolfo Chiesa; Tullio Pericoli. Bari-Roma: Laterza, 1990: 330p. *ISBN: 8842036668.* [Grandi opere.]
65 Societal values and their effect on the built environment in Saudi Arabia — a recent account. Tarik M. Al-Soliman. *J. Arch. Plan. Res.* **8:3** Autumn:1991 pp. 235 – 254
66 Sorting gender out in a children's museum. Zella Luria; Eleanor W. Herzog. *Gender Soc.* **5:2** 6:1991 pp. 224 – 232
67 Социальная роль книги: Сб.науч.тр *[In Russian]*; [The social role of the book — collection of scientific treatises]. N.F. Kodak *[Ed.]*. Kiev: Nauka Dumka, 1987: 159 p. [AN USSR. Центр.науч.б-ка.]

D.8: Art *[Art]*

68 Sowjetische Science-Fiction-Literatur als soziologisches Erkenntnismittel. Literarische Plattform und öffentliches Medium der wissenschaftlich-technischen Intelligenz *[In German]*; [Soviet science fiction as an instrument of sociological enquiry. Literary platform and public organ of the academic and technical intelligensia]. Ingrid Oswald. *Osteuropa* **41:4** 4:1991 pp. 393 – 405

69 Statsstödda samhällskritiker — författarautonomi och statsstyrning i Sverige *[In Swedish]*; [State subsidized critics of society — authors' autonomy and state control in Sweden]. Li Bennich-Björkman. [Stockholm]: Tidens förlag, c1991: 361 p. *ISBN: 9155037364; LofC: 91160839. swe: eng; Extra t.p. with thesis statement inserted; Summary in English; Includes bibliographical references (p. 333-353) and index.*

70 Studies in the morphology of the English building stock; *[French summary]*. P. Steadman; F. Brown; P. Rickaby. *Envir. Plan. B.* **18:1** 1:1991 pp. 85 – 98

71 Sur la fonction contradictoire de la culture *[In French]*; About the contradictory functions of culture *[Summary]*. David Wizenberg. *Pensée* **:283** 9-10:1991 pp. 33 – 42

72 Theater on the market. Marina L. Kniazeva. *J. Comm.* **41:2** Spring:1991 pp. 31 – 38

73 Традиционные виды искусства в эпоху СМК *[In Russian]*; [Traditional views of art in the age of "SMK"]. Y.A. Bogomolov *[Ed.]*. Moscow: , 1987: 209 p. *Bibliogr. at the end of article.*

74 Transforming features — double vision and the female reader. Gill Frith. *New Form.* **:15** Winter:1991 pp. 67 – 82

75 Transforming heroes — Hollywood and the demonization of women. Elizabeth G. Traube. *Publ. Cult.* **3:2** Spring:1991 pp. 1 – 28

76 Twentieth-century America — the intellectual and cultural context. Douglas Tallack. London: Longman, 1991: 432 p. *ISBN: 0582494540; LofC: 90041577. Includes bibliographical references and index.* [Longman literature in English series.]

77 Vietnamese cinema — first views. John Charlot. *J. SE. As. Stud.* **22:1** 3:1991 p. 33

78 War photography — realism in the press. John Taylor. London: Routledge, 1991: 199 p. (ill) *ISBN: 0415010640. Bibliography — p.107-139. Includes index.*

79 When art becomes news — portrayals of art and artists on network television news. John Ryan; Deborah A. Sim. *Soc. Forc.* **68:3** 3:1990 pp. 869 – 889

D.9: Education — *Éducation*

Sub-divisions: Education policy *[Politique de l'éducation]*; Education systems *[Systèmes d'enseignement]*; Educational sociology *[Sociologie de l'éducation]*; Primary education *[Enseignement primaire]*; Secondary education *[Enseignement secondaire]*; Tertiary education *[Enseignement post-scolaire]*

1 Adult literacy in the Third World — a review of objectives and strategies. Agneta Lind; Anton Johnston. Stockholm: Swedish International Development Authority, 1990: 144 p. *ISBN: 915867114.*

2 Computers, networks and education. Alan C. Kay. *Sci. Am.* **265:3** 9:1991 pp. 100 – 107

3 Continuity and change in Balinese society — an example from modern schooling. I Gde Widja. *Ind. Cir.* **:54** 3:1991 pp. 39 – 44

4 Cultural domain separation — two-way street or blind alley? Stephen Harris and the neo-Whorfians on Aboriginal education. Patrick McConvell. *Aust. Abor. S.* **:1** 1991 pp. 13 – 24

5 El desarrollo local y la práctica de la educación de adultos *[In Spanish]*; Local development and practice of adults' education *[Summary]*. Jose Rivero H.. *Soc. Part.* **:54** 6:1991 pp. 71 – 88

6 Early innovators in adult education. Huey Long. London: Routledge, 1991: 161 p. *ISBN: 0415005574. Includes bibliography and index.* [Theory and practice of adult education in North America series.]

7 La educación ignaciana *[In Spanish]*; [Ignatian education].*CIAS Vol.36; No.362 - 5: 1987.* pp. 129 – 142

8 Educating for a change. Rick Arnold; et al. Toronto: Doris Marshall Institute for Education and Action and Between the Lines, 1991: 206 p. *ISBN: 0921284470.*

9 Education for economic survival — from Fordism to post-Fordisim? Phillip Brown *[Ed.]*; Hugh Lauder *[Ed.]*. London: Routledge, 1991: 279 p. *ISBN: 0415049016; LofC: 91011175. Includes bibliographical references and index.*

D.9: Education *[Éducation]*

10 Education in the developing world — conflict and crisis. Sarah Graham-Brown. Harlow: Longman, 1991: 332 p. (ill) *ISBN: 0582064317. Includes bibliography and index.*
11 The election of blacks to school boards in North Carolina. Theodore S. Arrington; Thomas Gill Watts. *West. Pol. Q.* **44:4** 12:1991 pp. 1099 – 1105
12 Electronic links for learning. John Carey *[Contrib.]*; Jason Ohler *[Contrib.]*; Richard D. Lambert *[Contrib.]*; Sally M. Johnstone *[Contrib.]*; Kurt D. Moses *[Contrib.]*; David Edgerton *[Contrib.]*; Willard E. Shaw *[Contrib.]*; Ralph Grubb *[Contrib.]*; Lionel V. Baldwin *[Contrib.]*; Inabeth Miller *[Contrib.] and others. Collection of 12 articles.* **Ann. Am. Poli.** , *514*, 3:1991 pp. 11 – 173
13 The empirical correlates of action and structure — the transition from school to work. Derek Layder; David Ashton; Johnny Sung. *Sociology* **25:3** 8:1991 pp. 447 – 464
14 Language choice for Latino students. Rosalie Pedalino Porter. *Publ. Inter.* **:105** Fall:1991 pp. 48 – 60
15 Languages in school and society — policy and pedagogy. Mary E. McGroarty *[Ed.]*; Christian Faltis *[Ed.]*. Berlin: de Gruyter, 1991: 570 p. *ISBN: 3110125765.* [Contributions to the sociology of language. : No. 58]
16 Literacy scenario in India during 1991 — a march towards development of underdevelopment? Sheel C. Nuna. *Soc. Act.* **41:4** 10-12:1991 pp. 454 – 463
17 Magistero ecclesiastico e sottosviluppo *[In Italian]*; [Ecclesiastical education and underdevelopment]. Pio Cerocchi. *Civitas* **XLVII:3** 5-6:1991 pp. 65 – 76
18 Материальные стимулы как фактор самореализации научного работника *[In Russian]*; (Material incentives as a factor of self-realization of scholars). L.E. Dushatskiy. *Sot. Issle.* **:5** 1991 pp. 8 – 17
19 *[In Arabic]*; [The morale of teachers of handicapped children] *[Summary].Dirasat Ser. A.* **18A:2** 1991 pp. 62 – 79
20 Music and multicultural education. F. Murphy. *J. Multiling.* **12:5** 1991 pp. 383 – 392
21 O diretor de escola no Brasil — significados *[In Portuguese]*; [The headteacher in Brazil] *[Summary]*. Flávia Obino Corrêa Werle. *Est. Leop.* **27:124** 9-10:1991 pp. 23 – 36
22 Образование в современном мире *[In Russian]*; (Education in the modern world); (L'enseignement dans le monde contemporain: *Title only in French)*; (Bildungswesen in der Welt von heute: *Title only in German)*; (La instrucción en el mundo contemporaneo: *Title only in Spanish)*. V. Kuptsov. *Svobod. Mysl'* **:16** 1991 pp. 70 – 81
23 Participation in adult learning. Sean Courtney. London: Routledge, 1991: 191 p. *ISBN: 0415024803; LofC: 91010116. Includes bibliographical references (p.) and index.* [Routledge series on theory and practice of adult education in North America.]
24 Political learning and awareness among student teachers — a Caribbean case-study; *[Spanish summary]*. Rudolph W. Grant. *R. Eur. Lat.am. Caribe* **:51** 12:1991 pp. 67 – 90
25 The politics of life in schools — power, conflict, and cooperation. Joseph Blase *[Ed.]*. Newbury Park, Calif: Sage, c1991: xiv, 271 p. *ISBN: 0803938926; LofC: 91013614. Includes bibliographical references and index.* [Sage focus editions. : No. 134]
26 The politics of the textbook. Michael W. Apple *[Ed.]*; Linda K. Christian-Smith *[Ed.]*. New York: Routledge, 1991: 290 p. *ISBN: 0415902223; LofC: 90038277. Includes bibliographical references and index.*
27 Pragmatism or crude utility? A critique of the education with production movement in contemporary Africa; *[French summary]*. Gatian F. Lungu. *Quest* **V:2** 12:1991 pp. 74 – 89
28 Problématique de l'usage des images et affiches comme support d'éducation des adultes en milieu africain *[In French]*; [The problems of using images and posters to support adult education in Africa]. Mpey-Nka Ngub'usim. *Za-Afr.* **31:257** 8-9:1991 pp. 367 – 386
29 Regional disparities in literacy in India, 1981. Prem Sagar. *Asian Prof.* **19:3** 6:1991 pp. 253 – 268
30 The relevance of Habermas' communicative turn — some reflections on education as communicative action. J. Masschelein. *St. Philos. Educ.* **11:2** 1991 pp. 95 – 111
31 Research on telecommunicated learning — past, present, and future. Sally M. Johnstone. *Ann. Am. Poli.* **514** 3:1991 pp. 49 – 57
32 *[In Japanese]*; [Ritual named "school education"]. Yuji Yamamoto. *J. Ed. Soc. No.(49) - 1991.* pp. 94 – 113
33 School work and real work — economic and industrial understanding in the curriculum. Ian Jamieson. *Curric. J.* **2:1** Spring:1991 pp. 55 – 68
34 Second chances — adults returning to education. James Pye. Oxford: Oxford University Press, 1991: 276 p. *ISBN: 0192129902; LofC: 91011366. Includes bibliographical references and index.*

D.9: Education *[Éducation]*
35 Sheepskin effects in the returns to education in a developing country. Tayyeb Shabbir. *Pak. Dev. R.* **30:1** Spring:1991 pp. 1 – 20
36 Struggling with their histories — economic decline and educational improvement in four rural southeastern school districts. Alan J. DeYoung. Norwood, NJ.: Ablex, 1991: x, 288 p. (ill) *ISBN: 0893918172; LofC: 91016201. Includes bibliographical references and index.* [Interpretive perspectives on education and policy.]
37 Textbooks and tribalism in California. David L. Kirp. *Publ. Inter.* **:104** Summer:1991 pp. 20 – 36
38 Trends in gender and family background effects on school attainment — the case of Hong Kong. Suet-ling Pong; David Post. *Br. J. Soc.* **42:2** 6:1991 pp. 249 – 271

Education policy *[Politique de l'éducation]*
39 Aid and education in the developing world — the role of the donor agencies in educational analysis. Kenneth King. Harlow: Longman, 1991: 286 p. *ISBN: 0582052017.* [Education and development.]
40 Bildungsexpansion und betriebliche Informatisierungsprozesse — ein Drei-Länder-Vergleich *[In German]*; Educational expansion and industrial computerization — a comparison between three countries *[Summary]*. Martin Heidenreich. *Soz. Welt.* **42:1** :1991 pp. 46 – 67
41 Bilingual education. Ofelia García *[Ed.]*; Joshua A. Fishman *[Ed.]*. Amsterdam: J. Benjamins Pub. Co, 1991: viii, 348 p. (port) *ISBN: 1556191162; LofC: 91016166. Includes bibliographical references and index.* [Focusschrift in honor of Joshua A. Fishman on the occasion of his 65th birthday. : Vol. 1]
42 Chicano school failure and success — research and policy agendas for the 1990s. Richard R. Valencia *[Ed.]*. London: Falmer Press, 1991: 353 p. *ISBN: 1850008639.*
43 Connections — community service and school reform recommendations. Kate McPherson; Mary K. Nebgen. *Educ. Urban. Soc.* **23:3** 5:1991 pp. 326 – 334
44 Conservative agendas and progressive possibilities — understanding the wider politics of curriculum and teaching. Michael W. Apple. *Educ. Urban. Soc.* **23:3** 5:1991 pp. 279 – 291
45 Controlled choice — an alternative desegregation plan for minorities who feel betrayed. Charles V. Willie. *Educ. Urban. Soc.* **23:2** 2:1991 pp. 200 – 207
46 Curriculum issues for urban education. Francis P. Hunkins *[Contrib.]*; A. Harry Passow *[Contrib.]*; Kenneth A. Sirotnik *[Contrib.]*; Richard L. Andrews *[Contrib.]*; John Morefield *[Contrib.]*; Michael W. Apple *[Contrib.]*; Francis P. Hunkins *[Contrib.]*; Patricia A. Hammill *[Contrib.]*; Charles E. Bruckerhoff *[Contrib.]*; Thomas S. Popkewitz *[Contrib.]* and others. Collection of 10 articles. **Educ. Urban. Soc.** , *23:3*, 5:1991 pp. 235 – 341
47 Curriculum reform and the teacher. Andy Hargreaves *[Contrib.]*; Trish Stoddart *[Contrib.]*; John P. Neufeld *[Contrib.]*; Sandra Acker *[Contrib.]*; Gunnar Handal *[Contrib.]*; Freema Elbaz *[Contrib.]*; Liliana Pascual *[Contrib.]*; William Louden *[Contrib.]*. Collection of 8 articles. **Curric. J.** , *2:3*, Autumn:1991 pp. 249 – 374
48 Democracy and educational reforms in Argentina — possibilities and limitations. Liliana Pascual. *Curric. J.* **2:3** Autumn:1991 pp. 347 – 359
49 Deregulation and privatization of education — a flawed concept. Frank Brown; A. Reynaldo Contreras. *Educ. Urban. Soc.* **23:2** 2:1991 pp. 144 – 158
50 Development and reform of China's education. Dalin Tong. *Int. J. Soc. E.* **18:8-10** :1991 pp. 132 – 136
51 Education and social change — a study of tribal students. T. Lakshamaiah. *Man India* **71:4** 12:1991 pp. 587 – 599
52 Education for democratic citizenship — a challenge for multi-ethnic societies. Roberta S. Sigel *[Ed.]*; Marilyn B. Hoskin *[Ed.]*. Hillsdale, N.J: Lawrence Erlbaum Associates, 1991: vi, 226 p. (ill) *ISBN: 080580725x; LofC: 90049721. Papers originally presented at a conference sponsored by the Spencer Foundation of Chicago; Includes bibliographical references and indexes.*
53 Education in a future South Africa — policy issues for transformation. Thozamile Botha *[Ed.]*; Elaine Sara Unterhalter *[Ed.]*; Harold Wolpe *[Ed.]*. London: Heinenmann, 1991: 258 p. *ISBN: 0435916734.*
54 Education in South Africa — the present crisis and the problems of reconstruction. Alan Morris; Jonathan Hyslop. *Soc. Just.* **18:1-2** Spring-Summer:1991 pp. 259 – 289
55 Education, technological change and development — India, a case study. Priyatosh Maitra. *Ind. J. Soc. Sci.* **4:2** 4-6:1991 pp. 241 – 268

D.9: Education *[Éducation]* — Education policy *[Politique de l'éducation]*

56 Educational goals and political plans. Daniel Patrick Moynihan. *Publ. Inter.* **:102** Winter:1991 pp. 32 – 48

57 Гуманитаризация современного образования *[In Russian]*; (Humanization of modern education); (L'humanisation de l'enseignement moderne: *Title only in French*); (Geisteswissenschaftliche Durchdringung des modernen Bildungswesens: *Title only in German*); (La humanitarización de la enseñanza moderna: *Title only in Spanish*). V. Borzenkov; V. Kuptsov. *Kommunist* **:7(1377)** 1991 pp. 32 – 41

58 Improving urban schools in the age of "restructuring". Kenneth A. Sirotnik. *Educ. Urban. Soc.* **23:3** 5:1991 pp. 256 – 269

59 In the name of excellence — the struggle to reform the nation's schools, why it's failing, and what should be done. Thomas Toch. New York: Oxford University Press, 1991: viii, 325 p. *ISBN: 0195057619; LofC: 90041546. Includes bibliographical references (p. 277-312) and index.*

60 Increasing teacher effectiveness. Lorin W. Anderson. Paris: UNESCO International Institute for Educational Planning, 1991: 133 p. *ISBN: 9280311409. Bibliography — p.123-133.* [Fundamentals of educational planning. : No. 39]

61 Making the Indonesian state — the role of school texts. Barbara Leigh. *R. Ind. Malay. Aff.* **25:1** Winter:1991 pp. 17 – 43

62 The micropolitics of education. Catherine Marshall *[Contrib.]*; Jay D. Scribner *[Contrib.]*; Joseph J. Blase *[Contrib.]*; George Noblit *[Contrib.]*; Barnett Berry *[Contrib.]*; Van Dempsey *[Contrib.]*; Barbara A. Mitchell *[Contrib.]*; Susan Opotow *[Contrib.]*; Donald J. Willower *[Contrib.]*; Robert B. Everhart *[Contrib.] and others. Collection of 8 articles.* **Educ. Urban. Soc.** , *23:4*, 8:1991 pp. 347 – 471

63 Missing links — future policy for further education. Stuart Maclure. London: Policy Studies Institute, 1991: 93 p. *ISBN: 0853745110.*

64 Muslim matters — the educational needs of the Muslim child. Marie Parker-Jenkins. *New Comm.* **17:4** 7:1991 pp. 569 – 582

65 The organization and management of ministries of education in small states. M. Bray. *Publ. Adm. D.* **11:1** 1-2:1991 pp. 67 – 78

66 Österreichs Bildungspolitik — EG-harmonisch oder europareif? *[In German]*; Austrian education policies — in harmony with the EC or prepared for the new Europe? *[Summary]*. Susanne Dermutz; Peter Gstettner. *Öster. Z. Polit.* **:2** 1991 pp. 167 – 176

67 Plato at the keyboard — telecommunications technology and education policy. John Carey. *Ann. Am. Poli.* **514** 3:1991 pp. 11 – 21

68 Promoting girls' and women's education — lessons from the past. Rosemary T. Bellew; Elizabeth M. King. Washington, D.C.: Population and Human Resources Department, The World Bank, 1991: 59 p. *"July 1991"; Bibliography — p.47-55.* [Policy, research, and external affairs working papers.]

69 Развитие образования в мире. На каком же мы месте? *[In Russian]*; (Development of education in the world. Where are we?); (Le niveau d'instruction dans le monde — quelle place est la nôtre?: *Title only in French*); (Die Entwicklung des Bildungswesens in der Welt. An welcher Stelle stehen wir?: *Title only in German*); (El desarrollo de la enseñanza en el mundo. ¿Qué lugar ocupamos nosotros?: *Title only in Spanish*). Z. Mal'kova. *Kommunist* **:8(1378)** 1991 pp. 98 – 107

70 School choice plans. Frank Brown *[Ed.]*; Michael Martin *[Contrib.]*; Reynaldo Contreras *[Contrib.]*; J. John Harris *[Contrib.]*; Donna Y. Ford *[Contrib.]*; Patricia I. Wilson *[Contrib.]*; Rosetta F. Sandidge *[Contrib.]*; David G. Carter *[Contrib.]*; James P. Sandler *[Contrib.]*; Peter W. Cookson *[Contrib.] and others. Collection of 9 articles.* **Educ. Urban. Soc.** , *23:2*, 2:1991 pp. 115 – 227

71 Social purpose and schooling — alternatives, agendas, and issues. Jerald E. Paquette. London: Falmer Press, 1991: x, 196 p. (ill) *ISBN: 1850009201; LofC: 91014735. Includes bibliographical references (p. 182-187) and index.*

72 Teacher relationships and educational reform in England and Wales. Sandra Acker. *Curric. J.* **2:3** Autumn:1991 pp. 301 – 316

73 To change this house — popular education under the Sandinistas. Deborah Barndt. Toronto: Between the Lines, [1991]: 181 p. (ill) *ISBN: 0921284365; LofC: cn 90095584.*

74 Trading the known for the unknown — warning signs in the debate over schools of choice. Michael Martin. *Educ. Urban. Soc.* **23:2** 2:1991 pp. 119 – 142

75 Understanding educational reform in global context — economy, ideology, and the state. Mark B. Ginsburg *[Ed.]*. New York: Garland Pub, 1991: xx, 403 p. *ISBN: 0824068963; LofC: 91003812 //r92. Includes bibliographical references and index.* [Garland reference library of social science. : Vol. 663]

D.9: Education [Éducation] — Education policy [Politique de l'éducation]

76 L'unification du secondaire — un effet d'agrégation de la politique éducative au Portugal *[In French]*; Unification of secondary education — an aggregation effect in the educational policy in Portugal *[Summary]*; Die Vereinheitlichung des höheren Schulwesens — eine Aggregationswirkung der Erziehungspolitik in Portugal *[German summary]*; La unificación de la enseñanza secundaria — un resultado de amalgama de la política educativa en Portugal *[Spanish summary]*. Maria da Conceição Alves-Pinto. *Rev. Fr. Soc.* **XXXI:2** 4-6:1990 pp. 243 – 256

77 The University of Zimbabwe — university, national university, state university, or party university? A.P. Cheater. *Afr. Affairs* **90:359** 4:1991 pp. 189 – 206

78 Urban schools a second(?) or third(?) time around —priorities for curricular and instructional reform. A. Harry Passow. *Educ. Urban. Soc.* **23:3** 5:1991 pp. 243 – 255

79 W sprawie powrotu religii do szkół *[In Polish]*; (On reinstating religion as a subject of study at schools); (De la reprise de l'instruction religieuse à l'école: *Title only in French)*; (В деле возвращения религии в школу (Збигнев Струс): *Title only in Russian)*. Zbigniew Strus. *Pań. Prawo* **XLVI:11(549)** 1991 pp. 88 – 93

80 What should our public choose? The debate over school choice policy. J. John Harris; Donna Y. Ford; Patricia I. Wilson; Rosetta F. Sandidge. *Educ. Urban. Soc.* **23:2** 2:1991 pp. 159 – 173

81 Work, language and education in the industrial state. Michael Duane. London: Freedom Press, 1991: 35 p.

Education systems [Systèmes d'enseignement]

82 1992 — implications for teacher education in a different Europe. Hans Vonk *[Contrib.]*; Wolfgang Mitter *[Contrib.]*; Peter Szebenyi *[Contrib.]*; Michael Bruce *[Contrib.]*. Collection of 4 articles. **Br. J. Educ. S.** , *XXXIX:2,* 5:1991 pp. 117 – 172

83 The assumptive worlds of fledgling administrators. Catherine Marshall; Barbara A. Mitchell. *Educ. Urban. Soc.* **23:4** 8:1991 pp. 396 – 415

84 The blackboard debate — hurdles, options and opportunities in school integration. Monica Bot. Johannesburg: South African Institute of Race Relations, 1991: 150 p. *ISBN: 086982385x; LofC: 91124811. Includes bibliographical references (p. [137]-150).*

85 A blindfold removed — Ethiopia's struggle for literacy. Chris Searle. London: Karia Press, 1991: 112 p. (ill., facsim., fronts., maps, photos., ports) *ISBN: 1854650084. Includes bibliographical references.*

86 Decentralization and accountability in public education. Paul Thomas Hill; Josephine J. Bonan *[Ed.]*. Santa Monica, CA: Rand, 1991: xii, 93 p. *ISBN: 0833011510; LofC: 91200365 //r91. Includes bibliographical references.*

87 Democratization of South Korea's national universities. William W. Boyer; Nancy E. Boyer. *Kor. Stud.* **15** 1991 pp. 83 – 98

88 Determinants and consequences of the private-public school choice. Bruce W. Hamilton; Molly K. Macauley. *J. Urban Ec.* **29:3** 5:1991 pp. 282 – 294

89 Différenciation sexuelle et disparités sociales devant l'école en Afrique urbaine — une étude dans la banlieue de Dakar *[In French]*; Gender differentiation and social disparities of schooling in urban Africa — a study in the suburbs of Dakar *[Summary]*. D. Fassin; T. Calvez; J.L. Baudel; M. Tyrant; E. Jeannee. *Cah. Anthr. Bio. Hum.* **VVI:3-4** 1989 pp. 197 – 208

90 Education and society in Hong Kong — toward one country and two systems. Gerard A. Postiglione *[Ed.]*. Armonk, N.Y: M.E. Sharpe, c1991: xiv, 314 p. *ISBN: 0873327438; LofC: 90024658. Includes bibliographical references (p. 287-303) and index.* [Hong Kong becoming China.]

91 Educational transition in Hungary from the post-war period to the end of the 1980s. Péter Róbert. *Eur. Sociol. R.* **7:3** 12:1991 pp. 213 – 236

92 Growing-up modern — the Western state builds Third-World schools. Bruce Fuller. New York: Routledge, 1991: xxiv, 168 p. *ISBN: 0415902274; LofC: 90034232. Includes bibliographical references (p. 149-165) and index.* [Critical social thought.]

93 How did the British colonial policy influenced the contemporary system of Sri Lankan education. D. Thenuwara Gamage. *Asian Prof.* **19:5** 10:1991 pp. 473 – 484

94 Making the Indonesian state — the role of school texts. Barbara Leigh. *R. Ind. Malay. Aff.* **25:1** Winter:1991 pp. 17 – 43

95 Private schooling and equity — dilemmas of choice. Peter W. Cookson. *Educ. Urban. Soc.* **23:2** 2:1991 pp. 185 – 199

D.9: Education *[Éducation]* — Education systems *[Systèmes d'enseignement]*

96 Развитие образования в мире. На каком же мы месте? *[In Russian]*; (Development of education in the world. Where are we?); (Le niveau d'instruction dans le monde — quelle place est la nôtre?: *Title only in French)*; (Die Entwicklung des Bildungswesens in der Welt. An welcher Stelle stehen wir?: *Title only in German)*; (El desarrollo de la enseñanza en el mundo. ¿Qué lugar ocupamos nosotros?: *Title only in Spanish).* Z. Mal'kova. *Kommunist* :**8(1378)** 1991 pp. 98 – 107

97 *[In Japanese]*; [The social viewpoint for the "Dowa" education]. Haruhiko Kanegae. Tokyo: Akashi Shoten, 1991: 266 p.

98 Socialist education today — pessimism or optimism of the intellect? Marica Landy. *Rethink. Marx.* **4:3** Fall:1991 pp. 9 – 23

99 Le système éducatif *[In French]*; [The education system]. Claude Durand-Prinborgne *[Ed.]*. Paris: La Documentation française, 1991: 96 p. [Cahiers français. : No. 249]

100 Szkolnictwo państwowe we Francji a świecki charakter państwa *[In Polish]*; (The state school system in France and the lay nature of the state); (Les écoles publiques en France et le caractère laïc de l'Etat: *Title only in French)*; (Государственноя система просвешения и светский характер государства: *Title only in Russian).* Dorota Mazurkiewicz. *Pań. Prawo* **XLVI:10(548)** 1991 pp. 74 – 83

101 Társadalmi részvétel az iskolák irányításában *[In Hungarian]*; [The participation of people in directing schools]. Gábor Halász. *Mag. Köz. No.18 - [1991].* pp. 25 – 29

102 Trends in post-revolutionary Iranian education. Robert E. Rucker. *J. Cont. Asia* **21:4** 1991 pp. 455 – 468

103 Universitätsreform — vom Nutzen ihres Scheiterns oder vom Anfang ohne Ende — ein gesellschaftstheoretisches Panorama *[In German]*; The reform of the Austrian university *[Summary]*. Josef Melchior. *Öster. Z. Polit.* **20:1** 1991 pp. 19 – 42

104 The University of Zimbabwe — university, national university, state university, or party university? A.P. Cheater. *Afr. Affairs* **90:359** 4:1991 pp. 189 – 206

Educational sociology *[Sociologie de l'éducation]*

105 Adaptors and innovators — preference for educational procedures. Michael Kirton; Andrew Bailey; Walter Glendinning. *J. Psychol.* **125:4** 7:1991 pp. 445 – 456

106 Adolescent peer conflicts — implications for students and for schools. Susan Opotow. *Educ. Urban. Soc.* **23:4** 8:1991 pp. 416 – 441

107 Asian studies and social education — old and new imperatives. David Mahony. *Asian Stud. R.* **14:3** 4:1991 pp. 103 – 112

108 Attitudes towards race and poverty in the demand for private education — the case of Mississippi. John R. Conlon; Mwangi S. Kimenyi. *Rev. Bl. Pol. Ec.* **20:2** Fall:1991 pp. 5 – 22

109 Азиатское студенчество: Социал.-полит.п портр. *[In Russian]*; [Asiatic students — socialistic political portrait] *[Summary]*. I.E. Khomenko. Moscow: Nauka, 1987: 184 p. *Bibliogr. pp.172-181.*

110 Collective bargaining, teachers, and student achievement. Charles A. Register; Paul W. Grimes. *J. Labor Res.* **XII:2** Spring:1991 pp. 99 – 109

111 Cultural colonization and educational underdevelopment — changing patterns of American influence in Belizean schooling. Charles Rutheiser. *Beliz. St.* **19:1** 6:1991 pp. 18 – 29

112 Decentralization and accountability in public education. Paul Thomas Hill; Josephine J. Bonan *[Ed.]*. Santa Monica, CA: Rand, 1991: xii, 93 p. *ISBN: 0833011510; LofC: 91200365 //r91. Includes bibliographical references.*

113 L'échec scolaire des Polynésiens *[In French]*; [School failure in Polynesia]. Bernard Poirine. *Soc. Ét. Océan.* **XXI:253** 3:1991 pp. 69 – 109

114 Education and social class — revisiting the 1944 Education Act with fixed marginals. Robert Blackburn; Catherine Marsh. *Br. J. Soc.* **42:4** 12:1991 pp. 507 – 536

115 Education and the future of Japan. Michael D. Stephens. Folkestone: Japan Library, 1991: 120 p. *ISBN: 1873410107.* [Japan library.]

116 Effects of reward structures on academic performance and group processes in a classroom setting. Brian P. Niehoff; Debra J. Mesch. *J. Psychol.* **125:4** 7:1991 pp. 457 – 468

117 Environment, schools and active learning. Kathleen Kelley-Lainé; Peter Posch. Paris: Organisation for Economic Co-operation and Development, 1991: 146 p. (ill) *ISBN: 9264135693. "This study was prepared within the framework of the CERI project, Ènvironment and School Initiatives', in co-operation with experts from OECD Member countries."--Foreword; At head of title — Centre for Educational Research and Innovation; Includes bibliographical references.*

D.9: Education *[Éducation]* — Educational sociology *[Sociologie de l'éducation]*

118 Family structure, parental practices, and high school completion. Nan Marie Astone; Sara S. McLanahan. *Am. Sociol. R.* **56:3** 6:1991 pp. 309 – 320

119 From mono-cultural myopia to multi-cultural vision — the role of Jesuit secondary education in maintaining cultural pluralism in Belize. Charles T. Hunter. *Beliz. St.* **19:1** 6:1991 pp. 5 – 17

120 How education affects attitude to protest — a further test. Mark J. Rodeghier; Robert L. Hall; Bert Useem. *Sociol. Q.* **32:2** Summer:1991 pp. 277 – 288

121 Illiberal education — the politics of race and sex on campus. Dinesh d' Souza. New York: Free Press, c1991: ix, 319 p. *ISBN: 0029081009; LofC: 90047055.* Includes bibliographical references (p. 258-304) and index.

122 Individuen, gezinnen en buurten — sociale determinanten van het onderwijsniveau *[In Dutch]*; Individuals, families and neighbourhoods — social determinants of educational attainment *[Summary]*. Rolf van der Velden; Roel Bosker. *Mens Maat.* **66:3** 8:1991 pp. 277 – 295

123 Inequality in education. Chinnappan Gasper. *Art. Vij.* **XXXIII:1** 3:1991 pp. 56 – 64

124 An investigation of junior middle school student culture in Guangzhou. Guolin Li; Zibiao Li. *Soc. Sci. China* **XII:3** 9:1991 pp. 169 – 187

125 The iron law of inequality — different paths, but same results? Some comparisons between Lithuania and Norway. Gudmund Hernes; Knud Knudsen. *Eur. Sociol. R.* **7:3** 12:1991 pp. 192 – 211

126 Jesus says, "Order, children!" — ethnography of a Catholic classroom; *[French summary]*. Jacques Zylberberg; Yuki Shiose. *Soc. Compass* **38(4)** 1991 pp. 417 – 432

127 Knowledge for the masses — world models and national curricula, 1920-1986. Aaron Benavot; Yun-Kyung Cha; David Kamens; John W. Meyer; Suk-Ying Wong. *Am. Sociol. R.* **56:1** 2:1991 pp. 85 – 100

128 Learning and "leisure" — a study of adult participation in learning and its policy implications. Naomi Sargant. Leicester: National Institute of Adult Continuing Education, 1991: 132 p. *ISBN: 1872941117.*

129 Micropolitics and the sociology of school organizations. Donald J. Willower. *Educ. Urban. Soc.* **23:4** 8:1991 pp. 442 – 454

130 Muslim matters — the educational needs of the Muslim child. Marie Parker-Jenkins. *New Comm.* **17:4** 7:1991 pp. 569 – 582

131 A new network representation of a "classic" school districting problem. O. Benjamin Schoepfle; Richard L. Church. *Socio. Econ.* **25:3** 1991 pp. 189 – 198

132 Nierówności w dostępie do wykształcenia *[In Polish]*; Inequalities in access to education *[Summary]*. Ireneusz Białecki. *Prz. Soc.* **39** 1991 pp. 45 – 68

133 Papers on the sociology of education. Karuna Chanana *[Contrib.]*; M.K. Bacchus *[Contrib.]*; N. Jayaram *[Contrib.]*; Padma Velaskar *[Contrib.]*; Mala Khullar *[Contrib.]*. Collection of 5 articles. **Sociol. Bul.** , *39:1-2*, 3-9:1990 pp. 75 – 165

134 Parental characteristics, supply of schools, and child school-enrolment in Pakistan. Nadeem A. Burney; Mohammad Irfan. *Pak. Dev. R.* **30:1** Spring:1991 pp. 21 – 62

135 Participation in a TVEI programme in relation to self-perception and self-evaluation of pupils. W. Peter Robinson; Keith Williams; Carol A. Tayler. *Curric. J.* **2:1** Spring:1991 pp. 69 – 78

136 Political responses to reform — a comparative case study. George Noblit; Barnett Berry; Van Dempsey. *Educ. Urban. Soc.* **23:4** 8:1991 pp. 379 – 395

137 Power and politics in education. David Dawkins *[Ed.]*. London: Falmer, 1991: 290 p. *ISBN: 1850008892.* [Deakin studies in education series. : No. 8]

138 Los problemas de educación de las poblaciones marginadas de América Latina *[In Spanish]*; [Problems in educating the neglected population of Latin America]. Anne Bar Din. *Cuad. Am.* **1:25** 1-2:1991 pp. 127 – 138

139 Protests by pupils — empowerment, schooling and the state. Robert Adams. London: Falmer, 1991: 245 p. *ISBN: 1850008795.*

140 Radical agendas? — the politics of adult education. Sallie Westwood *[Ed.]*; J. E. Thomas *[Ed.]*. London: National Institute of Adult Continuing Education, 1991: 173 p. *ISBN: 1872941079.*

141 Regional disparities of lower level educational development of Bangladesh. Rejuan Hossain Bhuiyan; Shipra Banarjee. *Ind. J. Reg. Sci.* **XXIII:1** 1991 pp. 41 – 52

142 Sibship size and educational attainment in nuclear and extended families — Arabs and Jews in Israel. Yossi Shavit; Jennifer L. Pierce. *Am. Sociol. R.* **56:3** 6:1991 pp. 321 – 330

143 The social facts of deviance in school — a study of mundane reason. Stephen Hester. *Br. J. Soc.* **42:3** 9:1991 pp. 443 – 463

D.9: Education *[Éducation]* — *Educational sociology [Sociologie de l'éducation]*
144 *[In Japanese]*; [Sociology of education in Weber (3) — in relation to the concept of value-free and German universities]. Kazuo Nishine. ***B. Sch. Ed. Hiroshima** No.1(13) - 1991.* pp. 13 – 24
145 Становление преподавателя вуза как социологическая проблема *[In Russian]*; The higher school teacher's development as a sociological problem *[Summary]*. O.K. Krokinskaya. *Vest. Lenin. Univ.* 6 **L:6** 5:1991 pp. 95 – 102
146 Társadalmi részvétel az iskolák irányitásában *[In Hungarian]*; [The participation of people in directing schools]. Gábor Halász. ***Mag. Köz.** No.18 - [1991].* pp. 25 – 29
147 *[In Japanese]*; [Trends of theory and study of school (4)]. Michio Ohno. ***Bulletin of Fukutake Education Research Institute** No.(3) - 1991.* pp. 78 – 85
148 We must take charge — our schools and our future. Chester E Finn. New York: Free Press, c1991: xvii, 365 p. *ISBN: 0029102758; LofC: 91006526. Includes bibliographical references (p. 313-354) and index.*

Primary education *[Enseignement primaire]*
149 Access, choice, quality, and integration. David G. Carter; James P. Sandler. *Educ. Urban. Soc.* **23:2** 2:1991 pp. 175 – 184
150 Les activités de rééducation GAPP à l'école primaire — analyse du fonctionnement et évaluation des effets *[In French]*; Re-education activities with the GAPP (psycho-pedagogic assistance groups) in the primary school *[Summary]*; Die Umschulungsaktivitäten der GAPP (Gruppen zur psychopädagogischer Hilfe) in der Grundschule *[German summary]*; Las actividades de reeducación GAPP (grupos de ayuda psyco-pedagógica) en la escuela primaria *[Spanish summary]*. Alain Mingat. *Rev. Fr. Soc.* **XXXII:4** 10-12:1991 pp. 515 – 549
151 Cognitive attainment among firstborn children of adolescent mothers. Kristin A. Moore; Nancy O. Snyder. *Am. Sociol. R.* **56:5** 10:1991 pp. 612 – 624
152 Curricular content, educational expansion, and economic growth. Aaron Benavot. Washington, D.C.: Population and Human Resources Department, The World Bank, 1991: 22,8 p. *Bibliography — p..19-22.* [Policy, research, and external affairs working papers.]
153 La educación elemental en Hispanoamérica — desde la independencia hasta la centralización de los sistemas educativos nacionales *[In Spanish]*; [Elementary education in Latin America — from independence to the centralization of national educative systems]. Carlos Newland. *Hisp. Am. Hist. Rev.* **71:2** 5:1991 pp. 335 – 363
154 Education for young children in inner-city classrooms. Judith J. Carta. *Am. Behav. Sc.* **34:4** 3/4:1991 pp. 440 – 453
155 Educational performance assessment — a new framework of analysis. David J. Mayston; David St. J. Jesson. *Policy Pol.* **19:2** 4:1991 pp. 99 – 108
156 *[In Arabic]*; [The factor structure of the Jordanian Version of the Preschool and Kindergarten Interest Descriptor (JVPRIDE), designed for gifted children] *[Summary]*.*Dirasat Ser. A.* **18A:2** 1991 pp. 113 – 133
157 Improving primary education in developing countries. Marlaine E. Lockheed; Adriaan Verspoor *[Ed.]*; Deborah Bloch; et al. Washington, D.C: Published for the World Bank, Oxford University Press, c1991: xix, 429 p. (ill) *ISBN: 0195208722; LofC: 91030421. Includes bibliographical references (p. 389-415) and index.*
158 The myth of a myth? An assessment of two ethnographic studies of option choice schemes. Martyn Hammersley. *Br. J. Soc.* **42:1** 3:1991 pp. 61 – 94
159 W sprawie powrotu religii do szkół *[In Polish]*; (On reinstating religion as a subject of study at schools); (De la reprise de l'instruction religieuse à l'école: *Title only in French*); (В деле возвращения религии в школу (Збигнев Струс): *Title only in Russian*). Zbigniew Strus. *Pań. Prawo* **XLVI:11(549)** 1991 pp. 88 – 93

Secondary education *[Enseignement secondaire]*
160 Автоматизация: Методол.и социал.пробл. М-во высш. и сред.спец.образования РСФСР *[In Russian]*; [Automation — methodological and social problems. Ministry of higher and middle schools of specialist education in the Russian Soviet Federal Socialist Republic (RSFSR)]. I.F. Kefeli. Leningrad: Leningrad University Publishers, 1987: 134 p.
161 "Fear of success" and Jamaican adolescents; La peur de réussir parmi les jeunes Jamaïcains *[French summary]*; El miedo de enteuer éxito entre los adolescentes *[Spanish summary]*. Mary Richardson. *Soc. Econ. S.* **40:2** 1991 pp. 63 – 82

D.9: Education *[Éducation]* — *Secondary education [Enseignement secondaire]*
162 From mono-cultural myopia to multi-cultural vision — the role of Jesuit secondary education in maintaining cultural pluralism in Belize. Charles T. Hunter. *Beliz. St.* **19:**1 6:1991 pp. 5 – 17
163 The impact of school-based drug education; L'impact de la prévention de la drogue en milieu scolaire *[French summary]*; El impacto de una educacion escolar sobre drogas *[Spanish summary]*. N. Coggans; D. Shewan; M. Henderson; J.B. Davies. *Br. J. Addict.* **86:**9 9:1991 pp. 1099 – 1109
164 The PC bypass — multiculturalism in the public schools. Herbert Kohl. *Soc. Pol.* **22:**1 Summer:1991 pp. 33 – 41
165 Per la riforma. Idee sulla scuola secondaria superiore *[In Italian]*; (For a reform. Some ideas on the secondary school). Aureliana Alberici *[Contrib.]*; Giancarlo Aresta *[Contrib.]*; Giuseppe Cotturri *[Contrib.]*; Fiorenza Farinelli *[Contrib.]*; Roberto Maragliano *[Contrib.]*; Vincenzo Magni *[Contrib.]*; Paola Gaiotti de Biase *[Contrib.]*; Giuseppe Chiarante *[Contrib.]*; Lorenzo Cillario *[Contrib.]*; Giorgio Franchi *[Contrib.]* and others. Collection of 22 articles. **Crit. Marx.** , *29:4-5,* 7-10:1991 pp. 5 – 323
166 La pratique évaluative en classe terminale — consensus etillusion *[In French]*; Grades in the last year of secondary school — consensus and illusion *[Summary]*. Pierre Merle. *Sociol. Trav.* **XXXIII:**2 1991 pp. 277 – 292
167 Pre-vocational schooling in Europe today. S. J. Prais; Elaine Beadle. London: National Institute of Economic and Social Research, 1991: 60 p. [Report series.]
168 Resilience, schooling, and development in African-American youth. Linda F. Winfield *[Contrib.]*; Angela R. Taylor *[Contrib.]*; Sharon Nelson-Le Gall *[Contrib.]*; Elaine Jones *[Contrib.]*; Maxine L. Clark *[Contrib.]*; Diane Scott-Jones *[Contrib.]*; Valerie E. Lee *[Contrib.]*; Thomas C. Wilson *[Contrib.]*; Karen R. Wilson-Sadberry *[Contrib.]*; Deirdre A. Royster *[Contrib.]* and others. Collection of 11 articles. **Educ. Urban. Soc.** , *24:1,* 11:1991 pp. 5 – 162
169 Staying on in full-time education — the educational participation rate of 16-year-olds. Keith Whitfield; R.A. Wilson. *Economica* **58:231** 8:1991 pp. 391 – 404
170 Undereducation in America — the demography of high school dropouts. Dorothy Waggoner. New York: Auburn House, 1991: xxiv, 233 p. (ill) *ISBN: 086569043x; LofC: 91003980. Includes bibliographical references (p. [219]-222) and index.*
171 L'unification du secondaire — un effet d'agrégation de la politique éducative au Portugal *[In French]*; Unification of secondary education — an aggregation effect in the educational policy in Portugal *[Summary]*; Die Vereinheitlichung der höheren Schulwesens — eine Aggregationswirkung der Erziehungspolitik in Portugal *[German summary]*; La unificación de la enseñanza secundaria — un resultado de amalgama de la política educativa en Portugal *[Spanish summary]*. Maria da Conceição Alves-Pinto. *Rev. Fr. Soc.* **XXXI:**2 4-6:1990 pp. 243 – 256
172 W sprawie powrotu religii do szkół *[In Polish]*; (On reinstating religion as a subject of study at schools); (De la reprise de l'instruction religieuse à l'école: *Title only in French*); (В деле возвращения религии в школу (Збигнев Струс): *Title only in Russian*). Zbigniew Strus. *Pań. Prawo* **XLVI:11(549)** 1991 pp. 88 – 93

Tertiary education *[Enseignement post-scolaire]*

173 L'avenir de l'enseignement supérieur au Japon *[In French]*; The future of higher education in Japan *[Summary]*. Kazuyuki Kitamura. *Sociol. Trav.* **XXXIII:**1 1991 pp. 51 – 62
174 Bias in university enrolments — a regional analysis. Anthony Hoare. *Reg. Stud.* **25:**5 10:1991 pp. 459 – 470
175 The changing university — how increased demand for scientists and technology is transforming academic institutions internationally. Dorothy S. Zinberg *[Ed.]*. Dordrecht: Kluwer, in cooperation with NATO Scientific Affairs Division, 1991: 182 p. *ISBN: 0792312813. "Papers written for a NATO Advanced Research Workshop held at Harvard University in March 1990, entitled "The changing university and the education of scientists and engineers — an international workshop".* [NATO ASI series.]
176 College in black and white — African American students in predominantly white and in historically black public universities. Walter R. Allen *[Ed.]*; Edgar G. Epps *[Ed.]*; Nesha Z. Haniff *[Ed.]*. Albany, N.Y: State University of New York Press, c1991: xx, 322 p. *ISBN: 0791404854; LofC: 90032306. Includes bibliographical references (p.285-304) and index.* [SUNY series, frontiers in education.]
177 The conflicts of postmodern and traditional epistemologies in curricular reform — a dialogue. Grant Cornwell; Baylor Johnson. *St. Philos. Educ.* **11:**2 1991 pp. 149 – 166

D.9: Education [Éducation] — Tertiary education [Enseignement post-scolaire]

178 *[In Japanese]*; [The Danish university system — from a perspective of research environment]. Yukio Wakamatsu. **Historical Studies Higher Education** *No.(7) - 1991.* pp. 54 – 62

179 Defending the humanities — Weber, instrumentalism, and values in the politics of Australian higher education. Geoff Stokes. *Aust. J. Poli.* **37:1** 1991 pp. 1 – 20

180 Democratization of South Korea's national universities. William W. Boyer; Nancy E. Boyer. *Kor. Stud.* **15** 1991 pp. 83 – 98

181 Diplôme et entrée dans la vie active *[In French]*; [Diploma and entry to working life]. Alain Charlot; Jean-François Lochet; François Pottier; Thierry Pouch. *Regar. Actual.* **:167** 1:1991 pp. 17 – 41

182 Economic challenges in higher education. Charles T. Clotfelter *[Ed.]*. Chicago: University of Chicago Press, 1991: x, 422 p. (ill) *ISBN: 0226110508; LofC: 91023330.* Tertiary education; Includes bibliographical references (p. [393]-410) and indexes. [A National Bureau of Economic Research monograph.]

183 Education for young adults — international perspectives. Karen Evans *[Ed.]*; Ian Haffenden *[Ed.]*. London: Routledge, 1991: 159 p. *ISBN: 0415005779.* Includes bibliography and index. [International perspectives on adult and continuing education.]

184 Enrollment management and strategic planning — resolving a classic tension in higher education. Julie Gowen; Virginia Lee Owen. *Non. Manag. Leader.* **2:2** Winter:1991 pp. 143 – 158

185 The future of higher education. Tom Schuller *[Ed.]*. Buckingham: SRHE & Open University Press, 1991: 131p. *ISBN: 0335097944.* [Society for Research into Higher Education. Open University Press series.]

186 The great transformation in higher education, 1960-1980. Clark Kerr *[Foreword]*. Albany: SUNY Press, 1991: - *ISBN: 0791405125.* [SUNY series, frontiers in education.]

187 A guide to higher education systems and qualifications in the European Community. Anita Wijnaendts van Resandt *[Ed.]*. London: Kogan Page for the European Communities, 1991: 425 p. *ISBN: 074940387x.*

188 Harassment policies in the university. Alan Charles Kors. *Society* **28:4(192)** 5-6:1991 pp. 22 – 30

189 Higher education, industry and the journey of learning. Patrick Coldstream. Hull: Hull University Press, 1991: 14 p. *ISBN: 0859584984.* [Annual open lecture.]

190 Higher-education partnerships in engineering and science. Lionel V. Baldwin. *Ann. Am. Poli.* **514** 3:1991 pp. 76 – 91

191 Implications of internationalization for the university. Stanislav P. Merkur'ev. *Am. Behav. Sc.* **35:1** 9-10:1991 pp. 43 – 54

192 Industry training and education at a distance — the IBM approach. Charles L. Bruce; Elizabeth J. Katz; James A. Tomsic. *Ann. Am. Poli.* **514** 3:1991 pp. 119 – 132

193 Industry-academic links — the case of Oxford University. H. Lawton Smith. *Envir. Plan. C.* **9:4** 11:1991 pp. 403 – 416

194 International learning and national purposes in higher education. Clark Kerr. *Am. Behav. Sc.* **35:1** 9-10:1991 pp. 17 – 42

195 Internationalizing higher education. Peter A. Wollitzer *[Contrib.]*; Clark Kerr *[Contrib.]*; Stanislav P. Merkur'ev *[Contrib.]*; William H. Allaway *[Contrib.]*; Neil J. Smelser *[Contrib.]*. Collection of 5 articles. **Am. Behav. Sc.**, *35:1*, 9-10:1991 pp. 5 – 91

196 De invloed van kennisproduktie aan universiteiten op het investeringsgedrag in de nijverheid *[In Dutch]*; [The effect of the investment behaviour of industry of the production of knowledge at universities]. R.J.G.M. Florax; H. Folmer. *Maan. Econ.* **55:6** 1991 pp. 429 – 441

197 Learning in Europe — the ERASMUS experience — a survey of the 1988-89 ERASMUS students. Friedhelm Maiworm; Wolfgang Steube; Ulrich Teichler. London: Jessica Kingsley Publishers, 1991: 160 p. *ISBN: 1853025275.* [Higher education policy series. : No. 14]

198 Missing the boat — the disconnection between America's universities and its world role. Craufurd D. W. Goodwin; Michael Nacht *[Ed.]*. Cambridge: Cambridge University Press, 1991: 130 p. *ISBN: 0521402131.* Includes index.

199 More than an academic question — universities, government, and public policy in Canada. David M Cameron. Halifax, N.S: Institute for Research on Public Policy, c1991: xxxi, 472 p. *ISBN: 0886451345; LofC: 92180326.* eng: fre; Foreword in English and French; Includes bibliographical references and index.

200 Other routes — part-time higher education policy. David M. Smith; Michael R. Saunders. Buckingham: Society for Research into Higher Education, 1991: xii,106p. (ill) *ISBN: 033515199x.* Bibliography — p.92-99. Includes index. [The cutting edge.]

D.9: Education *[Éducation]* — *Tertiary education [Enseignement post-scolaire]*

201 Part-time students and their experience of higher education. Tom Bourner. Milton Keynes: Society for Research into Higher Education & Open University Press, 1991: 146 p. *ISBN: 0335093515. Includes bibliography and index.* [The cutting edge.]

202 PC and the decline of the American empire. Tim Brennan. *Soc. Pol.* **22:1** Summer:1991 pp. 16 – 32

203 The proletarianisation of academic labour; La prolétarisation du travail academique *[French summary]*. Tom Wilson. *Ind. Relat. J.* **22:4** Winter:1991 pp. 250 – 262

204 Quality and access in higher education — comparing Britain and the United States. Robert Oliver Berdahl *[Ed.]*; Graeme C. Moodie *[Ed.]*; Irving J. Spitzberg *[Ed.]*. Milton Keynes: Society for Reseach into Higher Education, 1991: 176 p. *ISBN: 0335096476; LofC: 90014236. Includes index.*

205 The racial crisis in American higher education. Philip G. Altbach *[Ed.]*; Kofi Lomotey *[Ed.]*. Albany: SUNY Pr., 1991: 275 p. *ISBN: 0791405206.* [SUNY series, frontiers in education.]

206 Religion and politics among the students of the Najah National University. Iyad Barghouti. *Middle E. Stud.* **27:2** 4:1991 pp. 203 – 218

207 La riforma dell'università italiana e il problema dell'occupazione *[In Italian]*; [The reform of the Italian university and the problem of employment]. Mario Arpea. *Aff. Soc. Int.* **XIX:2** 1991 pp. 89 – 98

208 Risk-taking behaviors of college students. Dona Schneider; Joyce Morris. *Envir. Behav.* **23:5** 9:1991 pp. 575 – 591

209 The role of universities in training for development. Jan K. Coetzee. *Develop. S. Afr.* **8:1** 2:1991 pp. 35 – 46

210 Should employers fund undergraduates? A study of employers' views and experiences of undergraduate sponsorship. Geoffrey Pike; Richard Pearson. Brighton: University of Sussex, Institute of Manpower Studies, 1991: 81 p. *ISBN: 1851841318.* [IMS report. : No. 214]

211 Thinking about American higher education — the 1990s and beyond. J. Wade Gilley. New York: American Council on Education, c1991: ix, 214 p. *ISBN: 0028971620; LofC: 90020406. Includes bibliographical references (p. 201-207) and index.* [American Council on Education/Macmillan series on higher education.]

212 Toward an ethic of higher education. Mortimer R Kadish. Stanford, Calif: Stanford University Press, 1991: viii, 205 p. *ISBN: 0804718830; LofC: 90027058. Includes bibliographical references (p. [191]-201) and index.*

213 Trinity College Dublin and the idea of a university. C. H. Holland *[Ed.]*. Dublin: Trinity College Dublin Press, 1991: 384 p.

214 The uneasy public triangle in higher education — quality, diversity, and budgetary efficiency. David H Finifter *[Ed.]*; Roger G Baldwin *[Ed.]*; John R Thelin *[Ed.]*. New York: American Council on Education, c1991: xix, 198 p. (ill) *ISBN: 0028971450; LofC: 90020407. Includes bibliographical references and index.* [American Council on Education/Macmillan series on higher education.]

215 Universitätsreform — vom Nutzen ihres Scheiterns oder vom Anfang ohne Ende — ein gesellschaftstheoretisches Panorama *[In German]*; The reform of the Austrian university *[Summary]*. Josef Melchior. *Öster. Z. Polit.* **20:1** 1991 pp. 19 – 42

216 Universités 2000 — quelle université pour demain? *[In French]*; [Universities in the year 2000 — which university for tomorrow?]. Martine Poulain *[Ed.]*. Paris: La Documentation française, 1991: 334 p. *ISBN: 2110026111.*

217 University and society — essays on the social role of research and higher education. Martin Trow *[Ed.]*; Thorsten Nybom *[Ed.]*. London: Jessica Kingsley, 1991: 251 p. *ISBN: 1853025259.* [Higher education policy series. : No. 12]

218 The University of Zimbabwe — university, national university, state university, or party university? A.P. Cheater. *Afr. Affairs* **90:359** 4:1991 pp. 189 – 206

219 Het wetenschappelijk onderwijs — egalitair of utilitair? De externe democratisering en verschuivende legitimaties in het beleid *[In Dutch]*; University education — egalitarian or utilitarian? *[Summary]*. Jan Karel Koppen. *Mens Maat.* **66:2** 5:1991 pp. 115 – 140

220 Wyższe wykształcenie w strategiach zyciowych studentów (na przykładzie badań nad łódzkimi studentami z 1986 r.) *[In Polish]*; University education in life strategies of students (on the example of survey of Lódź students in 1986) *[Summary]*. Anna Kubiak; Ilona Przybyłowska. *Acta Univ. Łódz. Folia Soc.* **20** 1991 pp. 169 – 177

E: Social structure — *Structure sociale*

E.1: Social system — *Système social*

1 America at century's end. Alan Wolfe *[Ed.]*. Berkeley: University of California Press, c1991: xv, 579 p. (ill) *ISBN: 0520074769; LofC: 91014455 //r91*. Includes bibliographical references (pp. 473-554) and index.
2 Asia and the Pacific. Robert H. Taylor *[Ed.]*. Oxford: Facts on File, 1991: - *ISBN: 0816016224*. [Handbooks to the modern world.]
3 Die Autopoiesis sozialer Systeme *[In German]*; The autopoiesis of social systems *[Summary]*. Wil Martens. *Kölner Z. Soz. Soz. psy.* **43**:4 1991 pp. 625 – 646
4 Controversies in Soviet social thought — democratization, social justice, and the erosion of official ideology. Murray Yanowitch. Armonk, N.Y: M.E. Sharpe, c1991: ix, 155 p. *ISBN: 0873325583; LofC. 91014600*. Includes bibliographical references (p. 141-149) and index.
5 *[In Japanese]*; [The emperor system in the 1990s and its continuity with the pre-war period and its relationship with the people]. Yasuko Muramatsu. **Shin. Hy.** *No.(40) - 1991.* pp. 193 – 211
6 Формирование социально-экономической структуры японской деревни *[In Russian]*; [The formation of the socio-economic structure of a Japanese village]. V.A. Popov. Moscow: Nauka, 1987: 187 p. pp.182-187 Bibliogr.
7 La France de l'intégration — sociologie de la nation en 1990 *[In French]*; [Integration and France — sociology of the nation in 1990]. Dominique Schnapper. Paris: Gallimard, 1991: 367 p. *ISBN: 2070721744*. [Bibliothèque des sciences humaines.]
8 *[In Japanese]*; [Logic and strategies of Africa as a complex society]. Haruka Wazaki. *J. Orient. Stud.* No.30(3) - 1991. pp. 38 – 75
9 Markets, hierarchies and networks — the coordination of social life. Grahame Thompson *[Ed.]*. London: Sage Publications, 1991: 306 p. *ISBN: 0803985894*.
10 *[In Japanese]*; [Modern social system]. Yukio Shirakura *[Ed.]*. Tokyo: Gakujutsu-tosho Shuppansha, 1991
11 Neugriechische Regionalproblematik — Vorstudien zu einer Sozialstrukturanalyse *[In German]*; [Regional problems in Greece — towards an analysis of social structure]. Theodor P. Ikonomu. New York: Lang, 1990: 162 p. *ISBN: 3820401431*. [Europäische Hochschulschriften. : No. 148]
12 Parsons, Hobbes und das Problem sozialer Ordnung — eine theoriegeschichtliche Notiz in systematischer Absicht *[In German]*; Parsons, Hobbes and the problem of social order *[Summary]*. Gerhard Wagner. *Z. Soziol.* **20**:2 4:1991 pp. 115 – 123
13 *[In Japanese]*; [Possibility of approaching social order problem from an individualistic standpoint]. Toshitake Kuji. **Riron to Hoho** No.6(1) - 1991. pp. 1 – 30
14 Rethinking utopia — from "Metropolis" to "Batman". Patty Lee Parmalee. *Rethink. Marx.* **4**:2 Summer:1991 pp. 79 – 92
15 Social Europe — in search of a common culture. Centro Studi Investimenti Sociali. : Franco Angeli for Censis, 1991: 275 p. *ISBN: 8820468557-*.
16 Social organization and social process — essays in honor of Anselm Strauss. David R. Maines *[Ed.]*. New York: A. de Gruyter, c1991: x, 398 p. (port) *ISBN: 020230390x; LofC: 91002770 //r91*. "The scholarly writings of Anselm L. Strauss"--P. 383-394; Includes bibliographical references and index. [Communication and social order.]
17 Social semigroups — a unified theory of scaling and blockmodelling as applied to social networks. John Paul Boyd. Fairfax, Va: George Mason University Press, 1991: 267 p. *ISBN: 0913969346; LofC: 90025957*. Includes index.
18 Society and politics in India — essays in a comparative perspective. André Béteille. London: Athlone Press, 1991: 317 p. *ISBN: 0485195631; LofC: 91023882*. Includes bibliographical references and index. [Monographs on social anthropology. : No. no. 63]
19 Sociology of the global system. Leslie Sklair. London: Harvester Wheatsheaf, 1991: 269 p. *ISBN: 0745009328*. [Social change in global perspectives.]
20 Sow what you know — the struggle for social reproduction in rural Sudan. Cindi Katz. *Ann. As. Am. G.* **81**:3 9:1991 pp. 488 – 513

E.1: Social system [Système social]

21 State and society in Lebanon. Leila Tarazi Fawaz *[Ed.]*; Fida Bahige Nasrallah *[Ed.]*; Nadim Shehadi *[Ed.]*. Oxford: Centre for Lebanese Studies, 1991: 108p. *ISBN: 1870552237*.
22 La technique, le marché et l'histoire — crise et conscience ouvrière *[In French]*; Technique, market and history — crises and worker consciousness *[Summary]*. Guy Groux. *Pensée* :**284** 11-12:1991 pp. 57 – 66
23 Une théorie de la société polonaise *[In French]*; (The theory of Polish society). Adam Podgórecki. *Rev. Ét. Comp.* **XXII:4** 12:1991 pp. 49 – 75
24 The underside of Malaysian history — pullers, prostitutes, plantation workers. Peter James Rimmer *[Ed.]*; Lisa M. Allen *[Ed.]*. Singapore: Singapore University Press for the Malaysia Society of the Asian Studies Association of Australia, c1990: xiv, 259 p., 8 leaves of plates (ill) *ISBN: 9971691272. Based on papers from a colloquium held at the Australian National University, 1985; Includes bibliographical references (p. 232-250) and index.*
25 Die Wissenschaft der Gesellschaft *[In German]*; [The science of society]. Niklas Luhmann. Frankfurt am Main: Suhrkamp, 1990: 732 p. *ISBN: 3518580655; LofC: 91119481. Includes bibliographical references and index.*

E.2: Social stratification — *Stratification sociale*

Sub-divisions: Class *[Classe]*

1 The anti-caste movement and the discourse of power. Gail Omvedt. *Race Class* **33:2** 10-12:1991 pp. 15 – 28
2 A biosocial theory of social stratification derived from the concepts of pro/antisociality and r/K selection. Lee Ellis. *Polit. Life* **10:1** 8:1991 pp. 5 – 23
3 Blacks in the white establishment? — a study of race and class in America. Richard L. Zweigenhaft; G. William Domhoff. London: Yale University Press, c1991: 198 p. *ISBN: 0300047886; LofC: 90038640. Includes bibliographical references and index.*
4 Chile's middle class — a struggle for survival in the face of neoliberalism. Larissa Adler de Lomnitz; Ana Melnick. Boulder: L. Rienner Publishers, 1991: ix, 161 p. (ill) *ISBN: 1555872581; LofC: 91019118. eng; Includes bibliographical references (p. 151-153) and index.* [LACC studies on Latin America and the Caribbean.]
5 Dekompozycja tablic ruchliwości społecznej *[In Polish]*; Decomposition of social mobility tables *[Summary]*. Grzegorz Lissowski. *Prz. Soc.* **39** 1991 pp. 167 – 210
6 *[In Japanese]*; [Differentiation and evaluation criterion of social stratification in a traditional industrial city]. Miyoshi Kikuchi. *Teikyo Shakaigaku No.(4) - 1991.* pp. 47 – 75
7 The division and integration of the Chinese social structure during the present stage. Beijing University, "Social Division" Study Group. *Soc. Sci. China* **XII:3** 9:1991 pp. 156 – 168
8 Educating the body — physical capital and the production of social inequalities. Chris Shilling. *Sociology* **25:4** 11:1991 pp. 653 – 672
9 Életút és származás *[In Hungarian]*; [Life-history and social origin]. Zsuzsa Solymosi; Mária Székelyi. *Szociologia Vol.16; No.4 - 1987.* pp. 457 – 468
10 Elite integration in stable democracies — a reconsideration. John Higley; Ursula Hoffmann-Lange; Charles Kadushin; Gwen Moore. *Eur. Sociol. R.* **7:1** 5:1991 pp. 35 – 53
11 The end of the Enlightenment and modernity — the irrational ironies of rationalization. Arthur J. Vidich. *Int. J. Pol. C. S.* **4:3** Spring:1991 pp. 269 – 284
12 Exploitation and exclusion — race and class in contemporary US society. Abebe Zegeye *[Ed.]*; Leonard Harris *[Ed.]*; Julia Maxted *[Ed.]*. London: Hans Zell, 1991: 277 p. *ISBN: 0905450671; LofC: 91031148. Includes bibliographical references and index.* [African discourse series. : No. 3]
13 A falusi társadalom rétegződéséről.(Töprengések egy történeti rétegződés-modell megalkotása közben) *[In Hungarian]*; [Stratification of rural society. Meditation in the course of building a historical model of stratification]. Tamás Faragó. *Szociologia Vol.16; No.3 - 1987.* pp. 395 – 418
14 From localised social structures to localities as agents. K.R. Cox; A. Mair. *Envir. Plan.A.* **23:2** 2:1991 pp. 197 – 213
15 From middle income to poor — downward mobility among displaced steelworkers. Allison Zippay. New York: Praeger, 1991: 144 p. *ISBN: 0275937917; LofC: 91011077. Includes bibliographical references (p. [133]-140) and index.*
16 La Grande-Bretagne et la logique sociale du pluralisme *[In French]*; [Great Britain and the social logic of pluralism]. Bhiku Parekh. *Temps Mod.* **46:540-541** 7-8:1991 pp. 83 – 110

E.2: Social stratification *[Stratification sociale]*

17 The impact of social and human capital on the income attainment of Dutch managers. A.W. Boxman *[Ed.]*; Paul M. de Graaf; Hendrik D. Flap. *Soc. Networks* **13:1** 3:1991 pp. 51 – 74

18 Inequality in Northern Ireland. David J. Smith; Gerald Chambers *[Ed.]*. Oxford: Clarendon Press, 1991: 401 p. *ISBN: 0198275544; LofC: 90007741. Includes bibliographical references and index.*

19 Integrációs kategóriák alkalmazási lehetőségei a társadalmi tagozódás kutatásában *[In Hungarian]*; [Possibilities of adopting integrated categories in the research of social stratification]. Dániel Deák. *Tarsad. Kozl.* Vol.17; No.1 - 1987. pp. 57 – 70

20 Israel's bureaucratic elite — social structure and patronage. David Nachmias. *Publ. Adm. Re.* **51:5** 9-10:1991 pp. 413 – 420

21 Job mobility and social ties — social resources, prior job, and status attainment. Bernd Wegener. *Am. Sociol. R.* **56:1** 2:1991 pp. 60 – 71

22 Knowledge and power — the case of India's ethnic intellectuals. Asoke Basu. *New Que.* **:86** 3-4:1991 pp. 99 – 104

23 Kozelebb a mobilitás valódi dimenzióihoz *[In Hungarian]*; [Nearer to the real dimensions of mobility]. Imre Kovách; Péter Róbert; Tamás Rudas. *Szociologia* Vol.16; No.1 - 1987. pp. 79 – 100

24 Las "malas" castas ayer y hoy *[In Spanish]*; ["Bad" castes yesterday and today]. Victor González Selanio. *Nueva Soc.* **:111** 1-2:1991 pp. 141 – 147

25 Mixed blessings — disruption and organization among peasant unions in Costa Rica. Leslie Anderson. *Lat. Am. Res. R.* **26:1** 1991 pp. 111 – 143

26 Mobility and social stratification. Richard Jenkins. *Br. J. Soc.* **42:4** 12:1991 pp. 557 – 580

27 Moral economists, subalterns, new social movements and the (re-) emergence of a (post-) modernised (middle) peasant. Tom Brass. *J. Peasant Stud.* **18:2** 1:1991 pp. 173 – 205

28 The new US class struggle — financial industry power vs. grassroots populism. Patrick Bond. *Cap. Class* **40** Spring:1990 pp. 150 – 181

29 Nierówności społeczne w Polsce — zamiast podsumowania *[In Polish]*; Social inequalities in Poland — instead of summing up *[Summary]*. Joanna Sikorska; Andrzej Rychard; Edmund Wnuk-Lipiński. *Prz. Soc.* **39** 1991 pp. 139 – 146

30 Nierówności społeczne — wstępne sformułowanie problemu *[In Polish]*; Social inequalities — preliminary formulation of problem *[Summary]*. Edmund Wnuk-Lipiński. *Prz. Soc.* **39** 1991 pp. 9 – 18

31 Nierówności społeczne w aspekcie międzygeneracyjnym *[In Polish]*; Social inequalities in their intergenerational aspect *[Summary]*. Wielislawa Warzywoda-Kruszynska. *Prz. Soc.* **39** 1991 pp. 241 – 262

32 Nierówności w procesie osiągania pozycji społecznej *[In Polish]*; Influence in the process of attaining social position *[Summary]*. Krystyna Janicka. *Prz. Soc.* **39** 1991 pp. 85 – 104

33 Pride, purdah, or paychecks — what maintains the gender division of labor in rural Egypt. James Toth. *Int. J. M.E. Stud.* **23:2** 5:1991 pp. 213 – 236

34 *[In Japanese]*; [A primitive model of distributional image of a stratification system]. Kenji Kosaka. *Kwansei Gakuin Sociology Department Studies* No.(63) - 1991. pp. 319 – 336

35 The process of status attainment among men in Poland, the U.S., and West Germany. Daniel H. Krymkowski. *Am. Sociol. R.* **56:1** 2:1991 pp. 46 – 59

36 Rola pochodzenia społecznego i wykształcenia w procesie osiągania pozycji społeczno-ekonomicznych w Polsce i w Finlandii *[In Polish]*; The role of social origin and education in the process of attaining the socio-economic position in Poland and in Finland *[Summary]*. Michał Pohoski; Seppo Pontinen. *Prz. Soc.* **39** 1991 pp. 211 – 226

37 Social mobility among the scheduled castes in Bihar — a case study of Barh block. Joseph Benjamin. *Soc. Act.* **41:4** 10-12:1991 pp. 442 – 453

38 Social resources and occupational status attainment in Spain — a cross- national comparison with the United States and the Netherlands. Felix Requena. *Int. J. Comp. Soc* **32:3-4** 9-12:1991 pp. 233 – 242

39 Status homogamy in the United States. Matthijs Kalmijn. *A.J.S.* **97:2** 9:1991 pp. 496 – 522

40 A státusinkonzisztencia mérése *[In Hungarian]*; [Measuring status inconsistency]. Tamás Kolosi. *Szociologia* Vol.16; No.1 - 1987. pp. 1 – 20

41 The structure of social stratification and the modernisation process in contemporary China. Lulu Li; Xiao Yang; Fengyu Wang. *Int. Sociol.* **6:1** 3:1991 pp. 25 – 35

42 Tagolt társadalom. Struktúra, rétegződés, egyenlőtlenség Magyarországon *[In Hungarian]*; [Divided society. Structure, stratification, inequality in Hungary]. Tamás Kolosi. Budapest: Gondolat, 1987: 356 p.

E.2: Social stratification *[Stratification sociale]*

43 Twilight of the state bourgeoisie? John Waterbury. *Int. J. M.E. Stud.* **23:1** 2:1991 pp. 1 – 17
44 Understanding social inequality — modeling allocation processes. Hubert M. Blalock. Newbury Park, CA: Sage Publications, c1991: xiv, 258 p. (ill) *ISBN: 0803943393; LofC: 91022015. Includes bibliographical references (p. 246-250) and indexes.* [Sage library of social research. : Vol. 188]
45 Von Bewegungen in zur Beweglichkeit von Strukturen. Provisorische Überlegungen zur Sozialstrukturanalyse im vereinten Deutschland *[In German]*; From movements within structures to moving structures *[Summary]*. Peter A. Berger. *Soz. Welt.* **42:1** :1991 pp. 68 – 92
46 The women elite in India. Anand Arora. London: Sangam, 1991: 201 p. *ISBN: 0861322525; LofC: gb 91036137. Bibliography — p.. 184-190.-Includes index.* [Women in the Third World.]
47 Wpływ systemu poiitycznego i gospodarczego na nierówności społeczne. Propozycja schematu analizy *[In Polish]*; Influence of political and economic system on social inequalities. Proposition of scheme for analysis *[Summary]*. Andrzej Rychard. *Prz. Soc.* **39** 1991 pp. 105 – 118
48 Zagadnienia nierówności społecznych w mieście szybko rozwijającym się pod wpływem budowanego kompleksu przemysłowego *[In Polish]*; Problem of social inequalities in town expanding rapidly under influence of industrial complex in construction *[Summary]*. Irena Machaj. *Prz. Soc.* **39** 1991 pp. 299 – 310

Class *[Classe]*

49 The accidental proletariat — workers, politics, and crisis in Gorbachev's Russia. Walter D. Connor. Princeton, N.J: Princeton University Press, c1991: xv, 374 p. *ISBN: 0691077878; LofC: 91008557. Includes bibliographical references (p. [323]-368) and index.*
50 The archaeology of inequality. Randall H. McGuire *[Ed.]*; Robert Paynter *[Ed.]*. Oxford: Blackwell, 1991: 295 p. *ISBN: 0631160434.* [Social archaeology.]
51 Are social classes dying?; Les classes sociales sont-elles en voie de disparition? *[French summary]*. Terry Nichols Clark; Seymour Martin Lipset. *Int. Sociol.* **6:4** 12:1991 pp. 397 – 412
52 Bringing class back in — contemporary and historical perspectives. Scott G McNall *[Ed.]*; Rhonda F Levine *[Ed.]*; Rick Fantasia *[Ed.]*. Boulder: Westview Press, 1991: vii, 344 p. *ISBN: 0813310490; LofC: 90044536. Includes bibliographical references and index.*
53 Citrus and the state — factions and class formation in rural Belize. M. Moberg. *Am. Ethn.* **18:2** 5:1991 pp. 215 – 233
54 Class and rationality — Olson's critique of Marx. J.M. Barbalet. *Sci. Soc.* **55:4** Winter:1991-1992 pp. 446 – 468
55 Class beyond the nation-state. David Ruccio; Stephen Resnick; Richard Wolff. *Cap. Class* **:43** Spring:1991 pp. 25 – 42
56 The class location of families — a refined classification and analysis. Brian Graetz. *Sociology* **25:1** 2:1991 pp. 101 – 118
57 Class structure and status hierarchies in contemporary Japan. Hiroshi Ishida. *Eur. Sociol. R.* **5:1** 5:1989 pp. 65 – 80
58 Class structure in Europe — new findings from East-West comparisons of social structure and mobility. Max Haller *[Ed.]*. Armonk, N.Y: M.E. Sharpe, c1990: xxii, 271 p. (ill) *ISBN: 0873327225; LofC: 90037798. Includes bibliographical references and index.*
59 Classes are states of affairs. David Armstrong. *Mind* **100 (2):398** 4:1991 pp. 189 – 200
60 The classification of social class in sociological research. Sheelagh Drudy. *Br. J. Soc.* **42:1** 3:1991 pp. 21 – 41
61 Collapse and convergence in class theory — the return of the social in the analysis of stratification arrangements. Malcolm Waters. *Theory Soc.* **20:2** 4:1991 pp. 141 – 172
62 A continuation of the underclass debate. Harold M. Rose *[Ed.]*; Anne M. Santiago *[Contrib.]*; Margaret G. Wilder *[Contrib.]*; Donald R. Deskins *[Contrib.]*; Richard P. Greene *[Contrib.]*; James H. Johnson *[Contrib.]*; Melvin L. Oliver *[Contrib.]*. Collection of 5 articles. **Urban Geogr.** , *12:6,* 11-12:1991 pp. 491 – 562
63 Culture, class, and development in Pakistan — the emergence of an industrial bourgeoisie in Punjab. Anita M. Weiss. Boulder: Westview Press, 1991: xii, 288 p. (ill) *ISBN: 0813379105; LofC: 90041303. Includes bibliographical references (p. 177-196) and index.* [Westview special studies on South and Southeast Asia.]
64 The development of an Irish census-based social class scale. Aileen O'Hare; Christopher J. Whelan; Patrick Commins. *Econ. Soc. R.* **22:2** 1:1991 pp. 135 – 156

E.2: Social stratification [Stratification sociale] — Class [Classe]

65 Elites, the rural masses and land in Paraguay — the subordination of the rural masses to the ruling class. J.M.G. Kleinpenning; E.B. Zoomers. *Develop. Cha.* **22:2** 4:1991 pp. 279 – 296

66 In their own interests — race, class, and power in twentieth-century Norfolk, Virginia. Earl Lewis. Berkeley: University of California Press, c1991: xv, 270 p. (ill., maps) *ISBN: 0520066448; LofC: 90042819. Includes bibliographical references (pp. 209-262) and index.*

67 Intergenerational class mobility in postwar Japan. Hiroshi Ishida; John H. Goldthorpe; Robert Erikson. *A.J.S.* **96:4** 1:1991 pp. 954 – 992

68 It's a working man's town — male working-class culture in Northwestern Ontario. Thomas W. Dunk. London: McGill-Queen's University Press, 1991: 191 p. *ISBN: 0773508619; LofC: cn 91090220. Includes bibliographical references and index.*

69 Legal resources of striking miners — notes for a study of class conflict and law. Frank Munger. *Soc. Sci. Hist.* **15:1** Spring:1991 pp. 1 – 34

70 Middle classes, democratization, and class formation — the case of South Korea. Hagen Koo. *Theory Soc.* **20:4** 8:1991 pp. 485 – 509

71 On the usefulness of class analysis in research on social mobility and socioeconomic inequality. Aage B. Sørenson. *Acta Sociol.* **34:2** 1991 pp. 71 – 88

72 The re-making of the English working class? Marc W. Steinberg. *Theory Soc.* **20:2** 4:1991 pp. 173 – 197

73 The reproduction of inequality — occupation, caste and family. André Béteille. *Contr. I. Soc.* **25:1** 1-6:1991 pp. 3 – 28

74 The rise and decline of the English working classes,1918-1990 — a social history. Eric Hopkins. London: Weidenfeld & Nicolson, 1991: 295 p. *ISBN: 0297820753.*

75 Searching for ideal types — the potentialities of latent class analysis. Jacques A. Hagenaars; Loek C. Halman. *Eur. Sociol. R.* **5:1** 5:1989 pp. 81 – 96

76 Shake it and break it — class and politics in Britain, 1979-1989. David Brown; Henri Simon. London: Echanges et Mouvement, 1991: 38 p. *[two texts, comprising Myths of Thatcherism by David Brown and Winter of Discontent by Henri Simon].*

77 Social class and social support — the same or different? Ann Oakley; Lynda Rajan. *Sociology* **25:1** 2:1991 pp. 31 – 59

78 Social class in Singapore. Stella R. Quah; Chiew Seen Kong; Ko Yiu Chung; Sharon Mengchee Lee; et al. Singapore: published by Times Academic Press for the Centre for Advanced Studies, National University of Singapore, 1991: xvii, 286 p. *ISBN: 9812100032; LofC: 92940212. Includes bibliographical references.*

79 Social stratification. Dipankar Gupta *[Ed.]*. New Delhi: Oxford University Press, 1991: 496p. *ISBN: 0195628012.* [Oxford in India readings in sociology and social and cultural anthropology.]

80 Сословно-классовое общество в истории Китая: (Опыт сист.-структур.анализа) *[In Russian]*; [Class society in the history of China — (the experience of system structural analysis)]. V.P. Iliushechkin. Moscow: Nauka, 1986: 396 p. *Bibliogr. pp.377-391.*

81 Trabalhadores no Brasil — imigracão e industrializacão *[In Portuguese]*; [Workers in Brazil — immigration and industrialization]. José Luiz del Roio *[Ed.]*. Sao Paulo: Icone, 1990: 156 p. *ISBN: 8527401479.*

82 View from below — working-class consciousness in Argentina. Peter Ranis. *Lat. Am. Res. R.* **26:2** 1991 pp. 133 – 156

83 Why 50 years? Working-class formation and long economic cycles. Jerry Lembcke. *Sci. Soc.* **55:4** Winter:1991-1992 pp. 417 – 445

84 Wybrane problemy klas a stan badań nad drobnomieszczaństwem współczesnym w Polsce *[In Polish]*; Social problems of classes and state of studies on contemporary middle class in Poland *[Summary]*. Zdziaław Zagórski. *Prz. Soc.* **39** 1991 pp. 311 – 332

E.3: Social change — *Changement social*

1 After the wall — East meets West in the new Berlin. John Borneman. New York, N.Y.: Basic Books, c1991: x, 258 p., 8 p. of plates (ill., maps) *ISBN: 0465000835; LofC: 90055589. Includes bibliographical references (p. 255-258).*
2 A biocultural analysis of revolution. Penny Anthon Green. *J. Soc. Biol. Struct.* **14:4** 1991 pp. 435 – 454
3 The boundaries of humanity — humans, animals, machines. James J. Sheehan *[Ed.]*; Morton Sosna *[Ed.]*. Berkeley: University of California Press, c1991: x, 274 p. (ill) *ISBN: 0520071530; LofC: 90022378. Includes bibliographical references and index.*
4 Bursting the dams — politics and society in the USSR since the coup. George W. Breslauer. *Probl. Commu.* **XL** 11-12:1991 pp. 2 – 12
5 Le cas d'une sociologie aliénée, témoin et acteur d'un changement social global *[In French]*; The case of an alienated sociology as a witness and an agent of macro-social change *[Summary]*. Adam Podgorecki. *Rev. Ét. Comp.* **XXII:1** 3:1991 pp. 123 – 142
6 Change in societal institutions. Maureen T. Hallinan *[Ed.]*; David M. Klein *[Ed.]*; Jennifer Glass *[Ed.]*. New York: Plenum Press, c1990: xv, 277 p. (ill) *ISBN: 0306435411; LofC: 90007464. Includes bibliographical references and index.* [The language of science.]
7 Changes in life-course patterns and behavior of three cohorts of Italian women. Chiara Saraceno. *Signs* **16:3** Spring:1991 pp. 502 – 521
8 De l'égalitarisme à l'enrichissement illégitime — colères et frustrations paysannes en Chine *[In French]*; [From egalitarianism to illegitimate wealth — rural fits and frustrations in China]. Isabelle Thireau. *Soc. Sci. Info.* **30:1** :1991 pp. 5 – 27
9 Development and social change in Sweden. Villy Bergstrom. *CEPAL R.* **:40** 4:1991 pp. 153 – 160
10 Divisions of homeownership — housing tenure and social change. A. Murie. *Envir. Plan.A.* **23:3** 3:1991 pp. 349 – 370
11 Dual dependency and property vacuum — social change on the state socialist semiperiphery. József Böröcz. *Theory Soc.* **21:1** 2:1991 pp. 77 – 104
12 Długookresowe przemiany struktury społecznej (szanse i zagrożenia dla transformacji systemowej) *[In Polish]*; (Долгосрочные перемены социальной структуры (шансы и угрожения для системной трансформации): *Title only in Russian)*; (Long-term changes of social structure (chances and threats for system transformation)). Zdzisława Czyżowska. *Pra. Zab. Społ.* **:11-12** 1991 pp. 1 – 6
13 *[In Japanese]*; [The end of messianism — the fall of socialism]. Tetsuo Sakurai. Tokyo: Chikuma Shobo, [1991]: 231 p.
14 Enfants et patriarches, politique des générations dans la Chine des années 80 *[In French]*; [Children and patriarchs, the politics of generations in China in the 1980s]. Joël Thoraval. *Temps Mod.* **46:534** 1:1991 pp. 97 – 116
15 Evaluation of social development projects. David Marsden *[Contrib.]*; Peter Oakley *[Contrib.]*; David Brown *[Contrib.]*; Laura Vargas Vargas *[Contrib.]*; Norman Uphoff *[Contrib.]*; K. Damodaram *[Contrib.]*; Philip Harding *[Contrib.]*; Kathryn McPhail *[Contrib.]*; Iara Altafin *[Contrib.]*; Hunger Project *and others. Collection of 10 articles.* **Comm. Dev. J.**, 26:4, 10:1991 pp. 257 – 336
16 Fourth world conflicts — communism and rural societies. Janusz Bugajski. Boulder, Colo: Westview Press, 1991: xi, 308 p. *ISBN: 0813380723; LofC: 90042561. Includes bibliographical references (p. 255-293) and index.*
17 From tribe to peasant? The Limbus and Nepalese state. Lionel Caplin. *J. Peasant Stud.* **18:2** 1:1991 pp. 305 – 321
18 Future issues and perspectives in the evaluation of social development. David Marsden; Peter Oakley. *Comm. Dev. J.* **26:4** 10:1991 pp. 315 – 328
19 Gender and sociopolitical change in twentieth-century Latin America. Sandra McGee Deutsch. *Hisp. Am. Hist. Rev.* **71:2** 5:1991 pp. 259 – 305
20 Global social change — a new agenda for social science? David L. Cooperrider; William A. Pasmore. *Human Relat.* **44:10** 10:1991 pp. 1037 – 1056
21 Grundsätze einer kritischen Theorie der Modernisierung *[In German]*; [Foundations of a critical theory of modernization] *[Summary]*. H.C.F. Mansilla. *J. Entwick.pol.* **VII:4** 1991 pp. 31 – 42
22 Hungary at the end of communism — an economic prescription and a political summary — really radical reform — economic citizenship in Hungary. Robin Archer. *Slovo* **4:1** 6:1991 pp. 37 – 46

E.3: Social change [Changement social]

23 Intragenerational stability of postmaterialism in Germany, the Netherlands and the United States. Nan Dirk De Graaf; Jacques Hagenaars; Ruud Luijkx. *Eur. Sociol. R.* **5:2** 9:1989 pp. 183 – 202

24 Jefas de familia. Otro rostro del deterioro *[In Spanish]*; [Family heads. The other face of deterioration]. Nena Delpino. *Nueva Soc.* **:114** 7-8:1991 pp. 50 – 56

25 *[In Japanese]*; ["Johoka" as a driving force of social change]. Youichi Ito. *Keio Communication Review No.(12) - 1991.* pp. 33 – 58

26 Legitimation from the top to civil society — politico-cultural change in Eastern Europe. Giuseppe Di Palma. *World Polit.* **44:1** 10:1991 pp. 49 – 80

27 Liberalization and democratization in the Soviet Union and Eastern Europe. Nancy Bermeo *[Contrib.]*; Timur Kuran *[Contrib.]*; Giuseppe Di Palma *[Contrib.]*; Andrew C. Janos *[Contrib.]*; Russell Bova *[Contrib.]*. Collection of 4 articles. **World Polit.** , *44:1*, 10:1991 pp. 7 – 137

28 Major problems in minor irrigation — social change and tank irrigation in Chitoor district of Andhra Pradesh. Uma Shankari. *Contr. I. Soc.* **25:1** 1-6:1991 pp. 85 – 112

29 Measurement issues in the study of social change. Stanley Presser. *Soc. Forc.* **68:3** 3:1990 pp. 856 – 868

30 Methodological consideration in the evaluation of social development programmes — an alternative approach. David Brown. *Comm. Dev. J.* **26:4** 10:1991 pp. 259 – 265

31 Методологические проблемы социальной революции и общественного прогресса: Межвуз.сб.науч.тр *[In Russian]*; [Methodological problems of social revolution and social progress — inter-college symposium]. Iu.N. Nazarov *[Ed.]*. Vladimir: Vladimir State Pedagogical Institute in the name of Lebedeva-Polianskogo, 1986: 92 p.

32 Мир нашего завтра *[In Russian]*; [The world of our tomorrows]. I.V. Bestuzhev-Lada. Moscow: Mysl', 1986: 269 p.

33 Mortalité et changement social en Espagne (1975-1988) *[In French]*; Mortality and social changes in Spain (1975-1988) *[Summary]*. A. Higueras-Arnal. *Espace Pop. Soc.* **1** 1991 pp. 143 – 150

34 The new social history in the Federal Republic of Germany. Gerhard A. Ritter. London: German Historical Institute, 1991: 102 p. *ISBN: 0951148575. Includes bibliographical references.*

35 О социальных процессах перестройки *[In Russian]*; (Of social processes under perestroika); (Processus sociaux de la perestroïka: *Title only in French*); (Über die sozialen Prozesse der Perestroika: *Title only in German*); (Acerca de los procesos sociales de la reestructuración: *Title only in Spanish*). V. Yadov. *Kommunist* **:6(1376)** 4:1991 pp. 58 – 71

36 Обозримое будущее: Социал. последствия НТР: г.2000 *[In Russian]*; [The surveyable future — social consequences of the scientific and technological revolution — year 2000]. E.A. Arab-Ogly. Moscow: Mysl', 1986: 205 p.

37 Большие перемены на трех континентах *[In Russian]*; [Great changes on three continents]. P.I. Pol'shchikov. Moscow: Mysl', 1987: 175 p. pp.171-175 Bibliogr.

38 The opening of Amish society — cottage industry as Trojan Horse. Marc A. Olshan. *Human. Org.* **50:4** Winter:1991 pp. 378 – 384

39 Oppositionelle Gruppen und alternative Milieus in Leipzig im Prozeß der Umgestaltung in Ostdeutschland *[In German]*; Opposition groups and alternative milieus in Leipzig and the process of change in eastern Germany]. Dieter Rink; Michael Hofmann. *Deut. Arch.* **24:9** 9:1991 pp. 940 – 948

40 Освободившиеся страны к 2000 году *[In Russian]*; [Liberated countries by the year 2000]. A.A. Iskenderov. Moscow: Mezhdunar. otnosheniia, 1986: 69 p. *Bibliogr. p.60.*

41 Pacific Island movement and socioeconomic change — metaphors of misunderstanding. Murray Chapman. *Pop. Dev. Rev.* **17:2** 6:1991 pp. 263 – 292

42 Philanthropy and the dynamics of change in east and southeast Asia. Barnett F. Baron *[Ed.]*. New York, N.Y: East Asian Institute, Columbia University, c1991: iv, 181 p. *ISBN: 0913418056; LofC: 91071259. Includes bibliographical references.* [Occasional papers of the East Asian Institute.]

43 Planning-in-action — an innovative approach to human development. Hunger Project. *Comm. Dev. J.* **26:4** 10:1991 pp. 329 – 336

44 *[In Japanese]*; [Post-materialistic values and new social movements]. Shin'ichi Watanabe. ***Nen. Shak. Ron.*** *No.(4) - 1991.* pp. 69 – 80

45 Powershift — knowledge, wealth and violence in the 21st century. Alvin Toffler. London: Bantam, 1991: 585 p. *ISBN: 0593022424.*

E.3: Social change *[Changement social]*

46 Прнятие развития и актуальные проблемы теории социального прогресса: Межвуз.сб.науч.тр *[In Russian]*; [The concept of development and current problems of the theory of social progress — inter-college symposium]. V.V. Orlov *[Ed.]*. Perma: , 1987: 154 p. E:F32

47 Promises not kept — the betrayal of social change in the Third World. John Isbister. West Hartford, CT, USA: Kumarian Press, c1991: x, 240 p. *ISBN: 0931816637; LofC: 91024458. Includes bibliographical references (p. 228-234) and index.* [Kumarian Press library of management for development.]

48 Qualitative indicators and the project framework. Philip Harding. *Comm. Dev. J.* **26:4** 10:1991 pp. 294 – 305

49 Рабочиай класс и революционные изменения в социальной структуре общества *[In Russian]*; [The working class and revolutionary changes in the social structure of society]. A.K. Sokolov. Moscow: Moscow University Publishers, 1987: 227 p.

50 Recent social trends in the United States — 1960-1990. Theodore Caplow *[Ed.]*. Montréal: McGill-Queen's University Press, 1991: 590 p. *ISBN: 0773508724; LofC: cn 91090103. "Prepared for the International Research Group on the Comparative Charting of Social Change in Advanced Industrial Societies"; Includes bibliographical references and index.*

51 Research on social movements — the state of the art in Western Europe and the USA. Dieter Rucht *[Ed.]*. Frankfurt am Main: Campus Verlag, 1991: 464 p. *ISBN: 3593342987; LofC: 90012777. Includes bibliographical references.*

52 Resource mobilization and political opportunity in the Nicaraguan revolution — the praxis. A.G. Cuzán. *Am. J. Econ. S.* **50:1** 1:1991 pp. 71 – 83

53 *[In Japanese]*; [Restructuring world society — a Japanese road to "world citizenship"]. Kokichi Shoji. *Soc. Econ. Sys. St. No.(10) - 1991.* pp. 23 – 30

54 Rewriting the past — trends in contemporary Romanian historiography. Dennis Deletant. *Ethn. Racial* **14:1** 1:1991 pp. 64 – 86

55 A Sinhala village in a time of trouble — politics and change in rural Sri Lanka. Jonathan Spencer. Delhi: Oxford University Press, 1990: xi, 285 p. (ill.) *ISBN: 0195624955.* [Oxford University south Asian studies series.]

56 Social breakdown. Fred Siegel *[Ed.]*; Irving Howe *[Contrib.]*; Nicolaus Mills *[Contrib.]*; Jim Chapin *[Contrib.]*; Paul Berman *[Contrib.]*; Maxine Phillips *[Contrib.]*; Lenny Glynn *[Contrib.]*; William Kornblum *[Contrib.]*; Robert Kuttner *[Contrib.]*; Cornel West *[Contrib.] and others. Collection of 25 articles.* **Dissent** ,Spring:1991 pp. 165 – 304

57 Social causation and interpretative processes — Herbert Blumer's theory of industrialization and social change. David R. Maines; Thomas J. Morrione. *Int. J. Pol. C. S.* **4:4** Summer:1991 pp. 535 – 548

58 Social change and collective memory — the democratization of George Washington. Barry Schwartz. *Am. Sociol. R.* **56:2** 4:1991 pp. 221 – 236

59 Social change, social welfare and social science. Peter Taylor-Gooby. London: Harvester Wheatsheaf, 1991: 240 p. *ISBN: 0745008690.*

60 *[In Japanese]*; [Social changes in contemporary Japan]. Tsutomu Shiobara *[Ed.]*; et al. Kyoto: Sekai-Shiso-Sha, 1991: 221 p.

61 Social formation and the problem of change. Surendra Munshi. *Sci. Soc.* **55:2** Summer:1991 pp. 175 – 196

62 Social history and historical science. A. Gurevich. *Soc. Sci.* **XXII:4** 1991 pp. 76 – 90

63 Social mobility and growing resistance — a study of social development and ethnic conflicts in India. Satish K. Sharma. *Soc. Act.* **41:1** 1-3:1991 pp. 64 – 77

64 Social movements — a cognitive approach. Ron Eyerman; Andrew Jamison *[Ed.]*. Cambridge: Polity Press in association with Basil Blackwell, 1991: 184 p. *ISBN: 0745607624. Includes bibliography and index.*

65 Social theory for a changing society. Pierre Bourdieu *[Ed.]*; James Samuel Coleman *[Ed.]*. Boulder: Westview Press, 1991: vii, 389 p. *ISBN: 0813311934; LofC: 91012563. Includes bibliographical references.*

66 La société québécoise après trente ans de changements *[In French]*; [Quebecan society following 30 years of change]. Fernand Dumont *[Ed.]*. Québec: Institut québécois de recherche sur la culture, 1991: 358 p. *ISBN: 2892241324.*

67 Society, culture, development. Ramkrishna Mukherjee. New Delhi: Sage Publications, 1991: 265 p. (ill) *ISBN: 0803991029; LofC: 91024457. Includes bibliographical references (p. [252]-263) and index.*

68 Sociologia dello sviluppo e questione meridionale oggi *[In Italian]*; Sociology of development and «southern question» today *[Summary]*. Antonio Mutti. *Rass. It. Soc.* **XXXII:2** 4-6:1991 pp. 155 – 180

E.3: Social change [Changement social]

69 Социальный прогресс и культурное наследие *[In Russian]*; [Social progress and cultural legacy]. N.S. Zlobin *[Ed.]*; E.A. Baller. Moscow: Nauka, 1987: 160 p. Науч.-попул.лит.; [Scientific popular literature].

70 Sotsial'nye revoliutsii i obshchestvennyĭ progress — teoriia, istoriia, sovremennost' *[In Russian]*; [Social revolutions and social progress — theory, history and the contemporary scene]. S.A. Lansov. Leningrad: Izd-vo Leningradskogo universiteta, 1991: 160 p. *ISBN: 5288005540. Includes bibliographical references.*

71 The South moves into its future — studies in the analysis and prediction of social change. Joseph S Himes *[Ed.]*. Tuscaloosa: University of Alabama Press, c1991: xvi, 322 p. (ill) *ISBN: 0817304614; LofC: 90010803. Includes bibliographical references (p. 286-309) and index.*

72 Советский народ — новая интернациональная общность людей *[In Russian]*; [Soviet people — a new international community]. M.P. Kim *[Ed.]*. Kishinev: Shtiintsa, 1987: 279 p. *Bibliogr.*

73 Die soziologische Interpretation der europäischen Revolutionen im Werk Eugen Rosenstock-Huessys *[In German]*; [The sociological interpretation of the European revolutions in Eugen Rosenstock-Huessys' work]. Viktor Beyfuss München: Kyrill-und-Method-Verl., 1991: 242 p. *ISBN: 3927527335.*

74 Stability of prestige hierarchies in the face of social changes — Poland, 1958-1987; *[French summary]*. Zbigniew Sawinski; Henryk Domanski. *Int. Sociol.* **6:2** 6:1991 pp. 227 – 241

75 Las transformaciones agrarias, las luchas y los movimientos campesinos en el Paraguay *[In Spanish]*; [Agrarian transformations, peasant movements and struggles in Paraguay]. Luis A. Galeano. *Rev. Parag. Sociol.* **28:80** 1-4:1991 pp. 39 – 62

76 The uses of history in sociology — reflections on some recent tendencies. John H. Goldthorpe. *Br. J. Soc.* **42:2** 6:1991 pp. 211 – 230

F: Population. Family. Gender. Ethnic group —
Population. Famille. Sexe. Groupe ethnique

F.1: Demography — *Démographie*

1 Afghanistan — demographic consequences of war, 1978-1987. Noor Ahmad Khalidi. *C.Asian Sur.* **10:3** 1991 pp. 101 – 125

2 Ajuste de una función expologística a la evolución de la población total de México, 1930-1985 *[In Spanish]*; Adjustment of an expologistic function to the evolution of Mexico's total population, 1930-1985 *[Summary]*. Manuel Ordorica Mellado. *Est. Demog. Urb.* **5:3** 9-12:1990 pp. 373 – 386

3 Analysis and prediction of the population in Spain — 1910-2000. A. Garcia-Ferrer; J. del Hoyo. *J. Forecast.* **10:4** 7:1991 pp. 347 – 370

4 An analysis of housing careers in Cardiff. R.B. Davies; A.R. Pickles. *Envir. Plan.A.* **23:5** 1991 pp. 629 – 650

5 Analysis of urban-rural population dynamics for China. J. Shen. *Envir. Plan.A.* **23:12** 12:1991 pp. 1797 – 1810

6 Applied demography — an introduction to basic concepts, methods, and data. Steve H. Murdock; David R. Ellis *[Ed.]*. Boulder, Colo: Westview Press, 1991: xx, 299 p. (ill) *ISBN: 0813383722; LofC: 91035208. Includes bibliographical references (p. [275]-287) and index.*

7 Assessing state population projections with transparent multiregional demographic models. A. Rogers; J.A. Woodward. *Pop. Res. Pol. R.* **10:1** 1991 pp. 1 – 26

8 Birthweight and sociobiological factors in Ilorin, Nigeria. Ehigie Ebomoyi; Olalekan O. Adetoro; Ananda R. Wickremasinghe. *J. Biosoc. Sc.* **23:4** 10:1991 pp. 417 – 424

9 The challenge facing population geography. Allan M. Findlay; Elspeth Graham. *Prog. H. Geog.* **15:2** 6:1991 pp. 149 – 162

10 Changes in the demographic behaviour of migrants in Australia and the transition between generations. Christabel M. Young. *Pop. Stud.* **45:1** 3:1991 pp. 67 – 89

11 Consistency of ancestry reporting between parents and children in the 1986 census. Siew-Ean Khoo. *J. Aust. Pop. Ass.* **8:2** 11:1991 pp. 129 – 139

F.1: Demography [Démographie]

12 The continental population structure of Europe. Robert R. Sokal. *Ann. R. Anthr.* **20:** 1991 pp. 119 – 140
13 Демографическая ситуация в СССР в 80-е годы *[In Russian]*; (Demographical situation in the Soviet Union in 1980s). O.D. Zakharova. *Sot. Issle.* **:4** 1991 pp. 43 – 52
14 Demographic analysis — a stochastic approach. N. Krishnan Namboodiri. San Diego: Academic Press, c1991: xii, 370 p. (ill) *ISBN: 012513830x; LofC: 90000742. Includes bibliographical references(p. 321-348) and indexes.*
15 Demographic currents — trends and issues that face the United States, the United Kingdom and Canada. Richard S. Belous; Thomas H.B. Symons *[Foreword]*. London: British-North American Committee, 1991: 46 p. [Occasional paper.]
16 Demographic indices as social indicators. J. Anson. *Envir. Plan.A.* **23:3** 3:1991 pp. 433 – 446
17 The demographic revolution. Jane McLoughlin. London: Faber, 1991: 159 p. *ISBN: 0571161146.*
18 The demography of the Caucasus according to 1989 Soviet census data. Paul B. Henze. *C.Asian Sur.* **10:1/2** 1991 pp. 147 – 170
19 Early modern population theory — a reassessment. Philip Kreager. *Pop. Dev. Rev.* **17:2** 6:1991 pp. 207 – 228
20 Elusive cycles — are there dynamically possible Lee-Easterlin models for U.S. births? K.W. Wachter. *Pop. Stud.* **45:1** 3:1991 pp. 109 – 135
21 The European demographic crisis — rhetoric versus reality. A. Rajan. *Inter. R. Strat. Manag.* **2:2** 1991 pp. 15 – 40
22 European population. Jean-Louis Rallu *[Ed.]*; Alain Blum *[Ed.]*. London: John Libbey and Company Ltd., 1991: 450 p. *ISBN: 0861963369. Published for the European Population Conference, Paris - October 21-25, 1991; Sponsored by the European Association for Population Studies.* [Congresses & colloquia. : No. 8]
23 Evaluating small-area population projections. Steve H. Murdock; Rita R. Hamm; Paul R. Voss; Darrell Fannin; Beverly Pecotte. *J. Am. Plann.* **57:4** Autumn:1991 pp. 432 – 443
24 Evaluation of procedures for improving population estimates for small areas. Kirk M. Wolter; Beverley D. Causey. *J. Am. Stat. Ass.* **86:414** 6:1991 pp. 278 – 284
25 An evolutionary perspective on the patterning of maternal investment in pregnancy. Nadine Peacock. *Hum. Nature* **2:4** 1991 pp. 351 – 386
26 The first universal nation — leading indicators and ideas about the surge of America in the 1990s. Ben J. Wattenberg. New York: Free Press, c1991: xiv, 418 p. (ill) *ISBN: 0029340012; LofC: 90003803. "Notes to indicators " — p. 390-391; Includes index.*
27 Future demographic trends in Europe and North America — what can we assume today? Wolfgang Lutz *[Ed.]*. London: Academic Press, 1991: 585 p. *ISBN: 0124604455.* [Studies in population.]
28 The gender stratification of income inequality among lawyers. John Hagan. *Soc. Forc.* **68:3** 3:1990 pp. 835 – 855
29 Household modelling and forecasting — dynamic approaches with use of linked census data. M. Murphy. *Envir. Plan.A.* **23:6** 6:1991 pp. 885 – 902
30 The impact of forecasting methodology on the accuracy of national population forecasts — evidence from the Netherlands and Czechoslovakia. N. Keilman; T. Kučera. *J. Forecast.* **10:4** 7:1991 pp. 371 – 398
31 Infectious disease and the demography of the Atlantic peoples. Alfred W. Crosby. *J. World. Hist.* **2:2** Fall:1991 pp. 119 – 134
32 Konzepte, Theorien und empirische Ergebnisse zur Eingliederung von Ausländern. Ein Bericht zur Literatur *[In German]*; Concepts, theories and empirical results regarding the integration of foreigners. A reply on the literature *[Summary]*. Christel Bals. *Inf. Raum.* **:7/8** 1991 pp. 513 – 522
33 Land, fertility, and the population establishment. Neil Thomas. *Pop. Stud. Egy.* **45:3** 11:1991 pp. 379 – 398
34 Life in black America. James S. Jackson *[Ed.]*. Newbury Park, Calif: Sage, c1991: xi, 311 p. (ill) *ISBN: 0803935374; LofC: 91006934. Includes bibliographical references (p. 274-295) and indexes.*
35 Locality studies and the household. L.D. Morris. *Envir. Plan.A.* **23:2** 2:1991 pp. 165 – 177
36 Mainland China's fourth census — a preliminary analysis. Fang Shan. *Iss. Stud.* **27:3** 3:1991 pp. 116 – 127
37 Méthodes de cartographie statistique des populations *[In French]*; (Methods of statistical population mapping). J. Désiré *[Contrib.]*; G. Palsky *[Contrib.]*; J.C. Muller *[Contrib.]*; C.

F.1: Demography *[Démographie]*

Cauvin *[Contrib.]*; H. Reymond *[Contrib.]*; C. Enaux *[Contrib.]*; P. Waniez *[Contrib.]*; Hu Yuju *[Contrib.]*; H. Rentao *[Contrib.]*; F. Lifan *[Contrib.]* *and others*. Collection of 11 articles. **Espace Pop. Soc.** , :*3*, 1991 pp. 445 – 538

38 Un método para proyectar la población según tamaño de la localidad. (Aplicación al caso de la población urbana de México en 1990) *[In Spanish]*; One method for projecting the population according to the size of the locality (application to the case of Mexico's urban population in 1990) *[Summary]*. Virgilio Partida Bush. *Est. Demog. Urb.* **5**:3 9-12:1990 pp. 387 – 412

39 The missing girls of China — a new demographic account; Les filles disparues en Chine — un nouveau compte rendu démographique *[French summary]*; Las niñas de China que faltan — una consideración demográfica nueva *[Spanish summary]*. Sten Johansson; Ola Nygren. *Pop. Dev. Rev.* **17**:1 3:1991 pp. 35 – 51

40 The nature of nurture — genetic influence on "environmental" measures. R. Plomin; C.S. Bergeman. *Behav. Brain Sci.* **14**:3 9:1991 pp. 373 – 414

41 Обострение национальных отношений в СССР (размышления по поводу предварительных итогов переписи населения 1989 г.) *[In Russian]*; (Aggravation of cross-national relations in the USSR. (Reflections over preliminary results of 1989 All-Union population census)). M.N. Rutkevich. *Sot. Issle.* **:1** 1991 pp. 27 – 39

42 Occupational endogeneity and gender wage differentials for young workers — an empirical analysis using Irish data. Barry Reilly. *Econ. Soc. R.* **21**:3 4:1990 pp. 311 – 328

43 On the demography of South Asian famines, part I. Tim Dyson. *Pop. Stud.* **45**:1 3:1991 pp. 5 – 25

44 Overpopulation and poverty in Africa. Bernard I. Logan. *J. Econ. Soc. Geogr.* **82**:1 1991 pp. 40 – 57

45 People and food. Anne H. Ehrlich. *Popul. Envir.* **12**:3 Spring:1991 pp. 221 – 229

46 Population and development in the central American isthmus. Andras Uthoff. *CEPAL R.* **:40** 4:1991 pp. 133 – 151

47 Population and the energy problem. John P. Holdren. *Popul. Envir.* **12**:3 Spring:1991 pp. 231 – 255

48 Population change in Canada — the challenges of policy adaptation. Roderic P. Beaujot. Toronto: McClelland & Stewart, 1991: 379 p. (ill) *ISBN: 077101158x; LofC: cn 91093728. Includes indexes; Includes bibliographical references — p. 324-366.*

49 Population change in Iran, 1966-86 — a stalled demographic transition? Akbar Aghajanian. *Pop. Dev. Rev.* **17**:4 12:1991 pp. 703 – 716

50 Population changes in Europe — demographic and social prospects and problems. Antonio Golini; Bruno Cantalini; Agostino Lori. *Labour [Italy]* **5**:2 Autumn:1991 pp. 3 – 36

51 Population research in Britain. Michael Murphy *[Ed.]*; John Hobcraft *[Ed.]*. London: Population Investigation Committee at the London School of Economics, 1991: 206 p. *ISBN: 090580404x.* [Population studies. : Vol. 45]

52 Population research in the Netherlands during the eighties — an overview. Nico van Nimwegen. *Bevolk. Gez.* **:1** 1991 pp. 123 – 131

53 Les populations du Brésil *[In French]*; Populations in Brazil. H. Théry; P. Waniez. *Espace Pop. Soc.* **:2** 1991 pp. 409 – 421

54 Pourquoi un déficit de plus de cent millions de femmes? *[In French]*; [Why is there a deficit of more than a hundred million women?]. Amartya Sen. *Esprit* **:174** 9:1991 pp. 42 – 53

55 Public policy and aboriginal population mobility — insights from the Katherine region, Northern Territory. J. Taylor. *Aust. Geogr.* **20**:1 5:1989 pp. 46 – 52

56 Race of parents and infant birthweight in the United States. William D. Mangold; Eve Powell-Griner. *Soc. Biol.* **38**:1-2 Spring-Summer:1991 pp. 13 – 27

57 Réflexions sur la conjoncture *[In French]*; Some reflections on the study of demographic situations ("conjonctural demography"). Louis Henry. *Population* **46**:6 11-12:1991 pp. 1577 – 1588

58 Researching the household — methodological and empirical issues. Naila Kabeer *[Ed.]*; Susan Joekes *[Ed.]*; Lawrence Haddad *[Contrib.]*; Simon Appleton *[Contrib.]*; Caroline Moser *[Contrib.]*; Peter Sollis *[Contrib.]*; Gail Wilson *[Contrib.]*; Sue Fleming *[Contrib.]*; Melissa Leach *[Contrib.]*; Alison Evans *[Contrib.]* *and others*. Collection of 8 articles. **IDS Bull.** , *22:1*, 1:1991 pp. 1 – 66

59 Seasonality of births in human populations. David A. Lam; Jeffrey A. Miron. *Soc. Biol.* **38**:1-2 Spring-Summer:1991 pp. 51 – 78

F.1: Demography *[Démographie]*

60 Secular trends in human sex ratios — their influence on individual and family behavior. Frank A. Pedersen. *Hum. Nature* **2**:3 1991 pp. 271 – 291

61 Showing off — tests of an hypothesis about men's foraging goals. Kirsten Hawkes. *Ethol. Socio.* **12**:1 1991 pp. 29 – 54

62 Socio-demografska struktura i dinamika regija Hrvatske *[In Serbo-Croatian]*; Социо-демографическая структура и динамизм регий Хорватии *[Russian summary]*; Socio-demographic structure and dynamics of regions in Croatia *[Summary]*. Maria Oliviera-Roca; et al. *Ekon. Preg.* **42**:1-2 1991 pp. 17 – 45

63 A structural approach to the form of the population density function. Oscar Fisch. *Geogr. Anal.* **23**:3 8:1991 pp. 261 – 275

64 Towards a regional geography of gender. Janet G. Townsend. *Geogr. J.* **157**:1 3:1991 pp. 25 – 35

65 Tracking the baby boom, the baby bust, and the echo generations — how age composition regulates US migration. David A. Plane; Peter A. Rogerson. *Prof. Geogr.* **43**:4 11:1991 pp. 416 – 430

66 Transition démographique et système coutumier dans les Pyrénées Occidentales *[In French]*; [Demographic transition and the usual system in the western Pyrenees]. André Etchelecou. Paris: PUF, 1991: 260 p. *ISBN: 2733201298. Bibliography — p227-249.* [Travaux et documents.]

67 Two-sex demographic models. Robert A. Pollak. *J. Polit. Ec.* **98**:2 4:1990 pp. 399 – 420

68 Le vieillissement de la population sera plus important que prévu *[In French]*; The population will age more than anticipated *[Summary]*; El envejecimiento de la población será más importante de lo que se ha previsto *[Spanish summary]*. Quang Chi Dinh. *E & S* **:243** 5:1991 pp. 53 – 60

69 What population studies can do for business. Graham Hugo. *J. Aust. Pop. Ass.* **8**:1 5:1991 pp. 1 – 22

70 World and United States population prospects. Carl Haub. *Popul. Envir.* **12**:3 Spring:1991 pp. 297 – 310

71 Zaïre — un aperçu démographique — résultats du recensement scientifique *[In French]*; [Zaire — a demographic survey — results of the scientific survey]. Document INS; PNUD. *Za-Afr.* **31**:255 5:1991 pp. 227 – 262

F.2: Age groups — *Groupes d'âges*

Sub-divisions: Ageing *[Vieillissement]*; Childhood *[Enfance]*; Youth *[Jeunesse]*

1 The changing age distribution in Indonesia and some consequences. Charles B. Nam; Gouranga Lal Dasvarma; Sri Pamoedjo Rahardjo. *B. Ind. Econ. St.* **27**:1 4:1991 pp. 121 – 136

2 Development change in speed of processing during childhood and adolescence. Robert Kail. *Psychol .B.* **109**:3 5:1991 pp. 490 – 501

3 Developmental disabilities and poverty. Travis Thompson *[Contrib.]*; Norman Garmezy *[Contrib.]*; James J. Gallagher *[Contrib.]*; Judith J. Carta *[Contrib.]*; Susan C. Hupp *[Contrib.]*; Alfred A. Baumeister *[Contrib.]*; Frank D. Kupstas *[Contrib.]*; Luann M. Klindworth *[Contrib.]*. *Collection of 6 articles.* **Am. Behav. Sc.** , *34:4, 3/4:1991* pp. 414 – 500

4 Factional conflict through generations. E.H. Mantell. *Am. J. Econ. S.* **50**:4 10:1991 pp. 407 – 420

5 The formation of religious attitudes and world views; *[French summary]*. Helena Helve. *Soc. Compass* **38(4)** 1991 pp. 373 – 392

6 Generaties en hun cohorten *[In Dutch]*; [Generations and their cohorts]. Henk A. Becker *[Contrib.]*; Leo B. van Snippenburg *[Contrib.]*; A. Benine van Berkel-van Schaik *[Contrib.]*; R.J.T. van Rijsselt *[Contrib.]*; P.L.J. Hermkens *[Contrib.]*; Rolf Becker *[Contrib.]*; Hans-Peter Blossfeld *[Contrib.]*. *Collection of 5 articles.* **Sociol. Gids** , *XXXVIII:4*, 7-8:1991 pp. 210 – 283

7 Generations in conflict. Paul Waller *[Contrib.]*; Victor R. Fuchs *[Contrib.]*; Barbara L. Wolfe *[Contrib.]*; Daniel Callahan *[Contrib.]*; Karl Hinrichs *[Contrib.]*; Eric R. Kingson *[Contrib.]*; John B. Williamson *[Contrib.]*. *Collection of 6 articles.* **Society** , *28:6*, 9/10:1991 pp. 6 – 41

F.2: Age groups [Groupes d'âges]

8 Inter-generational relations — conflict or consensus in the 21st century. Chris Phillipson. *Policy Pol.* **19:1** 1:1991 pp. 27 – 36
9 Intergenerational transmission of violence. Pamela C. Alexander; Sharon Moore; Elmore R. Alexander. *J. Marriage Fam.* **53:3** 8:1991 pp. 657 – 668
10 Inventory of longitudinal studies in the social sciences. Copeland H. Young; Kristen L. Savola [Ed.]; Erin Phelps [Ed.]. Newbury Park, Calif: Sage Publications, c1991: viii, 567 p. *ISBN: 0803943156; LofC: 91011195. Includes bibliographical references (p. 543-551) and indexes.*
11 Long-term projections of the AIDS epidemic. Thomas R. Sexton; Jennifer Feinstein. *Interfaces* **21:3** 5-6:1991 pp. 64 – 79
12 Measuring age as a structural concept. Ronald S. Burt. *Soc. Networks* **13:1** 3:1991 pp. 1 – 34
13 Models of intergenerational relations in mid-life. Joan Aldous; David Klein. *J. Marriage Fam.* **53:3** 8:1991 pp. 595 – 608
14 The nature of a person-stage. Peter K. McInerney. *Am. Phil. Q.* **28:3** 7:1991 pp. 227 – 236
15 Predicting the everyday life events of older adults. Alex J. Zautra; John F. Finch; John W. Reich; Charles A. Guarnaccia. *J. Personal.* **59:3** 9:1991 pp. 507 – 538
16 Prognosis after AIDS — a severity index based on experts' judgments. Farrokh Alemi; Barbara Turner; Leona Markson; Richard Szorady; Tom McCarron. *Interfaces* **21:3** 5-6:1991 pp. 105 – 116
17 Social research on children and adolescents — ethical issues. Barbara Stanley [Ed.]; Joan E. Sieber [Ed.]. Newbury Park, Calif: Sage Publications, c1991: 205 p. *ISBN: 0803943334; LofC: 91013620. "The work of a task force on research on minors that was organized by the Office for Protection from Research Risk of the National Institutes of Health"--Ch. 1; Includes bibliographical references and indexes.* [Sage focus editions.]
18 Социология девиантного поведения как специальная социологическая теория *[In Russian]*; (Sociology of deviant behaviour as a special sociological theory). Ya.I. Gilinskiy. *Sot. Issle.* **:4** 1991 pp. 72 – 78
19 South Asian Muslims in Hong Kong — creation of a "local boy" identity. Anita M. Weiss. *Mod. Asian S.* **25:3** 8:1991 pp. 417 – 454
20 Subiektywna przestrzeń społeczna młodego i starszego pokolenia (z badań nad systemem identyfikacji społecznej) *[In Polish]*; Subjective social space of young and old generations (from the research on system of social identification) *[Summary]*. Anita Wojciechowska-Miszalska. *Acta Univ. Łódz. Folia Soc.* **21** 1991 pp. 33 – 56
21 *[In Japanese]*; [Toward a change of conceptions — mass employment and promotion of middle and old age]. Yasuaki Muto. Tokyo: Chukei Shuppan, 1991: 205 p.
22 Use of a log-linear model to compute the empirical survival curve from interval-censored data, with application to data on tests for HIV positivity. Niels G. Becker; Mads Melbye. *Aust. J. Statist.* **33:2** 8:1991 pp. 125 – 134

Ageing [Vieillissement]

23 The activities of the elderly in rural Bangladesh. Mead T. Cain. *Pop. Stud. Egy.* **45:2** 7:1991 pp. 189 – 202
24 Ageing and economic performance. Paul Johnson. London: London School of Economics and Political science, 1991: 26 p. [Discussion paper.]
25 Ageing and urbanization — proceedings of the United Nations International Conference on Ageing Populations in the Context of Urbanization, Sendai (Japan), 12-16 September 1988. United Nations. Department of International Economic and Social Affairs. New York: United Nations, 1991: viii, 461 p. (ill) *ISBN: 9211512336. "ST/ESA/SER.R/109."; "United Nations publication sales no. E.91.XIII.12."; Includes bibliographical references.*
26 Ageing populations in the north and south of Europe. John A. Vincent; Zeljka Mudrovcic. *Int. J. Comp. Soc* **32:3-4** 9-12:1991 pp. 261 – 288
27 Aging and attitude change. Tom R. Tyler; Regina A. Schuller. *J. Pers. Soc. Psychol.* **61:5** 11:1991 pp. 689 – 697
28 *[In Japanese]*; [Aging and death among family members]. Hiroko Takahashi. *Japanese Journal of Geriatric Psychiatry No.2(8) - 1991.* pp. 961 – 971
29 Aging and ethics — philosophical problems in gerontology. Nancy Ann Silbergeld Jecker [Ed.]. Clifton, N.J: Humana Press, c1991: xi, 394 p. *ISBN: 0896032019; LofC: 91010792. Includes bibliographical references and indexes.* [Contemporary issues in biomedicine, ethics, and society.]
30 Aging in rural Canada. Norah Christine Keating. Toronto: Butterworths, 1991: 139 p. *ISBN: 0409888559; LofC: cn 91094097. Includes bibliographical references and index.* [Butterworths perspectives on individual and population aging.]

INTERNATIONAL BIBLIOGRAPHY OF SOCIOLOGY — 1991

F.2: Age groups *[Groupes d'âges]* — *Ageing [Vieillissement]*

31 *[In Japanese]*; [Aging society and gender]. Shihomi Amaki. ***Hyoron Shakaigaku, Doshisha University*** *No.(43) - 1991.* pp. 36 – 55
32 *[In Japanese]*; [Aging society and the middle-aged worker in Japanese business organization]. Masahide Maki. ***Kwansei Gakuin Sociology Department Studies*** *No.(63) - 1991.* pp. 413 – 429
33 Aging, cohorts, and the stability of sociopolitical orientations over the life span. Duane F. Alwin; Jon A. Krosnick. *A.J.S.* **97:1** 7:1991 pp. 169 – 194
34 Ältere Menschen und räumliche Forschung *[In German]*; [Elderly people and spatial studies]. Hansjörg Bucher *[Contrib.]*; Martina Kocks *[Contrib.]*; Gerhard Stiens *[Contrib.]*; Helmut Janich *[Contrib.]*; Uwe-Jens Walther *[Contrib.]*; Andrea Gaube *[Contrib.]*; Bernd Breuer *[Contrib.]*; Manfred Fuhrich *[Contrib.]*; Christel Bals *[Contrib.]*; Ingolf Heiland *[Contrib.] and others. Collection of 10 articles.* **Inf. Raum.**, :3/4, 1991 pp. 111 – 252
35 Australia's ageing population — policy options. Christabel Young. Canberra, ACT: Australian Government Publishing Service, 1990: 94 p. (ill) *ISBN: 0644128976.* Includes bibliographical references (p. 83-89) and index.
36 Centenarians, the new generation. Nera K. Wilson *[Ed.]*; Albert J. E. Wilson *[Ed.]*. New York: Greenwood Press, 1991: xxi, 281 p. *ISBN: 0313274797; LofC: 90040899. Ageing;* Includes bibliographical references (p. [271]-278) and index. [Contributions to the study of aging.]
37 *[In Japanese]*; [Comparative study of environment impact assessment and aging society impact assessment]. Kiyoshi Adachi. ***Annual Report of the Social Work Research Institute*** *No.(26) - 1991.* pp. 99 – 127
38 La composition des ménages des personnes âgées en Italie (1981) *[In French]*; Household composition of the elderly in Italy (1981) *[Summary]*. F. Bartiaux. *Eur. J. Pop.* **7:1** 4:1991 pp. 59 – 98
39 Critical perspectives on aging — the political and moral economy of growing old. Meredith Minkler *[Ed.]*; Carroll Lynn Estes *[Ed.]*. Amityville: Baywood Publ., 1991: 362 p. *ISBN: 0895030764.* [Policy, politics, health and medicine series.]
40 Customary physical activity — psychological well-being and successful ageing. Kevin Morgan; Helen Dallosso; E. Joan Bassey; Shah Ebrahim; P.H. Fentem; T.H.D. Arie. *Age. Soc.* **11:4** 12:1991 pp. 399 – 415
41 Den svenska äldreomsorgen — om ideologi och ekonomi *[In Swedish]*; [Care of the elderly in Sweden — on ideology and economy]. Per Gunnar Edebalk; Jan Petersson. *Ekon. Deb.* **7** 1987 pp. 566 – 572
42 The dynamics of population aging — demography and policy analysis. Kenneth G. Manton. *Milbank Q.* **69:2** 1991 pp. 309 – 338
43 Economics of population aging — the "graying" of Australia, Japan, and the United States. James H. Schulz; Allan Borowski *[Ed.]*; William H. Crown *[Ed.]*. New York: Auburn House, 1991: xiv, 364 p. (graphs) *ISBN: 0865690081; LofC: 90000437.* Includes bibliographical references (p. [349]-354) and index.
44 Generation sets — stability and change with special reference to Toposa and Turkana societies. Harald K. Müller-Dempf. *B. Sch. Orient. Afr. Stud.* **LIV:3** 1991 p. 554
45 Generativity in cultural context — the self, death and immortality as experienced by older American women. Baine B. Alexander; Robert L. Rubinstein; Marcene Goodman; Mark Luborsky. *Age. Soc.* **11:4** 12:1991 pp. 417 – 442
46 Health care provision and distributive justice — end stage renal disease and the elderly in Britain and America. Derek G. Gill; Stanley R. Ingman; James Campbell. *Soc. Sci. Med.* **32:5** 1991 pp. 565 – 577
47 How the death of a spouse affects economic well-being after retirement — a hazard model approach. Richard V. Burkhauser; J.S. Butler; Karen C. Holden. *Soc. Sci. Q.* **72:3** 9:1991 pp. 504 – 519
48 *[In Japanese]*; [Instrumental activities of daily living among elderly community residents — social functional disability and associated factors]. Wataru Koyano. ***Social Gerontology*** *No.(33) - 1991.* pp. 68 – 76
49 The invisibility of age — gender and class in later life. Sara Arber; Jay Ginn. *Sociol. Rev.* **39:2** 5:1991 pp. 260 – 291
50 Life after work — the arrival of the ageless society. Michael Young; Tom Schuller. London: HarperCollins, 1991: x,198p. *ISBN: 0002159295. Bibliography — p190-192. - Includes index.*
51 Living dangerously — risk-taking, safety and older people. Deirdre Wynne-Harley. London: Centre for Policy on Ageing, 1991: 54 p. *ISBN: 0904139794.* Includes bibliographical references. [CPA reports. : No. 16]

F.2: Age groups [Groupes d'âges] — Ageing [Vieillissement]

52 Loneliness — its effects on older persons in congregate housing. Larry C. Mullins. *Social Soc. Res.* **75:3** 4:1991 p. 170

53 Ludzie starzy w Łodzi *[In Polish]*; Elderly people in Lodz. B. Nowakowska *[Contrib.]*; W. Obraniak *[Contrib.]*; St. Bartczak *[Contrib.]*; Z. Zarzycka *[Contrib.]*; K. Nowak-Sapota *[Contrib.]*; A. Sztaudynger-Kaliszewicz *[Contrib.]*. Collection of 9 articles. **Acta Univ. Łódz.**, *108*, 1991 pp. 9 – 265

54 La maturescence — période critique d'âge entre 40-65 ans. Santé, maladie, vieillissement et âges sociaux *[In French]*; [Maturescence — a critical phase between ages 40 and 65, and its effects on health and ageing] *[Summary]*. Maryvonne Gognalons-Nicolet; Anne Bardet Blochet. *San. Ment. Qué* **XVI:1** 6:1991 pp. 191 – 212

55 Older women in the post-Reagan era. Terry Arendell; Carroll L. Estes. *Int. J. Health. Ser.* **21:1** 1991 pp. 59 – 73

56 *[In Japanese]*; [On public policies for the elderly in Japanese communities]. Haruro Sagaza. *Aging No.9(1) - 1991.* pp. 9 – 10

57 Az öregedés elemzése a nyers népmozgalmi arányszámok és a népmozgalmi eseményeket átélők átlagos életkorának függvényében *[In Hungarian]*; (The analysis of ageing considering vital rates and the mean age of individuals producing vital events). Valkovics Emil. *Demográfia* **34:3-4** 1991 pp. 432 – 460

58 Patterns of aging in Thailand and Côte d'Ivoire. Angus Deaton; Christina H. Paxson *[Ed.]*. Washington, D.C: World Bank, c1991: viii, 46 p. (ill) *ISBN: 0821318659; LofC: 91024154. Includes bibliographical references (p. 45-46).* [LSMS working paper.]

59 Quand la continuité nous est contée. Santé mentale et symbolisation de la règle de filiation chez les personnes âgées *[In French]*; The story of continuity — mental health and symbolization of the rule of filiality with elderly *[Summary]*. Louise Tassé. *San. Ment. Qué* **XVI:2** Automne:1991 pp. 41 – 66

60 Remarkable survivors — insights into successful aging among women. Alice Taylor Day. Washington, D.C: Urban Institute Press, c1991: xxv, 314 p. (ill) *ISBN: 0877664927; LofC: 90026598. Includes bibliographical references (p. [299]-311).*

61 Rethinking worklife options for older persons. Jack Habib *[Ed.]*; Charlotte Nusberg *[Ed.]*. Jerusalem, Israel: JDC-Brookdale Institute of Gerontology and Adult Human Development in Israel, c1990: ix, 268 p. (ill) *ISBN: 9653530062.* "Based primarily on papers that were presented at the XIV Congress of the International Association of Gerontology in Acapulco, Mexico in June 1989"--Introd; Includes bibliographical references.

62 The role of kinship in aging Chinese society. L. Rabušic. *Arch. Orient.* **59:1** 1991 pp. 26 – 32

63 *[In Japanese]*; [Social participation of aging in Okitama Yamagata Prefecture]. Hiromi Fujii. **Bulletin of Yamagata Prefecture Aging Social Laboratory** *No.10(4) - 1991.* pp.65-86.

64 The spatial isolation of elderly single-room-occupancy hotel tenants. Paul A. Rollinson. *Prof. Geogr.* **43:4** 11:1991 pp. 456 – 464

65 *[In Japanese]*; [A theory of a quality of life, positive research of raising quality and continuing goal of life for the aged]. Sachiko Kikuchi. **Journal of Well-being Society** *No.(8) - 1991.* pp. 1 – 8

66 Transitions in home experience in later life. Andrew J. Sixsmith; Judith A. Sixsmith. *J. Arch. Plan. Res.* **8:3** Autumn:1991 pp. 181 – 191

67 Vieillesse et représentations, effets du sexe et du niveau socioculturel *[In French]*; Old age and representation — effects of sex and sociocultural level *[Summary]*. F. Neto; F. Raveau; J. Chiche. *Cah. Anthr. Bio. Hum.* **VVI:3-4** 1989 pp. 209 – 228

Childhood [Enfance]

68 Abuse and neglect in nonparental child care. Leslie Margolin. *J. Marriage Fam.* **53:3** 8:1991 pp. 694 – 703

69 Adults' perceptions of children's videotaped truthful and deceptive statements. Helen L. Westcott; Graham M. Davies; Brian R. Clifford. *Child. Soc.* **5:2** Summer:1991 pp. 123 – 135

70 Adults' responses to infants varying in appearance of age and attractiveness. Jean M. Ritter; Rita J. Casey; Judith H. Langlois. *Child. Devel.* **62:1** 2:1991 pp. 68 – 82

71 Attachment across the life cycle. Colin Murray Parkes *[Ed.]*; Peter Marris *[Ed.]*; Joan Stevenson-Hinde *[Ed.]*. London: Routledge, 1991: 307 p. (ill) *ISBN: 0415056500. Includes bibliography and index.*

72 Baby observation — emotional relationships during the first year of life. Manuel Pérez-Sanchez. Scotland: Clunie, 1990: 219 p. *ISBN: 0902965263.*

F.2: Age groups *[Groupes d'âges]* — *Childhood [Enfance]*

73 Birthparent romances and identity formation in adopted children. Elinor B. Rosenberg; Thomas A. Horner. *Am. J. Orthopsy.* **61:1** 1:1991 pp. 70 – 77
74 Bullying — the child's view. J. S. la Fontaine. London: Calouste Gulbenkian Foundation, 1991: 35 p. *ISBN: 0903319586.*
75 Child welfare within law — the emergence of a hybrid discourse. Michael King. *J. Law Soc.* **18:3** Autumn:1991 pp. 303 – 322
76 Childhood antecedents of conventional social accomplishment in midlife adults — a 36-year prospective study. Carol E. Franz; David C. McClelland; Joel Weinberger. *J. Pers. Soc. Psychol.* **60:4** 4:1991 pp. 586 – 595
77 Children and young people as abusers — an agenda for action. Arnon Bentovim; Eileen Vizard *[Ed.]*; Anne Hollows *[Ed.]*; Helen Armstrong *[Ed.]*. London: National Children's Bureau, 1991: 97 p. *ISBN: 0902817566.*
78 Children in bondage — slaves of the subcontinent. Hope Hay Hewison *[Ed.]*. London: Anti-Slavery International, 1991: - *ISBN: 0900918276.* [Child labour series. : No. 10]
79 Children of alcoholics — a critical appraisal of theory and research. Kenneth J. Sher. Chicago: University of Chicago Press, 1991: x, 226 p. *ISBN: 0226752712; LofC: 91002414. Includes bibliographical references (p. 176-210) and indexes.* [The John D. and Catherine T. MacArthur Foundation series on mental health and development.]
80 Children of the cities. Jo Boyden; Pat Holden *[Ed.]*. London: Zed, 1991: 152 p. *ISBN: 0862329566. Includes bibliography and index.*
81 Children on trial? Psychology, videotechnology and the law. Graham Davies. *Howard J. Crim. Just.* **30:3** 8:1991 pp. 177 – 191
82 The child's voice. Peter M. Smith. *Child. Soc.* **5:1** Spring:1991 pp. 58 – 66
83 A comparative study of successful and disrupted adoptions. Susan Livingston Smith; Jeanne A. Howard. *Soc. Ser. R.* **65:2** 06:1991 pp. 248 – 265
84 Corporal punishment and psychological adjustment of children in the West Indies. Ronald P. Rohner; Kevin J. Kean; David E. Cournoyer. *J. Marriage Fam.* **53:3** 8:1991 pp. 681 – 693
85 Demographic models for child survival and implications for health intervention programmes. W. Henry Mosley; Stan Becker. *Health Pol. Plan.* **6:3** 9:1991 pp. 218 – 233
86 Determinants of the nutrition and health status of preschool children — an analysis with longitudinal data. Benjamin Senauer; Marito Garcia. *Econ. Dev. Cult. Change* **39:2** 1:1991 pp. 371 – 389
87 Developmental effects of infant care — the mediating role of gender and health. Frank L. Mott. *J. Soc. Issues* **47:2** 1991 pp. 139 – 158
88 Dimensions of childhood — essays on the history of children and youth in Canada. Russell Charles Smandych *[Ed.]*; Gordon Dodds *[Ed.]*; Alvin A. J. Esau *[Ed.]*. Winnipeg: Legal Research Institute of the University of Manitoba, 1991: 287 p. *ISBN: 0921242220; LofC: cn 91097152.*
89 Early and extensive maternal employment and young children's socioemotional development — children of the National Longitudinal Survey of Youth. Jay Belsky; David Eggebeen. *J. Marriage Fam.* **53:4** 11:1991 pp. 1083 – 1098
90 L'enfance en danger. 1. Les professionnels *[In French]*; [Children in danger. 1. The professionals]. Pierre Grelley *[Contrib.]*; Jacqueline Rubellin-Devichi *[Contrib.]*; Hervé Hamon *[Contrib.]*; Michel Allaix *[Contrib.]*; Dominique Barthe *[Contrib.]*; Patrick Tillie *[Contrib.]*; Claire Batton *[Contrib.]*; Frédérique Gruyer *[Contrib.]*; Pierre Bourreau *[Contrib.]*; Françoise Corvazier *[Contrib.] and others. Collection of 14 articles.* **Inf. Soc.**, *1*, 1-2:1990 pp. 2 – 83
91 Estimating the implicit value of a young child's life. Paul S. Carlin; Robert Sandy. *S. Econ. J.* **58:1** 7:1991 pp. 186 – 202
92 From property to person status — historical perspective on children's rights. Stuart N. Hart. *Am. Psychol.* **46:1** 1:1991 pp. 53 – 59
93 A home is not a school — the effects of child care on children's development. K. Alison Clarke-Stewart. *J. Soc. Issues* **47:2** 1991 pp. 205 – 123
94 Infanzia abbandonata di Calcutta (seguito) *[In Italian]*; [The deserted children of Calcutta (continuation)]. Vincenzo Del Corso. *Aff. Soc. Int.* **XIX:1** 1991 pp. 153 – 159
95 Kashmiri carpet children — exploited village weavers. Peter Cross. London: Anti-Slavery International, 1991: 32 p. *ISBN: 0900918187.*
96 The landscapes of childhood — the reflection of childhood's environment in adult memories and in children's attitudes. Rachel Sebba. *Envir. Behav.* **23:4** 7:1991 pp. 395 – 421
97 Learning to act — the Children Act 1989. Gillian Loughran. *Child. Soc.* **5:1** Spring:1991 pp. 11 – 20

F.2: Age groups *[Groupes d'âges]* — Childhood *[Enfance]*

98 Maintaining the links in adoption. John Triseliotis. *Br. J. Soc. W.* **21:4** 8:1991 pp. 401 – 414

99 Maltreated children's self-concept — effects of a comprehensive treatment program. Rex E. Culp; Vicki Little; Dana Letts; Harriet Lawrence. *Am. J. Orthopsy.* **61:1** 1:1991 pp. 114 – 121

100 Multimethod assessment of a child-care demonstration project for AFDC recipient families — the genesis of an evaluation. Peter A Neenan; Gary L. Bowen. *Eval. Rev.* **15:2** 4:1991 pp. 219 – 232

101 O massacre dos inocentes — a criança sem infância no Brasil *[In Portuguese]*; [The slaughter of the innocents — children without a childhood in Brazil]. José de Souza Martins *[Ed.]*; Ethel Volfzon Kosminsky *[Ed.]*; et al. São Paulo: Editora Hucitec, 1991: 216 p. (map) *ISBN: 8527101645; LofC: 90744832. Includes bibliographical references (p. 209-216).* [Ciências sociais. : No. 30]

102 Reaction times and intelligence — a comparison of Japanese and British children. Richard Lynn; T. Shigehisa. *J. Biosoc. Sc.* **23:4** 10:1991 pp. 409 – 416

103 The rights of the child in Malawi — an agenda for research on the impact of the United Nations Convention in a poor country. Garton Sandifolo Kamchedzera. *Int. J. Law Fam.* **5:3** 12:1991 pp. 241 – 257

104 Screening child survivors for post-traumatic stress disorders — experiences from the "Jupiter" sinking. William Yule; Orlee Udwin. *Br. J. Clin. Psycho.* **30:2** 5:1991 pp. 131 – 138

105 Separation from a parent during childhood and adult socioeconomic attainment. Paul R. Amato; Bruce Keith. *Soc. Forc.* **70:1** 9:1991 pp. 187 – 206

106 Strict and inconsistent discipline in childhood — consequences for adolescent mental health. Michael Feehan; Rob McGee; Warren R. Stanton; Phil A. Silva. *Br. J. Clin. Psycho.* **30:4** 11:1991 pp. 325 – 331

107 A study in economic psychology — children's saving in a play economy. Paul Webley; Mark Levine; Alan Lewis. *Human Relat.* **44:2** 2:1991 pp. 127 – 146

108 Taking children seriously — a proposal for a Children's Rights Commissioner. Martin Rosenbaum; Peter Newell *[Ed.]*. London: Calouste Gulbenkian Foundation, 1991: 76 p. *ISBN: 0903319551.*

109 Temperamental factors in human development. Jerome Kagan; Nancy Snidman. *Am. Psychol.* **46:8** 8:1991 pp. 856 – 862

110 A three-component model of children's teasing — aggression, humor and ambiguity. Jeremy P. Shapiro; Roy F. Baumeister; Jane W. Kessler. *J. Soc. Clin. Psychol.* **10:4** Winter:1991 pp. 459 – 472

111 The UN convention and children's rights in the UK. Peter Newell. London: National Children's Bureau, 1991: 219 p. *ISBN: 0902817779.*

112 The United Nations convention on the rights of the child. Dominic McGoldrick. *Int. J. Law Fam.* **5:2** 8:1991 pp. 132 – 169

113 The United Nations convention on the rights of the child — a British view. Bernadette Walsh. *Int. J. Law Fam.* **5:2** 8:1991 pp. 170 – 193

114 United Nations convention on the rights of the child — individual rights concepts and their significance for social scientists. Cynthia Price Cohen; Hedwin Naimark. *Am. Psychol.* **46:1** 1:1991 pp. 60 – 65

115 Variation in child care quality and its implications for children. Martha J. Zaslow. *J. Soc. Issues* **47:2** 1991 pp. 125 – 138

116 Vulnerability and competence — a review of research on resilience in childhood. Suniya S. Luthar; Edward Zigler. *Am. J. Orthopsy.* **61:1** 1:1991 pp. 6 – 22

117 Who's calling the shots — how to respond effectively to children's fascination with war play and war toys. Nancy Carlsson-Paige; Diane E. Levin *[Ed.]*. Philadelphia, PA: New Society Publishers, c1990: xv, 188 p. (ill) *ISBN: 086571164x. Includes bibliographical references and index.*

Youth *[Jeunesse]*

118 Acabar con la obsesión juvenil (1) *[In Spanish]*; [Putting an end to youth obsession]. Josep M. Lozano i Soler. *Rev. Fom. Soc.* **46:181** 1-3:1991 pp. 23 – 36

119 Adolescent competence and the shaping of the life course. John S. Clausen. *A.J.S.* **96:4** 1:1991 pp. 805 – 842

120 Adolescent stress — causes and consequences. Mary Ellen Colten *[Ed.]*; Susan Gore *[Ed.]*. New York: Aldine de Gruyter, c1991: xii, 330 p. (ill) *ISBN: 0202304205; LofC: 90047963. Adolescents; Includes bibliographical references and indexes.* [Social institutions and social change.]

F.2: Age groups [Groupes d'âges] — Youth [Jeunesse]

121 *[In Japanese]*; [Asian students and Japanese students — with research into Asian students in Japan and comparative study of youth culture in Japan, Taiwan and Korea]. Tsuyoshi Tsuboi. **Komazawa Journal of Sociology** *No.(23) - 1991.* pp. 115 – 144

122 De betekenis van jeugdstijlen voor de politieke meningsvorming van jongeren *[In Dutch]*; The relevance of group styles or youth subcultures for the attitude of youngsters *[Summary]*. Joep de Hart; Jacques Janssen. *Sociol. Gids* **38**:6 11-12:1991 pp. 372 – 397

123 Destiny and drift — subcultural preferences, status attainments, and the risk and rewards of youth. John Hagan. *Am. Sociol. R.* **56**:5 10:1991 pp. 567 – 582

124 *[In Japanese]*; [The diffusion of media in youth culture]. Masayuki Fujimura. **Kodomo to Katei** *No.27(11) - 1991.* pp. 6 – 10

125 Dimensions of childhood — essays on the history of children and youth in Canada. Russell Charles Smandych *[Ed.]*; Gordon Dodds *[Ed.]*; Alvin A. J. Esau *[Ed.]*. Winnipeg: Legal Research Institute of the University of Manitoba, 1991: 287 p. *ISBN: 0921242220; LofC: cn 91097152.*

126 Gangs, neighborhoods, and public policy. John M. Hagedorn. *Soc. Prob.* **38**:4 11:1991 pp. 529 – 542

127 I giovani del Mezzogiorno *[In Italian]*; [Youth in southern Italy]. Alessandro Cavalli *[Ed.]*. Bologna: Società editrice il Mulino, c1990: 396 p. *ISBN: 8815027750. Bibliography — p. 391-396.* [Studi e ricerche.]

128 Homeless youths and HIV infection. Cheryl Koopman; Anke A. Ehrhardt. *Am. Psychol.* **46**:11 11:1991 pp. 1188 – 1197

129 Identifying mechanisms of adoption of tobacco and alcohol use among youth — the Bogalusa heart study. Saundra Hunter; Igor A. Vizelberg; Gerald S. Berenson. *Soc. Networks* **13**:1 3:1991 pp. 91 – 104

130 Influence of sensation seeking on general deviance and specific problem behaviors from adolescence to young adulthood. Michael D. Newcomb; Linda McGee. *J. Pers. Soc. Psychol.* **61**:4 10:1991 pp. 614 – 628

131 Les jeunes et le mariage religieux — une émancipation du sacré *[In French]*; [Youth and religious marriage — the emancipation of the sacred] *[Summary]*. Liliane Voye. *Soc. Compass* **38**(4) 1991 pp. 405 – 416

132 Jeunes et socialisations religieuses *[In French]*; Youth and religious socializations. Dieter Ari Lenzen *[Contrib.]*; Yves Lambert *[Contrib.]*; Helena Helve *[Contrib.]*; Jean-Paul Montminy *[Contrib.]*; Réginald Richard *[Contrib.]*; Liliane Voye *[Contrib.]*; Jacques Zylberberg *[Contrib.]*; Yuki Shiose *[Contrib.]*. *Collection of 6 articles.* **Soc. Compass** , *38(4),* 1991 pp. 245 – 432

133 Jeunesses et marginalités *[In French]*; [Youth and marginal groups]. François Dubet. *Regar. Actual.* **:172** 7:1991 pp. 3 – 10

134 Juventud y cultura — niveles y horizontes culturales del universitario panameño — estudio exploratorio *[In Spanish]*; [Youth and culture — cultural levels and horizons of the Panamanian university — an exploratory study]. Alfredo Figueroa Navarro. Panamá: Imp. Roysa, 1990: 73 p. *BNB: 91153981; LofC: 91153981. "Avances de sociología de la cultura y de los medios de comunicación social."; Includes bibliographical references.*

135 Молодежь в условиях перехода к рыночным отношениям *[In Russian]*; (The youth under conditions of transfer to market economy). A.A. Mironov. *Sot. Issle.* **:3** 1991 pp. 39 – 45

136 Молодое поколение *[In Russian]*; [The young generation]. M. Kh. Titma; E.A. Saar. Moscow: Mysl', 1986: 255 p. [Социология и жизнь; [Sociology and life].]

137 Ostdeutsche Jugend 1990 *[In German]*; [Eastern German youth in 1990]. Walter Friedrich; Peter Förster. *Deut. Arch.* **24**:4 4:1991 p. 349

138 Perception de la religion chez les jeunes au Québec *[In French]*; [Religious perception in the youth of Quebec] *[Summary]*. Jean-Paul Montminy; Réginald Richard. *Soc. Compass* **38**(4) 1991 pp. 393 – 404

139 Perpetuated youth and self-sanctification; *[French summary]*. Dieter Ari Lenzen. *Soc. Compass* **38**(4) 1991 pp. 345 – 356

140 Preference changes among American youth — family, work, and goods aspirations, 1976-86; Les changements au niveau des préférences parmi la jeunesse des Etats-Unis concernant la famille, le travail et les aspirations aux biens matériels, de 1976 à 1986 *[French summary]*; Cambios de preferencia entre jóvenes americanos — aspiraciones de familia, trabajo y bienes, 1976-86 *[Spanish summary]*. Eileen M. Crimmins; Richard A. Easterlin; Yasuhiko Saito. *Pop. Dev. Rev.* **17**:1 3:1991 pp. 115 – 133

F.2: Age groups [Groupes d'âges] — Youth [Jeunesse]

141 Private materialism, personal self-fulfillment, family life, and public interest — the nature, effects, and causes of recent changes in the values of American youth. Richard A. Easterlin; Eileen M. Crimmins. *Publ. Opin. Q.* **55:4** Winter:1991 pp. 499 – 533

142 Problematische Lebenssituationen und Symptome der psychosozialen Belastung bei polnischen und deutschen Jugendlichen. Eine kulturvergleichende jugendsoziologische Analyse *[In German]*; Problematic life situations and symptoms of psychosocial stress among Polish and German adolescents *[Summary]*. Jürgen Mansel; Klaus Hurrelmann; Jan Wlodarek. *Kölner Z. Soz. Soz. psy.* **43:1** 1991 pp. 44 – 69

143 The relationship of hardiness, gender, and stress to health outcomes in adolescents. James A. Shepperd; Javad H. Kashani. *J. Personal.* **59:4** 12:1991 pp. 747 – 768

144 La religion et la recompositition du symbolique chez les jeunes Français *[In French]*; [Religion and the reconstruction of the symbolic for the French youth] *[Summary]*. Yves Lambert. *Soc. Compass* **38(4)** 1991 pp. 357 – 372

145 Short term labour market consequences of teenage pregnancy. D.M. Byrne; S.C. Myers; R.H. King. *Appl. Econ.* **23:12** 12:1991 pp. 1819 – 1827

146 Smoking behaviour from pre-adolescence to young adulthood. Anthony Victor Swan; Michael Murray; Linda Jarrett. Aldershot: Avebury, 1991; 231 p. *ISBN: 1856280330.*

147 Some research notes on living conditions and perceptions among Indonesian students in Cairo. Mona Abaza. *J. SE. As. Stud.* **22:2** 9:1991 pp. 347 – 360

148 Станаўленне духоўнага аблічча моладзі: здабыткі і страты *[In Belorussian]*; *[Russian summary]*; [Formation of the spiritual character of youth — possessions and losses] *[Summary]*. S.U. Talapina. *V. Aka. BSSR* **2** 1991 pp. 79 – 86

149 Structurele en culturele verscheidenheid onder jonge volwassenen *[In Dutch]*; Structural and cultural diversity among young adults *[Summary]*. Brigitte van Dam. *Sociol. Gids* **:2** 3-4:1991 pp. 111 – 122

150 Társadalmi folyamatok a magyar ifjuság körében *[In Hungarian]*; [Social processes among Hungarian youth]. Ferenc Gazsó. **Tarsad. Kozl.** *Vol.17; No.3 - 1987.* pp. 360 – 370

151 Work attitudes and life goals of Zambian youth. Kwaku Osei-Hwedie. *J. Soc. Devel. Afr.* **6:1** 1991 pp. 63 – 73

152 Young adults — self-perceptions and life contexts. Glen Evans; Millicent E. Poole. London: Falmer, 1991: xii, 325 p. (ill) *ISBN: 1850009384. Bibliography — p.291-307. Includes index.*

153 Young Europeans and changing living arrangements — some social and demographic effects. Hein Moors; Nico van Nimwegen. *Bevolk. Gez.* **:1** 1991 pp. 17 – 38

154 Young people's understanding of society. Adrian Furnham; Barrie Stacey *[Ed.]*. London: Routledge, 1991: 215 p. *ISBN: 0415017084; LofC: 90-40790. Includes bibliography and index.* [Adolescence and society.]

155 Youth and change. Jaana Lähteenmaa *[Ed.]*; Lasse Siurala *[Ed.]*. Helsinki: Tilastokeskus, 1991: 129 p. *ISBN: 9514753909.* [Youth Research Society.]

156 Youth and the Cuban Revolution — notes on the road traversed and its perspectives. Juan Luis Martín. *Lat. Am. Pers.* **18:2(69)** Spring: 1991 pp. 95 – 100

157 Youth gangs — continuity and change. Irving A. Spergel. *Crime Just.* **12** 1990 pp. 171 – 276

158 Ёшларнинг хуқуқий тарбиялаш муаммосига оид *[In Uzbek]*; К проблеме правовой социализации молодежи *[In Russian]*; [The problem of finding a legally-defined place in society for young people]. D. Madalieva. *Obshch. N. Usbek.* **:4** 1991 pp. 24 – 30

F.3: Demographic trends and population policy — *Tendances démographiques et politique démographique*

Sub-divisions: Family planning *[Planification de la famille]*; Fertility *[Fécondité]*; Morbidity *[Morbidité]*; Mortality *[Mortalité]*; Population growth *[Croissance démographique]*

1 The British population — patterns, trends and processes. D. A. Coleman; John Salt *[Ed.]*. Oxford: Oxford University Press, 1991: 680 p. (ill) *ISBN: 0198740972. Includes bibliography and index.*

2 Commons without tragedy — protecting the environment from overpopulation. Robert V. Andelson *[Ed.]*. London: Shepheard-Walwyn, 1991: 198 p. *ISBN: 0389209589; LofC: 91019511.*

F.3: Demographic trends and population policy *[Tendances démographiques et politique démographique]*

3 A demográfiai helyzet Lengyelországban és ennek hatása a népesedéspolitikára *[In Hungarian]*; (The demographic situation in Poland and its influence on population policy). Jerzy Z. Holzer. *Demográfia* **34:3-4** 1991 pp. 351 – 358

4 Disabled people in Britain and discrimination — a case for anti-discrimination legislation. Colin Barnes. Calgary: University of Calgary Press, 1991: 264 p. *ISBN: 1895176093; LofC: cn 91091711. Includes bibliographical references and index.*

5 Frauen der DDR im Spiegel der Demographie (ein Rückblick) *[In German]*; [GDR women in the mirror of demography] *[Summary]*. Juliane Roloff; Wulfram Speigner. *Konjunkturpolitik* **37:3** 1991 pp. 183 – 197

6 Guyana and the demographic transition. Trevor Noble. *Transition* **:18** 1991 pp. 5 – 19

7 Human resources information systems — concepts, functions and objectives. G.A. Abbink; K. Tejani; Sabur Ghayur *[Comments by]*. *Pak. Dev. R.* **30:4** Winter:1991 pp. 707 – 718

8 L'interattraction spatiale — analyse historique, 1871-1985 *[In French]*; [Spatial interattraction — historical analysis, 1871-1985] *[Summary]*. Daniel Fournier. *Rech. Soc.graph* **XXXII:2** 5-8: 1991 pp. 151 – 174

9 Interpreting spatial patterns from the 1990 China census. Clifton W. Pannell; Jeffrey S. Torguson. *Geogr. Rev.* **81:3** 7:1991 pp. 304 – 317

10 Ist der Weg in die multikulturelle Gesellschaft vorgezeichnet? *[In German]*; Is the route to the multicultural society mapped out? *[Summary]*. Stefanie Wahl. *Inf. Raum.* **:7/8** 1991 pp. 387 – 393

11 Mass education, Islamic revival, and the population problem in Egypt. Kimberly Faust; Rebecca Bach; Saad Gadalla; Hind Khattab; John Gulick. *J. Comp. Fam. Stud.* **XXII:3** Autumn:1991 pp. 329 – 341

12 Maternal and infant demographics and health status — a comparison of black, caucasian, and hispanic families. Judith H. Langlois; Jean M. Ritter; Rita J. Casey. *J. Biosoc. Sc.* **23:1** 1:1991 pp. 91 – 105

13 A methodological review of the sex ratio — alternatives for comparative research. Mark A. Fossett; K. Jill Kiecolt. *J. Marriage Fam.* **53:4** 11:1991 pp. 941 – 957

14 Několik úvah o současném a budoucím populačním vývoji *[In Czech]*; Reflection on recent and future population development *[Summary]*; Некоторые соображения о современной и будущей динамике народонаселения *[Russian summary]*. Pavel Vereš. *Demografie* **XXXIII:2** 1991 pp. 97 – 105

15 Perspectives on rural population change in Europe. M. Berlan-Darqué; P. Collomb *[Contrib.]*; B. Kayser *[Contrib.]*; W.J. Serow *[Contrib.]*; M. Štambuk *[Contrib.]*; B. Hervieu *[Contrib.]*; A. Etchelecou *[Contrib.]*; G.J. Lewis *[Contrib.]*; P. McDermott *[Contrib.]*; K.B. Sherwood *[Contrib.] and others. Collection of 7 articles.* **Sociol. Rur.**, *XXXI:4*, 1991 pp. 252 – 320

16 Population change in the suburbanized areas of the Federal Republic of Germany with special reference to Hamburg (1970-1987); Les changements de la population dans les zones suburbaines de la République Fédérale Allemande, en particulier autour de Hambourg (1970-1987) *[French summary]*. P. Gans. *Espace Pop. Soc.* **:2** 1991 pp. 293 – 307

17 Population distribution and urbanization in Spain. Manuel Ferrer Regales. *J. Reg. Pol.* **11:2** 4-6:1991 pp. 215 – 232

18 Population movements in post-Cold War Europe. François Heisbourg. *Survival* **XXXIII:1** 1-2:1991 pp. 31 – 44

19 Population policy in South Africa — a critical perspective. Barbara Klugman. *Develop. S. Afr.* **8:1** 2:1991 pp. 19 – 34

20 Population regions of a trans-Himalayan tribal tract — a case study of Kinnaur district of Himachal Pradesh. S.S. Chib. *Ind. J. Reg. Sci.* **XXIII:2** 1991 pp. 57 – 66

21 *[In Japanese]*; [Population trends and community life of inner Tokyo]. Hideki Takenaka. *Tos. Mon. No.82(7) - 1991.* pp. 43 – 57

22 *[In Japanese]*; [Population trends of local cities and local vitalizations]. Masao Saito. *Tos. Mon. No.82(7) - 1991.* pp. 59 – 73

23 *[In Japanese]*; [Relationship between pronatalist policy and immigration policy]. Hiroshi Kojima. ***Jinko Mondai Kenkyu*** *No.46(3) - 1991.* pp. 49 – 55

24 Residential density patterns in London — any role left for the exponential density gradient? G.R. Crampton. *Envir. Plan.A.* **23:7** 7:1991 pp. 1007 – 1024

25 The second demographic transition — fact or fiction ? Robert L. Cliquet. Strasbourg: Council of Europe, 1991: 115 p. *ISBN: 9287119635. Bibliography — p.99-115.* [Population studies (Council of Europe).: No. 23]

F.3: Demographic trends and population policy *[Tendances démographiques et politique démographique]*

26 The six questions that do not go away. Karol J. Krotki; Naushin Mahmood *[Comments by]. Pak. Dev. R.* **30:4** Winter:1991 pp. 649 – 666
27 *[In Japanese]*; [A sociological study of life and death]. Shigefumi Kurahashi. *Bulletin of Sociological Studies, Bukkyo University No.(12) - 1991.* pp. 1 – 11
28 Társadalompolitikai válaszok a népességszám csökkenésére a 21. évszázadban — pronatalista népesedéspolitika, bevándorlási politika, a foglalkoztatottság növelése vagy más alternatívák? *[In Hungarian]*; Policy responses to population decline in the twenty-first century — pronatalism, migration policy, growing labour force participation or other alternatives? *[Summary]*. Rudolf Andorka. *Demográfia* **XXXIII:1-2** 1990 pp. 7 – 23
29 Techniques for modelling population-related raster databases. D. Martin; I. Bracken. *Envir. Plan.A.* **23:7** 7:1991 pp. 1069 – 1075

Family planning *[Planification de la famille]*

30 Abortion in Canada — religious and ideological dimensions of women's attitudes. Vijaya Krishnan. *Soc. Biol.* **38:3-4** Fall-Winter:1991 pp. 249 – 257
31 Abortion in South Australia, 1971-86 — an update. Farhat Yusuf; Dora Briggs. *J. Biosoc. Sc.* **23:3** 7:1991 pp. 285 – 296
32 Artificial reproduction and reproductive rights. Athena Liu. Aldershot: Dartmouth, c1991: xi, 223 p. *ISBN: 1855210223. Bibliography — p.208-218. Includes index.*
33 Can women remember how many children they have borne? Data from the east Caribbean. Ann W. Brittain. *Soc. Biol.* **38:3-4** Fall-Winter:1991 pp. 219 – 232
34 Choix des cohortes et des sous-cohortes — règles générales et application à l'avortement *[In French]*; The choice of cohorts and sub cohorts for the study of demographic events. General rules and their application to abortion. Chantal Blayo. *Population* **46:6** 11-12:1991 pp. 1379 – 1404
35 Creating new traditions in modern Chinese populations — aiming for birth in the year of the dragon. Daniel M. Goodkind. *Pop. Dev. Rev.* **17:4** 12:1991 pp. 663 – 686
36 Családtervezés, gyermekvállalás, ideális gyermekszám a sokgyermekes anyák körében *[In Hungarian]*; (Family planning, childbearing and ideal number of children as expressed by mothers of large families). Pongrácz Tiborné; S. Molnár Edit. *Demográfia* **34:3-4** 1991 pp. 383 – 410
37 Current contraception among programme beneficiaries. Simeen Mahmud. *Bang. Dev. Stud.* **XIX:3** 9:1991 pp. 35 – 62
38 Differences in race, marital status, and education among women obtaining abortions. Katherine Trent; Eve Powell-Griner. *Soc. Forc.* **69:4** 6:1991 pp. 1121 – 1143
39 Does better access to contraceptives increase their use? Key policy and methodological issues. Susan Hill Cochrane; Laura Gibney. Washington, D.C.: Population and Human Resources Department, The World Bank, 1991: 26,4 p. [Policy, research, and external affairs working papers.]
40 Family planning and fertility in southern Appalachia — a community study. Donald L. Hochstrasser; Gerry A. Gairola. *Human. Org.* **50:4** Winter:1991 pp. 393 – 405
41 Family planning in the legacy of Islam. Abdel R. Omran. London: Routledge, 1990: 284 p. *ISBN: 0415055415.*
42 Family planning practice and the law. Kenneth McK. Norrie. Aldershot: Dartmouth, 1991: 203 p. *ISBN: 1855210355. Includes bibliography and index.* [Medico-legal series.]
43 Family planning programs — efforts and results, 1982-89. W. Parker Mauldin; John A. Ross *[Ed.]*. New York, NY: Population Council, 1991: 42 p. (ill) *ISBN: oc25352647. Includes bibliographical references (p. 39-42).* [Research Division working papers.]
44 Fertility control — new techniques, new policy issues. Robert H. Blank. New York: Greenwood Press, 1991: 164 p. *ISBN: 0313276404; LofC: 91013115. Includes bibliographical references (p. 145-154) and index.* [Contributions in medical studies.]
45 In vitro fertilization and embryo transfer — medical technology + social values = legislative solutions. Marvin F. Milich. *J. Fam. Law* **30:4** 1991-1992 pp. 875 – 901
46 Intervals between marriage and first birth in mothers and daughters. Bertrand Desjardins; Alain Bideau; Evelyne Heyer; Guy Brunet. *J. Biosoc. Sc.* **23:1** 1:1991 pp. 49 – 54
47 The investigation of parameter drift by expanded regressions — generalities, and a 'family-planning' example. E. Casetti. *Envir. Plan.A.* **23:7** 7:1991 pp. 1045 – 1061
48 The KAP-gap and the unmet need for contraception. John Bongaarts. *Pop. Dev. Rev.* **17:2** 6:1991 pp. 293 – 313

F.3: Demographic trends and population policy *[Tendances démographiques et politique démographique]* — Family planning *[Planification de la famille]*

49 Legal regulation of abortion in Poland. Małgorzata Fuszara. *Signs* **17:1** Autumn:1991 pp. 117 – 128
50 Mizuko kuyō — notulae on the most important "new religion" of Japan. R.J. Zwi Werblowsky. *Jap. J. Relig. St.* **18:4** 12:1991 pp. 295 – 354
51 Modernization and changing fertility behaviour — a study in a Rajasthan village. Tulsi Patel. *Sociol. Bul.* **39:1-2** 3-9:1990 pp. 53 – 73
52 Multilevel analysis of attitudes to abortion. R.D. Wiggins; K. Ashworth; C.A. O'Muircheartaigh; J.I. Galbraith. *Statistician* **40:2** 1991 pp. 225 – 234
53 The one child certificate in Hebei province, China — acceptance and consequence, 1979-1988. R.S. Cooney; J. Wei; M.G. Powers. *Pop. Res. Pol. R.* **10:2** 1991 pp. 137 – 156
54 Paraguayan pharmacies and the sale of pseudoabortifacients. Nelly Krayacich de Oddone; Michele G. Shedlin; Michael Welsh; Malcolm Potts; Paul Feldblum. *J. Biosoc. Sc.* **23:2** 4:1991 pp. 201 – 109
55 Planned parenthood and the new right — onslaught and opportunity? Sandra Whitworth. *Stud. Pol. Ec.* **35:** Summer:1991 pp. 73 – 102
56 População reprodução e saúde — anotações sobre a questão de uma política social *[In Portuguese]*; [Population, reproduction and health — notes on a social policy issue] *[Summary]*. Maria Isabel Baltar da Rocha. *Rev. Brasil. Est. Popul.* **5:2** 7-12:1988 pp. 21 – 33
57 The pro-choice movement — organization and activism in the abortion conflict. Suzanne Staggenborg. New York: Oxford University Press, 1991: xiv, 229 p. *ISBN: 0195065964; LofC: 90023877.* Includes bibliographical references and index.
58 The Profamilia family planning program, Colombia — an economic perspective. Jesus Amadeo; Dov Chernichovsky; Gabriel Ojeda. Washington, D.C.: Population and Human Resources Department, The World Bank, 1991: 113 p. *"August 1991".* [Policy, research, and external affairs working papers.]
59 Public attitudes toward genetic testing. E. Singer. *Pop. Res. Pol. R.* **10:3** 1991 pp. 235 – 255
60 Reproductive decisions among HIV-infected, drug using women — the importance of mother/child coresidence. Anitra Pivnick; Audrey Jacobson; Kathleen Eric; Michael Mulvihill; Ming Ann Hsu; Ernest Drucker. *Med. Anthr. Q.* **5:2** 6:1991 pp. 153 – 187
61 Risk-taking, control over partner choice and intended use of condoms by virgins. G.M. Breakwell; C. Fife-Schaw; K. Clayden. *J. Comm. App. Soc. Psychol.* **1:2** 6:1991 pp. 173 – 187
62 Scoring attitudes to abortion. Martin Knott; Maria Teresa Albanese; Jane Galbraith. *Statistician* **40:2** 1991 pp. 217 – 224
63 Servidores públicos versus profesionales liberales *[In Spanish]*; [Public servants versus liberal professionals]. Carmen Barroso; Sonia Correa. *Est. Sociol.* **IX:25** 1-4:1991 pp. 75 – 104
64 Son preference and contraception in Egypt. Hassan Y. Aly; Michael P. Shields. *Econ. Dev. Cult. Change* **39:2** 1:1991 pp. 353 – 370
65 Trend změn živě narozených mimo manželství v České republice *[In Czech]*; The trend of changes of illegitimate live births in the Czech Republic *[Summary]*; Тенденции изменений незаконно рожденных детей в Чешской Республике *[Russian summary]*. Augustin Syrovátka; Jiří Vondráček; Jaroslava Skutliová. *Demografie* **33:3** 1991 pp. 193 – 199
66 Turkey-baster babies — the demedicalization of artificial insemination. Daniel Wikler; Norma J. Wikler. *Milbank Q.* **69:1** 1991 pp. 5 – 40
67 Virtue theory and abortion. Rosalind Hursthouse. *Philos. Pub.* **20:3** Summer:1991 pp. 223 – 246
68 Voluntary childlessness among American men and women in the late 1980s. Cardell K. Jacobson; Tim B. Heaton. *Soc. Biol.* **38:1-2** Spring-Summer:1991 pp. 79 – 93
69 Voluntary sterilisation among Canadian women. Margaret De Wit; Fernando Rajulton. *J. Biosoc. Sc.* **23:3** 7:1991 pp. 263 – 274
70 Whose foetus is it? Celia Wells; Derek Morgan. *J. Law Soc.* **18:4** Winter:1991 pp. 431 – 447
71 Women and new reproductive technologies — medical, psychosocial, legal, and ethical dilemmas. Judith Rodin *[Ed.]*; Aila Collins *[Ed.]*. Hillsdale, NJ: L. Erlbaum, 1991: viii, 171 p. *ISBN: 0805809198; LofC: 90014148.* Based on a conference sponsored by the John D. and Catherine T. MacArthur Foundation Network on the Determinants and Consequences of Health Promoting and Health Damaging Behavior, held June 16-18, 1987 in Key Biscayne, Florida; Includes bibliographical references and index.

F.3: Demographic trends and population policy *[Tendances démographiques et politique démographique]* — **Family planning** *[Planification de la famille]*
72 Women, sexuality, and the changing social order — the impact of government policies on reproductive behavior in Kenya. Beth Maina Ahlberg. Philadelphia: Gordon and Breach, c1991: xiv, 274 p. *ISBN: 2881244998; LofC: 91012553.* Includes bibliographical references (p. 251-265) and index. [International studies in global change.]

Fertility *[Fécondité]*
73 Adolescent childbearing — risks and resilience. Diane Scott-Jones. *Educ. Urban. Soc.* **24:1** 11:1991 pp. 53 – 64
74 Age at first intercourse and the timing of marriage and childbirth. Brent C. Miller; Tim B. Heaton. *J. Marriage Fam.* **53:3** 8:1991 pp. 719 – 732
75 An alternative model of the impact of the proximate determinants on fertility change — evidence from Latin America. Lorenzo Moreno. *Pop. Stud. Egy.* **45:2** 7:1991 pp. 313 – 338
76 Anticipated child loss to migration and sustained high fertility in an East Caribbean population. Ann W. Brittain. *Soc. Biol.* **38:1-2** Spring-Summer:1991 pp. 94 – 112
77 La baisse de la fécondité dans le monde *[In French]*; [The world-wide fall in fecundity]. D. Noin. *Ann. Géogr.* **100:559** 5-6:1991 pp. 257 – 272
78 Birth spacing and infant mortality in Brazil. Siân L. Curtis; John W. McDonald. *J. Biosoc. Sc.* **23:3** 7:1991 pp. 343 – 352
79 Breastfeeding and fertility — a comparative analysis. Deborah Guz; John Hobcraft. *Pop. Stud.* **45:1** 3:1991 pp. 91 – 108
80 Breast-feeding, birth interval and child mortality in Bangladesh. Abdul Kashem Majumder. *J. Biosoc. Sc.* **23:3** 7:1991 pp. 297 – 312
81 Changes in contraceptive use and fertility — El Salvador, 1978-88. Richard S. Monteith; Charles W. Warren; Jose Mario Caceres; Howard I. Goldberg. *J. Biosoc. Sc.* **23:1** 1:1991 pp. 79 – 89
82 The childbearing family in sub-Saharan Africa — structure, fertility, and the future. Odile Frank. Washington, D.C.: Population and Human Resources Department, The World Bank, 1991: 54 p. *Bibliography* — *p.48-54.* [Policy, research, and external affairs working papers.]
83 China's strategic demographic initiative. H. Yuan Tien. New York: Praeger, 1991: xvii, 312 p. *ISBN: 0275938247; LofC: 90020614 //r91.* Includes bibliographical references (p. [283]-303) and index.
84 Convergence on the two-child family norm in Australia. Abbas Y. Adam. *J. Aust. Pop. Ass.* **8:2** 11:1991 pp. 77 – 91
85 Cuba — population et développement (essai sur la fécondité) *[In French]*; [Cuba — population and development (fertility study)]. Maryse Roux. *Cah. Amer. Lat.* **:11** 1991 pp. 83 – 101
86 Desired and excess fertility in Europe and the United States — indirect estimates from World Fertility Survey data; Naissances désirées et non désirées en Europe et aux États-Unis — estimations indirectes issues des données de l'Enquête Mondiale sur la Fécondité *[French summary]*. Ch. A. Calhoun. *Eur. J. Pop.* **7:1** 4:1991 pp. 29 – 57
87 Direct and indirect effects of religion on birth timing — a decomposition exercise using discrete-time hazard-rate models. Jay D. Teachman; Paul T. Schollaert. *Sociol. Q.* **32:1** Spring:1991 pp. 151 – 159
88 Educational attainment, age at first birth and lifetime fertility — an anlysis of Canadian fertility survey data; *[French summary]*. Carl F. Grindstaff; T.R. Balakrishnan; David J. Dewitt. *Can. R. Soc. A.* **28:3** 8:1991 pp. 324 – 339
89 Effect of infertility on the population structure of the Herero and Mbanderu of Southern Africa. Renee Pennington; Henry Harpending. *Soc. Biol.* **38:1-2** Spring-Summer:1991 pp. 127 – 139
90 Effects of selected socio-economic and demographic factors on fertility — a path analysis. S.M. Shafiqul Islam; H.T. Abdullah Khan. *Asian Prof.* **19:6** 12:1991 pp. 561 – 574
91 Événements politiques et fécondité en Chine *[In French]*; Political events and birth rates in China since 1950. Yves Blayo. *Population* **46:6** 11-12:1991 pp. 1589 – 1616
92 L'évolution après 1975 du célibat agricole masculin *[In French]*; Changes after 1975 in the numbers of single male farmers *[Summary]*; La evolución despues de 1975 del celibato masculino en zonas rurales *[Spanish summary]*. Guenhaël Jegouzo. *Population* **46:1** 1-2:1991 pp. 41 – 64

F.3: Demographic trends and population policy *[Tendances démographiques et politique démographique]* — Fertility *[Fécondité]*

93 Family planning and fertility in southern Appalachia — a community study. Donald L. Hochstrasser; Gerry A. Gairola. *Human. Org.* **50:4** Winter:1991 pp. 393 – 405

94 La fécondité en début de mariage. Réflexions sur le calcul des taux *[In French]*; Fertility at early durations of marriage. Some reflections on the calculation of rates. France Prioux. *Population* **46:6** 11-12:1991 pp. 1491 – 1512

95 Female labour force participation and fertility — an aggregate analysis; *[Italian summary]*; *[French summary]*. Vijaya Krishnan. *Genus* **XLVII:1-2** 1-6:1991 pp. 177 – 192

96 Female labour market behaviour and fertility — a rational-choice approach — proceedings of a workshop organized by the Netherlands Interdisciplinary Demographic Institute (NIDI) in collaboration with the Economic Institute, Centre for Interdisciplinary Re; search on Labour Market and Distribution Issues (CIAV) of Utrecht University held in The Hague, the Netherlands, April 20-22, 1989. Jacques J. Siegers *[Ed.]*; E. van Imhoff *[Ed.]*; J. de Jong-Gierveld *[Ed.]*. Berlin: Springer-Verlag, c1991: 301 p. *ISBN: 0387538968; LofC: 91013752. Includes bibliographical references and index.* [Population economics.]

97 Fertility change in contemporary Japan. Robert William Hodge; Naohiro Ogawa *[Ed.]*. Chicago: University of Chicago Press, 1991: xvii, 344 p. (ill) *ISBN: 0226346501; LofC: 91017767. Includes bibliographical references (p. 327-335) and index.* [Population and development.]

98 Fertility change in rural China, 1949-1982. Q. Yang. *Pop. Res. Pol. R.* **10:2** 1991 pp. 157 – 182

99 Fertility desires and fertility outcomes. Michael Bracher; Gigi Santow. *J. Aust. Pop. Ass.* **8:1** 5:1991 pp. 33 – 49

100 Fertility differentials in rural Sierra Leone — demographic and socioeconomic effects; Fécondité rurale différentielle en Sierra Leone, composantes démographiques et socio-économiques *[French summary]*; *[Italian summary]*. Mohamed Bailey; William J. Serow. *Genus* **XLVII:3-4** 7-12:1991 pp. 171 – 182

101 Fertility in England — a long-term perspective. Chris Wilson; Robert Woods. *Pop. Stud. Egy.* **45:3** 11:1991 pp. 399 – 416

102 Fertility in Larsmo — the effect of laestadianism. Fjalar Finnäs. *Pop. Stud. Egy.* **45:2** 7:1991 pp. 339 – 352

103 Fertility levels and trends in Arsi and Shoa regions of central Ethiopia. Assefa Hailemariam. *J. Biosoc. Sc.* **23:4** 10:1991 pp. 387 – 400

104 Fertility transition — the social dynamics of population change. Loraine Donaldson. Cambridge, Mass., USA: B. Blackwell, 1991: 227 p. *ISBN: 1557860904; LofC: 90043941*.

105 Husbands' participation in fertility treatment — they also serve who only stand and wait. Liz Meerabeau. *Sociol. Health Ill.* **13:3** 9:1991 pp. 396 – 410

106 Individual and aggregate influences on the age at first birth. N.L. Maxwell. *Pop. Res. Pol. R.* **10:1** 1991 pp. 27 – 46

107 Infecundity and subfertility among the rural population of Ethiopia. Habtemariam Tesfaghiorghis. *J. Biosoc. Sc.* **23:4** 10:1991 pp. 461 – 476

108 Infertility, sexuality, and health — toward a new world for women. Jocelynne A. Scutt. *Iss. Repro. Gen. Engin.* **4:1** :1991 pp. 17 – 26

109 Intervals between marriage and first birth in mothers and daughters. Bertrand Desjardins; Alain Bideau; Evelyne Heyer; Guy Brunet. *J. Biosoc. Sc.* **23:1** 1:1991 pp. 49 – 54

110 Lactation, birth spacing and maternal work-loads among two castes in rural Nepal. Catherine Panter-Brick. *J. Biosoc. Sc.* **23:2** 4:1991 pp. 137 – 154

111 Law, fertility and reproduction. Gillian Douglas. London: Sweet & Maxwell, 1991: 216 p. *ISBN: 0421420200*. [Modern legal studies.]

112 The link between black teen pregnancy and economic restructuring in Detroit — a neighborhood scale analysis. Harold M. Rose; Donald R. Deskins. *Urban Geogr.* **12:6** 11-12:1991 pp. 508 – 525

113 Mate selection and fertility in urban Nigeria. Bamikale J. Feyisetan; Akinrinola Bankole. *J. Comp. Fam. Stud.* **XXII:3** Autumn:1991 pp. 273 – 292

114 Un metodo di stima degli intervalli generici *[In Italian]*; [An evaluation method for general intervals] *[Summary]*. Moreno Ventisette. *Statistica* **LI:2** 4-6:1991 pp. 229 – 246

115 The mode of reproduction in transition — a Marxist-feminist analysis of the effects of reproductive technologies. Martha E. Gimenez. *Gender Soc.* **5:3** 9:1991 pp. 334 – 350

116 Modernization and changing fertility behaviour — a study in a Rajasthan village. Tulsi Patel. *Sociol. Bul.* **39:1-2** 3-9:1990 pp. 53 – 73

F.3: Demographic trends and population policy [Tendances démographiques et politique démographique] — Fertility [Fécondité]

117 Mortality and fertility in Germany — cointegration and causality tests for rural and urban Prussia and modern Germany. Horst Entorf; Klaus F. Zimmermann. *J. Interd. Ec.* **4:1** 1991 pp. 17 – 31

118 Mother's age, birth order and health status in a British national sample. Bernice A. Kaplan; C.G.N. Mascie-Taylor. *Med. Anthrop.* **13:4** 1991 pp. 353 – 368

119 Not yet pregnant — infertile couples in contemporary America. Arthur L Greil. New Brunswick [N.J.]: Rutgers University Press, c1991: viii, 243 p. *ISBN: 081351682x; LofC: 90021142.* Includes bibliographical references (p. 213-236) and index.

120 Objects, processes, and female infertility in Chinese medicine. Judith Farquhar. *Med. Anthr. Q.* **5:4** 12:1991 pp. 370 – 399

121 The parity structure of fertility decline in Thailand, 1953-1979; [Italian summary]; [French summary]. Norman Y. Luther; Chintana Pejaranonda. *Genus* **XLVII:1-2** 1-6:1991 pp. 63 – 88

122 Period-cohort fertility differentials in Bangladesh. S.M. Shafiqul Islam. *Asian Prof.* **19:4** 8:1991 pp. 369 – 377

123 Productive and reproductive decisions in Turkey — the role of domestic bargaining. Nilüfer A. İsvan. *J. Marriage Fam.* **53:4** 11:1991 pp. 1057 – 1070

124 Recent trends in timing of first birth in the United States. Renbao Chen; S. Philip Morgan. *Demography* **28:4** 11:1991 pp. 513 – 533

125 The relationship between sociodemographic variables and pregnancy loss in a rural area of Bangladesh. G. Mostafa; B. Wojtyniak; V. Fauveau; A. Bhuiyan. *J. Biosoc. Sc.* **23:1** 1:1991 pp. 55 – 63

126 Relationship of perceived maternal acceptance-rejection in childhood and social support networks of pregnant adolescents. Barry R. Sherman; Barry R. Donovan. *Am. J. Orthopsy.* **61:1** 1:1991 pp. 103 – 113

127 Relationships between women's work and demographic behaviour — some research evidence in West Africa. Christine Oppong. Geneva: International Labour Office, 1991: v, 53 p. *ISBN: 9221079899.* "April 1991."; Includes bibliographical references (p. 32-42). [World Employment Programme research working papers.]

128 Returns to parental investment in children in Benguet province, Philippines. Jean Treloggen Peterson. *J. Comp. Fam. Stud.* **XXII:3** Autumn:1991 pp. 313 – 328

129 A reversal of fertility trends in Singapore. Kuldip Singh; Yoke Fai Fong; S.S. Ratnam. *J. Biosoc. Sc.* **23:1** 1:1991 pp. 73 – 78

130 Serdülőkorú terhesek demografiai jellemzői és a családi környezet szocializáló hatása *[In Hungarian]*; [Demographic characteristics of pregnant teenagers and the socializing impact of family background]. Tiborné Pongrácz. *Demográfia* Vol.30; No.2-3 - 1987. pp. 273 – 290

131 Social structure and fertility — a study of population dynamics in Haryana. Gomti Arora. New Delhi: National Book Organization, 1990: 250 p. *ISBN: 8185135509.*

132 Social structure and the timing of first birth — the case of Ghana. Acheampong Yaw Amoateng. *S.Afr. Sociol. R.* **3:2** 4:1991 pp. 29 – 39

133 The sociocultural implications of modernizing childbirth among Greek women on the island of Rhodes. Mary P. Lefkarites. *Med. Anthrop.* **13:4** 1991 pp. 385 – 412

134 Socio-economic development and fertility decline — an application of the Easterlin synthesis approach to data from the world fertility survey — Colombia, Costa Rica, Sri Lanka, and Tunisia. John Persons McHenry. New York: United Nations, 1991: ix, 115 p. *ISBN: 9211512352.* Pref; At head of title — Department of International Economic and Social Affairs; "ST/ESA/SER.R/101."; "United Nations publication Sales No. E.91.XIII.14" --cover p. [4]; Includes bibliographical references (p. 114-115).

135 Stérilité et hypofertilité — du silence à l'impatience? *[In French]*; Sterility and sub-fecundity — from silence to impatience *[Summary]*; Esterilidad y subfertilidad — del silencio a la impaciencia *[Spanish summary]*. Henri Leridon. *Population* **46:2** 3-4:1991 pp. 225 – 248

136 A stochastic dynamic analysis of parental sex preferences and fertility. Siu Fai Leung. *Q. J. Econ.* **CVI:4** 11:1991 pp. 1063 – 1088

137 A termékenység alakulása a népesedéspolitikai intézkedések tükrében *[In Hungarian]*; (Changes in fertility, in view of population policy measures). Kamarás Ferenc. *Demográfia* **34:3-4** 1991 pp. 359 – 382

138 The transition from high to low marital fertility — cultural or socioeconomic determinants? Dov Friedlander; Jona Schellekens; Eliahu Ben-Moshe. *Econ. Dev. Cult. Change* **39:2** 1:1991 pp. 331 – 351

F.3: Demographic trends and population policy *[Tendances démographiques et politique démographique]* — *Fertility [Fécondité]*

139 Value of son(s) & fertility in rural Andhra Pradesh. P. Vinayaga Murthy. *East. Anthrop.* **44:1** 1-3:1991 pp. 69 – 76

140 Vývoj plodnosti neprovdaných žen v Československu v 80. letech *[In Czech]*; The fertility of unmarried women in the Czech and the Slovak Republics in the 1980s *[Summary]*; Динамика плодовитости незамужных женщин в Чешской и Словацкой Республиках в 80-ые годы *[Russian summary]*. Dagmar Bartoňová. *Demografie* **33:3** 1991 pp. 200 – 209

141 Women and fertility in Bangladesh. Alia Ahmad. New Delhi: Sage Publications, 1991: 184 p. *ISBN: 0803996829; LofC: 91006973. Includes bibliographical references and index.*

142 Women's bodies — the site for the ongoing conquest by reproductive technologies. Jyotsna Agnihotri Gupta. *Iss. Repro. Gen. Engin.* **4:2** :1991 pp. 93 – 108

Morbidity *[Morbidité]*

143 Age-specific incidence and prevalence — a statistical perspective (with discussion). N. Keiding. *J. Roy. Stat. Soc. A.* **154:3** :1991 pp. 371 – 412

144 AIDS and criminal justice. Arthur J. Lurigio *[Ed.]*; Mark Blumberg *[Contrib.]*; Denny Langston *[Contrib.]*; Anna T. Laszlo *[Contrib.]*; Barbara E. Smith *[Contrib.]*; Eugene Griffin *[Contrib.]*; Bruce Johnson *[Contrib.]*; Sandra Baxter *[Contrib.]*; Lawrence J. Ouellet *[Contrib.]*; Antonio D. Jimenez *[Contrib.] and others. Collection of 9 articles.* **Crime Delin.** , *37:1*, 1:1991 pp. 3 – 153

145 AIDS and the moral climate. Ian Sneddon; John Kremer. *Soc. Attit. N.Ire.* 1990-1991 pp. 120 – 141

146 AIDS and the news media. Dorothy Nelkin. *Milbank Q.* **69:2** 1991 pp. 293 – 308

147 AIDS and the public work force — local government preparedness in managing the epidemic. James D. Slack. Tuscaloosa: University of Alabama Press, c1991: xii, 182 p. *ISBN: 0817305483; LofC: 91002769. Includes bibliographical references p. [169]-177) and index.*

148 AIDS and the social sciences — common threads. Richard Ulack *[Ed.]*; William Francis Skinner *[Ed.]*. Lexington, Ky: University Press of Kentucky, c1991: xiii, 177 p. (ill) *ISBN: 0813117607; LofC: 91013348. Proceeding of a symposium held in October 1989 on the University of Kentucky campus; Includes bibliographical references (p. [158]-175).*

149 The AIDS epidemic and its demographic consequences — proceedings of the United Nations/World Health Organization Workshop on Modelling the Demographic Impact of the AIDS Epidemic in Pattern II countries — progress to date and policies for the future, New; York, 13-15 December 1989. International Economic and Social Affairs; World Health Organization. New York: United Nations, c1991: ix, 140 p. (ill) *ISBN: 9211512247. "ST/ESA/SER.A/119."; "Sales No. E.91.XIII.5"--T. p. verso."; Includes bibliographical references.*

150 AIDS impact on the number of intervenous drug users. Jonathan P. Caulkins; Edward H. Kaplan. *Interfaces* **21:3** 5-6:1991 pp. 50 – 63

151 AIDS in Africa — its present and future impact. Tony Barnett; Piers M. Blaikie. London: Belhaven Press, 1991: 193 p. *ISBN: 1852931159.*

152 Aids in Japan *[In German]*; [AIDS in Japan]. Roland Domenig. *Beit. Japan.* **29** 1991 pp. 506 – 525

153 AIDS modeling. Shan Cretin *[Contrib.]*; Richard C. Larson *[Contrib.]*; Margaret L. Brandeau *[Contrib.]*; Hau L. Lee *[Contrib.]*; Douglas K. Owens *[Contrib.]*; Carol H. Sox *[Contrib.]*; Robert M. Watcher; Jack B. Homer *[Contrib.]*; Christian L. St. Clair *[Contrib.]*; Jonathan P. Caulkins *[Contrib.] and others. Collection of 8 articles.* **Interfaces** , *21:3*, 5-6:1991 pp. 5 – 138

154 AIDS social representations — contents and processes. D. Páez; A. Echebarria; J. Valencia; I. Romo; C. San Juan; A. Vergara. *J. Comm. App. Soc. Psychol.* **1:2** 6:1991 pp. 89 – 104

155 AIDS — no greater challenge, solving the mysteries. David Spurgeon. [Ottawa]: Medical Research Council of Canada, [1990?]: 63 p. (ill., ports) *ISBN: oc23048794; LofC: cn 91070368. Issued also in French under title — SIDA, un défi sans précédent, à la recherche de solutions; Includes bibliographical references.*

156 AIDS — predicting the next map. Peter Gould; Joseph Kabel; Wilpen Gorr; Andrew Golub. *Interfaces* **21:3** 5-6:1991 pp. 80 – 92

157 AIDS — responses, interventions and care. Graham Hart *[Ed.]*; Peter Davies *[Ed.]*; Peter Aggleton *[Ed.]*. London: Falmer Press, 1991: vii, 286 p. (ill) *ISBN: oc22907031;*

F.3: Demographic trends and population policy *[Tendances démographiques et politique démographique]* — Morbidity *[Morbidité]*

LofC: 90026419. Contains many of the papers presented at the fourth conference on Social aspects of AIDS, held at South Bank Polytechnic, London, Mar. 1990; Includes bibliographical references and index. [Social aspects of AIDS.]

158 AIDS — women, drugs and social care. Nicholas Dorn *[Ed.]*; Sheila Henderson *[Ed.]*; Nigel South *[Ed.]*. Bristol, Pa: Falmer Press, 1991: 135 p. *ISBN: 1850008736; LofC: 90020419*. Includes index. [Social aspects of AIDS. : Vol. 1]

159 Aids, travel and migration — legal and human rights aspects; Aspects juridiques et humanitaires en matiére de voyage et de migration le défi des mesures de restriction liées au SIDA/VIH *[French summary]*; Aspectos jurídicos y de derechos humanos en viajes y migraciones — el desafio de las restricciones en relación con el VIH/SIDA *[Spanish summary]*. K. Tomasevski. *Int. Migr.* **XXIX:1** 3:1991 pp. 33 – 50

160 AIDS-related knowledge, attitudes, beliefs, and behaviors in Los Angeles County. David E. Kanouse *[Ed.]*. Santa Monica, CA: Rand, 1991: xx, 89 p. (ill) *ISBN: 0833011421; LofC: 91018295*. "Rand library collection"--Label on cover; Includes bibliographical references (p. 85-89),

161 Aspects of contemporary disease problems — are chronic diseases "genetic"? K.M. Weiss. *Coll. Antrop.* **15:1** 6:1991 pp. 87 – 100

162 Die Bestimmung von Gesundheit aus der Sicht der Dialektik des menschlichen Lebens *[In German]*; Defining health in a dialectical perspective on human life *[Summary]*. B. Rieske. *Medi. Mensch Gesell.* **16:3** 9:1991 pp. 218 – 226

163 Bioethics and public health in the 1980s — resource allocation and AIDS. R.R. Faden; N.E. Kass. *Ann. R. Pub. H.* **12** :1991 pp. 335 – 360

164 Blacks and AIDS — causes and origins. Samuel V. Duh. Newbury Park, Calif: Sage Publications, c1991: x, 153 p. *ISBN: 0803943466; LofC: 91015553*. Includes bibliographical references. [Sage series on race and ethnic relations. : Vol. 3]

165 The Box-Jenkins forecast of HIV seropositive population in Finland, 1991-1993. M. Löytönen. *Geog.ann. B.* **73:2** 1991 pp. 121 – 132

166 Cancer, control, and causality — talking about cancer in a working-class community. M. Balshem. *Am. Ethn.* **18:1** 2:1991 pp. 152 – 172

167 A cohort analysis of chronic morbidity and unemployment in the General Household Survey. David Winter. London: Suntory-Toyota International Centre for Economics and Related Disciplines, London School of Economics and Political Science, 1991: 33 p. [Welfare State Programme; Discussion paper. : No. WSP/59]

168 Continuity or change — inequalities in health in later life. Christina Victor. *Age. Soc.* **11:1** 3:1991 pp. 23 – 39

169 Différences selon le sexe dans l'âge d'apparition, la symptomatologie et l'évolution de la schizophrénie *[In French]*; [Gender differences in age at onset, symptomatology and course of schizophrenia] *[Summary]*. Heinz Häfner; Brigitte Fätkenheuer; Wolfram an der Heiden; Walter Löffler; Kurt Maurer; Povl Munk-Jorgensen; Anita Riecher. *San. Ment. Qué* **XVI:1** 6:1991 pp. 77 – 98

170 Disability in the United States — a portrait from national data. Inez Fitzgerald Storck *[Ed.]*; Susan Thompson-Hoffman *[Ed.]*. New York: Springer Pub. Co, c1991: xx, 260 p. (ill) *ISBN: 0826167705; LofC: 91010826 //r91*. Includes bibliographical references and index. [Springer series on rehabilitation. : Vol. 8]

171 Disease and mortality in sub-Saharan Africa. Richard George Feachem; Dean T. Jamison *[Ed.]*. Oxford: Oxford University Press for the World Bank, 1991: xv,356 p. *ISBN: 0195208269*.

172 A disease of society — cultural and institutional responses to AIDS. Dorothy Nelkin *[Ed.]*; David Willis *[Ed.]*; Scott Parris *[Ed.]*. Cambridge: Cambridge University Press, 1991: 287 p. *ISBN: 0521404118*.

173 Egypt's other wars — epidemics and the politics of public health. Nancy Elizabeth Gallagher. Syracuse: Syracuse University Press, 1991: 234p. (ill) *ISBN: 0815625073*. Includes bibliography and index. [Contemporary issues in the Middle East.]

174 Empirical status of cognitive theory of depression. David A.F. Haaga; Murray J. Dyck; Donald Ernst. *Psychol .B.* **110:2** 9:1991 pp. 215 – 236

175 Eßstörungen — Erklärung und Behandlung *[In German]*; Dietary disorders — explanation and treatment. I. Diedrichsen *[Contrib.]*; R.G. Laessle *[Contrib.]*; H. Feiereis *[Contrib.]*; I. Haisch *[Contrib.]*; J. Haisch *[Contrib.]*. Collection of 4 articles. **Medi. Mensch Gesell.** , *16:4*, 12:1991 pp. 227 – 275

F.3: Demographic trends and population policy [Tendances démographiques et politique démographique] — Morbidity [Morbidité]

176 Forecasting the number of AIDS cases in Brazil. Dan Gamerman; Hélio S. Migon. *Statistician* **40:4** 1991 pp. 427 – 442

177 Forum on AIDS disease in Africa. Philippe Engelhard *[Contrib.]*; Moussa Seck *[Contrib.]*; Adebowale Akande *[Contrib.]*; Sara Tallis *[Contrib.]*; Scott Harris *[Contrib.]*; A.I. Odebiyi *[Contrib.]*; Sola Olowu *[Contrib.]*; Franklin Vivekananda *[Contrib.]*; O. Okediji *[Contrib.]*; E.O. Ojofeitimi and others. Collection of 11 articles. **Scand. J. Devel. Altern.**, *X:1&2*, 3-6:1991 pp. 5 – 136

178 From authoritarianism to political democracy in Grenada — questions for U.S. policy. W. Marvin Will. *Stud. Comp. ID.* **26:3** Fall:1991 pp. 29 – 58

179 From TB to AIDS — epidemics among urban blacks since 1900. David McBride. Albany: State University of New York Press, c1991: x, 234 p. *ISBN: 0791405281; LofC: 90009758. by David McBride; Includes index; Includes bibliographical references (p. [177]-226).* [SUNY series in Afro-American studies.]

180 Un gramme cinq de latex — les hétérosexuels face au risque du SIDA et la prévention *[In French]*; [One and half grams of latex — heterosexuals facing up to the risk of AIDS and its prevention]. Hugues Lagrange. *Temps Mod.* **46:536-537** 3-4:1991 pp. 117 – 146

181 Health care workers' reactions to AIDS victims — perception of risk and attribution of responsibility. L. Mannetti; A. Pierro. *J. Comm. App. Soc. Psychol.* **1:2** 6:1991 pp. 133 – 142

182 HIV, AIDS and children — a cause for concern. Naomi Honigsbaum. London: National Children's Bureau in association with the National AIDS Trust, 1991: 179 p. *ISBN: 0902817639.*

183 Human Immunodeficiency Virus in Cuba — the public health response of a Third World country. Sarah Santana; Lily Faas; Karen Wald. *Int. J. Health. Ser.* **21:3** :1991 pp. 511 – 537

184 The illness experience — dimensions of suffering. Janice M. Morse *[Ed.]*; Joy L. Johnson *[Ed.]*. Newbury Park, Calif: Sage Publications, c1991: x, 350 p. (ill) *ISBN: 080394053x; LofC: 90009226. Includes bibliographical references and index.*

185 In time of plague — the history and social consequences of lethal epidemic disease. Arien Mack *[Ed.]*. New York: New York University Press, c1991: xii, 206 p. *ISBN: 0814754678; LofC: 91013750. Includes bibliographical references; Contents — AIDS and traditions of homophobia / Richard Poirier -- Plagues and morality / Anthony Quinton -- Human rights, public health, and the idea of moral plague / David A.J. Richards.*

186 The invisible epidemic — teenagers and AIDS — why teens are at risk, and what we can do to help. Andy Humm; Frances Kunreuther. *Soc. Pol.* **21:4** Spring:1991 pp. 40 – 47

187 Judging by appearances — audience understandings of the look of someone with HIV. J. Kitzinger. *J. Comm. App. Soc. Psychol.* **1:2** 6:1991 pp. 155 – 164

188 Life with AIDS. Rose Weitz. New Brunswick, NJ.: Rutgers University Press, c1991: x, 225 p. *ISBN: 0813516293; LofC: 90036219. Includes bibliographical references (p. 199-218) and index.*

189 Living in the real world — families speak out about Down's Syndrome. C. F. Goodey *[Ed.]*. London: Twenty-one Press, 1991: 135 p. *ISBN: 0951783807.*

190 Living with cystic fibrosis — the well sibling's perspective. Myra Bluebond-Langner. *Med. Anthr. Q.* **5:2** 6:1991 pp. 133 – 152

191 Lyme disease — the social construction of a new disease and its social consequences. Robert A. Aronowitz. *Milbank Q.* **69:1** 1991 pp. 79 – 112

192 La maladie mentale — une illusion *[In French]*; The illusion of mental illness *[Summary]*. Kate Millett. *San. Ment. Qué* **XVI:1** 6:1991 pp. 287 – 294

193 The male street prostitute — a vector for transmission of HIV infection into the heterosexual world. Edward V. Morse; Patricia M. Simon; Howard J. Osofsky; Paul M. Balson; H. Richard Gaumer. *Soc. Sci. Med.* **32:5** 1991 pp. 535 – 539

194 Les mécanismes d'adaptation des malades mentaux chroniques à la vie quotidienne *[In French]*; Day-to-day life adaptation mechanisms of chronically ill mental patients *[Summary]*. Yves Lecomte. *San. Ment. Qué* **XVI:2** Automne:1991 pp. 99 – 120

195 Mediating illness — newspaper coverage of tranquilliser dependence. Jonathan Gabe; Ulla Gustafsson; Michael Bury. *Sociol. Health Ill.* **13:3** 9:1991 pp. 332 – 353

196 Mental health and deviance in inner cities. Nicolas Queloz *[Ed.]*; William L. Parry-Jones *[Ed.]*. Geneva: World Health Organization, 1991: - *ISBN: 0119513927.*

197 Mental health, sensation seeking and drug use patterns — a longitudinal study; *[French summary]*; *[Spanish summary]*. Willy Pedersen. *Br. J. Addict.* **86:2** 2:1991 pp. 195 – 204

F.3: Demographic trends and population policy [Tendances démographiques et politique démographique] — Morbidity [Morbidité]

198 A model of HIV transmission through needle sharing. Jack B. Homer; Christian L. St. Clair. *Interfaces* **21:**3 5-6:1991 pp. 26 – 49

199 Modern death — taboo or not taboo? Tony Walter. *Sociology* **25:**2 5:1991 pp. 293 – 310

200 Mortalité et morbidité infantiles et juvéniles dans les grandes villes du Zaïre en 1986-1987 *[In French]*; [Infant and child morbidity and mortality in Zaire's cities 1986-1987]. Iman Ngondo a Pitshandenge. *Za-Afr.* **31:**251 1:1991 pp. 49 – 60

201 A multiperiod compartmental model of the HIV pandemic in the United States. Allan M. Salzberg; Stanley L. Dolins; Carol Salzberg. *Socio. Econ.* **25:**3 1991 pp. 167 – 178

202 Multiple stigma and AIDS — illness stigma and attitudes toward homosexuals and IV drug users in AIDS-related stigmatization. C.S. Crandall. *J. Comm. App. Soc. Psychol.* **1:**2 6:1991 pp. 165 – 172

203 A necessary end — attitudes to death. Julia Neuberger *[Ed.]*; John A. White *[Ed.]*. Basingstoke: Macmillan London, 1991: 178 p. *ISBN: 033348276x.*

204 Negotiating reality after physical loss — hope, depression, and disability. Timothy R. Elliott; Thomas E. Witty; Stephen Herrick; Josephine T. Hoffman. *J. Pers. Soc. Psychol.* **61:**4 10:1991 pp. 608 – 613

205 The new morbidity — a national plan of action. Alfred A. Baumeister; Frank D. Kupstas; Luann M. Klindworth. *Am. Behav. Sc.* **34:**4 3/4:1991 pp. 468 – 500

206 Performance of long-stay schizophrenics after drug withdrawal on matched immediate and delayed recall tasks. Avraham Calev; Doron Nigal; Sol Kugelmass; Malcolm P.I. Weller; Bernard Lerer. *Br. J. Clin. Psycho.* **30:**3 9:1991 pp. 241 – 246

207 Perspectives on AIDS — ethical and social issues. Christine Overall *[Ed.]*; William P Zion *[Ed.]*. Toronto: Oxford University Press, 1991: xi, 179 p. (ill) *ISBN: 0195407490; LofC: cn 91093127.* Includes bibliographical references and index.

208 Pilgrimage of pain — the illness experiences of women with repetition strain injury and the search for credibility. Janice Reid; Christine Ewan; Eva Lowy. *Soc. Sci. Med.* **32:**5 1991 pp. 601 – 612

209 The politics of AIDS. Jonathan Neale. *Int. Soc.* **:**53 Winter:1991 pp. 3 – 28

210 Public opinion about AIDS before and after the 1988 U.S. government public information campaign. Eleanor Singer; Theresa F. Rogers; Marc B. Glassman. *Publ. Opin. Q.* **55:**2 Summer:1991 pp. 161 – 179

211 Reproductive decisions among HIV-infected, drug using women — the importance of mother/child coresidence. Anitra Pivnick; Audrey Jacobson; Kathleen Eric; Michael Mulvihill; Ming Ann Hsu; Ernest Drucker. *Med. Anthr. Q.* **5:**2 6:1991 pp. 153 – 187

212 Response to the AIDS epidemic — a survey of homosexual and bisexual men in Los Angeles County. David E. Kanouse *[Ed.]*. Santa Monica, CA: Rand, 1991: xxii, 88 p. (ill) *ISBN: 0833011545.* Includes bibliographical references (p. 79-88).

213 A review of methods for the statistical analysis of spatial patterns of disease. R.J. Marshall. *J. Roy. Stat. Soc. A.* **154:**3 :1991 pp. 421 – 442

214 Revised understandings of psychogenic autism; *[French summary]*; *[German summary]*; *[Spanish summary]*. Frances Tustin. *Int. J.Psy.* **72:**4 1991 pp. 585 – 591

215 Sexually transmitted diseases and migration; Les maladies sexuellement transmissibles et la migration *[French summary]*; Las enfermedades transmitidas por via sexual y la migración *[Spanish summary]*. A. de Schryver; A. Meheus. *Int. Migr.* **XXIX:1** 3:1991 pp. 13 – 32

216 Sexually transmitted diseases and the reproductive health of women in developing countries. Christopher Elias. New York, NY: Population Council, Programs Division, 1991: viii, 54 p. *ISBN: oc25118489.* Includes bibliographical references (p. 47-54). [Working papers — Population Council, Programs Division.]

217 Le Sida — un défi aux droits *[In French]*; [AIDS — a challenge to human rights]. Michel Vincineau *[Ed.]*. Bruxelles: Émile Bruylant S.A., 1991: 888 p. *ISBN: 2802704974. Actes du colloque organisé à l'Université Libre de Bruxelles les 10, 11 et 12 mai 1990; At head of title — Institut de Sociologie et A.S.B.L. Aide Info Sida.*

218 Le SIDA — une pandémie *[In French]*; [AIDS — a pandemic]. Maurice Torrelli. *R. Gén. Droit Inter.* **95:**1 1991 pp. 93 – 107

219 Social dimensions of AIDS. D Abrams *[Ed.]*; D. Rosenthal *[Contrib.]*; S. Moore *[Contrib.]*; I. Flynn *[Contrib.]*; D. Páez *[Contrib.]*; A. Echebarria *[Contrib.]*; J. Valencia *[Contrib.]*; I. Romo *[Contrib.]*; C. San Juan *[Contrib.]*; A. Vergara *[Contrib.]* and others. Collection of 10 articles. **J. Comm. App. Soc. Psychol.** , *1:*2, 6:1991 pp. 77 – 187

220 Social structure, stress, and mental health — competing conceptual and analytic models. Carol S. Aneshensel; Carolyn M. Rutter; Peter A. Lachenbruch. *Am. Sociol. R.* **56:**2 4:1991 pp. 166 – 178

F.3: Demographic trends and population policy *[Tendances démographiques et politique démographique]* — **Morbidity** *[Morbidité]*

221 The sociology of health and illness; *[French summary]*. Kevin White. *Curr. Sociol.* **39:**2 Autumn:1991 pp. 1 – 82

222 The spatial diffusion of Human Immunodeficiency Virus type 1 in Finland, 1982-1997. Markku Löytönen. *Ann. As. Am. G.* **81:**1 3:1991 pp. 127 – 151

223 The spatial spread of the AIDS epidemic in Ohio — empirical analyses using the expansion method. E. Cassetti; C.C. Fan. *Envir. Plan.A.* **23:**11 11:1991 pp. 1589 – 1608

224 СПИД и вокруг него *[In Russian]*; (AIDS and related issues); (Attention — SIDA: *Title only in French)*; (AIDS und Umfeld: *Title only in German)*; (El SIDA y en torno a este: *Title only in Spanish)*. L. Milovanova. *Kommunist* **:**4(1374) 3:1991 pp. 89 – 99

225 Stress and adaptation in the context of culture — depression in a Southern Black community. William W. Dressler. Albany, N.Y: State University of New York Press, c1991: xv, 354 p. (ill) *ISBN: 0791404137; LofC: 89026307. Includes bibliographical references (p. 332-349) and index.*

226 Suomalaisten aikuisten mielenterveys ja mielenterveyden häiriöt *[In Finnish]*; Mental health and mental health disorders in the Finnish adult population *[Summary]*. Ville Lehtinen; Matti Joukamaa; Teela Jyrkinen; Kari Lahtela; Raimo Raitasalo; Jouni Maatela; Arpo Aromaa. *Kansan. Julk.* **:**33 1991 pp. 1 – 351

227 Symposium on international and comparative AIDS policy. Elizabeth A. Preble *[Contrib.]*; Carole K. Kauffman *[Contrib.]*; A. David Brandling-Bennett *[Contrib.]*; Edward J. Lynch *[Contrib.]*; Ana María Linares *[Contrib.]*; Lois E. Bradshaw *[Contrib.]*; Fernando Chang-Muy *[Contrib.]*; Ronald Bayer *[Contrib.]*; Lisa Bloom *[Contrib.]*; Günter Frankenberg *[Contrib.]* and others. *Collection of 10 articles.* **N.Y.U. J. Int'l. L. & Pol.** , **23:**4, Summer:1991 pp. 959 – 1110

228 Systemic HIV/AIDS counselling — creating balance in client belief systems. Robert Bor; Riva Miller; Isobel Scher; Heather Salt. *Practice* **5:**1 :1991 pp. 65 – 75

229 There was never really any choice — the experience of mothers of disabled children in the United Kingdom. Janet Read. *Wom. St. Inter. For.* **14:**6 1991 pp. 561 – 571

230 Traffic congestion, perceived control, and psychophysiological stress among urban bus drivers. Gary W. Evans; Sybil Carrère. *J. Appl. Psychol.* **76:**5 10:1991 pp. 658 – 663

231 We are all people living with AIDS — myths and realities of AIDS in Brazil. Herbert Daniel. *Int. J. Health. Ser.* **21:**3 :1991 pp. 539 – 551

232 Women and disability. Esther Boylan *[Ed.]*. London: Zed Books, 1991: 111 p. *ISBN: 0862329868; LofC: 91012443. Includes bibliographical references and index.* [Women and world development series.]

233 Znak „vzdělání" v epidemiologických studiích *[In Czech]*; Indicator of "education" in epidemiological studies *[Summary]*; Знак »образование« в эпидемиологических студиях *[Russian summary]*. Drahoslava Hrubá. *Demografie* **XXXIII:**2 1991 p. 134

Mortality *[Mortalité]*

234 AIDS deaths in the Bronx 1983-1988 — spatiotemporal analysis from a sociogeographic perspective. R. Wallace; M.T. Fullilove. *Envir. Plan.A.* **23:**12 12:1991 pp. 1701 – 1723

235 Assessment of cause of death in the Matlab demographic surveillance system. Vincent Fauveau *[Ed.]*. London: LSHTM, 1991: 52 p. in various pagings *ISBN: 0902657372. Bibliography — p 14-18.* [Research paper.]

236 Birth spacing and infant mortality in Brazil. Siân L. Curtis; John W. McDonald. *J. Biosoc. Sc.* **23:**3 7:1991 pp. 343 – 352

237 Birth weight and other determinants of infant and child mortality in three provinces of China. G. Dankert; J. van Ginneken. *J. Biosoc. Sc.* **23:**4 10:1991 pp. 477 – 490

238 Black-white mortality inequalities. Jere R. Behrman; Robin Sickles; Paul Taubman; Abdo Yazbeck. *J. Economet.* **50:**1/2 1991 pp. 183 – 203

239 Breast-feeding, birth interval and child mortality in Bangladesh. Abdul Kashem Majumder. *J. Biosoc. Sc.* **23:**3 7:1991 pp. 297 – 312

240 The centenarian question — old-age mortality in the Soviet Union, 1897-1970. Lea Keil Garson. *Pop. Stud. Egy.* **45:**2 7:1991 pp. 265 – 279

241 Changes in mortality in Pakistan 1960-88. Zeba A. Sathar; M.D. Mallick *[Comments by]*. *Pak. Dev. R.* **30:**4 Winter:1991 pp. 669 – 678

242 Child mortality in developing countries — socio-economic differentials, trends and implications. United Nations. Department of International Economic and Social Affairs. New York: United Nations, 1991: ix, 129 p. (ill) *ISBN: 9211512336. "Sales no. E.91.XIII.13" --T.p. verso; Includes bibliographical references.* [Document.]

F.3: Demographic trends and population policy *[Tendances démographiques et politique démographique]* — Mortality *[Mortalité]*

243 Détermination d'une table de mortalité — la conversion des taux en quotients *[In French]*; Life table construction. Conversion of rates into probabilities of dying. Gérard Calot; Graziella Caselli. *Population* **46:6** 11-12:1991 pp. 1441 – 1490

244 Différences de mortalité par sexe de la naissance à la puberté en Italie — un siècle d'évolution *[In French]*; Difference between the death rates of boys and girls below the age of puberty in Italy. A century of change. Antonella Pinnelli; Paola Mancini. *Population* **46:6** 11-12:1991 pp. 1651 – 1676

245 The differential effect of mothers' education on mortality of boys and girls in India. Katherine L. Bourne; George M. Walker. *Pop. Stud. Egy.* **45:2** 7:1991 pp. 203 – 220

246 Différentiation sociale et spatiale de la mortalité au Saguenay (Québec) *[In French]*; Social and spatial differenciation of mortality in the Saguenay (Quebec) *[Summary]*. M. Perron; S. Vieillette; M. Rainville; G. Hebert; C. Bouchard; C. Tremblay; J.-C. Otis. *Espace Pop. Soc.* **1** 1991 pp. 223 – 234

247 Disease and mortality in sub-Saharan Africa. Richard George Feachem; Dean T. Jamison *[Ed.]*. Oxford: Oxford University Press for the World Bank, 1991: xv,356 p. *ISBN: 0195208269.*

248 Les disparités géographiques de la mortalité en Tchécoslovaquie *[In French]*; Geographical mortality disparities in Czechoslovakia *[Summary]*. J. Rychtarikova; D. Dzúrová. *Espace Pop. Soc.* **1** 1991 pp. 183 – 190

249 Disparités régionales de la mortalité — le cas de la Rhénanie-Nord-Westphalie et de la Rhénanie-Palatinat *[In French]*; Regional disparities in mortality — the case of North-Rhine-Westphalia and Rhineland-Palatinate *[Summary]*. F. Heins. *Espace Pop. Soc.* **1** 1991 pp. 101 – 111

250 Les disparités régionales de mortalité en République Fédérale d'Allemagne *[In French]*; Regional disparities of mortality in the Federal Republic of Germany *[Summary]*. F.-J. Kemper; G. Thieme. *Espace Pop. Soc.* **1** 1991 pp. 93 – 100

251 Dissemblances de structure et contrastes régionaux de la mortalité en France *[In French]*; Structure dissimilarities and regional contrasts of mortality in France *[Summary]*. B. Kostrubiec. *Espace Pop. Soc.* **1** 1991 pp. 37 – 45

252 Effect of education and household characteristics on infant and child mortality in urban Nepal. Prakash Dev Pant. *J. Biosoc. Sc.* **23:4** 10:1991 pp. 437 – 444

253 Egyptian child mortality — a household, proximate determinants approach. Hassan Y. Aly. *J. Dev. Areas* **25:4** 7:1991 pp. 541 – 552

254 Estimation of adult mortality from orphanhood before and since marriage. Ian Timæus. *Pop. Stud. Egy.* **45:3** 11:1991 pp. 455 – 472

255 Estimation with heteroscedastic and correlated errors — a spatial analysis of intra-urban mortality data. Robert Haining. *Pap. Reg. Sci.* **70:3** 7:1991 pp. 223 – 246

256 Food habits, childhood mortality, growth and nutritional status of the rural Kisans of Sambalpur, Orissa. A.K. Mohanty; P.N. Sahu. *Man India* **71:4** 12:1991 pp. 601 – 610

257 Fun with Gompertz; *[Italian summary]*; *[French summary]*. John H. Pollard. *Genus* **XLVII:1-2** 1-6:1991 pp. 1 – 20

258 Géographie de la mortalité au Québec *[In French]*; The geography of mortality in the province of Quebec *[Summary]*. R. Pampalon. *Espace Pop. Soc.* **1** 1991 pp. 215 – 221

259 A halandóság néhány jellegzetessége Magyarországon az 1980-as években *[In Hungarian]*; (Selected features of mortality in Hungary in the 1980s). Józan Péter. *Demográfia* **34:3-4** 1991 pp. 339 – 350

260 Hijos de la deuda — un análisis de la situación de la infancia en el Ecuador *[In Spanish]*; [Children of debt — an analysis of infants in Ecuador]. Grupo de Trabajo sobre Deuda Externa y Desarollo. Quito: , 1990: 113 p.

261 The impact of public health interventions on sex differentials in childhood mortality in rural Punjab, India. Anne R. Pebley; Sajeda Amin. New York: The Population Council, 1991: 39 p. [Working papers.]

262 Les inégalités géographiques de la mortalité (II) *[In French]*; The geographical inequalities of mortality (II). Pierre-Jean Thumerelle *[Ed.]*; Nicole Thumerelle-Delaney *[Ed.]*; F. Tonnelier *[Contrib.]*; B. Kostrubiec *[Contrib.]*; Y. Chauviré *[Contrib.]*; P.-J. Thumerelle *[Contrib.]*; J.-M. Decroly *[Contrib.]*; J.-P. Grimmeau *[Contrib.]*; A.E. Kunst *[Contrib.]*; C.W.N. Looman *[Contrib.] and others. Collection of 21 articles.* **Espace Pop. Soc.**, *1*, 1991 pp. 29 – 234

263 Les inégalités géographiques de la mortalité selon la cause de décès en Pologne *[In French]*; Geographical inequalities of mortality according to cause of death in Poland *[Summary]*. B. Pulaska-Turyna. *Espace Pop. Soc.* **1** 1991 pp. 191 – 200

F.3: Demographic trends and population policy [Tendances démographiques et politique démographique] — Mortality [Mortalité]

264 Infant mortality in Bangladesh — a review of recent evidence. M. Faroque Ahmed. *J. Biosoc. Sc.* **23:3** 7:1991 pp. 327 – 336

265 Infant mortality, its components and correlates — findings from a longitudinal study in rural Karnataka, India; *[Italian summary]*; *[French summary]*. V.S. Badari; Y.S. Gopal; S.C. Devaramani. *Genus* **XLVII:1-2** 1-6:1991 pp. 89 – 108

266 Infant welfare services and infant mortality — a historian's view. Philippa Mein Smith. *Aust. Ec. Rev.* **93:1** 1-3:1991 pp. 22 – 34

267 Life span perspectives of suicide — time-lines in the suicide process. Antoon A. Leenaars *[Ed.]*. New York: Plenum Press, c1991: xvii, 325 p. (ill) *ISBN: 0306436205; LofC: 90049557.* Includes bibliographical references and index.

268 Limits to human life expectancy — evidence, prospects, and implications. Kenneth G. Manton; Eric Stallard; H. Dennis Tolley. *Pop. Dev. Rev.* **17:4** 12:1991 pp. 603 – 638

269 Marital transitions, poverty, and gender differences in mortality. Cathleen D. Zick; Ken R. Smith. *J. Marriage Fam.* **53:2** 5:1991 pp. 327 – 336

270 Measuring child mortality from maternity histories collected at time of childbirth. Case of EMIS surveys; *[Italian summary]*; *[French summary]*. Cheikh S.M. Mbacke. *Genus* **XLVII:1-2** 1-6:1991 pp. 109 – 130

271 Model mortality patterns — a parametric evaluation. Jon Anson. *Pop. Stud.* **45:1** 3:1991 pp. 137 – 184

272 Les modèles régionaux de mortalité des Pays-Bas sont-ils déterminés culturellement? *[In French]*; Are regional mortality patterns in the Netherlands culturally determined? *[Summary]*. A.E. Kunst; C.W.N. Looman; J.P. Mackenbach. *Espace Pop. Soc.* **1** 1991 pp. 85 – 91

273 La mortalité dans le Nord-Pas-de-Calais — un exemple de la stabilité des modèles régionaux de mortalité *[In French]*; Mortality in the Nord-Pas-de-Calais region — an example of the stability of regional models of mortality *[Summary]*. P.-J. Thumerelle. *Espace Pop. Soc.* **1** 1991 pp. 55 – 72

274 La mortalité des zones rurales et montagnardes en Catalogne *[In French]*; Mortality in rural and mountainous areas in Catalonia *[Summary]*. E. Mendizabal; A. Mompart; I. Pujadas. *Espace Pop. Soc.* **1** 1991 pp. 161 – 164

275 La mortalité en Italie selon des facteurs socio-économiques *[In French]*; Mortality and socio-economic conditions in Italy *[Summary]*. G. Meneghel. *Espace Pop. Soc.* **1** 1991 pp. 173 – 180

276 Mortality and fertility in Germany — cointegration and causality tests for rural and urban Prussia and modern Germany. Horst Entorf; Klaus F. Zimmermann. *J. Interd. Ec.* **4:1** 1991 pp. 17 – 31

277 Mortality in the two Germanies in 1986 and trends 1976-1986; La mortalité dans les deux Allemagnes en 1986 et les tendances 1976-1986 *[French summary]*. Ch. Höhn; J. Pollard. *Eur. J. Pop.* **7:1** 4:1991 pp. 1 – 28

278 Mortality of Hispanic populations — Mexicans, Puerto Ricans, and Cubans in the United States and in the home countries. Ira Rosenwaike *[Ed.]*. New York: Greenwood Press, 1991: xvi, 221 p. *ISBN: 0313275009; LofC: 91000002.* Mortality; Includes bibliographical references (p. 203-215) and index. [Studies in population and urban demography.]

279 Mortality reductions from health interventions — the case of immunization in Bangladesh; Les réductions des taux de mortalité à la suite d'interventions sanitaires — l'immunisation au Bangladesh *[French summary]*; Disminuyendo la mortalidad con intervenciones de salud — el caso de la inmunización en Bangladesh *[Spanish summary]*. Michael A. Koenig; Vincent Fauveau; Bogdan Wojtyniak. *Pop. Dev. Rev.* **17:1** 3:1991 pp. 87 – 104

280 Mothers' education and survival of female children in a rural area of Bangladesh. Abbas Bhuiya; Kim Streatfield. *Pop. Stud. Egy.* **45:2** 7:1991 pp. 253 – 264

281 Niveaux et causes de mortalité dans les provinces espagnoles *[In French]*; Mortality levels and causes in the Spanish provinces *[Summary]*. M. Blanco; M. Farre. *Espace Pop. Soc.* **1** 1991 pp. 151 – 160

282 Parental education and child mortality in Burundi. Josephine O'Toole; Robert E. Wright. *J. Biosoc. Sc.* **23:3** 7:1991 pp. 255 – 262

283 The politics of children's survival. George Kent. New York: Praeger, 1991: 204 p. *ISBN: 0275937232.*

284 The prevalence of chronic diseases during mortality increase — Hungary in the 1980s. James C. Riley. *Pop. Stud. Egy.* **45:3** 11:1991 pp. 489 – 496

F.3: Demographic trends and population policy [Tendances démographiques et politique démographique] — Mortality [Mortalité]

285 Příspěvek k regionální diferenciaci úmrtnosti *[In Czech]*; Contribution to regional mortality differentiation *[Summary]*; Региональная дифференциация смертности *[Russian summary]*. Jaroslav Kraus. *Demografie* **33**:3 1991 pp. 210 – 221

286 Proximate determinants of child mortality in Liberia. Omar B. Ahmad; Isaac W. Eberstein; David F. Sly. *J. Biosoc. Sc.* **23**:3 7:1991 pp. 313 – 326

287 Race or class or race and class — growing mortality differentials in the United States. Vicente Navarro. *Int. J. Health. Ser.* **21**:2 1991 pp. 229 – 236

288 Regional inequalities in mortality. Raymond Illsley; Christine Mullings; Julian le Grand. London: Suntory-Toyota International Centre for Economics and Related Disciplines, London School of Economics and Political Science, 1991: 41 p. [Welfare State Programme; Discussion paper. : No. WSP/57]

289 Social class as a risk factor for infant mortality in an Australian population. Susan Quine. *J. Biosoc. Sc.* **23**:1 1:1991 pp. 65 – 72

290 Socio-economic correlates of infant mortality in India; Correlazioni socioeconomiche della mortalità infantile in India *[Italian summary]*. Jandhyala B.G. Tilak. *Rev. Int. Sci. Ec. Com.* **38**:2 2:1991 pp. 169 – 192

291 Socio-economic development and the dynamics of child mortality among sedentarizing Bedouin in Israel. Avinoam Meir; Yosef Ben-David. *J. Econ. Soc. Geogr.* **82**:2 1991 pp. 139 – 147

292 Socioeconomic, demographic and environmental determinants of infant mortality in Nepal. Bhakta Gubhaju; Kim Streatfield; Abul Kashem Majumder. *J. Biosoc. Sc.* **23**:4 10:1991 pp. 425 – 436

293 Surmortalité féminine chez les musulmans en Yougoslavie — Islam ou culture méditerranéenne? *[In French]*; Excess mortality rates of Moslem women in Yugoslavia — Islam or the Mediterranean culture? *[Summary]*; Sobremortalidad femenina en los musulmanes yugoslavos — ¿Islam o cultura mediterránea? *[Spanish summary]*. Youssef Courbage. *Population* **46**:2 3-4:1991 pp. 299 – 326

294 Les tendances actuelles et la répartition spatiale de la mortalité en Pologne *[In French]*; Recent trends and spatial patterns of mortality in Poland *[Summary]*. A. Potrykowska. *Espace Pop. Soc.* **1** 1991 pp. 201 – 213

295 Trends, age patterns and differentials in childhood mortality in Haiti (1960-1987). George Bicego; Anouch Chahnazarian; Kenneth Hill; Michel Cayemittes. *Pop. Stud. Egy.* **45**:2 7:1991 pp. 235 – 252

296 Two centuries of mortality change in central Japan — the evidence from a temple death register. Ann Bowman Jannetta; Samuel H. Preston. *Pop. Stud. Egy.* **45**:3 11:1991 pp. 417 – 436

297 Variations intercommunales de la mortalité par âge en Belgique *[In French]*; Mortality per age variations within villages in Belgium *[Summary]*. J.-M. Decroly; J.-P. Grimmeau. *Espace Pop. Soc.* **1** 1991 pp. 75 – 83

298 Variations régionales de la mortalité en République d'Irlande *[In French]*; Regional variations of mortality in the Republic of Ireland *[Summary]*. D. Creton; D. Pringle. *Espace Pop. Soc.* **1** 1991 pp. 113 – 125

299 Writers die young — the impact of work and leisure on longevity. D.E. Kaun. *J. Econ. Psyc.* **12**:2 6:1991 pp. 381 – 400

Population growth [Croissance démographique]

300 Concise report on the world population situation in 1989 — with a special report on population trends and policies in the least developed countries. United Nations. Department of International Economic and Social Affairs. New York: United Nations, 1991: 31 p. (ill) *ISBN: 9211512190. "ST/ESA/SER.A/118."; "United Nations publication sales no. E.90.XIII.32"--T.p. verso.* [Population studies.]

301 Conséquences de la croissance démographique rapide dans les pays en développement *[In French]*; [The consequences of rapid demographic growth in developing countries]. Didier Blanchet *[Ed.]*; D.E. Horlacher *[Ed.]*; Georges Photios Tapinos *[Ed.]*. Paris: Institut national des études démographiques, 1991: 367 p. *ISBN: 2733240056. Bibliography — p.363-367.* [Congrès et colloques.]

302 Cuba — population et développement (essai sur la fécondité) *[In French]*; [Cuba — population and development (fertility study)]. Maryse Roux. *Cah. Amer. Lat.* :**11** 1991 pp. 83 – 101

F.3: Demographic trends and population policy [Tendances démographiques et politique démographique] — Population growth [Croissance démographique]

303 Downtown population growth and commuting trips — recent experience in Toronto. David M. Nowlan; Greg Stewart. *J. Am. Plann.* **57**:2 Spring:1991 pp. 165 – 182

304 Forecasting state and local population growth with limited data — the use of employment-migration relationships and trends in vital rates. M.J. Greenwood; G.L. Hunt. *Envir. Plan.A.* **23**:7 7:1991 pp. 987 – 1005

305 Népesedés és népesedéspolitika Magyarországon — a XXI. század kihívása és kockázata *[In Hungarian]*; [Population and population policy in Hungary. The challenge and risk of the 21st century]. István Monigl. ***Demográfia*** *Vol.30; No.4 - 1987.* pp. 369 – 396

306 On interpreting observed relationships between population growth and economic growth — a graphical exposition; Interpréter les relations observées entre la croissance démographique et la croissance économique — un exposé graphique *[French summary]*; Sobre interpretar relaciones observadas entre el crecimiento de la población y el crecimiento económico — una exposición gráfica *[Spanish summary]*. Didier Blachet. *Pop. Dev. Rev.* **17**:1 3:1991 pp. 105 – 114

307 Osservazioni sulle politiche di popolazione *[In Italian]*; [Observations on population policy]. Raimondo Cagiano de Azevedo. *Aff. Soc. Int.* **XIX**:2 1991 pp. 5 – 30

308 Overpopulation in India and the educational imperative. Kul Bhushan Suri. *Soc. Ser. R.* **65**:1 3:1991 pp. 22 – 42

309 Populační vývoj v Československu v roce 1990 *[In Czech]*; Population development of Czechoslovakia in 1990 *[Summary]*; Динамнка народонаселения в Чехословакии в 1990 году *[Russian summary]*. Jaroslav Kraus. *Demografie* **XXXIII**:4 1991 pp. 289 – 299

310 Population growth and nitrogen — an exploration of critical existential link. Vaclav Smil. *Pop. Dev. Rev.* **17**:4 12:1991 pp. 569 – 602

311 Population growth and policies in mega-cities. United Nations. Department of International Economic and Social Affairs. New York: United Nations, 1991: vi, 34 p. (map) *ISBN: 9211512220. "ST/ESA/SER.R/105."; "United Nations Publication. Sales No. E.91.XIII.3"--T.p. verso; Includes bibliographical references (p. 33-34).* [Population policy paper. : No. 32]

312 Population policies and programmes — lessons learned from two decades of experience. Nafis Sadik *[Ed.]*. New York: Published for United Nations Population Fund by New York University Press, c1991: xxiv, 464 p. (ill) *ISBN: 0814785530; LofC: 91012388. Includes bibliographical references (p. 404-432) and index.*

313 Rapid population growth and environmental stress. Barry Commoner. *Int. J. Health. Ser.* **21**:2 1991 pp. 199 – 227

F.4: Marriage and family — *Mariage et famille*

Sub-divisions: Divorce *[Divorce]*; Domestic violence and child abuse *[Violence domestique et enfants martyrs]*; Family law *[Droit de la famille]*; Marriage and cohabitation *[Mariage et cohabitation]*; Parenthood and parent-child relations *[Paternité-maternité et relations parents-enfants]*; Siblings and family structure *[Fratrie et structure de la famille]*

1 Abduction of children by family members. David Finkelhor; Gerald Hotaling; Andrea Sedlak. *J. Marriage Fam.* **53**:3 8:1991 pp. 805 – 817

2 *[In Japanese]*; [About LOVE — analysis of modern family (1)]. Shinya Tateiwa. ***Sociologos*** *No.(15) - 1991.* pp. 35 – 52

3 The American dream of family in film — from decline to a comeback. Emanuel Levy. *J. Comp. Fam. Stud.* **XXII**:2 Summer:1991 pp. 187 – 203

4 The American dream of family — ideals and changing realities. Suzanne Keller *[Contrib.]*; Vincent N. Parrillo *[Contrib.]*; Elizabeth Huttman *[Contrib.]*; Emanuel Levy *[Contrib.]*; Muriel G. Cantor *[Contrib.]*; David Halle *[Contrib.]*; Margaret L. Andersen *[Contrib.]*; Rosanna Hertz *[Contrib.]*. *collection of 7 articles.* **J. Comp. Fam. Stud.** , *XXII:2*, Summer:1991 pp. 129 – 265

5 The American family on television — from Molly Goldberg to Bill Cosby. Muriel G. Cantor. *J. Comp. Fam. Stud.* **XXII**:2 Summer:1991 pp. 205 – 216

6 The American upper class family — precarious claims on the future. Suzanne Keller. *J. Comp. Fam. Stud.* **XXII**:2 Summer:1991 pp. 159 – 183

F.4: Marriage and family [Mariage et famille]

7 Association models in family research. Masako Ishii-Kuntz. *J. Marriage Fam.* **53:2** 5:1991 pp. 337 – 347
8 A bereavement model for working with families of handicapped children. June Stewart; Gloria Pollack. *Child. Soc.* **5:3** Autumn:1991 pp. 241 – 253
9 Beyond the family — the social organization of human reproduction. A. F. Robertson. Oxford: Polity Press in association with Basil Blackwell, 1991: 231 p. *ISBN: 074560885x.*
10 *[In Japanese]*; [Beyond the future of family]. Kazuo Aoi. *Kikaku-joho No.(15) - 1991.* pp. 1 – 26
11 The "cession" of a child, potentially leading to an "alteration of the ego"; *[French summary]*; *[German summary]*; *[Spanish summary]*. José Rallo; Angeles de Miguel. *Int. Rev. Psy.* **18:2** 1991 pp. 241 – 248
12 *[In Japanese]*; [Changes in family ideology in post-war Japan — based on the results of nation-wide public-opinion polls]. Megumi Matsunari. *Kazoku Shakaigaku Kenkyu No.(3) - 1991.* pp. 85 – 97
13 The changing family in South Africa. Anna F. Steyn. *S.Afr. J. Sociol.* **22:1** 3:1991 pp. 23 – 30
14 *[In Japanese]*; [The changing life pattern of Japanese farm families]. Sonoko Kumagai. *Kazoku Shakaigaku Kenkyu No.(3) - 1991.* pp. 28 – 40
15 Child support in Australia — children's rights or public interest? Stephen Parker. *Int. J. Law Fam.* **5:1** 4:1991 pp. 24 – 57
16 Children of China — an inquiry into the relationship between Chinese family life and academic achievement in modern Taiwan. Douglas C. Smith. *Asian Cult. (Asian-Pac. Cult.) Q.* **XIX:1** Spring:1991 pp. 1 – 29
17 Chronicle — trends in population and family in the Low Countries. Joop de Beer; Gijs Beets; Erwin Bosman; Paul Willems. *Bevolk. Gez.* **:1** 1991 pp. 133 – 211
18 "Close to home" in Johannesburg — oppression in township households. Caroline White. *Agenda* **:11** 1991 pp. 78 – 89
19 Código familiar — uma versão sobre o significado da família em camadas médias urbanas *[In Portuguese]*; The family code — on the meaning of family in urban middle strata *[Summary]*. Tania Dauster. *Rev. Brasil. Est. Popul.* **5:1** 1-7:1988 pp. 103 – 125
20 The concept of caring in feminist research — the case of domestic service. Hilary Graham. *Sociology* **25:1** 2:1991 pp. 61 – 78
21 Cost/benefit oriented parental investment by high status families — the Krummhörn case. Eckart Voland; Eva Siegelkow; Claudia Engel. *Ethol. Socio.* **12:2** 1991 pp. 105 – 118
22 Couple strengths and stressors in Australian stepfamilies. Noel C. Schultz; Cynthia L. Schultz; David H. Olson. *J. Marriage Fam.* **53:3** 8:1991 pp. 555 – 564
23 Cultural elements of northern provenance in the family customs of Japan. Emori Itsuo. *Acta Asia.* **:61** 1991 pp. 83 – 102
24 Custodianship — relatives as carers and social worker assessments. Ellen Malos. *Adopt. Fost.* **15:2** 1991 pp. 28 – 35
25 The decline in men's labor force participation and income and the changing structure of family economic support. Jane Riblett Wilkie. *J. Marriage Fam.* **53:1** 2:1991 pp. 111 – 122
26 Demographic effects on household formation patterns. Karen Leppel. *J. Real Est. Res.* **6:2** Summer:1991 pp. 191 – 206
27 Determining children's home environments — the impact of maternal characteristics and current occupational and family conditions. Elizabeth G. Menaghan; Toby L. Parcel. *J. Marriage Fam.* **53:2** 5:1991 pp. 417 – 431
28 Displaying the dream — the visual presentation of family and self in the modern American household. David Halle. *J. Comp. Fam. Stud.* **XXII:2** Summer:1991 pp. 217 – 231
29 Dual-career couples and the American dream — self-sufficiency and achievement. Rosanna Hertz. *J. Comp. Fam. Stud.* **XXII:2** Summer:1991 pp. 247 – 265
30 Economic costs and rewards of two-earner, two-parent families. Sandra L. Hanson; Theodora Ooms. *J. Marriage Fam.* **53:3** 8:1991 pp. 622 – 634
31 Economic stress in the family and children's emotional and behavioral problems. David T. Takeuchi; David R. Williams; Russell K. Adair. *J. Marriage Fam.* **53:4** 11:1991 pp. 1031 – 1041
32 The effect of parental resources on patterns of leaving home among young adults in the Netherlands. Jenny de Jong-Gierveld; Aart C. Liefbroer; Erik Beekink. *Eur. Sociol. R.* **7:1** 5:1991 pp. 55 – 71
33 The effects of child mortality changes on fertility choice and parental welfare. Raaj K. Sah. *J. Polit. Ec.* **99:3** 6:1991 pp. 582 – 606

F.4: Marriage and family *[Mariage et famille]*

34 Egy új szempont a családi munkamegosztás vizsgálatához az időmérlegvizsgálatok tükrében *[In Hungarian]*; [A new aspect to the research of family labour division reflected in time-budget surveys]. Dávid Biró. *Szociologia Vol.16; No.1 - 1987.* pp. 129 – 139

35 Embarazo y parto entre la tradición y la modernidad — el caso de Ocuituco *[In Spanish]*; [Pregnancy and birth between tradition and modernity — the case of Ocuituco]. Roberto Castro; Mario Bronfman; Martha Loya. *Est. Sociol.* **IX:27** 9-12:1991 pp. 583 – 606

36 Estudis sobre la família *[In Catalan]*; [Family studies]. M. Jesús Izquierdo *[Contrib.]*; Dolors Comas d'Argemir *[Contrib.]*; Joan Josep Pujadas Munoz *[Contrib.]*; Lluís Flaquer *[Contrib.]*; Joan Bestard *[Contrib.]*; Xavier Coller *[Contrib.]*. Collection of 6 articles. **Papers** , *:36,* 1991 pp. 7 – 116

37 Ethnicity, family environment and social-status attainment — a follow-up analysis; *[French summary]*; *[Spanish summary]*. Kevin Marjoribanks. *J. Comp. Fam. Stud.* **XXII:1** Spring:1991 pp. 15 – 24

38 Evaluating the Milan approach. Alan Carr *[Contrib.]*; Matteo Selvini *[Contrib.]*; Lel Simpson *[Contrib.]*; Oded Manor *[Contrib.]*. Collection of 3 articles. **J. Fam. Ther.** , *13:3,* 8:1991 pp. 237 – 294

39 An exploratory path analysis of the stress process for dual-career men and women. Maureen G. Guelzow; Gloria W. Bird; Elizabeth H. Koball. *J. Marriage Fam.* **53:1** 2:1991 pp. 151 – 164

40 Família na transição demográfica — o caso de São Paulo *[In Portuguese]*; [The family in demographic transition — the case of São Paulo] *[Summary]*. Neide Lopes Patarra; Rosana Baeninger. *Rev. Brasil. Est. Popul.* **5:2** 7-12:1988 pp. 35 – 61

41 Families and delinquency — a meta-analysis of the impact of broken homes. L. Edward Wells; Joseph H. Rankin. *Soc. Prob.* **38:1** 2:1991 pp. 71 – 93

42 Families and hazard rates that change over time — some methodological issues in analyzing transitions. Sam Vuchinich; Jay Teachman; Lynn Crosby. *J. Marriage Fam.* **53:4** 11:1991 pp. 898 – 912

43 Families we choose — lesbians, gays, kinship. Kath Weston. New York: Columbia University Press, c1991: 261 p. *ISBN: 0231072880; LofC: 90049349.* Includes bibliographical references and index. [Between men--between women.]

44 *[In Hungarian]*; [The family and its culture — an investigation in seven East and West European countries for the European Coordination Centre for the Research and Documentation in Social Sciences]. Manfred Biskup *[Ed.]*; Vassilis Filias *[Ed.]*; Iván Vitányi *[Ed.]*. Budapest: Akadémiai Kiadó, 1987: xvi, 496 p.

45 Family and the state of theory. David Cheal. London: Harvester Wheatsheaf, 1991: 213 p. *ISBN: 0745005144.* Includes index.

46 The family context of nonorganic failure to thrive. Dennis Drotar. *Am. J. Orthopsy.* **61:1** 1:1991 pp. 23 – 34

47 Family decline in the Swedish welfare state. David Popenoe. *Publ. Inter.* **:102** Winter:1991 pp. 65 – 77

48 Family development cycle, social class, and inequality in Rwanda. Daniel C. Clay; Jim McAllister. *Rural Sociol.* **56:1** Spring:1991 pp. 22 – 40

49 Family diversity and the life cycle; *[French summary]*; *[Spanish summary]*. D.T. Rowland. *J. Comp. Fam. Stud.* **XXII:1** Spring:1991 pp. 1 – 14

50 The family in Italy from antiquity to the present. David I. Kertzer *[Ed.]*; Richard P. Saller *[Ed.]*. New Haven: Yale University Press, c1991: xiii, 399 p. *ISBN: 0300050372; LofC: 91012478.* Includes bibliographical references (p. 355-385) and index.

51 Family life quality — theory and assessment in economically stressed farm families. Kathryn D. Rettig; Sharon M. Danes; Jean W. Bauer. *Soc. Ind.* **24:3** 5:1991 pp. 269 – 299

52 Family policy in the EC countries — a general overview. Wilfried Dumon. *Bevolk. Gez.* **:1** 1991 pp. 1 – 16

53 *[In Japanese]*; [Family sociology and the social history of the family]. Kazue Muta. *Kazoku Shakaigaku Kenkyu No.(3) - 1991.* pp. 50 – 60

54 Family support for the elderly — the international experience. Hal L. Kendig *[Ed.]*; Akiko Hashimoto *[Ed.]*; Larry C. Coppard *[Ed.]*. Oxford [England]: Oxford University Press, 1991: 323 p. *ISBN: 0192621734; LofC: 91027405.* "A monograph sponsored by the Global Program for Health of the Elderly, World Health Organization.". [Oxford medical publications.]

55 Family support for the Nigerian elderly; *[French summary]*; *[Spanish summary]*. Margaret Peil. *J. Comp. Fam. Stud.* **XXII:1** Spring:1991 pp. 85 – 99

F.4: Marriage and family [Mariage et famille]

56 Family support networks, welfare, and work among young mothers. William L. Parish; Lingxin Hao; Dennis P. Hogan. *J. Marriage Fam.* **53:1** 2:1991 pp. 203 – 215
57 Family types and response to stress. Yoav Lavee; David H. Olson. *J. Marriage Fam.* **53:3** 8:1991 pp. 786 – 798
58 Feminism and the American family ideal. Margaret L. Andersen. *J. Comp. Fam. Stud.* **XXII:2** Summer:1991 pp. 235 – 246
59 Gender, work-family roles, and psychological well-being of blacks. Clifford L. Broman. *J. Marriage Fam.* **53:2** 5:1991 pp. 509 – 520
60 Genealogy and sociology — a preliminary set of statements and speculations. Michael Erben. *Sociology* **25:2** 5:1991 pp. 275 – 292
61 The God-market alliance in defence of family and community — the case of the new right in the United States. Banu Helvacioglu. *Stud. Pol. Ec.* **35:** Summer:1991 pp. 103 – 134
62 The history of widowhood — a bibliographic overview. Ida Blom. *J. Fam. Hist.* **16:2** 1991 pp. 191 – 210
63 Human capital investments or norms of role transition? how women's schooling and career affect the process of family formation. Hans-Peter Blossfeld; Johannes Huinink. *A.J.S.* **97:1** 7.1991 pp. 143 – 168
64 The immigrant family — securing the American dream. Vincent N. Parrillo. *J. Comp. Fam. Stud.* **XXII:2** Summer:1991 pp. 131 – 146
65 The impact of social and economic factors on the size of Israeli Jewish families. Yochanan Peres; Ilana Brosch. *J. Comp. Fam. Stud.* **XXII:3** Autumn:1991 pp. 367 – 378
66 *[In Japanese]*; [Impurity and social structure in Braham families of Nepal]. Kiyotomo Mikame. *Minzokugaku Kenkyu No.55(4) - 1991.* pp. 383 – 405
67 Intention versus behaviour in parental sex preferences among the Mukogodo of Kenya. Lee Cronk. *J. Biosoc. Sc.* **23:2** 4:1991 pp. 229 – 240
68 Intergenerational solidarity in aging families — an example of formal theory construction. Vern L. Bengtson; Robert E.L. Roberts. *J. Marriage Fam.* **53:4** 11:1991 pp. 856 – 870
69 *[In Japanese]*; [An investigation of the model family images]. Kazue Sakamoto. ***Tokei** No.42(5) - 1991.* pp. 27 – 34
70 Közvélemény-kutatás népesedési kérdésekről — 1989 *[In Hungarian]*; Public opinion poll concerning population issues, 1989 *[Summary]*. Edit Molnár. *Demográfia* **XXXIII:1-2** 1990 pp. 38 – 57
71 The Latin American family — familism vs machismo; *[French summary]*; *[Spanish summary]*. Bron B. Ingoldsby. *J. Comp. Fam. Stud.* **XXII:1** Spring:1991 pp. 57 – 62
72 The linkage between theory and research in family science. Yoav Lavee; David C. Dollahite. *J. Marriage Fam.* **53:2** 5:1991 pp. 361 – 373
73 A longitudinal analysis of sibling correlations in economic status. Gary Solon; Mary Corcoran; Roger Gordon; Deborah Laren. *J. Hum. Res.* **XXVI:3** Summer:1991 pp. 509 – 534
74 Marital quality and satisfaction with the division of household labor across the family life cycle. J. Jill Suitor. *J. Marriage Fam.* **53:1** 2:1991 pp. 221 – 230
75 Marriage, family, and the life course. John S. Clausen *[Contrib.]*; Daniel T. Lichter *[Contrib.]*; Felicia B. LeClere *[Contrib.]*; Diane K. McLaughlin *[Contrib.]*; Arland Thornton *[Contrib.]*; Judith A. Seltzer *[Contrib.]*; Linda J. Waite *[Contrib.]*; Lee A. Lillard *[Contrib.]*; Hiroshi Ishida *[Contrib.]*; John H. Goldthorpe *[Contrib.]* and others. Collection of 6 articles. *A.J.S.* , 96:4, 1:1991 pp. 805 – 992
76 Młode pokolenie a świat wartości życia rodzinnego *[In Polish]*; Young generation and the world values of the family life *[Summary]*. Anita Wojciechowska-Miszalska. *Acta Univ. Łódz. Folia Soc.* **21** 1991 pp. 57 – 72
77 New conceptions — biosocial innovations and the family. John N. Edwards. *J. Marriage Fam.* **53:2** 5:1991 pp. 349 – 360
78 *[In Japanese]*; [A note on the change in the craftman's "ie" and the family]. Maskazu Yamamoto. *Social Science No.(47) - 1991.* pp. 307 – 325
79 Obligations of kinship in contemporary Britain — is there normative agreement? Janet Finch; Jennifer Mason. *Br. J. Soc.* **42:3** 9:1991 pp. 344 – 367
80 Parental background, educational attainments and returns to schooling and to marriage — the case of Israel. S. Neuman. *Appl. Econ.* **23:8** 8:1991 pp. 1325 – 1334
81 Parental perceptions of the family and children's peer relations. Janis R. Bullock. *J. Psychol.* **125:4** 7:1991 pp. 419 – 426
82 Perceived stress and adjustment in religious Jewish families with a child who is disabled. Yona Leyser; Gad Dekel. *J. Psychol.* **125:4** 7:1991 pp. 427 – 438

F.4: Marriage and family [Mariage et famille]

83 Persian Gulf sojourn — stereotypes of family separation. Richard L. Dukes; Janice Naylor. *Social Soc. Res.* **76:1** 10:1991 pp. 29 – 34

84 Politique familiale et construction sociale de la famille *[In French]*; Family policy and the social construction of the family *[Summary]*. Remi Lenoir. *R. Fr. Sci. Pol.* **41:6** 12:1991 pp. 781 – 807

85 Power in family discourse. Richard J. Watts. Berlin: Mouton de Gruyter, 1991: xiv, 299 p. (ill) *ISBN: 3110132281; LofC: 91039289. Includes bibliographical references (p. [273]-288) and index.* [Contributions to the sociology of language. : No. 63]

86 Prescribing the model home. Gwendolyn Wright. *Soc. Res.* **58:1** Spring:1991 pp. 213 – 225

87 The prevalence of husband-centered migration — employment consequences for married mothers. Edward S. Shihadeh. *J. Marriage Fam.* **53:2** 5:1991 pp. 432 – 444

88 Příjmy mladých domácností v Československu (1970-1988) *[In Czech]*; Earnings of young families in Czechoslovakia (1970-1980) *[Summary]*; Доходы молодых домохозяйств в Чехословакии (1970-1988гг.) *[Russian summary]*. Miroslav Hiršl. *Demografie* **33:3** 1991 pp. 222 – 229

89 Produire la domus — une affaire de famille — niveaux et formes d'investissement des familles dans l'espace domestique *[In French]*; Home-making — a family concern — levels and forms of the investment in the home *[Summary]*. Philippe Bonnin. *Soc. Contemp.* **:5** 3:1991 pp. 145 – 162

90 Promjene u obitelji i specifični problemi migrantica *[In Serbo-Croatian]*; Changes in the family and the specific problems of women migrants *[Summary]*. Mirjana Oklobdžija. *Migrac. Teme* **6:4** 1990 pp. 39 – 46

91 Psychological distress and the recall of childhood family characteristics. Paul R. Amato. *J. Marriage Fam.* **53:4** 11:1991 pp. 1011 – 1020

92 Receipt of child support in the United States. Jay D. Teachman. *J. Marriage Fam.* **53:3** 8:1991 pp. 759 – 772

93 Relationship of children's ethnicity, gender, and social status to their family environments and school-related outcomes. Kevin Marjoibanks. *J. Soc. Psychol.* **131:1** 2:1991 pp. 83 – 91

94 Relationships among given names in the Scilly Isles. Pamela Raspe; Gabriel Lasker. *J. Biosoc. Sc.* **23:2** 4:1991 pp. 241 – 247

95 *[In Japanese]*; [Report on family's capacity for care of elderly]. Masashi Adachi. Kobe, Hyogo: Institute for study of Family Issues, 1991: 109 p.

96 A research note on dreams and aspirations of black families. Elizabeth Huttman. *J. Comp. Fam. Stud.* **XXII:2** Summer:1991 pp. 147 – 158

97 Reziprozität und Streß in "support"-Netzwerken — neue Perspektiven in der familiensoziologischen Netzwerkforschung *[In German]*; Reciprocity and stress in support-networks — new perspectives in family research *[Summary]*. Sylvia Gräbe. *Kölner Z. Soz. Soz. psy.* **43:2** 1991 pp. 344 – 356

98 A rokonság szerepe a mai magyar társadalomban *[In Hungarian]*; [The role of kinship in contemporary Hungarian society]. László Cseh-Szombathy. *Mag. Tud. Vol.32; No.5 - 1987.* pp. 348 – 358

99 The second child — family transition and adjustment. Robert B. Stewart. Newbury Park, Calif: Sage Publications, c1991: 251 p. *ISBN: 0803935196; LofC: 90043949. "May 1990."; Includes bibliographical references and indexes.* [New perspectives on family.]

100 Семья и религия *[In Russian]*; [The family and religion]. M.M. Usenova; N.P. Krasnikov *[Ed.]*. Alma-Ata: Mektets, 1986: 254 p.

101 Sex and politics — the family and morality in the Thatcher years. Martin Durham. London: Macmillan, 1991: 209 p. *ISBN: 0333498496.*

102 Sex preferences for offspring among men in the western area of Sierra Leone. Eugene K. Campbell. *J. Biosoc. Sc.* **23:3** 7:1991 pp. 337 – 342

103 *[In Japanese]*; Socializational factors of individual's achievement motivation in family *[Summary]*. Yu An-bang. *B. Inst. Ethn. Ac. Sin.* **:71** Spring:1991 pp. 87 – 132

104 *[In Japanese]*; [Sociology of contemporary family]. Kiyomi Morioka. Tokyo: University of Air Society for the Promotion of Education, 1991: 131 p.

105 *[In Japanese]*; [Solidarity through and among Japanese families — Taiaki case]. Kiyohide Seki; et al. ***Regional survey report on the attitude and behavior of the contemporary Japanese family, Nihon University*** *Vol.1991.* pp. 5 – 32

106 The Soviet family in the period of the decay of socialism. Vladimir Shlapentokh. *J. Comp. Fam. Stud.* **XXII:2** Summer:1991 pp. 267 – 279

F.4: Marriage and family [Mariage et famille]

107 Spouses' influence strategies in purchase decisions as dependent on conflict type and relationship characteristics. Erich Kirchler. *J. Econ. Psyc.* **11:1** 3:1990 pp. 101 – 118
108 Studying families. Anne P. Copeland; Kathleen M. White *[Ed.]*. Newbury Park, Calif: Sage Publications, c1991: ix, 116 p. *ISBN: 0803932472; LofC: 91011125. Includes bibliographical references (p. 105-113) and index.* [Applied social research methods series. : Vol. 27]
109 *[In Japanese]*; [Tendencies in German family sociology during the 1980s]. Ulrich Mohwald. *Kazoku Shakaigaku Kenkyu No.(3) - 1991.* pp. 98 – 103
110 A tie that blinds — family and ideology in Ireland. Ciaran McCullagh. *Econ. Soc. R.* **22:3** 4:1991 pp. 199 – 211
111 Time distributions in the process to marriage and pregnancy in Japan. Kenji Otani. *Pop. Stud. Egy.* **45:3** 11:1991 pp. 473 – 488
112 Using egocentered networks in survey research. A methodological preview on an application of social network analysis in the area of family research. W. Bien; J. Marcach; F. Neyer. *Soc. Networks* **13:1** 3:1991 pp. 75 – 90
113 Warm hearts and cold cash — the intimate dynamics of families and money. Marcia Millman. New York: Free Press, c1991: xi, 191 p. *ISBN: 0029212855; LofC: 90025094. Includes bibliographical references (p. 183-185) and index.*
114 Wives' off-farm employment, farm family economic status, and family relationships. Deborah D. Godwin; Peggy S. Draughn; Linda F. Little; Julia Marlowe. *J. Marriage Fam.* **53:2** 5:1991 pp. 389 – 402
115 Work/family conflicts — private lives - public responses. Bradley K. Googins. New York: Auburn House, 1991: xiv, 328 p. (ill) *ISBN: 0865690030; LofC: 90036656. Includes bibliographical references (p. [309]-319) and index.*
116 Youth unemployment and the family — voices of disordered times. Patricia Allatt; Susan Yeandle *[Ed.]*. New York: Routledge, 1991: 190 p. *ISBN: 041501851x; LofC: 91002708. Includes bibliographical references and index.*

Divorce [Divorce]

117 After marriage ends — economic consequences for midlife women. Leslie A. Morgan. Newbury Park, Calif: Sage Publications, c1991: 169 p. *ISBN: 080393548x; LofC: 90019472. "Published in cooperation with the National Council on Family Relations."; Includes bibliographical references.* [New perspectives on family.]
118 Age at first marriage, education and divorce — the case of the U.S.A. Pedro Telhado Pereira. *Economia [Lisbon]* **XV:1** 1:1991 pp. 21 – 50
119 Bestimmungsgründe des Ehescheidungsrisikos. Eine empirische Untersuchung mit Daten des soziöökonomischen Panels *[In German]*; Social determinants of the risk of divorce. An event in history analysis of retrospective data *[Summary]*. Andreas Diekmann; Thomas Klein. *Kölner Z. Soz. Soz. psy.* **43:2** 1991 pp. 271 – 290
120 Children and divorce — educational performance and behaviour before and after parental separation. B. Jane Elliott; Martin P.M. Richards. *Int. J. Law Fam.* **5:3** 12:1991 pp. 258 – 276
121 Consequences of parental divorce and marital unhappiness for adult well-being. Paul R. Amato; Alan Booth. *Soc. Forc.* **69:3** 3:1991 pp. 895 – 914
122 Contributions to children by divorced fathers. Jay D. Teachman. *Soc. Prob.* **38:3** 8:1991 pp. 358 – 370
123 The demographic dimensions of divorce — the case of Finland. Wolfgang Lutz; Anne B. Wils; Mauri Nieminen. *Pop. Stud. Egy.* **45:3** 11:1991 pp. 437 – 454
124 Divided families — what happens to children when parents part. Frank F. Furstenberg; Andrew J. Cherlin *[Ed.]*. Cambridge, Mass: Harvard University Press, c1991: 142 p. *ISBN: 0674655761; LofC: 90048171. Includes index.*
125 Divorce — an American tradition. Glenda Riley. New York: Oxford University Press, 1991: xi, 262 p. *ISBN: 0195061233; LofC: 90047746. Includes bibliographical references (p. 191-200) and index.*
126 Divorce — crisis, challenge, or relief? David A. Chiriboga; Linda S. Catron *[Ed.]*; H.B. Wilder *[Contrib.]*; Barbara Yee *[Contrib.]*. New York: New York University Press, c1991: xvi, 319 p. *ISBN: 0814714501; LofC: 90022219. Includes bibliographical references (p. 293-311) and index.*
127 Divorce, the law and social context — families of nations and the legal dissolution of marriage. Francis G. Castles; Michael Flood. *Acta Sociol.* **34:4** 1991 pp. 279 – 297

F.4: Marriage and family [Mariage et famille] — Divorce [Divorce]

128 Economic consequences of divorce — the international perspective. Lenore J Weitzman [Ed.]; Mavis Maclean [Ed.]. Oxford: Clarendon Press, 1991: 443 p. *ISBN: 0198254210; LofC: 91014739. Includes index.* [Oxford socio-legal studies.]

129 Hledání vysvětlujících faktorů rozvodovosti (regionální aplikace analýzy rozptylu) *[In Czech]*; Looking for explanatory divorce factors (a regional application of dispersion analysis) *[Summary]*; Поиск объясняющих факторов разводимости (региональное применение анализа рассеяния) *[Russian summary]*. Jaromír Běláček. *Demografie* **XXXIII:4** 1991 pp. 309 – 310

130 The illusion of equality — the rhetoric and reality of divorce reform. Martha A. Fineman. Chicago: University of Chicago Press, 1991: vii, 252 p. *ISBN: 0226249565; LofC: 90011274 //r91. Divorce; Includes bibliographical references (p. 191-248) and index.*

131 The legal and moral ordering of child custody. Carol Smart. *J. Law Soc.* **18:4** Winter:1991 pp. 485 – 500

132 The long shadow of marital conflict — a model of children's postdivorce adjustment. Marsha Kline; Janet R. Johnston; Jeanne M. Tschann. *J. Marriage Fam.* **53:2** 5:1991 pp. 297 – 309

133 The mediation alternative — process dangers for women. Trina Grillo. *Yale Law J.* **100:6** 4:1991 pp. 1545 – 1610

134 Parental divorce and adult well-being — a meta-analysis. Paul R. Amato; Bruce Keith. *J. Marriage Fam.* **53:1** 2:1991 pp. 43 – 58

135 Possible explanations for child sexual abuse allegations in divorce. Kathleen Coulborn Faller. *Am. J. Orthopsy.* **61:1** 1:1991 pp. 86 – 91

136 Postdivorce relationships between ex-spouses — the roles of attachment and interpersonal conflict. Carol Masheter. *J. Marriage Fam.* **53:1** 2:1991 pp. 103 – 110

137 Premarital sex and the risk of divorce. Joan R. Kahn; Kathryn A. London. *J. Marriage Fam.* **53:4** 11:1991 pp. 845 – 855

138 Provando e riprovando — matrimonio, famiglia e divorzio in Italia e in altri paesi occidentali *[In Italian]*; [Trying and trying again — marriage, family and divorce in Italy and in other Western countries]. Marzio Barbagli. Bologna: Il Mulino, c1990: 270 p. *ISBN: 8815025006; LofC: 90214767. Includes bibliographical references.* [Contemporanea.]

139 Regulating divorce. John Eekelaar. Oxford: Clarendon Press, 1991: 190 p. *ISBN: 0198257015; LofC: 91012532. Includes bibliographical references and index.* [Oxford socio-legal studies.]

140 The relations between reported well-being and divorce history, availability of a proximate adult, and gender. Lawrence R. Kurdek. *J. Marriage Fam.* **53:1** 2:1991 pp. 71 – 78

141 Single custodial females and their families — housing and coping strategies after divorce. Dana G. Stewart. *Int. J. Law Fam.* **5:3** 12:1991 pp. 296 – 317

142 Social integration and divorce. Alan Booth; John N. Edwards; David R. Johnson. *Soc. Forc.* **70:1** 9:1991 pp. 207 – 224

143 Social problems, political issues — marriage and divorce in the USSR. Andrea Stevenson Sanjian. *Eur.-Asia Stud.* **43:4** :1991 pp. 629 – 650

144 La standardisation indirecte améliorée et son application à la divortialité en Suède (1971-1989) *[In French]*; Improved indirect standardisation and patterns of divorce risks in Sweden (1971- 1989). Jan M. Hoem. *Population* **46:6** 11-12:1991 pp. 1551 – 1568

145 Surviving divorce — women's resources after separation. Mavis Maclean. London: Macmillan, 1991: 151 p. *ISBN: 0333465334. Divorce.* [Women in society.]

146 Time-related determinants of marital dissolution. Tim B. Heaton. *J. Marriage Fam.* **53:2** 5:1991 pp. 285 – 295

147 Zum gegenwärtigen Stand der Scheidungsursachenforschung Forschungsschwerpunkte und Erklärungsansätze über die verursachenden Bedingungen und den Anstieg der Ehescheidungen *[In German]*; On the present status of research on divorce and its causes *[Summary]*. Gitta Scheller. *Soz. Welt.* **42:3** 1991 pp. 323 – 348

Domestic violence and child abuse [Violence domestique et enfants martyrs]

148 Abused and battered — social and legal responses to family violence. Dean D. Knudsen [Ed.]; JoAnn L. Miller [Ed.]. New York: A. de Gruyter, c1991: xvi, 232 p. *ISBN: 0202304132; LofC: 90022716 //r91. Domestic violence and child abuse; Includes bibliographical references (p. 211-230) and index.* [Social institutions and social change.]

F.4: Marriage and family [Mariage et famille] — Domestic violence and child abuse [Violence domestique et enfants martyrs]

149 Black family violence — current research and theory. Robert L. Hampton *[Ed.]*. Lexington, Mass: Lexington Books, c1991: xv, 216 p. *ISBN: 0669218588; LofC: 90023280. Includes index.*
150 Child abuse in Sierra Leone — normative disparities. Bankole Thompson. *Int. J. Law Fam.* **5:1** 4:1991 pp. 13 – 23
151 Child sexual abuse in the Eastern Health Board region of Ireland in 1988 — an analysis of 512 confirmed cases. Kieran McKeown; Robbie Gilligan. *Econ. Soc. R.* **22:2** 1:1991 pp. 101 – 134
152 Child training practices and violent conflict management. Ursula Wagner. *Z. Ethn.* **115** 1990 pp. 67 – 72
153 Coping with an abusive relationship — I. How and why do women stay? Tracy Bennett Herbert; Roxane Cohen Silver; John H. Ellard. *J. Marriage Fam.* **53:2** 5:1991 pp. 311 – 325
154 Domestic violence — a nonrandom affair. Helen V. Tauchen; Ann Dryden Witte; Sharon K. Long. *Int. Econ. R.* **32:2** 5:1991 pp. 491 – 511
155 The effects of child abuse and neglect — issues and research. Raymond Starr *[Ed.]*; David A Wolfe *[Ed.]*. London: Guilford, 1991: xiv, 304 p. *ISBN: 0898627591; LofC: 91020247. Includes bibliographical references and index.*
156 Factors moderating physical and psychological symptoms of battered women. Diane R. Follingstad; Anne F. Brennan; Elizabeth S. Hause; Darlene S. Polek; Larry L. Rutledge. *J. Fam. Viol.* **6:1** 3:1991 pp. 81 – 96
157 Family sexual abuse — frontline research and evaluation. Michael Quinn Patton *[Ed.]*. Newbury Park: Sage, 1991: viii, 246 p. *ISBN: 0803939604; LofC: 90-19706.*
158 Intervening in child sexual abuse — learning from American experience. Kathleen Murray *[Ed.]*; David A. Gough *[Ed.]*. Edinburgh: Scottish Academic Press, 1991: xi, 212 p.,7p of plates (ill(some col.)) *ISBN: 0707305667. Includes bibliographies and index.*
159 Intrafamilial sexual abuse — family-of origin and family-of-procreation characteristics of female adult victims. David K. Carson; Linda M. Gertz; Mary Ann Donaldson; Stephen A. Wonderlich. *J. Psychol.* **125:5** 9:1991 pp. 579 – 597
160 Knowledge of spouse abuse in the community — a comparison across locations. Leslie W. Kennedy; David R. Forde; Michael D. Smith; Donald G. Dutton. *J. Fam. Viol.* **6:3** 9:1991 pp. 303 – 317
161 Legal images of battered women — redefining the issue of separation. Martha R. Mahoney. *Ml. law. R.* **90:1** 10:1991 pp. 1 – 94
162 Low and high deviance analogue assessment of parent-training with physically abusive parents. Virginia M. MacMillan; Ralph L. Olson; David J. Hansen. *J. Fam. Viol.* **6:3** 9:1991 pp. 279 – 302
163 New theory and old canards about family violence research. Murray A. Straus. *Soc. Prob.* **38:2** 5:1991 pp. 180 – 198
164 The other victim — the falsely accused parent in a sexual abuse custody case. Deborah H. Patterson. *J. Fam. Law* **30:4** 1991-1992 pp. 919 – 941
165 Overcoming barriers to the integration of practice and research in the field of domestic violence. Nanci Burns; Peggy Kieschnick. *Resp. Victim. Women Child.* **14:3(80)** 1991 pp. 9 – 17
166 The phenomenon of family murder in South Africa — an exploratory study — summary. L. Olivier *[Ed.]*. Pretoria: Human Sciences Research Council, 1991: 104 p. *ISBN: 079690989x.* [Report.]
167 Pre-program attrition in batterer programs. Edward W. Gondolf; Robert A. Foster. *J. Fam. Viol.* **6:4** 12:1991 pp. 337 – 350
168 Preventing of wife battering — insights from cultural analysis. Jacquelyn C. Campbell. *Resp. Victim. Women Child.* **14:3(80)** 1991 pp. 18 – 24
169 Le rôle de la relation conjugale dans l'abus et la négligence d'enfants. Vers une étude écologique *[In French]*; [The role of marital relations in the abuse and neglect of children — toward an ecological approach] *[Summary]*. Marc-André Provost; Joanne Dubé. *San. Ment. Qué* **XVI:1** 6:1991 pp. 213 – 234
170 Sexueller Mißbrauch von Kindern — Verbreitung, Phänomenologie und Prävention *[In German]*; Child sexual abuse — prevalence, phenomenology, intervention and prevention *[Summary]*. Berl Kutchinsky. *Z. Sexual.* **4:1** 3:1991 pp. 33 – 44
171 Treatment of sexual abuse which occurred in childhood — a review. C. Cahill; S.P. Llewelyn; C. Pearson. *Br. J. Clin. Psycho.* **30:1** 2:1991 pp. 1 – 12

F.4: Marriage and family *[Mariage et famille]* — **Domestic violence and child abuse** *[Violence domestique et enfants martyrs]*

172 True and false disclosures, true and false denials — believing and disbelieving children's allegations of abuse. Brian Minty. *Practice* **5**:3 1991 pp. 196 – 213

173 What changes the societal prevalence of domestic violence? Lance C. Egley. *J. Marriage Fam.* **53**:4 11:1991 pp. 885 – 897

174 With the best of intentions — the child sexual abuse prevention movement. Jill Duerr Berrick; Neil Gilbert. New York: Guilford Press, c1991: xiv, 210 p. *ISBN: 0898625645; LofC: 91024680. Includes bibliographical references (p. 125-153) and index.*

175 Woman battering — policy responses. Michael Steinman *[Ed.]*. Highland Heights, KY: Academy of Criminal Justice Sciences, Northern Kentucky University, c1991: v, 264 p. *ISBN: 0870848070; LofC: 90084733. Includes bibliographical references.* [ACJS/Anderson monograph series.]

176 Working for change — the movement against domestic violence. Andrew Hopkins; Heather McGregor. North Sydney: Allen & Unwin, c1991: xxiv, 150 p. *ISBN: 1863730192. Includes bibliographical references (p. 144-150).*

Family law *[Droit de la famille]*

177 Conditioning child support payments on visitation acess — a proposal. Alison Kitch. *Int. J. Law Fam.* **5**:3 12:1991 pp. 318 – 350

178 Court-ordered prenatal intervention — a final means to the end of gestational substance abuse. Michael T. Flannery. *J. Fam. Law* **30**:3 1991-1992 pp. 519 – 604

179 Divorce, the law and social context — families of nations and the legal dissolution of marriage. Francis G. Castles; Michael Flood. *Acta Sociol.* **34**:4 1991 pp. 279 – 297

180 The economics of wifing services — law and economics on the family. Belinda Bennett. *J. Law Soc.* **18**:2 Summer:1991 pp. 206 – 218

181 Die Ehe für Lesben und Schwule aus rechtspolitischer Sicht *[In German]*; Marriage for lesbians and gays from the legal point of view. Manfred Bruns; Volker Beck. *Z. Sexual.* **4**:3 9:1991 pp. 192 – 204

182 Eheliches Sonderrecht oder privatautonome Beziehungen *[In German]*; Special laws for marriage or autonomous relationships between individuals? *[Summary]*. Monika Frommel. *Z. Sexual.* **4**:3 9:1991 pp. 181 – 191

183 The European family and canon law; La famille européenne et le droit canon *[French summary]*; Die europäische Familie und das kanonische Recht *[German summary]*. Michael M. Sheehan. *Contin. Change* **6**:3 12:1991 pp. 347 – 360

184 Family ideology and political transition in Spain. Julio Iglesias de Ussel. *Int. J. Law Fam.* **5**:3 12:1991 pp. 277 – 295

185 The family in UK law and the International Convenant on Civil and Political Rights 1966. P.R. Ghandhi; E. MacNamee. *Int. J. Law Fam.* **5**:2 8:1991 pp. 104 – 131

186 Law and the family. Herbert Jacob *[Contrib.]*; Thomas B. Marvell *[Contrib.]*; Jessica Pearson *[Contrib.]*; Nancy Thoennes *[Contrib.]*; Patricia Tjaden *[Contrib.]*; Kirk R. Williams *[Contrib.]*; Richard Hawkins; David Greatbatch *[Contrib.]*; Robert Dingwall *[Contrib.]*. Collection of 5 articles. **Law Soc. Rev.** , *23:4*, 1989 pp. 539 – 641

187 Law reform and the family — the new South African rape-in-marriage legislation. Felicity Kaganas; Christina Murray. *J. Law Soc.* **18**:3 Autumn:1991 pp. 287 – 302

188 Legal custody arrangements and children's economic welfare. Judith A. Seltzer. *A.J.S.* **96**:4 1:1991 pp. 895 – 929

189 Looking for a family resemblance — the limits of the functional approach to the legal definition of family. *Harv. Law. Rev.* **104**:7 5:1991 pp. 1640 – 1659

190 Les manquements au droit de la famille en Afrique noire *[In French]*; [Breaches of family law in black Africa] *[Summary]*. Nicole-Claire Ndoko. *Rev. Int. D. C.* **43**:1 1-3:1991 pp. 87 – 104

191 Procedural due process rights of incarcerated parents in termination of parental rights proceedings — a fifty state analysis. Philip M. Genty. *J. Fam. Law* **30**:4 1991-1992 pp. 757 – 846

192 What does the Children Act mean for family members? Jo Tunnard; Mary Ryan. *Child. Soc.* **5**:1 Spring:1991 pp. 67 – 75

F.4: Marriage and family [Mariage et famille] —

Marriage and cohabitation [Mariage et cohabitation]

193 Une aide à l'analyse — les lignes d'isoquotients. L'exemple de la nuptialité [In French]; An aid to analysis. Isoquotients — nuptiality. Jean-Paul Sardon. *Population* **46:6** 11-12:1991 pp. 1405 – 1428

194 Are "worlds of pain" crosscultural? Korean working class marriages. Sook-Hyun Choi; Patricia M. Keith. *J. Comp. Fam. Stud.* **XXII:3** Autumn:1991 pp. 293 – 312

195 Assimilation oder Emanzipation? [In German]; Assimilation or emancipation? [Summary]. Jutta Oesterle-Schwerin. *Z. Sexual.* **4:3** 9:1991 pp. 205 – 212

196 Attachment in marriage — effects of security and accuracy of working models. R. Rogers Kobak; Cindy Hazan. *J. Pers. Soc. Psychol.* **60:6** 6:1991 pp. 861 – 869

197 [In Japanese]; [Attitudes toward marital and intergenerational relationships]. Toru Suzuki. *Journal of Population Problems* No.47(3) - 1991. pp. 28 – 40

198 Christianity and endogamy; Christianisme et endogamie [French summary]; Christentum and Endogamie [German summary]. Michael Mitterauer. *Contin. Change* **6:3** 12:1991 pp. 295 – 334

199 Common law union as a differentiating factor in the failure of marriage in Canada, 1984. S.S. Halli; Zachary Zimmer. *Soc. Ind.* **24:4** 6:1991 pp. 329 – 345

200 Commuter marriages — personal, family and career issues. Melissa M. Groves; Diane M. Horm-Wingerd. *Social Soc. Res.* **75:4** 7:1991 pp. 212 – 217

201 Conflict in married couples — personality predictors of anger and upset. David M. Buss. *J. Personal.* **59:4** 12:1991 pp. 663 – 688

202 Les défis de la psychologie face aux phénomènes conjugaux contemporains [In French]; [Psychology's challenges in view of contemporary marital phenomena] [Summary]. Carl Lacharité. *San. Ment. Qué* **XVI:1** 6:1991 pp. 17 – 26

203 Economic pressure and marital quality — an illustration of the method variance problem in the causal modeling of family processes. Frederick O. Lorenz; Rand D. Conger; Ronald L. Simons; Les B. Whitbeck; Glen H. Elder. *J. Marriage Fam.* **53:2** 5:1991 pp. 375 – 373

204 Economics and sociology of bride-price and dowry in eastern Rajasthan. V. Dixit. *Int. J. S. Law* **19:3** 8:1991 pp. 341 – 354

205 Effect of economic resources on marital quality for black couples. Patricia Clark-Nicolas; Bernadette Gray-Little. *J. Marriage Fam.* **53:3** 8:1991 pp. 645 – 656

206 Endogamia ed esogamia nel matrimonio dei cugini paralleli [In Italian]; Endogamy and exogamy in parallel cousin marriages [Summary]. Maria Arioti. *Rass. It. Soc.* **32:1** 1-3:1991 pp. 47 – 79

207 Ethnic intermarriage in Australia, 1950-52 to 1980- 82 — models or indices? F.L. Jones. *Pop. Stud.* **45:1** 3:1991 pp. 27 – 42

208 [In Japanese]; [Fertility and increasing age at time of first marriage — an interpretation on cross-sectional statistical data]. Taizo Egashira. *Hiroshima Hogaku* No.14(3) - 1991. pp. 71 – 109

209 Five decades of educational assortative mating. Robert D. Mare. *Am. Sociol. R.* **56:1** 2:1991 pp. 15 – 32

210 For better or for worse — the experience of caring for an early dementing spouse. Penelope Pollitt; I. Anderson; D.W. O'Connor. *Age. Soc.* **11:4** 12:1991 pp. 443 – 469

211 Gender and changing generational relations — spouse choice in Indonesia. Anju Malhotra. *Demography* **28:4** 11:1991 pp. 549 – 570

212 Group differences in economic opportunity and the timing of marriage — blacks and whites in the rural south, 1910. Nancy S. Landale; Stewart E. Tolnay. *Am. Sociol. R.* **56:1** 2:1991 pp. 33 – 45

213 Guidance, counselling, therapy — responses to "marital problems" 1950-90. David Clark. *Sociol. Rev.* **39:4** 11:1991 pp. 765 – 798

214 Les indices du moment de la nuptialité des célibataires [In French]; Period indices of nuptiality for single individuals. Yves Péron. *Population* **46:6** 11-12:1991 pp. 1429 – 1440

215 Influence of the marital history of parents on the marital and cohabitational experiences of children. Arland Thornton. *A.J.S.* **96:4** 1:1991 pp. 868 – 894

216 Intermarriage — effects on personality, adjustment, and intergroup relations in two samples of students. Walter G. Stephan; Cookie White Stephan. *J. Marriage Fam.* **53:1** 2:1991 pp. 241 – 250

217 Legal status and the stability of coresidential unions. Jay Teachman; Jeffrey Thomas; Kathleen Paasch. *Demography* **28:4** 11:1991 pp. 571 – 586

F.4: Marriage and family [Mariage et famille] — Marriage and cohabitation [Mariage et cohabitation]

218 Local marriage markets and the marital behavior of black and white women. Daniel T. Lichter; Felicia B. LeClere; Diane K. McLaughlin. *A.J.S.* **96:4** 1:1991 pp. 843 – 867

219 Marital mobility within Shahrestan Nowshahr, northern Iran. Haideh Mehrai; Eric Sunderland. *J. Biosoc. Sc.* **23:3** 7:1991 pp. 275 – 284

220 Marital status and personal happiness — an analysis of trend data. Gary R. Lee; Karen Seccombe; Constance L. Shehan. *J. Marriage Fam.* **53:4** 11:1991 pp. 839 – 844

221 Marriage and the sense of control. Catherine E. Ross. *J. Marriage Fam.* **53:4** 11:1991 pp. 831 – 838

222 Marriage duration and relational control. Paul H. Zietlow; C. Arthur Van Lear. *J. Marriage Fam.* **53:3** 8:1991 pp. 773 – 785

223 Marriage in an institutionalized life course — first marriage among American men in the twentieth century. Teresa M. Cooney; Dennis P. Hogan. *J. Marriage Fam.* **53:1** 2:1991 pp. 178 – 190

224 The marriage squeeze on high-caste Rajasthani women. Michael S. Billig. *J. Asian St.* **50:2** 5:1991 pp. 341 – 360

225 Marriage trends in the Italo-Greeks of Italy. G. Biondi; E. Perrotti. *J. Biosoc. Sc.* **23:2** 4:1991 pp. 129 – 135

226 Matrimonio e intercomunicación *[In Spanish]*; [Marriage and intercommunication]. Alfredo H. Altamira. *CIAS Vol.36; No.362 - 5: 1987.* pp. 147 – 158

227 ¿El mercado matrimonial en desbalance? El caso de México en 1980 *[In Spanish]*; Is the marriage market unbalanced? The case of Mexico in 1980 *[Summary]*. Norma Patricia Pavón. *Est. Demog. Urb.* **5:3** 9-12:1990 pp. 503 – 534

228 Monogamy and polygyny in southeast Arnhem Land — male coercion and female choice. James S. Chisholm; Victoria K. Burbank. *Ethol. Socio.* **12:4** 1991 pp. 291 – 314

229 Muslim Maghrebian marriages in France — a problem for legal pluralism. Edwige Rude-Antoine. *Int. J. Law Fam.* **5:2** 8:1991 pp. 93 – 163

230 Patterns of entry into cohabitation and marriage among mainland Puerto Rican women. Nancy S. Landale; Renata Forste. *Demography* **28:4** 11:1991 pp. 587 – 608

231 Polygyny in Istanbul. Cem Behar. *Middle E. Stud.* **27:3** 7:1991 pp. 477 – 486

232 Poverty and choice of marital status — a self-selection model. J.R. Rodgers. *Pop. Res. Pol. R.* **10:1** 1991 pp. 67 – 87

233 Przedmałżeńskie perspektywy sukcesu rodzinnego młodzieży miejskiej *[In Polish]*; Antenuptial perspectives of successful married life *[Summary]*. Jerzy Krzyszkowski. *Acta Univ. Łódz. Folia Soc.* **21** 1991 pp. 125 – 144

234 The recent trend in marital success in the United States. Norval D. Glenn. *J. Marriage Fam.* **53:2** 5:1991 pp. 261 – 270

235 Recht fertigen. Über die Einführung „homosexueller Ehen" in Dänemark *[In German]*; Some justifications. On the introduction of "homosexual marriages" in Denmark *[Summary]*. Henning Bech. *Z. Sexual.* **4:3** 9:1991 pp. 213 – 224

236 Reflections on a dissident Balinese marriage. Andrew Duff-Cooper. *Ind. Cir.* **:55** 6:1991 pp. 17 – 33

237 Rites of marrying — a Scottish study. S. R. Charsley. Manchester: Manchester University Press, 1991: - *ISBN: 0719028736. Includes index.* [Anthropological studies of Britain. : No. 5]

238 The role of cohabitation in declining rates of marriage. Larry L. Bumpass; James A. Sweet; Andrew Cherlin. *J. Marriage Fam.* **53:4** 11:1991 pp. 913 – 927

239 Role of social isolation in aggression among cohabiting partners. Jan E. Stets. *J. Marriage Fam.* **53:3** 8:1991 pp. 669 – 680

240 The roles of the wife and marital reality construction in the narrative interview. Uta Gerhardt. *Sociol. Health Ill.* **13:3** 9:1991 pp. 411 – 428

241 Sex differences in marital conflict — social psychophysiological versus cognitive explanations. Mary Anne Fitzpatrick. *Text* **11:3** 1991 pp. 341 – 364

242 *[In Japanese]*; [Sex education and marriage in Sweden]. Kyoko Yoshizumi. *Japanese Journal of Family-Relations No.(10) - 1991.* pp. 139 – 150

243 Shifting boundaries — trends in religious and educational homogamy. Matthijs Kalmijn. *Am. Sociol. R.* **56:6** 12:1991 pp. 786 – 800

244 Сколько стоит невеста *[In Russian]*; How much does the fiancee cost? F.N. Ilyasov. *Sot. Issle.* **:6** 1991 pp. 67 – 78

245 Social and family characteristics of marriage in England and Wales — information derived from marriage registration records. John C. Haskey. *J. Biosoc. Sc.* **23:2** 4:1991 pp. 179 – 200

F.4: Marriage and family [Mariage et famille] — Marriage and cohabitation [Mariage et cohabitation]

246 Social comparison and the drive upward revisited — affiliation as a response to marital stress. B.P. Buunk; N.W. Vanyperen; S.E. Taylor; R.L. Collins. *Eur. J. Soc. Psychol.* **21**:6 11-12:1991 pp. 529 – 546

247 Sociodemographic differentials in mate selection preferences. Scott J. South. *J. Marriage Fam.* **53**:4 11:1991 pp. 928 – 940

248 Socioeconomic and cultural differentials in age at marriage and the effect on fertility in Nepal. Ram Hari Aryal. *J. Biosoc. Sc.* **23**:2 4:1991 pp. 167 – 178

249 Socioeconomic correlates of age difference between spouses in the eastern province of Saudi Arabia. Abu Jafar Mohammad Sufian. *Social Soc. Res.* **75**:3 4:1991 pp. 164 – 169

250 Spheres of exchange and spheres of law — identity and power in Chinese marriage agreements. A. Riles. *Int. J. S. Law* **19**:4 11:1991 pp. 501 – 523

251 Stable unhappy marriages. Tim B. Heaton; Stan L. Albrecht. *J. Marriage Fam.* **53**:3 8:1991 pp. 747 – 758

252 Stress transmission — the effects of husbands' job stressors on the emotional health of their wives. Karen Rook; David Dooley; Ralph Catalano. *J. Marriage Fam.* **53**:1 2:1991 pp. 165 – 177

253 Synagogue marriages in Britain in the 1980s. Marlena Schmool. *Jew. J. Socio.* **XXXIII**:2 12:1991 pp. 107 – 116

254 Treue in Paarbeziehungen. Theoretische Aspekte, Bedeutungswandel und Milieu-Differenzierung *[In German]*; Fidelity in couple relationships — theoretical aspects, changes in meaning and differences between "milieus" *[Summary]*. Günter Burkart. *Soz. Welt.* **42**:4 1991 pp. 489 – 509

255 The varieties of other Caucasian intramarriage in Hawaii — 1987; *[French summary]*; *[Spanish summary]*. Joseph J. Leon; Michael G. Weinstein. *J. Comp. Fam. Stud.* **XXII**:1 Spring:1991 pp. 63 – 74

256 La vinculación de eventos demográficos — un estudio sobre los patrones de nupcialidad *[In Spanish]*; The link between demographic events — a study on the patterns of nuptiality *[Summary]*. Fátima Juárez. *Est. Demog. Urb.* **5**:3 9-12:1990 pp. 453 – 478

257 Violent emotions — shame and rage in marital quarrels. Suzanne M. Retzinger. Newbury Park, Calif: Sage Publications, c1991: xxiii, 238 p. *ISBN: 0803941838; LofC: 91003310.* Includes bibliographical references (p. 215-226) and indexes.

258 Von der Ehe als Institution zur individuellen Partnerschaft? Einstellungen zur Ehe und Familie in Österreich *[In German]*; From marriage as an institution to individual partnership? Attitudes towards marriage and the family in Austria *[Summary]*. Christine Goldberg. *Z. Soziol.* **20**:4 8:1991 p. 323

259 Whom God hath joined together — the work of marriage guidance. Jane Lewis; David Clark *[Ed.]*; David Morgan *[Ed.]*. London: Tavistock/Routledge, 1991: 308 p. *ISBN: 0415055539; LofC: 91013910.* Includes bibliographical references and index.

260 Why do women married to unemployed men have low participation rates? John Micklewright; Gianna Giannelli. Badia Fiesolana: European University Institute, 1991: 20 p. Bibliography — p.19-20. [EUI working paper.]

261 Women without husbands — an exploration of the margins of marriage. Joan Chandler. London: Macmillan, 1991: 188 p. *ISBN: 0333513657.* Includes bibliography and index. [Women in society.]

262 Women's confidants outside marriage — shared or competing sources of intimacy? Pat O'Connor. *Sociology* **25**:2 5:1991 pp. 241 – 254

263 Women's experience of power within marriage — an inexplicable phenomenon? Pat O'Connor. *Sociol. Rev.* **39**:4 11:1991 pp. 823 – 841

Parenthood and parent-child relations [Paternité-maternité et relations parents-enfants]

264 Adoption seeking in the United States, 1988. Christine A. Bachrach; Kathryn A. London; Penelope L. Maza. *J. Marriage Fam.* **53**:3 8:1991 pp. 705 – 718

265 Adult daughter-parent relationships and their associations with daughters' subjective well-being and psychological distress. Rosalind C. Barnett; Nazli Kibria; Grace K. Baruch; Joseph H. Pleck. *J. Marriage Fam.* **53**:1 2:1991 pp. 29 – 42

266 Affectionate touch between fathers and preadolescent sons. Robert E. Salt. *J. Marriage Fam.* **53**:3 8:1991 pp. 545 – 554

F.4: Marriage and family *[Mariage et famille]* — Parenthood and parent-child relations *[Paternité-maternité et relations parents-enfants]*

267 The affective organization of parenting — adaptive and maladaptative processes. Theodore Dix. *Psychol .B.* **110:1** 7:1991 pp. 3 – 25
268 Are breastfeeding patterns in Pakistan changing? Zubeda Khan. *Pak. Dev. R.* **30:3** 8:1991 pp. 297 – 311
269 Are fathers fungible? Patterns of coresident adult men in maritally disrupted families and young children's well-being. Alan J. Hawkins; David J. Eggebeen. *J. Marriage Fam.* **53:4** 11:1991 pp. 958 – 972
270 Assessing the costs and benefits of children — gender comparisons among childfree husbands and wives. Karen Seccombe. *J. Marriage Fam.* **53:1** 2:1991 pp. 191 – 202
271 Attachment to mother/attachment to father — a meta-analysis. Nathan A. Fox; Nancy L. Kimmerly; William D. Schafer. *Child. Devel.* **62:1** 2:1991 pp. 210 – 225
272 Birth parents and negotiated adoption agreements. Margaret Van Keppel. *Adopt. Fost.* **15:4** 1991 pp. 81 – 90
273 Black teenage mothers — pregnancy and child rearing from their perspective. Constance Willard Williams. Lexington, Mass: Lexington Books, c1991: xiii, 184 p. (ill) *ISBN: 0669243132; LofC: 90041347. Includes bibliographical references (p. [173]-177) and index.*
274 The child as project and the child as being — parents' ideas as frames of reference. Gunilla Halldén. *Child. Soc.* **5:4** Winter:1991 pp. 334 – 346
275 Child care — love, work and exploitation. Uta Enders-Dragässer. *Wom. St. Inter. For.* **14:6** 1991 pp. 551 – 556
276 Children and marital disruption. Linda J. Waite; Lee A. Lillard. *A.J.S.* **96:4** 1:1991 pp. 930 – 953
277 Competent child-focused practice — working with lesbian and gay carers. Helen Cosis Brown. *Adopt. Fost.* **15:2** 1991 pp. 11 – 17
278 Concepts of parenthood and their application to adoption. Malcolm Hill. *Adopt. Fost.* **15:4** 1991 pp. 16 – 23
279 Consistency and change in maternal child-rearing practices and values — a longitudinal study. Sandra McNally; Nancy Eisenberg; Jerry D. Harris. *Child. Devel.* **62:1** 2:1991 pp. 190 – 198
280 *[In Japanese]*; [Coping behaviors of working couples to their first child birth]. Miyoko Nagatsu. ***Kaseigaku Zasshi*** *No.42(2) - 1991.* pp. 25 – 37
281 Correlates of satisfaction for parents in stepfather families. Lawrence A. Kurdek; Mark A. Fine. *J. Marriage Fam.* **53:3** 8:1991 pp. 565 – 572
282 Cultural and psychological influences on the father's role in infant development. J. Kevin Nugent. *J. Marriage Fam.* **53:2** 5:1991 pp. 475 – 485
283 Daughters' help to mothers — intergenerational aid versus caregiving. Alexis J. Walker; Clara C. Pratt. *J. Marriage Fam.* **53:1** 2:1991 pp. 3 – 12
284 Dependency, self-criticism, and recollections of parenting — sex differences and the role of depressive affect. Valerie E. Whiffen; Teresa M. Sasseville. *J. Soc. Clin. Psychol.* **10:2** Summer:1991 pp. 121 – 133
285 Do men's adult life concerns affect their fathering orientations? Mary F. de Luccie; Albert J. Davis. *J. Psychol.* **125:2** 3:1991 pp. 175 – 188
286 Do parent-child relationships change during puberty? Roberta L. Paikoff; Jeanne Brooks-Gunn. *Psychol .B.* **110:1** 7:1991 pp. 47 – 66
287 Effects of adult children's problems on elderly parents. Karl Pillemer; J.Jill Suitor. *J. Marriage Fam.* **53:3** 8:1991 pp. 585 – 594
288 Effects of mothers' employment experiences on children's behaviour. Karyl E. MacEwen; Julian Barling. *J. Marriage Fam.* **53:3** 8:1991 pp. 635 – 644
289 The family life cycle in adoptive families. Fady Hajal; Elinor B. Rosenberg. *Am. J. Orthopsy.* **61:1** 1:1991 pp. 78 – 85
290 Fatherhood and families in cultural context. Frederick W Bozett *[Ed.]*; Shirley M. H Hanson *[Ed.]*. New York: Springer Pub. Co, c1991: xxiv, 290 p. (ill) *ISBN: 0826165702; LofC: 90009955. Includes bibliographical references and indexes.* [Springer series, focus on men. : Vol. 6]
291 Fathers' involvement in parenting sons and daughters. Kathleen Mullen Harris; S. Philip Morgan. *J. Marriage Fam.* **53:3** 8:1991 pp. 531 – 544
292 The fluctuating image of the 20th century American father. Ralph LaRossa; Betty Anne Gordon; Ronald Jay Wilson; Annette Bairan; Charles Jaret. *J. Marriage Fam.* **53:4** 11:1991 pp. 987 – 998

F.4: Marriage and family [Mariage et famille] — Parenthood and parent-child relations [Paternité-maternité et relations parents-enfants]

293 Images of parenthood in the United Kingdom and Japan. Robert Dingwall; Hiroko Tanaka; Satoshi Minamikata. *Sociology* **25:3** 8:1991 pp. 423 – 446

294 L'influence des conflits conjugaux sur l'enfant — revue des recherches, des théories et des pratiques *[In French]*; [The influence of marital conflict on the child — review of research, theory and practice] *[Summary]*. Marc Bigras; Diane Dubeau; Peter la Freniere. *San. Ment. Qué* **XVI:1** 6:1991 pp. 251 – 268

295 Interactions of middle-aged Japanese with their parents. Linda G. Martin; Noriko O. Tsuya. *Pop. Stud. Egy.* **45:2** 7:1991 pp. 299 – 312

296 De invloed van materiële en immateriële ouderlijke hulpbronnen op het verlaten van het ouderlijk huis *[In Dutch]*; The impact of material and immaterial parental resources on leaving home *[Summary]*. Jenny de Jong-Gierveld; Aart C. Liefbroer; Erik Beekink. *Mens Maat.* **66:1** 2:1991 pp. 25 – 53

297 Like parent like child? Associations between drinking and smoking behaviour of parents and their children; Tel père, tel fils? Corrélation entre les comportements de boisson et de tabagisme des parents et de leurs enfants *[French summary]*; ¿De tal palo tal astilla? Asociaciones entre la conducta bebedora y fumadora de padres e hijos *[Spanish summary]*. Gill Green; Sally Macintyre; Patrick West; Russell Ecob. *Br. J. Addict.* **86:6** 6:1991 pp. 745 – 758

298 Lone parenthood — coping with constraints and making opportunities. Michael Hardey *[Interviewer]*; Graham Crow *[Ed.]*. Hemel Hempstead: Harvester-Wheatsheaf, 1991: 200 p. *ISBN: 0745009654*.

299 Motherhood — meanings, practices and ideologies. Eva Lloyd *[Ed.]*; Ann Phoenix *[Ed.]*; Anne Woollett *[Ed.]*. London: Sage Publications, 1991: 240 p. *ISBN: 0803983131*. [Gender and psychology.]

300 Mothers and daughters — the distortion of a relationship. Vivien E. Nice; Jo Campling *[Ed.]*. London: Macmillan Academic and Professional, 1991: 256 p. *ISBN: 0333525280*.

301 Mothers' and fathers' perceptions of daily hassles of parenting across early childhood. Keith Crnic; Cathryn L. Booth. *J. Marriage Fam.* **53:4** 11:1991 pp. 1042 – 1050

302 Multiple determinants of father involvement during infancy in dual-earner and single-earner families. Brenda L. Volling; Jay Belsky. *J. Marriage Fam.* **53:2** 5:1991 pp. 461 – 474

303 Non-genetic mothers and their "own" children — infertility and IVF donor ova birth. Erica L. Hallebone. *Aust. J. Soc. Iss.* **26:2** 5:1991 pp. 123 – 137

304 Le nouveau-né et la couple — adversaires ou partenaires? *[In French]*; [The newborn and the couple — adversaries or partners?] *[Summary]*. Marc-André Provost; Serge Tremblay. *San. Ment. Qué* **XVI:1** 6:1991 pp. 235 – 250

305 On surrogacy — morality, markets, and motherhood. Michele M. Moody-Adams. *Publ. Aff. Q.* **5:2** 4:1991 pp. 175 – 190

306 One parent or two? The intertwining of American marriage and fertility patterns. Ronald R. Rindfuss; Jo Ann Jones. *Sociol. For.* **6:2** 6:1991 pp. 311 – 326

307 Parental absence during childhood and depression in later life. Paul R. Amato. *Sociol. Q.* **32:4** Winter:1991 pp. 543 – 556

308 Parental obligations and the ethics of surrogacy — a causal perspective. James Lindemann Nelson. *Publ. Aff. Q.* **5:1** 1:1991 pp. 49 – 61

309 Parent-child relations and parents' satisfaction with living arrangements when adult children live at home. William S. Aquilino; Khalil R. Supple. *J. Marriage Fam.* **53:1** 2:1991 pp. 13 – 28

310 Parent-offspring and sibling adoption analyses of parental ratings of temperament in infancy and childhood. Robert Plomin; Hilary Coon; Gregory Carey; J.C. DeFries; David W. Fulker. *J. Personal.* **59:4** 12:1991 pp. 705 – 732

311 Parents' attitudes towards the death of infants in the traditional Jewish-Oriental family; *[French summary]*; *[Spanish summary]*. Abraham Stahl. *J. Comp. Fam. Stud.* **XXII:1** Spring:1991 pp. 75 – 84

312 Partnership with parents — fantasy or reality? Jane Aldgate. *Adopt. Fost.* **15:2** 1991 pp. 5 – 10

313 Paternal engagement activities with minor children. William Marsiglio. *J. Marriage Fam.* **53:4** 11:1991 pp. 973 – 986

314 Patterns of marital change and parent-child interaction. Jay Belsky; Lise Youngblade; Michael Rovine; Brenda Volling. *J. Marriage Fam.* **53:2** 5:1991 pp. 487 – 498

315 Permanent family placement — a decade of experience. Joan Fratter *[Ed.]*. London: British Agencies for Adoption & Fostering, c1991: 125 p. (ill) *ISBN: 0903534967*. [Research series. : No. 8]

F.4: Marriage and family *[Mariage et famille]* — **Parenthood and parent-child relations** *[Paternité-maternité et relations parents-enfants]*

316 Preclusion, children and paternity — why are the children caught in the middle? John H. Grieve. *J. Fam. Law* **30:3** 1991-1992 pp. 629 – 640

317 Preferential parental investment in daughters over sons. Lee Cronk. *Hum. Nature* **2:4** 1991 pp. 387 – 417

318 Preventive intervention and outcome with anxiously attached dyads. Alicia F. Lieberman; Donna R. Weston; Jeree H. Pawl. *Child. Devel.* **62:1** 2:1991 pp. 199 – 209

319 Prisoners' children — what are the issues? Roger Shaw *[Ed.]*. London: Routledge, c1991: 207 p. *ISBN: 0415060672; LofC: 91009630. Includes bibliographical references and index.*

320 The quality of family time among young adolescents in single-parent and married-parent families. Linda Asmussen; Reed Larson. *J. Marriage Fam.* **53:4** 11:1991 pp. 1021 – 1030

321 Reforms for women — on male terms — the example of the Swedish legislation on parental leave. K. Widerberg. *Int. J. S. Law* **19:1** 2:1991 pp. 27 – 44

322 Les relations parents-enfants dans un contexte d'immigration ce que nous savons et ce que nous devrions savoir *[In French]*; [Parent-child relationships within the context of immigration what we know and what we should know] *[Summary]*. Colette Sabatier. *San. Ment. Qué* **XVI:1** 6:1991 pp. 165 – 190

323 Relationships between fathers and children who live apart — the father's role after separation. Judith A. Seltzer. *J. Marriage Fam.* **53:1** 2:1991 pp. 79 – 102

324 School-age child care and equal opportunities. Pat Petrie. *Wom. St. Inter. For.* **14:6** 1991 pp. 527 – 537

325 *[In Japanese]*; [Searching for the framework and key concepts of comparative sociology on childbirth and child rearing]. Keiko Funabashi. *Obirin Review of International Studies No.(3) - 1991.* pp. 143 – 158

326 Stepparents — wicked or wonderful? Christina Hughes. Aldershot: Avebury, c1991: x, 160 p. *ISBN: 1856281450. Bibliography — p.156-160..*

327 Subjection and the ethics of anguish — the Nepalese Parbatya parent-daughter relationship. Vivienne Kondon. *Contr. I. Soc.* **25:1** 1-6:1991 pp. 113 – 134

328 "Train up a child" — conceptions of child- rearing in Christian conservative social thought. Michael Lienesch. *Comp. Soc. Res.* **13** 1991 pp. 203 – 224

329 Work and family — should parents feel guilty? Lynn Sharp Paine. *Publ. Aff. Q.* **5:1** 1:1991 pp. 81 – 99

Siblings and family structure *[Fratrie et structure de la famille]*

330 Changing family structure and fertility patterns — an Indian case. G.N. Ramu. *J. As. Afr. S.* **XXVI:3-4** 7-10:1991 pp. 189 – 206

331 Children at risk — the role of family structure in Latin America and West Africa. Sonalde Desai. New York, N.Y: Population Council, 1991: 41 p. (ill) *ISBN: oc25065917. Includes bibliographical references (p. 37-41).*

332 Dynamics of family development — a theoretical perspective. James M. White; Roy H. Rodgers *[Ed.]*. London: Guilford Press, 1991: 254 p. *ISBN: 0898620805.* [Perspectives on marriage and the family.]

333 Family dynamics in China — a life table analysis. Yi Zeng. Madison, Wis: University of Wisconsin Press, c1991: xxi, 197 p. (ill., map) *ISBN: 0299126307; LofC: 90050102. Includes bibliographical references (p. 183-192) and indexes.* [Life course studies.]

334 Family structure and age at marriage — evidence from a South Indian village. P.H. Reddy. *J. As. Afr. S.* **XXVI:3-4** 7-10:1991 pp. 253 – 266

335 Family structure and children's health and well-being. Deborah A. Dawson. *J. Marriage Fam.* **53:3** 8:1991 pp. 573 – 583

336 Family structure and home-leaving — a further specification of the relationship. William S. Aquilino. *J. Marriage Fam.* **53:4** 11:1991 pp. 999 – 1010

337 Family structure, parental practices, and high school completion. Nan Marie Astone; Sara S. McLanahan. *Am. Sociol. R.* **56:3** 6:1991 pp. 309 – 320

338 Family structure, welfare spending, and child homicide in developed democracies. Rosemary Gartner. *J. Marriage Fam.* **53:1** 2:1991 pp. 231 – 240

339 Family structures and the moral politics of caring. John J. Rodger. *Sociol. Rev.* **39:4** 11:1991 pp. 799 – 821

340 The influence of the family environment on personality — accounting for sibling differences. Lois Wladis Hoffman. *Psychol .B.* **110:2** 9:1991 pp. 187 – 203

341 The intergenerational flow of income — family structure and the status of black Americans. Frances K. Goldscheider; Calvin Goldscheider. *J. Marriage Fam.* **53:2** 5:1991 pp. 499 – 508

F.4: Marriage and family [Mariage et famille] — Siblings and family structure [Fratrie et structure de la famille]

342 Junge Familien in der Bundesrepublik — Familienalltag-Familienumwelt-Familienpolitik *[In German]*; [Young families in the Federal Republic. Everyday family life — family environment — family policy]. Volker Teichert *[Ed.]*. Opladen: Leske und Budrich, 1991: 287 p. *ISBN: 3810008079.*

343 Living arrangements in Flanders in the eighties. Freddy Deven. *Bevolk. Gez.* :**1** 1991 pp. 39 – 52

344 La monoparentalité — un concept moderne, une réalité ancienne *[In French]*; One-parent families. A modern concept or an old reality? Jacques Légaré; Bertrand Desjardins. *Population* **46:6** 11-12:1991 pp. 1677 – 1688

345 A népesség öregedésének hatása az idősek családösszetételére *[In Hungarian]*; (The impact of population ageing on the family structure of the elderly). Dooghe Gilbert. *Demográfia* **XXXIII:1-2** 1990 pp. 24 – 37

346 Number of siblings and sociability. Judith Blake; Barbra Richardson; Jennifer Bhattacharya. *J. Marriage Fam.* **53:2** 5:1991 pp. 271 – 283

347 Race, family structure, and changing poverty among American children. David J. Eggebeen; Daniel T. Lichter. *Am. Sociol. R.* **56:6** 12:1991 pp. 801 – 817

348 Race, kin networks, and assistance to mother-headed families. Dennis P. Hogan; Ling-Xin Hao; William L. Parish. *Soc. Forc.* **68:3** 3:1990 pp. 797 – 812

349 Sibling structure and intergenerational relations. Glenna Spitze; John R. Logan. *J. Marriage Fam.* **53:4** 11:1991 pp. 871 – 884

350 Sibship size and educational attainment in nuclear and extended families — Arabs and Jews in Israel. Yossi Shavit; Jennifer L. Pierce. *Am. Sociol. R.* **56:3** 6:1991 pp. 321 – 330

351 Types de familles, conditions de vie, fonctionnement du système familial et inadaptation sociale au cours de la latence et de l'adolescence *[In French]*; [Family types, living conditions, operation of family systems and social maladjustment during latency and adolescence in underprivileged districts] *[Summary]*. Marc le Blanc; Pierre McDuff; Richard Tremblay. *San. Ment. Qué* **XVI:1** 6:1991 pp. 45 – 76

352 Urbanisation et structures familiales en Algérie (1948-1987) *[In French]*; Urbanization and family structures in Algeria (1948-1987) *[Summary]*; Verstädterung und Familienstrukturen in Algerien (1948-1987) *[German summary]*; Urbanización y estructuras familiares en Argelia (1948-1987) *[Spanish summary]*. Maurice Guetta. *Rev. Fr. Soc.* **XXXII:4** 10-12:1991 pp. 577 – 597

353 Vliv počtu dětí na celkový rozsah a strukturu práce rodiny (francouzsko-česká komparace) *[In Czech]*; Influence of the number of children on total extent and structure of the family work (French and Czech comparison) *[Summary]*; Влияние численности детей на общий объем и структуру работы семьи (сравнение Франция — ЧСФР) *[Russian summary]*. Zuzana Miková. *Demografie* **XXXIII:4** 1991 pp. 317 – 326

354 Zurück zur postmodernen Familie — Geschlechterverhältnisse, Verwandtschaft und soziale Schicht im Silicon Valley *[In German]*; Backwards toward the postmodern family *[Summary]*. Judith Stacey. *Soz. Welt.* **42:3** 1991 pp. 300 – 322

F.5: Gender — *Sexe*

Sub-divisions: Feminism *[Féminisme]*; Gender differentiation *[Différenciation sexuelle]*; Gender roles *[Rôles de sexe]*

1 Accounting for cosmetic surgery — the accomplishment of gender. Diana Dull; Candace West. *Soc. Prob.* **38:1** 2:1991 pp. 54 – 70

2 Age at marriage, divorce, fertility and labour force participation of women — a time series perspective. Naci H. Mocan. *J. Interd. Ec.* **4:1** 1991 pp. 1 – 16

3 Class, gender, and machismo — the "treacherous-woman" folklore of Mexican male workers. Manuel Peña. *Gender Soc.* **5:1** 3:1991 pp. 30 – 46

4 Conflict, complement, and control — family and religion among Middle Eastern Jewish women in Jerusalem. Susan Starr Sered. *Gender Soc.* **5:1** 3:1991 pp. 10 – 29

5 The effect of emigration of husbands on the status of their wives — an Egyptian case. Judy H. Brink. *Int. J. M.E. Stud.* **23:2** 5:1991 pp. 201 – 211

6 The feminization of poverty — the demographic factor and the composition of economic growth. Emily M. Northrop. *J. Econ. Iss.* **XXIV:1** 3:1990 pp. 145 – 160

F.5: Gender [Sexe]

7 From Mao to Deng — life satisfaction among rural women in an emigrant community in South China. Yuen-fong Woon. *Aust. J. Chin. Aff.* **25** 1:1991 pp. 139 – 169
8 Gender and migration — geographical mobility and the wife's sacrifice. Norman Bonney; John Love. *Sociol. Rev.* **39:2** 5:1991 pp. 335 – 348
9 Gender and poverty in India. World Bank. Washington, D.C., U.S.A: The World Bank, 1991: 373 p. *ISBN: 0821318969; LofC: 91027720. Includes bibliographical references.* [A World Bank country study.]
10 Gender and publishing in sociology. Linda Grant; Kathryn B. Ward. *Gender Soc.* **5:2** 6:1991 pp. 207 – 223
11 Gender and the state in Japan. Jennifer Robertson *[Ed.]*; Nancy Rosenberger *[Contrib.]*; Anne Allison *[Contrib.]*. Collection of 4 articles. **Anthr. Quart.**, *64:4*, 10:1991 pp. 163 – 207
12 Gender and work orientation — values and satisfaction. David de Vaus; Ian McAllister. *Work Occup.* **18:1** 2:1991 pp. 72 – 93
13 Gender dilemmas in sexual harassment policies and procedures. Stephanie Riger. *Am. Psychol.* **46:5** 5:1991 pp. 497 – 505
14 Gender, production and well-being — rethinking the household economy. Naila Kabeer. Brighton: University of Sussex, Institute of Development Studies, 1991: 50 p. *ISBN: 0903715422. Bibl.*
15 Hearing other voices — Christian women and the coming of Islam. Eleanor A. Doumato. *Int. J. M.E. Stud.* **23:2** 5:1991 pp. 177 – 199
16 Honour and shame — women in modern Iraq. Sana al- Khayyat. London: Saqi, 1991: 232 p. *ISBN: 0863560946. Includes bibliography.*
17 How employment affects women's gender attitudes — the workplace as a locus of contextual effects. Lee Ann Banaszak; Jan E. Leighley. *Polit. Geogr. Q.* **10:2** 4:1991 pp. 174 – 185
18 Immigrant women in Los Angeles. Rebecca Morales; Paul Ong. *Econ. Ind. Dem.* **12:1** 2:1991 pp. 65 – 81
19 The integration of women into professional personnel and labor relations work. Einar Hardin. *Ind. Lab. Rel.* **44:2** 1:1991 pp. 229 – 240
20 *[In Japanese]*; [Japanese women as votes]. Joji Watanuki. ***Leviatán*** *No.(8) - 1991.* pp. 23 – 40
21 Leading lives — Irish women in Britain. Rita Wall. Dublin: Attic, 1991: 143 p. (ill) *ISBN: 1855940205.*
22 The menopause industry — medicine's 'discovery' of the mid-life woman. Sandra Coney. Auckland: Penguin, 1991: 307p. *ISBN: 0140152490.*
23 Migracije jugoslavenskih žena *[In Serbo-Croatian]*; Migration of Yugoslav women *[Summary]*. Melita Švob. *Migrac. Teme* **6:4** 1990 pp. 3 – 11
24 Modernisation in agriculture and rural women. Mita Majumdar. *Soc. Act.* **41:4** 10-12:1991 pp. 367 – 381
25 More than mothers and whores — redefining the AIDS prevention needs of women. Kathryn Carovano. *Int. J. Health. Ser.* **21:1** 1991 pp. 131 – 142
26 My love, she speaks like silence — men, sex, and subjectivity. Jock Norton. *Mel. J. Pol.* **20** 1991 pp. 148 – 188
27 Never married older women — the life experience. Mary O'Brien. *Soc. Ind.* **24:3** 5:1991 pp. 301 – 315
28 NGOs and women's development in rural south India — a comparative analysis. Vanita Viswanath. Boulder: Westview Press, 1991: xv, 179 p. (ill) *ISBN: 0813381045; LofC: 91008524. Includes bibliographical references and index.*
29 Older women in the post-Reagan era. Terry Arendell; Carroll L. Estes. *Int. J. Health. Ser.* **21:1** 1991 pp. 59 – 73
30 On the man question — gender and civic virtue in America. Mark E. Kann. Philadelphia: Temple University Press, 1991: xi, 364 p. *ISBN: 0877228078; LofC: 90045668. Includes bibliographical references (p. [317]-355) and index.*
31 Overemancipation? Liberation? Soviet women in the Gorbachev period. Ester Reiter; Meg Luxton. *Stud. Pol. Ec.* **:34** Spring:1991 pp. 53 – 74
32 Persons and powers of women in diverse cultures — essays in commemoration of Audrey I. Richards, Phyllis Kaberry, and Barbara E. Ward. Shirley Ardener *[Ed.]*; Audrey Isabel Richards *[Ed.]*; Phyllis Mary Kaberry *[Ed.]*; Barbara E. Ward *[Ed.]*. New York: Berg, 1991: 219 p. *ISBN: 0854967443; LofC: 91024663. Includes bibliographical references and index.* [Cross-cultural perspectives on women.]
33 The pornography "problem" — disciplining women and young girls. Wai-Teng Leong. *Media Cult. Soc.* **13:1** 1:1991 pp. 91 – 117

F.5: Gender *[Sexe]*

34 The progressive verification method — toward a feminist methodology for studying women cross-culturally. Janet Mancini Billson. *Wom. St. Inter. For.* **14:3** 1991 pp. 201 – 215
35 The restructuring of gender relations in an aging society. Annemette Sørensen. *Acta Sociol.* **34:1** 1991 pp. 45 – 55
36 Sewing clothes and sorting cashew nuts — factories, families, and women in Beira, Mozambique. Kathleen Sheldon. *Wom. St. Inter. For.* **14:1/2** 1991 pp. 27 – 36
37 Sex and nation — women in Irish culture and politics. Gerardine Meaney. Dublin: Attic, 1991: 22 p. *ISBN: 1855940159.*
38 Sex preference in Bangladesh, India, and Pakistan, and its effect on fertility. Moni Nag. New York, N.Y: Population Council, 1991: 43 p. *ISBN: oc25066357. Includes bibliographical references (p. 37-43).* [Research Division working papers.]
39 Time, the life course and work in women's lives — reflections from Newfoundland. Marilyn Porter. *Wom. St. Inter. For.* **14:1/2** 1991 pp. 1 – 14
40 Transcending boundaries — multi-disciplinary approaches to the study of gender. Pamela R. Frese *[Ed.]*; John M. Coggeshall *[Ed.]*. New York: Bergin & Garvey, 1991: xvi, 208 p. (ill) *ISBN: 0897892305; LofC: 90039154. Includes bibliographical references and index.*
41 Unequal participation by women in the working world. Irma Arriagada. *CEPAL R* **:40** 4:1991 pp. 83 – 98
42 Veiling the unveiled — the politics of purdah in a Muslim sect. Rehana Ghadially. *S. Asia* **XII:2** 12:1989 pp. 33 – 48
43 Voices from within — early personal narratives of Bengali women. Malavika Karlekar. Delhi: Oxford University Press, 1991: 227 p. (ill) *ISBN: 0195628365. Bibliography pp.199-212.*
44 Washing our linen — one year of women against fundamentalism. Clara Connolly. *Feminist R.* **37** Spring:1991 pp. 68 – 77
45 Women and AIDS in Zimbabwe — the making of an epidemic. Mary T. Bassett; Marvellous Mhloyi. *Int. J. Health. Ser.* **21:1** 1991 pp. 143 – 156
46 Women and economic empowerment. Dawn-Marie Driscoll *[Ed.]*. Boston: Massachusetts U.P., 1991: 269 p. *This special issue is vol.6, no.1 of the New England Journal of Public Policy.*
47 Women and health in Africa. Meredeth Turshen *[Ed.]*. Trenton, N.J: Africa World Press, 1991: vi, 250 p. *ISBN: 0865431809. Includes bibliographical references and index.*
48 Women and the environment — a reader — crisis and development in the Third World. Sally Sontheimer *[Ed.]*. London: Earthscan Publications, 1991: 192 p. *ISBN: 1853831115. Gender roles.*
49 Women and the "Kerala model" — four lives, 1870s-1980s. Robin Jeffrey. *S. Asia* **XII:2** 12:1989 pp. 13 – 32
50 Women and the law — commentary and materials. Jocelynne A. Scutt. Perth, W.A: Law Book Co, 1990: lii, 596 p. *ISBN: 0455209847; LofC: 91179555. Includes bibliographical references and indexes.*
51 Women and the private domain — a symbolic interactionist perspective. Efrat Tseëlon. *J. Theory Soc. Behav.* **21:1** 3:1991 pp. 111 – 124
52 Women at the turning-point — the socio-economic situation and prospects of women in the former GDR. Sabine Hübner. *Pol. Soc. Ger. Aust. Swit.* **3:3** Spring:1991 pp. 23 – 33
53 Women caregivers, women wage earners — social policy perspectives in Norway. Kris Kissman. *Wom. St. Inter. For.* **14:3** 1991 pp. 193 – 199
54 Women in the German-speaking countries. Eva Kolinsky *[Contrib.]*; Sabine Hübner *[Contrib.]*; Cheryl Benard *[Contrib.]*; Edit Schlaffer *[Contrib.]*; Claudia Kaufmann *[Contrib.]*; Sibylle Knauss *[Contrib.]*; Brigid Haines *[Contrib.]*. Collection of 6 articles. **Pol. Soc. Ger. Aust. Swit.** , *3:3,* Spring:1991 pp. 1 – 60
55 Women in the new Germany. Eva Kolinsky. *Pol. Soc. Ger. Aust. Swit.* **3:3** Spring:1991 pp. 1 – 22
56 Women of the intifada — gender, class and national liberation. Nahla Abdo. *Race Class* **32:4** 4-6:1991 pp. 19 – 34
57 Women, weight and eating disorders — a socio-cultural and political-economic analysis. Sharlene Hesse-Biber. *Wom. St. Inter. For.* **14:3** 1991 pp. 173 – 191
58 Women's health matters. Helen Roberts *[Ed.]*. London: Routledge, 1991: 200 p. *ISBN: 0415066859; LofC: 91012746. Includes bibliographical references and index.*
59 Women's madness — misogyny or mental illness? Jane M. Ussher. Hemel Hempstead: Harvester-Wheatsheaf, 1991: 341 p. *ISBN: 0745008313.*
60 The women's movement during the intifada. Joost R. Hiltermann. *J. Pal. Stud.* **XX:3(79)** Spring:1991 pp. 48 – 57

F.5: Gender *[Sexe]*
61 Women's work and food — a comparative perspective. C.E. Sachs. *J. Rural St.* **7:1-2** 1991 pp. 49 – 56

Feminism *[Féminisme]*

62 Against the grain — the contemporary women's movement in Northern Ireland. Eileen Evason. Dublin: Attic, 1991: 63 p. *ISBN: 1855940191*.
63 Apprenticeship in liberty — sex, feminism and sociobiology. Beatrice Faust. North Ryde, NSW: Angus & Robertson, c1991: 402 p., 8 p. of plates (ill) *ISBN: 0207157375*.
64 Between feminism and labor — the significance of the comparable worth movement. Linda M. Blum. Berkeley: University of California Press, c1991: x, 249 p. *ISBN: 0520070321; LofC: 90037561. Includes bibliographical references (pp. 219-242) and index.*
65 Beyond accommodation — ethical feminism, deconstruction, and the law. Drucilla Cornell. New York: Routledge, 1991: ix, 239 p. *ISBN: 0415901057; LofC: 91008554. Includes bibliographical references (p. 207-233) and index.* [Thinking gender.]
66 Beyond methodology — feminist scholarship as lived research. Mary Margaret Fonow *[Ed.]*; Judith A. Cook *[Ed.]*. Bloomington: Indiana University Press, c1991: vi, 310 p. *ISBN: 0253323452; LofC: 90043508. Includes bibliographical references and index.*
67 Beyond the pale — white women, racism, and history. Vron Ware. London: Verso, 1991: 263 p. *ISBN: 0860913368; LofC: 91035739. Includes index.* [Questions for feminism.]
68 Black women, sexism and racism — black or antiracist feminism? Gemma Tang Nain. *Feminist R.* **37** Spring:1991 pp. 1 – 22
69 Canadian feminism and the law — the Women's Legal Education and Action Fund and the pursuit of equality. Sherene Razack. Toronto: Second Story Press, 1991: - *ISBN: 0929005198; LofC: cn 91093462. Includes bibliographical references and index.*
70 The contemporary U.S. women's movement — an empirical example of competition theory. Rachel A. Rosenfeld; Kathryn B. Ward. *Sociol. For.* **6:3** 9:1991 pp. 471 – 500
71 Contradictions of feminist methodology. Sherry Gorelick. *Gender Soc.* **5:4** 12:1991 pp. 459 – 477
72 The democratic potential of mothering. Patricia Boling. *Polit. Theory* **19:4** 11:1991 pp. 606 – 625
73 Dharma's daughters — contemporary Indian women and Hindu culture. Sara S. Mitter. New Brunswick, NJ.: Rutgers University Press, c1991: xi, 198 p. *ISBN: 0813516773; LofC: 90019387. Includes bibliographical references (p. [187]-190) and index.*
74 Disciplining Foucault — feminism, power, and the body. Jana Sawicki. New York: Routledge, 1991: xiii, 130 p. *ISBN: 0415901871; LofC: 91000142. Includes bibliographical references and index.*
75 Does the sex of your children matter? Support for feminism among women and men in the United States and Canada. Rebecca L. Warner. *J. Marriage Fam.* **53:4** 11:1991 pp. 1051 – 1056
76 Eco-feminism — lessons for feminism from ecology. Sue V. Rosser. *Wom. St. Inter. For.* **14:3** 1991 pp. 143 – 151
77 Los estuidos de la mujery su inesercíon en la educacíon superior en Centroamérica *[In Spanish]*; [Women's studies — its insertion into higher education in Central America]. Helga Jiménez. *Vop. Ist.* **:55** 1-4:1991 pp. 15 – 26
78 Feminine language — contradictory textual politics. Sinikka Tuohimaa. *Semiotica* **87:** 3-4:1991 pp. 371 – 380
79 Feminism & political theory. Cass R. Sunstein *[Ed.]*. Chicago: University of Chicago Press, 1990: vii, 317 p. *ISBN: 0226780082; LofC: 90030656. Includes bibliographical references and index.*
80 Feminism and cultural studies — pasts, presents, futures. Sarah Franklin; Celia Lury; Jackie Stacey. *Media Cult. Soc.* **13:2** 4:1991 pp. 171 – 192
81 Feminism and Eastern Europe. Ines Rieder. Dublin: Attic Press, 1991: 23 p. *ISBN: 1855940175*.
82 Feminism and liberal theory. Richard C. Sinopoli; Nancy J. Hirschmann. *Am. Poli. Sci.* **85:1** 3:1991 pp. 221 – 234
83 Feminism and philosophy — perspectives on difference and equality. Moira Gatens. Oxford: Polity Press, 1991: 162 p. *ISBN: 0745604692. Includes index.*
84 Feminism and pornography. Ronald J. Berger; Patricia Searles; Charles E. Cottle. New York: Praeger, 1991: x, 178 p. *ISBN: 0275938190; LofC: 90024125. Includes bibliographical references (p. [143]-168) and index.*

F.5: Gender [Sexe] — Feminism [Féminisme]

85 Feminism and sexual harassment. Nicholas Davidson. *Society* **28:4(192)** 5-6:1991 pp. 39 – 49
86 Feminism and the contradictions of law reform. M. Thornton. *Int. J. S. Law* **19:4** 11:1991 pp. 453 – 474
87 Feminism and the gender gap — a second look. Elizabeth Adell Cook; Clyde Wilcox. *J. Polit.* **53:4** 11:1991 pp. 1111 – 1122
88 The feminism of T.H. Green — a late Victorian success story? O. Anderson. *Hist. Polit. Thou.* **XII:4** Winter:1991 pp. 671 – 694
89 Feminism without women. Tania Modleski. New York: Routledge, 1991: xi, 188 p. *ISBN: 0415904161; LofC: 91013126. Includes bibliographical references and index.*
90 Feminist ethics. Claudia Card *[Ed.]*. Lawrence, Kansas: University Press of Kansas, 1991: 300 p. *ISBN: 0700604820.*
91 Feminist groupwork. Sandra Butler; Claire Wintram *[Ed.]*. London: Sage Publications, 1991: 224 p. *ISBN: 0803982097.* [Gender and psychology.]
92 Feminist scholarship in sociology — transformation from within? Susan A. McDaniel. *Can. J. Soc.* **16:3** Summer:1991 pp. 303 – 312
93 Feminist theorizing and communication ethics. Linda Steiner. *Communication* **12:3** :1991 pp. 157 – 174
94 Finding our way — rethinking eco-feminist politics. Janet Biehl. Montréal: Black Rose Books, 1991: 159 p. *ISBN: 0921689799; LofC: cn 91090134.*
95 Flexible sexism. D. Massey. *Envir. Plan. D* **9:1** 3:1991 pp. 31 – 57
96 Glass slippers and tough bargains — women,men and power. Maureen Gaffney. Dublin: Attic, 1991: 24 p. *ISBN: 1855940167.*
97 Hearing the difference — First and Third World feminisms. Chilla Bulbeck. *Asian Stud. R.* **15:1** 7:1991 pp. 77 – 90
98 The hysterical male — new feminist theory. Arthur Kroker *[Ed.]*; Marilouise Kroker *[Ed.]*. Basingstoke: Macmillan Education, 1991: 272 p. *ISBN: 0333557344.*
99 Images of power and contradiction — feminist theory and post-processual archaeology. Ericka Engelstad. *Antiquity* **65:248** 9:1991 pp. 502 – 514
100 Interpretation and genealogy in feminism. Kathy E. Ferguson. *Signs* **16:2** Winter:1991 pp. 322 – 339
101 Italian feminist thought — a reader. Paola Bono *[Ed.]*; Sandra Kemp *[Ed.]*. Oxford: Basil Blackwell, 1991: 458 p. *ISBN: 0631171150. Includes bibliography and index.*
102 Luce Irigaray's "contradictions" — poststructuralism and feminism. Maggie Berg. *Signs* **17:1** Autumn:1991 pp. 50 – 70
103 Male designs — feminism and technology. Judy Wajcman. Cambridge: Polity, 1991: 184 p. *ISBN: 0745607772. Includes bibliography and index.*
104 Marxism, feminism, and the struggle for democracy in Latin America. Norma Stoltz Chinchilla. *Gender Soc.* **5:3** 9:1991 pp. 291 – 310
105 Memories of origin — sexual difference and feminist polity. Francoise Vergès. *Iss. Repro. Gen. Engin.* **4:1** :1991 pp. 3 – 15
106 Moving the mountain — the women's movement in America since 1960. Flora Davis. New York: Simon & Schuster, c1991: 604 p. *ISBN: 0671602071; LofC: 91025144. Includes bibliographical references (p. [574]-581) and index.*
107 Nicaragua, revolución y feminismo (1977-89) *[In Spanish]*; [Nicaragua, revolution and feminism (1977-98)]. Clara Murguialday. Madrid: Editorial Revolución, c1990: 314 p. (ill) *ISBN: 8485781864; LofC: 90183505. Includes bibliographical references (p. 299-312).* [Hablan las mujeres. : No. 4]
108 The "no-problem" problem — feminist challenges and cultural change. Deborah L. Rhode. *Yale Law J.* **100:6** 4:1991 pp. 1731 – 1794
109 Off-centre — feminism and cultural studies. Sarah Franklin *[Ed.]*; Celia Lury *[Ed.]*; Jackie Stacey *[Ed.]*. Hammersmith, London, UK: HarperCollins Academic, 1991: x, 334 p., 8 p. of plates (ill) *ISBN: 0044456662; LofC: 90027327. Includes bibliographical references (p. [305]-320) and index.* [Cultural studies Birmingham.]
110 Out of the margins — women's studies in the nineties. Jane Aaron *[Ed.]*; Sylvia Walby *[Ed.]*. London: Falmer Press, 1991: 244 p. *ISBN: 1850009686; LofC: 91009617. Includes bibliographical references and index.*
111 Parità uomo-donna — sviluppo teorico e realizzazione pratica. Il contributo delle Nazioni Unite *[In Italian]*; [Sex equality — the theoretical development and practical realization. The contribution of the United Nations]. Giuseppe Scognamiglio. *Aff. Soc. Int.* **XIX:3** 1991 pp. 11 – 16

F.5: Gender [Sexe] — Feminism [Féminisme]

112 Passion and politics in women's studies in the nineties. Renate D. Klein. *Wom. St. Inter. For.* **14**:3 1991 pp. 125 – 134

113 The politics of reproduction. Faye Ginsburg; Rayna Rapp. *Ann. R. Anthr.* **20**: 1991 pp. 311 – 343

114 Pornography and feminism — the case against censorship. Gillian Rodgerson *[Ed.]*; Elizabeth Wilson *[Ed.]*. London: Lawrence & Wishart, 1991: 79 p. *ISBN: 0853157421.*

115 "Postfeminism" and popular culture. Suzanna D. Walters. *New Polit.* **III**:2 Winter:1991 pp. 103 – 112

116 Preferences in family politics — women's consciousness or family context? Eric Plutzer. *Polit. Geogr. Q.* **10**:2 4:1991 pp. 162 – 173

117 Reaching for global feminism — approaches to curriculum change in the southwestern United States. Janice Monk *[Ed.]*; Anne Betteridge *[Ed.]*; Amy W. Newhall *[Ed.]*; Carole Boyce Davies *[Contrib.]*; Tessie Liu *[Contrib.]*; Judy Nolte Lensink *[Contrib.]*; Kate Begnal *[Contrib.]*; Janet Owens Frost *[Contrib.]*; Amal Kawar *[Contrib.]*; Marie Cort Daniels *[Contrib.]* and others. Collection of 11 articles. **Wom. St. Inter. For.** , *14:4*, 1991 pp. 239 – 356

118 Recreating sexual politics — men, feminism and politics. Victor J. Seidler. London: Routledge, 1991: 311 p. *ISBN: 0415058538.*

119 Reflections on the women's movement in Trinidad — calypsos, changes and sexual violence. Patricia Mohammed. *Feminist R.* :**38** Summer:1991 pp. 33 – 47

120 Representations of difference — the varieties of French feminism. Jane Jenson. *New Left R.* **180** 1990 pp. 127 – 160

121 Science, feminism and animal natures I — extending the boundaries. Lynda I.A. Birke. *Wom. St. Inter. For.* **14**:5 :1991 pp. 443 – 449

122 Science, feminism and animal natures II — feminist critiques and the place of animals in science. Lynda I.A. Birke. *Wom. St. Inter. For.* **14**:5 :1991 pp. 451 – 458

123 Sexual democracy — women, oppression, and revolution. Ann Ferguson. Boulder, Colo: Westview Press, 1991: ix, 293 p. *ISBN: 0813307465; LofC: 90021084.* Includes bibliographical references (p. 255-274) and index. [Feminist theory and politics.]

124 Shifting territories — feminism and Europe. Helen Crowley *[Contrib.]*; Barbara Einhorn *[Contrib.]*; Catherine Hall *[Contrib.]*; Maxine Molyneux *[Contrib.]*; Lynne Segal *[Contrib.]*; Irene Dölling *[Contrib.]*; Frigga Haug *[Contrib.]*; Yudit Kiss *[Contrib.]*; Nira Yuval-Davis *[Contrib.]*; Mirjana Morokvasic *[Contrib.]* and others. Collection of 23 articles. *Feminist R.* , :*39*, Autumn:1991 pp. 1 – 186

125 Social action theory and the women's movement — an analysis of assumptions. Bill Lee; Wendy Weeks. *Comm. Dev. J.* **26**:3 7:1991 pp. 220 – 226

126 Space, sexual violence and social control — integrating geographical and feminist analyses of women's fear of crime. Rachel Pain. *Prog. H. Geog.* **15**:4 12:1991 pp. 415 – 431

127 Structure and agency in socialist-feminist theory. Amy S. Wharton. *Gender Soc.* **5**:3 9:1991 pp. 373 – 389

128 Taking stock of planning, space, and gender. Beth Moore Milroy. *J. Plan. Lit.* **6**:1 8:1991 pp. 3 – 15

129 *[In Japanese]*; [The theory of feminism concerning the system of capitalism and the system of patriarchy]. Seiko Higuchi. *Tohoku Fukushi University Bulletin 1991.* pp. 1 – 14

130 Third World women and the politics of feminism. Chandra Talpade Mohanty *[Ed.]*; Ann Russo *[Ed.]*; Lourdes Torres *[Ed.]*. Bloomington: Indiana University Press, 1991: 338 p. *ISBN: 0253338735.*

131 Toward a feminist regrounding of constitutional law. Gayle Binion. *Soc. Sci. Q.* **72**:2 6:1991 pp. 207 – 220

132 The trouble with subjects — feminism, Marxism and the questions of poststructuralism. Eleanor MacDonald. *Stud. Pol. Ec.* **35**: Summer:1991 pp. 43 – 72

133 Unsettling relations — the university as a site of feminist struggles. Himani Bannerji; et al. Toronto: Women's Press, 1991: 159 p. *ISBN: 0889611602; LofC: cn 91094010.* Includes bibliographical references.

134 Walking to the edge — essays of resistance. Margaret Randall. Boston: South End Press, c1991: xiii, 207 p. (ill) *ISBN: 0896083985; LofC: 90048221.* Includes bibliographical references.

135 The way forwards to the emancipation of women. Pat Horn. *Agenda* **10**: :1991 pp. 53 – 66

136 What can she know? — feminist theory and the construction of knowledge. Lorraine Code. Ithaca: Cornell University Press, 1991: xiv, 349 p. *ISBN: 0801424763; LofC: 90055755.* Includes bibliographical references (p. 325-338) and index.

F.5: Gender [Sexe] — Feminism [Féminisme]

137 When the moon waxes red — representation, gender and cultural politics. T. Minh-Ha Trinh. London: Routledge, 1991: ix, 251 p. *ISBN: 0415904307.*

138 Women organising. Helen Brown. New York: Routledge, 1991: 211 p. *ISBN: 0415048516; LofC: 91012107. Includes bibliographical references and index.*

139 Women's archaeology? Political feminism, gender theory and historical revision. Roberta Gilchrist. *Antiquity* **65:248** 9:1991 pp. 495 – 501

140 Women's caring — feminist perspectives on social welfare. Carol Baines *[Ed.]*; Patricia M. Evans *[Ed.]*; Sheila M. Neysmith *[Ed.]*. Toronto, Ontario: McClelland & Stewart, c1991: 310 p. *ISBN: 077101046x; LofC: 91167786. Includes bibliographical references and index.*

141 Women's life stories and reciprocal ethnography as feminist and emergent. Elaine J. Lawless. *J. Folk. Res.* **28:1** 1-4:1991 pp. 35 – 60

142 The women's movement in the United States — theory and practice. S. Farganis. *Int. J. Moral Soc. S.* **6:3** Autumn:1991 pp. 217 – 232

143 Women's movements in America — their successes, disappointments, and aspirations. Rita James Simon; Gloria Danziger. New York: Praeger, 1991: 171 p. *ISBN: 0275939480; LofC: 91008619. Includes bibliographical references (p. [147]-161) and index.*

144 Women's words — the feminist practice of oral history. Sherna Berger Gluck *[Ed.]*; Daphne Patai *[Ed.]*. New York: Routledge, 1991: 234 p. *ISBN: 0415903718. Includes bibliography and index.*

Gender differentiation [Différenciation sexuelle]

145 Accommodating protest — working women, the new veiling, and change in Cairo. Arlene Elowe Macleod. New York: Columbia University Press, c1991: xxiv, 206 p. *ISBN: 0231072805; LofC: 90002435. Includes bibliographical references (p. 187--202) and index.*

146 *[In Arabic]*; [The attitudes of male administrators in Jordan's public sector towards working women on the same level] *[Summary].Dirasat Ser. A.* **18A:2** 1991 pp. 212 – 236

147 The attitudes of subordinates to the gender of superiors in a managerial hierarchy. K. Cannings; C. Montmarquette. *J. Econ. Psyc.* **12:4** 12:1991 pp. 707 – 724

148 Austria — can women's capitalism have a social conscience? Cheryl Benard; Edit Schlaffer. *Pol. Soc. Ger. Aust. Swit.* **3:3** Spring:1991 pp. 34 – 39

149 „Autonomie" und „Institutionalisierung" — zwei konkurrierende politische Strategien *[In German]*; „Autonomy" versus „institutionalization" — a political controversy *[Summary]*. Erna Appelt. *Öster. Z. Polit.* **:2** 1991 pp. 131 – 142

150 De betekenis van arbeid in het levensplan van jonge mannen en vrouwen *[In Dutch]*; The meaning of work in the life plan of young men and women *[Summary]*. Frans Meijers. *Sociol. Gids* **XXXVIII** 9-10:1991 pp. 308 – 323

151 Conceiving selves — a case study of changing identities during the transition to motherhood. J. Smith. *J. Lang. Soc. Psychol.* **10:4** 1991 pp. 225 – 243

152 Convergence and divergence in the status of Moslem women — the cases of Turkey and Saudi Arabia; Convergence et divergence dans le statut des femmes musulmanes — les cas de la Turquie et de l'Arabie Saoudite *[French summary]*. Yakin Ertürk. *Int. Sociol.* **6:3** 9:1991 pp. 307 – 320

153 The decline of sex segregation and the wage gap, 1970-80. Judith Fields; Edward N. Wolff. *J. Hum. Res.* **XXVI:4** Fall:1991 pp. 608 – 622

154 Diritti umani. Alcune considerazioni sui diritti delle donne *[In Italian]*; [Human rights. Some thoughts on women's rights]. Pier Marcello Masotti. *Aff. Soc. Int.* **XIX:3** 1991 pp. 3 – 10

155 Discrimination against female-headed households in rental housing — theory and exploratory evidence. George Galster; Peter Constantine. *R. Soc. Econ.* **XLIX:1** Spring:1991 pp. 76 – 100

156 Do women receive compensating wages for risks of dying on the job? J. Paul Leigh; Andrew M. Gill. *Soc. Sci. Q.* **72:4** 12:1991 pp. 727 – 737

157 Dualism in biology — the case of sex hormones. Nelly Oudshoorn; Marianne van den Wijngaard. *Wom. St. Inter. For.* **14:5** :1991 pp. 459 – 471

158 L'égalité des femmes n'est pas pour demain *[In French]*; [Women's equality is not just around the corner]. Jean-Claude Bodson. *Socialisme* **38:224** 3-4:1991 pp. 99 – 109

159 Empowering women — self, autonomy, and responsibility. Barbara Rowland-Serdar; Peregrine Schwartz-Shea. *West. Pol. Q.* **44:3** 9:1991 pp. 605 – 624

160 Equal rights fails American mothers — the limitations of an equal rights strategy in family law and the workplace. Mary Ann Mason. *Int. J. Law Fam.* **5:3** 12:1991 pp. 211 – 240

INTERNATIONAL BIBLIOGRAPHY OF SOCIOLOGY — 1991

F.5: Gender *[Sexe]* — *Gender differentiation [Différenciation sexuelle]*

161 Equality politics and gender. Elizabeth M. Meehan *[Ed.]*; Selma Sevenhuijsen *[Ed.]*. London: Sage Publications, 1991: 200 p. *ISBN: 0803984820*. [Sage modern politics series. : No. 29]

162 Espace public et participation féminine — paysannes et commerce dans le nord-est du Brésil *[In French]*; [Public space and womens' participation — peasants and trade in north-east Brazil]. Marie France Garcia. *Soc. Sci. Info.* **30:**3 9:1991 pp. 523 – 554

163 An experimental investigation of gender bias in the use of management information. Ralph Estes. *J. Psychol.* **125:**4 7:1991 pp. 479 – 488

164 Feeding the family — the social organization of caring as gendered work. Marjorie L. DeVault. Chicago: University of Chicago Press, 1991: xii, 270 p. *ISBN: 0226143597; LofC: 91014447. Gender differentiation; Includes bibliographical references (p. 247-257) and index.* [Women in culture and society.]

165 Femmes et insertion dans les quartiers en développement social — étude-bilan 1982-1989 *[In French]*; [Women and integration in areas of social development — study for 1982-1989]. Isabelle Mahiou; Dominique Poggi *[Ed.]*. Paris: La Documentation française, 1991: 139 p. *ISBN: 2110024437*. [Droits des femmes.]

166 Forms and functions of female space — interrelationships with women's paid and unpaid work — a south Asian paradigm. Deipica Bagchi. *Asian Prof.* **19:**3 6:1991 pp. 269 – 282

167 Gender and distance learning. Cornelia Brunner. *Ann. Am. Poli.* **514** 3:1991 pp. 133 – 145

168 Gender and later life — a sociological analysis of resources and constraints. Sara Arber; Jay Ginn *[Ed.]*. London: Sage Publications, 1991: 230 p. *ISBN: 0803983964.*

169 Gender and small business success — an inquiry into women's relative disadvantage. Karyn A. Loscocco; Joyce Robinson; Richard H. Hall; John K. Allen. *Soc. Forc.* **70:1** 9:1991 pp. 65 – 86

170 Gender and university teaching — a negotiated difference. Anne Statham; Laurel Richardson *[Ed.]*; Judith A. Cook *[Ed.]*. Albany: State University of New York Press, c1991: viii, 202 p. *ISBN: 0791407039; LofC: 90044786. Includes bibliographical references (p. 179-194) and indexes.* [SUNY series in gender and society.]

171 Gender anthropology in the Middle East — the politics of Muslim women's misrepresentation. Saddeka Arebi. *Am. J. Islam. Soc. Sci.* **8:1** 3:1991 p. 99

172 Gender differences in ego defenses in adolescence — sex roles as one way to understand the differences. David B. Levit. *J. Pers. Soc. Psychol.* **61:6** 12:1991 pp. 992 – 999

173 Gender differences in health related behaviour — some unanswered questions. Mary-Anne Kandrack; Karen R. Grant; Alexander Segall. *Soc. Sci. Med.* **32:5** 1991 pp. 579 – 590

174 Gender differences in household resource allocations. Duncan Thomas. Washington, D.C: World Bank, c1991: vii, 33 p. *ISBN: 0821318233; LofC: 91018694. Includes bibliographical references (p. 27-31).* [LSMS working paper.]

175 Gender differences in schooling in Indonesia. Mayling Oey-Gardiner. *B. Ind. Econ. St.* **27:1** 4:1991 pp. 57 – 80

176 Gender differences in wage rates, work histories, and occupational segregation. Brian G.M. Main. *J. Econ. Stud.* **18:2** 1991 pp. 22 – 38

177 Gender differences — their impact on public policy. Mary Lou Kendrigan *[Ed.]*. New York: Greenwood Press, 1991: vi, 249 p. *ISBN: 0313248753; LofC: 90043381. Includes bibliographical references (p. [235]-237) and index.* [Contributions in women's studies.]

178 Gender divisions and gentrification — a critique. Liz Bondi. *Trans. Inst. Br. Geogr.* **16:2** 1991 pp. 190 – 198

179 Gender gaps — who needs to be explained? Dale T. Miller; Brian Taylor; Michelle B. Buck. *J. Pers. Soc. Psychol.* **61:1** 7:1991 pp. 5 – 12

180 Gender inequality and the division of household labor in the United States and Sweden — a socialist-feminist approach. Toni M. Calasanti; Carol A. Bailey. *Soc. Prob.* **38:1** 2:1991 pp. 34 – 53

181 The gender of power. Kathy Davis *[Ed.]*; Monique Leijenaar *[Ed.]*; Jantine Oldersma *[Ed.]*. London: Sage Publications, 1991: 198 p. *ISBN: 0803985428.*

182 Gender, science and methodological preferences. Sheldon Goldenberg; Frank Grigel. *Soc. Sci. Info.* **30:3** 9:1991 pp. 429 – 443

183 Gender, social location and feminist politics in South Africa. Shireen Hassim. *Transformation* **:15** 1991 pp. 65 – 82

184 Gender, social reproduction, and women's self-organization — considering the U.S. welfare state. Johanna Brenner; Barbara Laslett. *Gender Soc.* **5:3** 9:1991 pp. 311 – 333

185 Gendered mobility patterns in industrial economies — the case of Japan. Mary C. Brinton; Hang-Yue Ngo; Kumiko Shibuya. *Soc. Sci. Q.* **72:4** 12:1991 pp. 807 – 816

F.5: Gender *[Sexe]* — Gender differentiation *[Différenciation sexuelle]*

186 Girls and young women in education — a European perspective. Maggie Wilson *[Ed.]*. Oxford [England]: Pergamon, 1991: viii, 240 p. (ill) *ISBN: 008037266x; LofC: 90041074*. Includes bibliographical references and index. [Comparative and international education series. : Vol. 10]

187 Guatemala — donde la mitad de la población es discriminada como minoría *[In Spanish]*; [Guatemala — where half the population is discriminated against as a minority]. Azzo Ghidinelli. *Nueva Soc.* :**111** 1-2:1991 pp. 119 – 127

188 Guatemalan women speak. Margaret Hooks. London: Catholic Institute for International Relations, 1991: 128 p. *ISBN: 1852870818.*

189 Half the power, half the income and half the glory, the use of microeconomic theory in women's emancipation research. S.S. Gustafsson. *Economist [Leiden]* **139**:4 1991 pp. 515 – 529

190 The health of women in Papua New Guinea. Joy E. Gillett. Goroka: Papua New Guinea Institute of Medical Research, 1990: 180 p. (ill.) *ISBN: 998071008x.*

191 Identity and its discontents — women and the nation. Deniz Kandiyoti. *Millennium* **20**:3 Winter:1991 pp. 429 – 444

192 The impact of Islam on women in Senegal. Lucy E. Creevey. *J. Dev. Areas* **25**:3 4:1991 pp. 347 – 368

193 In the way of women — men's resistance to sex equality in organizations. Cynthia Cockburn. Basingstoke: Macmillan Education, 1991: 260 p. *ISBN: 0333549120. Includes bibliography and index.*

194 Income and dowry — some revealing connections. K. Saroja; S.M. Chandrika. *Indian J. Soc. W.* **LII**:2 4:1991 pp. 205 – 214

195 Indian women and the changing character of the working class Indian household in Natal 1860-1990. Bill Freund. *J. S.Afr. Stud.* **17**:3 9:1991 pp. 414 – 429

196 The influence of technology on the politics of motherhood — an overview of the United States. Laura R. Woliver. *Wom. St. Inter. For.* **14**:5 :1991 pp. 479 – 490

197 Intergenerational mobility in the Republic of Ireland — does gender make a difference? Bernadette C. Hayes; Robert L. Miller. *Sociol. Q.* **32**:4 Winter:1991 pp. 621 – 647

198 Law, custom, and crimes against women — the problem of dowry death in India. John van Willigen; V.C. Channa. *Human. Org.* **50**:4 Winter:1991 pp. 369 – 377

199 Law, gender, and injustice — a legal history of U.S. women. Joan Hoff-Wilson. New York: New York University Press, c1991: xi, 525 p. *ISBN: 0814734677; LofC: 90040553. Includes bibliographical references (489-507) and index.* [Feminist crosscurrents.]

200 The legal status of women in Guyana. Josephine Whitehead. *Transition* :**18** 1991 pp. 73 – 90

201 Male-female wage differentials in Australia — a reassessment. Paul Miller; Sarah Rummery. *Aust. Econ. P.* **30**:56 6:1991 pp. 50 – 69

202 Managerial momentum — a simultaneous model of the career progress of male and female managers. Kathy Cannings; Claude Montmarquette. *Ind. Lab. Rel.* **44**:2 1:1991 pp. 212 – 228

203 Meanderings around "strategy" — a research note on strategic discourse in the lives of women. Rosalind Edwards; Jane Ribbens. *Sociology* **25**:3 8:1991 pp. 477 – 489

204 Memories of origin — sexual difference and feminist polity. Francoise Vergès. *Iss. Repro. Gen. Engin.* **4**:1 :1991 pp. 3 – 15

205 Men's and women's consciousness of gender inequality — Austria, West Germany, Great Britain, and the United States. Nancy J. Davis; Robert V. Robinson. *Am. Sociol. R.* **56**:1 2:1991 pp. 72 – 84

206 Nouvelles cultures, nouveaux droits *[In French]*; [New cultures, new rights]. Renée David. *Inf. Soc.* :**14** 10-11:1991 pp. 68 – 77

207 Older women, stout-hearted women, women of substance. Francoise Heritier-Auge. *J. Soc. Stud. Dhaka* :**54** 10:1991 pp. 70 – 91

208 The outer circle — women in the scientific community. Harriet Zuckerman *[Ed.]*; Jonathan R. Cole *[Ed.]*; John T. Bruer *[Ed.]*. New York: Norton, 1991: 351 p. *ISBN: 0393027732; LofC: 90040018.*

209 *[In Japanese]*; [The participation of Japanese women in political and public life]. Sumiko Yazawa. ***International Women*** No.91(2) - 1991. pp. 63 – 67

210 The politics of gender — negotiating liberation. Andrew Charman; Cobus de Swardt; Mary Simons. *Transformation* :**15** 1991 pp. 40 – 64

211 Politics, women and well-being — how Kerala became a "model". Robin Jeffrey. London: Macmillan Academic and Professional, 1991: 320 p. *ISBN: 0333548086.* [Cambridge Commonwealth series.]

INTERNATIONAL BIBLIOGRAPHY OF SOCIOLOGY — 1991

F.5: Gender *[Sexe]* — *Gender differentiation [Différenciation sexuelle]*

212 The position of women in Switzerland — the bumpy road to equal opportunities. Claudia Kaufmann. *Pol. Soc. Ger. Aust. Swit.* **3:3** Spring:1991 pp. 40 – 47

213 Post-apartheid South Africa — what about women's emancipation? Patricia Horn. *Transformation* **:15** 1991 pp. 26 – 39

214 Pronatalism and women's equality policies; Natalisme et politiques d'égalité des femmes *[French summary]*. A. Heitlinger. *Eur. J. Pop.* **7:4** 1991 pp. 343 – 376

215 The public/private dichotomy — gendered and discriminatory. Margaret Thornton. *J. Law Soc.* **18:4** Winter:1991 pp. 448 – 463

216 Reading the letters of Edith Wharton. Annette Zilversmit *[Contrib.]*; Gloria C. Erlich *[Contrib.]*; Susan Goodman *[Contrib.]*; Alan Price *[Contrib.]*; Julie Olin-Ammentorp *[Contrib.]*; Kathleen Pfeiffer *[Contrib.]*; Clare Colquitt *[Contrib.]*; Jean Frantz Blackall *[Contrib.]*; Denise Witzig *[Contrib.]*; Carol J. Singley *[Contrib.] and others. Collection of 10 articles.* **Wom. Stud.** , *20:2,* 1991 pp. 93 – 204

217 The reproduction of gender inequality in Muslim societies — a case study of Iran in the 1980s. V.M. Moghadam. *World Dev.* **19:10** 10:1991 pp. 1335 – 1349

218 Rethinking men and gender relations — an investigation of men, their changing roles within the household, and the implications for gender relations in Kisii district, Kenya. Margrethe Silberschmidt. Copenhagen: Centre for Development Research, 1991: 91 p. *ISBN: 8788467198*. [CDR research report. : No. 16]

219 La revolución no da la solución. La mujer en la Nicaragua sandinista *[In Spanish]*; [The revolution offers no solutions. Women in Sandinista Nicaragua. Alicia Garriazu. *Nueva Soc.* **:113** 5-6:1991 p. 50

220 Satisfaction? The psychological impact of gender segregation on women at work. Amy S. Wharton; James N. Baron. *Sociol. Q.* **32:3** Fall:1991 pp. 365 – 388

221 Schwerpunkt — frauenpolitische Aspekte der Gesundheitsversorgung und der Sozialversicherung *[In German]*; Focal point — aspects of women-oriented policies in the health care and insurance systems *[Summary]*. A. Goeschel *[Ed.]*; H. Steinweber *[Contrib.]*; M. Landenberger *[Contrib.]*; G.-U. Watzlawczik *[Contrib.]*; A. Fette *[Contrib.]*; S. Gassner *[Contrib.]*; A. Mayfarth *[Contrib.]*. *Collection of 4 articles.* **Medi. Mensch Gesell.** , *16:3,* 9:1991 pp. 151 – 193

222 Self-selection and sexual politics — locals, cosmopolitans and the end of ERA. Elliott White. *Soc. Sci. Info.* **30:3** 9:1991 pp. 381 – 428

223 Sex selective eugenic abortion — prospects in China and India. Elizabeth Moen. *Iss. Repro. Gen. Engin.* **4:3** 1991 pp. 231 – 249

224 Sexual selection, parental investment, and sexism. Cheryl Brown Travis; C.P. Yeager. *J. Soc. Issues* **47:3** 1991 pp. 117 – 130

225 Shock therapy — GDR women in transition from a socialist welfare state to a social market economy. Dorothy J. Rosenberg. *Signs* **17:1** Autumn:1991 pp. 129 – 151

226 Sind Betriebsgründerinnen in der Minderheit benachteiligt? Überprüfung der „Token"-These von Rosabeth M. Kanter am Beispiel von Betriebsgründerinnen *[In German]*; Are female business founders tokens? A test of Rosabeth Kanter's thesis *[Summary]*. Monika Jungbauer-Gans; Rolf Ziegler. *Kölner Z. Soz. Soz. psy.* **43:4** 1991 pp. 720 – 738

227 Social justice for women — the International Labor Organization and women. Carol Riegelman Lubin; Anne Winslow *[Ed.]*. Durham: Duke University Press, 1991: xvii, 328 p. (ill) *ISBN: 0822310627; LofC: 90002003. Includes bibliographical references (p. 299-319) and index.*

228 Space, sexual violence and social control — integrating geographical and feminist analyses of women's fear of crime. Rachel Pain. *Prog. H. Geog.* **15:4** 12:1991 pp. 415 – 431

229 Status of women in Islam. M.T. Mesbah; M. J. Bahonar *[Ed.]*; L.Lamya Al-Faruqi *[Ed.]*. London: Sangam Books by arrangement with Radiant Publishers, New Delhi, 1991: 61 p. *ISBN: 0861322614.*

230 Strategies for strengthening women's participation in trade union leadership. Anne Trebilcock. *Int. Lab. Rev.* **130:4** 4:1991 pp. 407 – 426

231 Strategies of organisation and resistance — women workers in Sri Lankan free trade zones. Kumudhini Rosa. *Cap. Class* **:45** Autumn:1991 pp. 27 – 34

232 The structure of the female/male wage differential — is it who you are, what you do, or where you work? Erica L. Groshen. *J. Hum. Res.* **XXVI:3** Summer:1991 pp. 457 – 472

233 The Swedish gender model — productivity, pragmatism and paternalism. Maud L. Eduards. *W. Eur. Pol.* **14:3** 7:1991 pp. 166 – 181

234 "Sy is die Baas van die Huis" — women's position in the coloured working class family. Sean Field. *Agenda* **:9** 1991 pp. 60 – 70

**F.5: Gender *[Sexe]* — *Gender differentiation [Différenciation sexuelle]*
235 Thinking about wages — the gendered wage gap in Swedish banks. Joan Acker. *Gender Soc.* **5:3** 9:1991 pp. 390 – 407
236 Trabajo, fecundidad y condición femenina en México *[In Spanish]*; Work, fertility and the condition of women in Mexico *[Summary]*. Orlandina de Oliveira; Brígida García. *Est. Demog. Urb.* **5:3** 9-12:1990 pp. 693 – 710
237 Tribal female literacy — factors in differentiation among Munda religious communities. Dominic Bara; Ratnaker Bhengra; Boniface Minz. *Soc. Act.* **41:4** 10-12:1991 pp. 399 – 415
238 The uneven advance of Norwegian women. Hege Skjeie. *New Left R.* **:187** 5/6:1991 pp. 79 – 102
239 Veiled half truths — Western travellers' perceptions of Middle Eastern women. Judy Mabro. London: Tauris, 1991: 275 p. *ISBN: 1850430977. Includes bibliography and index.*
240 Whatever's happening to women? — promises, practices and pay offs. Julia Neuberger. London: Kyle Cathie, 1991: 218 p. *ISBN: 1856260461.*
241 Women and change. Amna E. Badri *[Ed.]*; Sarra M.S. Akrat *[Contrib.]*; Amna O. El Musharaf *[Contrib.]*; Sunita Pitamber *[Contrib.]*; Zubeida Abdalla Salim *[Contrib.]*. *Collection of 4 articles.* **Ahfad J.** , *8:2,* 12:1991 pp. 1 – 84
242 Women and computing — some response to falling numbers in higher education. Julia Dain. *Wom. St. Inter. For.* **14:3** 1991 pp. 217 – 225
243 Women and development in the Third World. Janet Henshall Momsen. London: Routledge, 1991: 115 p. (ill) *ISBN: 0415016959. Includes bibliographic references and index.* [Routledge introductions to development.]
244 Women and economic development. Clare Rigg; Miranda Miller. *Local. Ec.* **6:3** 11:1991 pp. 196 – 210
245 Women and rights. Cynthia Fuchs Epstein *[Ed.]*; Jean L. Cohen *[Contrib.]*; Frances Olsen *[Contrib.]*; Susan Moller Okin *[Contrib.]*; Wendy Kaminer *[Contrib.]*; Alida Brill *[Contrib.]*; Drucilla Cornell *[Contrib.]*; David Miller *[Contrib.]*. *Collection of 7 articles.* **Dissent** ,Summer:1991 pp. 369 – 405
246 Women and sovereignty in Balinese lombok and in Japan; Frauen und Herrschaft im balinesischen Lombok und in Japan *[German summary]*. Andrew Duff-Cooper. *Sociologus* **41:2** 1991 pp. 150 – 172
247 Women as entrepreneurs — a study of female business owners, their motivations, experiences and strategies for success. Sara Carter; Tom Cannon *[Ed.]*. London: Academic Press, 1991: ix, 171 p. (ill) *ISBN: 0121617556; LofC: gb 91087295.*
248 Women immigrants — what is the "problem"? Wuokko Knocke. *Econ. Ind. Dem.* **12:4** 11:1991 pp. 469 – 486
249 Women in local goverment — towards a future South Africa. Nolulamo Gwagwa. *Agenda* **10:** :1991 pp. 67 – 76
250 Women in the informal enterprise — empowerment or exploitation? Susan Greenhalgh. New York, NY.: Population Council, 1991: 43 p. *ISBN: oc25352932. Includes bibliographical references (p. 39-43).*
251 Women on the verge — winners and losers in German unification. Gertrude Schaffner Goldberg. *Soc. Pol.* **22:2** Fall:1991 pp. 35 – 44
252 The 'women question' in the age of perestroika. Maxine Molyneux. *Agenda* **10:** :1991 pp. 89 – 108
253 Women, men, and the division of power — a study of gender stratification in Kenya. Lisa A. Cubbins. *Soc. Forc.* **69:4** 6:1991 pp. 1063 – 1084
254 Women's autobiographies. Shari Benstock *[Contrib.]*; Thomas Dukes *[Contrib.]*; Mary M. O'Brien *[Contrib.]*; Doris Sommer *[Contrib.]*; Aleine Austin *[Contrib.]*. *Collection of 6 articles.* **Wom. Stud.** , *20:1,* 1991 pp. 5 – 90
255 *[In Japanese]*; [Women's cultural reproduction and social stratification]. Emi Kataoka. **Bulletin of Kanto Gakuin University** *No.(59) - 1991.* pp. 63 – 93
256 Women's persistence in undergraduate majors — the effects of gender-disproportionate representation. Stacy J. Rogers; Elizabeth G. Menaghan. *Gender Soc.* **5:4** 12:1991 pp. 549 – 564
257 Women's role in maintaining households — poverty and gender inequality in Ghana. Cynthia B. Lloyd; Anastasia Brandon. New York: The Population Council, 1991: 55 p. [Working Papers.]
258 Women's social standing — the empirical problem of female social class. Roy Carr-Hill; Colin Pritchard. London: Macmillan, 1991: 140 p. *ISBN: 0333389700.*

F.5: Gender *[Sexe] — Gender differentiation [Différenciation sexuelle]*

259 Working women and the law — equality and discrimination in theory and practice. Anne E. Morris; Susan M. Nott *[Ed.]*. London: Routledge, 1991: 237 p. *ISBN: 0415057396*.

260 Zaposlenost, uvjeti rada, položaj na poslu i doškolovanje jugoslavenskih radnica u SR Njemačkoj *[In Serbo-Croatian]*; Employment, working conditions and the position at work of migrant women *[Summary]*. Karmen Brčić. *Migrac. Teme* **6**:4 1990 pp. 21 – 31

261 Zhenshchiny v obshchestve — realii, problemy, prognozy *[In Russian]*; [Women in society — reality, problems and prognosis]. Natalia Mikhaĭlovna Rimashevskay a *[Ed.]*. Moskva: Nauka, 1991: 125 p. *ISBN: 5020133973*.

Gender roles *[Rôles de sexe]*

262 The Achilles heel reader — men, sexual politics and socialism. Victor J. Seidler *[Ed.]*. London: Routledge, 1991: 216 p. (ill) *ISBN: 0415063507. Collection of articles from Achilles Heel; Includes bibliography and index.*

263 Asian self-effacement or feminine modesty? Attributional patterns of women university students in Taiwan. Kathleen S. Crittenden. *Ann. Rep. Shiz., Hamam. Coll.* **5**:1 3:1991 pp. 98 – 117

264 Body guards — the cultural politics of gender ambiguity. Julia Epstein *[Ed.]*; Kristina Straub *[Ed.]*. New York: Routledge, 1991: viii, 382 p. (ill) *ISBN: 0415903882; LofC: 91014070. Includes bibliographical references and index.*

265 Ces femmes qui nous gouvernent *[In French]*; [These women in government]. Catherine Mangin; Elizabeth Martichoux *[Ed.]*. Paris: A. Michel, c1991: 256 p. *ISBN: 2226049096*.

266 Contested identities — gender and kinship in modern Greece. Peter Loizos *[Ed.]*; Euthymios Papataxiarchis *[Ed.]*. Princeton, N.J: Princeton University Press, 1991: 259 p. *ISBN: 0691094608; LofC: 90047780. Includes bibliographical references and index.* [Princeton modern Greek studies.]

267 Corporatism and gender equality — a comparative study of two Swedish labour market organisations. C. Bergqvist. *Eur. J. Pol. R.* **20**:2 9:1991 pp. 107 – 126

268 The cultural politics of masculinity — towards a social geography. Peter Jackson. *Trans. Inst. Br. Geogr.* **16**:2 1991 pp. 199 – 213

269 Disciplining women? Rice, mechanization, and the evolution of Mandinka gender relations in Senegambia. Judith Carney; Michael Watts. *Signs* **16**:4 Summer:1991 pp. 651 – 681

270 Disparities of embodiment — gender models in the context of the new reproductive technologies. Marilyn Strathern. *Cam. Anthrop.* **15**:2 1991 pp. 25 – 43

271 Dissonante Stereotypisierung (2). Das Männerbild in *[In German]*; »Brigitte«, »Neue Post«, »Emma« und »Playboy«; Dissonant stereotypization (2). The image of men in Brigitte, Neue Post, Emma, and Playboy *[Summary]*; Stereotypisation dissonante (2). L'image de l'homme dans »Brigitte«, »Neue Post«, »Emma« et »Playboy« *[French summary]*; Estereotipización disonante (2). El imagen viril en les revista »Brigitte«, »Neue Post«, »Emma« y »Playboy« *[Spanish summary]*. Joachim Friedrich Staah; Monika I. Birk; Andrea Hans; Birte Petersen. *Publizistik* **36**:4 10-12:1991 pp. 446 – 453

272 The domestic paradigm — violence, nurturance and stereotyping of the sexes. Jocelynne A. Scutt. *Wom. St. Inter. For.* **14**:3 1991 pp. 163 – 172

273 The emerging role of Muslim women. Luis Q. Lacar. *Phil. Stud.* **39** first quarter: 1991 pp. 3 – 22

274 Family, household and gender relations in Latin America. Elizabeth Jelin *[Ed.]*. London: Kegan Paul, 1991: 229 p. *ISBN: 0710303998*.

275 Female life careers — a pattern approach. Sigrid B. Gustafson; David Magnusson *[Ed.]*. Hillsdale, N.J: L. Erlbaum Associates, 1991: x, 221 p. *ISBN: 0805809481; LofC: 90013923. Includes bibliographical references (p. 207-213) and indexes.* [Paths through life. : No. 3]

276 Feminism without women. Tania Modleski. New York: Routledge, 1991: xi, 188 p. *ISBN: 0415904161; LofC: 91013126. Includes bibliographical references and index.*

277 Foucault and affirmative action. Peter Hadreas. *Prax. Int.* **11**:2 7:1991 pp. 214 – 226

278 Frauenerwerbstätigkeit und Wandel der Geschlechtsrollen im internationalen Vergleich *[In German]*; Female employment and changing sex-roles. An international comparison *[Summary]*. Franz Höllinger. *Kölner Z. Soz. Soz. psy.* **43**:4 1991 pp. 753 – 771

279 Gender and citizenship. Diana Owen; Linda M.G. Zerilli. *Society* **28**:5 7-8:1991 pp. 27 – 34

280 Gender and development — a practical guide. Lise Østergaard *[Ed.]*. London: Routledge, 1991: 220 p. *ISBN: 0415071313; LofC: 91016824. Includes bibliographical references and index.*

F.5: Gender *[Sexe]* — Gender roles *[Rôles de sexe]*

281 Gender and romantic-love roles. Jerold Heiss. *Sociol. Q.* **32:4** Winter:1991 pp. 575 – 591
282 Gender ideology and township politics in the 1980s. Jeremy Seekings. *Agenda* **10:** :1991 pp. 77 – 88
283 Gender matters from school to work. Jane Gaskell. Milton Keynes: Open University Press, 1991: 168 p. *ISBN: 0335096921.* [Modern education thought.]
284 Gender paradox and the otherness of God. Megan McLaughlin. *Gend. Hist.* **3:2** Summer:1991 pp. 147 – 159
285 Gender role portrayal analysis of children's television programming in Japan. David R. Rolandelli. *Human Relat.* **44:12** 12:1991 pp. 1273 – 1300
286 Gender stereotypes and the relationship between masculinity and femininity — a developmental analysis. Monica Biernat. *J. Pers. Soc. Psychol.* **61:3** 9:1991 pp. 351 – 365
287 Gender, power and sexuality. Pamela Abbott *[Ed.]*; Claire Wallace *[Ed.]*. Basingstoke: Macmillan, 1991: 199 p. *ISBN: 0333542770.* [Explorations in sociology. : No. 34]
288 Gender, work, and stress — the potential impact of role-identity salience and commitment. Mary Glenn Wiley. *Sociol. Q.* **32:4** Winter:1991 pp. 495 – 510
289 Geschlechtsspezifische Strukturen sozialer Unterstützungsnetzwerke *[In German]*; (Gender-specific structures of social support networks). Hans O.F. Veiel; Johannes Herrle. *Z. Soziol.* **20:3** 6:1991 pp. 237 – 245
290 Grateful slaves and self-made women — fact and fantasy in women's work orientations. Catherine Hakim. *Eur. Sociol. R.* **7:2** 9:1991 pp. 101 – 122
291 The HIT LIST and other horror stories — sex roles and school transfer. Sara Delamont. *Sociol. Rev.* **39:2** 5:1991 pp. 238 – 259
292 Indias y Ladinas. Los ásperos caminos de las mujeres en Guatemala *[In Spanish]*; [Indians and Ladinas. Rough roads for women in Guatemala]. Ana Lorena Carrillo. *Nueva Soc.* **:111** 1-2:1991 pp. 109 – 118
293 Innovative agricultural extension for women — a case study in Cameroon. S. Tjip Walker. Washington, D.C.: Population and Human Resources Department, World Bank, 1990: iv, 53 p. (map) *BNB: 90213323; LofC: 90213323.* Includes bibliographical references (p. [47]-53). [Policy, research, and external affairs working papers.]
294 Live fast and die young — the construction of masculinity among young working-class men on the margin of the labour market. R.W. Connell. *Aust. N.Z. J. Soc.* **27:2** 8:1991 pp. 141 – 171
295 The macho eunuch — the politics of masculinity in Jia Pingwa's "Human Extremities". Kam Louie. *Mod. Chi.* **17:2** 4:1991 pp. 163 – 187
296 Mutterschaft im Vaterland *[In German]*; Motherhood in the fatherland *[Summary]*. Susanne Dermutz. *Öster. Z. Polit.* **:2** 1991 pp. 143 – 153
297 Political philosophers and the trouble with polygamy — patriarchal reasoning on modern natural law. U. Vogel. *Hist. Polit. Thou.* **XII:2** Summer:1991 pp. 229 – 251
298 The politics of gender — negotiating liberation. Andrew Charman; Cobus de Swardt; Mary Simons. *Transformation* **:15** 1991 pp. 40 – 64
299 Position sociale et statut féminin dans les activités quotidiennes *[In French]*; Social position and feminine status in daily activities. Yannick Lemel; Caroline Roy. *Soc. Contemp.* **:7** 9:1991 pp. 113 – 127
300 Pouvoirs sexuels. Le juge Thomas, la Cour suprême et la société américaine *[In French]*; [Sexual power. Judge Thomas, the Supreme Court and American society]. Éric Fassin. *Esprit* **:177** 12:1991 pp. 102 – 130
301 Productivity of men and women and the sexual division of labor in peasant agriculture of the Peruvian Sierra. H.G. Jacoby. *J. Dev. Econ.* **37:1/2** 11:1991 pp. 265 – 287
302 The quest for national identity — women, Islam and the state in Bangladesh. Naila Kabeer. *Feminist R.* **37** Spring:1991 pp. 38 – 58
303 Ranking and linking as a function of sex and gender role attitudes. Jim Sidanius; B.J. Cling; Felicia Pratto. *J. Soc. Issues* **47:3** 1991 pp. 131 – 150
304 The rites of man — love, sex and death in the making of the male. Rosalind Miles. London: Grafton, 1991: 261 p. *ISBN: 0246134747.* Includes bibliography and index.
305 Skirting the competence issue — effects of sex-based preferential selection on task choices of women and men. Madeline E. Heilman; J. Carlos Rivero; Joan F. Brett. *J. Appl. Psychol.* **76:1** 2:1991 pp. 99 – 105
306 *[In Japanese]*; [Social phenomenology of "sex discrimination" — sex-role stereotype in advertisements and anti-"miss contest" movement]. Koichi Ichikawa. ***Bulletin of Living Science*** *No.(13) - 1991.* pp. 23 – 38

F.5: Gender *[Sexe]* — *Gender roles [Rôles de sexe]*

307 Some aspects of the changing situation of women in Hungary. Julia Szalai. *Signs* **17:**1 Autumn:1991 pp. 152 – 170

308 Soviet women — walking the tightrope. Francine du Plessix Gray. London: Virago, 1991: 213 p. *ISBN: 1853814652.*

309 Subversive potential, coercive intent — women, work and welfare in the '90s. Felicia Kornblub. *Soc. Pol.* **21:**4 Spring:1991 pp. 23 – 39

310 Support for gender equality in West Europe — a longitudinal analysis. C. Wilcox. *Eur. J. Pol. R.* **20:**2 9:1991 pp. 127 – 148

311 The tea ceremony — a transformed Japanese ritual. Barbara Lynne Rowland Mori. *Ann. Rep. Shiz., Hamam. Coll.* **5:**1 3:1991 pp. 86 – 97

312 Tibetan women (then and now) — a faithful and vivid account of the status and role of Tibetan women who lived in ancient Tibet as well as those who are living today in and outside Tibet. Indra Majupuria. Lashkar (Gwalior), India: M. Devi, 1990: 280 p. *ISBN: 9747315203.*

313 Transitions in the mid-life — women's work and family roles in the 1970s. Phyllis Moen. *J. Marriage Fam.* **53:**1 2:1991 pp. 135 – 150

314 Try, try again — incorporating international perspectives into a course on sex roles and social change. Vella Neil Evans. *Wom. St. Inter. For.* **14:**4 1991 pp. 335 – 343

315 Unwed mothers and household reputation in a Spanish Galician community. H. Kelley. *Am. Ethn.* **18:**3 8:1991 pp. 565 – 580

316 Urbanisation, coping mechanisms and slum women's status. Walter Fernandes. *Soc. Act.* **41:**4 10-12:1991 pp. 382 – 398

317 Veranderinen in de beroepsoriëntatie van vrouwen — een vergelijking tussen opeenvolgende generaties *[In Dutch]*; Changes in job orientation of women — a comparison between successive generations *[Summary]*. J. Dessens; J. van Doorne-Huiskes; E. Mertens. *Mens Maat.* **66:**2 5:1991 pp. 180 – 199

318 Was bedeutet die Umgestaltung für Frauen in Osteuropa — Traditionalisierung versus Modernisierung der Geschlechterverhältnisse *[In German]*; What does perestroika mean for the women in Eastern Europe — traditionalisation versus modernisation of gender relationships? *[Summary]*. Krisztina Mänicke-Gyöngyösi. *Öster. Z. Polit.* :2 1991 pp. 117 – 129

319 The wingless eros of socialism — nationalism and sexuality in Hungary. László Kürti. *Anthr. Quart.* **64:**2 04:1991 pp. 55 – 67

320 A woman's place in Northern Ireland. Pamela Montgomery; Celia Davies. *Soc. Attit. N.Ire. 1990-1991* pp. 74 – 95

321 Women and food security — the experience of the SADCC countries. Marilyn Carr *[Ed.]*. London: IT, 1991: vi, 210 p. (ill) *ISBN: 1853391182. Includes bibliographies.*

322 Women have no affines and men no kin — the politics of the Jivaroan gender relation. Charlotte Seymour-Smith. *Man* **26:**4 12:1991 pp. 629 – 649

323 Women in Britain since 1945 — women, family, work, and the state in the post-war years. Jane Lewis. Oxford: Basil Blackwell, 1991: 149 p. *ISBN: 063116975x; LofC: 91027521. Includes bibliographical references and index.* [Making contemporary Britain.]

324 Women in decision-making — case-study on Costa Rica. United Nations Office. Centre for Social Development and Humani. New York: United Nations, 1991: vii, 59 p. *ISBN: 9211301467. "... Third in a series on the participation of women in decision-making processes related to peace and disarmament ..."--p. iii; "Sales no. E.91.IV.5"--T.p. verso; Includes bibliographical references.*

325 Women in decision-making — case-study on Greece. United Nations. Centre for Social Development and Humanitarian Affairs. New York: United Nations, 1991: iv, 28 p. (ill) *ISBN: 9211301475. "... Second in a series on the participation of women in decision-making processes related to peace and disarmament ..."--P. iv; "United Nations publication sales no. E.91.IV.6"--T.p. verso; "ST/CSDHA/10"--T.p. verso; Includes bibliographical references.*

326 Women, family, state, and economy in Africa. Judith Carney *[Contrib.]*; Michael Watts *[Contrib.]*; Kristin Mann *[Contrib.]*; Elizabeth A. Eldredge *[Contrib.]*; Elizabeth Schmidt *[Contrib.]*; Nakanyike B. Musisi *[Contrib.]*; Carol Summers *[Contrib.]*; Patricia Stamp *[Contrib.]*. *Collection of 7 articles.* **Signs** , *16:4*, Summer:1991 pp. 651 – 845

327 Women's caring — feminist perspectives on social welfare. Carol Baines *[Ed.]*; Patricia M. Evans *[Ed.]*; Sheila M. Neysmith *[Ed.]*. Toronto, Ontario: McClelland & Stewart, c1991: 310 p. *ISBN: 077101046x; LofC: 91167786. Includes bibliographical references and index.*

F.5: Gender *[Sexe]* — *Gender roles [Rôles de sexe]*
328 Women's self-growth groups and empowerment of the "uterine family" in Taiwan. Hwei-syin Lu. *B. Inst. Ethn. Ac. Sin.* :**71** Spring:1991 pp. 29 – 62

F.6: Sexual behaviour — *Comportement sexuelle*

1 Adolescent self-efficacy, self-esteem and sexual risk-taking. D. Rosenthal; S. Moore; I. Flynn. *J. Comm. App. Soc. Psychol.* **1:2** 6:1991 pp. 77 – 88
2 Against nature — essays on history, sexuality and identity. Jeffrey Weeks. London: Rivers Oram Press, 1991: 224 p. *ISBN: 1854890042.*
3 Autonomy, equality, community — the question of lesbian and gay rights. Morris B. Kaplan. *Prax. Int.* **11:2** 7:1991 pp. 195 – 213
4 Bisexuality & HIV/AIDS — a global perspective. Rob Tielman *[Ed.]*; Manuel Carballo *[Ed.]*; Aart Hendriks *[Ed.]*. Buffalo, N.Y: Prometheus Books, 1991: 253 p. *ISBN: 0879756667; LofC: 91016625. Includes bibliographical references (p. 245-248) and index.* [New concepts in human sexuality series.]
5 Bodies, pleasures, and passions — sexual culture in contemporary Brazil. Richard G. Parker. Boston: Beacon Press, c1991: x, 203 p. *ISBN: 0807041025; LofC: 90052586. Includes bibliographical references (p. 183-198) and index.*
6 Careful maneuvers — mediating sexual harassment. Howard Gadlin. *Negot. J.* **7:2** 4:1991 pp. 139 – 153
7 Célibats en Europe du Sud *[In French]*; [Celibacy in Southern Europe]. Pierre Bourdieu *[Contrib.]*; Brian Juan O'Neill *[Contrib.]*; Raúl Iturra *[Contrib.]*; Jesús Contreras *[Contrib.]*. Collection of 5 articles. **Rural Stud.** , *113-114*, 1-6:1989 pp. 9 – 116
8 Constitutional barriers to civil and criminal restrictions on pre- and extramarital sex.*Harv. Law. Rev.* **104:7** 5:1991 pp. 1660 – 1680
9 The destabilization of the traditional Yoruba sexual system. John C. Caldwell; I.O. Orubuloye; Pat Caldwell. *Pop. Dev. Rev.* **17:2** 6:1991 pp. 229 – 262
10 Discarnate desires — thoughts on sexuality and poststructuralist discourse. Somer Brodribb. *Wom. St. Inter. For.* **14:3** 1991 pp. 135 – 142
11 Disclosure of sexual orientation by lesbians and gay men — a comparison of private and public processes. Rachel Franke; Mark R. Leary. *J. Soc. Clin. Psychol.* **10:3** Fall:1991 pp. 262 – 269
12 The drive to possess and control as a motivation for sexual behavior — applications to the study of rape. Lee Ellis. *Soc. Sci. Info.* **30:4** 12:1991 pp. 663 – 676
13 An "epidemic" model of adolescent sexual intercourse — applications to national survey data. David C. Rowe; Joseph L. Rodgers. *J. Biosoc. Sc.* **23:2** 4:1991 pp. 211 – 219
14 Factors affecting condom use among adolescents. R. Richard; J. van der Pligt. *J. Comm. App. Soc. Psychol.* **1:2** 6:1991 pp. 105 – 116
15 Geschlecht und Sexualität. Feministische Kritik biologischer Theorien *[In German]*; Gender and sexuality. Feminist critiques of biological theories *[Summary]*. Lynda I.A. Birke. *Z. Sexual.* **4:2** 6:1991 pp. 109 – 118
16 Getting to know you...young people's knowledge of their partners at first intercourse. R. Ingham; A. Woodcock; K. Stenner. *J. Comm. App. Soc. Psychol.* **1:2** 6:1991 pp. 117 – 132
17 Growing up gay in the South — race, gender, and journey of the spirit. James T. Sears. New York: Haworth, 1990: 530 p. *ISBN: 0866569111.*
18 Hostile environment sexual harassment — a clearer view. Dawn D. Bennett-Alexander. *Lab. Law J.* **42:3** 3:1991 pp. 131 – 143
19 Human sexuality and gender — a course of study. Richley H. Crapo. *Wom. St. Inter. For.* **14:4** 1991 pp. 321 – 333
20 Individual differences in sociosexuality — evidence for convergent and discriminant validity. Jeffry A. Simpson; Steven W. Gangestad. *J. Pers. Soc. Psychol.* **60:6** 6:1991 pp. 870 – 883
21 The influence of religion on attitudes toward non-marital sexuality — a preliminary assessment of reference group therapy. John K. Cochran; Leonard Beeghley. *J. Sci. S. Relig.* **30:1** 3:1991 pp. 45 – 62
22 Inside out — lesbian theories, gay theories. Diana Fuss *[Ed.]*. London: Routledge, 1991: 426 p. *ISBN: 0415902363.*
23 Looks can kill — pornographic business. Leeds: I Spy Productions, [1991?]: 75 p.
24 Love without ties — a new phase in the sexual life course. Ron van der Vliet. *Neth. J. Soc. Sci.* **27:2** 10:1991 pp. 67 – 79

F.6: Sexual behaviour [Comportement sexuelle]

25 Mandlig prostitution og seksuel identitet *[In Danish]*; Male prostitution and sexual identity *[Summary]*. Anders Dahl. *Tids. Antrop.* **:24** 1991 pp. 59 – 74
26 The meanings of lesbianism in post-war America. Donna Penn. *Gend. Hist.* **3:2** Summer:1991 pp. 190 – 203
27 Neglected fathers in the aetiology and treatment of sexual deviations; *[French summary]*; *[German summary]*; *[Spanish summary]*. A. Limentani. *Int. J.Psy.* **72:4** 1991 pp. 573 – 584
28 Negotiating respectability in ambigous commerce — selling sex paraphernalia at home parties; *[French summary]*. Eleen A. Baumann. *Can. R. Soc. A.* **28:3** 8:1991 pp. 377 – 391
29 Le nombre de partenaires sexuels — les hommes en ont-ils plus que les femmes? *[In French]*; Do men have more sexual partners than women? *[Summary]*; El número de compañeros sexuales — ¿los hombres tienen más que las mujeres? *[Spanish summary]*. Hugues Lagrange. *Population* **46:2** 3-4:1991 pp. 249 – 278
30 Onabasulu male homosexuality — cosmology, affect and prescribed male homosexual activity among the Onabasulu of the Great Papuan Plateau. Thomas M. Ernst. *Oceania* **62:1** 9:1991 pp. 1 – 11
31 Patterns of deception in intersexual and intrasexual mating strategies. William Tooke; Lori Camire. *Ethol. Socio.* **12:5** 1991 pp. 345 – 364
32 Perceived benefits and consistency of condom use by adolescent males. Joseph H. Pleck; Freya L. Sonenstein; Leighton C. Ku. *J. Marriage Fam.* **53:3** 8:1991 pp. 733 – 746
33 Pink Samurai — the pursuit and politics of sex in Japan. Nicholas Bornoff. London: Grafton Books, 1991: 492 p. *ISBN: 0246134534*.
34 Policing and prostitution. Sibusio Mavolwane; Susan Miller; Judy Watson; Eileen Cadman *[Ed.]*. London: Rights of Women, 1991: 45,2,3,12,5,1,2 p.
35 Porn — myths for the twentieth century. Robert J. Stoller. New Haven: Yale University Press, c1991: ix, 228 p. *ISBN: 0300050925; LofC: 91013623. Includes bibliographical references and index.*
36 Pornography — private right or public menace? Robert M. Baird *[Ed.]*; Stuart E. Rosenbaum *[Ed.]*. Buffalo, N.Y: Prometheus Books, 1991: 248 p. *ISBN: 087975690x; LofC: 91029627. Includes bibliographical references.* [Contemporary issues.]
37 Pressure, resistance, empowerment — young women and the negotiation of safer sex. Janet Holland *[Ed.]*; et al. London: Tufnell Press [for] Women, Risk, and AIDS Project, 1991: 28 p. *ISBN: 1872767753*.
38 Prostitution i Helsingfors — en studie i kvinnokontroll *[In Swedish]*; [Prostitution in Helsinki]. Margaretha Järvinen. Abo: Abo Akademis Förlag, 1990: 285 p. (ill) *ISBN: 9519498710; LofC: 91133384. swe: eng; Summary in English; Includes bibliographical references (p. 257-276).*
39 Religious heritage and premarital sex — evidence from a national sample of young adults. Scott H. Beck; Bettie S. Cole; Judith A. Hammond. *J. Sci. S. Relig.* **30:2** 2-6:1991 pp. 173 – 180
40 The right to privacy — gays, lesbians, and the constitution. Vincent Joseph Samar. Philadelphia: Temple University Press, 1991: xiv, 254 p. *ISBN: 0877227969; LofC: 90021937. Includes bibliographical references (p. [237]-248) and index.*
41 Sex and danger in Buenos Aires — prostitution, family, and nation in Argentina. Donna J. Guy. Lincoln: University of Nebraska Press, 1991: 260 p. (ill., maps) *ISBN: 0803221398; LofC: 91008664. Includes bibliographical references (p. 235-260) and index.* [Engendering Latin America. : Vol. 1]
42 Sex and virtue. D. Putman. *Int. J. Moral Soc. S.* **6:1** Spring:1991 pp. 47 – 56
43 Sex, God, and liberalism. Ron Replogle. *Millennium* **20:3** Winter:1991 pp. 937 – 960
44 Sexual aggression, masulinity, and fathers. David Lisak. *Signs* **16:2** Winter:1991 pp. 238 – 262
45 Sexual dissidence — Augustine to Wilde, Freud to Foucault. Jonathan Dollimore. Oxford: Clarendon Press, 1991: 388 p. *ISBN: 0198112254; LofC: 91008339. Includes bibliographical references and index.*
46 Sexual harassment in the church. Linda C. Majka. *Society* **28:4(192)** 5-6:1991 pp. 13 – 21
47 Sexual offending and dysfunctional social relationship in a homosexual couple. Heather Young. *J. For. Psy.* **2:1** 5:1991 pp. 37 – 48
48 Sexualität als Gegenstand der Sexualforschung *[In German]*; Sexuality as a subject for sex research *[Summary]*. Martin Dannecker. *Z. Sexual.* **4:4** 12:1991 pp. 281 – 293
49 Sexuality and identity — the contribution of object relations theory to a constructionist sociology. Steven Espstein. *Theory Soc.* **20/6** 12:1991 pp. 825 – 876

F.6: Sexual behaviour *[Comportement sexuelle]*

50 Sexually aggressive tactics in dating relationships — personality and attitudinal correlates. Janet T. Spence; Michael Losoff; Ann S. Robbins. *J. Soc. Clin. Psychol.* **10:**3 Fall:1991 pp. 289 – 304

51 Sexualwissenschaft und die Beschwörung des Natürlichen *[In German]*; Sexual biology and the symbolism of the natural *[Summary]*. Leonore Tiefer. *Z. Sexual.* **4:**2 6:1991 pp. 97 – 108

52 Die Stellung des Sexuellen in Holzkamps Kritischer Psychologie *[In German]*; The sexual in Holzkamp's critical psychology *[Summary]*. Roland Härdtle. *Z. Sexual.* **4:**2 6:1991 pp. 133 – 150

53 Die transsexuellen und unser nosomorpher Blick. Teil 1 — zur Enttotalisierung des Transsexualismus *[In German]*; The transsexuals and our nosomorphic view. Part 1 — against the totalitaristic viewpoint of transsexualism *[Summary]*. Volkmar Sigusch. *Z. Sexual.* **4:**3 9:1991 pp. 225 – 256

54 Die Transsexuellen und unser nosomorpher Blick. Teil II — Zur Entpathologisierung des Transsexualismus *[In German]*; The transsexuals and our nosomorphic view. Part II — against the psychopathologic viewpoint of transsexualism *[Summary]*. Volkmar Sigusch. *Z. Sexual.* **4:**4 12:1991 pp. 309 – 343

55 Zonas de tolerancia on the northern Mexican border. James R. Curtis; Daniel D. Arreola. *Geogr. Rev.* **81:**3 7:1991 pp. 333 – 346

56 Zur Dechiffrierung des Freudschen Triebbegriffs *[In German]*; On deciphering the psychoanalytical concept of drive *[Summary]*. Ralph J. Butzer. *Z. Sexual.* **4:**1 3:1991 pp. 1 – 32

57 Die Zweischneidigkeit der Medikalisierung männlicher Sexualität *[In German]*; The medicalisation of male sexuality — a "mixed blessing" *[Summary]*. John Bancroft. *Z. Sexual.* **4:**4 12:1991 pp. 294 – 308

F.7: Ethnic groups — *Groupes ethniques*

Sub-divisions: Ethnicity *[Ethnicité]*; Race relations *[Relations raciales]*; Racial discrimination *[Discrimination raciale]*

1 Achterstand van allochtonen in het onderwijs — sociaal milieu en migratie-achtergronden *[In Dutch]*; Education, ethnic minorities and inequality — social class and migration *[Summary]*. Theo Roelandt; Edwin Martens; Justus Veenman. *Mens Maat.* **65:**2 1990 pp. 103 – 125

2 Ain't gonna let nobody turn me round — the pursuit of racial justice in the rural South. Richard A. Couto. Philadelphia: Temple University Press, c1991: xi, 421 p. (ill., map) *ISBN: 087722806x; LofC: 90020645. Richard A. Couto; Includes bibliographical references (p. 353-405) and index.*

3 Andinos, criollos y mestizos en la formación de la cultura de trabajo *[In Spanish]*; Andeans, creoles and mestizos and their place in the work culture *[Summary]*. Rafael Tapia. *Soc. Part.* **:55** 9:1991 pp. 75 – 86

4 Blacks and whites in São Paulo, Brazil, 1888-1988. George Reid Andrews. Madison, Wis: University of Wisconsin Press, c1991: xiii, 369 p. (map) *ISBN: 0299131009; LofC: 91050320. Includes bibliographical references (p. 339-356) and index.*

5 Breaking bread — insurgent black intellectual life. Bell Hooks; Cornel West. Boston, MA: South End Press, c1991: 174 p. *ISBN: 0896084159; LofC: 91022027. Includes bibliographical references (p. 165-174).*

6 A brief survey of present-day Karaite communities in Europe. Emanuela Trevisan Semi. *Jew. J. Socio.* **XXXIII:**2 12:1991 pp. 97 – 106

7 Caribbean immigrants — a black success story? Suzanne Model. *Int. Migr. Rev.* **XXV:**2 Summer:1991 pp. 248 – 276

8 The closing door — conservative policy and black opportunity. Gary Orfield; Carole Ashkinaze *[Ed.]*; Andrew Young *[Foreword]*. Chicago: University of Chicago Press, 1991: xx, 254 p. (ill., maps) *ISBN: 0226632725; LofC: 90048542. Includes bibliographical references (p. 235-244) and index.*

9 Colouring California — new Asian immigrant households, social networks and the local state; *[French summary]*. Michael P. Smith; Bernadette Tarallo; George Kagiwada. *Int. J. Urban* **15:**2 6:1991 pp. 250 – 268

F.7: Ethnic groups *[Groupes ethniques]*

10 Continuous versus episodic change — the impact of civil rights policy on the economic status of blacks. John J. Donohue; James Heckman. *J. Econ. Lit.* **XXIX:4** 12:1991 pp. 1603 – 1643

11 Cultural endowment, disadvantaged status and economic niche — the development of an ethnic trade. Ronald Tadao Tsukashima. *Int. Migr. Rev.* **XXV:2** Summer:1991 pp. 333 – 354

12 Demands and constraints — ethnic minorities and social services in Scotland. Alison Bowes *[Ed.]*; Duncan Sim *[Ed.]*. Scotland: Scottish Cncl. Voluntary Orgs., 1991: 199 p. *ISBN: 1870904214.*

13 Démocratie et minorités ethniques — le cas anglais *[In French]*; [Democracy and ethnic minorities — the English case]. Didier Lapeyronnie *[Contrib.]*; Andrew Gamble *[Contrib.]*; John Solomos *[Contrib.]*; Bhiku Parekh *[Contrib.]*; Tariq Modood *[Contrib.]*; Robert Miles *[Contrib.]*; Paul Gilroy *[Contrib.]*; Stuart Holland *[Contrib.]*; Daniele Joly *[Contrib.]*; Catherine Neveu *[Contrib.] and others. Collection of 13 articles.* **Temps Mod.** , *46:540-541,* 7-8:1991 pp. 10 – 332

14 Education and the social construction of "race". Peter Figueroa. London: Routledge, 1991: 216 p. *ISBN: 0415009146. Includes bibliography and index.*

15 Ethnic minority elderly people — helping the community to care. Benjamin Bowling. *New Comm.* **17:4** 7:1991 pp. 645 – 653

16 Ethnic Turks from Bulgaria — an assessment of their employment and living conditions in Turkey. Wolf Scott. Geneva: International Labour Office, 1991: 45 p. *ISBN: 9221079465.* [World Employment Programme research working papers.]

17 Ethnies et politique en Asie centrale *[In French]*; [Ethnic groups and politics in Central Asia]. O. Roy. *R. Mon. Musul. Med.* **59-60** 1-2:1991 pp. 17 – 36

18 The evolution of protracted ethnic conflict — group dominance and political underdevelopment in Northern Ireland and Lebanon. Elizabeth Crighton; Martha Abele MacIver. *Comp. Polit.* **23:2** 1:1991 pp. 127 – 142

19 La famille soninke en France — mode de reproduction et ruptures *[In French]*; [The Soninke family in France — reproduction and ruptures]. Mahamet Timera. *Islam Soc. S.Sah.* **:5** 11:1991 pp. 57 – 68

20 A framework for comparative study of minority-group aspirations. Marvin W. Mikesell; Alexander B. Murphy. *Ann. As. Am. G.* **81:4** 12:1991 pp. 581 – 604

21 From ethnocentrism to Euro-racism. Frances Webber. *Race Class* **32:3** 1-3:1991 pp. 11 – 17

22 From negro to black to African American — the power of names and naming. Ben L. Martin. *Pol. Sci. Q.* **106:1** Spring:1991 pp. 83 – 108

23 The gypsies of Eastern Europe. John Kolsti *[Ed.]*; David M. Crowe *[Ed.]*. Armonk: M.E. Sharpe, 1991: 250 p. *ISBN: 0873326717.*

24 The health status and health beliefs of two London migrant communities; L'État sanitaire et les pratiques de santé de deux communautes londoniennes de migrants *[French summary]*; Situación sanitaria y creencias en materia de salud de dos comunidades de migrantes en Londres *[Spanish summary]*. G. Karmi. *Int. Migr.* **XXIX:1** 3:1991 pp. 5 – 12

25 Hungary's disappearing Romanian minority. G. James Patterson. *E. Eur. Quart.* **XXV:1** Spring:1991 pp. 117 – 123

26 Immigrant second and third-generation Chinese in Australia — a profile drawn from the 1986 census. Kee Pookong; Arthur Huck. *Asian Stud. R.* **14:3** 4:1991 pp. 43 – 70

27 Immigration et minorités ethniques au Royaume-Uni *[In French]*; [Immigration and ethnic minorities in the United Kingdom]. John Crowley. *Esprit* **169** 2:1991 pp. 60 – 72

28 Indians in South Africa — tradition vs. westernization. Sabita Jithoo. *J. Comp. Fam. Stud.* **XXII:3** Autumn:1991 pp. 343 – 357

29 Indians of the professions in Australia — some theoretical and methodological considerations. Arthur W. Helweg. *Popul. R.* **35:1&2** 1-12:1991 pp. 75 – 89

30 Institutions and the economic welfare of black Americans in the 1980s. John T. Harvey. *J. Econ. Iss.* **XXV: 1** 3:1991 pp. 115 – 135

31 Intragroup differences in the health of Hispanic children. Ronald J. Angel; Jacqueline Lowe Worobey. *Soc. Sci. Q.* **72:2** 6:1991 pp. 361 – 378

32 The Italian factor — the Italian community in Great Britain. Terri Colpi. Edinburgh: Mainstream, 1991: 300 p. *ISBN: 1851583440.*

33 The Kurds — a contemporary overview. Philip G. Kreyenbroek *[Ed.]*; Stefan Sperl *[Ed.]*. London: Routledge, 1991: 250 p. *ISBN: 0415072654.*

34 Minority business and the hidden dimension — the influence of urban contexts on the development of ethnic enterprise. Martin J. Dijst; Ronald van Kempen. *J. Econ. Soc. Geogr.* **82:2** 1991 pp. 128 – 138

F.7: Ethnic groups *[Groupes ethniques]*

35 Negros y chinos en la historia peruana contemporánea *[In Spanish]*; Blacks and Chinese in Peruvian contemporary history *[Summary]*. Humberto Rodríguez Pastor. *Soc. Part.* :**55** 9:1991 pp. 69 – 74

36 Die neue/alte Legende Vom Komplott der Juden und Freimaurer. Zur Renaissance des antisemitisch-antifreimaurerischen Verschwörungsmythos in der Sowjetunion *[In German]*; [The new/ old legend of the plot of the Jews and Freemasons. The renaissance of the antisemitic-antimasonic conspiracy myth in the USSR]. Armin Pfahl-Traughber. *Osteuropa* **41:2** 2:1991 pp. 122 – 133

37 The politics of black patients' identity — ward-rounds on the "black side" of a South African psychiatric hospital. Leslie Swartz. *Cult. Medic. Psych.* **15:2** 6:1991 pp. 217 – 244

38 Los pueblos indios de América *[In Spanish]*; [Indigenous peoples of Latin America]. José Matos Mar. *Pen. Iber.* :**19** 1-7:1991 pp. 181 – 200

39 Racialisation and public policy. Syd Jeffers *[Ed.]*; Robin Means *[Ed.]*; John Solomos *[Contrib.]*; Karl Atkin *[Contrib.]*; Jim Baker *[Contrib.]*; Tariq Modood *[Contrib.]*; Philip Nanton *[Contrib.]*; Martin Baldwin-Edwards *[Contrib.]*. Collection of 6 articles. **Policy Pol.** , *19:3,* 7:1991 pp. 147 – 212

40 Social distance among Australian ethnic groups. Ian McAllister; Rhonda Moore. *Social Soc. Res.* **75:2** 1:1991 pp. 95 – 100

41 Southeast Asian migrants to Australia. Richard T. Jackson. *Asian Stud. R.* **14:3** 4:1991 pp. 71 – 87

42 Spatial assimilation models — a micro-macro comparison. Andrew B. Gross; Douglas S. Massey. *Soc. Sci. Q.* **72:2** 6:1991 pp. 347 – 360

43 The way of the WASP — how it made America, and how it can save it, so to speak. Richard Brookhiser. New York: Free Press, c1991: xiii, 171 p. *ISBN: 0029047218; LofC: 90038965. Includes bibliographical references (p. 155-164) and index.*

44 William Isaac Thomas and the Helen Culver Fund for Race Psychology — the beginnings of scientific sociology at the University of Chicago, 1910- 1913. Rudolf K. Haerle. *J. Hist. Beh. Sci.* **XXVII:1** 1:1991 pp. 21 – 41

45 Zur Situation der Nordafrikaner in Frankreich *[In German]*; The situation of North Africans in France *[Summary]*. Cathérine Wihtol de Wenden. *Inf. Raum.* :**7/8** 1991 pp. 459 – 468

Ethnicity *[Ethnicité]*

46 The Afrikaners of South Africa. V. A February. London: K. Paul International, 1991: x, 296 p. (ill., maps) *ISBN: 071030353x; LofC: 90046346. Includes bibliographical references (p. 274-278) and index.* [Monographs from the African Studies Center, Leiden.]

47 Les Arabes d'Asie centrale soviétique — maintenance et mutations de l'identité ethnique *[In French]*; [Arabs in Soviet Central Asia — maintenance and change of ethnic identity]. V. Fourniau. *R. Mon. Musul. Med.* **59-60** 1-2:1991 p.83-100

48 Aspects of ethnicity. Richard Bosworth *[Ed.]*; Des Storer *[Contrib.]*; Katrin Wilson *[Contrib.]*; Jan Ryan *[Contrib.]*; Margot Melia *[Contrib.]*; Bobbie Oliver *[Contrib.]*; John N. Yiannakis *[Contrib.]*; Enallić Czeladka *[Contrib.]*; Richard Bosworth *[Contrib.]*; Beverley Hooper *[Contrib.]* and others. Collection of 7 articles. **Stud. W.Aust. Hist.** , *XII:,* 4:1991 pp. 1 – 102

49 Atlas des diasporas *[In French]*; [An atlas of diasporas]. Gérard Chaliand; Jean-Pierre Rageau *[Ed.]*. Paris: O. Jacob, c1991: XXI-182 p. (ill., cartes) *ISBN: 2738101038.*

50 Bhutan — ethnic identity and national dilemma. A. C. Sinha. New Delhi: Reliance, 1991: xix, 258 p. *ISBN: 8185047820. Bibliography — pp. 243-254.* [Sociological publications in honour of Dr. K. Ishwaran. : Vol. X]

51 Black entrepreneurship in 52 metropolitan areas. Robert A. Boyd. *Social Soc. Res.* **75:3** 4:1991 pp. 158 – 163

52 Blacks in the white establishment? — a study of race and class in America. Richard L. Zweigenhaft; G. William Domhoff. London: Yale University Press, c1991: 198 p. *ISBN: 0300047886; LofC: 90038640. Includes bibliographical references and index.*

53 Burying Otieno — the politics of gender and ethnicity in Kenya. Patricia Stamp. *Signs* **16:4** Summer:1991 pp. 808 – 845

54 The Cajunization of French Louisiana — forging a regional identity. Cécyle Trépanier. *Geogr. J.* **157:2** 7:1991 pp. 161 – 171

55 Castellorizian participation and influence within Perth's Greek community. John N. Yiannakis. *Stud. W.Aust. Hist.* **XII:** 4:1991 pp. 40 – 51

56 The changing significance of ethnic and class resources in immigrant businesses — the case of Korean immigrant businesses in Chicago. In-Jin Yoon. *Int. Migr. Rev.* **XXV:2** Summer:1991 pp. 303 – 331

F.7: Ethnic groups [Groupes ethniques] — Ethnicity [Ethnicité]

57 China and the Chinese overseas. Gungwu Wang. Singapore: Times Academic Press, 1991: 312 p. *ISBN: 9810019947.*

58 Chinese minority policy and the meaning of minority culture — the example of Bai in Yunnan, China. David Y.H. Wu. *Human. Org.* **49:1** Spring:1990 pp. 1 – 13

59 The color of strangers, the color of friends — the play of ethnicity in school and community. Alan Peshkin. Chicago: University of Chicago Press, c1991: xiii, 304 p. *ISBN: 0226662004; LofC: 90019765. Includes bibliographical references (p. 297-301) and index.*

60 Community care in a multi-racial society — incorporating the user view. Karl Atkin. *Policy Pol.* **19:3** 7:1991 pp. 159 – 166

61 Comparative study of Muslim minorities — a preliminary framework. R. Hrair Dekmejian. *Am. J. Islam. Soc. Sci.* **8:2** 9:1991 pp. 307 – 315

62 Containing political instability in a poly-ethnic society — the case of Mauritius. Eliphas G. Mukonoweshuro. *Ethn. Racial* **14:2** 4:1991 pp. 199 – 224

63 Cross-ethnic identifications and misidentifications by Israelis. Arye Rattner; Gabriel Weimann; Gideon Fishman. *Social Soc. Res.* **74:2** 1:1990 pp. 73 – 79

64 Cultural and economic boundaries of Korean ethnicity — a comparative analysis. Pyong Gap Min. *Ethn. Racial* **14:2** 4:1991 pp. 225 – 240

65 Defining the limits of tolerance — U.K. government policy on gypsies. T.A. Acton. *Roma* **:35** 7:1991 pp. 20 – 33

66 Détours et retours de la tradition chez les Juifs de France aujourd'hui — essai d'analyse et d'interprétation *[In French]*; [Turnabouts and roundabouts in the Jewish tradition in today's France — an analytical and interpretive essay] *[Summary]*. Régine Azria. *Soc. Compass* **38:1** 1991 pp. 55 – 62

67 Erin's heirs — Irish bonds of community. Dennis Clark. Lexington, KY: University Press of Kentucky, c1991: 238 p. (1 map) *ISBN: 0813117526; LofC: 90025249. Includes bibliographical references (p. [221]-232) amd index.*

68 Ethnic and racial identity in adoption within the United Kingdom. John Small. *Adopt. Fost.* **15:4** 1991 pp. 61 – 69

69 Ethnic enclosure or ethnic competition? Ethnic identification among Hispanics in Texas. Sean-Shong Hwang; Steven H. Murdock. *Sociol. Q.* **32:3** Fall:1991 pp. 469 – 476

70 Ethnic identities and indigenous psychologies in pluralist societies. Peter Weinreich. *Psychol. Devel. Soc.* **3:1** 1-6:1991 pp. 73 – 92

71 Ethnic identity and ethnic relations among the Jews of non-European USSR. Zvi Gitelman. *Ethn. Racial* **14:1** 1:1991 pp. 24 – 54

72 Ethnic minority identity — a social psychological perspective. N Hutnik. Oxford: Oxford University Press, 1991: 205 p. *ISBN: 0198521936; LofC: 91014317. Includes bibliographical references and index.*

73 Ethnicité, bandes et communautarisme *[In French]*; [Ethnicity, gangs and community]. Olivier Roy. *Esprit* **169** 2:1991 pp. 37 – 47

74 Ethnicity and the state — constitutional provisions in some Pacific Island states. Graham Hassall. *Eth. Groups* **9:2** :1991 pp. 83 – 106

75 Ethnicity, nationalism, race, minority — a semantic/onomantic exercise (part one); Ethnicite, nationalisme, race, minorité — une analyse semantique/onomantique *[French summary]*. Fred W. Riggs. *Int. Sociol.* **6:3** 9:1991 pp. 281 – 306

76 Ethnicity, nationalism, race, minority — a semantic/onomantic exercise (part two); Ethnicité, nationalisme, race, minorité — une analyse semantique/ontologique (seconde partie) *[French summary]*. Fred W. Riggs. *Int. Sociol.* **6:4** 12:1991 pp. 443 – 463

77 L'ethnologue daghestanais, agent de l'intégration soviétique ou vecteur de l'identité? *[In French]*; [Daghestanian ethnology, agent of Soviet integration or identity vector?]. F. Longuet-Marx. *R. Mon. Musul. Med.* **59-60** 1-2:1991 pp. 123 – 132

78 Etniczność, naród i państwo narodowe jako kategorie analizy współczesnych społeczeństw *[In Polish]*; Ethnicity, nation and nation state as categories of modern societies *[Summary]*. Friedrich Heckmann. *Prz. Pol.* **XVII:1** 1991 pp. 5 – 12

79 Etnisitet, nasjonalisme og minoriteter — begrepsavklaring og noen kritiske refleksjoner *[In Norwegian]*; Ethnicity, nationalism and minorities — definitions and some critical reflections *[Summary]*. Thomas Hylland Eriksen. *Int. Pol.* **49:4** 1991 pp. 479 – 488

80 Factors in the marital assimilation of ethno-religious populations in Canada, 1871 and 1971; *[French summary]*. Madeline A. Richard. *Can. R. Soc. A.* **28:1** 2:1991 pp. 99 – 111

81 Family environment and cognitive correlates of young adults' social status attainment — ethnic group differences. Kevin Marjoribanks. *J. Biosoc. Sc.* **23:4** 10:1991 pp. 491 – 498

F.7: Ethnic groups *[Groupes ethniques]* — Ethnicity *[Ethnicité]*

82 Der Gebrauchswert von Selbstund Fremdethnisierung in Strukturen sozialer Ungleichheit *[In German]*; [The practical use of defining oneself and of being defined as an ethnic community in structures of social inequality]. Michael Bommes; Albert Scherr. *Prokla* **21:2(83)** 1991 pp. 291 – 316

83 Government, nationalities and the Jews of Russia, 1772-1990 — proceedings of a conference convened by the Institute of Jewish Studies University College, London. John D. Klier *[Contrib.]*; Anthony D. Smith *[Contrib.]*; Chimen Abramsky *[Contrib.]*; John A. Armstrong *[Contrib.]*; Michael Zand *[Contrib.]*; Dov Levin *[Contrib.]*; Georgy A. Kumanev *[Contrib.]*; Nataliya V. Yukhneva *[Contrib.]*; John B. Dunlop *[Contrib.]*; Theodore H. Friedgut *[Contrib.] and others. Collection of 12 articles.* **Sov. Jew. Aff.** , *21:1*, Summer:1991 pp. 7 – 117

84 Have they passed the cricket test? A "qualitative" study of Asian adolescents. P. Avtar Singh Ghuman. *J. Multiling.* **12:5** 1991 pp. 327 – 346

85 Ich Hab' Noch einen Koffer in Berlin — German-Jewish identity in Argentina, 1933-1985. Jack Twiss Quarles van Ufford; Joep Merkx (Jozef). *Jew. Soc. Stud.* **L:1-2** Winter-Spring:1988/1992 pp. 99 – 110

86 Identification and separatism — religious involvement and racial orientations among black Americans. Christopher G. Ellison. *Sociol. Q.* **32:3** Fall:1991 pp. 477 – 494

87 L'identité azérie à l'épreuve de l'indépendance *[In French]*; [Azer identity testing independence]. C. Urjewicz. *R. Mon. Musul. Med.* **59-60** 1-2:1991 pp. 117 – 122

88 Identité ethnique et identité régionale en Iran et en Asie centrale *[In French]*; [Ethnic identity and regional identity in Iran and Central Asia]. M. Bazin. *R. Mon. Musul. Med.* **59-60** 1-2:1991 p. 101-116

89 *[In Japanese]*; [Identity crisis of young Koreans in Japan]. Yasunori Fukuoka; et al. Tokyo: Shinkansha, 1991: 221 p.

90 Immigration and ethnicity — the case of Argentina; Immigration et ethnicité — le cas de l'Argentine *[French summary]*; Inmigración y etnicidad — el caso de la Argentina *[Spanish summary]*. Brian M. du Toit. *Int. Migr.* **XXIX:1** 3:1991 pp. 77 – 88

91 In their own interests — race, class, and power in twentieth-century Norfolk, Virginia. Earl Lewis. Berkeley: University of California Press, c1991: xv, 270 p. (ill., maps) *ISBN: 0520066448; LofC: 90042819. Includes bibliographical references (pp. 209-262) and index.*

92 *[In Japanese]*; [Integration of refugees from Southeast Asia in the Federal Republic of Germany and in Japan]. Fumiko Kosaka-Isleif. Saarbrucken: Breitenbach Pub., 1991: 364 p.

93 Integration of the Gypsies in Czechoslovakia. Otto Ulč. *Eth. Groups* **9:2** :1991 pp. 107 – 118

94 Is America different? A new look at American exceptionalism. Byron E Shafer *[Ed.]*. Oxford: Clarendon Press, 1991: xi, 266 p. *ISBN: 0198277342; LofC: 90019691. Includes bibliographical references and index.*

95 Issues on creating an autonomous region for the Cordillera, Northern Philippines. Steven Rood. *Ethn. Racial* **14:4** 10:1991 pp. 516 – 543

96 Japanese American ethnicity — the persistence of community. Stephen Fugita; David J. O'Brien. Seattle: University of Washington Press, c1991: x, 207 p. *ISBN: 0295970537; LofC: 90025584 //r91. Includes bibliographical references (p. 187-204) and index.*

97 The Jewish heritage in British history — Englishness and Jewishness. Tony Kushner *[Contrib.]*; David Cesarani *[Contrib.]*; Colin Richmond *[Contrib.]*; David S. Katz *[Contrib.]*; Lara Marks *[Contrib.]*; Bill Williams *[Contrib.]*; Sharman Kadish *[Contrib.]*; Susie Barson *[Contrib.]*; Judy Glasman *[Contrib.]. Collection of 10 articles.* **Imm. Minor.** , *10:1&2*, 3/7:1991 pp. 1 – 211

98 Jewish settlement and community in the modern western world. Ronald L. Dotterer *[Ed.]*; Deborah Dash Moore *[Ed.]*; Steven M. Cohen *[Ed.]*. Selinsgrove: Susquehanna University Press, 1991: 218 p. *ISBN: 094563613x. Includes index and bibliographical references.* [Susquehanna University Studies.]

99 The living tree — the changing meaning of being Chinese today. Wei-ming Tu *[Contrib.]*; Mark Elvin *[Contrib.]*; Ambrose Yeo-chi King *[Contrib.]*; Vera Schwarcz *[Contrib.]*; Myron L. Cohen *[Contrib.]*; Gungwu Wang *[Contrib.]*; David Yen-ho Wu *[Contrib.]*; L. Ling-chi Wang *[Contrib.]*; Leo Ou-fan Lee *[Contrib.]. Collection of 9 articles.* **Dædalus** , *120:2*, Spring:1991 pp. 1 – 226

100 Made or re-made in America? Nationality and identity formation among Carpatho-Rusyn immigrants and their descendants. P.R. Magocsi. *Coexistence* **28:2** 6:1991 pp. 335 – 348

F.7: Ethnic groups *[Groupes ethniques]* — *Ethnicity [Ethnicité]*

101 Media and changing metaphors of ethnicity and identity. Thomas K. Fitzgerald. *Media Cult. Soc.* **13**:2 4:1991 pp. 193 – 214

102 Međimurje — povijest, identitet i seobe *[In Serbo-Croatian]*; Međimurje — history, identity and migrations *[Summary]*. Emil Heršak; Joža Šimunko. *Migrac. Teme* **6**:4 1990 pp. 569 – 591

103 The myth of ethnic division — township conflict on the Reef. Rupert Taylor. *Race Class* **33**:2 10-12:1991 pp. 1 – 14

104 National integration and ethnicity in Balochistan, Pakistan. Arbab M. Jahangir. *Asian Prof.* **19**:6 12:1991 pp. 541 – 550

105 Native Americans and cumulative voting — the Sisseton-Wahpeton Sioux. Richard L. Engstrom; Charles J. Barrilleaux. *Soc. Sci. Q.* **72**:2 6:1991 pp. 388 – 393

106 New immigrants and democratic society — minority integration in western democracies. Marilyn B. Hoskin. New York: Praeger, 1991: xi, 164 p. *ISBN: 0275940047; LofC: 91010586. Includes bibliographical references (p. [151]-158) and index.*

107 Out of the barrio — toward a new politics of Hispanic assimilation. Linda Chavez. [New York, N.Y.]: BasicBooks, c1991: x, 208 p. *ISBN: 0465054307; LofC: 91070060. Includes bibliographical references (p. 173-196) and index.*

108 Politics in an American lifeboat — the case of Loatian immigrants. John C. Harles. *J. Am. Stud.* **25**:3 12:1991 pp. 419 – 442

109 Post mortem — Juifs et Baltes *[In French]*; [Post mortem — Jews and Baltic peoples]. Yves Plasseraud. *Esprit* **169** 2:1991 pp. 102 – 113

110 Pour une intégration communautaire *[In French]*; [For a community integration]. Philippe Genestier. *Esprit* **169** 2:1991 pp. 48 – 59

111 The power of definition. Stigmatisation, minoritisation and ethnicity illustrated by the history of Gypsies in the Netherlands. Leo Lucassen. *Neth. J. Soc. Sci.* **27**:2 10:1991 pp. 80 – 91

112 Predicting Vietnamese refugee adjustment to western Canada; Comment prevoir l'adaptation des réfugiés Vietnamiens au Canada occidental *[French summary]*; Predicción del ajuste de los refugiados Vietnamitas en el oeste del Canada *[Spanish summary]*. R. Montgomery. *Int. Migr.* **XXIX**:1 3:1991 pp. 89 – 118

113 Das Problem der deutschen Minderheit in Oberschlesien *[In German]*; The problem of the German minority in Upper Silesia *[Summary]*. Danuta Berlinska; Krzysztof Frysztacki. *Inf. Raum.* :**7/8** 1991 pp. 469 – 480

114 Protektzia — the roots of organizational biculturalism among Israeli Jews. Brenda Danet. *Soc. Forc.* **68**:3 3:1990 pp. 909 – 932

115 Punjabi pioneers in California — political skills on a new frontier. Karen Leonard. *S. Asia* **XII**:2 12:1989 pp. 69 – 81

116 Race and the issue of national identity in Israel. Roselle Tekiner. *Int. J. M.E. Stud.* **23**:1 2:1991 pp. 39 – 55

117 Race differences in the determinants of support for legalized abortion. Karen Dugger. *Soc. Sci. Q.* **72**:3 9:1991 pp. 570 – 587

118 Race differences — an overview. Michael Levin. *J. Soc. Pol. E.* **16**:2 Summer:1991 pp. 195 – 216

119 Religious or ethnic self-identification over the telephone — a pilot study of Manchester Jewry. Marlena Schmool. *Jew. J. Socio.* **XXXIII**:1 6:1991 pp. 21 – 34

120 Los rituales públicos y la politización de la etnicidad en Nueva York *[In Spanish]*; [Public rituals and ethnic politicization in New York]. Judith Freidenberg; Philip Kasinitz. *Desar. Econ.* **30**:117 4-6:1990 pp. 109 – 132

121 The role of the school in maintenance and change of ethnic group affiliation. Adeline Becker. *Human. Org.* **49**:1 Spring:1990 pp. 48 – 55

122 The salience of ethnicity in modernization — evidence from India. S.L. Sharma. *Sociol. Bul.* **39**:1-2 3-9:1990 pp. 33 – 51

123 A sense of belonging — dilemmas of British Jewish identity. Howard J. Cooper; Paul Morrison. London: Weidenfeld and Nicholson in association with Channel four, 1991: 223 p. *ISBN: 0297810979.*

124 Shades of black — diversity in African-American identity. William E. Cross. Philadelphia: Temple University Press, 1991: xix, 272 p. (ill) *ISBN: 0877227594; LofC: 90036170. Includes bibliographical references (p. 237-265) and index.*

125 Significance of ethnic and racial identity in inter-country adoption within the United States. Ruth G. McRoy. *Adopt. Fost.* **15**:4 1991 pp. 53 – 61

F.7: Ethnic groups *[Groupes ethniques]* — **Ethnicity** *[Ethnicité]*

126 Somalis in London's East End — a community striving for recognition. Camillia Fawzi El-Solh. *New Comm.* **17:4** 7:1991 pp. 539 – 552
127 Soviet Jews in the glasnost era. Semyon E. Reznik. *Society* **28:4(192)** 5-6:1991 pp. 73 – 83
128 Stains on my name, war in my veins — Guyana and the politics of cultural struggle. Brackette F. Williams. Durham: Duke University Press, 1991: xix, 322 p. (ill) *ISBN: 0822311194; LofC: 90047529. Includes bibliographical references (p. 301-315) and index.*
129 State policies, land control, and an ethnic minority — the Arabs in the Galilee region, Israel. O. Yiftachel. *Envir. Plan. D* **9:3** 9:1991 pp. 329 – 362
130 Study on the rights of persons belonging to ethnic, religious and linguistic minorities. Francesco Capotorti. New York: United Nations, 1991: 114 p. *ISBN: 9211540836.* [Human rights study series. : No. 5]
131 Understanding and managing multiculturalism — some possible implications of research in Canada. J.W. Berry. *Psychol. Devel. Soc.* **3:1** 1-6:1991 pp. 17 – 50
132 En Venezuela todos somos minoría *[In Spanish]*; [In Venezuela we're all a minority]. Enrique González O. *Nueva Soc.* **:111** 1-2:1991 pp. 128 – 140
133 «Le vent qui descend du Nord» — les Kurdes d'Irak *[In French]*; The wind which comes from the north — the Kurds in Iraq *[Summary]*. Patrick Ribau. *Pensée* **:281** 5-6:1991 pp. 95 – 108
134 The Welsh in Patagonia — the state and the ethnic community. Glyn Williams. Cardiff: University of Wales Press, 1991: 285 p. *ISBN: 0708310893. Includes bibliography and index.*
135 When ethnic groups do not assimilate — the case of Basque-American resistance. Catherine M. Petrissans. *Eth. Groups* **9:2** :1991 pp. 61 – 82
136 Who is black? — one nation's definition. Fanny Davis. University Park: Pennsylvania State UP., 1991: 204 p. *ISBN: 0271007397.*
137 Žumberčani — subetnička grupa u hrvata *[In Serbo-Croatian]*; Žumberčani — a Croatian sub-ethnic group *[Summary]*. Nada Hranilović. *Migrac. Teme* **6:4** 1990 pp. 593 – 612
138 ¿Por qué no existe el Poder Negro en America Latina? *[In Spanish]*; [Why does black power not exist in Latin America?]. Andrés Serbin. *Nueva Soc.* **:111** 1-2:1991 pp. 148 – 157

Race relations *[Relations raciales]*

139 Anglo-Jewry revisited. Max Beloff. *Jew. J. Socio.* **XXXIII:1** 6:1991 pp. 35 – 42
140 An Arab segregated neighborhood in Tel-Aviv — the case of Adjami. Juval Portugali. *Geogr. Res. For.* **11:** 1991 pp. 37 – 50
141 Arabes et Turquie — le cas jordanien *[In French]*; [Arabs and Turkey — the Jordanian case]. Louis-Jean Duclos. *Cah. Ét. Méd. Ori. Tur-Iran.* **11** 1991 pp. 119 – 139
142 *[In Japanese]*; [Asian foreigners in Ikebukuro — a sociological study]. Junko Tajima *[Ed.]*; et al. Tokyo: Mekon, 1991
143 Ausländer im Westen der Bundesrepublik Deutschland — Alltagsprobleme, Kontakte und Konflikte *[In German]*; Foreigners in Western Germany — everyday problems, contacts and conflicts *[Summary]*. Ferdinand Böltken. *Inf. Raum.* **:7/8** 1991 pp. 481 – 499
144 "Balanced multiculturalism" and the challenge of peaceful co-existence in pluralistic societies. Fathali M. Moghaddam; Elizabeth A. Solliday. *Psychol. Devel. Soc.* **3:1** 1-6:1991 pp. 51 – 72
145 Black Americans' views of racial inequality — the dream deferred. Lee Sigelman; Susan Welch *[Ed.]*. Cambridge [England]: Cambridge University Press, 1991: xi, 214 p. (ill) *ISBN: 0521400155; LofC: 90041558. Includes bibliographical references (p. 189-204) and indexes.*
146 Black-white housing segregation in the city of St. Louis — a 1988 update. John E. Farley. *Urban Aff. Q.* **26:3** 3:1991 pp. 442 – 450
147 Bull Connor. William A Nunnelley. Tuscaloosa: University of Alabama Press, c1991: x, 225 p. (ill) *ISBN: 0817304959; LofC: 89078196. Includes bibliographical references (p. [208]-212) and index.*
148 Center-periphery relations and ethnic conflict in Pakistan — Sindhis, Muhajirs, and Punjabis. Theodore P. Wright. *Comp. Polit.* **23:3** 4:1991 pp. 299 – 312
149 Class, gender and race struggles in a Portuguese neighbourhood in London. Wenona Giles. *Int. J. Urban* **15:3** 9:1991 pp. 432 – 442
150 Community care in a multi-racial society — incorporating the user view. Karl Atkin. *Policy Pol.* **19:3** 7:1991 pp. 159 – 166
151 Community relations in Northern Ireland — attitudes to contact and integration. A.M. Gallagher; S. Dunn. *Soc. Attit. N.Ire.* 1990-1991 pp. 7 – 22

F.7: Ethnic groups [Groupes ethniques] — Race relations [Relations raciales]

152 Conflict and harmony in pluralistic societies. R.C. Tripathi *[Ed.]*; Thomas F. Pettigrew *[Contrib.]*; J.W. Berry *[Contrib.]*; Fathali M. Moghaddam *[Contrib.]*; Elizabeth A. Solliday *[Contrib.]*; Peter Weinreich *[Contrib.]*; Emmanuel S.K. Ghosh *[Contrib.]*; Rashmi Kumar *[Contrib.]*; Michael T. Lynskey *[Contrib.]*; Colleen Ward *[Contrib.]* and others. Collection of 7 articles. **Psychol. Devel. Soc.** , **3**:1, 1-6:1991 pp. 1 – 127

153 Containing political instability in a poly-ethnic society — the case of Mauritius. Eliphas G. Mukonoweshuro. *Ethn. Racial* **14**:2 4:1991 pp. 199 – 224

154 Contextual aspects of ethnic stereotypes and interethnic evaluations. G. Kleinpenning; L. Hagendoorn. *Eur. J. Soc. Psychol.* **21**:4 7-8:1991 pp. 331 – 348

155 Du pluriculturel en général et des Espagnols en France en particulier *[In French]*; On the multicultural in general and the Spanish in France in particular *[Summary]*. Nicole Beaurain. *Hom. Soc.* **XXV**:4(102) 1991 pp. 93 – 112

156 Eigene und das Fremde — neuer Rassismus in der alten Welt? *[In German]*; [One's own and the stranger — new racism in the old world?]. Uli Bielefeld *[Ed.]*. Hamburg: Junius, 1991: 338 p. *ISBN: 3885061902.*

157 Этнические процессы в современном мире *[In Russian]*; [Ethnic processes in contemporary world]. Iu.V. Bromulei *[Ed.]*. Moscow: Nauka, 1987: 447 p. *Bibliogr.*

158 Ethnic conflict in the Soviet Union. Charles Tilly *[Contrib.]*; Algis Prazauskas *[Contrib.]*; Valery A. Tishkov *[Contrib.]*; A.N. Yamskov *[Contrib.]*; John Comaroff *[Contrib.]*; Andrus Park *[Contrib.]*; V.M. Sergeev *[Contrib.]*; Zvi Gitelman *[Contrib.]*; Gail W. Lapidus *[Contrib.]*; Lee Walker *[Contrib.]* and others. Collection of 10 articles. **Theory Soc.** , **20**:5, 10:1991 pp. 569 – 722

159 Ethnic differences among Israeli Jews — a new look. U. O. Schmelz; Uri Avnery; Sergio della Pergola. Jerusalem: Institute of Contemporary Jewry, Hebrew University of Jerusalem, 1991: 204 p. *ISBN: 9652222151; LofC: 91165192. Includes bibliographical references.* [Jewish population studies.]

160 Ethnic differences in migration patterns — disparities among Arabs and Jews in the peripheral regions of Israel. Gabriel Lipshitz. *Prof. Geogr.* **43**:4 11:1991 pp. 445 – 455

161 Ethnicity and nationalism in post-imperial Britain. Harry Goulbourne. Cambridge: Cambridge University Press, 1991: 271 p. *ISBN: 0521400848. Includes bibliography and index.* [Comparative ethnic and race relations series.]

162 Europe and 1992 — focus on racial issues. Ann Dummett. London: Catholic Association for Racial Justice, 1991: 27 p. [CARJ cross currents.]

163 The evolution of protracted ethnic conflict — group dominance and political underdevelopment in Northern Ireland and Lebanon. Elizabeth Crighton; Martha Abele MacIver. *Comp. Polit.* **23**:2 1:1991 pp. 127 – 142

164 Exil, relations interethniques et identité dans la crise afghane *[In French]*; [Exile, interethnic relations and identity in the Afghan crisis]. P. Centlivres. *R. Mon. Musul. Med.* **59-60** 1-2:1991 pp. 70 – 82

165 Explaining ethnic antagonism in Yugoslavia. Sergej Flere. *Eur. Sociol. R.* **7**:3 12:1991 pp. 183 – 193

166 Exploitation and exclusion — race and class in contemporary US society. Abebe Zegeye *[Ed.]*; Leonard Harris *[Ed.]*; Julia Maxted *[Ed.]*. London: Hans Zell, 1991: 277 p. *ISBN: 0905450671; LofC: 91031148. Includes bibliographical references and index.* [African discourse series. : No. 3]

167 Hasta que la Argentina nos una — reconsiderando las pautas matrimoniales de los inmigrantes, el crisol de razas y el pluralismo cultural *[In Spanish]*; [Until Argentina unites us — immigrant marriage, the racial melting pot and cultural pluralism revisited]. Eduardo José Míguez; María Elba Argeri; María Mónica Bjerg; Hernán Otero. *Hisp. Am. Hist. Rev.* **71**:4 11:1991 pp. 781 – 808

168 Hindu-Muslim intergroup relations in India — applying socio-psychological perspectives. Emmanuel S.K. Ghosh; Rashmi Kumar. *Psychol. Devel. Soc.* **3**:1 1-6:1991 pp. 93 – 112

169 The historic dispossession of the American Indian — did it violate American ideals? Dwight Murphey. *J. Soc. Pol. E.* **16**:3 Fall:1991 pp. 347 – 367

170 In and out of Chinatown — residential mobility and segregation of New York City's Chinese. Min Zhou; John R. Logan. *Soc. Forc.* **70**:2 12:1991 pp. 387 – 408

171 The Indian economic success — a challenge to some race relations assumptions. Tariq Modood. *Policy Pol.* **19**:3 7:1991 pp. 177 – 190

172 Ingroup/outgroup balance and interdependent interethnic behavior. Raymond T. Garza; Silvia J. Santos. *J. Exp. S. Psychol.* **27**:2 3:1991 pp. 124 – 137

F.7: Ethnic groups *[Groupes ethniques]* — Race relations *[Relations raciales]*

173 Intergroup bullying and racial harassment in the Netherlands. Marianne Junger. *Social Soc. Res.* **74:2** 1:1990 pp. 65 – 72

174 International issues and domestic ethnic relations — African Americans, American Jews, and the Israel-South Africa debate. Yvonne D. Newsome. *Int. J. Pol. C. S.* **5:1** Fall:1991 pp. 19 – 48

175 Is there a future for local authority race advisers? Jim Baker. *Policy Pol.* **19:3** 7:1991 pp. 167 – 176

176 Issues on creating an autonomous region for the Cordillera, Northern Philippines. Steven Rood. *Ethn. Racial* **14:4** 10:1991 pp. 516 – 543

177 La jeunesse pakistanaise musulmane de Birmingham *[In French]*; [Pakistani Muslim youth in Birmingham]. Daniele Joly. *Temps Mod.* **46:540-541** 7-8:1991 pp. 202 – 237

178 The Jews of Arab lands in modern times. Norman A. Stillman. Philadelphia: The Jewish Publication Society, 1991: xxviii, 604 p., 16 p. of plates (ill., col. maps) *ISBN: 0827603703; LofC: 90005341. Includes bibliographical references (p. 565-582) and index.*

179 К вопросу о современных таджикско-узбекских межнациональных отношениях *[In Russian]*; On current Tadshik-Uzbek interethnic relations *[Summary]* R R Rakhimov. *Sovet. Etno.* **:1** 1991 pp. 13 – 24

180 Living together separately — Arabs and Jews in contemporary Jerusalem. Michael Romann; Alex Weingrod. Princeton: Princeton U.P., 1991: xiii, 258, 1p. *ISBN: 0691094551.* [Princeton studies on the Near East.]

181 The measurement of segregation change through integration and deconcentration, 1970-1980. Richard A. Smith. *Urban Aff. Q.* **26:4** 6:1991 pp. 477 – 496

182 Миллат ва миллатлараро муносабатларни мохиятининг хусусиятларига оид *[In Uzbek]*; К характеристике сущности нации и межнациональных отношений *[In Russian]*; [Defining the essence of the concepts of nation and interethnic relations]. B.R. Karimov. *Obshch. N. Usbek.* **:9** 1991 pp. 27 – 33

183 Minorities in the middle — a cross-cultural analysis. Walter P. Zenner. Albany: State University of New York Press, c1991: xv, 224 p. *ISBN: 0791406423; LofC: 90039846. Includes bibliographical references (p. 155-210) and indexes.* [SUNY series in ethnicity and race in American life.]

184 Minorities on India's West Coast — history & society. Anirudha Gupta *[Ed.]*. Delhi: Kalinga Publications, 1991: xix, 231 p. *ISBN: 8185163227. Includes bibliographies.*

185 Les musulmans de Grand-Bretagne et l'affaire Rushdie *[In French]*; [British Muslims and the Rushdie affair]. Tariq Modood. *Temps Mod.* **46:540-541** 7-8:1991 pp. 111 – 132

186 National and racial minorities in total war. Panikos Panayi. *Imm. Minor.* **9:2** 7:1991 pp. 178 – 194

187 Natsional′naia politika KPSS — istoricheskii opyt, protivorechiia i problemy perestroiki *[In Russian]*; [The nationalities policy of the USSR — historical experience, controversy and the problems of perestroika]. M. V. Rumiantsev *[Ed.]*; et al. Cheboksary: Chuvashskii gos. universitet, 1990: 132 p. *ISBN: 5230180064.*

188 New minority groups in the citadel of Europe. Jacques Berque. Strasbourg: Council for Cultural Co-operation, School and Out-of-school Education Section, 1991: 58 p. *ISBN: 0119839687.*

189 No crooked death — Coatesville, Pennsylvania, and the lynching of Zachariah Walker. Dennis B Downey; Raymond M. Hyser *[Ed.]*. Urbana: University of Illinois Press, c1991: xv, 174 p. (ill., maps) *ISBN: 0252017390; LofC: 90010853. Includes bibliographical references (p. 163-169) and index.* [Blacks in the New World.]

190 Opening doors — perspectives on race relations in contemporary America. Harry J. Knopke *[Ed.]*; Robert J. Norrell *[Ed.]*; Ronald W. Rogers *[Ed.]*. Tuscaloosa: University of Alabama Press, c1991: xviii, 234 p. (ill) *ISBN: 0817304975; LofC: 90036167. Papers presented at a national symposium held at the University of Alabama, June 11-13, 1988; Includes bibliographical references (p. 223-225) and index.*

191 Paradoxes of multiculturalism — essays on Swedish society. Aleksandra Alund; Carl-Ulrik Schierup. Aldershot: Avebury, 1991: 192 p. *ISBN: 1856282333.* [Research in ethnic relations series.]

192 The political impasse in South Africa and Northern Ireland — a comparative perspective. Adrian Guelke. *Comp. Polit.* **23:2** 1:1991 pp. 143 – 162

193 The pragmatics of minority politics in Belgium. J. Blommaert; J. Verschueren. *Lang. Soc.* **20:4** 12:1991 pp. 503 – 532

F.7: Ethnic groups [Groupes ethniques] — Race relations [Relations raciales]

194 Publieke opinies over etnische minderheden in Nederland en West-Duitsland *[In Dutch]*; Public opinions about ethnic minorities in the Netherlands and West Germany *[Summary]*. Paul Dekker. *Mens Maat.* **66:3** 8:1991 pp. 296 – 314

195 Race and reflexivity — the black other in contemporary Japanese mass culture. John Russell. *Cult. Anthro.* **6:1** 2:1991 pp. 3 – 25

196 The race relations problematic. Michael Banton. *Br. J. Soc.* **42:1** 3:1991 pp. 115 – 130

197 Race talk and common sense — patterns in Pakeha discourse on Maori/Pakeha relations in New Zealand. R.G. Nairn; T.N. McCreanor. *J. Lang. Soc. Psychol.* **10:4** 1991 pp. 245 – 262

198 Racial rhetoric at the United Nations. Michael Banton. *Int. J. Pol. C. S.* **5:1** Fall:1991 pp. 5 – 18

199 Racialised relations in Liverpool — a contemporary anomaly. Steven Small. *New Comm.* **17:4** 7:1991 pp. 511 – 538

200 Racism in Canada. Ormond Knight McKague *[Ed.]*. Saskatoon, Sask: Fifth House Publishers, c1991: x, 230 p. *ISBN: 0920079733; LofC: 92123107. Includes bibliographical references (p. 207-230).* [Fifth House reader. : No. 1]

201 Le racisme dans les relations interethniques *[In French]*; Racism in interethnic relations *[Summary]*. Véronique De Rudder. *Hom. Soc.* **XXV:4(102)** 1991 pp. 75 – 92

202 Il razzista democratico *[In Italian]*; [Democratic racism]. Fiamma Nirenstein. Milano: Mondadori, 1990: 191 p. *ISBN: 8804340029.*

203 Remedying environmental racism. Rachel D. Godsil. *MI. law. R.* **90:2** 11:1991 pp. 394 – 427

204 Restructuring for ethnic peace — a public debate at the University of Hawai'i. Majid Tehranian *[Ed.]*. Honolulu, Hawai'i: Spark M. Matsunaga Institute for Peace, University of Hawai'i, 1991: 187 p. *ISBN: 1880309033; LofC: 91043404. Papers from a series of seven public forums held in the spring of 1991 at the University of Hawaii; Includes bibliographical references.*

205 The resurgence of racial conflict in post industrial America. Antoine Joseph. *Int. J. Pol. C. S.* **5:1** Fall:1991 pp. 81 – 94

206 The role of evolution in ethnocentric conflict and its management. Marc Howard Ross. *J. Soc. Issues* **47:3** 1991 pp. 167 – 186

207 Shadows of race and class. Raymond S Franklin. Minneapolis: University of Minnesota Press, c1991: xxvii, 189 p. *ISBN: 0816619565; LofC: 90032446. Includes bibliographical references (p. 157-178) and index.*

208 Social integration of low-income black adults in middle-class white suburbs. James E. Rosenbaum; Susan J. Popkin; Julie E. Kaufman; Jennifer Rusin. *Soc. Prob.* **38:4** 11:1991 pp. 448 – 461

209 Stereotypes and intergroup attributions in New Zealand. Michael T. Lynskey; Colleen Ward; Garth J.O. Fletcher. *Psychol. Devel. Soc.* **3:1** 1-6:1991 pp. 113 – 127

210 Training for equality — a study of race relations and equal opportunities training. Colin Brown; Jean Lawton *[Ed.]*. London: Policy Studies Institute, 1991: 109 p. *ISBN: 0853745269. Includes bibliography.*

211 Understanding everyday racism — an interdisciplinary theory. Philomena Essed. Newbury Park: Sage Publications, c1991: x, 322 p. *ISBN: 0803942559; LofC: 91022025. Includes bibliographical references (p. 297-318) and index.* [Sage series on race and ethnic relations. : Vol. 2]

212 What do the Maori want? — new Maori political perspectives. R.K. Vasil. Auckland, N.Z: Random Century, 1990: 174 p. *ISBN: 1869410858; LofC: 91158177. Includes bibliographical references (p. 144-145).*

213 Who is black? — one nation's definition. Fanny Davis. University Park: Pennsylvania State UP., 1991: 204 p. *ISBN: 0271007397.*

214 ¿Por qué no existe el Poder Negro en Ameica Latina? *[In Spanish]*; [Why does black power not exist in Latin America?]. Andrés Serbin. *Nueva Soc.* **:111** 1-2:1991 pp. 148 – 157

Racial discrimination [Discrimination raciale]

215 Against a rising tide — racism, Europe and 1992. Mel Read; Al Simpson *[Ed.]*. Nottingham: Spokesman, 1991: 100 p. (ill) *ISBN: 0851245250. Includes bibliography.* [Elfbooks. : Vol. 3]

216 Anti-Judaism and antisemitism. Geoffrey Alderman. *Jew. J. Socio.* **XXXIII:2** 12:1991 pp. 107 – 122

217 Anti-semitism in the 1990 Polish presidential election. Konstanty Gebert. *Soc. Res.* **58:4** Winter:1991 pp. 723 – 756

F.7: Ethnic groups [Groupes ethniques] — Racial discrimination [Discrimination raciale]

218 Anti-semitism — the longest hatred. Robert S. Wistrich. London: Methuen, 1991: 341 p. *ISBN: 041365320x.*

219 Ausländerfeindliche und rechtsextreme Orientierungen bei ostdeutschen Jugendlichen. Eine empirische Studie *[In German]*; [Xenophobic and extreme right orientations among youths in eastern Germany. An empirical study]. Walter Friedrich; Wilfried Schubarth. *Deut. Arch.* **24:10** 10:1991 pp. 1052 – 1065

220 Black people's experience of criminal justice. Eric Smellie; Iain Crow *[Ed.]*. London: NACRO, 1991: 52 p. *ISBN: 0850690447.*

221 Black political mobilisation and the struggle for equality. John Solomos; Les Back. *Sociol. Rev.* **39:2** 5:1991 pp. 215 – 237

222 Consensual racism and career track — some implications of social dominance theory. Jim Sidanius; Felicia Pratto; Michael Martin; Lisa M. Stallworth. *Polit. Psych.* **12:4** 12:1991 pp. 691 – 721

223 The continuing significance of race — antiblack discrimination in public places. Joe R. Feagin. *Am. Sociol. R.* **56:1** 2:1991 pp. 101 – 116

224 The continuing significance of race — racial conflict and racial discrimination in construction. Roger Waldinger; Thomas Bailey. *Polit. Soc.* **19:3** 9:1991 pp. 291 – 324

225 David Duke and the race for the Governor's mansion. Mary Ellison. *Race Class* **33:2** 10-12:1991 pp. 71 – 79

226 Deadly silence — black deaths in custody. A. Sivanandan *[Ed.]*. London: Institute of Race Relations, 1991: 75 p. *ISBN: 0850010381.*

227 The decline of discrimination against colored people in South Africa, 1970-1980. P.G. Moll. *J. Dev. Econ.* **37:1/2** 11:1991 pp. 289 – 307

228 The development of ethnic prejudice — an analysis of Australian immigrants. Ian McAllister; Rhonda Moore. *Ethn. Racial* **14:2** 4:1991 pp. 127 – 151

229 Discrimination in professional sports — a survey of the literature. Lawrence M. Kahn. *Ind. Lab. Rel.* **44:3** 4:1991 pp. 395 – 418

230 Education and the ideologies of racism. Madan Sarup. Stoke on Trent: Trentham Books, 1991: - *ISBN: 0948080469.*

231 L'Espace du racisme *[In French]*; [Space of racism]. Michel Wieviorka. Paris: Seuil, 1991: 255 p. *ISBN: 2020125676.*

232 Exploitation and exclusion — race and class in contemporary US society. Abebe Zegeye *[Ed.]*; Leonard Harris *[Ed.]*; Julia Maxted *[Ed.]*. London: Hans Zell, 1991: 277 p. *ISBN: 0905450671; LofC: 91031148. Includes bibliographical references and index.* [African discourse series. : No. 3]

233 Exploring the meaning and implications of deracialization in African-American urban politics. Huey L. Perry *[Contrib.]*; Carol A. Pierannunzi *[Contrib.]*; John D. Hutcheson *[Contrib.]*; Mary E. Summers *[Contrib.]*; Philip A. Klinkner *[Contrib.]*; Robert T. Starks *[Contrib.]*. *Collection of 5 articles.* **Urban Aff. Q.** , 27:2, 12:1991 pp. 181 – 226

234 Fair driving — gender and race discrimination in retail car negotiations. Ian Ayres. *Harv. Law. Rev.* **104:4** 2:1991 pp. 817 – 872

235 La fin l'antiracisme *[In French]*; [The end of anti-racism]. Paul Gilroy. *Temps Mod.* **46:540-541** 7-8:1991 pp. 166 – 189

236 Les formes contemporaines de l'idéologie raciale dans la société britannique *[In French]*; [Modern forms of racial ideology in British society]. John Solomos. *Temps Mod.* **46:540-541** 7-8:1991 pp. 65 – 82

237 De huisvestingspositie van allochtonen — sociaal-economische positie, lokale woningvoorraad, migratie-achtergronden en ongelijke kansen *[In Dutch]*; The housing situation of ethnic minorities — socio-economic position, local housing stock, migration and unequalities in opportunities *[Summary]*. Jaco Dagevos; Theo Roelandt. *Sociol. Gids.* **:2** 3-4:1991 pp. 95 – 110

238 Incarceration and nonincarceration of African-American men raised in black Christian churches. Naida M. Parson; James K. Mikawa. *J. Psychol.* **125:2** 3:1991 pp. 163 – 174

239 International action against racial discrimination. Michael Banton. *Ethn. Racial* **14:4** 10:1991 pp. 545 – 555

240 Marginalisierung statt multikultureller Gesellschaft? Ausländer in Frankfurt a.M. *[In German]*; Marginalization instead of a multicultural society? Foreigners in Frankfurt a.M. *[Summary]*. Bernd Hausmann. *Inf. Raum.* **:7/8** 1991 pp. 439 – 445

241 „Mir ist das Thema Juden irgendwie unangenehm". Kommunikationslatenz und die Wahrnehmung des Meinungsklimas im Fall des Antisemitismus *[In German]*; "I feel

F.7: Ethnic groups [Groupes ethniques] — Racial discrimination [Discrimination raciale]

uneasy talking about Jews at all". Social latency and the perception of the climate of opinion concerning anti-semitism [Summary]. Werner Bergmann; Rainer Erb. *Kölner Z. Soz. Soz. psy.* **43:**3 1991 pp. 502 – 519

242 Modernity — all "niggers" now? Or new slaves for old? Preston King. *New Comm.* **17:**4 7:1991 pp. 489 – 510

243 The new racism. Paul M. Sniderman; Thomas Piazza; Philip E. Tetlock; Ann Kendrick. *Am. J. Pol. Sc.* **35:**2 5:1991 pp. 423 – 447

244 Polish intellectuals and anti-semitism. Abraham Brumberg. *Dissent Winter:1991* pp. 72 – 77

245 Political economy of racial discrimination. Hillel Ticktin. London: Pluto, 1991: 115 p. *ISBN: 074530494x.*

246 The politics of race and housing. John Solomos. *Policy Pol.* **19:**3 7:1991 pp. 147 – 158

247 Prejudice with and without compunction. Patricia G. Devine; Margo J. Monteith; Julia R. Zuwerink; Andrew J. Elliot. *J. Pers. Soc. Psychol.* **60:**6 6:1991 pp. 817 – 830

248 A pyramid of complaints — the handling of complaints about racial discrimination in the Netherlands. Anita Böcker. *New Comm.* **17:**4 7:1991 pp. 603 – 615

249 Racial discrimination and the public sector. A.W. Bradley. *Publ. Law Autumn:1991* pp. 317 – 325

250 Racial occupational inequality in southern metropolitan areas, 1940-1980 — revisiting the visibility-discrimination hypothesis. Jeffrey A. Burr; Omer R. Galle; Mark A. Fossett. *Soc. Forc.* **69:**3 3:1991 pp. 831 – 850

251 Racial segregation in Major League baseball. Satya R. Pattnayak; John Leonard. *Social Soc. Res.* **76:**1 10:1991 pp. 3 – 9

252 Racism and antiracism — inequalities, opportunities and policies. Peter Braham *[Ed.]*; Ali Rattansi *[Ed.]*; Richard Skellington *[Ed.]*. London: Sage Publications, 1991: 304 p. *ISBN: 0803985819; LofC: gb 91087241.*

253 Racism and education — structures and strategies. Dawn Gill *[Ed.]*; Barbara Mayor *[Ed.]*; Maud Blair *[Ed.]*. London: Sage Publications, 1991: 336 p. *ISBN: 0803985770.*

254 Racism and the incorporation of foreign labour — farm labour migration to Canada since 1945. Vic Satzewich. London: Routledge, 1991: 241 p. *ISBN: 0415043964. Includes bibliography and index.* [Critical studies in racism and migration.]

255 Racism in America and in other race-centered nation-states — synchronic considerations. John H. Stanfield. *Int. J. Comp. Soc* **32:**3-4 9-12:1991 pp. 243 – 260

256 Racism in baseball card collecting — fact or fiction? Bob Regoli. *Human Relat.* **44:**3 3:1991 pp. 255 – 264

257 Le racisme dans les relations interethniques *[In French]*; Racism in interethnic relations *[Summary]*. Véronique De Rudder. *Hom. Soc.* **XXV:4(102)** 1991 pp. 75 – 92

258 Razzismo e immigrazione — il caso Italia *[In Italian]*; [Racism and immigration — the Italian case]. Leone Iraci Fedeli; Giorgio la Malfa *[Foreword]*. Italy: Acropoli, 1990: 175 p. *ISBN: 8885355013.*

259 The resistable rise of Jean-Marie Le Pen. Daniel Singer. *Ethn. Racial* **14:**3 7:1991 pp. 368 – 381

260 Scientific racism — the cloak of objectivity. Halford H. Fairchild. *J. Soc. Issues* **47:**3 1991 pp. 101 – 116

261 Skin tone and stratification in the black community. Verna M. Keith; Cedric Herring. *A.J.S.* **97:**3 11:1991 pp. 760 – 778

262 Social categorization and person memory — the pervasiveness of race as an organizing principle. M. Hewstone; A. Hantzi; L. Johnston. *Eur. J. Soc. Psychol.* **21:**6 11-12:1991 pp. 517 – 528

263 Sport, racism and ethnicity. Grant Jarvie *[Ed.]*. London: Falmer, 1991: 202 p. *ISBN: 1850009163. Includes bibliographies and index.*

264 The support for the Front National — analyses and findings. Christopher T. Husbands. *Ethn. Racial* **14:**3 7:1991 pp. 382 – 416

265 Training for equality — a study of race relations and equal opportunities training. Colin Brown; Jean Lawton *[Ed.]*. London: Policy Studies Institute, 1991: 109 p. *ISBN: 0853745269. Includes bibliography.*

266 The unbreakable thread — non-racialism in South Africa. Julie Frederikse. Johannesburg: Ravan, 1990: 294 p. *ISBN: 0869754025.*

267 Understanding everyday racism — an interdisciplinary theory. Philomena Essed. Newbury

F.7: Ethnic groups *[Groupes ethniques]* — **Racial discrimination** *[Discrimination raciale]*
Park: Sage Publications, c1991: x, 322 p. *ISBN: 0803942559; LofC: 91022025. Includes bibliographical references (p. 297-318) and index.* [Sage series on race and ethnic relations. : Vol. 2]

268 Von heruntergekommenen Altbauquartieren zu abgewerteten Sozialwohnungen. Ethnische Minderheiten in Frankreich, Deutschland und dem Vereinigten Königreich *[In German]*; From run-down accommodation in old buildings to degraded public housing. Ethnic minorities in France, Germany and the United Kingdom *[Summary]*. Maurice Blanc. *Inf. Raum.* :**7/8** 1991 pp. 447 – 457

269 'Wat reg is, is reg' — 'n Inhoudsontleding van sosiologika by 'n kleurinsident *[In Afrikaans]*; "What's right, is right" — content-analysis of socio-logic in an incident of race discrimination *[Summary]*. Dian Joubert. *S.Afr. J. Sociol.* **22:2** 5:1991 pp. 59 – 72

F.8: Migration — *Migration*

Sub-divisions: Immigrant adaptation *[Adaptation des immigrants]*; Internal migration *[Migration interne]*; International migration *[Migration internationale]*

1 Access to homeownership among immigrant groups in Canada; *[French summary]*. Brian K. Ray; Eric Moore. *Can. R. Soc. A.* **28:1** 2:1991 pp. 1 – 29
2 Are immigrants overrepresented in the Australian social security system? Peter Whiteford. *J. Aust. Pop. Ass.* **8:2** 11:1991 pp. 93 – 109
3 Behind the bamboo hedge — the impact of homeland politics in the Parisian Vietnamese community. Gisele L. Bousquet. Ann Arbor Mich: University of Michison Press, c1991: 196 p. *ISBN: 0472101749. Bibliography — pp.179-186. - Includes index.*
4 Bessemer — a sociological perspective of the Chicano barrio. Irene I. Blea. New York, NY: AMS Press, c1991: x, 211 p. *ISBN: 0404194230; LofC: 87045778. Includes index.* [Immigrant communities & ethnic minorities in the United States & Canada. : No. 13]
5 Borders and boundaries of state and self at the end of empire. Michael Kearney. *J. Hist. Soc.* **4:1** 3:1991 pp. 52 – 74
6 Central American migration — a framework for analysis. Nora Hamilton; Norma Stoltz Chinchilla. *Lat. Am. Res. R.* **26:1** 1991 pp. 75 – 110
7 The Cherkess on Yugoslav territory (a supplement to the article "Cherkess" in the Encyclopaedia of Islam). Alexandre Popovic. *C.Asian Sur.* **10:1/2** 1991 pp. 65 – 80
8 Citizenship and the nation-state. Maxim Silverman. *Ethn. Racial* **14:3** 7:1991 pp. 333 – 349
9 Collective assertion strategies of immigrants in Switzerland; Strategies d'affirmation collective des immigrés en Suisse *[French summary]*. Caludio Bolzman; Rosita Fibbi. *Int. Sociol.* **6:3** 9:1991 pp. 321 – 342
10 Comparative studies of migration and exclusion on the grounds of "race" and ethnic background in western Europe — a critical appraisal. Frank Bovenkerk; Robert Miles; Gilles Verbunt. *Int. Migr. Rev.* **XXV:2** Summer:1991 pp. 375 – 390
11 Composition of the personal voice — violence and migration. Das Veena. *Stud. Hist.* **7:1** 1-6:1991 pp. 65 – 78
12 The deconcentration theoretical perspective as an explanation for recent changes in the West German migration system. T. Kontuly. *Geoforum* **22:3** 1991 pp. 299 – 318
13 Deutsche Arbeiten in Israel — Motive, Möglichkeiten und Grenzen sozialer Arbeit in einem komplizierten Land *[In German]*; [Germans working in Israel — motives, possibilities and limits of social work in a complicated country]. Bernd Pfeifer; Ralf-H. Rehfeldt. Frankfurt am Main: R.G. Fischer, 1990: 113 p. *ISBN: 3894062509; LofC: 91216629. Includes bibliographical references (p. 111-112).*
14 Les diplômées *[In French]*; [Graduates]. Zaihia Zeroulou. *Inf. Soc.* :**14** 10-11:1991 pp. 54 – 63
15 Duration of residence in the United States and the fertility of U.S. immigrants. Kathleen Ford. *Int. Migr. Rev.* **XXIV:1** Spring:1990 pp. 34 – 68
16 Explicando la migración — la teoría en la encrucijada *[In Spanish]*; Explaining migration theory at the crossroads *[Summary]*. Alan B. Simmons. *Est. Demog. Urb.* **6:1** 1-4:1991 pp. 5 – 32
17 Familias migrantes — reproducción de la identidad y del sentimiento de pertenencia *[In*

F.8: Migration *[Migration]*

Spanish]; *[Catalan summary]*; [Migrant families — reproduction of identity and a sense of belonging] *[Summary]*. Dolors Comas d'Argemir; Joan Josep Pujadas Munoz. *Papers* :**36** 1991 pp. 33 – 56

18 Family migration in a developing country. Brenda Davis Root; Gordon F. de Jong. *Pop. Stud. Egy.* **45:2** 7:1991 pp. 221 – 234

19 La France et la Grande-Bretagne face à leurs minorités immigrées *[In French]*; [France and Great Britain in the face of their immigrant minorities]. Didier Lapeyronnie. *Temps Mod.* **46:540-541** 7-8:1991 pp. 10 – 45

20 The gender-specific terror of El Salvador and Guatemala — post-traumatic stress disorder in Central American refugee women. Adrianne Aron; Shawn Corne; Anthea Fursland; Barbara Zelwer. *Wom. St. Inter. For.* **14:1/2** 1991 pp. 37 – 48

21 Human immunodeficiency virus and migrant labor in South Africa. Karen Jochelson; Monyaola Mothibeli; Jean-Patrick Leger. *Int. J. Health. Ser.* **21:1** 1991 pp. 157 – 173

22 Ils feront de bons Français — enquête sur l'assimilation des Maghrébins *[In French]*; [They will make good French people — survey into the assimilation of North Africans]. Christian Jelen. Paris: Laffont, 1991: 235 p. *ISBN: 2221070836.*

23 Immigrant suicide in Australia, Canada, England and Wales, and the United States. Erich Kliewer. *J. Aust. Pop. Ass.* **8:2** 11:1991 pp. 111 – 128

24 L'immigration africaine au féminin *[In French]*; [Immigration and African women]. Jacques Barou. *Inf. Soc.* :**14** 10-11:1991 pp. 26 – 33

25 Immigration and the family. George J. Borjas; Stephen G. Bronars. *J. Labor Ec.* **9:2** 4:1991 pp. 123 – 148

26 L'immigration prise aux mots — les immigrés dans la presse au tournant des années 80 *[In French]*; [Immigrants in the media in the 80's]. Simone Bonnafous. Paris: Editions Kimé, c1991: 301 p. *ISBN: 2908212064. Notes et bibliographie.* [Argumentation et sciences du langage.]

27 Immigration, classe ouvrière et salariat *[In French]*; Immigration, working class and wage earning people *[Summary]*. Jean Magniadas. *Pensée* :**284** 11-12:1991 pp. 29 – 46

28 Les jeunes d'origine immigrée en Grand-Bretagne *[In French]*; [Young people with immigrant origins in Great Britain]. Robert Miles. *Temps Mod.* **46:540-541** 7-8:1991 pp. 133 – 165

29 The mainstream right and the politics of immigration in France — developments in the 1980s. Christopher T. Husbands. *Ethn. Racial* **14:2** 4:1991 pp. 170 – 198

30 Migrability — a diffusion model of migration; *[Italian summary]*; *[French summary]*. Fernando Rajulton. *Genus* **XLVII:1-2** 1-6:1991 pp. 31 – 48

31 Migracije i zdravlje *[In Serbo-Croatian]*; Migration and health *[Summary]*. Sonja Podgorelec. *Migrac. Teme* **6:4** 1990 pp. 69 – 78

32 Migración y ciudad intermedia — Hidalgo del Parral, México *[In Spanish]*; [Migration and medium sized cities — Hidalgo del Parral, Mexico]. Wouter Hoenderdos; Wim de Regt. *Rev. Int.Am. Plan.* **XXIV:93** 1-3:1991 pp. 86 – 107

33 I migranti e i diritti umani *[In Italian]*; [Migrants and human rights]. Pier Marcello Masotti. *Aff. Soc. Int.* **XIX:1** 1991 pp. 31 – 42

34 Migration and circulation in Ecuador. Jorge A. Brea. *J. Econ. Soc. Geogr.* **82:3** 1991 pp. 206 – 219

35 Migration and recession — Arab labor mobility in the Middle East, 1982-89; La migration et la récession — la mobilité de la main-d'oeuvre arabe au Moyen-Orient, de 1982 á 1989 *[French summary]*; Migración y recesión — la mobilidad laboral árabe en el Medio Oriente, 1982-89 *[Spanish summary]*. Gil Feiler. *Pop. Dev. Rev.* **17:1** 3:1991 pp. 134 – 155

36 Migration consequences for household energy consumption in a nonmetropolitan recreation-retirement area. Glenn V. Fuguitt; Thomas A. Heberlein; Pamela R. Rathbun. *Rural Sociol.* **56:1** Spring:1991 pp. 56 – 69

37 Migration impacts of trade and foreign investment — Mexico and Caribbean Basin countries. Sidney Weintraub *[Ed.]*; Sergio Diaz-Briquets *[Ed.]*. Boulder: Westview Press, 1991: xv, 301 p. *ISBN: 0813383390; LofC: 91008057. Includes bibliographical references.* [Series on development and international migration in Mexico, Central America, and the Caribbean Basin. : No. 3]

38 Migration of Hispanic youth and poverty status — a logit analysis. Maria Wilson-Figueroa; E. Helen Berry; Michael B. Toney. *Rural Sociol.* **56:2** Summer:1991 pp. 189 – 203

F.8: Migration *[Migration]*

39 Migration, gender and social change. Marta Tienda; Karen Booth. *Int. Sociol.* **6:1** 3:1991 pp. 51 – 71
40 Migration, remittances, and small business development — Mexico and Caribbean Basin countries. Sidney Weintraub *[Ed.]*; Sergio Diaz-Briquets *[Ed.]*. Boulder: Westview Press, 1991: xv, 209 p. (ill) *ISBN: 0813383404; LofC: 91008691. Includes bibliographical references.* [Series on development and international migration in Mexico, Central America, and the Caribbean Basin. : No. 4]
41 Migration, sense of place, and nonmetropolitan vitality. Gundars Rudzitis. *Urban Geogr.* **12:1** 1-2:1991 pp. 80 – 88
42 Le migrazioni — che cosa interessa conoscere *[In Italian]*; Migration — a few points of significance *[Summary]*; *[French summary]*. Nora Federici. *Genus* **XLVII:1-2** 1-6:1991 pp. 153 – 162
43 Mobility and the single homeless. David K. Whynes. *Area* **23:2** 6:1991 pp. 111 – 118
44 New directions in migration research. Perspectives from some North American regional science disciplines. M.J. Greenwood; P.R. Mueser; D.A. Plane; A.M. Schlottmann. *Ann. Reg. Sci.* **25:4** 1991 pp. 237 – 270
45 Open borders — a global-humanist approach to the refugee crisis. M. Gurtov. *World Dev.* **19:5** 5:1991 pp. 485 – 496
46 Patterns of immigrant enterprise in six metropolitan areas. Constance A. Hoffman; Martin N. Marger. *Social Soc. Res.* **75:3** 4:1991 pp. 144 – 157
47 Perspectives avec migrations *[In French]*; Projections that include migration. Daniel Courgeau. *Population* **46:6** 11-12:1991 pp. 1513 – 1530
48 The political mobilization of the North African community in France. Alec G. Hargreaves. *Ethn. Racial* **14:3** 7:1991 pp. 350 – 367
49 A probability model for the distribution of the number of migrants at the household level; *[Italian summary]*; *[French summary]*. Kedar N.S. Yadava; Ram B. Singh. *Genus* **XLVII:1-2** 1-6:1991 pp. 49 – 62
50 The public finance impact of immigrant population on host nations — some Canadian evidence. Ather H. Akbari. *Soc. Sci. Q.* **72:2** 6:1991 pp. 334 – 346
51 Reconciling the pattern of trade with the pattern of migration. James E. Rauch. *Am. Econ. Rev.* **81:4** 9:1991 pp. 775 – 796
52 Refugees from revolution — U.S. policy and Third-World migration. Peter H. Koehn. Boulder: Westview Press, 1991: xiv, 463 p. *ISBN: 0813377196; LofC: 91031275. Includes bibliographical references. (p. [458]-460) and index.*
53 Regional and sectoral development in Mexico as alternatives to migration. Sidney Weintraub *[Ed.]*; Sergio Diaz-Briquets *[Ed.]*. Boulder: Westview Press, 1991: xvii, 393 p. *ISBN: 0813381436; LofC: 90025257. Includes bibliographical references.* [Series on development and international migration in Mexico, Central America, and the Caribbean Basin.]
54 Secondary earner strategies and family poverty — immigrant-native differentials, 1960-1980. Leif Jensen. *Int. Migr. Rev.* **XXV:1** Spring:1991 pp. 113 – 140
55 Sequential migration theory and evidence from Peru. C. Pessino. *J. Dev. Econ.* **36:1** 7:1991 pp. 55 – 88
56 Social characteristics and destinations of recent emigrants from selected regions in the west of Ireland. J. MacLaughlin. *Geoforum* **22:3** 1991 pp. 319 – 332
57 Speaking, reading, and earnings among low- skilled immigrants. Barry R. Chiswick. *J. Labor Ec.* **9:2** 4:1991 pp. 149 – 170
58 The status of the Spanish language in the United States at the beginning of the 21st century. Calvin Veltman. *Int. Migr. Rev.* **XXIV:1** Spring:1990 pp. 108 – 123
59 Towards an authoritarian European state. Tony Bunyan. *Race Class* **32:3** 1-3:1991 pp. 19 – 27
60 Uma pobreza "exótica" — a imigração argelina na França *[In Portuguese]*; "Exotic" poverty — Algerian immigrants in France *[Summary]*; Une pauvreté "exotique " — l'immigration algérienne en France *[French summary]*. Abdelmalek Sayad. *Rev. Bras. Ciên. Soc.* **6:17** 10:1991 pp. 84 – 107
61 Understanding intra-ethnic attitude variations — Mexican origin population views of immigration. Rodolfo O. de la Garza; Jerry L. Polinard; Robert D. Wrinkle; Thomás Longoria. *Soc. Sci. Q.* **72:2** 6:1991 pp. 379 – 387
62 Undocumented immigration and unemployment of U.S. youth and minority workers — econometric evidence. C.R. Winegarden; Lay Boon Khor. *Rev. Econ. St.* **LXXIII:1** 2:1991 pp. 105 – 112

F.8: Migration *[Migration]*

63 Who forgets? An analysis of memory effects in a retrospective survey on migration history; Qui oublie? Une analyse des effets de mémoire dans une enquête rétrospective sur la biographie migratoire *[French summary]*. N. Auriat. *Eur. J. Pop.* **7:4** 1991 pp. 311 – 342

64 Wir sind immer die Fremden — Aussiedler in Deutschland *[In German]*; [We are always aliens — immigrants in Germany]. Lothar Ferstl; Harald Hetzel. Bonn: Dietz, 1990: 207 p. *ISBN: 3801230376; LofC: 91147409.* [Dietz Taschenbuch.]

Immigrant adaptation *[Adaptation des immigrants]*

65 Assimilation in American life — an Islamic perspective. Mazen Hashem. *Am. J. Islam. Soc. Sci.* **8:1** 3:1991 pp. 83 – 98

66 Der berufliche und soziale Eingliederungsprozeß der ersten und zweiten Generation türkischer Arbeitnehmer in Nordrhein-Westfalen *[In German]*; The process of occupational and social integration of first and second generation Turkish employees in North-Rhine Westphalia *[Summary]*. Günther Schultze. *Inf. Raum.* **:7/8** 1991 pp. 421 – 427

67 Chinese immigrant families in Australia — a variety of experiences; *[French summary]*; *[Spanish summary]*. Lawrence W. Crissman. *J. Comp. Fam. Stud.* **XXII:1** Spring:1991 pp. 25 – 38

68 A comparative study of Mauritian immigrants in two European cities, London and Paris — an investigation into the problems of adaptation. Sam Lingayah. London: Mauritians' Welfare Association, 1991: 162 p. *ISBN: 0951350315.*

69 Demele, "making it" — migration and adaptation among Haitian boat people in the United States. Rose-Marie Cassagnol Chierici. New York: AMS Press, c1991: xviii, 333 p. *ISBN: 040419480x; LofC: 89018506. Includes bibliographical references (p. 314-328) and index.* [Immigrant communities & ethnic minorities in the United States & Canada.]

70 Femmes bangladeshi à Londres *[In French]*; [Bangladeshi women in London]. Catherine Neveu. *Temps Mod.* **46:540-541** 7-8:1991 pp. 238 – 257

71 Foreign-born Canadian emigrants and their characteristics (1981-1986). Margaret Michalowski. *Int. Migr. Rev.* **XXV:1** Spring:1991 pp. 28 – 59

72 Formation et différenciation du marché des travailleurs étrangers au Japon *[In French]*; The labour market for immigrant workers *[Summary]*. Akihiro Ishikawa. *Sociol. Trav.* **XXXIII:1** 1991 pp. 173 – 188

73 Household and family among Lebanese immigrants in Nova Scotia — continuity, change and adaptation; *[French summary]*; *[Spanish summary]*. Nancy W. Jabbra. *J. Comp. Fam. Stud.* **XXII:1** Spring:1991 pp. 39 – 56

74 Immigration and living arrangements — elderly women in Canada. Monica Boyd. *Int. Migr. Rev.* **XXV:1** Spring:1991 pp. 4 – 27

75 L'intégration des Maghrébins en France *[In French]*; [The integration of North Africans in France]. Mohand Khellil. Paris: PUF, 1991: 182 p. *ISBN: 2130435483.* [Sociologie d'aujourd'hui.]

76 Minorities, immigrants and refugees — the problems of integration. Maurice Zinkin. *Int. Rel.* **X:3** 5:1991 pp. 267 – 276

77 Refugee adaptation and community structure —the Indochinese in Quebec City, Canada. Louis-Jacques Dorais. *Int. Migr. Rev.* **XXV:3** Fall:1991 pp. 551 – 573

78 Rehabilitating the returning migrants from the Gulf. Prakash C. Jain. *Int. Stud.* **28:3** 7-9:1991 pp. 307 – 316

79 The relative economic progress of male foreign workers in Kuwait. Sulayman S. Al-Qudsi; Nasra M. Shah. *Int. Migr. Rev.* **XXV:1** Spring:1991 pp. 141 – 166

80 Remittances behaviour of a section of Bangladeshi migrants living in Scotland; Le comportement d'un groupe de travailleurs bangladeshis residant en Écosse, dans le transfert de leurs revenus *[French summary]*. Dipak Ghosh. *Sav. Develop.* **XV:3** 1991 pp. 261 – 272

81 Socijalizacijska uloga porodice u razvoju druge generacije Jugoslavena u Francuskoj *[In Serbo-Croatian]*; The sociolizational role of the family in the development of second generation Yugoslavs in France *[Summary]*. Jadranka Čačić. *Migrac. Teme* **6:4** 1990 pp. 55 – 64

82 Sprawy Polaków na Litwie w opinii „Czerwonego Sztandaru" Świadomość narodowa i język *[In Polish]*; The problems of Poles in Lithuania in the opinion of „Czerwony Sztandar". National awareness and language *[Summary]*. Monika Szpiczakowska. *Prz. Pol.* **XVII:2** 1991 pp. 89 – 104

83 Stratégies d'intégration *[In French]*; [Integration strategies]. Isabelle Taboada-Léonetti. *Inf. Soc.* **:14** 10-11:1991 pp. 11 – 19

F.8: Migration *[Migration]* — Immigrant adaptation *[Adaptation des immigrants]*

84 Voices from Southeast Asia — the refugee experience in the United States. John Tenhula. New York: Holmes & Meier, 1991: xix, 247 p. (ill., map) *ISBN: 084191110x; LofC: 90040696.* Includes bibliographical references. [Ellis Island series.]

Internal migration *[Migration interne]*

85 Aged migration to coastal and inland centres in NSW. R. Drysdale. *Aust. Geogr. Stud.* **29:2** 10:1991 pp. 268 – 284

86 Bauern und Migranten — Über den Zusammenhang zwischen sozio-ökonomischer Organisation andiner Dörfer und Stadtmigration in Peru *[In German]*; Peasants and migrants *[Summary]*. Harald Moßbrucker. *Z. Soziol.* **20:1** 2:1991 pp. 50 – 63

87 Black exodus — the great migration from the American South. Alferdteen Harrison *[Ed.]*. Jackson: University Press of Mississippi, c1991: xviii, 107 p. *ISBN: 087805491x; LofC: 90019216.* Includes index.

88 The determinants of migrating with a pre-arranged job and of the initial duration of urban unemployment — an analysis based on Indian data on rural-to-urban migrants. B. Banerjee. *J. Dev. Econ.* **36:2** 10:1991 pp. 337 – 351

89 Differences in migratory spatial patterns in Israel's national periphery — theoretical ramifications. Gabriel Lipshitz. *Geogr. Res. For.* **11:** 1991 pp. 66 – 77

90 Gender, households and seasonal migration in Guanacaste, Costa Rica. Sylvia Chant. *R. Eur. Lat.am. Caribe* **:50** 6:1991 pp. 51 – 86

91 How "sticky" is urbanward migration? Evidence for the United States, 1850-1980. Brian J.L. Berry. *Urban Geogr.* **12:3** 5-6:1991 pp. 283 – 290

92 Immigration and internal migration as a mechanism of polarization and dispersion of population and development — the Israeli case. Gabriel Lipshitz. *Econ. Dev. Cult. Change* **39:2** 1:1991 pp. 391 – 404

93 Information flow, job search, and migration. T. Vishwanath. *J. Dev. Econ.* **36:2** 10:1991 pp. 313 – 335

94 Interregional migration of labor in Ghana, West Africa — determinants, consequences and policy intervention. John A. Arthur. *Rev. Bl. Pol. Ec.* **20:2** Fall:1991 pp. 89 – 104

95 Interregional migration patterns of Chicanos — the core, periphery, and frontier. Rogelio Saenz. *Soc. Sci. Q.* **72:1** 3:1991 pp. 135 – 148

96 Japanese migration in contemporary Japan — economic segmentation and interprefectural migration. Hiroshi Fukurai. *Soc. Biol.* **38:1-2** Spring-Summer:1991 pp. 28 – 50

97 La migración a la ciudad de México — un proceso multifacético *[In Spanish]*; Migration to Mexico City. A multifaceted process *[Summary]*. María Eugenia Negrete Salas. *Est. Demog. Urb.* **5:3** 9-12:1990 pp. 641 – 654

98 Migrations and development in rural Latin America. Solon Barraclough. *Econ. Ind. Dem.* **12:1** 2:1991 pp. 43 – 63

99 Migratsiia naseleniia v bol´shikh gorodakh SSSR i stran Vostochnoĭ Evropy *[In Russian]*; [Population migrations to the large cities and Eastern Europe]. Włodzimierz Mirowski; G. Morozova. Moskva: Nauka, 1990: 109 p. *ISBN: 5020133655; LofC: 92119907.* Includes bibliographical references.

100 On the road again — seasonal migration to a sunbelt metropolis. Kevin E. McHugh; Robert C. Mings. *Urban Geogr.* **12:1** 1-2:1991 pp. 1 – 18

101 Permanent and temporary migration differentials in China. Sidney Goldstein; Alice Goldstein *[Ed.]*. Honolulu, Hawaii: East-West Center, [1991]: vii, 52 p. *ISBN: 0866381376; LofC: 91007663.* Includes bibliographical references (p. 51-52). [Papers of the East-West Population Institute.]

102 Recent trends and future prospects for urban-rural migration in Europe; Tendances récentes et projections futures des migrations urbaines-rurales en Europe *[French summary]*; Neueste Trends und Zukunftsaussichten der Stadt-Land-Wanderung in Europa *[German summary]*. W.J. Serow. *Sociol. Rur.* **XXXI:4** 1991 pp. 269 – 280

103 Regional migration in Britain — an analysis of gross flows using NHS central register data. Richard Jackman; S. Savouri. London: London School of Economics and Political Science, 1991: 88 p. [Discussion paper.]

104 Relative deprivation and migration — theory, evidence, and policy implications. Oded Stark; J. Edward Taylor. Washington, D.C.: Population and Human Resources Department and Agriculture and Rural Development Department, The World Bank, 1991: 42 p. [Policy, research, and external affairs working papers.]

105 Residential mobility differences among developed countries. Larry Long. *Int. Reg. Sci. R.* **14:2** 1991 pp. 133 – 148

F.8: Migration *[Migration]* — Internal migration *[Migration interne]*

106 Die Rolle der Pädagogik in der westdeutschen Migrations- und Minderheitenforschung. Bemerkungen aus wissenschaftssoziologischer Sicht *[In German]*; The role of pedagogics in migration and minority research. Comments from a sociology of knowledge perspective *[Summary]*. Frank-Olaf Radtke. *Soz. Welt.* **42:1** :1991 pp. 93 – 108

107 Rural-urban migration in Zambia and migrant ties to home villages. Mitsuo Ogura. *Develop. Eco.* **XXIX:2** 6:1991 pp. 145 – 165

108 Social and geographical mobility in the non-metropolitan south of England; La mobilité social et géographique dans le sud non métropolitain de l'Angleterre *[French summary]*. A.J. Fielding. *Espace Pop. Soc.* **:2** 1991 pp. 395 – 408

109 South Africa's labor empire — a history of black migrancy to the gold mines. Jonathan Scott Crush; Alan H. Jeeves *[Ed.]*; David Yudelman *[Ed.]*. Boulder: Westview Press, 1991: xvi, 266 p. (ill) *ISBN: 0813374170; LofC: 91014141. Includes bibliographical references (p. 239-250) and index.* [African modernization and development series.]

110 Urban-rural migration — effects of a change in agricultural uncertainty. Charles A. Ingene. *Pap. Reg. Sci.* **70:1** 1:1991 pp. 81 – 95

International migration *[Migration internationale]*

111 African emigres in the United States — a missing link in Africa's social and economic development. Kofi K. Apraku. New York: Praeger, 1991: xxiv, 162 p. *ISBN: 0275937992.*

112 Asian immigration to Australia — past and current trends. Laksiri Jayasuriya; David Sang. *Popul. R.* **35:1&2** 1-12:1991 pp. 35 – 56

113 Between two islands — Dominican international migration. Sherri Grasmuck; Patricia R. Pessar *[Ed.]*. Berkeley: University of California Press, c1991: xviii, 247 p. (ill) *ISBN: 0520071492; LofC: 90050924. Includes bibliographical references (p. 209-238) and index.*

114 Cent ans d'immigration, étrangers d'hier français d'aujord'hui — apport démographique, dynamique familiale et économique de l'immigrant étrangère *[In French]*; [100 years of immigration, yesterday, foreigners, today's French people — demographic, social and economic study of immigrants]. Michèle Tribalat *[Ed.]*. Paris: INED, 1991: 301 p. *ISBN: 273320131x. Bibliography — p[293]-301.* [Travaux et documents.]

115 The "century of the refugee", a European century? Hans Arnold. *Aussenpolitik* **42:3** 1991 pp. 271 – 280

116 The chains that bind — family reunion migration to Australia in the 1980s. Robert Birrell. Canberra: Australian Government Publishing Service, c1990: 57 p. *ISBN: 0644098848.*

117 "Cradle of freedom on earth" — refugee immigration and ethnic pluralism. Tomas Hammar. *W. Eur. Pol.* **14:3** 7:1991 pp. 182 – 196

118 Deciding who gets in — decisionmaking by immigration inspectors. Janet A. Gilboy. *Law Soc. Rev.* **25:3** 1991 pp. 571 – 599

119 Demele, "making it" — migration and adaptation among Haitian boat people in the United States. Rose-Marie Cassagnol Chierici. New York: AMS Press, c1991: xviii, 333 p. *ISBN: 040419480x; LofC: 89018506. Includes bibliographical references (p. 314-328) and index.* [Immigrant communities & ethnic minorities in the United States & Canada.]

120 Determinants of emigration from Mexico, Central America, and the Caribbean. Sidney Weintraub *[Ed.]*; Sergio Diaz-Briquets *[Ed.]*. Boulder: Westview Press, c1991: xix, 356 p. (ill) *ISBN: 0813381428; LofC: 90021311. Includes bibliographical references.* [Series on development and international migration in Mexico, Central America, and the Caribbean Basin. : No. 1]

121 Differential economic opportunity, transferability of skills, and immigration to the United States and Canada. Michael J. Greenwood; John M. McDowell. *Rev. Econ. St.* **LXXIII:4** 11:1991 pp. 612 – 623

122 Dual chain migration — post-1965 Filipino immigration to the United States. John M. Liu; Paul M. Ong; Carolyn Rosenstein. *Int. Migr. Rev.* **XXV:3** Fall:1991 pp. 487 – 513

123 The effect of maquiladora employment on the monthly flow of Mexican undocumented immigration to the U.S., 1978-1982. Davila Alberto; Rogelio Saenz. *Int. Migr. Rev.* **XXIV:1** Spring:1990 pp. 96 – 107

124 The effects of receiving country policies on migration flows. Sidney Weintraub *[Ed.]*; Sergio Díaz-Briquets *[Ed.]*. Boulder: Westview Press, 1991: xv, 303 p. (ill) *ISBN: 0813383420; LofC: 91008644. Includes bibliographical references.* [Series on development and international migration in Mexico, Central America, and the Caribbean Basin. : No. 6]

125 Emigration from the French Caribbean — the origins of an organized migration; *[French summary]*. Stephanie A. Condon; Philip E. Ogden. *Int. J. Urban* **15:4** 12:1991 pp. 505 – 523

F.8: Migration *[Migration]* — **International migration** *[Migration internationale]*

126 The emigrations from Eastern Europe and the Soviet Union to the United States after the Second World War (1945-1980). The Romanian contribution. Radu Toma. *Rev. Roumaine EInt.* **XXV:1-2(111-112)** 1-4:1991 pp. 15 – 22

127 European immigration and ethnicity in Latin America — a bibliography. Oliver Marshall. London: Institute of Latin American Studies, 1991: 165 p. *ISBN: 0901145726.* Includes bibliography and index.

128 Festung Europa. Grenzziehungen in der Ost-West-Migration *[In German]*; [Fortress Europe. Erecting barriers to East-West migration]. Erhard Stölting. *Prokla* **21:2(83)** 1991 pp. 249 – 263

129 Foreign media and the desire to emigrate from Belize. Leslie Snyder; Connie Roser; Steven Chaffee. *J. Comm.* **41:1** Winter:1991 pp. 117 – 132

130 Immigration after 1992. Martin Baldwin-Edwards. *Policy Pol.* **19:3** 7:1991 pp. 199 – 212

131 L'immigration au pays des droits de l'homme — politique et droit *[In French]*; [Immigration to human rights countries — policy and law]. Alain Bockel. Paris: Publisud, 1991: 273 p. *ISBN: 286600440x.* [L'Avenir de la politique.]

132 L'immigration comparée en France et an Allemagne *[In French]*; [Comparing immigration in France and Germany]. William R. Brubaker. *Temps Mod.* **46:540-541** 7-8·1991 pp. 293 – 332

133 Immigration policy and the issue of nationality. Catherine Wihtol de Wenden. *Ethn. Racial* **14:3** 7:1991 pp. 319 – 332

134 La inmigración — un problema para los Estados Unidos. Particularidades sobre el caso cubano *[In Spanish]*; [Immigration — a problem for the United States. Details of the Cuban case]. María Teresa Miyar Bolio. *Cuad. Am.* **1:25** 1-2:1991 pp. 139 – 151

135 Integration and immigration pressures in Western Europe. W.R. Böhning. *Int. Lab. Rev.* **130:4** 4:1991 pp. 445 – 458

136 International labor migration patterns in West Africa. John A. Arthur. *Afr. Stud. R.* **34:3** 12:1991 pp. 65 – 88

137 International migration and the "moral" economy of the "Barani" peasantry. Azfar F. Khan; Zafar Mahmood *[Comments by]*. *Pak. Dev. R.* **30:4** Winter:1991 pp. 1087 – 1100

138 International migration and welfare in the source-country. Bharati Basu; G. Bhattacharyya. *Scand. J. Devel. Altern.* **X:4** 12:1991 pp. 63 – 76

139 International migration under incomplete information — a microeconomic approach. Siegfried Berninghaus; Hans-Günther Seifert-Vogt *[Ed.]*. Berlin: Springer-Verlag, c1991: viii, 115 p. (ill) *ISBN: 3540540911; LofC: 91021089.* Includes bibliographical references (p. 113-115). [Studies in international economics and institutions.]

140 International migration — challenge for the nineties. Reginald T. Appleyard. Geneva: International Organization for Migration, 1991: 84 p. *ISBN: 9290680369.* "Published for the 40th anniversary of IOM"--t.p..

141 The international mobility of labor — North African migrant workers in France. Ann M. Oberhauser. *Prof. Geogr.* **43:4** 11:1991 pp. 431 – 444

142 Iranian refugees and exiles since Khomeini. Asghar Fathi *[Ed.]*. Costa Mesa, CA: Mazda Publishers, 1991: 296 p. (ill) *ISBN: 0939214687; LofC: 91001999.* Includes bibliographical references.

143 Les jeunes réfugiés majeurs isolés du Sud- Est Asiatique en France. Parcours et problématique psychologique *[In French]*; [Young adult refugees from Southeast Asia living without parents in France. Case history and psychological problems]. Didier Bertrand. *AWR B.* **29(38):1** :1991 pp. 21 – 27

144 Labour demand and immigration in Italy. Giovanni Ancona. *J. Reg. Pol.* **11:1** 1-3:1991 pp. 143 – 148

145 Labour migration to the Middle East — a case study of Sri Lanka. F. Eelens *[Ed.]*; Toon Schampers *[Ed.]*. London: K. Paul International, 1991: 259 p. *ISBN: 0710304269; LofC: 90025157.* Includes bibliographical references and indexes. [Spectacular Times pocketbook series.]

146 Long-term immigration to the United States — new approaches to measurement. Ellen Percy Kraly; Robert Warren. *Int. Migr. Rev.* **XXV:1** Spring:1991 pp. 60 – 92

147 Measuring the net migration of immigrants to U.S. metropolitan areas. M.J. Greenwood; S.E. Ragland. *J. Econ. Soc.* **17:3-4** 1991 pp. 233 – 248

148 Međunarodna migracija u arapskoj regiji *[In Serbo-Croatian]*; International migrations in the Arab region *[Summary]*. Ružica Čičak-Chand. *Migrac. Teme* **6:4** 1990 pp. 481 – 495

149 Migración internacional de miembros de clases sociales media y alta hacia La Paz, Bolivia *[In Spanish]*; [The international migration of members of the middle and upper classes to La Paz, Bolivia]. Gerrit Köster. *Rev. Int.Am. Plan.* **XXIV:93** 1-3:1991 pp. 108 – 126

F.8: Migration *[Migration]* — International migration *[Migration internationale]*

150 Migration and migrants in France. Robert Miles *[Contrib.]*; Jeanne Singer-Kérel *[Contrib.]*; Philip E. Ogden *[Contrib.]*; Catherine Wihtol de Wenden *[Contrib.]*; Maxim Silverman *[Contrib.]*; Alec G. Hargreaves *[Contrib.]*; Daniel Singer *[Contrib.]*; Christopher T. Husbands *[Contrib.]*. Collection of 8 articles. **Ethn. Racial** , *14:3,* 7:1991 pp. 265 – 416

151 Migration from Northern Ireland — a survey of new year travellers as a means of identifying emigrants; La migration en provenance de l'Irlande du Nord — une enquête des voyageurs de nouvel an comme mode d'établir l'identité des émigrants *[French summary]*; Auswanderung aus Nordirland — eine Aufnahme Neujahrsreisender als Methode der Identifizierung von Auswanderern *[German summary]*. Paul A. Compton; John Power. *Reg. Stud.* **25:1** 2:1991 pp. 1 – 11

152 Migration to the Arab world — experience of returning migrants. Godfrey Gunatilleke *[Ed.]*. Tokyo: United Nations University Press, 1991: 352 p. *ISBN: 9280807455*. *"HSDB-47/UNUP-745"*; *Includes bibliographical references.*

153 Migratsiia naseleniia v bol´shikh gorodakh SSSR i stran Vostochnoĭ Evropy *[In Russian]*; [Population migrations to the large cities and Eastern Europe]. Włodzimierz Mirowski; G. Morozova. Moskva: Nauka, 1990: 109 p. *ISBN: 5020133655; LofC: 92119907. Includes bibliographical references.*

154 Migrazioni internazionali e intervento politico *[In Italian]*; [International migration and political intervention]. Raimondo Cagiano de Azevedo. *Aff. Soc. Int.* **XIX:1** 1991 pp. 5 – 30

155 The New filipino immigrants to the United States — increasing diversity and change. Benjamin V. Cariño *[Ed.]*; et al. Honolulu, Hawaii: East-West Center, 1990: ix, 92 p. *ISBN: 0866381244; LofC: 90003725. Includes bibliographical references (p. 89-92).* [Papers of the East-West Population Institute.]

156 The normative and the factual — an analysis of emigration factors among the Jews of India. Margaret Abraham. *Jew. J. Socio.* **XXXIII:1** 6:1991 pp. 5 – 20

157 A parametric failure time model of international return migration. Brigitte S. Waldorf; Adrian Esparza. *Pap. Reg. Sci.* **70:4** 10:1991 pp. 419 – 438

158 Polacy w Hiszpanii *[In Polish]*; Poles in Spain *[Summary]*. Maria-Paula Malinowski-Rubio. *Prz. Pol.* **XVII:2** 1991 pp. 73 – 88

159 Потенциальные ремигранты России *[In Russian]*; (Possible remigrants in Russia). V.R. Belenkiy. *Sot. Issle.* **:4** 1991 pp. 57 – 53

160 The price of commitment — return migration and citizenship. Constance Lever-Tracy. *J. Aust. Stud.* **:28** 3:1991 pp. 40 – 55

161 Proletarianisation of Patagonia — reassessing the rationale for the Afrikaner migration to Argentina, 1902-6. David Fig. *Soc. Dyn.* **17:2** 12:1991 pp. 103 – 125

162 Realtà dell'immigrazione extracomunitaria in Italia. Problemi e prospettive *[In Italian]*; [Immigration from outside the Community in Italy. Problems and prospects]. Peter Schatzer. *Aff. Soc. Int.* **XIX:1** 1991 pp. 67 – 72

163 Refugee and migration movements. Peter J. Opitz. *Aussenpolitik* **42:3** 1991 pp. 261 – 270

164 Refugees and displaced persons — geographical perspectives and research directions. Richard Black. *Prog. H. Geog.* **15:3** 9:1991 pp. 281 – 297

165 Relative deprivation and migration — theory, evidence, and policy implications. Oded Stark; J. Edward Taylor. Washington, D.C.: Population and Human Resources Department and Agriculture and Rural Development Department, The World Bank, 1991: 42 p. [Policy, research, and external affairs working papers.]

166 El sector informal y la migración internacional. El caso de los dominicanos en Puerto Rico *[In Spanish]*; The informal sector and international migration. The case of Dominicans in Puerto Rico. Jorge Duany. *Nueva Soc.* **:113** 5-6:1991 pp. 16 – 27

167 Small country development and international labor flows — experiences in the Caribbean. A. P. Maingot *[Ed.]*. Boulder: Westview Press, 1991: xv, 266 p. *ISBN: 0813383412; LofC: 91008634. Includes bibliographical references.* [Series on development and international migration in Mexico, Central America, and the Caribbean Basin. : No. 5]

168 South-north migration. Reginald T. Appleyard. *Int. Migr. Rev.* **XXV:3** Fall:1991 pp. 610 – 619

169 Temporal and spatial patterns of geographically indirect immigration to the United States. Michael J. Greenwood; Eloise Trabka. *Int. Migr. Rev.* **XXV:1** Spring:1991 pp. 93 – 112

170 To the United States and into the labor force — occupational expectations of Filipino and Korean immigrant women. Maruja Milagros B. Asis. Honolulu, Hawaii: East-West Center, [1991]: vii, 59 p. *ISBN: 0866381368; LofC: 91004467. Includes bibliographical references (p. 51-59).* [Papers of the East-West Population Institute. : No. 118]

F.8: Migration *[Migration]* — *International migration [Migration internationale]*

171 Ukrajinska imigracija u Kanadi — neki aspekti socijalno-demografske integracije *[In Serbo-Croatian]*; Ukrainian immigration in Canada — some aspects of social-demographic integration *[Summary]*; Украинская иммиграция в Канаде: некоторые аспекты социально-демографической интеграции *[Russian summary]*. Vladimir B. Jevtuh. *Migrac. Teme* **6:4** 1990 pp. 497 – 510

172 The unfinished story — Turkish labour migration to Western Europe with special reference to the Federal Republic of Germany. Philip L. Martin. Geneva: International Labour Office, 1991: 123p. *ISBN: 9221072924*. *"Published with the financial support of the United Nations Development Programme"; On cover — "World Employment Programme"*.

173 Van gerepatrieerdenzorg tot allochtonenbeleid. Wetenschap en beleid met betrekking tot immigranten in Nederland *[In Dutch]*; Dutch policy with regard to immigrants *[Summary]*. J.M.M. van Amersfoort. *Sociol. Gids* **XXXVIII:1** 1-2:1991 pp. 24 – 36

174 Voices from Southeast Asia — the refugee experience in the United States. John Tenhula. New York: Holmes & Meier, 1991: xix, 247 p. (ill., map) *ISBN: 084191110x; LofC: 90040696*. Includes bibliographical references. [Ellis Island series.]

175 Wanderungen von Ausländern in der Bundesrepublik Deutschland der 80er Jahre *[In German]*; Migrations of foreigners in the Federal Republic of Germany during the '80s *[Summary]*. Hansjörg Bucher; Martina Kocks; Mathias Siedhoff. *Inf. Raum.* **:7/8** 1991 pp. 501 – 511

176 Współczesne migracje zarobkowe mieszkańców Podhala do USA. Raport z badań terenowych w latach 1987-1988 *[In Polish]*; Contemporary economic migration of the inhabitants of the Podhale region in Poland to the USA. A report on field research conducted in the years 1987-1988 *[Summary]*. Ryszard Kantor. *Prz. Pol.* **XVII:1** 1991 pp. 13 – 32

177 Die Zukunft der internationalen Migrationsbewegungen *[In German]*; [The future of international migration]. Aristide R. Zollberg. *Prokla* **21:2(83)** 1991 pp. 189 – 221

G: Environment. Community. Rural. Urban —
Environment. Communauté. Rural. Urbain

G.1: Ecology. Geography. Human settlements — *Écologie. Géographie. Établissements humains*

Sub-divisions: Geography *[Géographie]*

1 Aquatic habitat measurement and valuation — inputing social benefits to instream flow levels. A.J. Douglas; R.L. Johnson. *J. Environ. Manag.* **32:3** 4:1991 pp. 267 – 280

2 At odds with progress — Americans and conservation. Bret Wallach. Tucson: University of Arizona Press, c1991: xiv, 255 p. (maps) *ISBN: 0816509174; LofC: 90011296*. *[maps by Allan Yokisaari]; Includes bibliographical references (p. [215]-241) and index*.

3 Biosocial influences on stature — a review. C.G. Nicholas Mascie-Taylor. *J. Biosoc. Sc.* **23:1** 1:1991 pp. 113 – 128

4 "Build, therefore, your own world" — the New England village as settlement ideal. Joseph S. Wood. *Ann. As. Am. G.* **81:1** 3:1991 pp. 32 – 50

5 Changing international gaze on environment and health issues. K.R. Nayar. *Soc. Act.* **41:1** 1-3:1991 pp. 54 – 63

6 Coastal economies, cultural accounts — human ecology and Icelandic discourse. Gisli Pálsson. Manchester: Manchester University Press, c1991: 202 p. *ISBN: 0719035430; LofC: 90029067. Includes bibliographical references and index*. [Themes in social anthropology.]

7 Coastal zone management in Bahrain — an analysis of social, economic and environmental impacts of dredging and reclamation. I.M. Al-Madany; M.A. Abdalla; A.S.E. Abdu. *J. Environ. Manag.* **32:4** 6:1991 pp. 335 – 348

8 Communes and the green vision — counterculture, lifestyle and the new age. David Pepper. London: Green Print, 1991: 243 p. *ISBN: 1854250515*.

9 Conservation — a secondary environmental consideration. Lynda M. Warren. *J. Law Soc.* **18:1** Spring:1991 pp. 64 – 80

G.1: Ecology. Geography. Human settlements [Écologie. Géographie. Établissements humains]

10 Controlling earth's resources — markets or socialism? Richard L. Stroup. *Popul. Envir.* **12**:3 Spring:1991 pp. 265 – 284

11 The cost of edible fish — effects on the Swedish and Finnish forest industries from the imposition of effluent charges on chlorine residuals in Sweden. Lars Hultkrantz. *J. Environ. Manag.* **32**:2 3:1991 pp. 145 – 164

12 Development and environment — a view from the South. N. Shanmugaratnam. *Race Class* **XXX**:3 1-3:1989 pp. 13 – 30

13 Differences in the attitudes of farmers and conservationists and their implications. S. Carr; J. Tait. *J. Environ. Manag.* **32**:3 4:1991 pp. 281 – 294

14 Ecologia sanitaria. Aspetti del rapporto tra etica dell'ambiente e della salute *[In Italian]*; [Health ecology. Aspects of the relationship between the ethics of environment and health]. Adriano Bompiani. *Civitas* **XLII**:6 11-12:1991 pp. 13 – 32

15 The ecological self. Freya Mathews. London: Routledge, 1991: 192 p. (ill) *ISBN: 0415052521*. Includes bibliography and index.

16 Ecology, economics, ethics — the broken circle. F. Herbert Bormann *[Ed.]*; Stephen R. Kellert *[Ed.]*. New Haven: Yale University Press, c1991: 233 p. *ISBN: 0300049765; LofC: 91015191*. Includes bibliographical references and index.

17 Elusive societies — a regional-cartographical approach to the study of human relatedness. Martin W. Lewis. *Ann. As. Am. G.* **81**:4 12:1991 pp. 605 – 626

18 Environmental change in the Baliem valley, montane Irian Jaya, Republic of Indonesia. S.G. Haberle; G.S. Hope; Y. DeFretes. *J. Biogeogr.* **18**:1 1:1991 pp. 25 – 40

19 Environmental ethics — man's relationship with nature, interactions with science — Sixth Economic Summit Conference on Bioethics, Val Duchesse, Brussels, 10-12 May 1989. Philippe Bourdeau *[Ed.]*; P.M. Fasella *[Ed.]*; A. Teller *[Ed.]*. Luxembourg: Commission of the European Communities, 1990: iii, 325 p. (ill) *ISBN: 9282613984. eng, fre; "Catalogue number — CD-NA-12848-EN-C." --T.p. verso;* Includes bibliographical references.

20 Evaluation of mail and in-person contingent value surveys — results of a study of recreational boaters. Gregory Mannesto; John B. Loomis. *J. Environ. Manag.* **32**:2 3:1991 p. 177

21 Factors influencing household recycling behavior. Stuart Oskamp; Maura J. Harrington; Todd C. Edwards; Deborah L. Sherwood; Shawn M. Okuda; Deborah C. Swanson. *Envir. Behav.* **23**:4 7:1991 pp. 494 – 519

22 The green case — a sociology of environmental issues, arguments and politics. Steven Yearley. London: Unwin Hyman, 1991: 197 p. *ISBN: 0044457529*. Includes bibliography.

23 High and low in the townscapes of Dutch South America and South Africa — the dialectics of material culture. Martin Hall. *Soc. Dyn.* **17**:2 12:1991 pp. 41 – 75

24 The integration of pollution control. John Gibson. *J. Law Soc.* **18**:1 Spring:1991 pp. 18 – 31

25 On a clear day you can see Barnsley Town Hall — attitudes to our environment. Ian Clayton *[Ed.]*. Castleford: Yorkshire Art Circus, c1990: 115 p. (ill) *ISBN: 0947780564; LofC: gb 91028708.*

26 The organization of hazardous waste production in the U.S. — social and ecological performance. Robert L. Swinth. *Human Relat.* **44**:2 2:1991 pp. 147 – 174

27 The politics of Amazonian deforestation. Andrew Hurrell. *J. Lat. Am. St.* **23**:1 2:1991 pp. 197 – 215

28 Population, territory, environment. A new challenge for social regulation; Population, territoire, environnement. Un nouveau défi en matière de régulation sociale *[French summary]*; Bevölkerung, Territorium, Umwelt. Eine neue Herausforderung für die soziale Regulierung *[German summary]*. A. Etchelecou. *Sociol. Rur.* **XXXI**:4 1991 pp. 300 – 308

29 Postmodernism, language, and the strains of modernism. Michael R. Curry. *Ann. As. Am. G.* **81**:2 6:1991 pp. 210 – 228

30 Power, politics, and locality. Barney Warf. *Urban Geogr.* **12**:6 11-12:1991 pp. 563 – 569

31 Recycling as altruistic behavior — normative and behavioral strategies to expand participation in a community recycling program. Joseph R. Hopper; Joyce McCarl Nielsen. *Envir. Behav.* **23**:2 3:1991 pp. 195 – 220

32 Reflexive pollution. R.E. Kohn. *J. Environ. Manag.* **32**:3 4:1991 pp. 221 – 226

33 Resident peoples and national parks — social dilemmas and strategies in international conservation. Patrick C. West *[Ed.]*; Steven R. Brechin *[Ed.]*. Tucson: University of Arizona Press, c1991: xxiv, 443 p. (ill., maps) *ISBN: 0816511284; LofC: 90011300.* Includes bibliographical references (p. [401]-426) and index.

34 Social impact assessment and resource development — issues from the Australian experience. Richard Howitt. *Aust. Geogr.* **20**:1 5:1989 pp. 153 – 166

G.1: Ecology. Geography. Human settlements [Écologie. Géographie. Établissements humains]

35 Spatial ontology and explanation. Theodore R. Schatzki. *Ann. As. Am. G.* **81:4** 12:1991 pp. 650 – 670
36 Spatial price competition — a network approach. Timothy J. Fik; Gordon F. Mulligan. *Geogr. Anal.* **23:1** 1:1991 pp. 79 – 89
37 Standing on Earth — selected essays. Wendell Berry; Jonathon Porritt *[Foreword]*; Brian Keeble *[Intro.]*. Ipswich: Golgonooza, 1991: 225 p. *ISBN: 0903880458.*
38 A study of water vending and willingness to pay for water in Onitsha, Nigeria. D. Whittington; D.T. Lauria; Xinming Mu. *World Dev.* **19:2-3** 2-3:1991 pp. 179 – 198
39 Tides of war. Michael McKinnon; Peter Vine. London: Boxtree, 1991: 192 p. *ISBN: 1852831588.*
40 Tomorrow will be too late — East meets West on global ecology. Rolf Edberg; Alexei Yablokov *[Ed.]*. Tucson: University of Arizona Press, 1991: 220 p. *ISBN: 0816512175.*
41 Towards watering the Bangladeshi Sundarbans. Alan Potkin. *J. Soc. Stud. Dhaka* **51** 1:1991 pp. 40 – 58
42 Towns of the Nile Delta and the potential for damage from aggressive saline groundwater. H.A.M. Ibrahim; J.C. Doornkamp. *Third Wor, P.* **13:1** 2:1991 pp. 83 – 90
43 Toxic waste dumping in the Third World. Third World Network. *Race Class* **XXX:3** 1-3:1989 pp. 47 – 56
44 The twinning of the world — sister cities in geographic and historical perspective. Wilbur Zelinsky. *Ann. As. Am. G.* **81:1** 3:1991 pp. 1 – 31
45 Uneven and combined development and ecological crisis — a theoretical introduction. James O'Connor. *Race Class* **XXX:3** 1-3:1989 pp. 1 – 12
46 Valuation of pollution abatement benefits — direct and direct measurement. M. Shechter; M. Kim. *J. Urban Ec.* **30:2** 9:1991 pp. 133 – 151
47 What's in a place? An approach to the concept of place as illustrated by the British National Union of Mineworkers strike 1984-85. M.J. Griffiths; R.J. Johnston. *Antipode* **23:2** 4:1991 pp. 185 – 213
48 Women and the environment. Annabel Rodda. London: Zed Books, 1991: 180 p. *ISBN: 0862329841.*
49 Ziemia w społeczności wiejskiej — studium wsi Południowo-wschodniego mazowsza (koniec XIX i XX wiek) *[In Polish]*; Land and the rural community. A study of a village community in central Poland (since the end of the 19th century till now) *[Summary]*. Mirosława Drozd-Piasecka. *Bibl. Etnogr. Pol.* **:44** 1991 pp. 7 – 172
50 Zur Ermittlung der Kosten des Straßenverkehrslärms mit Hilfe von Zahlungsbereitschaftsanalysen *[In German]*; Assessing the costs of road traffic noise using willingness-to-pay analyses *[Summary]*. Marius Weinberger. *Z. Verkehr.* **62:2** :1991 pp. 62 – 92

Geography [Géographie]

51 Behind the locality debate — deconstructing geography's dualisms. A. Sayer. *Envir. Plan.A.* **23:2** 2:1991 pp. 283 – 308
52 Geographic aspects of the new thinking. V. Kotlyakov. *Soc. Sci.* **XXII:2** 1991 pp. 214 – 225
53 Geographic perspectives on Soviet Central Asia. Robert Lewis *[Ed.]*. London: Routledge, 1991: 323 p. *ISBN: 0415075920.*
54 The geography of borderlands — the case of the Quebec-US borderlands. Peter M. Slowe. *Geogr. J.* **157:2** 7:1991 pp. 191 – 198
55 History, geography, and historical geography. Richard Dennis. *Soc. Sci. Hist.* **15:2** Summer:1991 pp. 265 – 288
56 Insignificant others — lesbian and gay geographies. David J. Bell. *Area* **23:4** 12:1991 pp. 323 – 329
57 Interventions in the historical geography of modernity — social theory, spatiality and the politics of representation. D. Gregory. *Geog.ann. B.* **73 B:1** 1991 pp. 17 – 44
58 Mapping meaning, denoting difference, imagining identity — dialectical images and postmodern geographies. M.J. Watts. *Geog.ann. B.* **73 B:1** 1991 pp. 7 – 16
59 On the geography of Borneo. M.C. Cleary; F.J. Lian. *Prog. H. Geog.* **15:2** 6:1991 pp. 163 – 178
60 On the measure of geographic segregation. Richard L. Morrill. *Geogr. Res. For.* **11:** 1991 pp. 25 – 36
61 On the possibility of ethics in geography — writing, citing, and the construction of intellectual property. Michael R. Curry. *Prog. H. Geog.* **15:2** 6:1991 pp. 125 – 148

INTERNATIONAL BIBLIOGRAPHY OF SOCIOLOGY — 1991

G.1: Ecology. Geography. Human settlements [Écologie. Géographie. Établissements humains] — Geography [Géographie]

62 Person-environment theories in contemporary perceptual and behavioural geography I — personality, attitudinal and spatial choice theories. Stuart C. Aitken. *Prog. H. Geog.* **15:**2 6:1991 pp. 179 – 193

63 Pigouvian taxation and the geographic dispersion of emissions in an economy of identical polluting firms. Robert E. Kohn. *Geogr. Anal.* **23:**1 1:1991 pp. 74 – 79

64 Power, modernity, and historical geography. Cole Harris. *Ann. As. Am. G.* **81:**4 12:1991 pp. 671 – 683

G.2: Community — *Communauté*

1 Between the household — researching community organisation and networks. Sue Fleming. *IDS Bull.* **22:**1 1:1991 pp. 37 – 43

2 Building community organization — the history of a squatter settlement and its own organizations in Buenos Aires; La construction d'une organisation communautaire — l'histoire d'un établissement de squatters et de ses propres organisations à Buenos Aires *[French summary]*; Construyendo una organización comunitaria — la historia de una barriada y su organización comunitaria en Buenos Aires (Argentina) *[Spanish summary]*. Ana Hardoy; Jorge E. Hardoy; Ricardo Schusterman. *Environ. Urban.* **3:**2 10:1991 pp. 104 – 120

3 Class as community — the new dynamics of social change. J. Fitzgerald. *Envir. Plan. D* **9:**1 3:1991 pp. 117 – 128

4 Class, ethnicity, and the Kenyan state — community mobilization in the context of global politics. Barbara P. Thomas-Slayter. *Int. J. Pol. C. S.* **4:**3 Spring:1991 pp. 301 – 321

5 Community at loose ends. Miami Theory Collective. Minneapolis: University of Minnesota Press, c1991: xxvi, 139 p. (ill) *ISBN: 0816619212; LofC: 90011131 //r91. Includes bibliographical references (p. 131-134) and index.*

6 Community development in five European countries. Charlie McConnell. *Comm. Dev. J.* **26:**2 4:1991 pp. 103 – 111

7 Community development in Greece. George A. Daoutopoulos. *Comm. Dev. J.* **26:**2 4:1991 pp. 131 – 138

8 The community in rural America. Kenneth P. Wilkinson. New York: Greenwood Press, 1991: x, 141 p. *ISBN: 0313264678; LofC: 90047534. Under the auspices of the Rural Sociological Society; Includes bibliographical references (p. [119]-134) and index.* [Contributions in sociology.]

9 Community structure and delinquency — a typology. Josefina Figueira-McDonough. *Soc. Ser. R.* **65:**1 3:1991 pp. 68 – 91

10 Community through exclusion and illusion — the creation of social worlds in an American shopping mall. George H. Lewis. *J. Pop. Cult.* **24:**2 Fall:1990 pp. 121 – 136

11 Community — the tie that binds. Mary F. Rousseau. Lanham, Md: University Press of America, 1991: xiv, 173 p. *ISBN: 0819182095; LofC: 91007430. Includes bibliographical references.*

12 Contested ground — collective action and the urban neighborhood. John Emmeus Davis. Ithaca, N.Y: Cornell University Press, 1991: x, 356 p. (ill., maps) *ISBN: 0801422159; LofC: 90042034. Includes bibliographical references (p. 333-345) and index.*

13 Delivery and management of basic services to the urban poor — the role of the urban basic services, Delhi. Ashok Kumar. *Comm. Dev. J.* **26:**1 1:1991 pp. 50 – 60

14 Ecuadorian promotors learn to "facilitate" rather than to "direct". Judi Aubel; Bill Hanson; Napoleon Cevallos; Homero Morales. *Comm. Dev. J.* **26:**1 1:1991 pp. 35 – 42

15 The European dimension. Marilyn Taylor *[Contrib.]*; John Benington *[Contrib.]*; Wim Van Rees *[Contrib.]*; Charlie McConnell *[Contrib.]*; Lesley Karen Smith *[Contrib.]*; Paul Henderson *[Contrib.]*; Lars Qvortrup *[Contrib.]*; George A. Daoutopoulos *[Contrib.]*; Diarmuid O'Cearbhaill *[Contrib.]*; Ward Govaerts *[Contrib.] and others. Collection of 9 articles.* *Comm. Dev. J.* , 26:2, 4:1991 pp. 81 – 154

16 Factors motivating community participation in regional water-allocation planning — a test of an expectancy-value model. G.J. Syme; D.K. Macpherson; C. Seligman. *Envir. Plan.A.* **23:**12 12:1991 pp. 1779 – 1795

17 *[In Japanese]*; [The formal institutionalization of "Chonaikai" and the community administration]. Naoki Yoshihara. *Gekkan Jichiken No.33(385) - 1991.* pp. 54 – 60

G.2: Community *[Communauté]*

18 Grass-root mobilisation and citizen participation — issues and challenges. F. Vasoo. *Comm. Dev. J.* **26:1** 1:1991 pp. 1 – 7
19 Help or hindrance towards 1992? The impact of local administrative and political structures on neighbourhood development in Ireland. Diarmuid O'Cearbhaill. *Comm. Dev. J.* **26:2** 4:1991 pp. 139 – 146
20 *[In Japanese]*; [Housing maintenance association and community life]. Akio Tanosaki; et al. *Chuo Daogaku Bungakubu Kiyo No.(142) - 1991.* pp. 91 – 134
21 *[In Japanese]*; [The human estrangement and its conquest in the community]. Haruo Yamagishi. *Kyshu Journal of Educational Research No.(18) - 1991.* pp. 2 – 6
22 Innovative participation in neighbourhood service organizations. Barry Checkoway. *Comm. Dev. J.* **26:1** 1:1991 pp. 14 – 23
23 An integrated approach to urban infrastructure development — a review of the Indonesian experience. Harry T. Dimitriou. *Cities* **8:3** 8:1991 pp. 193 – 208
24 Linking the micro- and microlevel dimensions of community social organization. Robert J. Sampson. *Soc. Forc.* **70:1** 9:1991 pp. 43 – 64
25 Marking transgressions — the use of style in a women-only community in London. Sarah Green. *Cam. Anthrop.* **15:2** 1991 pp. 71 – 87
26 Politics in place — social power relations in an Australian country town. Ian Gray. Cambridge [England]: Cambridge University Press, 1991: ix, 214 p. (ill., maps) *ISBN: 0521404266; LofC: 91021381. Includes bibliographical references and index.*
27 Raymond Williams and local cultures. B. Longhurst. *Envir. Plan.A.* **23:2** 2:1991 pp. 229 – 238
28 Reclaiming capital — democratic initiatives and community development. Christopher Eaton Gunn; Hazel Dayton Gunn *[Ed.]*. Ithaca: Cornell University Press, 1991: ix, 179 p. *ISBN: 0801423236; LofC: 90055725. Includes bibliographical references (p. [167]-173) and index.*
29 Regional institutes for community development in Flanders, Belgium — their relationship to regional land local authories. Ward Govaerts. *Comm. Dev. J.* **26:2** 4:1991 pp. 147 – 152
30 Religiöse und sozialutopische Siedlungsgemeinschaften in den USA *[In German]*; [Religious and social utopian communities in the USA]. Justin Stagl. *Geogr. Rund.* **43:7-8** 7-8:1991 pp. 466 – 472
31 The social impact of the single European market — the challenges facing voluntary and community organisations. John Benington. *Comm. Dev. J.* **26:2** 4:1991 pp. 85 – 95
32 *[In Japanese]*; [The sociological meaning of neighbourhood in community care]. Fujio Tomita. *Shak. Ron. No.(112) - 1991.* pp. 53 – 62
33 Squatters in the United States and Latin America — the discourse of community development. Jeff D. Peterson. *Comm. Dev. J.* **26:1** 1:1991 pp. 28 – 34
34 The struggle for community. Allan David Heskin. Boulder: Westview Press, 1991: vi, 195 p. (ill) *ISBN: 0813383382; LofC: 91015786. Includes bibliographical references (p. [167]-177) and index.*
35 Theory and practice in voluntary social action. Chris L. Clark. Aldershot: Avebury, 1991: 184 p. (ill) *ISBN: 1856281132. Includes bibliography.* [Avebury studies of care in the community.]
36 Women and community action. Lena Dominelli. Birmingham: Venture Press, 1990: 156 p. *ISBN: 0900102772. Includes bibliography and index.*

G.3: Rural and urban sociology — *Sociologie rurale et urbaine*

1 The counter-urbanization process — demographic restructuring and policy response in rural England; Les processus de rurbanisation — restructuration démographique et réponse politique dans l'Angleterre rurale *[French summary]*; Der Prozeß der Gegenurbanisierung — demographische Umstrukturierung und politische Reaktionen im ländlichen England *[German summary]*. G.J. Lewis; P. McDermott; K.B. Sherwood. *Sociol. Rur.* **XXXI:4** 1991 pp. 309 – 320
2 Deconstructing regions — notes on the scales of spatial life. A. Paasi. *Envir. Plan.A.* **23:2** 2:1991 pp. 239 – 256
3 The future of the periphery of the periphery. The case of a Sicilian agrotown; L'avenir de la périphérie de la périphérie. Le cas d'une agroville sicilienne *[French summary]*; Die Zukunft der Peripherie der Peripherie. Das Beispiel einer sizilianischen Agrarstadt *[German summary]*. A.J. Jansen. *Sociol. Rur.* **XXXI:2-3** 1991 pp. 122 – 139

G.3: Rural and urban sociology *[Sociologie rurale et urbaine]*

4 Life in a dual system revisited — urban-rural ties in Enugu, Nigeria, 1961-87. J. Gugler. *World Dev.* **19:5** 5:1991 pp. 399–410

5 Metropolitan dominance versus decentralization in the information age. Annabel Kirschner Cook; Donald M. Beck. *Soc. Sci. Q.* **72:2** 6:1991 pp. 284–298

6 New perspectives on the locality debate. S. Duncan *[Contrib.]*; M. Savage *[Contrib.]*; L.D. Morris *[Contrib.]*; I. Elander *[Contrib.]*; T. Strömberg *[Contrib.]*; B. Danermark *[Contrib.]*; B. Söderfeldt *[Contrib.]*; K.R. Cox *[Contrib.]*; A. Mair *[Contrib.]*; P. Jackson *[Contrib.]* and others. Collection of 10 articles. **Envir. Plan.A.** , 23:2, 2:1991 pp. 155–308

7 De regionale metamorfose van Nederland vanaf het midden van de vorige eeuw *[In Dutch]*; The regional metamorphosis of the Netherlands since the 1850s *[Summary]*. B. de Pater. *Volks. Bul.* **17:1** 3:1991 pp. 15–40

8 Regions as social constructs — the gap between theory and practice. Alexander B. Murphy. *Prog. H. Geog.* **15:1** 3:1991 pp. 23–35

9 Une revue de la littérature scientifique sur l'étalement urbain et sur les relations urbaines-agricoles dans la frange urbaine — le cas de la région métropolitaine de Montréal, dans le contexte nord-américain *[In French]*; A review of the scientific literature about the urban sprawl and about the urban-agriculture interactions within the fringe — the case of the Montreal metropolitan region, within the Northern-American context *[Summary]*. C. Marois; P. Deslauriers; C. Bryant. *Espace Pop. Soc.* :**2** 1991 pp. 325–334

10 Rural-urban differences — the migrants' perspective. Sarita Kamra. *Indian J. Soc. W.* **LII:2** 4:1991 pp. 215–228

11 Urban and rural settlements. Harold Carter. London: Longman, 1990: 189 p. (ill) *ISBN: 0582355850. Includes bibliography and index.* [Longman modular geography series.]

G.3.1: Rural sociology — *Sociologie rurale*

Sub-divisions: Peasant studies *[Études paysannes]*; Rural development *[Développement rurale]*

1 Agricultural economics and rural sociology — the contemporary core literature. Wallace C. Olsen; Margot A. Bellamy *[Contrib.]*; B. F. Stanton *[Contrib.]*. Ithaca, N.Y: Cornell University Press, 1991: xi, 346 p. *ISBN: 0801426774; LofC: 91055261. Includes bibliographical references and index.* [Literature of the agricultural sciences.]

2 Die Arbeitswelt in Agrargesellschaften *[In German]*; Work in agrarian societies *[Summary]*. Gerd Spittler. *Kölner Z. Soz. Soz. psy.* **43:1** 1991 pp. 1–17

3 Changing gender roles in Hungarian agriculture. H. Repassy. *J. Rural St.* **7:1-2** 1991 pp. 23–30

4 Changing gender roles in productionist and post-productionist capitalist agriculture. D. Symes. *J. Rural St.* **7:1-2** 1991 pp. 85–90

5 The changing role of rural women in Malaysia — a case study. Noor Rahamah Hj. Abu Bakar. *Asian Prof.* **19:1** 2:1991 pp. 21–38

6 Chinese village, socialist state. Edward Friedman; Paul Pickowicz; Mark Selden. New Haven: Yale University Press, 1991: 336 p. *ISBN: 0300046553; LofC: 90071877. Includes bibliographical references and index.*

7 Conceptualising the Indian village — an overview of the village studies tradition. Seemanthini Niranjana. *Ind. J. Soc. Sci.* **4:3** 7-9:1991 pp. 371–386

8 Contemporary land struggles in rural Transvaal. Aninka Claassens. *Antipode* **23:1** 1:1991 pp. 142–157

9 A country that has gone downhill. Bradley H. Baltensperger. *Geogr. Rev.* **81:4** 10:1991 pp. 433–443

10 The dearth of data on Irish farm wives — a critical review of the literature. Sally Shortall. *Econ. Soc. R.* **22:4** 7:1991 pp. 311–332

11 Désintégration et intégration des relations agriculture-élevage dans les régions méditerranéennes *[In French]*; [Disintegration and integration of relations between breeders and farmers in Mediterranean regions] *[Summary]*. B. Kayser. *Ann. Géogr.* **100:557** 1-2:1991 pp. 18–29

12 Determinants of rural service use among households in Gazaland district, Zimbabwe. Sudhir Wanmali. *Econ. Geogr.* **67:4** 10:1991 pp. 346–360

G.3.1: Rural sociology *[Sociologie rurale]*

13 Dynamismes ruraux et contrastes fonciers dans Madagascar en crise *[In French]*; (Rural dynamics and landholding discrepancies in Madagascar in a time of crisis); (Agrardynamik und Konflikte um Grund und Boden — Madagaskar in der Krise: *Title only in German)*; (Dinamismos rurales y contrastes en la propiedad agrícola en Madagascar en crisis: *Title only in Spanish)*. Jean-Pierre Raison. *R. T-Monde* **32:128** 10-12:1991 pp. 901 – 916

14 L'économie rurale viêtnamienne — bilan du IVe plan quinquennal (1986-1990) *[In French]*; [Vietnamese rural economy — consequences of the IV quinquennial plan (1986-1990)]. L. Thanh Liêm. *Ann. Géogr.* **100:560** 7-8:1991 pp. 438 – 454

15 *[In Japanese]*; [Elementary structure of rural social organizations]. Yoshihiko Aikawa. Tokyo: Ochanomizu Shobo, 1991: 482 p.

16 Emerging urban forms in rural South Africa. Dhiru Soni; Brij Maharaj. *Antipode* **23:1** 1:1991 pp. 47 – 67

17 The empirical dimension of multiple job-holding agriculture in Greece; Pluriactivité dans l'agriculture grècque — étude empirique *[French summary]*; Empirische Aspekte der Mehrfachbeschäftigung in der griechischen Landwirtschaft *[German summary]*. D. Damianos; M. Demoussis; C. Kasimis. *Sociol. Rur.* **XXXI:1** 1991 pp. 37 – 47

18 The estimates and trends in rural poverty in Pakistan. Shahnawaz Malik. *Ind. J. Soc. Sci.* **4:3** 7-9.1991 pp. 407 – 414

19 The farmed landscape and the occupancy change process. T.K. Marsden; R.J.C. Munton. *Envir. Plan.A.* **23:5** 1991 pp. 663 – 676

20 Farming patterns, rural restructuring, and poverty — a comparative regional analysis. Linda M. Lobao; Michael D. Schulman. *Rural Sociol.* **56:4** Winter:1991 pp. 565 – 602

21 For a rural people's Europe. Paul Henderson. *Comm. Dev. J.* **26:2** 4:1991 pp. 118 – 123

22 Formulating and evaluating agricultural zoning programs. Robert E. Coughlin. *J. Am. Plann.* **57:2** Spring:1991 pp. 183 – 192

23 From Mao to Deng — life satisfaction among rural women in an emigrant community in South China. Yuen-fong Woon. *Aust. J. Chin. Aff.* **25** 1:1991 pp. 139 – 169

24 Gender and agricultural production in Samia, Kenya — strategies and complaints. Joyce M. Olenja. *J. As. Afr. S.* **XXVI:3-4** 7-10:1991 pp. 267 – 275

25 Growth linkages, the nonfarm sector, and rural inequality — a study in southern Sri Lanka. Kristian Stokke; Lakshman S. Yapa; Hiran D. Dias. *Econ. Geogr.* **67:3** 7:1991 pp. 223 – 239

26 Homelessness in rural places — perspectives from upstate New York. Janet M. Fitchen. *Urban Anthro.* **20:2** Summer:1991 pp. 177 – 210

27 Household productivity in new rural settlements in Egypt — perspectives on kitchen gardens. M. Tarek Shalaby. *Third Wor. P.* **13:3** 8:1991 pp. 237 – 260

28 Ilocano irrigation — the corporate resolution. Henry T. Lewis. Honolulu, HI: University of Hawaii Press, c1991: x, 159 p. (ill., maps) *ISBN:* 082481357x; *LofC:* 90047736. Includes bibliographical references (p. 151-154) and index. [Asian studies at Hawaii. : No. 37]

29 Initial results of strengthening the two-tier management system in rural areas of Yutian county. Shiyi Zhang; Xuesheng Liu; Baowen Li; Zeting Yang. *Soc. Sci. China* **XII:1** 3:1991 pp. 114 – 125

30 The Javanese village as a Cheshire Cat — the Java debate against a European and Latin American background. Peter Boomgaard. *J. Peasant Stud.* **18:2** 1:1991 pp. 288 – 304

31 Justicia agraria. La tierra para el que atropella *[In Spanish]*; [Agrarian justice. Land for he who grabs it]. T. Miguel Pressburger. *Nueva Soc.* **:112** 3-4:1991 pp. 115 – 123

32 Lessons on European integration — watching agricultural policies from the fringe; Leçons sur l'intégration en Europe — remarques sur les politiques agricoles à partir de la périphérie *[French summary]*; Lektionen zur europäischen Integration — Agrarpolitik vom Rande Europas aus betrachtet *[German summary]*. E.B. Haney; R. Almas. *Sociol. Rur.* **XXXI:2-3** 1991 pp. 99 – 121

33 Life cycle or patriarchy? Gender divisions in family farming. S. Whatmore. *J. Rural St.* **7:1-2** 1991 pp. 71 – 76

34 The life experience and status of Chinese rural women from observation of three age groups. Dai Kejing. *Int. Sociol.* **6:1** 3:1991 pp. 5 – 23

35 Local factors in changing land-tenure patterns. Janel M. Curry-Roper; John Bowles. *Geogr. Rev.* **81:4** 10:1991 pp. 443 – 456

36 Measuring the quality of life in rural community development. Pieter Barnard; J.N.K. van der Merwe. *Soc. Ind.* **24:1** 2:1991 pp. 57 – 70

37 Migrations de population et enracinement dans un village irrigué de l'Inde du sud —

G.3.1: Rural sociology *[Sociologie rurale]*

Mottahalli *[In French]*; [Population migration and entrenchment in an irrigated village in South India — Mottahalli]. Frédéric Landy. *Cah. Outre-mer* **44:174** 4-6:1991 pp. 129 – 166

38 The military regime and restructuring of land tenure. Patricio Silva. *Lat. Am. Pers.* **18:1** Winter:1991 pp. 15 – 32

39 Minorities in rural society. Jess Gilbert *[Ed.]*; Gene F. Summers *[Contrib.]*; Maria Wilson-Figueroa *[Contrib.]*; E. Helen Berry *[Contrib.]*; Michael B. Toney *[Contrib.]*; Rogelio Saenz *[Contrib.]*; John K. Thomas *[Contrib.]*; Bruce H. Rankin *[Contrib.]*; William W. Falk *[Contrib.]*; Phyllis A. Gray *[Contrib.]* and others. Collection of 8 articles. **Rural Sociol.** , *56:2*, Summer:1991 pp. 177 – 297

40 Modelling the seamless web — economic linkages and rural policy; Pour une modélisation du tissue économique — système économique et politique rurale *[French summary]*; Das nahtlose Netz formen — ökonomische Verflechtungen und ländliche Politik *[German summary]*. A. Errington. *Sociol. Rur.* **XXXI:1** 1991 pp. 17 – 26

41 Models of the land-development process — a critical review. T. Gore; D. Nicholson. *Envir. Plan.A.* **23:5** 1991 pp. 705 – 730

42 Movilidad y estabilidad en una sociedad rural en México (Veracruz) *[In Spanish]*; [Mobility and stability in rural Mexican society (Veracruz)]. Odile Hoffmann. *Est. Sociol.* **IX:27** 9-12:1991 pp. 607 – 621

43 New activities in rural areas; Les nouvelles activités en région rurale *[French summary]*; Neue Aktivitäten im ländlichen Raum *[German summary]*. J. Oksa. *Sociol. Rur.* **XXXI:1** 1991 pp. 9 – 16

44 Norwegian farm women and the cultural meaning of food. L.E. Thorsen. *J. Rural St.* **7:1-2** 1991 pp. 63 – 66

45 Norwegian gender roles in transition — the masculinization hypothesis in the past and in the future. R. Almås; M.S. Haugen. *J. Rural St.* **7:1-2** 1991 pp. 79 – 84

46 Occupancy change and the farmed landscape — an analysis of farm-level trends, 1970-85. R.J.C. Munton; T.K. Marsden. *Envir. Plan.A.* **23:4** 4:1991 pp. 499 – 510

47 On "methodological monism" in rural sociology. Douglas Harper. *Rural Sociol.* **56:1** Spring:1991 pp. 70 – 88

48 People in the countryside — studies of social change in rural Britain. Tony Champion *[Ed.]*; Charles Watkins *[Ed.]*. London: Paul Chapman, 1991: 210 p. *ISBN: 1853961280. Includes bibliography and index.*

49 Place of origin — the repopulation of rural El Salvador. Beatrice E. Edwards; Gretta Tovar Siebentritt. Boulder, Colorado: Lynne Riener, 1991: vii, 158 p. *ISBN: 1555872417.*

50 A place of their own — family farming in eastern Finland. Ray Abrahams. Cambridge [England]: Cambridge University Press, 1991: xi, 210 p. (ill., maps) *ISBN: 0521381002; LofC: 90024168. Includes bibliographical references (pp. [194]-200) and indexes.* [Cambridge studies in social and cultural anthropology. : No. 81]

51 The planning of rural settlement in Romania. David Turnock. *Geogr. J.* **157:3** 11:1991 pp. 251 – 264

52 Pluriactivity, structural change and farm household vulnerability in Western Europe; Pluriactivité, changements structurels et vulnérabilité des ménages agricoles en Europe de l'Ouest *[French summary]*; Mehrfachbeschäftigung, Strukturwandel und Unsicherheit landwirtschaftlicher Haushalte in Westeuropa *[German summary]*. N. Mackinnon; J. Bryden; C. Bell; A. Fuller; M. Spearman. *Sociol. Rur.* **XXXI:1** 1991 pp. 58 – 71

53 Promise to the land — essays on rural women. Joan M. Jensen. Albuquerque: New Mexico University Press, 1991: 319 p. *ISBN: 0826312470.*

54 Una propuesta metodologica para medicion y analisis del empleo rural y resultados de su aplicacion en paises Latinoamericanos *[In Spanish]*; [A methodological approach to the measurement and analysis of rural employment. Results for Latin American countries]. José Ferreira Irmão. Pernambuco, Brazil: Universidade Federal de Pernambuco, 1990: 24 p.

55 Psychology and rural America — current status and future directions. J. Dennis Murray; Peter A. Keller. *Am. Psychol.* **46:3** 3:1991 pp. 220 – 231

56 A regional analysis of enterprise substitution in Irish agriculture in the context of a changing common agricultural policy. James A. Walsh. *Irish Geogr.* **24:1** :1991 pp. 10 – 23

57 Les ruptures du monde agricole *[In French]*; [The breakdown of the agricultural world].*Regar. Actual.* **:168** 2:1991 pp. 23 – 35

G.3.1: Rural sociology *[Sociologie rurale]*

58 Rural families and income from migration — Honduran households in the world economy. Susan C. Stonich. *J. Lat. Am. St.* **23:1** 2:1991 pp. 131 – 161

59 Rural mental health in America. Jeffrey Human; Cathy Wasem. *Am. Psychol.* **46:3** 3:1991 pp. 232 – 239

60 Rural women in Latin America — directions for future research. Lynne Phillips. *Lat. Am. Res. R.* **XXV:3** 1990 pp. 89 – 107

61 Rurality and well-being during the middle years of life. Donald M. Crider; Fern K. Willits; Conrad L. Kanagy. *Soc. Ind.* **24:3** 5:1991 pp. 253 – 268

62 Securing the future — "survival strategies' amongst Somerset dairy farmers. Steve Pile. *Sociology* **25:2** 5:1991 pp. 255 – 274

63 Shifts in rural population patterns and changes in the agriculture of the central regions of the European USSR. G.V. Ioffe. *Geoforum* **22:1** :1991 pp. 91 – 97

64 A Sinhala village in a time of trouble — politics and change in rural Sri Lanka. Jonathan Spencer. Delhi: Oxford University Press, 1990: xi, 285 p. (ill.) *ISBN: 0195624955*. [Oxford University south Asian studies series.]

65 The social networks of leaders in more and less viable rural communities. David J. O'Brien; Edward W. Hassinger; Ralph B. Brown; James R. Pinkerton. *Rural Sociol.* **56:4** Winter:1991 pp. 699 – 716

66 Social theory and the de/reconstruction of agricultural science — local knowledge for an alternative agriculture. Jack Kloppenburg. *Rural Sociol.* **56:4** Winter:1991 pp. 519 – 548

67 Socioeconomic differentiation among small cultivators on Paraguay's eastern frontier. Beverly Y. Nagel. *Lat. Am. Res. R.* **26:2** 1991 pp. 103 – 131

68 Socio-economic measures of quality of rural life — an alternative approach for measuring rural poverty. K. Dhanasekaran. *Ind. J. Agri. Eco.* **XLVI:1** 1-3:1991 pp. 34 – 45 .

69 *[In Japanese]*; [Some trends of Japanese village studies]. Mishiharu Matsumoto. *Kenkyu Tsushin, Chiikishakaigakkai No.(166) - 1991*. pp. 30 – 36

70 Strangers and gifts — hostility and hospitality in rural Greece. Juliet du Boulay. *J. Mediter. St.* **1:1** 1991 pp. 37 – 53

71 Theoretical issues of women's non-agricultural employment in rural areas, with illustrations from the U.K. J. Little. *J. Rural St.* **7:1-2** 1991 pp. 99 – 106

72 *[In Japanese]*; [Toward a paradigm shift of rural sociology — rethinking some basic categories]. Kanji Ikeda. *Chiikishakaigaku Nenpo No.(5) - 1991*. pp. 29 – 57

73 A tragédia da terra *[In Portuguese]*; [The tragedy of the land]. Francisco Graziano Neto. São Paulo, SP: IGLU, c1991: 93 p. *BNB: 90744251; LofC: 90744251*. "O fracasso da reforma agrária no Brasil"--Cover; Based on the author's thesis (doctoral)--Fundação Getúlio Vargas, São Paulo.

74 Transforming women's roles in Pakistan's rural sector — donor policy and local response. S.S. Saulniers. *J. Rural St.* **7:1-2** 1991 pp. 107 – 114

75 U.S. farm women, politics and policy. W.G. Haney; L.C. Miller. *J. Rural St.* **7:1-2** 1991 pp. 115 – 122

76 The use of court records in the reconstruction of village networks — a comparative perspective. Karen Barkey. *Int. J. Comp. Soc* **XXXII: 1-2** 1-4:1991 pp. 195 – 216

77 Very small farm holdings and the rural economy; Micro-exploitations agricoles et économie rurale *[French summary]*; Landwirtschaftliche Kleinstbetriebe und die ländliche Wirtschaft *[German summary]*. M. Turner. *Sociol. Rur.* **XXXI:1** 1991 pp. 72 – 81

78 Les villages-centres du Sénégal *[In French]*; [Village centres of Senegal]. Alain Galaup. *Cah. Outre-mer* **44:174** 4-6:1991 pp. 187 – 206

79 What work is real? Changing roles of farm and ranch wives in south-eastern Ohio. V.S. Fink. *J. Rural St.* **7:1-2** 1991 pp. 17 – 22

80 Women and the reproduction of family farms — change and continuity in the region of Thessaly, Greece. A. Gourdomichalis. *J. Rural St.* **7:1-2** 1991 pp. 57 – 62

81 Women in agriculture. M. Berlan Darqué *[Ed.]*; R. Gasson *[Ed.]*; S.J. Rennie *[Contrib.]*; M. Kaur *[Contrib.]*; M.L. Sharma *[Contrib.]*; V.S. Fink *[Contrib.]*; H. Repassy *[Contrib.]*; N. Nevo *[Contrib.]*; F.M. Shaver *[Contrib.]*; C.E. Sachs *[Contrib.]* and others. Collection of 17 articles. **J. Rural St.** , *7:1-2,* 1991 pp. 5 – 121

82 Women's off-farm work and gender stratification. F.A. Deseran; N.R. Simpkins. *J. Rural St.* **7:1-2** 1991 pp. 91 – 98

G.3.1: Rural sociology *[Sociologie rurale]* —

Peasant studies *[Études paysannes]*

83 "Chercher la vie" — migrations et stratégies de subsistance dans la paysannerie haïtienne *[In French]*; "To find life" — migration and subsistence strategies in the Haitian peasantry *[Summary]*. Raymond Baril. *Labour Cap. Soc.* **24:1** 4:1991 pp. 40 – 65

84 Communities of grain — rural rebellion in comparative perspective. Victor V. Magagna. Ithaca: Cornell University Press, 1991: xii, 277 p. *ISBN: 0801423619; LofC: 90055720. Includes bibliographical references and index.* [The Wilder house series in politics, history, and culture.]

85 Constraints and incentives in "successful" Zimbabwean peasant agriculture — the interaction between gender and class. Donna Pankhurst. *J. S.Afr. Stud.* **17:4** 12:1991 pp. 611 – 632

86 Cultivating workers — peasants and capitalism in a Sudanese village. Victoria Bernal. New York: Columbia University Press, c1991: xv, 224 p. (maps) *ISBN: 0231071728; LofC: 90047686. Includes bibliographical references (p. 209-217) and index.*

87 Dans l'Amérique des Cordillères — le bref été des mouvements paysans indiens (1970-1991) *[In French]*; (The short summer of Indian peasant movements in the Cordillera (1970-1990)); (Der kurze Sommer der indianischen Bauernbewegungen in den Kordillieren (1970-1990): *Title only in German)*; (El breve verano de los movimientos campesinos indios en la América de las Cordilleras (1970-1990): *Title only in Spanish).* Yvon le Bot. *R. T-Monde* **32:128** 10-12:1991 pp. 831 – 850

88 Investing in tradition. Peasants and rural institutions in post-revolution Ethiopia; En s'appuyant sur la tradition. Paysans et institutions rurales dans l'Ethiopie post-révolutionnaire *[French summary]*; In Tradition investieren. Bäuerliche Bevölkerung und ländliche institutionen im nachrevolutionären Äthiopien *[German summary]*. D. Rahmato. *Sociol. Rur.* **XXXI:2-3** 1991 pp. 169 – 183

89 Krest´ianskii vopros vchera i segodnia *[In Russian]*; [The peasant question yesterday and today]. A. P. Lanshchikov; A. S. Salutskii. Moskva: Sovremennik, 1990: 396 p. *ISBN: 5270011441.*

90 Landholding and commercial agriculture in the Middle East. Çağlar Keyder *[Ed.]*; Faruk Tabak *[Ed.]*. Albany (NY): State University of New York Press, 1991: vi, 1, 260 p. *ISBN: 0791405508.*

91 Mir tainstvennyi — razmyshleniia o krest´ianstve *[In Russian]*; [The secretive world — reflections on the peasantry]. P. I. Simush. Moskva: Politizdat, 1991: 254 p. *ISBN: 5250007589.*

92 New rural institutions built on tradition? Ethiopian peasants need a democratic reconstruction; De nouvelles institutions agricoles créées à partir de traditions? Les paysans éthiopiens ont besoin de reconstruire la démocratie *[French summary]*; Neue ländliche Institutionen auf Tradition aufbauen? Die äthiopischen Bäuerinnen und Bauern brauchen einen demokratischen Wiederaufbau *[German summary]*. S. Pausewang. *Sociol. Rur.* **XXXI:2-3** 1991 pp. 184 – 198

93 Pouvoir et paysannerie en Amérique latine *[In French]*; [Power and peasantry in Latin America]. Danièle Dehouve *[Contrib.]*; François Lartigue *[Contrib.]*; Elena Lazos Chavero *[Contrib.]*; Lourdes Villers Ruiz *[Contrib.]*; Maxime Haubert *[Contrib.]*; Michel Bertrand *[Contrib.]*. Collection of 5 articles. **Rural Stud.** , *113-114*, 1-6:1989 pp. 119 – 199

94 Le retour des paysans — mythes et réalités *[In French]*; (The return of the peasants — myths and realities); (Die Rückkehr der Bauern — Mythos und Wirklichkeit: *Title only in German)*; (El retorno de los campesinos — mitos y realidades: *Title only in Spanish)*. Maxime Haubert. *R. T-Monde* **32:128** 10-12:1991 pp. 725 – 740

95 The rise and decline of an Indian peasantry in Natal. Bill Freund. *J. Peasant Stud.* **18:2** 1:1991 pp. 263 – 287

96 L'Union centrale des Coopératives agricoles de l'Ouest du Cameroun (UCCAO) — de l'entreprise commerciale à l'organisation paysanne *[In French]*; (The Central Union of Agricultural Cooperatives of Western Cameroon (UCCAO) — from commercial enterprise to peasant organization); (Die Union Centrale des Coopératives Agricoles in West-Kamerun (UCCAO) — vom Handelsbetrieb zur Bauernorganisation: *Title only in German)*; (La Unión Central de Cooperativas Agrícolas del Oeste del Camerún (UCCAO) — de la empresa comercial a la organización campesina: *Title only in Spanish)*. Georges Courade; P. Eloundou-Enyègue; I. Grangeret. *R. T-Monde* **32:128** 10-12:1991 pp. 887 – 899

G.3.1: Rural sociology *[Sociologie rurale]* —

Rural development *[Développement rurale]*

97 Agricultural depopulation in Croatia; Exode agricole en Croatie *[French summary]*; Die Abwanderung der landwirtschaftlichen Bevölkerung in Kroatien *[German summary]*. M. Štambuk. *Sociol. Rur.* **XXXI:4** 1991 pp. 281 – 289

98 Change and adaptation in four rural communities in New England, NSW. Philippa Hudson. *Aust. Geogr.* **20:1** 5:1989 pp. 53 – 63

99 Changes in ways of making a living among Norwegian farmers 1975-1990; Transformation des moyens de subsistance chez les agriculteurs norvégiens (1975-1990) *[French summary]*; Wandel der Strategien norwegischer Landwirte, sich ihren Lebensunterhalt zu verdienen, 1975-1990 *[German summary]*. A. Blekesaune. *Sociol. Rur.* **XXXI:1** 1991 pp. 48 – 57

100 Community teleservice centres and the future of rural society. Lars Qvortrup. *Comm. Dev. J.* **26:2** 4:1991 pp. 124 – 130

101 De la Loire au Saint-Laurent — des régions rurales face aux recompositions socio-territoriales *[In French]*; [From the Loire to Saint-Laurant — on rural areas faced with socio-territorial reconstruction]. J. Chevalier *[Ed.]*; et al. Rimouski, Québec: Université du Québec à Rimouski, Groupe de recherche interdisciplinaire en développement de l'Est du Québec (GRIDEQ), 1991: 354 p. *ISBN: 2920270478.*

102 De l'importance des systèmes d'information dans les programmes d'infrastructures rurales dans les pays en développement *[In French]*; (The importance of information systems in rural infrastructure programmes in developing countries); (Zur Bedeutung der Informatik in den Programmen der landwirtschaftlichen Infrastruktur in den Entwicklungsländern: *Title only in German)*; (O važnosti sistem informacii v programmakh sel'skokhozjajstvennykh infrastruktur v razvivajuščikhsja stranakh: *Title only in Russian)*; (De la importancia de los sistemas de información en los programas de infraestructuras rurales en los países en desarrollo: *Title only in Spanish)*. Jacques Gaude; Réjean Tremblay. *R. T-Monde* **XXXII:127** 7-9:1991 pp. 597 – 616

103 A decade of integrated rural development planning — an assessment of PRODERM experiences in Cusco, Peru. E.B. Zoomers; G.N. Geurten. *J. Econ. Soc. Geogr.* **82:3** 1991 pp. 195 – 205

104 El desarrollo regional en la selva Peruana — el proyecto Pichis-Palcazú *[In Spanish]*; [Regional development in the Peruvian forest — the Pichis-Palcazú project]. Klaus Gierhake. *Rev. Int.Am. Plan.* **XXIV:93** 1-3:1991 pp. 159 – 171

105 Endangered spaces, enduring places — change, identity, and survival in rural America. Janet M. Fitchen; Sandra Rosenzweig Gittelman *[Illus.]*. Boulder: Westview Press, 1991: xvi, 314 p. (ill) *ISBN: 0813311144; LofC: 90019908. Includes bibliographical references (p. 289-302) and index.*

106 From structural conflict to agrarian stalemate — agrarian reforms in South India. Ronald J. Herring. *J. As. Afr. S.* **XXVI:3-4** 7-10:1991 pp. 169 – 188

107 The future of rural America — anticipating policies for constructive change. Kenneth E. Pigg *[Ed.]*. Boulder: Westview Press, 1991: viii, 285 p. (ill) *ISBN: 0813383641; LofC: 91016084. Includes bibliographical references and index.* [Rural studies series of the rural sociological society.]

108 Ghana under structural adjustment — the impact of agriculture and the rural poor. Hadi Shams; Alexander Sarris *[Ed.]*. New York: New York University Press, c1991: 269 p. *ISBN: 0814779328; LofC: 91017007. Includes index.* [IFAD studies in poverty alleviation. : No. 2]

109 The human factor in rural development. Tom Gabriel. London: Belhaven Press, 1991: 159 p. *ISBN: 1852931221; LofC: 90028762. Includes bibliographical references and index.*

110 Impact evaluation of World Bank agriculture and rural development projects — methodology and selected findings. Kathryn McPhail. *Comm. Dev. J.* **26:4** 10:1991 pp. 306 – 311

111 Investing in tradition. Peasants and rural institutions in post-revolution Ethiopia; En s'appuyant sur la tradition. Paysans et institutions rurales dans l'Ethiopie post-révolutionnaire *[French summary]*; In Tradition investieren. Bäuerliche Bevölkerung und ländliche institutionen im nachrevolutionären Äthiopien *[German summary]*. D. Rahmato. *Sociol. Rur.* **XXXI:2-3** 1991 pp. 169 – 183

112 Jornaleros andaluces — el Plan de Empleo Rural ¿solución o problema? *[In Spanish]*; [Andalucian labourers — the Rural Employment Plan — problem or solution?]. Rafael Yeste Moyano. *Rev. Fom. Soc.* **46:182** 4-6:1991 pp. 201 – 212

G.3.1: Rural sociology *[Sociologie rurale]* — *Rural development [Développement rurale]*

113 Land, labor & capital in modern Yucatán — essays in regional history and political economy. Jeffery Brannon *[Ed.]*; G. M. Joseph *[Ed.]*. Tuscaloosa: University of Alabama Press, c1991: x, 322 p. (ill., map) *ISBN: 0817305556; LofC: 90046746. Includes bibliographical references (p. [301]-313) and index.*

114 Local development in the global economy — the case of Pakistan. Pervaiz Nazir. Aldershot, England: Avebury, c1991: ix, 210 p. *ISBN: 185628106x; LofC: 90027547. Includes bibliographical references (p. 203-210).*

115 Migrations and development in rural Latin America. Solon Barraclough. *Econ. Ind. Dem.* **12:1** 2:1991 pp. 43 – 63

116 Models and means for a rural future — papers from the 14th ESRS Congress for Rural Sociology, Giessen, 1990. R. Gasson *[Contrib.]*; J. Oksa *[Contrib.]*; A. Errington *[Contrib.]*; M. Rønningen *[Contrib.]*; D. Damianos *[Contrib.]*; M. Demoussis *[Contrib.]*; C. Kasimis *[Contrib.]*; A. Blekesaune *[Contrib.]*; N. Mackinnon *[Contrib.]*; J. Bryden *[Contrib.]* *and others*. Collection of 9 articles. **Sociol. Rur.**, *XXXI:1*, 1991 pp. 3 – 88

117 Norwegian policies for rural development — beliefs, visions facts; Les politiques de développement rural en Norvège — les croyances, les perspectives et les faits *[French summary]*; Norwegische Strategien zur ländlichen Entwicklung. Überzeugungen, Vorstellungen und Tatsachen *[German summary]*. M. Rønningen. *Sociol. Rur.* **XXXI:1** 1991 pp. 27 – 36

118 Not seeing the wood for the trees — searching for indigenous non goverment organisations in the forest of voluntary "self-help" associations. Gary Salole. *J. Soc. Devel. Afr.* **6:1** 1991 pp. 5 – 17

119 Planned technology development and local initiative. Computer-supported enterprise comparisons among Dutch horticulturists; Développement technologique planifié et initiative locale — comparaisons d'entreprises horticoles informatisées aux Pays-Bas *[French summary]*; Geplante Technologieentwicklung und lokale initiative — computer-unterstützte Unternehmensvergleiche unter niederländischen Gärtnern *[German summary]*. C. Leeuwis; M. Arkesteyn. *Sociol. Rur.* **XXXI:2-3** 1991 pp. 140 – 162

120 The politics of harmony — land dispute strategies in Swaziland. Laurel L. Rose. Cambridge: Cambridge University Press, 1991: - *ISBN: 0521392969. Includes bibliography and index.* [African studies series.]

121 The recomposition of rural Europe — a review; *[French summary]*. H. Clout. *Ann. Géogr.* **:561-562** 1991 pp. 714 – 729

122 Role of women in rural development. M. Kaur; M.L. Sharma. *J. Rural St.* **7:1-2** 1991 pp. 11 – 16

123 Rural and regional restructuring in South Africa. John Pickles *[Ed.]*; Daniel Weiner *[Ed.]*; John Pickles *[Contrib.]*; Alan Mabin *[Contrib.]*; Dhiru Soni *[Contrib.]*; Brij Maharaj *[Contrib.]*; Richard Levin *[Contrib.]*; Ben Wisner *[Contrib.]*; Aninka Claassens *[Contrib.]*. Collection of 11 articles. **Antipode**, *23:1*, 1:1991 pp. 1 – 184

124 Rural change — Britain and the USSR. D.J.B. Shaw *[Contrib.]*; A.W. Gilg *[Contrib.]*; P.T. Gaskell *[Contrib.]*; M.F. Tanner *[Contrib.]*; G.V. Ioffe *[Contrib.]*; B.S. Zhikharevich *[Contrib.]*; R. Munton *[Contrib.]*; T. Marsden *[Contrib.]*. Collection of 6 articles. **Geoforum**, *22:1*, :1991 pp. 71 – 117

125 Rural development and planning in Zimbabwe. A. H. J. Helmsing *[Ed.]*; N. D. Mutizwa-Mangiza *[Ed.]*. Aldershot: Avebury, 1991: 481 p. (ill) *ISBN: 1856281426. Includes bibliography.*

126 Rural development in South Korea — a socio-political analysis. William W Boyer; Pyŏng-man An *[Ed.]*. Newark: University of Delaware Press, c1991: 155 p. (ill., map) *ISBN: 0874134315; LofC: 90050708. Includes bibliographical references (p. 138-148) and index.*

127 Rural development in Sudan — the Dutch aid experience. P. O'Keefe; J. Kirkby; J. Harnmeijer. *Publ. Adm. D.* **11:4** 7-8:1991 pp. 325 – 240

128 Rural development policy in Sri Lanka, 1935 to 1989. S. Sathananthan. *J. Cont. Asia* **21:4** 1991 pp. 433 – 454

129 Rural health transformation — the need for involvement. Anita D. Aetugbo; A.I. Odebiyi. *Scand. J. Devel. Altern.* **X:4** 12:1991 pp. 91 – 100

130 The rural labour market in Zimbabwe. Jennifer Adams. *Develop. Cha.* **22:2** 4:1991 pp. 297 – 320

131 Shaping modern times in rural France — the transformation and reproduction of an

G.3.1: Rural sociology *[Sociologie rurale]* — **Rural development** *[Développement rurale]*

Aveyronnais community. Susan Carol Rogers. Princeton, N.J: Princeton University Press, 1991: 231 p. *ISBN: 0691094586; LofC: 90008989. Includes bibliographical references and index.*

132 Social class differentials in the impact of repression and guerrilla war on rural population and development in Zimbabwe. Robert E. Mazur. *J. Dev. Areas* **25:4** 7:1991 pp. 509 – 528

133 Social science agricultural agendas and strategies. Glenn L. Johnson *[Ed.]*; James T. Bonnen *[Ed.]*; Darrell Fienup *[Ed.]*; et al. East Lansing: Michigan State University Press, 1991: - *ISBN: 087013289x.*

134 *[In Japanese]*; [Theoretical framework for rural revitalization]. Yoshio Kawamura. *Nogyo to Keizai No.57(1) - 1991.* pp. 5 – 13

135 Training for rural development in Thailand — content or process model? N. Martwanna; S. Chamala. *Comm. Dev. J.* **26:1** 1:1991 pp. 43 – 49

136 *[In Japanese]*; [The transformation in rural community in urban phenomenon and the changing process on "the collecting standard of KUHI"]. Ichizo Goto. *Shak. Hyor. No.42(3) - 1991.* pp. 31 – 50

G.3.2: Urban sociology — *Sociologie urbaine*

Sub-divisions: Housing *[Logement]*; Spatial and social differentiation *[Différenciation spatio-sociale]*; Urban planning and development *[Aménagement et développement urbain]*; Urbanization *[Urbanisation]*

1 Los Angeles en 1990 — une nouvelle capitale mondiale *[In French]*; [Los Angles in 1990 — a new world capital]. B. Marchand; A. Scott. *Ann. Géogr.* **100:560** 7-8:1991 pp. 406 – 426

2 Anxiety as a cost of commuting to work. Bruce H. Smith. *J. Urban Ec.* **29:2** 03:1991 pp. 260 – 266

3 Apprehending the city — the view from above, below, and behind. Anthony M. Orum. *Urban Aff. Q.* **26:4** 6:1991 pp. 589 – 609

4 The APRA government and the urban poor — the PAIT programme in Lima's pueblos jóvenes. Carol Graham. *J. Lat. Am. St.* **23:1** 2:1991 pp. 91 – 130

5 Architecture and townscape in today's Cairo — the relevance of tradition. Florian Steinberg. *Ekistics* **58:346/ 347** 1/2-3/4:1991 pp. 75 – 86

6 Changing Japanese suburbia — a study of two present-day localities. Eyal Ben-Ari. London: Kegan Paul International, 1991: 328 p. *ISBN: 0710303815; LofC: 90043778. Includes bibliographical references and index.* [Japanese studies.]

7 Citoyenneté et urbanité *[In French]*; [Citizenship and urbanism]. Jean Baudrillard *[Ed.]*; et al. Paris: Esprit, 1991: 175 p. *ISBN: 2909210030.* [Série société.]

8 City and crisis — the case of Oaxaca, Mexico. Arthur D. Murphy *[Contrib.]*; Martha W. Rees *[Contrib.]*; Earl W. Morris *[Contrib.]*; Mary Winter *[Contrib.]*; Pedro D. Pacheco Vasquez *[Contrib.]*; Henry A. Selby *[Contrib.]*; Alex Stepick *[Contrib.]*. Collection of 7 articles. **Urban Anthro.** , *20:1,* Spring:1991 pp. 1 – 107

9 *[In Japanese]*; [The city and the power]. Hiroo Fujita. Tokyo: Sobunsha, 1991: 360 p.

10 A city of farmers — informal urban agriculture in the open spaces of Nairobi, Kenya. Donald B. Freeman. Montréal: McGill-Queen's University Press, 1991: xv, 159 p., 8 p. of plates (ill., maps) *ISBN: 0773508228; LofC: cn 90090431. Includes bibliographical references (p. [149]-153) and index.*

11 Las ciudades en el desarrollo regional de America Latina — los casos de Venezuela y Brasil *[In Spanish]*; [Cities and regional development in Latin America — the cases of Venezuela and Brazil]. Andrzej Bonasewicz. *Rev. Int.Am. Plan.* **XXIV:93** 1-3:1991 pp. 21 – 32

12 *[In Japanese]*; [Classifying cities by population fluidity in Kanto area]. Yukio Mori. *Sociologica No.16(1) - 1991.* pp. 21 – 46

13 *[In Japanese]*; [Collective means of consumption-triad and communal society — a case of K-district in Kobe city]. Hidehiro Takahashi. *Shak. Hyor. No.41(4) - 1991.* pp. 16 – 33

14 Company towns and class processes — a study of the coal towns of Central Queensland. K. Gibson. *Envir. Plan. D* **9:3** 9:1991 pp. 285 – 308

15 *[In Japanese]*; [Co-operative community theory for residences in central city]. Yaeko Nishiyama. *Tos. Mon. No.82(1) - 1991.* pp. 65 – 77

G.3.2: Urban sociology *[Sociologie urbaine]*

16 *[In Japanese]*; [The creation of city-orientated resort community from a viewpoint of social development]. Morio Onda. *Tos. Mon. No.82(4) - 1991.* pp. 69 – 80

17 Crise des banlieues — le béton n'est pas en cause *[In French]*; [Crisis in the suburbs — the concrete is not the cause]. Jean-François Laé. *Regar. Actual.* **:172** 7:1991 pp. 23 – 34

18 A critical evaluation of the city life cycle idea. Susan Roberts. *Urban Geogr.* **12:5** 9-10:1991 pp. 431 – 449

19 Cross-national urban structure in the era of global cities — the US-Mexico transfrontier metropolis. Lawrence A. Herzog. *Urban Stud.* **28:4** 8:1991 pp. 519 – 534

20 Dinámica de los centros de ciudad y del conjunto urbano-turístico Maldonado-Punta del este y San Carlos (Uruguay) *[In Spanish]*; [Dynamics of city centres of the urban-tourist conglommeration of Maldonado-Punta in the East and San Carlos (Uruguay)]. Anne Collin Delavaud. *Rev. Int.Am. Plan.* **XXIV:93** 1-3:1991 pp. 195 – 217

21 Les entreprises étrangères dans les villes françaises *[In French]*; [Foreign enterprises in French cities]. C. Rozenblat. *Ann. Géogr.* **100:559** 5-6:1991 pp. 295 – 310

22 Экологическая перспектива города *[In Russian]*; [The ecological perspective of the town]. O.N. Ianitskii. Moscow: Mysl', 1987: 280 p. *Bibliogr. pp.269-279.*

23 Equity, equality and appropriate distribution — multiple interpretations and Zimbabwean usages. D.R. Gasper. *R. Rur. Urb. Plan. S.& E.Afr.* **:1** 1991 p. 1

24 The European city street, part 2 — relating form and function. Cliff Moughtin. *Town Plan. R.* **62:2** 4:1991 pp. 153 – 200

25 Les faubourgs de la cité *[In French]*; [The suburbs of the city] *[Summary]*. Michel-Louis Rouquette. *Cah. Int. Soc.* **XCI:** 7-12:1991 pp. 395 – 402

26 Les franges périurbaines en Belgique, quelques éléments de recherche concernant leur délimitation, leur population et leurs caractéristiques sociales *[In French]*; The periurban fringes, in Belgium, some research elements about their delimitation, their population and their social characteristics *[Summary]*. H. van der Haegen. *Espace Pop. Soc.* **:2** 1991 pp. 259 – 270

27 From barn to royal cottage — the planning of Old Farms Forest — Devonwood, USA. James Bischoff. *Ekistics* **58:346/ 347** 1/2-3/4:1991 pp. 97 – 109

28 From rag trade to real estate in New York's garment center — remaking the labor landscape in a global city. Andrew Herod. *Urban Geogr.* **12:4** 7-8:1991 pp. 324 – 338

29 Las funciones de los centros urbanos en el desarrollo regional — la región Huetar Norte en Costa Rica *[In Spanish]*; [The function of urban centres in regional development — the north Heutar region of Costa Rica]. Arie Romein; Jur Schuurman. *Rev. Int.Am. Plan.* **XXIV:93** 1-3:1991 pp. 127 – 158

30 The future of cities in Britain and Canada — proceedings of a Canada/UK Colloquium, Val Morin, Quebec, Canada. Ian Jackson *[Ed.]*. Ottawa: Institute for Research on Public Policy, c1991: ix, 149 p. *ISBN: 0886451280; LofC: cn 92003052. Colloquium held in 1990; Includes bibliographical references.*

31 Generating urban forms from diffusive growth. M. Batty. *Envir. Plan.A.* **23:4** 4:1991 pp. 511 – 544

32 The gentrification of paradise — St. John's, Antigua. Gerald A. Thomas. *Urban Geogr.* **12:5** 9-10:1991 pp. 469 – 487

33 Geography and the political economy of urban transportation. David C. Hodge. *Urban Geogr.* **11:1** 1-2:1990 pp. 87 – 100

34 Getting ahead in urban China. Nan Lin; Yanjie Bian. *A.J.S.* **97:3** 11:1991 pp. 657 – 688

35 Global finance and urban living — a study of metropolitan change. Leslie Budd *[Ed.]*; Sam Whimster *[Ed.]*. New York, NY: Routledge, 1991: 367 p. *ISBN: 041507097x; LofC: 91014751. Includes bibliographical references and index.* [The international library of sociology.]

36 Городская среда: в поисках здравого смысла *[In Russian]*; (City environment — a search for common sense); (Milieu urbain — à la recherche du bon sens: *Title only in French*); (Die Stadtumwelt — Auf der Suche nach gesundem Menschenverstand: *Title only in German*); (El medio urbano — en busca del sentido común: *Title only in Spanish*). V. Glazychev. *Svobod. Mysl'* **:18(1388)** 1991 pp. 77 – 84

37 Grocery shopping patterns of the ambulatory urban elderly. Geoffrey C. Smith. *Envir. Behav.* **23:1** 1:1991 pp. 86 – 114

38 Household and business firm densities in the Danish urban pattern. Gustav Kristensen. *Geogr. Res. For.* **11:** 1991 pp. 51 – 65

39 Human growth and urban pollution. L.M. Schell. *Coll. Antrop.* **15:1** 6:1991 pp. 59 – 72

G.3.2: Urban sociology *[Sociologie urbaine]*

40 If you lived here — the city in art, theory, and social activism. Martha Rosler; Brian Wallis *[Ed.]*. Seattle: Bay Press, 1991: 312 p. (ill) *ISBN: 0941920186; LofC: 89650815. Bibliography — p.. 306-311.* [Discussions in contemporary culture. : No. 6]

41 Innovation and urban population dynamics — a multi-level process. Christian Matthiessen *[Ed.]*; K. P. Strohmeier *[Ed.]*. Aldershot: Avebury, 1991: 310 p. *ISBN: 1856281434.* [Urban Europe series. : No. 6]

42 Interhousehold exchange of goods and services in the city of Oaxaca. Mary Winter. *Urban Anthro.* **20:1** Spring:1991 pp. 67 – 86

43 La investigación urbana en América Latina. Una aproximación *[In Spanish]*; [An approach to urban investigation in Latin America]. Fernando Carrión. *Nueva Soc.* **:114** 7-8:1991 pp. 113 – 123

44 Locational conflict in metropolitan areas — Melbourne and Sydney, 1989. J.S. Humphreys; D.J. Walmsley. *Aust. Geogr. Stud.* **29:2** 10:1991 pp. 313 – 328

45 The long-term trend toward increased dispersion in the distributions of city sizes. B.M. Roehner. *Envir. Plan.A.* **23:12** 12:1991 pp. 1725 – 1740

46 The making of the urban landscape. J. W. R. Whitehand. Oxford: Basil Blackwell, 1991: 239 p. *ISBN: 0631176349; LofC: 91013425.* [The Institute of British Geographers special publications series.]

47 Method and theory in comparative urban studies. David A. Smith. *Int. J. Comp. Soc* **XXXII: 1-2** 1-4:1991 pp. 39 – 58

48 Mill town decline ten years later — the limits of corporate civic leadership. Roger S. Ahlbrandt. *J. Am. Plann.* **57:2** Spring:1991 pp. 193 – 203

49 A model for the representation of urban knowledge; *[French summary]*. P. Quintrand; J. Zoller; R. de Filippo; S. Faure. *Envir. Plan. B.* **18:1** 1:1991 pp. 71 – 83

50 Modeling suburbanization as an evolutionary system dynamic. Debra Straussfogel. *Geogr. Anal.* **23:1** 1:1991 pp. 1 – 24

51 Modernism is dead. Rod Hackney. *Ekistics* **58:346/ 347** 1/2-3/4:1991 pp. 110 – 117

52 Mrs Thatcher's vision of the "new Britain" and the other sides of the Cambridge phenomenon. P. Crang; R.L. Martin. *Envir. Plan. D* **9:1** 3:1991 pp. 91 – 116

53 Neighbourhoods, the state and collective action. Wim Van Rees. *Comm. Dev. J.* **26:2** 4:1991 pp. 96 – 102

54 The Oaxacan urban household and the crisis. Henry A. Selby. *Urban Anthro.* **20:1** Spring:1991 pp. 87 – 98

55 Omgaan met stedelijk gevaar *[In Dutch]*; Coping with urban insecurities *[Summary]*. Lodewijk Brunt. *Sociol. Gids* **:2** 3-4:1991 pp. 74 – 94

56 On anti-suburban orthodoxy. Brett W. Hawkins; Stephen L. Percy. *Soc. Sci. Q.* **72:3** 9:1991 pp. 478 – 490

57 *[In Japanese]*; [On urban strangers]. Yuiche Yoshise. ***Transactions of Humanities*** *No.(14) - 1991.* pp. 69 – 84

58 Organización y funcionamiento de las áreas metropolitanas — un análisis comparado *[In Spanish]*; [Organisation and function of metropolitan areas — a comparative analyses]. Montserrat Cuchillo; Francesc Morata *[Ed.]*. Madrid: Ministerio Para Las Administraciones Públicas, 1991: 279 p. *ISBN: 8470885480. Bibliography — p263-271.* [Colección estudios. Serie administraciones territoriales.]

59 El papel de las ciudades intermedias en el desarrollo regional — una comparación de cuatro ciudades de Ecuador *[In Spanish]*; [The role played by intermediate cities in regional development — comparing four cities in Ecuador]. Stella Lowder. *Rev. Int.Am. Plan.* **XXIV:93** 1-3:1991 pp. 45 – 60

60 The perimetropolitan bow wave. John Fraser Hart. *Geogr. Rev.* **81:1** 1:1991 pp. 35 – 51

61 The politics and pragmatism of urban containment — Belfast since 1940. Michael Murray. Aldershot, Hants, England: Avebury, c1991: viii, 280 p. (ill., maps) *ISBN: 1856282457; LofC: 91032765. Revision of the author's doctoral thesis; Includes bibliographical references (p. 269-280) and index.*

62 Prisoners of the city — whatever could a postmodern city be? Kevin Robins. *New Form.* **:15** Winter:1991 pp. 1 – 22

63 Problems of hawkers in Calcutta — a case study. K.P. Bhattacharya; P. Dey. *Ind. J. Soc. Sci.* **4:2** 4-6:1991 pp. 307 – 319

64 Realidad múltiple de la gran ciudad. Una visión desde Caracas *[In Spanish]*; [The multiple reality of the big city. A view from Caracas]. Marco Negrón. *Nueva Soc.* **:114** 7-8:1991 pp. 76 – 83

G.3.2: Urban sociology *[Sociologie urbaine]*

65 Resettlement and famine in Ethiopia — the villagers' experience. Alula Pankhurst. Manchester, England: Manchester University Press, c1991: 290 p. *ISBN: 0719035376; LofC: 91018748. Includes bibliographical references and index.*

66 The restless urban landscape — economic and sociocultural change and the transformation of metropolitan Washington, D.C. Paul L. Knox. *Ann. As. Am. G.* **81:2** 6:1991 pp. 181 – 209

67 The role and structure of metropolises in China's urban economy. Won Bae Kim. *Third Wor. P.* **13:2** 5:1991 pp. 155 – 178

68 Sectoral-level employment multipliers in small urban settlements — a comparison of five models. Gordon F. Mulligan; Hak-Hoon Kim. *Urban Geogr.* **12:3** 5-6:1991 pp. 240 – 259

69 Символика Петербурга и проблемы семиотики города *[In Russian]*; [The symbolism of St. Petersburg and the problems of the city's semiotics]. Iurii Lotman. *Raduga* **:5** 5:1991 pp. 29 – 44

70 A small town in modern times — Alexandria, Ontario. David M. Rayside. Montreal: McGill-Queen's University Press, 1991: 336 p. *ISBN: 0773508260; LofC: cn 90090516. Includes index; Bibliography.*

71 Socioenvironmental determinants of community formation. Carl Keane. *Envir. Behav.* **23:1** 1:1991 pp. 27 – 46

72 *[In Japanese]*; [Sociology on citylife]. Kazutaka Hashimoto, et al. Tokyo: Jichosha, 1991: 213 p.

73 Some problems relating to the numerical simulation of urban ambient environments; *[French summary]*. J.-P. Peneau. *Envir. Plan. B.* **18:1** 1:1991 pp. 107 – 117

74 Die sozialistische Stadt in Mitteleuropa — der Modellfall Halle a.d. Saale. Zustand und Struktur am Ende einer Epoche *[In German]*; [The Central European socialist town — the model case of Halle a.d. Saale. Conditions and structure at the end of an era]. Martin Seger; Doris Wastl-Walter. *Geogr. Rund.* **43:10** 10:1991 pp. 570 – 579

75 Steeltown, USSR — Soviet society in the Gorbachev era. Stephen Kotkin. London: Weidenfeld & Nicolson, 1991: 269 p. (ill) *ISBN: 0297820826. Includes bibliography and index.*

76 Subcenters in the Los Angeles region. G. Giuliano; K.A. Small. *Reg. Sci. Urb. Econ.* **21:2** 7:1991 pp. 163 – 182

77 Tags et zoulous, une nouvelle violence urbaine *[In French]*; [Tags and "zulus", a new urban violence]. Michel Kokoreff. *Esprit* **169** 2:1991 pp. 23 – 36

78 Towards the simulation of urban morphology; *[French summary]*. J. Rabie. *Envir. Plan. B.* **18:1** 1:1991 pp. 57 – 70

79 Le transport urbain en Afrique au sud du Sahara *[In French]*; [Urban transportation in sub-Saharan Africa] *[Summary]*. L. Bonnamour. *Afr. Cont.* **:158(2)** 1991 pp. 14 – 30

80 TRAPU — a tool for data capture and visualisation of the urban fabric; *[French summary]*. Y. Egels. *Envir. Plan. B.* **18:1** 1:1991 pp. 19 – 24

81 *[In Japanese]*; [Urban environmental problems in modern Japan]. Nobuko Ijima. *Tos. Mon. No.43(6) - 1991.* pp. 95 – 107

82 The urban experience. Bruno Bettelheim. *Free Assoc.* **2:22** 1991 pp. 175 – 190

83 The urban factor — sociology of Canadian cities. Leo Driedger. Don Mills, Ont: Oxford University Press, 1991: xiv, 319 p. (ill) *ISBN: 0195407881; LofC: cn 91093237. Includes index; Includes bibliographical references — p. [286]-309.*

84 Urban farming practices in Tanzania. A.R. Mosha. *R. Rur. Urb. Plan. S.& E.Afr.* **:1** 1991 pp. 83 – 92

85 Urban flood protection post-project appraisal in England and Wales. P.M. Thompson; A. H. Wigg; D. J. Parker. *Proj. App.* **6:2** 6:1991 pp. 84 – 92

86 Urban liveability in context. David Ley. *Urban Geogr.* **11:1** 1-2:1990 pp. 31 – 35

87 Urban origin and form in central New York. Richard H. Schein. *Geogr. Rev.* **81:1** 1:1991 pp. 52 – 69

88 *[In Japanese]*; [Urban society and the multi-layer meaning structures]. Ken Arisue. *Chiikishakaigaku Nenpo No.(5) - 1991.* pp. 59 – 89

89 Urban subcenter formation. R.W. Helsley; A.M. Sullivan. *Reg. Sci. Urb. Econ.* **21:2** 7:1991 pp. 255 – 276

90 Urban theory and the treatment of differences — administrative practices, social sciences and the difficulties of specifics; *[French summary]*. Antonio Tosi. *Int. J. Urban* **15:4** 12:1991 pp. 594 – 609

91 Urbanism, migration, and tolerance — a reassessment. Thomas C. Wilson. *Am. Sociol. R.* **56:1** 2:1991 pp. 117 – 123

G.3.2: Urban sociology *[Sociologie urbaine]*
92 Whose cities? Mark Fisher *[Ed.]*; Ursula Owen *[Ed.]*. London: Penguin, 1991: 194 p. *ISBN: 014015793x*.
93 Значение города в интеграции бытовой культуры (по материалам русского города 1970-1980-х гг.) *[In Russian]*; City as a factor of cultural integration (the Russian experience of 1970s-1980s) *[Summary]*. O.R. Budina; M.N. Shmeleva. *Sovet. Etno.* :**4** 4:1991 pp. 17 – 27

Housing *[Logement]*
94 Affordable housing in London. C.M.E. Whitehead; D.T. Cross. *Plan. Pract. Res.* **6:**2 Summer:1991 pp. 7 – 87
95 The aims and methods of comparative housing research. M. Oxley. *Scand. Hous. Plan. R.* **8:**2 1991 pp. 67 – 77
96 An analysis of house price differentials between English regions; Une analyse des écarts de prix des maisons suivant les régions en Angleterre *[French summary]*; Eine Analyse des Hauspreisgefälles von einer Region Englands zur anderen *[German summary]*. David Forrest. *Reg. Stud.* **25:**3 6:1991 pp. 231 – 238
97 Comparing Karachi's informal and formal housing delivery systems. David E. Dowall. *Cities* **8:**3 8:1991 pp. 217 – 227
98 Counting the homeless — the methodologies, policies, and social significance behind the numbers. David S. Cordray *[Contrib.]*; Georgine M. Pion *[Contrib.]*; Christopher Walker *[Contrib.]*; Anna Kondratas *[Contrib.]*; Barrett A. Lee *[Contrib.]*; Bruce G. Link *[Contrib.]*; Paul A. Toro *[Contrib.]*; Eleanor Chelimsky *[Contrib.]*; Michael L. Dennis *[Contrib.]*; Franklin J. James *[Contrib.]* and others. Collection of 17 articles. **Hous. Pol. Deb.** , 2:3, 1991 pp. 587 – 1094
99 *[In Japanese]*; [Covert prejudice and resistance in housing discrimination in contemporary America — measurement and theoretical speculation]. Hidenori Kimura. ***Bulletin of the Faculty of Letters of Aichi Gakuin University** No.(20) - 1991*. pp. 149 – 160
100 The crisis of public housing in Sweden — economic reality or organizational myth? B. Bengtsson. *Scand. Hous. Plan. R.* **8:**2 1991 pp. 113 – 127
101 The DDA and the housing scenario in Delhi — the controversial role. Sipra Maitra. *Ind. J. Reg. Sci.* **XXIII:1** 1991 pp. 27 – 40
102 The demand for housing in Sweden — equilibrium choice of tenure and type of dwelling. David Brownstone; Peter Englund. *J. Urban Ec.* **29:**3 5:1991 pp. 267 – 281
103 Deterioration of the public sector housing stock. Diane Diacon. Aldershot: Avebury, c1991: xi, 268 p. *ISBN: 1856281108. Housing; Bibliography — p.253-262. Includes index.*
104 Developing institutional capacity to meet the housing needs of the urban poor — experience in Kenya, Tanzania and Zambia. Carole Rakodi. *Cities* **8:**3 8:1991 pp. 228 – 243
105 Difficulties for home-ownership in Iceland. J.R. Sveinsson. *Scand. Hous. Plan. R.* **8:**1 2:1991 pp. 37 – 43
106 The empirical analysis of housing careers — a review and a general statistical modelling framework. A.R. Pickles; R.B. Davies. *Envir. Plan.A.* **23:**4 4:1991 pp. 465 – 484
107 Ethnographic methods in the development of census procedures for enumerating the homeless. Matt T. Salo; Pamela C. Campanelli. *Urban Anthro.* **20:**2 Summer:1991 pp. 127 – 140
108 Ethnographic perspectives on homelessness. Rob Rosenthal *[Contrib.]*; Matt T. Salo *[Contrib.]*; Pamela C. Campanelli; Michael Owen Robertson *[Contrib.]*; Kim Hopper *[Contrib.]*; Janet M. Fitchen *[Contrib.]*. Collection of 5 articles. **Urban Anthro.** , *20:2*, Summer:1991 pp. 109 – 210
109 Una evaluación de la vivienda en condominio — el caso de Monterrey *[In Spanish]*; An evaluation of housing in condominiums — the case of Monterrey *[Summary]*. Alma del Rosario García Cavazos. *Est. Demog. Urb.* **6:1** 1-4:1991 pp. 117 – 148
110 The fractured metropolis — political fragmentation and metropolitan segregation. Gregory Weiher. Albany, N.Y: State University of New York Press, c1991: xi, 225 p. (ill) *ISBN: 0791405648; LofC: 90009878. Includes bibliographical references (p. 197-221) and index.* [SUNY series, the new inequalities.]
111 Galloping bungalows — the rise and demise of the American house trailer. David A Thornburg. Hamden, Conn: Archon Books, 1991: 197 p. (ill) *ISBN: 0208022775; LofC: 90041214. Includes bibliographical references (p. 193-194) and index.*
112 Gentrification as consumption — issues of class and gender. A. Warde. *Envir. Plan. D* **9:**2 6:1991 pp. 223 – 232
113 High-density housing in Harare — commodification and overcrowding. Deborah Potts; C.C. Mutambirwa. *Third Wor. P.* **13:**1 2:1991 pp. 1 – 26

G.3.2: Urban sociology [Sociologie urbaine] — Housing [Logement]

114 High-rise housing clusters in Soweto — (the views of a group of Sowetans on the desirability of erecting a large, high-rise complex in Soweto). Toni Lamont. Pretoria: Human Sciences Research Council, 1991: 56 p. *ISBN: 0796909520*. [Report.]

115 Household, kin and nonkin sources of assistance in home building — the case of the city of Oaxaca. Earl W. Morris. *Urban Anthro.* **20:1** Spring:1991 pp. 49 – 66

116 Households in action — on access to housing in a regulated private rental market. O. Siksiö; L.-E. Borgegård. *Scand. Hous. Plan. R.* **8:1** 2:1991 pp. 1 – 12

117 Houses-now! — building for hope in Costa Rica. Fernando Zumbado Jimenez. Leicestershire: Building and Social Housing Foundation, 1991: 76 p. *ISBN: 0951278363*.

118 Housing action. Diane Diacon *[Contrib.]*; Marcelo Ebrard *[Contrib.]*; Jorge Gamboa de Buen *[Contrib.]*; Kosta Mathéy *[Contrib.]*; Magdy Tewfik *[Contrib.]*; A. Faruk Göksu *[Contrib.]*; Swapna Banerjee-Guha *[Contrib.]*; Lee Ogunshakin *[Contrib.]*; Olatokunbo Osasona *[Contrib.]*; Florian Steinberg *[Contrib.]* and others. Collection of 11 articles. **Ekistics**, *58:346/ 347*, 1/2-3/4:1991 pp. 4 – 117

119 Housing and social theory. J. Kemeny. London: Routledge, 1991: 192 p. *ISBN: 041506273x*. Housing.

120 Housing discrimination and urban poverty of African-Americans. George C. Galster. *J. Hous. Res.* **2:2** 1991 pp. 87 – 124

121 Housing famine and homelessness — how the low-income housing crisis affects families with inadequate supports. R. Wallace; E. Bassuk. *Envir. Plan.A.* **23:4** 4:1991 pp. 485 – 498

122 Housing for blacks — a challenge for Kansas. William E. Robertson. *Rev. Bl. Pol. Ec.* **19:3-4** Winter/Spring:1991 pp. 195 – 210

123 Housing inequalities under socialism — the case of Poland. K. J. Zaniewski. *Geoforum* **22:1** :1991 pp. 39 – 53

124 Housing obsolescence and depreciation. William C. Baer. *J. Plan. Lit.* **5:4** 5:1991 pp. 323 – 332

125 Housing policy — goals, rhetoric, information and regularity. U. Torgersen. *Scand. Hous. Plan. R.* **8:2** 1991 pp. 105 – 111

126 Housing problems and prospects for blacks in Houston. Robert D. Bullard. *Rev. Bl. Pol. Ec.* **19:3-4** Winter/Spring:1991 pp. 175 – 194

127 The housing provision chain as a comparative analytical framework. P.J. Ambrose. *Scand. Hous. Plan. R.* **8:2** 1991 pp. 91 – 104

128 Housing the poor in the developing world — methods of analysis, case studies, and policy. A. Graham Tipple *[Ed.]*; K. G Willis *[Ed.]*. London: Routledge, 1991: 287 p. *ISBN: 0415055393; LofC: 90027271*. Includes bibliographical references and index.

129 The impact of rental properties on the value of single-family residences. Ko Wang; Terry V. Grissom; James R. Webb; Lewis Spellman. *J. Urban Ec.* **30:2** 9:1991 pp. 152 – 166

130 The impact of the minkatsu policy on Japanese housing and land use. K. Hayakawa; Y. Hirayama. *Envir. Plan. D* **9:2** 6:1991 pp. 151 – 164

131 Innovative and successful solutions to global housing problems. Diane Diacon. *Ekistics* **58:346/ 347** 1/2-3/4:1991 pp. 4 – 17

132 Interpreting homelessness — the influence of professional and non-professional service providers. Michael Owen Robertson. *Urban Anthro.* **20:2** Summer:1991 pp. 141 – 154

133 The Italian housing market — its failures and their causes. Ireneus L.M. van Hees. *Urban Stud.* **28:1** 2:1991 pp. 15 – 39

134 Logement *[In French]*; [Housing]. Pierre Durif *[Contrib.]*; Claude Taffin *[Contrib.]*; Gérard Curci *[Contrib.]*; André Massot *[Contrib.]*; Michel Jacod *[Contrib.]*; Colette Pavageau *[Contrib.]*; Martine Eenschooten *[Contrib.]*; Ibtissam Haehnel *[Contrib.]*; Sylvie le Laidier *[Contrib.]*; J. Bosvieux *[Contrib.]* and others. Collection of 10 articles. **E & S**, :240, 2:1991 pp. 3 – 95

135 Le logement à la Réunion — entre tradition et modernité *[In French]*; Housing in Reunion — caught between tradition and modernism *[Summary]*; La vivienda en la isla de La Reunión — entre la tradición y la modernidad *[Spanish summary]*. Michel Jacod; Colette Pavageau. *E & S* **:240** 2:1991 pp. 47 – 57

136 Low-income shelter strategies in Latin America. Jorge L. Arrigone. *Unisa Lat.Am. Rep.* **7:2** 1991 pp. 16 – 29

137 The maze of urban housing markets — theory, evidence, and policy. Jerome Rothenberg *[Ed.]*; et al. Chicago: University of Chicago Press, 1991: viii, 549 p. (ill) *ISBN: 0226729516; LofC: 90022756*. Includes bibliographical references (p. [523]-539) and indexes.

G.3.2: Urban sociology *[Sociologie urbaine]* — Housing *[Logement]*

138 Measuring housing and environmental quality as indicator of quality of urban life — a case of traditional city of Benin, Nigeria. Leonard N. Muoghalu. *Soc. Ind.* **25:1** 8:1991 pp. 63 – 98

139 Middle-class multi-apartment housing in Nigeria — development perspectives. Lee Ogunshakin; Olatokunbo Osasona. *Ekistics* **58:346/ 347** 1/2-3/4:1991 pp. 65 – 74

140 Movers and stayers on the housing market in the post-parental stage — the Swedish case. L. Lundin. *Scand. Hous. Plan. R.* **8:1** 2:1991 pp. 19 – 24

141 Movildad residencial en una ciudad planificada — Brasilia, D.F. *[In Spanish]*; [Residential mobility in a planned city — Brasilia, D.F.]. Aldo Paviani; Neido Campos; Ricardo Farret. *Rev. Int.Am. Plan.* **XXIV:94** 4-6:1991 pp. 155 – 175

142 Neighborhood type, housing and housing characteristics in Oaxaca. Pedro D. Pacheco Vasquez; Earl W. Morris; Mary Winter; Arthur D. Murphy. *Urban Anthro.* **20:1** Spring:1991 pp. 31 – 48

143 Obstacles for the young Swedes to find a home of their own. A.-L Lindén. *Scand. Hous. Plan. R.* **11:1990** pp. 195 – 205

144 Opération 20,000 logements et l'espace social de Montréal *[In French]*; [Operation 20,000 homes and the social space of Montréal] *[Summary]*. François Charbonneau; René Parenteau. *Rech. Soc.graph* **XXXII:2** 5-8; 1991 pp. 237 – 254

145 L'opinion des Français sur leur logement *[In French]*; What the French think of their homes *[Summary]*; La opinión de los franceses acerca de su vivienda *[Spanish summary]*. Martine Eenschooten. *E & S* **:240** 2:1991 pp. 59 – 68

146 Politics and representation in Melbourne slum clearance. S.E. Morrissey. *Mel. J. Pol.* **20** 1991 pp. 68 – 85

147 Poor people, council housing and the right to buy. Simon James; Bill Jordan; Helen Kay. *J. Soc. Pol.* **20:1** 1:1991 pp. 27 – 40

148 Portrait du locataire *[In French]*; Portrait of a tenant *[Summary]*; Retrato del inquilino tipo *[Spanish summary]*. Gérard Curci. *E & S* **:240** 2:1991 pp. 19 – 28

149 Public housing in Charlottesville — the black experience in a small southern city. William M. Harris; Nancy Olmsted. *Rev. Bl. Pol. Ec.* **19:3-4** Winter/Spring:1991 pp. 161 – 174

150 Recent changes in the housing status of blacks in Los Angeles. J. Eugene Grigsby; Mary L. Hruby. *Rev. Bl. Pol. Ec.* **19:3-4** Winter/Spring:1991 pp. 211 – 253

151 Reconstruction in central Mexico City after the 1985 earthquakes. Marcelo Ebrard; Jorge Gamboa de Buen. *Ekistics* **58:346/ 347** 1/2-3/4:1991 pp. 18 – 27

152 Residential spatial growth with perfect foresight and multiple income groups. Ralph M. Braid. *J. Urban Ec.* **30:3** 11:1991 pp. 385 – 407

153 Rolling stones for the resurrection of policy as the focus of comparative housing research. L.J. Lundqvist. *Scand. Hous. Plan. R.* **8:2** 1991 pp. 79 – 90

154 Scapegoating rent control — masking the causes of homelessness. Richard P. Appelbaum; Michael Dolny; Peter Dreier; John I. Gilderbloom. *J. Am. Plann.* **57:2** Spring:1991 pp. 153 – 164

155 Segmentation of the home-buyer market — a Cincinnati study. David P. Varady. *Urban Aff. Q.* **26:4** 6:1991 pp. 549 – 566

156 Segregation in the second ghetto — racial and ethnic segregation in American public housing, 1977. Adam Bickford; Douglas S. Massey. *Soc. Forc.* **69:4** 6:1991 pp. 1011 – 1036

157 Self-building in the urban housing market. Richard Harris. *Econ. Geogr.* **67:1** 1:1991 pp. 1 – 21

158 Sites and services for low income housing — Turner and the World Bank. G. Magutu. *R. Rur. Urb. Plan. S.& E.Afr.* **:1** 1991 pp. 35 – 56

159 Social housing in the 1980s and 1990s — past experience and future trends. Mark P. Kleinman. Cambridge: University of Cambridge. Department of Land Economy, 1991: 38 p.

160 Straighter from the source — alternative methods of researching homelessness. Rob Rosenthal. *Urban Anthro.* **20:2** Summer:1991 pp. 109 – 126

161 Tenure choice in a West African city. A. Graham Tipple; Kenneth G. Willis. *Third Wor. P.* **13:1** 2:1991 pp. 27 – 46

162 Trends in the housing status of black Americans across selected metropolitan areas. Wilhelmina A. Leigh. *Rev. Bl. Pol. Ec.* **19:3-4** Winter/Spring:1991 pp. 43 – 64

163 Urban and regional planning of Nigeria. Ademola T. Salau *[Ed.]*; K.P. Moseley *[Contrib.]*; J.I. Ighalo *[Contrib.]*; I.A. Animashaun *[Contrib.]*; Layi Egunjobi *[Contrib.]*; S.I. Abumere *[Contrib.]*; W.J. Okowa *[Contrib.]*; Tunde Agbola *[Contrib.]*; C.O. Olatubara *[Contrib.]*; Tade Akin Aina *[Contrib.]* *and others*. Collection of 13 articles. **Afr. Urb. Q.** , *4:1-2*, 1-5:1989 pp. 1 – 144

G.3.2: Urban sociology *[Sociologie urbaine]* — Housing *[Logement]*

164 Urban growth and housing policy in Algeria — a case study of a migrant community in the city of Constantine. Rabah Boudebaba. Aldershot: Avebury, 1991: 303 p. *ISBN: 1856282473.*
165 Urban growth and housing-market change — Aberdeen 1968 to 1978. C. Jones; D. Maclennan. *Envir. Plan.A.* **23:4** 4:1991 pp. 571-590
166 Urban housing in Nigeria. Poju Onibokun *[Ed.]*. Ibadan: University of Ibadan. Nigerian Institute of Social and Economic Research (NISER), 1990: 425 p.
167 Urban housing segregation of minorities in Western Europe and the United States. Elizabeth D Huttman *[Ed.]*; Wim Blauw *[Ed.]*; Juliet Saltman *[Ed.]*. Durham: Duke University Press, 1991: xiii, 431 p. (ill., maps) *ISBN: 0822310600; LofC: 90003221.* Includes bibliographical references and index.
168 Urban low income housing in Zimbabwe. Christopher J. C. Mafico. Aldershot: Avebury, 1991: 175 p. *ISBN: 1856282260.*
169 Vivienda y familia en la China urbana contemporánea *[In Spanish]*; Housing and family in contemporary urban China *[Summary]*. Flora Botton Beja; Romer Cornejo Bustamante. *Est. Demog. Urb.* **6:1** 1-4:1991 pp. 187-208
170 Wheel estate — the rise and decline of mobile homes. Allan D Wallis. New York: Oxford University Press, 1991: x, 283 p. (ill) *ISBN: 0195061837; LofC: 90031275.* Includes bibliographical references (p. 257-273) and index.
171 Who lives in condominiums and cooperatives? Valerie Preston. *J. Econ. Soc. Geogr.* **82:1** 1991 pp. 2-14
172 Жилищная проблема: поиск выхода *[In Russian]*; (Housing problem — search for a way to resolve). N.I. Gaydukova. *Sot. Issle.* **:4** 1991 pp. 83-91

Spatial and social differentiation *[Différenciation spatio-sociale]*

173 Banlieues, relégations ou citoyenneté *[In French]*; [The suburbs, banishment or citizenship]. Didier la Peyronnie *[Contrib.]*; Jeannette Colombel *[Contrib.]*; Alain Battegay *[Contrib.]*; Jacques Rey *[Contrib.]*; Maurice Charrier *[Contrib.]*; Farid *[Contrib.]*; Pascal Bavoux *[Contrib.]*; Fayssad Hachani *[Contrib.]*; Azouz Begag *[Contrib.]*; Claude Jacquier *[Contrib.]* and others. Collection of 15 articles. **Temps Mod.** , *47:545-546*, 12-1:1991-1992 pp. 2-235
174 Changing gender relations in urban space. J. Regulska *[Contrib.]*; L. McDowell *[Contrib.]*; K.V.L. England *[Contrib.]*; G. Pratt *[Contrib.]*; S. Hanson *[Contrib.]*; J.E. Kodras *[Contrib.]*; J.P. Jones *[Contrib.]*; A. Herod *[Contrib.]*; D. Rose *[Contrib.]*; N. Chicoine *[Contrib.]* and others. Collection of 8 articles. **Geoforum** , *22:2,* 1991 pp. 119-236
175 Coexistence and segregation of two groups in a metropolitan area through externalities. Kazuo Kishimoto. *J. Urban Ec.* **30:3** 11:1991 pp. 293-309
176 A comparative perspective on the underclass — questions of urban poverty, race, and citizenship. Barbara Schmitter Heisler. *Theory Soc.* **20:4** 8:1991 pp. 455-484
177 Comparing preferences of neighbors and a neighborhood design review board. Arthur E. Stamps. *Envir. Behav.* **23:5** 9:1991 pp. 616-629
178 Consistency and differential impact in urban social dimensionality — intraurban variations in the 24 metropolitan areas of Canada. Wayne K.D. Davies; Robert A. Murdie. *Urban Geogr.* **12:1** 1-2:1991 pp. 55-79
179 Contribuciones al modelo de diferenciación socioespacial de ciudades intermedias de América Latina — ejemplos colombianos *[In Spanish]*; [Contributions to the socio-spatial differentiation model of intermediate Latin American cities — Colombian examples]. Günter Mertins. *Rev. Int.Am. Plan.* **XXIV:93** 1-3:1991 pp. 172-194
180 Crowding and residential satisfaction in the urban environment — a contextual approach. Mirilia Bonnes; Marino Bonaiuto; Anna Paola Ercolani. *Envir. Behav.* **23:5** 9:1991 pp. 531-552
181 Developing the spatial mismatch hypothesis — problems of accessibility to employment for low-wage central city labor. Thomas J. Cooke; J. Matthew Shumway. *Urban Geogr.* **12:4** 7-8:1991 pp. 310-323
182 Distance, space and the organisation of urban life. Charles L. Leven. *Urban Stud.* **28:3** 6:1991 pp. 319-325
183 The dynamics of work and survival for the urban poor — a gender analysis of panel data from Madras. Helzi Noponen. *Develop. Cha.* **22:2** 4:1991 pp. 233-260
184 The effects of distance on intra-urban social movements in the metropolitan region of Lagos, Nigeria. F.G.I. Omiunu. *J. Econ. Soc. Geogr.* **82:3** 1991 pp. 185-194

G.3.2: Urban sociology *[Sociologie urbaine]* — *Spatial and social differentiation [Différenciation spatio-sociale]*

185 Этническая группа в современном советском городе: Социол.очерки *[In Russian]*; [Ethnic groups in the contemporary Soviet town — sociological essays]. K.V. Chistov *[Ed.]*; G.V. Starovoitova. Moscow: Nauka. Leningr. Department, 1987: 174 p. [AN USSR. Institute of Ethography in the name of N.N. Miklukho-Maklaia.]

186 L'équilibre spatial résidentiel dans les villes multicentriques *[In French]*; [Spatial residential equilibrium in multicentre urban areas] *[Summary]*. C. Maurice-Baumont. *R. Ec. Reg. Urb.* :**5** 1991 pp. 539 – 564

187 Firm location and land use in discrete urban space — a study of the spatial structure of Dallas-Fort Worth. V. Shukla; P. Waddell. *Reg. Sci. Urb. Econ.* **21:2** 7:1991 pp. 255 – 276

188 La France des banlieues *[In French]*; [Suburban France]. Alain Touraine *[Contrib.]*; Hervé Vieillard-Baron *[Contrib.]*; Michel Kokoreff *[Contrib.]*; Olivier Roy *[Contrib.]*; Philippe Genestier *[Contrib.]*; John Crowley *[Contrib.]*; Daniel Mothé *[Contrib.]*. Collection of 7 articles. **Esprit**, *169*, 2:1991 pp. 7 – 91

189 Les franges périurbaines *[In French]*; (Periurban fringes). H. van der Haegen *[Contrib.]*; P. Bruyelle *[Contrib.]*; J. Steinberg *[Contrib.]*; P. Gans *[Contrib.]*; A. Garcia Ballesteros *[Contrib.]*; E. Pozo Rivera *[Contrib.]*; C. Marois *[Contrib.]*; P. Deslauriers *[Contrib.]*; C. Bryant *[Contrib.]*; C. Chevigne *[Contrib.]* and others. Collection of 12 articles. **Espace Pop. Soc.**, :*2*, 1991 pp. 259 – 408

190 Getto's of concentratiegebieden — goudkusten versus steenpuisten? *[In Dutch]*; Ghetto or concentration — gold coasts against slums? *[Summary]*. Rene Teule; Ronald van Kempen. *Sociol. Gids* **XXXVIII:1** 1-2:1991 pp. 48 – 59

191 Городская среда: феномен престижности *[In Russian]*; (Urban environment — phenomenon of residence place prestige). B.A. Portnov. *Sot. Issle.* :**1** 1991 pp. 69 – 74

192 Insurance redlining, agency location, and the process of urban disinvestment. Gregory D. Squires; William Velez; Karl E. Taeuber. *Urban Aff. Q.* **26:4** 6:1991 pp. 567 – 588

193 An international city going "global" — spatial change in the city of London. M. Pryke. *Envir. Plan. D* **9:2** 6:1991 pp. 197 – 222

194 Is neighborhood racial succession inevitable? Forty years of evidence. Peter B. Wood; Barrett A. Lee. *Urban Aff. Q.* **26:4** 6:1991 pp. 610 – 620

195 Is the Burgess concentric zonal theory of spatial differentiation still applicable to urban Canada?; *[French summary]*. T.R. Balakrishnan; George K. Jarvis. *Can. R. Soc. A.* **28:4** 11:1991 pp. 526 – 539

196 Islands in the street — gangs and American urban society. Martín Sánchez Jankowski. Berkeley: University of California Press, c1991: xiv, 382 p. *ISBN: 0520072642; LofC: 90048641*. Includes bibliographical references (pp. 363-371) and index.

197 Lokale Politik und ethnische Identität — Minderheiten im Modernisierungsprozeß *[In German]*; Local politics and ethnic identity *[Summary]*. Albert F. Reiterer. *Öster. Z. Polit.* **20:4** 1991 pp. 383 – 399

198 Maintaining racially diverse neighborhoods. Juliet Saltman. *Urban Aff. Q.* **26:3** 3:1991 pp. 416 – 441

199 Metropolitan spatial structure and its determinants — a case-study of Tokyo. Xiao-Ping Zheng. *Urban Stud.* **28:1** 2:1991 pp. 87 – 104

200 Migrants to and in Oaxaca City. Martha W. Rees; Arthur D. Murphy; Earl W. Morris; Mary Winter. *Urban Anthro.* **20:1** Spring:1991 pp. 15 – 30

201 Migrations et franges périurbaines — l'exemple du Nord-Pas-de-Calais *[In French]*; Migrations and periurban fringes — the example of Nord-Pas-de-Calais region *[Summary]*. P. Bruyelle. *Espace Pop. Soc.* :**2** 1991 pp. 271 – 282

202 Movimentos sociais urbanos (MSU) em Porto Alegre, 1982/ 84 *[In Portuguese]*; [Urban social movements in Porto Alegre, 1982/ 84 *[Summary]*. Maria Thereza Rosa Ribeiro. *Est. Leop.* **27:123** 6-8:1991 pp. 101 – 121

203 Moving up or staying down? Migrant-native differential mobility in La Paz. Paul van Lindert. *Urban Stud.* **28:3** 6:1991 pp. 433 – 463

204 Neighbourhood change in Amsterdam. Sako Musterd. *J. Econ. Soc. Geogr.* **82:1** 1991 pp. 30 – 39

205 The outer suburbs and metropolitan social change — a case study of London; Les banlieues et l'évolution sociale d'une métropole — le cas de Londres *[French summary]*. P. Congdon. *Espace Pop. Soc.* :**2** 1991 pp. 381 – 394

206 The perception of spatial inequalities in a traditional Third World city. Boyowa Anthony Chokor. *Urban Stud.* **28:2** 4:1991 pp. 233 – 253

G.3.2: Urban sociology *[Sociologie urbaine]* — **Spatial and social differentiation** *[Différenciation spatio-sociale]*

207 Le peuplement des bidonvilles d'Alger — emploi et mobilité socio-professionnelle *[In French]*; The population of the shanty-towns of Algiers — jobs and socio-professional mobility *[Summary]*; Die Bevölkerung der Bidonvilles (Elendsviertel) von Alger — Arbeitsverhältnisse und sozioprofessionelle Mobilität *[German summary]*; El pueblo de los barrios de las latas de Argel — empleos y movilidad socio-profesional *[Spanish summary]*. Maurice Guetta; Cyrille Megdiche. *Rev. Fr. Soc.* **XXXI:2** 4-6:1990 pp. 297 – 313

208 Phoenix in flux — household instability, residential mobility and neighborhood change. Patricia Gober; Kevin E. McHugh; Neil Reid. *Ann. As. Am. G.* **81:1** 3:1991 pp. 80 – 88

209 Poverty area diffusion — the depopulation hypothesis examined. Richard P. Greene. *Urban Geogr.* **12:6** 11-12:1991 pp. 526 – 541

210 Poverty concentration measures and the urban underclass. Richard Greene. *Econ. Geogr.* **67:3** 7:1991 pp. 240 – 252

211 Racial differences in urban neighboring. Barrett A. Lee; Karen E. Campbell; Oscar Miller. *Sociol. For.* **6:3** 9:1991 pp. 525 – 550

212 Reflections on neighbourhood decentralization in Tower Hamlets. Gerry Stoker *[Ed.]*; Sean Baine; Susan Carlyle; Steve Charters; Tony Du Sautoy. *Publ. Admin.* **69** Autumn:1991 pp. 373 – 384

213 Reflections on the absence of squatter settlements in West African cities — the case of Kumasi, Ghana. Kwadwo O. Konadu-Agyemang. *Urban Stud.* **28:1** 2:1991 pp. 139 – 151

214 Residential differentiation and social production — the interrelations of class, gender, and space. M. Huxley; H.P.M. Winchester. *Envir. Plan. D* **9:2** 6:1991 pp. 233 – 240

215 Residential spatial growth with perfect foresight and multiple income groups. Ralph M. Braid. *J. Urban Ec.* **30:3** 11:1991 pp. 385 – 407

216 Le risque du ghetto *[In French]*; [The risk of a ghetto]. Hervé Vieillard-Baron. *Esprit* **169** 2:1991 pp. 14 – 22

217 Sectoral clustering and growth in American metropolitan areas. Breandán Ó Huallacháin. *Reg. Stud.* **25:5** 10:1991 pp. 411 – 426

218 Site value taxation in a declining city. P.S. Kochanowski. *Am. J. Econ. S.* **50:1** 1:1991 pp. 45 – 58

219 Spatial disparities of urban socio-economic development in the People's Republic of China. Y. Xie; A. K. Dutt. *Geoforum* **22:1** :1991 pp. 55 – 67

220 The spatial mismatch hypothesis — what has the evidence shown? Harry J. Holzer. *Urban Stud.* **28:1** 2:1991 pp. 105 – 122

221 Spatial orientation and the angularity of urban routes — a field study. Daniel R. Montello. *Envir. Behav.* **23:1** 1:1991 pp. 47 – 69

222 Spatial transformation in cities of the developing world — multinucleation and land-capital substitution in Bogotá, Colombia. D.E. Dowall; P.A. Treffeisen. *Reg. Sci. Urb. Econ.* **21:2** 7:1991 pp. 201 – 254

223 Studying inner-city social dislocations — the challenge of public agenda research. William Julius Wilson. *Am. Sociol. R.* **56:1** 2:1991 pp. 1 – 14

224 Symptoms, survival, and the redefinition of public space — a feasibility study of homeless people in a metropolitan airport. Kim Hopper. *Urban Anthro.* **20:2** Summer:1991 pp. 155 – 176

225 Urban children's access to their neighborhood — changes over three generations. Sanford Gaster. *Envir. Behav.* **23:1** 1:1991 pp. 70 – 85

226 The watta-dwellers — a sociological study of selected urban low-income communities in Sri Lanka. Kalinga Tudor Silva; Karunatissa Athukorala *[Ed.]*. Lanham, Md: University Press of America, c1991: xv, 223 p. (ill., 11 maps) *ISBN: 0819181064; LofC: 90024260.* *Includes bibliographical references (p. 205-218) and index.*

227 Die Weltstadt zwischen globaler Gesellschaft und Lokalitäten *[In German]*; The world city between global society and localities *[Summary]*. Rüdiger Korff. *Z. Soziol.* **20:5** 10:1991 pp. 357 – 368

Urban planning and development *[Aménagement et développement urbain]*

228 Aesthetics in US planning — from billboards to design controls. J. Barry Cullingworth. *Town Plan. R.* **62:4** 10:1991 pp. 399 – 413

229 America's downtowns — growth, politics & preservation. Richard C. Collins; Elizabeth B. Waters; Anthony Bruce Dotson; Constance Epton Beaumont *[Ed.]*. Washington, D.C: Preservation Press, c1991: 159 p. (ill) *ISBN: 0891331778; LofC: 90048661.*

G.3.2: Urban sociology *[Sociologie urbaine]* — **Urban planning and development** *[Aménagement et développement urbain]*

230 Analyzing urban decentralization — the case of Houston. P. Mieszkowski; B. Smith. *Reg. Sci. Urb. Econ.* **21:2** 7:1991 pp. 183 – 200

231 Application of new town concepts in developing countries — the case of Abu Nuseir, Amman. Magdy Tewfik. *Ekistics* **58:346/ 347** 1/2-3/4:1991 pp. 42 – 49

232 Asi camina lo urbano — el derrotero. Ciudad y tecnologiá en el postmodernismo *[In Spanish]*; [The way of the city — a plan of action. Cities and technology in postmodernism]. Ester Limonad. *Rev. Int.Am. Plan.* **XXIV:95** 7-9:1991 pp. 96 – 115

233 Asian urban development policies in the 1990s — from growth control to urban diffusion. D.A. Rondinelli. *World Dev.* **19:7** 7:1991 pp. 791 – 804

234 The blind men and the elephant — the explanation of gentrification. Chris Hamnett. *Trans. Inst. Br. Geogr.* **16:2** 1991 pp. 173 – 189

235 The booming towns studies — methodological issues. A.E. Green; A.G. Champion. *Envir. Plan.A.* **23:10** 10:1991 pp. 1393 – 1408

236 British town planning education — a comparative perspective. Austín Rodríguez-Bachiller. *Town Plan. R.* **62:4** 10:1991 pp. 431 – 445

237 Canadian cities in transition. Trudi E Bunting *[Ed.]*; Pierre Filion *[Ed.]* Toronto: Oxford University Press, 1991: 553 p. (ill) *ISBN: 0195407946; LofC: cn 91093347. Includes bibliographical references and index.*

238 The Canadian city. Kent Gerecke *[Ed.]*. Montréal: Black Rose Books, 1991: 268 p. *ISBN: 0921689934; LofC: cn 91090086.*

239 Capital restructuring and the new built environment of global cities — New York and Los Angeles. Robert A. Beauregard. *Int. J. Urban* **15:1** 3:1991 pp. 90 – 105

240 Causes and consequences of the changing urban form. H.F. Ladd *[Contrib.]*; W. Wheaton *[Contrib.]*; G. Giuliano *[Contrib.]*; K.A. Small *[Contrib.]*; P. Mieszkowski *[Contrib.]*; B. Smith *[Contrib.]*; D.E. Dowall *[Contrib.]*; P.A. Treffeisen *[Contrib.]*; V. Shukla *[Contrib.]*; P. Waddell *[Contrib.]* and others. Collection of 7 articles. **Reg. Sci. Urb. Econ.** , *21:2,* 7:1991 pp. 157 – 315

241 Challenging uneven development — an urban agenda for the 1990s. Philip W. Nyden *[Ed.]*; Wim Wiewel *[Ed.]*. New Brunswick, N.J: Rutgers University Press, c1991: xii, 233 p. *ISBN: 0813516587; LofC: 90045221 //r92. Includes bibliographical references and index.*

242 Changing roles and positions of planners. Louis Albrechts. *Urban Stud.* **28:1** 2:1991 pp. 123 – 137

243 China's city hierarchy, urban policy and spatial development in the 1980s. Xiangming Chen. *Urban Stud.* **28:3** 6:1991 pp. 341 – 367

244 Cities and people — towards a gender-aware urban planning process? C. Rakodi. *Publ. Adm. D.* **11:6** 11-12:1991 pp. 541 – 559

245 Cities in transition — the regeneration of Britain's inner cities. Michael Middleton. London: Michael Joseph, 1991: 336 p. *ISBN: 0718132424.*

246 Cities of the 21st century — new technologies and spatial systems. John F. Brotchie *[Ed.]*; et al. Melbourne, Australia: Longman Cheshire, 1991: xiii, 446 p. (ill) *ISBN: 0582871263; LofC: 91000187. Includes bibliographical references (pp. [397]-429) and index.*

247 City development and planning in the Berlin conurbation — current situation and future perspectives. Dieter Frick. *Town Plan. R.* **62:1** 1:1991 pp. 37 – 49

248 Ciudad and ciudadanía. Metrópolis del subdesarrollo industrializado *[In Spanish]*; [The city and citizens. The metropolis of industrialized underdevelopment]. Lúcio Kowarick. *Nueva Soc.* **:114** 7-8:1991 pp. 84 – 93

249 A computer package to facilitate inhabitants' participation in urban renewal; *[French summary]*. A. Dupagne. *Envir. Plan. B.* **18:1** 1:1991 pp. 119 – 134

250 Computers in the modelling and simulation of urban built form. E. Rubio Royo *[Contrib.]*; J.M. Padron Hdez *[Contrib.]*; J.A. Montiel Nelson *[Contrib.]*; P. Marabelli *[Contrib.]*; A. Polistina *[Contrib.]*; R. Verona *[Contrib.]*; C. Cicconetti *[Contrib.]*; E. Gasparini *[Contrib.]*; M. Mastretta *[Contrib.]*; E. Morten *[Contrib.]* and others. Collection of 14 articles. **Envir. Plan. B.** , *18:1,* 1:1991 pp. 1 – 134

251 The context of urban planning in secondary cities — examples from Andean Ecuador. Stella Lowder. *Cities* **8:1** 2:1991 pp. 54 – 65

252 Customer service — a new philosophy towards effective city planning. Bruce McClendon. *J. Am. Plann.* **57:2** Spring:1991 pp. 205 – 211

253 Desarrollo metropolitano y democratización en Santiago *[In Spanish]*; [Metropolitan development and democratization in Santiago]. Andres Necochea. *Rev. Int.Am. Plan.* **XXIV:96** 10-12:1991 pp. 42 – 63

G.3.2: Urban sociology *[Sociologie urbaine]* — Urban planning and development *[Aménagement et développement urbain]*

254 Developing the capacity for urban management in Africa — the technical assistance and training approach to urban development. Richard Martin. *Cities* **8:2** 5:1991 pp. 134 – 141

255 The development of the small town and China's modernization. Ma Rong. *Soc. Sci. China* **XII:1** 3:1991 pp. 90 – 113

256 Development of urban management capacities — training for integrated urban infrastructure development in Indonesia. Parulian Sidabutar; Nana Rukmana; der van Hoff; Florian Steinberg. *Cities* **8:2** 5:1991 pp. 142 – 150

257 Downtown plans of the 1980s — the case for more equity in the 1990s. W. Dennis Keating; Norman Krumholz. *J. Am. Plann.* **57:2** Spring:1991 pp. 136 – 152

258 Energy and urban development in an archetypal English town. P.A. Rickaby. *Envir. Plan. B.* **18:(2)** 4:1991 pp. 153 – 175

259 Establishing a Zionist metropolis — alternative approaches to building Tel-Aviv. S. Ilan Troen. *J. Urban Hist.* **18:1** 11:1991 pp. 10 – 36

260 An evaluation of socially responsive planning in a new resource town. Alison M. Gill. *Soc. Ind.* **24:2** 3:1991 pp. 177 – 204

261 A fistful of dollars — legitimation, production and debate in Hong Kong; *[French summary]*. Alexander R. Cuthbert. *Int. J. Urban* **15:2** 6:1991 pp. 234 – 249

262 For a few dollars more — urban planning and the legitimation process in Hong Kong; *[French summary]*. Alexander R. Cuthbert. *Int. J. Urban* **15:4** 12:1991 pp. 575 – 593

263 A framework for speculating about future urban growth patterns in the US. Benjamin Chinitz. *Urban Stud.* **28:6** 12:1991 pp. 939 – 959

264 Gearing up for effective management of urban development. Forbes Davidson. *Cities* **8:2** 5:1991 pp. 120 – 133

265 Gender, migration and urban development in Costa Rica — the case of Guanacaste. S. Chant. *Geoforum* **22:3** 1991 pp. 237 – 254

266 The gentrification-social structure dialectic — a Toronto case study; *[French summary]*. Pierre Filion. *Int. J. Urban* **15:4** 12:1991 pp. 553 – 574

267 Gesundheit, Stadtplanung und Modernisierung *[In German]*; Public health, urban planning, and modernization *[Summary]*; Santé, aménagement urbain et modernisation *[French summary]*. Marianne Rodenstein. *Arc. Kommunal.* **30:1** 1991 pp. 47 – 63

268 GIS and their role in urban development. Peter F. Dale. *Cities* **8:1** 2:1991 pp. 10 – 16

269 GIS and urban management. Morris Juppenlatz *[Contrib.]*; Peter F. Dale *[Contrib.]*; Theo Bogaerts *[Contrib.]*; Rebecca Somers *[Contrib.]*. *Collection of articles.* **Cities** , *8:1, 2*:1991 pp. 2 – 32

270 Großbritannien. Aspekte der Wirtschafts- , Regional- und Stadtentwicklung in der Thatcher-Ära *[In German]*; [Great Britain. Aspects of economic, regional and urban development in the Thatcher era]. Heinz Heineberg. *Geogr. Rund.* **43:1** 1:1991 pp. 4 – 13

271 Impact fees, exlusionary zoning, and the density of new development. Joseph Gyourko. *J. Urban Ec.* **30:2** 9:1991 pp. 242 – 256

272 Industrial change and regional development — the transformation of new industrial spaces. Georges Benko *[Ed.]*; Michael Dunford *[Ed.]*. London: Belhaven Press, 1991: 329 p. *ISBN: 1852931205; LofC: 90024902. Revised papers, chiefly translations from French, German, and Italian, originally presented at a conference held Mar. 21-22, 1984, at the University of Paris I--Panthéon-Sorbonne; Includes bibliographical references and index.*

273 Land reclamation — an end to dereliction? M. C. R. Davies *[Ed.]*. London: Elsevier Applied Science, 1991: 422 p. *ISBN: 1851666583. Urban planning and development.*

274 *[In Japanese]*; [Local urban renewal and resident's responses in inner city area — the case of Mano, Kobe City]. Hiroaki Konno. **Memoires of College of Education, Akita University** *No.(42) - 1991.* pp. 113 – 130

275 The London Docklands Development Corporation (LDDC), 1981-1991 — a perspective on the management of urban regeneration. Taner Oc; Steven Tiesdell. *Town Plan. R.* **62:3** 7:1991 pp. 311 – 330

276 London. Positive und negative Entwicklungstendenzen *[In German]*; [London. Positive and negative trends in development]. Wolf Gaebe; John Hall. *Geogr. Rund.* **43:1** 1:1991 pp. 14 – 20

277 A Markov chain model of zoning change. Daniel P. McMillen; John F. Mcdonald. *J. Urban Ec.* **30:2** 9:1991 pp. 257 – 270

278 *[In Japanese]*; [Metropolitan redevelopment for the city dwellers]. Kohzo Iwao. **International Management Review, Kanagawa University** *No.(2) - 1991.* pp. 97 – 124

G.3.2: Urban sociology [Sociologie urbaine] — Urban planning and development [Aménagement et développement urbain]

279 Modernism and the vernacular — transformation of public spaces and social life in Singapore. Beng-Huat Chua. *J. Arch. Plan. Res.* **8:3** Autumn:1991 pp. 203 – 221

280 Modernizing the Brazilian city. Brian J. Godfrey. *Geogr. Rev.* **81:1** 1:1991 pp. 18 – 34

281 The myth of the master builder — Robert Moses, New York, and the dynamics of metropolitan development since World War II. Leonard Wallock. *J. Urban Hist.* **17:4** 8:1991 pp. 339 – 362

282 Native and newcomer — making and remaking a Japanese city. Jennifer Ellen Robertson. Berkeley: University of California Press, c1991: xvii, 235 p. (ill., maps) *ISBN: 0520072960; LofC: 90027918 //r91. Includes bibliographical references (pp. 215-226) and index.*

283 Neighbourhood regeneration — an international evaluation. Rachelle Alterman *[Ed.]*; Göran Cars *[Ed.]*. London: Mansell, 1991: 230 p. (ill) *ISBN: 072012073x. Includes index.*

284 Our changing cities. John Fraser Hart *[Ed.]*. Baltimore: Johns Hopkins University Press, c1991: xv, 261 p. (ill) *ISBN: 0801840872; LofC: 91009226. Includes bibliographical references and index.*

285 Out of site — a social criticism of architecture. Diane Ghirardo *[Ed.]* Seattle: Bay Press, 1991: 251 p. (ill) *ISBN: 0941920208; LofC: 90048948. Includes bibliographical references.*

286 Overview of Kenya's urban development policy. M. Kiamba. *R. Rur. Urb. Plan. S.& E.Afr.* **:1** 1991 pp. 93 – 100

287 Pededstrian streets in Sweden's city centres. Kent A. Robertson. *Cities* **8:4** 11:1991 pp. 301 – 314

288 A planimetric model of Milan's urban master plan; *[French summary]*. P. Marabelli; A. Polistina; R. Verona. *Envir. Plan. B.* **18:1** 1:1991 pp. 7 – 18

289 Planning and development of industrial estates in Singapore. Belinda Yuen. *Third Wor. P.* **13:1** 2:1991 pp. 47 – 68

290 Planning appeals — a critique. Michael Purdue. Milton Keynes, England: Open University Press, 1991: 66 p. *ISBN: 0335096301; LofC: 91013347. Includes index.* [Studies in law and politics.]

291 Planning Belfast — a case study of public policy and community action. Tim Blackman. Aldershot: Avebury, c1991: ix, 234 p. *ISBN: 1856281825; LofC: gb 91035504. Includes index; Bibliography — p.. 222-229.*

292 Planning for a change in Belfast — the urban economy, urban regeneration and the Belfast Urban Area Plan 1988. F. Gaffikin; S. Mooney; M. Morrissey. *Town Plan. R.* **62:4** 10:1991 pp. 415 – 430

293 Planning for serfdom — legal economic discourse and downtown development. Robin Paul Malloy. Philadelphia: University of Pennsylvania Press, c1991: xi, 183 p. *ISBN: 0812230558; LofC: 90029188. Includes bibliographical references (p. [143]-180) and index.*

294 Planning inquiries — a socio-legal study. Tim Blackman. *Sociology* **25:2** 5:1991 pp. 311 – 327

295 Política regional y urbana en Chile *[In Spanish]*; [Regional and urban policy in Chile]. Juan Braun L.. Santiago: Pontificia Universidad Católica de Chile, Instituto de Economía, Oficina de Publicaciones, 1990: 33 leaves (ill) *BNB: 91140831; LofC: 91140831. Includes bibliographical references.* [Documento de trabajo.]

296 Politics and representation in Melbourne slum clearance. S.E. Morrissey. *Mel. J. Pol.* **20** 1991 pp. 68 – 85

297 Popular music and urban regeneration — the music industries of Merseyside. Sara Cohen. *Cult. St.* **5:3** 10:1991 pp. 332 – 346

298 El proceso de desconcentración — una alternativa de desarrollo de las ciudades medianas y pequeñas *[In Spanish]*; [The decentralization process — alternative development in medium and small cities]. Miroslawa Czerny. *Rev. Int.Am. Plan.* **XXIV:93** 1-3:1991 pp. 61 – 72

299 Public and private responses to hypergrowth in Third World metropolitan areas. Samuel V. Noe. *Third Wor. P.* **13:3** 8:1991 pp. 217 – 236

300 Public/private partnership schemes in UK urban regeneration — the role of joint enabling agencies. Tony Gore. *Cities* **8:3** 8:1991 pp. 209 – 216

301 *[In Japanese]*; [The real phase of internationalization and its development in a local city]. Kaname Tsutumi-Yoshida. *Soc. Anal. No.(19) - 1991.* pp. 227 – 258

G.3.2: Urban sociology *[Sociologie urbaine]* — *Urban planning and development [Aménagement et développement urbain]*

302 Recycling urban systems and metropolitan areas — a geographical agenda for the 1990s and beyond. L.S. Bourne. *Econ. Geogr.* **67:3** 7:1991 pp. 185 – 209

303 Reflections on neighbourhood decentralization in Tower Hamlets. Gerry Stoker *[Ed.]*; Sean Baine; Susan Carlyle; Steve Charters; Tony Du Sautoy. *Publ. Admin.* **69** Autumn:1991 pp. 373 – 384

304 Researching planning practice. Patsy Healey. *Town Plan. R.* **62:4** 10:1991 pp. 447 – 459

305 The rise of the industrial metropolis — the myth and the reality. David R. Meyer. *Soc. Forc.* **68:3** 3:1990 pp. 731 – 752

306 Some effects of urbanism on black networks. Zhong Deng; Phillip Bonacich. *Soc. Networks* **13:1** 3:1991 pp. 35 – 50

307 Spatial disparities of urban socio-economic development in the People's Republic of China. Y. Xie; A. K. Dutt. *Geoforum* **22:1** :1991 pp. 55 – 67

308 A stochastic model of the propagation of local fire fronts in New York City — implications for public policy. R. Wallace. *Envir. Plan.A.* **23:5** 1991 pp. 651 – 662

309 Strategic planning and urban restructuring — the case of Pyrmont-Ultimo. Morgan Sant; Susan Jackson. *Aust. Geogr.* **22:2** 11:1991 pp. 136 – 146

310 Street geometry and flows. Sandra L. Arlinghaus; John D. Nystuen. *Geogr. Rev.* **81:2** 4:1991 pp. 206 – 214

311 The study of power mechanisms — an interactive and generative approach to a case study of Swedish urban renewal. M. Ekström; B. Danermark. *Scand. Hous. Plan. R.* **8:3** 1991 pp. 153 – 170

312 Telecity — information technology and its impact on city form. Tarik A. Fathy. New York: Praeger, 1991: xiv, 155 p. (ill) *ISBN: 027593814x; LofC: 91000443. Includes bibliographical references (p. [133]-152) and index.*

313 Telford — the making of Shropshire's new town. Maurice De Soissons. Shrewsbury: Swan Hill, 1991: 208 p. *ISBN: 1853102539.*

314 Town planning responses to city change. Vincent Nadin *[Ed.]*; Joe Doak *[Ed.]*. Aldershot: Avebury, 1991: 238 p. (ill) *ISBN: 1856281612. Includes bibliography.*

315 Traffic calming policy and performance — the Netherlands, Denmark and Germany. Tim M. Pharoah; John R.E. Russell. *Town Plan. R.* **62:1** 1:1991 pp. 79 – 105

316 Traffic growth — the problems and the solutions. Stephen Joseph. *J. Law Soc.* **18:1** Spring:1991 pp. 126 – 134

317 Transit joint development in the USA — an inventory and policy assessment. J. Landis; R. Cervero; P. Hall. *Envir. Plan. C.* **9:4** 11:1991 pp. 431 – 452

318 Urban design practice in socialist China. Yichun Xie; Frank J. Costa. *Third Wor. P.* **13:3** 8:1991 pp. 277 – 296

319 Urban environment — expert contributions. Commission of the European Communities. Luxembourg: Office for Official Publications of the European Communities, 1991: 92 p. *ISBN: 9282618005. Catalogue no. — CD-NA-13145-EN-C; "1990"--t.p.; Directorate-General Environment, Nuclear Safety and Civil Protection.* [EUR. : No. 13145]

320 Urban growth coalitions and urban development policy — postwar growth and the politics of annexation in metropolitan Columbus. Andrew E.G. Jonas. *Urban Geogr.* **12:3** 5-6:1991 pp. 197 – 225

321 Urban growth in India — demographic and sociocultural prospects. Jay Weinstein. *Stud. Comp. ID.* **26:4** Winter:1991-92 pp. 29 – 44

322 Urban growth management in Jeddah. A.-M.I. Daghistani. *Plan. Out.* **34:1** 1991 pp. 3 – 9

323 Urban industrial reform in China — problems and prospects. Roger F. Riefler. *Int. Reg. Sci. R.* **14:1** 1991 pp. 95 – 107

324 Urban management in developing countries — a critical role. Giles Clarke. *Cities* **8:2** 5:1991 pp. 93 – 107

325 Urban management in the Third World — developing the capacity. Forbes Davidson *[Ed.]*; Peter Nientied *[Ed.]*; Mirjam Zaaijer *[Contrib.]*; Giles Clarke *[Contrib.]*; Maria Clara Echeverria *[Contrib.]*; Richard Martin *[Contrib.]*; Parulian Sidabutar *[Contrib.]*; Nana Rukmana *[Contrib.]*; Robert van der Hoff *[Contrib.]*; Florian Steinberg *[Contrib.] and others. Collection of 6 articles.* **Cities** , *8:2,* 5:1991 pp. 82 – 150

326 Urban networking in Europe — I — concepts, intentions and new realities. Yannis N. Pyrgiotis *[Contrib.]*; Jean Gottmann *[Contrib.]*; Klaus R. Kunzmann *[Contrib.]*; Michael Wegener *[Contrib.]*; Alain Sallez *[Contrib.]*; Pierre Verot *[Contrib.]*; Michael Parkinson

G.3.2: **Urban sociology** *[Sociologie urbaine]* — *Urban planning and development [Aménagement et développement urbain]*
[Contrib.]; Georges Mercadal [Contrib.]; Sergio Conti [Contrib.]; Giorgio Spriano [Contrib.] *and others*. Collection of 15 articles. **Ekistics** , *58:350/351*, 9/10-11/12:1991 pp. 272 – 381

327 Urban participation in Caracas — an unbalanced encounter. Giulietta Fadda. *Third Wor. P.* **13:4** 11:1991 pp. 319 – 334

328 Urban redevelopment of greenbelt-area villages — a case study of Seoul, Korea. Kim Joochul. *B. Concern. Asia. Schol.* **23:2** 4-6:1991 pp. 20 – 29

329 Urban reform in Colombia — a tool for democratic development? Maria Clara Echeverria. *Cities* **8:2** 5:1991 pp. 108 – 119

330 Urban regeneration and the development industry. Patsy Healey. *Reg. Stud.* **25:2** 4:1991 pp. 97 – 110

331 Urban renewal planning versus local values — a study of modern urban policy and renewal processes and of their impact on a local community — with reference to the case of Gröna Gatan in Göteborg. A. Reza Kazemian. Göteborg, Sweden: Chalmers University of Technology, School of Architecture, Department of Design Methodology, 1991: 226 p. (ill) *ISBN: 9170325626. Includes bibliographical references (p. [212]-226).*

332 Urban renewal — the case of Buffalo, NY. Alfred D. Price. *Rev. Bl. Pol. Ec.* **19:3-4** Winter/Spring:1991 pp. 125 – 160

333 US urban policy evaluation in the 1980s — lessons from practice. D. Hart. *Reg. Stud.* **25:3** 6:1991 pp. 255 – 260

334 The use of central place theory in Kenya's development strategies. Roddy Fox. *J. Econ. Soc. Geogr.* **82:2** 1991 pp. 106 – 127

Urbanization *[Urbanisation]*

335 Aspects of urbanization. Chris Mathieu. Maseru: Physical Planning Division, Department of Lands, Surveys and Physical Planning, 1990: 111 p. (ill., maps) [National settlement policy working paper. : No. 12]

336 Black suburbanization — has it changed the relative location of races? George C. Galster. *Urban Aff. Q.* **26:4** 6:1991 pp. 621 – 628

337 Characteristics and patterns of urbanisation in Algeria. Kaddour Boukhemis; Anissa Zeghiche. *Orient* **32:1** 1991 pp. 45 – 58

338 Chinese urban reform — what model now? R. Yin-Wang Kwok *[Ed.]*; Grant Blank *[Ed.]*. Armonk, N.Y: M.E. Sharpe, c1990: xii, 258 p. (ill) *ISBN: 0873325893; LofC: 89024315. "An East gate book."; Based on a 1987 conference on urban development at the Centre for Urban Planning and Development at Hong Kong University; Includes bibliographical references (p. 243-254) and index.* [Studies on contemporary China.]

339 Cities and development in the Third World. Robert B. Potter *[Ed.]*; A. T. Salau *[Ed.]*. London: Mansell in association with the Commonwealth Foundation, 1991: 200 p. (ill) *ISBN: 0720120667. Includes index.*

340 Un département de la périphérie parisienne en voie de périurbanisation — la Seine-et-Marne *[In French]*; A department of the Paris periphery in the process of periurbanization — the Seine-et-Marne *[Summary]*. J. Steinberg. *Espace Pop. Soc.* **:2** 1991 pp. 283 – 291

341 The differentiation of the urbanization process under apartheid. J. May; S. Rankin. *World Dev.* **19:10** 10:1991 pp. 1351 – 1365

342 Dimensions of urban growth in Pakistan. M. Framurz Kiani; H.B. Siyal. *Pak. Dev. R.* **30:4** Winter:1991 pp. 681 – 691

343 The extended metropolis — settlement transition in Asia. Norton Ginsburg *[Ed.]*; Bruce Koppel *[Ed.]*; T. G. McGee *[Ed.]*. Honolulu: University of Hawaii Press, c1991: xviii, 339 p. (ill., maps) *ISBN: 0824812972; LofC: 90046252. Papers from a conference held Sept. 1988 under the auspices of the Environment and Policy Institute of the East-West Center; Includes bibliographical references and index.*

344 Italian urban geography — counterurbanization versus peripheral development. Calogero Muscarà. *Urban Geogr.* **12:4** 7-8:1991 pp. 363 – 380

345 Lagos — the city is the people. Margaret Peil. London: Belhaven, 1991: 213 p. (ill) *ISBN: 1852931035. Includes bibliography and index.* [World cities series.]

346 The Mediterranean city in transition — social change and urban development. Lila Leontidou. Cambridge: Cambridge University Press, 1990: 296 p. (ill) *ISBN: 0521344670. Includes bibliography and index.* [Cambridge human geography.]

G.3.2: Urban sociology *[Sociologie urbaine]* — Urbanization *[Urbanisation]*

347 The new suburbanization — challenge to the central city. Thomas M. Stanback. Boulder: Westview Press, 1991: xv, 126 p. *ISBN: 0813380510; LofC: 90039827. Includes bibliographical references and index.* [The Eisenhower Center for the Conservation of Human Resources studies in the new economy.]

348 The new urban frontier — urbanisation and city building in Australasia and the American West. Lionel Frost. Randwick,NSW: New South Wales University Press, 1991: 226 p. *ISBN: 0868402680.*

349 The pace of Indian urbanization. Vibhooti Shukla; Brian J.L. Berry. *Geogr. Anal.* **23**:3 8:1991 pp. 185 – 209

350 The political urbanization fringe development in Copenhagen; Politique et évolution de l'urbanisation dans la banlieue de Copenhague *[French summary]*. H.T. Anderson. *Espace Pop. Soc.* :**2** 1991 pp. 367 – 379

351 Rural-to-urban transition and the division of labor — evidence from Saudi Arabia. W. Parker Frisbie; Abdullah H.M. Al-Khalifah. *Rural Sociol.* **56**:4 Winter:1991 pp. 646 – 659

352 Services and metropolitan development. P. W. Daniels *[Ed.]*. London: Routledge, 1991: 331 p. *ISBN: 0415008522. Includes bibliography and index.*

353 Some aspects of urbanization and the environment in southeast Asia. Ernesto M. Pernia. Manila: Asian Development Bank, 1991: 27 p. [Economics and Development Resource Center report series. : No. 54]

354 The suburbanization in the USSR — case analysis by taking the example the Moscow region; La suburbanisation en URSS — analyse du problème d'après l'exemple de la région de Moscou *[French summary]*. G.A. Gornostayeva. *Espace Pop. Soc.* :**2** 1991 pp. 349 – 357

355 Third World urbanization — reappraisals and new perspectives. Satya Brata Datta. Stockholm: Swedish Council for Research in the Humanities and Social Sciences, 1990: 282 p. [Urban studies.]

356 Tourism urbanization; *[French summary]*. Patrick Mullins. *Int. J. Urban* **15**:3 9:1991 pp. 326 – 342

357 Urban and regional planning of Nigeria. Ademola T. Salau *[Ed.]*; K.P. Moseley *[Contrib.]*; J.I. Ighalo *[Contrib.]*; I.A. Animashaun *[Contrib.]*; Layi Egunjobi *[Contrib.]*; S.I. Abumere *[Contrib.]*; W.J. Okowa *[Contrib.]*; Tunde Agbola *[Contrib.]*; C.O. Olatubara *[Contrib.]*; Tade Akin Aina *[Contrib.] and others. Collection of 13 articles.* **Afr. Urb. Q.** , *4:1-2*, 1-5:1989 pp. 1 – 144

358 Urbanisation in China. Zhang Xing Quan. *Urban Stud.* **28**:1 2:1991 pp. 41 – 51

359 Urbanización y cambios en las ciudades medianas del interior del estado de Sao Paulo, Brasil *[In Spanish]*; [Urbanization and change in medium sized cities in inland Sao Paulo state, Brazil]. Ma. Teresa Miceli Kervauy. *Rev. Int.Am. Plan.* **XXIV**:93 1-3:1991 pp. 33 – 44

360 Urbanization and development in sub-Saharan Africa. M. Lang; M. Kamiar. *R. Rur. Urb. Plan. S.& E.Afr.* :**1** 1991 pp. 57 – 82

361 Urbanization and regional disparities in post-revolutionary Iran. Ahmad Sharbatoghlie. Boulder: Westview Press, 1991: xvii, 235 p. (ill., maps) *ISBN: 0813383587; LofC: 91012672. Includes bibliographical references (p. [217]-227) and index.*

362 Urbanization and urban change in Southern Africa region with special emphasis on the Republic of South Africa. C.M. Rogerson *[Ed.]*; Gibson O. Aduwo *[Contrib.]*; R.A. Obudho *[Contrib.]*; A.C. Mosha *[Contrib.]*; William F. Banyikwa *[Contrib.]*; J.R.N. Mlia *[Contrib.]*; Ben M. Kaluwa *[Contrib.]*; Mpanjilwa P. Mulwanda *[Contrib.]*; I.J. Van Der Merwe *[Contrib.]*; H.S. Geyer *[Contrib.] and others. Collection of 15 articles.* **Afr. Urb. Q.** , *4:3-4*, 8-11:1989 pp. 207 – 348

363 Urbanization and urban water problems in Southeast Asia — a case of unsustainable development. K.S. Low; G. Balamurugan. *J. Environ. Manag.* **32**:3 4:1991 pp. 195 – 210

364 Urbanization dynamics in the eastern Caribbean — focus on the Windward Islands. Len Ishmael. *Cities* **8**:3 8:1991 pp. 174 – 192

365 Urbanization in South Africa — priorities for the 1990s. Gina Saayman; Heston Phillips *[Ed.]*; Pieter C. Kok *[Ed.]*. Pretoria: Human Sciences Research Council, 1991: 40 p. *ISBN: 0796909326.* [Report.]

366 Urbanization in the Hong Kong-South China region. Jeffrey Henderson *[Ed.]*; Jonathan R. Schiffer *[Contrib.]*; Leslie Sklair *[Contrib.]*; Josephine Smart *[Contrib.]*; Alan Smart *[Contrib.]*; Alexander R. Cuthbert *[Contrib.]*. *Collection of 5 articles.* **Int. J. Urban** , *15:2*, 6:1991 pp. 169 – 249

367 Urbanization issues in the Asian-Pacific region. Gavin W. Jones. *Asian-Pacific Ec. Lit.* **5**:2 9:1991 pp. 5 – 34

G.3.2: Urban sociology *[Sociologie urbaine]* — *Urbanization [Urbanisation]*
368 Urbanization policy — lessons from South America for South Africa. Vanessa Watson. *Soc. Dyn.* **17:2** 12:1991 pp. 155 – 167

H: Economic life — *Vie économique*

H.1: Economic sociology — *Sociologie économique*

1 Consumo versus trabajo en la teoría del valor económico *[In Spanish]*; [Consumption versus work in the theory of economic worth]. José Juan Franch Meneu. *Rev. Fom. Soc.* **46:181** 1-3:1991 pp. 37 – 44
2 Economic growth in East Asia and the Confucian ethic. Joseph A. Martellaro. *Asian Prof.* **19:1** 2:1991 pp. 81 – 90
3 Explaining Asian economic organization — toward a Weberian institutional perspective. Nicole Woolsey Biggart. *Theory Soc.* **20:2** 4:1991 pp. 199 – 232
4 History and economics. Hugh Rockoff. *Soc. Sci. Hist.* **15:2** Summer:1991 pp. 239 – 264
5 Schumpter on Schmoller and Weber — a methodology of economic sociology. Yuichi Shionoya. *Hist. Polit. Ec.* **23:2** Summer:1991 pp. 193 – 219

H.2: Economic systems — *Systèmes économiques*

1 American enterprise in Japan. Tomoko Hamada. Albany, N.Y: State University of New York Press, c1991: xi, 294 p. (ill) *ISBN: 0791406385; LofC: 90038186. Includes bibliographical references (p. 259-281) and index.* [SUNY series in the anthropology of work.]
2 The economic system and the work situation — a comparison of Finland and Estonia; Systémé économique et situation de travail — une comparaison entre la Finlande et l'Estonie Sovietique *[French summary]*. Raimo Blom; Markku Kivinen; Harri Melin; Erkki Rannik. *Int. Sociol.* **6:3** 9:1991 pp. 343 – 360
3 The emerging Europe of the 1990s. Alexander B. Murphy. *Geogr. Rev.* **81:1** 1:1991 pp. 1 – 17
4 Los enfoques teóricos para la explicación de la economía informal y sus implancias socio-políticas *[In Spanish]*; [Theoretical approaches for explaining the informal economy and their socio-political implication]. H.C.F. Mansilla. *Rev. Parag. Sociol.* **28:80** 1-4:1991 pp. 115 – 130
5 Flexible specialization versus post-Fordism — theory, evidence and policy implications. Paul Hirst; Jonathan Zeitlin. *Econ. Soc.* **20:1** 2:1991 pp. 1 – 56
6 Fragmented societies — a sociology of economic life beyond the market paradigm. Enzo Mingione. Oxford: Basil Blackwell, 1991: 512 p. *ISBN: 0631163999. Includes bibliography and index.*
7 The free market in a republic. Ryszard Legutko. *Crit. Rev.* **5:1** Winter:1991 pp. 37 – 52
8 The free market is not readily transferable — reflection on the links between market, social relations, and moral norms. Jean-Philippe Platteau. Namur: Facultés Universitaires Notre-Dame de la Paix, 1991: 91 p. [Cahiers de la Faculté des Sciences Économiques et Sociales de Namur.]
9 From peasants to petty commodity producers — a theoretical debate. M. Giura-Longo. *Int. J. Moral Soc. S.* **6:1** Spring:1991 pp. 57 – 76
10 Gibt es eine befreiungstheologische Wirtschaftsethik? Beispiele aus der katholischen Kirche Mexikos *[In German]*; [Is there an economic ethic of liberation theology? Examples from the Catholic Church of Mexico]. Gerhard Kruip. *Jahr. Christ. Sozialwiss.* **31** 1990 pp. 156 – 178
11 Global capitalism — theories of societal development. Richard Peet. London: Routledge, 1991: 206 p. (ill) *ISBN: 0415013143. Includes bibliography and index.*
12 The humane economy — populism, capitalism, and democracy. Norman Pollack. New Brunswick [N.J.]: Rutgers University Press, c1990: xiv, 215 p. *ISBN: 0813515998; LofC: 90031078. Includes bibliographical references (p. [201]-207) and index.*
13 Jewish economics in the light of Maimonides. Walter Block. *Int. J. Soc. E.* **17:3** 1990 pp. 60 – 68

H.2: Economic systems [Systèmes économiques]

14 The new household economy. William James Booth. *Am. Poli. Sci.* **85:1** 3:1991 pp. 59 – 75
15 Ota Siks Mitarbeitergesellschaft und das ihr zugrundeliegende Menschenbild im Licht einer christlichen Sozialethik *[In German]*; [Ota Sik's co-operative and it's basic humanist conception in the light of a Christian social ethic]. Rafael Fernandes. *Jahr. Christ. Sozialwiss.* **31** 1990 pp. 115 – 135
16 The power axis — Bowles, Gordon and Weisskopf's theory of postwar US accumulation. Bruce Norton. *Soc. Scient.* **19:1-2** 1-2:1991 pp. 47 – 80
17 Problems of socialist development — the significance of Shenzhen special economic zone for China's open door development strategy; *[French summary]*. Leslie Sklair. *Int. J. Urban* **15:2** 6:1991 pp. 197 – 215
18 The social market economy in Germany and in Europe — principles and perspectives. Hubertus Dessloch. *Relig. Comm. Lands* **19:1-2** Summer:1991 pp. 112 – 118
19 Socio-economic security and insecurity in socialist and capitalist political economies — a survey study of two European cities. Roberta Garner; Larry Garner. *Sci. Soc.* **55:1** Spring:1991 pp. 5 – 25
20 Tax evasion — an experimental approach. Paul Webley *[Ed.]*. Cambridge: Cambridge University Press, 1991: 160 p. *ISBN: 0521374596. Includes index.* [European monographs in social psychology.]

H.3: Economic conditions and living standards — *Conditions économiques et niveau de vie*

Sub-divisions: Income *[Revenu]*

1 Les acteurs du développement local *[In French]*; [The actors of local development]. Odile Benoit-Guilbot *[Contrib.]*; Dominique Lorrain *[Contrib.]*; Soledad Garcia *[Contrib.]*; Patrick Le Galès *[Contrib.]*; Jean Saglio *[Contrib.]*. Collection of 5 articles. **Sociol. Trav.**, *XXXIII:4*, 1991 pp. 453 – 543
2 Amenities and regional differences in returns to worker characteristics. Patricia E. Beeson. *J. Urban Ec.* **30:2** 9:1991 pp. 224 – 241
3 Basisdaten für die Beschreibung und Analyse des sozio-ökonomishen Wandels der DDR *[In German]*; Basic data for the description and analysis of socio-economic change in the GDR *[Summary]*. Jürgen Schupp; Gert Wagner. *Kölner Z. Soz. Soz. psy.* **43:2** 1991 pp. 322 – 333
4 Belief in action — economic philosophy and social change. Eduardo Giannetti da Fonseca. Cambridge: Cambridge University Press, 1991: 256 p. *ISBN: 052139306x. Includes bibliography and index.*
5 Birth order, family size, and achievement — family structure and wage determination. Daniel Kessler. *J. Labor Ec.* **9:4** 10:1991 pp. 413 – 426
6 Children's living arrangements in developing countries. Cynthia B. Lloyd; Sonalde Desai. New York, N.Y: Population Council, 1991: 41 p. *ISBN: oc25066431. Includes bibliographical references (p. 37-41).*
7 Consumptieongelijkheid — consumptieve bestedingen als basis voor ongelijkheidsmeting in landenvergelijkend onderzoek *[In Dutch]*; Consumption inequality — consumer expenditure as a basis for measurement of inequality in cross-national studies *[Summary]*. Marcel van Dam; Gerbert Kraaykamp. *Acta Pol.* **XXVI** 1:1991 pp. 85 – 109
8 A contextual examination of the feminization of poverty. J.E. Kodras; J.P. Jones. *Geoforum* **22:2** 1991 pp. 159 – 172
9 Contrasts and commonalities — Hispanic and Anglo farming in Conejos County, Colorado. Paul Gutierrez; Jerry Eckert. *Rural Sociol.* **56:2** Summer:1991 pp. 247 – 263
10 Crisis y comercio domiciliario en México *[In Spanish]*; [Crisis and home trade in Mexico]. Fernando Cortés; Marcela Benites. *Est. Sociol.* **IX:25** 1-4:1991 pp. 165 – 187
11 A critique of the ZPG urban stress test — on the uses and misuses of social indicators. Edward G. Stockwell; Arthur G. Neal. *Soc. Ind.* **24:4** 6:1991 pp. 393 – 402
12 The culture of economic development. Augusto Graziani. *J. Reg. Pol.* **11:3-4** 7-12:1991 pp. 459 – 466
13 Developing human resources — quality of life. Meera Bapat. *Ind. J. Soc. Sci.* **4:4** 10-12:1991 pp. 503 – 520

H.3: Economic conditions and living standards [Conditions économiques et niveau de vie]

14 Development data constraints and the human development index. Christopher J. L. Murray. Geneva, Switzerland: United Nations Research Institute for Social Development, [1991]: iv, 25 p. (ill) *ISBN: oc25154779. "May 1991."; Includes bibliographical references (p. 21-25).* [Discussion paper.]
15 Does marriage really make men more productive? Sanders Korenman; David Neumark. *J. Hum. Res.* **XXVI:2** Spring:1991 pp. 282 – 307
16 Les écarts de loyer *[In French]*; Differences in rents *[Summary]*; Las disparidades de los alquilieres *[Spanish summary]*. Gérard Curci; Claude Taffin. *E & S* **:240** 2:1991 pp. 29 – 36
17 Economic development and African Americans in the Mississippi Delta. Phyllis A. Gray. *Rural Sociol.* **56:2** Summer:1991 pp. 238 – 246
18 Economic growth and popular well-being in Taiwan — a time series examination of some preliminary hypotheses. Steve Chan; Cal Clark. *West. Pol. Q.* **44:3** 9:1991 pp. 560 – 582
19 The economics of the family. Alessandro Cigno. Oxford: Clarendon Press, 1991: 212 p. *ISBN: 0198287097; LofC: 91006319.*
20 The effect of immigration on Australian living standards. John Nevile. Canberra: Australian Government Publishing Service, 1990: 24 p. *ISBN: 0644131861.*
21 The effects of international remittances on poverty, inequality, and development in rural Egypt. Richard H. Adams. Washington, D.C: International Food Policy Research Institute, c1991: 88 p. *ISBN: 0896290891; LofC: 91017816. Includes bibliographical references (p. 83-88).* [Research report. International Food Policy Research Institute.]
22 Families and inflation — who was hurt in the last high-inflation period? Joan Aldous; Rodney Ganey; Scott Trees; Lawrence C. Marsh. *J. Marriage Fam.* **53:1** 2:1991 pp. 123 – 134
23 The gap between market rewards and economic well-being in modern societies. Johan Fritzell. *Eur. Sociol. R.* **7:1** 5:1991 pp. 19 – 33
24 Household production, consumption and time allocation in Peru. John K. Dagsvik; Rolf Aaberge *[Ed.]*. Oslo: Central Bureau of Statistics, 1991: 54 p. *Bibliography — p54.* [Discussion paper.]
25 The IMF and the south — the social impact of crisis and adjustment. Dharam Ghai *[Ed.]*. London: Zed Books, c1991: 273 p. *ISBN: 0862329507; LofC: 90039961. Includes bibliographical references and index.*
26 The impact of metropolitan opportunity structure on the economic status of blacks and Hispanics in Newark. Anne M. Santiago; Margaret G. Wilder. *Urban Geogr.* **12:6** 11-12:1991 pp. 494 – 507
27 Industrial development and Arab-Jewish economic gaps in the Galilee region, Israel. Oren Yiftachel. *Prof. Geogr.* **43:2** 5:1991 pp. 163 – 179
28 Inequality in distributions of hours of work and consumption in Peru. Rolf Aaberge; John K. Dagsvik *[Ed.]*. Oslo: Central Bureau of Statistics, 1991: 41 p. *Bibliography — p41.* [Discussion paper.]
29 La inflación y los pactos sociales en Brasil y en México *[In Spanish]*; [Inflation and social contracts in Brazil and Mexico]. Ian Roxborough. *Foro Int.* **XXXII:2** 10-12:1991 pp. 165 – 198
30 Living in anonymity — conditions of life in the hostels of Cape Town. Julia Segar. *S.Afr. Sociol. R.* **3:2** 4:1991 pp. 40 – 61
31 Measurement and determinants of socioeconomic development — a critical conspectus. Habibullah Khan. *Soc. Ind.* **24:2** 3:1991 pp. 153 – 175
32 Measures and meaning in comparisons of wealth equality. Courtland L. Smith. *Soc. Ind.* **24:4** 6:1991 pp. 367 – 392
33 Measuring living standards using existing national data sets. Sandra Hutton. *J. Soc. Pol.* **20:2** 4:1991 pp. 237 – 258
34 Measuring the quality of life across countries — a multidimensional analysis. Daniel Slottje *[Ed.]*. Boulder: Westview Press, 1991: ix, 278 p. (ill., maps) *ISBN: 0813312361; LofC: 91010213. Includes bibliographical references (p. 275-278).*
35 Non-employed women, marriage and the sisyphus syndrome. Julia A. Heath. *J. Econ. Iss.* **XXIV:1** 3:1990 pp. 103 – 114
36 Perceptions of poverty. Eileen Evason. *Soc. Attit. N.Ire.* 1990-1991 pp. 62 – 73
37 Переход к рынку в зеркале общественного мнения *[In Russian]*; (The transition to the market in the mirror of social opinion). E.M. Babosov. *Sot. Issle.* **:4** 1991 pp. 25 – 33
38 The persistence of the black farmer — the contemporary relevance of the Lenin-Chayanov debate. Michael D. Schulman; Barbara A. Newman. *Rural Sociol.* **56:2** Summer:1991 pp. 264 – 283

H.3: Economic conditions and living standards [Conditions économiques et niveau de vie]

39 Personal relations and divergent economies — a case study of Hong Kong investment in South China; [French summary]. Josephine Smart; Alan Smart. *Int. J. Urban* **15:2** 6:1991 pp. 216 – 233
40 Pessimistic rumination in popular songs and news magazines predict economic recession via decreased consumer optimism and spending. H.M. Zullow. *J. Econ. Psyc.* **12:3** 9:1991 pp. 501 – 526
41 Promoting economic development. Gary P. Green; Arnold Fleischmann. *Urban Aff. Q.* **27:1** 9:1991 pp. 145 – 154
42 Quality of life in rural areas with special reference to Korea and some developing countries. In Keun Wang. *Korea Obs.* **XXII:1** Spring:1991 pp. 75 – 138
43 La recomposition du salariat, vers la fin du ghetto ouvrier? *[In French]*; The recomposition of wage-earning at the end of the workers ghetto *[Summary]*. Jean Lojkine. *Pensée* **:284** 11-12:1991 pp. 5 – 28
44 Regional inequalities in France. D. Ian Scargill. *Geography* **76:4** 10:1991 p. 343
45 Regional well-being in Australia revisited. T. Sorensen; H. Weinand. *Aust. Geogr. Stud.* **29:1** 4:1991 pp. 42 – 70
46 Relative deprivation and social mobility — structural constraints on distributive justice judgments. Bernd Wegener. *Eur. Sociol. R.* **7:1** 5:1991 pp. 3 – 18
47 The role of intergovernmental grants in underpopulated regions. Kiyoko Hagihara; Yoshimi Hagihara. *Reg. Stud.* **25:2** 4:1991 pp. 163 – 171
48 Some issues of regional inequality in the USSR under Gorbachev. Gennady I. Ozornoy. *Reg. Stud.* **25:5** 10:1991 pp. 381 – 393
49 Soviet perceptions of economic conditions during the period of stagnation — evidence from two diverse emigrant surveys. Paul Gregory; Barbara Dietz. *Eur.-Asia Stud.* **43:3** 1991 pp. 535 – 551
50 Structural adjustment and multiple modes of social livelihood in Nigeria. Abdul Raufu Mustapha. Geneva: United Nations Research Institute for Social Development, 1991: 27 p. [Discussion paper.]
51 Substitution bias and cost of living variability for U.S. demographic groups. S.A. Cobb. *Am. J. Econ. S.* **50:1** 1:1991 pp. 85 – 98
52 Technological development and the improvement of living and working conditions — options for the future. Federico Butera *[Ed.]*; Eberhard Köhler *[Ed.]*; Vittorio di Martino *[Ed.]*. London: Kogan Page, 1989: 400 p. (ill) *ISBN: 1850917957.* European Foundation for the Improvement of Living and Working Conditions; Catalogue no. — SY-5-88-293-EN-C; "EF/88/10/EN"--t.p. verso; Includes bibliography and index.
53 Toward a new political economy of metropolitan regions. W.R. Barnes; L.C. Ledebur. *Envir. Plan. C.* **9:2** 5:1991 pp. 127 – 141
54 The upgrading of squatter settlements in Tanzania — the role of security of land tenure and the provision of amenities in housing improvement. Sababu Kaitilla. *J. As. Afr. S.* **XXVI:3-4** 7-10:1991 pp. 220 – 236
55 Urban-rural cost-of-living differentials in a developing economy. Martin Ravallion; Dominique van de Walle. *J. Urban Ec.* **29:1** 1:1991 pp. 113 – 127
56 Die Verteilungswirkungen von Wirtschaftskrise und Anpassungspolitik in Mexiko *[In German]*; [The distributive effects of economic crisis and structural adjustment policy in Mexico] *[Summary]*. Andreas Schedler. *J. Entwick.pol.* **VII:4** 1991 pp. 63 – 85
57 Women and the world economic crisis. Jeanne Vickers *[Ed.]*. London: Zed, 1991: 146 p. (ill) *ISBN: 0862329744.* Includes bibliography and index. [Women and world development.]
58 Women, recession and adjustment in the Third World. Carolyne Dennis *[Ed.]*; Haleh Afshar *[Ed.]*. London: Macmillan, 1991: 271 p. *ISBN: 0333537432.*

Income [Revenu]

59 Childhood influences on adult male earnings in a longitudinal study. Diana Kuh; Michael Wadsworth. *Br. J. Soc.* **42:4** 12:1991 pp. 537 – 556
60 Compensation for commuts in labor and housing markets. Jeffrey S. Zax. *J. Urban Ec.* **30:2** 9:1991 pp. 192 – 207
61 Conceptions of fair pay — theoretical perspectives and empirical research. Miriam Dornstein. New York: Praeger, 1991: x, 221 p. *ISBN: 0275934047; LofC: 91008609.* Includes bibliographical references (p. 191-209) and indexes.
62 Defining and measuring poverty in the nonmetropolitan United States using the survey of income and program participation. Robert A. Hoppe. *Soc. Ind.* **24:2** 3:1991 pp. 123 – 151

H.3: Economic conditions and living standards [Conditions économiques et niveau de vie] — Income [Revenu]

63 Disparités linguistiques de revenu au Canada selon la langue parlée à la maison *[In French]*; [Income differentials by language spoken at home in Canada] *[Summary]*. Marc Lavoie; Maurice Saint-Germain. *Act. Econ.* **67:3** 9:1991 pp. 356 – 380

64 Distributive justice and occupational incomes — perceptions of justice determine perceptions of fact. Bruce Headey. *Br. J. Soc.* **42:4** 12:1991 pp. 581 – 596

65 The earnings assimilation of immigrants. Renato Aguilar; Björn Gustafsson. *Labour [Italy]* **5:2** Autumn:1991 pp. 37 – 58

66 Earnings distribution in Czechoslovakia — intertemporal changes and international comparison. Jiří Večerník. *Eur. Sociol. R.* **7:3** 12:1991 pp. 237 – 252

67 The effect of illicit drug use on the wages of young adults. Robert Kaestner. *J. Labor Ec.* **9:4** 10:1991 pp. 381 – 412

68 Estimating short and long run income elasticities of foods and nutrients for rural south India. A. Bhargava. *J. Roy. Stat. Soc. A.* **154:1** :1991 pp. 157 – 173

69 Explaining the male-female wage gap — job segregation and solidarity wage bargaining in Sweden. Carl le Grand. *Acta Sociol.* **34:4** 1991 pp. 261 – 278

70 Five reasons why wages vary among employers. Erica L. Groshen. *Ind. Relat.* **30:3** Fall:1991 pp. 350 – 381

71 The gender salary gap — do academic achievement, internship experience, and college major make a difference? Rex Fuller; Richard Schoenberger. *Soc. Sci. Q.* **72:4** 12:1991 pp. 715 – 726

72 The gender stratification of income inequality among lawyers. John Hagan. *Soc. Forc.* **68:3** 3:1990 pp. 835 – 855

73 Gender, class and income inequalities in later life. Jay Ginn; Sara Arber. *Br. J. Soc.* **42:3** 9:1991 pp. 369 – 396

74 Government wage differentials revisited. William J. Moore; John Raisian. *J. Labor Res.* **XII:1** Winter:1991 pp. 13 – 33

75 Haushalts- und Erwerbsein kommen in der DDR *[In German]*; Household income and income from employment in the GDR *[Summary]*. Joachim Frick; Peter Krause; Johannes Schwarze. *Kölner Z. Soz. Soz. psy.* **43:2** 1991 pp. 334 – 343

76 The impact of unionization, right-to-work laws, and female labor force participation on earnings inequality across states. Michael Nieswiadomy; Daniel J. Slottje; Kathy Hayes. *J. Labor Res.* **XII:2** Spring:1991 pp. 185 – 195

77 Income and the idea of justice — principles, judgments, and their framing. W. Arts; P. Hermkens; P. van Wijck. *J. Econ. Psyc.* **12:1** 3:1991 pp. 121 – 140

78 Income inequality and economic development — geographic divergence. Denny Braun. *Soc. Sci. Q.* **72:3** 9:1991 pp. 520 – 536

79 Industrial change and local economic fragmentation — the case of Stoke-on-Trent. R. Imrie. *Geoforum* **22:4** 1991 pp. 433 – 453

80 Internal and external referents as predictors of pay satisfaction among employees of a two-tier wage setting. Raymond T. Lee; James E. Martin. *J. Occup. Psychol.* **64:1** 3:1991 pp. 57 – 66

81 Market forces, trade union ideology and trends in Swedish wage dispersion. Douglas A. Hibbs. *Acta Sociol.* **34:2** 1991 pp. 89 – 102

82 Market-like forces and social stratification — how neoclassical theories of wages can survive recent sociological critiques. Samuel Cohn. *Soc. Forc.* **68:3** 3:1990 pp. 714 – 730

83 Pension benefits and male-female wage differentials; Allocations de retraite et différentiels de salaires entre hommes et femmes *[French summary]*. James E. Pesando; Morley Gunderson; John McLaren. *Can. J. Econ.* **XXIV:3** 8:1991 pp. 536 – 550

84 Poverty, inequality, and prices in rural India. Nikhilesh Bhattacharya. New Delhi: Sage Publications, 1991: 236 p. *ISBN: 0803996853; LofC: 91006965. Includes bibliographical references.*

85 Poverty, per capita income and per worker sectoral incomes. K.C. Singhal; H.S. Gill. *Ind. J. Reg. Sci.* **XXIII:2** 1991 pp. 1 – 10

86 Prawo pracownic do jednakowego wynagrodzenia *[In Polish]*; Право сотрудниц до одинаковой зарплаты: *Title only in Russian*); (Employees' right to the same equal fee). Irena Boruta. *Pra. Zab. Społ.* **:11-12** 1991 pp. 7 – 14

87 Problemy kształtowania płacy minimalnej *[In Polish]*; (Проблемы образования минимальной заплаты: *Title only in Russian*); (The problems of subsistence level wages formation). Henryk Zarychta. *Pra. Zab. Społ.* **33:1** 1:1991 pp. 1 – 8

H.3: Economic conditions and living standards *[Conditions économiques et niveau de vie]* — **Income** *[Revenu]*

88 Race, region, and earnings — blacks and whites in the South. Bruce H. Rankin; William W. Falk. *Rural Sociol.* **56:2** Summer:1991 pp. 224 – 237
89 Regional earnings differences in Great Britain — evidence from the new earnings survey. Philip J. Hemmings. *Reg. Stud.* **25:2** 4:1991 pp. 123 – 134
90 Wage subsidies as an anti-discrimination policy. S.B. Isbell; L.H. Smith. *Pop. Res. Pol. R.* **10:3** 1991 pp. 257 – 271
91 Women, work and wages in two Arab villages. Nicholas S. Hopkins. *East. Anthrop.* **44:2** 4-6:1991 pp. 103 – 123

H.4: Enterprises and production systems — *Entreprises et systèmes de production*

Sub-divisions: Enterprises *[Entreprises]*; Technology *[Technologie]*

1 Bäuerliche Tradition im sozialen Wandel *[In German]*; Cultural tradition and social change in agriculture *[Summary]*. Hans Pongratz. *Kölner Z. Soz. Soz. psy.* **43:2** 1991 pp. 235 – 246
2 Berufsstruktureller Wandel und soziale Ungleichheit. Entsteht in der Bundesrepublik Deutschland ein neues Dienstleistungsproletariat? *[In German]*; Expansion of the tertiary sector and social inequality. Is there a new service proletariat emerging in the Federal Republic of Germany? *[Summary]*. Hans-Peter Blossfeld; Karl-Ulrich Mayer. *Kölner Z. Soz. Soz. psy.* **43:4** 1991 pp. 671 – 696
3 Beyond the farmgate — factors related to agricultural performance in two dairy communities. James Cruise; Thomas A. Lyson. *Rural Sociol.* **56:1** Spring:1991 pp. 41 – 55
4 Centralization and experimentation in the implementation of a national monitoring and evaluation system — the experience of Malawi. Michael Useem; Graham Chipande. *Eval. Rev.* **15:2** 4:1991 pp. 233 – 253
5 Les commerçants dans la modernisation de la distribution *[In French]*; Shopkeepers in modernized distribution *[Summary]*; Die Händler innerhalb der sich modernisierenden Distribution *[German summary]*; Los comerciantes en la modernización de la distribución *[Spanish summary]*. René Peron. *Rev. Fr. Soc.* **XXXII:2** 4-6:1991 pp. 179 – 207
6 La Communauté européenne et la fin de l'exception agricole *[In French]*; The European Community and the end of an agricultural exception *[Summary]*; Die Europäische Gemeinschaft und das Ende der Agrarausnahme *[German summary]*; La Communidad europea y el fin de la excepción agrícola *[Spanish summary]*. Palcide Rambaud. *Rev. Fr. Soc.* **XXXII:2** 4-6:1991 pp. 157 – 177
7 Control during corporate crisis — asbestos and the Manville bankruptcy. Kevin J. Delaney. *Int. J. Health. Ser.* **21:4** 1991 pp. 697 – 716
8 Deindustrialisation and the reality of the post-industrial city. W.F. Lever. *Urban Stud.* **28:6** 12:1991 pp. 983 – 999
9 Density bonuses, exactions, and the supply of affordable housing. Jeffrey I. Rubin; Joseph J. Seneca. *J. Urban Ec.* **30:2** 9:1991 pp. 208 – 223
10 Density dependence in organizational mortality — legitimacy or unobserved heterogeneity? Trond Petersen; Kenneth W. Koput. *Am. Sociol. R.* **56:3** 6:1991 pp. 399 – 409
11 The development of China's peasant economy — a new formulation of old problems. R. Bin Wong. *Peasant Stud.* **XVIII:1** Fall:1990 pp. 5 – 26
12 Discontinuities in the French farming world; Les ruptures du monde agricole *[French summary]*; Diskontinuitäten in der Welt der französischen Landwirtschaft *[German summary]*. B. Hervieu. *Sociol. Rur.* **XXXI:4** 1991 pp. 290 – 299
13 Dominican sugar plantations — production and foreign labor integration. Martin F. Murphy. New York: Praeger, 1991: xii, 186 p. *ISBN: 0275931137; LofC: 90048704. Includes bibliographical references and index.*
14 Engineering as a social enterprise. Hedy E. Sladovich; J. Herbert Hollomon. Washington, D.C: National Academy Press, 1991: vii, 113 p. (ill) *ISBN: 0309044316; LofC: 91061730. "Papers presented during the 1990 Meeting of the National Academy of Engineering in a symposium dedicated to the memory of J. Herbert Hollomon."; Includes bibliographical references.*
15 Fordism and flexibility — divisions and change. Nigel Gilbert *[Ed.]*; Roger Burrows *[Ed.]*; Anna Pollert *[Ed.]*. Basingstoke: Macmillan Academic and Professional, 1991: 160 p. *ISBN: 0333565355.* [Explorations in sociology. : No. 41]

H.4: Enterprises and production systems [Entreprises et systèmes de production]

16 Framework for comparative studies of management in post-socialist economies. Andrzej K. Kozminski. *Stud. Comp. Commun.* **XXIV:4** 12:1991 pp. 413 – 424

17 Gender, power and postindustrialism; *[French summary]*. Monica Boyd; Mary Ann Mulvihill; John Myles. *Can. R. Soc. A.* **28:4** 11:1991 pp. 407 – 436

18 Gestion publique — gestion privée *[In French]*; [Public management — private management]. Michel Franc *[Ed.]*; Michel Crozier *[Contrib.]*; Claude Riveline *[Contrib.]*; Simon Booth *[Contrib.]*; Jean-Claude Cohen *[Contrib.]*; Guy Crespy *[Contrib.]*; Michel Ghertman *[Contrib.]*; Jacques Maisonrouge *[Contrib.]*; Ambroise Laurent *[Contrib.]*; Luc Rouban *[Contrib.] and others*. Collection of 10 articles. *R. Fr. Admin. Publ.* , :**59**, 7-9:1991 pp. 345 – 444

19 Green meanings — what might "sustainable agriculture" sustain? Christopher Hamlin. *Sci. Cult.* **2:4(13)** 1991 pp. 507 – 537

20 Impact of management by objectives on organizational productivity. Robert Rodgers; John E. Hunter. *J. Appl. Psychol.* **76:2** 4:1991 pp. 322 – 336

21 Indigenous management. David Marsden. *Int. J. Hum. Res. Man.* **2:1** 5:1991 pp. 21 – 38

22 Internal assessment of organizational health and effectiveness — an empirical study. Omer Bin Sayeed. *Ind. J. Ind. Rel.* **26:3** 1:1991 pp. 227 – 243

23 Interorganizational relations of nonprofit organizations — an exploratory study. Judith R. Blau; Gordana Rabrenovic. *Sociol. For.* **6:2** 6:1991 pp. 327 – 348

24 Intraurban location effects on firm performance — some evidence from the Leeds engineering sector. S. Dobson; B. Gerrard. *Envir. Plan.A.* **23:5** 1991 pp. 757 – 764

25 Just the working life — opposition and accommodation in daily industrial life. Marc Lendler. Armonk, N.Y: M.E. Sharpe, c1990: x, 227 p. *ISBN: 0873326083; LofC: 89070267. Includes bibliographical references (p. 211-220) and index.*

26 Die Logik der Koordination des verarbeitenden Gewerbes in Amerika *[In German]*; The logic of coordinating American manufacturing sectors *[Summary]*. J. Rogers Hollingsworth. *Kölner Z. Soz. Soz. psy.* **43:1** 1991 pp. 18 – 43

27 Metrological control — industrial measurement management. Hiroshi Yano. Tokyo: Asian Productivity Organization, 1991: 477 p. *ISBN: 9283311078.*

28 Northern Ireland's productivity failure — a matched plant comparison with West Germany. D.M.W.N. Hitchens; K. Wagner; J.E. Birnie. *Reg. Stud.* **25:2** 4:1991 pp. 111 – 122

29 O modelo japonês em debate — pós-fordismo ou japonização do fordismo *[In Portuguese]*; Debating the Japanese model — post-Fordism or Japanization of Fordism *[Summary]*; Le modèle japonaise en question — post-fordisme ou japonaisation du fordisme *[French summary]*. Stephen Wood. *Rev. Bras. Ciên. Soc.* **6:17** 10:1991 pp. 28 – 43

30 L'organisation corporative des chauffeurs de taxis collectifs à Bamako et Lomé *[In French]*; [The corporative organization of a taxi drivers' collective in Bamako and Lomé]. J.C. Pradeilles; G. Garcia-Oriol; I. Tall. *Afr. Cont.* :**158(2)** 1991 pp. 4 – 13

31 L'organisation de la societe paysanne et la situation du mouvement cooperatif dans le Bas-Zaire *[In French]*; [The organization of peasant society and the situation of the cooperative movement in Lower Zaire]. Ngiyene Amena Lubana. Collection of 6 articles. **Cah. CEDAF** , *3-4*, 4-8:1990 pp. 7 – 158

32 Un point de vue d'ingénieur sur la gestion des organisation *[In French]*; An engineer's point of view on organization management *[Summary]*. Claude Riveline. *R. Fr. Admin. Publ.* :**59** 7-9:1991 pp. 355 – 366

33 Power and accountability. Robert A. G Monks; Nell Minow. London: HarperCollins, c1991: x, 292 p. *ISBN: 0887305121; LofC: 91008959. Includes bibliographical references (p. 267-283) and index.*

34 Проблемы оптимизации управленческих решений *[In Russian]*; [Problems of optimization of management decisions]. V.A. Pirozhkov. Sverdlovsk: Izd-vo Ural. un-ta, 1987: 166 p. p.165 Bibliogr.

35 Production domestique *[In French]*; (Home production). Yannick Lemel *[Contrib.]*; Alain Degenne *[Contrib.]*; Marie-Odile Lebeaux; James Cécora *[Contrib.]*; Claude Bonnette-Lucat *[Contrib.]*; Bernard Picon *[Contrib.]*; Véronique Beillan *[Contrib.]*. Collection of 6 articles. **Soc. Contemp.** , :*8*, 1991 pp. 7 – 106

36 Profit, loss, and fate — the entrepreneurial ethic and practice of gambling in an overseas Chinese community. Ellen Oxfeld Basu. *Mod. Chi.* **17:2** 4:1991 pp. 227 – 259

37 Психология менеджмена *[In Russian]*; (Management psychology). G.S. Nikiforov; Iu.N. Slivkin. *Ves. Lenin. Univ. Ser. 5* :**2(13)** 7:1991 pp. 59 – 70

38 Public construction expenditures in the United States — are there structural breaks in the 1921-1987 period? Lata Chatterjee; Syed Abu Hasnath. *Econ. Geogr.* **67:1** 1:1991 pp. 42 – 53

H.4: Enterprises and production systems [Entreprises et systèmes de production]

39 Reconsidering innovation policy for small and medium sized enterprises — the Canadian case. J.N.H. Britton. *Envir. Plan. C.* **9:2** 5:1991 pp. 189 – 206

40 The regional dimension of competitiveness in manufacturing — productivity, employment and wages in Northern Ireland and the United Kingdom; La compétitivité de l'industrie manufacturière sous un optique régional — productivité, emploi et salaires en Irlande du Nord et au Royaume-Uni *[French summary]*; Die regionale Dimension industrieller Konkurrenzfähigkeit — Produktivität, Erwerbsätigkeit und Löhne in Nordirland und im Vereinigten Königreich *[German summary]*. Vani K. Borooah; Kevin C. Lee. *Reg. Stud.* **25:3** 6:1991 pp. 219 – 229

41 Regional formation of high-technology service industries — the software industry in Washington State. P. Haug. *Envir. Plan.A.* **23:6** 6:1991 pp. 869 – 884

42 Retail activity allocation modeling with endogenous retail prices and shopping travel costs. N. Oppenheim. *Envir. Plan.A.* **23:5** 1991 pp. 731 – 744

43 Social forestry perspective and Bangladesh. Muhammad Hasan Imam. *Asian Prof.* **19:2 4**:1991 pp. 185 – 192

44 The social side of sustainability — class, gender and race. Patricia L. Allen; Carolyn E. Sachs. *Sci. Cult.* **2:4(13)** 1991 pp. 569 – 590

45 Subsistence agriculture versus cash cropping — the social repercussions. S.J. Rennie. *J. Rural St.* **7:1-2** 1991 pp. 5 – 10

46 Toward a systemic crisis management strategy — learning from the best examples in the US, Canada and France. T.C. Pauchant; I.I. Mitroff; P. Lagadec. *Ind. Crisis Q.* **5:3** :1991 p. 209

47 Traditional versus modern and co-evolutionary development potential — the case of marine fisheries in India. John Kurien. *Soc. Act.* **41:1** 1-3:1991 pp. 29 – 41

48 Trajectoires d'évolution de la sous-traitance japonaise *[In French]*; Trajectories of the evolution of subcontracting in Japan *[Summary]*. Masayoshi Ikeda. *Sociol. Trav.* **XXXIII:1** 1991 pp. 135 – 147

49 Transplanted organizations — the transfer of Japanese industrial organization to the U.S. Richard Florida; Martin Kenney. *Am. Sociol. R.* **56:3** 6:1991 pp. 381 – 398

50 The UK whiteware industry — Fordism, flexibility or somewhere in between?; La fabrication de produits blancs au Royaume-Uni — s'agit-il du Fordisme, de la flexibilité ou d'une situation intermédiaire? *[French summary]*; Die "Weisse" Industrie Grossbritanniens — Fordismus, Elastizität oder ein Mittelding? *[German summary]*. Simon Milne. *Reg. Stud.* **25:3** 6:1991 pp. 239 – 253

51 Understanding plant closures — the UK brewing industry. H. Douglas Watts. *Geography* **76:4** 10:1991 pp. 315 – 330

52 Union rents and market structure revisited. William F. Chappell; Walter J. Mayer; William F. Shughart. *J. Labor Res.* **XII:1** Winter:1991 pp. 35 – 46

53 Value added productivity measurement and practical approach to management improvement. Masayoshi Shimizu; Kiyoshi Wainai; Kazuo Nagai. Tokyo: Asian Productivity Organization, 1991: 231 p. *ISBN: 9283317130.* [Productivity series. : No. 23]

54 We build the road as we travel. Roy Morrison. Philadelphia, PA.: New Society Publishers, c1991: x, 276 p. (ill) *ISBN: 0865711720. Includes bibliographical references (p. 265-270) and index.*

55 Women, work and the evolution of agriculture. F.M. Shaver. *J. Rural St.* **7:1-2** 1991 pp. 37 – 44

56 Work and the enterprise culture. Malcolm Cross *[Ed.]*; Geoff Payne *[Ed.]*. London: Falmer Press, 1991: 236 p. *ISBN: 1850007993; LofC: 90048865. Includes bibliographical references and index.*

57 A world of services? P.W. Daniels. *Geoforum* **22:4** 1991 pp. 359 – 376

58 Zur Doppelstruktur planwirtschaftlichen Handelns in der DDR *[In German]*; The double structure of economic activites in the former German Democratic Republic *[Summary]*. Martin Heidenreich. *Z. Soziol.* **20:6** 12:1991 pp. 411 – 429

59 Zur Politischen Ökonomie des »post-fordistischen« Telekommunikationssektors — der Fall USA *[In German]*; [On the political economy of post-Fordian telecommunications sector — the case of the USA]. Boy Lüthje. *Prokla* **21** 12:1991 pp. 636 – 658

60 Zwischen Geschäftspolitik und persönlichem Anstand — ein kompliziertes Spannungsfeld *[In German]*; [Between business policy and personal integrity — a complex relationship]. Jan Kerkhofs. *Jahr. Christ. Sozialwiss.* **31** 1990 pp. 75 – 90

H.4: Enterprises and production systems [Entreprises et systèmes de production]

Enterprises [Entreprises]

61 L'aventure d'une multinationale au Bangladesh — ethnologie d'une entreprise [In French]; [The venture of a multinational enterprise in Bangladesh — ethnology of an enterprise]. Monique Sélim. Paris: L'Harmattan, [1991]: 254 p. *BNB: 91133828; LofC: 91133828.*

62 Barriers to women's small-business success in the United States. Karyn A. Loscocco; Joyce Robinson. *Gender Soc.* **5:4** 12:1991 pp. 511 – 532

63 Beyond success — corporations and their critics in the 1990s. James W Kuhn; Donald W Shriver *[Ed.].* New York: Oxford University Press, 1991: viii, 336 p. *ISBN: 019506433x; LofC: 90007084.* Includes bibliographical references and index. [The Ruffin series in business ethics.]

64 A comparative study of corporatist development. Bruce Western. *Am. Sociol. R.* **56:3** 6:1991 pp. 283 – 294

65 Corporate performance and CEO turnover — a comparison of performance indicators. Sheila M. Puffer; Joseph B. Weintrop. *Adm. Sci. Qua.* **36:1** 3:1991 pp. 1 – 19

66 Corporate responsibility and legitimacy — an interdisciplinary analysis. James J. Brummer. New York: Greenwood Press, 1991: xi, 323 p. *ISBN: 0313247269; LofC: 90025223 //r91.* Includes bibliographical references and indexes. [Contributions in philosophy.]

67 The desperate need for new values in Japanese corporate behavior. Haruo Shimada. *J. Jpn. Stud.* **17:1** Winter:1991 pp. 107 – 126

68 Director interlocks and the political behavior of corporations and corporate elites. Val Burris. *Soc. Sci. Q.* **72:3** 9:1991 pp. 537 – 551

69 Japanese motor industry transplants — the West European dimension. Philip N. Jones; John North. *Econ. Geogr.* **67:2** 4:1991 pp. 105 – 123

70 Jobs, land, and urban development — the economic success of small manufacturers in East Delhi, India. Solomon J. Benjamin. Cambridge, Mass: Lincoln Institute of Land Policy, c1991: xviii, 130 p., xxiv p. of plates (ill) *ISBN: 1558441107; LofC: 90028671.* Includes bibliographical references (p. 129-130).

71 New firm formation in the British counties with special reference to Scotland. Brian Ashcroft; James H. Love; Eleanor Malloy. *Reg. Stud.* **25:5** 10:1991 pp. 395 – 409

72 Los problemas de representación en los organismos empresariales [In Spanish]; [Representation problems in business institutions]. Rogelio Hernández Rodríguez. *Foro Int.* **XXXI:3** 1-3:1991 pp. 446 – 471

73 Size, concentration, and corporate networks — determinants of business collective action. Mark S. Mizruchi; Thomas Koenig. *Soc. Sci. Q.* **72:2** 6:1991 pp. 299 – 313

74 Small firms, business services growth and regional development in the United Kingdom — some empirical findings. David Keeble; John Bryson; Peter Wood. *Reg. Stud.* **25:5** 10:1991 pp. 439 – 457

75 Small firms, industrial reorganisation, and space — the case of the UK high-fidelity audio sector. S. Milne. *Envir. Plan.A.* **23:6** 6:1991 pp. 833 – 852

76 Die soziale Welt kleiner Betriebe — Wirtschaften, Arbeiten und Leben im mittelständischen Industriebetrieb [In German]; [The social world of small enterprises — economics, work and life in a medium-sized industrial entreprise]. Hermann Kotthoff. Göttingen: Schwartz, 1990: 400 p. *ISBN: 3509015495.*

77 Sweaters — gender, class and workshop - based industry in Mexico. Fiona Wilson. London: Macmillan, 1991: 224 p. *ISBN: 0333538293.* [Macmillan international political economy series.]

78 Who wants to be an entrepreneur? A study of adolescents interested in a young enterprise scheme. C. Bonnett; A. Furnham. *J. Econ. Psyc.* **12:3** 9:1991 pp. 465 – 478

Technology [Technologie]

79 Action into nature — an essay on the meaning of technology. Barry Cooper. Notre Dame: University of Notre Dame Press, c1991: xvi, 291 p. *ISBN: 0268006296; LofC: 90050975.* Includes bibliographical references (p. 265-287) and index. [Loyola lectures in political analysis.]

80 Aiming for the discursive high ground — Monsanto and the biotechnology controversy. Daniel Lee Kleinman; Jack Kloppenburg. *Sociol. For.* **6:3** 9:1991 pp. 427 – 448

81 Automação e racionalidade técnica [In Portuguese]; Automation and technical rationality [Summary]; Automation et rationalité technique [French summary]. Rogério Valle. *Rev. Bras. Ciên. Soc.* **6:17** 10:1991 pp. 53 – 67

H.4: Enterprises and production systems [Entreprises et systèmes de production] — Technology [Technologie]

82 Cleaning up on the farm. Les Levidow. *Sci. Cult.* **2:4(13)** 1991 pp. 538 – 568
83 Communication and control — networks and the new economies of communication. G. J Mulgan. Cambridge: Polity Press, 1991: 302 p. *ISBN: 0745605370; LofC: gb 90010486. Includes index.*
84 Diffusion of technologies and social behavior. Arnulf Grübler *[Ed.]*; Nebojsa Nakicenovic *[Ed.]*. Berlin: Springer-Verlag, c1991: 604 p. *ISBN: 0387538461; LofC: 91011741.*
85 The dynamics of just-in-time; *[French summary]*. Nick Oliver. *New Tech. Work. Empl.* **6:1** Spring:1991 pp. 19 – 27
86 Az elektronizáció társadalmi feltételei és következményei *[In Hungarian]*; [Social conditions and consequences of development of electronics]. Ildikó Szpirulisz. **Tarsad. Kozl.** *Vol.17; No.2 - 1987.* pp. 191 – 203
87 Los estudios sociales de la tecnología en la región latinoamericano, diagnóstico y perspectivas *[In Spanish]*; [Social studies of technology in Latin America, analysis and perspectives]. Enrique Oteiza. *Rev. Parag. Sociol.* **28:81** 5-8:1991 pp. 21 – 82
88 Feminism confronts technology. Judy Wajcman. University Park, Pa: Pennsylvania State University Press, 1991: x, 184 p. (ill) *ISBN: 0271008016; LofC: 91018539. Includes bibliographical references (p. [168]-179) and index.*
89 Философия и социология науки и техники: Ежегодник *[In Russian]*; [Philosophy and sociology of science and technology — yearbook]. I.T. Frolov *[Ed.]*; V.L. Rabinovich *[Ed.]*. Moscow: Nauka, 1987
90 Gender relations, technology and employment change in the contemporary textile industry. Roger Penn; Ann Martin; Hilda Scattergood. *Sociology* **25:4** 11:1991 pp. 569 – 587
91 La gestion de l'innovation — un modèle général *[In German]*; Managing innovation — a general model *[Summary]*. Simon Booth. *R. Fr. Admin. Publ.* **:59** 7-9:1991 pp. 367 – 377
92 Impact of science and technology on everyday life — an African perspective. Andrew O. Urevbu. *Impact Sci.* **41:1(161)** :1991 pp. 69 – 79
93 Innovation als rekursiver Prozeß — zur Theorie und Empirie der Technikgenese am Beispiel der Produktionstechnik *[In German]*; Innovation as a recurrent process — a theoretical model of the generation of machine tool technologies *[Summary]*. Jupp Asdonk; Udo Bredeweg; Uli Kowol. *Z. Soziol.* **20:4** 8:1991 p. 290
94 Listening to a long conversation — an ethnographic approach to the study of information and communication technologies in the home. Roger Silverstone; Eric Hirsch; David Morley. *Cult. St.* **5:2** 5:1991 pp. 204 – 227
95 The new telecommunications — infrastructure for the information age. Frederick Williams. New York: Free Press, c1991: 247 p. *ISBN: 0029352819; LofC: 91011635. Includes bibliographical references and index.* [Series in communication technology and society.]
96 Organisationen und Institutionen in der Technikentwicklung — Organisationskultur, Leitbilder und „Stand der Technik" *[In German]*; Organizations and institutions in technology development — organizational culture, "leitbilder" and "golden standard" of technology *[Summary]*. Andreas Knie; Sabine Helmers. *Soz. Welt.* **42:4** 1991 pp. 427 – 444
97 Risk, organizations, and society. Martin Shubik *[Ed.]*. Boston: Kluwer Academic, c1991: vi, 239 p. (ill) *ISBN: 0792391187; LofC: 90004692. Includes bibliographical references (p. 219-221) and index.* [Studies in risk and uncertainty.]
98 The social context of technological change — the case of the retail food industry. John P. Walsh. *Sociol. Q.* **32:3** Fall:1991 pp. 447 – 467
99 Социальные и методологические проблемы НТР и технического хнания: Сборник *[In Russian]*; [Social and methodological problems of the scientific and cultural revolution and technical knowedge]. I.A. Negodaev *[Ed.]*. Rostov/ Leningrad: Rostov University Publishers, 1986: 153 p. [Rostov/Leningrad Mechanical Engineering Institute.]
100 Les techniques — enjeux humains et sociaux *[In French]*; [Technology — human and social issues]. G. Balandier *[Contrib.]*; J. Neirynck *[Contrib.]*; P. Feschotte *[Contrib.]*; E. Ascher *[Contrib.]*; J.-Cl Piguet *[Contrib.]*; J. Grineveld *[Contrib.]*; G. Busino *[Ed.]*; D. Bourg *[Contrib.]*; G. Berthoud *[Ed.]*; J. Freund *[Contrib.]* and others. Collection of 16 articles. **Rev. Eur. Sci. Soc.**, *XXIX:91*, 1991 pp. 1 – 210
101 Technological change — scale biases in the distribution of output and employment gains in India's dairy farming sector. Mahesh Lalwani. *Soc. Act.* **41:1** 1-3:1991 pp. 42 – 53
102 Technology as a factor in gender differentiation of work roles — a case study of Israel's smallholder cooperative villages. N. Nevo. *J. Rural St.* **7:1-2** 1991 pp. 31 – 36

H.4: Enterprises and production systems *[Entreprises et systèmes de production]*
— **Technology** *[Technologie]*

103 Technology control, global warming and environmental colonialism — the WRI report. Anil Agarwal; Sunita Narain. *Soc. Act.* **41:1** 1-3:1991 pp. 3 – 28
104 Zur Computerkritik in Japan *[In German]*; [On critical attitudes towards computers in Japan]. Ilse Lenz. *Beit. Japan.* **29** 1991 pp. 482 – 499

H.5: Markets and consumption — *Marchés et consommation*

1 Acceso al mercado en municipios del estado de México, México *[In Spanish]*; [Market access in towns in Mexico, F.D. Mexico]. Arthur Morris. *Rev. Int.Am. Plan.* **XXIV:93** 1-3:1991 pp. 73 – 85
2 Accession — l'ancien réhabilité *[In French]*; The ownership of property — the trend toward old homes *[Summary]*; Acceso a la propiedad — rehabilitación de lo antiguo *[Spanish summary]*. Claude Taffin. *E & S* :**240** 2:1991 pp. 5 – 18
3 Advertising bans — consequences for consumers. Mark Bentley; Mai Fyfield. London: Social Affairs Unit, 1991: 51 p, *ISBN: 0907631452*
4 Affective reactions to consumption situations — a pilot investigation. Ch. Derbaix; M.T. Pham. *J. Econ. Psyc.* **12:2** 6:1991 pp. 325 – 356
5 Aggregate consumer behaviour without exact aggregation; Le comportement agrégé des consommateurs en l'absence d'agrégation exacte *[French summary]*. Christopher J. Nicol. *Can. J. Econ.* **XXIV:3** 8:1991 pp. 578 – 594
6 Attributions, baseball and consumer behavior. Peter Stratton. *J. Market R.* **33:3** 7:1991 pp. 163 – 178
7 Changing retail structure in southern Sydney. D.J. Walmsley; H.C. Weinand. *Aust. Geogr.* **22:1** 5:1991 pp. 57 – 66
8 Changing suburban retail patterns in metropolitan Los Angeles. William J. Lloyd. *Prof. Geogr.* **43:3** 8:1991 pp. 335 – 344
9 Children and money — getting an allowance, credit versus cash, and knowledge of pricing. R. Abramovitch; J.L. Freedman; P. Pliner. *J. Econ. Psyc.* **12:1** 3:1991 pp. 27 – 45
10 Civic culture and consumption in Eastern Europe. Alexander J. Matejko. *Social. Int.* **29:1** 1991 pp. 75 – 102
11 Le consommateur — agent économique et acteur politique *[In French]*; The consumer — scholarly category and slogan *[Summary]*; Der Verbraucher — Wissenschaftskategorie und Parole *[German summary]*; El consumidor — categoría erudita y contraseña *[Spanish summary]*. Louis Pinto. *Rev. Fr. Soc.* **XXXI:2** 4-6:1990 pp. 179 – 198
12 La consommation du vin en France — évolutions tendancielles et diversité des comportements *[In French]*; [The consumption of wine in France — changing trends and diversity of behaviour] *[Summary]*. P. Aigrain; D. Boulet; J.L. Lambert; J.P. Laporte. *R.E.M.* **39:155-156** 3-4:1991 pp. 19 – 52
13 Consumer attitudes, buying intentions and consumption expenditures — an analaysis of the Swedish household survey data. Anders Agren; Bo Jonsson *[Ed.]*. Stockholm: Konjunkturinstitutet, 1991: 27p. *Bibliography — p23-24.* [Working paper.]
14 Consumerism reconsidered — buying and power. Mica Nava. *Cult. St.* **5:2** 5:1991 pp. 157 – 173
15 Consumption and American culture. David E. Nye *[Ed.]*; Carl Pedersen *[Ed.]*. Amsterdam: VU University Press, 1991: 239 p. *ISBN: 9062569595.* [European contributions to American studies. : No. 21]
16 Consumption and class — divisions and change. Catherine Marsh *[Ed.]*; Roger Burrows *[Ed.]*. London: Macmillan, 1991: 263 p. *ISBN: 0333565363.* [Explorations in sociology. : No. 40]
17 Cross-country alcohol consumption comparison — an application of the Rotterdam system. E.A. Selvanathan. *Appl. Econ.* **23:10** 10:1991 pp. 1613 – 1622
18 Distinction by consumption in Czechoslovakia, Hungary, and the Netherlands. Nan Dirk de Graaf. *Eur. Sociol. R.* **7:3** 12:1991 pp. 267 – 290
19 Duality in consumer post-purchase attitude. A. Geva; A. Goldman. *J. Econ. Psyc.* **12:1** 3:1991 pp. 141 – 164
20 The economic organization of the household. W. Keith Bryant. Cambridge: Cambridge University Press, 1991: 286 p. *ISBN: 0521391873.*
21 An economic-psychological model of scrapping behavior. G. Antonides. *J. Econ. Psyc.* **12:2** 6:1991 pp. 357 – 380

H.5: Markets and consumption *[Marchés et consommation]*

22 A framework for comparing customer satisfaction across individuals and product categories. M.D. Johnson; C. Fornell. *J. Econ. Psyc.* **12:2** 6:1991 pp. 267 – 286

23 Handbook of consumer behavior. Tom Robertson *[Ed.]*; Harold H Kassarjian *[Ed.]*. Englewood Cliffs, N.J: Prentice-Hall, c1991: x, 614 p. (ill) *ISBN: 0133727491; LofC: 90040459. Includes bibliographical references and indexes; Contents — Behavioral methods / Jerry Wind, Vithala R. Rao, Paul E. Green -- Philosophical tensions in consumer inquiry / J. Paul Peter -- Postmodern alternatives — the interpretive turn in consumer research / John F. Sherry, Jr.*

24 Influence of price on aspects of consumers' cognitive process. Jerry B. Gotlieb; Alan J. Dubinsky. *J. Appl. Psychol.* **76:4** 8:1991 pp. 541 – 549

25 Live and automated telephone surveys — a comparison of human interviewers and an automated technique. Michael J. Havice; Mark J. Banks. *J. Market R.* **33:2** 4:1991 pp. 91 – 102

26 The local employment impact of a hypermarket — a modified multiplier analysis incorporating the effect of lower retail prices. Rhona L. MacDonald; J.K. Swales. *Reg. Stud.* **25:2** 4:1991 pp. 155 – 162

27 *[In Japanese]*; [Marketing strategic information system under personal consumption society]. Terue Ohashi. Tokyo: TBS Buritanika, 1991

28 Opis nierówności społecznych w konsumpcji *[In Polish]*; Description of social inequalities in consumption *[Summary]*. Joanna Sikorska. *Prz. Soc.* **39** 1991 pp. 119 – 130

29 Patronage rates of supermarket shopping centers, San Antonio, Texas. Richard C. Jones. *Prof. Geogr.* **43:3** 8:1991 pp. 345 – 355

30 Price patterns in competitively clustered markets. T.J. Fik. *Envir. Plan.A.* **23:11** 11:1991 pp. 1545 – 1560

31 A propensity to protect — butter, margarine and the rise of urban culture in Canada. W. H. Heick. Waterloo, Ont: Wilfrid Laurier University Press, c1991: viii, 229 p. (ill) *ISBN: 0889209944; LofC: cn 90095512. Includes bibliographical references and index.*

32 Remembering and dating past prices. S. Kemp. *J. Econ. Psyc.* **12:3** 9:1991 pp. 431 – 445

33 Rethinking resource allocation in modern society — a meanings-based approach. S.D. Roberts; R.P. Dant. *J. Econ. Psyc.* **12:3** 9:1991 pp. 411 – 430

34 Shop til you drop — shopping as recreational and laborious activity. Robert Prus; Lorne Dawson. *Can. J. Soc.* **16:2** Spring:1991 pp. 145 – 164

35 Shopping orientation segmentation of in-home electronic shoppers. Soyeon Shim; Marianne Y. Mahoney. *Int. R. Ret. Dist. Res.* **1:4** 7:1991 pp. 437 – 454

36 Spatiotemporal sequencing processes of pedestrians in urban retail environments. Xavier van der Hagen; Aloys Borgers; Harry Timmermans. *Pap. Reg. Sci.* **70:1** 1:1991 pp. 37 – 52

37 Thoughts on the cooperative conflict model of the household in relation to economic method. Gail Wilson. *IDS Bull.* **22:1** 1:1991 pp. 31 – 36

38 A transaction cost approach to consumer dissatisfaction and complaint actions. K. Grønhaug; M.C. Gilly. *J. Econ. Psyc.* **12:1** 3:1991 pp. 165 – 183

39 Trans-border outshopping — an Arabian Gulf study. Ugur Yavas; Abdulla Abdul-Gader. *Int. R. Ret. Dist. Res.* **1:4** 7:1991 pp. 455 – 468

40 Validation in marketing models. David Coates; Paul Finlay; John Wilson. *J. Market R.* **33:2** 4:1991 pp. 83 – 90

41 Wettbewerb und Moral *[In German]*; [Competition and ethics]. Karl Homann. *Jahr. Christ. Sozialwiss.* **31** 1990 pp. 34 – 56

H.6: Finance — *Finance*

1 Banks and society. Robert Scott Alexander *[Ed.]*; et al. London: Chartered Institute of Bankers, 1991: 77 p. *ISBN: 0852972962.* [Gilbart lectures on banking. : No. 1990]
2 Constraints on the use of money as a gift at Christmas — the role of status and intimacy. C.B. Burgoyne; D.A. Routh. *J. Econ. Psyc.* **12:1** 3:1991 pp. 47 – 69
3 Flexibility, surveillance and hype in New Zealand financial retailing. Terry Austrin. *Work Emp. Soc.* **5:2** 6:1991 pp. 201 – 221
4 Framing justice — taxpayer evaluations of personal tax burdens. Karyl A. Kinsey; Harold G. Grasmick; Kent W. Smith. *Law Soc. Rev.* **25:4** 1991 pp. 845 – 874
5 How do loan officers make their decisions about credit risks? A study of parallel distributed processing. W. Rodgers. *J. Econ. Psyc.* **12:2** 6:1991 pp. 243 – 266
6 Images de la finance *[In French]*; Images of finance *[Summary]*; Bilder der Finanzwelt *[German summary]*; Imágenes de las finanzas *[Spanish summary]*. Jean-François Baré. *Homme* **XXXI:119** 7-9:1991 pp. 23 – 40
7 In search of explanations for bank performance — some Finnish data. Risto Tainio; Pekka J. Korhonen; Timo J. Santalainen. *Organ. Stud.* **12:3** 1991 pp. 425 – 550
8 Neighborhood development and local credit markets. Richard C. Hula. *Urban Aff. Q.* **27:2** 12:1991 pp. 249 – 267
9 Race, class, and the differential application of bank bailouts. Davita Silfen Glasberg. *Crit. Sociol.* **18:2** Summer: 1991 pp. 51 – 76
10 The sacred meanings of money. Russell W. Belk; Melanie Wallendorf. *J. Econ. Psyc.* **11:1** 3:1990 pp. 35 – 67
11 The theory of credit money — a structural analysis. Costas Lapavitsas. *Sci. Soc.* **55:3** Fall:1991 pp. 291 – 322

H.7: Economic policy and planning — *Politique économique et planification*

1 Contradictions in policy making for urbanization and economic development — planning in Papua New Guinea. David King. *Cities* **8:1** 2:1991 pp. 44 – 53
2 Creating an enterprise culture in the North East? The impact of urban and regional policies of the 1980s. A. Amin; J. Tomaney. *Reg. Stud.* **25:5** 10:1991 pp. 479 – 488
3 Crisis de legitimidad en el estado planificador *[In Spanish]*; [A legitimacy crisis in the planning state]. Martin Hopenhayn. *Rev. Int.Am. Plan.* **XXIV:96** 10-12:1991 pp. 5 – 24
4 Disparités internes et politique de développement régional au Brésil *[In French]*; [Internal disparity and regional development policy in Brazil]. J.M.G. Kleinpenning. *Cah. Outre-mer* **44:174** 4-6:1991 pp. 113 – 128
5 Economic reform in Australia — geographical perspectives. R.H. Fagan *[Contrib.]*; G.J.R. Linge *[Contrib.]*; Phillip M. O'Neill *[Contrib.]*; Hilary P.M. Winchester *[Contrib.]*; Richard Howitt *[Contrib.]*; Michael Taylor *[Contrib.]*; John V. Langdale *[Contrib.]*; Peter Crabb *[Contrib.]*; Blair Badcock *[Contrib.]*; Ruth Fincher *[Contrib.] and others*. Collection of 10 articles. *Aust. Geogr.* , 22:2, 11:1991 pp. 102 – 135
6 Economic restructuring and regional change in Australia. M. Taylor. *Aust. Geogr. Stud.* **29:2** 10:1991 pp. 255 – 267
7 Electric utility least-cost planning — making it work within a multiattribute decision-making framework. Mark Hanson; Stephen Kidwell; Dennis Ray; Rodney Stevenson. *J. Am. Plann.* **57:1** Winter:1991 pp. 34 – 43
8 Geografía, desarrollo regional y política exterior — el caso de la frontera tripartita colombo-venezolana-brasileña en la intendencia del guainia. Una perspectiva desde Colombia *[In Spanish]*; [Geography, regional development and foreign policy — the case of the tripartite Colombian-Venezuelan-Brazilian border in the administration of Guyana. A Colombian perspective]. Juan Gabriel Tokatlian; Cristina Barrera. *Est. Inter.* **XXIV:93** 1-3:1991 pp. 53 – 80
9 La gestión regional — un enfoque sistémico *[In Spanish]*; [Regional management — a systematic approach]. Sergio Boisier. *Rev. Int.Am. Plan.* **XXIV:96** 10-12:1991 pp. 105 – 126

H.7: Economic policy and planning *[Politique économique et planification]*

10 GIS in rural environmental planning — visual and land use analysis of major development proposals. Paul Selman; Donald Davidson; Alistair Watson; Sandra Winterbottom. *Town Plan. R.* **62:2** 4:1991 pp. 215 – 224

11 The impact of credentials, skill levels, worker training, and motivation on employment outcomes — sorting out the implications for economic development policy. Harold Wolman; Cary Lichtman; Suzie Barnes. *Econ. Devel. Q.* **5:2** 5:1991 pp. 140 – 151

12 Impacto regional de los parques y ciudades industriales en México *[In Spanish]*; Regional impact of industrial parks and cities in Mexico *[Summary]*. Gustavo Garza. *Est. Demog. Urb.* **5:3** 9-12:1990 pp. 655 – 676

13 Local environments and plant closures by multi-locational firms — a cross-cultural analysis. H.A. Stafford; H.D. Watts. *Reg. Stud.* **25:5** 10:1991 pp. 427 – 438

14 Physical planning in the Grenada revolution — achievement and legacy. Brian Hudson. *Third Wor. P.* **13:2** 5:1991 pp. 179 – 190

15 Planned colonisation in Bolivian and Ecuadorian Amazonia — the need for a re-assessment of successful planning policy. David A. Eastwood. *R. Eur. Lat.am. Caribe* **:50** 6:1991 pp. 115 – 134

16 Planning and chaos theory. T.J. Cartwright. *J. Am. Plann.* **57:1** Winter:1991 pp. 44 – 56

17 A practical guide for managing planning projects. Terry Moore. *J. Am. Plann.* **57:2** Spring:1991 pp. 212 – 222

18 The practice of land use planning in Spain. Pere Riera; Ian Munt; John Keyes. *Plan. Pract. Res.* **6:2** Summer:1991 pp. 11 – 18

19 Promoting economic development — urban planning in the United States and Great Britain. Susan S. Fainstein. *J. Am. Plann.* **57:1** Winter:1991 pp. 22 – 33

20 Racionalidad, mercado y desarrollo — un análisis sociológico de la privatización *[In Spanish]*; [Rationality, market and development — a sociological analysis of privatization]. Alejandro Vial. *Rev. Parag. Sociol.* **28:81** 5-8:1991 pp. 7 – 20

21 Regional development and planning in Madhya Pradesh. Rolee Kanchan. *Ind. J. Reg. Sci.* **XXIII:1** 1991 pp. 95 – 106

22 Regional policy and planning in south west Germany. D. Scott. *Geoforum* **22:3** 1991 pp. 287 – 298

23 Revitalizing the urban south — neighborhood preservation and planning since the 1920s. Christopher Silver. *J. Am. Plann.* **57:1** Winter:1991 pp. 69 – 84

24 Сельская социальная инфраструктура в среднеазиатском регионе (проблемы управления) *[In Russian]*; (Rural social infrastructure in Soviet Central Asia region (problems of planning and development control)). A.P. Mironenkov. *Sot. Issle.* **:4** 1991 pp. 104 – 110

25 State policy and economic growth — a note on the Hong Kong model; *[French summary]*. Jonathan R. Schiffer. *Int. J. Urban* **15:2** 6:1991 pp. 180 – 196

26 Strategic planning for tribal economic development — a culturally appropriate model for consensus building. Benjamin J. Broome; Irene L. Cromer. *Int. J. Confl. Manag.* **2:3** 7:1991 pp. 217 – 234

27 Sviluppo del Mezzogiorno e capitale umano *[In Italian]*; Development of the south of Italy and human capital *[Summary]*. Paolo Sestito. *Ec. Lav.* **XXV:4** 10-12:1991 pp. 3 – 14

28 Using a metropolitan-area econometric model to analyse economic development proposals. Paul Coomes; Dennis Olson; John Merchant. *Urban Stud.* **28:3** 6:1991 pp. 369 – 382

I: Labour — *Travail*

I.1: Sociology of industry and work — *Sociologie de l'industrie et du travail*

1 Além de Braverman, depois de Burawoy — vertentes analíticas na sociologia do trabalho *[In Portuguese]*; Beyond Braverman, after Burawoy — analytical lines in labor sociology *[Summary]*; Au-delà Braverman, après Burawoy — tendances analytiques dans la sociologie du travail *[French summary]*. Nadya Araújo Castro; Antônio Sérgio Alfredo Guimarães. *Rev. Bras. Ciên. Soc.* **6:17** 10:1991 pp. 44 – 52

2 Alemania — ¿Un nuevo paradigma de empresa? *[In Spanish]*; [Germany — a new enterprise paradigm?]. Alberto Lopez Caballero. *Rev. Fom. Soc.* **46:181** 1-3:1991 pp. 81 – 89

3 Aspects of time in organization. John Hassard. *Human Relat.* **44:2** 2:1991 pp. 105 – 125

4 Del trabajo como vocación al trabajo como elemento de estructura *[In Spanish]*; [From work as vocation to work as a structural element]. Antonio Marzal Fuentes. *Rev. Fom. Soc.* **46:181** 1-3:1991 pp. 61 – 79

5 Ideology, solidarity, and work values — the case of the Histadrut enterprises. Aviad Bar-Hayim; Gerald S. Berman. *Human Relat.* **44:4** 4:1991 pp. 357 – 370

6 Industrial sociology and economic crisis. J. E. T. Eldridge; J. MacInnes *[Ed.]*; P. Cressey *[Ed.]*. Hemel Hempstead: Harvester Wheatsheaf, 1991: 236 p. *ISBN: 0710807775*. Includes bibliography and index.

7 Interdisciplinary teams and the control of clients — a sociotechnical perspective. Eli Teram. *Human Relat.* **44:4** 4:1991 pp. 343 – 356

8 Japon — nouveaux défis *[In French]*; [Japan — new challenges]. Marc Maurice *[Contrib.]*; Shojiro Ujihara *[Contrib.]*; Takeshi Inagami *[Contrib.]*; Kazuyuki Kitamura *[Contrib.]*; Kazuo Koike *[Contrib.]*; Koichiro Imano *[Contrib.]*; Scott T. Davis *[Contrib.]*; Minoru Ito *[Contrib.]*; Michio Nitta *[Contrib.]*; Masayoshi Ikeda *[Contrib.] and others.* Collection of 12 articles. **Sociol. Trav.**, *XXXIII:1*, 1991 pp. 1 – 212

9 Magical work — firefighters in New York. Miriam Lee Kaprow. *Human. Org.* **50:1** Spring:1991 pp. 97 – 103

10 Quality of working life and the level of economic and industrial democracy in Latin America. Azril Bacal *[Ed.]*; Gert Rosenthal *[Contrib.]*; Stefan de Vylder *[Contrib.]*; Rodolfo Stavenhagen *[Contrib.]*; Solon Barraclough *[Contrib.]*; Rebecca Morales *[Contrib.]*; Paul Ong *[Contrib.]*; Leslie Howard *[Contrib.]*; Björn Feuer *[Contrib.]*; Azril Bacal *[Contrib.] and others.* Collection of 8 articles. **Econ. Ind. Dem.**, *12:1*, 2:1991 pp. 5 – 135

11 Regional industrial analysis and vintage dynamics. B. Johansson. *Ann. Reg. Sci.* **25:1** :1991 pp. 1 – 18

12 Restructuring or destructuring? Deindustrialization in two industrial heartland cities. Douglas Koritz. *Urban Aff. Q.* **26:4** 6:1991 pp. 497 – 511

13 The sociology of work — an introduction. Keith Grint. Oxford: Polity, 1991: 358 p. *ISBN: 0745606067*.

14 The value and costs of work — a study of the consequences of wage labour for the individual. Michael Tåhlin. *Eur. Sociol. R.* **5:2** 9:1989 pp. 115 – 132

15 Work psychology — understanding human behaviour in the workplace. John Arnold; Ivan T. Robertson; Cary L. Cooper. London: Pitman Publishing, 1991: 53 p. *ISBN: 0273034413*.

16 A world city and flexible specialization — restructuring of the Tokyo metropolis; *[French summary]*. Kuniko Kujita. *Int. J. Urban* **15:2** 6:1991 pp. 269 – 284

I.2: Employment and labour market — *Emploi et marché du travail*

Sub-divisions: Gender issues *[Questions de sexe]*; Labour force *[Main d'oeuvre]*; Labour policy and employment policy *[Politique du travail et politique de l'emploi]*; Unemployment *[Chômage]*

1 The 1987 crash and the spatial incidence of employment changes in the New York metropolitan region. Joseph C. Cox; Valerie Preston; Barney Warf. *Urban Stud.* **28**:3 6:1991 pp. 327 – 339
2 Australian evidence on the exit-voice model of the labor market. Paul Miller; Charles Mulvey. *Ind. Lab. Rel.* **45**:1 10:1991 pp. 44 – 57
3 Beloning en allocatie op een informele arbeidsdeelmarkt *[In Dutch]*; Wages and allocation on an informal labour market *[Summary]*. Rudi Wielers; Siegwart Lindenberg. *Mens Maat.* **66**:1 2:1991 pp. 5 – 24
4 Career employment and job stopping. Christopher J. Ruhm. *Ind. Relat.* **30**:2 Spring:1991 pp. 193 – 208
5 Croissance urbaine et restructuration du marché du travail en Côte d'Ivoire *[In French]*; [Urban growth and restructuring of the labour market in the Ivory Coast]. Aka Kouamé. *Can. J. Afr. St.* **25**:3 1991 pp. 396 – 417
6 The decline and rise of self-employment. Udo Staber; Dieter Bögenhold. *Work Emp. Soc.* **5**:2 6:1991 pp. 223 – 239
7 Dinamiche migratorie e dinamiche territoriali dei mercati del lavoro *[In Italian]*; Migration trends and geographical trends in the labour market *[Summary]*. Enrico del Colle. *Ec. Lav.* **XXV**:2 4-6:1991 pp. 107 – 115
8 The effect of job access on black and white youth employment — a cross-sectional analysis. Keith R. Ihlanfeldt; David L. Sjoquist. *Urban Stud.* **28**:2 4:1991 pp. 255 – 265
9 Empleo temporario y empleo incierto — dos caras del trabajo "temporario" en la Argentina *[In Spanish]*; [Temporary employment and uncertain employment — the two faces of temporary work in Argentina]. Adriana Marshall. *Desar. Econ.* **31**:122 7-9:1991 pp. 265 – 277
10 Employment and changing technology in the postwar railroad industry. Gilbert Yochum; G. Steven Rhiel. *Ind. Relat.* **30**:1 Winter:1991 pp. 116 – 127
11 Employment and the labour market. John Wrench. *New Comm.* **17**:4 7:1991 pp. 617 – 623
12 Employment changes and input-output linkages in key technology industries — a comparative analysis; L'évolution de l'emploi et les échanges inter-industriels dans les industries technologiques clé — une analyse comparative *[French summary]*; Beschäftigungsveranderungen und Input-Output- Verflechtungen in Schlüsseltechnologie-Industrien — eine vergleichende Analyse *[German summary]*. Harald Bathelt. *Reg. Stud.* **25**:1 2:1991 pp. 31 – 43
13 Employment changes in central London in the 1980s. II — understanding recent forces for change and future development constraints. M.E. Frost; N.A. Spence. *Geogr. J.* **157**:2 7:1991 pp. 125 – 135
14 Employment changes in central London. I. The record of the 1980s. M.E. Frost; N.A. Spence. *Geogr. J.* **157**:1 3:1991 pp. 1 – 12
15 Employment in India's organised sector. Suzan Hazra. *Soc. Scient.* **19**:7 7:1991 pp. 39 – 54
16 Etnicidad y mercado de trabajo en Ciudad de Guatemala — una aproximación *[In Spanish]*; [Ethnicity and the labour market in Guatemala City]. J.P. Perez Sainz. *An. Est. Cent.Am.* **16**:2/**17**:1 1990/1991 pp. 7 – 20
17 Explaining variations in employment growth — structural and cyclical change among states and local areas. David G. Terkla; Peter B. Doeringer. *J. Urban Ec.* **29**:3 5:1991 pp. 329 – 348
18 Farewell to flexibility? Anna Pollert *[Ed.]*. Oxford: Basil Blackwell, 1991: 316 p. *ISBN: 0631177965. Includes bibliographies and index.* [Warwick studies in industrial relations.]
19 Fidélité et rupture *[In French]*; [Reliability and rupture]. François Gaudu. *Droit Soc.* **:5** 5:1991 pp. 419 – 429
20 Formation et différenciation du marché des travailleurs étrangers au Japon *[In French]*; The labour market for immigrant workers *[Summary]*. Akihiro Ishikawa. *Sociol. Trav.* **XXXIII**:1 1991 pp. 173 – 188

I.2: Employment and labour market [Emploi et marché du travail]

21 Les garanties contractuelles de stabilité d'emploi *[In French]*; [Contract guarantees and employment stability]. Jean Savatier. *Droit Soc.* :**5** 5:1991 pp. 413 – 418

22 Getting a good job — mobility in a segmented labor market. Howard Wial. *Ind. Relat.* **30:3** Fall:1991 pp. 396 – 416

23 Giovani diplomati e successo nella ricerca di un lavoro stabile *[In Italian]*; (Young school-leavers and success in the search for a stable job position). Federico Rappelli. *Ec. Lav.* **XXV:4** 10-12:1991 pp. 129 – 148

24 Growth, technology, and the demand for scientists and engineers. Kevin F. Forbes; Ernest M. Zampelli. *Ind. Relat.* **30:2** Spring:1991 pp. 294 – 301

25 High-technology agglomeration and the labor market — the case of Silicon Valley. D.P. Angel. *Envir. Plan.A.* **23:10** 10:1991 pp. 1501 – 1516

26 Hiring, promotion, and pay in a corporate head office — an internal labour market in action? Richard B. Bernard; Michael R. Smith. *Can. J. Soc.* **16:4** Fall:1991 pp. 353 – 374

27 Homework and the fragmentation of space — challenges for the labor movement. A. Herod. *Geoforum* **22:2** 1991 pp. 173 – 184

28 Income redistribution in a common labor market. David E. Wildasin. *Am. Econ. Rev.* **81:4** 9·1991 pp. 757 – 774

29 Inequality and attainment in a dual labor market. Arthur Sakamoto; Meichu D. Chen. *Am. Sociol. R.* **56:3** 6:1991 pp. 295 – 308

30 Изменение характера и содэржания труда на современном этапе развития социализма *[In Russian]*; [Change in the character and the maintenance of labour in the current stage in the development of socialism]. R.K. Ivanova *[Ed.]*; D.N. Karpukhin *[Ed.]*; N.A. Glodnykh. Moscow: Nauka, 1987: 272 p.

31 Job search behavior of employed youth. Donald O. Parsons. *Rev. Econ. St.* **LXXIII:4** 11:1991 pp. 597 – 604

32 A la recherche des synergies perdues *[In French]*; [In search of lost synergies]. Jean-Louis Laville. *Inf. Soc.* :**13** 8-9:1991 pp. 8 – 17

33 Labor market access and labor market outcomes for urban youth. K.M. O'Regan; J.M. Quigley. *Reg. Sci. Urb. Econ.* **21:2** 7:1991 pp. 277 – 294

34 Labour market flexibility — the case of part-time employment in Canada; La flexibilité du marché du travail — le cas de l'emploi à temps partiel au Canada *[French summary]*. Olive Robinson. *Ind. Relat. J.* **22:1** Spring:1991 pp. 46 – 58

35 Labour market inequality between men and women — allocational differences versus wage rate differences. Joop J. Schippers; Jacques J. Siegers. *Economist [Leiden]* **139:3** :1991 pp. 401 – 427

36 Labour market transitions of husbands and wives in the Netherlands between 1980 and 1986. Paul M. de Graaf; Wout C. Ultee. *Neth. J. Soc. Sci.* **27:1** 4:1991 pp. 43 – 59

37 Le licenciement, à raison de ses mœurs, d'un salarié d'une association à caractère religieux *[In French]*; [Redundancy, due to the morals of a worker in a religious company]. Jean Savatier. *Droit Soc.* :**6** 6:1991 pp. 485 – 490

38 Le marché du travail *[In French]*; [The labour market]. Olivier Marchand *[Contrib.]*; Michel Cézard *[Contrib.]*; Monique Meron *[Contrib.]*; Nicole Roth *[Contrib.]*; Constance Torelli *[Contrib.]*; Sylvie Dumartin *[Contrib.]*; Yves Bourdet *[Contrib.]*; Inga Persson *[Contrib.]*; Dominique Rouault-Galdo *[Contrib.]*; Hervé Huyghues Despointes *[Contrib.]* and others. Collection of 10 articles. **E & S**, 249, 12:1991 pp. 7 – 119

39 Matching processes in the labor market. James S. Coleman. *Acta Sociol.* **34:1** 1991 pp. 3 – 12

40 Matching samples and analysing their differences in a cross-national study of labour market entry in England and West Germany. John Bynner; Walter Heinz. *Int. J. Comp. Soc* **XXXII: 1-2** 1-4:1991 pp. 137 – 153

41 Measuring discrimination by direct experimental methods — seeking gunsmoke. Peter A. Riach; Judith Rich. *J. Post. Keyn. Ec.* **14:2** Winter:1991/92 pp. 143 – 150

42 Los mecanismos de discriminación racial en el mercado de trabajo *[In Spanish]*; [Mechanisms of racial discrimination in the labour market]. Salvador A.M. Sandoval. *Est. Sociol.* **IX:25** 1-4:1991 pp. 35 – 60

43 Modelling hours of work in a labour services function. Derek Leslie. *Scot. J. Poli.* **38:1** 02:1991 pp. 19 – 31

44 National business cycles and community competition for jobs. John D. Kasarda; Michael D. Irwin. *Soc. Forc.* **69:3** 3:1991 pp. 733 – 761

45 Nationalismus und Arbeitsmarktintegration in der BRD *[In German]*; Nationalism and labor market integration in (pre-unification) Germany *[Summary]*. David Baker; Gero Lenhardt. *Z. Soziol.* **20:6** 12:1991 pp. 463 – 478

I.2: Employment and labour market *[Emploi et marché du travail]*

46 New approaches to economic and social analyses of discrimination. Richard R. Cornwall *[Ed.]*; Phanindra V. Wunnava *[Ed.]*. New York: Praeger, 1991: xvii, 412 p. (ill) ISBN: 0275935817; LofC: 91015504. Rev. papers from the eleventh annual Middlebury Conference on Economic Issues held April 6-8, 1989; Includes bibliographical references (p. [365]-390) and index.

47 Occupational differentiation approach to public service remuneration. D. Sing. *S. Afr. J. Labour Relat.* **15:2** 6:1991 pp. 27 – 33

48 On the links between home and work — family-household strategies in a buoyant labour market. Geraldine Pratt; Susan Hanson. *Int. J. Urban* **15:1** 3:1991 pp. 55 – 74

49 "Overeducation" in the labor market. Nachum Sicherman. *J. Labor Ec.* **9:2** 4:1991 pp. 101 – 122

50 Palestinian national identity and the Israeli labor market — Q-analyses. Juval Portugali; Michael Sonis. *Prof. Geogr.* **43:3** 8:1991 pp. 265 – 279

51 Patterns of human resource development in Saudi Arabia. Robert E. Looney. *Middle E. Stud.* **27:4** 10:1991 pp. 668 – 678

52 Prejudice, discrimination, and the labor market — attainments of immigrants in Australia. M.D.R. Evans; Jonathan Kelley. *A.J.S.* **97:3** 11:1991 pp. 721 – 759

53 Public employee unions, reformism, and black employment in 1,200 American cities. Kenneth R. Mladenka. *Urban Aff. Q.* **26:4** 6:1991 pp. 532 – 548

54 Redistribution of work and income in the crisis — actors' problems of working time reduction and a guaranteed basic income. Georg Vobruba. *Cr. Law Soc. Chan.* **14:1** 3:1990 pp. 57 – 67

55 Residential segregation and the economic status of black workers — new evidence for an old debate. Mark Alan Hughes; Janice Fanning Madden. *J. Urban Ec.* **29:1** 1:1991 pp. 28 – 49

56 Roles familiares y mercado de trabajo *[In Spanish]*; *[Catalan summary]*; [Family roles and the labour market] *[Summary]*. Xavier Coller. *Papers* **:36** 1991 pp. 93 – 116

57 Search for nonwage job characteristics — a test of the reservation wage hypothesis. David M. Blau. *J. Labor Ec.* **9:2** 4:1991 pp. 186 – 205

58 Les services de proximité *[In French]*; [Services in demand]. Bernard Eme. *Inf. Soc.* **:13** 8-9:1991 pp. 34 – 42

59 Short term labour market consequences of teenage pregnancy. D.M. Byrne; S.C. Myers; R.H. King. *Appl. Econ.* **23:12** 12:1991 pp. 1819 – 1827

60 A simultaneous wage and labor supply model with hours restrictions. Martijn P. Tummers; Isolde Woittiez. *J. Hum. Res.* **XXVI:3** Summer:1991 pp. 393 – 423

61 Sponsorship and employment status among Indochinese refugees in the United States. Thanh V. Tran. *Int. Migr. Rev.* **XXV:3** Fall:1991 pp. 536 – 550

62 Studying work in China. Robert Storey. *Can. J. Soc.* **16:3** Summer:1991 pp. 241 – 264

63 Temporary work in Western Europe — threat or complement to permanent employment? A.S. Bronstein. *Int. Lab. Rev.* **130:3** 1991 pp. 291 – 310

64 Testing for racial discrimination in the labour market. Peter A. Riach; Judith Rich. *Camb. J. Econ.* **15:3** 9:1991 pp. 239 – 256

65 Trapped in poverty? — labour-market decisions in low-income households. Bill Jordan *[Ed.]*. London: Routledge, 1991: 350 p. ISBN: 0415068673; LofC: 91010046. Labour force; Includes bibliographical references and index.

66 Turkse HTS'ers zoeken werk. Verslag van een sollicitatie-experiment *[In Dutch]*; Turkish civil engineers look for jobs *[Summary]*. Ömer Büyükbozkoyum; Michael Stamatiou; Margo Stolk. *Sociol. Gids* **38:3** 5/6:1991 pp. 187 – 192

67 U.N. International Convention on the Protection of the Rights of All Migrant Workers and Members of their Families. Michael Hasenau *[Contrib.]*; Roger Böhning *[Contrib.]*; Juhani Lönnroth *[Contrib.]*; Linda S. Bosniak *[Contrib.]*; James A.R. Nafziger *[Contrib.]*; Barry C. Bartel *[Contrib.]*; Shirley Hune *[Contrib.]*; Giovanni Kojanec *[Contrib.]*; Tugrul Ansay *[Contrib.]*; Arthur C. Helton *[Contrib.]* and others. Collection of 14 articles. **Int. Migr. Rev.**, *XXV:4*, Winter:1991 pp. 687 – 957

68 Urban structure and the labour market — worker mobility, commuting, and underemployment in cities. Wayne Simpson. Oxford: Clarendon Press, 1991: 198 p. ISBN: 019828358x; LofC: 91032146. Includes bibliographical references and index.

69 Use of family rhetoric in a work incentive program. Gale Miller. *J. Marriage Fam.* **53:3** 8:1991 pp. 609 – 621

70 The use of multiple regression analysis in employment discrimination cases. C. Connolly. *Pop. Res. Pol. R.* **10:2** 1991 pp. 117 – 136

I.2: Employment and labour market *[Emploi et marché du travail]*
71 YTS and the labour market. I.G. Begg; A.P. Blake; B.M. Deakin. *Br. J. Ind. R.* **29:2** 6:1991 pp. 223 – 236

Gender issues *[Questions de sexe]*
72 L'activité féminine — une affaire de familles *[In French]*; Women's labor force participation — a family affair *[Summary]*. Françoise Bloch; Monique Buisson; Jean-Claude Mermet. *Sociol. Trav.* **XXXIII:2** 1991 pp. 255 – 276
73 Analyse biographique du travail féminin *[In French]*; The life history analysis of women's work *[Summary]*. M. Kempeneers; E. Lelièvre. *Eur. J. Pop.* **7:4** 1991 pp. 377 – 400
74 Asian women workers in Kuwait. Nasra M. Shah; Sulayman S. Al-Qudsi; Makhdoom A. Shah. *Int. Migr. Rev.* **XXV:3** Fall:1991 pp. 464 – 486
75 Attractions of male blue-collar jobs for black and white women — economic need, exposure, and attitudes. Irene Padavic. *Soc. Sci. Q.* **72:1** 3:1991 pp. 33 – 49
76 Career orientations in women from rural and urban backgrounds. Millicent E. Poole; Janice Langan-Fox; Mary Omodei. *Human Relat.* **44:9** 9:1991 pp. 983 – 1006
77 Child-care expenditures and women's employment turnover. David J. Maume. *Soc. Forc.* **70:2** 12:1991 pp. 495 – 508
78 Contradictions in the gender subtext of the war on poverty — the community work and resistance of women from low income communities. Nancy A. Naples. *Soc. Prob.* **38:3** 8:1991 pp. 316 – 332
79 Contrasting perspectives on women's access to prestigious occupations — a cross-national investigation. Roger Clark. *Soc. Sci. Q.* **72:1** 3:1991 pp. 20 – 32
80 Culture, gender, and labor force participation — a cross-national study. Roger Clark; Thomas W. Ramsbey; Emily Stier Adler. *Gender Soc.* **5:1** 3:1991 pp. 47 – 66
81 Dealing with poverty — self-employment for poor, rural women. Usha Jumani. New Delhi: Sage Publications, 1991: 246 p. *ISBN: 0803996918; LofC: 91013755.*
82 The determinants of female recruitment. F. Green. *Appl. Econ.* **23:4B** 4:1991 pp. 709 – 716
83 Determinants of the supply of women in the labour market — a micro analysis. Shahnaz Hamid; S. Zia Al-Jalali *[Comments by]*. *Pak. Dev. R.* **30:4** Winter:1991 pp. 755 – 765
84 La discontinuité professionnelle des femmes au Canada — permanance et changements *[In French]*; Career breaks among Canadian women. Permanance and change *[Summary]*; Discontinuidad profesional de las mujeres en Canada — permanencia y Cambio *[Spanish summary]*. Marianne Kempeneers. *Population* **46:1** 1-2:1991 pp. 9 – 28
85 Discrimination in the Pakistan labour market — myth and reality. Yasmeen Mohiuddin; Shahnaz Kazi *[Comments by]*. *Pak. Dev. R.* **30:4** Winter:1991 pp. 965 – 977
86 Duality of female employment in Pakistan. Shahnaz Kazi; Bilquees Raza; Ann Duncan *[Comments by]*. *Pak. Dev. R.* **30:4** Winter:1991 pp. 733 – 741
87 Earnings and assimilation of female immigrants. E. Field-Hendrey; E. Balkan. *Appl. Econ.* **23:10** 10:1991 pp. 1665 – 1672
88 Earnings and percentage female — a longitudinal study. Barry Gerhart; Nabil El Cheikh. *Ind. Relat.* **30:1** Winter:1991 pp. 62 – 78
89 Employed mothers — the impact of class and marital status on the prioritizing of family and work. Beverly H. Burris. *Soc. Sci. Q.* **72:1** 3:1991 pp. 50 – 66
90 Employment versus empowerment — a case study of the nature of women's work in Ecuador. Anne H. Faulkner; Victoria A. Lawson. *J. Dev. Stud.* **27:4** 7:1991 pp. 16 – 47
91 The experiences of Canadian women in trades and technology. Frances Cherry; Nancy McIntyre; Deborah Jaggernathsingh. *Wom. St. Inter. For.* **14:1/2** 1991 pp. 15 – 26
92 Exploring the reasons behind the narrowing gender gap in earnings. Elaine Joy Sorensen. Washington, D.C: Urban Institute Press, 1991: xi, 163 p. (ill) *ISBN: 0877665079; LofC: 90026783.* Includes abstract; Includes bibliographical references (p. [159]-163). [Urban Institute report.]
93 Female labor supply — labor force participation, market wage rate and working hours of married and unmarried women in the Federal Republic of Germany; Das Arbeitsangebot von Frauen — Erwerbsbeteiligung, Marktlohnsatz und Arbeitszeit verheirateter und unverheirateter Frauen in der Bundesrepublik Deutschland *[German summary]*. Joachim Merz. *Jahrb. N. St.* **207:3** 5:1990 pp. 240 – 270
94 Female wage labor in rural Zimbabwe. J.M. Adams. *World Dev.* **19:2-3** 2-3:1991 pp. 163 – 177
95 Flexibility, gender and local labour markets — some examples from Denmark. Lise Drewes Nielsin. *Int. J. Urban* **15:1** 3:1991 pp. 42 – 54

I.2: Employment and labour market [Emploi et marché du travail] — Gender issues [Questions de sexe]

96 The gender and labor politics of postmodernity. Aihwa Ong. *Ann. R. Anthr.* **20:** 1991 pp. 279 – 301
97 Gender and off-farm employment in two farming systems — responses to farm crisis in the Cornbelt and the Mississippi Delta. Max J. Pfeffer; Jess Gilbert. *Sociol. Q.* **32:4** Winter:1991 pp. 593 – 610
98 Gender and population in the adjustment of African economies — planning for change. Ingrid Palmer. Geneva: International Labour Office, 1991: 187 p. *ISBN: 922107739x*. [Women, work and development. : No. 19]
99 Gender considerations in economic enterprises — report of a workshop held in the Philippines. Eugenia Piza Lopez *[Ed.]*; Candida March *[Ed.]*. Oxford: Oxfam, 1991: 40 p. *ISBN: 085598189x*. [Oxfam discussion paper. : No. 2]
100 Gender differences in work-family conflict. Linda Elizabeth Duxbury; Christopher Alan Higgins. *J. Appl. Psychol.* **76:1** 2:1991 pp. 60 – 74
101 Gender differentials in labour force participation in Bangladesh. Nilufar Ahmad. *Bang. J. Pol. Econ.* **11:2B** 1991 pp. 247 – 258
102 Gender discrimination in the British labour market — a reassessment. R.E. Wright; J.F. Ermisch. *Econ. J.* **101:406** 5:1991 pp. 508 – 522
103 Gender, family, and economy — the triple overlap. Rae Lesser Blumberg *[Ed.]*. London: Sage Publications, 1991: 311 p. *ISBN: 0803937563. Includes bibliographical references.* [Sage focus editions. : No. 125]
104 The gendered economy — work, careers, and success. Rita Mae Kelly. London: Sage Publications, 1991: 304 p. *ISBN: 080394215x; LofC: gb 91091697.*
105 Growth in service sector employment and MSA gender earnings inequality — 1970-1980. Jon Lorence. *Soc. Forc.* **69:3** 3:1991 pp. 763 – 783
106 Home investment in husband's human capital and the wife's decision to work. P.S. Carlin. *J. Pop. Ec.* **4:1** 1991 pp. 71 – 86
107 Immigrant women go to work — analysis of immigrant wives' labor supply for six Asian groups. Haya Stier. *Soc. Sci. Q.* **72:1** 3:1991 pp. 67 – 82
108 The impact of employer-sponsored child care on female labor supply behavior — evidence from the nursing profession. E.L. Lehrer; T. Santero; S. Mohan-Neill. *Pop. Res. Pol. R.* **10:3** 1991 pp. 197 – 212
109 Impact of male and female wages on labour force participation. Juanita M. Firestone; Beth Anne Shelton. *Social Soc. Res.* **74:2** 1:1990 pp. 127 – 136
110 Impact of the equal employment opportunity and affirmative action programs on the employment of women in the US. Noel D. Uri; J. Wilson Mixon. *Labour [Italy]* **5:2** Autumn:1991 pp. 89 – 104
111 The incentive effects of Medicaid on women's labor supply. Anne E. Winkler. *J. Hum. Res.* **XXVI:2** Spring:1991 pp. 308 – 337
112 Increasing women's participation in technical fields. A pilot project in Africa. Sue Leigh-Doyle. *Int. Lab. Rev.* **130:4** 4:1991 pp. 427 – 444
113 An interdisciplinary approach to analyzing the managerial gender gap. Kathleen Cannings. *Human Relat.* **44:7** 7:1991 pp. 679 – 696
114 Job search and the occupational segregation of women. Susan Hanson; Geraldine Pratt. *Ann. As. Am. G.* **81:2** 6:1991 pp. 229 – 253
115 Just wages — a feminist assessment of pay equity. Judy Fudge *[Ed.]*; Patricia McDermott *[Ed.]*. Toronto: University of Toronto Press, c1991: 307 p. *ISBN: 0802059376; LofC: 92143913. Includes bibliographical references (p. [289]-303).*
116 Labor market participation, returns to education, and male-female wage differences in Peru. Shahidur R. Khandker. Washington, D.C.: Population and Human Resources Department, the World Bank, 1990: 51 p. *BNB: 91155380; LofC: 91155380. Includes bibliographical references (p. 46-47).* [Policy, research, and external affairs working papers.]
117 Labour force status of older men and women in the Netherlands. Kène Henkens; Jacques Siegers. *Bevolk. Gez.* **:1** 1991 pp. 77 – 94
118 De loopbaanontwikkeling van vrouwen en mannen in de rechterlijke macht — beeld en werkelijkheid *[In Dutch]*; Careers of women and men in the Dutch judiciary — self-perception and reality *[Summary]*. L.E. de Groot-van Leeuwen; C.C.M. Kester; J.G.C. Kester. *Mens Maat.* **66:1** 2:1991 pp. 54 – 64
119 Married womens' tastes and the decision to participate in the labour market — results from a fixed effects model. C.F. Miller. *Appl. Econ.* **23:9** 9:1991 pp. 1499 – 1510

I.2: Employment and labour market *[Emploi et marché du travail]* — Gender issues *[Questions de sexe]*

120 Men managers and women workers — women employees as an under-used resource. L. Ashburner. *Br. J. Manag.* **2:1** 4:1991 pp. 3 – 15
121 Men, women, and the culture of engineering. J. Gregg Robinson; Judith S. McIlwee. *Sociol. Q.* **32:3** Fall:1991 pp. 403 – 421
122 "More and more women work" — inquiries into the work patterns of adult Swiss women. Ursula Streckeisen. *Wom. St. Inter. For.* **14:1/2** 1991 pp. 77 – 84
123 New technologies, employment shifts and gender divisions within the textile industry; *[French summary]*. Louise Crewe. *New Tech. Work. Empl.* **6:1** Spring:1991 pp. 43 – 53
124 Nők a munkaerőpiacon *[In Hungarian]*; [Women in the labour market]. Katalin Koncz. Budapest: Közgazdasági és Jogi Könyvkiadó, 1987: 391 p.
125 Occupational differences in the ability of men to delay retirement. Thomas N. Chirikos; Gilbert Nestel. *J. Hum. Res.* **XXVI:1** Winter:1991 pp. 1 – 26
126 L'offerta di lavoro femminile — persistenza e partecipazione *[In Italian]*; Female labour supply — persistence and paticipation *[Summary]*. Monica Giulietti; M. Meloria Meschi. *Ec. Lav.* **XXV:4** 10-12:1991 pp. 57 – 72
127 On measuring the progress of women's quest for economic equality. Joyce M. Manchester; David C. Stapleton. *J. Hum. Res.* **XXVI:3** Summer:1991 pp. 562 – 577
128 Part-time work — women count the cost. Linda Grant. Bradford: WYCROW, 1991: 92 p. (ill) *ISBN: 1851430504. Includes bibliography.* [Wycrow working paper. : No. 2]
129 The patriarchal restructuring of gender segregation — a case study of the hotel and catering industry. Paul Bagguley. *Sociology* **25:4** 11:1991 pp. 607 – 625
130 Pregnancy discrimination — an empirical analysis of a continuing problem. William M. Slonaker; Ann C. Wendt. *Lab. Law J.* **42:6** 6:1991 pp. 343 – 350
131 The promise and the price — the struggle for equal opportunity in women's employment. Clare Burton. North Sydey, NSW, Australia: Allen & Unwin, 1991: xiv, 184 p. *ISBN: 0044422865; LofC: 90082309. Includes bibliographical references (p. 153-154) and index.*
132 Race, gender, and work — a multicultural economic history of women in the United States. Teresa L. Amott; Julie A. Matthaei. Boston, MA: South End Press, c1991: xiii, 433 p. (ill) *ISBN: 0896083764; LofC: 90048222. Includes bibliographical references (p. 357-394) and index.*
133 Rational versus gender role explanations for work-family conflict. Barbara A. Gutek; Sabrina Searle; Lilian Klepa. *J. Appl. Psychol.* **76:4** 8:1991 pp. 560 – 568
134 Rethinking tokenism — looking beyond numbers. Janice D. Yoder. *Gender Soc.* **5:2** 6:1991 pp. 178 – 192
135 Rhythm and flexiblity — a temporal approach to employment, age and gender. Tom Schuller. *Soc. Sci. Info.* **30:4** 12:1991 pp. 727 – 737
136 Serving hamburgers and selling insurance — gender, work, and identity in interactive service jobs. Robin Leidner. *Gender Soc.* **5:2** 6:1991 pp. 154 – 177
137 Sex discrimination and non-random sampling in the Australian labour market. Michael P. Kidd; Rosalie Viney. *Aust. Econ. P.* **30:56** 6:1991 pp. 28 – 49
138 Sex, employment and the law. Simon Honeyball. Oxford: Blackwell Law, 1991: 174 p. *ISBN: 0632025190. Includes bibliography and index.*
139 Sharing of home responsibilities between professionally employed women and their husbands. Monica Biernat; Camille B. Wortman. *J. Pers. Soc. Psychol.* **60:6** 6:1991 pp. 844 – 860
140 Socio-economic conditions of women workers in selected handloom and khadi units in Uttar Pradesh.*Indian. Lab. J.* **32:8** 8:1991 pp. 1139 – 1149
141 Sources of earnings inequality in the black and white female labor forces. Shelley A. Smith. *Sociol. Q.* **32:1** Spring:1991 pp. 117 – 138
142 Status of women employees in government. G. Vidya Rani. New Delhi: Mittal, 1990: 355 p.
143 Structural adjustment and African women farmers. Christina H. Gladwin *[Ed.]*. Gainesville: Florida University Press, 1991: 413 p. *ISBN: 0813010632.*
144 Suburban labor markets, urban labor markets, and gender inequality in earnings. Moshe Semyonov; Noah Lewin-Epstein. *Sociol. Q.* **32:4** Winter:1991 pp. 611 – 620
145 Talking shop(ping) — office conversations and women's dual labour; *[French summary]*. Melody Hessing. *Can. J. Soc.* **16:7** Winter:1991 pp. 23 – 50
146 Les transformations des structures du cycle de la vie des femmes au Japon *[In French]*; Changes in life cycle trends of women in Japan *[Summary]*. Machiko Osawa. *Sociol. Trav.* **XXXIII:1** 1991 pp. 163 – 172

I.2: Employment and labour market *[Emploi et marché du travail]* — Gender issues *[Questions de sexe]*

147 Transforming the debate about child care and maternal employment. Louise B. Silverstein. *Am. Psychol.* **46:10** 10:1991 pp. 1025 – 1032

148 When men are the minority — the case of men in nursing. E. Joel Heikes. *Sociol. Q.* **32:3** Fall:1991 pp. 389 – 402

149 Womanpower — managing in times of demographic turbulence. Uma Sekaran *[Ed.]*; Frederick T. L. Leong *[Ed.]*. London: Sage, 1991: xvii, 286 p. *ISBN: 0803941056; LofC: 91014324. Includes bibliographical references and index.*

150 Women and working lives — divisions and change. Nigel Gilbert *[Ed.]*; Sara Arber *[Ed.]*. London: Macmillan, 1991: 215 p. *ISBN: 0333565347.* [Explorations in sociology.]

151 Women in science — token women or gender equality? Veronica Stolte-Heiskanen *[Ed.]*; et al; Ruža First-Dilić *[Ed.]*. New York: Berg, 1991: 256 p. *ISBN: 0854967427; LofC: 90028894. "International Social Science Council in co-operation with Unesco."; Includes bibliographical references.*

152 Women into engineering and science — employers' practices and policies. Susan McRae; Fiona Devine *[Ed.]*; Jane Lakey *[Ed.]*. London: Policy Studies Institute, 1991: 113 p. *ISBN: 0853745196; LofC: gb 91003663.*

153 Women on the board. Elspeth Rosamund Morton Howe; Susan McRae *[Ed.]*. London: Policy Studies Institute, 1991: 14 p. *ISBN: 0853745145.*

154 Women workers and flexible specialization — the case of Tokyo. Kuniko Fujita. *Econ. Soc.* **20:3** 8:1991 pp. 260 – 282

155 Women working in nontraditional fields — references and resources, 1963-1988. Carroll Wetzel Wilkinson. Boston, Mass: G.K. Hall, 1991: xxiv, 213 p. *ISBN: 081618934x; LofC: 90026655. Includes indexes.* [G.K. Hall women's studies publications.]

156 Women, employment and social policy in Northern Ireland — a problem postponed? Celia Davies *[Ed.]*; Eithne McLaughlin *[Ed.]*. Belfast: Policy Research Institute, The Queen's University of Belfast and the University of Ulster, c1991: vii,174 p. (ill) *ISBN: 1870654110. Includes bibliographies and index.*

157 Women, training and the skills shortage — the case for public investment. Joan Payne. London: Policy Studies Institute, 1991: 190 p. *ISBN: 0853745056.*

158 Women's employment and technology. U.H. Rasheda Akhtar Khanam. *Bang. J. Pol. Econ.* **11:2B** 1991 pp. 259 – 267

159 Women's employment during pregnancy and after the first birth — occupational characteristics and work commitment. Sonalde Desai; Linda J. Waite. [New York]: Population Council Research Division, 1991: 40 p. *ISBN: oc24311438. Includes bibliographical references (p. 38-40).* [Working papers.]

160 Women's work, education, and family welfare in Peru. Barbara Knapp Herz *[Ed.]*; Shahidur R. Khandker *[Ed.]*. Washington, D.C: World Bank, c1991: xvi, 280 p. (ill) *ISBN: 0821317741; LofC: 91006831. Includes bibliographical references (p. 269-280).* [World Bank discussion papers.]

161 Work engendered — toward a new history of American labor. Ava Baron *[Ed.]*. Ithaca: Cornell University Press, 1991: viii, 385 p. (ill) *ISBN: 0801422566; LofC: 91002281. Includes bibliographical references and index.*

162 The world views of export processing workers in northern Mexico — a study of women, consciousness, and the new international division of labor. Robert Fiala; Susan Tiano. *Stud. Comp. ID.* **26:3** Fall:1991 pp. 3 – 27

Labour force *[Main d'oeuvre]*

163 Au-delà de l'an 2000, s'adapter à une pénurie de main-d'oeuvre *[In French]*; Adapting to a shortage of labor beyond the year 2000 *[Summary]*; Adaptarse a una penuria de mano de obra al principio del siglo XXI *[Spanish summary]*. Didier Blanchet; Olivier Marchand. *E & S* **:243** 5:1991 pp. 61 – 68

164 Ausländische Selbständige auf dem bundesdeutschen Arbeitsmarkt. Ein Beispiel für den wirtschaftlichen und sozialen Aufstieg ehemaliger ausländischer Arbeitnehmer *[In German]*; Self-employed foreigners on the Federal German labour market. An example of the economic and upward social mobility of former foreign employees *[Summary]*. Andreas Goldberg. *Inf. Raum.* **:7/8** 1991 pp. 411 – 419

165 British employment in the eighties — the spatial, structural and compositional change of the workforce. Martin Frost *[Contrib.]*; Nigel Spence *[Contrib.]*. Collection of 3 articles. *Prog. Plan.*, **35:2**, 1991 pp. 75 – 168

I.2: Employment and labour market [Emploi et marché du travail] — Labour force [Main d'oeuvre]

166 Career plans and expectations of young women and men — the earnings gap and labor force participation. Francine D. Blau; Marianne A. Ferber. *J. Hum. Res.* **XXVI:4** Fall:1991 pp. 581 – 607

167 Child labour in Zimbabwe and the rights of the child. Rene Loewenson. *J. Soc. Devel. Afr.* **6:1** 1991 pp. 19 – 31

168 Comparative managerial perceptions of progress made in black advancement in South Africa. K.B. Hofmeyr; A.J. Templer. *S. Afr. J. Labour Relat.* **15:2** 6:1991 pp. 3 – 11

169 The determinants of interdistrict labour in-migration in Pakistan. Andrew P. Barkley. *Pak. Dev. R.* **30:3** 8:1991 pp. 275 – 296

170 Determinants of the supply of women in the labour market — a micro analysis. Shahnaz Hamid; S. Zia Al-Jalali *[Comments by]*. *Pak. Dev. R.* **30:4** Winter:1991 pp. 755 – 765

171 Determinants of urban labour force participation in Kenya. G.M. Barber; W.J. Milne; G. Ongile. *E. Afr. Econ. Rev.* **6:2** 1990 pp. 83 – 94

172 The experience of refugees in the Australian labor market. Mark Wooden. *Int. Migr. Rev.* **XXV:3** Fall:1991 pp. 514 – 535

173 Female labor force participation in urban and rural China. Richard E. Barrett; William P. Bridges; Moshe Semyonov; Xiaoyuan Gao. *Rural Sociol.* **56:1** Spring:1991 pp. 1 – 21

174 The first "real" job — a study of young workers. Kathryn M. Borman. Albany: State University of New York Press, c1991: xi, 153 p. *ISBN: 0791405982; LofC: 90009910. Includes bibliographical references (p. 137-144) and index.* [SUNY series, the new inequalities.]

175 Gender differentials in labour force participation in Bangladesh. Nilufar Ahmad. *Bang. J. Pol. Econ.* **11:2B** 1991 pp. 247 – 258

176 Die gestremde werknemer in perspektief *[In Afrikaans]*; The disabled person as employee in perspective *[Summary]*. R. Uys. *S. Afr. J. Labour Relat.* **15:1** 3:1991 pp. 37 – 51

177 Health and labour force participation — "stress", selection and the reproduction costs of labour power. Mel Bartley. *J. Soc. Pol.* **20:3** 7:1991 pp. 327 – 364

178 Hispanics in the labor force — issues and policies. Edwin Melendez *[Ed.]*; Clara Rodriguez *[Ed.]*; Janis Barry Figueroa *[Ed.]*. New York: Plenum Press, 1991: xviii, 310 p. (ill) *ISBN: 0306437996; LofC: 91020344. Includes bibliographical references and index.* [Environment, development, and public policy.]

179 Human capital investments and labor mobility. Göran Eriksson. *J. Labor Ec.* **9:3** 7:1991 pp. 236 – 254

180 Immigrant women go to work — analysis of immigrant wives' labor supply for six Asian groups. Haya Stier. *Soc. Sci. Q.* **72:1** 3:1991 pp. 67 – 82

181 Impact of male and female wages on labour force participation. Juanita M. Firestone; Beth Anne Shelton. *Social Soc. Res.* **74:2** 1:1990 pp. 127 – 136

182 An integrated analysis of the individual and societal division of labour. Walter van Dongen. *Bevolk. Gez.* **:1** 1991 pp. 53 – 76

183 Die Kehrseite der Mode — Migranten als Flexibilisierungsquelle in der Pariser Bekleidungsproduktion *[In German]*; [The flipside of fashion — migrants as a source of flexibilization in the Paris clothing industry]. Mirjana Morokvasic. *Prokla* **21:2(83)** 1991 pp. 264 – 284

184 Labor force participation of women and the sex ratio — a cross-country analysis. Marianne A. Ferber; Helen M. Berg. *R. Soc. Econ.* **XLIX:1** Spring:1991 pp. 2 – 19

185 Labor market segmentation — African American and Puerto Rican labor in New York City, 1960-1980. Andrés Torres. *Rev. Bl. Pol. Ec.* **20:1** Summer:1991 pp. 59 – 78

186 The labour force of the Maghreb countries. Eleonore Jacob. *Asien. Af. Lat.am.* **19:3** 1991 pp. 501 – 516

187 Legal foundations of human capital markets. Dan Jacoby. *Ind. Relat.* **30:2** Spring:1991 pp. 229 – 250

188 Literacy and less skilled jobs. John Atkinson; Rachel Papworth. Brighton: University of Sussex, Institute of Manpower Studies, 1991: 111 p. *ISBN: 1851841288. Labour force; Based on Manpower commentary no.48 in the IMS manpower commentary programme undertaken for the Employment Department Group.* [IMS report. : No. 211]

189 Meer, minder of gelijk? Over de arbeidskansen van hoog opgeleide leden van etnische groepen *[In Dutch]*; More, less or equal *[Summary]*. Frank Bovenkerk; Bertien den Brok; Loes Ruland. *Sociol. Gids* **38:3** 5/6:1991 pp. 174 – 186

190 Municipal labor demand in the presence of uncertainty — an econometric approach. Douglas Holtz-Eakin; Harvey S. Rosen. *J. Labor Ec.* **9:3** 7:1991 pp. 276 – 293

I.2: Employment and labour market [Emploi et marché du travail] — Labour force [Main d'oeuvre]

191 Occupational mobility in segmented labour markets — the experience of immigrant workers in Melbourne. Iain Campbell; Ruth Fincher; Michael Webber. *Aust. N.Z. J. Soc.* **27:2** 8:1991 pp. 172 – 194

192 The operation of regional labor markets for highly trained manufacturing workers in the United States. Richard Barff; Mark Ellis. *Urban Geogr.* **12:4** 7-8:1991 pp. 339 – 362

193 Le peuplement des bidonvilles d'Alger — emploi et mobilité socio-professionnelle *[In French]*; The population of the shanty-towns of Algiers — jobs and socio-professional mobility *[Summary]*; Die Bevölkerung der Bidonvilles (Elendsviertel) von Alger — Arbeitsverhältnisse und sozioprofessionnelle Mobilität *[German summary]*; El pueblo de los barrios de las latas de Argel — empleos y movilidad socio-profesional *[Spanish summary]*. Maurice Guetta; Cyrille Megdiche. *Rev. Fr. Soc.* **XXXI:2** 4-6:1990 pp. 297 – 313

194 Protecting working children. William E. Myers *[Ed.]*. London: Zed Books in association with United Nations Children's Fund, New York, c1991: 173 p. *ISBN: 1856490068; LofC: 91013767. Includes index.*

195 Race, gender, and work — a multicultural economic history of women in the United States. Teresa L. Amott; Julie A. Matthaei. Boston, MA: South End Press, c1991: xiii, 433 p. (ill) *ISBN: 0896083764; LofC: 90048222. Includes bibliographical references (p. 357-394) and index.*

196 Racial differences in intersegment mobility. Jeffrey Waddoups. *Rev. Bl. Pol. Ec.* **20:2** Fall:1991 pp. 23 – 44

197 Rhythm and flexiblity — a temporal approach to employment, age and gender. Tom Schuller. *Soc. Sci. Info.* **30:4** 12:1991 pp. 727 – 737

198 La sous-utilisation des ressources humaines et ses causes — quelques hypothèses sur le cas ivoirien *[In French]*; The under-utilization of human resources and its causes — some hypotheses on the Ivorian case *[Summary]*. Aka Kouamé. *Labour Cap. Soc.* **24:1** 4:1991 pp. 110 – 134

199 Soviet workers — a new beginning? Leo Panitch; Sam Gindin. *Mon. Rev.* **42:11** 4:1991 pp. 17 – 35

200 The U-Curve adjustment hypothesis revisited — a review and theoretical framework. J. Stewart Black; Mark Mendenhall. *J. Int. Bus. Stud.* **22:2** 1991 pp. 225 – 247

201 Why people work — an examination of interstate variations in labor force participation. Lowell Gallaway; Richard Vedder; Robert Lawson. *J. Labor Res.* **XII:1** Winter:1991 pp. 47 – 59

202 Work and family — policies for a changing work force. Marianne A. Ferber *[Ed.]*; Brigid O'Farrell *[Ed.]*; LaRue Allen *[Ed.]*. Washington, DC: National Academy Press, 1991: ix, 260 p. *ISBN: 0309042771; LofC: 91025484. Panel on Employer Policies and Working Families, Committee on Women's Employment and Related Social Issues, Commission on Behavioral and Social Sciences and Education, National Research Council; Includes bibliographical references (p. 202-232) and index.*

203 Zur Entwicklung der Situation und zur beruflichen Integration von Ausländern in der Bundesrepublik Deutschland *[In German]*; Developments in the situation of foreigners in the Federal Republic of Germany and their integration into working life *[Summary]*. Bernhard Bruno Schmidt. *Inf. Raum.* **:7/8** 1991 pp. 405 – 409

Labour policy and employment policy [Politique du travail et politique de l'emploi]

204 Affirmative talk, affirmative action — a comparative study of the politics of affirmative action. Augustus J. Jones. New York: Praeger, 1991: xiv, 186 p. *ISBN: 0275936813; LofC: 90024157. Labour policy and employment policy; Includes bibliographical references (p. [175]-182) and index.*

205 California's radical proposal — a model for the fifty states? Nancy Kubasek; Andrea Giampetro-Meyer. *Lab. Law J.* **42:3** 3:1991 pp. 173 – 178

206 The effect of government incentives and assistance on location and job growth in manufacturing; L'effet des incitations et des aides gouvernementales sur la localisation et la croissance de l'emploi dans l'industrie *[French summary]*; Die Auswirkung von Regierungsanreizen und- beihilfen auf Standort und Stellenzuwachs in der herstellenden Industrie *[In German]*. Robert Walker; David Greenstreet. *Reg. Stud.* **25:1** 2:1991 pp. 13 – 30

I.2: Employment and labour market *[Emploi et marché du travail]* — Labour policy and employment policy *[Politique du travail et politique de l'emploi]*

207 Flexible employment strategies in British industry — evidence from the UK "sunbelt"; Stratégies d'emploi souples dans l'industrie en Grand-Bretagne — des preuves provenant de la zone "ensoleillée' au Royaume-Uni *[French summary]*; Elastische Arbeitseinsatztaktiken in der britischen Industrie — Beweismaterial vom "sunbelt" *[German summary]*. S. Pinch; C. Mason; S. Witt. *Reg. Stud.* **25:3** 6:1991 pp. 207 – 218

208 Generalized social attitudes and perceptions of youth unemployment policy-making — a cross-cultural comparison of adolescents in Denmark, Finland, Norway, and Sweden. Tom Bryder. *Polit. Psych.* **12:3** 9:1991 pp. 431 – 445

209 Hiring strategies, racial bias, and inner-city workers. Kathryn M. Neckerman; Joleen Kirschenman. *Soc. Prob.* **38:4** 11:1991 pp. 433 – 447

210 Human resource implications of new technology — a case study of automobiles in Spain. Kuriakose Mamkoottam; Emil Herbolzeimer. *Ind. J. Ind. Rel.* **26:3** 1:1991 pp. 205 – 226

211 The Japanese permanent employment system — empirical findings. Man Tsun Cheng. *Work Occup.* **18:2** 5:1991 pp. 148 – 171

212 Legal mobilization as a social movement tactic — the struggle for equal employment opportunity. Paul Burstein. *A.J.S.* **96:5** 3:1991 pp. 1201 – 1225

213 Maternity rights in Britain — the experience of women and employers. Susan McRae; W.W. Daniel *[Foreword]*. London: Policy Studies Institute, 1991: 276 p. *ISBN: 0853745242.*

214 Ochrona zatrudnienia we włoskim prawie pracy *[In Polish]*; (Охрана занятости в итальянском праве труда: *Title only in Russian)*; (Employment protection in Italian labour law). Beata Pałka. *Pra. Zab. Społ.* :**11-12** 1991 pp. 33 – 42

215 Poor work — disadvantage and the division of labour. Richard Scase *[Ed.]*; Phillip Brown *[Ed.]*. Milton Keynes: Open University Press, 1991: 168 p. *ISBN: 0335099416.*

216 Rethinking tokenism — looking beyond numbers. Janice D. Yoder. *Gender Soc.* **5:2** 6:1991 pp. 178 – 192

217 Rice bowls and job security — the urban contract labour system. Pat Howard. *Aust. J. Chin. Aff.* **25** 1:1991 pp. 93 – 114

218 Sex, employment and the law. Simon Honeyball. Oxford: Blackwell Law, 1991: 174 p. *ISBN: 0632025190. Includes bibliography and index.*

219 Some evidence of the effects of labour market policies on workers' attitudes toward change in Canada and Sweden. Joseph Smucker; Axel van den Berg. *Can. J. Soc.* **16:7** Winter:1991 pp. 51 – 74

220 Sozialpartnerschaft und Beschäftigungspolitik in Österreich — eine Untersuchung vor dem Hintergrund der beschäftigungspolitischen Diskussion in der Bundesrepublik *[In German]*; [Social partnership and business policy in Austria — an investigation against the background of the business policy debate in Germany]. Reinhard Christl. Frankfurt am Main: P. Lang, 1990: iv, 222 p. *ISBN: 3631431333; LofC: 91198684. Originally presented as the author's thesis (doctoral)--Universität Passau, 1990; Includes bibliographical references (p. 193-222).* [Europäische Hochschulschriften.]

221 Time for retirement — comparative studies of early exit from the labor force. Martin Kohli *[Ed.]*; et al. Cambridge: Cambridge University Press, 1991: vii, 398 p. *ISBN: 0521400538; LofC: 91010462.*

222 Vulnerable workers — psychosocial and legal issues. Marilyn J. Davidson *[Ed.]*; Jill Earnshaw *[Ed.]*. Chichester: J. Wiley, c1991: viii, 341 p. *ISBN: 0471927597; LofC: 90012597. Includes bibliographical references and index.* [Wiley series on studies in occupational stress.]

223 Welfare benefits and lone parents' employment in Great Britain. John F. Ermisch; Robert E. Wright. *J. Hum. Res.* **XXVI:3** Summer:1991 pp. 424 – 456

Unemployment *[Chômage]*

224 Het aanbod van zwarte arbeid door werkloze uitkeringsgerechtigden *[In Dutch]*; [Unemployment benefits and "black" labour supply] *[Summary]*. Wim Groot. *Mens Maat.* **65:2** 1990 pp. 145 – 164

225 De arbeidsmarktpositie van werkzoekenden na scholing — een vergelijking van allochtonen met autochtonen *[In Dutch]*; The unemployment rate between Dutch and ethnic people after finishing an educational program *[Summary]*. P. Scheepers; T. Speller; A. Willems. *Sociol. Gids* **38:3** 5/6:1991 pp. 162 – 173

226 Brytyjskie doświadczenia w organiczeniu bezrobocia — możliwość ich wykorzystania w Polsce *[In Polish]*; (Опыт Великобритании в ограничивании безработницы:

I.2: Employment and labour market [Emploi et marché du travail] — Unemployment [Chômage]

возможность его использования в Польше: Title only in Russian); (British experience of reduction of unemployment — possibility of its utilization in Poland). Grażyna Koptas. *Pra. Zab. Społ.* **33**:2-3 2-3:1991 pp. 36 – 42

227 La disoccupazione di lunga durata in Italia — un'analisi dell'evidenza empirica nel periodo 1977-1989 *[In Italian]*; Long-term unemployment in Italy — an empirical analysis of the period 1977-1989 *[Summary]*. Livia Ricciardi. *Ec. Lav.* **XXV**:2 4-6:1991 pp. 69 – 94

228 Economic restructuring and black male joblessness in U.S. metropolitan areas. James H. Johnson; Melvin L. Oliver. *Urban Geogr.* **12**:6 11-12:1991 pp. 542 – 562

229 Facing the future — young people and unemployment around the world. Alain Touraine. Paris: United Nations Educational, Scientific and Cultural Organisation, 1991: viii, 250 p. *ISBN: 9231024922. Includes bibliographical references (p. 249-250).*

230 Generalized social attitudes and perceptions of youth unemployment policy-making — a cross-cultural comparison of adolescents in Denmark, Finland, Norway, and Sweden. Tom Bryder. *Polit. Psych.* **12**:3 9:1991 pp. 431 – 445

231 Graduate unemployment and the job search process — a theoretical and empirical analysis from a developing country. Sola Fajana. *Ind. J. Ind. Rel.* **26**:4 4:1991 pp. 367 – 383

232 Impact du chômage sur la santé mentale — premiers résultats d'une analyse de réseaux *[In French]*; Unemployment and mental health — first results of a network analysis *[Summary]*. Sébastien Reichmann. *Soc. Contemp.* :5 3:1991 pp. 99 – 116

233 Job displacement — consequences and implications for policy. John T. Addison *[Ed.]*. Detroit: Wayne State University Press, c1991: 306 p. *ISBN: 0814322859; LofC: 90022623. Includes bibliographical references and indexes.* [Labor economics and policy series.]

234 A longitudinal study of the psychological effects of unemployment and unsatisfactory employment on young adults. Anthony H. Winefield; Helen R. Winefield; Marika Tiggemann; Robert D. Goldney. *J. Appl. Psychol.* **76**:3 6:1991 pp. 424 – 431

235 Long-term follow-up and benefit-cost analysis of the jobs program — a preventive intervention for the unemployed. Amiram D. Vinokur; Michelle van Ryn; Edward M. Gramlich; Richard H. Price. *J. Appl. Psychol.* **76**:2 4:1991 pp. 213 – 219

236 On the causes of Ireland's unemployment. Frank Barry; John Bradley. *Econ. Soc. R.* **22**:4 7:1991 pp. 253 – 286

237 Potential output and the natural rate of unemployment — an empirical analysis in the UK. Giorgio Radaelli. *Bus. Econ.* **23**:1 Winter:1991 pp. 7 – 20

238 Problemy bezrobocia w dużym ośrodku przemysłowym na przykładzie województwa łódzkiego *[In Polish]*; (Проблеиы безработицы в большом промышленном центре (на примере Лодзенского воеводства): Title only in Russian); (Problems of unemployment in big industrial centres, the examples of Lodz Voivodship). Henryk Retkiewicz. *Pra. Zab. Społ.* **33**:2-3 2-3:1991 pp. 30 – 35

239 A qualitative analysis of unemployment in Spain. Mercedes Gracia-Díez. *Labour [Italy]* **5**:2 Autumn:1991 pp. 159 – 174

240 Recession, restructuring and workplace reform — unemployment and the underclass in Australia in the 1990s. Hilary P.M. Winchester. *Aust. Geogr.* **22**:2 11:1991 pp. 112 – 116

241 La relation chômage-santé — une étude longtitudinale *[In French]*; Unemployment and mental health — a longitudinal analysis *[Summary]*. Francine Mayer; Paul-Martel Roy. *Can. J. Econ.* **XXIV**:3 8:1991 pp. 551 – 562

242 Rynek pracy. Szanse powodzenia walki z bezrobociem *[In Polish]*; (Рынок рабочей силы. Шанс успеха борьбы с безработицей: Title only in Russian); (Labour market. Chances of success of fight against unemployment). Stanisława Borkowska. *Pra. Zab. Społ.* **33**:2-3 2-3:1991 pp. 10 – 17

243 A survey of employment security law — determining eligibility for unemployment compensation benefits. Patricia S. Wall. *Lab. Law J.* **42**:3 3:1991 pp. 179 – 185

244 La transaction — ses effets au regard de l'indemnisation du chômage *[In French]*; [Transaction — its effects on unemployment insurance]. Albert Arseguel; Philippe Isoux. *Droit Soc.* :5 5:1991 pp. 438 – 446

245 Unemployment and local labour markets. Peter Robinson *[Ed.]*. Aldershot: Avebury, 1991: 119 p. *ISBN: 1856281256. Includes bibliography.*

246 Unemployment, poverty and psychological distress. Christopher T. Whelan; Damian F. Hannan; Sean Creighton. Dublin: Economic and Social Research Institute, 1991: xv, 153 p. (ill) *ISBN: 0707001161. Bibl.* [General research series paper.]

I.2: Employment and labour market [Emploi et marché du travail] — Unemployment [Chômage]

247 Werkloosheid, arbeidsplicht en sociale rechtvaardigheid. Oordelen over de rechten en plichten van werklozen *[In Dutch]*; Unemployment, the obligation to work and social justice — judgements on the rights and duties of the unemployed *[Summary]*. Dick Houtman. *Sociol. Gids* **38**:3 5/6:1991 pp. 144 – 161

I.3: Personnel management and working conditions — Administration du personnel et conditions de travail

Sub-divisions: Job satisfaction *[Satisfaction au travail]*; Occupational safety *[Sécurité du travail]*; Personnel management *[Gestion du personnel]*

1 The 5S's — five keys to a total quality environment. Takashi Osada. Tokyo: Asian Productivity Organization, 1991: 211 p. (ill) *ISBN: 9283311167.*
2 Administration, domination and "organisation theory" — the political foundations of surveillance at work. David Binns. Dagenham: Polytechnic of East London, 1991: 74 p. *ISBN: 187353115x.* [Occasional papers on business, economy and society.]
3 Antecedents and consequences of emotional exhaustion in the airline reservations service sector. Mary Jane Saxton; James S. Phillips; Roger N. Blakeney. *Human Relat.* **44**:6 6:1991 pp. 583 – 595
4 Arbeit ohne Integration? Formen und Folgen systemischer Rationalisierung in der westdeutschen Bauwirtschaft *[In German]*; Labour without integration? *[Summary]*. Gerd Syben. *Soz. Welt.* **42**:3 1991 pp. 371 – 386
5 Arbeit, Vergesellschaftung, Identität — zur zunehemenden normativen Subjektivierung der Arbeit *[In German]*; Labor, socialization, identity — on the increasingly normative subjective attitude towards labor *[Summary]*. Martin Baethge. *Soz. Welt.* **42**:1 :1991 pp. 6 – 19
6 Ascriptive influences on pay and employment conditions — a survey of British multinationals and indigenous employers in Nigeria. Sola Fajana. *Int. J. Hum. Res. Man.* **2**:3 12:1991 pp. 345 – 358
7 Assessing self-appraisal of job performance as an evaluation device — are the poor results a function of method or methodology? Mark John Somers; Dee Birnbaum. *Human Relat.* **44**:10 10:1991 pp. 1081 – 1092
8 An assessment of measurement error bias for estimating the effect of mental distress on income. Richard Frank; Paul Gertler. *J. Hum. Res.* **XXVI**:1 Winter:1991 pp. 154 – 164
9 The barriers to flexibility — flexible rostering on the railways. Andrew Pendleton. *Work Emp. Soc.* **5**:2 6:1991 pp. 241 – 257
10 Changes in working practices in British manufacturing industry in the 1980s — a study of employee concessions made during wage negotiations. Peter N. Ingram. *Br. J. Ind. R.* **29**:1 3:1991 pp. 1 – 13
11 Changing the workplace to fit human needs — the Norwegian work environment act. Mike Otten. *Econ. Ind. Dem.* **12**:4 11:1991 pp. 487 – 500
12 Child care as an adult work environment. Deborah Phillips; Carollee Howes; Marcy Whitebook. *J. Soc. Issues* **47**:2 1991 pp. 49 – 70
13 A comparison of job stability in Germany and the US. Jonathan Leonard; Ronald Schettkat. *Labour [Italy]* **5**:2 Autumn:1991 pp. 143 – 158
14 Concepts of discrimination in "general ability" job testing. Mark Kelman. *Harv. Law. Rev.* **104**:6 4:1991 pp. 1158 – 1247
15 Control theory and social behavior in the workplace. Lloyd Sandelands; Mary Ann Glynn; James R. Larson. *Human Relat.* **44**:10 10:1991 pp. 1107 – 1130
16 Corporate social responsibilities and housing in South Africa — the role of the employer. P.S. Reddy; S. Moodley. *S. Afr. J. Labour Relat.* **15**:2 6:1991 pp. 34 – 41
17 Creating a family in the workplace. Howell S. Baum. *Human Relat.* **44**:11 11:1991 pp. 1137 – 1159
18 Determinants and consequences of salary negotiations by male and female MBA graduates. Barry Gerhart; Sara Rynes. *J. Appl. Psychol.* **76**:2 4:1991 pp. 256 – 262
19 Discrepancies in the working times of community workers. Lionel van Reenen. *Comm. Dev. J.* **26**:3 7:1991 pp. 210 – 219

I.3: Personnel management and working conditions [Administration du personnel et conditions de travail]

20 Effect of self-relevance of an event on hindsight bias — the foreseeability of a layoff. Melvin M. Mark; Steven Mellor. *J. Appl. Psychol.* **76:4** 8:1991 pp. 569 – 577
21 Effects of grievance activity on absenteeism. Brian S. Klaas; Herbert G. Heneman; Craig A. Olson. *J. Appl. Psychol.* **76:6** 12:1991 pp. 818 – 824
22 The effects of individual power on earnings. Jeffrey Pfeffer; Alison M. Konrad. *Work Occup.* **18:4** 11:1991 pp. 385 – 414
23 Effects of minimum wage on the employment status of youths — an update. Alison J. Wellington. *J. Hum. Res.* **XXVI:1** Winter:1991 pp. 27 – 46
24 The effects of overtime pay regulation on worker compensation. Stephen J. Trejo. *Am. Econ. Rev.* **81:4** 9:1991 pp. 719 – 740
25 Effects of supervisor age and subordinate age on rating congruence. Lynn McFarlane Shore; Linda M. Bleicken. *Human Relat.* **44:10** 10:1991 pp. 1093 – 1106
26 Employee response to compulsory short-time work. Victor R. Fuchs; Joyce P. Jacobsen. *Ind. Relat.* **30:3** Fall:1991 pp. 501 – 513
27 Employee responses to technologically-driven change — the implementation of office automation in a service organization. Charles K. Parsons; Robert C. Liden; Edward J. O'Connor; Dennis H. Nagao. *Human Relat.* **44:12** 12:1991 pp. 1331 – 1356
28 Employee turnover intentions — implications from a national sample. Jacob Weisberg; Alan Kirschenbaum. *Int. J. Hum. Res. Man.* **2:3** 12:1991 pp. 359 – 375
29 An employer's perspective on monitoring telemarketing calls — invasion of privacy or legitimate business practice? Ann K. Bradley. *Lab. Law J.* **42:5** 5:1991 pp. 259 – 272
30 Employment effects of working time reductions in the former Federal Republic of Germany. Hartmut Seifert. *Int. Lab. Rev.* **130:4** 4:1991 pp. 495 – 510
31 Empresa y medio ambiente. Una aproximación necesaria *[In Spanish]*; [Businesses and their environment. A necessary approximation]. Paul Remy. *Apuntes* **28** Primer Semestre: 1991 pp. 45 – 54
32 Encouraging long-term tenure — wage tilt or pensions? Richard A. Ippolito. *Ind. Lab. Rel.* **44:3** 4:1991 pp. 520 – 535
33 Fear, unemployment and pay flexibility. D.G. Blanchflower. *Econ. J.* **101:406** 5:1991 pp. 483 – 496
34 Flexible men and women. The changing temporal organization of work and culture — an empirical analysis. Mark Elchardus. *Soc. Sci. Info.* **30:4** 12:1991 pp. 701 – 726
35 From linear to integrative logics — characteristics of workplace development as illustrated by projects in large mail centers. Bjørn Gustavsen; Horst Hart; Bernd Hofmaier. *Human Relat.* **44:4** 4:1991 pp. 309 – 332
36 The impact of occupational segregation on working conditions. Jennifer Glass. *Soc. Forc.* **68:3** 3:1990 pp. 779 – 796
37 Influence of job characteristics on the acceptibility of employee drug testing. Kevin S. Murphy; George C. Thornton; Kristin Prue. *J. Appl. Psychol.* **76:3** 6:1991 pp. 447 – 453
38 Interdisciplinary examination of the costs and benefits of enlarged jobs — a job design quasi-experiment. Michael A. Campion; Carol L. McClelland. *J. Appl. Psychol.* **76:2** 4:1991 pp. 186 – 198
39 Interrelationships of work commitment constructs. Donna M. Randall; Joseph A. Cote. *Work Occup.* **18:2** 5:1991 pp. 194 – 211
40 Job duration in the Netherlands — the co-existence of high turnover and permanent job attachment. Maarten Lindeboom; Jules Theeuwes. *Ox. B. Econ. S.* **53:3** 8:1991 pp. 243 – 264
41 Job-related threats to control among older employees. Jacqueline H. Remondet; Robert O. Hansson. *J. Soc. Issues* **47:4** 1991 pp. 129 – 142
42 Law of dismissal and employment practices in Japan; Les procédures et les indemnités de licenciement au Japon *[French summary]*. Fumito Komiya. *Ind. Relat. J.* **22:1** Spring:1991 pp. 59 – 66
43 Layoffs and lemons. Robert Gibbons; Lawrence F. Katz. *J. Labor Ec.* **9:4** 10:1991 pp. 351 – 380
44 Male-female differences in hourly wages — the role of human capital, working conditions, and housework. Joni Hersch. *Ind. Lab. Rel.* **44:4** 7:1991 pp. 746 – 758
45 Manufacturing employees and technological change. Brian Bemmels; Yonatan Reshef. *J. Labor Res.* **XII:3** Summer:1991 pp. 231 – 246
46 Meaning and measurement of turnover — comparison of alternative measures and recommendations for research. Michael A. Campion. *J. Appl. Psychol.* **76:2** 4:1991 pp. 199 – 212

I.3: Personnel management and working conditions [Administration du personnel et conditions de travail]

47 Les mouvements du personnel comme vecteurs des transferts de technologie et de la compétitivité des entreprises japonaises *[In French]*; The RD system behind Japan's high technology products — human network organisations *[Summary]*. Minoru Ito. *Sociol. Trav.* **XXXIII:1** 1991 pp. 105 – 117

48 Negotiating a flexible retirement — further-paid work and the quality of life in retirement. Dallas Cliff. *Age. Soc.* **11:3** 9:1991 pp. 319 – 340

49 Neutral job titles and occupational stereotypes — when legal and psychological realities conflict. Jack P. Lipton; Maureen O'Connor; Craig Terry; Elizabeth Bellamy. *J. Psychol.* **125:2** 3:1991 pp. 129 – 152

50 Numerically controlled machine tools and worker skills. Jeffrey H. Keefe. *Ind. Lab. Rel.* **44:3** 4:1991 pp. 503 – 519

51 On the effectiveness of individual wage incentive plans in manufacturing firms. Arie Shirom; Emmie Mar. *Int. J. Hum. Res. Man.* **2:3** 12:1991 pp. 327 – 344

52 On the extent and reduction of avoidable absenteeism — an assessment of absence policy provisions. Dan R. Dalton; Debra J. Mesch. *J. Appl. Psychol.* **76:6** 12:1991 pp. 810 – 817

53 Organization vs. culture — Japanese automotive transplants in the US; Organisation et culture — les transplantations automobiles japonaises aux les Etats- Unis *[French summary]*. Richard Florida; Martin Kenney. *Ind. Relat. J.* **22:3** Autumn:1991 pp. 181 – 196

54 Organizational commitment, job involvement, and turnover — a substantive and methodological analysis. Mark A. Huselid; Nancy E. Day. *J. Appl. Psychol.* **76:3** 6:1991 pp. 380 – 391

55 The organizational context of women's and men's pay satisfaction. Karyn A. Loscocco; Glenna Spitze. *Soc. Sci. Q.* **72:1** 3:1991 pp. 3 – 19

56 Organizations, relationships, markets and labor discipline in craft production — a Tiffany-style lamp workshop in Tijuana, Mexico. Leslie Howard. *Econ. Ind. Dem.* **12:1** 2:1991 pp. 83 – 96

57 Pay for performance — evaluating performance appraisal and merit pay. George T. Milkovich *[Ed.]*; Alexandra K. Wigdor *[Ed.]*. Washington, D.C: National Academy Press, 1991: viii, 210 p. *ISBN: 0309044278; LofC: 90025995. Committee on Performance Appraisal for Merit Pay, Commission on Behavioral and Social Sciences and Education, National Research Council; Includes bibliographical references (p. 167-187) and index.*

58 Perceived fairness of employee drug testing as a predictor of employee attitudes and job performance. Mary A. Konovsky; Russell Cropanzano. *J. Appl. Psychol.* **76:5** 10:1991 pp. 698 – 707

59 La philosophie du travail en milieu salarié kinois *[In French]*; [The work ethic among salaried Kinois]. Révérien Gahinyuza. *Za-Afr.* **30:249-250** 11-12:1990 pp. 465 – 478

60 Les pratiques d'emploi japonaises au Japon et en Europe *[In French]*; Paper — Japanese employment practices at home and in Europe *[Summary]*. Peter Buckley *[Contrib.]*; Sushil Wadhwani *[Contrib.]*; Ian Gow *[Contrib.]*; Antony Cassidy *[Contrib.]*; Peter Wickens *[Contrib.]*. Collection of 5 articles. **Gestion**, *7:1*, 2-3:1991 pp. 155 – 208

61 Predictors and outcomes of reactions to pay-for-performance plans. Marcia P. Miceli; Iljae Jung; Janet P. Near; David B. Greenberger. *J. Appl. Psychol.* **76:4** 8:1991 pp. 508 – 521

62 Production and the welfare state — the political context of reforms. Vicente Navarro. *Int. J. Health. Ser.* **21:4** 1991 pp. 585 – 614

63 A proportional hazards regression analysis of employee turnover among nurses in New Zealand. Sik Hung Ng; Fiona Cram; Lesley Jenkins. *Human Relat.* **44:12** 12:1991 pp. 1313 – 1330

64 Protection and oppression — a case study of domestic service in Jamaica; *[French summary]*. Patricia Anderson. *Labour Cap. Soc.* **24:1** 4:1991 pp. 10 – 39

65 The psychological impact of expatriate relocation on partners. Helen De Cieri; Peter J. Dowling; Keith F. Taylor. *Int. J. Hum. Res. Man.* **2:3** 12:1991 pp. 377 – 413

66 Put up and shut up — workplace sexual assaults. Beth E. Schneider. *Gender Soc.* **5:4** 12:1991 pp. 533 – 548

67 Qualità e consenso. L'evoluzione del lavoro operaio alla Fiat Mirafiori (1980-1990) *[In Italian]*; Quality and consent. The evolution of manual work at Fiat Mirafiori *[Summary]*. Giuseppe Bonazzi. *Rass. It. Soc.* **32:1** 1-3:1991 pp. 3 – 24

68 Quality of work life and human resource outcomes. Stephen J. Havlovic. *Ind. Relat.* **30:3** Fall:1991 pp. 469 – 479

69 Race, amenities, and psychic income. Mwangi S. Kimenyi. *Rev. Bl. Pol. Ec.* **20:1** Summer:1991 pp. 49 – 58

I.3: Personnel management and working conditions [Administration du personnel et conditions de travail]

70 The reality of workplace flexibility. John Tomaney. *Cap. Class* **40** Spring:1990 pp. 29 – 60

71 Recruiter beware — the oral promise of lifetime employment may be more than a mere inducement. Nancy K. Kubasek; M. Neil Browne. *Lab. Law J.* **42:5** 5:1991 pp. 273 – 284

72 A re-examination of autonomy in light of new manufacturing practices. Janice A. Klein. *Human Relat.* **44:1** 1:1991 pp. 21 – 38

73 Relations of job characteristics from multiple data sources with employee affect, absence, turnover intentions, and health. Paul E. Spector; Steve M. Jex. *J. Appl. Psychol.* **76:1** 2:1991 pp. 46 – 53

74 A response to arguments against mandated parental leave — findings from the Connecticut survey of parental leave policies. Eileen Trzcinski; Matia Finn-Stevenson. *J. Marriage Fam.* **53:2** 5:1991 pp. 445 – 460

75 Self-reported versus objective measures of health in retirement models. John Bound. *J. Hum. Res.* **XXVI:1** Winter:1991 pp. 106 – 138

76 Sexual harassment in America and South Africa — nature, relief and employer liability. L. Dancaster. *S. Afr. J. Labour Relat.* **15:2** 6:1991 pp. 12 – 26

77 Shabashniki — the Soviet Union's "wild brigades". Hans Oversloot. *Neth. J. Soc. Sci.* **27:1** 4:1991 pp. 17 – 28

78 Smoking and absenteeism. R. Ault; R.B. Ekelund; J.D. Jackson; R.S. Saba; D.S. Saurman. *Appl. Econ.* **23:4B** 4:1991 pp. 743 – 754

79 Social theory for action — how individuals and organizations learn to change. William Foote Whyte. Newbury Park: Sage Publications, c1991: vii, 301 p. (ill) *ISBN: 0803941668; LofC: 91006941. Includes bibliographical references (p. 288-293) and index.*

80 Some differences make a difference — individual dissimilarity and group heterogeneity as correlates of recruitment, promotions, and turnover. Susan E. Jackson; Joan F. Brett; Valerie I. Sessa; Dawn M. Cooper; Johan A. Julin; Karl Peyronnin. *J. Appl. Psychol.* **76:5** 10:1991 pp. 675 – 689

81 „Der Sozialismus braucht den ganzen Menschen". Zum Verhältnis vertraglicher und nichtvertraglicher Beziehungen in einem VEB *[In German]*; "Socialism needs the whole person" — on the relationship between contractual and non-contractual work in a socialistic company *[Summary]*. Richard Rottenburg. *Z. Soziol.* **20:4** 8:1991 p. 305

82 State or trait — effects of positive mood on prosocial behaviors at work. Jennifer M. George. *J. Appl. Psychol.* **76:2** 4:1991 pp. 299 – 307

83 Structural changes in U.S. labor markets — causes and consequences. Randall W. Eberts *[Ed.]*; Erica L. Groshen *[Ed.]*. Armonk, NY.: M.E. Sharpe, c1991: 234 p. *ISBN: 0873328256; LofC: 91011478. Includes bibliographical references and index.*

84 Taking time off — leave provision in the European Community for parents of school-age children. Bronwen Cohen. *Wom. St. Inter. For.* **14:6** 1991 pp. 585 – 598

85 Task and job — the promise of transactional analysis. A. Papathanasis; C. Vasillopulos. *Am. J. Econ. S.* **50:2** 4:1991 pp. 169 – 181

86 Task interdependence and extrarole behavior — a test of the mediating effects of felt responsibility. Jone L. Pearce; Hal B. Gregersen. *J. Appl. Psychol.* **76:6** 12:1991 pp. 838 – 844

87 Technological change in an auto assembly plant — the impact on workers' tasks and skills. Ruth Milkman; Cydney Pullman. *Work Occup.* **18:2** 5:1991 pp. 123 – 147

88 Textile workers in Brazil and Argentina — a study of the interrelationships between work and households. Liliana Acero *[Ed.]*; Claudia Minoliti *[Ed.]*; Alejandra Rotania *[Ed.]*; Irma Nora Perez Vichich. Tokyo: United Nations University Press, 1991: xiv, 305 p. *ISBN: 9280807536. "HGA-2/UNUP-753."; Includes bibliographical references.*

89 Towards an efficient and effective approach in managing public sector organisations — reflections from a development context. Johnnie Palmer. *Cah. Afr. Admin. Pub.* **:36** 1991 pp. 17 – 34

90 Trends in the growth and distribution of skills in the U.S. workplace, 1960-1985. David R. Howell; Edward N. Wolff. *Ind. Lab. Rel.* **44:3** 4:1991 pp. 486 – 502

91 Whistleblowing — the law of retaliatory discharge. Daniel P. Westman. Washington, DC: Bureau of National Affairs, c1991: xvi, 232 p. *ISBN: 0871796619; LofC: 90023947. Includes bibliographical references and index.*

92 Why quality circles failed but total quality management might succeed. Stephen Hill. *Br. J. Ind. R.* **29:4** 12:1991 pp. 541 – 568

93 Working time reductions in the former Federal Republic of Germany — a dead end for employment policy. Elisabeth Neifer-Dichmann. *Int. Lab. Rev.* **130:4** 4:1991 pp. 511 – 522

I.3: Personnel management and working conditions *[Administration du personnel et conditions de travail]*

94 La Yougoslavie autogestionnaire — bilan critique d'une époque prestigieuse *[In French]*; [Yugoslavia under joint worker-management control — a critical assessment of a prestigious era]. Georges Guezennec. Nonette: Creer, 1991: 181 p.
95 "Zen-Mystik" als "Wirtschaftsethik"? Zur funktion zen- buddisthischer Übungen in heutigen japanischen Unternehmen *[In German]*; ["Zen mysticism" as "business ethics"? On the function of Zen Buddhist exercises in Japanese enterprises today]. Thomas Frischkorn. *Beit. Japan.* **29** 1991 pp. 396 – 402

Job satisfaction *[Satisfaction au travail]*

96 An assessment of extrinsic feedback on participation, role perceptions, motivation, and job satisfaction in a self-managed system for monitoring group achievement. C.A.L. Pearson. *Human Relat.* **44:5** 5:1991 pp. 517 – 537
97 Attachments to work — Russians in Israel. Robert Dubin; Amira Galin. *Work Occup.* **18:2** 5:1991 pp. 172 – 193
98 Behavioral intentions as predictors of job attitudes — the role of economic choice. Lucinda I. Doran; Veronica K. Stone; Arthur P. Brief; Jennifer M. George. *J. Appl. Psychol.* **76:1** 2:1991 pp. 40 – 45
99 Cause and effect explanations of job satisfaction and commitment — the case of exchange commitment. Meni Koslowsky; Tamir Caspy; Menachem Lazar. *J. Psychol.* **125:2** 3:1991 p. 153
100 A current look at the job satisfaction/life satisfaction relationship — review and future considerations. Jeffrey S. Rain; Irving M. Lane; Dirk D. Steiner. *Human Relat.* **44:3** 3:1991 pp. 287 – 307
101 Differences in employee attitudes and behaviors based on Rotter's (1966) internal-external locus of control — are they all valid? Robert W. Renn; Robert J. Vandenberg. *Human Relat.* **44:11** 11:1991 pp. 1161 – 1178
102 Facet importance and job satisfaction. Robert W. Rice; Douglas A. Gentile; Dean B. McFarlin. *J. Appl. Psychol.* **76:1** 2:1991 pp. 31 – 39
103 Is job satisfaction an antecedent or a consequence of psychological burnout? Jacob Wolpin; Ronald J. Burke; Esther R. Greenglass. *Human Relat.* **44:2** 2:1991 pp. 193 – 209
104 Race in the workplace — black/white differences in the antecedents of job satisfaction. Steven A. Tuch; Jack K. Martin. *Sociol. Q.* **32:1** Spring:1991 pp. 103 – 116
105 Social networks, social circles, and job satisfaction. Jeanne S. Hurlbert. *Work Occup.* **18:4** 11:1991 pp. 415 – 430
106 Unionism and changing employees views towards work. Paul Jarley; Jack Fiorito. *J. Labor Res.* **XII:3** Summer:1991 pp. 223 – 229

Occupational safety *[Sécurité du travail]*

107 The aftermath of injury — cultural factors in compensation seeking in Canada and the United States. Herbert M. Kritzer; W.A. Bogart; Nei Vidmar. *Law Soc. Rev.* **25:3** 1991 pp. 499 – 543
108 Gender-based fetal protection policies — impermissible sex discrimination. George M. Sullivan; William A. Nowlin. *Lab. Law J.* **42:7** 7:1991 pp. 387 – 397
109 The growth of occupational welfare in Britain — evolution and harmonization of modern personnel practice. Alice Russell. Aldershot: Avebury, c1991: 299 p. *ISBN: 1856281213.*
110 Industrial injuries in British manufacturing industry and cyclical effects — continuities and discontinuities in industrial injury research. Theo Nichols. *Sociol. Rev.* **39:1** 2:1991 pp. 131 – 139
111 Injury and ill-health in the chemical industry — decentring the accident-prone victim. S. Tombs. *Ind. Crisis Q.* **5:1** 3:1991 pp. 59 – 75
112 Labour intensification, work injuries and the measurement of percentage utilization of labour (PUL). Theo Nichols. *Br. J. Ind. R.* **29:4** 12:1991 pp. 569 – 592
113 Life and death at work — industrial accidents as a case of socially produced error. Tom Dwyer. New York: Plenum Press, c1991: xv, 318 p. *ISBN: 0306439492; LofC: 91022166. Includes bibliographical references and index.* [Plenum studies in work and industry.]
114 No evidence of compensating wages for occupational fatalities. J. Paul Leigh. *Ind. Relat.* **30:3** Fall:1991 pp. 382 – 395
115 Occupational stress, social support, and the buffer hypothesis. Valerie A. Haines; Jeanne S. Hurlbert; Catherine Zimmer. *Work Occup.* **18:2** 5:1991 pp. 212 – 235

I.3: Personnel management and working conditions [Administration du personnel et conditions de travail] — Occupational safety [Sécurité du travail]

116 Odszkodowawcza odpowiedzialność zakładu pracy za wypadki przy pracy [In Polish]; (Compensational enterprise responsibility of accidents at work); (Маря Рафач-Кжижановска - Компенсационная ответственность преддириятия из-за несчастливых случаев на роботе: Title only in Russian). Maria Rafacz-Krzyżanowska. Pra. Zab. Społ. **33**:7 7:1991 pp. 47 – 54

117 Production control and chronic stress in work organizations. Gerard J. Houben. Int. J. Health. Ser. **21**:2 1991 pp. 309 – 327

118 La protection de la santé et de la sécurité du travailleur — la Suisse face au droit de la Communauté européenne [In French]; [The protection of health and industrial safety. Switzerland and European Community law]. Gabriel Aubert [Ed.]; Florence Aubry Girardin [Ed.]; Pascale Byrne-Sutton [Ed.]. Zürich: Schulthess, 1991: 179 p. ISBN: 3725528659. [Le droit du travail en pratique.]

119 Risky business — genetic testing and exclusionary practices in the hazardous workplace. Elaine Draper. Cambridge [England]: Cambridge University Press, 1991: xv, 315 p. ISBN: 0521370272; LofC: 90028112. Includes bibliographical references (pp. 253-296) and index. [Cambridge studies in philosophy and public policy.]

120 Sterilization of workers from pesticide exposure — the causes and consequences of DBCP-induced damage in Costa Rica and beyond. Lori Ann Thrupp. Int. J. Health. Ser. **21**:4 1991 pp. 731 – 757

121 Stress reduction in transition — conceptual problems in the design, implementation, and evaluation of worksite stress management interventions. Shirley Reynolds; David A. Shapiro. Human Relat. **44**:7 7:1991 pp. 717 – 734

122 Työterveyshuollon toteuttaminen ja muutostarpeita — tutkimus työterveyshuollon kehittämisestä 1980-luvulla erityistarkastelussa rakennusala ja pienet työpaikat [In Finnish]; Implementation and need for improvement in occupational health care in Finland — a study of occupational health care in the 1980s, in the construction industry and at small workplaces in particular [Summary]. Esko Kalimo; Timo Klaukka; Risto Lehtonen; Kauko Nyman; Raimo Raitasalo. Kansan. Julk. :**78** 1991 pp. 1 – 129

Personnel management [Gestion du personnel]

123 Affirmative action at work — law, politics, and ethics. Bron Raymond Taylor. Pittsburgh, PA.: University of Pittsburgh Press, c1991: xvii, 251 p. ISBN: 0822936747; LofC: 90024450. Includes bibliographical references (p. 239-245) and index. [Pitt series in policy and institutional studies.]

124 Beyond traditional paternalistic and developmental approaches to organizational change and human resource strategies. Doug A. Stace; Dexter C. Dunphy. Int. J. Hum. Res. Man. **2**:3 12:1991 pp. 263 – 284

125 Biodata in selection — issues in practice. Marie Strebler. Brighton: Institute of Manpower Studies, University of Sussex, 1991: 54 p. ISBN: 1851841121. Bibliography — p.50-53. [IMS paper. : No. 160]

126 The climate of workplace relations. Ali Dastmalchian; Paul Blyton [Ed.]; Ray Adamson [Ed.]. London: Routledge, 1991: 215 p. ISBN: 0415037387. Includes bibliography and index.

127 Competitive strategy, flexibility and selection — the case of Caledonian Paper; Stratégie compétitive, flexibilité et selection — le cas de Caledonian Paper [French summary]. P.B. Beaumont; L.C. Hunter. Ind. Relat. J. **22**:3 Autumn:1991 pp. 222 – 228

128 Developing Japan's R&D staff — in search of a new personnel management; [French summary]. Kevin McCormick. New Tech. Work. Empl. **6**:1 Spring:1991 pp. 1 – 18

129 The development of human resources. K.T. Li. Ind. Free China **LXXV**:3 3:1991 pp. 47 – 54

130 Diversification industrielle et stratégie de gestion des ressources humaines dans l'industrie japonaise du textile synthétique [In French]; Industrial diversification and human resource management strategy in Japanese synthetic textiles companies [Summary]. Michio Nitta. Sociol. Trav. **XXXIII**:1 1991 pp. 119 – 134

131 Elastyczny czas pracy i elastyczne zatrudnienie jako instrument zarządzania przedsiębiorstwem w okresie reformowania gospodarki w Polsce [In Polish]; (Эластичное рабочее время и эластичное затруднение как инструмент управления предприятием во время преобразовывания экономики в Польше: Title only in Russian); (Elastic work time and elastic employment as a tool of enterprise managing in the period of economic reform in Poland). Helena Strzemińska. Pra. Zab. Społ. **33**:1 1:1991 pp. 19 – 26

I.3: Personnel management and working conditions [Administration du personnel et conditions de travail] — Personnel management [Gestion du personnel]

132 Foreign competition in Japan — human resource strategies. Robert J Ballon. New York: Routledge, 1991: 174 p. *ISBN: 0415069807; LofC: 91002818. Includes bibliographical references and index.*

133 Gendering jobs — corporate strategies, managerial control and dynamics of job segregation. Glenn Morgan; David Knights. *Work Emp. Soc.* **5:2** 6:1991 pp. 181 – 200

134 The growth of occupational welfare in Britain — evolution and harmonization of modern personnel practice. Alice Russell. Aldershot: Avebury, c1991: 299 p. *ISBN: 1856281213.*

135 Human resource management. S. Pandey *[Ed.]*; Udai Pareek *[Contrib.]*; Rabindra N. Kanungo *[Contrib.]*; Ishwar Dayal *[Contrib.]*; N. Sastry *[Contrib.]*; P.K. Nag *[Contrib.]*; A. Monappa *[Contrib.]*; M. Alimullah Miyan *[Contrib.]*; R. d' Souza *[Contrib.]*; Gouranga P. Chattopadhyay *[Contrib.] and others. Collection of 16 articles.* **Indian J. Soc. W.**, *LII:4*, 10:1991 pp. 447 – 658

136 Human resource strategies. Graeme Salaman *[Ed.]*. London: Sage Publications, 1991: 336p. *ISBN: 0803986262.*

137 De ideale sollicitant is een vrouw. Onderzoek naar sekseverschillen in het (personeels) selectieproces *[In Dutch]*; The ideal applicant is a woman — sex biased selection of employees *[Summary]*. Albertine Veldman; Roel Wittink. *Mens Maat.* **66:2** 5:1991 pp. 141 – 160

138 The impact of personnel selection and assessment methods on candidates. Ivan T. Robertson; Paul A. Iles; Lynda Gratton; David Sharpley. *Human Relat.* **44:9** 9:1991 pp. 963 – 982

139 Is reinstatement a remedy suitable to at-will employees? Gilles Trudeau. *Ind. Relat.* **30:2** Spring:1991 pp. 302 – 315

140 Management selection — a comparative survey of methods used in top British and French companies. Viv Shackleton; Sue Newell. *J. Occup. Psychol.* **64:1** 3:1991 pp. 23 – 36

141 Mastery and frequency of managerial behaviors relative to sub-unit effectiveness. Frank Shipper. *Human Relat.* **44:4** 4:1991 pp. 371 – 388

142 Die meting van personeelbestuur in 'n boerdery-onderneming *[In Afrikaans]*; Measurement of staff management in a farm firm *[Summary]*. L.K. Oosthuizen; A.J. Radley. *Agrekon* **30:1** 3:1991 pp. 18 – 28

143 La modernisation de la gestion des ressources humaines du secteur public *[In French]*; Modernizing public sector human resource management *[Summary]*. Institut de l'entreprise. *R. Fr. Admin. Publ.* **:59** 7-9:1991 pp. 413 – 426

144 'n Diagnose van die personeelbestuurstelsel in 'n boerdery-onderneming *[In Afrikaans]*; A diagnosis of the staff management system in a farm firm *[Summary]*. L.K. Oosthuizen; L. Coetzee. *Agrekon* **30:2** 6:1991 pp. 61 – 73

145 One foot in hell — on self-destructive staff dynamics. Clemens Janzing. *Inter. J. Therap. Comm.* **12:1** 1991 pp. 5 – 12

146 Organisational stress — concept, determinants and management. Upinder Dhar. *Ind. J. Ind. Rel.* **26:3** 1:1991 pp. 278 – 289

147 Personnel management — the end of orthodoxy. David E. Guest. *Br. J. Ind. R.* **29:2** 6:1991 pp. 149 – 176

148 Predicting the perceived fairness of parental leave policies. Steven L. Grover. *J. Appl. Psychol.* **76:2** 4:1991 pp. 247 – 255

149 Psychometric properties of performance ratings by self and superior. K.K. Mathew. *Ind. J. Ind. Rel.* **26:3** 1:1991 pp. 290 – 299

150 Relative effect of applicant work experience and academic qualification on selection interview decisions — a study of between-sample generalizability. Ming S. Singer; Chris Bruhns. *J. Appl. Psychol.* **76:4** 8:1991 pp. 550 – 559

151 Succession planning — a critical look at some organisations. E.C. Aduaka. *Cah. Afr. Admin. Pub.* **:36** 1991 pp. 1 – 15

152 TQM and the management of labour. Adrian Wilkinson; Peter Allen; Ed Snape. *Employ. Relat.* **13:1** 1991 pp. 24 – 31

153 Validity and generalizability of a role-play test to select telemarketing representatives. Paul Squires; Steven J. Torkel; James W. Smither; Margaret R. Ingate. *J. Occup. Psychol.* **64:1** 3:1991 pp. 37 – 47

154 Zróżnicowany i elastyczny czas pracy jako czynnik lepszego wykorzystania potencjału przedsiębiorstw — sprawozdanie z międzynarodowego seminarium zorganizowanego przez IPiSS *[In Polish]*; (Дифференцированное и эластичное рабочее время как фактор лучшего использования потенциала на предприятии - отчёт из

I.3: Personnel management and working conditions *[Administration du personnel et conditions de travail]* — **Personnel management** *[Gestion du personnel]*
международной семинарии: *Title only in Russian)*; (Flexible working time management as a factor of better utilization of enterprise potential — a report from international seminar). Lucyna Machol. *Pra. Zab. Społ.* **33**:1 1:1991 pp. 33 – 38

I.4: Vocational training, occupations and careers — *Formation professionnelle, professions et carrières*

Sub-divisions: Career development *[Déroulement de carrière]*; Managers *[Cadres]*; Professional workers *[Travailleurs professionnels]*; Vocational training *[Formation professionnelle]*

1 Alchimie ouvrière *[In French]*; Working class alchemy — technicians and "peoes" in the petrochemical industry at Salvador de Bahia, Brazil *[Summary]*. Michel Agier; Antonio Sergio Guimaraes. *Sociol. Trav.* :3 1991 pp. 351 – 374
2 Automated technologies, institutional environments, and skilled labor processes — toward an institutional theory of automation outcomes. James R. Zetka. *Sociol. Q.* **32**:4 Winter:1991 pp. 557 – 574
3 The availability of information and awareness of procedures. Tim Rollinson; Willy Bendix. *Ind. Rel. J. S.Afr.* **11**:2 1991 pp. 21 – 30
4 Die betriebliche Produktion von Wirklichkeit im Arbeitshandeln *[In German]*; The manufacture of reality in factory work *[Summary]*. Ludger Pries. *Z. Soziol.* **20**:4 8:1991 pp. 257 – 274
5 Careers and identities. Michael Banks. Milton Keynes: Open University Press, 1991: 219 p. *ISBN: 0335097154; LofC: 91021346. Includes bibliographical references and index.*
6 Close coupling in work-family relationships — making and implementing decisions in a new family business and at home. Alan W. Wicker; Kim A. Burley. *Human Relat.* **44**:1 1:1991 pp. 77 – 92
7 A comparison of the occupational distributions of native- and foreign-born males. P.E. Gabriel. *Am. J. Econ. S.* **50**:3 7:1991 pp. 351 – 364
8 Competing philosophies in the circuits regarding post-contract grievances — an employer's perspective. Paul F. Hodapp. *Lab. Law J.* **42**:1 1:1991 pp. 35 – 44
9 The contradictions of class and ideology among Argentine laborers and employees. Peter Ranis. *Stud. Comp. ID.* **26**:4 Winter:1991-92 pp. 3 – 28
10 Countering resume fraud within and beyond banking — no excuse for not doing more. Arthur A. Sloane. *Lab. Law J.* **42**:5 5:1991 pp. 303 – 310
11 The decomposition of inequality by class and by occupation. Scott H. Beck. *Sociol. Q.* **32**:1 Spring:1991 pp. 139 – 150
12 Defining occupational groupings by educational structure. A. de Grip; L.F.M. Groot; J.A.M. Heijke. *Envir. Plan.A.* **23**:1 1:1991 pp. 59 – 85
13 La déontologie des statisticiens *[In French]*; The deontology of statisticians. René Padieu. *Soc. Contemp.* :7 9:1991 pp. 35 – 62
14 Dissensus in assessments of occupational prestige — the case of Poland. Zbigniew Sawińskim; Henryk Domański. *Eur. Sociol. R.* **7**:3 12:1991 pp. 253 – 265
15 Education and entrepreneurs. Michael D. Stephens. Nottingham: Dept of Adult Education, University of Nottingham, 1991: 187 p. *ISBN: 1850410410.*
16 Education and the ethnic division of labor in reform-minded societies. D. John Grove. *Comp. Poli. S.* **24**:1 4:1991 pp. 56 – 75
17 The effect of unions on the innovative behaviour of firms in Canada; L'effet des syndicats sur le comportement innovateur des firmes au Canada *[French summary]*. Gordon Betcherman. *Ind. Relat. J.* **22**:2 Summer:1991 pp. 142 – 151
18 Effects of skill and attitudes on employee performance and earnings. Stanley D. Nollen; Karen N. Gaertner. *Ind. Relat.* **30**:3 Fall:1991 pp. 435 – 455
19 An empirical analysis of occupational expectations. S. Bradley. *Appl. Econ.* **23**:7 7:1991 pp. 1159 – 1174
20 Equality in Israeli occupational ratings and preferences at age 12 — kibbutz vs. town. Shmuel Shamai; Zipora Margalit. *Social Soc. Res.* **75**:2 1:1991 pp. 66 – 72

I.4: Vocational training, occupations and careers [Formation professionnelle, professions et carrières]

21 Functiestructuurveranderingen als gevolg van automatisering [In Dutch]; Job structure changes due to automation [Summary]. Ronald S. Batenburg. *Mens Maat.* **65:2** 1990 pp. 126 – 144

22 Gerações operárias — rupturas e continuidades na experiência de metalúrgicos no Rio de Janeiro [In Portuguese]; Worker generations — breaks and continuities in the experiences of Rio de Janeiro metalworkers [Summary]; Générations ouvrières — ruptures et perennité dans l'expérience des métallurgistes à Rio de Janeiro [French summary]. Elina G. da Fonte Pessanha; Regina Lúcia de Moraes Morel. *Rev. Bras. Ciên. Soc.* **6:17** 10:1991 pp. 68 – 83

23 How Indonesian lecturers have adjusted to civil service compensation. David H. Clark; Mayling Oey-Gardiner. *B. Ind. Econ. St.* **27:3** 12:1991 pp. 129 – 148

24 The impact of race and gender on correctional officers' orientation to the integrated environment. Patricia van Voorhis; Francis T. Cullen; Bruce G. Link; Nancy Travis Wolfe. *J. Res. Crim. Delin.* **28:4** 11:1991 pp. 472 – 500

25 The impact of surplus schooling on worker productivity. Mun C. Tsang; Russell W. Rumberger; Henry M. Levin. *Ind. Relat.* **30:2** Spring:1991 pp. 209 – 228

26 Industrial harmony in modern Japan — the invention of a tradition. W. Dean Kinzley. London: Routledge, 1991: 190 p. *ISBN: 0415051673*. Includes bibliography and index.

27 Jerarquía de valores en la mujer trabajadora [In Spanish]; [The hierarchy of value in working women]. Lopez Caballero. *Rev. Fom. Soc.* **46:182** 4-6:1991 pp. 183 – 200

28 Job mobility among Ontario nursing professionals, 1984-1989. Robert D. Hiscott. *Social Soc. Res.* **75:4** 7:1991 pp. 189 – 197

29 A logit model of labour market influences on the choice of occupation. G.V. Crockett. *J. Ind. Relat.* **33:3** 9:1991 pp. 309 – 328

30 Marché du travail artistique et socialisation du risque — le cas des arts du spectacle [In French]; The artist job market and risk socialization — concerning actors in particular [Summary]; Arbeitsmarkt der Künstler und Sozialisation des Risikos. Der Fall der Schaukünste [German summary]; Mercado del trabajo artístico y socialización del riesgo. El caso de las artes del espectáculo [Spanish summary]. Pierre-Michel Menger. *Rev. Fr. Soc.* **XXXII:1** 1-3:1991 pp. 61 – 74

31 Matching people and organizations — selection and socialization in public accounting firms. Jennifer A. Chatman. *Adm. Sci. Qua.* **36:3** 9:1991 pp. 459 – 484

32 Mítoszok a munkáról — gyárak összchasonlítása egy szocialista és egy fejlett tőkés orszagban [In Hungarian]; [Myths of work — the comparison of factories in a socialist and in an advanced capitalist country]. Michel Burawoy; János Lukács. *Tarsadalomkutatás* Vol.5; No.2 - 1987. pp. 43 – 62

33 Mobility aspirations among racial minorities, controlling for SES. Daniel G. Solorzano. *Social Soc. Res.* **75:4** 7:1991 pp. 182 – 188

34 Moonlighting and mobility. John W. Langford. *Can. Publ. Ad.* **34:1** Spring:1991 pp. 62 – 72

35 Occupational change over childbirth — evidence from a national survey. Susan McRae. *Sociology* **25:4** 11:1991 pp. 589 – 605

36 Occupational segregation and selectivity bias in occupational wage equations — an empirical analysis using Irish data. B. Reilly. *Appl. Econ.* **23:1A** 1:1991 pp. 1 – 7

37 L'ouvrier qualifié à l'ère de la mécatronique — bricoleur et artisan [In French]; The skilled worker in the area of mechatronics — handy-man and artisan [Summary]. Kenji Okuda. *Sociol. Trav.* **XXXIII:1** 1991 pp. 149 – 161

38 People, cases, and stereotypes — a study of staff practice in a DSS benefit office. Sandra Cullen; Leo Howe. *Cam. Anthrop.* **15:1** 1991 pp. 1 – 26

39 Professionalism and rationality — a study in misapprehension. Michael Fores; Ian Glover; Peter Lawrence. *Sociology* **25:1** 2:1991 pp. 79 – 100

40 Race and post-deplacement earnings among high-tech workers. Paul M. Ong. *Ind. Relat.* **30:3** Fall:1991 pp. 456 – 468

41 Reforms of work practices and IR procedures in the maritime industry — an Australian- U.S. comparison; Les reformes des pratiques de travail et des procédures en matière de relations industrielles dans l'industrie maritime — une comparison Australie-Etats Unis [French summary]. Cliff Donn; Richard Morris; Gerry Phelan. *Ind. Relat. J.* **22:2** Summer:1991 pp. 130 – 141

42 The role of space in determining the occupations of black and white workers. K.R. Ihlanfeldt; D.L. Sjoquist. *Reg. Sci. Urb. Econ.* **21:2** 7:1991 pp. 295 – 311

43 Rural households, labor flows and the housing construction industry in Bandung, Indonesia. Tommy Firman. *J. Econ. Soc. Geogr.* **82:2** 1991 pp. 94 – 105

I.4: Vocational training, occupations and careers [Formation professionnelle, professions et carrières]

44 Segregation curves, Lorenz curves, and inequality in the distribution of people across occupations. R.M. Hutchens. *Math. Soc. Sc.* **21:1** 2:1991 pp. 31 – 51
45 Self-employment and occupational structure in an industrializing city — Detroit, 1880. Melanie Archer. *Soc. Forc.* **69:3** 3:1991 pp. 785 – 809
46 The silviculture labor force in eastern Ontario — a socio-economic profile. Lorenzo Rugo. Ottawa: Forestry Canada, 1991: 62 p. (ill. (some col.)) *ISBN: 0662185307; LofC: 91173414*. [Information report.]
47 The social dimension — convergence or diversification of IR in the single European market; La dimension sociale — convergence ou divergence des relations industrielles dans le marché unique européen? *[French summary]*. Jesper Due; Jørgen Steen Madsen; Carsten Strøby Jensen. *Ind. Relat. J.* **22:2** Summer:1991 pp. 85 – 102
48 Stress and contradiction in psychiatric nursing. Jocelyn Handy. *Human Relat.* **44:1** 1:1991 pp. 39 – 53
49 Structural equation models for ordinal variables — an analysis of occupational destination. Yu Xie. *Sociol. Meth.* **17:4** 5:1989 pp. 325 – 352
50 A study of bank jobs in relation to work motivation, job and work involvement. K.B. Akhilesh; Mary Mathew. *Ind. J. Ind. Rel.* **26:3** 1:1991 pp. 244 – 261
51 Tax evasion and occupational choice. Pierre Pestieau; Uri M. Possen. *J. Publ. Ec.* **45:1** 6:1991 pp. 107 – 125
52 Travail et compétences — récapitulation critique des approches des savoirs au travail *[In French]*; Work and skills — a critical summary of approaches to knowledge in work *[Summary]*; Arbeit und Kompetenzen — kritische Zusammenfassung der Forschungsrichtung — Kenntnisse in der Arbeitswelt *[German summary]*. Marcelle Stroobants. *Form. Emp.* **:33** 1-3:1991 pp. 31 – 42
53 When married men lose jobs — income replacement within the family. Adam D. Seitchik. *Ind. Lab. Rel.* **44:4** 7:1991 pp. 692 – 707
54 When the lifetime employment strategy fails — case studies on the Japanese shipbuilding and coal mining industries. Nichio Nitta. *Ann. Inst. Soc. Sci.* **:33** 1991 pp. 67 – 86
55 Work experience and control orientation in adolescence. Michael D. Finch; Michael J. Shanahan; Jeylan T. Mortimer; Seongryeol Ryu. *Am. Sociol. R.* **56:5** 10:1991 pp. 597 – 611
56 Worker learning and compensating differentials. W. Kip Viscusi; Michael J. Moore. *Ind. Lab. Rel.* **45:1** 10:1991 pp. 80 – 96
57 Worker ownership, ideology and social structure in "third-way" work organizations. Menachem Rosner. *Econ. Ind. Dem.* **12:3** 8:1991 pp. 369 – 384
58 Worker representation on boards of directors — a study of competing roles. Tove H. Hammer; Steven C. Currall; Robert N. Stern. *Ind. Lab. Rel.* **44:4** 7:1991 pp. 661 – 680

Career development [Déroulement de carrière]

59 *[In Japanese]*; [The career pattern of female teachers in nursing school]. Kenji Moriya. *Japanese Journal of Nursing Education No.32(4) - 1991*. pp. 221 – 225
60 The development of career identity in Cyprus — a family systems approach. Stellos N. Georgiou. *Cyprus Rev.* **3:2** Fall:1991 pp. 27 – 56
61 Enforcing the work ethic — rhetoric and everyday life in a work incentive program. Gale Miller. Albany: SUNY Press, 1991: 252 p. *ISBN: 0791404234*. [SUNY series in the sociology of work.]
62 Features of educational attainment and job promotion prospects. Seymour Spilerman; Tormod Lunde. *A.J.S.* **97:3** 11:1991 pp. 689 – 720
63 Histoires de vies professionnelles — mobilités externes *[In French]*; [Stories about professional lives — external mobility]. Anne Flottes Lerolle. Paris: CEREQ, 1991: 132 p. *Bibliography — p[131]-132*. [Documents de travail.]
64 Innerbetriebliche Mobilitätsprozesse — Individuelle und strukturelle Determinanten der Karrieredynamik von Beschäftigten eines bundesdeutschen Großbetriebes *[In German]*; Mobility within the firm. Individual and structural factors determining career mobility among employees of a large West German firm *[Summary]*. Josef Brüderl; Peter Preisendörfer; Rolf Ziegler. *Z. Soziol.* **20:5** 10:1991 pp. 369 – 384
65 Perspektiven der beruflichen Beratung in den osteuropäischen Ländern und der Volksrepublik China *[In German]*; [Prospects for career advice in Eastern Europe and China]. Bernd-Joachim Ertelt *[Ed.]*; András Zakar *[Ed.]*. Nürnberg: Institut für Arbeitsmarkt- und Berufsforschung, 1991: 126 p. [Beiträge zur Arbeitsmarkt und Berufsforschung. : No. 151]

I.4: Vocational training, occupations and careers *[Formation professionnelle, professions et carrières]* — **Career development** *[Déroulement de carrière]*

66 Trajectoires d'ingénieurs et territoire — l'exemple des hautes technologies à Toulouse *[In French]*; Engineers trajectories and territory — the example of the high technology at Toulouse *[Summary]*. Michel]Grossetti. *Soc. Contemp.* :**6** 6:1991 pp. 65 – 80

67 Trying work — gender, youth and work experience. Anne Stafford. Edinburgh: Edinburgh University Press, 1991: 118 p. *ISBN: 0748602054. Includes bibliography and index.* [Edinburgh education and society series.]

68 Wages, benefits, and the promotion process for Chinese university faculty. Todd M. Johnson. *China Quart.* :**125** 1991 pp. 137 – 155

Managers *[Cadres]*

69 Attitudes towards women as managers — the case of Greece. Nancy Papalexandris; Dimitris Bourantas. *Int. J. Hum. Res. Man.* **2:2** 9:1991 pp. 133 – 148

70 Chinese workers' high expectations of enterprise managers. Jianhua Lu. *Int. Sociol.* **6:1** 3:1991 pp. 37 – 50

71 Dimensions of success and motivation needs among managers. Bernadette M. Ruf; Leonard H. Chusmir. *J. Psychol.* **125:6** 11:1991 pp. 631 – 640

72 The ethics of managing a diverse workforce in government. Mary Margaret Dauphinee; Ceta Ramkhalawansingh. *Can. Publ. Ad.* **34:1** Spring:1991 pp. 50 – 56

73 Expected managerial careers within growing and declining R&D establishments. Yehouda Shenhav. *Work Occup.* **18:1** 2:1991 pp. 46 – 71

74 How Chinese managers learn — management and industrial training in China. Malcolm Warner. : Macmillan Academic and Professional, 1991: 188 p. *ISBN: 0333527070.* [Studies on the Chinese economy.]

75 The impact of spouse's career-orientation on managers during international transfers. Gregory K. Stephens; Stewart Black. *J. Manag. Stu.* **28:4** 7:1991 pp. 417 – 428

76 Managementsoziologie — ein Desiderat der Industriesoziologie? Theoretische Perspektiven einer Soziologie des Managements *[In German]*; Sociology of management — a desideratum of industrial sociology? Theoretical perspectives of a sociology of management *[Summary]*. Gerd Schienstock. *Soz. Welt.* **42:3** 1991 pp. 349 – 370

77 Managerial activities, competence and effectiveness — manager and subordinate perceptions. Michael P. O'Driscoll; Maria Humphries; Henrik H. Larsen. *Int. J. Hum. Res. Man.* **2:3** 12:1991 pp. 313 – 325

78 Managers' employment issues — international comparisons between Australia and Britain. Russell D. Lansbury; Greg J. Bamber. *Int. J. Hum. Res. Man.* **2:3** 12:1991 pp. 285 – 312

79 Motivation of public sector managers — a comparative study. Baldev R. Sharma; Sarita Bhasker. *Ind. J. Ind. Rel.* **26:4** 4:1991 pp. 319 – 340

80 Munificent compensations as disincentives — the case of American CEOs. Jacques Delacroix; Shahrokh M. Saudagaran. *Human Relat.* **44:7** 7:1991 pp. 665 – 678

81 Quelques aspects de l'approche SCOP du management *[In French]*; [Some aspects of the SCOP approach to management]. Andrianjaka Bezanahary. *R. Et. Coop. Mut. Ass.* :**37** 1-3:1991 pp. 35 – 48

82 A race and gender-group analysis of the early career experience of MBAs. Taylor H. Cox; Stella M. Nkomo. *Work Occup.* **18:4** 11:1991 pp. 431 – 446

83 Relationship between managers' power and the perception of their non-managers' behaviour. Jai B.P. Sinha; Sunita Singh-Sengupta. *Ind. J. Ind. Rel.* **26:4** 4:1991 pp. 341 – 351

84 Le sort du contrat de travail des directeurs généraux *[In French]*; [The fate of labour contracts for general managers]. Bruno Petit. *Droit Soc.* :**6** 6:1991 pp. 463 – 468

85 Status consistency and work satisfaction among professional and managerial women and men. Margaret L. Cassidy; Bruce O. Warren. *Gender Soc.* **5:2** 6:1991 pp. 193 – 206

Professional workers *[Travailleurs professionnels]*

86 The accounting profession in South Korea. Steven F. Moliterno. New York: American Institute of Certified Public Accountants, 1990: 87 p. [Professional accounting in foreign countries series.]

87 Bénévoles et professionnels de la réinsertion sociale — conflits éthiques et conflits pratiques — note de recherche *[In French]*; Volunteers and professionals in social reintegration — ethical and practical conflicts. Research note. Dominique Lebleux. *Soc. Contemp.* :**7** 9:1991 pp. 103 – 112

I.4: Vocational training, occupations and careers *[Formation professionnelle, professions et carrières]* — *Professional workers [Travailleurs professionnels]*

88 Career commitment in human service professionals — a biographical study. Cary Cherniss. *Human Relat.* **44:5** 5:1991 pp. 419 – 437

89 La chronique de jurisprudence du CERIT — la requalification judiciaire de stages d'initiation à la vie professionelle *[In French]*; [Jurisprudence news from CERIT — a judicial requalification of the initiation stages in professional life]. Philippe Enclos. *Droit Soc.* **:6** 6:1991 pp. 500 – 510

90 Le développement professionnel des «cols blancs» diplômés d'université *[In French]*; The professional development of "white collar" university graduates *[Summary]*. Kazuo Koike. *Sociol. Trav.* **XXXIII:1** 1991 pp. 63 – 82

91 The economics of professional ethics — should the professions be more like business? R.C.O. Matthews. *Econ. J.* **101:407** 7:1991 pp. 737 – 750

92 Emergence d'un groupe professionnel et travail de légitimation — le cas des médecins de la douleur *[In French]*; Appearance of a professional group and its legitimation. The case of the pain doctors *[Summary]*; Das Hervortreten einer Berufsgruppe und Legitimierungsarbeit. Der Fall der «Schmerzärzte» *[German summary]*; Aparición de un grupo profesional y trabajo de legitimación. El caso de los médicos del dolor *[Spanish summary]*. Isabelle Baszanger. *Rev. Fr. Soc.* **XXXI:2** 4-6:1990 pp. 257 – 282

93 Éthique professionnelle *[In French]*; [Professional ethics. Jean-Paul Terrenoire *[Contrib.]*; René Padieu *[Contrib.]*; Gwen Terrenoire *[Contrib.]*; Pierre Bonte *[Contrib.]*; Jacques Commaille *[Contrib.]*; Dominique Lebleux *[Contrib.]*; Yannick Lemel *[Contrib.]*; Caroline Roy *[Contrib.]*. Collection of 7 articles. **Soc. Contemp.** , :7, 9:1991 pp. 7 – 127

94 Histoires de vies professionnelles — mobilités externes *[In French]*; [Stories about professional lives — external mobility]. Anne Flottes Lerolle. Paris: CEREQ, 1991: 132 p. *Bibliography — p[131]-132.* [Documents de travail.]

95 Les ingénieurs des années 1990 — mutations professionnelles et identité sociale *[In French]*; The engineers of the 1990s — professional change and social identity *[Summary]*. Jean-Marie Duprez; André Grelon; Catherine Marry. *Soc. Contemp.* **:6** 6:1991 pp. 41 – 63

96 Les ingénieurs en Pologne — formation, place et rôle dans la transformation du système socio-économique dans les années 1990 *[In French]*; Engineers in Poland — formation, position and role in the transformation of the socio-economic system in the 1990s *[Summary]*. Andrzej Matczewski; Ewa Okon-Horodynska. *Soc. Contemp.* **:6** 6:1991 pp. 93 – 106

97 Ingénieurs et développement au Proche-Orient — Liban, Syrie, Jordanie *[In French]*; Engineers and development in the Middle East — Lebanon, Syria, Jordan *[Summary]*. Elisabeth Longuenesse. *Soc. Contemp.* **:6** 6:1991 pp. 9 – 40

98 La maestra universitaria — doble jornada laboral *[In Spanish]*; [The university teacher — a double working day]. Rosa María Barrientos Granda. *Est. Sociol.* **IX:26** 5-8:1991 pp. 235 – 252

99 The micropolitical orientation of teachers toward closed school principals. Joseph J. Blase. *Educ. Urban. Soc.* **23:4** 8:1991 pp. 356 – 378

100 Notaires et huissiers de justice — du patrimoine à l'entreprise *[In French]*; Solicitors and bailiffs — from patrimony to the enterprise *[Summary]*; Notare und Gerichtsvollzieher — vom Erbgut zum Unternehmen *[German summary]*; Notarios y porteros de estrados — del patrimonio a la empresa *[Spanish summary]*. Christian Thuderoz. *Rev. Fr. Soc.* **XXXII:2** 4-6:1991 pp. 209 – 239

101 Physicians' choices of specialty, location, and mode — a reexamination within an interdependent decision framework. Jeremiah E. Hurley. *J. Hum. Res.* **XXVI:1** Winter:1991 pp. 47 – 71

102 Professional culture and organizational morality — an ethnographic account of a therapeutic organization. Mia Nijsmans. *Br. J. Soc.* **42:1** 3:1991 pp. 1 – 19

103 Профессиональная занятость (региональный аспект) *[In Russian]*; [Professional employment — the regional aspect]. Iu. Bogumolov; L. Dobrynina. *Plan. Khoz.* **:5** :1991 pp. 108 – 113

104 Professions and patriarchy. Anne Witz. London: Routledge, 1991: 233 p. *ISBN: 0415050081; LofC: 91013905. Includes bibliographical references and index.* [The international library of sociology.]

105 Professions and the state — expertise and autonomy in the Soviet Union and Eastern Europe. Anthony Jones *[Ed.]*. Philadelphia: Temple University Press, 1991: 256p. *ISBN: 0877228019.* [Labor and social change.]

I.4: Vocational training, occupations and careers [Formation professionnelle, professions et carrières] — Professional workers [Travailleurs professionnels]

106 La recherche-développement et la formation des chercheurs et ingénieurs au Japon *[In French]*; The RD organisation and the management of scientists and engineers in Japan *[Summary]*. Koichiro Imano; Scott T. Davis. *Sociol. Trav.* **XXXIII:1** 1991 pp. 83 – 104

107 School choice plans and the professionalization of teaching. Camilla A. Heid; Lawrence E. Leak. *Educ. Urban. Soc.* **23:2** 2:1991 pp. 219 – 227

108 Sex discrimination in the legal profession — a study of promotion. Stephen J. Spurr. *Ind. Lab. Rel.* **43:4** 4:1990 pp. 406 – 417

109 *[In Japanese]*; [Sociological approach to the social role of lawyers]. Tomohiko Otani. **Hiroshima Hogaku No.14(4) - 1991**. pp. 575 – 610

110 Sociologie de l'éthique professionnelle — contribution à la réflexion théorique *[In French]*; Sociology of professional ethics — a contribution to theory. Jean-Paul Terrenoire. *Soc. Contemp.* **:7** 9:1991 pp. 7 – 34

111 Status consistency and work satisfaction among professional and managerial women and men. Margaret L. Cassidy; Bruce O. Warren. *Gender Soc.* **5:2** 6:1991 pp. 193 – 206

112 Teacher education and the social conditions of schooling. Daniel P. Liston. London: Routledge, 1991: 293 p. *ISBN: 0415900719* [Critical social thought.]

113 Technical workers in a newly industrialising economy — the work experience of engineers in Singapore. Hing Ai Yun. *Int. J. Comp. Soc* **32:3-4** 9-12:1991 pp. 321 – 332

114 Tenure for Socrates — a study in the betrayal of the American professor. Jon Huer. New York: Bergin & Garvey, 1991: xvi, 211 p. *ISBN: 0897892445; LofC: 90-38827. Includes bibliographical references (p.205-206) and index..*

115 Thinking like an engineer — the place of a code of ethics in the practice of a profession. Michael Davis. *Philos. Pub.* **20:2** Spring:1991 pp. 150 – 167

Vocational training *[Formation professionnelle]*

116 Assessing the effectiveness of training and temporary employment schemes — some results from the youth labour market. Richard Breen. *Econ. Soc. R.* **22:3** 4:1991 pp. 177 – 198

117 European trends in training and development. Len Holden. *Int. J. Hum. Res. Man.* **2:2** 9:1991 pp. 113 – 132

118 La formation expérientielle des adultes *[In French]*; [The training experience of adults]. B. Courteau *[Ed.]*; Guy Pineau *[Ed.]*. Paris: La Documentation française, 1991: 348 p. *ISBN: 2110026359. Bibliography — p333-337*. [Recherche en formation continue.]

119 The impact of gender and working life cycle position on the likelihood and accumulation of formal on-the-job training. A.J. Field; A.H. Goldsmith. *Pop. Res. Pol. R.* **10:1** 1991 pp. 47 – 66

120 L'insertion professionnelle a l'issue des CAP et des BEP (1980-1988) *[In French]*; Job integration after short technical training *[Summary]*; Die berufliche Eingliederung mit berufsqualifizierendem Abschluß *[German summary]*. Yvette Grelet; Xavier Viney. *Form. Emp.* **:33** 1-3:1991 pp. 64 – 77

121 International comparisions of vocational education and training for intermediate skills. Paul Ryan *[Ed.]*. London: The Falmer Press, 1991: 301 p. *ISBN: 185000899x*.

122 Job-related formal training — who receives it and what is it worth? Alison L. Booth. *Ox. B. Econ. S.* **53:3** 8:1991 pp. 281 – 294

123 Job-training and relocation experiences among displaced industrial workers. Allison Zippay. *Eval. Rev.* **15:5** 10:1991 pp. 555 – 570

124 Local systems of vocational education and job training — diversity, interdependence, and effectiveness. W. Norton Grubb; Lorraine M. McDonnell. Santa Monica, CA: Rand, 1991: xv, 92 p. *ISBN: oc24577775. Includes bibliographical references (p. 89-92)*.

125 Meeting trainees' expectations — the influence of training fulfillment on the development of commitment, self-efficacy, and motivation. Scott I. Tannenbaum; John E. Mathieu; Eduardo Salas; Janis A. Cannon-Bowers. *J. Appl. Psychol.* **76:6** 12:1991 pp. 759 – 769

126 A quasi-experimental evaluation of the Vocational Training Centre for Adults. J. de Koning; M. Koss; A. Verkaik. *Envir. Plan. C.* **9:2** 5:1991 pp. 143 – 153

127 Recent developments in the German apprenticeship system. Bernard Casey. *Br. J. Ind. R.* **29:2** 6:1991 pp. 205 – 222

128 Skills for life — experiences of training in three developing countries. Dennis Frost *[Ed.]*. London: Intermediate Technology Publications, 1991: 192 p. *ISBN: 185339081x*. Vocational training.

129 Training and education for the voluntary sector — the needs and the problems. Margaret Harris; Gill Davies *[Ed.]*; Carli Lessof *[Ed.]*. London: London School of Economics and Political Science. Centre for Voluntary Organisation, 1991: 39 p. *ISBN: 0853281262*.

I.4: Vocational training, occupations and careers *[Formation professionnelle, professions et carrières]* — *Vocational training [Formation professionnelle]*

130 Vocational and technical education and training. John Middleton *[Ed.]*; Adrian Ziderman *[Ed.]*; Arvil Van Adams *[Ed.]*. Washington, D.C: World Bank, c1991: 83 p. *ISBN: 0821317806; LofC: 91002760*. Includes bibliographical references (p. 73-83). [A World Bank policy paper.]

131 Worker characteristics, job characteristics, and the receipt of on-the-job training. Joseph G. Altonji; James R. Spletzer. *Ind. Lab. Rel.* **45:1** 10:1991 pp. 58 – 79

132 Youth training and the local reconstruction of skill — evidence from the engineering industry of North West England, 1981-88. J.A. Peck; G.F. Haughton. *Envir. Plan.A.* **23:6** 6:1991 pp. 813 – 832

133 Youth training in the United States, Britain, and Australia. Hong W. Tan *[Ed.]*; et al. Santa Monica, Calif: RAND, 1991: 47 p. *ISBN: 0833011634.* [Rand report.4022-ED]

I.5: Labour relations — *Relations du travail*

Sub-divisions: Collective bargaining *[Négociation collective]*; Labour disputes *[Conflits du travail]*; Labour law *[Droit du travail]*; Trade unions *[Syndicats]*; Workers' participation *[Participation des travailleurs]*

1 Arrangement im Status quo minus. Deregulierung der Beschäftigungsverhältnisse in Frankreich und der Bundesrepublik Deutschland und ihre Verarbeitung im System der industriellen Beziehungen *[In German]*; Arrangements in status quo minus *[Summary]*. Ingo Bode; Hanns-Georg Brose; Stephan Voswinkel. *Soz. Welt.* **42:1** :1991 pp. 20 – 45

2 The attitudes of factory workers in Malaysia. Fatimah Daud. *Asian Prof.* **19:5** 10:1991 pp. 423 – 434

3 Attribution theory and discipline arbitration. Brian Bemmels. *Ind. Lab. Rel.* **44:3** 4:1991 pp. 548 – 562

4 Britain in a social Europe — industrial relations and 1992; Les relations professionnelles en Europe *[French summary]*. Jeff Bridgford; John Stirling. *Ind. Relat. J.* **22:4** Winter:1991 pp. 263 – 272

5 The changing character of employee relations. Robert T. Thompson. *J. Labor Res.* **XII:4** Fall:1991 pp. 311 – 321

6 Common interests — women organising in global electronics. Women Working Worldwide. London: Women Working Worldwide, 1991: 237 p. (ill) *ISBN: 0951707507.*

7 Comparative industrial relations in Japan and India. John Zechariah. *Ind. J. Ind. Rel.* **26:4** 4:1991 pp. 352 – 366

8 The construction of social communities in work — the case of a Nigerian factory. Jimi Adesina. *Cap. Class* **40** Spring:1990 pp. 115 – 149

9 Customer racial discrimination in major league baseball. Torben Andersen; Sumner J. La Croix. *Econ. Inq.* **XXIX:4** 10:1991 pp. 665 – 677

10 Customers, competitors and choice — employee relations in food retailing; Clients, concurrents et choix — les relations professionnelles dans le commerce de détail alimentaire *[French summary]*. Mick Marchington; Eric Harrison. *Ind. Relat. J.* **22:4** Winter:1991 pp. 286 – 299

11 Democracy in the workplace — the French experience. Frank L. Wilson. *Polit. Soc.* **19:4** 12:1991 pp. 439 – 462

12 Des relations industrielles comme objet théorique *[In French]*; Industrial relations as a subject of theory *[Summary]*. Guy Caire. *Sociol. Trav.* **:3** 1991 pp. 375 – 402

13 Determinants of effectiveness in industrial relations. F.M. Horwitz. *S. Afr. J. Labour Relat.* **15:1** 3:1991 pp. 3 – 20

14 Determination of leadership style and style range. J. Ramkanth. *Ind. J. Ind. Rel.* **26:4** 4:1991 pp. 395 – 411

15 The dilemmas of social democracies. The case of Norway and Sweden. Gudmund Hernes. *Acta Sociol.* **34:4** 1991 pp. 239 – 260

16 Employee relations at work in urban government — a study. Rama Prasada Rao; P. Subba Rao. *Ind. J. Ind. Rel.* **26:3** 1:1991 pp. 262 – 270

17 Employment relations and the labour market — integrating institutional and market perspectives. William P. Bridges; Wayne J. Villemez. *Am. Sociol. R.* **56:6** 12:1991 pp. 748 – 764

I.5: Labour relations [Relations du travail]

18 Engendering everyday resistance — gender, patronage and production politics in rural Malaysia. Gillian Hart. *J. Peasant Stud.* **19:1** 10:1991 pp. 93 – 123
19 Environment, corporate ideology, and involvement programs. Irene Goll. *Ind. Relat.* **30:1** Winter:1991 pp. 138 – 149
20 Essai sur la transformation historique des pratiques d'emploi et des relations professionnelles au Japon *[In French]*; Essay on the historical transformation of employment practices and industrial relations in Japan *[Summary]*. Shojiro Ujihara. *Sociol. Trav.* **XXXIII:1** 1991 pp. 19 – 25
21 The European Community as an integrated area for international tourism. Gabriele Gaetani d' Aragona. *J. Reg. Pol.* **11:1** 1-3:1991 pp. 77 – 90
22 L'evoluzione delle relazioni industriali — mutamenti profondi e un futuro incerto *[In Italian]*; Industrial relations developments during the 1980s *[Summary]*. Corrado Squarzon. *Ec. Lav.* **XXV:2** 4-6:1991 pp. 55 – 68
23 La forme coordination — une catégorie sociale révélatrice de sens *[In French]*; The "coordination" — a new form of social organization that reveals meaning *[Summary]*. Patrick Rozenblatt. *Sociol. Trav.* **XXXIII:2** 1991 pp. 239 – 254
24 Free enterprise and socialized labor. John McDermott. *Sci. Soc.* **55:4** Winter:1991-1992 pp. 388 – 416
25 Gerencia estrategica y relaciones industriales *[In Spanish]*; [Strategic management and industrial relations]. Pablo Lira. *Invest. Ger.* **8:4(37)** 1991 pp. 183 – 194
26 The impact on economic performance of a transformation in workplace relations. Joel Cutcher-Gershenfeld. *Ind. Lab. Rel.* **44:2** 1:1991 pp. 241 – 260
27 Industrial councils in jeopardy? A focus on iron and steel. Melvin Goldberg. *Ind. Rel. J. S.Afr.* **11:2** 1991 pp. 31 – 46
28 Industrial relations in Australia and Sweden — strategies for change in the 1990s. Russell D. Lansbury. *Econ. Ind. Dem.* **12:4** 11:1991 pp. 527 – 534
29 Industrial restructuring and industrial relations in Canada and the United States. Noah M. Meltz; Michael J. Piore; Elaine B. Willis. Kingston, Ont: Industrial Relations Centre, Queen's University, 1991: vi, 32 p. *ISBN: 0888862873; LofC: cn 91094783. Two papers presented at a conference held at Queen's University, 1989; Includes bibliographical references.*
30 Die industriellen Beziehungen in der Bundesrepublik jenseits eines kulturellen Verteilungskampfes? *[In German]*; [Labour relations in the FRG beyond a cultural struggle for fair distribution?]. Jürgen Hoffmann. *Gewerk. Monat.* **42:2** 2:1991 pp. 89 – 102
31 The influence of member role preferences and leader characteristics on the effectiveness of quality circles. Peter Makin; Colin Eveleigh; Barrie Dale. *Int. J. Hum. Res. Man.* **2:2** 9:1991 pp. 193 – 204
32 Information sharing and firm performance in Japan. Motohiro Morishima. *Ind. Relat.* **30:1** Winter:1991 pp. 37 – 61
33 Information sharing of sensitive business data with employees. Morris M. Kleiner; Marvin L. Bouillon. *Ind. Relat.* **30:3** Fall:1991 pp. 480 – 491
34 Labor relations — current issues and future prospects. James T. Bennett *[Contrib.]*; Robert T. Thompson *[Contrib.]*; Francis A. O'Connell *[Contrib.]*; Elmer Chatak *[Contrib.]*; Herbert R. Northrup *[Contrib.]*; Don Bellante *[Contrib.]*; Peter Feuille *[Contrib.]*; Joseph D. Reid *[Contrib.]*; John Thomas Delaney *[Contrib.]*; Thomas J. DiLorenzo *[Contrib.]* and others. Collection of 12 articles. **J. Labor Res.** , *XII:4*, Fall:1991 pp. 307 – 409
35 Labour movements, employers, and the state — conflict and co-operation in Britain and Sweden. James Fulcher. Oxford: Clarendon Press, 1991: 367 p. *ISBN: 0198272898; LofC: 91002920. Includes bibliographical references and index.*
36 Labour relations in Israel (part I). W. Backer. *S. Afr. J. Labour Relat.* **15:4** 12:1991 pp. 6 – 22
37 Locus of control as a moderator of the relationship between perceived influence and procedural justice. Paul D. Sweeney; Dean B. McFarlin; John L. Cotton. *Human Relat.* **44:4** 4:1991 pp. 333 – 342
38 Management dilemmas and decisions — impact of framing and anticipated responses. William C. McDaniel; Francis Sistrunk. *Confl. Resolut.* **35:1** 3:1991 pp. 21 – 42
39 Managerial issues and responsibilities in the use of integrity tests. Carolyn Wiley; Docia L. Rudley. *Lab. Law J.* **42:3** 3:1991 pp. 152 – 159
40 Managerial prerogrative and industrial democracy. Barney Jordaan. *Ind. Rel. J. S.Afr.* **11:3** 1991 pp. 1 – 10

I.5: Labour relations [Relations du travail]

41 The meaning of job security. Hugh Collins. *Ind. Law J.* **20:4** 12:1991 pp. 227 – 239
42 New technology and the restructuring of pit-level industrial relations in the British coal industry; *[French summary]*. Steve Leman; Jonathan Winterton. *New Tech. Work. Empl.* **6:1** Spring:1991 pp. 54 – 64
43 Organisationsentwicklung — Barrieren und Chancen der Veränderung von Arbeitsorganisationen *[In German]*; [Organizational development — obstacles to, and chances for, change in productive organizations]. Irene Raehlmann. *Gewerk. Monat.* **42:8** 8:1991 pp. 496 – 505
44 Privatisation and the management of IR in electricity distribution; La privatisation offre-t-elle de nouvelles chances? La gestion des relations industrielles dans l'industrie de l'electricité *[French summary]*. Trevor Colling. *Ind. Relat. J.* **22:2** Summer:1991 pp. 117 – 129
45 Privatization, regulation and industrial relations. Anthony Ferner; Trevor Colling. *Br. J. Ind. R.* **29:3** 9:1991 pp. 391 – 410
46 Problemy negocjowania polityki socjalnej w zakładach pracy *[In Polish]*; (Problems of social policy negotiation in works enterprise); (Проблемы негоциации социальной политики на предприятиях: *Title only in Russian*). Henryk Zarychta. *Pra. Zab. Społ.* **33:7** 7:1991 pp. 6 – 12
47 Productive forces and industrial citizenship — an evolutionary perspective on labour relations. Walther Müller-Jentsch. *Econ. Ind. Dem.* **12:4** 11:1991 pp. 439 – 467
48 Profit sharing and public policy — insights for the United States. Gary W. Florkowski. *Ind. Relat.* **30:1** Winter:1991 pp. 96 – 115
49 Reforming industrial relations — law, politics, and power. Roy Lewis. *Ox. R. Econ. Pol.* **7:1** Spring:1991 pp. 60 – 75
50 Salaire d'efficience, contrat implicite et théorie des organisations *[In French]*; Efficiency wage, implicit contract and organizational theory *[Summary]*; Effizienzgerechtes Gehalt, stillschweigender Vertrag und Theorie der Organisation *[German summary]*; Salario de eficiencia, contrato implícito y teoría de las organizaciones *[Spanish summary]*. Jean-François Amadieu. *Rev. Fr. Soc.* **XXXI:2** 4-6:1990 pp. 225 – 242
51 Simulazione e intelligenza artificiale nello studio delle relazioni industriali *[In Italian]*; Simulation and artificial intelligence in the study of industrial relations *[Summary]*. Giancarlo Provasi. *Ec. Lav.* **XXV:2** 4-6:1991 pp. 3 – 38
52 Strategic management development — an industrial relations perspective. K. Jowell. *S. Afr. J. Labour Relat.* **15:3** 9:1991 pp. 5 – 15
53 Taiwan — an exploration of labour relations in transition. Archie Kleingartner; Hsueh-yu Peng (Shara). *Br. J. Ind. R.* **29:3** 9:1991 pp. 427 – 446
54 Testing the survey method — continuity and change in British industrial relations. Tim Morris; Stephen Wood. *Work Emp. Soc.* **5:2** 6:1991 pp. 259 – 282
55 "Them and us" — social psychology and "the new industrial relations". John Kelly; Caroline Kelly. *Br. J. Ind. R.* **29:1** 3:1991 pp. 25 – 48
56 Transforming industrial relations. Michael Easson *[Ed.]*; Jeff Shaw *[Ed.]*. Leichardt, New South Wales: Pluto Press, 1990: 207 p. *ISBN: 0949138495*.
57 Workers are working harder — effort and shop-floor relations in the 1980s. P.K. Edwards; Colin Whitston. *Br. J. Ind. R.* **29:4** 12:1991 pp. 593 – 602
58 Workers, firms, and the dominant ideology — hegemony and consciousness in the monopoly core. Steven Peter Vallas. *Sociol. Q.* **32:1** Spring:1991 pp. 61 – 83
59 Workplace IR in British Rail — change and continuity in the 1980s; Les relations industrielles sur le lieu de travail à British Rail — changement et continuité dans les années 1980 *[French summary]*. Andrew Pendleton. *Ind. Relat. J.* **22:3** Autumn:1991 pp. 209 – 221

Collective bargaining [Négociation collective]

60 Arbeitsbeziehungen und Tarifpolitik in Europa *[In German]*; [Labour relations and collective bargaining in Europe]. Wolfgang Lecher. *Gewerk. Monat.* **42:11** 11:1991 pp. 700 – 710
61 Arbitrator decisions in Wisconsin teacher wage disputes. Craig A. Olson; Paul Jarley. *Ind. Lab. Rel.* **44:3** 4:1991 pp. 536 – 547
62 Collective bargaining in the public sector — the effect of legal structure on dispute costs and wages. Janet Currie; Sheena McConnell. *Am. Econ. Rev.* **81:4** 9:1991 pp. 693 – 718
63 La contrattazione collettiva nel pubblico impiego *[In Italian]*; (Collective bargaining in the public sector). Carmine Russo. *Ec. Lav.* **XXV:2** 4-6:1991 pp. 117 – 129
64 The debate over levels of bargaining (a legal approach). M.H. Marcus. *S. Afr. J. Labour Relat.* **15:4** 12:1991 pp. 31 – 43

I.5: Labour relations [Relations du travail] — Collective bargaining [Négociation collective]

65 The decollectivisation of trade unionism? Ballots and collective bargaining in the 1980s; La décollectivisation des syndicats? Scrutins et négociation collective dans les années 80 *[French summary]*. Roderick Martin; Patricia Fosh; Huw Morris; Paul Smith; Roger Undy. *Ind. Relat. J.* **22:3** Autumn:1991 pp. 197 – 208

66 Implementing a mutual gains approach to collective bargaining. Lawrence E. Susskind; Elaine M. Landry. *Negot. J.* **7:1** 1: 1991 pp. 5 – 10

67 Informal shopfloor bargaining, custom and practice in industrial relations — a systematisation. A.S. Kritzinger. *Ind. Rel. J. S.Afr.* **11:4** 1991 pp. 1 – 14

68 Information sharing and collective bargaining in Japan — effects on wage negotiation. Motohiro Morishima. *Ind. Lab. Rel.* **44:3** 4:1991 pp. 469 – 485

69 Kształtowanie zbiorowych stosunków pracy w Polsce — doświadczenia i przyszłość *[In Polish]*; (Formation of collective working relations in Poland — experiences and future); (Формирование коллективных трудовых отношений в Польше: опыт и будущее: *Title only in Russian)*. Stanisława Borkowska. *Pra. Zab. Społ.* **XXXIII:8-9** 8-9:1991 pp. 7 – 15

70 Labor's inequality of bargaining power — myth or reality? Bruce E. Kaufman. *J. Labor Res.* **XII:2** Spring:1991 pp. 151 – 166

71 The nature and role of local bargaining in South African industrial relations — a comparative view on structures and mechanisms. A.S. Kritzinger. *S. Afr. J. Labour Relat.* **15:1** 3:1991 pp. 21 – 36

72 Patterns of teacher bargaining in Canada and the United States. Kenneth Wm. Thornicroft. *Lab. Law J.* **42:12** 12:1991 pp. 779 – 791

73 Resolving conflict through explicit bargaining. Elizabeth Heger Boyle; Edward J. Lawler. *Soc. Forc.* **69:4** 6:1991 pp. 1183 – 1204

74 Rethinking labour-management relations — the case for arbitration. C. J. Bruce; Joseph Roger Carby-Hall *[Ed.]*. London: Routledge, 1991: ix, 206 p. *ISBN: 0415022134; LofC: 90026703. Includes bibliographical references (p. [169]-196) and index.*

75 Towards an employee's charter and away from collective bargaining. Nicholas Finney; Graham Brady. London: Centre for Policy Studies, 1991: 36 p. *ISBN: 1870265858.* [Policy study.]

Labour disputes [Conflits du travail]

76 A century of UK strike activity — an alternative perspective. Simon Milner; David Metcalf. London: London School of Economics and Political Science, 1991: 25 p. [Discussion paper.]

77 Conflict management and negotiations in South Africa — lessons from industrial relations. Frank Horwitz. *Ind. Rel. J. S.Afr.* **11:1** 1991 pp. 61 – 78

78 Crossing the picket line — violence in industrial conflict. E. Webster; G. Simpson. *Ind. Rel. J. S.Afr.* **11:4** 1991 pp. 15 – 32

79 Economie politique d'une grève *[In French]*; The "political economy" of a strike *[Summary]*. Salvador Aguilar; Jordi Roca. *Sociol. Trav.* **XXXIII:2** 1991 pp. 217 – 238

80 The European Convention on Human Rights, the Employment Act of 1988 and the right to refuse to strike. Sheldon Leader. *Ind. Law J.* **20:1** 3:1991 pp. 39 – 59

81 Farm workers, boycotts, and free speech. Mark M. Hager. *Lab. Law J.* **42:12** 12:1991 pp. 792 – 799

82 Gender effects in grievance arbitration. Brian Bemmels. *Ind. Relat.* **30:1** Winter:1991 pp. 150 – 162

83 Grievance procedure strength and teacher quits. Daniel I. Rees. *Ind. Lab. Rel.* **45:1** 10:1991 pp. 31 – 43

84 The "isolated mass" revisited — strikes in British coal mining. Roy Church; Quentin Outram; David N. Smith. *Sociol. Rev.* **39:1** 2:1991 pp. 55 – 87

85 Калектыўныя працоўныя спрэчкі і забастоўкі: праблемы рэгламентацыі *[In Belorussian]*; *[Russian summary]*; [Collective labour disputes and strikes — regulatory problems] *[Summary]*. A.P. Dubavets. *V. Aka. BSSR* **:4** :1991 pp. 44 – 50

86 The "macho" management debate and the dismissal of employees during industrial disputes. David Denham. *Sociol. Rev.* **39:2** 5:1991 pp. 349 – 364

87 Predictors of strike voting behavior — the case of university faculty. Ignace Ng. *J. Labor Res.* **XII:2** Spring:1991 pp. 123 – 134

88 Professional mediators' judgments of mediation tactics — multidimensional scaling and cluster analyses. Mary E. McLaughlin; Peter Carnevale; Rodney G. Lim. *J. Appl. Psychol.* **76:3** 6:1991 pp. 465 – 472

I.5: Labour relations *[Relations du travail]* — Labour disputes *[Conflits du travail]*

89 Rola młodej generacji pracowników w kryzysie i konflikcie społecznym *[In Polish]*; Young generation of employees in crisis and conflict situations *[Summary]*. Wielisława Warzywoda-Kruszyńska. *Acta Univ. Łódz. Folia Soc.* **21** 1991 pp. 7 – 31

90 The roles of supervisors, employees, and stewards in grievance initiation. Brian Bemmels; Yonatan Reshef; Kay Stratton-Devine. *Ind. Lab. Rel.* **45:1** 10:1991 pp. 15 – 30

91 State mediation of conflicts over work refusals — the role of the Ontario Labour Relations Board. Vivienne Walters. *Int. J. Health. Ser.* **21:4** 1991 pp. 717 – 729

92 Strike durations in the United States — selected comparisons from the public and private sectors. Beth A. Rubin; Brian T. Smith. *Sociol. Q.* **32:1** Spring:1991 pp. 85 – 101

93 Ten ways to work more effectively with volunteer mediators. Susan J. Rogers. *Negot. J.* **7:2** 4:1991 pp. 201 – 211

94 When Hollywood strikes. Jan Wilson. *Lab. Law J.* **42:10** 10:1991 pp. 693 – 707

95 Why do strikes turn violent? Don Sherman Grant; Michael Wallace. *A.J.S.* **96:5** 3:1991 pp. 1117 – 1150

96 Workplace dispute resolution and gender inequality. Patricia A. Gwartney-Gibbs; Denise H. Lach. *Negot. J.* **7:2** 4:1991 pp. 187 – 200

97 Workplace justice outcomes "in the name of the union" — a field assessment. Debra J. Mesch; Dan R. Dalton. *Int. J. Confl. Manag.* **2:1** 1:1991 pp. 45 – 54

Labour law *[Droit du travail]*

98 Les accords de groupe, quelques difficultés juridiques *[In French]*; [Group agreements, some judicial difficulties]. Marie-Armelle Rotschild-Souriac. *Droit Soc.* **:6** 6:1991 pp. 491 – 496

99 AIDS-related dementia and treatment of AIDS-affected individuals under changing employment law. David C. Wyld; Sam D. Cappel. *Lab. Law J.* **42:4** 4:1991 pp. 204 – 213

100 Are terminations precipitated by an invasion of privacy wrongful? David S. Hames. *Lab. Law J.* **42:6** 6:1991 pp. 371 – 375

101 The courts and compulsory arbitration in Pennsylvania. J. Joseph Loewenberg. *Lab. Law J.* **42:5** 5:1991 pp. 296 – 302

102 Le droit international du travail en mouvement — déploiement et approches nouvelles *[In French]*; [International labour law in flux — deployment and new approaches]. Jean-Michel Servais. *Droit Soc.* **:5** 5:1991 pp. 447 – 452

103 The Employment Act 1990 — still fighting the industrial cold war. Hazel Carty. *Ind. Law J.* **20:1** 3:1991 pp. 1 – 20

104 Employment rights in Britain and Europe — selected papers in labour law. Kenneth William Wedderburn. London: Lawrence and Wishart, 1991: 431 p. *ISBN: 0853157448*.

105 Equal employment opportunity law and firm profitability. Joni Hersch. *J. Hum. Res.* **XXVI:1** Winter:1991 pp. 139 – 152

106 Equal employment opportunity on campus — strengthening the commitment. William T. Burke; Frank J. Cavaliere. *Lab. Law J.* **42:1** 1:1991 pp. 19 – 27

107 The evolution of unjust-dismissal legislation in the United States. Alan B. Krueger. *Ind. Lab. Rel.* **44:4** 7:1991 pp. 644 – 660

108 The Irish Industrial Relations Act 1990 — corporatism and conflict control. Brian Wilkinson. *Ind. Law J.* **20:1** 3:1991 pp. 21 – 37

109 Irish industrial relations legislation — consensus not compulsion. Tony Kerr. *Ind. Law J.* **20:4** 12:1991 pp. 240 – 257

110 Is there a purpose of workplace participation? Liv Tørres. *Ind. Rel. J. S.Afr.* **11:2** 1991 pp. 1 – 20

111 Making the case for a national commission on American labor law and competitiveness. Steve Gunderson. *Lab. Law J.* **42:9** 9:1991 pp. 587 – 595

112 Negligent hiring and criminal record information — a muddled area of employment law. Gary D. Miller; James W. Fenton. *Lab. Law J.* **42:3** 3:1991 pp. 186 – 192

113 Neuere Entwicklungen im britischen Arbeitsrecht *[In German]*; [Recent developments in British labour law]. Christopher Docksey. *Recht Int. Wirst.* **37:9** 9:1991 pp. 722 – 728

114 Potential for flexibility in EC countries. Regina Konle-Seidl; Ulrich Walwei. *Labour [Italy]* **5:2** Autumn:1991 pp. 175 – 193

115 Redundancy rights — rights for whom? D.H. Simpson. *Employ. Relat.* **13:1** 1991 pp. 4 – 11

116 Right-to-work laws, free riders, and unionization in the local public sector. Casey Ichniowski; Jeffrey S. Zax. *J. Labor Ec.* **9:3** 7:1991 pp. 255 – 275

117 El sindicalismo en el derecho español — modelo, problemas y perspectivas *[In Spanish]*; [Trade unionism in Spanish law — models, problems and outlooks]. Antonio Marzal. *Rev. Fom. Soc.* **46:183** 7-9:1991 pp. 303 – 318

I.5: Labour relations [Relations du travail] —

Trade unions [Syndicats]

118 Die Angst vor dem Individuum — Gewerkschaften und ihr blockiertes Verhältnis zu einem vielschichtigen Thema [In German]; [Fear of the individual — trade unions and the deadlocked position on a complex subject]. Klaus Pumberger. *Gewerk. Monat.* **42:8** 8:1991 pp. 485 – 496

119 L'arena delle relazioni industriali e il rapporto tra sindacati partiti [In Italian]; The industrial relations arena and the union-party relationship [Summary]. Paolo Feltrin. *Ec. Lav.* **XXV:2** 4-6:1991 pp. 39 – 54

120 The attitude of employee association members toward union mergers — the effect of socioeconomic status. Daniel B. Cornfield. *Ind. Lab. Rel.* **44:2** 1:1991 pp. 334 – 348

121 The break-up of an international labour union — uneven development in the North American auto industry and the schism in the UAW. J. Holmes; A. Rusonik. *Envir. Plan.A.* **23:1** 1:1991 pp. 9 – 35

122 British unions — dissolution or resurgence? David Metcalf. *Ox. R. Econ. Pol.* **7:1** Spring:1991 pp. 18 – 32

123 Caste, class and trade unionism among industrial workers. R. Maruthakutti; U.R. Kallappan; T. Chandramohan Reddy. *Ind. J. Ind. Rel.* **26:4** 4:1991 pp. 384 – 394

124 Changes in union status, increased competition and wage growth in the 1980s. Paul Gregg; Stephen Machin. *Br. J. Ind. R.* **29:4** 12:1991 pp. 603 – 612

125 Changes in wage-setting arrangements and trade union presence in the 1980s. Paul Gregg; Anthony Yates. *Br. J. Ind. R.* **29:3** 9:1991 pp. 361 – 376

126 Company or trade union — which wins workers' allegiance? A study of commitment in the UK electronics industry. David E. Guest; Philip Dewe. *Br. J. Ind. R.* **29:1** 3:1991 pp. 75 – 96

127 Contract curve or implicit contract — which will a union choose? Walter J. Wessels. *J. Labor Res.* **XII:1** Winter:1991 pp. 73 – 89

128 COSATU Congress — elections, voting, new blocs — what does it all mean? Karl von Holdt. *S.Afr. Lab. B.* **16:1** 7/8:1991 pp. 12 – 22

129 Determinants of decertification activity — an interstate analysis. C. Timothy Koeller. *Ind. Relat.* **30:1** Winter:1991 pp. 128 – 137

130 Determinants of trade union growth and decline in the Federal Republic of Germany. Claus Schnabel. *Eur. Sociol. R.* **5:2** 9:1989 pp. 133 – 146

131 Determinants of trade union membership in Australia. Stephen Deery; Helen De Cieri. *Br. J. Ind. R.* **29:1** 3:1991 pp. 59 – 73

132 The determinants of union membership growth in Taiwan. Basu Sharma; Peter Sephton. *J. Labor Res.* **XII:4** Fall:1991 pp. 429 – 438

133 Determinants of union recognition and employee involvement — evidence from London Docklands. Simon Milner; Edward Richards. *Br. J. Ind. R.* **29:3** 9:1991 pp. 377 – 390

134 Discriminating characteristics of union members' attitudes toward drug testing in the workplace. Michael H. LeRoy. *J. Labor Res.* **XII:4** Fall:1991 pp. 453 – 465

135 Do members' services packages influence trade union recruitment?; Les services offerts aux membres influencent-ils le recrutement syndical? [French summary]. Simon Sapper. *Ind. Relat. J.* **22:4** Winter:1991 pp. 309 – 316

136 Do unions contract for added employment? Walter J. Wessels. *Ind. Lab. Rel.* **45:1** 10:1991 pp. 181 – 193

137 Do unions influence the diffusion of technology? Jeffrey H. Keefe. *Ind. Lab. Rel.* **44:2** 1:1991 pp. 261 – 274

138 Dual commitment among unionized faculty — a longitudinal investigation. Laura L. Beauvais; Richard W. Scholl; Elizabeth A. Cooper. *Human Relat.* **44:2** 2:1991 pp. 175 – 192

139 L'échange politique difficile — les stratégies syndicales en Italie 1975-1990 [In French]; Difficult political bargaining — labor union strategies in Italy, 1975-1990 [Summary]. Udo Rehfeldt. *Sociol. Trav.* **:3** 1991 pp. 323 – 350

140 Economic dissatisfaction, potential unionism, and attitudes toward unions in Canada; [French summary]. Douglas E. Baer; Edward Grabb; William A. Johnston. *Can. R. Soc. A.* **28:1** 2:1991 pp. 67 – 83

141 The economic effects of faculty unions. Randall G. Kesselring. *J. Labor Res.* **XII:1** Winter:1991 pp. 61 – 72

142 Economie politique d'une grève [In French]; The "political economy" of a strike [Summary]. Salvador Aguilar; Jordi Roca. *Sociol. Trav.* **XXXIII:2** 1991 pp. 217 – 238

I.5: Labour relations *[Relations du travail]* — Trade unions *[Syndicats]*

143 Enforcing OSHA — the role of labor unions. David Weil. *Ind. Relat.* **30**:1 Winter:1991 pp. 20 – 36

144 Explaining union destiny in twentieth-century Britain. W.C. Runciman. *Sociology* **25**:4 11:1991 pp. 697 – 712

145 Feminizing unions — challenging the gendered structure of wage labor. Marion Crain. *Ml. law. R.* **89**:5 3:1991 pp. 1155 – 1220

146 The future of unions as political organizations. John Thomas Delaney. *J. Labor Res.* **XII**:4 Fall:1991 pp. 373 – 387

147 ICFTU conference for African trade unionists — international solidarity or paternalism? Dot Keet. *S.Afr. Lab. B.* **16**:1 7/8:1991 pp. 70 – 82

148 Insiders and trade union wage bargaining. Ian M. McDonald. *Manch. Sch. E.* **LIX**:4 12:1991 pp. 395 – 407

149 Is unionization compatible with professionalism? David M. Rabban. *Ind. Lab. Rel.* **45**:1 10:1991 pp. 97 – 112

150 Locating South Africa in the Third World — comparative perspectives on patterns of industrialisation and political trade unionism in South America. David Cooper. *Soc. Dyn.* **17**:2 12:1991 pp. 1 – 40

151 Le long chemin vers l'unité syndicale Africaine *[In French]*; [The long road towards African trade union unity] *[Summary]*; *[French summary]*; *[German summary]*. George Martens. *Genève-Afrique* **XXIX**:1 1991 pp. 7 – 32

152 Long-run international trends in aggregate unionization. G. Neumann; P.J. Pedersen; N. Westergård-Nielsen. *Eur. J. Pol. Ec.* **7**:3 :1991 pp. 249 – 274

153 Mining unionism, political democracy and revealed preferences — the quid pro quo of labour relations in Bolivia, Chile and Peru, 1950-80. Björn Feuer. *Econ. Ind. Dem.* **12**:1 2:1991 pp. 97 – 118

154 More uncertainties — German unions facing 1992. Wolfgang Streeck. *Ind. Relat.* **30**:3 Fall:1991 pp. 317 – 349

155 New evidence on unions and layoff rates. Mark Montgomery. *Ind. Lab. Rel.* **44**:4 7:1991 pp. 708 – 721

156 "New" union approaches to membership decline — reviving the policies of the 1920s? Herbert R. Northrup. *J. Labor Res.* **XII**:4 Fall:1991 pp. 333 – 347

157 Les ouvriers communistes — sociologie de l'adhésion ouvrière au PCF *[In French]*; [Communist workers — the sociology of worker cohesion in the French Communist Party (PCF)]. Jean-Paul Molinari. Thonon-les-Bains: L'Albaron, c1991 *ISBN: 2908528185.* Includes bibliographies.

158 Pratiques représentatives et construction identitaire. Une approche des coordinations *[In French]*; Representational practices and identity construction — a study of "coordinations" *[Summary]*. Patrick Hassenteufel. *R. Fr. Sci. Pol.* **41**:1 2:1991 pp. 5 – 27

159 Private sector unions — the myth of decline. James T. Bennett. *J. Labor Res.* **XII**:1 Winter:1991 pp. 1 – 12

160 Probleme und Perspektiven des Deutschen Gewerkschaftsbundes *[In German]*; [Problems and perspectives of the German trade unions]. Joachim Wiemeyer. *Jahr. Christ. Sozialwiss.* **31** 1990 pp. 91 – 114

161 Public sector unions and municipal employment. Stephen J. Trejo. *Ind. Lab. Rel.* **45**:1 10:1991 pp. 166 – 180

162 Race, ethnicity, union attitudes, and voting predilections. Ronnie Silverblatt; Robert J. Amann. *Ind. Relat.* **30**:2 Spring:1991 pp. 271 – 285

163 "Red" unions and "bourgeois" contracts? Judith Stepan-Norris; Maurice Zeitlin. *A.J.S.* **96**:5 3:1991 pp. 1151 – 1200

164 Relative deprivation and union participation. K. Pradeep Kumar. *Ind. J. Ind. Rel.* **26**:3 1:1991 pp. 271 – 277

165 The reserve army effect, unions, and nominal wage growth. Tsuyoshi Tsuru. *Ind. Relat.* **30**:2 Spring:1991 pp. 251 – 270

166 Right-to-work laws, free riders, and unionization in the local public sector. Casey Ichniowski; Jeffrey S. Zax. *J. Labor Ec.* **9**:3 7:1991 pp. 255 – 275

167 Sindacato e cambiamento tecnologico — una verifica empirica *[In Italian]*; [Trade unionism and technological change — an empirical analysis]. Laura Solimene. *Industria* **XII**:3 7-9:1991 pp. 369 – 396

168 El sindicalismo en el derecho español — modelo, problemas y perspectivas *[In Spanish]*; [Trade unionism in Spanish law — models, problems and outlooks]. Antonio Marzal. *Rev. Fom. Soc.* **46**:183 7-9:1991 pp. 303 – 318

I.5: Labour relations [Relations du travail] — Trade unions [Syndicats]

169 Smithfield meat market — the ultimate pre-entry closed shop. David Metcalf. *Work Emp. Soc.* **5:2** 6:1991 pp. 159 – 179

170 Some structural determinants of union participation among women workers. T. Chandramohan Reddy; S.V. Udayakumar; R. Tamilselvi. *Soc. Act.* **41:2** 4-6:1991 pp. 205 – 212

171 Strategy and circumstance — the success of the NUJ's new technology policy. Mike Noon. *Br. J. Ind. R.* **29:2** 6:1991 pp. 259 – 267

172 Technological choice and union-management cooperation. Robert J. Thomas. *Ind. Relat.* **30:2** Spring:1991 pp. 167 – 192

173 Tendances récentes du système japonais de relations industrielles — néo-corporatisme et nouvelle «identité syndicale» *[In French]*; Recent trends in the Japanese system of industrial systems — neocorporatism and new trade union identities *[Summary]*. Takeshi Inagami. *Sociol. Trav.* **XXXIII:1** 1991 pp. 27 – 49

174 Theoretical generality, case particularity — qualitative comparative analysis of trade union growth and decline. Larry J. Griffin; Christopher Botsko; Ana-Maria Wahl; Larry W. Issac. *Int. J. Comp. Soc* **XXXII: 1-2** 1-4:1991 pp. 110 – 136

175 A theory of trade union membership retention. Paul Lewis; Liam Murphy. *Br. J. Ind. R.* **29:2** 6:1991 pp. 277 – 294

176 Trabajo, sindicalismo y reconversión industrial en Brasil *[In Spanish]*; [Work, trade unionism and industrial rationalization in Brazil]. Nadia Araujo Castro; Antonio Sergio Guimaraes. *Est. Sociol.* **IX:25** 1-4:1991 pp. 105 – 126

177 The trade union campaign against water privatisation; La campagne syndicale contre la privatisation de l'eau *[French summary]*. Stuart Ogden. *Ind. Relat. J.* **22:1** Spring:1991 pp. 20 – 35

178 *[In Japanese]*; [Trade union identity — reconstruction of strategies]. Takashi Kawakita *[Ed.]*; et al. Tokyo: Sogorodo Kenkyusyo, 1991: 251 p.

179 Trade union recognition and employment contraction. Britain, 1980-1984. P.B. Beaumont; R.I.D. Harris. *Br. J. Ind. R.* **29:1** 3:1991 pp. 49 – 58

180 Trade union recruitment strategies — facing the 1990's; Les stratégies syndicales de recrutement — faire face aux années 90 *[French summary]*. Bob Mason; Peter Bain. *Ind. Relat. J.* **22:1** Spring:1991 pp. 36 – 45

181 Trade unions and HRM; Les syndicats et la gestion des ressources humaines *[French summary]*. P.B. Beaumont. *Ind. Relat. J.* **22:4** Winter:1991 pp. 300 – 308

182 Trade unions and productivity — opening the Harvard "black boxes". Peter J. Turnbull. *J. Labor Res.* **XII:2** Spring:1991 pp. 135 – 150

183 Trade unions and productivity — the German evidence. Claus Schnabel. *Br. J. Ind. R.* **29:1** 3:1991 pp. 15 – 24

184 Trade unions and workplace technical change in Europe. Hugo Levie; Åke Sandberg. *Econ. Ind. Dem.* **12:2** 5:1991 pp. 231 – 258

185 Trade unions under changing conditions — the West German experience, 1950-1985. Klaus Armingeon. *Eur. Sociol. R.* **5:1** 5:1989 pp. 1 – 24

186 The trade-off between precommitment and flexibility in trade union wage setting. Simon P. Anderson; Michael B. Devereux. *Ox. Econ. Pap.* **43:4** 10:1991 pp. 549 – 569

187 Unionism in the public sector — the joy of protected markets. Peter Feuille. *J. Labor Res.* **XII:4** Fall:1991 pp. 351 – 367

188 Unionization and cost of production — compensation, productivity, and factor-use effects. Randall W. Eberts; Joe A. Stone. *J. Labor Ec.* **9:2** 4:1991 pp. 171 – 185

189 Unions and the U.S. comparative advantage. Thomas Karier. *Ind. Relat.* **30:1** Winter:1991 pp. 1 – 19

190 Unions, bureaucracy, and change — old dogs learn new tricks very slowly. James A. Craft. *J. Labor Res.* **XII:4** Fall:1991 pp. 393 – 405

191 Voting rules and election outcomes — when does the true majority win? James R. Fain; James B. Dworkin. *J. Labor Res.* **XII:3** Summer:1991 pp. 247 – 260

192 WARN — the rights, duties, and obligations of employers, employees, and unions. T.S. Lough. *Lab. Law J.* **42:5** 5:1991 pp. 285 – 295

193 When does union-management cooperation work? A look at NUMMI and GM-Van Nuys. Clair Brown; Michael Reich. *Calif. Manag. R.* **31:4** Summer:1989 pp. 26 – 44

194 When is a union not a union? Good-faith doubt by an employer. Robert W. Schupp. *Lab. Law J.* **42:6** 6:1991 pp. 357 – 365

195 Who joins the union? Determinants of trade union membership in West Germany 1976-1984. Paul Windolf; Joachim Haas. *Eur. Sociol. R.* **5:2** 9:1989 pp. 147 – 166

I.5: Labour relations [Relations du travail] —

Workers' participation [Participation des travailleurs]

196 Democracy as "organizational divorce" and how the postmodern democracy is stifled by unity and majority. Ann Westenholtz. *Econ. Ind. Dem.* **12:2** 5:1991 pp. 173 – 186
197 Democratic producerism — enlisting American politics for workplace flexibility. Stephen Amberg. *Econ. Soc.* **20:1** 2:1991 pp. 57 – 78
198 The determinants of participatory management. Robert Drago; Mark Wooden. *Br. J. Ind. R.* **29:2** 6:1991 pp. 177 – 204
199 The impact on absenteeism and quits of profit-sharing and other forms of employee participation. Nicholas Wilson; Michael J. Peel. *Ind. Lab. Rel.* **44:3** 4:1991 pp. 454 – 468
200 Is there a purpose of workplace participation? Liv Tørres. *Ind. Rel. J. S.Afr.* **11:2** 1991 pp. 1 – 20
201 A participatory organizational and training strategy for the self-management sector — a case study of action-research in Peru. Azril Bacal. *Econ. Ind. Dem.* **12:1** 2:1991 pp. 119 – 135
202 Predictors and moderators of employee responses to employee participation programs. Jill W. Graham; Anil Verma. *Human Relat.* **44:6** 6:1991 pp. 551 – 568
203 Work, politics and power — an international perspective on workers' control and self-management. Assef Bayat. London: Zed Books, 1991: 243 p. *ISBN: 0862329760.*
204 Workers' participation and self-management in developing countries. Janez Prašnikar. Boulder: Westview Press, c1991: vi, 156 p. (ill) *ISBN: 081338172x; LofC: 90026929. Includes bibliographical references (p. [143]-149) and index.*

I.6: Leisure — *Loisir*

1 An analysis of the demand for and value of outdoor recreation in the United States. John C. Bergstrom; H. Ken Cordell. *J. Leis. Res.* **23:1** 1991 pp. 67 – 86
2 An attitudinal based model of pricing for recreation services. Geoff N. Kerr; Michael J. Manfredo. *J. Leis. Res.* **23:1** 1991 pp. 37 – 50
3 Better betting with a decent feller — bookmakers, betting and the British working class, 1750-1990. Carl Chinn. Hemel Hempstead: Harvester-Wheatsheaf, 1991: 306 p. *ISBN: 0710812884.*
4 Birth-order and participation in high and low dangerous sports among selected Nigerian elite athletes. A.S. Sohi; K.B. Yusuff. *J. As. Afr. S.* **XXVI:3-4** 7-10:1991 pp. 276 – 282
5 British football and social change — getting into Europe. John Williams *[Ed.]*; Stephen Wagg *[Ed.]*. London: Leicester University Press, 1991: 258 p. *ISBN: 0718514106.*
6 Coastal zone tourism — a potent force affecting environment and society. Marc L. Miller; Jan Auyong. *Mar. Pol.* **15:2** 3:1991 pp. 75 – 99
7 Contribution à une sociologie historique du loisir *[In French]*; [Contribution to a historical sociology of leisure] *[Summary]*. Roger Sue. *Cah. Int. Soc.* **XCI:** 7-12:1991 pp. 273 – 300
8 Cultural aspects of football. Gary Armstrong *[Contrib.]*; Rosemary Harris *[Contrib.]*; Eric Dunning *[Contrib.]*; Patrick Murphy *[Contrib.]*; Ivan Waddington *[Contrib.]*; Steve Redhead *[Contrib.]*; H.F. Moorhouse *[Contrib.]*; Richard Giulianotti *[Contrib.]*; Roman Horak *[Contrib.]*; Dick Hobbs *[Contrib.] and others. Collection of 10 articles.* **Sociol. Rev.** , *39:3*, 8:1991 pp. 427 – 645
9 Equity theory versus expectancy theory — the case of major league baseball free agents. Joseph W. Harder. *J. Appl. Psychol.* **76:3** 6:1991 pp. 458 – 464
10 Essays on leisure — human and policy issues. Max Kaplan. Rutherford: Fairleigh Dickinson U.P., 1991: 181 p. *ISBN: 0838634176.*
11 *[In Japanese]*; [Family education for formation of subject in leisure]. Hideo Yoshikane. **Kankyo-Bunka-Institute Kenkyu Kiyo** *No.(2) - 1991.* pp. 1 – 11
12 Football "fanzines" and football culture — a case of successful "cultural contestation". David Jary; John Horne; Tom Bucke. *Sociol. Rev.* **39:3** 8:1991 pp. 581 – 598
13 The government and politics of sport. Barrie Houlihan. London: Routledge, 1991: 295 p. *ISBN: 0415054028. Includes bibliography and index.*
14 Government and the economics of sport. Chris Gratton; Peter Taylor *[Ed.]*. Harlow: Longman, 1991: 224 p. *ISBN: 0582078040.*
15 The impact of tourism on Wales — inaugural lecture. Stephen F. Witt. Swansea: University College of Swansea, 1991: 25 p. *ISBN: 0860760723. Lecture delivered at the college, 11 February 1991; Bibliographical references — p25.*

I.6: Leisure *[Loisir]*

16 *[In Japanese]*; [Increases in free time and family leisure]. Akira Takatori. *Shak. Ron.* No.(112) - 1991. pp. 119 – 132

17 The influence of past experience on wilderness choice. Alan E. Watson; Joseph W. Roggenbuck; Daniel R. Williams. *J. Leis. Res.* **23:1** 1991 pp. 21 – 36

18 Is Sport Kultur? *[In German]*; Is sport culture? *[Summary]*. Ronald Hitzler. *Z. Soziol.* **20:6** 12:1991 pp. 479 – 487

19 Istoriia vodki *[In Russian]*; [The history of vodka]. V.V. Pokhlebkin. Moska: Inter-verso, 1991: 285 p. *ISBN: 5852170127.*

20 Изменения в использовании свободного времени городского населения за двадцать лет (1965-1986) *[In Russian]*; (Alteration in using of leisure-time by urban residents during 20 years (1965-1986)). V.D. Patrushev. *Sot. Issle.* **:3** 1991 pp. 24 – 32

21 Leisure behavior and styles of tourism in a Maghrebi society (e.g. Morocco) — neither traditional nor modern; (Styles et comportement touristiques d'une société maghrébine (le cas du Maroc) — ni-tradition ni-modernité): *Title only in French).* Mohamed Berriane. *Orient* **32:1** 1991 pp. 69 – 84

22 Massenexodus oder Erneuerung der jüdischen Kultur? Die jüdische Bewegung in der Sowjetunion *[In German]*; [Mass exodus or revival of Jewish culture? The Jewish movement in the USSR]. Verena Dohrn. *Osteuropa* **41:2** 2:1991 pp. 105 – 121

23 The meaning of baseball in 1992 (with notes on the post-American). Bill Brown. *Publ. Cult.* **4:1** Fall:1991 pp. 43 – 70

24 Merit, equity, and test validity — a new look at an old problem. Norma M. Riccucci. *Admin. Soc.* **23:1** 5:1991 pp. 74 – 93

25 A model for assessing the effects of communication on recreationists. Michael J. Manfredo; Alan D. Bright. *J. Leis. Res.* **23:1** 1991 pp. 1 – 20

26 Modeling and forecasting demand in tourism. Stephen F. Witt *[Ed.]*; Christine A. Witt *[Ed.]*. London: Academic Press, 1991: 192 p. *ISBN: 0127607404.*

27 Nature tourism — managing for the environment. Tensie Whelan *[Ed.]*. Washington, D.C: Island Press, c1991: xii, 223 p. (ill., maps) *ISBN: 155963037x; LofC: 91002646. Includes bibliographical references and index.*

28 Nonconsumptive wildlife recreation. Mark L. Rockel; Mary Jo Kealy. *Land Econ.* **67:4** 11:1991 pp. 422 – 434

29 Occupations in the hotel tourist sector within the European Community — a comparative analysis. Giovanni Peroni; Duccio Guerra *[Ed.]*. Luxembourg: OOPEC, 1991: 101 p. *ISBN: 9282629864.*

30 The price of affluence — the political economy of Japanese leisure. Gavan McCormack. *Rev. F. Braudel. Ctr.* **:188** 7/8:1991 pp. 121 – 135

31 Recreational tourism — a social science perspective. Chris Ryan. London: Routledge, 1991: 227 p. *ISBN: 0415054230. Includes bibliography and index.*

32 The reserve clause in professional sports — legality and effect on competitive balance. Alan Balfour; Philip K. Porter. *Lab. Law J.* **42:1** 1:1991 pp. 8 – 18

33 Scotland's tartan army in Italy — the case for the carnivalesque. Richard Giulianotti. *Sociol. Rev.* **39:3** 8:1991 pp. 503 – 527

34 The sociology of football — a research agenda for the 1990s. Vic Duke. *Sociol. Rev.* **39:3** 8:1991 pp. 627 – 646

35 Социальное время: Пробл. изуч. и использ *[In Russian]*; [Social time — problems of study and exploration]. F.M. Borodkin *[Ed.]*; V.A. Artemov. Novosibirsk: Nauka.Sib. otd-nie, 1987: 240 p.

36 Sport e civilizzazione *[In Italian]*; Sport and civilization *[Summary]*. Antonio Roversi. *Rass. It. Soc.* **32:4** 12:1991 pp. 477 – 494

37 Sport ed economia in Italia. Un'analisi macroeconomica *[In Italian]*; Sport and economics in Italy. A macroeconomic analysis *[Summary]*. Marco Brunelli; Marco Spinedi. *Industria* **XII:4** 10-12:1991 pp. 633 – 666

38 Sport in Canadian society. Ann Hall *[Ed.]*; et al. Toronto: McClelland & Stewart, c1991: ix, 281 p. (ill) *ISBN: 077103783x; LofC: cn 91093367. Includes indexes; Includes bibliographical references — p. 250-273.*

39 The story of gardening. Martin Hoyles. London: Journeyman, 1990: 313 p. *ISBN: 1851720286.*

40 Testing the involvement profile (IP) scale in the context of selected recreational and touristic activities. Frederic Dimanche; Mark E. Havitz; Dennis R. Howard. *J. Leis. Res.* **23:1** 1991 pp. 51 – 66

I.6: Leisure [Loisir]

41 Tourism and economic development in Eastern Europe and the Soviet Union. Derek R. Hall [Ed.]. London: Belhaven Press, c1991: 321 p. *ISBN: 0470217588; LofC: 91009122. Includes bibliographical references and index.*
42 Video kids — making sense of Nintendo. Eugene F. Provenzo. Cambridge, Mass: Harvard University Press, 1991: xii, 184 p. *ISBN: 0674937082; LofC: 91011697. Includes bibliographical references and index.*
43 Взгляд на арену *[In Russian]*; (A look at arena of stadium). V.A. Ponomarchuk; V.A. Vinnik. *Sot. Issle.* :**5** 1991 pp. 68 – 74
44 Взгляд на трибуны: социальный портрет болельщика *[In Russian]*; (A look at stadium's stand — sociological picture of a supporter). V.A. Viktorov; S.I. Platonov. *Sot. Issle.* :**5** 1991 pp. 75 – 83
45 Waiting for the weekend. Witold Rybczynski. New York, N.Y., U.S.A: Viking, 1991: ix, 260 p. *ISBN: 0670830011; LofC: 90050760. Includes bibliographical references (p. 237-249) and index.*
46 The wilderness as a source of recreation and renewal. W.C. Hendon. *Am. J. Econ. S.* **50:1** 1:1991 pp. 105 – 112

J: Politics. State. International relations — *Politique. État. Relations internationales*

J.1: Political sociology — *Sociologie politiques*

1 Chaos in Europe. An inquiry into the nature of social systems and the methodology of the behavioral sciences. Johan K. de Vree. *Acta Pol.* **XXVI** 1:1991 pp. 25 – 63
2 Cohort trends in attitudes about law and order — who's leading the conservative wave? Nicholas L. Danigelis; Stephen J. Cutler. *Publ. Opin. Q.* **55:1** Spring:1991 pp. 24 – 49
3 Configurazioni di potere e conseguenze non pianificate dell'azione. Un'applicazione della teoria del potere di Norbert Elias *[In Italian]*; Configurations and power differentials in Norbert Elias' theory *[Summary]*. Hans-Günther Heiland; Christian Lüdemann. *Rass. It. Soc.* **32:4** 12:1991 pp. 443 – 464
4 The crisis of movements — the enabling state as quisling. Peter J. Taylor. *Antipode* **23:2** 4:1991 pp. 214 – 228
5 The cult of the divine America — ritual, symbol, and mystification in American political culture. J.R. McLeod. *Int. J. Moral Soc. S.* **6:2** Summer:1991 pp. 93 – 116
6 Cultural politics/political culture — an interview with Stanley Aronowitz. David Kallick. *Soc. Pol.* **21:4** Spring:1991 pp. 15 – 22
7 The current situation in Cuba and the process of change. Julio Carranza Valdés. *Lat. Am. Pers.* **18:2(69)** Spring: 1991 pp. 10 – 17
8 Dismembering and remembering the nation — the semantics of political violence in Venezuela. Fernando Coronil; Julie Skurski. *Comp. Stud. S.* **33:2** 4:1991 pp. 288 – 337
9 Game theories? Spatial divisions of labour and rational choice Marxism. Peter Sunley. *Antipode* **23:2** 4:1991 pp. 229 – 239
10 The hidden link between internal political culture and cross-national perceptions — divergent images of the Soviet Union in the United States and the Federal Republic of Germany. Stephen Kalberg. *Theory Cult. Soc.* **8:2** 5:1991 pp. 31 – 56
11 Intellectuals and politics — social theory in a changing world. Charles C. Lemert [Ed.]. Newbury Park, Calif: Sage Publications, c1991: x, 188 p. *ISBN: 0803937318; LofC: 90021368. Most of the essays were originally presented at a colloquium sponsored by the Theory Section of the American Sociological Association in San Francisco on Aug. 13, 1989; Includes bibliographical references.* [Key issues in sociological theory. : No. 5]
12 Le jardin des délices démocratiques — pour une lecture psycho-affective des régimes pluralistes *[In French]*; [The garden of democratic delights — for a psycho-affective reading of pluralist regimes]. Philippe Braud. Paris: Presses de la Fondation nationale des sciences politiques, c1991: 273 p. *ISBN: 2724605888. Includes index; Bibliography — p. 263-268.*
13 A measure of Thatcherism — a sociology of Britain. Stephen Edgell; Vic Duke. London: Unwin Hyman, 1991: 271 p. *ISBN: 0043012477.*

J.1: Political sociology [Sociologie politiques]

14 Political behavior and the local context. John W. Books; Charles L. Prysby. New York: Praeger Publishers, 1991: 184 p. *ISBN: 0275936295.*
15 *[In Japanese]*; [The political sociology of Emile Durkheim (1)]. Tada'aki Kitagawa. *Bulletin of the Yamagata University (Social Science) No.21(2) - 1991.* pp. 141 – 178
16 Political trust — its biological roots. James Chowning Davies. *J. Soc. Biol. Struct.* **12:1** 1:1989 pp. 37 – 52
17 Politics between the positive and the negative. Jean A. Laponce. *Soc. Sci. Info.* **30:2** 1991 pp. 257 – 267
18 The powerless in power — political identity in post-communist Eastern Europe. Tomaž Mastnak. *Media Cult. Soc.* **13:3** 7:1991 pp. 399 – 406
19 Racially based changes in political alienation in America. Cedric Herring; James S. House; Richard P. Mero. *Soc. Sci. Q.* **72:1** 3:1991 pp. 123 – 134
20 The renaissance of strategic planning? M.J. Breheny. *Envir. Plan. B.* **18:(2)** 4:1991 pp. 233 – 249
21 Sequential patterns of strategic group formation and political change in Southeast Asia. Hans-Dieter Evers. *J. Soc. Stud. Dhaka* **51** 1:1991 pp. 59 – 78
22 Sociología política puertorriqueña *[In Spanish]*; [Puertorican political sociology]. A. Frambes-Buxeda. San Juan de Puerto Rico: Editorial Tortuga Verde, c1990-: 180 p. (ill) *BNB: 91218498; LofC: 91218498. Includes bibliographical references.* [Colleción Libros Tortuga Verde.]

J.2: Political thought — *Pensée politique*

1 The antinomies of abstract nationalism — Durkheim and Weber. Paul James. *Mel. J. Pol.* **20** 1991 pp. 3 – 22
2 Back to Sarajevo or beyond Trianon? Some thoughts on the problem of nationalism in Eastern Europe. Koen Koch. *Neth. J. Soc. Sci.* **27:1** 4:1991 pp. 29 – 42
3 Capitalism by democratic design? Democratic theory facing the triple transition in East Central Europe. Claus Offe. *Soc. Res.* **58:4** Winter:1991 pp. 865 – 892
4 Civic republicans and liberal individualists — the case of Britain. David Marquand. *Eur. J. Soc.* **XXXII:2** 1991 pp. 329 – 344
5 La democracia entre dos épocas. América Latina 1990 *[In Spanish]*; [Democracy between two eras. Latin America 1990]. Manuel Antonio Garretón. *Rev. Parag. Sociol.* **28:80** 1-4:1991 pp. 23 – 38
6 Democracy and violence. Renata Salecl. *New Form.* **:14** Summer:1991 pp. 17 – 26
7 Ethical and jurisprudence aspects of development. Edward D. Re. *J. Reg. Pol.* **11:3-4** 7-12:1991 pp. 569 – 579
8 "An experiment that failed"? E.M.S. Namboodiripad. *Soc. Scient.* **19:12** 12:1991 pp. 3 – 19
9 Grundaspekte der Nation. Eine begrifflich- systematische Untersuchung *[In German]*; Fundamental aspects of nation *[Summary]*. Bernd Estel. *Soz. Welt.* **42:2** 1991 pp. 208 – 231
10 The hour of eugenics — race, gender, and nation in Latin America. Nancy Stepan. Ithaca: Cornell University Press, 1991: viii, 210 p. *ISBN: 0801425697; LofC: 91055051. Includes bibliographical references and index.*
11 Ideology — an introduction. Terry Eagleton. London: Verso, 1991: 242 p. *ISBN: 0860913198. Includes bibliography and index.*
12 Культура і дэмакратыя: асноўныя напрамкі ўзаемадзеяння ва ўмовах перабудовы *[In Belorussian]*; *[Russian summary]*; [Culture and democracy — basic directions of interaction in conditions of perestroika] *[Summary]*. L.G. Mashukova. *V. Aka. BSSR* **:4** :1991 pp. 16 – 22
13 Más allá de las transiciones a la democracia en América Latina *[In Spanish]*; [Beyond democratization in Latin America]. Marcelo Cavarozzi. *Rev. Parag. Sociol.* **28:80** 1-4:1991 pp. 131 – 154
14 The methodologies of positivism and Marxism — a sociological debate. Norma R. A. Romm. Basingstoke: Macmillan, 1991: 208 p. *ISBN: 0333543386. Includes index.*
15 Modelle des öffentlichen Raums — Hannah Arendt, die liberale Tradition und Jürgen Habermas *[In German]*; Models of public space — Hannah Arendt, the liberal tradition and Jürgen Habermas *[Summary]*. Seyla Benhabib. *Soz. Welt.* **42:2** 1991 pp. 147 – 165
16 Money, the mountain, and state power in a Naxi village. Erik Mueggler. *Mod. Chi.* **17:2** 4:1991 pp. 188 – 226

J.2: Political thought [Pensée politique]

17 Nationalism in Central and Eastern Europe. Jerzy Szacki *[Contrib.]*; Konstanty Gebert *[Contrib.]*; Adam Michnik *[Contrib.]*; Jiřina Šiklová *[Contrib.]*; Jan Urban *[Contrib.]*; Ferenc Miszlivetz *[Contrib.]*; Pavel Campeanu *[Contrib.]*; Nicolae Gheorghe *[Contrib.]*; Frank Sysyn *[Contrib.]*; Claus Offe *[Contrib.] and others*. Collection of 11 articles. *Soc. Res.*, *58:4*, Winter:1991 pp. 711 – 901

18 On democracy. Chantal Mouffe *[Contrib.]*; Renata Salecl *[Contrib.]*; Joan Copjec *[Contrib.]*; Mladen Dolar *[Contrib.]*; Zdravko Kobe *[Contrib.]*; Slavoj Žižek *[Contrib.]*. Collection of 6 articles. *New Form.*, *:14*, Summer:1991 pp. 1 – 86

19 Pluralism and modern democracy — around Carl Schmitt. Chantal Mouffe. *New Form.* **:14** Summer:1991 pp. 1 – 16

20 The politics of postmodernity. G.B. Madison. *Crit. Rev.* **5:1** Winter:1991 pp. 53 – 79

21 Post-Fordism and social form — a Marxist debate on the post-Fordist state. Werner Bonefeld *[Ed.]*; John Holloway *[Ed.]*. London: Macmillan, 1991: 212 p. *ISBN: 0333543939*.

22 Presentación. Sobre la domocracia en Brasil *[In Spanish]*; [Introduction. Democracy in Brazil]. Vania Salles. *Est. Sociol.* **IX:25** 1-4:1991 pp. 3 – 14

23 Renewal of ideology and the ideology of renewal. G. Shakhnazarov. *Soc. Sci.* **XXII:2** 1991 pp. 15 – 32

24 Sentiments of nationalism among Nigerian students attending an American university; *[French summary]*. John Crittenden. *Can R. Stud. N.* **XVIII:1-2** 1991 pp. 145 – 164

25 Le « socialisme réel » un avenir disparu *[In French]*; ["Real socialism" — a vanished future] *[Summary]*. Lilly Marcou. *Temps Mod.* **47:543** 10:1991 pp. 47 – 57

26 Soviet interpretations of collectivization. E. Economakis. *Slav. E.Eur. Rev.* **69:2** 4:1991 pp. 257 – 281

27 A theory and practice of regions — the case of Europe. P.J. Taylor. *Envir. Plan. D* **9:2** 6:1991 pp. 183 – 196

28 The unfinished revolutions of 1989 — the decline of the nation-state? Ferenc Miszlivetz. *Soc. Res.* **58:4** Winter:1991 pp. 781 – 804

29 The Unvermögender other — hysteria and democracy in America. Joan Copjec. *New Form.* **:14** Summer:1991 pp. 27 – 42

30 War der reale Sozialismus modern? Versuch einer strukturellen Bestimmung *[In German]*; Was the real socialism modern? An attempt to a structural determination *[Summary]*. Ilja Srubar. *Kölner Z. Soz. Soz. psy.* **43:3** 1991 pp. 415 – 432

31 Западный марксизм: социальный аспект *[In Russian]*; (Western Marxism — social aspect). E.V. Osipova. *Sot. Issle.* **:4** 1991 pp. 111 – 122

J.3: Political systems — *Systèmes politique*

Sub-divisions: Police *[Police]*

1 Authoritarian and democratic transitions in national political systems. Robert M. Marsh. *Int. J. Comp. Soc* **32:3-4** 9-12:1991 pp. 219 – 232

2 Beyond law and order — criminal justice policy and politics into the 1990s. Robert Reiner *[Ed.]*; Malcolm Cross *[Ed.]*. Basingstoke: Macmillan, 1991: 254 p. *ISBN: 0333542800*. Includes index. [Explorations in sociology. : No. 35]

3 Ce que déclarer des droits veut dire. L'exemple de la Déclaration des Droits de l'Homme et du Citoyen de 1789 *[In French]*; [What a declaration of rights means. The example of the Declaration of the Rights of Man and the Citizen of 1789] *[Summary]*. Christine Fauré. *Cah. Int. Soc.* **XCI:** 7-12:1991 pp. 259 – 272

4 A challenge to political transition in South Africa — majority vs minority rights. Lawrence Schlemmer. *S.Afr. J. Sociol.* **22:1** 3:1991 pp. 16 – 23

5 Changing perspectives. On theoretical explanations of democratisation in the Netherlands. Huub Spoormans. *Neth. J. Soc. Sci.* **27:1** 4:1991 pp. 3 – 16

6 Ciudadanía y participación popular dentro de la nueva Constitución brasileña *[In Spanish]*; [Citizenship and popular participation in the new Brazilian constitution]. José Álvaro Moisés. *Est. Sociol.* **IX:25** 1-4:1991 pp. 15 – 34

7 The collapse of actually prevailing socialism — some lessons. Azizur Rahman Khan. *Soc. Scient.* **19:7** 7:1991 pp. 3 – 17

8 Contribution à l'analyse du phénomène associatif au Maroc *[In French]*; [A contribution to the analysis of the associative phenomenon in Morocco]. Ahmed Ghazali. *Ann. Afr. Nord* **XXVIII** 1989 pp. 243 – 260

J.3: Political systems [Systèmes politique]

9 La crisis de la justicia penal y la defensa social — modelos de control social *[In Spanish]*; [The crisis in criminal justice and social defence — social control models] *[Summary]*; *[Spanish summary]*. E.R. Zaffaroni. *Ann. Inter. Crimin.* **29:1&2** 1991 pp. 61 – 70

10 *[In Japanese]*; [The ethos and image of man in the modern civil society]. Naoharu Shimoda. *Journal of Applied Sociology No.(33) - 1991.* pp. 19 – 32

11 From rags to robes. E. Digby Baltzell; Howard G. Schnelderman. *Society* **28:4(192)** 5-6:1991 pp. 45 – 54

12 The Islamic state — a conceptual framework. Louay M. Safi. *Am. J. Islam. Soc. Sci.* **8:2** 9:1991 pp. 221 – 234

13 Justice by geography — urban, suburban, and rural variations in juvenille justice administration. Barry C. Feld. *J. Crim. Law* **82:1** Spring:1991 pp. 156 – 210

14 The king is a thing. Slavoj Žižek. *New Form.* **:13** Spring:1991 pp. 19 – 38

15 The law-based state — society and the individual. V. Kudryavtsev. *Soc. Sci.* **XXII:2** 1991 pp. 7 – 14

16 Legal discourse, media discourse, and speech rights — the shift from content to identity — the case of Israel. R. Shamir. *Int. J. S. Law* **19:1** 2:1991 pp. 45 – 66

17 Models of liberty — Berlin's "two concepts". Alan Haworth. *Econ. Soc.* **20:3** 8:1991 pp. 245 – 259

18 Organizational citizenship — a review, proposed model, and research agenda. Mel Schnake. *Human Relat.* **44:7** 7:1991 pp. 735 – 749

19 Parliamentary supremacy versus judicial review — is a compromise possible? Douglas V. Verney. *J. Comm. C. Pol.* **XXVII:2** 7:1989 pp. 185 – 200

20 *[In Japanese]*; [Parson's orientation to civil society]. Kazuyoshi Takagi. *Shisō No.(799) - 1991.* pp. 77 – 104

21 The perculiarities of the English state. G.E. Aylmer. *J. Hist. Soc.* **3:2** 6:1990 pp. 91 – 108

22 Le phénomène associatif en Algérie — genèse et perspectives *[In French]*; [The associative phenomenon in Algeria — genesis and perspectives]. Ramdane Babadji. *Ann. Afr. Nord* **XXVIII** 1989 pp. 229 – 242

23 Political geography and state formation — disputed territory. Felix Driver. *Prog. H. Geog.* **15:3** 9:1991 pp. 268 – 280

24 A politics of virtue — Hinduism, sexuality, and countercolonial discourse in Fiji. John Dunham Kelly. Chicago: University of Chicago Press, 1991: xvi, 266 p. ISBN: 0226430308; LofC: 91017326. Includes bibliographical references (p. 249-257) and index.

25 The production of guilt in the juvenile justice system — the pressures to "plead". Joy Wundersitz; Ngaire Naffine; Fay Gale. *Howard J. Crim. Just.* **30:3** 8:1991 pp. 192 – 206

26 Rede- und Schweigeverbote *[In German]*; Prohibitions of speech and silence *[Summary]*. Alois Hahn. *Kölner Z. Soz. Soz. psy.* **43:1** 1991 pp. 86 – 105

27 Symposium — civil liberties versus political agendas. William A. Donohue *[Contrib.]*; Samuel Walker *[Contrib.]*; Sylvia A. Law *[Contrib.]*; Fred Siegel *[Contrib.]*. Collection of 4 articles. *Society*, 28:2, 1-2:1991 pp. 5 – 22

28 Time binding and theory building in personal attribute models of Supreme Court voting behavior, 1916-88. C. Neal Tate; Roger Handberg. *Am. J. Pol. Sc.* **35:2** 5:1991 pp. 460 – 480

29 The unplanned society — Poland during and after communism. Janine Wedel *[Ed.]*. New York, N.Y: Columbia University Press, 1991: viii, 271 p. ISBN: 0231073720; LofC: 91029307. Includes bibliographical references and index.

30 Les voies du politique en URSS. L'exemple de l'écologie *[In French]*; Development of political debate in the USSR — the ecological controversies *[Summary]*. Marie-Hélène Mandrillon. *Annales* **46:6** 11-12:1991 pp. 1375 – 1388

31 Wandel durch Auflehnung — Thesen zum Verfall bürokratischer Herrschaft in der DDR *[In German]*; (Changes through rebellion — theses on the decay of bureaucratic rule in the G.D.R.). Sigrid Meuschel. *Berl. J. Soziol.* **Special issue** 1991 pp. 15 – 27

32 What's left? A lot's left. Neil Smith. *Antipode* **23:4** 10:1991 pp. 406 – 418

33 World capitalist system and developing countries. V. Volsky. *Soc. Sci.* **XXII:2** 1991 pp. 59 – 64

34 The world, the free market and the left. Robert Pollin; Alexander Cockburn. *Soc. Scient.* **19:7** 7:1991 pp. 18 – 38

J.3: Political systems *[Systèmes politique]* —

Police *[Police]*

35 Complaints against the police — the trend to external review. Andrew Goldsmith *[Ed.]*. Oxford: Clarendon, 1991: 331 p. *ISBN: 0198252579. Bibliography — pxvi-xvii. - Includes index.*

36 Complaints amongst the police — the new procedure of informal resolution. C.L. Corbett. *Poli. Soc.* **2:1** :1991 pp. 47 – 60

37 The computer game — detectives, suspects, and technology. R.R. Harper. *Br. J. Crimin.* **31:3** Summer:1991 pp. 292 – 307

38 Hercules, Hippolyte and the Amazons — or policewomen in the RUC. John D. Brewer. *Br. J. Soc.* **42:2** 6:1991 pp. 231 – 247

39 An inside job — policing and police culture in Britain. Malcolm Young. Oxford: Clarendon Press, 1991: 424 p. (ill) *ISBN: 019825296x. Bibliography — p498-525. - Includes index.*

40 A piece of business — the moral economy of detective work in the East-End of London. Dick Hobbs. *Br. J. Soc.* **42:4** 12:1991 pp. 596 – 608

41 Police and public perception of the seriousness of traffic offences. Claire Corbett; Frances Simon. *Br. J. Crimin.* **31:2** Spring:1991 pp. 153 – 164

42 Police as problem solvers. Hans Toch; James Douglas Grant. New York: Plenum Press, c1991: xv, 303 p. (ill) *ISBN: 0306438453; LofC: 91010619. Includes bibliographical references (p. 293-297) and indexes.*

43 Police, crime and the media — an Australian tale. S.E. Hatty. *Int. J. S. Law* **19:2** 5:1991 pp. 171 – 191

44 The police, space and society — the geography of policing. Nicholas R. Fyfe. *Prog. H. Geog.* **15:3** 9:1991 pp. 249 – 267

45 Power and restraint — the moral dimension of police work. Howard Cohen; Michael Feldberg. New York: Praeger, 1991: xvii, 166 p. *ISBN: 0275938565; LofC: 90028100. Includes bibliographical references (p. [159]-161) and index.*

46 Situational and attitudinal explanations of police behavior — a theoretical reappraisal and empirical assessment. Robert E. Worden. *Law Soc. Rev.* **23:4** 1989 pp. 667 – 711

J.4: Public administration — *Administration publique*

1 After excellence — models of organisational culture for the public sector. Amanda Sinclair. *Aust. J. Publ.* **50:3** 9:1991 pp. 321 – 332

2 The constitution and administrative ethics in America. William D. Richardson; Lloyd G. Nigro. *Admin. Soc.* **23:3** 11:1991 pp. 275 – 287

3 Descentralización, integración y principios de vinculació en las relaciones centro-locales *[In Spanish]*; [Decentralization, integration and the principles of linkage in central-local relations]. Miguel Ángel González Block. *Est. Sociol.* **IX:27** 9-12:1991 pp. 439 – 462

4 Effectiveness and quality of service data — public sector "affluence", private sector "squalor"? Michael Howard. *Aust. J. Publ.* **50:3** 9:1991 pp. 264 – 273

5 Fire alarms, garbage cans, and the administrative presidency. Robert F. Durant. *Admin. Soc.* **23:1** 5:1991 pp. 94 – 122

6 The geography of trade union responses to local government privatization. Joe Painter. *Trans. Inst. Br. Geogr.* **16:2** 1991 pp. 214 – 226

7 El gobierno municipal en la planificación *[In Spanish]*; [Local government and planning]. Jaime Ahumada Pacheco. *Rev. Parag. Sociol.* **28:80** 1-4:1991 pp. 89 – 114

8 Impact fees — a new funding source for local growth. Jean Carter Ryan. *J. Plan. Lit.* **5:4** 5:1991 pp. 401 – 407

9 The management of legitimacy and politics in public sector administration. Mark A. Covaleski; Mark W. Dirsmith. *J. Acc. Pub. Pol.* **10:2** Summer:1991 pp. 135 – 156

10 Managerial thinking. A study of public managers from developing countries. S. Rahman; F. Norling. *Publ. Adm. D.* **11:2** 3-4:1991 pp. 111 – 126

11 The nature of managerial work in the public sector — an African perspective. R. Vengroff; M. Belhaj; M. Ndiaye. *Publ. Adm. D.* **11:2** 3-4:1991 pp. 95 – 110

12 The place of constitutionalism in the education of public administrators. Donald J. Maletz. *Admin. Soc.* **23:3** 11:1991 pp. 374 – 394

13 La politique scientifique comme représentation construite en contexte bureaucratique — le cas de À l'heure des biotechnologies *[In French]*; [Science and technology policy as a construct in bureaucratic activity] *[Summary]*. Camille Limoges; Alberto Cambrosio; Denyse Pronovost. *Rech. Soc.graph* **XXXII:1** 1-4:1991 pp. 69 – 82

J.4: Public administration [Administration publique]

14 Power and money — a Marxist theory of bureaucracy. Ernest Mandel. London: Verso, 1991: 252 p. *ISBN: 086091321x.*
15 Privatizing government service delivery — theory, evidence, and implications. K.P. Voytek. *Envir. Plan. C.* **9:2** 5:1991 pp. 155 – 171
16 The public administrator as hero. Christopher Bellavita. *Admin. Soc.* **23:2** 8:1991 pp. 155 – 185
17 Public-sector applications of the analytic hierarchy process. Edward A. Wasil *[Contrib.]*; Bruce L. Golden *[Contrib.]*; Erhan Erkut *[Contrib.]*; Stephen R. Moran *[Contrib.]*; Keith Willett *[Contrib.]*; Ramesh Sharda *[Contrib.]*; Susan Imber *[Contrib.]*; Cluney Stagg *[Contrib.]*; William R. Stewart *[Contrib.]*; Evan R. Horowitz *[Contrib.] and others.* Collection of 8 articles. **Socio. Econ.**, *25:2*, 1991 pp. 87 – 162
18 Reinventing rationality — the role of regulatory analysis in the federal bureaucracy. Thomas O. McGarity. Cambridge: Cambridge University Press, 1991: - *ISBN: 0521402565.* Includes bibliography and index.
19 De relatie tussen aantal en type sleutelinformanten en de volledigheid van informatie *[In Dutch]*; The relationship between number and type of key informants and completeness of data *[Summary]*. N.Y. Kuiper; H. van Goor. *Sociol. Gids* **38:6** 11-12:1991 pp. 398 – 413
20 Situations tendues et sens ordinaires de la justice au sein d'une administration municipale *[In French]*; Tense situations and the ordinary senses of justice within a local council *[Summary]*; Spannungssituationen und Gewohnheitsbegriff der Justiz in einer Gemeindeverwaltung *[German summary]*; Situaciones críticas y sentidos ordinarios de la justicia en el seno de una administración municipal *[Spanish summary]*. Claudette Lafaye. *Rev. Fr. Soc.* **XXXI:2** 4-6:1990 pp. 199 – 223
21 Das sowjetische Privilegiensystem. Entstehung und Auflösung *[In German]*; [The Soviet system of privileges — origins and disintegration]. René Ahlberg. *Osteuropa* **41:12** 12:1991 pp. 1135 – 1157
22 Thatcherism, class politics, and urban development in London. Chris Toulouse. *Crit. Sociol.* **18:1** Spring:1991 pp. 55 – 76
23 Theoretical foundations of ethics in public administration — approaches to understanding moral action. Debra W. Stewart. *Admin. Soc.* **23:3** 11:1991 pp. 357 – 373
24 Toward a theory of the public for public administration. H. George Frederickson. *Admin. Soc.* **22:4** 2:1991 pp. 395 – 417
25 Women in management and public administration; *[Arabic summary]*. Amna E. Badri. *Ahfad J.* **8:2** 12:1991 pp. 5 – 24
26 Women, politics and place — spatial patterns of representation in New Jersey. J. Regulska; S. Fried; J. Tiefenbacher. *Geoforum* **22:2** 1991 pp. 203 – 222

J.5: Political parties, pressure groups and political movements — *Partis politiques, groupes de pression et mouvements politiques*

1 All-or-nothing games in the civil rights movement. Dennis Chong. *Soc. Sci. Info.* **30:4** 12:1991 pp. 677 – 697
2 The American peace movement — references and resources. Charles F. Howlett. Boston, MA.: G.K. Hall, 1991: lxii, 416 p. *ISBN: 0816118361; LofC: 91002992.* Includes bibliographical references and indexes. [Reference publications on American social movements.]
3 Black organisations, planning and access to premises. Ian Munt. *New Comm.* **17:4** 7:1991 pp. 583 – 602
4 Building movements, educating citizens — Myles Horton and the Highlander Folk School. Julius Lester *[Contrib.]*; Lucy Massie Phenix *[Contrib.]*; Cynthia Stokes Brown *[Contrib.]*; Anne Braden *[Contrib.]*; Frank Adams *[Contrib.]*; Herbert Kohl *[Contrib.]*; Guy Carawan *[Contrib.]*; Candie Carawan *[Contrib.]*; Aleine Austin *[Contrib.] and others.* Collection of 14 articles. **Soc. Pol.**, *21:3*, Winter:1991 pp. 8 – 77
5 Communist party education in Finland — from red flags to wine tasting. Marja van Diggelen. *J. Commun. S.* **7:4** 12:1991 pp. 477 – 500
6 Community action for social justice — grassroots organizations in India. Shashi Ranjan Pandey. New Delhi: Sage Publications, 1991: 294p. *ISBN: 0803996748; LofC: 90023116.* Includes bibliographical references.

J.5: Political parties, pressure groups and political movements [Partis politiques, groupes de pression et mouvements politiques]

7 Cultural preservation of the Sea Island Gullah — a black social movement in the post-civil rights era. John P. Smith. *Rural Sociol.* **56:2** Summer:1991 pp. 284 – 298

8 DDR '89. Zu den Ursachen einer spontanen Revolution *[In German]*; GDR '89. Some notes on the causes of a spontaneous revolution *[Summary]*. Karl-Dieter Opp. *Kölner Z. Soz. Soz. psy.* **43:2** 1991 pp. 302 – 321

9 Environmental movements — some conceptual issues in East-West comparisons; *[French summary]*. Oleg Yanitsky. *Int. J. Urban* **15:4** 12:1991 pp. 524 – 541

10 From consumption to production — labor participation in grass-roots movements in Pittsburgh and Hartford. Joan Fitzgerald; Louise Simmons. *Urban Aff. Q.* **26:4** 6:1991 pp. 512 – 531

11 The greening of British politics? C.A. Rootes. *Int. J. Urban* **15:2** 6:1991 pp. 287 – 297

12 The impact of the Intifada on the Palestinians in Israel. E. Zureik; A. Haider. *Int. J. S. Law* **19:4** 11:1991 pp. 475 – 499

13 Kollektives Handeln und politische Gelegenheitsstruktur in Mobilisierungswellen —Theoretische Perspektiven *[In German]*; Collective action and political opportunity structure in waves of mobilization — some theoretical perspectives *[Summary]*. Sidney Tarrow. *Kölner Z. Soz. Soz. psy.* **43:4** 1991 pp. 647 – 670

14 The Kraken Wakes — corporate social responsibility and the political dynamics of the hazardous waste issue. D. Smith. *Ind. Crisis Q.* **5:3** :1991 pp. 189 – 207

15 Die Leipziger Montagsdemonstration — Aufstieg und Wandel einer basisdemokratischen Institution des friedlichen Umbruchs im Spiegel empirischer Meinungsforschung *[In German]*; (The Leipzig Monday demonstration — rise and change of a basis-democratic institution of the peaceful revolution as seen in empirical opinion research). Kurt Mühler; Steffen H. Wilsdorf. *Berl. J. Soziol.* **Special issue** 1991 pp. 37 – 45

16 Mobilization at the grassroots — shantytowns and resistance in authoritarian Chile. Cathy Schneider. *Lat. Am. Pers.* **18:1** Winter:1991 pp. 92 – 112

17 Los movimientos agrarios de la década de los años ochenta — la coordinación de los centros de movimientos locales *[In Spanish]*; [Agrarian movements in the 1980s — the coordination of centres of local movements] *[Summary]*; *[French summary]*. Patrick H. Mooney. *Agr. Soc.* **:60** 9:1991 pp. 93 – 118

18 The Muslimeen insurrection in Trinidad. Chris Searle. *Race Class* **33:2** 10-12:1991 pp. 29 – 43

19 O gênero da representação — movimento de mulheres e representação política no Brasil (1980-1990) *[In Portuguese]*; The gender of representation — the women's movement and political representation in Brazil (1980-1990) *[Summary]*; Le genre de la représentation — mouvements de femmes et représentation politique au Brésil (1980-1990) *[French summary]*. Elisabeth Souza-Lobo. *Rev. Bras. Ciên. Soc.* **6:17** 10:1991 pp. 7 – 14

20 Perceptions of the causes of the troubles in Northern Ireland. Michelle Dillon. *Econ. Soc. R.* **21:3** 4:1990 pp. 299 – 310

21 Political activism and feminist spirituality. Nancy J. Finley. *Sociol. Anal.* **52:4** Winter:1991 pp. 349 – 362

22 The popular sector response to an authoritarian regime — shantytown organizations since the military coup. Philip Oxhorn. *Lat. Am. Pers.* **18:1** Winter:1991 pp. 66 – 91

23 Prostitutes' rights in the United States — the failure of a movement. Ronald Weitzer. *Sociol. Q.* **32:1** Spring:1991 pp. 23 – 41

24 Public opinion toward environmental groups in western Europe — one movement or two? Robert Rohrschneider. *Soc. Sci. Q.* **72:2** 6:1991 pp. 251 – 266

25 Religious movements and social movements. John A. Hannigan *[Contrib.]*; Scott Thumma *[Contrib.]*; Nancy J. Finley *[Contrib.]*; Carl Latkin *[Contrib.]*; Henry C. Finney *[Contrib.]*; Armand L. Mauss *[Contrib.]*; Philip L. Barlow *[Contrib.]*. Collection of 6 articles. **Sociol. Anal.**, *52:4*, Winter:1991 pp. 311 – 413

26 Resource mobilization and political opportunity in the Nicaraguan revolution — the theory. A.G. Cuzán. *Am. J. Econ. S.* **49:4** 10:1990 pp. 401 – 412

27 Die Revolution in der DDR. Eine strukturellindividualistische Erklärungsskizze *[In German]*; The revolution in the GDR. A structural- individualistic explanation *[Summary]*. Bernhard Prosch; Martin Abraham. *Kölner Z. Soz. Soz. psy.* **43:2** 1991 pp. 291 – 301

28 Revolution in spiritless times. An essay on Michel Foucault's enquiries into the Iranian revolution; La revolution en cette epoque sans spitirualité — un essai sur les travaux de Michel Foucault sur la revolution Iranienne *[French summary]*. George Stauth. *Int. Sociol.* **6:3** 9:1991 pp. 259 – 280

J.5: Political parties, pressure groups and political movements [Partis politiques, groupes de pression et mouvements politiques]

29 The role of religious organizations in social movements. Barbara M. Yarnold *[Ed.]*; Andrew S. McFarland; William R. Marty; Steven H. Haeberle; Mel Hailey. New York: Praeger Publishers, c1991: xii, 133 p. *ISBN: 0275940179; LofC: 91007206.* Includes bibliographical references and index.

30 The roots of Solidarity — a political sociology of Poland's working-class democratization. Roman Laba. Princeton, N.J: Princeton University Press, c1991: xii, 247 p. (ill) *ISBN: 0691078629; LofC: 90042595.* Includes bibliographical references (p. [183]-241) and index.

31 Social movements during cycles of issue attention — the decline of the anti-nuclear energy movements in West Germany and the USA. Christian Joppke. *Br. J. Soc.* **42:1** 3:1991 pp. 43 – 60

32 Stability of equilibria in multi-party political systems. I. Petersen. *Math. Soc. Sc.* **21:1** 2:1991 pp. 81 – 93

33 Studying collective action. Mario Diani *[Ed.]*; Ron Eyerman *[Ed.]*. London: Sage Publications, 1991: 263 p. *ISBN: 080398524x*. [Sage modern politics series. : No. 30]

34 *[In Japanese]*; [Two stages theory of social movement involvement — a case of local protest against construction of the railroad "Rokko Liner"]. Shinji Katagiri. **Momoyama Gakuin Daigaku Shakaigaku Ronshu** *No.25(2) - 1991.* pp. 1 – 36

35 Urban restructuring and the emergence of new political groupings — women and neighborhood activism in Tucson, Arizona. S.A. Marston; M. Saint-Germain. *Geoforum* **22:2** 1991 pp. 223 – 236

36 Vielfalt oder strukturierte Komplexität? Zur Institutionalisierung politischer Spannungslinien im Verbände- und Parteiensystem in der Bundesrepublik *[In German]*; Diversity or structured complexity? The interest groups, parties, and cleavage patterns in West Germany *[Summary]*. Bernhard Weßels. *Kölner Z. Soz. Soz. psy.* **43:3** 1991 pp. 454 – 475

37 Violence and the sacred in the modern world. Mark Juergensmeyer *[Contrib.]*; Mark R. Anspach *[Contrib.]*; Martin Kramer *[Contrib.]*; Ehud Sprinzak *[Contrib.]*; Emmanuel Sivan *[Contrib.]*; Bruce B. Lawrence *[Contrib.]*; David C. Rapoport *[Contrib.]*; René Girard *[Contrib.]*. Collection of 10 articles. **Terror. Pol. Viol.** , *3:3*, Autumn:1991 pp. 1 – 157

38 The women's movement and local politics — the influence on councillors in London. Jim Barry. Aldershot: Avebury, c1991: xiii, 234 p. *ISBN: 1856282856; LofC: 91044536.* Based on the author's thesis (Ph.D.)--Birkbeck College, University of London; Includes bibliographical references (p. 211-228) and index.

J.6: Political behaviour and elections — *Comportement politique et élections*

Sub-divisions: Elections *[Elections]*

1 The acquisition of partisanship by Latinos and Asian Americans. Bruce E. Cain; D. Roderick Kiewiet; Carole J. Uhlaner. *Am. J. Pol. Sc.* **35:2** 5:1991 pp. 390 – 422

2 The attitudinal bases for responsiveness to public opinion among American foreign policy officials. Philip J. Powlick. *Confl. Resolut.* **35:4** 12:1991 pp. 611 – 641

3 Außenseiter als Politiker — Rekrutierung und Identitäten neuer lokaler Eliten in einer ostdeutschen Gemeinde *[In German]*; Outsiders as politicians. Recruiting and identities of new local elites in an East German community *[Summary]*. Helmuth Berking; Sighard Neckel. *Soz. Welt.* **42:3** 1991 pp. 283 – 299

4 Charisma — a blighted concept and an alternative formula. William Spinrad. *Pol. Sci. Q.* **106:2** Summer:1991 p. 295

5 China's reforms — a study in the application of historical materialism. Paul Bowles; Tony Stone. *Sci. Soc.* **55:3** Fall:1991 pp. 261 – 290

6 Clases populares, cultura política y democracia *[In Spanish]*; Popular classes, political culture, and democracy *[Summary]*. Wálter Alarcón Glasinovich. *Soc. Part.* **:54** 6:1991 pp. 1 – 14

7 Continuity and change in Russian political culture. Jeffrey W. Hahn. *Br. J. Poli. S.* **21:4** 10:1991 pp. 393 – 422

J.6: Political behaviour and elections *[Comportement politique et élections]*

8 Critical essays on Israeli society, politics, and culture. Ian Lustick *[Ed.]*; Barry Rubin *[Ed.]*. Albany: State University of New York Press, c1991: xi, 204 p. *ISBN: 0791406466; LofC: 90010055. "A publication from the Association for Israel Studies."; Includes bibliographical references.* [Books on Israel; SUNY series in Israeli studies. : Vol. 2]

9 Del poder social al poder político *[In Spanish]*; [From social power to political power]. John Friedmann. *Vop. Ist.* **:55** 1-4:1991 pp. 61 – 72

10 Economic and political effects on presidential popularity in Costa Rica. Alfred C. Cuzan; Charles M. Bundrick. *J. Dev. Soc.* **VII:2** 7-9:1991 pp. 269 – 276

11 The effects of the 1960s political generation on former left- and right-wing youth activist leaders. Margaret M. Braungart; Richard G. Braungart. *Soc. Prob.* **38:3** 8:1991 pp. 297 – 315

12 The formation and development of party loyalties — patterns among Australian immigrants. Ian McAllister; Toni Makkai. *Aust. N.Z. J. Soc.* **27:2** 8:1991 pp. 195 – 217

13 Gender and political participation in Australia. Clive Bean. *Aust. J. Soc. Iss.* **26:4** 12:1991 pp. 276 – 293

14 Grenada — the lessons of losing power. Barbara Creecy. *S.Afr. Lab. B.* **15:8** 6:1991 pp. 64 – 71

15 Ideology, constituent interests, and senatorial voting — the case of abortion. George A. Chressanthis; Kathie S. Gilbert; Paul W. Grimes. *Soc. Sci. Q.* **72:3** 9:1991 pp. 588 – 600

16 Image, issues, and ideology — the processing of information about political candidates. Robert S. Wyer; Thomas Lee Budesheim; Sharon Shavitt; Ellen D. Riggle; R. Jeffrey Melton; James H. Kuklinski. *J. Pers. Soc. Psychol.* **61:4** 10:1991 pp. 533 – 545

17 Immigrant background and political participation — examining generational patterns. Tina W.L. Chui; James E. Curtis; Ronald D. Lambert. *Can. J. Soc.* **16:4** Fall:1991 pp. 375 – 396

18 Improving legal compliance by noncoercive means — coproducing order in Washington state. Craig Curtis; Quint C. Thurman; David C. Nice. *Soc. Sci. Q.* **72:4** 12:1991 pp. 645 – 660

19 Independent necessary and sufficient conditions for approval voting. N. Baigent; Y.-S. Xu. *Math. Soc. Sc.* **21:1** 2:1991 pp. 21 – 29

20 "Just what needed to be done" — the political practice of women community workers in low-income neighborhoods. Nancy A. Naples. *Gender Soc.* **5:4** 12:1991 pp. 478 – 494

21 Justice, democracy, litigation, and political participation. Susan E. Lawrence. *Soc. Sci. Q.* **72:3** 9:1991 pp. 464 – 477

22 Личность в политике: «кто играет короля?» *[In Russian]*; (Personality in politics — "who plays the king?"). M.V. Ilyin; B.I. Koval. *Polis* **:6** 1991 pp. 127 – 138

23 Lifetimes of commitment — aging, politics, psychology. Molly Andrews. Cambridge [England]: Cambridge University Press, 1991: 229 p. *ISBN: 0521402808; LofC: 90024161. Includes bibliographical references and index.*

24 Local government in Bangladesh —recent changes and people's participation. Muhiuddin Khan Alamgir. *J. Soc. Stud. Dhaka* **51** 1:1991 pp. 79 – 93

25 Local political practice in response to a manufacturing plant closure — how geography complicates class analysis. Andrew Herod. *Antipode* **23:4** 10:1991 pp. 385 – 402

26 Majority tournaments — sincere and sophisticated voting decisions under amendment procedure. K.B. Reid. *Math. Soc. Sc.* **21:1** 2:1991 pp. 1 – 19

27 Modern political ritual — ethnography of an inauguration and a pilgrimage by President Mitterrand. Marc Abeles. *J. Soc. Stud. Dhaka* **:54** 10:1991 pp. 48 – 69

28 Modernization and political instability — coups d'Etat in Africa 1955-85. Tormod K. Lunde. *Acta Sociol.* **34:1** 1991 pp. 13 – 32

29 Participation ideologies in Israeli planning. S. Gertel; H. Law-Yone. *Envir. Plan. C.* **9:2** 5:1991 pp. 173 – 188

30 Periphery praetorianism in cliometric perspective 1855-1985. David Kowalewski. *Int. J. Comp. Soc* **32:3-4** 9-12:1991 pp. 289 – 303

31 Personality and charisma in the U.S. presidency — a psychological theory of leader effectiveness. Robert J. House; William D. Spangler; James Woycke. *Adm. Sci. Qua.* **36:3** 9:1991 pp. 364 – 396

32 The political attitudes of Australian voters and candidates. Ian McAllister. *Aust. J. Soc. Iss.* **26:3** 8:1991 pp. 163 – 190

33 Political culture and popular participation in Cuba. Rafael Hernández; Haroldo Dilla. *Lat. Am. Pers.* **18:2(69)** Spring: 1991 pp. 38 – 54

34 The political economy of public participation — the case of Zimbabwe. Christopher Rambanapasi. *Ind. J. Soc. Sci.* **4:2** 4-6:1991 pp. 269 – 286

J.6: Political behaviour and elections *[Comportement politique et élections]*

35 Political leadership in Cuba — background and current projections. Georgina Suárez Hernández. *Lat. Am. Pers.* **18:2(69)** Spring: 1991 pp. 55 – 68
36 The politics of identity — community and ethnicity in a pro-Sandinista enclave on Nicaragua's Atlantic coast. Pamela Perry. *Berkeley J. Soc.* **36** 1991 pp. 115 – 136
37 Politische Orientierungen im Übergang. Eine Analyse politischer Einstellungen der Bürger in West- und Ostdeutschland 1990/ 1991 *[In German]*; Political orientations in transition. An analysis of political attitudes of the citizens in West and East Germany 1990/ 91 *[Summary]*. Petra Bauer. *Kölner Z. Soz. Soz. psy.* **43:3** 1991 pp. 433 – 453
38 Die politischen Veränderungen im Erleben von Patienten mit affektiven Psychosen in Ost-und Westberlin 1989/90 *[In German]*; The political changes in East and West Berlin in 1989/90 as experienced by patients with affective psychoses *[Summary]*. J. Bohlken; S. Priebe; E. Umann. *Medi. Mensch Gesell.* **16:4** 12:1991 pp. 285 – 290
39 Polityczne poglądy i postawy aktywistów ZSMP (wyniki sondażu) *[In Polish]*; Political views and attitudes of PSYU activists. Research results *[Summary]*. Jolanta Grotowska-Leder. *Acta Univ. Łódz. Folia Soc.* **21** 1991 pp. 87 – 106
40 Popular culture and political change in modern America. Ronald William Edsforth; Larry Bennett. Albany: State University of New York Press, c1991: x, 222 p. *ISBN: 0791407659; LofC: 90047621.* Includes bibliographical references (p. [177]-211) and index. [SUNY series in popular culture and political change.]
41 Postawy polityczne młodzieży szkolnej i studenckiej *[In Polish]*; Political attitudes of school and student youth *[Summary]*. Ewa Rokicka. *Acta Univ. Łódz. Folia Soc.* **21** 1991 pp. 73 – 85
42 Postmaterialisme en stemgedrag *[In Dutch]*; Postmaterialism and voting *[Summary]*. Hendriks P.G.J. Vettehen. *Mens Maat.* **65:2** 1990 pp. 165 – 178
43 Presidential effectiveness and the leadership motive profile. William D. Spangler; Robert J. House. *J. Pers. Soc. Psychol.* **60:3** 3:1991 pp. 439 – 455
44 Provincial elite in post-Mao China. Xiaowei Zang. *Asian Sur.* **XXXI:6** 6:1991 pp. 512 – 525
45 The psychological bases of regime support among urban workers in Venezuela and Mexico — instrumental or expressive? Charles L. Davis; John G. Speer. *Comp. Poli. S.* **24:3** 10:1991 pp. 319 – 343
46 Social currents in Eastern Europe — the sources and meaning of the great transformation. Sabrina P. Ramet. Durham, North Carolina: Duke University Press, 1991: xii, 434 p. *ISBN: 0822311488; LofC: 90024049.* Includes bibliographical references (p. [357]-413) and index.
47 Stability and change in the U.S. public's knowledge of politics. Michael X. Delli Carpini; Scott Keeter. *Publ. Opin. Q.* **55:4** Winter:1991 pp. 583 – 612
48 Tenured radicals, the new McCarthyism and "PC". Bruce Robbins. *Rev. F. Braudel. Ctr.* **:188** 7/8:1991 pp. 151 – 157
49 Threat and authoritarianism in the United States, 1978-1987. Richard M. Doty; Bill E. Peterson; David G. Winter. *J. Pers. Soc. Psychol.* **61:4** 10:1991 pp. 629 – 640
50 Toward a general theory of occupational regulation. Elizabeth Graddy. *Soc. Sci. Q.* **72:4** 12:1991 pp. 676 – 695
51 Tráfico de esperanzas *[In Spanish]*; [Trafficking in hope]. José Arthur Giannotti. *Est. Sociol.* **IX:25** 1-4:1991 pp. 127 – 144
52 Die unvollendete Republik *[In German]*; [The unfinished republic]. Lutz Hoffmann. *Gewerk. Monat.* **42:9** 9:1991 pp. 595 – 600
53 Voting, parties and social change in Finland. Tuomo Martikainen; Risto Yrjönen. Helsinki: Tilastokeskus, 1991: 105 p. *ISBN: 9514753836.* Bibliography — p103-105. [Tutkimuksia.]
54 Watch on the right — conservative intellectuals in the Reagan era. J. David Hoeveler. Madison, Wis: University of Wisconsin Press, c1991: xiii, 333 p. *ISBN: 0299128105; LofC: 90013021.* Includes bibliographical references (p. 287-321) and index. [History of American thought and culture.]
55 Women and political participation in Africa — broadening the scope of research. D. Hirschmann. *World Dev.* **19:12** 12:1991 pp. 1679 – 1694
56 Zur Bedeutung von Alters-, Perioden-, und Generationseinflüssen für den Wandel politischer Werte in der Bundesrepublik *[In German]*; The significance of age, period and cohort effects for changing political values in the F.R.G. *[Summary]*. Thomas Klein. *Z. Soziol.* **20:2** 4:1991 pp. 138 – 146
57 Eine zweite „Entnazifizierung"? Zur Verarbeitung politischer Umwälzungen in Deutschland 1945 und 1989 *[In German]*; [A second "denazification"? On the German response to the political upheavals in 1945 and 1989]. Alexander von Plato. *Gewerk. Monat.* **42:7** 7:1991 pp. 415 – 428

J.6: Political behaviour and elections *[Comportement politique et élections]* —

Elections *[Elections]*

58 "Achievement" and "ascription" in admission to an elite college — a political-organizational analysis. David Karen. *Sociol. For.* **6:2** 6:1991 pp. 349 – 380
59 The class basis of late teenage voting preferences. Christopher R. Fife-Schaw; Glynis M. Breakwell. *Eur. Sociol. R.* **7:2** 9:1991 pp. 135 – 148
60 Elettori in Italia — riflessioni sulle vicende elettorali degli anni ottanta *[In Italian]*; [Voters in Italy — reflections on electoral events in the 1980s]. Roberto Cartocci. Bologna: Il Mulino, c1990: 234 p. (ill., maps) *ISBN: 8815027874; LofC: 91117726. Includes bibliographical references.* [Ricerca — Il Mulino.]
61 Historia de una ausencia. Notas acerca de la participación electoral en el Paraguay *[In Spanish]*; [The story of absence. Notes on electoral participation in Paraguay]. Victor-jacinto Flecha. *Rev. Parag. Sociol.* **28:80** 1-4:1991 pp. 63 – 88
62 The influence of racial transition on incumbency advantage in local elections. James M. Vanderleeuw. *Urban Aff. Q.* **27:1** 9:1991 pp. 36 – 50
63 Making sense of middle-class politics — a secondary analysis of the 1987 British general election survey. Mike Savage. *Sociol. Rev.* **39:1** 2:1991 pp. 26 – 54
64 Многопартийные выборы в Грузии *[In Russian]*; (Multiparty elections in Georgia). R.G. Gachechiladse. *Sot. Issle.* **:5** 1991 pp. 53 – 63
65 Political action committees — how much influence will. Tim Brightbill. *Int. J. Health. Ser.* **21:2** 1991 pp. 285 – 290
66 Self-reported turnout and voter validation. Donald Granberg; Sören Holmberg. *Am. J. Pol. Sc.* **35:2** 5:1991 pp. 448 – 459
67 St. Louis's black-white elections. Lana Stein; Carol W. Kohfeld. *Urban Aff. Q.* **27:2** 12:1991 pp. 227 – 248

J.7: Armed forces — *Forces armées*

1 African-American women in the U.S. military. Brenda L. Moore. *Arm. Forces Soc.* **17:3** Spring:1991 pp. 363 – 384
2 Aspetti sociologici della riconversione dell'industria bellica *[In Italian]*; [Sociological aspects of defence industry conversion]. Fabrizio Battistelli. *Sociologia [Rome]* **XXV:1** :1991 pp. 191 – 215
3 Campfollowing — a history of the military wife. Betty Sowers Alt; Bonnie Domrose Stone. New York: Praeger, 1991: xiii, 164 p. *ISBN: 0275937216; LofC: 90024999. Includes bibliographical references (p. [153]-160) and index.*
4 Card games and an Israeli army unit — an interpretive case study. Michael Feige; Eyal Ben-Ari. *Arm. Forces Soc.* **17:3** Spring:1991 pp. 429 – 448
5 Civil military interaction in Asia and Africa. Charles H. Kennedy *[Ed.]*; David J. Louscher *[Ed.]*. Leiden: E.J. Brill, 1991: 154 p. *ISBN: 9004093591; LofC: 90024887. Includes bibliographical references and index.* [International studies in sociology and social anthropology.]
6 Civilian job opportunities and naval re-enlistment behavior. B.R. Schiller; B.G. Kroetch; P.R. Flacco. *J. Econ. Soc.* **17:2** 1991 pp. 69 – 86
7 Civil-military relations in South Asia — Pakistan, Bangladesh, and India. Veena Kukreja. New Delhi: Sage Publications, 1991: 306 p. *ISBN: 0803996993; LofC: 91015168. Includes bibliographical references and index.*
8 Codes and conflict — toward a theory of war as ritual. Philip Smith. *Theory Soc.* **20/1** 2:1991 pp. 103 – 138
9 Ethnicity, integration, and the military. Henry A. Dietz *[Ed.]*; Jerrold Elkin *[Ed.]*; Maurice M. Roumani *[Ed.]*. Boulder: Westview Press, 1991: xi, 227 p. *ISBN: 0813311063; LofC: 91010233. Includes bibliographical references.* [IUS special editions on armed forces and society. : No. 3]
10 Evidence, ideology and miscalculation — public opinion and the 1987 military coups in Fiji. Deryck Scarr. *J. Soc. Océan.* **92-93:1&2** 1991 pp. 69 – 88
11 Exterminating angels — morality, violence and technology in the Gulf War. Asu Aksoy; Kevin Robins. *Sci. Cult.* **2:3(12)** 1991 pp. 322 – 336
12 "Feminization" and the French military — an anthropological approach. Jean Boulègue. *Arm. Forces Soc.* **17:3** Spring:1991 pp. 343 – 362

J.7: Armed forces [Forces armées]

13 The impact of military life on spouse labor force outcomes. J. Brad Schwartz; Lisa L. Wood; Janet D. Griffith. *Arm. Forces Soc.* **17:3** Spring:1991 pp. 385 – 408

14 Left face — soldier unions and resistance movements in modern armies. David Cortright; Max Watts. New York: Greenwood Press, 1991: x, 282 p. (ill) *ISBN: 0313276269; LofC: 90046702. Includes bibliographical references (p. [253]-272) and index.* [Contributions in military studies.]

15 Legitimacy and the military — the Yugoslav crisis. James Gow. London: Pinter, 1991: 208 p. *ISBN: 1855670313.*

16 Making and breaking enemy images. William Eckhardt. *Secur. Dial.* **22:1** 3:1991 pp. 87 – 95

17 Mates & muchachos — unit cohesion in the Falklands/Malvinas War. Nora Kinzer Stewart. Washington [D.C.]: Brassey's (US), c1991: xiii, 192 p. *ISBN: 0080374395; LofC: 90048771. Includes bibliographical references (p. 167-179) and index.*

18 Militarism and politics in Latin America — Peru from Sánchez Cerro to Sendero Luminoso. Daniel M. Masterson. New York: Greenwood Press, 1991: xiii, 345 p. (ill., map) *ISBN: 0313272131; LofC: 90023010. Includes bibliographical references (p. [307]-334) and index.* [Contributions in military studies.]

19 Politischer Pluralismus und die jugoslawischen Berufsmilitärs *[In German]*; Political pluralism and the Yugoslav professional military *[Summary]*. Anton Bebler. *Öster. Z. Polit.* **20:3** 1991 pp. 257 – 274

20 Response to strategy and communication in an arms race-disarmament dilemma. Brian Betz. *Confl. Resolut.* **35:4** 12:1991 pp. 678 – 690

21 Stress and suicide in the U.S. army — effects of relocation on service member's mental health. Joseph M. Rothberg. *Arm. Forces Soc.* **17:3** Spring:1991 pp. 449 – 458

22 Technological cultures of weapons design. Perry Morrison; Stephen Little. *Sci. Cult.* **2(2):11** :1991 pp. 227 – 258

23 The United States military under the constitution of the United States, 1789-1989. Richard H. Kohn *[Ed.]*. New York: New York University Press, 1991: 424 p. *ISBN: 0814746152.*

24 The warlord — twentieth-century Chinese understandings of violence, militarism, and imperialism. Arthur Waldron. *Am. Hist. Rev.* **96:4** 10:1991 pp. 1073 – 1100

J.8: International relations — Relations internationales

1 Australian university students' views of the nuclear arms race — comparative and qualitative analyses. Jeanette A. Lawrence; Philip Jennings; Agnes E. Dodds; Irene M. Styles. *Aust. J. Soc. Iss.* **26:3** 8:1991 pp. 191 – 209

2 Bridging organizations and sustainable development. L. David Brown. *Human Relat.* **44:8** 8:1991 pp. 807 – 832

3 Civil religion and the arms race; *[French summary]*. Sheldon Ungar. *Can. R. Soc. A.* **28:4** 11:1991 pp. 503 – 525

4 Considerations on the European Community and the new world order. Lucio Levi. *Federalist* **XXXIII:1** 1991 pp. 8 – 27

5 East-West, North-South. Iu. Krasin. *Soc. Sci.* **XXII:2** 1991 pp. 33 – 46

6 Europa 1992 — z problematyki integracji społecznej w ramach Wspólnoty Europejskiej *[In Polish]*; (Europe 1992 — problems of social integration in European Community); (Европа 1992 — из проблематики социальной интеграции в рамках Европейского Общества: *Title only in Russian*). Elżbieta Sobótka. *Pra. Zab. Społ.* **33:7** 7:1991 pp. 13 – 21

7 Europe and the European Community 1992. Christopher G.A. Bryant. *Sociology* **25:2** 5:1991 pp. 189 – 207

8 Formational and civilizational approaches. E. Pozdnyakov. *Soc. Sci.* **XXII:4** 1991 pp. 63 – 75

9 El largo y difícil camino hacia la Europa Social (primera parte) *[In Spanish]*; [The long and winding road towards European social union (part one)]. Gaspar Rul-Lan Buades. *Rev. Fom. Soc.* **46:182** 4-6:1991 pp. 121 – 136

10 New world order or neo-colonialism? Environment, EC, detente and Gulf War. Walter Fernandes. *Soc. Act.* **41:1** 1-3:1991 pp. 78 – 93

11 The old and new transnationalism — an evolutionary perspective. Elise Boulding. *Human Relat.* **44:8** 8:1991 pp. 789 – 806

12 Psychoanalytic concepts in international politics — the role of shame and humiliation; *[French summary]*; *[German summary]*; *[Spanish summary]*. Blema S. Steinberg. *Int. Rev. Psy.* **18:1** 1991 pp. 65 – 85

J.8: International relations *[Relations internationales]*

13 The psychodynamics of international relationships. Vamik D Volkan *[Ed.]*; Demetrios A Julius *[Ed.]*; Joseph V Montville *[Ed.]*. Lexington, Mass: Lexington Books, c1991: 2 v. ill *ISBN: 0669243663; LofC: 90005889. Includes bibliographical references and indexes.*

14 The psychology of war and peace — the image of the enemy. R. W. Rieber *[Ed.]*. New York: Plenum Press, c1991: xx, 282 p. (ill) *ISBN: 0306435438; LofC: 91010481. Includes bibliographical references and index.*

15 Socjologiczne ujęcie pokoju *[In Polish]*; (A sociological approach to peace); (Социологический подход к миру: *Title only in Russian*); (La conception sociologique de la paix: *Title only in French*). Stanisław Bieleń. *Spr. Między.* **XLIV:7-8** 1991 pp. 117 – 126

16 Sovereignty, identity, sacrifice. Jean Bethke Elshtain. *Millennium* **20:3** Winter:1991 pp. 395 – 406

17 The transfrontier organization of space along the U.S.-Mexico border. L.A. Herzog. *Geoforum* **22:3** 1991 pp. 255 – 270

18 Understanding war. W. B. Gallie. London: Routledge, 1991: 116 p. *ISBN: 041505639x. Includes index.* [Points of conflict.]

19 The wall of mirrors — nationalism and perceptions of the border at Niagara Falls. Patrick McGreevy; Chris Merrit. [Orono, Me.]: Borderlands Project, c1991: v, 55 p. (ill., maps) *ISBN: 0962505544. Includes bibliographical references.* [Borderlands monograph series. : No. 5]

20 War-related stress — addressing the stress of war and other traumatic events. Stevan E. Hobfoll; Charles D. Spielberger; Shlomo Breznitz; Charles Figley; Susan Folkman; Bonnie Lepper-Green; Donald Meichenbaum; Norman A. Milgram; Irwin Sandler; Irwin Sarason *and others.Am. Psychol.* **46:8** 8:1991 pp. 848 – 855

21 Women and war. Janna Thompson. *Wom. St. Inter. For.* **14:1/2** 1991 pp. 63 – 76

22 Zwischen machtpolitischem Realismus und pazifistischer Utopie — Krieg und Frieden als Thema der soziologischen Theorie *[In German]*; (Between power-political realism and pacifist utopia — war and peace as subject of sociological theory). Hans Joas. *Berl. J. Soziol.* **Special issue** 1991 pp. 59 – 71

K: Social problems. Social services. Social work — *Problèmes sociaux. Services sociaux. Travail social*

K.1: Social problems — *Problèmes sociaux*

Sub-divisions: Child neglect and abuse *[Enfants martyrs et abandon d'enfant]*; Crime *[Délits]*; Criminal justice *[Justice criminelle]*; Poverty *[Pauvreté]*; Substance abuse *[Usage des stupéfiants]*; Suicide *[Suicide]*; Violence *[Violence]*

1 Chernobyl — taking stock. Konstantin I. Massik *[Contrib.]*; Abel J. González *[Contrib.]*; Fred A. Mettler *[Contrib.]*; Jonathan E. Briggs *[Contrib.]*; Vladimir K. Savchenko *[Contrib.]*; William C. Potter *[Contrib.]*; Bruno Lefèvre *[Contrib.]*; Pierre Fayard *[Contrib.]*. Collection of 7 articles. **Impact Sci.**, *41:163*, 3:1991 pp. 201 – 288

2 Coping with catastrophe — a handbook of disaster management. Peter E. Hodgkinson; Michael Stewart *[Ed.]*. London: Routledge, 1991: 230 p. (ill) *ISBN: 0415040973. Includes bibliography and index.*

3 The death penalty and gender discrimination. Elizabeth Rapaport. *Law Soc. Rev.* **25:2** 1991 pp. 367 – 384

4 The emergence of premenstrual syndrome as a social problem. C. Amanda Rittenhouse. *Soc. Prob.* **38:3** 8:1991 pp. 412 – 425

5 Emergency Planning in the 90's — proceedings of the second conference, University of Bradford, september 1990. A. Z. Keller *[Ed.]*; H. C. Wilson *[Ed.]*. Letchworth: Technical Communications, 1991: 322 p.

6 Grey policing — a theoretical framework. B. Hoogenboom. *Poli. Soc.* **2:1** :1991 pp. 17 – 30

7 La liberté individuelle — une responsabilité sociale *[In French]*; [Individual freedom — a social responsibility]. Amartya Sen. *Esprit* **170** 3-4:1991 pp. 5 – 25

K.1: Social problems [Problèmes sociaux]

8 A longitudinal test of social control theory and delinquency. Robert Agnew. *J. Res. Crim. Delin.* **28:**2 5:1991 pp. 126 – 156

9 The observational study of adolescent gambling in UK amusement arcades. M. Griffiths. *J. Comm. App. Soc. Psychol.* **1:**4 11:1991 pp. 309 – 320

10 The origins of black hostility to the police. D.J. Smith. *Poli. Soc.* **2:**1 :1991 pp. 1 – 16

11 Les paysans de Cordillères andines face aux mouvements de guérilla et à la drogue — victimes ou acteurs? *[In French]*; (The peasants of the Andean Cordillera in the face of guerrilla movements and drugs — victims or agents?); (Die Andenbauern gegenüber den Guerilla-Bewegungen und der Droge — Opfer oder Mittäter?: *Title only in German)*; (Los campesinos de las Cordilleras Andinas frente a los movimientos de guerrilla y a la droga — ¿víctimas o actores?: *Title only in Spanish)*. Christian Gros. *R. T-Monde* **32:**128 10-12:1991 pp. 811 – 830

12 Police amongst adolescent black, white and Asian boys. P.A.J. Waddington; Q. Braddock. *Poli. Soc.* **2:**1 :1991 pp. 31 – 46

13 Police and government in the 1990s. Barry Loveday. *Soc. Pol. Admin.* **25:**4 12:1991 pp. 311 – 328

14 Police communication programmes aimed at burglary victims — a review of studies and an experimental evaluation. F.W. Winkel. *J. Comm. App. Soc. Psychol.* **1:**4 11:1991 pp. 275 – 289

15 Postpartum psychosis, infanticide and the law. D. Maier-Katkin. *Cr. Law Soc. Chan.* **15:**2 3:1991 pp. 109 – 123

16 The rebels — a brotherhood of outlaw bikers. Daniel R. Wolf. Toronto: University of Toronto Press, c1991: 372 p., 8 p. of plates (ill) *ISBN: 0802027245; LofC:* cn 90095849. *Includes index; Includes bibliographical references — p. [365]-366.*

17 Reflections, sketches, and provocations — essays and commentary, 1981-1987. Bob Avakian. Chicago: RCP Publications, c1990: vi, 242 p. *ISBN: 089851102x; LofC: 89039782.*

18 Risk factors and predictability of famine in Ethiopia. Theodore M. Vestal. *Polit. Life* **9:**2 2:1991 pp. 187 – 203

19 Size at birth and some sociodemographic factors in gypsies in Hungary. Kálmán Joubert. *J. Biosoc. Sc.* **23:**1 1:1991 pp. 39 – 47

20 Social networks, social support, and their relationship to depression among immigrant Mexican women. William A. Vega; Bohdan Kolody; Ramon Valle; Judy Weir. *Human. Org.* **50:**2 Summer:1991 pp. 154 – 162

21 Soviet social problems. Anthony Jones *[Ed.]*; Walter D. Connor *[Ed.]*; David E Powell *[Ed.]*. Boulder: Westview Press, 1991: 337p. *ISBN: 0813376904; LofC: 90020685. Includes index.* [The John M. Olin critical issues series.]

22 Studies in New Zealand social problems. Paul F. Green *[Ed.]*. Palmerston North, New Zealand: The Dunmore Press Limited, 1990: 261 p. *ISBN: 0864691106.*

23 The victim syndrome. Jean Bethke Elshtain. *Society* **28:**4(192) 5-6:1991 pp. 31 – 38

24 Women partners of prisoners. Moira Peelo; John Stewart; Gill Stewart; Ann Prior. *Howard J. Crim. Just.* **30:**4 1991 pp. 311 – 327

Child neglect and abuse [Enfants martyrs et abandon d'enfant]

25 The abuse of children in out of home care. Michael Nunno; Nolan Rindfleisch. *Child. Soc.* **5:**4 Winter:1991 pp. 295 – 305

26 Brazil — war on children. Gilberto Dimenstein. London: The Latin America Bureau, 1991: 100 p. *ISBN: 0906156637.*

27 Child abuse and neglect in Micronesia. Mariano N. Marcus. *J. Pacific Soc.* **14:**3(52) 10:1991 pp. 110 – 103

28 Child abuse in India — a theoretical overview. Uma A. Segal. *Indian J. Soc. W.* **LII:**3 7:1991 pp. 293 – 302

29 Child labour in the Indian subcontinent — dimensions and implications. Ramesh Kanbargi. New Delhi: Sage Publications, 1991: 184 p. *ISBN: 0803996934; LofC: 91014988. Includes index.*

30 Child sexual abuse — whose problem? — reflections from Cleveland. Sue Richardson *[Ed.]*; Heather Bacon *[Ed.]*. Birmingham: Venture, 1991: 170 p. *ISBN: 0900102861.*

31 Children at risk — how different are children on child abuse registers? Mark Campbell. *Br. J. Soc. W.* **21:**3 6:1991 pp. 259 – 276

32 A comprehensive 5-year evaluation of project 12-ways — an ecobehavioral program for treating and preventing child abuse and neglect. David Wesch; John R. Lutzker. *J. Fam. Viol.* **6:**1 3:1991 pp. 17 – 36

K.1: Social problems *[Problèmes sociaux]* — **Child neglect and abuse** *[Enfants martyrs et abandon d'enfant]*

33 False allegations in child sexual abuse — the pattern of referral in an area where reporting is not mandatory. Graham Anthony; Jane Watkeys. *Child. Soc.* **5:2** Summer:1991 pp. 111 – 122

34 Family environments of victims of intrafamilial and extrafamilial child sexual abuse. Kelle Chandler Ray; Joan L. Jackson; Ruth M. Townsley. *J. Fam. Viol.* **6:4** 12:1991 pp. 365 – 374

35 Female victims of child sexual abuse — adult adjustment. Seymour Parker; Hilda Parker. *J. Fam. Viol.* **6:2** 6:1991 pp. 183 – 198

36 Integrating affect in treatment with adult survivors of physical and sexual abuse. William F. Cornell; Karen A. Olio. *Am. J. Orthopsy.* **61:1** 1:1991 pp. 59 – 69

37 Issues in school-based child sexual abuse prevention. Robert Webster. *Child. Soc.* **5:2** Summer:1991 pp. 146 – 164

38 Long-term effects of sexual abuse which occurred in childhood — a review. C. Cahill; S.P. Llewelyn; C. Pearson. *Br. J. Clin. Psycho.* **30:2** 5:1991 pp. 117 – 130

39 Niño abandonado, niño delincuente *[In Spanish]*; [Abandoned child, delinquent child]. Emilio García Méndez. *Nueva Soc.* **:112** 3-4:1991 pp. 124 – 135

40 The politics of law and order — case study evidence for a conflict model of the criminal law formation process. Thomas C. Castellano; Edmund F. McGarrell. *J. Res. Crim. Delin.* **28:3** 8:1991 pp. 304 – 329

41 Problems in the assessment and management of Munchausen syndrome by proxy abuse. Brenda Neale; Christopher Bools; Roy Meadow. *Child. Soc.* **5:4** Winter:1991 pp. 324 – 333

42 The relationship of abuse and witnessing violence on the child abuse potential inventory with black adolescents. Trisha R. Miller; Paul J. Handal; Frank H. Gilner; John F. Cross. *J. Fam. Viol.* **6:4** 12:1991 pp. 351 – 364

43 Social work and police response to child sexual abuse in Scotland. Lorraine Waterhouse; James Carnie. *Br. J. Soc. W.* **21:4** 8:1991 pp. 373 – 380

44 Theories of child abuse and neglect — differential perspectives, summaries, and evaluations. Oliver C. S. Tzeng; Jay W Jackson; Henry C. Karlson. New York: Praeger, 1991: xxi, 355 p. (ill) *ISBN: 0275938328; LofC: 90046516. Includes bibliographical references (p. [315]-338) and index.*

45 Undergraduate students' perceptions of child sexual abuse — the impact of victim sex, perpetrator sex, respondent sex, and victim response. Sylvia Broussard; William G. Wagner; Richard Kazelskis. *J. Fam. Viol.* **6:3** 9:1991 pp. 267 – 278

Crime *[Délits]*

46 Acquaintance rape — the hidden crime. Andrea Porter *[Ed.]*; Laurie Bechhofer *[Ed.]*. New York: Wiley, 1991: 401 p. *ISBN: 0471510238.* [Wiley series in personality processes.]

47 Age, gender, and crime across three historical periods — 1935, 1960, and 1985. Darrell Steffensmeier; Cathy Steifel. *Soc. Forc.* **69:3** 3:1991 pp. 869 – 894

48 Análisis de un problema de definiciones — la criminalidad en Puerto Rico *[In Spanish]*; [Analysis of a problem of definitions — criminality in Puerto Rico]. Angie Vázquez. *Homines* **14/15:1/2** 9/9:1990/1991 pp. 120 – 126

49 An analysis of American Indian homicide — a test of social disorganization and economic deprivation at the reservation county level. Ronet Bachman. *J. Res. Crim. Delin.* **28:4** 11:1991 pp. 456 – 471

50 Apparel as one factor in sex crimes against young females — professional opinions of U.S. psychiatrists. Donna Vali; Nicholas D. Rizzo. *Int. J. Offen.* **35:2** Summer:1991 pp. 167 – 181

51 Are there multiple paths to delinquency? David Huizinga; Finn-Aage Esbensen; Anne Wylie Weiher. *J. Crim. Law* **82:1** Spring:1991 pp. 83 – 118

52 "Beyond the 'thorny question'" — feminism, Foucault and the desexualisation of rape. V. Bell. *Int. J. S. Law* **19:1** 2:1991 pp. 83 – 100

53 Big men, small men — some comments on urban crime and inequality in PNG. Sinclair Dinnen. *Melan. Law J.* **19** 1991 pp. 79 – 100

54 British and U.S. left realism — a critical comparison. Walter S. DeKeseredy; Martin D. Schwartz. *Int. J. Offen.* **35:3** Fall:1991 pp. 248 – 262

55 Bűnözés és társadalompolitika *[In Hungarian]*; [Crime and societal policy]. Katalin Gönczöl. Budapest: Akadémiai Kiadó, 1987: 188 p.

K.1: Social problems [Problèmes sociaux] — Crime [Délits]

56 A bűnözés szociológiája *[In Hungarian]*; [Sociology of crime]. Denis Szabó. *Tarsadalomkutatás* Vol.5; No.4 - 1987. pp. 65 – 87

57 Burglary. Neal Shover. *Crime Just.* **14** 1991 pp. 73 – 114

58 Canadian immigrants and criminality; Immigrants canadiens et criminalité *[French summary]*; Los inmigrantes en el Canada y la tasa de delincuencia *[Spanish summary]*. T.J. Samuel; R. Faustino-Santos. *Int. Migr.* **XXIX:1** 3:1991 pp. 51 – 76

59 Casinos, crime, and real estate values — do they relate? Andrew J. Buck; Simon Hakim; Uriel Spiegel. *J. Res. Crim. Delin.* **28:3** 8:1991 pp. 288 – 303

60 Changing patterns of delinquency and crime — a longitudinal study in Racine. Lyle W Shannon; Judith L. McKilm *[Contrib.]*; Kathleen R. Anderson *[Contrib.]*; William E. Murph *[Contrib.]*. Boulder: Westview Press, 1991: xi, 174 p. (ill) *ISBN: 0813382882; LofC: 90025337*. Includes bibliographical references (p. [155]-165) and index.

61 Characteristics of U.S. cities with extreme (high or low) crime rates — results of discriminant analyses of 1960, 1970, and 1980 data. Kenneth C. Land; Patricia L. McCall; Lawrence E. Cohen. *Soc. Ind.* **24:3** 5:1991 pp. 209 – 231

62 The Chinese laundry — international drug trafficking and Hong Kong's banking industry. Mark S. Gaylord. *Cr. Law Soc. Chan.* **14:1** 3:1990 pp. 23 – 37

63 Cognitive and interpersonal factors in woman abuse. Jeffrey L. Edleson; Zvi C. Eisikovits; Edna Guttmann; Michal Sela-Amit. *J. Fam. Viol.* **6:2** 6:1991 pp. 167 – 167

64 Crime free housing. Barry Poyner; Barry Webb *[Ed.]*. Oxford: Butterworth-Architecture, 1991: 128 p. *ISBN: 0750612738*.

65 Crime placement, displacement, and deflection. Robert Barr; Ken Pease. *Crime Just.* **12** 1990 pp. 277 – 318

66 Crime prevention through environmental design — applications of architectural design and space management concepts. Timothy D. Crowe. Boston: Butterworth-Heinemann, 1991: xii, 241 p. (ill) *ISBN: 0750690585; LofC: 90029031*. Includes bibliographical references (p. 223-231) and index.

67 Crime, criminological research, and criminal policy in West and East Germany before and after their unification. Hans Joachim Schneider. *Int. J. Offen.* **35:4** Winter:1991 pp. 283 – 295

68 Crimes of the middle classes — white collar offenders in the federal courts. David Weisburd; et al. New Haven, Connecticut: Yale University Press, 1991: 211 p. *ISBN: 0300049528*.

69 Criminal behavior and rapid community growth — examining the evidence. William R. Freudenburg; Robert Emmett Jones. *Rural Sociol.* **56:4** Winter:1991 pp. 619 – 645

70 Criminologia y religion *[In Spanish]*; *[Portuguese summary]*; Criminology and religion *[Summary]*. Antonio Beristain. *Est. Juríd.* **23:62** 9-12:1991 pp. 5 – 54

71 Criminologie et défense sociale — dialogue à voix multiples *[In French]*; [Criminology and social defence] *[Summary]*; *[Spanish summary]*; *[French summary]*. D. Szabo. *Ann. Inter. Crimin.* **29:1&2** 1991 pp. 71 – 82

72 Criminology as peacemaking. Harold Eugene Pepinsky *[Ed.]*; Richard Quinney *[Ed.]*. Bloomington: Indiana University Press, c1991: ix, 339 p. (ill) *ISBN: 0253343577; LofC: 90042361*. Includes bibliographical references and index.

73 A cross-national assessment of a criminological perspective. Richard R. Bennett. *Soc. Forc.* **70:1** 9:1991 pp. 147 – 164

74 The cycle of crime and socialization practices. Joan McCord. *J. Crim. Law* **82:1** Spring:1991 pp. 211 – 228

75 Delinquency prevention — where's the beef? Ira M. Schwartz. *J. Crim. Law* **82:1** Spring:1991 pp. 132 – 140

76 Delivery of services to crime victims — a national survey. Albert R. Roberts. *Am. J. Orthopsy.* **61:1** 1:1991 pp. 128 – 137

77 Development and crime — a cross-national, time-series analysis of competing models. Richard R. Bennett. *Sociol. Q.* **32:3** Fall:1991 pp. 343 – 363

78 Developments in crime and crime control research — German studies on victims, offenders, and the public. Klaus Sessar *[Ed.]*; Hans-Jürgen Kerner *[Ed.]*. New York: Springer Verlag, c1991: 192p. *ISBN: oc20722932; LofC: 89026185*. [Research in criminology.]

79 Did crime rise or fall during the Reagan presidency? The effects of an "aging" U.S. population on the nation's crime rate. Darrell Steffensmeier; Miles D. Harer. *J. Res. Crim. Delin.* **28:3** 8:1991 pp. 330 – 359

80 Dimensions of delinquency — exploring the correlates of participation, frequency, and persistence of deliquent behavior. Douglas A. Smith; Christy A. Visher; G. Roger Jarjoura. *J. Res. Crim. Delin.* **28:1** 02:1991 pp. 6 – 32

K.1: Social problems [Problèmes sociaux] — Crime [Délits]

81 Discipline and deviance — physical punishment of children and violence and other crime in adulthood. Murray A. Straus. *Soc. Prob.* **38:2** 5:1991 pp. 133 – 154
82 A Dutch perspective on some of the effects of alternative sanctions. A.R. Hauber. *Cr. Law Soc. Chan.* **15:2** 3:1991 pp. 91 – 108
83 The effectiveness of a police-initiated fear-reducing strategy. Trevor Bennett. *Br. J. Crimin.* **31:1** Winter:1991 pp. 1 – 14
84 Essays on crime and development. Uglješa Zvekić *[Ed.]*. Rome: United Nations Interregional Crime and Justice Research Institute, 1990: 377 p. (ill) *ISBN: 929078010x; LofC: 91170007.* eng, fre; English and French; Includes bibliographical references. [Publication.]
85 Explaining crime ideology — an exploration of the parental sociological perspective. R. Gregory Dunaway; Francis T. Cullen. *Crime Delin.* **37:4** 10:1991 pp. 536 – 554
86 Exploring the gender, race and class dimensions of victimization — a left realist critique of the Canadian urban victimization. Walter S. DeKeseredy; Brian D. MacLean. *Int. J. Offen.* **35:2** Summer:1991 pp. 143 – 161
87 Factors affecting rapists and non rapists' perceptions of the likelihood of sexual activity. Garfield A. Harmon; R. Glynn Owens; Michael E. Dewey. *Int. J. Offen.* **35:3** Fall:1991 pp. 217 – 224
88 Fear of crime in urban residential neighborhoods — implications of between- and within-neighborhood sources for current models. Jeannette M. Covington; Ralph B. Taylor. *Sociol. Q.* **32:2** Summer:1991 pp. 231 – 249
89 Fear of school-related predatory crime. Frank S. Pearson; Jackson Toby. *Social Soc. Res.* **75:3** 4:1991 pp. 117 – 125
90 Firearm availability and homicide rates in Detroit, 1951-1986. David McDowall. *Soc. Forc.* **69:4** 6:1991 pp. 1085 – 1102
91 General deterrence in a longitudinal perspective. A Swedish case — theft, 1841-1985. Hanns von Hofer; Henrik Tham. *Eur. Sociol. R.* **5:1** 5:1989 pp. 25 – 46
92 Homicide in urban Canada — testing the impact of economic inequality and social disorganization. Leslie W. Kennedy; Robert A. Silverman; David R. Forde. *Can. J. Soc.* **16:4** Fall:1991 pp. 397 – 410
93 In partial defense of socialist realism. Some theoretical and methodological concerns of the local crime survey. B.D. MacLean. *Cr. Law Soc. Chan.* **15:3** 5:1991 pp. 213 – 254
94 Initiation, education and desistance in juvenile offending and their correlations. Rolf Loeber; Magda Stouthamer-Loeber; Welmoet Van Kammen; David P. Farrington. *J. Crim. Law* **82:1** Spring:1991 pp. 36 – 82
95 The intangible rewards from crime — the case of domestic marijuana cultivation. Ralph A. Weisheit. *Crime Delin.* **37:4** 10:1991 pp. 506 – 527
96 Interest groups and criminal behavior. Gregory G. Brunk; Laura Ann Wilson. *J. Res. Crim. Delin.* **28:2** 5:1991 pp. 157 – 173
97 Intraracial rape revisited — on forging a feminist future beyond factions and frightening politics. Diane Bell. *Wom. St. Inter. For.* **14:5** :1991 pp. 385 – 412
98 The investigation of crime — a guide to police powers. Vaughan Bevan; K. W. Lidstone. London: Butterworths, 1991: 570 p. *ISBN: 0406104018.*
99 Issues in realist criminology. Roger Matthews *[Ed.]*; Jock Young *[Ed.]*. London: Sage Publications, 1991: 176 p. *ISBN: 0803986246; LofC: gb 91087377.* [Sage contemporary criminology series.]
100 Juvenile sexual offending — causes, consequences, and correction. Gail Ryan *[Ed.]*; Sandra L. Lane *[Ed.]*. Lexington, Mass: Lexington Books, c1991: x, 435 p. *ISBN: 0669194646; LofC: 90022355.*
101 Left realist criminology — strengths weaknesses and the feminist critique. M.D. Schwartz; W.S. DeKeseredy. *Cr. Law Soc. Chan.* **15:1** 1:1991 pp. 51 – 72
102 Lethal police response as a crime deterrent. D.O. Cloninger. *Am. J. Econ. S.* **50:1** 1:1991 pp. 59 – 70
103 The life and death of the care order (criminal). Robert Harris. *Br. J. Soc. W.* **21:1** 2:1991 pp. 1 – 17
104 The living conditions of law violators in Denmark. Britta Kyvsgaard. *Int. J. Offen.* **35:3** Fall:1991 pp. 235 – 247
105 Measuring crime seriousness — lessons from the national survey of crime severity. David A. Parton; Mark Hansel; John R. Stratton. *Br. J. Crimin.* **31:1** Winter:1991 pp. 72 – 85
106 The media politics of crime and criminal justice. Philip Schlesinger; Howard Tumber; Graham Murdock. *Br. J. Soc.* **42:3** 9:1991 pp. 397 – 420

K.1: Social problems [Problèmes sociaux] — Crime [Délits]

107 The mentally disordered offender. Katia Gilhome Herbst *[Ed.]*; John Gunn *[Ed.]*. London: Heinemann Medical in association with Mental Health Foundation, 1991: 257 p. *ISBN: 0750600284. Includes index.*

108 Models for bivariate count data with an application to teenage delinquency and paternity. David H. Good; Maureen A. Pirog-Good. *Sociol. Meth.* **17**:4 5:1989 pp. 409 – 431

109 Monoamine oxidase and criminality — identifying an apparent biological marker for antisocial behavior. Lee Ellis. *J. Res. Crim. Delin.* **28**:2 5:1991 pp. 227 – 251

110 The motivation of the persistent robber. Jack Katz. *Crime Just.* **14** 1991 pp. 277 – 306

111 The nature of crime — is cheating necessary for cooperation? Richard Machalek; Lawrence E. Cohen. *Hum. Nature* **2**:3 1991 pp. 215 – 234

112 The needs and rights of victims of crime. Mike Maguire. *Crime Just.* **14** 1991 pp. 363 – 433

113 Negative social sanctions and juvenile delinquency — effects of labeling in a model of deviant behavior. Howard B. Kaplan; Robert J. Johnson. *Soc. Sci. Q.* **72**:1 3:1991 pp. 98 – 122

114 A neighborhood business area is hurting — crime, fear of crime, and disorders take their toll. Bonnie Fisher. *Crime Delin.* **37**:3 7:1991 pp. 363 – 373

115 The neuropsychology of juvenile delinquency — a critical review. Terrie E. Moffitt. *Crime Just.* **12** 1990 pp. 99 – 170

116 O crime na historiografia brasileira — uma revisão da pesquisa recente *[In Portuguese]*; [Crime in Brazilian historiography — a review of recent research]. Marcos Liuz Bretas. *Bol. Inf. Bibl. Soc.* :32 1991 pp. 49 – 62

117 Об организованной преступности на Западе и в СССР *[In Russian]*; On organised crime in western countries and in the USSR *[Summary]*; (La criminalité organisée en Occident et en URSS: *Title only in French*). A.S. Nikiforov. *Sovet. Gos. Pr.* :4 1991 pp. 48 – 57

118 On the nature of rape. J.H. Bogart. *Publ. Aff. Q.* **5**:2 4:1991 pp. 117 – 136

119 Организация расследования преступлений как вид социального управления *[In Russian]*; ("Investigation engineering" — of crimes as a sort of social control activity). B.Ya. Petelin. *Sot. Issle.* :4 1991 pp. 66 – 71

120 Pecunia non olet — cleansing the money-launderers from the temple. M. Levi. *Cr. Law Soc. Chan.* **16**:3 11:1991 pp. 217 – 302

121 Personal meaning in the lives of a shoplifting population. Frank J. McShane; John Lawless; Barrie A. Noonan. *Int. J. Offen.* **35**:3 Fall:1991 pp. 190 – 204

122 The phantom epidemic of sexual assault. Neil Gilbert. *Publ. Inter.* :**103** Spring:1991 pp. 54 – 65

123 The Philadelphia birth cohort and selective incapacitation. Thomas J. Bernard; R. Richard Ritti. *J. Res. Crim. Delin.* **28**:1 02:1991 pp. 33 – 54

124 Police attitudes to crime and punishment — certainties and dilemmas. Nigel Fielding; Jane Fielding. *Br. J. Crimin.* **31**:1 Winter:1991 pp. 39 – 53

125 Police officers' definitions of rape — a prototype study. B. Krahé. *J. Comm. App. Soc. Psychol.* **1**:3 9:1991 pp. 223 – 244

126 Police, victims, and crime prevention — some research-based recommendations on victim-orientated interventions. Frans Willem Winkel. *Br. J. Crimin.* **31**:3 Summer:1991 pp. 250 – 265

127 The politics of crime control. Kevin Stenson *[Ed.]*; David Cowell *[Ed.]*. London: Sage Publications, 1991: 226 p. *ISBN: 0803983417.*

128 Престчпность в СССР: основные тенденции и закономерности *[In Russian]*; (Crime in the USSR — main trends and regularities); (La criminalité en URSS — principales tendances et lois: *Title only in French*). V.V. Luneev. *Sovet. Gos. Pr.* :8 1991 pp. 90 – 97

129 Преступность и психические аномалии *[In Russian]*; [Criminality and mental abnormality]. V.H. Kudryavtsev *[Ed.]*; Iu. M. Antonian; S.V. Borodin. Moscow: Nauka, 1987: 208 p.

130 Processing of criminal homicide cases in a large southern city. James L. Williams; Daniel G. Rodeheaver. *Social Soc. Res.* **75**:2 1:1991 pp. 80 – 88

131 Prostitution, criminal law and morality in the Netherlands. J.C.J. Boutellier. *Cr. Law Soc. Chan.* **15**:3 5:1991 pp. 201 – 211

132 The psychological experience of crime — a test of the mediating role of beliefs in explaining the distress of victims. Fran H. Norris; Krzysztof Kaniasty. *J. Soc. Clin. Psychol.* **10**:3 Fall:1991 pp. 239 – 260

133 Punishment, crime and market forces. Leslie T. Wilkins. Aldershot: Dartmouth, 1991: 180 p. *ISBN: 1855212285.*

K.1: Social problems [Problèmes sociaux] — Crime [Délits]

134 De quelques réflexions sur la victimologie en tant que nouvelle approche du phénomène criminel *[In French]*; [Reflections on victimology — a new approach to the criminal phenomenon] *[Summary]*. Abdelhamid Berchiche. *Rev. Algér.* **XXIX:1-2:** 1991 pp. 37 – 46

135 Rape and child sexual abuse in Soweto — an interview with community leader Mary Mabaso. Diana E.H. Russell. *S.Afr. Sociol. R.* **3:2** 4:1991 pp. 62 – 82

136 Les recherches sur les femmes criminalisées. Questions actuelles et nouvelles questions de recherche *[In French]*; [Research on criminalized women. Current issues and new questions] *[Summary]*; *[Spanish summary]*. D. Laberge. *Ann. Inter. Crimin.* **29:1&2** 1991 pp. 21 – 41

137 The reduction of violent crimes through economic equality for women. Jim Hackler. *J. Fam. Viol.* **6:2** 6:1991 pp. 199 – 216

138 Relationship between illicit drug enforcement policy and property crimes. Bruce L. Benson; David W. Rasmussen. *Cont. Policy* **IX:4** 10:1991 pp. 106 – 115

139 The relationship between social skills deficits and juvenile delinquency. Stanley Renwick; Nicholas Emler. *Br. J. Clin. Psycho.* **30:1** 2:1991 pp. 61 – 71

140 Riding the underground dragon — crime control and public order on Hong Kong's mass transit railway. Mark S. Gaylord; John F. Galliher. *Br. J. Crimin.* **31:1** Winter:1991 pp. 15 – 26

141 Sex crime in the news. Keith Soothill; Sylvia Walby *[Ed.]*. London: Routledge, 1991: 181 p. *ISBN: 0415018153. Includes bibliography and index.*

142 Sex crimes. Ronald M. Holmes. Newbury Park: Sage Publications, c1991: x, 146 p. (ill) *ISBN: 0803939523; LofC: 90019480. Includes bibliographical references (p. 129-138) and index.*

143 The sex ratio, family disruption, and rates of violent crime — the paradox of demographic structure. Steven F. Messner; Robert J. Sampson. *Soc. Forc.* **69:3** 3:1991 pp. 693 – 713

144 Sex-offender risk assessment and disposition planning — a review of empirical and clinical findings. Robert J. McGrath. *Int. J. Offen.* **35:4** Winter:1991 pp. 328 – 350

145 Singularidade, igualdade e transcendência — um ensaio sobre o significado social do crime *[In Spanish]*; Singularity, equality, and transcendence — an essay on the social meaning of crime *[Summary]*; Singularité, égalité et transcendance — essai sur la signification sociale du crime *[French summary]*. Sérgio Carrara. *Rev. Bras. Ciên. Soc.* **6:16** 7:1991 pp. 80 – 88

146 Social area influences on delinquency — a multilevel analysis. Denise C. Gottfredson; Richard J. McNeil; Gary D. Gottfredson. *J. Res. Crim. Delin.* **28:2** 5:1991 pp. 197 – 226

147 Social change and crime rates — an evaluation of alternative theoretical approaches. Terance D. Miethe; Michael Hughes; David McDowall. *Soc. Forc.* **70:1** 9:1991 pp. 165 – 186

148 Sociological perspectives on punishment. David Garland. *Crime Just.* **14** 1991 pp. 115 – 166

149 The sociology of crime and deviance in France. Philippe Robert. *Br. J. Crimin.* **31:1** Winter:1991 pp. 27 – 38

150 Соучастие и организованная преступность *[In Russian]*; (Participation and organized crime). N.A. Beyaev. *Vest. Lenin. Univ. 6* **6:3** 9:1991 pp. 89 – 96

151 The Soviet mafia. Arkady Vaksberg; John Roberts *[Tr.]*; Elizabeth Roberts *[Tr.]*. London: Weidenfeld and Nicolson, 1991: 275 p. *ISBN: 0297812025.*

152 Soviet narcotics trade. Rensselaer W. Lee. *Society* **28:5** 7-8:1991 pp. 46 – 52

153 Specifying the SES/delinquency relationship by social characteristics of contexts. Charles R. Tittle; Robert F. Meier. *J. Res. Crim. Delin.* **28:4** 11:1991 pp. 430 – 455

154 Structural correlates of juvenile property crime — a cross-national, time- series analysis. Richard R. Bennett; P. Peter Basiotis. *J. Res. Crim. Delin.* **28:3** 8:1991 pp. 262 – 287

155 *[In Japanese]*; [A study on delinquent careers of the 1970 birth cohort (2) — an event history analysis on the effect of school maladjustment]. Yutaka Harada. ***Report of the National Research Institute of Police Science** No.32(1) - 1991.* pp. 38 – 52

156 Sunbelt effects on homicide rates. Gregory S. Kowaslski; Thomas A. Petee. *Social Soc. Res.* **75:2** 1:1991 pp. 73 – 79

157 Testing the relationship between unemployment and crime — a methodological comment and empirical analysis using time series data from England and Wales. Chris Hale; Dima Sabbagh. *J. Res. Crim. Delin.* **28:4** 11:1991 pp. 400 – 417

158 Toward a developmental criminology. Rolf Loeber; Marc Le Blanc. *Crime Just.* **12** 1990 pp. 375 – 473

159 Transient crowding and crime — some crimes rates change. S. Jarrell; R.M. Howsen. *Am. J. Econ. S.* **49:4** 10:1990 pp. 483 – 494

K.1: Social problems [Problèmes sociaux] — Crime [Délits]

160 Understanding crime incidence statistics — why the UCR diverges from the NCS. Albert D. Biderman; James P. Lynch. New York: Springer-Verlag, c1991: xii, 132 p. (ill) *ISBN: 0387970452; LofC: 89011576*. Includes bibliographical references (p. 123-128) and index. [Research in criminology.]

161 Urban crime, criminals, and victims — the Swedish experience in an Anglo-American comparative perspective. Per-Olof H. Wikström. New York: Springer-Verlag, c1991: viii, 269 p. (ill., maps) *ISBN: 0387974059; LofC: 90010124*. Includes bibliographical references (p. 246-259). [Research in criminology.]

162 Voldtægt — sex eller misogyni? *[In Danish]*; Rape — sex or misogyny? *[Summary]*. Britta Mogensen. *Tids. Antrop.* :**24** 1991 pp. 25 – 40

163 Whiter than white collar crime — tax, fraud insurance and the management of stigma. Doreen McBarnet. *Br. J. Soc.* **42:3** 9:1991 pp. 324 – 343

164 Young people and crime — costs and prevention. Ivan Potas; Aidan Vining *[Ed.]*; Paul R. Wilson *[Ed.]*. Canberra: Australian Institue of Criminology, 1990: 82,10,22 p. *ISBN: 0642155380*.

Criminal justice [Justice criminelle]

165 AIDS and criminal justice. Arthur J. Lurigio *[Ed.]*; Mark Blumberg *[Contrib.]*; Denny Langston *[Contrib.]*; Anna T. Laszlo *[Contrib.]*; Barbara E. Smith *[Contrib.]*; Eugene Griffin *[Contrib.]*; Bruce Johnson *[Contrib.]*; Sandra Baxter *[Contrib.]*; Lawrence J. Ouellet *[Contrib.]*; Antonio D. Jimenez *[Contrib.]* and others. Collection of 9 articles. **Crime Delin.** , *37:1*, 1:1991 pp. 3 – 153

166 The boot camp program for offenders — does the shoe fit? Rudolf E.S. Mathias; James W. Mathews. *Int. J. Offen.* **35:4** Winter:1991 pp. 322 – 327

167 Calling on the experts — the financial management initiative (FMI), private sector management consultants and the probation service. Christopher Humphrey. *Howard J. Crim. Just.* **30:1** 2:1991 pp. 1 – 18

168 Certainty vs. severity of punishment. Jeffrey Grogger. *Econ. Inq.* **XXIX:2** 4:1991 pp. 297 – 309

169 Community service work placements. Gill McIvor. *Howard J. Crim. Just.* **30:1** 2:1991 pp. 19 – 29

170 Community treatment orders — do we need them? John Dunn. *J. For. Psy.* **2:2** 9:1991 pp. 153 – 166

171 Correlates of jail overcrowding — a case study of a county detention center. Randall G. Shelden; William B. Brown. *Crime Delin.* **37:3** 7:1991 pp. 347 – 362

172 Counting youth in trouble in institutions — bringing the United States up to date. Paul Lerman. *Crime Delin.* **37:4** 10:1991 pp. 465 – 480

173 Courts and the poor. Christopher E. Smith. Chicago: Nelson-Hall, 1991: 177 p. *ISBN: 0830412964*.

174 The crimes women commit, the punishments women receive. Rita James Simon; Jean Landis *[Ed.]*. Lexington, Mass: Lexington Books, c1991: xx, 136 p. *ISBN: 0669202363; LofC: 90006432 //r912*. Includes bibliographical references (p.[125]-130) and index.

175 *[In Japanese]*; [Current constructionist studies on crime, criminal justice and social problems in the United States]. Nobuyoshi Nakagawa. **Han. Shak. Kenk.** *No.(16) - 1991*. pp. 152 – 157

176 The death penalty in the nineties — an examination of the modern system of capital punishment. Welsh S. White. Ann Arbor: University of Michigan Press, 1991: 223 p. *ISBN: 0472094610. Includes index*.

177 Differential effects of juvenile justice reform on incarceration rates of the states. Edmund F. McGarrell. *Crime Delin.* **37:2** 4:1991 pp. 262 – 280

178 A Dutch perspective on some of the effects of alternative sanctions. A.R. Hauber. *Cr. Law Soc. Chan.* **15:2** 3:1991 pp. 91 – 108

179 Early release of prisoners in France — plus ça change plus c'est la même chose. Margaret Gwynne Lloyd. *Howard J. Crim. Just.* **30:3** 8:1991 pp. 231 – 237

180 An evaluation of intensive probation in California. Joan Petersilia; Susan Turner. *J. Crim. Law* **82:3** Fall:1991 p. 610

181 The evolution of criminal policy and prevention from the perspective of social defense and enlightenment through criminological research; *[French summary]*; *[Spanish summary]*. A.J. Reiss. *Ann. Inter. Crimin.* **29:1&2** 1991 pp. 9 – 20

182 Excluded — the current status of African-American scholars in the field of criminolgy and criminal justice. Vernetta Young; Anne Thomas Sulton. *J. Res. Crim. Delin.* **28:1** 02:1991 pp. 101 – 116

K.1: Social problems [Problèmes sociaux] — Criminal justice [Justice criminelle]

183 Federal criminal sentencing — some measurement issues with application to pre-guideline sentencing disparity. William Rhodes. *J. Crim. Law* **81:4** Winter:1991 pp. 1002 – 1033

184 From crime policy to victim policy. The need for a fundamental policy change; *[French summary]*; *[Spanish summary]*. E.A. Fattah. *Ann. Inter. Crimin.* **29:1&2** 1991 pp. 43 – 60

185 Gender bias in juvenile justice handling of seriously crime-involved youths. Ruth Horowitz; Anne E. Pottieger. *J. Res. Crim. Delin.* **28:1** 02:1991 pp. 75 – 100

186 The human costs of "giving the kid another chance". Waln K. Brown; Richard L. Jenkins; Timothy P. Miller; Warren A. Rhodes. *Int. J. Offen.* **35:4** Winter:1991 pp. 296 – 302

187 The "immaterial" prison — custody as a factory for the manufacture of handicaps. E. Gallo; V. Ruggiero. *Int. J. S. Law* **19:3** 8:1991 pp. 273 – 292

188 Inmate classification — a correctional program that works? John E. Berecochea; Joel B. Gibbs. *Eval. Rev.* **15:3** 6:1991 pp. 333 – 363

189 Inside — rethinking Scotland's prisons. Andrew Coyle. Edinburgh: Scottish Child, 1991: 304 p. (ill) *ISBN: 187339201x. Includes bibliography and index.*

190 Jails versus mental hospitals — a social dilemma. George B. Palermo; Maurice B. Smith; Frank J. Liska. *Int. J. Offen.* **35:2** Summer:1991 pp. 97 – 106

191 Justice for victims and offenders — a restorative response to crime. Martin Wright. Milton Keynes, England: Open University Press, 1991: 159 p. *ISBN: 0335096972; LofC: 90026086. Includes bibliographical references.*

192 Juvenile justice — history and policy. Donna C. Hale *[Contrib.]*; Alexander W. Pisciotta *[Contrib.]*; Mary E. Odem *[Contrib.]*; Steven Schlossman; Theodore N. Ferdinand *[Contrib.]*; Kathleen J. Block *[Contrib.]*; Arnold Binder *[Contrib.]*; Susan L. Polan *[Contrib.]*; Edmund F. McGarrell *[Contrib.]*; Prue Rains *[Contrib.]* and others. *Collection of 7 articles.* **Crime Delin.** , *37:2*, 4:1991 pp. 163 – 299

193 Knowledge and death penalty opinion — a test of the Marshall hypotheses. Robert M. Bohm; Louise J. Clark; Adrian F. Aveni. *J. Res. Crim. Delin.* **28:3** 8:1991 pp. 360 – 387

194 Массовое освобождение спецпоселенцев и ссыльных *[In Russian]*; (Mass release of "special convicts" and exiles). V.N. Zemskov. *Sot. Issle.* **:1** 1991 pp. 5 – 26

195 Maximum-security custody in Britain and the USA — a study of Gartree and Oak Park Heights. Roy D. King. *Br. J. Crimin.* **31:2** Spring:1991 pp. 126 – 152

196 The media politics of crime and criminal justice. Philip Schlesinger; Howard Tumber; Graham Murdock. *Br. J. Soc.* **42:3** 9:1991 pp. 397 – 420

197 No escape — the future of American corrections. John J. DiIulio. [New York]: BasicBooks, c1991: xii, 301 p. *ISBN: 0465051111; LofC: 90055596. Includes bibliographical references (p. 273-288) and index.*

198 Noch einmal — Geschlechtsspezifische Kriminalisierung im Jugendstrafrecht? *[In German]*; Once again — is there a relationship between gender and criminalization in juvenile justice? *[Summary]*. Wolfgang Ludwig-Mayerhofer; Dorothea Rzepka. *Kölner Z. Soz. Soz. psy.* **43:3** 1991 pp. 542 – 557

199 Out of jail — the reduction in the use of penal custody for male juveniles 1981-88. Rob Allen. *Howard J. Crim. Just.* **30:1** 2:1991 pp. 30 – 52

200 Pipe dream blues — racism and the war on drugs. Clarence Lusane; Jesse Jackson *[Contrib.]*; Dennis Desmond *[Contrib.]*. Boston, MA: South End Press, c1991: 293 p. *ISBN: 0896084108; LofC: 90027575. Includes bibliographical references (p. 225-254) and index.*

201 Prison discipline — the case for implementing Woolf. Rod Morgan; Helen Jones. *Br. J. Crimin.* **31:3** Summer:1991 pp. 280 – 291

202 Private corporate justice — store police, shoplifters, and civil recovery. Melissa G. Davis; Richard J. Lundman; Ramiro Martinez. *Soc. Prob.* **38:3** 8:1991 pp. 395 – 410

203 Prostitution, criminal law and morality in the Netherlands. J.C.J. Boutellier. *Cr. Law Soc. Chan.* **15:3** 5:1991 pp. 201 – 211

204 Psychological treatment as an alternative to prosecution — a form of primary diversion. David J. Cooke. *Howard J. Crim. Just.* **30:1** 2:1991 pp. 53 – 65

205 Punishment under pressure — the probation service in the inner city. Bob Broad. London: Kingsley, 1991: 238 p. *ISBN: 1853020907. Includes bibliography and index.*

206 Punitive attitudes toward criminals — racial consensus or racial conflict? Steven F. Cohn; Steven E. Barkan; William A. Halteman. *Soc. Prob.* **38:2** 5:1991 pp. 287 – 296

207 Reexamining community corrections models. Richard Lawrence. *Crime Delin.* **37:4** 10:1991 pp. 449 – 464

208 Reform through community — resocializing offenders in the kibbutz. Michael Fischer; Brenda Geiger. New York: Greenwood Press, 1991: xv, 228 p. *ISBN: 0313279314;*

K.1: Social problems *[Problèmes sociaux]* — *Criminal justice [Justice criminelle]*
LofC: 91012837. "Prepared under the auspices of the Institute for Research and Study of the Kibbutz and the Cooperative Idea, University of Haifa."; Includes bibliographical references (p. [209]-221) and index. [Kibbutz studies series.]

209 The response of the criminal justice system to prison overcrowding — recidivism patterns among four successive parolee cohorts. William R. Kelly; Sheldon Ekland-Olson. *Law Soc. Rev.* **25:3** 1991 pp. 601 – 620

210 The scale of imprisonment. Franklin E Zimring; Gordon Hawkins *[Ed.]*. Chicago: University of Chicago Press, c1991: xiv, 244 p. (ill) *ISBN: 0226983536; LofC: 90044613.* Includes bibliographical references (p. 223-234) and index. [Studies in crime and justice.]

211 The scope and purposes of corrections — exploring alternative responses to crowding. Richard Rosenfeld; Kimberly Kempf. *Crime Delin.* **37:4** 10:1991 pp. 481 – 505

212 Sociological perspectives on punishment. David Garland. *Crime Just.* **14** 1991 pp. 115 – 166

213 Tags, taggers, taggage *[In French]*; [Tags, taggers, tagging]. Christian Ruby. *Regar. Actual.* **:172** 7:1991 pp. 11 – 22

214 The transformation of strategies for controlling admissions — professionalization and youth processing organizations. Prue Rains; Eli Teram *Crime Delin.* **37:2** 4:1991 pp. 281 – 299

215 Treating the sexual offender. Barry Maletzky; Kevin B. McGovern *[Ed.]*. Newbury Park, Calif: Sage Publications, c1991: 357 p. (ill) *ISBN: 0803936621; LofC: 90008863.* Includes bibliographical references (p. 331-344) and indexes.

216 The Young Offenders Act — a revolution in Canadian juvenile justice. Alan Winfield Leschied *[Ed.]*; Peter Jaffe *[Ed.]*; Wayne Willis *[Ed.]*. Toronto: University of Toronto Press, c1991: xvi, 300 p. *ISBN: 0802026230; LofC: cn 90095935.* Includes bibliographical references.

Poverty *[Pauvreté]*

217 Adolescence and poverty — challenge for the 1990s. Peter B. Edelman *[Ed.]*; Joyce A. Ladner *[Ed.]*. Washington, D.C: Center for National Policy Press, c1991: 164 p. (ill) *ISBN: 0944237312; LofC: 91016446.* Includes bibliographical references.

218 Alte und neue Armut in der Bundesrepublik Deutschland *[In German]*; [Old and new poverty in the Federal Republic of Germany]. Beate Werth. Berlin: VWB, c1991: 344 p. (ill) *ISBN: 3927408581; LofC: 92112249.* Includes bibliographical references (p. 330-344).

219 American refugees. Jim Hubbard; Jonathan Kozol *[Foreword]*. Minneapolis: University of Minnesota Press, c1991: 108 p. (ill) *ISBN: 0816618968; LofC: 90049448.*

220 Armoede en gettovorming in Nederland *[In Dutch]*; [Poverty and ghetto formation in the Netherlands]. Lodewijk Brunt *[Ed.]*; Jan Godschalk *[Ed.]*; Godfried Engbersen *[Contrib.]*; J.M.M. van Amersfoort *[Contrib.]*; H.B. Entzinger *[Contrib.]*; Rene Teule *[Contrib.]*; Ronald van Kempen *[Contrib.]*. Collection of 4 articles. *Sociol. Gids*, **XXXVIII:1, 1-2:**1991 pp. 7 – 59

221 Between Verwoerd and the ANC — profiles of contemporary repression, deprivation, and poverty in South Africa's "Bantustans". Eliphas G. Mukonoweshuro. *Soc. Just.* **18:1-2** Spring-Summer:1991 pp. 171 – 185

222 Children in poverty — child development and public policy. Aletha C. Huston *[Ed.]*. Cambridge: Cambridge University Press, 1991: x, 331 p. (ill) *ISBN: 0521391628; LofC: 91009814.* Includes bibliographical references and indexes.

223 Community attitudes toward the homeless. Michael Dear; Brandan Gleeson. *Urban Geogr.* **12:2** 3-4:1991 pp. 155 – 176

224 Comparing poverty rates internationally — lessons from recent studies in developed countries. Anthony B. Atkinson. *W.B. Econ. R.* **5:1** 1:1991 pp. 3 – 21

225 Consuming credit — debt & poverty in the UK. Janet Ford. London: CPAG, 1991: 107 p. *ISBN: 0946744327.*

226 Deadly connections — culture, poverty, and the direction of lethal violence. Lin Huff-Corzine; Jay Corzine; David C. Moore. *Soc. Forc.* **69:3** 3:1991 pp. 715 – 732

227 Deprivation, social welfare and expertise. Juhani Lehto *[Ed.]*. Finland: VAPK-Publishing, 1991: 237 p.

228 La disqualification sociale — essai sur la nouvelle pauvreté *[In French]*; [Social disqualification — an essay on the new poor]. Serge Paugam; Dominique Schnapper *[Foreword]*. Paris: Presses universitaires de France, c1991: 254 p. *ISBN: 2130432263; LofC: 91129499.* Includes bibliographical references (p. 249-254). [Sociologies.]

229 Does the choice of poverty index matter in practice? J.R. Rodgers. *Soc. Ind.* **24:3** 5:1991 pp. 233 – 252

K.1: Social problems [Problèmes sociaux] — Poverty [Pauvreté]

230 The economic correlates of homelessness in sixty cities. Cecil Bohanon. *Soc. Sci. Q.* **72:**4 12:1991 pp. 817 – 825

231 The epidemic theory of ghettos and neighborhood effects on dropping out and teenage childbearing. Jonathan Crane. *A.J.S.* **96:**5 3:1991 pp. 1226 – 1259

232 Etnische minderheden, stedelijke armoede, gettovorming *[In Dutch]*; Ethnic minorities — urban poverty — ghettoisation *[Summary]*. H.B. Entzinger. *Sociol. Gids* **XXXVIII:**1 1-2:1991 pp. 37 – 47

233 Exposure to panhandling and beliefs about poverty causation. George Wilson. *Social Soc. Res.* **76:**1 10:1991 pp. 14 – 19

234 Gimme shelter — a social history of homelessness in contemporary America. Gregg Barak. New York: Praeger, 1991: xiv, 212 p. *ISBN: 0275933202; LofC: 90024567. Includes bibliographical references (p. [197]-199) and index.*

235 Homeless children and youth — a new American dilemma. Lester M. Salamon *[Ed.]*; Janice Marie Molnar *[Ed.]*; Julee H. Kryder-Coe *[Ed.]*. New Brunswick, N.J., U.S.A: Transaction Publishers, c1991: xviii, 323 p. (ill) *ISBN: 0887383866; LofC: 90042495. Papers prepared for a conference held in Washington, D.C. in April 1989, sponsored by the Johns Hopkins Institute for Policy Studies; Includes bibliographical references and indexes.*

236 Homeless women — moving toward a comprehensive model. Norweeta Milburn; Ann D' Ercole. *Am. Psychol.* **46:**11 11:1991 pp. 1161 – 1169

237 Homeless young people and runaways — agency definitions and processes. Mark Liddiard; Susan Hutson. *J. Soc. Pol.* **20:**3 7:1991 pp. 365 – 388

238 Homelessness. Jennifer R. Wolch *[Ed.]*; Robin Law *[Contrib.]*; Charles Hoch *[Contrib.]*; Michael Dear *[Contrib.]*; Brendan Gleeson *[Contrib.]*; Gerald Daly *[Contrib.]*. Collection of 5 articles. *Urban Geogr.* , *12:2*, 3-4:1991 pp. 99 – 193

239 Homelessness. James M. Jones *[Ed.]*; Irene S. Levine *[Ed.]*; Allison A. Rosenberg *[Ed.]*; Paul A. Toro *[Ed.]*; Melissa G. Warren *[Ed.]*; Ann D' Ercole *[Ed.]*; Robert B. Huebner *[Ed.]*; Norweeta Milburn *[Ed.]*; Pamela J. Fischer *[Contrib.]*; William R. Breakey *[Contrib.]* and others. Collection of 15 articles. *Am. Psychol.* , *46:11*, 11:1991 pp. 1108 – 1252

240 Homelessness and economic restucturing. Robin Law; Jennifer R. Wolch. *Urban Geogr.* **12:**2 3-4:1991 pp. 105 – 136

241 Homelessness and health — what do we know?what should be done? Anne-Marie Barry; Julie Glanville; Roy Carr-Hill. York: Centre for Health Economics, University of York, 1991: 34 p.

242 Homelessness in Britain. John Greve. York: Joseph Rowntree Foundation, 1991: 60 p. *ISBN: 1872470440.*

243 Homelessness in the United States — an ecological perspective. Paul A. Toro; Edison J. Trickett; David D. Wall; Deborah A. Salem. *Am. Psychol.* **46:**11 11:1991 pp. 1208 – 1218

244 Homelessness — an empirical assessment of poverty amongst plenty in Nevada, U.S.A. Edward W. Davis. *Indian J. Soc. W.* **LII:**2 4:1991 pp. 169 – 178

245 Hunger and poverty in Iraq. Jean Dreze; Haris Gazdar. London: London School of Economics, 1991: 65 p. [Development economics research programme discussion paper series. : No. 32]

246 Institutional dimensions of poverty reduction. Lawrence F. Salmen. Washington, D.C.: Country Economics Department, World Bank, 1990: 38 p. *BNB: 90206430; LofC: 90206430. Cover title; "May 1990."; Includes bibliographical references.* [Policy, research, and external affairs working papers.]

247 Is American business working for the poor? Mary Jo Bane; David T. Ellwood. *Harv. Bus. Re.* **69:**5 9-10:1991 pp. 58 – 66

248 Les maisons d'hébergement pour femmes sens abri — plus qu'un toit *[In French]*; Shelter for homeless women — more than just a roof overhead *[Summary]*. Guylaine Racine. *San. Ment. Qué* **XVI:**2 Automne:1991 pp. 67 – 88

249 Measuring changes in poverty — a methodological case study of Indonesia during an adjustment period. Martin Ravallion; Monika Huppi. *W.B. Econ. R.* **5:**1 1:1991 pp. 57 – 82

250 Measuring the intensity of poverty among subpopulations — applications to the United States. John L. Rodgers; Joan R. Rodgers. *J. Hum. Res.* **XXVI:**2 Spring:1991 pp. 338 – 361

251 Minority poverty in nonmetropolitan Texas. Rogelio Saenz; John K. Thomas. *Rural Sociol.* **56:**2 Summer:1991 pp. 204 – 223

252 Moderne armoede — feit en fictie *[In Dutch]*; Modern poverty — fact and fiction *[Summary]*. Godfried Engbersen. *Sociol. Gids* **XXXVIII:**1 1-2:1991 pp. 7 – 23

253 The new homeless — the crisis of youth homelessness and the reponse of the local housing authorities. Rosy Thornton. London: SHAC, 1990: 86 p. *ISBN: 094885748x.*

K.1: Social problems *[Problèmes sociaux]* — *Poverty [Pauvreté]*

254 "New" structural poverty? Jimy M. Sanders. *Sociol. Q.* **32:2** Summer:1991 pp. 179 – 199

255 On the demography of South Asian famines part II. Tim Dyson. *Pop. Stud. Egy.* **45:2** 7:1991 pp. 279 – 298

256 Pauvreté santé mentale et stratégies d'existence *[In French]*; [Poverty, mental health and existence strategies] *[Summary]*. Louise Blais; Lorraine Guay. *San. Ment. Qué* **XVI:1** 6:1991 pp. 117 – 138

257 Peasants in distress — poverty and unemployment in the Dominican Republic. Rosemary Vargas-Lundius. Boulder: Westview Press, 1991: xxi, 387 p. (ill., map) *ISBN: 0813379725; LofC: 90032923. Includes bibliographical references (p. [353]-369) and index.* [Series in political economy and economic development in Latin America.]

258 People, plans, and policies — essays on poverty, racism, and other national urban problems. Herbert J Gans. New York: Columbia University Press, 1991: 383 p. *ISBN: 0231074026; LofC: 90023224. Includes bibliographical references and index.* [Columbia history of urban life.]

259 Persistent poverty — the American dream turned nightmare. Richard H. Ropers; Wayne K. Hinton *[Foreword]*. New York: Plenum Press, c1991: xvi, 251 p. (ill) *ISBN: 0306437643; LofC: 91000014. "Insight books"; Includes bibliographical references and index.*

260 The physical and mental health status of homeless adults. Deborah L. Dennis; Irene S. Levine; Fred C. Osher. *Hous. Pol. Deb.* **2:3** 1991 pp. 815 – 836

261 Las poblaciones marginales en el Perú *[In Spanish]*; [Marginalized people in Peru]. Oscar Gómez Peralta. [Lince]: E.F. Gómez e hijos, 1990: 198 p. (ill., maps, ports) *ISBN: oc22066654. Includes bibliographical references.*

262 La pobreza en América Central *[In Spanish]*; [Poverty in Central America]. Rafael Menjívar; Juan Diego Trejos S. *[Ed.]*. San José, Costa Rica: FLACSO, 1990: 146 p. (ill) *ISBN: 9977680183; LofC: 91146951. Includes bibliographical references (p. 131-140).*

263 A poor apart — the distancing of homeless men in New York's history. Kim Hopper. *Soc. Res.* **58:1** Spring:1991 pp. 107 – 132

264 The poor in ASEAN cities — perspectives in health care management. Trinidad S. Osteria *[Ed.]*. Singapore: Institute of Southeast Asian Studies, 1991: x, 186 p. (ill) *ISBN: 9813035765. eng.*

265 The poor in the inner city — stability and change in two Parisian neighborhoods. Paul White; Hilary P.M. Winchester. *Urban Geogr.* **12:1** 1-2:1991 pp. 35 – 54

266 Poverty alleviation programmes in rural India — an assessment. Raghav Gaiha. *Develop. Cha.* **22:1** 1:1991 pp. 117 – 54

267 Poverty amidst affluence — Britain and the United States. Victor George; Irving Howards. Aldershot: Edward Elgar, c1991: ix, 206 p. (ill) *ISBN: 1852783370; LofC: 91009952. Includes bibliographical references and index.*

268 Poverty and health — working with families. Clare Blackburn. Milton Keynes [England]: Open University Press, 1991: 170 p. *ISBN: 0335097359; LofC: 91021914. Inlcudes index.*

269 Poverty and income distribution. K. S. Krishnaswamy *[Ed.]*. Bombay: Oxford University Press for Sameeksha Trust, 1990: viii, 420 p. *ISBN: 019562680x.*

270 Poverty and the distribution of income in Northern Ireland. Pat P.L. McGregor; Vani K. Borooah. *Econ. Soc. R.* **22:2** 1:1991 pp. 81 – 100

271 Poverty in Palanpur. Peter Lanjouw; Nicholas Stern. *W.B. Econ. R.* **5:1** 1:1991 pp. 23 – 55

272 Poverty measurement and the within-household distribution — agenda for action. Stephen P. Jenkins. *J. Soc. Pol.* **20:4** 10:1991 pp. 457 – 484

273 Poverty monitoring in the rural sector. Hamid Tabatabai. Geneva: International Labour Office, 1991: 51 p. *ISBN: 9221082407.* [World Employment Programme research working papers.]

274 Predicting chronic homelessness. Robert J. Calsyn; Gary A. Morse. *Urban Aff. Q.* **27:1** 9:1991 pp. 155 – 164

275 Public transfers — safety net or inducement into poverty. Jimy M. Sanders. *Soc. Forc.* **68:3** 3:1990 pp. 813 – 834

276 Reducing poverty. L. Salmen. *Publ. Admin.* **11:3** 5-6:1991 pp. 295 – 302

277 Relationele onbekwaamheid van thuislozen? *[In Dutch]*; Social incompetence of the homeless? *[Summary]*. Frans Spierings. *Sociol. Gids* **38:6** 11-12:1991 pp. 414 – 423

278 Resiliency and vulnerability to adverse developmental outcomes associated with poverty. Norman Garmezy. *Am. Behav. Sc.* **34:4** 3/4:1991 pp. 416 – 430

279 Running away during adolescence as a precursor to adult homelessness. Ronald L. Simons; Les B. Whitbeck. *Soc. Ser. R.* **65:2** 06:1991 pp. 224 – 247

K.1: Social problems *[Problèmes sociaux]* — Poverty *[Pauvreté]*

280 Saving children at risk — poverty and disabilities. Travis Thompson *[Ed.]*; Susan C. Hupp *[Ed.]*. Newbury Park: Sage Publications, 1991: xiii, 190 p. (ill) *ISBN: 0803939671; LofC: 91010630*. Includes bibliographical references and index. [Sage focus editions. : No. 131]

281 Secondary earner strategies and family poverty — immigrant-native differentials, 1960-1980. Leif Jensen. *Int. Migr. Rev.* **XXV:1** Spring:1991 pp. 113 – 140

282 Sobre la pobreza en España, 1965-1990 *[In Spanish]*; [On poverty in Spain, 1965-1990]. Demetrio Casado. Barcelona: Editorial Hacer, c1990: 285 p. (ill) *ISBN: 8485348796; LofC: 91193008*. Includes bibliographical references.

283 Social science research and problem of poverty. Tarlok Singh *[Ed.]*. New Delhi: Concept Publishing, 1990: 468 p. *ISBN: 8170222311*.

284 Socio-demographic changes, income distribution, and poverty. Bea Cantillon. *Bevolk. Gez.* **:1** 1991 pp. 95 – 122

285 The spatial organization of the urban homeless — a case study of Chicago. Charles Hoch. *Urban Geogr.* **12:2** 3-4:1991 pp. 137 – 154

286 Les statuts de la pauvreté assistée *[In French]*; The status of assisted poverty *[Summary]*; Die Statuten der unterstützten Armut *[German summary]*; Los estatutos de la probeza socorrida *[Spanish summary]*. Serge Paugam. *Rev. Fr. Soc.* **XXXII:1** 1-3:1991 pp. 75 – 101

287 Street kids — the tragedy of Canada's runaways. Marlene Webber. Toronto: University of Toronto Press, 1991: xi, 261 p. (ill) *ISBN: 0802057896; LofC: cn 90095663*. Includes bibliographical references.

288 Structural determinants of homelessness in the United States. Marta Elliott; Lauren J. Krivo. *Soc. Prob.* **38:1** 2:1991 p. 113

289 Szegénység a mai Magyarországon *[In Hungarian]*; [Poverty in contemporary Hungary]. Ágnes Bokor. Budapest: Magvető, 1987: 281 p.

290 The underclass in the United States. Katherine O'Sullivan See *[Contrib.]*; Kathryn M. Neckerman *[Contrib.]*; Joleen Kirschenman *[Contrib.]*; James E. Rosenbaum *[Contrib.]*; Susan J. Popkin *[Contrib.]*; Julie E. Kaufman *[Contrib.]*; Jennifer Rusin *[Contrib.]*; Kathryn Edin *[Contrib.]*; Paul Osterman *[Contrib.]*; Anne M. Santiago *[Contrib.]* and others. Collection of 9 articles. *Soc. Prob.* , *38:4*, 11:1991 pp. 427 – 561

291 Urban homelessness — an agenda for research. Jennifer R. Wolch. *Urban Geogr.* **12:2** 3-4:1991 pp. 99 – 104

292 The urban underclass and the poverty paradox. Paul E. Peterson. *Pol. Sci. Q.* **106:4** Winter:1991-1992 pp. 617 – 638

293 Welfare and poverty in the Europe of the 1990s — social progress or social dumping? Peter E. Abrahamson. *Int. J. Health. Ser.* **21:2** 1991 pp. 237 – 264

294 Wherever I lay my hat — young women and homelessness. Jane Dibblin. London: Shelter, 1991: 101 p. (ill) *ISBN: 1870767101*.

295 Women, health and poverty — an introduction. Sarah Payne. London: Harvester Wheatsheaf, 1991: 236 p. *ISBN: 0745008747*.

Substance abuse *[Usage des stupéfiants]*

296 А.А. — Анонимные алкоголики *[In Russian]*; (Alcoholics Anonymous).*Sot. Issle.* **:5** 1991 pp. 123 – 132

297 Adolescent perceptions of help-seeking resources for substance abuse. Michael Windle; Carol Miller-Tutzauer; Grace M. Barnes; John Welte. *Child. Devel.* **62:1** 2:1991 pp. 179 – 189

298 Advertising, price, income and publicity effects on weekly cigarette sales in New Zealand supermarkets; Effets de la publicité, des prix et de la réclame sur les venteshebdomadaires de cigarettes dans les supermarchés néo- zelandais *[French summary]*; Efectos de la publicidad, el precio y los ingresos en las ventas semanales de cigarrillos en los supermercados de Nueva Zelanda *[Spanish summary]*. Murray Laugesen; Chris Meads. *Br. J. Addict.* **86:1** 1:1991 pp. 83 – 89

299 Alcohol and alcohol problems research 16. Northern Ireland; Revue de presse internationale — recherches sur l'alcool et les problèmes d'alcool — Irlande du Nord *[French summary]*; Series de revision internacionales — alcohol e investigación en problemas alcoholicos — Irlanda del Norte *[Spanish summary]*. Robin Davidson. *Br. J. Addict.* **86:7** 7:1991 pp. 829 – 835

300 Alcohol and drug use in a Scottish cohort — 10 years on; Consommation d'alcool et de drogue dans une cohorte en Ecosse sur 10 ans *[French summary]*; Consumo de alcohol y drogas en una cohorte escocesa — a lo largo de 10 años *[Spanish summary]*. Gellisse Bagnall. *Br. J. Addict.* **86:7** 7:1991 pp. 895 – 904

K.1: Social problems [Problèmes sociaux] — Substance abuse [Usage des stupéfiants]

301 Alcohol and other drug problems among the homeless — research, practice, and future directions. James Baumohl; Robert B. Huebner. *Hous. Pol. Deb.* **2:3** 1991 pp. 837 – 868

302 Alcohol education and young offenders — medium and short term effectivenss of education programs. Steve Baldwin. New York: Springer-Verlag, c1991: ix, 152 p. *ISBN: 0387975071; LofC: 90025252. Includes bibliographical references (p. 137-152).* [Recent research in psychology.]

303 Alcohol in America — drinking practices and problems. Walter B. Clark *[Ed.]*; Michael E. Hilton *[Ed.]*. Albany: State University of New York Press, c1991: xi, 380 p. *ISBN: 0791406954; LofC: 90045048. Includes bibliographical references (p. 351-370) and index.* [SUNY series in new social studies on alcohol and drugs.]

304 Alcohol in human violence. Kai Pernanen; Dwight B. Heath *[Ed.]*. New York: Guilford, 1991: xiii, 280 p. (ill) *ISBN: 0898621712; LofC: 91016338. Includes bibliographical references (p. 259-272) and index.* [The Guilford substance abuse series.]

305 Alcohol problems among women in a general hospital ward; Problèmes d'alcool parmi les femmes d'un pavillon d'hôpital général *[French summary]*; Problemas relacionados con el alcohol entre mujeres ingresadas en una sala de un hospital general *[Spanish summary]*. Hazel E. Watson; Peter W. Kershaw; John B. Davies. *Br. J. Addict.* **86:7** 7:1991 pp. 889 – 894

306 Alcohol problems and relapse — can the clinic combat the community. B. Saunders; S. Allsop. *J. Comm. App. Soc. Psychol.* **1:3** 9:1991 pp. 213 – 222

307 Alcohol, social factors and mortality among young men; Alcool, facteurs sociaux et mortalité chez les hommes jeunes *[French summary]*; Alcohol, factores sociales y mortalidad entre hombres jovenes *[Spanish summary]*. Sven Andréasson; Anders Romelsjö; Peter Allebeck. *Br. J. Addict.* **86:7** 7:1991 pp. 877 – 887

308 Alcoholism and memory — broadening the scope of alcohol-expectancy research. Mark S. Goldman; Sandra A. Brown; Bruce A. Christiansen; Gregory T. Smith. *Psychol .B.* **110:1** 7:1991 pp. 137 – 146

309 Alcoholism, antisocial behavior and family history; *[French summary]*; *[Spanish summary]*. Collins E. Lewis; Kathleen K. Bucholz. *Br. J. Addict.* **86:2** 2:1991 pp. 177 – 194

310 Alcoholism, drug abuse, and the homeless. Dennis McCarty; Milton Argeriou; Robert B. Huebner; Barbara Lubran. *Am. Psychol.* **46:11** 11:1991 pp. 1139 – 1148

311 Beneficiaries of the illicit drug trade — political consequences and international policy at the intersection of supply and demand. LaMond Tullis. Geneva: United Nations Research Institute for Social Development, [1991]: ii, 33 p. (ill) *ISBN: oc24273205. "March 1991."; Includes bibliographical references (p. 17-33).* [Discussion paper.]

312 Beware the first drink! — the Washington temperance movement and Alcoholics Anonymous. Leonard U. Blumberg; William Pittman. Seattle, Wash: Glen Abbey Books, c1991: xxi, 278 p. *ISBN: 0934125228; LofC: 90019639. Includes bibliographical references (p. [261]-273) and index.*

313 Cannabis psychosis following bhang ingestion; Psychoses au cannabis secondaires à l'ingestion de bhang *[French summary]*; Zpsicosis cannabica tras una ingestión de bhang *[Spanish summary]*. Haroon Rashid Chaudry; Howard B. Moss; Amir Bashir; Tahir Suliman. *Br. J. Addict.* **86:9** 9:1991 pp. 1075 – 1081

314 The case for legalizing drugs. Richard Lawrence Miller. New York: Praeger, 1991: xi, 247 p. *ISBN: 0275934594; LofC: 90007379. Includes bibliographical references (p. [215]-241) and index.*

315 Changes in the use of drugs among Norwegian youth year by year from 1968 to 1989; Changements dans la consommation de drogues parmi le jeunes Norvégiens année par année de 1968 à 1989 *[French summary]*; Cambios anuales en el consumo de drogas entre la juventud Noreuga, desde 1968 hasta 1989 *[Spanish summary]*. Olav Irgens-Jensen. *Br. J. Addict.* **86:11** 11:1991 pp. 1449 – 1458

316 Changes over time in heroin and cocaine use among injecting drug users in Amsterdam, The Netherlands, 1985-1989; Evolution dans la consommation d'héroïne et de cocaïne parmi les toxicomanes intraveineux à Amsterdam, aux Pays-Bas 1985-1989 *[French summary]*; Cambios a largo plazo en el consumo de heroina y cocaina entre consumidores de drogas inyectadas en Amsterdam, Holanda, 1985-1989 *[Spanish summary]*. Christina Hartgers; Anneke van den Hoek; Pieta Krijnen; Giel H.A. van Brussel; Roel A. Coutinho. *Br. J. Addict.* **86:9** 9:1991 pp. 1091 – 1097

317 Changing cocaine smoking rituals in the Dutch heroin addict population; *[French summary]*; *[Spanish summary]*. Jean-Paul C. Grund; Nico F.P. Adriaans; Charles D. Kaplan. *Br. J. Addict.* **86:4** 4:1991 pp. 439 – 448

K.1: Social problems [Problèmes sociaux] — Substance abuse [Usage des stupéfiants]

318 The Chinese laundry — international drug trafficking and Hong Kong's banking industry. Mark S. Gaylord. *Cr. Law Soc. Chan.* **14:1** 3:1990 pp. 23 – 37

319 Clinical testing of drug abuse liability. Jordi Camí *[Ed.]*; Fernando García Alonso *[Contrib.]*; Frank J. Vocci *[Contrib.]*; Jack H. Mendelson *[Contrib.]*; Robert L. Balster *[Contrib.]*; Donald R. Jasinski *[Contrib.]*; Marian W. Fischman *[Contrib.]*; Richard W. Foltin *[Contrib.]*; Jack E. Henningfield *[Contrib.]*; Caroline Cohen *[Contrib.] and others. Collection of 20 articles.* **Br. J. Addict.** , *86:12*, 12:1991 pp. 1525 – 1652

320 La coca nostra *[In Spanish]*; [Our cocaine]. Fabio Castillo. Bogotá: Editorial Documentos Periodísticos, 1991: 347p. *ISBN: 9589515525*.

321 Coca-Cocaina — entre el derecho y la guerra — politica criminal de la droga en los paises andinos *[In Spanish]*; [Coca-cocaine — between law and war criminal policies in the Andes drugs war]. Juan Bustos Ramirez. Barcelona: PPU, 1990: 146 p. *ISBN: 8476657617.* [Derecho y estado.]

322 Cocaine today — its effects on the individual and society. Francesco Bruno *[Ed.]*. [Rome]: UNICRI, 1991: 419 p. (ill. (some col.)) *ISBN: 9290780185. Includes bibliographical references.* [Publication.]

323 Coherence of the dependence syndrome in cocaine users; Cohérence du syndrome de dépendance chez les consommateurs de cocaine *[French summary]*; La coherencia del síndrome de dependencia en consumidores de cocaina *[Spanish summary]*. Kendall J. Bryant; Bruce J. Rounsaville; Thomas F. Babor. *Br. J. Addict.* **86:10** 10:1991 pp. 1299 – 1310

324 Confronting drug policy — part 1. Ronald Bayer *[Contrib.]*; Denise B. Kandel *[Contrib.]*; William Kornblum *[Contrib.]*; Charles Winick *[Contrib.]*; Harry G. Levine *[Contrib.]*; Craig Reinarman *[Contrib.]*; Gerald M. Oppenheimer *[Contrib.]. Collection of 6 articles.* **Milbank Q.** , *69:3*, 1991 pp. 341 – 526

325 Confronting drug policy — part 2. Mark H. Moore *[Contrib.]*; Lawrence O. Gostin *[Contrib.]*; Patricia A. King *[Contrib.]*; Robert J. Levine *[Contrib.]*; Kenneth E. Warner *[Contrib.]. Collection of 5 articles.* **Milbank Q.** , *69:4*, 1991 pp. 529 – 661

326 Contextual factors related to the drinking behaviors of American business and professional women; *[French summary]*; *[Spanish summary]*. Elsie R. Shore; Steve Batt. *Br. J. Addict.* **86:2** 2:1991 pp. 171 – 176

327 Crack — the broken promise. David Allen; James F. Jekel. London: Macmillan, 1991: 115 p. *ISBN: 0333499727. Includes index.*

328 Criminal justice responses to crack. Steven Belenko; Jeffrey Fagan; Ko-Lin Chin. *J. Res. Crim. Delin.* **28:1** 02:1991 pp. 55 – 74

329 The cue-responsivity phenomenon in dependent drinkers — "personality" vulnerability and anxiety as intervening variables; Le phénomène signal-réponse chez les buveurs dépendants — personnalité vulnérable et anxiété intervenant comme variables *[French summary]*; Capacidad de respuesta a estimulos condicionados en alcohlicos. Personalidad vulnerable y ansiedad como variables asociadas *[Spanish summary]*. C.G. McCusker; K. Brown. *Br. J. Addict.* **86:7** 7:1991 pp. 905 – 912

330 Demographic characteristics of cigarette smokers in the United States. Richard G. Rogers. *Soc. Biol.* **38:1-2** Spring-Summer:1991 pp. 1 – 12

331 Determinants of teenage smoking, with special reference to non-standard family background; *[French summary]*; *[Spanish summary]*. Matti Isohanni; Irma Moilanen; Paula Rantakallio. *Br. J. Addict.* **86:4** 4:1991 pp. 391 – 398

332 The development and initial validation of a questionnaire on smoking urges; Développement et validation initiale d'un questionnaire sur les besoins tabagiques *[French summary]*; Desarrollo y validación inicial de un cuestionario sobre el ansia de fumar *[Spanish summary]*. Stephen T. Tiffany; David J. Drobes. *Br. J. Addict.* **86:11** 11:1991 pp. 1467 – 1476

333 Drink-driving and adolescent lifestyles — re-thinking policy. Elim Papadakis; Anya Moore. *Aust. J. Soc. Iss.* **26:2** 5:1991 pp. 83 – 106

334 Drogensucht und Kriminalität in der Sowjetunion *[In German]*; [Drug addiction and criminality in the Soviet Union]. René Ahlberg. *Osteuropa* **40:4** 4:1990 pp. 318 – 335

335 Drogues — le défi hollandais *[In French]*; [Drugs — the Dutch challenge]. Isabelle Stengers; Olivier Ralet *[Ed.]*. Paris: Laboratoires Delagrange, 1991: 117 p. *ISBN: 2908602083.* [Les empêcheurs de penser en rond.]

336 The drug legalization debate. James A. Inciardi *[Ed.]*. Newbury Park, Calif: Sage Publications, c1991: 230 p. (ill) *ISBN: 080393677x; LofC: 90041441. Includes bibliographical references and indexes.* [Studies in crime, law, and justice. : Vol. 7]

K.1: Social problems *[Problèmes sociaux]* — **Substance abuse** *[Usage des stupéfiants]*

337 Drug problems and drug policies in Ireland — a quarter of a century reviewed. Shane Butler. *Administration* **39:3** 1991 pp. 210 – 233
338 Drug-control policies in Britain. Geoffrey Pearson. *Crime Just.* **14** 1991 pp. 167 – 228
339 Drugs and drug policy in the Netherlands. Ed Leuw. *Crime Just.* **14** 1991 pp. 229 – 276
340 Drugs in society — causes, concepts, and control. Michael D. Lyman; Gary W. Potter *[Ed.]*. Cincinnati, Ohio: Anderson Pub. Co, c1991: xiv, 423 p. (ill., maps) *ISBN: 0870845489; LofC: 90084732. Includes bibliographical references (p. 405-412) and index.*
341 Drugs, crime, and social policy — research, issues, and concern. Thomas Mieczkowski *[Ed.]*. Boston: Allyn and Bacon, 1991: xiv, 322 p. (ill) *ISBN: 0205132057; LofC: 91025426. Includes bibliographical references.*
342 L'effet du travail sur la consommation d'alcool et de drogue dans une usine de pâtes et papiers *[In French]*; [The effects of work on alcohol and drug consumption in a pulp and paper plant] *[Summary]*. Marie-France Maranda. *Rech. Soc.graph* **XXXII:1** 1-4:1991 pp. 55 – 68
343 Effetti perversi del proibizionismo *[In Italian]*; [Perverse effects of prohibition]. Giancarlo Arnao. *Volonta* **XLV:1** 5:1991 pp. 49 – 58
344 Employer response to the Drug-free Workplace Act of 1988 — a preliminary look. Donald J. Petersen; Douglas Massengill. *Lab. Law J.* **42:3** 3:1991 pp. 144 – 151
345 Enabling dependent drug users — a cognitive behavioural assessment. Julian Buchanan. *Practice* **5:1** :1991 pp. 34 – 46
346 Environmental economics and the social cost of smoking. Dwight R. Lee. *Cont. Policy* **IX:1** 1:1991 pp. 83 – 92
347 The epidemiology of alcohol, drug, and mental disorders among homeless persons. Pamela J. Fischer; William R. Breakey. *Am. Psychol.* **46:11** 11:1991 pp. 1115 – 1128
348 Estimating hidden populations — a new method of calculating the prevalence of drug-injecting and non-injecting female street prostitution; Evaluer les populations cachées — une nouvelle méthode de calcul de la prévalence de la consommation de drogues injectables chez les femmes prostituées *[French summary]*; La estimacion de poblaciones no controladas — un nuevo metodo para calcular la prevalencia de prostitutas que se inyectan drogas *[Spanish summary]*. Michael Bloor; Alastair Leyland; Marina Barnard; Neil McKeganey. *Br. J. Addict.* **86:11** 11:1991 pp. 1477 – 1483
349 Examining personal control beliefs as a mediating variable in the health-damaging behavior of substance use — an alternative approach. Pamela Carlisle-Frank. *J. Psychol.* **125:4** 7:1991 pp. 381 – 398
350 Explaining racial/ethnic differences in adolescent drug use — the impact of background and lifestyle. John M. Wallace; Jerald G. Bachman. *Soc. Prob.* **38:3** 8:1991 pp. 333 – 357
351 Functioning, life context, and help-seeking among late-onset problem drinkers — comparisons with nonproblem and early-onset problem drinkers; Fonctionnement, contexte de vie et demande d'assistance parmi les buveurs à problèmes tardifs comparés aux non-buveurs et aux buveurs à problèmes précoces *[French summary]*; Funcionamiento, contexto vital y busqueda de ayuda entre bebedores problemáticos tardios. Comparaciones con bebedores no problemáticos y con problematicas precoces *[Spanish summary]*. Penny L. Brennan; Rudolf H. Moos. *Br. J. Addict.* **86:9** 9:1991 pp. 1139 – 1150
352 Gender differences in drinking motivations and outcomes. Rebecca C. Bailly; Roderick S. Carman; Morris A. Forslund. *J. Psychol.* **125:6** 11:1991 pp. 649 – 656
353 Gender roles, suicide attempts, and substance abuse. Silvia S. Canetto. *J. Psychol.* **125:6** 11:1991 pp. 605 – 620
354 Heroin policy and deficit models — the limits of left realism. S.K. Mugford; P. O'Malley. *Cr. Law Soc. Chan.* **15:1** 1:1991 pp. 19 – 36
355 *[In Japanese]*; [Homeless people and alcohol problems]. Shinji Shimizu. *Arukohru Iryo Kenkyu* No.8(1) - 1991. pp. 31 – 35
356 Homeless women with children — the role of alcohol and other drug abuse. Marjorie J. Robertson. *Am. Psychol.* **46:11** 11:1991 pp. 1198 – 1204
357 Homelessness among injecting drug users — implications for the spread of AIDS. H. Klee. *J. Comm. App. Soc. Psychol.* **1:2** 6:1991 pp. 143 – 154
358 How drugs affect decisions by burglars. Paul F. Cromwell; D'Aunn W. Avary; James N. Olson; Alan Marks. *Int. J. Offen.* **35:4** Winter:1991 pp. 310 – 321
359 Identification of alcohol-related problems in a general hospital setting — a cost-effectiveness evaluation; *[French summary]*; *[Spanish summary]*. Keith Tolley; Nancy Rowland. *Br. J. Addict.* **86:4** 4:1991 pp. 429 – 438

K.1: Social problems [Problèmes sociaux] — Substance abuse [Usage des stupéfiants]

360 Illicit drug taking and prohibition laws — public consequences and the reform of public policy in the United States. LaMond Tullis. Geneva: United Nations Research Institute for Social Development, [1991]: 43 p. *ISBN: oc24273308. "April 1991."; Includes bibliographical references (p. 23-43).* [Discussion paper.]

361 Individual and family characteristics of middle class adolescents hospitalized for alcohol and other drug abuse; Caractéristiques individuelles et familiales d'adolescents issus de classe moyenne, hospitalisés pour consommation d'alcool ou d'autres drogues *[French summary]*; Caracteristicas individuales y familiares de adolescentes de clase media hospitalizados por abuso de alcohol y otras drogas *[Spanish summary]*. Irving Maltzman; Avraham Schweiger. *Br. J. Addict.* **86:11** 11:1991 pp. 1435 – 1447

362 Institutional and organizational dynamics in community-based drug abuse treatment. Mark Peyrot. *Soc. Prob.* **38:1** 2:1991 pp. 20 – 33

363 Interpersonal versus technological orientation and alcohol abuse in future physicians; Orientations interpersonnelle et technologique, et abus d'alcool chez les futurs médecins *[French summary]*; Orientaciones interpersonales versus tecnologicas frente al abuso de alcohol en futuros medicos *[Spanish summary]*. Judith A. Richman; Charlene E. Pyskoty. *Br. J. Addict.* **86:9** 9:1991 pp. 1133 – 1138

364 A longitudinal study of New Zealand children's experience with alcohol. Sally Casswell; Joanna Stewart; Gary Connolly; Phil Silva. *Br. J. Addict.* **86:3** 3:1991 pp. 277 – 285

365 La lucha mundial contra la droga, ¿una batalla perdida? *[In Spanish]*; [The global battle against drugs — a lost cause?]. José Paniagua Gil. *Rev. Fom. Soc.* **46:183** 7-9:1991 pp. 247 – 270

366 A meta-analysis of life-course variation in drinking; Une méta-analyse des variations de consommation d'alcool au cours de la vie *[French summary]*; Meta-análisis de las variaciones en la conducta bebedora a lo largo de la vida *[Spanish summary]*. Kaye Middleton Fillmore; Elizabeth Hartka; Bryan M. Johnstone; E. Victor Leino; Michelle Motoyoshi; Mark T. Temple. *Br. J. Addict.* **86:10** 10:1991 pp. 1221 – 1268

367 Needle access as an AIDS prevention strategy for IV drug users — a research perspective. Merrill Singer; Ray Irizarry; Jean J. Schensul. *Human. Org.* **50:2** Summer:1991 pp. 142 – 153

368 Opiate dependents and their babies. Patricia Kearney; Marcelle Ibbetson. *Br. J. Soc. W.* **21:2** 4:1991 pp. 105 – 126

369 Parents noticing teenage drinking — evidence from college freshmen. Celia C. Lo; Gerald Globetti. *Social Soc. Res.* **76:1** 10:1991 pp. 20 – 28

370 Patterns of cocaine use in Australia, 1985-88. Ian McAllister; Toni Makkai. *Aust. J. Soc. Iss.* **26:2** 5:1991 pp. 107 – 122

371 La piste blanche — l'Afrique sous l'emprise de la drogue *[In French]*; [The white trail — Africa under the drug trade]. Eric Fottorino. Paris: Editions Balland, 1991: 174 p. (cartes, graph) *ISBN: 2715808879.*

372 Policing and prescribing — the British system of drug control. David K. Whynes *[Ed.]*; Philip T. Bean *[Ed.]*. London: Macmillan, 1991: 282 p. *ISBN: 033352229x.*

373 Predisposing effects of cigarette advertising on children's intention to smoke when older; *[French summary]*; *[Spanish summary]*. P.P. Aitken; D.R. Eadie; G.B. Hastings; A.J. Haywood. *Br. J. Addict.* **86:4** 4:1991 pp. 383 – 390

374 Problem drinking and family history; Problèmes d'alcool et histoire familiale *[French summary]*; Habitos de bebida problematicos e historia familiar *[Spanish summary]*. Keron D. Fletcher; David K. Price; Christopher C.H. Cook. *Br. J. Addict.* **86:10** 10:1991 pp. 1335 – 1342

375 Punishing drug addicts who have babies — women of color, equality, and the right of privacy. Dorothy E. Roberts. *Harv. Law. Rev.* **104:7** 5:1991 pp. 1419 – 1482

376 Quantity-frequency measures of alcohol consumption — beverage-specific vs global questions; *[French summary]*; *[Spanish summary]*. Marcia Russell; John W. Welte; Grace M. Barnes. *Br. J. Addict.* **86:4** 4:1991 pp. 409 – 418

377 The reduction of drug-related harm. P. A O'Hare *[Ed.]*. London: Routledge, 1991: 214 p. *ISBN: 0415066921; LofC: 91015436. Includes bibliographical references and index.*

378 The relationship between stressful life situations and changes in alcohol consumption in a general population sample; *[French summary]*; *[Spanish summary]*. Anders Romelsjö; Nancy B. Lazarus; George A. Kaplan; Richard D. Cohen. *Br. J. Addict.* **86:2** 2:1991 pp. 157 – 169

K.1: Social problems [Problèmes sociaux] — Substance abuse [Usage des stupéfiants]

379 Sense and nonsense about IQ — the case for uniqueness. C.M. Locurto. New York: Praeger, 1991: xviii, 196 p. (ill) *ISBN: 0275938034; LofC: 90023133. Includes bibliographical references (p. [187]-191) and index.*

380 Sexual lifestyles in injecting drug users in Italy — potential for HIV infection transmission; Pratiques sexuelles parmi les toxicomanes intraveineux en Italie — un potentiel de transmission de l'infection à VIH *[French summary]*; Formas de vida sexual en consumidores de drogas inyectadas en Italia — un potencial para el sida *[Spanish summary]*. Hartmut Sasse; Stefania Salmaso; Susanna Conti; Giovanni Rezza. *Br. J. Addict.* **86:9** 9:1991 pp. 1083 – 1089

381 Shooting dope — career patterns of hard-core heroin users. Charles E. Faupel. Gainesville: Florida University Press, 1991: 220 p. *ISBN: 0813010705.* [American social problems.]

382 Social and cultural preconditions of Alcoholics Anonymous (AA) and factors associated with the strength of AA; Préconditions sociales et culturelles des Alcooliques Anonymes (AA) et facteurs associés à l'activité des AA *[French summary]*; Precondiciones sociales y culturales de los alcoholicos anonimos (AA) y factores asociados a su fuerzo como grupo *[Spanish summary]*. Klaus Mäkelä. *Br. J. Addict.* **86:11** 11·1991 pp. 1405 – 1413

383 Le social saisi par la drogue *[In French]*; [Society in the grip of drugs]. Martine Xiberras *[Contrib.]*; Christian Bachman *[Contrib.]*; Victor Girard *[Contrib.]*; Françoise Gailliard *[Contrib.]*; Chantal Debock *[Contrib.]*; Bruno Tanche *[Contrib.]*; Marc Krawczyk *[Contrib.]*; Laurent Elghozi *[Contrib.]*; Philippe Macquet *[Contrib.]*; Lia Calvalcanti-Tavares *[Contrib.] and others. Collection of 13 articles.* **Inf. Soc.** , :15, 11-12:1991 pp. 4 – 78

384 Gli Stati Uniti contro la droga *[In Italian]*; [The United States against drugs]. Thomas Szasz. *Volonta* **XLV:1** 5:1991 pp. 11 – 28

385 The street addict role — a theory of heroin addiction. Richard C. Stephens. Albany, N.Y: State University of New York Press, c1991: xix, 223 p. *ISBN: 0791406199; LofC: 90039205.* [SUNY series, the new inequalities.]

386 Der Streit um das Rauchen — zur Genese eines Risikokonflikts *[In German]*; The smoking debate — on the origins of a risk conflict *[Summary]*. Karin Stiehr. *Soz. Welt.* **42:4** 1991 pp. 510 – 521

387 Substance use and problems among Toronto street youth; Consommation et problèmes de drogues parmi les adolescents des rues de Toronto *[French summary]*; El consumo de sustancias psicoactivas y sus problemas asociados en la juventud callejera de Toronto *[Spanish summary]*. Reginald G. Smart; Edward M. Adlaf. *Br. J. Addict.* **86:8** 8:1991 pp. 999 – 1010

388 Tráfico y consumo de drogas en el Campo de Gibraltar — estudio criminológico *[In Spanish]*; [Drug traficking and consumption in the Campo de Gibraltar region]. Luis M. Sánchez Tostado. [Cádiz]: Servicio de Publicaciones, Universidad de Cádiz, [1990?]: 290 p. (ill., maps) *ISBN: 8477860173; LofC: 91157398. Includes related legislation; Includes bibliographical references.*

389 Undoing drugs — beyond legalization. Daniel K. Benjamin; Roger LeRoy Miller *[Ed.]*. [New York]: Basic Books, 1991: viii, 296 p. *ISBN: 0465088538; LofC: 91070407. Includes bibliographical references (p. 269-285) and index.*

390 An unwinnable war against drugs — the politics of decriminalisation. Terry Carney; et al. Leichhardt, NSW: Pluto Press Australia, 1991: 73 p. *ISBN: 0949138479.* [Australia, strategies for renewal.]

391 Variations in risk perceptions and smoking decisions. W. Kip Viscusi. *Rev. Econ. St.* **LXXIII:4** 11:1991 pp. 577 – 588

392 The war on drugs — commentary and critique. Mark Rabine *[Contrib.]*; Rosa del Olmo *[Contrib.]*; Pat O'Malley *[Contrib.]*; Stephen Mugford *[Contrib.]*; Edward S. Herman *[Contrib.]*; Henry H. Brownstein *[Contrib.]*; Franklin E. Zimring *[Contrib.]*; Gordon Hawkins *[Contrib.]*; Christina Johns *[Contrib.]*; Elizabeth Martínez *[Contrib.] and others. Collection of 9 articles.* **Soc. Just.** , *18:4*, Winter:1991 pp. 1 – 173

393 Who stopped smoking? Results from a panel survey of living conditions in Sweden. O. Lundberg; B. Rosén; M. Rosén. *Soc. Sci. Med.* **32:5** 1991 pp. 619 – 622

K.1: Social problems [Problèmes sociaux] —

Suicide [Suicide]

394 Effects of socioeconomic factors on secular trends in suicide in Japan, 1953-86. Y. Motohashi. *J. Biosoc. Sc.* **23**:2 4:1991 pp. 221 – 228

395 Gender roles, suicide attempts, and substance abuse. Silvia S. Canetto. *J. Psychol.* **125**:6 11:1991 pp. 605 – 620

396 *[In Japanese]*; [Measuring mutual causation — effects of suicide news on suicides in Japan]. Ken'ichi Ishi'i. *Social Science Research No.(20) - 1991.* pp. 188 – 195

397 Prodromal states of suicide — thoughts on the death of Ann France. Nini Herman. *Free Assoc.* **2:22** 1991 pp. 249 – 258

398 Social images of suicide. Realino Marra; Marco Orrù. *Br. J. Soc.* **42**:2 6:1991 pp. 273 – 288

399 The social structure of suicide. Peter S. Bearman. *Sociol. For.* **6**:3 9:1991 pp. 501 – 524

400 Suicide in rural areas — the case of Japan 1960- 1990. Satomi Kurosu. *Rural Sociol.* **56**:4 Winter:1991 pp. 603 – 618

401 Triage model for suicidal runaways. Mary Jane Rotheram-Borus; John Bradley. *Am. J. Orthopsy.* **61**:1 1:1991 pp. 122 – 127

402 Zur Interpretation suizidalen Verhaltens im Kontext sozialer und politischer Ursachen — auf dem Hintergrund sozialer Erfahrungen in der DDR *[In German]*; Towards the interpretation of suicidal behaviour in the context of social and political factors — on the background of former developments in the G.D.R. *[Summary]*. D. Belau. *Medi. Mensch Gesell.* **16**:4 12:1991 pp. 276 – 284

Violence [Violence]

403 Adaptability and cohesion — implications for understanding the violence-prone system. Ron F. Lehr; George Fitzsimmons. *J. Fam. Viol.* **6**:3 9:1991 pp. 255 – 265

404 Anthropological versus sociological approaches to the study of soccer hooliganism — some critical notes. Eric Dunning; Patrick Murphy; Ivan Waddington. *Sociol. Rev.* **39**:3 8:1991 pp. 459 – 478

405 Australian violence — contemporary perspectives. Duncan Chappell *[Ed.]*; Peter Grabosky *[Ed.]*; Heather Strang *[Ed.]*. Canberra: Australian Institute of Criminology, 1991: 325 p. (ill) *ISBN: 0642157634; LofC: 91205925. Includes bibliographical references (p. [303]-320) and index.*

406 The boy done good — football violence, changes and continuities. Dick Hobbs; David Robins. *Sociol. Rev.* **39**:3 8:1991 pp. 551 – 580

407 Corporal punishment and adult use of violence — a critique of "discipline and deviance". Demie Kurz. *Soc. Prob.* **38**:2 5:1991 pp. 155 – 161

408 Courtship violence and social control — does gender matter? Susan L. Miller; Sally S. Simpson. *Law Soc. Rev.* **25**:2 1991 pp. 335 – 366

409 Deadly connections — culture, poverty, and the direction of lethal violence. Lin Huff-Corzine; Jay Corzine; David C. Moore. *Soc. Forc.* **69**:3 3:1991 pp. 715 – 732

410 Deadly consequences — how violence is destroying our teenage population and a plan to begin solving the problem. Deborah Prothrow-Stith; Michaele Weissman. New York, N.Y: HarperCollins, c1991: xviii, 269 p. *ISBN: 0060163445; LofC: 90055938. Includes bibliographical references (p. 204-225) and index.*

411 The effects of weaponry on human violence. Gary Kleck; Karen McElrath. *Soc. Forc.* **69**:3 3:1991 pp. 669 – 692

412 Elder abuse — major issues from a national perspective. Blossom T. Wigdor. Ottawa: National Advisory Council on Aging, 1991: 17, 19 p. *ISBN: 0662581571; LofC: ce 91072519. Text in English and French with French text on inverted pages — La violence faite aux aînées, une perspective nationale; Includes bibliographical references — p. 14 (1st group).* [Forum collection.]

413 An eye for an eye? A note on the southern subculture of violence thesis. Christopher G. Ellison. *Soc. Forc.* **69**:4 6:1991 pp. 1223 – 1240

414 Football hooligans — old bottle, new whines? H.F. Moorhouse. *Sociol. Rev.* **39**:3 8:1991 pp. 489 – 502

415 Football hooligans — theory and evidence. Gary Armstrong; Rosemary Harris. *Sociol. Rev.* **39**:3 8:1991 pp. 427 – 458

416 The geometry of violence and democracy. Harold Eugene Pepinsky. Bloomington: Indiana University Press, c1991: xii, 139 p. *ISBN: 0253343437; LofC: 90004704. Includes bibliographical references (p. [133]-139).*

K.1: Social problems *[Problèmes sociaux]* — *Violence [Violence]*

417 Hostility and stress as mediators of aggression in violent men. Ola W. Barnett; Ronald W. Fagan; Jolyne M. Booker. *J. Fam. Viol.* **6:3** 9:1991 pp. 217 – 241

418 Innovations in the policing of domestic violence in London, England. J. Sheptycki. *Poli. Soc.* **2:2** 1991 pp. 117 – 138

419 Overcoming endemic violence against women in South Africa. Lloyd Vogelman; Gillian Eagle. *Soc. Just.* **18:1-2** Spring-Summer:1991 pp. 209 – 229

420 People and violence in South Africa. Brian McKendrick *[Ed.]*; Wilma Hoffmann *[Ed.]*. Oxford: Oxford University Press, 1991: 495 p. *ISBN: 0195705815*. [Contemporary South African debates.]

421 Perceptions of domestic violence against women — a cross-cultural survey of international students. Elisabeth Reichert. *Resp. Victim. Women Child.* **14:1(78)** 1991 pp. 13 – 18

422 Point blank — guns and violence in America. Gary Kleck. New York: A. de Gruyter, c1991: xv, 512 p. (ill) *ISBN: 0202304191; LofC: 91016780*. Includes bibliographical references (p. 477-505) and index. [Social institutions and social change.]

423 Priming aggressive thoughts — the effect of the anticipation of a violent movie upon the aggressive behaviour of the spectators. J.-P. Leyens; M. Dunand. *Eur. J. Soc. Psychol.* **21:6** 11-12:1991 pp. 507 – 516

424 Punishment and violence. Murray A. Straus *[Contrib.]*; Demie Kurz *[Contrib.]*; Donileen R. Loseke *[Contrib.]*; Joan Mccord *[Contrib.]*; Robert M. Emerson *[Contrib.]*; Lisa Frohmann *[Contrib.]*; Phillip W. Davis *[Contrib.]*; Celesta A. Albonetti *[Contrib.]*; Martha A. Myers *[Contrib.]*; James L. Massey *[Contrib.] and others. Collection of 11 articles.* **Soc. Prob.**, *38:2*, 5:1991 pp. 133 – 296

425 The sex ratio, family disruption, and rates of violent crime — the paradox of demographic structure. Steven F. Messner; Robert J. Sampson. *Soc. Forc.* **69:3** 3:1991 pp. 693 – 713

426 Some reflections on discourses on football hooliganism. Steve Redhead. *Sociol. Rev.* **39:3** 8:1991 pp. 479 – 488

427 The technology of personal violence. Philip J. Cook. *Crime Just.* **14** 1991 pp. 1 – 72

428 Things change — trends in Austrian football hooliganism from 1977-1990. Roman Horak. *Sociol. Rev.* **39:3** 8:1991 pp. 531 – 548

429 Violence against lesbians and gay men. Gary Comstock. New York: Columbia University Press, 1991: 319 p. *ISBN: 0231073305; LofC: 90047126*. Includes bibliographical references and index. [Between men--between women.]

430 Violent heights in an Andean community of Southern Peru; *[French summary]*. Christiane Paponnet-Cantat. *Can. R. Soc. A.* **28:3** 8:1991 pp. 340 – 356

K.2: Social security — *Sécurité sociale*

Sub-divisions: Child care *[Aide à l'enfance]*; Welfare services *[Services de bien-être]*

1 Algunas sugerencias para la investigación en políticas sociales *[In Spanish]*; [Some suggestions for research in social policy]. Dolores María Refian Lizana. *Rev. Parag. Sociol.* **28:80** 1-4:1991 pp. 7 – 22

2 The bigger the better? On the dimensions of welfare state development. Olli Kangas. *Acta Sociol.* **34:1** 1991 pp. 33 – 44

3 Cash and caring in Brugge. Patrick Moenaert. *Soc. Pol. Admin.* **25:3** 9:1991 pp. 202 – 210

4 The confluence of sociology, statistics and public policy in the quality control of the food stamps, AFDC, and Medicaid family assistance programs. S. James Press; Judith M. Tanur. *Eval. Rev.* **15:3** 6:1991 pp. 315 – 332

5 Expanding urban homesteading — lessons from the local property demonstration. William M. Rohe. *J. Am. Plann.* **57:4** Autumn:1991 pp. 444 – 455

6 Exploring the "need" for family centres. J.R. Fells; S. de Gruchy. *Br. J. Soc. W.* **21:2** 4:1991 pp. 173 – 184

7 Filtering in socialist housing systems — results of vacancy chain surveys in Hungary. József Hegedüs; Ivan Tosics. *Urban Geogr.* **12:1** 1-2:1991 pp. 19 – 34

8 From "bringing" to "putting" — the state in late twentieth-century social theory. Rianne Mahon. *Can. J. Soc.* **16:2** Spring:1991 pp. 119 – 144

9 The future of basic and supplementary pension schemes in the European Community — 1992 and beyond. Winfried Schmähl *[Ed.]*. Baden Baden: Nomos Verlagsgesellschaft, 1991: 269 p. *ISBN: 3789024910.*

K.2: Social security [Sécurité sociale]

10 Housing costs and subsidies in the Glasgow travel-to-work-area. Karen Hancock; et al. York: Joseph Rowntree Foundation, 1991: 117 p.
11 Implementation of social policy revisited. Yeheskel Hasenfeld; Thomas Brock. *Admin. Soc.* **22:4** 2:1991 pp. 451 – 479
12 Informal care of the dependent elderly at home — some Swedish experiences. Lennarth Johansson. *Age. Soc.* **11:1** 3:1991 pp. 41 – 58
13 Local programs designed to address the homelessness crisis — a comparative assessment of the United States, Canada, and Britain. Gerald Daly. *Urban Geogr.* **12:2** 3-4:1991 pp. 177 – 193
14 Lone parent families in the UK. Jonathan Bradshaw; Jane Millar. London: HMSO, 1991: vii, 101 p. *ISBN: 0117618683*. [Research report.]
15 Middle axioms in social policy in Australia. Michael Horsburgh. *Soc. Pol. Admin.* **25:2** 6:1991 pp. 121 – 135
16 The new German Children and Young People Act. Walter Lorenz. *Br. J. Soc. W.* **21:4** 8:1991 pp. 329 – 340
17 Problems and treatment of the aged among the plain Bhuiyans of Orissa. D.K. Behera; M. Parida; S.S. Mohanty. *Soc. Act.* **41:4** 10-12:1991 pp. 428 – 441
18 Les régimes de sécurité sociale du travailleur migrant africain *[In French]*; [Social security systems for migrant African workers]]. Raymond Lemesle. Paris: CHEAM, 1991: 126 p. *ISBN: 2903182329. Bibliography — p.127.* [Notes africaines, asiatiques et caraïbes.]
19 Russia, before the coup and after. Andrzej Walicki. *Crit. Rev.* **5:1** Winter:1991 pp. 1 – 35
20 La sécurité sociale face a l'Europe de 1992 *[In French]*; [Social security facing the Europe of 1992]. Herman Deleeck. *Droit Soc.* **2** 2:1991 pp. 166 – 176
21 Siting ambulances and fire companies — new tools for planners. Charles Revelle. *J. Am. Plann.* **57:4** Autumn:1991 pp. 471 – 484
22 *[In Japanese]*; [Social change as diffusion phenomenon — a case study of social security system]. Teruya Oda. ***Nen. Shak. Ron.*** *No.(4) - 1991.* pp. 129 – 141
23 Social policy and social security in Australia, Britain and the USA. Helen Bolderson. Aldershot, Hants: Avebury, 1991: 196 p. *ISBN: 1856282120.*
24 Social security in the 1980s. Ruth Lister. *Soc. Pol. Admin.* **25:2** 6:1991 pp. 91 – 107
25 *[In Japanese]*; [Social support for the elderly — the concept and its measurement]. Yuji Noguchi. ***Social Gerontology*** *No.(34) - 1991.* pp. 37 – 48
26 The sociology of social security. Michael Adler *[Ed.]*. Edinburgh: Edinburgh University Press, 1991: 288 p. *ISBN: 0748602585.* [Edinburgh education and society series.]
27 Soziale Sicherung im EG-Binnenmarkt — Aufgaben und Probleme aus deutscher Sicht *[In German]*; [Social security in the single European market — challenges and problems from the German perspective]. Winfried Schmähl *[Ed.]*. Baden-Baden: Nomos, 1990: 205 p. (ill) *ISBN: 3789021911.*
28 States, labor markets, and the future of old age policy. John Myles *[Ed.]*; Jill S. Quadagno *[Ed.]*. Philadelphia: Temple University Press, 1991: 324 p. *ISBN: 087722790x; LofC: 91009678. Includes bibliographical references and index.*
29 Support for income maintenance benefits — attitudes of a group of non-recipients. T.C. Puckett. *Aust. J. Soc. Iss.* **26:2** 5:1991 pp. 138 – 152
30 Transorganizational development in urban policy coalitions. David W. Sink. *Human Relat.* **44:11** 11:1991 pp. 1179 – 1195
31 Возможен ли социальный дизэйн? *[In Russian]*; Is a social design possible? I.V. Bestuzhev-Lada. *Sot. Issle.* **:5** 1991 pp. 84 – 91
32 Welfare rights work into the 1990s — a changing agenda. Pete Alcock; Jane Shepherd; Gill Stewart; John Stewart. *J. Soc. Pol.* **20:1** 1:1991 pp. 41 – 63
33 Who cares for the elderly? — public policy and the experiences of adult daughters. Emily K Abel. Philadelphia: Temple University Press, 1991: viii, 220 p. *ISBN: 0877228140; LofC: 90011244. Includes bibliographical references (p. 185-208) and index.* [Women in the political economy.]
34 Zoning, rent control, and affordable housing. William Tucker. Washington, D.C: Cato Institute, c1991: 72 p. (ill) *ISBN: 093279078x; LofC: 91029205. Includes bibliographical references.*

K.2: Social security *[Sécurité sociale]* —

Child care *[Aide à l'enfance]*

35 Access to school daycare services — class, family, ethnicity and space in Montreal's old and inner city. D. Rose; N. Chicoine. *Geoforum* **22:2** 1991 pp. 185 – 202
36 Age structure and public expenditures on children. Scott J. South. *Soc. Sci. Q.* **72:4** 12:1991 pp. 661 – 675
37 Caring for troubled children in Flanders, the Netherlands, and the United Kingdom. Matthew Colton; Walter Hellinckx; Roger Bullock; Benedikte van den Bruel. *Br. J. Soc. W.* **21:4** 8:1991 pp. 381 – 392
38 Caseload dynamics and foster care reentry. Fred Wulczyn. *Soc. Ser. R.* **65:1** 3:1991 pp. 133 – 156
39 Child care policies and programs — an international overview. Sheila B. Kamerman. *J. Soc. Issues* **47:2** 1991 pp. 179 – 196
40 Child care policy research. Sandra L. Hofferth; Deborah A. Phillips. *J. Soc. Issues* **47:2** 1991 pp. 1 – 13
41 Child care policy research. Sandra L. Hofferth *[Contrib.]*; Deborah A. Phillips *[Contrib.]*; Freya L. Sonenstein *[Contrib.]*; Douglas A. Wolf *[Contrib.]*; Linda J. Waite *[Contrib.]*; Arleen Leibowitz *[Contrib.]*; Christina Witsberger *[Contrib.]*; Carollee Howes *[Contrib.]*; Marcy Whitebook *[Contrib.]*; Mary Culkin *[Contrib.] and others. Collection of 11 articles.* **J. Soc. Issues**, *47:2,* 1991 pp. 1 – 196
42 Child care utilization by disadvantaged teenage mothers. Ellen Eliason Kisker; Marsha Silverberg. *J. Soc. Issues* **47:2** 1991 pp. 159 – 177
43 Child protection law. Linda Feldman. London: Longman, 1991: 302 p. *ISBN: 0851218024.*
44 Childcare in a modern welfare system — towards a new national policy. Bronwen Cohen; Neil Fraser. London: Institute for Public Policy Research, 1991: 134 p.
45 Childcare in rural communities — Scotland in Europe. Julia Palmer. Edinburgh: HMSO, 1991: 129 p. *ISBN: 0114941572.*
46 The Children Act — looking forward, looking back. Jean Packman; Bill Jordan. *Br. J. Soc. W.* **21:4** 8:1991 pp. 315 – 328
47 Custodianship — caring for other people's children. Emma Bullard; Ellen Malos *[Ed.]*; R. A. Parker *[Ed.]*. London: HMSO, 1991: xi, 251 p. *ISBN: 0113213484.*
48 Developing outcome measures in child care. Harriet Ward; Sonia Jackson. *Br. J. Soc. W.* **21:4** 8:1991 pp. 393 – 399
49 The effect of child support enforcement on child support payments. A.H. Beller; J.W. Graham. *Pop. Res. Pol. R.* **10:2** 1991 pp. 91 – 116
50 Estimating nonresponse and response bias — resident and nonresident parents, reports about child support. Nora Cate Schaeffer; Judith A. Seltzer; Marieka Klawitter. *Sociol. Meth.* **210:1** 8:1991 pp. 30 – 59
51 Examining profit and nonprofit child care — an odyssey of quality and auspices. Sharon L. Kagan. *J. Soc. Issues* **47:2** 1991 pp. 87 – 104
52 Family preservation services — research and evaluation. David E. Biegel *[Ed.]*; Kathleen Wells *[Ed.]*. Newbury Park, CA: Sage, 1991: 261 p. *ISBN: 0803935153; LofC: 90024568. Includes bibliographical references.* [Sage focus editions.]
53 Foster care policy and permanency — an analysis of the context for practice. Jan Mason. *Aust. J. Soc. Iss.* **26:4** 12:1991 pp. 242 – 256
54 Governing the family — child care, child protection and the state. Nigel Parton. London: Macmillan Education, 1991: 251 p. *ISBN: 0333541219. Includes bibliography and index.*
55 Irish child care services — policy, practice and provision. Robbie Gilligan. Dublin: Institute of Public Administration, 1991: 263 p.
56 Models of school-age child care — a review of current research on implications for women and their children. Michelle Seligson. *Wom. St. Inter. For.* **14:6** 1991 pp. 577 – 584
57 Parental leave and child care — setting a research and policy agenda. Janet Shibley Hyde *[Ed.]*; Marilyn Essex *[Ed.]*. Philadelphia: Temple University Press, 1991: 511 p. *ISBN: 0877227322.* [Women in the political economy.]
58 Patterns & outcomes in child placement — messages from current research and their implications. Wendy Rose *[Ed.]*; Jane Rowe *[Ed.]*. London: HMSO, 1991: 138 p. *ISBN: 0113213573.*
59 Perspectives in child care policy. Lorraine Fox Harding. Harlow: Longman, 1991: xiii, 246 p. *ISBN: 0582083451. Bibliography — pp.235-241.-Includes index.*
60 Quality and the true cost of child care. Mary Culkin; John R. Morris; Suzanne W. Helburn. *J. Soc. Issues* **47:2** 1991 pp. 71 – 86

K.2: Social security *[Sécurité sociale]* — **Child care** *[Aide à l'enfance]*
61 Researching childcare in a multi-ethnic society. Berry Mayall. *New Comm.* **17:4** 7:1991 pp. 553 – 568
62 A review of risk factors assessed in child protective services. Thomas McDonald; Jill Marks. *Soc. Ser. R.* **65:1** 3:1991 pp. 112 – 132
63 Romania's poor orphans — civil and information societies. Peter Gross. *Media Cult. Soc.* **13:3** 7:1991 pp. 407 – 413
64 Satisfaction with child care — perspectives of welfare mothers. Freya L. Sonenstein; Douglas A. Wolf. *J. Soc. Issues* **47:2** 1991 pp. 15 – 31
65 School-age child care in the Western northern hemisphere. Pat Petrie *[Ed.]*; Ria Meijvogel *[Ed.]*; Uta Enders-Dragässer *[Ed.]*; Peter Moss *[Contrib.]*; Janet Read *[Contrib.]*; Christine Orton *[Contrib.]*; Michelle Seligson *[Contrib.]*; Bronwen Cohen *[Contrib.]*; Hettie A. Pott-Buter *[Contrib.]*; Jytte Juul Jensen *[Contrib.]* *and others. Collection of 10 articles.* **Wom. St. Inter. For.** , *14:6,* 1991 pp. 525 – 612
66 The social policy contents of prevention in child care. Pauline Hardiker; Ken Exton; Mary Barker. *Br. J. Soc. W.* **21:4** 8:1991 pp. 341 – 360
67 A voice for children — speaking out as their ombudsman. Malfrid Grude Flekkoy. London: Jessica Kingsley Publishers, 1991: 249 p. *ISBN: 1853021199.*
68 What parents pay for — child care characteristics, quality, and costs. Linda J. Waite; Arleen Leibowitz; Christina Witsberger. *J. Soc. Issues* **47:2** 1991 pp. 33 – 48
69 Who pays for the children? — a first look at the operation of Australia's new child support scheme. Margaret Harrison; Gregg Snider *[Ed.]*; Rosangela Merlo *[Ed.]*. Melbourne, Australia: Australian Institute of Family Studies, c1990: xvi, 166 p. (ill) *ISBN: 0642154805; LofC: 91154995. Includes bibliographical references (p. 163-166).* [Monograph.]

Welfare services *[Services de bien-être]*
70 *[In Japanese]*; [About-face on the way of welfare thinking]. Nobuhiro Ito. **Ann. Rep. Shiz., Hamam. Coll.** *No.(5) - 1991.* pp. 21 – 36
71 Care for elderly people in Ireland. Bob Carroll. *Soc. Pol. Admin.* **25:3** 9:1991 pp. 238 – 248
72 Care for elderly people in the European Community. Jean-Claude Henrard. *Soc. Pol. Admin.* **25:3** 9:1991 pp. 184 – 192
73 The CDEP scheme — administrative and policy issues. Jon Altman; Will Sanders. *Aust. J. Publ.* **50:4** 12:1991 pp. 515 – 525
74 Change in local authority services for the elderly in England, 1979-88. K. Hoggart; T.A. Smith. *Envir. Plan.A.* **23:12** 12:1991 pp. 1741 – 1757
75 The costs and benefits of social support in families. Elizabeth B. Robertson; Glen H. Elder; Martie L. Skinner; Rand D. Conger. *J. Marriage Fam.* **53:2** 5:1991 pp. 403 – 416
76 The creation and development of social welfare in the Nordic countries. Guy Backman. Abo, Finland: Abo Akademi, 1991: 48 p. *ISBN: 9516498310.* [Meddelanden fran ekonomisk-statsvetenskapliga fakulteten vid Abo Akademi. Socialpolitiska institutionen.]
77 Distributive mechanisms of the welfare state — a formal analysis and an empirical application. Rune Åberg. *Eur. Sociol. R.* **5:2** 9:1989 pp. 167 – 182
78 Evictions in the welfare state — an unintended consequence of the Swedish policy? Sten-Åke Stenberg. *Acta Sociol.* **34:2** 1991 pp. 103 – 114
79 A gyermekek után járó arányos, esélyegyenlő és értékállandó családtámogatás kialakításának egy lehetséges módja *[In Hungarian]*; A possible way of developing a proportionate, equal chances and constant value system of assistance to families with children *[Summary]*. László Szabó. *Demográfia* **XXXIII:1-2** 1990 pp. 95 – 109
80 The ideology of "age/race wars" — deconstructing a social problem. Meredith Minkler; Ann Robertson. *Age. Soc.* **11:1** 3:1991 pp. 1 – 22
81 Immigrants, natives, and the French welfare state — explaining different interactions with a social welfare program. Jeremy Hein. *Int. Migr. Rev.* **XXV:3** Fall:1991 pp. 592 – 609
82 Individualisering en bereidheid om hulp te geven *[In Dutch]*; Individualization and the attitude to social support *[Summary]*. Bart Gubbels; Alphons A.M. Fiselier; Harry J.M. Hüttner. *Sociol. Gids* **XXXVIII** 9-10:1991 pp. 324 – 342
83 Making the most of a case study — theories of the welfare state and the American experience. Edwin Armenta. *Int. J. Comp. Soc* **XXXII: 1-2** 1-4:1991 pp. 172 – 194
84 The moral construction of poverty — welfare reform in America. Joel F. Handler; Yeheskel Hasenfeld *[Ed.]*. Newbury Park, Calif: Sage Publications, 1991: 269 p. *ISBN: 0803941978; LofC: 91006939. Includes bibliographical references.*

K.2: Social security *[Sécurité sociale]* — Welfare services *[Services de bien-être]*

85 The myth of the Woopie? Incomes, the elderly and targeting welfare. Jane Falkingham; Christina Victor. *Age. Soc.* **11:4** 12:1991 pp. 471 – 493

86 Una politica sanitaria e sociale a favore degli anziani *[In Italian]*; [A health and social policy favourable to the aged]. A. Ardigò *[Contrib.]*; M. Marotta *[Contrib.]*; G. Chiapella *[Contrib.]*; M. Trabucchi *[Contrib.]*; M.L. Maniscalco *[Contrib.]*; A. Bartoli *[Contrib.]*; G. Nervo *[Contrib.]*; F. Fabris *[Contrib.]*; G. Vecchi *[Contrib.]*; S. Burgalassi *[Contrib.]* and others. Collection of 3 articles. **Sociologia [Rome]**, *XXV:1*, :1991 pp. 5 – 110

87 The politics of welfare policy in Sweden — structural determinants and attitudinal cleavages. Stefan Svallfors. *Br. J. Soc.* **42:4** 12:1991 pp. 609 – 634

88 Poor citizens — the state and the poor in twentieth century Britain. David Vincent. New York: Longman, 1991: 258 p. *ISBN: 0582494699*. [Studies in modern history.]

89 Power to the people — the key responsive services in health & social care. Liz Winn *[Ed.]*. London: Kings Fund, 1990: 92 p.

90 Los problemas de la seguridad social española *[In Spanish]*; [Problems of social security in Spain]. Ma. de la Concepción González Rabanal. Madrid: Tecnos, c1990: 175 p. (ill) *ISBN: 8430919430; LofC: 91154219. Includes bibliographical references (p. 171-175).*

91 The radical right and the welfare state — an international assessment. Howard Glennerster *[Ed.]*; James Midgley *[Ed.]*. Hemel Hempstead: Harvester Wheatsheaf, 1991: 224 p. *ISBN: 0745009778.* [Studies in international social policy and welfare.]

92 Une remise en cause de la démocratie dans la gestion de la sécurité sociale? *[In French]*; [A reduction of democracy in social welfare management]. Jean Bordeloup. *Droit Soc.* :**6** 6:1991 pp. 528 – 536

93 Restructuring Canada's welfare state. Ernie Lightman; Allan Irving. *J. Soc. Pol.* **20:1** 1:1991 pp. 65 – 86

94 The rise of the ideas of the welfare state. Judith Buber Agassi. *Philos. S. Sc.* **21:4** 12:1991 pp. 444 – 457

95 Social policy and social work — critical essays on the welfare state. Robert Moroney. New York: Aldine de Gruyter, c1991: xiii, 257 p. (ill) *ISBN: 020236061x; LofC: 90049124. Includes bibliographical references (p. 239-249) and indexes.* [Modern applications of social work.]

96 Social policy and the European Commission. Graham Room. *Soc. Pol. Admin.* **25:3** 9:1991 pp. 175 – 183

97 Social services and the ageing population. Raymond Jack. *Soc. Pol. Admin.* **25:4** 12:1991 pp. 284 – 299

98 The social services perspective. Jim Carlton. *Child. Soc.* **5:1** Spring:1991 pp. 21 – 27

99 Social welfare in India. H.Y. Siddiqui *[Ed.]*. New Delhi: Harnam Publications, 1990: 261 p. *ISBN: 8185247056.*

100 Social welfare services for Israel's Arab population. Aziz Haidar. Boulder: Westview Press, 1991: xiii, 175 p. *ISBN: 0813377609; LofC: 89025078.* "*Published in cooperation with the International Center for Peace in the Middle East, Tel Aviv*"--P. [ii]; *Includes bibliographical references (p. [163]-168) and index.* [Westview special studies on the Middle East.]

101 The state and social welfare — the objectives of policy. Thomas Wilson *[Ed.]*; Dorothy Wilson *[Ed.]*. London: Longman, 1991: 311 p. *ISBN: 0582085136; LofC: 91011335. Chiefly papers presented at a workshop, held Jan. 1989, University College, Oxford; Includes bibliographical references and index.*

102 Subsidiarity in social services in Germany. Dirk Jarré. *Soc. Pol. Admin.* **25:3** 9:1991 pp. 211 – 217

103 Surviving the welfare system — how AFDC recipients make ends meet in Chicago. Kathryn Edin. *Soc. Prob.* **38:4** 11:1991 pp. 462 – 474

104 Unprotected by the Swedish welfare state — a survey of battered women and the assistance they received. R. Amy Elman; Maud L. Eduards. *Wom. St. Inter. For.* **14:5** :1991 pp. 413 – 421

105 Volunteers in welfare. Cora V. Baldock. North Sydney, NSW: Allen & Unwin, 1990: 171 p. *ISBN: 004442213x.* [Studies in society.]

106 Welfare durations and the marriage market — evidence from survey of income and program participation. John Fitzgerald. *J. Hum. Res.* **XXVI:3** Summer:1991 pp. 545 – 561

107 Welfare participation in a full employment economy. Paul Osterman. *Soc. Prob.* **38:4** 11:1991 pp. 475 – 491

108 The welfare state in Israel — the evolution of social security policy and practice. Avraham

K.2: Social security *[Sécurité sociale] — Welfare services [Services de bien-être]*
Doron; Ralph M. Kramer *[Ed.]*. Boulder, Colo: Westview Press, 1991: xiv, 194 p. *ISBN: 0813380553; LofC: 91022137. Includes bibliograpbhical references and index.* [Westview special studies on the Middle East.]
109 What is a family? Benefit models and social realities. Jo Roll. London: Family Policy Studies Centre, 1991: 98 p. *ISBN: 0907051596.*
110 When the bough breaks — the cost of neglecting our children. Sylvia Ann Hewlett. New York, NY.: Basic Books, c1991: x, 346 p. (ill) *ISBN: 0465091652; LofC: 90055663. Includes bibliographical references (p. 285-327) and index.*
111 The world of social welfare — social welfare and services in an international context. Doreen Elliott; Nazneen S. Mayadas; Thomas D. Watts. Springfield, Ill., U.S.A: Charles C. Thomas, c1990: xviii, 309 p. (ill) *ISBN: 0398057109; LofC: 90011218. Includes bibliographical references and index.*

K.3: Social work — *Travail social*

1 A 24 hour duty system — using practitioner research to manage the stress. Helen Masson; Tony Morrison. *Br. J. Soc. W.* **21:4** 8:1991 pp. 361 – 372
2 AIDS and social work in Africa. Helen Jackson. *J. Soc. Devel. Afr.* **6:1** 1991 pp. 47 – 62
3 Anti-discriminatory and anti-oppressive practice. Pat Taylor *[Contrib.]*; Mark Baldwin *[Contrib.]*; Wynetta Devore *[Contrib.]*; Margaret Boushel *[Contrib.]*. Collection of 4 articles. **Soc. Work. Ed.** , *10:3*, 1991 pp. 5 – 69
4 Case finding and screening for social work in acute general hospitals. Paul Bywaters. *Br. J. Soc. W.* **21:1** 2:1991 pp. 19 – 39
5 Client access to records — participation in social work. David Shemmings. Aldershot: Avebury, 1991: 400 p. *ISBN: 1856281078.*
6 Competencies and values. Bill Jordan. *Soc. Work. Ed.* **10:1** 1991 pp. 5 – 10
7 Crossing the frontiers — a discussion of some of the implications of integrating community work and child protection. Jennifer Sayer; Kathleen Heaton. *App. Commun. Stud.* **1:1** 1991 pp. 39 – 63
8 Description of a course model designed to develop advanced practice skills in supervision and consultation for qualified and experienced staff. Celia Downes; Jenny Smith. *Soc. Work. Ed.* **10:1** 1991 pp. 30 – 47
9 The development of therapeutic consultations in child-focused family work. Eddy Street; Jim Downey; Anna Brazier. *J. Fam. Ther.* **13:3** 8:1991 pp. 311 – 334
10 Discourse analysis and social relationships in social work. John J. Rodger. *Br. J. Soc. W.* **21:1** 2:1991 pp. 63 – 79
11 Drawing the line — life, death, and ethical choices in an American hospital. Samuel Gorovitz. New York: Oxford University Press, 1991: xiv, 195 p. *ISBN: 0195044282; LofC: 90007089. Includes bibliographical references (p. 187-188) and index.*
12 Efficiency,economy and the quality of care. Colin Palfrey; Ceri Phillips; Paul Thomas. Norwich: Social Work Monographs, 1991: 37 p. (ill) *ISBN: 0946751803. Bibliography — p.36-37.* [Social work monographs. : No. 95]
13 Enhancing the durability of intervention gains — a challenge for the 1990s. Tina L. Rzepnicki. *Soc. Ser. R.* **65:1** 3:1991 pp. 92 – 111
14 Ethnically sensitive social work — the obstacle race. Brendah Malahleka; Sylvia Woolfe. *Practice* **5:1** :1991 pp. 47 – 64
15 Families in crisis — the impact of intensive family preservation services. Mark W. Fraser *[Ed.]*; Peter J. Pecora *[Ed.]*; David Haapala *[Ed.]*. New York: A. de Gruyter, c1991: xiv, 354 p. (ill) *ISBN: 0202360695; LofC: 91006430. Includes bibliographical references and index.* [Modern applications of social work.]
16 Feminist social work practice in clinical settings. Nancy R. Hooyman *[Ed.]*; Naomi Gottlieb *[Ed.]*; Mary Bricker-Jenkins *[Ed.]*. Newbury Park: Sage Publications, c1991: xi, 308 p. *ISBN: 0803936257; LofC: 90027897. Includes bibliographical references.* [Sage sourcebooks for the human services series. : No. 19]
17 From values to rights in social work. Nina Biehal; Eric Sainsbury. *Br. J. Soc. W.* **21:3** 6:1991 pp. 245 – 258
18 Group counseling with juvenile delinquents — the limit and lead approach. Matthew L. Ferrara. Newbury Park, CA: Sage Publications, 1991: xi, 156 p. (ill) *ISBN: 0803938853; LofC: 91007627. "Published in cooperation with the University of Michigan School of Social Work."; Includes bibliographical references.* [Sage human service guides. : Vol. 65]

K.3: Social work *[Travail social]*

19 Groupwork with offenders. Allan Brown *[Ed.]*; Brian Caddick *[Ed.]*; Marion Jones *[Contrib.]*; Mary Mordecai *[Contrib.]*; Frances Rutter *[Contrib.]*; Linda Thomas *[Contrib.]*; Judith Earnshaw *[Contrib.]*; Kathryn Hutchins *[Contrib.]*; Catherine Mulvie *[Contrib.]*; Jane Mackintosh *[Contrib.] and others. Collection of 9 articles.* **Groupwork**, **4**:3, 1991 pp. 197 – 299

20 Joint police and social worker investigations in child abuse — a practice example from Central Scotland. Colin Findlay. *Child. Soc.* **5**:3 Autumn:1991 pp. 225 – 231

21 Keeping families together — the homebuilders model. Jill Kinney; David Haapala *[Ed.]*; Charlotte Booth *[Ed.]*. New York: A. de Gruyter, c1991: xi, 235 p. *ISBN: 0202360679; LofC: 90019973. Includes bibliographical references (p. 227-230) and index.* [Modern applications of social work.]

22 The long reach of childhood; *[French summary]*; *[Spanish summary]*. J. McCord. *Ann. Inter. Crimin.* **29**:1&2 1991 pp. 89 – 96

23 Male youth prostitution — perspectives, policy and practice. Claire Foster. Norwich: University of East Anglia, 1991: 44 p. *ISBN: 0946751862.* [Social work monographs. : No. 100]

24 A model for learning — some notes from a practice teacher training programme. L. Humphreys; J. Morton. *Soc. Work. Ed.* **10**:1 1991 pp. 48 – 61

25 Monitoring interventions with young Israeli families. Rami Benbenishty; Anat Ben-Zaken; Hanna Yekel. *Br. J. Soc. W.* **21**:2 4:1991 pp. 143 – 155

26 Moral reasoning in social work practice. Ann Fleck-Henderson. *Soc. Ser. R.* **65**:2 06:1991 pp. 185 – 202

27 On acquiring law competence for social work — teaching, practice and assessment. Suzie Braye; Michael Preston-Shoot. *Soc. Work. Ed.* **10**:1 1991 pp. 12 – 29

28 Organization and professionalism — the social work agenda in the 1990s. Richard Hugman. *Br. J. Soc. W.* **21**:3 6:1991 pp. 199 – 216

29 Parole and its problems — a Canadian-English comparison. Natalie Polvi; Ken Pease. *Howard J. Crim. Just.* **30**:3 8:1991 pp. 218 – 230

30 Post-abortion adjustment of health care professionals in training. Jeanne Parr Lemkau. *Am. J. Orthopsy.* **61**:1 1:1991 pp. 92 – 102

31 Power in caring professions. Richard Hugman. London: Macmillan, 1991: 250 p. *ISBN: 0333498550.*

32 The referral process — a study of working relationships between antenatal clinic nursing staff and hospital social workers and their impact on Asian women. Randhir Auluck; Paul Iles. *Br. J. Soc. W.* **21**:1 2:1991 pp. 41 – 61

33 The rise of the therapeutic state. Andrew Joseph Polsky. Princeton, New Jersey: Princeton University Press, c1991: x, 287 p. *LofC: 91009363; ISBN: 0691078785 (alk. paper). Includes bibliographical references (p. [225]-281) and index.* [The city in the twenty-first century book series.]

34 Self-determination — lessons to be learned from social work practice in India. Farida Kassim Ejaz. *Br. J. Soc. W.* **21**:2 4:1991 pp. 127 – 142

35 Sibling groups and social work — a study of children referred for permanent substitute family placement. Peter Wedge; Greg Mantle. Aldershot: Avebury, c1991: ix, 96 p. *ISBN: 1856281957. Bibliography — p.85-90. Includes index.*

36 Social change & social welfare practice. Judy Petruchenia *[Ed.]*; Rosamund Thorpe *[Ed.]*. Sydney, NSW: Hale & Iremonger, c1990: 217 p. *ISBN: 086806386x; LofC: 91170029. Includes bibliographical references (p. 197-211) and index.*

37 Social prevention and the social sciences — theoretical controversies, research problems, and evaluation strategies. Günter Albrecht *[Ed.]*; Hans-Uwe Otto *[Ed.]*. Berlin: Walter de Gruyter, 1991: xii, 638 p. (ill) *ISBN: 3110123878; LofC: 91030026. Includes bibliographical references and indexes.* [Prevention and intervention in childhood and adolescence.]

38 Social work and the European Community — the social policy and practice contexts. Malcolm Hill *[Ed.]*. London: Jessica Kingsley, 1991: 208 p. *ISBN: 1853020915.* [Research highlights in social work. : No. 23]

39 Social work practice in health care. Mieke Badawi *[Ed.]*; Brenda Biamonti *[Ed.]*. New York: Woodhead-Faulkner, 1990: 199 p. *ISBN: 0859416496; LofC: gb 90029679.*

40 Social work practice in Zimbabwe. Eddie Kaseke. *J. Soc. Devel. Afr.* **6**:1 1991 pp. 33 – 45

41 Social work, modernity and post modernity. Graham B. McBeath; Stephen A. Webb. *Sociol. Rev.* **39**:4 11:1991 pp. 745 – 764

K.3: Social work *[Travail social]*

42 Social workers, old women and female carers — feminist reflections on the relevance of gender. Catherine Rees. Norwich: Social Work Monographs, 1991: 40 leaves *ISBN: 0946751846. Bibliography — p.37-39.* [Social work monographs. : No. 99]
43 Sozialarbeit in Europa *[In German]*; [Social work in Europe]. Claus Mühlfeld *[Ed.]*; et al. Neuweid: Luchterhand, 1990: - *ISBN: 3472004967.* [Brennpunkte sozialer Arbeit.]
44 Stressors and strains amongst social workers — demands, supports, constraints, and psychological health. Fiona Jones; Ben C. Fletcher; Keith Ibbetson. *Br. J. Soc. W.* **21:**5 10:1991 pp. 443 – 470
45 Towards a new sociology of social work. Roger Sibeon. Aldershot, Hants, England: Avebury, 1991: 188 p. *ISBN: 1856280284; LofC: 90028098.*
46 Training in AIDS/HIV counselling in India. Indira Kapoor; Kamini Puthran. *Indian J. Soc. W.* **LII:**2 4:1991 pp. 137 – 150
47 Volunteers as witnesses — the mobilization of AIDS volunteers in New York City, 1981-1988. Susan M. Chambré. *Soc. Ser. R.* **65:**4 12:1991 pp. 531 – 547
48 What is probation? Phyllida Parsloe. *Soc. Work. Ed.* **10:**2 1991 pp. 50 – 59

K.4: Health care — *Soins médicaux*

Sub-divisions: Community care *[Garde communitaire]*; Geriatrics *[Gériatrie]*; Health economics *[Économie de la santé]*; Health policy *[Politique sanitaire]*; Medical ethics *[Code déontologique médical]*

1 Adapting to the social fund. Meg Huby; Robert Walker. *Soc. Pol. Admin.* **25:**4 12:1991 pp. 329 – 349
2 Afro Caribbeans and schizophrenia — how does psychiatry deal with issues of race, culture and ethnicity? Caroline Knowles. *J. Soc. Pol.* **20:**2 4:1991 pp. 173 – 190
3 "Between a rock and a hard place" — women's professional organizations in nursing and class, racial, and ethnic inequalities. Nona Y. Glazer. *Gender Soc.* **5:**3 9:1991 pp. 351 – 372
4 Boundary encroachment and task delegation — clinical pharmacists on the medical team. Mark A. Mesler. *Sociol. Health Ill.* **13:**3 9:1991 pp. 310 – 331
5 Changing perspectives in the study of the social role of medicine. David Mechanic. *Milbank Q.* **69:**2 1991 pp. 215 – 232
6 Characteristics of physicians practicing in alternative primary care settings — a Quebec study of local community service center physicians. Raynald Pineault; Brigitte Maheux; Jean Lambert; François Béland; Anne Lévesque. *Int. J. Health. Ser.* **21:**1 1991 pp. 49 – 58
7 Chemical deception — the toxic threat to health and the environment. Marc Lappé. San Francisco: Sierra Club Books, c1991: xiv, 360 p. (ill) *ISBN: 0871566036; LofC: 90009043. Includes bibliographical references (p. 270-333) and index.*
8 CHESS — providing decision support for reducing health risk behavior and improving access to health services. Kris Bosworth; David H. Gustafson. *Interfaces* **21:**3 5-6:1991 pp. 93 – 104
9 Childhood living conditions, health status, and social mobility — a contribution to the health selection debate. Olle Lundberg. *Eur. Sociol. R.* **7:**2 9:1991 pp. 149 – 161
10 Clinical issues in mental health service delivery to refugees. Elizabeth Gong-Guy; Richard B. Cravens; Terence E. Patterson. *Am. Psychol.* **46:**6 6:1991 pp. 642 – 648
11 Communicating to promote health. Gary L. Kreps *[Contrib.]*; Charles Atkin *[Contrib.]*; John C. McGrath *[Contrib.]*; William J. Brown *[Contrib.]*; Byron R. Reeves *[Contrib.]*; John Newhagen *[Contrib.]*; Edward Maibach *[Contrib.]*; Michael Basil *[Contrib.]*; Kathleen Kurz *[Contrib.]*; Leigh Arden Ford *[Contrib.]* and others. Collection of 9 articles. *Am. Behav. Sc.*, *34:*6, 7-8:1991 pp. 648 – 767
12 Communication between Spanish-speaking patients and their doctors in medical encounters. Sharry Erzinger. *Cult. Medic. Psych.* **15:**1 3:1991 pp. 91 – 110
13 Community genetics services in Europe — report on a survey. Bernadette Modell; A. M. Kuliev; M. Wagner. Copenhagen, Denmark: World Health Organization, Regional Office for Europe, 1991: x, 137 p. (ill) *ISBN: 928901301x. Includes bibliographical references (p. 123-132).* [WHO regional publications.]
14 Community participation in health — a case study of the World Health Organisation's Healthy Cities Project in Barcelona and Sheffield. Lesley Karen Smith. *Comm. Dev. J.* **26:**2 4:1991 pp. 112 – 117

K.4: Health care [Soins médicaux]

15 The cultural geography of health care. Wilbert M. Gesler. Pittsburgh, Pa: University of Pittsburgh Press, c1991: ix, 245 p. (ill., maps) *ISBN: 082293664x; LofC: 90044299 //r91*. Includes bibliographical references (p. 219-240) and index.

16 The development of high technology and its medical applications in Cuba. Manuel Limonta Vidal; Guillermo Padrón. *Lat. Am. Pers.* **18:2**(69) Spring: 1991 pp. 101 – 112

17 A disaggregation model of a flexible nurse scheduling support system. Irem Ozkarahan. *Socio. Econ.* **25:1** 1991 pp. 9 – 26

18 Distributive effects of location — government hospitals in Ibadan. S.I. Okafor. *Area* **23:2** 6:1991 pp. 128 – 135

19 Dwuinstancyjne postępowanie sądowe w sprawach ubezpieczeń społecznych a problem ustalania inwalidztwa (wybrane zagadnienia) *[In Polish]*; (Двуинстанцийное судопроизводство по делам социальных обеспечений и проблема определения инвалидности (избранные вопросы): *Title only in Russian*); (Two-instance legal proceedings in issues regarding social services and the problem of ascertainment of disability). Jan Brol. *Pra. Zab. Społ.* **33:1** 1:1991 pp. 9 – 18

20 Economic crisis, structural adjustment, and health in Africa. Francois Pathé Diop; Ken Hill; Ismail Abdel-Hamid Sirageldin. Washington, D.C.: Population and Human Resources Department, the World Bank, 1991: 74 p. (ill) *BNB. 92126623, LofC. 92126623*. Cover title; "September 1991."; Includes bibliographical references (p. 52-54). [Policy, research, and external affairs working papers.]

21 The effect of population density on welfare participation. Thomas A. Hirschl; Mark R. Rank. *Soc. Forc.* **70:1** 9:1991 pp. 225 – 235

22 The effects on formalization on departments of a multi-hospital system. Robert W. Hetherington. *J. Manag. Stu.* **28:2** 3:1991 pp. 103 – 141

23 Emerging themes in the history of medicine. Allan M. Brandt. *Milbank Q.* **69:2** 1991 pp. 199 – 214

24 L'enfance en danger. 1. Les professionnels *[In French]*; [Children in danger. 1. The professionals]. Pierre Grelley *[Contrib.]*; Jacqueline Rubellin-Devichi *[Contrib.]*; Hervé Hamon *[Contrib.]*; Michel Allaix *[Contrib.]*; Dominique Barthe *[Contrib.]*; Patrick Tillie *[Contrib.]*; Claire Batton *[Contrib.]*; Frédérique Gruyer *[Contrib.]*; Pierre Bourreau *[Contrib.]*; Françoise Corvazier *[Contrib.]* and others. Collection of 14 articles. **Inf. Soc.**, *1*, 1-2:1990 pp. 2 – 83

25 Estimation concerns for family level analysis in national longitudinal health care surveys. S.B. Cohen. *J. Econ. Soc.* **17:2** 1991 pp. 57 – 68

26 Evaluating referral and agency coordination with a computerized client-tracking system. Russell G. Schuh; Laura C. Leviton. *Eval. Rev.* **15:5** 10:1991 pp. 533 – 554

27 An evaluation of a developing community mental health service. Jackie Powell; Robin Lovelock *[Ed.]*. Southampton: Centre for Evaluative & Developmental Research, Department of Social Work Studies, University of Southampton, 1991: xi, 170 p. *ISBN: 0854323899.*

28 Evaluation of behavioral demand models of consumer choice in health care. Kris Siddharthan. *Eval. Rev.* **15:4** 8:1991 pp. 455 – 470

29 Evaluation of outreach as a project element. Laura C. Leviton; Russell G. Schuh. *Eval. Rev.* **15:4** 8:1991 pp. 420 – 440

30 Examining doctors — medicine in the 1990s. Donald Gould. London: Faber, 1991: x, 148 p. *ISBN: 0571143601.*

31 Examining the world of the depressed — do depressed people prefer others who are depressed? Abram Rosenblatt; Jeff Greenberg. *J. Pers. Soc. Psychol.* **60:4** 4:1991 pp. 620 – 629

32 Explaining variations in hospital death rates — randomness, severity of illness, quality of care. Rolla Edward Park *[Ed.]*. Santa Monica, CA: Rand, 1991: xvi, 110 p. (ill) *ISBN: 0833010980; LofC: 90009213*. Includes bibliographical references (p. 107-110).

33 Factors influencing the use of health evaluation research in Congress. John F. Boyer; Laura I. Langbein. *Eval. Rev.* **15:5** 10:1991 pp. 507 – 532

34 Family caregiving — autonomous and paternalistic decision making. Victor G. Cicirelli. Newbury Park, CA: Sage Publications, 1991: xii, 252 p. *ISBN: 080393906x; LofC: 91011256*. Includes bibliographical references and index. [Sage library of social research. : Vol. 186]

35 "A fit person to be removed" — personal accounts of life in a mental deficiency institution. Maggie Potts; Rebecca Fido *[Ed.]*. Plymouth: Northcote House Publishers, 1991: 128 p. *ISBN: 074630580x.*

K.4: Health care *[Soins médicaux]*

36 General practice, social work, and mental health sections — the social control of women. Michael Sheppard. *Br. J. Soc. W.* **21:6** 12:1991 pp. 663 – 684

37 The genetics of mental illness. Barbara A. Cornblatt *[Contrib.]*; Richard S.E. Keefe *[Contrib.]*; Kenneth K. Kidd *[Contrib.]*; Miron Baron *[Contrib.]*; Anne S. Bassett *[Contrib.]*; Jeremy M. Silverman *[Contrib.]*; Larry J. Siever *[Contrib.]*. Collection of 5 articles. **Soc. Biol.**, *38:3-4*, Fall-Winter:1991 pp. 1 – 218

38 Gesundheit und Gesellschaft in der DDR *[In German]*; Health and society in the GDR. A. Schuller *[Contrib.]*; K. Volpp *[Contrib.]*; J. Düllings *[Contrib.]*; P. Wiesenhütter *[Contrib.]*; P. Apelt *[Contrib.]*. Collection of 4 articles. **Medi. Mensch Gesell.**, *61:1*, 3:1991 pp. 1 – 33

39 The health and social functions of black midwives on the Texas Brazos Bottom, 1920-1985. Ruth C. Schaffer. *Rural Sociol.* **56:1** Spring:1991 pp. 89 – 105

40 Health and social services. Mark R.D. Johnson. *New Comm.* **17:4** 7:1991 pp. 624 – 632

41 Health behavior, health knowledge, and schooling. Donald S. Kenkel. *J. Polit. Ec.* **99:2** 4:1991 pp. 287 – 305

42 Health care for Asians. Brian R. McAvoy *[Ed.]*; L. J. Donaldson *[Ed.]*. Oxford: Oxford University Press, 1990: 331p. (ill(some col.)) *ISBN: 0192617338. Includes bibliography and index.* [Oxford general practice series. : No. 18]

43 Health plan choice and the utilization of health care services. Bryan Dowd; Roger Feldman; Steven Cassou; Michael Finch. *Rev. Econ. St.* **LXXIII:1** 2:1991 pp. 85 – 93

44 Health professionals and the act. Rosalynde Lowe. *Child. Soc.* **5:1** Spring:1991 pp. 52 – 57

45 Health protection and medical assistance in disaster situations. Peter Macalister-Smith *[Contrib.]*; Rémi Russbach *[Contrib.]*; Hernán Reyes *[Contrib.]*; Robin Charles Gray *[Contrib.]*; Robin Michael Coupland *[Contrib.]*; Alain Garachon *[Contrib.]*; Pierre Perrin *[Contrib.]*; Claude de Ville de Goyet *[Contrib.]*; Bruce Dick *[Contrib.]*. Collection of 9 articles. **Int. R. Red Cross**, :*284*, 9-10:1991 pp. 440 – 532

46 A health risk index for assessing PHC coverage in urban India. Venkatalakshmi Srilatha; Iain W. Aitken. *Health Pol. Plan.* **6:3** 9:1991 pp. 234 – 243

47 Homelessness and dual diagnosis. Robert E. Drake; Fred C. Osher; Michael A. Wallach. *Am. Psychol.* **46:11** 11:1991 pp. 1149 – 1158

48 Homelessness as psychological trauma — broadening perspectives. Lisa Goodman; Leonard Saxe; Mary Harvey. *Am. Psychol.* **46:11** 11:1991 pp. 1219 – 1225

49 Hospitals in transition — the resource management experiment. Tim Packwood; Justin Keen; Martin Buxton. Milton Keynes: Open University Press, 1991: 160 p. *ISBN: 0335099513.* [State of health series.]

50 Housing for health. Susan J. Smith *[Ed.]*; Anne McGuckin *[Ed.]*; Robin Knill-Jones *[Ed.]*. Harlow: Longman, 1991: xi, 235 p. *ISBN: 0582078326.*

51 How does mother's education affect child height? Duncan Thomas; John Strauss; Maria-Helena Henriques. *J. Hum. Res.* **XXVI:2** Spring:1991 pp. 183 – 211

52 The implications for residential care. Dudley Roach. *Child. Soc.* **5:1** Spring:1991 pp. 87 – 95

53 Independent living schemes. D. Phillips; T. Booth; S. Berry; D. Jones; M. Lee; A. McGlade; J. Matthews; C. Melotte; J. Pritlove. *Br. J. Soc. W.* **21:2** 4:1991 pp. 157 – 172

54 Inequality and access to health care. Karen Davis. *Milbank Q.* **69:2** 1991 pp. 253 – 274

55 L'influence de la médecine arabe médiévale sur la médecine moderne *[In French]*; The influence of medieval Arabian medicine upon modern medicine *[Summary]*. Jacques Roux. *Pensée* **280** 3-4:1991 pp. 39 – 54

56 Information-giving in medical consultations — the influence of patients' communicative styles and personal characteristics. Richard L. Street. *Soc. Sci. Med.* **32:5** 1991 pp. 541 – 548

57 Into the valley — death and the socialization of medical students. Frederic W. Hafferty. New Haven: Yale University Press, c1991: xix, 234 p. *ISBN: 0300051441; LofC: 91015096. Includes bibliographical references (p. 217-227) and index.*

58 Invisibility and selective avoidance — gender and ethnicity in psychiatry and psychiatric nursing staff interaction. Kathryn Hopkins Kavanagh. *Cult. Medic. Psych.* **15:2** 6:1991 pp. 245 – 274

59 The location of health centers in a rural region using a decision support system — a Zambian case study. Bryan H. Massam; Jacek Malczewski. *Geogr. Res. For.* **11:** 1991 pp. 1 – 24

60 The measurement of health — concepts and indicators. James S. Larson. New York: Greenwood Press, 1991: xii, 175 p. (forms) *ISBN: 0313273391; LofC: 90044840. Health policy; Includes bibliographical references (p. [101]-109) and index.* [Contributions in medical studies.]

K.4: Health care [Soins médicaux]

61 Measures of need and outcome for primary health care. David Wilkin; Lesley Hallam *[Ed.]*; Marie-Anne Doggett *[Ed.]*. Oxford: Oxford University Press, 1991: 301 p. *ISBN: 0192618180; LofC: 91031914. Includes bibliographical references and index.*

62 Measuring health — a review of quality of life measurement scales. Ann Bowling. Milton Keynes: Open University Press, 1991: 199 p. *ISBN: 0335154360. Includes bibliography.*

63 Medical malpractice on trial. Paul C Weiler. Cambridge, Mass: Harvard University Press, 1991: xiii, 240 p. (ill) *ISBN: 0674561201; LofC: 90015600. Includes bibliographical references (p. 165-232) and indexes.*

64 Mental disorder and the tutelary relationship — from pre- to post-carceral legal order. Clive Unsworth. *J. Law Soc.* **18:2** Summer:1991 pp. 254 – 278

65 Midwifery — an appropriate(d) symbol of women's reproductive rights? Annette Burfoot. *Iss. Repro. Gen. Engin.* **4:2** :1991 pp. 119 – 128

66 A new approach to optimal selection of services in health care organizations. Donald L. Adolphson; Mark L. Baird; Kenneth D. Lawrence. *Socio. Econ.* **25:1** 1991 pp. 35 – 48

67 Nursing histories — reviving life in abandoned selves. Marian McMahon. *Feminist R.* **37** Spring:1991 pp. 23 – 37

68 Origine et évolution du concept du médicament essentiel promu par l'OMS *[In French]*; (Origin and evolution of the concept of essential drugs promoted by WHO); (Ursprung und Entwicklung eines Konzepts für ein von OMS gefördertes wesentliches Heilmeittl: *Title only in German)*; (Proiskhoždenie i evoljuciaj concepcii «osnovnogo lekarstva» obeščannogo OMS: *Title only in Russian)*; (Origen y evolución del concepto de medicamento esencial promovido por la OMS: *Title only in Spanish*). Germán Velásquez. *R. T-Monde* **XXXII:127** 7-9:1991 pp. 673 – 680

69 Outpatient commitment as both social control and least restrictive alternative. Theresa L. Scheid-Cook. *Sociol. Q.* **32:1** Spring:1991 pp. 43 – 60

70 Paediatricians and the Children Act. Marion Miles; David Harvey. *Child. Soc.* **5:1** Spring:1991 pp. 34 – 39

71 Le paiement symbolique, monnaie du désir *[In French]*; [The symbolic payment — a worthwhile investment] *[Summary]*. Daniel Puskas. *San. Ment. Qué* **XVI:1** 6:1991 pp. 139 – 148

72 The patient as diagnostician — intracultural differences in illness etiology in a Mexican neighborhood. Michael B. Whiteford. *J. Dev. Soc.* **VII:2** 7-9:1991 pp. 256 – 268

73 Pflegenotstand in Akutkrankenhäusern — die Entwicklung des Pflegeaufwands in bundesdeutschen Akutkrankenhäusern zwischen 1980 und 1989 *[In German]*; Hospital nursing in emergency — the development of nursing input in the F.R.G. between 1980 and 1989 *[Summary]*. R.H. Dinkel; E. Görtler; I. Milenovic. *Medi. Mensch Gesell.* **16:3** 9:1991 pp. 194 – 201

74 Political violence in the Third World — a public health issue. Anthony Zwi; Antonio Ugalde. *Health Pol. Plan.* **6:3** 9:1991 pp. 203 – 217

75 The politics of medical encounters — how patients and doctors deal with social problems. Howard Waitzkin. New Haven: Yale University Press, c1991: xvi, 311 p. (ill) *ISBN: 0300049498; LofC: 90045611. Includes bibliographical references (p. 279-304) and index.*

76 Postmodernism, rationality and the evaluation of health care. Nicholas J. Fox. *Sociol. Rev.* **39:4** 11:1991 pp. 709 – 744

77 Premiums without benefits — waste and inefficiency in the commercial health insurance industry. Robert M. Brandon; Michael Podhorzer; Thomas H. Pollak. *Int. J. Health. Ser.* **21:2** 1991 pp. 265 – 284

78 Primary-care decentralization in the Southern cone — shantytown health care as urban social movement. Joseph L. Scarpaci. *Ann. As. Am. G.* **81:1** 3:1991 pp. 103 – 126

79 Private health care in South Africa — should the unions intervene? Jonathan Broomberg; Cedric de Beer; Max Price. *Int. J. Health. Ser.* **21:4** 1991 pp. 779 – 791

80 Psychiatric care in relation to the development of the contemporary state — the case of Catalonia. Josep M. Comelles. *Cult. Medic. Psych.* **15:2** 6:1991 pp. 193 – 215

81 The psychology of health — an introduction. Marian Pitts *[Ed.]*; Keith Phillips *[Ed.]*. London: Routledge, 1991: xvi, 308 p. (ill) *ISBN: 0415041147; LofC: 90008514. Includes bibliographical references (p. [248]-287) and indexes.*

82 Quality assurance for long-term care providers. William Ammentorp; Ken Gossett *[Ed.]*; Nancy Euchner Poe *[Ed.]*. Newbury Park, Calif: Sage Publications, c1991: 163 p. *ISBN: 0803940246; LofC: 90021377. Includes bibliographical references.* [Sage human services guides.]

K.4: Health care [Soins médicaux]

83 Receipt of information and influence over decisions in hospitals by the board, Chief Executive Officer and medical staff. Keith G. Provan. *J. Manag. Stu.* **28**:3 5:1991 pp. 281 – 298
84 The role of female doctors in health services in the Sudan; [Arabic summary]. Amna O. El Musharaf; Sunita Pitamber. *Ahfad J.* **8**:2 12:1991 pp. 37 – 57
85 Sairausvakuutuksen pientä päivärahaa saavat [In Finnish]; Recipients of small sickness allowances [Summary]. H. Niemelä. *Kansan. Julk.* :**79** 1991 pp. 1 – 73
86 Schwerpunkt — medizinsoziologische und -psychologische Implikationen der Musiktherapie [In German]; Focal point — medicosociological and medicopsychological implications of music therapy. S. Evers [Contrib.]; H. Gembris [Contrib.]; R. Burkhardt [Contrib.]; H.V. Bolay [Contrib.]. Collection of 5 articles. **Medi. Mensch Gesell.** , *16:2*, 6:1991 pp. 81 – 114
87 Social and economic disparities under Canadian health care. Robin F. Badgley. *Int. J. Health. Ser.* **21**:4 1991 pp. 659 – 671
88 The social construction of noncompliance — a study of health care and social service providers in everyday practice. Norman Fineman. *Sociol. Health Ill.* **13**:3 9:1991 pp. 354 – 374
89 South African health care in change. H.C.J. van Rensburg. *S.Afr. J. Sociol.* **22**:1 3:1991 pp. 1 – 10
90 Sozialistische Gesundheits- und Lebensreformverbände [In German]; [Socialist groups for the reform of health and lifestyle]. Franz Walter; Viola Denecke; Cornelia Regin. Bonn: J.H.W. Dietz, c1991: 428 p. (ill) ISBN: 380124010x. Includes bibliographical references and index. [Reihe Politik- und Gesellschaftsgeschichte; Solidargemeinschaft und Milieu. : No. 24]
91 La spécificité du champ médical "moderne" dans un pays en développement, le cas du Burkina Faso — d'une transposition à une automatisation [In French]; The specificity of the "modern" medical field within a developing country the case of Burkina Faso — from the transposition to the autonomy [Summary]. I. Gobatto. *Cah. Anthr. Bio. Hum.* **VVI**:3-4 1989 pp. 259 – 268
92 The state, violence and race in psychiatry. Janis Hunter Jenkins [Contrib.]; Pablo J. Farias [Contrib.]; Josep M. Comelles [Contrib.]; Leslie Swartz [Contrib.]; Kathryn Hopkins Kavanagh [Contrib.]. Collection of 5 articles. **Cult. Medic. Psych.** , *15:2*, 6:1991 pp. 139 – 274
93 Staying fit and staying well — physical fitness as a moderator of life stress. Jonathon D. Brown. *J. Pers. Soc. Psychol.* **60**:4 4:1991 pp. 555 – 561
94 Stellenwert psychosozialer Aspekte chronischer Erkrankungen in Arztzeitschriften. Eine inhaltsanalytische Untersuchung der Berichterstattung in medizinischen Fachzeitschriften [In German]; The role of psychosocial aspects of chronic diseases in medical journals — a content analysis of reporting in medical journals [Summary]. D. Haberstroh; H. Haaser; F.A. Muthny. *Medi. Mensch Gesell.* **16**:4 12:1991 pp. 291 – 301
95 Die Stellung der Ärzteschaft im sich wandelnden Gesundheitswesen der USA [In German]; The status of the medical profession in the changing U.S. health care system [Summary]. H. Müller; A. Wessen. *Medi. Mensch Gesell.* **16**:4 12:1991 pp. 302 – 312
96 Studenci medycyny wobec alternatywnych sposobów leczenia [In Polish]; Medical students and alternative methods of medical treatment [Summary]. Agnieszka Golczyńska-Grondas. *Acta Univ. Łódz. Folia Soc.* **21** 1991 pp. 159 – 179
97 Technical cooperation in research on the development of malaria control measures. Akira Ishii. *Tech. Devel.* **4** 1:1991 pp. 41 – 55
98 The technology of medicine. P.K. Sethi. *Soc. Act.* **41**:1 1-3:1991 pp. 94 – 102
99 Time and health. Ronald Frankenberg [Ed.]. London: Sage Publications, 1991: 160 p. ISBN: 0803986785.
100 The transfer of sentenced prisoners to hospital 1960-1983 — a study in one special hospital. Adrian Grounds. *Br. J. Crimin.* **31**:1 Winter:1991 pp. 54 – 71
101 Transparenz oder Ambiguität? Kulturspezifische Formen der Aneignung von Informationstechniken im Krankenhaus [In German]; Transparency vs ambiguity? Cultural differences in putting information technology in hospitals into use [Summary]. Ina Wagner. *Z. Soziol.* **20**:4 8:1991 pp. 275 – 289
102 Using medical malpractice data to predict the frequency of claims — a study of Poisson process models with random effects. Bruce Cooil. *J. Am. Stat. Ass.* **86**:414 6:1991 pp. 285 – 295
103 Which direction for health care in Nigeria? Ibukun-Oluwa O. Ogunbekun. *Health Pol. Plan.* **6**:3 9:1991 pp. 254 – 261

K.4: Health care [Soins médicaux]

104 Who receives medical care? Income, implicit prices, and the distribution of medical services among pregnant women in the United States. Mark R. Rosenzweig; T. Paul Schultz. *J. Hum. Res.* **XXVI:3** Summer:1991 pp. 473 – 508

105 Women, health, and medicine. Agnes Miles. Milton Keynes, Pa: Open University Press, 1991: 234 p. *ISBN: 0335099068; LofC: 91022711*. Includes bibliographical references and index.

106 Zdrowotny wymiar nierówności społecznych *[In Polish]*; Health dimension of social inequalities *[Summary]*. Magdalena Sokołowska. *Prz. Soc.* **39** 1991 pp. 241 – 262

Community care [Garde communitaire]

107 After the asylums — community care for the mentally ill. Elaine Murphy. London: Faber & Faber, 1991: 248 p. *ISBN: 0571163572.*

108 Beyond community care — normalisation and integration work. Shulamit Ramon *[Ed.]*. London: Macmillan Education, 1991: 202 p. *ISBN: 0333514009.* [Issues in mental health.]

109 Caring in our communities — the management agenda. Norman Flynn; Clive Miller *[Ed.]*. London: National Institute for Social Work, 1991: 50 p. *ISBN: 0902789724.* [Briefing paper.]

110 Community care and frail elderly people. Peggy Foster. *Soc. Pol. Admin.* **25:2** 6:1991 pp. 108 – 120

111 The community in focus. Donal O Shea. *Administration* **39:2** :1991 pp. 133 – 146

112 Community involvement in rehabilitation programmes for disabled children — a Guyanese experience. Brian O'Toole. *Comm. Dev. J.* **26:3** 7:1991 pp. 202 – 209

113 Community-based long-term care — innovative models. Judith Ann Miller. Newbury Park, Calif: Sage Publications, c1991: 253 p. *ISBN: 0803939191; LofC: 90009223. Materials from a study conducted for the Health Care Financing Administration by a research team from the Center for Health Services Research at the University of Colorado Health Sciences Center; Includes indexes; Includes bibliographical references.*

114 Culture and the restructuring of community mental health. William Vega; John W. Murphy. New York: Greenwood Press, 1990: 162 p. *ISBN: 0313268878; LofC: 90003158.* Includes bibliographical references (p. [155]-158) and index. [Contributions in psychology.]

115 Home and away — respite care in the community. Carol Robinson. Birmingham: Venture Press, 1991: 111 p. *ISBN: 0900102810.*

116 Home care for older people in Europe — a comparison of policies and practices. Anne Jamieson *[Ed.]*. Oxford: Oxford University Press, c1991: 356 p. *ISBN: 0192620509; LofC: 91003530.* Includes bibliographical references and index. [Commission of the European Communities health services research series; Oxford medical publications. : No. 7]

117 Home care for the elderly — an international perspective. Abraham Monk; Carole B. Cox *[Ed.]*. New York: Auburn House, 1991: xii, 171 p. *ISBN: 0865690057; LofC: 90001280.* Includes bibliographical references (p. [161]-165) and index.

118 Home-bound — crisis in the care of young people with severe learning difficulties. Jane Hubert. London: King's Fund Centre, 1991: 122 p. *ISBN: 0903060876.* Bibl.

119 Homelessness and mental illness — the dark side of community care. Martin Page *[Ed.]*; Robin Powell *[Ed.]*. London: Concern Publications, 1991: 50 p. *ISBN: 0951826905.*

120 Homes of their own — a community care initiative for children with learning difficulties. Anne Leonard. Aldershot: Avebury, 1991: 151 p. (ill) *ISBN: 1856281566.* Includes bibliography and index. [Studies in cash and care.]

121 The identification and provision of care for the terminally ill at home by "family" members. Maura Hunt. *Sociol. Health Ill.* **13:3** 9:1991 pp. 375 – 395

122 The impact of centralisation upon geographical variations in the provision of aged care services — a comparison of outcomes in Melbourne and Adelaide. S. Pinch. *Aust. Geogr. Stud.* **29:1** 4:1991 pp. 26 – 41

123 Informal welfare in Belfast — caring communities? Fred St. Leger; Norman Gillespie. Aldershot: Avebury, 1991: 249 p. *ISBN: 185628154x.* [Avebury studies of care in the community.]

124 Mental health work in the community — theory and practice in community psychiatric nursing. Michael Sheppard. London: Falmer, 1991: vii, 202 p. *ISBN: 1850009783.* Bibliography — p.185 - 198 .Includes index.

125 Multi-disciplinary teamwork — community mental handicap teams. Morag McGrath. Aldershot: Avebury, 1991: 211 p. (ill) *ISBN: 1856281523. Community care;* Includes bibliography and index. [Care in the community.]

INTERNATIONAL BIBLIOGRAPHY OF SOCIOLOGY — 1991

K.4: Health care *[Soins médicaux]* — Community care *[Garde communitaire]*

126 No place like home — intergenerational homesharing through social exchange. Nicholas L Danigelis; Alfred P. Fengler *[Ed.]*. New York: Columbia University Press, c1991: x, 322 p. *ISBN: 0231074042; LofC: 91011460. Includes bibliographical references and index.* [Columbia studies of social gerontology and aging.]

127 Normalisation — a reader for the nineties. Hilary Brown *[Ed.]*; Helen Smith *[Ed.]*; Linda Ward *[Foreword]*. London: Tavistock, 1991: 189 p. *ISBN: 0415070791; LofC: 91012881.*

128 Peer group counseling — a normalized residential alternative to the specialized treatment of adolescent sex offenders. James M. Brannon; Richard Troyer. *Int. J. Offen.* **35:3** Fall:1991 pp. 225 – 234

129 Planning for community care — the community placement questionnaire. P. Clifford; A. Charman; Y. Webb; T.J.K. Craig; D. Cowan. *Br. J. Clin. Psycho.* **30:3** 9:1991 pp. 193 – 212

130 Rehabilitation and community care. Stephen Pilling. London: Routledge, 1991: 167 p. *ISBN: 0415058171. Includes bibliography and index.* [Strategies for mental health.]

131 Utopia, community care, and the retreat from the asylums. Dylan Ronald Tomlinson. Milton Keynes [England]: Open University Press, 1991: 176 p. *ISBN: 0335096239; LofC: 91022585. Includes bibliographical references and index.*

132 Worlds of the mentally ill — how deinstitutionalization works in the city. Dan A Lewis *[Ed.]*. Carbondale: Southern Illinois University Press, c1991: xii, 198 p. *ISBN: 0809314770; LofC: 89010056. Includes index; Bibliography — p. 189-193.*

Geriatrics *[Gériatrie]*

133 The aging of the Canadian population. Neena L. Chappell. Ottawa: Department of the Secretary of State, 1991: 32, 35 p. *ISBN: 0662572130. eng, fre; Bibliography — p32.* [About Canada.]

134 Beiträge zu einer neuen Dienstleistungkultur — Beispiele aus dem Bereich der Altenpflege in den Niederlanden, Schweden und England *[In German]*; Contributing to a new service culture — significant examples from the sector of elderly care in the Netherlands, Sweden and England *[Summary]*. John Baldock; Adalbert Evers. *Soz. Welt.* **42:2** 1991 pp. 232 – 257

135 Care for the elderly — significant innovations in three European countries. Robbert J. Kraan *[Ed.]*. Frankfurt am Main: Campus Verlag, 1991: x, 248 p. (ill) *ISBN: 3593343991; LofC: 90071891. Includes bibliographical references.* [Public policy and social welfare. : Vol. 6]

136 Clinicians and residential home assessments. Neil P. McKeganey. *Soc. Pol. Admin.* **25:2** 6:1991 pp. 149 – 159

137 Day care in the United Kingdom and the Netherlands — a comparative study. Henk Nies; Susan Tester; Jan Maarten Nuijens. *Age. Soc.* **11:3** 9:1991 pp. 245 – 273

138 The economics of care of the elderly. Jozef Pacolet *[Ed.]*; Celeste Wilderom *[Ed.]*. Aldershot: Avebury, 1991: 225 p. *ISBN: 1856281965.*

139 Financing home care — improving protection for disabled elderly people. Diane Rowland *[Ed.]*; Barbara Lyons *[Ed.]*. Baltimore: Johns Hopkins University Press, c1991: xviii, 256 p. (ill) *ISBN: 0801842565; LofC: 91020809. Includes bibliographical references and index.* [Johns Hopkins studies in health care finance and administration. : No. 4]

140 Health and health care in later life. Christina Victor. Milton Keynes: Open University Press, 1991: 182 p. *ISBN: 0335092845; LofC: 91002692. Includes index.*

141 The health problems of the elderly living in institutions and homes in Zimbabwe. A. C. Nyanguru. *J. Soc. Devel. Afr.* **6:2** 1991 pp. 71 – 90

142 Helping elderly tenants of housing associations to stay in their own homes. Heather Clark; Helen Enevoldson; John Lansley; Ann Smith. *App. Commun. Stud.* **1:1** 1991 pp. 23 – 38

143 The impact of centralisation upon geographical variations in the provision of aged care services — a comparison of outcomes in Melbourne and Adelaide. S. Pinch. *Aust. Geogr. Stud.* **29:1** 4:1991 pp. 26 – 41

144 Informal and formal care — exploring the complementarity. Neena Chappell; Audrey Blandford. *Age. Soc.* **11:3** 9:1991 pp. 299 – 317

145 L'insomnie et son traitement chez les personnes âgées — une nouvelle approche *[In French]*; [A new look at the complaint of insomnia and its treatment in elderly] *[Summary]*. Catherine S. Fichten; Eva Libman. *San. Ment. Qué* **XVI:1** 6:1991 pp. 99 – 116

146 Multicultural health care and rehabilitation of older people. Amanda J. Squires *[Ed.]*. London: Edward Arnold, 1991: 256 p. *ISBN: 0340543620.*

K.4: Health care [Soins médicaux] — Geriatrics [Gériatrie]

147 Psychiatric morbidity and service use among elderly people. Ann Bowling. *Age. Soc.* **11**:3 9:1991 pp. 275 – 297
148 Set no limits — a rebuttal to Daniel Callahan's proposal to limit health care for the elderly. Robert Laurence Barry *[Ed.]*; Gerard V. Bradley *[Ed.]*; Nat Hentoff *[Foreword]*. Urbana: University of Illinois Press, c1991: xix, 134 p. (ill) *ISBN: 0252018605; LofC: 91010448*. *Includes bibliographical references*.
149 Too old for health care? — controversies in medicine, law, economics, and ethics. Robert H. Binstock *[Ed.]*; Stephen Garrard Post *[Ed.]*. Baltimore: Johns Hopkins University Press, c1991: xv, 209 p. *ISBN: 0801841658; LofC: 90023237*. *Includes bibliographical references and index*. [The Johns Hopkins series in contemporary medicine and public health.]

Health economics [Économie de la santé]

150 Auswirkungen der Kostendämpfungspolitik auf die Frauenbeschäftigung in der Gesundheitswirtschaft *[In German]*; Cost containment policies and their effects on female employment in the health economy *[Summary]*. M. Landenberger; G.-U. Watzlawczik. *Medi. Mensch Gesell.* **16**:3 9:1991 pp. 166 – 177
151 Balancing act — the new medical ethics of medicine's new economics. E. Haavi Morreim. Dordrecht: Kluwer Academic Publishers, c1991: xiii, 184 p. *ISBN: 0792311701. Includes bibliographical references (p. 155-175) and index*. [Clinical medical ethics. : Vol. 3]
152 Capital budgeting in hospital management using the analytic hierarchy process. M. Murat Tarimcilar; Shahriar Z. Khaksari. *Socio. Econ.* **25**:1 1991 pp. 27 – 34
153 The costs of poor health habits. Willard G. Manning *[Ed.]*; et al. Cambridge, Mass: Harvard University Press, 1991: ix, 223 p. *ISBN: 0674174852; LofC: 91007043*. "*A RAND study.*"; *Includes bibliographical references (p. [209]-218) and index*.
154 The economics of care of the elderly. Jozef Pacolet *[Ed.]*; Celeste Wilderom *[Ed.]*. Aldershot: Avebury, 1991: 225 p. *ISBN: 1856281965*.
155 The economics of child care. David Blau *[Ed.]*. New York: Russell Sage Foundation, c1991: xi, 192 p. (ill) *ISBN: 0871541181; LofC: 91017321*.
156 The economics of health. A.J. Culyer *[Ed.]*. Aldershot: Elgar, c1991: - *ISBN: 1852781769. Includes index*. [The international library of critical writings in economics; An Elgar reference collection. : No. 12]
157 Health care funding. Stephen Birch. *Soc. Pol. Admin.* **25**:4 12:1991 pp. 300 – 310
158 Health economics and policy — problems and prescriptions. Malcolm C. Brown. Toronto: McClelland & Stewart, c1991: 268 p. (ill) *ISBN: 0771017022; LofC: cn 91093727*. *Includes bibliographical references and index*.
159 Health, health expenditures and equity. A. J. Culyer. York: Centre for Health Economics, University of York, 1991: 34 p.
160 Income and health. Allison Quick; Richard G. Wilkinson *[Ed.]*. London: Socialist Health Association, 1991: 79p. (ill) *ISBN: 0900687177*.
161 The profit motive and patient care — the changing accountability of doctors and hospitals. Bradford H. Gray. Cambridge, Mass.: Harvard University Press, 1991: 440 p. *ISBN: 0674713370*. "*A Twentieth Century Fund report*"; *Index*.
162 Serious and unstable condition — financing America's health care. Henry J. Aaron. Washington, D.C: Brookings Institution, 1991: 158p. *ISBN: 0815700512; LofC: 91018516*. *Includes bibliographical references and index*.
163 A system of health statistics — toward a new conceptual framework for integrating health data. Michael C. Wolfson. *R. In. Weal.* **37**:1 3:1991 pp. 81 – 104
164 What cost case management in long term care? Rosalie A. Kane; Joan D. Penrod; Gestur Davidson; Ira Moscovice; Eugene Rich. *Soc. Ser. R.* **65**:2 06:1991 pp. 281 – 303

Health policy [Politique sanitaire]

165 Access to health and social services records in Denmark. Anne Petersen. *App. Commun. Stud.* **1**:1 1991 pp. 16 – 22
166 Un acercamiento a la problemática de salud en México a fines de los ochenta *[In Spanish]*; [An approach to Mexico's health problems at the close of the 1980s]. Carolina Martínez S.; Alejandro Córdova C.; Gustavo Leal F.. *Est. Sociol.* **IX**:26 5-8:1991 pp. 253 – 178
167 Addressing the contradictions — health promotion and community health action in the United Kingdom. Wendy Farrant. *Int. J. Health. Ser.* **21**:3 :1991 pp. 423 – 439

K.4: Health care [Soins médicaux] — Health policy [Politique sanitaire]

168 AIDS and health care deficiencies. Anselm L. Strauss; Shizuko Fagerhaugh; Barbara Suczek; Carolyn Wiener. *Society* **28:**5 7-8:1991 pp. 63 – 73
169 AIDS and the health of nations — the contraditions of public health. Alan Sears. *Crit. Sociol.* **18:**2 Summer: 1991 pp. 31 – 50
170 An AIDS prevention campaign — effects on attitudes, beliefs and communication behavior. William J. Brown. *Am. Behav. Sc.* **34:**6 7-8:1991 pp. 666 – 678
171 AIDS, women, and the next generation — towards a morally acceptable public policy for HIV testing of pregnant women and newborns. Ruth R. Faden *[Ed.]*; Gail Geller *[Ed.]*; Madison Powers *[Ed.]*. New York: Oxford University Press, 1991: xix, 374 p. *ISBN: 0195065727; LofC: 90014328. Includes bibliographical references and index.*
172 AIDSPLAN — a decision support model for planning the provision of HIV/AIDS- related services. E. Rizakou; J. Rosenhead; K. Reddington. *Interfaces* **21:**3 5-6:1991 pp. 117 – 138
173 Allocating resources to health care — is the QALY (quality adjusted life year) a technical solution to a political problem? Roy A. Carr-Hill. *Int. J. Health. Ser.* **21:**2 1991 pp. 351 – 363
174 America's infant-mortality puzzle. Nicholas Eberstadt. *Publ. Inter.* **:**105 Fall:1991 pp. 30 – 47
175 Analysing health systems — a modular approach. Avi Yacar Ellencweig. Oxford: Oxford University Press, 1991: 348 p. *ISBN: 0192620851; LofC: 91028870. Includes index.* [Oxford medical publications.]
176 An analysis of the American Medical Association's recommendations for change in the medical care sector of the United States. Vicente Navarro. *Int. J. Health. Ser.* **21:**4 1991 pp. 685 – 696
177 Anthropometric indicators of children's nutrition in two Nigerian communities. E.W. Ebomoyi; A.R. Wickremasinghe; Flora F. Cherry. *J. Biosoc. Sc.* **23:**1 1:1991 pp. 33 – 38
178 The autopsy crisis reexamined — the case for a national autopsy policy. Rolla B. Hill; Robert E. Anderson. *Milbank Q.* **69:**1 1991 pp. 51 – 78
179 Die Bedeutung der Frauen für das gegliederte System der gesetzlichen Krankenversicherung *[In German]*; Women's significance for the structured system of mandatory health insurance *[Summary]*. A Goeschel; H. Steinweber. *Medi. Mensch Gesell.* **16:**3 9:1991 pp. 153 – 165
180 Business management as the way to resolve the public/private polarity in the national health system. Elio Borgonovi. *Rev. Ec. Con. It.* **:**2 5-8:1991 pp. 137 – 164
181 Chancen und Probleme der Gesundheitswissenschaften in der Bundesrepublik *[In German]*; The health sciences in the Federal Republic of Germany — opportunities and problems *[Summary]*. D. Braun. *Medi. Mensch Gesell.* **16:**2 6:1991 pp. 114 – 122
182 Clinical psychology as a strategy for dealing with psychosocial issues in a South African neurosurgery ward. Tracey Miller; Leslie Swartz. *Sociol. Health Ill.* **13:**3 9:1991 pp. 293 – 309
183 Community action for health promotion — a strategy to empower individuals and communities. E. Richard Brown. *Int. J. Health. Ser.* **21:**3 :1991 pp. 441 – 456
184 A community development approach to Chagas' disease — the Sucre health project, Bolivia. John Renshaw; Daniel Rivas. *Health Pol. Plan.* **6:**3 9:1991 pp. 244 – 253
185 The community in focus. Donal O Shea. *Administration* **39:**2 :1991 pp. 133 – 146
186 Comparative health policy and the new right — from rhetoric to reality. Christa Altenstetter *[Ed.]*; Stuart Haywood *[Ed.]*. London: Macmillan, c1991: 332 p. *ISBN: 0333531841. Includes index.*
187 Coping with cutbacks and managing retrenchment in health. Rob Flynn. *J. Soc. Pol.* **20:**2 4:1991 pp. 215 – 236
188 Culture and the restructuring of community mental health. William Vega; John W. Murphy. New York: Greenwood Press, 1990: 162 p. *ISBN: 0313268878; LofC: 90003158. Includes bibliographical references (p. [155]-158) and index.* [Contributions in psychology.]
189 A decade of research and services for homeless mentally ill persons — where do we stand? Deborah L. Dennis; John C. Buckner; Frank R. Lipton; Irene S. Levine. *Am. Psychol.* **46:**11 11:1991 pp. 1129 – 1138
190 The dialogue on health care reform. Louis W. Sullivan. *Lab. Law J.* **42:**10 10:1991 pp. 651 – 657
191 Dimensions of state mental health policy. Christopher G. Hudson *[Ed.]*; Arthur J. Cox *[Ed.]*; David Mechanic *[Foreword]*. New York: Praeger, 1991: xiv, 301 p. *ISBN: 0275932524; LofC: 90007595. Includes bibliographical references (p. [255]-280) and indexes.*

K.4: Health care [Soins médicaux] — Health policy [Politique sanitaire]

192 Emerging trends in the Swedish health system. Richard B. Saltman. *Int. J. Health. Ser.* **21**:4 1991 pp. 615 – 623

193 Ethics and equity in Canadian health care — policy alternatives. Samuel Wolfe. *Int. J. Health. Ser.* **21**:4 1991 pp. 673 – 680

194 Evaluating national health communication campaigns — formative and summative research issues. John C. McGrath. *Am. Behav. Sc.* **34**:6 7-8:1991 pp. 652 – 665

195 The evaluation of national health systems. George E Cumper. Oxford: Oxford University Press, 1991: 218 p. *ISBN: 0192618032; LofC: 90007666.*

196 Externalities and compulsory vaccinations. Dagobert L. Brito; Eytan Sheshinski; Michael D. Intriligator. *J. Publ. Ec.* **45**:1 6:1991 pp. 69 – 90

197 Food and health data — their use in nutrition policy-making. W. Becker; Elisabet Helsing *[Ed.]*. Copenhagen: World Health Organization, Regional Office for Europe, 1991: xii, 171 p. (ill) *ISBN: 9289011254. Includes bibliographical references.* [WHO regional publications.]

198 From asylum to community — mental health policy in modern America. Gerald N Grob. Princeton, N.J: Princeton University Press, c1991: xv, 406 p., 8 p. of plates (ill) *ISBN: 0691047901; LofC: 90009178. Includes bibliographical references (p. [375]-391) and index.*

199 Health and health care in later life. Christina Victor. Milton Keynes: Open University Press, 1991: 182 p. *ISBN: 0335092845; LofC: 91002692. Includes index.*

200 Health and health care in South Africa — the challenge for a majority ruled state. Ben Wisner. *Antipode* **23**:1 1:1991 pp. 121 – 136

201 Health and social services — the new relationship. Isobel Allen *[Ed.]*. London: Policy Studies Institute, 1991: 80 p. *ISBN: 0853745315.*

202 *[In Japanese]*; [Health care reforms in the world — does the change of regime reform health care?]. Shohei Anesaki; et al. Tokyo: Keiso Shobo, 1991: 205 p.

203 Health check — health care reforms in an international context. Christopher Ham; Ray Robinson *[Ed.]*; Michaela Benzeval *[Ed.]*. London: King's Fund Institute, c1990: 112 p. *ISBN: 187060718x.*

204 Health economics and policy — problems and prescriptions. Malcolm C. Brown. Toronto: McClelland & Stewart, c1991: 268 p. (ill) *ISBN: 0771017022; LofC: cn 91093727. Includes bibliographical references and index.*

205 Health policy reform in the People's Republic of China. Pei-lin Yang; Vivian Lin; James Lawson. *Int. J. Health. Ser.* **21**:3 :1991 pp. 481 – 491

206 Health promotion research — towards a new social epidemiology. Bernhard Badura; Ilona Kickbusch *[Ed.]*. Copenhagen: World Health Organization, Regional Office for Europe, c1991: x, 496 p. (ill) *ISBN: 9289011289. Includes bibliographical references.* [WHO regional publications.]

207 The health security partnership — an equitable, pragmatic, and passable national health program. Melvin A. Glasser. *Int. J. Health. Ser.* **21**:2 1991 pp. 345 – 350

208 Health services and space utilisation in urban and rural communities — a case study of Ile-Ife, Nigeria. K. Ajibola. *Third Wor. P.* **13**:3 8:1991 pp. 297 – 307

209 Healthy cities. John Ashton *[Ed.]*. Milton Keynes [England]: Open University Press, 1991: 235 p. *ISBN: 0335094775; LofC: 91021246. Includes index.*

210 HIV-AIDS and social care. Keith Tolley; Alan Maynard; David Robinson. York: Centre for Health Economics University of York, 1991: 77 p. [Discussion paper.]

211 How do we value our children today? As reflected by children's health, health care, and policy? Zarrina Kurtz; John Tomlinson. *Child. Soc.* **5**:3 Autumn:1991 pp. 207 – 224

212 Identity and coping with mental illness in long-stay psychiatric rehabilitation. Kathryn E. Taylor; Rachel E. Perkins. *Br. J. Clin. Psycho.* **30**:1 2:1991 pp. 73 – 85

213 Implementing a new approach to urban health problems — the case of Addis Ababa; La réalisation d'une nouvelle approche aux problèmes de santé urbains — le cas de Addis Ababa *[French summary]*; Un nuevo enfoque para las problemas de salud en zonas urbanas — el caso de Addis Abeba *[Spanish summary]*. Wendmu Dejene. *Environ. Urban.* **3**:2 10:1991 pp. 127 – 135

214 The implications of the corporatization of health care delivery in Hong Kong. Peter P. Yuen. *Asian J. Pub. Admin.* **13**:1 6:1991 pp. 23 – 38

215 Improving access to health services for children and pregnant women. Joshua M. Wiener; Jeannie Engel *[Ed.]*. Washington, D.C: Brookings Institution, c1991: viii, 90 p. *ISBN: 0815793758; LofC: 91076610.* "This volume...reports on and amplifies

K.4: Health care *[Soins médicaux]* — Health policy *[Politique sanitaire]*
presentations made at a July 1989 conference sponsored by the Brookings Institution in conjunction with the National Commission to Prevent Infant Mortality." -- [vii]; Includes bibliographical references (p. 71-81). [Brookings dialogues on public policy.]

216 The internationalisation and commercialisation of health care in Britain. J. Mohan. *Envir. Plan.A.* **23:6** 6:1991 pp. 853 – 868

217 Jails versus mental hospitals — the Milwaukee approach to a social dilemma. Maurice B. Smith; Frank J. Liska. *Int. J. Offen.* **35:3** Fall:1991 pp. 205 – 216

218 Looking forward to the past? The politics of public health. Rob Baggott. *J. Soc. Pol.* **20:2** 4:1991 pp. 191 – 214

219 Mandated health care — issues and strategies. Donald L. Westerfield; Thomas B. Curtis *[Foreword]*. New York: Praeger, 1991: xiv, 202 p. (Ill) *ISBN: 0275938131; LofC: 90014331 //r92*. Includes bibliographical references (p. [181]-191) and index.

220 The marketing of empowerment and the construction of the health consumer — a critique of health promotion. Victoria M. Grace. *Int. J. Health. Ser.* **21:2** 1991 pp. 329 – 343

221 Mental disability in Scotland. Michael Titterton. *Soc. Pol. Admin.* **25:2** 6:1991 pp. 136 – 148

222 Mental health and the law in Scotland — philosphy, policy issues, application. Derek Ball; Mono Chakrabarti. Glasgow: Jordanhill College of Education, 1991: 144 p. *ISBN: 185098297x.*

223 Mental health care in Italy. Emma Fasolo; Renato Frisanco. *Soc. Pol. Admin.* **25:3** 9:1991 pp. 218 – 226

224 National health systems of the world. Milton Irwin Roemer. New York: Oxford University Press, 1991 *ISBN: 0195053206; LofC: 90007336 //r91*. Includes bibliographical references and index; Contents — v. 1. The countries.

225 On health. Silvia Edwards *[Contrib.]*; Simon Kinsey *[Contrib.]*; Jim Brown *[Contrib.]*; Jenny Corbett *[Contrib.]*; Tony Smythe *[Contrib.]*; Katy Andrews *[Contrib.]*; Caroline Hodgson *[Contrib.]*; M. Boustred *[Contrib.]*; Clio Bellenis *[Contrib.]*; Donald Rooum *[Contrib.]* and others. Collection of 17 articles. **Raven**, *4:3*, 7-9:1991 pp. 195 – 285

226 Paying the doctor — health policy and physician reimbursement. Jonathan D. Moreno *[Ed.]*. London: Auburn House, 1991: 194 p. *ISBN: 0865690065.*

227 Planning the health care system in a decade of economic decline — the Ghanaian experience. R. Quaye. *Cr. Law Soc. Chan.* **16:3** 11:1991 pp. 303 – 312

228 Policy administration in the Soviet health service. Michael Ryan. *Soc. Pol. Admin.* **25:3** 9:1991 pp. 227 – 237

229 A policy model of human immunodeficiency virus screening and intervention. Margaret L. Brandeau; Hau L. Lee; Douglas K. Owens; Carol H. Sox; Robert M. Wachter. *Interfaces* **21:3** 5-6:1991 pp. 5 – 25

230 Preventing coronary heart disease — prospects, policies and politics. Michael Calnan. London: Routledge, 1991: 226 p. *ISBN: 0415044901.*

231 Professional closure — the case of British nursing. Wai-Fong Chua; Stewart Clegg. *Theory Soc.* **19:2** 4:1990 pp. 135 – 172

232 Quelques réflexions en marge du regroupement des ressources alternatives en santé mentale du Québec (RRASMQ) *[In French]*; [Notions arising from the orientation congress of Québec's alternative mental health resource network] *[Summary]*. Yves Lecomte. *San. Ment. Qué* **XVI:1** 6:1991 pp. 7 – 16

233 Refugee children — theory, research, and services. Frederick L. Ahearn *[Ed.]*; Jean L. Athey *[Ed.]*. Baltimore: Johns Hopkins University Press, c1991: xii, 230 p. *ISBN: 0801841607; LofC: 90025554*. Includes bibliographical references and index. [The Johns Hopkins series in contemporary medicine and public health.]

234 Regionale Unterschiede in der Gesundheitslage der Frauen — Daten für eine regionalisierte geschlechtsspezifische Gesundheitberichterstattung *[In German]*; Regional differences in women's state of health — data for regionalized gender-specific health monitoring *[Summary]*. A. Fette; S. Gassner. *Medi. Mensch Gesell.* **16:3** 9:1991 pp. 178 – 187

235 La santé publique à l'épreuve du Sida — une approche systématique des processus décisionnels *[In French]*; Public health testing through AIDS — a systemic approach to decision-making processes *[Summary]*. Guy Setbon. *Sociol. Trav.* **:3** 1991 pp. 403 – 428

236 A six country survey of the content and structure of heroin treatment programmes using methadone; Une enquête sur le contenu et la structure des programmes de traitement de l'héroïnomanie utilisant la méthadone, dans six pays *[French summary]*; Un estudio prospectivo del contenido y la estructura de los programas de tratamiento con metadona en seis paises *[Spanish summary]*. Michael Gossop; Marcus Grant. *Br. J. Addict.* **86:9** 9:1991 pp. 1151 – 1160

K.4: Health care [Soins médicaux] — Health policy [Politique sanitaire]

237 Social action theory for a public health psychology. Craig K. Ewart. *Am. Psychol.* **46:9** 9:1991 pp. 931 – 964
238 Systemic crisis and the nonprofit sector — towards a political economy of the nonprofit health and social services sector. Carroll L. Estes; Robert R. Alford. *Theory Soc.* **19:2** 4:1990 pp. 173 – 198
239 A time for conceptual stocktaking; Un temp pour un inventaire conceptuel *[French summary]*; El momento indicado para realizar un balance conceputal *[Spanish summary]*. Martin J. Jarvis. *Br. J. Addict.* **86:5** 5:1991 pp. 643 – 647
240 Die Vergesellschaftung der Gesundheit. Eine Analyse der Regionalstrategie für „Gesundheit 2000" des Regionalkomitees für Europa der Weltgesundheitsorganisation *[In German]*; The socialization of health. An analysis of the regional strategy for "Health 2000" of the WHO European regional committee *[Summary]*. J. Bauch. *Medi. Mensch Gesell.* **61:1** 3:1991 pp. 33 – 44
241 Welfare and the state in Australia. Adam Graycar; Adam Jamrozik. *Soc. Pol. Admin.* **25:4** 12:1991 pp. 271 – 283
242 What has bioethics to offer health policy? Daniel Wikler. *Milbank Q.* **69:2** 1991 pp. 233 – 252
243 What's in a smear? Cervical screening, medical signs and metaphors. Tina Posner. *Sci. Cult.* **2(2):11** :1991 pp. 167 – 187
244 Working the markets — purchaser/provider separation in English health care. Stephen Harrison. *Int. J. Health. Ser.* **21:4** 1991 pp. 625 – 635

Medical ethics [Code déontologique médical]

245 AIDS — an epidemic of ethical puzzles. Hastings Centre. Aldershot: Dartmouth, 1991: 187 p. ISBN: 1855212064. Includes index. [Issues in bioethics. : No. 1]
246 AIDS, philosophy and beyond — philosophical dilemmas of a modern pandemic. Joseph Wayne Smith. Aldershot: Avebury, c1991: vi, 341 p. ISBN: 1856281388. Includes index. [Avebury series in philosophy.]
247 Balancing act — the new medical ethics of medicine's new economics. E. Haavi Morreim. Dordrecht: Kluwer Academic Publishers, c1991: xiii, 184 p. ISBN: 0792311701. Includes bibliographical references (p. 155-175) and index. [Clinical medical ethics. : Vol. 3]
248 *[In Japanese]*; [Brain death — organ transplantation and the Japanese society]. Jiro Nudeshima. Tokyo: Kobundo, 1991: 206 p.
249 Ethical and social aspects of the Human Genome Project. Santiago Grisolia. *Impact Sci.* **41:1(161)** :1991 pp. 37 – 44
250 Ethics and equity in U.S. health care — the data. Dorothy P. Rice. *Int. J. Health. Ser.* **21:4** 1991 pp. 637 – 651
251 L'éthique du généticien — les débuts de l'American Society of Human Genetics *[In French]*; Geneticists and their ethics — the beginnings of the American society of human genetics. Gwen Terrenoire. *Soc. Contemp.* **:7** 9:1991 pp. 63 – 72
252 Euthanasia — toward an ethical social policy. David C. Thomasma; Glenn C. Graber *[Ed.]*. New York: Continuum, 1991, c1990: x, 302 p. ISBN: 0826404707; LofC: 90030987. Includes bibliographical references and index.
253 Fetal neural transplantation — placing the ethical debate within the context of society's use of human material. D. Gareth Jones. *Bioethics* **5:1** 1991 pp. 23 – 43
254 Human embryos and research — proceedings of the European Bioethics Conference in Mainz, 7-9 November 1988. Umberto Bertazzoni *[Ed.]*. Frankfurt ; New York: Campus Verlag, c1990: 258 p. ISBN: 3593343185. Includes bibliographical references. [Gentechnologie; EUR. : No. 25]
255 The human genome project — where will the map lead us? Darryl Macer *[Contrib.]*; Dorothy C. Wertz *[Contrib.]*; John C. Fletcher *[Contrib.]*; Loane Skene *[Contrib.]*; Bo Andreassen Rix *[Contrib.]*. Collection of 4 articles. **Bioethics** , *5:3*, 7:1991 pp. 183 – 255
256 Just doctoring — medical ethics in the liberal state. Troyen A. Brennan. Berkeley: University of California Press, c1991: xiv, 287 p. ISBN: 0520073339; LofC: 91010146. Includes bibliographical references (p. 239-282) and index.
257 Künstliche Fortpflanzung — Heilmittel ungewollter Kinderlosigkeit? Historische, soziale, ethische und medizinisch-psychologische Aspekte der Reproduktionsmedizin *[In German]*; Artificial reproduction — is it a cure for unwanted infertility? Historical, social, ethical, and medico-psychological aspects of reproduction medicine *[Summary]*. G. Schilling. *Medi. Mensch Gesell.* **16:3** 9:1991 pp. 208 – 217

K.4: Health care *[Soins médicaux]* — Medical ethics *[Code déontologique médical]*

258 Life and death choices after Cruzan — case law and standards of professional conduct. Larry Gostin; Robert F. Weir. *Milbank Q.* **69:1** 1991 pp. 143 – 173

259 The limits of medical paternalism. Heta Häyry. London: Routledge, 1991: 208 p. *ISBN: 0415063205; LofC: 91009501. Includes bibliographical references and index.* [Social ethics and policy.]

260 Macro ethics and micro ethics — the case of health care. Martin Barkin. *Can. Publ. Ad.* **34:1** Spring:1991 pp. 30 – 36

261 Mapping the human genome — some thoughts for those who say "there should be a law on it". Loane Skene. *Bioethics* **5:3** 7:1991 pp. 233 – 248

262 Preventing prenatal harm — should the state intervene? Deborah Mathieu. Dordrecht: Kluwer Academic Publishers, c1991: viii, 153 p. *ISBN: 0792309847; LofC: 90015592. Includes bibliographical references (p. 137-148) and index.* [Clinical medical ethics. : Vol. 1]

263 Privacy and disclosure in medical genetics examined in an ethics of care. Dorothy C. Wertz; John C. Fletcher. *Bioethics* **5:3** 7:1991 pp. 212 – 231

264 Protecting the vulnerable — autonomy and consent in health care. Margaret Brazier *[Ed.]*; Mary Lobjoit *[Ed.]*. London: Routledge, 1991: 183 p. *ISBN: 0415046971; LofC: 91018609. Includes bibliographical references and index.* [Social ethics and policy.]

265 Right to self-determination — proceedings of the 8th World Conference of the International Federation of Right to Die Societies organized by the Nederlandse Vereniging voor Vrijwillige Euthanasie (NVVE) in Maastricht on June 7-10 1990. Aycke O. A. Smook *[Ed.]*; Bé de Vos-Schippers *[Ed.]*. Amsterdam: Free University Press, 1991: 148 p. *ISBN: 9062569307.*

266 Set no limits — a rebuttal to Daniel Callahan's proposal to limit health care for the elderly. Robert Laurence Barry *[Ed.]*; Gerard V. Bradley *[Ed.]*; Nat Hentoff *[Foreword]*. Urbana: University of Illinois Press, c1991: xix, 134 p. (ill) *ISBN: 0252018605; LofC: 91010448. Includes bibliographical references.*

267 Should ethical concerns regulate science? The European experience with the human genome project. Bo Andreassen Rix. *Bioethics* **5:3** 7:1991 pp. 250 – 255

268 Too old for health care? — controversies in medicine, law, economics, and ethics. Robert H. Binstock *[Ed.]*; Stephen Garrard Post *[Ed.]*. Baltimore: Johns Hopkins University Press, c1991: xv, 209 p. *ISBN: 0801841658; LofC: 90023237. Includes bibliographical references and index.* [The Johns Hopkins series in contemporary medicine and public health.]

269 What has bioethics to offer health policy? Daniel Wikler. *Milbank Q.* **69:2** 1991 pp. 233 – 252

270 Whose genome project? Darryl Macer. *Bioethics* **5:3** 7:1991 pp. 183 – 210

271 Zur Demokratieverträglichkeit von Bio- und Gentechnologie *[In German]*; Can biotechnology and genetic technology be reconciled with democracy? *[Summary]*. Heinz Theisen. *Soz. Welt.* **42:1** :1991 pp. 109 – 130

AUTHOR INDEX
INDEX DES AUTEURS

Aaberge, R: **H.3**: 24, 28.
Aaron, H: **K.4**: 162.
Aaron, J: **F.5**: 110.
Abaza, M: **F.2**: 147.
Abbink, G: **F.3**: 7.
Abbott, A: **A.1**: 14.
Abbott, P: **F.5**: 287.
Abdalla, M: **G.1**: 7.
Abdel Karim, R: **D.3**: 31.
Abdel-Kawi, O: **C.2**: 102.
Abdo, N: **F.5**: 56.
Abdu, A: **G.1**: 7.
Abdul-Gader, A: **H.5**: 39.
Abe, G: **D.5**: 117.
Abeele, Vanden, P: **D.7**: 115.
Abel, E: **K.2**: 33.
Abeles, M: **J.6**: 27.
Åberg, R: **K.2**: 77.
Aboulafia, M: **B.1**: 67.
Abraham, M: **F.8**: 156. **J.5**: 27.
Abraham, S: **C.3**: 78.
Abrahams, R: **G.3.1**: 50.
Abrahamson, E: **C.5**: 5.
Abrahamson, P: **K.1**: 293.
Abramovitch, R: **H.5**: 9.
Abrams, D: **C.3**: 78. **F.3**: 219.
Abramsky, C: **F.7**: 83.
Abu-Laban, S: **D.5**: 168.
Abumere, S: **G.3.2**: 163.
Acero, L: **I.3**: 88.
Achard, P: **B.1**: 24. **D.1**: 18.
Achuthan, M: **C.7**: 9.
Acker, J: **F.5**: 235.
Acker, S: **D.9**: 47, 72.
Acton, T: **F.7**: 65.
Adachi, K: **F.2**: 37.
Adachi, M: **F.4**: 95.
Adair, R: **F.4**: 31.
Adam, A: **F.3**: 84.

Adams, A: **I.4**: 130.
Adams, F: **J.5**: 4.
Adams, J: **G.3.1**: 130. **I.2**: 94.
Adams, R: **D.9**: 139. **H.3**: 21.
Adamson, R: **I.3**: 126.
Addi, L: **A.1**: 33.
Addison, J: **I.2**: 233.
Adelman, R: **D.7**: 77.
Adesina, J: **I.5**: 8.
Adetoro, O: **F.1**: 8.
Adilkariev, K: **D.4**: 25.
Adkins, C: **C.3**: 91.
Adlaf, E: **K.1**: 387.
Adler, E: **I.2**: 80.
Adler, M: **K.2**: 26.
Adolphson, D: **K.4**: 66.
Adriaans, N: **K.1**: 317.
Aduaka, E: **I.3**: 151.
Adulo, T: **D.1**: 27.
Aduwo, G: **G.3.2**: 362.
Aebischer, V: **C.7**: 36.
Aetugbo, A: **G.3.1**: 129.
Affleck, G: **C.2**: 200–201.
Afshar, H: **H.3**: 58.
Agar, K: **C.2**: 125.
Agar, M: **D.7**: 331.
Agarwal, A: **H.4**: 103.
Agassi, J: **K.2**: 94.
Agbola, T: **G.3.2**: 163.
Agelusz, R: **D.7**: 28.
Agger, B: **B.1**: 29.
Aggleton, P: **F.3**: 157.
Aghajanian, A: **F.1**: 49.
Agier, M: **I.4**: 1.
Agnew, R: **K.1**: 8.
Agnoli, F: **C.2**: 142.
Agren, A: **H.5**: 13.
Aguilar, R: **H.3**: 65.

Aguilar, S: **I.5**: 79.
Aguirre, A: **C.3**: 74.
Ahearn, F: **K.4**: 233.
Ahlberg, B: **F.3**: 72.
Ahlberg, R: **J.4**: 21. **K.1**: 334.
Ahlbrandt, R: **G.3.2**: 48.
Ahmad, A: **F.3**: 141.
Ahmad, N: **I.2**: 101.
Ahmad, O: **F.3**: 286.
Ahmed, M: **F.3**: 264.
Ahrens, A: **C.3**: 150.
Ahsan, M: **D.5**: 175.
Aiba, J: **A.1**: 5.
Aigrain, P: **H.5**: 12.
Aikawa, Y: **G.3.1**: 15.
Aina, T: **G.3.2**: 163.
Ainsworth, M: **C.2**: 183.
Aitken, I: **K.4**: 46.
Aitken, P: **K.1**: 373.
Aitken, S: **G.1**: 62.
Ajibola, K: **K.4**: 208.
Ajzen, I: **D.7**: 1.
Akande, A: **F.3**: 177.
Akbari, A: **F.8**: 50.
Aken, van, M: **C.2**: 182.
Akerlof, G: **C.7**: 50.
Akerström, M: **C.3**: 13.
Akhiezer, A: **D.1**: 100.
Akhilesh, K: **I.4**: 50.
Akrat, S: **F.5**: 241.
Aksoy, A: **J.7**: 11.
Al-Ahnaf, M: **A.1**: 33.
Al-Bdour, S: **D.5**: 159.
Al-Faruqi, L: **F.5**: 229.
Al-Jalali, S: **I.2**: 83.
Al-Khalifah, A: **G.3.2**: 351.
al-Khalil, S: **D.8**: 34.
Al-Madany, I: **G.1**: 7.
Al-Qudsi, S: **F.8**: 79. **I.2**: 74.
Al-Soliman, T: **D.8**: 65.
Alam, S: **D.5**: 177.
Albanese, M: **F.3**: 62.
Alberici, A: **D.9**: 165.
Albert, D: **C.2**: 24.
Alberto, D: **F.8**: 123.
Albonetti, C: **K.1**: 424.
Albrecht, G: **K.3**: 37.

Albrecht, S: **F.4**: 251.
Albrecht-Jensen, C: **D.5**: 12.
Albrechts, L: **G.3.2**: 242.
Albrow, M: **B.1**: 138.
Alcock, P: **K.2**: 32.
Alderman, G: **F.7**: 216.
Aldgate, J: **F.4**: 312.
Aldous, J: **F.2**: 13. **H.3**: 22.
Aldrich, J: **C.1**: 64.
Alemi, F: **F.2**: 16.
Alexander, A: **D.7**: 326.
Alexander, B: **F.2**: 45.
Alexander, E: **F.2**: 9.
Alexander, H: **B.1**: 32.
Alexander, J: **B.1**: 22.
Alexander, P: **F.2**: 9.
Alexander, R: **H.6**: 1.
Alford, C: **C.1**: 53.
Alford, R: **K.4**: 238.
Allaix, M: **F.2**: 90.
Allan, K: **C.2**: 93.
Allatt, P: **F.4**: 116.
Allaway, W: **D.9**: 195.
Allebeck, P: **K.1**: 307.
Allen, D: **K.1**: 327.
Allen, I: **K.4**: 201.
Allen, J: **F.5**: 169.
Allen, L: **E.1**: 24. **I.2**: 202.
Allen, P: **H.4**: 44. **I.3**: 152.
Allen, R: **K.1**: 199.
Allen, W: **D.9**: 176.
Alles, G: **D.5**: 59.
Alliger, G: **C.6**: 10.
Allison, A: **F.5**: 11.
Allison, P: **B.2**: 68.
Allman, A: **C.2**: 82.
Allott, R: **D.3**: 77.
Allsop, S: **K.1**: 306.
Almas, R: **G.3.1**: 32, 45.
Alonso, F: **K.1**: 319.
Alper, Y: **C.3**: 28.
Alt, B: **J.7**: 3.
Altafin, I: **E.3**: 15.
Altamira, A: **F.4**: 226.
Altbach, P: **D.9**: 205.
Altenstetter, C: **K.4**: 186.

Alterman, R: **G.3.2**: 283.
Altheide, D: **D.7**: 283.
Altman, J: **K.2**: 73.
Altonji, J: **I.4**: 131.
Altschuld, J: **B.2**: 97.
Alund, A: **F.7**: 191.
Alves-Pinto, M: **D.9**: 171.
Alvesson, M: **C.5**: 60.
Alwin, D: **B.2**: 20–21, 116. **D.7**: 144. **F.2**: 33.
Aly, H: **F.3**: 64, 253.
Amadeo, J: **F.3**: 58.
Amadieu, J: **I.5**: 50.
Amaki, S: **F.2**: 31.
Amann, R: **I.5**: 162.
Amariglio, J: **B.1**: 43.
Amaro, H: **C.1**: 83.
Amato, P: **F.2**: 105. **F.4**: 91, 121, 134, 307.
Amberg, S: **I.5**: 197.
Ambrose, P: **G.3.2**: 127.
Amersfoort, van, J: **F.8**: 173. **K.1**: 220.
Amico. d', R: **D.8**: 49.
Amin, A: **H.7**: 2.
Amin, S: **F.3**: 261.
Ammentorp, W: **K.4**: 82.
Amoateng, A: **F.3**: 132.
Amott, T: **I.2**: 132.
Ampofo-Boateng, K: **C.2**: 12.
An, P: **G.3.1**: 126.
An-bang, Y: **F.4**: 103.
Ancona, D: **C.4**: 22.
Ancona, G: **F.8**: 144.
Andelson, R: **F.3**: 2.
Andersen, M: **F.4**: 4, 58.
Andersen, T: **I.5**: 9.
Anderson, A: **C.2**: 16. **D.7**: 178.
Anderson, C: **C.1**: 91. **C.3**: 160. **C.7**: 33.
Anderson, H: **G.3.2**: 350.
Anderson, I: **F.4**: 210.
Anderson, J: **C.7**: 39.
Anderson, K: **K.1**: 60.
Anderson, L: **D.9**: 60. **E.2**: 25.
Anderson, M: **D.5**: 131.
Anderson, N: **C.2**: 145.
Anderson, O: **F.5**: 88.
Anderson, P: **I.3**: 64.
Anderson, R: **A.3**: 7. **K.4**: 178.
Anderson, S: **I.5**: 186.

Anderson, U: **C.7**: 5.
Anderson-Levitt, K: **D.1**: 3.
Andersson, P: **D.7**: 45.
Andorka, R: **A.1**: 16. **F.3**: 28.
Andrade, D', R: **C.7**: 8.
Andre, J: **D.3**: 82.
Andréasson, S: **K.1**: 307.
Andreenkov, V: **B.2**: 115.
Andrews, F: **C.2**: 96, 189. **D.2**: 2.
Andrews, G: **F.7**: 4.
Andrews, K: **K.4**: 225.
Andrews, M: **J.6**: 23.
Andrews, Π: **D.9**: 40.
Androunas, E: **D.7**: 379.
Anesaki, S: **K.4**: 202.
Aneshensel, C: **F.3**: 220.
Angel, D: **I.2**: 25.
Angel, R: **F.7**: 31.
Anheier, H: **D.8**: 30.
Animashaun, I: **G.3.2**: 163.
Ansart, P: **D.1**: 79.
Ansay, T: **I.2**: 67.
Anson, J: **F.1**: 16. **F.3**: 271.
Anson, O: **D.5**: 185.
Anspach, M: **D.5**: 178. **J.5**: 37.
Anspach, R: **C.5**: 24.
Anthony, G: **K.1**: 33.
Antolik, M: **D.7**: 318.
Antonian, I: **K.1**: 129.
Antonides, G: **C.1**: 125. **H.5**: 21.
Antonio, R: **B.1**: 22.
Antoun, R: **D.1**: 44.
Aoi, K: **F.4**: 10.
Apelt, P: **K.4**: 38.
Appelbaum, M: **B.2**: 45.
Appelbaum, R: **G.3.2**: 154.
Appelt, E: **F.5**: 149.
Apple, M: **D.9**: 26, 44, 46.
Appleton, S: **F.1**: 58.
Appleyard, R: **F.8**: 140, 168.
Apraku, K: **F.8**: 111.
Apter, M: **C.1**: 77.
Aquilino, W: **F.4**: 309, 336.
Arab-Ogly, E: **E.3**: 36.
Aragona, d', G: **I.5**: 21.
Arbatov, G: **D.1**: 105.

Arber, S: **B.2**: 35. **F.2**: 49. **F.5**: 168. **H.3**: 73. **I.2**: 150.
Archer, J: **C.1**: 106.
Archer, M: **A.1**: 38. **I.4**: 45.
Archer, R: **E.3**: 22.
Archer, S: **D.7**: 208.
Ardelt, M: **C.3**: 47.
Ardener, S: **F.5**: 32.
Ardigò, A: **K.2**: 86.
Arebi, S: **F.5**: 171.
Arendell, T: **F.2**: 55.
Aresta, G: **D.9**: 165.
Arestov, V: **D.5**: 56.
Argeri, M: **F.7**: 167.
Argeriou, M: **K.1**: 310.
Argyle, M: **D.2**: 23.
Arie, T: **F.2**: 40.
Arioti, M: **F.4**: 206.
Aristar, A: **D.7**: 216.
Arisue, K: **G.3.2**: 88.
Arkesteyn, M: **G.3.1**: 119.
Arkin, R: **C.2**: 7.
Arlinghaus, S: **G.3.2**: 310.
Armenta, E: **K.2**: 83.
Armingeon, K: **I.5**: 185.
Armstrong, D: **E.2**: 59.
Armstrong, G: **I.6**: 8. **K.1**: 415.
Armstrong, H: **F.2**: 77.
Armstrong, J: **F.7**: 83.
Arnao, G: **K.1**: 343.
Arnold, B: **D.4**: 9.
Arnold, H: **F.8**: 115.
Arnold, J: **I.1**: 15.
Arnold, R: **D.9**: 8.
Arnon, G: **C.1**: 124.
Aromaa, A: **F.3**: 226.
Aron, A: **C.3**: 15. **F.8**: 20.
Aron, E: **C.3**: 15.
Aronowitz, R: **F.3**: 191.
Arora, A: **E.2**: 46.
Arora, G: **F.3**: 131.
Arotçarena, G: **D.5**: 95.
Arpea, M: **D.9**: 207.
Arreola, D: **F.6**: 55.
Arriagada, I: **F.5**: 41.
Arrigone, J: **G.3.2**: 136.
Arrington, T: **D.9**: 11.
Arseguel, A: **I.2**: 244.
Artemov, V: **I.6**: 35.
Arthur, J: **F.8**: 94, 136.
Arts, W: **C.7**: 41. **H.3**: 77.
Aryal, R: **F.4**: 248.
Asch, S: **C.2**: 52.
Aschenbrenner, M: **C.2**: 24.
Ascher, E: **C.1**: 153. **H.4**: 100.
Asdonk, J: **H.4**: 93.
Asendorpf, J: **C.2**: 182.
Ash, M: **C.1**: 114.
Ashburner, L: **I.2**: 120.
Ashcroft, B: **H.4**: 71.
Ashkenazi, M: **D.2**: 11. **D.5**: 25, 122.
Ashkinaze, C: **F.7**: 8.
Ashmore, R: **C.3**: 92.
Ashton, D: **D.9**: 13.
Ashton, J: **K.4**: 209.
Ashworth, K: **F.3**: 52.
Asis, M: **F.8**: 170.
Asmussen, L: **F.4**: 320.
Assin, M: **C.1**: 44.
Astone, N: **F.4**: 118.
Astor, J: **C.1**: 137.
Astridge, C: **B.2**: 101.
Astroff, R: **D.7**: 243.
Atari, W: **B.1**: 54.
Athey, J: **K.4**: 233.
Athukorala, K: **G.3.2**: 226.
Atkin, C: **K.4**: 11.
Atkin, D: **D.7**: 361.
Atkin, K: **F.7**: 39, 150.
Atkinson, A: **K.1**: 224.
Atkinson, J: **I.2**: 188.
Atlas, J: **D.7**: 205.
Aubel, J: **G.2**: 14.
Aubert, G: **I.3**: 118.
Aubry Girardin, F: **I.3**: 118.
Audi, R: **D.3**: 21, 87.
Auge, M: **B.2**: 26.
Augoustinos, M: **C.7**: 20.
Augustin, G: **D.7**: 319.
Ault, R: **I.3**: 78.
Auluck, R: **K.3**: 32.
Auriat, N: **F.8**: 63.
Austin, A: **F.5**: 254. **J.5**: 4.

Austin, D: **C.5**: 9.
Austrin, T: **H.6**: 3.
Auyong, J: **I.6**: 6.
Avakian, B: **K.1**: 17.
Avary, D: **K.1**: 358.
Aveni, A: **K.1**: 193.
Avila, R: **D.7**: 226.
Avnery, U: **F.7**: 159.
Avruch, K: **C.3**: 109.
Ayish, M: **D.7**: 254.
Ayliffe, G: **C.1**: 32.
Aylmer, G: **J.3**: 21.
Ayres, I: **F.7**: 234.
Ayres, M: **B.1**: 142.
Azevedo, de, R: **F.3**: 307. **F.8**: 154.
Azria, R: **F.7**: 66.
Ba-Yunus, I: **B.1**: 140.
Baba, V: **C.2**: 218.
Babadji, R: **J.3**: 22.
Babaev, B: **B.2**: 12.
Babalola, E: **D.5**: 162.
Babor, T: **K.1**: 323.
Babosov, E: **H.3**: 37.
Bacal, A: **I.1**: 10. **I.5**: 201.
Bacchus, M: **D.9**: 133.
Bach, R: **F.3**: 11.
Bachmair, B: **D.7**: 146.
Bachman, C: **K.1**: 383.
Bachman, J: **K.1**: 350.
Bachman, R: **K.1**: 49.
Bachrach, C: **F.4**: 264.
Back, L: **F.7**: 221.
Backer, W: **I.5**: 36.
Backman, G: **K.2**: 76.
Bacon, H: **K.1**: 30.
Badalamenti, A: **B.2**: 43.
Badari, V: **F.3**: 265.
Badawi, M: **K.3**: 39.
Badcock, B: **H.7**: 5.
Baddeley, A: **C.2**: 156.
Badgley, R: **K.4**: 87.
Badri, A: **F.5**: 241. **J.4**: 25.
Badura, B: **K.4**: 206.
Baeck, L: **D.3**: 81.
Baeninger, R: **F.4**: 40.
Baer, D: **D.1**: 131. **I.5**: 140.
Baer, W: **G.3.2**: 124.

Baert, P: **B.1**: 23.
Baethge, M: **I.3**: 5.
Bafoil, F: **A.1**: 31.
Bagby, R: **C.2**: 191.
Bagchi, D: **F.5**: 166.
Baggott, R: **K.4**: 218.
Bagguley, P: **I.2**: 129.
Bagnall, G: **K.1**: 300.
Bagozzi, R: **C.5**: 2.
Bahonar, M: **F.5**: 229.
Baigent, N: **J.6**: 19.
Bailey, A: **D.9**: 105.
Bailey, C: **F.5**: 180.
Bailey, F: **D.5**: 42.
Bailey, M: **F.3**: 100.
Bailey, T: **F.7**: 224.
Bailie, W: **D.3**: 48.
Bailly, R: **K.1**: 352.
Bain, P: **I.5**: 180.
Bainbridge, W: **D.1**: 115.
Baine, S: **G.3.2**: 303.
Baines, C: **F.5**: 140.
Bairan, A: **F.4**: 292.
Baird, M: **K.4**: 66.
Baird, R: **D.3**: 63. **F.6**: 36.
Bakar, N: **G.3.1**: 5.
Baker, D: **I.2**: 45.
Baker, G: **C.1**: 50.
Baker, J: **F.7**: 39, 175.
Baker, K: **B.2**: 124, 129.
Baker, S: **C.2**: 32.
Baker, W: **D.8**: 62.
Bakker, H: **D.5**: 154.
Balakrishnan, T: **F.3**: 88. **G.3.2**: 195.
Balamurugan, G: **G.3.2**: 363.
Balandier, G: **H.4**: 100.
Baldock, C: **K.2**: 105.
Baldock, J: **K.4**: 134.
Baldwin, L: **D.9**: 12, 190.
Baldwin, M: **K.3**: 3.
Baldwin, R: **D.9**: 214.
Baldwin, S: **K.1**: 302.
Baldwin, T: **D.7**: 361.
Baldwin-Edwards, M: **F.7**: 39. **F.8**: 130.
Balen, van, R: **C.1**: 11.
Balfour, A: **I.6**: 32.

Balkan, E: **I.2**: 87.
Balkwell, J: **B.1**: 104.
Ball, D: **K.4**: 222.
Ball, M: **D.7**: 155.
Baller, E: **E.3**: 69.
Ballesteros, A: **G.3.2**: 189.
Ballon, R: **I.3**: 132.
Bals, C: **F.1**: 32. **F.2**: 34.
Balshem, M: **F.3**: 166.
Balson, P: **F.3**: 193.
Balster, R: **K.1**: 319.
Baltensperger, B: **G.3.1**: 9.
Baltzell, E: **J.3**: 11.
Bamber, G: **I.4**: 78.
Bamberger, E: **D.7**: 103.
Bamgbose, A: **D.7**: 337.
Ban'ko, V: **D.6**: 18.
Banarjee, S: **D.9**: 141.
Banaszak, L: **F.5**: 17.
Bancroft, J: **F.6**: 57.
Bandura, A: **C.1**: 131.
Bane, M: **K.1**: 247.
Banerjee, B: **F.8**: 88.
Banerjee-Guha, S: **G.3.2**: 118.
Banez, G: **C.2**: 73.
Bankole, A: **F.3**: 113.
Banks, M: **H.5**: 25. **I.4**: 5.
Bannerji, H: **F.5**: 133.
Bannister, R: **A.2**: 10.
Banton, M: **F.7**: 196, 198, 239.
Bantz, C: **C.3**: 20.
Banu, U: **D.5**: 164.
Banyikwa, W: **G.3.2**: 362.
Bapat, M: **H.3**: 13.
Bapi, R: **C.2**: 147.
Bar-Hayim, A: **I.1**: 5.
Bar-Tal, D: **C.3**: 155.
Bara, D: **F.5**: 237.
Barak, G: **K.1**: 234.
Baranow, U: **D.7**: 80.
Barbagli, M: **F.4**: 138.
Barbalet, J: **E.2**: 54.
Barber, G: **I.2**: 171.
Baré, J: **H.6**: 6.
Barff, R: **B.2**: 72. **I.2**: 192.
Bargh, J: **C.7**: 67.
Barghouti, I: **D.9**: 206.

Baril, R: **G.3.1**: 83.
Barkan, S: **K.1**: 206.
Barker, M: **K.2**: 66.
Barker, S: **D.7**: 200.
Barkey, K: **G.3.1**: 76.
Barkin, M: **K.4**: 260.
Barkley, A: **I.2**: 169.
Barley, S: **C.5**: 78.
Barling, J: **F.4**: 288.
Barlow, P: **D.5**: 53.
Barnard, M: **K.1**: 348.
Barnard, P: **G.3.1**: 36.
Barndt, D: **D.9**: 73.
Barnes, C: **F.3**: 4.
Barnes, G: **K.1**: 297, 376.
Barnes, S: **H.7**: 11.
Barnes, W: **H.3**: 53.
Barnett, O: **K.1**: 417.
Barnett, R: **F.4**: 265.
Barnett, T: **F.3**: 151.
Barnett, W: **C.5**: 78.
Barnhurst, K: **D.7**: 244.
Baron, A: **I.2**: 161.
Baron, B: **E.3**: 42.
Baron, D: **D.7**: 18.
Baron, J: **C.7**: 45. **F.5**: 220.
Baron, M: **D.3**: 12. **K.4**: 37.
Baron, R: **C.3**: 116.
Barou, J: **F.8**: 24.
Barr, R: **C.2**: 26. **K.1**: 65.
Barraclough, S: **F.8**: 98. **I.1**: 10.
Barrera, C: **H.7**: 8.
Barrett, F: **C.5**: 30.
Barrett, R: **I.2**: 173.
Barrilleaux, C: **F.7**: 105.
Barron, D: **C.5**: 3.
Barroso, C: **F.3**: 63.
Barry, A: **K.1**: 241.
Barry, F: **I.2**: 236.
Barry, J: **J.5**: 38.
Barry, R: **K.4**: 148.
Barson, S: **F.7**: 97.
Bartczak, S: **F.2**: 53.
Bartel, B: **I.2**: 67.
Barthe, D: **F.2**: 90.
Bartholomew, D: **B.2**: 19.

Bartholomew, K: **C.3**: 9.
Bartiaux, F: **F.2**: 38.
Bartley, M: **I.2**: 177.
Bartoli, A: **K.2**: 86.
Bartolome, C: **C.2**: 33.
Barton, D: **D.7**: 190.
Bartoňová, D: **F.3**: 140.
Baruch, G: **F.4**: 265.
Bashir, A: **K.1**: 313.
Basil, M: **D.7**: 369. **K.4**: 11.
Basinger, K: **D.3**: 73.
Basiotis, P: **K.1**: 154.
Bassett, A: **K.4**: 37.
Bassett, M: **F.5**: 45.
Bassey, E: **F.2**: 40.
Bassuk, E: **G.3.2**: 121.
Bast, C: **C.3**: 107.
Basu, A: **E.2**: 22.
Basu, B: **F.8**: 138.
Basu, E: **H.4**: 36.
Baszanger, I: **I.4**: 92.
Batalov, E: **B.1**: 78.
Batenburg, R: **I.4**: 21.
Bathelt, H: **I.2**: 12.
Batson, C: **C.3**: 98, 100.
Batson, J: **C.3**: 100.
Batt, S: **K.1**: 326.
Battegay, A: **G.3.2**: 173.
Battistelli, F: **J.7**: 2.
Batton, C: **F.2**: 90.
Batty, M: **G.3.2**: 31.
Batygin, G: **A.1**: 23.
Bauch, J: **K.4**: 240.
Baucom, D: **C.3**: 144.
Baudel, J: **D.9**: 89.
Baudrillard, J: **G.3.2**: 7.
Bauer, J: **F.4**: 51.
Bauer, P: **J.6**: 37.
Baum, H: **I.3**: 17.
Baum, J: **C.5**: 33.
Bauman, T: **C.7**: 52.
Bauman, Z: **B.1**: 13. **D.1**: 26.
Baumann, E: **F.6**: 28.
Baumeister, A: **F.2**: 3. **F.3**: 205.
Baumeister, R: **C.2**: 223. **F.2**: 110.
Baumgardner, A: **C.1**: 96.
Baumohl, J: **K.1**: 301.

Baumol, W: **D.3**: 54.
Bausell, R: **B.2**: 2.
Bautista, M: **D.7**: 8, 79.
Bavoux, P: **G.3.2**: 173.
Bawden, B: **D.3**: 57.
Baxi, U: **B.1**: 92.
Baxter, S: **F.3**: 144.
Bayat, A: **I.5**: 203.
Bayer, R: **F.3**: 227. **K.1**: 324.
Baylis, G: **C.2**: 125.
Bazerman, M: **C.2**: 114.
Bazin, M: **F.7**: 88.
Bazzanella, C. **D.7**. 89.
Beadle, E: **D.9**: 167.
Bean, C: **J.6**: 13.
Bean, P: **C.1**: 70. **K.1**: 372.
Bearman, P: **K.1**: 399.
Beattie, K: **C.7**: 79.
Beaudry, M: **C.1**: 59.
Beaujot, R: **F.1**: 48.
Beaumont, C: **G.3.2**: 229.
Beaumont, P: **I.3**: 127. **I.5**: 179, 181.
Beaurain, N: **F.7**: 155.
Beauregard, R: **G.3.2**: 239.
Beauvais, L: **I.5**: 138.
Bebler, A: **J.7**: 19.
Bech, H: **F.4**: 235.
Bechhofer, L: **K.1**: 46.
Beck, A: **C.2**: 119.
Beck, D: **G.3**: 5.
Beck, S: **F.6**: 39. **I.4**: 11.
Beck, V: **F.4**: 181.
Becker, A: **F.7**: 121.
Becker, H: **F.2**: 6.
Becker, K: **D.7**: 325.
Becker, N: **F.2**: 22.
Becker, R: **F.2**: 6.
Becker, S: **F.2**: 85.
Becker, W: **K.4**: 197.
Bécue Bertaut, M: **B.2**: 29.
Beech, A: **C.2**: 125.
Beeghley, L: **F.6**: 21.
Beekink, E: **F.4**: 32, 296.
Beer, de, C: **K.4**: 79.
Beer, de, J: **F.4**: 17.
Beeson, P: **H.3**: 2.

Beets, G: **F.4**: 17.
Begag, A: **G.3.2**: 173.
Begg, I: **I.2**: 71.
Begnal, K: **F.5**: 117.
Behar, C: **F.4**: 231.
Behera, D: **K.2**: 17.
Behrman, J: **F.3**: 238.
Beijing University, "Social Division" Study Group: **E.2**: 7.
Beillan, V: **H.4**: 35.
Beit-Hallahmi, B: **D.5**: 39.
Bekhradnia, S: **D.5**: 80.
Běláček, J: **F.4**: 129.
Béland, F: **K.4**: 6.
Belau, D: **K.1**: 402.
Belenkiy, V: **F.8**: 159.
Belenko, S: **K.1**: 328.
Belhaj, M: **J.4**: 11.
Belk, R: **H.6**: 10.
Belkin, P: **C.1**: 172.
Bell, A: **D.7**: 269.
Bell, C: **G.3.1**: 52.
Bell, D: **G.1**: 56. **K.1**: 97.
Bell, J: **B.2**: 125.
Bell, V: **K.1**: 52.
Bellamy, E: **I.3**: 49.
Bellamy, M: **G.3.1**: 1.
Bellante, D: **I.5**: 34.
Bellavita, C: **J.4**: 16.
Bellenis, C: **K.4**: 225.
Beller, A: **K.2**: 49.
Bellew, R: **D.9**: 68.
Beloff, M: **F.7**: 139.
Belous, R: **F.1**: 15.
Belsky, J: **F.2**: 89. **F.4**: 302, 314.
Bemmels, B: **I.3**: 45. **I.5**: 3, 82, 90.
Ben Rejeb, R: **C.1**: 43.
Ben-Ari, E: **G.3.2**: 6. **J.7**: 4.
Ben-David, Y: **F.3**: 291.
Ben-Moshe, E: **F.3**: 138.
Ben-Yehoshua, N: **C.3**: 28.
Ben-Zaken, A: **K.3**: 25.
Benard, C: **F.5**: 54, 148.
Benavot, A: **D.9**: 127, 152.
Benbenishty, R: **K.3**: 25.
Bendix, J: **D.7**: 250.
Bendix, W: **I.4**: 3.

Bendor, J: **C.3**: 93.
Benfer, R: **B.2**: 8.
Bengtson, V: **F.4**: 68.
Bengtsson, B: **G.3.2**: 100.
Benhabib, S: **B.1**: 51. **J.2**: 15.
Benington, J: **G.2**: 15, 31.
Benites, M: **H.3**: 10.
Benjamin, D: **K.1**: 389.
Benjamin, J: **E.2**: 37.
Benjamin, S: **H.4**: 70.
Benko, G: **G.3.2**: 272.
Bennett, B: **C.2**: 106. **F.4**: 180.
Bennett, J: **I.5**: 34, 159.
Bennett, L: **J.6**: 40.
Bennett, R: **K.1**: 73, 77, 154.
Bennett, T: **K.1**: 83.
Bennett-Alexander, D: **F.6**: 18.
Bennich-Björkman, L: **D.8**: 69.
Benoit-Guilbot, O: **H.3**: 1.
Benson, B: **K.1**: 138.
Benson, H: **D.5**: 18.
Benson, P: **C.7**: 12.
Benstock, S: **F.5**: 254.
Bentall, R: **C.1**: 50.
Bentler, P: **C.2**: 206.
Bentley, M: **H.5**: 3.
Benton, T: **A.1**: 4.
Bentovim, A: **F.2**: 77.
Benzel, K: **D.8**: 7.
Benzeval, M: **K.4**: 203.
Bérard, E: **D.2**: 16.
Berbeshkina, Z: **C.2**: 95.
Berchiche, A: **K.1**: 134.
Bercovitch, J: **C.3**: 117.
Berdahl, R: **D.9**: 204.
Berecochea, J: **K.1**: 188.
Berenson, F: **C.3**: 125.
Berenson, G: **F.2**: 129.
Berenstein, V: **C.2**: 236.
Berg, H: **I.2**: 184.
Berg, M: **F.5**: 102.
Bergan, T: **C.1**: 119.
Bergeman, C: **F.1**: 40.
Berger, A: **D.7**: 282.
Berger, J: **C.4**: 42.
Berger, P: **E.2**: 45.

Berger, R: **D.4**: 39. **F.5**: 84.
Bergin, A: **C.1**: 140.
Bergmann, W: **F.7**: 241.
Bergqvist, C: **F.5**: 267.
Bergstrom, J: **I.6**: 1.
Bergstrom, V: **E.3**: 9.
Berg, van den, A: **I.2**: 219.
Beristain, A: **K.1**: 70.
Berkel-van Schaik, van, A: **F.2**: 6.
Berking, H: **J.6**: 3.
Berlan-Darqué, M: **F.3**: 15.
Berlinska, D: **F.7**: 113.
Berman, G: **I.1**: 5.
Berman, H: **D.5**: 24.
Berman, L: **C.1**: 16.
Berman, P: **E.3**: 56.
Berman, R: **D.8**: 46, 49.
Bermeo, N: **E.3**: 27.
Bernal, V: **G.3.1**: 86.
Bernard, R: **I.2**: 26.
Bernard, T: **K.1**: 123.
Bernard, Y: **D.2**: 9.
Berninghaus, S: **F.8**: 139.
Bernstein, R: **B.1**: 14.
Berque, J: **F.7**: 188.
Berriane, M: **I.6**: 21.
Berrick, J: **F.4**: 174.
Berry, B: **D.9**: 62, 136. **F.8**: 91. **G.3.2**: 349.
Berry, D: **C.2**: 163. **C.3**: 147.
Berry, E: **F.8**: 38. **G.3.1**: 39.
Berry, J: **C.2**: 78. **F.7**: 131, 152.
Berry, S: **K.4**: 53.
Berry, W: **G.1**: 37.
Bertazzoni, U: **K.4**: 254.
Berthoud, G: **H.4**: 100.
Bertrand, D: **F.8**: 143.
Bertrand, M: **G.3.1**: 93.
Best, S: **B.1**: 18. **D.6**: 5.
Bestard, J: **F.4**: 36.
Bestuzhev-Lada, I: **E.3**: 32. **K.2**: 31.
Betcherman, G: **I.4**: 17.
Béteille, A: **E.1**: 18. **E.2**: 73.
Bettelheim, B: **G.3.2**: 82.
Bettenhausen, K: **C.4**: 11.
Betteridge, A: **F.5**: 117.
Bettoni, C: **D.7**: 39.
Betz, A: **C.2**: 164.

Betz, B: **J.7**: 20.
Bevan, V: **K.1**: 98.
Beyaev, N: **K.1**: 150.
Beyfuss, V: **E.3**: 73.
Bezanahary, A: **I.4**: 81.
Bhargava, A: **H.3**: 68.
Bhasker, S: **I.4**: 79.
Bhattacharya, J: **F.4**: 346.
Bhattacharya, K: **G.3.2**: 63.
Bhattacharya, N: **H.3**: 84.
Bhattacharyya, G: **F.8**: 138.
Bhengra, R: **F.5**: 237.
Bhuiya, A: **F.3**: 280.
Bhuiyan, A: **F.3**: 125.
Bhuiyan, R: **D.9**: 141.
Białecki, I: **D.9**: 132.
Biamonti, B: **K.3**: 39.
Bian, Y: **G.3.2**: 34.
Bicego, G: **F.3**: 295.
Bickford, A: **G.3.2**: 156.
Bickle, G: **D.4**: 20.
Bidart, C: **C.3**: 7. **C.4**: 49.
Bideau, A: **F.3**: 109.
Biderman, A: **K.1**: 160.
Biegel, D: **K.2**: 52.
Biehal, G: **D.7**: 104.
Biehal, N: **K.3**: 17.
Biehl, J: **F.5**: 94.
Bielefeld, U: **F.7**: 156.
Bieleń, S: **J.8**: 15.
Bien, W: **F.4**: 112.
Bierhoff, H: **C.2**: 184.
Biernat, M: **C.7**: 66. **F.5**: 286. **I.2**: 139.
Biggart, N: **H.1**: 3.
Bigras, M: **F.4**: 294.
Billig, M: **C.7**: 69. **F.4**: 224.
Billington, R: **D.1**: 13.
Billson, J: **F.5**: 34.
Binder, A: **K.1**: 192.
Binghao, A: **D.7**: 82.
Binion, G: **F.5**: 131.
Binns, D: **I.3**: 2.
Binstock, R: **K.4**: 149.
Biondi, G: **F.4**: 225.
Birch, S: **K.4**: 157.
Bird, G: **F.4**: 39.

Birk, M: **F.5**: 271.
Birke, L: **F.5**: 121–122. **F.6**: 15.
Birnbaum, D: **I.3**: 7.
Birnie, J: **H.4**: 28.
Biró, D: **F.4**: 34.
Birrell, R: **F.8**: 116.
Bischoff, J: **G.3.2**: 27.
Bishop, D: **D.7**: 56.
Biskup, M: **F.4**: 44.
Bisol, L: **D.7**: 80.
Bissonnette, V: **C.3**: 146.
Bizeul, Y: **D.5**: 115.
Bjerg, M: **F.7**: 167.
Blachet, D: **F.3**: 306.
Black, J: **C.3**: 57. **I.2**: 200.
Black, P: **C.3**: 109.
Black, R: **F.8**: 164.
Black, S: **I.4**: 75.
Blackall, J: **F.5**: 216.
Blackburn, C: **K.1**: 268.
Blackburn, R: **D.9**: 114.
Black, J, S: **D.1**: 52.
Blackman, S: **D.3**: 54.
Blackman, T: **G.3.2**: 291, 294.
Blaikie, P: **F.3**: 151.
Blair, E: **B.2**: 25.
Blair, M: **F.7**: 253.
Blais, A: **D.7**: 332.
Blais, L: **K.1**: 256.
Blake, A: **I.2**: 71.
Blake, J: **F.4**: 346.
Blakeney, R: **I.3**: 3.
Blalock, H: **E.2**: 44.
Blanc, M: **F.7**: 268.
Blanchet, D: **F.3**: 301. **I.2**: 163.
Blanchflower, D: **I.3**: 33.
Blanc, le, M: **F.4**: 351. **K.1**: 158.
Blanco, M: **F.3**: 281.
Blandford, A: **K.4**: 144.
Blank, G: **G.3.2**: 338.
Blank, R: **F.3**: 44.
Blase, J: **D.9**: 25, 62. **I.4**: 99.
Blasi, A: **C.2**: 225.
Blass, T: **C.2**: 219.
Blatz, C: **D.3**: 35.
Blau, D: **I.2**: 57. **K.4**: 155.
Blau, F: **I.2**: 166.

Blau, J: **C.6**: 12. **D.5**: 139. **H.4**: 23.
Blau, P: **C.3**: 47.
Blauw, W: **G.3.2**: 167.
Blayo, C: **F.3**: 34.
Blayo, Y: **F.3**: 91.
Blazhnov, E: **D.7**: 328.
Blea, I: **F.8**: 4.
Bleicken, L: **I.3**: 25.
Blekesaune, A: **G.3.1**: 99, 116.
Bloch, D: **D.9**: 157.
Bloch, F: **I.2**: 72.
Blochet, A: **F.2**: 54.
Block, J: **C.2**: 204.
Block, K: **K.1**: 192.
Block, R: **C.2**: 71.
Block, W: **H.2**: 13.
Blocker, T: **C.7**: 22.
Blockley, S: **C.7**: 25.
Blok, P: **D.7**: 205.
Blom, I: **F.4**: 62.
Blom, R: **H.2**: 2.
Blommaert, J: **F.7**: 193.
Bloom, L: **F.3**: 227.
Bloomfield, T: **D.8**: 25.
Bloor, M: **B.2**: 23. **K.1**: 348.
Blossfeld, H: **B.2**: 88. **F.2**: 6. **F.4**: 63. **H.4**: 2.
Bluebond-Langner, M: **F.3**: 190.
Blum, A: **F.1**: 22.
Blum, L: **D.3**: 74. **F.5**: 64.
Blum, M: **C.3**: 108.
Blumberg, L: **K.1**: 312.
Blumberg, M: **F.3**: 144.
Blumberg, R: **I.2**: 103.
Blumler, J: **D.7**: 323.
Blyton, P: **I.3**: 126.
Bockel, A: **F.8**: 131.
Bockenholt, U: **C.2**: 24.
Böcker, A: **F.7**: 248.
Bode, I: **I.5**: 1.
Bodson, J: **F.5**: 158.
Boeck, De, P: **C.2**: 48.
Bogaerts, T: **G.3.2**: 269.
Bogart, J: **K.1**: 118.
Bogart, L: **D.7**: 232.
Bogart, W: **I.3**: 107.
Bogemskaya, K: **D.8**: 41.

Bogen, D: **D.7**: 211.
Bögenhold, D: **I.2**: 6.
Boger, G: **B.1**: 122.
Bogomolov, A: **D.1**: 23.
Bogomolov, Y: **D.7**: 365. **D.8**: 59, 73.
Bogumolov, I: **I.4**: 103.
Bohanon, C: **K.1**: 230.
Bohlken, J: **J.6**: 38.
Bohm, R: **K.1**: 193.
Bohman, J: **B.1**: 65.
Böhning, R: **I.2**: 67.
Böhning, W: **F.8**: 135.
Bohrnstedt, G: **B.2**: 54.
Boiko, V: **C.1**: 174. **C.7**: 44.
Boisier, S: **H.7**: 9.
Boisvert, J: **C.1**: 59.
Boje, D: **C.3**: 86.
Bokor, A: **K.1**: 289.
Bolay, H: **K.4**: 86.
Bolderson, H: **K.2**: 23.
Bolger, N: **C.2**: 200, 203. **C.3**: 159.
Boling, P: **F.5**: 72.
Bolio, M: **F.8**: 134.
Bollen, K: **B.2**: 61.
Bollinger, L: **D.7**: 262.
Bolstein, R: **B.2**: 125.
Böltken, F: **F.7**: 143.
Bolton, K: **D.7**: 81.
Bolzman, C: **F.8**: 9.
Bommes, M: **F.7**: 82.
Bompiani, A: **G.1**: 14.
Bonacich, P: **C.4**: 54. **G.3.2**: 306.
Bonaiuto, M: **G.3.2**: 180.
Bonan, J: **D.9**: 112.
Bonasewicz, A: **G.3.2**: 11.
Bonazzi, G: **I.3**: 67.
Bond, D: **B.2**: 69, 124.
Bond, P: **E.2**: 28.
Bondi, L: **F.5**: 178.
Bonefeld, W: **J.2**: 21.
Bonfils, B: **A.1**: 32.
Bongaarts, J: **F.3**: 48.
Bonnafous, S: **F.8**: 26.
Bonnamour, L: **G.3.2**: 79.
Bonneh, D: **D.5**: 185.
Bonnen, J: **G.3.1**: 133.
Bonnes, M: **G.3.2**: 180.

Bonnett, C: **H.4**: 78.
Bonnette-Lucat, C: **H.4**: 35.
Bonney, N: **F.5**: 8.
Bonnin, P: **F.4**: 89.
Bono, P: **F.5**: 101.
Bonß, W: **D.1**: 102.
Bonte, P: **I.4**: 93.
Booker, J: **K.1**: 417.
Books, J: **J.1**: 14.
Bools, C: **K.1**: 41.
Boomgaard, P: **G.3.1**: 30.
Booth, A: **F.4**: 121, 142. **I.4**: 122.
Booth, C: **F.4**: 301. **K.3**: 21.
Booth, K: **F.8**: 39.
Booth, S: **H.4**: 18, 91.
Booth, T: **K.4**: 53.
Booth, W: **H.2**: 14.
Bor, R: **F.3**: 228.
Borchgrevink, C: **C.3**: 26.
Bordeloup, J: **K.2**: 92.
Borgegård, L: **G.3.2**: 116.
Borgers, A: **H.5**: 36.
Börgers, T: **C.7**: 76.
Borgida, E: **C.1**: 64.
Borgonovi, E: **K.4**: 180.
Borjas, G: **F.8**: 25.
Borkowska, S: **I.2**: 242. **I.5**: 69.
Borman, K: **I.2**: 174.
Bormann, F: **G.1**: 16.
Borneman, J: **E.3**: 1.
Bornoff, N: **F.6**: 33.
Böröcz, J: **E.3**: 11.
Borodin, S: **K.1**: 129.
Borodkin, F: **I.6**: 35.
Borooah, V: **H.4**: 40. **K.1**: 270.
Borowski, A: **F.2**: 43.
Bortoni, S: **D.7**: 80.
Boruta, I: **H.3**: 86.
Borzenkov, V: **D.9**: 57.
Bosker, R: **D.9**: 122.
Bosman, E: **F.4**: 17.
Bosniak, L: **I.2**: 67.
Bosvieux, J: **G.3.2**: 134.
Bosworth, K: **K.4**: 8.
Bosworth, R: **F.7**: 48.
Bot, M: **D.9**: 84.

Botha, T: **D.9**: 53.
Bot, le, Y: **G.3.1**: 87.
Botsko, C: **A.2**: 8. **I.5**: 174.
Botton Beja, F: **G.3.2**: 169.
Bouchard, C: **F.3**: 246.
Boudebaba, R: **G.3.2**: 164.
Boudon, R: **C.1**: 153.
Bouillon, M: **I.5**: 33.
Bouissac, P: **D.7**: 25, 72.
Boukhemis, K: **G.3.2**: 337.
Boulay, du, J: **G.3.1**: 70.
Boulding, E: **J.8**: 11.
Boulègue, J: **J.7**: 12.
Boulet, D: **H.5**: 12.
Boullata, K: **A.1**: 33.
Boulton, M: **C.3**: 58. **C.4**: 8.
Bouma, D: **C.6**: 15.
Bound, J: **I.3**: 75.
Bourantas, D: **I.4**: 69.
Bourdeau, P: **G.1**: 19.
Bourdet, Y: **I.2**: 38.
Bourdieu, P: **D.5**: 138. **E.3**: 65. **F.6**: 7.
Boureau, A: **D.7**: 6.
Bourg, D: **D.3**: 46. **H.4**: 100.
Bourhis, R: **C.4**: 44.
Bourne, K: **F.3**: 245.
Bourne, L: **G.3.2**: 302.
Bourner, T: **D.9**: 201.
Bourreau, P: **F.2**: 90.
Boushel, M: **K.3**: 3.
Bousquet, G: **F.8**: 3.
Boustred, M: **K.4**: 225.
Boutan, P: **D.8**: 52.
Boutellier, J: **K.1**: 131.
Bova, R: **E.3**: 27.
Bovenkerk, F: **F.8**: 10. **I.2**: 189.
Bowen, G: **F.2**: 100.
Bowerman, M: **D.7**: 210.
Bowes, A: **F.7**: 12.
Bowlby, J: **C.2**: 183.
Bowler, A: **D.8**: 45.
Bowles, J: **G.3.1**: 35.
Bowles, M: **C.5**: 52.
Bowles, P: **J.6**: 5.
Bowling, A: **K.4**: 62, 147.
Bowling, B: **F.7**: 15.
Boxman, A: **E.2**: 17.

Boyd, J: **E.1**: 17.
Boyd, M: **F.8**: 74. **H.4**: 17.
Boyd, R: **F.7**: 51.
Boyd, S: **D.7**: 45.
Boyden, J: **F.2**: 80.
Boyer, J: **K.4**: 33.
Boyer, N: **D.9**: 180.
Boyer, W: **D.9**: 180. **G.3.1**: 126.
Boylan, E: **F.3**: 232.
Boyle, E: **I.5**: 73.
Boyle, T: **D.5**: 120.
Bozett, F: **F.4**: 290.
Braaten, J: **B.1**: 107.
Bracher, M: **F.3**: 99.
Bracken, I: **F.3**: 29.
Bradac, J: **D.7**: 61.
Bradburn, N: **C.2**: 62.
Braddock, Q: **K.1**: 12.
Braden, A: **J.5**: 4.
Bradley, A: **F.7**: 249. **I.3**: 29.
Bradley, G: **K.4**: 148.
Bradley, J: **I.2**: 236. **K.1**: 401.
Bradley, S: **I.4**: 19.
Bradshaw, J: **K.2**: 14.
Bradshaw, L: **F.3**: 227.
Bradshaw, Y: **B.2**: 105.
Brady, G: **I.5**: 75.
Braham, P: **F.7**: 252.
Braid, R: **G.3.2**: 152.
Brandeau, M: **F.3**: 153. **K.4**: 229.
Brandling-Bennett, A: **F.3**: 227.
Brandon, A: **F.5**: 257.
Brandon, D: **C.1**: 67.
Brandon, R: **K.4**: 77.
Brandstätter, V: **C.3**: 42.
Brandt, A: **K.4**: 23.
Brandt, G: **D.1**: 21.
Brannon, J: **G.3.1**: 113. **K.4**: 128.
Brass, D: **C.5**: 78.
Brass, T: **E.2**: 27.
Braud, P: **J.1**: 12.
Braun, D: **H.3**: 78. **K.4**: 181.
Braun L., J: **G.3.2**: 295.
Braungart, M: **J.6**: 11.
Braungart, R: **J.6**: 11.
Bravo, M: **C.1**: 66.

Bray, M: **D.9**: 65.
Braye, S: **K.3**: 27.
Brazier, A: **K.3**: 9.
Brazier, M: **K.4**: 264.
Brčić, K: **F.5**: 260.
Brea, J: **F.8**: 34.
Breakey, W: **K.1**: 239, 347.
Breakwell, G: **C.1**: 169. **F.3**: 61. **J.6**: 59.
Brechin, S: **G.1**: 33.
Breckler, S: **C.2**: 131.
Bredeweg, U: **H.4**: 93.
Breen, R: **I.4**: 116.
Breheny, M: **J.1**: 20.
Brennan, A: **F.4**: 156.
Brennan, M: **B.2**: 101.
Brennan, P: **K.1**: 351.
Brennan, T: **D.9**: 202. **K.4**: 256.
Brenner, J: **F.5**: 184.
Brent, E: **A.3**: 7. **B.2**: 8.
Breslauer, G: **E.3**: 4.
Bresnahan, M: **D.7**: 96.
Bretas, M: **K.1**: 116.
Brets, R: **C.2**: 116.
Brett, J: **C.3**: 115. **C.4**: 40. **F.5**: 305. **I.3**: 80.
Breuer, B: **F.2**: 34.
Brewer, J: **J.3**: 38.
Brewer, M: **C.1**: 106.
Brewin, C: **C.1**: 99.
Breznitz, S: **J.8**: 20.
Bricker-Jenkins, M: **K.3**: 16.
Bridges, W: **I.2**: 173. **I.5**: 17.
Bridgford, J: **I.5**: 4.
Brief, A: **I.3**: 98.
Briggs, D: **F.3**: 31.
Briggs, J: **K.1**: 1.
Briggs, S: **C.3**: 146.
Bright, A: **I.6**: 25.
Brightbill, T: **J.6**: 65.
Brill, A: **F.5**: 245.
Brink, J: **F.5**: 5.
Brinkerhoff, M: **D.5**: 103.
Brinton, M: **F.5**: 185.
Brito, D: **K.4**: 196.
Brittain, A: **F.3**: 33, 76.
Britton, J: **H.4**: 39.
Broad, B: **K.1**: 205.
Brock, A: **C.1**: 42.

Brock, D: **D.1**: 36.
Brock, T: **K.2**: 11.
Brodribb, S: **F.6**: 10.
Brok, den, B: **I.2**: 189.
Brol, J: **K.4**: 19.
Broman, C: **F.4**: 59.
Bromley, D: **D.5**: 61.
Bromulei, I: **F.7**: 157.
Bronars, S: **F.8**: 25.
Bronfman, M: **F.4**: 35.
Bronstein, A: **I.2**: 63.
Brooke, J: **D.5**: 127.
Brookhiser, R: **F.7**: 43.
Brooks, J: **B.1**: 84.
Brooks-Gunn, J: **F.4**: 286.
Broomberg, J: **K.4**: 79.
Broome, B: **C.3**: 120. **H.7**: 26.
Brosch, I: **F.4**: 65.
Brose, H: **I.5**: 1.
Brosh, M: **C.3**: 155.
Brosius, H: **D.7**: 71.
Brotchie, J: **G.3.2**: 246.
Broussard, S: **K.1**: 45.
Brown, A: **K.3**: 19.
Brown, B: **I.6**: 23.
Brown, C: **F.7**: 265. **I.5**: 193. **J.5**: 4.
Brown, D: **D.1**: 78. **E.2**: 76. **E.3**: 15, 30.
Brown, E: **K.4**: 183.
Brown, F: **D.8**: 70. **D.9**: 49, 70.
Brown, H: **F.4**: 277. **F.5**: 138. **K.4**: 127.
Brown, J: **A.1**: 11. **C.3**: 70. **K.4**: 93, 225.
Brown, K: **D.5**: 188. **K.1**: 329.
Brown, L: **J.8**: 2.
Brown, M: **K.4**: 204.
Brown, P: **D.9**: 9. **I.2**: 215.
Brown, R: **G.3.1**: 65.
Brown, S: **D.4**: 28. **K.1**: 308.
Brown, W: **K.1**: 171, 186. **K.4**: 11, 170.
Browne, E: **B.2**: 73.
Browne, M: **I.3**: 71.
Brownfield, D: **B.2**: 110.
Brownstein, H: **K.1**: 392.
Brownstone, D: **G.3.2**: 102.
Brubaker, W: **F.8**: 132.
Bruce, C: **D.9**: 192. **I.5**: 74.
Bruce, M: **D.9**: 82.

Bruce, S: **D.7**: 375.
Bruce, V: **C.2**: 141. **C.3**: 68.
Bruckerhoff, C: **D.9**: 46.
Brüderl, J: **I.4**: 64.
Bruel, van den, B: **K.2**: 37.
Bruer, J: **F.5**: 208.
Bruhn, J: **A.3**: 3.
Bruhns, C: **I.3**: 150.
Brumberg, A: **F.7**: 244.
Brummer, J: **H.4**: 66.
Brunelli, M: **I.6**: 37.
Brunet, G: **F.3**: 109.
Brunk, G: **K.1**: 96.
Brunner, C: **F.5**: 167.
Bruno, F: **K.1**: 322.
Bruns, M: **F.4**: 181.
Brunt, L: **G.3.2**: 55. **K.1**: 220.
Brussel, van, G: **K.1**: 316.
Bruyelle, P: **G.3.2**: 189, 201.
Bryant, C: **G.3**: 9. **G.3.2**: 189. **J.8**: 7.
Bryant, K: **K.1**: 323.
Bryant, P: **D.7**: 56.
Bryant, W: **H.5**: 20.
Bryden, J: **G.3.1**: 52, 116.
Bryder, T: **I.2**: 208.
Bryson, J: **H.4**: 74.
Buchanan, C: **C.2**: 18.
Buchanan, J: **K.1**: 345.
Bucher, H: **F.2**: 34. **F.8**: 175.
Bucholz, K: **K.1**: 309.
Buck, A: **K.1**: 59.
Buck, M: **F.5**: 179.
Buck, N: **C.3**: 127.
Bucke, T: **I.6**: 12.
Buckingham, D: **D.7**: 392.
Buckley, P: **I.3**: 60.
Buckner, J: **K.4**: 189.
Buczkowski, P: **D.6**: 25.
Budd, L: **G.3.2**: 35.
Budesheim, T: **J.6**: 16.
Budina, O: **G.3.2**: 93.
Buell, S: **D.4**: 42.
Buen, de, J: **G.3.2**: 118, 151.
Büyükbozkoyum, O: **I.2**: 66.
Bugajski, J: **E.3**: 16.
Bugental, D: **C.3**: 11.
Buisson, M: **I.2**: 72.

Bulbeck, C: **F.5**: 97.
Bull, R: **B.2**: 96.
Bullard, E: **K.2**: 47.
Bullard, R: **G.3.2**: 126.
Buller, D: **C.3**: 110.
Bullock, J: **F.4**: 81.
Bullock, R: **K.2**: 37.
Bumpass, L: **F.4**: 238.
Bundrick, C: **J.6**: 10.
Bunting, T: **G.3.2**: 237.
Bunyan, T: **F.8**: 59.
Bunzel, J: **D.7**: 5.
Burawoy, M: **I.4**: 32.
Burbank, V: **F.4**: 228.
Burchell, R: **D.1**: 67.
Burchinal, M: **B.2**: 45.
Buren, van, J: **C.1**: 49.
Burfoot, A: **K.4**: 65.
Burgalassi, S: **K.2**: 86.
Burger, J: **C.1**: 119. **C.7**: 17.
Burgess, A: **C.2**: 79.
Burgess, J: **D.7**: 245.
Burgoyne, C: **H.6**: 2.
Burg, van der, W: **B.1**: 74.
Burkart, G: **F.4**: 254.
Burkart, R: **D.7**: 188.
Burke, P: **C.2**: 46.
Burke, R: **I.3**: 103.
Burke, W: **I.5**: 106.
Burkhardt, M: **C.5**: 78.
Burkhardt, R: **K.4**: 86.
Burkhauser, R: **F.2**: 47.
Burkitt, I: **C.1**: 170. **C.2**: 214.
Burley, K: **I.4**: 6.
Burney, N: **D.9**: 134.
Burns, N: **F.4**: 165.
Burns, T: **B.1**: 97.
Burr, J: **F.7**: 250.
Burris, B: **I.2**: 89.
Burris, V: **H.4**: 68.
Burroughs, W: **C.1**: 130.
Burrows, R: **H.4**: 15. **H.5**: 16.
Bursik, K: **C.2**: 3.
Bursik, R: **C.7**: 59. **D.5**: 57.
Burstein, P: **I.2**: 212.
Burston, D: **C.1**: 29.

Burt, R: **F.2**: 12.
Burton, A: **C.2**: 141.
Burton, C: **I.2**: 131.
Burton, M: **C.3**: 68.
Burton, S: **B.2**: 25.
Bury, M: **F.3**: 195.
Busch, J: **D.7**: 61.
Bush, A: **D.3**: 86.
Bushardt, S: **C.5**: 44.
Busino, G: **H.4**: 100.
Buss, D: **C.2**: 66. **F.4**: 201.
Bustos Ramirez, J: **K.1**: 321.
Butera, F: **H.3**: 52.
Butler, J: **B.1**: 3. **F.2**: 47.
Butler, R: **C.5**: 21, 27.
Butler, S: **F.5**: 91. **K.1**: 337.
Butt, N: **D.5**: 176.
Butzer, R: **F.6**: 56.
Buunk, B: **C.3**: 33. **F.4**: 246.
Buxton, M: **K.4**: 49.
Bybee, J: **C.2**: 238.
Bye, B: **B.2**: 59.
Bynner, J: **A.2**: 8. **I.2**: 40.
Byrne, B: **C.2**: 226.
Byrne, D: **I.2**: 145.
Byrne, R: **C.2**: 113.
Byrne-Sutton, P: **I.3**: 118.
Bywaters, P: **K.3**: 4.
Caballero, L: **I.4**: 27.
Çaceres, J: **F.3**: 81.
Čačić, J: **F.8**: 81.
Caddick, B: **K.3**: 19.
Cadiet, L: **D.4**: 16.
Cadman, E: **F.6**: 34.
Cahill, C: **F.4**: 171. **K.1**: 38.
Cain, B: **J.6**: 1.
Cain, M: **F.2**: 23.
Caire, G: **I.5**: 12.
Calasanti, T: **F.5**: 180.
Calcagno, E: **A.2**: 2.
Caldwell, J: **F.6**: 9.
Caldwell, L: **D.2**: 12.
Caldwell, P: **F.6**: 9.
Calev, A: **F.3**: 206.
Calhoun, C: **D.5**: 138. **F.3**: 86.
Calhoun, G: **C.2**: 65.
Callahan, D: **F.2**: 7.

Callari, A: **B.1**: 43.
Calleri, D: **D.7**: 89.
Callero, P: **C.3**: 73.
Calnan, M: **K.4**: 230.
Calot, G: **F.3**: 243.
Calsyn, R: **K.1**: 274.
Calvalcanti-Tavares, L: **K.1**: 383.
Calvez, T: **D.9**: 89.
Cambrosio, A: **J.4**: 13.
Cameron, D: **D.9**: 199.
Camí, J: **K.1**: 319.
Camire, L: **F.6**: 31.
Campanelli, P: **B.2**: 125. **G.3.2**: 107–108.
Campbell, C: **B.1**: 132.
Campbell, E: **F.4**: 102.
Campbell, G: **B.2**: 62.
Campbell, I: **I.2**: 191.
Campbell, J: **C.2**: 117. **F.2**: 46. **F.4**: 168.
Campbell, K: **C.4**: 39. **G.3.2**: 211.
Campbell, M: **K.1**: 31.
Campbell, R: **D.7**: 56.
Campeanu, P: **J.2**: 17.
Campion, M: **I.3**: 38, 46.
Campling, J: **F.4**: 300.
Campos, N: **G.3.2**: 141.
Campos Mello, de, V: **A.2**: 2.
Canetto, S: **K.1**: 395.
Caney, S: **B.1**: 19.
Canino, G: **C.1**: 66.
Cannings, K: **F.5**: 147, 202. **I.2**: 113.
Cannon, T: **F.5**: 247.
Cannon-Bowers, J: **I.4**: 125.
Cantalini, B: **F.1**: 50.
Cantillon, B: **K.1**: 284.
Cantor, M: **F.4**: 4–5.
Cantor, N: **C.2**: 59, 200.
Caplan, L: **C.2**: 26.
Caplin, L: **E.3**: 17.
Caplow, T: **E.3**: 50.
Caporael, L: **C.1**: 106.
Capotorti, F: **F.7**: 130.
Cappel, S: **I.5**: 99.
Cappelleri, J: **B.2**: 18.
Caputi, J: **D.7**: 214.
Carawan, C: **J.5**: 4.
Carawan, G: **J.5**: 4.

Carballo, M: **F.6**: 4.
Carby-Hall, J: **I.5**: 74.
Card, C: **F.5**: 90.
Cardano, M: **A.2**: 22.
Carey, G: **F.4**: 310.
Carey, J: **D.9**: 12, 67.
Carey, S: **C.1**: 41.
Cariño, B: **F.8**: 155.
Carley, K: **C.4**: 59. **C.5**: 20.
Carlin, P: **F.2**: 91. **I.2**: 106.
Carlisle-Frank, P: **K.1**: 349.
Carlo, G: **C.2**: 181. **C.3**: 132.
Carlsson-Paige, N: **F.2**: 117.
Carlton, J: **K.2**: 98.
Carlyle, S: **G.3.2**: 303.
Carman, R: **K.1**: 352.
Carmeli, Y: **D.7**: 72.
Carnevale, P: **C.3**: 114. **I.5**: 88.
Carney, J: **F.5**: 269, 326.
Carney, T: **K.1**: 390.
Carnie, J: **K.1**: 43.
Carovano, K: **F.5**: 25.
Carpendale, J: **D.3**: 86.
Carpini, M: **J.6**: 47.
Carr, A: **C.1**: 158. **F.4**: 38.
Carr, M: **F.5**: 321.
Carr, S: **G.1**: 13.
Carr-Hill, R: **F.5**: 258. **K.1**: 241. **K.4**: 173.
Carranza Valdés, J: **J.1**: 7.
Carrara, S: **K.1**: 145.
Carrère, S: **F.3**: 230.
Carrier, M: **D.6**: 32.
Carrillo, A: **F.5**: 292.
Carrión, F: **G.3.2**: 43.
Carroll, B: **K.2**: 71.
Carroll, G: **C.5**: 38.
Cars, G: **G.3.2**: 283.
Carson, D: **F.4**: 159.
Carta, J: **D.9**: 154. **F.2**: 3.
Carter, D: **D.9**: 70, 149.
Carter, H: **G.3**: 11.
Carter, S: **D.7**: 29. **F.5**: 247.
Cartocci, R: **J.6**: 60.
Cartwright, T: **H.7**: 16.
Carty, H: **I.5**: 103.
Casado, D: **K.1**: 282.
Casavola, F: **D.5**: 136.

Caselli, G: **F.3**: 243.
Casetti, E: **F.3**: 47.
Casey, B: **I.4**: 127.
Casey, J: **C.2**: 91.
Casey, R: **F.2**: 70. **F.3**: 12.
Caspi, A: **C.2**: 187.
Caspy, T: **I.3**: 99.
Cassetti, E: **F.3**: 223.
Cassia, P: **C.2**: 6.
Cassidy, A: **I.3**: 60.
Cassidy, M: **I.4**: 111.
Cassou, S: **K.4**: 43.
Casswell, S: **K.1**: 364.
Castellano, T: **D.4**: 22. **K.1**: 40.
Castillo, F: **K.1**: 320.
Castles, F: **F.4**: 127.
Castro, N: **I.1**: 1. **I.5**: 176.
Castro, R: **F.4**: 35.
Castro-Gómez, S: **D.1**: 71.
Catalano, R: **F.4**: 252.
Catanzaro, S: **C.3**: 2.
Catanzaro, de, D: **C.7**: 27.
Catron, L: **F.4**: 126.
Caulkins, J: **F.3**: 150, 153.
Causey, B: **F.1**: 24.
Cauvin, C: **F.1**: 37.
Cavaliere, F: **I.5**: 106.
Cavalli, A: **D.1**: 96. **F.2**: 127.
Cavarozzi, M: **J.2**: 13.
Cavell, M: **C.1**: 57.
Cayemittes, M: **F.3**: 295.
Cayer, N: **D.4**: 34.
Cécora, J: **H.4**: 35.
Centlivres, P: **F.7**: 164.
Centro Studi Investimenti Sociali: **E.1**: 15.
Cerezo, J: **C.1**: 102.
Cerocchi, P: **D.9**: 17.
Cervero, R: **G.3.2**: 317.
Cesa, I: **C.2**: 103.
Cesarani, D: **F.7**: 97.
Cevallos, N: **G.2**: 14.
Cézard, M: **I.2**: 38.
Cha, Y: **D.9**: 127.
Chachere, J: **D.7**: 249.
Chaffee, S: **D.7**: 270. **F.8**: 129.
Chahnazarian, A: **F.3**: 295.

Chaiken, S: **C.1**: 63. **C.2**: 236.
Chakrabarti, M: **K.4**: 222.
Chakravarty, P: **D.7**: 124, 128.
Chaliand, G: **F.7**: 49.
Chamala, S: **G.3.1**: 135.
Chambaz, J: **D.8**: 8.
Chambers, G: **E.2**: 18.
Chambré, S: **K.3**: 47.
Champagne, R: **D.3**: 50.
Champion, A: **G.3.2**: 235.
Champion, F: **D.5**: 21.
Champion, T: **G.3.1**: 48.
Chan, J: **D.7**: 305.
Chan, S: **H.3**: 18.
Chanana, K: **D.9**: 133.
Chandler, J: **F.4**: 261.
Chandler, M: **C.2**: 123.
Chandrika, S: **F.5**: 194.
Chang-Muy, F: **F.3**: 227.
Channa, V: **F.5**: 198.
Chant, D: **B.2**: 32.
Chant, S: **F.8**: 90. **G.3.2**: 265.
Chantraine, Y: **C.2**: 25.
Chapin, J: **E.3**: 56.
Chaplin, W: **C.2**: 194.
Chapman, M: **E.3**: 41.
Chappell, D: **K.1**: 405.
Chappell, N: **K.4**: 133, 144.
Chappell, W: **H.4**: 52.
Charbonneau, F: **G.3.2**: 144.
Charlesworth, W: **D.3**: 67. **D.4**: 3.
Charlot, A: **D.9**: 181.
Charlot, J: **D.8**: 77.
Charman, A: **F.5**: 210. **K.4**: 129.
Charon, J: **D.7**: 309.
Charon, R: **D.7**: 77.
Charrier, M: **G.3.2**: 173.
Charsley, S: **F.4**: 237.
Charters, S: **G.3.2**: 303.
Chatak, E: **I.5**: 34.
Chatman, J: **I.4**: 31.
Chatterjee, L: **H.4**: 38.
Chattopadhyay, G: **I.3**: 135.
Chaudry, H: **K.1**: 313.
Chauviré, Y: **F.3**: 262.
Chavero, E: **G.3.1**: 93.
Chaves, M: **D.5**: 46, 64.

Chavez, L: **F.7**: 107.
Chazine, J: **A.1**: 27.
Cheal, D: **F.4**: 45.
Cheater, A: **D.9**: 104.
Checkoway, B: **G.2**: 22.
Cheikh, N: **I.2**: 88.
Chelimsky, E: **G.3.2**: 98.
Chelle, D: **D.4**: 16.
Chen, A: **D.7**: 19.
Chen, C: **C.2**: 179. **C.6**: 1.
Chen, J: **D.7**: 16.
Chen, K: **D.1**: 92.
Chen, M. **I.2**. 29.
Chen, P: **C.1**: 37.
Chen, R: **F.3**: 124.
Chen, X: **G.3.2**: 243.
Cheng, M: **I.2**: 211.
Cherlin, A: **F.4**: 124, 238.
Chernichovsky, D: **F.3**: 58.
Cherniss, C: **I.4**: 88.
Chernyshev, V: **C.2**: 217.
Cherry, F: **I.2**: 91. **K.4**: 177.
Cherry, R: **B.1**: 128.
Cherulnik, P: **C.7**: 55.
Cheshire, J: **D.7**: 198.
Chevalier, J: **G.3.1**: 101.
Chevigné, C: **G.3.2**: 189.
Chew, B: **C.2**: 117.
Chiapella, G: **K.2**: 86.
Chiarante, G: **D.9**: 165.
Chiarucci, P: **C.7**: 47.
Chib, S: **F.3**: 20.
Chiche, J: **F.2**: 67.
Chicoine, N: **G.3.2**: 174. **K.2**: 35.
Chidester, D: **D.5**: 49, 65.
Chierici, R: **F.8**: 69.
Chiesa, A: **D.8**: 64.
Childers, T: **B.2**: 127.
Chin, K: **K.1**: 328.
Chinchilla, N: **F.5**: 104. **F.8**: 6.
Chinitz, B: **G.3.2**: 263.
Chinn, C: **I.6**: 3.
Chiodo, L: **C.2**: 66.
Chipande, G: **H.4**: 4.
Chiriboga, D: **F.4**: 126.
Chirikos, T: **I.2**: 125.

Chisholm, J: **F.4**: 228.
Chistov, K: **G.3.2**: 185.
Chiswick, B: **F.8**: 57.
Cho, J: **D.7**: 162.
Chock, P: **D.7**: 33.
Choi, S: **D.7**: 210. **F.4**: 194.
Chokor, B: **B.2**: 86. **G.3.2**: 206.
Chong, D: **J.5**: 1.
Choudhury, M: **C.7**: 61.
Chressanthis, G: **J.6**: 15.
Christian-Smith, L: **D.9**: 26.
Christiansen, B: **K.1**: 308.
Christiansson, P: **A.3**: 1.
Christl, R: **I.2**: 220.
Chua, B: **G.3.2**: 279.
Chua, W: **K.4**: 231.
Chuaqui, R: **D.4**: 18.
Chui, T: **J.6**: 17.
Chung, C: **D.5**: 7.
Chung, K: **E.2**: 78.
Church, R: **D.9**: 131. **I.5**: 84.
Churchill, M: **C.3**: 50.
Chusmir, L: **C.2**: 174. **I.4**: 71.
Çi, J: **C.2**: 14.
Čičak-Chand, R: **F.8**: 148.
Cicconetti, C: **G.3.2**: 250.
Cicirelli, V: **K.4**: 34.
Cieri, De, H: **I.3**: 65. **I.5**: 131.
Cigno, A: **H.3**: 19.
Cillario, L: **D.9**: 165.
Cioffi, D: **C.1**: 81.
Citro, C: **B.2**: 53.
Claassens, A: **G.3.1**: 8, 123.
Claridge, G: **C.1**: 128.
Clark, C: **G.2**: 35. **H.3**: 18.
Clark, D: **F.4**: 213, 259. **F.7**: 67. **I.4**: 23.
Clark, H: **C.2**: 209. **K.4**: 142.
Clark, I: **D.3**: 7.
Clark, K: **C.5**: 78.
Clark, L: **C.3**: 137. **K.1**: 193.
Clark, M: **C.3**: 133. **D.9**: 168.
Clark, R: **D.7**: 180. **I.2**: 79–80.
Clark, T: **E.2**: 51.
Clark, W: **K.1**: 303.
Clark-Nicolas, P: **F.4**: 205.
Clarke, G: **G.3.2**: 324–325.
Clarke, J: **D.1**: 86.

Clarke-Stewart, K: **F.2**: 93.
Clausen, J: **F.2**: 119. **F.4**: 75.
Clay, D: **F.4**: 48.
Clayden, K: **F.3**: 61.
Clayton, I: **G.1**: 25.
Cleary, M: **G.1**: 59.
Clegg, S: **K.4**: 231.
Clémence, A: **C.7**: 70.
Cliff, D: **I.3**: 48.
Clifford, B: **D.7**: 353. **F.2**: 69.
Clifford, P: **K.4**: 129.
Cling, B: **F.5**: 303.
Cliquet, R: **F.3**: 25.
Cloninger, D: **K.1**: 102.
Cloonan, J: **D.7**: 334.
Clotfelter, C: **D.9**: 182.
Clout, H: **G.3.1**: 121.
Clyne, M: **D.7**: 155.
Cmiel, K: **D.7**: 279.
Coates, D: **H.5**: 40.
Cobb, A: **C.5**: 81.
Cobb, S: **H.3**: 51.
Cochran, J: **D.5**: 9, 57. **F.6**: 21.
Cochran, S: **C.1**: 107.
Cochrane, S: **F.3**: 39.
Cockburn, A: **J.3**: 34.
Cockburn, C: **F.5**: 193.
Code, L: **F.5**: 136.
Codevilla, G: **D.5**: 4.
Coenen-Huther, J: **D.1**: 16.
Coetzee, J: **D.9**: 209.
Coetzee, L: **I.3**: 144.
Cogan, R: **C.1**: 9.
Coggans, N: **D.9**: 163.
Coggeshall, J: **F.5**: 40.
Cohe, S: **D.8**: 60.
Cohen, B: **C.3**: 85. **I.3**: 84. **K.2**: 44, 65.
Cohen, C: **F.2**: 114. **K.1**: 319.
Cohen, E: **D.5**: 83, 122.
Cohen, H: **J.3**: 45.
Cohen, J: **F.5**: 245. **H.4**: 18.
Cohen, L: **K.1**: 61, 111.
Cohen, M: **D.1**: 4. **F.7**: 99.
Cohen, R: **K.1**: 378.
Cohen, S: **D.8**: 48. **F.7**: 98. **K.4**: 25.
Cohen, W: **C.5**: 78.

Cohn, S: **H.3**: 82. **K.1**: 206.
Colasante, C: **C.3**: 30.
Coldstream, P: **D.9**: 189.
Cole, B: **F.6**: 39.
Cole, J: **D.1**: 57. **F.5**: 208.
Coleman, D: **F.3**: 1.
Coleman, G: **C.5**: 35.
Coleman, J: **D.5**: 69. **E.3**: 65. **I.2**: 39.
Coles, R: **B.1**: 52.
Colle, del, E: **I.2**: 7.
Coller, X: **F.4**: 36. **I.2**: 56.
Collier, G: **C.1**: 147.
Collin Delavaud, A: **G.3.2**: 20.
Colling, T: **I.5**: 44–45.
Collins, A: **C.1**: 151. **F.3**: 71.
Collins, H: **I.5**: 41.
Collins, R: **F.4**: 246. **G.3.2**: 229.
Collomb, P: **F.3**: 15.
Colombel, J: **G.3.2**: 173.
Colpi, T: **F.7**: 32.
Colquitt, C: **F.5**: 216.
Coltart, N: **C.1**: 2.
Colten, M: **F.2**: 120.
Colton, M: **K.2**: 37.
Colvin, C: **C.2**: 82, 207. **C.7**: 29.
Comaroff, J: **F.7**: 158.
Comas d'Argemir, D: **F.4**: 36. **F.8**: 17.
Comelles, J: **K.4**: 74, 80.
Cominos, A: **D.7**: 335.
Commaille, J: **D.3**: 45. **I.4**: 93.
Commins, P: **E.2**: 64.
Commission of the European Communities: **G.3.2**: 319.
Commoner, B: **F.3**: 313.
Compas, B: **C.2**: 73.
Compton, P: **F.8**: 151.
Comstock, G: **D.7**: 326, 381. **K.1**: 429.
Comstock, J: **C.3**: 110.
Condon, S: **F.8**: 125.
Coney, S: **F.5**: 22.
Congdon, P: **G.3.2**: 205.
Conger, R: **F.4**: 203. **K.2**: 75.
Conlon, D: **C.4**: 12.
Conlon, J: **D.9**: 108.
Connell, R: **F.5**: 294.
Connolly, C: **F.5**: 44. **I.2**: 70.
Connolly, G: **K.1**: 364.

Connor, W: **E.2**: 49. **K.1**: 21.
Constantine, P: **F.5**: 155.
Content, A: **D.7**: 56.
Conti, S: **G.3.2**: 326. **K.1**: 380.
Contreras, A: **D.9**: 49.
Contreras, J: **F.6**: 7.
Contreras, R: **D.9**: 70.
Conway, D: **D.7**: 163.
Conway, M: **C.2**: 159.
Cooil, B: **K.4**: 102.
Cook, A: **G.3**: 5.
Cook, C: **K.1**: 374.
Cook, E: **F.5**: 87.
Cook, J: **F.5**: 66, 170.
Cook, L: **D.7**: 29.
Cook, P: **K.1**: 427.
Cook, T: **B.2**: 9.
Cook-Flannagan, C: **C.2**: 59.
Cooke, D: **K.1**: 204.
Cooke, T: **G.3.2**: 181.
Cookson, P: **D.9**: 70, 95.
Coomes, P: **H.7**: 28.
Coon, H: **F.4**: 310.
Cooney, R: **F.3**: 53.
Cooney, T: **F.4**: 223.
Cooper, B: **H.4**: 79.
Cooper, C: **I.1**: 15.
Cooper, D: **I.3**: 80. **I.5**: 150.
Cooper, E: **I.5**: 138.
Cooper, H: **C.1**: 96. **F.7**: 123.
Cooperrider, D: **C.5**: 51. **E.3**: 20.
Copeland, A: **F.4**: 108.
Copjec, J: **J.2**: 18, 29.
Coppard, L: **F.4**: 54.
Corbett, C: **J.3**: 36, 41.
Corbett, J: **K.4**: 225.
Corbetta, G: **D.3**: 52.
Corbey, R: **C.2**: 221.
Corcoran, M: **F.4**: 73.
Cordell, H: **I.6**: 1.
Córdova C., A: **K.4**: 166.
Cordray, D: **G.3.2**: 98.
Corfield, P: **D.7**: 209.
Cornblatt, B: **K.4**: 37.
Corne, S: **F.8**: 20.
Cornejo Bustamante, R: **G.3.2**: 169.

Cornell, D: **C.2**: 232. **C.3**: 25. **F.5**: 65, 245.
Cornell, W: **K.1**: 36.
Corner, J: **D.1**: 2.
Cornfield, D: **I.5**: 120.
Cornille, C: **D.5**: 22.
Cornwall, R: **I.2**: 46.
Cornwell, G: **D.9**: 177.
Coronil, F: **J.1**: 8.
Correa, S: **F.3**: 63.
Corrigan, P: **B.1**: 26.
Corso, Del, V: **F.2**: 94.
Cort, J: **D.5**: 74.
Cortázar, J: **D.5**: 58.
Cortes, D: **C.1**: 75.
Cortés, F: **H.3**: 10.
Cortright, D: **J.7**: 14.
Corvazier, F: **F.2**: 90.
Corzine, J: **K.1**: 226.
Coser, R: **C.1**: 103.
Cossette, L: **C.1**: 95.
Cossu, G: **D.7**: 56.
Costa, F: **G.3.2**: 318.
Cote, J: **I.3**: 39.
Cottingham, J: **D.3**: 8.
Cottle, C: **F.5**: 84.
Cottle, S: **D.7**: 313.
Cotton, J: **I.5**: 37.
Cotturri, G: **D.9**: 165.
Coughlin, R: **G.3.1**: 22.
Coulmas, F: **D.7**: 16.
Coupland, J: **D.7**: 44, 77, 194.
Coupland, N: **C.1**: 156. **D.7**: 44, 77, 160, 194.
Coupland, R: **K.4**: 45.
Courade, G: **G.3.1**: 96.
Courbage, Y: **F.3**: 293.
Courgeau, D: **F.8**: 47.
Cournoyer, D: **F.2**: 84.
Courteau, B: **I.4**: 118.
Courtney, S: **D.9**: 23.
Coutinho, R: **K.1**: 316.
Couto, R: **C.5**: 29. **F.7**: 2.
Covaleski, M: **J.4**: 9.
Covey, E: **D.3**: 55.
Covington, C: **C.1**: 22.
Covington, J: **K.1**: 88.
Cowan, D: **K.4**: 129.
Cowell, D: **K.1**: 127.

Cowen, T: **C.2**: 92.
Cox, A: **K.4**: 191.
Cox, B: **C.2**: 191.
Cox, C: **K.4**: 117.
Cox, J: **I.2**: 1.
Cox, K: **E.2**: 14. **G.3**: 6.
Cox, T: **I.4**: 82.
Coyle, A: **K.1**: 189.
Crabb, P: **H.7**: 5.
Craft, J: **I.5**: 190.
Crago, M: **D.7**: 24.
Craig, T: **K.4**: 129.
Crain, M: **I.5**: 145.
Crain, S: **D.7**: 40.
Cram, F: **I.3**: 63.
Cramer, P: **C.2**: 4.
Crampton, G: **F.3**: 24.
Crandall, C: **F.3**: 202.
Crane, J: **K.1**: 231.
Crang, P: **G.3.2**: 52.
Crapo, R: **F.6**: 19.
Craven, I: **D.7**: 358.
Craven, J: **C.2**: 94.
Cravens, R: **K.4**: 10.
Crawford, J: **C.2**: 93.
Cray, D: **C.5**: 27.
Creecy, B: **J.6**: 14.
Creevey, L: **F.5**: 192.
Creighton, S: **I.2**: 246.
Cremer, R: **D.7**: 16.
Crespi, F: **C.3**: 63.
Crespy, G: **H.4**: 18.
Cressey, P: **I.1**: 6.
Cretin, S: **F.3**: 153.
Creton, D: **F.3**: 298.
Crewe, L: **I.2**: 123.
Crider, D: **G.3.1**: 61.
Crighton, E: **F.7**: 18.
Crimmins, E: **F.2**: 140–141.
Crissman, L: **F.8**: 67.
Crittenden, J: **J.2**: 24.
Crittenden, K: **F.5**: 263.
Crnic, K: **F.4**: 301.
Crocker, J: **C.3**: 80.
Crockett, G: **I.4**: 29.
Croix, La, S: **I.5**: 9.

Cromer, I: **H.7**: 26.
Cromley, R: **B.2**: 62.
Cromwell, P: **K.1**: 358.
Cronk, L: **F.4**: 67, 317.
Crook, S: **B.1**: 121.
Cropanzano, R: **C.3**: 116. **I.3**: 58.
Crosby, A: **F.1**: 31.
Crosby, L: **F.4**: 42.
Cross, D: **G.3.2**: 94.
Cross, J: **K.1**: 42.
Cross, M: **H.4**: 56. **J.3**: 2.
Cross, P: **F.2**: 95.
Cross, W: **F.7**: 124.
Croteau, D: **D.7**: 240.
Crow, G: **F.4**: 298.
Crow, I: **F.7**: 220.
Crowe, D: **F.7**: 23.
Crowe, T: **K.1**: 66.
Crowley, D: **D.7**: 126.
Crowley, H: **F.5**: 124.
Crowley, J: **F.7**: 27. **G.3.2**: 188.
Crowley, K: **C.2**: 127.
Crown, C: **C.3**: 22.
Crown, W: **F.2**: 43.
Crozier, M: **H.4**: 18.
Cruise, J: **H.4**: 3.
Crush, J: **F.8**: 109.
Csányi, V: **C.5**: 69.
Cseh-Szombathy, L: **F.4**: 98.
Csepeli, G: **D.1**: 58, 60.
Csikszentmihalyi, M: **C.2**: 172. **C.3**: 6.
Cubbins, L: **F.5**: 253.
Cuchillo, M: **G.3.2**: 58.
Culkin, M: **K.2**: 41, 60.
Cullen, F: **I.4**: 24. **K.1**: 85.
Cullen, S: **I.4**: 38.
Cullenberg, S: **B.1**: 43.
Cullingworth, J: **G.3.2**: 228.
Culp, R: **F.2**: 99.
Culyer, A: **K.4**: 156, 159.
Cumberbatch, G: **D.7**: 363.
Cumper, G: **K.4**: 195.
Cunningham, P: **D.2**: 5.
Curci, G: **G.3.2**: 134, 148. **H.3**: 16.
Curley, S: **C.7**: 12.
Currall, S: **I.4**: 58.
Curran, J: **D.1**: 2. **D.7**: 307.

Currie, J: **I.5**: 62.
Curry, M: **G.1**: 29, 61.
Curry-Roper, J: **G.3.1**: 35.
Curtis, C: **J.6**: 18.
Curtis, J: **F.6**: 55. **J.6**: 17.
Curtis, S: **F.3**: 78.
Curtis, T: **K.4**: 219.
Cushman, P: **C.2**: 230.
Cutcher-Gershenfeld, J: **I.5**: 26.
Cuthbert, A: **G.3.2**: 261–262, 366.
Cutler, S: **J.1**: 2.
Cutright, J: **C.3**: 25.
Cuzán, A: **E.3**: 52. **J.5**: 26. **J.6**: 10.
Czada, R: **C.5**: 45.
Czeladka, E: **F.7**: 48.
Czerny, M: **G.3.2**: 298.
Czyżowska, Z: **E.3**: 12.
Daft, R: **C.5**: 75.
Dagevos, J: **F.7**: 237.
Daghistani, A: **G.3.2**: 322.
Dagsvik, J: **H.3**: 24, 28.
Dahl, A: **F.6**: 25.
Dahlgren, P: **D.7**: 241.
Dahua, C: **D.5**: 87.
Dain, J: **F.5**: 242.
Dale, B: **I.5**: 31.
Dale, P: **G.3.2**: 268–269.
Daley, P: **D.7**: 315.
Dallosso, H: **F.2**: 40.
Dalton, D: **I.3**: 52. **I.5**: 97.
Daly, G: **K.1**: 238. **K.2**: 13.
Daly, J: **C.3**: 124.
Damianos, D: **G.3.1**: 17, 116.
Damodaram, K: **E.3**: 15.
Damon, M: **D.7**: 88.
Dam, van, B: **F.2**: 149.
Dam, van, M: **H.3**: 7.
Dancaster, L: **I.3**: 76.
Danermark, B: **G.3**: 6. **G.3.2**: 311.
Danes, S: **F.4**: 51.
Danet, B: **F.7**: 114.
Daniel, H: **F.3**: 231.
Daniel, W: **I.2**: 213.
Daniels, M: **F.5**: 117.
Daniels, P: **G.3.2**: 352. **H.4**: 57.
Danigelis, N: **J.1**: 2. **K.4**: 126.

Dankert, G: **F.3**: 237.
Dankov, V: **D.2**: 27.
Dannecker, M: **F.6**: 48.
Danner, V: **B.1**: 151.
Dant, R: **H.5**: 33.
Dant, T: **D.6**: 15.
Danziger, G: **F.5**: 143.
Danziger, K: **C.1**: 114.
Daoutopoulos, G: **G.2**: 7, 15.
Dard, F: **D.7**: 247.
Darley, J: **D.7**: 161, 176.
Darqué, M: **G.3.1**: 81.
Darré, J: **C.4**: 30, 49.
Dastmalchian, A: **I.3**: 126.
Dasvarma, G: **F.2**: 1.
Datta, S: **G.3.2**: 355.
Daud, F: **I.5**: 2.
Dauphinee, M: **I.4**: 72.
Dauster, T: **F.4**: 19.
David, R: **F.5**: 206.
Davidson, D: **H.7**: 10.
Davidson, F: **G.3.2**: 264, 325.
Davidson, G: **K.4**: 164.
Davidson, M: **I.2**: 222.
Davidson, N: **F.5**: 85.
Davidson, R: **K.1**: 299.
Davies, C: **F.5**: 117, 320. **I.2**: 156.
Davies, G: **C.2**: 105. **F.2**: 69, 81. **I.4**: 129.
Davies, I: **B.1**: 46.
Davies, J: **D.9**: 163. **J.1**: 16. **K.1**: 305.
Davies, M: **G.3.2**: 273.
Davies, P: **F.3**: 157.
Davies, R: **F.1**: 4. **G.3.2**: 106.
Davies, W: **G.3.2**: 178.
Davis, A: **F.4**: 285.
Davis, C: **J.6**: 45.
Davis, E: **K.1**: 244.
Davis, F: **F.5**: 106. **F.7**: 136.
Davis, J: **G.2**: 12.
Davis, K: **F.5**: 181. **K.4**: 54.
Davis, M: **I.4**: 115. **K.1**: 202.
Davis, N: **D.1**: 22. **F.5**: 205.
Davis, P: **C.3**: 87. **D.4**: 42. **K.1**: 424.
Davis, S: **I.1**: 8. **I.4**: 106.
Davydov, I: **B.1**: 111. **D.1**: 23.
Dawkins, D: **D.9**: 137.
Dawson, D: **F.4**: 335.

Dawson, L: **H.5**: 34.
Day, A: **F.2**: 60.
Day, N: **I.3**: 54.
Dayal, I: **I.3**: 135.
Deák, D: **E.2**: 19.
Deakin, B: **I.2**: 71.
Deane, G: **D.5**: 139.
Dear, M: **K.1**: 223, 238.
Deaton, A: **F.2**: 58.
Debock, C: **K.1**: 383.
Deconchy, J: **C.7**: 36.
DeCotiis, T: **C.1**: 104.
Decroly, J: **F.3**: 262, 297.
Dee, J: **D.7**: 326.
Deery, S: **I.5**: 131.
DeFretes, Y: **G.1**: 18.
DeFries, J: **F.4**: 310.
Degenne, A: **C.4**: 48–49. **H.4**: 35.
Dehouve, D: **G.3.1**: 93.
Dehue, T: **C.1**: 114.
Dejene, W: **K.4**: 213.
Dekel, G: **F.4**: 82.
DeKeseredy, W: **K.1**: 54, 86, 101.
Dekker, P: **F.7**: 194.
Dekmejian, R: **F.7**: 61.
Delacroix, J: **C.5**: 16. **I.4**: 80.
Delamont, S: **F.5**: 291.
Delaney, J: **I.5**: 34, 146.
Delaney, K: **H.4**: 7.
Deleeck, H: **K.2**: 20.
Delessert, A: **C.1**: 153.
Deletant, D: **D.1**: 84. **E.3**: 54.
Delpino, N: **E.3**: 24.
Delu, Z: **C.3**: 69.
Demoussis, M: **G.3.1**: 17, 116.
Dempsey, J: **B.2**: 17.
Dempsey, V: **D.9**: 62, 136.
Dench, N: **C.3**: 68.
Denecke, V: **K.4**: 90.
Deng, Z: **G.3.2**: 306.
Denham, D: **I.5**: 86.
Dennis, C: **H.3**: 58.
Dennis, D: **K.1**: 260. **K.4**: 189.
Dennis, E: **D.7**: 277.
Dennis, M: **G.3.2**: 98.
Dennis, R: **G.1**: 55.

Denton, K: **D.3**: 86.
Denzin, N: **D.8**: 20.
Derbaix, C: **H.5**: 4.
Dermutz, S: **D.9**: 66. **F.5**: 296.
Dertouzos, M: **D.7**: 129.
Desai, S: **F.4**: 331. **H.3**: 6. **I.2**: 159.
DeSarbo, W: **D.7**: 162.
Deseran, F: **G.3.1**: 82.
Desforges, D: **C.7**: 24, 75.
Désiré, J: **F.1**: 37.
Desjardins, B: **F.3**: 109. **F.4**: 344.
Deskins, D: **E.2**: 62. **F.3**: 112.
Deslauriers, P: **G.3**: 9. **G.3.2**: 189.
Desmond, D: **K.1**: 200.
Despointes, H: **I.2**: 38.
Dess, N: **C.2**: 53.
Dessens, J: **F.5**: 317.
Dessloch, H: **H.2**: 18.
Deutsch, S: **E.3**: 19.
Devaramani, S: **F.3**: 265.
DeVault, M: **F.5**: 164.
DeVellis, R: **B.2**: 70.
Deven, F: **F.4**: 343.
Devereux, M: **I.5**: 186.
Devine, F: **I.2**: 152.
Devine, P: **B.2**: 69. **F.7**: 247.
Devore, W: **K.3**: 3.
Devyatko, I: **C.7**: 40.
Dewaet, A: **D.7**: 115.
Dewe, P: **I.5**: 126.
Dewey, J: **C.3**: 25.
Dewey, M: **K.1**: 87.
Dewitt, D: **F.3**: 88.
Dewsbury, D: **C.1**: 123.
Dex, S: **B.2**: 56.
Dey, P: **G.3.2**: 63.
DeYoung, A: **D.9**: 36.
Dhanasekaran, K: **G.3.1**: 68.
Dhaouadi, M: **D.1**: 70.
Dhar, U: **I.3**: 146.
Diacon, D: **G.3.2**: 103, 118, 131.
Diamond, S: **D.4**: 8.
Diani, M: **J.5**: 33.
Dias, H: **G.3.1**: 25.
Diaz-Briquets, S: **F.8**: 37, 40, 53, 120, 124.
Díaz-Guerrero, R: **D.7**: 185.
Dibblin, J: **K.1**: 294.

Dick, B: **K.4**: 45.
Diedrichsen, I: **F.3**: 175.
Diehl, M: **C.4**: 47. **C.7**: 42.
Diekmann, A: **F.4**: 119.
Diener, E: **C.2**: 36, 82, 89.
Dienes, Z: **C.2**: 163.
Dietz, B: **H.3**: 49.
Dietz, H: **J.7**: 9.
Diggelen, van, M: **J.5**: 5.
Dilulio, J: **K.1**: 197.
Dijk, T: **D.7**: 310.
Dijst, M: **F.7**: 34.
Diligenoky, H: **B.1**: 57.
Dilla, H: **J.6**: 33.
Dillon, M: **J.5**: 20.
DiLorenzo, T: **I.5**: 34.
DiMaggio, P: **C.5**: 47. **D.8**: 42.
Dimanche, F: **I.6**: 40.
Dimenstein, G: **K.1**: 26.
Dimitriou, H: **G.2**: 23.
Din, A: **D.9**: 138.
Dingwall, R: **F.4**: 186, 293.
Dingyi, L: **D.6**: 19.
Dinh, Q: **F.1**: 68.
Dinkel, R: **K.4**: 73.
Dinnen, S: **K.1**: 53.
Diop, F: **K.4**: 20.
Dirsmith, M: **J.4**: 9.
Dix, T: **F.4**: 267.
Dixit, R: **D.7**: 228.
Dixit, V: **F.4**: 204.
Dixon, P: **C.7**: 77.
Dmozna, A: **D.1**: 38.
Doak, J: **G.3.2**: 314.
Dobbins, G: **C.5**: 54.
Dobrynina, L: **I.4**: 103.
Dobson, S: **H.4**: 24.
Docksey, C: **I.5**: 113.
Document INS: **F.1**: 71.
Dodds, A: **J.8**: 1.
Dodds, G: **F.2**: 125.
Doepel, D: **C.3**: 27.
Doeringer, P: **I.2**: 17.
Doggett, M: **K.4**: 61.
Doherty, K: **C.2**: 235.
Dohrn, V: **I.6**: 22.

Doise, W: **C.1**: 153.
Dolar, M: **B.1**: 114. **J.2**: 18.
Dolins, S: **F.3**: 201.
Dollahite, D: **F.4**: 72.
Dollimore, J: **F.6**: 45.
Dölling, I: **F.5**: 124.
Dollinger, S: **C.2**: 199.
Dolny, M: **G.3.2**: 154.
Domanski, H: **E.3**: 74. **I.4**: 14.
Domenig, R: **F.3**: 152.
Domhoff, G: **E.2**: 3.
Dominelli, L: **G.2**: 36.
Donaldson, L: **F.3**: 104. **K.4**: 42.
Donaldson, M: **F.4**: 159.
Dongen, van, W: **I.2**: 182.
Donn, C: **I.4**: 41.
Donnadieu, R: **D.4**: 16.
Donnelly, D: **C.1**: 85.
Donnerstein, E: **D.1**: 112.
Donohue, J: **F.7**: 10.
Donohue, W: **C.3**: 26. **J.3**: 27.
Donovan, B: **F.3**: 126.
Dooley, D: **F.4**: 252.
Doorne-Huiskes, van, J: **F.5**: 317.
Doornkamp, J: **G.1**: 42.
Dorais, L: **F.8**: 77.
Doran, L: **I.3**: 98.
Dorn, N: **F.3**: 158.
Dornstein, M: **H.3**: 61.
Doron, A: **K.2**: 108.
Dorr, D: **D.5**: 147.
Dotson, A: **G.3.2**: 229.
Dotterer, R: **F.7**: 98.
Doty, R: **J.6**: 49.
Douglas, A: **G.1**: 1.
Douglas, G: **F.3**: 111.
Douglas, M: **D.1**: 142. **D.7**: 72.
Doumato, E: **F.5**: 15.
Dovbush, M: **D.2**: 27.
Dovbush, P: **C.2**: 193.
Dowall, D: **G.3.2**: 97, 222, 240.
Dowd, B: **K.4**: 43.
Dowd, J: **C.1**: 167.
Dowling, P: **I.3**: 65.
Downes, C: **K.3**: 8.
Downey, D: **F.7**: 189.
Downey, J: **K.3**: 9.

Downie, B: **C.3**: 121.
Downing, J: **C.7**: 64.
Doyle, T: **C.3**: 68.
Dozier, J: **C.1**: 84.
Drago, R: **I.5**: 198.
Drake, R: **C.7**: 64. **K.4**: 47.
Draper, E: **I.3**: 119.
Draughn, P: **F.4**: 114.
Dreher, A: **C.1**: 3.
Dreher, G: **C.2**: 116.
Dreier, P: **G.3.2**: 154.
Dressler, W: **F.3**: 225.
Drews, D: **C.1**: 130.
Drews, S: **C.1**: 3.
Dreze, J: **K.1**: 245.
Driedger, L: **G.3.2**: 83.
Driscoll, D: **F.5**: 46.
Driskell, J: **C.4**: 25.
Driver, F: **J.3**: 23.
Drobes, D: **K.1**: 332.
Drobizheva, L: **D.1**: 37, 84.
Drotar, D: **F.4**: 46.
Droz, R: **C.1**: 153.
Drozd-Piasecka, M: **G.1**: 49.
Drucker, E: **F.3**: 60.
Druckman, D: **C.3**: 90, 120.
Drudy, S: **E.2**: 60.
Drummond, L: **C.1**: 44.
Dryer, D: **C.3**: 71.
Dryman, A: **B.2**: 54.
Drysdale, R: **F.8**: 85.
Duan, C: **C.4**: 14.
Duane, M: **D.9**: 81.
Duany, J: **F.8**: 166.
Dubavets, A: **I.5**: 85.
Dubé, J: **F.4**: 169.
Dubeau, D: **F.4**: 294.
Dubet, F: **F.2**: 133.
Dubin, R: **I.3**: 97.
Dubinsky, A: **H.5**: 24.
Dubrow, N: **C.2**: 108.
Ducatel, K: **D.7**: 91.
Ducharme, H: **D.3**: 89.
Duchesne-Guillemin, J: **D.5**: 75.
Duclos, L: **F.7**: 141.
Dudoignon, S: **D.7**: 34.

Due, J: **I.4**: 47.
Düllings, J: **K.4**: 38.
Duff-Cooper, A: **F.4**: 236. **F.5**: 246.
Dugger, K: **F.7**: 117.
Duh, S: **F.3**: 164.
Duke, V: **I.6**: 34. **J.1**: 13.
Dukes, R: **F.4**: 83.
Dukes, T: **F.5**: 254.
Dulany, D: **D.7**: 12.
Dull, D: **F.5**: 1.
Dumartin, S: **I.2**: 38.
Dummett, A: **F.7**: 162.
Dumon, W: **F.4**: 52.
Dumont, F: **E.3**: 66.
Dunand, F: **D.1**: 119.
Dunand, M: **K.1**: 423.
Dunaway, D: **B.2**: 16.
Dunaway, R: **K.1**: 85.
Duncan, A: **I.2**: 86.
Duncan, S: **G.3**: 6.
Dunford, M: **G.3.2**: 272.
Dunk, T: **E.2**: 68.
Dunlop, C: **D.1**: 109.
Dunlop, F: **B.1**: 73.
Dunlop, J: **F.7**: 83.
Dunn, J: **K.1**: 170.
Dunn, S: **F.7**: 151.
Dunning, D: **C.2**: 132.
Dunning, E: **I.6**: 8. **K.1**: 404.
Dunphy, D: **I.3**: 124.
Dupagne, A: **G.3.2**: 249.
Duprez, J: **I.4**: 95.
Duran, J: **B.1**: 42.
Durán, R: **D.7**: 19.
Durand-Prinborgne, C: **D.9**: 99.
Durant, R: **J.4**: 5.
Durden, G: **D.4**: 17.
Durham, M: **F.4**: 101.
Duriez, B: **B.2**: 106.
Durif, P: **G.3.2**: 134.
Duruoha, I: **D.8**: 19.
Dushatskiy, L: **D.9**: 18.
Dutt, A: **G.3.2**: 219.
Dutt, U: **D.8**: 22.
Dutton, D: **F.4**: 160.
Duval, S: **C.7**: 11.
Duxbury, L: **I.2**: 100.

Dworkin, J: **I.5**: 191.
Dwyer, T: **C.5**: 32. **I.3**: 113.
Dyck, M: **F.3**: 174.
Dyson, T: **F.1**: 43. **K.1**: 255.
Dzúrová, D: **F.3**: 248.
Eadie, D: **K.1**: 373.
Eagle, G: **K.1**: 419.
Eagleton, T: **J.2**: 11.
Eagly, A: **C.3**: 92. **C.6**: 3.
Earnshaw, J: **I.2**: 222. **K.3**: 19.
Eason, K: **A.1**: 30.
Easson, M: **I.5**: 56.
Easterlin, R: **F.2**: 140–141.
Eastwood, D: **H.7**: 15.
Eaton, W: **B.2**: 54.
Ebaugh, H: **D.5**: 140.
Eberstadt, N: **K.4**: 174.
Eberstein, I: **F.3**: 286.
Eberts, R: **I.3**: 83. **I.5**: 188.
Ebomoyi, E: **F.1**: 8. **K.4**: 177.
Ebrahim, S: **F.2**: 40.
Ebrard, M: **G.3.2**: 118, 151.
Eccles, J: **C.2**: 18.
Echebarria, A: **F.3**: 154, 219.
Echeverria, M: **G.3.2**: 325, 329.
Eckenrode, J: **C.3**: 159.
Eckert, J: **H.3**: 9.
Eckhardt, W: **J.7**: 16.
Ecob, R: **F.4**: 297.
Economakis, E: **J.2**: 26.
Edberg, R: **G.1**: 40.
Edebalk, P: **F.2**: 41.
Edelman, P: **K.1**: 217.
Edgell, S: **J.1**: 13.
Edgerton, D: **D.9**: 12.
Edin, K: **K.1**: 290. **K.2**: 103.
Edit, S: **F.3**: 36.
Edleson, J: **K.1**: 63.
Edsforth, R: **J.6**: 40.
Eduards, M: **F.5**: 233. **K.2**: 104.
Edwards, B: **G.3.1**: 49.
Edwards, J: **F.4**: 77, 142.
Edwards, P: **I.5**: 57.
Edwards, R: **F.5**: 203.
Edwards, S: **K.4**: 225.
Edwards, T: **G.1**: 21.

Eekelaar, J: **F.4**: 139.
Eelens, F: **F.8**: 145.
Eenschooten, M: **G.3.2**: 134, 145.
Eenwyk, Van, J: **C.1**: 4, 79.
Egashira, T: **F.4**: 208.
Egawa, N: **D.7**: 320.
Egels, Y: **G.3.2**: 80.
Eggebeen, D: **F.2**: 89. **F.4**: 269, 347.
Eghenter, C: **B.1**: 2.
Egley, L: **F.4**: 173.
Egunjobi, L: **G.3.2**: 163.
Ehmig, S: **D.7**: 295.
Ehrentraut, A: **D.8**: 17.
Ehrhardt, A: **F.2**: 128.
Ehrlich, A: **F.1**: 45.
Einhorn, B: **F.5**: 124.
Eisenberg, N: **C.2**: 181. **C.3**: 132. **F.4**: 279.
Eisenstadt, S: **D.5**: 138.
Eisikovits, Z: **K.1**: 63.
Eisinga, R: **D.1**: 6.
Eitzen, D: **A.1**: 29.
Ejaz, F: **K.3**: 34.
Ejizu, C: **D.5**: 40.
Ekelund, R: **I.3**: 78.
Ekland-Olson, S: **K.1**: 209.
Ekman, P: **C.3**: 161.
Ekström, M: **G.3.2**: 311.
El Musharaf, A: **K.4**: 84.
El-Solh, C: **F.7**: 126.
Elander, I: **G.3**: 6.
Elbaz, F: **D.9**: 47.
Elchardus, M: **I.3**: 34.
Elder, G: **F.4**: 203. **K.2**: 75.
Eldredge, E: **F.5**: 326.
Eldridge, J: **I.1**: 6.
Elfstrom, G: **D.3**: 53.
Elghozi, L: **K.1**: 383.
Elias, C: **F.3**: 216.
Elias, N: **B.1**: 143.
Elkin, J: **J.7**: 9.
Ellard, J: **F.4**: 153.
Ellemers, N: **C.3**: 42.
Ellencweig, A: **K.4**: 175.
Eller, C: **D.5**: 36.
Ellermeier, W: **C.2**: 68.
Ellickson, R: **D.4**: 31.
Elliot, A: **F.7**: 247.

Elliott, B: **F.4**: 120.
Elliott, C: **C.1**: 127.
Elliott, D: **K.2**: 111.
Elliott, M: **K.1**: 288.
Elliott, T: **F.3**: 204.
Ellis, D: **F.1**: 6.
Ellis, J: **C.3**: 84.
Ellis, L: **E.2**: 2. **F.6**: 12. **K.1**: 109.
Ellis, M: **I.2**: 192.
Ellis, N: **D.7**: 344.
Ellison, C: **D.5**: 31. **F.7**: 86. **K.1**: 413.
Ellison, G: **D.2**: 26.
Ellison, M: **F.7**: 225.
Ellwood, D: **K.1**: 247.
Elman, R: **K.2**: 104.
Eloundou-Enyègue, P: **G.3.1**: 96.
Elshtain, J: **J.8**: 16. **K.1**: 23.
Elster, J: **C.3**: 49. **D.1**: 124.
Elvers, G: **C.5**: 34.
Elvin, M: **F.7**: 99.
Ely, M: **D.7**: 351.
Eme, B: **I.2**: 58.
Emekianov, E: **C.1**: 172.
Emerson, R: **K.1**: 424.
Emil, V: **F.2**: 57.
Eminov, A: **D.7**: 193.
Emler, N: **K.1**: 139.
Emmons, R: **C.2**: 76.
Enaux, C: **F.1**: 37.
Enç, M: **D.7**: 224.
Enclos, P: **I.4**: 89.
Enders-Dragässer, U: **F.4**: 275. **K.2**: 65.
Endleman, R: **C.1**: 149.
Endler, N: **C.2**: 191.
Enevoldson, H: **K.4**: 142.
Engbersen, G: **K.1**: 220, 252.
Engel, C: **F.4**: 21.
Engel, J: **K.4**: 215.
Engelhard, P: **F.3**: 177.
Engelstad, E: **F.5**: 99.
England, K: **G.3.2**: 174.
Englund, P: **G.3.2**: 102.
Engstrom, R: **F.7**: 105.
Ennaji, M: **A.1**: 33.
Enninger, W: **D.7**: 145.
Enriquez, E: **C.1**: 153.

Entman, R: **D.7**: 256.
Entorf, H: **F.3**: 276.
Entzinger, H: **K.1**: 220, 232.
Enzle, M: **C.2**: 176.
Epinay, d', C: **C.2**: 50.
Epps, E: **D.9**: 176.
Epskamp, K: **D.8**: 10.
Epstein, C: **F.5**: 245.
Epstein, J: **F.5**: 264.
Epstein, S: **C.2**: 121.
Erb, R: **F.7**: 241.
Erben, M: **F.4**: 60.
Erber, R: **C.2**: 180. **C.3**: 89.
Ercolani, A: **G.3.2**: 180.
Ercole, D', A: **K.1**: 236, 239.
Erev, I: **C.3**: 8.
Eric, K: **F.3**: 60.
Ericson, R: **D.1**: 15. **D.7**: 273.
Eriksen, T: **F.7**: 79.
Erikson, R: **E.2**: 67.
Eriksson, G: **I.2**: 179.
Erkut, E: **J.4**: 17.
Erlich, G: **F.5**: 216.
Ermisch, J: **I.2**: 102, 223.
Ernst, D: **F.3**: 174.
Ernst, T: **F.6**: 30.
Errington, A: **G.3.1**: 40, 116.
Ertelt, B: **I.4**: 65.
Ertürk, Y: **F.5**: 152.
Erzinger, S: **K.4**: 12.
Esanov, M: **D.4**: 25.
Esau, A: **F.2**: 125.
Esbensen, F: **K.1**: 51.
Escobedo, E: **C.7**: 63.
Esparza, A: **F.8**: 157.
Espstein, S: **F.6**: 49.
Essed, P: **F.7**: 211.
Esser, H: **B.1**: 129.
Essex, M: **K.2**: 57.
Essien, O: **D.7**: 215.
Estel, B: **J.2**: 9.
Estes, C: **F.2**: 39, 55. **K.4**: 238.
Estes, R: **F.5**: 163.
Estes, W: **C.1**: 136.
Estroff, S: **C.2**: 228.
Estruch, J: **C.1**: 1.
Etchelecou, A: **F.1**: 66. **F.3**: 15. **G.1**: 28.

Etzioni, A: **D.3**: 43.
Evans, A: **F.1**: 58.
Evans, C: **D.2**: 10.
Evans, G: **C.1**: 148. **C.2**: 90. **F.2**: 152. **F.3**: 230.
Evans, J: **C.5**: 74.
Evans, K: **D.9**: 183.
Evans, M: **C.1**: 121. **I.2**: 52.
Evans, P: **F.5**: 140.
Evans, V: **F.5**: 314.
Evason, E: **F.5**: 62. **H.3**: 36.
Eveleigh, C: **I.5**: 31.
Everhart, R: **D.9**: 62.
Evers, A: **K.4**: 134.
Evers, H: **J.1**: 21.
Evers, S: **K.4**: 86.
Ewan, C: **F.3**: 208.
Ewart, C: **K.4**: 237.
Ewert, A: **C.4**: 27.
Exton, K: **K.2**: 66.
Eyerman, R: **E.3**: 64. **J.5**: 33.
Faas, L: **F.3**: 183.
Fabes, R: **C.3**: 132.
Fabianic, D: **A.1**: 6.
Fabre-Vassas, C: **D.5**: 187.
Fabris, F: **K.2**: 86.
Fadda, G: **G.3.2**: 327.
Faden, R: **F.3**: 163. **K.4**: 171.
Fagan, J: **K.1**: 328.
Fagan, R: **H.7**: 5. **K.1**: 417.
Fagerhaugh, S: **K.4**: 168.
Fagot-Largeault, A: **D.3**: 18.
Fain, J: **I.5**: 191.
Fainstein, S: **H.7**: 19.
Fair, J: **D.7**: 243.
Fairchild, E: **C.5**: 46.
Fairchild, H: **C.1**: 106. **F.7**: 260.
Fairfield, M: **C.2**: 237.
Fairholm, G: **C.6**: 16.
Fajana, S: **I.2**: 231. **I.3**: 6.
Falk, W: **G.3.1**: 39. **H.3**: 88.
Falkingham, J: **K.2**: 85.
Faller, K: **F.4**: 135.
Fals-Borda, O: **B.2**: 1.
Faltis, C: **D.9**: 15.
Fan, C: **F.3**: 223.
Fannin, D: **F.1**: 23.

Fantasia, R: **E.2**: 52.
Faragó, T: **E.2**: 13.
Farganis, S: **F.5**: 142.
Farghal, M: **D.6**: 1.
Farias, P: **C.2**: 28. **K.4**: 74.
Farid: **G.3.2**: 173.
Farina, A: **C.3**: 39.
Farinelli, F: **D.9**: 165.
Farkas, J: **D.6**: 30.
Farley, J: **F.7**: 146.
Farquhar, J: **F.3**: 120.
Farr, R: **C.1**: 157.
Farrant, W: **K.4**: 167.
Farre, M: **F.3**: 281.
Farrell, R: **D.4**: 38.
Farrell, T: **D.7**: 284.
Farret, R: **G.3.2**: 141.
Farrington, D: **C.2**: 42. **K.1**: 94.
Fasella, P: **G.1**: 19.
Fasolo, E: **K.4**: 223.
Fassin, D: **D.9**: 89.
Fassin, E: **F.5**: 300.
Fathi, A: **F.8**: 142.
Fathy, T: **G.3.2**: 312.
Fätkenheuer, B: **F.3**: 169.
Fattah, E: **K.1**: 184.
Faubion, J: **D.5**: 138.
Faulkner, A: **I.2**: 90.
Faulkner, K: **C.1**: 9.
Faulkner, R: **D.8**: 62.
Faupel, C: **K.1**: 381.
Fauré, C: **J.3**: 3.
Faure, S: **G.3.2**: 49.
Faust, B: **F.5**: 63.
Faust, K: **F.3**: 11.
Faustino-Santos, R: **K.1**: 58.
Fausto, D: **D.3**: 36.
Fauveau, V: **F.3**: 125, 235, 279.
Fawaz, L: **E.1**: 21.
Fay, R: **B.2**: 125.
Fayard, P: **K.1**: 1.
Feachem, R: **F.3**: 171.
Feagin, J: **B.1**: 90. **F.7**: 223.
Feather, N: **C.7**: 34.
February, V: **F.7**: 46.
Federici, N: **F.8**: 42.
Feehan, M: **F.2**: 106.

Feiereis, H: **F.3**: 175.
Feige, M: **J.7**: 4.
Feigelman, W: **D.5**: 146.
Feiler, G: **F.8**: 35.
Feinberg, B: **B.2**: 92.
Feinberg, S: **B.2**: 55.
Feinstein, J: **F.2**: 11.
Feitelson, E: **B.2**: 113.
Feld, B: **J.3**: 13.
Feldberg, M: **J.3**: 45.
Feldblum, P: **F.3**: 54.
Feldman, L: **K.2**: 43.
Feldman, R: **D.7**: 147. **K.4**: 43.
Feldwick, P: **D.7**: 29.
Fells, J: **K.2**: 6.
Felson, R: **C.4**: 5.
Felt, L: **C.2**: 40.
Feltrin, P: **I.5**: 119.
Fengler, A: **K.4**: 126.
Fentem, P: **F.2**: 40.
Fenton, J: **I.5**: 112.
Ferber, M: **I.2**: 166, 184, 202.
Ferdinand, T: **K.1**: 192.
Ferenc, K: **F.3**: 137.
Ference, R: **C.4**: 24.
Ferge, Z: **D.1**: 129.
Ferguson, A: **F.5**: 123.
Ferguson, H: **D.5**: 55.
Ferguson, K: **F.5**: 100.
Ferguson, M: **D.7**: 47.
Fernandes, R: **H.2**: 15.
Fernandes, W: **F.5**: 316. **J.8**: 10.
Fernández Santana, O: **B.2**: 29.
Fernando, S: **C.1**: 69.
Ferner, A: **I.5**: 45.
Ferrand, A: **C.3**: 18. **C.4**: 49.
Ferrara, M: **K.3**: 18.
Ferraro, K: **D.5**: 12.
Ferrié, J: **A.1**: 33.
Ferstl, L: **F.8**: 64.
Feschotte, P: **H.4**: 100.
Fetison, E: **C.3**: 56.
Fette, A: **F.5**: 221. **K.4**: 234.
Feucht, T: **B.2**: 46.
Feuchtwang, S: **D.5**: 20.
Feuer, B: **I.1**: 10. **I.5**: 153.

Feuille, P: **I.5**: 34, 187.
Feyereisen, P: **D.7**: 148.
Feyisetan, B: **F.3**: 113.
Fiala, R: **I.2**: 162.
Fibbi, R: **F.8**: 9.
Fichten, C: **K.4**: 145.
Fidanzi, P: **C.7**: 47.
Fido, R: **K.4**: 35.
Fiedler, K: **B.2**: 87.
Field, A: **I.4**: 119.
Field, N: **C.1**: 45.
Field, S: **F.5**: 234.
Field-Hendrey, E: **I.2**: 87.
Fielding, A: **F.8**: 108.
Fielding, J: **K.1**: 124.
Fielding, N: **K.1**: 124.
Fields, E: **D.5**: 46, 78.
Fields, J: **F.5**: 153.
Fienup, D: **G.3.1**: 133.
Fierman, W: **D.7**: 339.
Fife-Schaw, C: **F.3**: 61. **J.6**: 59.
Fig, D: **F.8**: 161.
Figley, C: **J.8**: 20.
Figueira, S: **C.1**: 38.
Figueira-McDonough, J: **G.2**: 9.
Figueroa, J: **I.2**: 178.
Figueroa, P: **F.7**: 14.
Figueroa Navarro, A: **F.2**: 134.
Fik, T: **G.1**: 36. **H.5**: 30.
Fikentscher, W: **D.4**: 3, 36.
Filias, V: **F.4**: 44.
Filion, P: **G.3.2**: 237, 266.
Filippo, de, R: **G.3.2**: 49.
Fillmore, K: **K.1**: 366.
Finch, J: **F.2**: 15. **F.4**: 79.
Finch, M: **I.4**: 55. **K.4**: 43.
Fincher, R: **H.7**: 5. **I.2**: 191.
Findlay, A: **F.1**: 9.
Findlay, C: **K.3**: 20.
Fine, G: **A.1**: 24.
Fine, M: **F.4**: 281.
Fineman, M: **F.4**: 130.
Fineman, N: **K.4**: 88.
Finifter, D: **D.9**: 214.
Fink, V: **G.3.1**: 79, 81.
Finkelhor, D: **F.4**: 1.
Finkelstein, J: **C.1**: 150.

Finlay, P: **H.5**: 40.
Finley, N: **D.5**: 53. **J.5**: 21.
Finn, C: **D.9**: 148.
Finn-Stevenson, M: **I.3**: 74.
Finnäs, F: **F.3**: 102.
Finney, H: **D.5**: 53, 81.
Finney, N: **I.5**: 75.
Fiorito, J: **I.3**: 106.
Firestone, J: **I.2**: 181.
Firkowska-Mankiewicz, A: **C.2**: 37.
Firman, T: **I.4**: 43.
First-Dilić, R: **I.2**: 151.
Fisch, O: **F.1**: 63.
Fischer, J: **D.3**: 19, 87.
Fischer, M: **K.1**: 208.
Fischer, P: **K.1**: 239, 347.
Fischman, M: **K.1**: 319.
Fischoff, B: **D.1**: 130.
Fischoff, S: **D.7**: 326.
Fişek, M: **C.4**: 42.
Fiselier, A: **K.2**: 82.
Fisher, B: **K.1**: 114.
Fisher, M: **G.3.2**: 92.
Fishman, G: **F.7**: 63.
Fishman, J: **D.7**: 338, 347. **D.9**: 41.
Fiske, A: **C.3**: 19.
Fiske, S: **C.3**: 19.
Fitchen, J: **G.3.1**: 26, 105. **G.3.2**: 108.
Fitzgerald, J: **G.2**: 3. **J.5**: 10. **K.2**: 106.
Fitzgerald, T: **D.1**: 2. **F.7**: 101.
Fitzpatrick, K: **C.3**: 37.
Fitzpatrick, M: **F.4**: 241.
Fitzsimmons, G: **K.1**: 403.
Flacco, P: **J.7**: 6.
Flament, C: **C.4**: 2, 49.
Flanagan, C: **C.2**: 18.
Flanagan, D: **C.2**: 30.
Flanagan, K: **D.5**: 148.
Flanagan, O: **C.2**: 220.
Flannery, M: **F.4**: 178.
Flap, H: **E.2**: 17.
Flaquer, L: **F.4**: 36.
Flecha, V: **J.6**: 61.
Fleck, K: **C.3**: 11.
Fleck-Henderson, A: **K.3**: 26.
Fleeson, W: **C.2**: 59.

Flege, J: **D.7**: 228.
Fleischman, S: **D.7**: 135.
Fleischmann, A: **H.3**: 41.
Flekkoy, M: **K.2**: 67.
Fleming, D: **D.7**: 111.
Fleming, J: **D.7**: 161, 176.
Fleming, S: **F.1**: 58. **G.2**: 1.
Flere, S: **D.5**: 10. **F.7**: 165.
Fletcher, B: **K.3**: 44.
Fletcher, G: **F.7**: 209.
Fletcher, J: **K.4**: 255, 263.
Fletcher, K: **K.1**: 374.
Flink, C: **C.3**: 41.
Flood, J: **D.4**: 15.
Flood, M: **F.4**: 127.
Florax, R: **D.9**: 196.
Flores, M: **D.2**: 16.
Florida, R: **C.5**: 57. **H.4**: 49. **I.3**: 53.
Florkowski, G: **I.5**: 48.
Flottes Lerolle, A: **I.4**: 63.
Flynn, I: **F.3**: 219. **F.6**: 1.
Flynn, N: **K.4**: 109.
Flynn, R: **K.4**: 187.
Fodor, J: **B.1**: 31.
Fokht-Babushkin, I: **D.8**: 26.
Folkman, S: **J.8**: 20.
Follingstad, D: **F.4**: 156.
Folmer, H: **D.9**: 196.
Foltin, R: **K.1**: 319.
Fonacier Bernabe, E: **D.7**: 79.
Fondacaro, R: **D.7**: 170, 176.
Fong, Y: **F.3**: 129.
Fonow, M: **F.5**: 66.
Fonseca, E: **H.3**: 4.
Fontaine, la, J: **F.2**: 74.
Fonte Pessanha, da, E: **I.4**: 22.
Forbes, K: **I.2**: 24.
Ford, D: **D.9**: 70, 80.
Ford, J: **C.2**: 161. **K.1**: 225.
Ford, K: **F.8**: 15.
Ford, L: **D.7**: 108. **K.4**: 11.
Ford, T: **C.7**: 4.
Forde, D: **F.4**: 160. **K.1**: 92.
Fordham, M: **C.1**: 138.
Forehand, R: **C.3**: 3.
Fores, M: **I.4**: 39.
Forgas, J: **C.3**: 5.

Fornell, C: **H.5**: 22.
Forrest, D: **G.3.2**: 96.
Forrest, R: **C.4**: 21.
Forsé, M: **C.4**: 10, 49.
Forslund, M: **K.1**: 352.
Forste, R: **F.4**: 230.
Förster, P: **F.2**: 137.
Forster, R: **C.1**: 71.
Fosh, P: **I.5**: 65.
Fossett, M: **F.3**: 13. **F.7**: 250.
Foster, C: **K.3**: 23.
Foster, G: **D.1**: 110.
Foster, P: **K.4**: 110.
Foster, R: **F.4**: 167.
Foster, S: **B.2**: 85.
Fottorino, E: **K.1**: 371.
Fouke, D: **B.1**: 75.
Fourniau, V: **F.7**: 47.
Fournier, D: **F.3**: 8.
Fournier, I: **C.4**: 48–49.
Fowler, R: **D.7**: 268.
Fox, N: **F.4**: 271. **K.4**: 76.
Fox, R: **G.3.2**: 334.
Fox-Genovese, E: **B.1**: 102.
Frambes-Buxeda, A: **J.1**: 22.
Franc, M: **H.4**: 18.
Franch Meneu, J: **H.1**: 1.
Franchi, G: **D.9**: 165.
Francis, J: **D.1**: 104.
Frank, J: **D.4**: 7.
Frank, O: **F.3**: 82.
Frank, R: **I.3**: 8.
Franke, R: **F.6**: 11.
Frankenberg, G: **F.3**: 227.
Frankenberg, R: **K.4**: 99.
Franklin, R: **F.7**: 207.
Franklin, S: **D.1**: 2. **F.5**: 80, 109.
Franz, C: **F.2**: 76.
Fraser, M: **K.3**: 15.
Fraser, N: **K.2**: 44.
Fratter, J: **F.4**: 315.
Frazer-Jans, J: **C.5**: 50.
Frederickson, H: **J.4**: 24.
Frederikse, J: **F.7**: 266.
Freedman, J: **H.5**: 9.
Freeman, D: **G.3.2**: 10.

Freeman, J: **D.7**: 196.
Freeman, S: **D.3**: 65.
Freeman, W: **C.2**: 77.
Freidenberg, J: **F.7**: 120.
Freniere, la, P: **F.4**: 294.
Frese, P: **F.5**: 40.
Fretwell, C: **C.5**: 44.
Freudenburg, W: **K.1**: 69.
Freund, B: **F.5**: 195. **G.3.1**: 95.
Freund, J: **H.4**: 100.
Frick, D: **G.3.2**: 247.
Frick, J: **H.3**: 75.
Fridlund, A: **C.3**: 81.
Fried, S: **J.4**: 26.
Friedgut, T: **F.7**: 83.
Friedlander, D: **F.3**: 138.
Friedman, E: **G.3.1**: 6.
Friedman, H: **C.2**: 196.
Friedman, J: **D.1**: 82.
Friedman, M: **D.3**: 17.
Friedman, N: **A.3**: 8.
Friedman, R: **C.4**: 22. **D.5**: 18.
Friedman, W: **C.2**: 155.
Friedmann, J: **J.6**: 9.
Friedrich, W: **F.2**: 137. **F.7**: 219.
Frisanco, R: **K.4**: 223.
Frisbie, W: **G.3.2**: 351.
Frischkorn, T: **I.3**: 95.
Frith, G: **D.8**: 74.
Fritz, A: **C.2**: 123. **D.7**: 149.
Fritzell, J: **H.3**: 23.
Frohmann, L: **K.1**: 424.
Frolov, I: **H.4**: 89.
Frommel, M: **F.4**: 182.
Frosh, S: **C.1**: 47.
Frost, D: **I.4**: 128.
Frost, J: **F.5**: 117.
Frost, L: **G.3.2**: 348.
Frost, M: **I.2**: 13–14, 165.
Frost, P: **C.5**: 67.
Frow, J: **A.2**: 11.
Frumkina, R: **D.7**: 48.
Frysztacki, K: **F.7**: 113.
Fuchs, V: **F.2**: 7. **I.3**: 26.
Fudge, J: **I.2**: 115.
Fuentes, A: **I.1**: 4.
Fugita, S: **F.7**: 96.

Fuguitt, G: **F.8**: 36.
Fuhrich, M: **F.2**: 34.
Fujii, H: **F.2**: 63.
Fujimura, M: **F.2**: 124.
Fujita, F: **C.2**: 36.
Fujita, H: **G.3.2**: 9.
Fujita, K: **I.2**: 154.
Fujiyama, Y: **B.1**: 47.
Fukada, H: **B.1**: 113.
Fukuoka, Y: **F.7**: 89.
Fukurai, H: **F.8**: 96.
Fulcher, J: **I.5**: 35.
Fuligni, A: **C.2**: 18.
Fulker, D: **F.4**: 310.
Fuller, A: **G.3.1**: 52.
Fuller, B: **D.9**: 92.
Fuller, D: **D.3**: 73.
Fuller, R: **H.3**: 71.
Fuller, S: **D.6**: 14.
Fullilove, M: **F.3**: 234.
Fulton, J: **D.5**: 41.
Funabashi, K: **F.4**: 325.
Funder, D: **C.2**: 207. **C.7**: 29.
Fung, K: **C.5**: 49.
Furbee-Losee, L: **B.2**: 8.
Furnham, A: **C.1**: 28. **C.7**: 51. **F.2**: 154. **H.4**: 78.
Fursland, A: **F.8**: 20.
Furstenberg, F: **F.4**: 124.
Furumoto, L: **C.1**: 110.
Fuss, D: **F.6**: 22.
Fussell, S: **C.2**: 2. **D.7**: 166, 176.
Fuszara, M: **F.3**: 49.
Fuyou, C: **D.7**: 225.
Fyfe, N: **J.3**: 44.
Fyfield, M: **H.5**: 3.
Gabe, J: **F.3**: 195.
Gabriel, P: **I.4**: 7.
Gabriel, T: **G.3.1**: 109.
Gabriel, Y: **C.5**: 48, 84.
Gachechiladse, R: **J.6**: 64.
Gadalla, S: **F.3**: 11.
Gadlin, H: **F.6**: 6.
Gaebe, W: **G.3.2**: 276.
Gaertner, K: **I.4**: 18.
Gaffikin, F: **G.3.2**: 292.
Gaffney, M: **F.5**: 96.

Gagnon, E: **A.2**: 3.
Gahinyuza, R: **I.3**: 59.
Gaidenko, P: **B.1**: 111. **D.1**: 23.
Gaiha, R: **K.1**: 266.
Gailliard, F: **K.1**: 383.
Gaiotti de Biase, P: **D.9**: 165.
Gairola, G: **F.3**: 40.
Galam, S: **C.4**: 61.
Galaskiewicz, J: **B.2**: 5.
Galaup, A: **G.3.1**: 78.
Galbraith, J: **F.3**: 52, 62.
Gale, F: **J.3**: 25.
Galeano, L: **E.3**: 75.
Galeriu, C: **D.5**: 76.
Galès, Le, P: **H.3**: 1.
Galin, A: **I.3**: 97.
Gallagher, A: **F.7**: 151.
Gallagher, D: **C.2**: 89.
Gallagher, J: **F.2**: 3.
Gallagher, N: **F.3**: 173.
Gallaway, L: **I.2**: 201.
Galle, O: **F.7**: 250.
Gallie, W: **J.8**: 18.
Galliher, J: **K.1**: 140.
Gallissot, R: **D.1**: 1, 18.
Gallo, E: **K.1**: 187.
Gallois, C: **D.7**: 55.
Galster, G: **F.5**: 155. **G.3.2**: 120, 336.
Gamage, D: **D.9**: 93.
Gaman, O: **C.2**: 193.
Gamble, A: **F.7**: 13.
Gambling, T: **D.3**: 31.
Game, A: **B.1**: 148.
Gamerman, D: **F.3**: 176.
Gane, M: **B.1**: 88–89.
Ganey, R: **H.3**: 22.
Gangestad, S: **F.6**: 20.
Gans, H: **K.1**: 258.
Gans, P: **F.3**: 16. **G.3.2**: 189.
Ganster, D: **C.2**: 195. **C.4**: 4.
Ganzach, Y: **C.1**: 126.
Ganzarain, R: **C.1**: 17.
Ganzen, V: **C.1**: 132.
Gao, G: **C.3**: 112.
Gao, X: **I.2**: 173.
Garachon, A: **K.4**: 45.
Garbarino, J: **C.2**: 108.

Garber, J: **C.1**: 141.
Garcia, A: **C.3**: 113.
García, B: **F.5**: 236.
Garcia, M: **F.2**: 86. **F.5**: 162.
García, O: **D.9**: 41.
Garcia, S: **C.3**: 146. **H.3**: 1.
García Cavazos, A: **G.3.2**: 109.
Garcia-Ferrer, A: **F.1**: 3.
Garcia-Oriol, G: **H.4**: 30.
Gardial, S: **D.7**: 104.
Gardin, J: **C.1**: 153. **D.6**: 4.
Garland, D: **K.1**: 212.
Garland, R: **D.7**: 51.
Garmezy, N: **F.2**: 3. **K.1**: 278.
Garner, L: **H.2**: 19.
Garner, R: **H.2**: 19.
Garnets, L: **C.1**: 107.
Garretón, M: **J.2**: 5.
Garriazu, A: **F.5**: 219.
Garson, L: **F.3**: 240.
Gartman, D: **D.1**: 14.
Gartner, R: **F.4**: 338.
Garza, G: **H.7**: 12.
Garza, R: **F.7**: 172.
Garza, de la, R: **F.8**: 61.
Gaskell, J: **F.5**: 283.
Gaskell, P: **G.3.1**: 124.
Gasparini, E: **G.3.2**: 250.
Gasper, C: **D.9**: 123.
Gasper, D: **G.3.2**: 23.
Gassner, S: **F.5**: 221. **K.4**: 234.
Gasson, R: **G.3.1**: 81, 116.
Gaster, S: **G.3.2**: 225.
Gatens, M: **F.5**: 83.
Gathercole, S: **C.2**: 156.
Gattiker, U: **C.5**: 26.
Gaube, A: **F.2**: 34.
Gaude, J: **G.3.1**: 102.
Gaudu, F: **I.2**: 19.
Gaumer, H: **F.3**: 193.
Gaviria, E: **C.3**: 42.
Gay, du, P: **D.1**: 17.
Gaydukova, N: **G.3.2**: 172.
Gaylord, M: **K.1**: 140, 318.
Gazdar, H: **K.1**: 245.
Gazsó, F: **F.2**: 150.

Gebert, K: **F.7**: 217. **J.2**: 17.
Gee, H: **C.1**: 115.
Gee, J: **D.7**: 227.
Gee, P: **D.5**: 41.
Gegeo, D: **D.7**: 35.
Geiger, B: **K.1**: 208.
Geißlinger, H: **D.6**: 29.
Gelder, de, B: **D.7**: 56.
Geller, G: **K.4**: 171.
Gellner, D: **D.5**: 86.
Gelman, S: **C.2**: 55.
Gembris, H: **K.4**: 86.
Gemes, K: **D.7**: 151.
Gemmill, G: **C.4**: 6.
Genestier, P: **F.7**: 110. **G.3.2**: 188.
Gentile, D: **I.3**: 102.
Genty, P: **F.4**: 191.
George, J: **C.1**: 173. **I.3**: 82, 98.
George, V: **K.1**: 267.
Georgiou, S: **I.4**: 60.
Gerecke, K: **G.3.2**: 238.
Gerhards, J: **D.8**: 30.
Gerhardt, U: **F.4**: 240.
Gerhart, B: **I.2**: 88. **I.3**: 18.
Germain, C: **C.1**: 154.
Gerrard, B: **H.4**: 24.
Gerrard, M: **C.1**: 134.
Gertel, S: **J.6**: 29.
Gerth, H: **C.1**: 111.
Gertler, P: **I.3**: 8.
Gertz, L: **F.4**: 159.
Gertz, N: **D.1**: 108.
Gesler, W: **K.4**: 15.
Geurten, G: **G.3.1**: 103.
Geva, A: **H.5**: 19.
Gewirth, A: **B.1**: 1.
Geyer, H: **G.3.2**: 362.
Ghadially, R: **F.5**: 42.
Ghai, D: **H.3**: 25.
Ghandhi, P: **F.4**: 185.
Ghannam, J: **C.3**: 71.
Ghayur, S: **F.3**: 7.
Ghazali, A: **J.3**: 8.
Gheorghe, N: **J.2**: 17.
Ghertman, M: **H.4**: 18.
Ghidinelli, A: **F.5**: 187.
Ghirardo, D: **G.3.2**: 285.

Ghosh, D: **F.8**: 80.
Ghosh, E: **F.7**: 29, 152.
Ghuman, P: **F.7**: 84.
Giampetro-Meyer, A: **I.2**: 205.
Giannelli, G: **F.4**: 260.
Giannotti, J: **J.6**: 51.
Gibbons, F: **C.1**: 134. **C.3**: 72.
Gibbons, P: **D.7**: 61.
Gibbons, R: **I.3**: 43.
Gibbs, J: **D.3**: 73. **K.1**: 188.
Gibney, L: **F.3**: 39.
Gibson, J: **G.1**: 24.
Gibson, K: **G.3.2**: 14.
Giedymin, J: **B.1**: 36.
Gierhake, K: **G.3.1**: 104.
Gifford, R: **D.7**: 159.
Gigerenzer, G: **C.2**: 208.
Gilbert, D: **C.2**: 124. **C.7**: 74. **F.4**: 345.
Gilbert, J: **G.3.1**: 39. **I.2**: 97.
Gilbert, K: **J.6**: 15.
Gilbert, N: **F.4**: 174. **H.4**: 15. **I.2**: 150. **K.1**: 122.
Gilbert, P: **C.3**: 38.
Gilboy, J: **F.8**: 118.
Gilchrist, R: **F.5**: 139.
Gilden, D: **C.2**: 69.
Gilderbloom, J: **G.3.2**: 154.
Giles, H: **C.1**: 156. **D.7**: 44, 77, 160, 194, 199.
Giles, W: **F.7**: 149.
Gilg, A: **G.3.1**: 124.
Gilhus, I: **D.5**: 48.
Gilinskiy, Y: **F.2**: 18.
Gill, A: **F.5**: 156. **G.3.2**: 260.
Gill, D: **F.2**: 46. **F.7**: 253.
Gill, H: **C.1**: 24. **H.3**: 85.
Gillespie, N: **K.4**: 123.
Gillett, J: **F.5**: 190.
Gilley, J: **D.9**: 211.
Gilligan, R: **F.4**: 151. **K.2**: 55.
Gilliland, D: **D.5**: 112.
Gilly, M: **H.5**: 38.
Gilner, F: **K.1**: 42.
Gilroy, P: **F.7**: 13, 235.
Gimenez, M: **F.3**: 115.
Gindin, S: **I.2**: 199.
Giner de Grado, C: **D.5**: 123.
Ginetsinsky, V: **B.1**: 70.

Ginn, J: **F.2**: 49. **F.5**: 168. **H.3**: 73.
Ginneken, van, J: **F.3**: 237.
Ginsberg, A: **C.5**: 5.
Ginsburg, C: **D.7**: 174.
Ginsburg, F: **F.5**: 113.
Ginsburg, M: **D.9**: 75.
Ginsburg, N: **G.3.2**: 343.
Giosue, F: **C.3**: 42.
Girard, R: **J.5**: 37.
Girard, V: **K.1**: 383.
Gitelman, Z: **D.1**: 84. **F.7**: 71, 158.
Gittelman, S: **G.3.1**: 105.
Giuliano, G: **G.3.2**: 76, 240.
Giulianotti, R: **I.6**: 8, 33.
Giulietti, M: **I.2**: 126.
Giura-Longo, M: **H.2**: 9.
Gjerde, P: **C.2**: 204.
Gladwin, C: **I.2**: 143.
Glanville, J: **K.1**: 241.
Glasberg, D: **H.6**: 9.
Glasinovich, W: **J.6**: 6.
Glasman, J: **F.7**: 97.
Glass, J: **E.3**: 6. **I.3**: 36.
Glasser, M: **K.4**: 207.
Glassman, M: **F.3**: 210.
Glassner, B: **D.7**: 287.
Glazer, N: **K.4**: 3.
Glazychev, V: **D.1**: 100. **G.3.2**: 36.
Gleason, J: **D.7**: 70.
Gleeson, B: **K.1**: 223, 238.
Gleichmann, P: **A.2**: 15.
Glendinning, W: **D.9**: 105.
Glenn, N: **F.4**: 234.
Glennerster, H: **K.2**: 91.
Glinert, L: **D.7**: 28.
Glisky, M: **C.2**: 1.
Globetti, G: **K.1**: 369.
Glodnykh, N: **I.2**: 30.
Glover, I: **I.4**: 39.
Gluck, S: **F.5**: 144.
Glynn, L: **E.3**: 56.
Glynn, M: **I.3**: 15.
Gobatto, I: **K.4**: 91.
Gobbicchi, A: **C.5**: 64.
Gober, P: **G.3.2**: 208.
Gochfeld, M: **C.1**: 119.
Godfrey, B: **G.3.2**: 280.

Godschalk, J: **K.1**: 220.
Godsil, R: **F.7**: 203.
Godwin, D: **F.4**: 114.
Goehring, B: **C.1**: 119.
Goeschel, A: **F.5**: 221. **K.4**: 179.
Gognalons-Nicolet, M: **F.2**: 54.
Göksu, A: **G.3.2**: 118.
Golczyńska-Grondas, A: **K.4**: 96.
Goldberg, A: **I.2**: 164.
Goldberg, C: **F.4**: 258.
Goldberg, E: **D.5**: 145.
Goldberg, G: **F.5**: 251.
Goldberg, H: **F.3**: 81.
Goldberg, M: **I.5**: 27.
Goldberg, R: **D.7**: 210.
Goldberg, S: **C.3**: 115.
Golden, B: **J.4**: 17.
Golden, M: **D.4**: 42.
Goldenberg, I: **C.5**: 39.
Goldenberg, S: **F.5**: 182.
Goldfarb, J: **D.1**: 65.
Goldman, A: **H.5**: 19.
Goldman, M: **K.1**: 308.
Goldman, R: **D.7**: 367.
Goldney, R: **C.2**: 97. **I.2**: 234.
Goldscheider, C: **F.4**: 341.
Goldscheider, F: **F.4**: 341.
Goldsmith, A: **I.4**: 119. **J.3**: 35.
Goldstein, A: **F.8**: 101.
Goldstein, H: **B.2**: 14.
Goldstein, S: **F.8**: 101.
Goldstone, J: **D.1**: 24.
Goldthorpe, J: **E.2**: 67. **E.3**: 76. **F.4**: 75.
Golik, N: **D.1**: 21.
Golini, A: **F.1**: 50.
Goll, I: **I.5**: 19.
Gollob, H: **C.4**: 38.
Golub, A: **F.3**: 156.
Gómez Peralta, O: **K.1**: 261.
Goncharenko, A: **C.2**: 193.
Gönczöl, K: **K.1**: 55.
Gondolf, E: **F.4**: 167.
Gong-Guy, E: **K.4**: 10.
Gonzalez, A: **D.7**: 79, 87. **K.1**: 1.
Gonzalez, G: **C.1**: 98.
González Block, M: **J.4**: 3.

González O, E: **F.7**: 132.
González Rabanal, M: **K.2**: 90.
Good, D: **K.1**: 108.
Goodchilds, J: **C.1**: 107.
Goodey, C: **F.3**: 189.
Goodkind, D: **F.3**: 35.
Goodman, D: **D.2**: 21.
Goodman, F: **D.5**: 11.
Goodman, L: **K.4**: 48.
Goodman, M: **F.2**: 45.
Goodman, N: **C.6**: 12.
Goodman, P: **C.4**: 17.
Goodman, S: **F.5**: 216.
Goodnow, J: **D.3**: 14.
Goodwin, A: **D.8**: 47.
Goodwin, C: **D.9**: 198.
Goody, J: **D.8**: 18.
Googins, B: **F.4**: 115.
Goor, van, H: **J.4**: 19.
Gopal, Y: **F.3**: 265.
Gopalakrishnan, S: **D.8**: 28.
Gopnik, M: **D.7**: 24.
Gordon, B: **C.3**: 107. **F.4**: 292.
Gordon, R: **F.4**: 73.
Gore, M: **D.5**: 85.
Gore, S: **F.2**: 120.
Gore, T: **G.3.1**: 41. **G.3.2**: 300.
Gorelick, S: **F.5**: 71.
Gori, F: **D.2**: 16.
Gorkin, M: **D.2**: 3.
Gorman, B: **D.5**: 146.
Gornostayeva, G: **G.3.2**: 354.
Gorovitz, S: **K.3**: 11.
Gorr, W: **F.3**: 156.
Gorsuch, R: **D.5**: 33.
Görtler, E: **K.4**: 73.
Gory, la, M: **C.3**: 37.
Gossett, K: **K.4**: 82.
Gossop, M: **K.4**: 236.
Gostin, L: **K.1**: 325. **K.4**: 258.
Goswami, U: **C.2**: 112.
Gotlieb, J: **H.5**: 24.
Goto, I: **G.3.1**: 136.
Gottfredson, D: **K.1**: 146.
Gottfredson, G: **K.1**: 146.
Gottlieb, N: **K.3**: 16.
Gottmann, J: **G.3.2**: 326.

Gough, D: **F.4**: 158.
Goulbourne, H: **F.7**: 161.
Gould, D: **K.4**: 30.
Gould, P: **F.3**: 156.
Gould, S: **C.1**: 106.
Gourdomichalis, A: **G.3.1**: 80.
Gourko, H: **D.7**: 298–299.
Govaerts, W: **G.2**: 15, 29.
Gow, I: **I.3**: 60.
Gow, J: **J.7**: 15.
Gowen, J: **D.9**: 184.
Goyet, de, C: **K.4**: 45.
Craaf, De, N: **E.3**: 23. **H.5**. 18.
Graaf, de, P: **E.2**: 17. **I.2**: 36.
Grabb, E: **D.1**: 131. **I.5**: 140.
Gräbe, S: **F.4**: 97.
Graber, G: **K.4**: 252.
Grabosky, P: **K.1**: 405.
Grace, J: **D.3**: 40.
Grace, V: **K.4**: 220.
Gracia-Díez, M: **I.2**: 239.
Grada, de, E: **D.7**: 207.
Graddy, E: **J.6**: 50.
Graetz, B: **E.2**: 56.
Graham, C: **G.3.2**: 4.
Graham, E: **F.1**: 9.
Graham, H: **F.4**: 20.
Graham, J: **C.3**: 76. **I.5**: 202. **K.2**: 49.
Graham, S: **C.2**: 100. **C.3**: 65.
Graham-Brown, S: **D.9**: 10.
Gramlich, E: **I.2**: 235.
Gramling, R: **B.2**: 95.
Granberg, D: **D.5**: 6. **J.6**: 66.
Granda, R: **I.4**: 98.
Grandin, E: **D.5**: 103.
Grand, le, C: **H.3**: 69.
Grand, le, J: **F.3**: 288.
Grangeret, I: **G.3.1**: 96.
Grant, D: **I.5**: 95.
Grant, J: **J.3**: 42.
Grant, K: **F.5**: 173.
Grant, L: **F.5**: 10. **I.2**: 128.
Grant, M: **K.4**: 236.
Grant, P: **C.4**: 15.
Grant, R: **D.9**: 24.
Grasmick, H: **C.7**: 59. **D.5**: 9, 57. **H.6**: 4.

Grasmuck, S: **F.8**: 113.
Gratton, C: **I.6**: 14.
Gratton, L: **I.3**: 138.
Gray, B: **K.4**: 161.
Gray, C: **C.7**: 25. **D.7**: 27.
Gray, D: **C.7**: 58.
Gray, I: **G.2**: 26.
Gray, P: **G.3.1**: 39. **H.3**: 17.
Gray, R: **K.4**: 45.
Gray, W: **D.1**: 101.
Gray-Little, B: **F.4**: 205.
Graycar, A: **K.4**: 241.
Graziani, A: **H.3**: 12.
Greatbatch, D: **F.4**: 186.
Greeley, A: **D.5**: 38.
Green, A: **G.3.2**: 235.
Green, E: **C.7**: 52.
Green, F: **I.2**: 82.
Green, G: **F.4**: 297. **H.3**: 41.
Green, K: **C.3**: 45.
Green, P: **E.3**: 2. **K.1**: 22.
Green, S: **G.2**: 25.
Greenberg, B: **D.7**: 361.
Greenberg, J: **K.4**: 31.
Greenberg, M: **B.2**: 120.
Greenberger, D: **I.3**: 61.
Greene, I: **D.3**: 47.
Greene, K: **D.5**: 13.
Greene, M: **D.7**: 77.
Greene, R: **E.2**: 62. **G.3.2**: 209–210.
Greene, de, K: **C.5**: 71.
Greenglass, E: **I.3**: 103.
Greenhalgh, S: **F.5**: 250.
Greenman, N: **A.2**: 12.
Greenstein, D: **B.2**: 78.
Greenstreet, D: **I.2**: 206.
Greenwood, J: **C.1**: 164.
Greenwood, M: **A.3**: 2. **F.3**: 304. **F.8**: 44, 121, 147, 169.
Gregersen, H: **C.3**: 57. **D.1**: 52. **I.3**: 86.
Gregg, P: **I.5**: 124–125.
Gregorich, S: **C.2**: 168.
Gregory, D: **G.1**: 57.
Gregory, P: **H.3**: 49.
Greil, A: **F.3**: 119.
Grelet, Y: **I.4**: 120.
Grelley, P: **F.2**: 90.

Grelon, A: **I.4**: 95.
Greve, J: **K.1**: 242.
Grieco, M: **C.5**: 61.
Grieve, J: **F.4**: 316.
Grieve, R: **C.2**: 140.
Griffeth, R: **B.2**: 81.
Griffin, E: **F.3**: 144.
Griffin, L: **A.2**: 8. **I.5**: 174.
Griffith, J: **J.7**: 13.
Griffiths, M: **G.1**: 47. **K.1**: 9.
Griffiths, P: **D.7**: 98.
Grigel, F: **F.5**: 182.
Grigsby, J: **G.3.2**: 150.
Grillo, T: **F.4**: 133.
Grimes, P: **D.9**: 110. **J.6**: 15.
Grimmeau, J: **F.3**: 262, 297.
Grindstaff, C: **F.3**: 88.
Grineveld, J: **H.4**: 100.
Grint, K: **I.1**: 13.
Grip, de, A: **I.4**: 12.
Griset, P: **D.4**: 14.
Grisolia, S: **K.4**: 249.
Grissom, T: **G.3.2**: 129.
Grob, G: **K.4**: 198.
Grobler, A: **D.6**: 31.
Groc, G: **D.7**: 252.
Groebel, J: **C.3**: 21.
Groenendijk, J: **D.7**: 197.
Grogger, J: **K.1**: 168.
Gronbeck, B: **D.7**: 284.
Gronbjerg, K: **C.5**: 31.
Grønhaug, K: **H.5**: 38.
Groot, L: **I.4**: 12.
Groot, W: **I.2**: 224.
Groot-van Leeuwen, de, L: **I.2**: 118.
Gropen, J: **D.7**: 210.
Gropper, R: **C.7**: 30.
Gros, C: **K.1**: 11.
Groshen, E: **F.5**: 232. **H.3**: 70. **I.3**: 83.
Gross, A: **F.7**: 42.
Gross, P: **K.2**: 63.
Grossetti, M: **I.4**: 66.
Grotowska-Leder, J: **J.6**: 39.
Grounds, A: **K.4**: 100.
Groux, G: **E.1**: 22.
Grove, D: **I.4**: 16.

Grover, S: **I.3**: 148.
Groves, M: **F.4**: 200.
Grubb, R: **D.9**: 12.
Grubb, W: **I.4**: 124.
Grube, J: **C.4**: 7.
Gruchy, de, S: **K.2**: 6.
Grübler, A: **H.4**: 84.
Gruenewald, P: **D.7**: 103.
Grund, J: **K.1**: 317.
Grupo de Trabajo sobre Deuda Externa y Desarollo: **F.3**: 260.
Gruter, M: **D.4**: 3, 27.
Gruyer, F: **F.2**: 90.
Gryb, V: **D.6**: 24.
Gstettner, P: **D.9**: 66.
Guarnaccia, C: **F.2**: 15.
Guarnaccia, P: **C.1**: 72.
Guay, L: **K.1**: 256.
Gubbels, B: **K.2**: 82.
Gubhaju, B: **F.3**: 292.
Gucht, D: **D.8**: 3.
Guelke, A: **F.7**: 192.
Guelzow, M: **F.4**: 39.
Günthner, S: **C.3**: 53.
Gueriviere, P: **D.7**: 124, 264.
Guerra, D: **I.6**: 29.
Guest, D: **I.3**: 147. **I.5**: 126.
Guetta, M: **F.4**: 352. **G.3.2**: 207.
Guezennec, G: **I.3**: 94.
Gugler, J: **G.3**: 4.
Guigo, D: **D.7**: 182.
Guille-Escuret, G: **B.1**: 34.
Guillemin, A: **D.7**: 112.
Guimarães, A: **I.1**: 1. **I.4**: 1. **I.5**: 176.
Gulick, J: **F.3**: 11.
Gullestad, M: **D.2**: 29.
Gunatilleke, G: **F.8**: 152.
Gunderson, M: **H.3**: 83.
Gunderson, S: **I.5**: 111.
Gunn, C: **G.2**: 28.
Gunn, H: **G.2**: 28.
Gunn, J: **K.1**: 107.
Gunn, P: **D.8**: 15.
Gunter, B: **D.7**: 353.
Gupta, A: **F.7**: 184.
Gupta, D: **E.2**: 79.
Gupta, J: **F.3**: 142.

Gurevich, A: **E.3**: 62.
Gurtov, M: **F.8**: 45.
Gustafson, D: **K.4**: 8.
Gustafson, S: **F.5**: 275.
Gustafsson, B: **H.3**: 65.
Gustafsson, S: **F.5**: 189.
Gustafsson, U: **F.3**: 195.
Gustavsen, B: **I.3**: 35.
Gutek, B: **I.2**: 133.
Gutierrez, P: **H.3**: 9.
Guttmann, E: **K.1**: 63.
Guy, C: **B.2**: 77.
Guy, D: **F.6**: 41.
Guy, J: **D.8**: 54.
Guz, D: **F.3**: 79.
Gwagwa, N: **F.5**: 249.
Gwartney-Gibbs, P: **I.5**: 96.
Gyourko, J: **G.3.2**: 271.
Haaga, D: **F.3**: 174.
Haapala, D: **K.3**: 15, 21.
Haarmann, H: **D.7**: 4.
Haas, H: **D.7**: 271.
Haas, J: **I.5**: 195.
Haaser, H: **K.4**: 94.
Haberle, S: **G.1**: 18.
Habermas, J: **B.1**: 91.
Haberstroh, D: **K.4**: 94.
Habib, J: **F.2**: 61.
Hachani, F: **G.3.2**: 173.
Hackler, J: **K.1**: 137.
Hackney, R: **G.3.2**: 51.
Hadaway, C: **D.5**: 113.
Hadda, J: **C.1**: 40.
Haddad, L: **F.1**: 58.
Haddad, Y: **D.5**: 171.
Hadreas, P: **F.5**: 277.
Haeberle, S: **J.5**: 29.
Haegen, van der, H: **G.3.2**: 26, 189.
Haehnel, I: **G.3.2**: 134.
Haerle, R: **F.7**: 44.
Haffenden, I: **D.9**: 183.
Hafferty, F: **K.4**: 57.
Häfner, H: **F.3**: 169.
Hagan, J: **D.4**: 9. **F.1**: 28. **F.2**: 123.
Hagedorn, J: **F.2**: 126.
Hagenaars, J: **E.2**: 75. **E.3**: 23.

Hagendoorn, L: **C.4**: 13. **C.7**: 21. **F.7**: 154.
Hagen, van der, X: **H.5**: 36.
Hager, M: **I.5**: 81.
Hagihara, K: **H.3**: 47.
Hagihara, Y: **H.3**: 47.
Hahn, A: **J.3**: 26.
Hahn, J: **J.6**: 7.
Haidar, A: **K.2**: 100.
Haider, A: **J.5**: 12.
Hailemariam, A: **F.3**: 103.
Hailey, M: **J.5**: 29.
Haines, B: **F.5**: 54.
Haines, V: **I.3**: 115.
Haining, R: **F.3**: 255.
Haisch, I: **F.3**: 175.
Haisch, J: **F.3**: 175.
Hajal, F: **F.4**: 289.
Hakim, C: **F.5**: 290.
Hakim, S: **K.1**: 59.
Haksar, V: **D.3**: 13.
Hakuta, K: **D.7**: 19.
Hala, S: **C.2**: 123.
Halász, G: **D.9**: 146.
Hale, C: **C.3**: 107. **K.1**: 157.
Hale, D: **K.1**: 192.
Halimi, S: **D.7**: 260.
Hall, A: **I.6**: 38.
Hall, C: **F.5**: 124.
Hall, D: **I.6**: 41.
Hall, J: **G.3.2**: 276.
Hall, M: **G.1**: 23.
Hall, P: **G.3.2**: 317.
Hall, R: **D.9**: 120. **F.5**: 169.
Hall, W: **D.7**: 21, 79.
Hallam, L: **K.4**: 61.
Hallden, G: **F.4**: 274.
Halle, D: **F.4**: 4, 28.
Halle, M: **D.7**: 68.
Hallebone, E: **F.4**: 303.
Haller, M: **E.2**: 58.
Halli, S: **F.4**: 199.
Halliday, M: **C.2**: 165.
Hallinan, M: **E.3**: 6.
Halman, L: **E.2**: 75.
Halpern, D: **C.1**: 110.
Halteman, W: **K.1**: 206.
Ham, C: **K.4**: 203.

Hamada, T: **H.2**: 1.
Hamberg, E: **D.5**: 28, 72.
Hamberger, L: **C.2**: 205.
Hamerle, A: **B.2**: 48, 63, 88.
Hames, D: **I.5**: 100.
Hamid, S: **I.2**: 83.
Hamilton, B: **D.9**: 88.
Hamilton, N: **F.8**: 6.
Hamilton, P: **B.1**: 118.
Hamlin, C: **H.4**: 19.
Hamm, B: **D.1**: 8.
Hamm, R: **D.7**: 175. **F.1**: 23.
Hammar, T: **F.8**: 117.
Hammer, T: **I.4**: 58.
Hammersley, M: **D.9**: 158.
Hammill, P: **D.9**: 46.
Hammond, J: **F.6**: 39.
Hammond, P: **C.7**: 37. **D.5**: 118.
Hamnett, C: **G.3.2**: 234.
Hamon, H: **F.2**: 90.
Hampton, R: **F.4**: 149.
Hancock, K: **C.1**: 107. **K.2**: 10.
Handal, G: **D.9**: 47.
Handal, P: **K.1**: 42.
Handberg, R: **J.3**: 28.
Handelman, D: **D.7**: 72.
Handler, J: **K.2**: 84.
Handy, J: **I.4**: 48.
Haney, E: **G.3.1**: 32.
Haney, W: **G.3.1**: 75.
Haniff, N: **D.9**: 176.
Hannah, T: **B.1**: 48.
Hannan, D: **I.2**: 246.
Hannan, M: **C.5**: 3, 79.
Hannigan, J: **D.5**: 53, 66.
Hans, A: **F.5**: 271.
Hans, V: **D.7**: 326.
Hansel, M: **K.1**: 105.
Hansen, A: **D.7**: 275.
Hansen, D: **F.4**: 162.
Hansen, G: **C.3**: 142.
Hansen, W: **C.3**: 76.
Hanson, B: **G.2**: 14.
Hanson, M: **H.7**: 7.
Hanson, S: **F.4**: 30, 290. **G.3.2**: 174. **I.2**: 48, 114.
Hansson, R: **I.3**: 41.

Hantzi, A: **F.7**: 262.
Hanushek, E: **B.2**: 53.
Hao, L: **F.4**: 56, 348.
Haq, I: **D.7**: 266.
Harada, Y: **K.1**: 155.
Harcum, E: **C.2**: 85.
Harder, J: **I.6**: 9.
Hardey, M: **F.4**: 298.
Hardiker, P: **K.2**: 66.
Hardin, E: **F.5**: 19.
Harding, L: **K.2**: 59.
Harding, P: **E.3**: 15, 48.
Harding, S: **C.3**: 157.
Hardoy, A: **G.2**: 2.
Hardoy, J: **G.2**: 2.
Härdtle, R: **F.6**: 52.
Hardy, L: **C.2**: 8.
Harer, M: **K.1**: 79.
Hargrave, A: **D.7**: 274.
Hargreaves, A: **D.9**: 47. **F.8**: 48, 150.
Harles, J: **F.7**: 108.
Harmon, G: **K.1**: 87.
Harnmeijer, J: **G.3.1**: 127.
Harpending, H: **F.3**: 89.
Harper, D: **C.1**: 129. **C.2**: 71. **G.3.1**: 47.
Harper, R: **J.3**: 37.
Harré, R: **C.6**: 17. **D.6**: 27.
Harrell, K: **C.3**: 100.
Harries-Jones, P: **B.1**: 38.
Harrington, M: **G.1**: 21.
Harris, B: **C.1**: 42.
Harris, C: **G.1**: 64.
Harris, J: **D.7**: 68, 202. **D.9**: 70, 80. **F.4**: 279.
Harris, K: **F.4**: 291.
Harris, L: **E.2**: 12.
Harris, M: **I.4**: 129.
Harris, R: **G.3.2**: 157. **I.5**: 179. **I.6**: 8. **K.1**: 103, 415.
Harris, S: **F.3**: 177.
Harris, W: **G.3.2**: 149.
Harrison, A: **C.3**: 151. **F.8**: 87.
Harrison, C: **D.7**: 245.
Harrison, E: **I.5**: 10.
Harrison, J: **C.5**: 38.
Harrison, M: **K.2**: 69.
Harrison, S: **K.4**: 244.
Hart, D: **G.3.2**: 333.

Hart, G: **F.3**: 157. **I.5**: 18.
Hart, H: **D.5**: 51. **I.3**: 35.
Hart, J: **G.3.2**: 60, 284.
Hart, P: **C.4**: 36.
Hart, R: **D.7**: 288.
Hart, S: **F.2**: 92.
Hart, de, J: **F.2**: 122.
Hartgers, C: **K.1**: 316.
Hartig, T: **C.2**: 90.
Hartka, E: **K.1**: 366.
Hartz, G: **C.2**: 44.
Harvey, B: **D.3**: 52.
Harvey, D: **B.1**: 116. **K.4**: 70.
Harvey, J: **F.7**: 30.
Harvey, M: **K.4**: 48.
Harvey, P: **D.7**: 333.
Harwood, J: **D.7**: 199.
Hasegawa, T: **C.2**: 61.
Hasenau, M: **I.2**: 67.
Hasenfeld, Y: **K.2**: 11, 84.
Hashem, M: **F.8**: 65.
Hashimoto, A: **F.4**: 54.
Hashimoto, K: **G.3.2**: 72.
Hashizume, D: **B.1**: 80.
Haskey, J: **F.4**: 245.
Haslam, N: **C.3**: 19.
Haslam, S: **C.3**: 154.
Hasnath, S: **H.4**: 38.
Hassall, G: **F.7**: 74.
Hassard, J: **I.1**: 3.
Hasselbach, S: **D.7**: 300.
Hassenteufel, P: **I.5**: 158.
Hassim, S: **F.5**: 183.
Hassinger, E: **G.3.1**: 65.
Hastings, G: **K.1**: 373.
Hastings, J: **C.2**: 205.
Hastings Centre: **K.4**: 245.
Hatim, B: **D.7**: 62.
Hatty, S: **J.3**: 43.
Haub, C: **F.1**: 70.
Hauber, A: **K.1**: 178.
Haubert, M: **G.3.1**: 93–94.
Haug, F: **F.5**: 124.
Haug, P: **H.4**: 41.
Haugen, M: **G.3.1**: 45.
Haughton, G: **I.4**: 132.

Hause, E: **F.4**: 156.
Hauser, R: **B.2**: 68.
Hausmann, B: **F.7**: 240.
Havers, S: **C.1**: 50.
Havice, M: **H.5**: 25.
Havitz, M: **I.6**: 40.
Havlovic, S: **I.3**: 68.
Hawkes, K: **F.1**: 61.
Hawkins, A: **F.4**: 269.
Hawkins, B: **G.3.2**: 56.
Hawkins, G: **K.1**: 210, 392.
Hawkins, K: **C.3**: 83.
Hawkins, R: **F.4**: 186.
Haworth, A: **J.3**: 17.
Hay, A: **D.3**: 4.
Hayakawa, K: **G.3.2**: 130.
Hayashi, R: **D.7**: 204.
Hayes, B: **F.5**: 197.
Hayes, K: **H.3**: 76.
Haynes, P: **C.1**: 32.
Häyry, H: **K.4**: 259.
Haythornthwaite, J: **C.2**: 150.
Haywood, A: **K.1**: 373.
Haywood, S: **K.4**: 186.
Hazan, C: **F.4**: 196.
Hazani, M: **C.2**: 107.
Hazlett, S: **C.2**: 237.
Hazra, S: **I.2**: 15.
Hdez, J: **G.3.2**: 250.
He, Z: **C.7**: 14.
Headey, B: **C.2**: 104. **H.3**: 64.
Healey, P: **G.3.2**: 304, 330.
Heath, D: **K.1**: 304.
Heath, J: **H.3**: 35.
Heatherton, T: **C.2**: 223–224.
Heaton, K: **K.3**: 7.
Heaton, T: **F.3**: 68, 74. **F.4**: 146, 251.
Heberlein, T: **F.8**: 36.
Hebert, G: **F.3**: 246.
Hechter, M: **B.1**: 134.
Heckman, J: **F.7**: 10.
Heckmann, F: **F.7**: 78.
Hedderley, D: **C.7**: 28.
Heer, de, W: **B.2**: 124, 128.
Heerschop, M: **B.2**: 125.
Hees, van, I: **G.3.2**: 133.
Heffernan, T: **C.2**: 165.

Hegedüs, J: **K.2**: 7.
Hegeman, S: **D.1**: 41.
Heick, W: **H.5**: 31.
Heid, C: **I.4**: 107.
Heiden, an der, W: **F.3**: 169.
Heidenfelder, M: **C.2**: 68.
Heidenreich, M: **C.5**: 63. **D.9**: 40. **H.4**: 58.
Heieck, S: **D.1**: 140.
Heijke, J: **I.4**: 12.
Heikes, E: **I.2**: 148.
Heil, J: **C.2**: 63.
Heiland, H: **J.1**: 3.
Heiland, I: **F.2**: 34.
Heilbroner, R: **A.1**: 10.
Heilman, M: **F.5**: 305.
Heim, I: **D.7**: 217, 222.
Hein, J: **K.2**: 81.
Heineberg, H: **G.3.2**: 270.
Heinrich, J: **D.7**: 330.
Heins, F: **F.3**: 249.
Heinz, W: **I.2**: 40.
Heisbourg, F: **F.3**: 18.
Heisler, B: **G.3.2**: 176.
Heiss, J: **F.5**: 281.
Heitlinger, A: **F.5**: 214.
Helburn, S: **K.2**: 60.
Hellinckx, W: **K.2**: 37.
Helmers, S: **H.4**: 96.
Helmsing, A: **G.3.1**: 125.
Helsing, E: **K.4**: 197.
Helsley, R: **G.3.2**: 89.
Helton, A: **I.2**: 67.
Helvacioglu, B: **F.4**: 61.
Helve, H: **F.2**: 5, 132.
Helweg, A: **F.7**: 29.
Hemmings, P: **H.3**: 89.
Hemphill, K: **C.1**: 135.
Henderson, J: **G.3.2**: 366.
Henderson, M: **D.9**: 163.
Henderson, P: **G.2**: 15. **G.3.1**: 21.
Henderson, R: **C.5**: 78.
Henderson, S: **F.3**: 158.
Hendon, W: **I.6**: 46.
Hendrick, C: **C.3**: 123.
Hendrick, S: **C.3**: 123.
Hendriks, A: **F.6**: 4.

Heneman, H: **I.3**: 21.
Henik, A: **B.2**: 83.
Henke, R: **C.4**: 13.
Henkens, K: **I.2**: 117.
Hennig, J: **D.1**: 117.
Henningfield, J: **K.1**: 319.
Henrard, J: **K.2**: 72.
Henriques, M: **K.4**: 51.
Henry, L: **F.1**: 57.
Hentoff, N: **K.4**: 148.
Henze, P: **F.1**: 18.
Hepworth, M: **D.7**: 91.
Herbert, T: **F.4**: 153.
Herbolzeimer, E: **I.2**: 210.
Herbst, K: **K.1**: 107.
Herek, G: **C.1**: 83.
Héritier-Augé, F: **D.8**: 35. **F.5**: 207.
Herman, B: **D.3**: 2.
Herman, E: **K.1**: 392.
Herman, N: **K.1**: 397.
Hermkens, P: **B.2**: 31. **F.2**: 6. **H.3**: 77.
Hernández, R: **J.6**: 33.
Hernes, G: **D.9**: 125. **I.5**: 15.
Herod, A: **G.3.2**: 28, 174. **I.2**: 27. **J.6**: 25.
Herr, T: **D.3**: 23.
Herrick, S: **F.3**: 204.
Herring, C: **F.7**: 261. **J.1**: 19.
Herring, R: **G.3.1**: 106.
Herrle, J: **F.5**: 289.
Heršak, E: **F.7**: 102.
Hersch, J: **I.3**: 44. **I.5**: 105.
Hertz, R: **F.4**: 4, 29.
Hervieu, B: **F.3**: 15. **H.4**: 12.
Herz, B: **I.2**: 160.
Herzog, E: **D.8**: 66.
Herzog, L: **G.3.2**: 19. **J.8**: 17.
Heskin, A: **G.2**: 34.
Hesse-Biber, S: **C.2**: 229. **F.5**: 57.
Hessing, M: **I.2**: 145.
Hester, S: **D.9**: 143.
Hestevold, H: **D.5**: 5.
Hetherington, R: **K.4**: 22.
Hetzel, H: **F.8**: 64.
Hewison, H: **F.2**: 78.
Hewitt, W: **D.5**: 142.
Hewlett, S: **K.2**: 110.
Hewstone, M: **F.7**: 262.

Heyer, E: **F.3**: 109.
Heyer, P: **D.7**: 126.
Heywood, J: **C.4**: 27.
Hibbs, D: **H.3**: 81.
Hickson, D: **C.5**: 27.
Higgins, C: **I.2**: 100.
Higgins, E: **C.2**: 236. **D.7**: 170, 176.
Higgs, N: **B.2**: 66, 124.
Higley, J: **E.2**: 10.
Higuchi, S: **F.5**: 129.
Higueras-Arnal, A: **E.3**: 33.
Hildebrandt, H: **D.7**: 16.
Hill, C: **C.3**: 136. **C.7**: 6.
Hill, K: **F.3**: 295. **K.4**: 20.
Hill, L: **D.1**: 5. **D.7**: 123.
Hill, M: **F.4**: 278. **K.3**: 38.
Hill, P: **D.9**: 112.
Hill, R: **K.4**: 178.
Hill, S: **I.3**: 92.
Hills, E: **D.1**: 25.
Hiltermann, J: **F.5**: 60.
Hilton, D: **D.7**: 12, 120, 176.
Hilton, M: **K.1**: 303.
Hilty, J: **C.3**: 67.
Himes, J: **E.3**: 71.
Hinde, R: **C.3**: 21.
Hinds, L: **D.7**: 390.
Hinrichs, K: **F.2**: 7.
Hinton, W: **K.1**: 259.
Hirano, H: **D.1**: 53.
Hirayama, Y: **G.3.2**: 130.
Hirochika, N: **D.5**: 22.
Hirsch, E: **H.4**: 94.
Hirschl, T: **K.4**: 21.
Hirschman, E: **D.8**: 50.
Hirschmann, D: **J.6**: 55.
Hirschmann, N: **F.5**: 82.
Hiršl, M: **F.4**: 88.
Hirst, P: **H.2**: 5.
Hirvela, A: **D.7**: 16.
Hiscott, R: **I.4**: 28.
Hitch, G: **C.2**: 165–166.
Hitchens, D: **H.4**: 28.
Hitzler, R: **I.6**: 18.
Hixon, J: **C.7**: 74.
Hoare, A: **D.9**: 174.

Hobbs, D: **I.6**: 8. **J.3**: 40. **K.1**: 406.
Hobcraft, J: **B.2**: 35. **F.1**: 51. **F.3**: 79.
Hobfoll, S: **J.8**: 20.
Hoch, C: **K.1**: 238, 285.
Hochstrasser, D: **F.3**: 40.
Hodapp, P: **I.4**: 8.
Hodge, D: **G.3.2**: 33.
Hodge, R: **F.3**: 97.
Hodgkinson, P: **K.1**: 2.
Hodgson, C: **K.4**: 225.
Hodgson, G: **D.1**: 74.
Hodyreva, N: **C.1**: 122.
Hoek, J: **B.2**: 101.
Hoeksema, J: **D.7**: 205.
Hoek, van den, A: **K.1**: 316.
Hoem, J: **F.4**: 144.
Hoenderdos, W: **F.8**: 32.
Hoerster, N: **D.3**: 11.
Hoeveler, J: **J.6**: 54.
Hof, H: **D.4**: 35.
Hofer, von, H: **K.1**: 91.
Hoff-Wilson, J: **F.5**: 199.
Hofferth, S: **K.2**: 40–41.
Hoffman, C: **F.8**: 46.
Hoffman, D: **C.2**: 106.
Hoffman, J: **F.3**: 204.
Hoffman, L: **F.4**: 340.
Hoffmann, J: **I.5**: 30.
Hoffmann, L: **D.1**: 103. **J.6**: 52.
Hoffmann, O: **G.3.1**: 42.
Hoffmann, S: **D.3**: 33.
Hoffmann, W: **K.1**: 420.
Hoffmann-Lange, U: **E.2**: 10.
Hoffrage, U: **C.2**: 208.
Hoff, van, D: **G.3.2**: 256.
Hoff, van der, R: **G.3.2**: 325.
Hofmaier, B: **I.3**: 35.
Hofmann, M: **E.3**: 39.
Hofmeyr, K: **I.2**: 168.
Hofstede, G: **C.5**: 18.
Hogan, D: **F.4**: 56, 223, 348.
Hogan, J: **C.7**: 48.
Hogan, R: **C.2**: 192, 231.
Hogg, M: **C.4**: 52.
Hoggart, K: **K.2**: 74.
Hoggart, R: **D.1**: 2.
Höhn, C: **F.3**: 277.

Holden, K: **F.2**: 47.
Holden, L: **I.4**: 117.
Holden, P: **F.2**: 80.
Holder, J: **D.7**: 114.
Holdnak, B: **C.5**: 44.
Holdren, J: **F.1**: 47.
Holdt, von, K: **I.5**: 128.
Holland, C: **C.2**: 154. **D.9**: 213.
Holland, J: **F.6**: 37.
Holland, S: **F.7**: 13.
Hollander, M: **D.7**: 210.
Höllinger, F: **F.5**: 278.
Hollingsworth, J: **H.4**: 26.
Hollomon, J: **H.4**: 14.
Hollon, S: **C.1**: 141.
Holloway, J: **J.2**: 21.
Hollows, A: **F.2**: 77.
Holm, N: **D.5**: 44.
Holmberg, S: **J.6**: 66.
Holmes, J: **I.5**: 121.
Holmes, L: **C.5**: 61.
Holmes, M: **D.4**: 38.
Holmes, R: **K.1**: 142.
Holmwood, J: **B.1**: 6.
Holtz-Eakin, D: **I.2**: 190.
Holub, R: **B.1**: 59.
Holzer, H: **G.3.2**: 220.
Holzer, J: **F.3**: 3.
Hom, P: **B.2**: 81.
Homan, R: **B.2**: 6.
Homann, K: **H.5**: 41.
Homer, J: **F.3**: 153, 198.
Honeyball, S: **I.2**: 138.
Honigsbaum, N: **F.3**: 182.
Honneth, A: **B.1**: 91.
Hoodbhoy, P: **D.5**: 163.
Hoogenboom, B: **K.1**: 6.
Hooks, B: **F.7**: 5.
Hooks, M: **F.5**: 188.
Hooper, B: **F.7**: 48.
Hooyman, N: **K.3**: 16.
Hope, G: **G.1**: 18.
Hopenhayn, M: **H.7**: 3.
Hopf, W: **B.1**: 133.
Hopkins, A: **F.4**: 176.
Hopkins, E: **E.2**: 74.

Hopkins, N: **H.3**: 91.
Hoppe, R: **H.3**: 62.
Hopper, J: **G.1**: 31.
Hopper, K: **C.1**: 73. **G.3.2**: 108, 224. **K.1**: 263.
Horak, R: **I.6**: 8. **K.1**: 428.
Horlacher, D: **F.3**: 301.
Horley, J: **C.7**: 65.
Horm-Wingerd, D: **F.4**: 200.
Horn, P: **F.5**: 135, 213.
Horne, J: **I.6**: 12.
Horner, T: **F.2**: 73.
Hornsby-Smith, M: **D.5**: 141.
Horowitz, E: **J.4**: 17,
Horowitz, L: **C.3**: 9, 71.
Horowitz, R: **K.1**: 185.
Horrel, J: **D.7**: 123.
Horsburgh, M: **K.2**: 15.
Horvath, B: **D.7**: 9.
Horwitz, F: **I.5**: 13, 77.
Horwitz, R: **D.7**: 253.
Hoskens, M: **C.2**: 48.
Hoskin, M: **D.9**: 52. **F.7**: 106.
Hosking, D: **C.1**: 168.
Hosotsuji, K: **C.3**: 61.
Hotaling, G: **F.4**: 1.
Houben, G: **I.3**: 117.
Houlihan, B: **I.6**: 13.
Hours, B: **D.5**: 179.
House, J: **J.1**: 19.
House, R: **J.6**: 31, 43.
Houston, D: **C.2**: 32.
Houtman, D: **I.2**: 247.
Hovav, M: **D.7**: 210.
Howard, D: **I.6**: 40.
Howard, G: **C.1**: 94.
Howard, J: **C.3**: 73. **F.2**: 83.
Howard, L: **I.1**: 10. **I.3**: 56.
Howard, M: **J.4**: 4.
Howard, P: **I.2**: 217.
Howards, I: **K.1**: 267.
Howe, E: **I.2**: 153.
Howe, I: **E.3**: 56.
Howe, L: **I.4**: 38.
Howell, D: **I.3**: 90.
Howell, J: **C.3**: 25.
Howes, C: **I.3**: 12. **K.2**: 41.
Howitt, D: **C.1**: 87.

Howitt, R: **G.1**: 34. **H.7**: 5.
Howlett, C: **J.5**: 2.
Howsen, R: **K.1**: 159.
Hox, J: **B.2**: 31.
Hoy, D: **D.6**: 12.
Hoyles, M: **I.6**: 39.
Hoynes, W: **D.7**: 240.
Hoyo, del, J: **F.1**: 3.
Hranilović, N: **F.7**: 137.
Hrubá, D: **F.3**: 233.
Hruby, M: **G.3.2**: 150.
Hsu, M: **F.3**: 60.
Hubbard, J: **K.1**: 219.
Huber, J: **A.1**: 18.
Hubert, J: **K.4**: 118.
Huby, M: **K.4**: 1.
Huck, A: **F.7**: 26.
Huck, G: **D.7**: 203.
Hudson, B: **H.7**: 14.
Hudson, C: **K.4**: 191.
Hudson, P: **G.3.1**: 98.
Huebner, R: **K.1**: 239, 301, 310.
Hübner, S: **F.5**: 52, 54.
Hünermann, P: **D.5**: 94.
Huer, J: **I.4**: 114.
Hüttner, H: **K.2**: 82.
Huff-Corzine, L: **K.1**: 226.
Hughes, C: **F.4**: 326.
Hughes, M: **C.2**: 140. **C.5**: 70. **I.2**: 55. **K.1**: 147.
Hugman, R: **K.3**: 28, 31.
Hugo, G: **F.1**: 69.
Huguet, P: **C.3**: 42.
Hui, C: **C.7**: 23.
Huinink, J: **F.4**: 63.
Huizinga, D: **K.1**: 51.
Hula, R: **H.6**: 8.
Hullot-Kentor, R: **D.8**: 21.
Hulme, C: **D.7**: 56.
Hultkrantz, L: **G.1**: 11.
Human, J: **G.3.1**: 59.
Humm, A: **F.3**: 186.
Humphrey, C: **K.1**: 167.
Humphreys, J: **G.3.2**: 44.
Humphreys, L: **K.3**: 24.
Humphries, M: **I.4**: 77.
Hund, J: **B.1**: 152.

Hune, S: **I.2**: 67.
Hunger Project: **E.3**: 15, 43.
Hunkins, F: **D.9**: 46.
Hunt, E: **C.2**: 142.
Hunt, G: **F.3**: 304.
Hunt, J: **C.6**: 9.
Hunt, M: **K.4**: 121.
Hunt, R: **C.2**: 44.
Hunter, C: **D.9**: 119.
Hunter, J: **H.4**: 20.
Hunter, L: **I.3**: 127.
Hunter, S: **F.2**: 129.
Huotari, V: **D.5**: 129.
Hupet, M: **C.2**: 25.
Hupp, S: **C.2**: 130. **F.2**: 3. **K.1**: 280.
Huppi, M: **K.1**: 249.
Hurbon, L: **D.5**: 22.
Hurford, J: **D.7**: 23.
Hurlbert, J: **I.3**: 105, 115.
Hurley, J: **C.2**: 84. **I.4**: 101.
Hurrell, A: **G.1**: 27.
Hurrelmann, K: **F.2**: 142.
Hursthouse, R: **B.1**: 44. **F.3**: 67.
Husbands, C: **F.7**: 264. **F.8**: 29, 150.
Husbands, J: **C.3**: 90.
Huselid, M: **I.3**: 54.
Huston, A: **K.1**: 222.
Huston, H: **C.1**: 98.
Huston, T: **C.3**: 140.
Hutchens, R: **I.4**: 44.
Hutcheson, J: **F.7**: 233.
Hutchins, K: **K.3**: 19.
Hutnik, N: **F.7**: 72.
Hutson, S: **K.1**: 237.
Huttman, E: **F.4**: 4, 96. **G.3.2**: 167.
Hutton, S: **H.3**: 33.
Huxley, M: **G.3.2**: 214.
Hwang, S: **D.7**: 183. **F.7**: 69.
Hyde, J: **K.2**: 57.
Hyman, H: **B.2**: 126.
Hyser, R: **F.7**: 189.
Hyslop, J: **D.9**: 54.
Hyslop, R: **D.3**: 9.
Iacono, W: **D.4**: 43.
Iakubanets, V: **C.2**: 197.
Ianitskii, O: **G.3.2**: 22.
Iannone, A: **D.3**: 66.

Iaroshevskii, M: **C.1**: 172.
Iarushkin, V: **C.2**: 188.
Ibbetson, K: **K.3**: 44.
Ibbetson, M: **K.1**: 368.
Ibrahim, F: **D.1**: 42.
Ibrahim, H: **G.1**: 42.
Ichikawa, K: **F.5**: 306.
Ichniowski, C: **I.5**: 116.
Ickes, W: **C.3**: 146.
Ighalo, J: **G.3.2**: 163.
Ihara, C: **C.2**: 21.
Ihlanfeldt, K: **I.2**: 8. **I.4**: 42.
Ijima, N: **G.3.2**: 81.
Ikeda, K: **G.3.1**: 72.
Ikeda, M: **H.4**: 48. **I.1**: 8.
Ikemiya, M: **D.7**: 76.
Ikonomu, T: **E.1**: 11.
Iles, P: **I.3**: 138. **K.3**: 32.
Iliushechkin, V: **E.2**: 80.
Illingworth, L: **C.2**: 228.
Illsley, R: **F.3**: 288.
Ilyasov, F: **F.4**: 244.
Ilyin, M: **J.6**: 22.
Imada, T: **A.1**: 13.
Imaeda, N: **B.1**: 17.
Imai, C: **D.2**: 19.
Imam, M: **H.4**: 43.
Imano, K: **I.1**: 8. **I.4**: 106.
Imber, S: **J.4**: 17.
Imhoff, van, E: **F.3**: 96.
Imrie, R: **H.3**: 79.
Inagami, T: **I.1**: 8. **I.5**: 173.
Inciardi, J: **K.1**: 336.
Ingate, M: **I.3**: 153.
Ingene, C: **F.8**: 110.
Ingham, R: **F.6**: 16.
Inglehart, R: **C.7**: 26.
Ingman, S: **F.2**: 46.
Ingoldsby, B: **F.4**: 71.
Ingram, P: **I.3**: 10.
Inoue, H: **D.7**: 352.
Institut de l'entreprise: **I.3**: 143.
International Economic and Social Affairs: **F.3**: 149.
Intriligator, M: **K.4**: 196.
Ioannou, Y: **D.7**: 63.
Ioffe, G: **G.3.1**: 63, 124.

Ion, J: **B.2**: 106.
Ioskebich, I: **D.8**: 23.
Ippolito, R: **I.3**: 32.
Iraci Fedeli, L: **F.7**: 258.
Ireton, F: **A.1**: 33.
Irfan, M: **D.9**: 134.
Irgens-Jensen, O: **K.1**: 315.
Iribarne, D', P: **D.1**: 61.
Irizarry, R: **K.1**: 367.
Irmão, J: **G.3.1**: 54.
Irving, A: **K.2**: 93.
Irwin, M: **I.2**: 44.
Isaac, L: **A.2**: 8.
Isbell, S: **H.3**: 90.
Isbister, J: **E.3**: 47.
Ishi'i, K: **K.1**: 396.
Ishida, H: **E.2**: 57, 67. **F.4**: 75.
Ishii, A: **K.4**: 97.
Ishii-Kuntz, M: **F.4**: 7.
Ishikawa, A: **F.8**: 72.
Ishitsuka, S: **B.1**: 112.
Ishmael, L: **G.3.2**: 364.
Iskenderov, A: **E.3**: 40.
Islam, S: **F.3**: 90.
Islei, G: **C.4**: 26.
Isohanni, M: **K.1**: 331.
Isoux, P: **I.2**: 244.
Issac, L: **I.5**: 174.
Isvan, N: **F.3**: 123.
Ito, M: **D.7**: 131. **I.1**: 8. **I.3**: 47.
Ito, N: **K.2**: 70.
Ito, Y: **E.3**: 25.
Itsuo, E: **F.4**: 23.
Iturra, R: **F.6**: 7.
Ivanic, R: **D.7**: 190.
Ivanov, M: **C.1**: 172.
Ivanov, V: **B.2**: 112, 115. **D.1**: 21.
Ivanova, R: **I.2**: 30.
Iversen, G: **C.4**: 9.
Iwao, K: **G.3.2**: 278.
Izquierdo, M: **F.4**: 36.
Jabbra, N: **F.8**: 73.
Jack, A: **C.2**: 93.
Jack, R: **K.2**: 97.
Jackendoff, R: **D.7**: 210.
Jackman, R: **F.8**: 103.

Jackson, F: **D.3**: 5.
Jackson, H: **K.3**: 2.
Jackson, I: **G.3.2**: 30.
Jackson, J: **F.1**: 34. **I.3**: 78. **K.1**: 34, 44, 200.
Jackson, M: **C.1**: 128.
Jackson, P: **D.1**: 118. **F.5**: 268. **G.3**: 6.
Jackson, R: **F.7**: 41.
Jackson, S: **G.3.2**: 309. **I.3**: 80. **K.2**: 48.
Jacob, E: **I.2**: 186.
Jacob, H: **F.4**: 186.
Jacob, J: **B.1**: 16. **C.1**: 113.
Jacob, M: **D.1**: 68.
Jacobs, J: **D.5**: 17. **D.7**: 205.
Jacobs, S: **A.2**: 18. **B.1**: 58.
Jacobsen, J: **I.3**: 26.
Jacobson, A: **F.3**: 60.
Jacobson, C: **F.3**: 68.
Jacobvitz, R: **D.7**: 326.
Jacoby, D: **I.2**: 187.
Jacoby, H: **F.5**: 301.
Jacoby, W: **B.2**: 41.
Jacod, M: **G.3.2**: 134–135.
Jacquier, C: **G.3.2**: 173.
Jaegel, D: **D.4**: 34.
Jaffe, P: **K.1**: 216.
Jagacinski, C: **C.2**: 151.
Jaggernathsingh, D: **I.2**: 91.
Jahangir, A: **F.7**: 104.
Jain, P: **F.8**: 78.
Jaiswal, S: **D.5**: 158.
Jamal, M: **C.2**: 218.
James, B: **D.7**: 308.
James, F: **G.3.2**: 98.
James, P: **B.2**: 73. **J.2**: 1.
James, S: **G.3.2**: 147.
Jameson, F: **D.1**: 93.
Jamieson, A: **K.4**: 116.
Jamieson, G: **C.2**: 81.
Jamieson, I: **D.9**: 33.
Jamison, A: **E.3**: 64.
Jamison, D: **D.7**: 360. **F.3**: 171.
Jamrozik, A: **K.4**: 241.
Janich, H: **F.2**: 34.
Janicka, K: **E.2**: 32.
Jankowski, M: **G.3.2**: 196.
Jankowski, N: **B.2**: 11. **D.7**: 297.
Jannetta, A: **F.3**: 296.

INTERNATIONAL BIBLIOGRAPHY OF SOCIOLOGY — 1991

Janoff-Bulman, R: **C.2**: 39.
Janos, A: **A.1**: 34. **E.3**: 27.
Janoski, T: **A.2**: 8. **B.1**: 144.
Jans, N: **C.5**: 50.
Jansen, A: **G.3**: 3.
Janssen, J: **F.2**: 122.
Janssen, R: **C.1**: 5.
Janzing, C: **I.3**: 145.
Jaret, C: **F.4**: 292.
Jarjoura, G: **K.1**: 80.
Jarley, P: **I.3**: 106. **I.5**: 61.
Jarré, D: **K.2**: 102.
Jarrell, S: **K.1**: 159.
Jarrett, L: **F.2**: 146.
Jarvie, G: **F.7**: 263.
Järvinen, M: **F.6**: 38.
Jarvis, G: **G.3.2**: 195.
Jarvis, M: **K.4**: 239.
Jary, D: **I.6**: 12.
Jasinski, D: **K.1**: 319.
Jaspaert, K: **D.7**: 75.
Jasso, G: **D.5**: 102.
Jatulis, L: **C.2**: 152.
Jayaram, N: **D.9**: 133.
Jayasuriya, L: **D.7**: 336. **F.8**: 112.
Jeannee, E: **D.9**: 89.
Jecker, N: **F.2**: 29.
Jeeves, A: **F.8**: 109.
Jeffers, S: **F.7**: 39.
Jeffrey, R: **F.5**: 49, 211.
Jegouzo, G: **F.3**: 92.
Jehn, K: **C.4**: 46.
Jekel, J: **K.1**: 327.
Jelen, C: **F.8**: 22.
Jelin, E: **F.5**: 274.
Jenkins, J: **D.1**: 98. **K.4**: 74.
Jenkins, L: **I.3**: 63.
Jenkins, R: **E.2**: 26. **K.1**: 186.
Jenkins, S: **K.1**: 272.
Jenkins-Hall, K: **C.1**: 97.
Jennings, P: **J.8**: 1.
Jensen, C: **I.4**: 47.
Jensen, J: **G.3.1**: 53. **K.2**: 65.
Jensen, K: **B.2**: 11.
Jensen, L: **F.8**: 54.
Jenson, J: **F.5**: 120.

Jepson, J: **D.7**: 186.
Jesson, D: **D.9**: 155.
Jevtuh, V: **F.8**: 171.
Jewsiewicki, B: **D.1**: 94.
Jex, S: **I.3**: 73.
Jimenez, A: **F.3**: 144.
Jiménez, H: **F.5**: 77.
Jithoo, S: **F.7**: 28.
Joas, H: **B.1**: 91. **J.8**: 22.
Jobert, A: **C.5**: 82.
Jochelson, K: **F.8**: 21.
Joekes, S: **F.1**: 58.
Johansson, B: **I.1**: 11.
Johansson, I: **B.1**: 68.
Johansson, L: **K.2**: 12.
Johansson, S: **F.1**: 39.
John, O: **C.3**: 148.
Johns, C: **K.1**: 392.
Johnson, B: **D.9**: 177. **F.3**: 144.
Johnson, C: **D.7**: 139.
Johnson, D: **D.3**: 48. **F.4**: 142.
Johnson, G: **G.3.1**: 133.
Johnson, J: **E.2**: 62. **F.3**: 184. **I.2**: 228.
Johnson, L: **B.1**: 135.
Johnson, M: **H.5**: 22. **K.4**: 40.
Johnson, P: **F.2**: 24.
Johnson, R: **G.1**: 1. **K.1**: 113.
Johnson, T: **I.4**: 68.
Johnston, A: **C.2**: 228. **D.7**: 370. **D.9**: 1.
Johnston, G: **C.5**: 6.
Johnston, J: **F.4**: 132.
Johnston, K: **C.3**: 90.
Johnston, L: **F.7**: 262.
Johnston, R: **B.2**: 47. **C.2**: 141. **G.1**: 47.
Johnston, W: **D.1**: 131. **I.5**: 140.
Johnstone, B: **D.7**: 36. **K.1**: 366.
Johnstone, S: **D.9**: 12, 31.
Jolly, L: **B.2**: 104.
Joly, D: **F.7**: 13, 177.
Jonas, A: **G.3.2**: 320.
Jonas, K: **C.7**: 42.
Jones, A: **I.2**: 204. **I.4**: 105. **K.1**: 21.
Jones, C: **G.3.2**: 165.
Jones, D: **K.4**: 53, 253.
Jones, E: **D.9**: 168.
Jones, F: **F.4**: 207. **K.3**: 44.
Jones, G: **G.3.2**: 367.

Jones, H: **K.1**: 201.
Jones, J: **B.2**: 85. **F.4**: 306. **G.3.2**: 174. **H.3**: 8. **K.1**: 239.
Jones, M: **K.3**: 19.
Jones, P: **H.4**: 69.
Jones, R: **H.5**: 29. **K.1**: 69.
Jong-Gierveld, de, J: **F.3**: 96. **F.4**: 32, 296.
Jong, de, G: **F.8**: 18.
Jonghe, de, F: **C.1**: 5.
Jonsson, B: **H.5**: 13.
Joó, R: **D.1**: 84.
Joochul, K: **G.3.2**: 328.
Joppke, C: **J.5**: 31.
Jordaan, B: **I.5**: 40.
Jordan, B: **G.3.2**: 147. **I.2**: 65. **K.2**: 46. **K.3**: 6.
Joseph, A: **F.7**: 205.
Joseph, G: **G.3.1**: 113.
Joseph, S: **G.3.2**: 316.
Joshi, P: **D.7**: 124.
Joubert, D: **F.7**: 269.
Joubert, K: **K.1**: 19.
Joukamaa, M: **F.3**: 226.
Joule, R: **C.7**: 49.
Jourden, F: **C.1**: 131.
Jowell, K: **I.5**: 52.
Juan, C: **F.3**: 219.
Juárez, F: **F.4**: 256.
Judd, C: **C.4**: 1. **C.7**: 64.
Juergensmeyer, M: **D.5**: 60. **J.5**: 37.
Juillard, C: **D.7**: 346.
Julin, J: **I.3**: 80.
Julius, D: **J.8**: 13.
Jumani, U: **I.2**: 81.
Jung, I: **I.3**: 61.
Jungbauer-Gans, M: **F.5**: 226.
Junger, M: **F.7**: 173.
Juppenlatz, M: **G.3.2**: 269.
Jurchenko, V: **C.1**: 132.
Jurs, S: **B.2**: 93.
Jyrkinen, T: **F.3**: 226.
Kabeer, N: **F.1**: 58. **F.5**: 14, 302.
Kabel, J: **F.3**: 156.
Kaberry, P: **F.5**: 32.
Kadish, M: **D.9**: 212.
Kadish, S: **F.7**: 97.
Kadri, A: **A.1**: 33.
Kadushin, C: **E.2**: 10.

Kadvany, J: **B.1**: 50.
Kaestner, R: **H.3**: 67.
Kagan, J: **F.2**: 109.
Kagan, M: **D.1**: 21. **D.8**: 24.
Kagan, S: **K.2**: 51.
Kaganas, F: **F.4**: 187.
Kagiwada, G: **F.7**: 9.
Kahn, J: **F.4**: 137.
Kahn, L: **F.7**: 229.
Kaid, L: **D.7**: 370.
Kail, R: **F.2**: 2.
Kaiser, M: **D.6**: 22.
Kaltilla, S: **H.3**: 54.
Kak, S: **A.1**: 15.
Kalberg, S: **J.1**: 10.
Kaliappan, U: **I.5**: 123.
Kalimo, E: **I.3**: 122.
Kallick, D: **J.1**: 6.
Kalma, A: **C.6**: 4.
Kalmijn, M: **E.2**: 39. **F.4**: 243.
Kalnoy, I: **C.3**: 56.
Kaluwa, B: **G.3.2**: 362.
Kamchedzera, G: **F.2**: 103.
Kameda, T: **C.4**: 45.
Kamens, D: **D.9**: 127.
Kamerman, S: **K.2**: 39.
Kamiar, M: **G.3.2**: 360.
Kaminer, W: **F.5**: 245.
Kammen, Van, W: **K.1**: 94.
Kamra, S: **G.3**: 10.
Kanagy, C: **G.3.1**: 61.
Kanbargi, R: **K.1**: 29.
Kanchan, R: **H.7**: 21.
Kandel, D: **K.1**: 324.
Kandiah, T: **D.7**: 143.
Kandiyoti, D: **F.5**: 191.
Kandrack, M: **F.5**: 173.
Kane, E: **B.2**: 111.
Kane, R: **K.4**: 164.
Kanegae, H: **D.9**: 97.
Kangas, O: **K.2**: 2.
Kaniasty, K: **K.1**: 132.
Kaniss, P: **D.7**: 272.
Kann, M: **F.5**: 30.
Kanouse, D: **F.3**: 160, 212.
Kanter, R: **C.5**: 76.

Kantor, R: **F.8**: 176.
Kanungo, R: **I.3**: 135.
Kapitza, S: **D.6**: 2.
Kaplan, B: **F.3**: 118.
Kaplan, C: **K.1**: 317.
Kaplan, E: **F.3**: 150.
Kaplan, G: **K.1**: 378.
Kaplan, H: **K.1**: 113.
Kaplan, M: **F.6**: 3. **I.6**: 10.
Kapoor, I: **K.3**: 46.
Kaprow, M: **I.1**: 9.
Kapur, N: **D.3**: 25.
Karamysheva, N: **A.1**: 40.
Karasawa, M: **C.4**: 60.
Karau, S: **C.6**: 3.
Karen, D: **J.6**: 58.
Karier, T: **I.5**: 189.
Karimov, B: **F.7**: 182.
Karlekar, M: **F.5**: 43.
Karlson, H: **K.1**: 44.
Karmi, G: **F.7**: 24.
Karoulla-Vrikkis, D: **D.7**: 43, 63.
Karpukhin, D: **I.2**: 30.
Kas'iana, V: **C.2**: 193.
Kasarda, J: **I.2**: 44.
Kaseke, E: **K.3**: 40.
Kashani, J: **F.2**: 143.
Kashioka, T: **C.3**: 88.
Kasimatis, M: **C.2**: 22, 200.
Kasimis, C: **G.3.1**: 17, 116.
Kasinitz, P: **F.7**: 120.
Käsler, D: **A.2**: 13.
Kaslow, F: **C.1**: 80.
Kass, J: **D.5**: 18.
Kass, N: **F.3**: 163.
Kassarjian, H: **H.5**: 23.
Katagiri, S: **J.5**: 34.
Kataoka, E: **F.5**: 255.
Katriel, T: **D.2**: 1.
Katz, C: **E.1**: 20.
Katz, D: **F.7**: 97.
Katz, E: **D.9**: 192.
Katz, J: **K.1**: 110.
Katz, L: **C.2**: 121. **I.3**: 43.
Kauffman, C: **F.3**: 227.
Kauffmann, M: **D.1**: 99.
Kaufman, B: **I.5**: 70.

Kaufman, J: **F.7**: 208. **K.1**: 290.
Kaufman, R: **B.2**: 104.
Kaufmann, C: **F.5**: 54, 212.
Kaun, D: **F.3**: 299.
Kaur, M: **G.3.1**: 81, 122.
Kavanagh, K: **K.4**: 58, 74.
Kawabata, A: **D.5**: 43.
Kawai, T: **A.2**: 5.
Kawakita, T: **I.5**: 178.
Kawamura, Y: **G.3.1**: 134.
Kawar, A: **F.5**: 117.
Kawka, Z: **D.3**: 90.
Kay, A: **D.9**: 2.
Kay, F: **D.4**: 9.
Kay, H: **G.3.2**: 147.
Kaye, D: **B.2**: 55.
Kaye, J: **D.4**: 42.
Kayser, B: **F.3**: 15. **G.3.1**: 11.
Kazelskis, R: **K.1**: 45.
Kazemian, A: **G.3.2**: 331.
Kazi, S: **I.2**: 85–86.
Kealy, M: **I.6**: 28.
Kean, K: **F.2**: 84.
Keane, C: **G.3.2**: 71.
Kearney, M: **F.8**: 5.
Kearney, P: **K.1**: 368.
Keating, N: **F.2**: 30.
Keating, W: **G.3.2**: 257.
Kecke, A: **D.7**: 302.
Keeble, B: **G.1**: 37.
Keeble, D: **H.4**: 74.
Keefe, J: **I.3**: 50. **I.5**: 137.
Keefe, R: **K.4**: 37.
Keen, J: **K.4**: 49.
Keenan, T: **C.5**: 28.
Keet, D: **I.5**: 147.
Keeter, S: **J.6**: 47.
Kefeli, I: **D.9**: 160.
Keiding, N: **F.3**: 143.
Keiji, I: **D.5**: 14.
Keilman, N: **F.1**: 30.
Keith, B: **F.2**: 105. **F.4**: 134.
Keith, P: **F.4**: 194.
Keith, V: **F.7**: 261.
Keith-Spiegel, P: **D.3**: 41.
Kejing, D: **G.3.1**: 34.

Keller, A: **K.1**: 5.
Keller, P: **G.3.1**: 55.
Keller, S: **F.4**: 4, 6.
Kellert, S: **G.1**: 16.
Kelley, H: **F.5**: 315.
Kelley, J: **I.2**: 52.
Kelley-Lainé, K: **D.9**: 117.
Kellner, D: **B.1**: 18.
Kelly, C: **I.5**: 55.
Kelly, J: **I.5**: 55. **J.3**: 24.
Kelly, R: **I.2**: 104.
Kelly, W: **K.1**: 209.
Kelman, M: **I.3**: 14.
Kelner, V: **D.7**: 265.
Kemeny, J: **G.3.2**: 119.
Kemerov, V: **A.1**: 17.
Kemp, S: **B.2**: 58. **F.5**: 101. **H.5**: 32.
Kempeneers, M: **I.2**: 73, 84.
Kempen, van, R: **F.7**: 34. **G.3.2**: 190. **K.1**: 220.
Kemper, F: **F.3**: 250.
Kempf, K: **K.1**: 211.
Kendig, H: **F.4**: 54.
Kendrick, A: **F.7**: 243.
Kendrigan, M: **F.5**: 177.
Kenkel, D: **K.4**: 41.
Kennedy, C: **J.7**: 5.
Kennedy, L: **F.4**: 160. **K.1**: 92.
Kennedy-Moore, E: **B.2**: 120.
Kenney, M: **C.5**: 57. **H.4**: 49. **I.3**: 53.
Kent, G: **F.3**: 283.
Keppel, Van, M: **F.4**: 272.
Kepplinger, H: **D.7**: 291.
Kerkhofs, J: **H.4**: 60.
Kernaghan, K: **D.3**: 29, 51.
Kernberg, O: **C.1**: 61.
Kerner, H: **K.1**: 78.
Kerr, C: **D.9**: 186, 194–195.
Kerr, G: **I.6**: 2.
Kerr, J: **C.1**: 77.
Kerr, N: **C.3**: 102.
Kerr, T: **I.5**: 109.
Kershaw, P: **K.1**: 305.
Kerstenetzky, I: **B.1**: 100.
Kertzer, D: **F.4**: 50.
Kesner, I: **C.5**: 77.
Kesselring, R: **I.5**: 141.
Kessler, D: **H.3**: 5.

Kessler, J: **F.2**: 110.
Kessler, R: **C.2**: 150.
Kester, C: **I.2**: 118.
Kester, J: **I.2**: 118.
Ketelaar, T: **C.2**: 202.
Keuren, van, D: **A.1**: 11.
Keyder, C: **G.3.1**: 90.
Keyes, C: **D.5**: 96, 122.
Keyes, J: **H.7**: 18.
Khaksari, S: **K.4**: 152.
Khalidi, N: **F.1**: 1.
Khan, A: **F.8**: 137. **J.3**: 7.
Khan, F: **D.5**: 161.
Khan, H: **F.3**: 90. **H.3**: 31.
Khan, Z: **F.4**: 268.
Khan Alamgir, M: **J.6**: 24.
Khanam, U: **I.2**: 158.
Khandker, S: **I.2**: 116, 160.
Khaniutin, A: **D.7**: 181.
Khattab, H: **F.3**: 11.
Khaykin, S: **B.2**: 107.
Khayyat, S: **F.5**: 16.
Khellil, M: **F.8**: 75.
Khomenko, I: **D.9**: 109.
Khoo, S: **F.1**: 11.
Khor, L: **F.8**: 62.
Khullar, M: **D.9**: 133.
Kiamba, M: **G.3.2**: 286.
Kiani, M: **G.3.2**: 342.
Kibria, N: **F.4**: 265.
Kickbusch, I: **K.4**: 206.
Kidd, K: **K.4**: 37.
Kidd, M: **I.2**: 137.
Kidwai, A: **D.5**: 175.
Kidwell, S: **H.7**: 7.
Kiecolt, K: **D.5**: 109. **F.3**: 13.
Kiel, L: **B.1**: 115.
Kierulff, S: **D.5**: 90.
Kieschnick, P: **F.4**: 165.
Kiesler, S: **D.7**: 11.
Kiewiet, D: **J.6**: 1.
Kihlstrom, J: **C.2**: 1.
Kikuchi, M: **E.2**: 6.
Kikuchi, S: **F.2**: 65.
Kilduff, M: **C.3**: 35.
Kilgore, S: **C.5**: 53.

Kilminster, R: **B.1**: 143.
Kim, H: **C.3**: 112. **G.3.2**: 68.
Kim, K: **D.7**: 189.
Kim, M: **E.3**: 72. **G.1**: 46.
Kim, W: **G.3.2**: 67.
Kimble, G: **C.1**: 110.
Kimenyi, M: **D.9**: 108. **I.3**: 69.
Kimmel, D: **C.1**: 83.
Kimmerly, N: **F.4**: 271.
Kimura, H: **G.3.2**: 99.
Kimura, K: **A.1**: 42.
King, A: **C.3**: 52. **D.1**: 63. **F.7**: 99.
King, D: **H.7**: 1.
King, E: **D.9**: 68.
King, G: **B.2**: 71.
King, K: **D.9**: 39.
King, M: **D.1**: 90. **F.2**: 75.
King, P: **F.7**: 242. **K.1**: 325.
King, R: **I.2**: 145. **K.1**: 195.
Kingson, E: **F.2**: 7.
Kinney, J: **K.3**: 21.
Kinsey, K: **C.7**: 59. **D.5**: 9. **H.6**: 4.
Kinsey, S: **K.4**: 225.
Kinzley, W: **I.4**: 26.
Kirchler, E: **C.3**: 29. **F.4**: 107.
Kiritani, S: **D.7**: 64.
Kirkbride, P: **C.3**: 106.
Kirkby, J: **G.3.1**: 127.
Kirkpatrick, J: **C.2**: 54.
Kirp, D: **D.9**: 37.
Kirschenbaum, A: **I.3**: 28.
Kirschenman, J: **I.2**: 209. **K.1**: 290.
Kirton, M: **D.9**: 105.
Kiselev, G: **D.1**: 126.
Kiser, E: **B.1**: 134.
Kishimoto, K: **G.3.2**: 175.
Kisker, E: **K.2**: 42.
Kiss, Y: **F.5**: 124.
Kissman, K: **F.5**: 53.
Kitagawa, T: **J.1**: 15.
Kitamura, K: **D.9**: 173. **I.1**: 8.
Kitayama, O: **C.2**: 110.
Kitch, A: **F.4**: 177.
Kitchener, R: **A.2**: 9.
Kitzinger, J: **F.3**: 187.
Kiva, A: **C.7**: 71.
Kivinen, M: **H.2**: 2.

Kivisto, P: **B.1**: 117.
Klaas, B: **I.3**: 21.
Klapp, O: **D.1**: 116.
Klaukka, T: **I.3**: 122.
Klawitter, M: **B.2**: 21. **K.2**: 50.
Kleck, G: **K.1**: 411, 422.
Klee, H: **K.1**: 357.
Klein, D: **E.3**: 6. **F.2**: 13.
Klein, H: **C.2**: 35.
Klein, J: **C.5**: 80. **I.3**: 72.
Klein, L: **A.1**: 30. **D.1**: 112.
Klein, R: **C.2**: 184. **F.5**: 112.
Klein, T: **F.4**: 119. **J.6**: 56.
Klein, U: **D.7**: 205.
Kleinbölting, H: **C.2**: 208.
Kleiner, M: **I.5**: 33.
Kleingartner, A: **I.5**: 53.
Kleinman, D: **H.4**: 80.
Kleinman, M: **G.3.2**: 159.
Kleinpenning, G: **C.7**: 21. **F.7**: 154.
Kleinpenning, J: **E.2**: 65. **H.7**: 4.
Klepa, L: **I.2**: 133.
Klieger, P: **D.5**: 84.
Klier, J: **F.7**: 83.
Kliewer, E: **F.8**: 23.
Klinck, D: **D.4**: 44.
Klindworth, L: **F.2**: 3. **F.3**: 205.
Kline, M: **F.4**: 132.
Kline, S: **C.2**: 17.
Kling, R: **D.1**: 109.
Klingemann, H: **C.2**: 173.
Klinkner, P: **F.7**: 233.
Klitzner, M: **D.7**: 103.
Kloppenburg, J: **G.3.1**: 66. **H.4**: 80.
Klüver, J: **B.1**: 103.
Klugman, B: **F.3**: 19.
Knauss, S: **F.5**: 54.
Knauth, B: **D.7**: 191.
Kneer, G: **B.1**: 25.
Kniazeva, B: **A.2**: 17.
Kniazeva, M: **D.8**: 72.
Knickman, J: **C.3**: 79.
Knie, A: **H.4**: 96.
Knights, D: **I.3**: 133.
Knill-Jones, R: **K.4**: 50.
Kniveton, B: **C.1**: 56.

Knoblauch, H: **D.7**: 156.
Knocke, W: **F.5**: 248.
Knopke, H: **F.7**: 190.
Knott, M: **F.3**: 62.
Knowles, C: **K.4**: 2.
Knox, P: **G.3.2**: 66.
Knudsen, D: **B.2**: 72. **F.4**: 148.
Knudsen, K: **D.9**: 125.
Kobak, R: **F.4**: 196.
Koball, E: **F.4**: 39.
Kobayashi, H: **D.1**: 121.
Kobe, Z: **J.2**: 18.
Koch, E: **C.1**: 112.
Koch, K: **J.2**: 2.
Kochanowski, P: **G.3.2**: 218.
Kocks, M: **F.2**: 34. **F.8**: 175.
Kodak, N: **D.8**: 67.
Kodras, J: **G.3.2**: 174. **H.3**: 8.
Koehn, P: **F.8**: 52.
Koeller, C: **I.5**: 129.
Koenig, M: **F.3**: 279.
Koenig, T: **H.4**: 73.
Koestner, R: **C.2**: 178.
Kogan, B: **D.3**: 59.
Kohfeld, C: **J.6**: 67.
Kohl, H: **D.9**: 164. **J.5**: 4.
Köhler, E: **H.3**: 52.
Kohli, M: **I.2**: 221.
Kohn, R: **G.1**: 32, 63. **J.7**: 23.
Koike, K: **I.1**: 8. **I.4**: 90.
Kojanec, G: **I.2**: 67.
Kojima, A: **D.7**: 121.
Kojima, H: **F.3**: 23.
Kojima, K: **A.2**: 19.
Kok, P: **G.3.2**: 365.
Kokoreff, M: **G.3.2**: 77, 188.
Kokoshin, A: **A.1**: 2.
Kolb, D: **C.4**: 22.
Kolesnik, S: **D.7**: 100.
Kolinsky, E: **F.5**: 54–55.
Koller, M: **C.3**: 55.
Kolody, B: **K.1**: 20.
Kolosi, T: **E.2**: 40, 42.
Kolpin, V: **C.7**: 43.
Kolsti, J: **F.7**: 23.
Komiya, F: **I.3**: 42.
Komorita, S: **C.3**: 67.

Konadu-Agyemang, K: **G.3.2**: 213.
Koncz, K: **I.2**: 124.
Kondon, V: **F.4**: 327.
Kondratas, A: **G.3.2**: 98.
Kong, C: **E.2**: 78.
Koning, de, J: **I.4**: 126.
Konle-Seidl, R: **I.5**: 114.
Konno, H: **G.3.2**: 274.
Konopacki, W: **B.2**: 30.
Konovsky, M: **I.3**: 58.
Konrad, A: **I.3**: 22.
Kontuly, T: **F.8**: 12.
Koo, H: **E.2**: 70.
Koopman, C: **F.2**: 128.
Koppel, B: **G.3.2**: 343.
Koppen, J: **D.9**: 219.
Koptas, G: **I.2**: 226.
Koput, K: **H.4**: 10.
Korenman, S: **H.3**: 15.
Korff, R: **G.3.2**: 227.
Korhonen, P: **H.6**: 7.
Koritz, D: **I.1**: 12.
Kornblub, F: **F.5**: 309.
Kornblum, W: **E.3**: 56. **K.1**: 324.
Kors, A: **D.9**: 188.
Korzenny, F: **D.7**: 132.
Kosaka, K: **E.2**: 34.
Kosaka-Isleif, F: **F.7**: 92.
Koshizuka, T: **B.2**: 44.
Koslowsky, M: **I.3**: 99.
Kosminsky, E: **F.2**: 101.
Koss, M: **I.4**: 126.
Kostelny, K: **C.2**: 108.
Köster, G: **F.8**: 149.
Kostomarova, V: **D.7**: 83.
Kostrubiec, B: **F.3**: 251, 262.
Kotkin, S: **G.3.2**: 75.
Kotlyakov, V: **G.1**: 52.
Kottak, C: **D.7**: 270, 388.
Kotthoff, H: **H.4**: 76.
Kouamé, A: **I.2**: 5, 198.
Kourilsky, C: **D.4**: 32.
Kovách, I: **E.2**: 23.
Koval, B: **J.6**: 22.
Kowalewski, D: **D.5**: 8. **J.6**: 30.
Kowarick, L: **G.3.2**: 248.

Kowaslski, G: **K.1**: 156.
Kowol, U: **H.4**: 93.
Kox, W: **D.5**: 51.
Koyano, W: **F.2**: 48.
Koys, D: **C.1**: 104.
Kozakaï, T: **D.1**: 139.
Kozlowski, S: **C.2**: 161.
Kozma, A: **B.1**: 48. **C.2**: 60.
Kozminski, A: **H.4**: 16.
Kozol, J: **K.1**: 219.
Kraan, R: **K.4**: 135.
Kraaykamp, G: **H.3**: 7.
Krackhardt, D: **C.3**: 35.
Krahé, B: **C.2**: 213. **K.1**: 125.
Kraly, E: **F.8**: 146.
Kramarz, F: **D.7**: 195.
Kramer, M: **D.5**: 174. **J.5**: 37.
Kramer, R: **C.3**: 93. **K.2**: 108.
Kramp, P: **C.2**: 184.
Kranich, K: **D.7**: 394.
Krantz, D: **C.1**: 126.
Krasin, I: **J.8**: 5.
Krasnikov, N: **F.4**: 100.
Kraus, J: **F.3**: 285, 309.
Krause, P: **H.3**: 75.
Krauss, R: **C.2**: 2. **C.3**: 30. **D.7**: 166, 176.
Krawczyk, M: **K.1**: 383.
Kreager, P: **F.1**: 19.
Krebs, D: **D.3**: 86.
Kreft, I: **B.2**: 31.
Krementsov, N: **C.1**: 106.
Kremer, J: **F.3**: 145.
Kreps, G: **K.4**: 11.
Kreveld, van, D: **C.4**: 36, 43.
Kreyenbroek, P: **F.7**: 33.
Krieken, van, R: **D.1**: 123.
Krijnen, P: **K.1**: 316.
Krippendorff, K: **D.7**: 169.
Krippes, K: **D.7**: 78.
Krisberg, B: **A.2**: 1.
Krishen, P: **D.8**: 27.
Krishnan, V: **F.3**: 30, 95.
Krishnaswamy, K: **K.1**: 269.
Kristensen, G: **G.3.2**: 38.
Kristiansen, T: **D.7**: 199.
Kritzer, H: **I.3**: 107.
Kritzinger, A: **I.5**: 67, 71.

Krivo, L: **K.1**: 288.
Kroetch, B: **J.7**: 6.
Kroger, R: **C.3**: 62.
Kroker, A: **F.5**: 98.
Kroker, M: **F.5**: 98.
Krokinskaya, O: **D.9**: 145.
Kroon, M: **C.3**: 42. **C.4**: 36, 43.
Kroon, S: **D.7**: 75.
Krosnick, J: **B.2**: 20–21. **C.7**: 64. **F.2**: 33.
Krotki, K: **F.3**: 26.
Krueger, A: **I.5**: 107.
Krueger, J: **C.7**: 1.
Kruglanski, A: **C.3**: 46. **C.4**: 28.
Kruip, G: **H.2**: 10.
Krumholz, N: **G.3.2**: 257.
Kryder-Coe, J: **K.1**: 235.
Krymkowski, D: **E.2**: 35.
Kryshtanovskii, A: **B.2**: 115.
Krzyszkowski, J: **F.4**: 233.
Ku, L: **F.6**: 32.
Kubasek, N: **I.2**: 205. **I.3**: 71.
Kubey, R: **D.7**: 326.
Kubiak, A: **B.2**: 130. **D.1**: 135. **D.9**: 220.
Kučera, T: **F.1**: 30.
Kudryavtsev, V: **A.1**: 35. **J.3**: 15. **K.1**: 129.
Kürti, L: **F.5**: 319.
Kugelmass, S: **F.3**: 206.
Kuh, D: **H.3**: 59.
Kuhl, P: **C.3**: 45.
Kuhn, J: **H.4**: 63.
Kuhrau-Neumärker, D: **D.5**: 156.
Kuiper, N: **J.4**: 19.
Kuji, T: **E.1**: 13.
Kujita, K: **I.1**: 16.
Kukalis, S: **C.5**: 22.
Kuklinski, J: **J.6**: 16.
Kukreja, V: **J.7**: 7.
Kukushkina, E: **D.1**: 120.
Kuliev, A: **K.4**: 13.
Kumagai, F: **D.1**: 54.
Kumagai, S: **F.4**: 14.
Kumanev, G: **F.7**: 83.
Kumar, A: **G.2**: 13.
Kumar, K: **I.5**: 164.
Kumar, R: **F.7**: 29, 152.
Kumar, S: **D.7**: 124.

Kunreuther, F: **F.3**: 186.
Kunst, A: **F.3**: 262, 272.
Kunzmann, K: **G.3.2**: 326.
Kupstas, F: **F.2**: 3. **F.3**: 205.
Kuptsov, V: **D.9**: 22, 57.
Kurahashi, S: **F.3**: 27.
Kuran, T: **E.3**: 27.
Kurdek, L: **C.3**: 141. **F.4**: 140, 281.
Kurien, J: **H.4**: 47.
Kurita, O: **B.2**: 44.
Kurosu, S: **K.1**: 400.
Kurt, R: **D.8**: 5.
Kűrti, L: **D.8**: 61.
Kurtz, Z: **K.4**: 211.
Kurz, D: **K.1**: 407, 424.
Kurz, K: **D.7**: 369. **K.4**: 11.
Kushner, T: **F.7**: 97.
Kutchinsky, B: **F.4**: 170.
Kutsenko, V: **B.1**: 40.
Kuttner, R: **E.3**: 56.
Kuzmics, H: **B.1**: 5.
Kwan-Terry, A: **D.7**: 16.
Kwok, H: **D.7**: 81.
Kwok, R: **G.3.2**: 338.
Kyvsgaard, B: **K.1**: 104.
Laaksonen, S: **B.2**: 28, 124.
Lab, S: **D.2**: 5.
Laba, R: **J.5**: 30.
Laberge, D: **K.1**: 136.
Labini, P: **D.3**: 34.
Lacar, L: **F.5**: 273.
Lach, D: **I.5**: 96.
Lacharité, C: **F.4**: 202.
Lachenbruch, P: **F.3**: 220.
Lachicotte, W: **C.2**: 228.
Lachman, M: **C.2**: 160.
Lacohée, H: **C.2**: 11.
Lacroix, J: **D.7**: 387.
Ladame, F: **C.1**: 76.
Ladd, H: **G.3.2**: 240.
Ladner, J: **K.1**: 217.
Laé, J: **G.3.2**: 17.
Laessle, R: **F.3**: 175.
Lafaye, C: **J.4**: 20.
Lagadec, P: **H.4**: 46.
Lagrange, H: **F.3**: 180. **F.6**: 29.
Lahiri, A: **D.7**: 213.

Lähteenmaa, J: **F.2**: 155.
Lahtela, K: **F.3**: 226.
Laidier, le, S: **G.3.2**: 134.
Laing, J: **C.4**: 62.
Laing, S: **D.1**: 2. **D.7**: 376.
Lakey, J: **I.2**: 152.
Lakey, P: **D.1**: 5.
Lakshamaiah, T: **D.9**: 51.
Lalwani, M: **H.4**: 101.
Lam, D: **F.1**: 59.
Lamal, P: **C.1**: 145.
Lamb, J: **B.2**: 84, 124.
Lambert, A: **C.3**: 158.
Lambert, J: **H.5**: 12. **K.4**: 6.
Lambert, R: **D.9**: 12. **J.6**: 17.
Lambert, W: **D.7**: 19.
Lambert, Y: **D.5**: 77. **F.2**: 132, 144.
Lambret, J: **C.2**: 10.
Lammers, H: **C.2**: 171.
Lammers, J: **D.1**: 6. **D.8**: 4.
Lamont, T: **G.3.2**: 114.
Lance, L: **D.1**: 112.
Land, K: **D.1**: 112. **D.5**: 139. **K.1**: 61.
Landale, N: **F.4**: 212, 230.
Landau, B: **C.2**: 138.
Landau, E: **C.6**: 14.
Landenberger, M: **F.5**: 221. **K.4**: 150.
Landis, J: **G.3.2**: 317. **K.1**: 174.
Lando, H: **C.1**: 134.
Landry, E: **I.5**: 66.
Landy, F: **G.3.1**: 37.
Landy, M: **D.9**: 98.
Lane, D: **C.1**: 82.
Lane, I: **C.5**: 54. **I.3**: 100.
Lane, S: **K.1**: 100.
Lang, M: **G.3.2**: 360.
Langan, J: **D.3**: 44.
Langan-Fox, J: **C.2**: 98. **I.2**: 76.
Langbein, L: **K.4**: 33.
Langdale, J: **H.7**: 5.
Langenhove, van, L: **C.6**: 17.
Lange, van, P: **D.1**: 128.
Langford, J: **I.4**: 34.
Langlois, J: **F.2**: 70. **F.3**: 12.
Langs, R: **B.2**: 43.
Langston, C: **C.2**: 59.

Langston, D: **F.3**: 144.
Lanjouw, P: **K.1**: 271.
Lannamann, J: **C.3**: 48.
Lannoy, de, J: **D.7**: 148.
Lanoue, G: **D.7**: 41.
Lansbury, R: **I.4**: 78. **I.5**: 28.
Lanshchikov, A: **G.3.1**: 89.
Lansley, J: **K.4**: 142.
Lansov, S: **E.3**: 70.
Lantz, P: **D.1**: 18. **D.8**: 63.
Lapavitsas, C: **H.6**: 11.
Lapeyronnie, D: **F.7**: 13. **F.8**: 19.
Lapidus, G: **F.7**: 158.
Laponce, J: **J.1**: 17.
Laporte, J: **H.5**: 12.
Lappé, M: **K.4**: 7.
Lardinois, R: **A.1**: 33.
Laren, D: **F.4**: 73.
LaRossa, R: **F.4**: 292.
Larrain, J: **C.7**: 68.
Larsen, H: **I.4**: 77.
Larsen, R: **C.2**: 22, 200, 202.
Larson, J: **I.3**: 15. **K.4**: 60.
Larson, R: **D.7**: 66. **F.3**: 153. **F.4**: 320.
Lartigue, F: **G.3.1**: 93.
Lash, S: **D.1**: 82.
Lasker, G: **F.4**: 94.
Laslett, B: **F.5**: 184.
Lasnik, H: **D.7**: 217, 222.
Laszlo, A: **F.3**: 144.
Latagan, B: **D.5**: 67.
Latiesa, M: **B.2**: 29.
Latkin, C: **C.4**: 20. **D.5**: 53.
Lauder, H: **D.9**: 9.
Laufer, E: **C.1**: 7.
Laugesen, M: **D.7**: 116. **K.1**: 298.
Launer, M: **D.7**: 312.
Laurent, A: **H.4**: 18.
Lauria, D: **G.1**: 38.
Laurie, H: **B.2**: 36.
Lavallée, I: **C.2**: 128.
Lavee, Y: **F.4**: 57, 72.
Lavery, J: **C.7**: 65.
Laville, J: **I.2**: 32.
Lavoie, M: **H.3**: 63.
Law, J: **D.6**: 26.
Law, R: **K.1**: 238, 240.

Law, S: **D.4**: 42. **J.3**: 27.
Law-Yone, H: **J.6**: 29.
Lawler, E: **I.5**: 73.
Lawless, E: **F.5**: 141.
Lawless, J: **K.1**: 121.
Lawrence, B: **D.5**: 166. **J.5**: 37.
Lawrence, D: **B.2**: 60.
Lawrence, H: **F.2**: 99.
Lawrence, J: **J.8**: 1.
Lawrence, K: **K.4**: 66.
Lawrence, P: **I.4**: 39.
Lawrence, R: **K.1**: 207.
Lawrence, S: **J.6**: 21.
Lawrence, W: **C.4**: 64.
Lawson, A: **D.3**: 62.
Lawson, J: **K.4**: 205.
Lawson, R: **I.2**: 201.
Lawson, V: **I.2**: 90.
Lawton, J: **F.7**: 265.
Layder, D: **D.9**: 13.
Lazar, J: **D.7**: 177.
Lazar, M: **I.3**: 99.
Lazarus, N: **K.1**: 378.
Lazarus, R: **C.2**: 129.
Lazear, E: **C.5**: 40.
Leach, M: **F.1**: 58.
Leader, S: **I.5**: 80.
Leak, L: **I.4**: 107.
Leal F., G: **K.4**: 166.
Learner, S: **C.6**: 10.
Lear, Van, C: **F.4**: 222.
Leary, M: **C.2**: 74. **C.3**: 64. **F.6**: 11.
Lebeaux, M: **H.4**: 35.
Lebleux, D: **I.4**: 87, 93.
Lebreuilly, J: **C.2**: 70.
Lebrun, J: **D.8**: 11.
Lecher, W: **I.5**: 60.
Lechner, F: **D.5**: 2.
Lechner, N: **A.2**: 24.
LeClere, F: **F.4**: 75, 218.
Lecomte, Y: **F.3**: 194. **K.4**: 232.
Ledebur, L: **H.3**: 53.
Lee, B: **C.4**: 39. **F.5**: 125. **G.3.2**: 98, 194, 211.
Lee, C: **D.7**: 305.
Lee, D: **D.7**: 130, 391. **K.1**: 346.
Lee, G: **F.4**: 220.

Lee, H: **C.3**: 111. **F.3**: 153. **K.4**: 229.
Lee, J: **B.2**: 37.
Lee, K: **D.7**: 58. **H.4**: 40.
Lee, L: **F.7**: 99.
Lee, M: **K.4**: 53.
Lee, P: **D.5**: 3.
Lee, R: **H.3**: 80. **K.1**: 152.
Lee, S: **E.2**: 78.
Lee, V: **D.9**: 168.
Leenaars, A: **F.3**: 267.
Leerssen, J: **C.2**: 221.
Leeuwen, Van, M: **C.7**: 24.
Leeuwis, C: **G.3.1**: 119.
Lefèvre, B: **K.1**: 1.
Lefkarites, M: **F.3**: 133.
Lefort, C: **C.1**: 153.
Légaré, J: **F.4**: 344.
Leger, J: **F.8**: 21.
Legutko, R: **H.2**: 7.
Lehman, D: **C.1**: 135.
Lehr, R: **K.1**: 403.
Lehrer, E: **I.2**: 108.
Lehtinen, V: **F.3**: 226.
Lehto, J: **K.1**: 227.
Lehtonen, R: **I.3**: 122.
Leibowitz, A: **K.2**: 41, 68.
Leidner, R: **I.2**: 136.
Leigh, B: **D.9**: 61.
Leigh, J: **F.5**: 156. **I.3**: 114.
Leigh, W: **G.3.2**: 162.
Leigh-Doyle, S: **I.2**: 112.
Leighley, J: **F.5**: 17.
Leijenaar, M: **F.5**: 181.
Leino, E: **K.1**: 366.
Leippe, M: **C.2**: 158.
Leitner, G: **D.7**: 22.
Lelièvre, E: **I.2**: 73.
Leman, S: **I.5**: 42.
Lembcke, J: **E.2**: 83.
Lemel, Y: **F.5**: 299. **H.4**: 35. **I.4**: 93.
Lemert, C: **B.1**: 22. **J.1**: 11.
Lemesle, R: **K.2**: 18.
Lemkau, J: **K.3**: 30.
Lendler, M: **H.4**: 25.
Leng, R: **D.4**: 4.
Lenhardt, G: **I.2**: 45.
Lenoir, R: **F.4**: 84.

Lenon, P: **D.7**: 20.
Lensink, J: **F.5**: 117.
Lenski, G: **B.1**: 127.
Lent, J: **D.7**: 184.
Lenz, I: **H.4**: 104.
Lenzen, D: **F.2**: 132, 139.
Leon, G: **C.1**: 119.
Leon, J: **F.4**: 255.
Leonard, A: **K.4**: 120.
Leonard, J: **F.7**: 251. **I.3**: 13.
Leonard, K: **F.7**: 115.
Léonard, Y: **A.1**: 7.
Leong, F: **I.2**: 149.
Leong, W: **F.5**: 33.
Leonhard, P: **C.7**: 9.
Leontidou, L: **G.3.2**: 346.
Lepore, S: **C.1**: 148.
Leppel, K: **F.4**: 26.
Lepper, M: **C.7**: 24, 75.
Lepper-Green, B: **J.8**: 20.
Lerer, B: **F.3**: 206.
Leridon, H: **B.1**: 30. **F.3**: 135.
Lerman, P: **K.1**: 172.
LeRoy, M: **I.5**: 134.
Leschied, A: **K.1**: 216.
Leserman, J: **D.5**: 18.
Leslie, D: **I.2**: 43.
Lessof, C: **I.4**: 129.
Lester, J: **J.5**: 4.
Letts, D: **F.2**: 99.
Leung, S: **F.3**: 136.
Leupin, A: **C.1**: 27.
Leuw, E: **K.1**: 339.
Leven, C: **G.3.2**: 182.
Levenson, A: **D.5**: 185.
Lever, W: **H.4**: 8.
Lever-Tracy, C: **F.8**: 160.
Lévesque, A: **K.4**: 6.
Levi, L: **J.8**: 4.
Levi, M: **D.1**: 107. **K.1**: 120.
Levidow, L: **H.4**: 82.
Levie, H: **I.5**: 184.
Levin, B: **D.7**: 210.
Levin, D: **F.2**: 117. **F.7**: 83.
Levin, H: **I.4**: 25.
Levin, M: **F.7**: 118.

Levin, R: **G.3.1**: 123.
Levine, D: **A.2**: 21. **C.2**: 147.
Levine, G: **C.7**: 63.
Levine, H: **K.1**: 324.
Levine, I: **K.1**: 239, 260. **K.4**: 189.
Levine, M: **F.2**: 107.
Levine, R: **E.2**: 52. **K.1**: 325.
Levinthal, D: **C.5**: 66, 78.
Levit, D: **F.5**: 172.
Leviton, L: **B.2**: 9. **K.4**: 26, 29.
Levy, E: **F.4**: 3–4.
Lew, R: **D.1**: 18.
Lewandowski, E: **D.5**: 37.
Lewin-Epstein, N: **I.2**: 144.
Lewis, A: **F.2**: 107.
Lewis, C: **K.1**: 309.
Lewis, D: **K.4**: 132.
Lewis, E: **E.2**: 66.
Lewis, G: **F.3**: 15. **G.2**: 10. **G.3**: 1.
Lewis, H: **G.3.1**: 28.
Lewis, J: **C.3**: 11. **D.7**: 362. **F.4**: 259. **F.5**: 323.
Lewis, L: **D.7**: 230.
Lewis, M: **G.1**: 17.
Lewis, P: **I.5**: 175.
Lewis, R: **A.1**: 12. **G.1**: 53. **I.5**: 49.
Lewis, S: **C.2**: 54.
Ley, D: **G.3.2**: 86.
Ley, R: **B.1**: 135.
Leyden, D: **C.4**: 17.
Leydesdorff, L: **B.2**: 79.
Leyens, J: **C.7**: 57. **K.1**: 423.
Leyland, A: **K.1**: 348.
Leyser, Y: **F.4**: 82.
Li, B: **G.3.1**: 29.
Li, G: **D.9**: 124.
Li, K: **I.3**: 129.
Li, L: **E.2**: 41.
Li, W: **D.7**: 7.
Li, X: **C.1**: 20. **D.7**: 355.
Li, Y: **D.7**: 348.
Li, Z: **D.9**: 124.
Lian, F: **G.1**: 59.
Liber, G: **D.1**: 84.
Liberman, A: **C.1**: 63.
Libman, E: **K.4**: 145.
Lichter, D: **F.4**: 75, 218, 347.
Lichtman, C: **H.7**: 11.

Liddiard, M: **K.1**: 237.
Liden, R: **I.3**: 27.
Lidstone, K: **K.1**: 98.
Lie, S: **D.7**: 212.
Lieberman, A: **F.4**: 318.
Lieberson, S: **B.2**: 74.
Liebler, C: **D.7**: 250.
Liebrand, W: **D.1**: 128.
Liedka, R: **C.5**: 87.
Liefbroer, A: **F.4**: 32, 296.
Liefstinck-Koeijers, C: **B.2**: 125.
Liêm, L: **G.3.1**: 14.
Lienesch, M: **D.5**: 138. **F.4**: 328.
Lietaer, G: **C.1**: 11.
Lievesley, D: **B.2**: 35.
Lifan, F: **F.1**: 37.
Lightman, E: **K.2**: 93.
Lillard, L: **F.4**: 75, 276.
Lim, R: **I.5**: 88.
Limentani, A: **F.6**: 27.
Limoges, C: **J.4**: 13.
Limonad, E: **G.3.2**: 232.
Limonta Vidal, M: **K.4**: 16.
Lin, N: **G.3.2**: 34.
Lin, S: **C.3**: 112.
Lin, V: **K.4**: 205.
Linares, A: **F.3**: 227.
Lind, A: **D.9**: 1.
Lindauer, M: **D.8**: 32.
Lindeboom, M: **I.3**: 40.
Lindén, A: **G.3.2**: 143.
Lindenberg, S: **I.2**: 3.
Lindert, van, P: **G.3.2**: 203.
Lindholm, K: **D.7**: 19.
Lindley, D: **B.2**: 82.
Lingayah, S: **F.8**: 68.
Linge, G: **H.7**: 5.
Link, B: **G.3.2**: 98. **I.4**: 24.
Linz, D: **D.1**: 112.
Lipe, M: **C.3**: 24.
Lipiansky, E: **C.7**: 36.
Lipkus, I: **C.3**: 1.
Lipset, S: **E.2**: 51.
Lipshitz, G: **F.7**: 160. **F.8**: 89, 92.
Lipton, F: **K.4**: 189.
Lipton, J: **I.3**: 49.

Lira, P: **I.5**: 25.
Lisak, D: **F.6**: 44.
Lisek-Michalska, J: **B.2**: 90.
Liska, F: **K.1**: 190. **K.4**: 217.
Lissowski, G: **E.2**: 5.
Lister, R: **K.2**: 24.
Liston, D: **I.4**: 112.
Little, C: **D.8**: 56.
Little, J: **G.3.1**: 71.
Little, L: **F.4**: 114.
Little, S: **J.7**: 22.
Little, V: **F.2**: 99.
Little, W: **D.7**: 72.
Llu, A: **F.3**: 32.
Liu, J: **D.7**: 16. **F.8**: 122.
Liu, T: **F.5**: 117.
Liu, X: **G.3.1**: 29.
Livingstone, S: **C.2**: 29.
Lizana, D: **K.2**: 1.
Llewellyn, J: **D.7**: 288.
Llewelyn, S: **F.4**: 171. **K.1**: 38.
Lloyd, C: **B.1**: 11. **F.5**: 257. **H.3**: 6.
Lloyd, E: **F.4**: 299.
Lloyd, M: **K.1**: 179.
Lloyd, W: **H.5**: 8.
Lo, C: **K.1**: 369.
Loaeza, S: **D.5**: 116.
Lobao, L: **G.3.1**: 20.
Lobjoit, M: **K.4**: 264.
Lochet, J: **D.9**: 181.
Lockard, C: **D.8**: 55.
Locke, K: **C.3**: 71.
Locke, S: **D.6**: 7.
Lockett, G: **C.4**: 26.
Lockheed, M: **D.9**: 157.
Locurto, C: **K.1**: 379.
Loeber, R: **K.1**: 94, 158.
Loewenberg, J: **I.5**: 101.
Loewenson, R: **I.2**: 167.
Löffler, W: **F.3**: 169.
Logan, B: **F.1**: 44.
Logan, J: **F.4**: 349. **F.7**: 170.
Loizos, P: **F.5**: 266.
Lojkine, J: **H.3**: 43.
Lomnitz, L: **E.2**: 4.
Lomonosova, M: **A.2**: 17.
Lomotey, K: **D.9**: 205.

London, K: **F.4**: 137, 264.
Long, H: **D.9**: 6.
Long, L: **F.8**: 105.
Long, S: **C.4**: 53, 57. **F.4**: 154.
Longhurst, B: **G.2**: 27.
Longo, L: **C.3**: 92.
Longoria, T: **F.8**: 61.
Longuenesse, E: **I.4**: 97.
Longuet-Marx, F: **F.7**: 77.
Lönnroth, J: **I.2**: 67.
Look, S: **C.2**: 176.
Looman, C: **F.3**: 262, 272.
Loomis, J: **G.1**: 20.
Looney, R: **I.2**: 51.
Lopez, E: **I.2**: 99.
Lopez Caballero, A: **I.1**: 2.
López Roldán, P: **B.2**: 29.
Lopukhin, I: **D.3**: 49.
Lord, C: **C.7**: 24, 75.
Lord, R: **C.6**: 8.
Lorence, J: **I.2**: 105.
Lorenz, F: **F.4**: 203.
Lorenz, W: **K.2**: 16.
Lorenzi-Cioldi, F: **C.2**: 239.
Lori, A: **F.1**: 50.
Lorrain, D: **H.3**: 1.
Loscocco, K: **F.5**: 169. **H.4**: 62. **I.3**: 55.
Loseke, D: **K.1**: 424.
Loshitzky, Y: **D.7**: 364.
Losoff, M: **F.6**: 50.
Lotman, I: **G.3.2**: 69.
Louden, W: **D.9**: 47.
Lough, T: **I.5**: 192.
Loughran, G: **F.2**: 97.
Louie, K: **F.5**: 295.
Louis, M: **C.2**: 139.
Louscher, D: **J.7**: 5.
Love, J: **F.5**: 8. **H.4**: 71.
Loveday, B: **K.1**: 13.
Lovelock, R: **K.4**: 27.
Low, K: **G.3.2**: 363.
Lowder, S: **G.3.2**: 59, 251.
Lowe, G: **D.5**: 16.
Lowe, R: **K.4**: 44.
Lowy, E: **F.3**: 208.
Loya, M: **F.4**: 35.

Löytönen, M: **F.3**: 165, 222.
Lozano i Soler, J: **F.2**: 118.
Lozares Colina, C: **B.2**: 29.
Lu, H: **F.5**: 328.
Lu, J: **I.4**: 70.
Lu, L: **C.2**: 20.
Lubana, N: **H.4**: 31.
Lubin, C: **F.5**: 227.
Luborsky, M: **F.2**: 45.
Lubran, B: **K.1**: 310.
Lucassen, L: **F.7**: 111.
Luccie, de, M: **F.4**: 285.
Lucich, P: **C.4**: 3.
Ludes, P: **D.7**: 377.
Ludwig-Mayerhofer, W: **K.1**: 198.
Lüdemann, C: **J.1**: 3.
Lüthje, B: **H.4**: 59.
Lugovaya, E: **D.1**: 21.
Luhmann, N: **A.1**: 1. **C.2**: 34. **D.5**: 47. **E.1**: 25.
Luijk, van, H: **D.3**: 52.
Luijkx, R: **E.3**: 23.
Lukács, J: **I.4**: 32.
Lukács, L: **D.5**: 128.
Lukes, S: **D.1**: 125.
Luksic, B: **D.1**: 133.
Lull, J: **D.7**: 354.
Lundberg, O: **K.1**: 393. **K.4**: 9.
Lunde, T: **I.4**: 62. **J.6**: 28.
Lundin, L: **G.3.2**: 140.
Lundman, R: **K.1**: 202.
Lundqvist, L: **G.3.2**: 153.
Luneev, V: **K.1**: 128.
Lungu, G: **D.9**: 27.
Lunt, P: **C.2**: 29. **C.3**: 60.
Luparev, G: **D.5**: 132.
Luria, Z: **D.8**: 66.
Lurigio, A: **F.3**: 144.
Lury, C: **D.1**: 2. **F.5**: 80, 109.
Lusane, C: **K.1**: 200.
Lustick, I: **J.6**: 8.
Luthans, F: **C.5**: 86.
Luthar, S: **F.2**: 116.
Luther, N: **F.3**: 121.
Lutyński, J: **B.2**: 123. **D.1**: 135.
Lutz, B: **D.7**: 302.
Lutz, W: **F.1**: 27. **F.4**: 123.
Lutzker, J: **K.1**: 32.

Luxton, M: **F.5**: 31.
Luyken, G: **D.7**: 372.
Luzio, di, A: **D.7**: 218.
Lyman, M: **K.1**: 340.
Lynch, E: **F.3**: 227.
Lynch, J: **K.1**: 160.
Lynn, P: **B.2**: 121.
Lynn, R: **F.2**: 102.
Lynn, S: **C.2**: 45.
Lynskey, M: **F.7**: 152, 209.
Lyon, J: **D.7**: 344.
Lyons, B: **K.4**: 139.
Lyson, T: **H.4**: 3.
Maass, A: **C.3**: 77.
Maatela, J: **F.3**: 226.
Mabin, A: **G.3.1**: 123.
Mabro, J: **F.5**: 239.
Mabry, T: **C.5**: 34.
Macalister-Smith, P: **K.4**: 45.
Macauley, M: **D.9**: 88.
MacDonald, E: **F.5**: 132.
MacDonald, R: **H.5**: 26.
Macer, D: **K.4**: 255, 270.
MacEwen, K: **F.4**: 288.
Machaj, I: **E.2**: 48.
Machalek, R: **K.1**: 111.
Machicado Saravia, F: **C.7**: 2.
Machin, S: **I.5**: 124.
Machol, L: **I.3**: 154.
MacInnes, J: **I.1**: 6.
Macintyre, S: **F.4**: 297.
MacIver, M: **F.7**: 18.
Mack, A: **F.3**: 185.
MacKay, D: **B.2**: 42.
Mackenbach, J: **F.3**: 272.
Mackinnon, N: **G.3.1**: 52, 116.
Mackintosh, J: **K.3**: 19.
MacLaughlin, J: **F.8**: 56.
MacLaury, R: **C.2**: 134. **D.7**: 220.
MacLean, B: **K.1**: 86, 93.
Maclean, M: **F.4**: 128, 145.
Maclennan, D: **G.3.2**: 165.
Macleod, A: **F.5**: 145.
Maclure, S: **D.9**: 63.
MacMillan, V: **F.4**: 162.
MacNamee, E: **F.4**: 185.

Macpherson, D: **G.2**: 16.
Macquet, P: **K.1**: 383.
Macrae, C: **C.3**: 149.
Macy, M: **C.3**: 54. **C.7**: 16.
Madalieva, D: **F.2**: 158.
Madan, T: **D.5**: 45.
Madden, J: **I.2**: 55.
Madden, T: **D.7**: 1.
Madison, G: **J.2**: 20.
Mádr, O: **D.5**: 151.
Madsen, J: **I.4**: 47.
Maffessoli, M: **D.2**: 25.
Mafico, C: **G.3.2**: 168.
Magagna, V: **G.3.1**: 84.
Magalhães, M: **D.7**: 80.
Magni, V: **D.9**: 165.
Magniadas, J: **F.8**: 27.
Magnusson, D: **F.5**: 275.
Magocsi, P: **F.7**: 100.
Maguire, B: **B.2**: 118.
Maguire, M: **K.1**: 112.
Magutu, G: **G.3.2**: 158.
Maharaj, B: **G.3.1**: 16, 123.
Maharishi, M: **D.8**: 13.
Maher, K: **C.6**: 8.
Maheux, B: **K.4**: 6.
Mahiou, I: **F.5**: 165.
Mahmood, N: **F.3**: 26.
Mahmood, Z: **F.8**: 137.
Mahmud, S: **F.3**: 37.
Mahon, R: **K.2**: 8.
Mahoney, M: **F.4**: 161. **H.5**: 35.
Mahony, D: **D.9**: 107.
Mai, H: **D.7**: 119.
Maibach, E: **D.7**: 369. **K.4**: 11.
Maier, M: **B.2**: 99.
Maier-Katkin, D: **K.1**: 15.
Maier-Rabler, U: **D.7**: 171.
Main, B: **F.5**: 176.
Maines, D: **E.1**: 16. **E.3**: 57.
Maingot, A: **F.8**: 167.
Mainzer, L: **D.3**: 61.
Mair, A: **E.2**: 14. **G.3**: 6.
Maïs, J: **D.5**: 95.
Maisonrouge, J: **H.4**: 18.
Maiteny, P: **D.7**: 245.
Maitra, P: **D.9**: 55.

Maitra, S: **G.3.2**: 101.
Maiworm, F: **D.9**: 197.
Majka, L: **F.6**: 46.
Major, B: **C.3**: 80.
Majumdar, M: **F.5**: 24.
Majumder, A: **F.3**: 80, 292.
Majupuria, I: **F.5**: 312.
Mäkelä, K: **K.1**: 382.
Makhijani, M: **C.3**: 92.
Maki, M: **F.2**: 32.
Makin, P: **I.5**: 31.
Makkai, T: **J.6**: 12. **K.1**: 370.
Mal'kova, Z: **D.9**: 96.
Malahleka, B: **K.3**: 14.
Malcarne, V: **C.2**: 73.
Malczewski, J: **K.4**: 59.
Maletz, D: **J.4**: 12.
Maletzky, B: **K.1**: 215.
Malfa, la, G: **F.7**: 258.
Malgady, R: **C.1**: 75.
Malgesini, F: **C.7**: 63.
Malhotra, A: **F.4**: 211.
Malik, S: **G.3.1**: 18.
Malinowski-Rubio, M: **F.8**: 158.
Malitz, J: **D.4**: 18.
Mallick, M: **F.3**: 241.
Mallory, G: **C.5**: 27.
Malloy, E: **H.4**: 71.
Malloy, R: **G.3.2**: 293.
Malone, T: **D.7**: 10.
Malos, E: **F.4**: 24. **K.2**: 47.
Maltzman, I: **K.1**: 361.
Mamada, T: **C.2**: 87.
Mamkoottam, K: **I.2**: 210.
Man, P: **C.3**: 43.
Mana, K: **D.5**: 106.
Manabe, K: **D.1**: 33.
Manaev, O: **D.7**: 263.
Manchester, J: **I.2**: 127.
Mancini, P: **F.3**: 244.
Mancino, S: **D.3**: 29.
Mandel, E: **J.4**: 14.
Mander, W: **D.6**: 9.
Mandrillon, M: **J.3**: 30.
Manfredo, M: **I.6**: 2, 25.
Mang, M: **C.2**: 90.

Mangin, C: **F.5**: 265.
Mangold, W: **F.1**: 56.
Mänicke-Gyöngyösi, K: **F.5**: 318.
Manion, A: **C.2**: 158.
Manis, M: **C.7**: 66.
Maniscalco, M: **K.2**: 86.
Manktelow, K: **C.6**: 13.
Mann, K: **F.5**: 326.
Mannari, H: **C.5**: 12.
Mannesto, G: **G.1**: 20.
Mannetti, L: **D.7**: 207. **F.3**: 181.
Manning, W: **K.4**: 153.
Mannix, E: **C.4**: 50.
Manor, O: **F.4**: 38.
Mansel, J: **F.2**: 142.
Mansilla, H: **D.5**: 114. **E.3**: 21. **H.2**: 4.
Mansingh, S: **D.5**: 71.
Manski, C: **B.2**: 109.
Mantell, E: **F.2**: 4.
Mantle, G: **K.3**: 35.
Manton, K: **B.2**: 54. **F.2**: 42. **F.3**: 268.
Manuel, P: **D.7**: 270. **D.8**: 29.
Maoz, B: **D.5**: 185.
Mar, E: **I.3**: 51.
Mar, J: **F.7**: 38.
Marabelli, P: **G.3.2**: 250, 288.
Maragliano, R: **D.9**: 165.
Maranda, M: **K.1**: 342.
Marc, V: **C.1**: 6.
Marcach, J: **F.4**: 112.
March, C: **I.2**: 99.
Marchand, B: **G.3.2**: 1.
Marchand, O: **I.2**: 38, 163.
Marchant, G: **C.7**: 5.
Marchi, de, B: **D.7**: 138.
Marchington, M: **I.5**: 10.
Marchman, V: **D.7**: 73.
Marcou, L: **J.2**: 25.
Marcus, G: **C.2**: 122.
Marcus, M: **I.5**: 64. **K.1**: 27.
Mare, R: **F.4**: 209.
Margalit, Z: **I.4**: 20.
Marger, M: **F.8**: 46.
Margolin, L: **F.2**: 68.
Marín, B: **B.2**: 22.
Marín, G: **B.2**: 22.
Marino, M: **C.2**: 229.

Marjoibanks, K: **F.4**: 93.
Marjoribanks, K: **F.4**: 37. **F.7**: 81.
Mark, M: **I.3**: 20.
Marks, A: **K.1**: 358.
Marks, D: **C.3**: 78.
Marks, G: **C.3**: 76. **C.7**: 11.
Marks, J: **K.2**: 62.
Marks, L: **F.7**: 97.
Markson, L: **F.2**: 16.
Marlowe, J: **F.4**: 114.
Marois, C: **G.3**: 9. **G.3.2**: 189.
Marotta, M: **K.2**: 86.
Marquand, D: **J.2**: 4.
Marra, R: **K.1**: 398.
Marriott, H: **D.2**: 8.
Marris, P: **F.2**: 71.
Marry, C: **C.4**: 48–49. **I.4**: 95.
Marsden, D: **E.3**: 15, 18. **H.4**: 21.
Marsden, T: **G.3.1**: 19, 46, 124.
Marsh, C: **B.2**: 35. **D.9**: 114. **H.5**: 16.
Marsh, H: **C.2**: 226.
Marsh, L: **H.3**: 22.
Marsh, R: **J.3**: 1.
Marshall, A: **I.2**: 9.
Marshall, C: **D.9**: 62, 83.
Marshall, D: **D.7**: 338.
Marshall, J: **D.7**: 56.
Marshall, O: **F.8**: 127.
Marshall, R: **F.3**: 213.
Marsiglio, W: **F.4**: 313.
Marske, C: **C.5**: 8.
Marslen-Wilson, W: **D.7**: 213.
Marston, S: **J.5**: 35.
Martellaro, J: **H.1**: 2.
Martens, E: **F.7**: 1.
Martens, G: **I.5**: 151.
Martens, W: **E.1**: 3.
Martichoux, E: **F.5**: 265.
Martijn, C: **C.7**: 15.
Martikainen, T: **J.6**: 53.
Martin, A: **H.4**: 90.
Martin, B: **F.7**: 22.
Martin, D: **D.5**: 62. **F.3**: 29.
Martin, E: **B.2**: 125. **D.6**: 8.
Martin, J: **C.2**: 137. **F.2**: 156. **H.3**: 80. **I.3**: 104.
Martin, L: **F.4**: 295.

Martin, M: **D.7**: 150. **D.9**: 70, 74. **F.7**: 222.
Martin, P: **A.2**: 2. **F.8**: 172.
Martin, R: **B.1**: 69. **G.3.2**: 52, 254, 325. **I.5**: 65.
Martin-Jones, M: **D.7**: 349.
Martínez, E: **K.1**: 392.
Martinez, R: **K.1**: 202.
Martínez S., C: **K.4**: 166.
Martini, M: **D.5**: 130.
Martinić, T: **D.2**: 28.
Martino, di, V: **H.3**: 52.
Martins, J: **F.2**: 101.
Martwanna, N: **G.3.1**: 135.
Marty, M: **D.5**: 126.
Marty, W: **J.5**: 29.
Maruthakutti, R: **I.5**: 123.
Marvell, T: **F.4**: 186.
Marwell, G: **B.2**: 67.
Marwick, A: **D.1**: 62.
Marzal, A: **I.5**: 168.
Marzano, F: **D.3**: 60.
Masayuki, O: **D.5**: 22.
Mascie-Taylor, C: **F.3**: 118. **G.1**: 3.
Masheter, C: **F.4**: 136.
Mashiko, H: **D.7**: 84.
Mashukova, L: **J.2**: 12.
Mason, B: **I.5**: 180.
Mason, C: **I.2**: 207.
Mason, J: **C.7**: 24. **F.4**: 79. **K.2**: 53.
Mason, M: **F.5**: 160.
Masotti, P: **F.5**: 154. **F.8**: 33.
Massam, B: **K.4**: 59.
Massaro, T: **D.4**: 37.
Masschelein, J: **D.9**: 30.
Massengill, D: **K.1**: 344.
Massey, D: **F.5**: 95. **F.7**: 42. **G.3.2**: 156.
Massey, J: **K.1**: 424.
Massik, K: **K.1**: 1.
Masson, H: **K.3**: 1.
Massot, A: **G.3.2**: 134.
Masters, R: **C.6**: 5. **D.4**: 3, 29.
Masterson, D: **J.7**: 18.
Mastnak, T: **J.1**: 18.
Mastretta, M: **G.3.2**: 250.
Matczewski, A: **I.4**: 96.
Matejko, A: **H.5**: 10.
Mathew, K: **I.3**: 149.
Mathew, M: **I.4**: 50.

Mathews, F: **G.1**: 15.
Mathews, H: **C.7**: 6.
Mathews, J: **K.1**: 166.
Mathéy, K: **G.3.2**: 118.
Mathias, R: **K.1**: 166.
Mathieu, C: **G.3.2**: 335.
Mathieu, D: **K.4**: 262.
Mathieu, J: **I.4**: 125.
Matsui, K: **B.1**: 95.
Matsumoto, K: **B.1**: 105.
Matsumoto, M: **G.3.1**: 69.
Matsunari, M: **F.4**: 12.
Matsuoka, M: **B.1**: 108.
Mattelart, A: **D.7**: 101.
Matthaei, J: **I.2**: 132.
Matthews, J: **K.4**: 53.
Matthews, R: **I.4**: 91. **K.1**: 99.
Matthiessen, C: **G.3.2**: 41.
Matz, D: **C.3**: 4.
Mauldin, W: **F.3**: 43.
Maume, D: **I.2**: 77.
Maurer, K: **F.3**: 169.
Maurice, M: **I.1**: 8.
Maurice-Baumont, C: **G.3.2**: 186.
Mauss, A: **D.5**: 53.
Mautner, B: **C.1**: 18.
Mavolwane, S: **F.6**: 34.
Maxted, J: **E.2**: 12.
Maxwell, N: **F.3**: 106.
May, J: **G.3.2**: 341.
May, L: **D.3**: 33.
May, R: **D.7**: 217, 222.
Mayadas, N: **K.2**: 111.
Mayall, B: **K.2**: 61.
Mayer, F: **I.2**: 241.
Mayer, K: **H.4**: 2.
Mayer, W: **H.4**: 52.
Mayes, B: **C.2**: 195.
Mayfarth, A: **F.5**: 221.
Maylor, E: **C.7**: 38.
Maynard, A: **K.4**: 210.
Maynard, D: **D.7**: 154.
Mayor, B: **F.7**: 253.
Mayrhauser, Von, R: **C.1**: 114.
Mayston, D: **D.9**: 155.
Maza, P: **F.4**: 264.

Mazur, R: **G.3.1**: 132.
Mazurkiewicz, D: **D.9**: 100.
Mbacke, C: **F.3**: 270.
McAleer, J: **D.7**: 353.
McAllister, I: **F.5**: 12. **F.7**: 40, 228. **J.6**: 12, 32. **K.1**: 370.
McAllister, J: **F.4**: 48.
McAllister, P: **C.2**: 16.
McAuley, E: **C.2**: 166.
McAvoy, B: **K.4**: 42.
McBarnet, D: **K.1**: 163.
McBeath, G: **K.3**: 41.
McBride, D: **F.3**: 179.
McCabe, A: **D.7**: 26.
McCabe, M: **C.2**: 185.
McCall, P: **D.1**: 112. **K.1**: 61.
McCann, C: **C.2**: 131. **D.7**: 170, 176.
McCann, H: **C.2**: 133.
McCarron, T: **F.2**: 16.
McCarty, D: **K.1**: 310.
McCay, B: **B.1**: 2.
McClelland, C: **I.3**: 38.
McClelland, D: **C.2**: 178. **F.2**: 76.
McClendon, B: **G.3.2**: 252.
McClendon, M: **B.2**: 21, 91.
McClure, J: **D.1**: 137.
McConkey, K: **C.2**: 1.
McConnell, C: **G.2**: 6, 15.
McConnell, S: **I.5**: 62.
McConvell, P: **D.9**: 4.
McConville, M: **D.4**: 4.
McCord, J: **K.1**: 74, 424. **K.3**: 22.
McCormack, G: **I.6**: 30.
McCormick, A: **C.5**: 65.
McCormick, K: **I.3**: 128.
McCoy, S: **C.3**: 72.
McCreanor, T: **F.7**: 197.
McCrickard, J: **D.5**: 92.
McCullagh, C: **C.7**: 32. **F.4**: 110.
McCusker, C: **K.1**: 329.
McCutcheon, A: **B.2**: 54.
McDaniel, S: **F.5**: 92.
McDaniel, W: **I.5**: 38.
McDermott, J: **I.5**: 24.
McDermott, P: **F.3**: 15. **G.3**: 1. **I.2**: 115.
McDonald, I: **I.5**: 148.
McDonald, J: **F.3**: 78. **G.3.2**: 277.

McDonald, M: **D.3**: 26.
McDonald, T: **C.2**: 23. **K.2**: 62.
McDonnell, L: **I.4**: 124.
McDowall, D: **K.1**: 90, 147.
McDowell, J: **A.3**: 2. **F.8**: 121.
McDowell, L: **G.3.2**: 174.
McDuff, P: **F.4**: 351.
McElrath, K: **K.1**: 411.
McFarland, A: **J.5**: 29.
McFarlin, D: **I.3**: 102. **I.5**: 37.
McGarity, T: **J.4**: 18.
McGarrell, E: **D.4**: 22. **K.1**: 40, 177, 192.
McGee, L: **F.2**: 130.
McGee, R: **F.2**: 106.
McGee, T: **G.3.2**: 343.
McGill, A: **C.2**: 51.
McGlade, A: **K.4**: 53.
McGoldrick, D: **F.2**: 112.
McGovern, K: **K.1**: 215.
McGovern, P: **C.1**: 134.
McGovern, T: **C.1**: 110.
McGrath, J: **K.4**: 11, 194.
McGrath, M: **K.4**: 125.
McGrath, R: **K.1**: 144.
McGraw, K: **D.4**: 1.
McGreevy, P: **J.8**: 19.
McGregor, G: **D.7**: 7.
McGregor, H: **F.4**: 176.
McGregor, P: **K.1**: 270.
McGroarty, M: **D.9**: 15.
McGuckin, A: **K.4**: 50.
McGuire, M: **D.3**: 76. **D.4**: 3.
McGuire, R: **E.2**: 50.
McHenry, J: **F.3**: 134.
McHugh, K: **F.8**: 100. **G.3.2**: 208.
McIlwee, J: **I.2**: 121.
McIlwraith, R: **D.7**: 326.
McInerney, P: **F.2**: 14.
McIntyre, N: **I.2**: 91.
McIvor, G: **K.1**: 169.
McKague, O: **F.7**: 200.
McKeachie, W: **C.1**: 110.
McKeganey, N: **B.2**: 23. **K.1**: 348. **K.4**: 136.
McKelvey, C: **B.1**: 45.
McKendrick, B: **K.1**: 420.
McKeown, K: **F.4**: 151.

McKevitt, C: **D.5**: 153.
McKilm, J: **K.1**: 60.
Mckim, W: **B.1**: 48.
McKinnon, M: **G.1**: 39.
McLachlan, A: **C.3**: 31.
McLanahan, S: **F.4**: 118.
McLaren, J: **H.3**: 83.
McLaughlin, D: **F.4**: 75, 218.
McLaughlin, E: **B.1**: 123. **I.2**: 156.
McLaughlin, M: **F.5**: 284. **I.5**: 88.
McLeay, S: **D.7**: 208.
McLeod, J: **D.7**: 316. **J.1**: 5.
McLoughlin, J: **F.1**: 17.
McMahon, C: **D.3**: 15.
McMahon, M: **K.4**: 67.
McManus, D: **C.2**: 125.
McMillen, D: **G.3.2**: 277.
McNair, B: **D.7**: 259.
McNall, S: **E.2**: 52.
McNally, S: **F.4**: 279.
McNeil, R: **K.1**: 146.
McPhail, K: **E.3**: 15. **G.3.1**: 110.
McPherson, J: **C.5**: 25.
McPherson, K: **D.9**: 43.
McRae, S: **I.2**: 152–153, 213. **I.4**: 35.
McRobbie, A: **D.1**: 32.
McRoy, R: **F.7**: 125.
McShane, F: **K.1**: 121.
Meadow, R: **K.1**: 41.
Meadows, S: **C.3**: 64.
Meads, C: **D.7**: 116. **K.1**: 298.
Meaney, G: **F.5**: 37.
Means, R: **F.7**: 39.
Mearns, J: **C.3**: 23.
Mechanic, D: **K.4**: 5, 191.
Medvedkov, O: **C.2**: 38.
Meehan, E: **F.5**: 161.
Meerabeau, L: **F.3**: 105.
Meeus, W: **D.5**: 51.
Megdiche, C: **G.3.2**: 207.
Meghnagi, D: **C.3**: 51.
Meglino, B: **C.3**: 91.
Meheus, A: **F.3**: 215.
Mehrai, H: **F.4**: 219.
Mehta, S: **C.3**: 39.
Meichenbaum, D: **J.8**: 20.
Meier, R: **D.7**: 53. **K.1**: 153.

Meijer, de, M: **C.7**: 10.
Meijers, F: **F.5**: 150.
Meijvogel, R: **K.2**: 65.
Meindl, J: **C.6**: 1.
Meir, A: **F.3**: 291.
Melbye, M: **F.2**: 22.
Melchior, J: **D.9**: 215.
Mele, A: **C.2**: 63.
Melendez, E: **I.2**: 178.
Melia, M: **F.7**: 48.
Melin, H: **H.2**: 2.
Mellor, S: **I.3**: 20.
Melnick, A: **E.2**: 4.
Melotte, C: **K.4**: 53.
Melton, G: **C.1**: 83.
Melton, R: **J.6**: 16.
Meltz, N: **I.5**: 29.
Meltzoff, A: **C.3**: 45.
Memon, A: **B.2**: 96.
Men, A: **D.5**: 133.
Menaghan, E: **F.4**: 27. **F.5**: 256.
Menard, S: **B.2**: 57.
Mendelson, J: **K.1**: 319.
Mendenhall, M: **I.2**: 200.
Méndez, E: **K.1**: 39.
Mendizabal, E: **F.3**: 274.
Meneghel, G: **F.3**: 275.
Menger, P: **I.4**: 30.
Menjívar, R: **K.1**: 262.
Menkel-Meadow, C: **D.4**: 8.
Mercadal, G: **G.3.2**: 326.
Mercer, C: **D.2**: 18.
Merchant, J: **H.7**: 28.
Merelman, R: **D.1**: 91.
Merezhinskaia, E: **D.5**: 26.
Merkur'ev, S: **D.9**: 191, 195.
Merkx, J: **F.7**: 85.
Merle, P: **D.9**: 166.
Merlo, R: **K.2**: 69.
Merluzzi, T: **C.3**: 40.
Mermet, J: **I.2**: 72.
Mero, R: **J.1**: 19.
Meron, M: **I.2**: 38.
Merrell, F: **D.7**: 90.
Merrill, J: **D.7**: 277.
Merrill, K: **B.1**: 56.

Merrit, C: **J.8**: 19.
Merten, K: **D.7**: 233.
Mertens, E: **F.5**: 317.
Mertins, G: **G.3.2**: 179.
Merwe, Van Der, I: **G.3.2**: 362.
Merwe, van der, J: **G.3.1**: 36.
Merz, J: **I.2**: 93.
Mesbah, M: **F.5**: 229.
Mesch, D: **D.9**: 116. **I.3**: 52. **I.5**: 97.
Meschi, M: **I.2**: 126.
Mesler, M: **K.4**: 4.
Messeri, P: **C.7**: 47.
Messner, S: **K.1**: 425.
Mestrovic, S: **D.5**: 79.
Metcalf, D: **I.5**: 76, 122, 169.
Metcalfe, J: **C.2**: 162.
Mettler, F: **K.1**: 1.
Meulemann, H: **C.2**: 58.
Meuschel, S: **J.3**: 31.
Mey, de, S: **D.7**: 205.
Meyer, D: **G.3.2**: 305.
Meyer, H: **D.5**: 104.
Meyer, J: **D.9**: 127.
Mhloyi, M: **F.5**: 45.
Miami Theory Collective: **G.2**: 5.
Miceli, M: **C.1**: 84. **I.3**: 61.
Miceli Kervauy, M: **G.3.2**: 359.
Michaels, L: **D.7**: 85.
Michaelsen, L: **C.4**: 37.
Michalos, A: **C.1**: 101.
Michalowski, M: **F.8**: 71.
Michener, H: **B.2**: 37.
Michnik, A: **J.2**: 17.
Mickiewicz, E: **D.7**: 360.
Micklewright, J: **F.4**: 260.
Midden, C: **C.3**: 16.
Middleton, J: **I.4**: 130.
Middleton, L: **B.2**: 84, 124.
Middleton, M: **G.3.2**: 245.
Midgley, C: **C.2**: 18.
Midgley, J: **K.2**: 91.
Midwinter, E: **D.7**: 294.
Mieczkowski, T: **K.1**: 341.
Mieszkowski, P: **G.3.2**: 230, 240.
Miethe, T: **K.1**: 147.
Migon, H: **F.3**: 176.
Miguel, de, A: **D.2**: 7. **F.4**: 11.

Míguez, E: **F.7**: 167.
Mikame, K: **F.4**: 66.
Mikawa, J: **F.7**: 238.
Mikesell, M: **F.7**: 20.
Miková, Z: **F.4**: 353.
Mikulincer, M: **C.2**: 212. **C.3**: 8, 10.
Milano, M: **C.2**: 45.
Milburn, N: **K.1**: 236, 239.
Milenovic, I: **K.4**: 73.
Miles, A: **K.4**: 105.
Miles, M: **K.4**: 70.
Miles, R: **F.5**: 304. **F.7**: 13. **F.8**: 10, 28, 150.
Milgram, N: **J.8**: 20.
Milich, M: **F.3**: 45.
Milkman, R: **I.3**: 87.
Milkovich, G: **I.3**: 57.
Millar, J: **K.2**: 14.
Miller, A: **B.1**: 55. **D.6**: 13.
Miller, B: **F.3**: 74.
Miller, C: **I.2**: 119. **K.4**: 109.
Miller, D: **F.5**: 179, 245.
Miller, G: **I.2**: 69. **I.4**: 61. **I.5**: 112.
Miller, I: **D.9**: 12.
Miller, J: **C.5**: 41. **F.4**: 148. **K.4**: 113.
Miller, L: **G.3.1**: 75.
Miller, M: **B.2**: 73. **F.5**: 244. **I.6**: 6.
Miller, O: **G.3.2**: 211.
Miller, P: **C.3**: 132. **D.7**: 223. **F.5**: 201. **I.2**: 2.
Miller, R: **F.3**: 228. **F.5**: 197. **K.1**: 314, 389.
Miller, S: **F.6**: 34. **K.1**: 408.
Miller, T: **K.1**: 42, 186. **K.4**: 182.
Miller-Herringer, T: **C.2**: 196.
Miller-Tutzauer, C: **K.1**: 297.
Millett, K: **C.1**: 68. **F.3**: 192.
Milliken, F: **C.4**: 56.
Millman, M: **F.4**: 113.
Mills, N: **E.3**: 56.
Millward, N: **B.2**: 119, 124.
Milne, S: **H.4**: 50, 75.
Milne, W: **I.2**: 171.
Milner, S: **I.5**: 76, 133.
Milovanova, L: **F.3**: 224.
Milroy, B: **F.5**: 128.
Milton, K: **C.2**: 225.
Min, P: **F.7**: 64.
Minami, M: **D.7**: 26.

Minamikata, S: **F.4**: 293.
Miner, A: **C.5**: 56.
Miner, J: **C.2**: 179.
Mingat, A: **D.9**: 150.
Mingione, E: **H.2**: 6.
Mings, R: **F.8**: 100.
Minkler, M: **F.2**: 39. **K.2**: 80.
Minoliti, C: **I.3**: 88.
Minow, N: **H.4**: 33.
Minsk, E: **C.7**: 45.
Minson, J: **D.4**: 41.
Minton, H: **C.1**: 147.
Minty, B: **F.4**: 172.
Minz, B: **F.5**: 237.
Miron, J: **F.1**: 59.
Mironenkov, A: **H.7**: 24.
Mironov, A: **F.2**: 135.
Mirowski, W: **F.8**: 99.
Mis'kevich, U: **D.6**: 18.
Misra, G: **D.3**: 85.
Misumi, J: **D.7**: 94.
Miszlivetz, F: **J.2**: 17, 28.
Mitchell, B: **D.9**: 62, 83.
Mitchell, C: **C.3**: 94.
Mitchell, P: **C.2**: 11.
Mitchell, T: **C.2**: 167.
Mitroff, I: **H.4**: 46.
Mitter, S: **F.5**: 155.
Mitter, W: **D.9**: 82.
Mitterauer, M: **F.4**: 198.
Mixon, J: **I.2**: 110.
Miyadai, S: **D.7**: 278.
Miyajima, T: **B.1**: 21.
Miyamoto, K: **B.1**: 33.
Miyan, M: **I.3**: 135.
Miyanaga, K: **C.2**: 19.
Mizruchi, M: **H.4**: 73.
Mkrtchan, A: **D.3**: 70, 83.
Mladenka, K: **I.2**: 53.
Mlia, J: **G.3.2**: 362.
Moberg, M: **E.2**: 53.
Mocan, N: **F.5**: 2.
Mocellin, J: **C.1**: 119.
Mochizuki-Sudo, M: **D.7**: 64.
Model, S: **F.7**: 7.
Modell, B: **K.4**: 13.
Modleski, T: **F.5**: 276.

Modood, T: **F.7**: 13, 39, 171, 185.
Moeketsi, R: **D.7**: 311.
Moen, E: **F.5**: 223.
Moen, P: **F.5**: 313.
Moenaert, P: **K.2**: 3.
Moffitt, T: **C.2**: 187. **K.1**: 115.
Mogensen, B: **K.1**: 162.
Moghadam, V: **F.5**: 217.
Moghaddam, F: **F.7**: 144, 152.
Mohammed, P: **F.5**: 119.
Mohan, J: **K.4**: 216.
Mohan-Neill, S: **I.2**: 108.
Mohanty, A: **F.3**: 256.
Mohanty, C: **F.5**: 130.
Mohanty, S: **K.2**: 17.
Mohiuddin, Y: **I.2**: 85.
Mohwald, U: **F.4**: 109.
Moilanen, I: **K.1**: 331.
Moin, V: **B.2**: 94.
Moisés, J: **J.3**: 6.
Molchanov, V: **D.1**: 80.
Molinari, J: **I.5**: 157.
Moliterno, S: **I.4**: 86.
Moll, P: **F.7**: 227.
Molnár, E: **F.4**: 70.
Molnar, J: **K.1**: 235.
Molyneux, M: **F.5**: 124, 252.
Momigliano, L: **C.1**: 48.
Mompart, A: **F.3**: 274.
Momsen, J: **F.5**: 243.
Monappa, A: **I.3**: 135.
Mongin, P: **B.1**: 71.
Monigl, I: **F.3**: 305.
Monk, A: **K.4**: 117.
Monk, J: **F.5**: 117.
Monks, R: **H.4**: 33.
Monnier, A: **D.1**: 55.
Monroe, L: **C.3**: 40.
Monteil, J: **C.2**: 136.
Monteith, M: **F.7**: 247.
Monteith, R: **F.3**: 81.
Montello, D: **G.3.2**: 221.
Montgomery, M: **I.5**: 155.
Montgomery, P: **F.5**: 320.
Montgomery, R: **D.5**: 70. **F.7**: 112.
Montmarquette, C: **F.5**: 147, 202.

Montminy, J: **F.2**: 132, 138.
Montville, J: **J.8**: 13.
Moodie, G: **D.9**: 204.
Moodley, S: **I.3**: 16.
Moody-Adams, M: **F.4**: 305.
Mooney, L: **B.2**: 95.
Mooney, P: **J.5**: 17.
Mooney, S: **G.3.2**: 292.
Moore, A: **K.1**: 333.
Moore, B: **J.7**: 1.
Moore, D: **F.7**: 98. **K.1**: 226.
Moore, E: **F.8**: 1.
Moore, G: **E.2**: 10.
Moore, K: **D.9**: 151.
Moore, M: **I.4**: 56. **K.1**: 325.
Moore, R: **F.7**: 40, 228.
Moore, S: **C.7**: 3. **F.2**: 9. **F.3**: 219. **F.6**: 1.
Moore, T: **H.7**: 17.
Moore, W: **H.3**: 74.
Moorhead, G: **C.4**: 24.
Moorhouse, H: **I.6**: 8. **K.1**: 414.
Moorman, R: **C.5**: 68.
Moors, H: **F.2**: 153.
Moos, R: **K.1**: 351.
Moraes, E: **D.7**: 80.
Moraes Morel, de, R: **I.4**: 22.
Morales, H: **G.2**: 14.
Morales, R: **F.5**: 18. **I.1**: 10.
Moran, M: **C.1**: 8.
Moran, S: **J.4**: 17.
Morata, F: **G.3.2**: 58.
Morawska, E: **D.5**: 138.
Morchain, P: **C.3**: 42.
Mordecai, M: **K.3**: 19.
Morefield, J: **D.9**: 46.
Moreno, J: **D.3**: 69. **K.4**: 226.
Moreno, L: **F.3**: 75.
Morey, N: **C.5**: 86.
Morf, C: **C.2**: 237.
Morgan, D: **F.3**: 70. **F.4**: 259.
Morgan, G: **I.3**: 133.
Morgan, K: **F.2**: 40.
Morgan, L: **F.4**: 117.
Morgan, M: **C.4**: 7. **D.7**: 270, 326, 382.
Morgan, R: **K.1**: 201.
Morgan, S: **F.3**: 124. **F.4**: 291.
Morgas Spà, de, M: **D.7**: 292.

Mori, B: **F.5**: 311.
Mori, Y: **G.3.2**: 12.
Morioka, K: **F.4**: 104.
Morishima, M: **I.5**: 32, 68.
Moriya, K: **I.4**: 59.
Morley, D: **H.4**: 94.
Morley, I: **C.1**: 168.
Morokvasic, M: **F.5**: 124. **I.2**: 183.
Moroney, R: **K.2**: 95.
Morozova, G: **F.8**: 99.
Morreim, E: **K.4**: 247.
Morrel-Samuels, P: **C.3**: 30.
Morrill, C: **C.5**: 13, 19.
Morrill, R: **G.1**: 60.
Morrione, T: **E.3**: 57.
Morris, A: **D.9**: 54. **F.5**: 259. **H.5**: 1.
Morris, D: **C.1**: 93.
Morris, E: **G.3.2**: 8, 115, 142, 200.
Morris, H: **I.5**: 65.
Morris, J: **D.9**: 208. **K.2**: 60.
Morris, L: **F.1**: 35. **G.3**: 6.
Morris, R: **I.4**: 41.
Morris, T: **I.5**: 54.
Morrison, F: **C.2**: 93.
Morrison, P: **F.7**: 123. **J.7**: 22.
Morrison, R: **H.4**: 54.
Morrison, T: **K.3**: 1.
Morrissey, M: **G.3.2**: 292.
Morrissey, S: **G.3.2**: 146.
Morrow, J: **C.2**: 80.
Morse, E: **F.3**: 193.
Morse, G: **K.1**: 274.
Morse, J: **F.3**: 184.
Morse, M: **C.3**: 71.
Morten, E: **G.3.2**: 250.
Mortimer, J: **I.4**: 55.
Morton, A: **C.2**: 146.
Morton, J: **K.3**: 24.
Moscovice, I: **K.4**: 164.
Moscovici, S: **C.4**: 61. **D.1**: 43.
Moseley, K: **G.3.2**: 163.
Moser, C: **F.1**: 58.
Moses, K: **D.9**: 12.
Mosha, A: **G.3.2**: 84, 362.
Mosley, W: **F.2**: 85.
Moss, H: **K.1**: 313.

Moss, P: **K.2**: 65.
Moßbrucker, H: **F.8**: 86.
Mostafa, G: **F.3**: 125.
Mostovaya, A: **D.7**: 48.
Mothé, D: **G.3.2**: 188.
Mothibeli, M: **F.8**: 21.
Motobayashi, Y: **D.5**: 32.
Motohashi, Y: **K.1**: 394.
Motojima, K: **C.5**: 10.
Motoyoshi, M: **K.1**: 366.
Mott, F: **F.2**: 87.
Mouffe, C: **J.2**: 18–19.
Moughtin, C: **G.3.2**: 24.
Mounier, L: **C.4**: 48–49.
Mouzelis, N: **B.1**: 87.
Moynihan, D: **D.9**: 56.
Mu, X: **G.1**: 38.
Mucchi-Faina, A: **C.3**: 77.
Mudrovcic, Z: **F.2**: 26.
Mueggler, E: **J.2**: 16.
Mühler, K: **J.5**: 15.
Mühlfeld, C: **K.3**: 43.
Müller, H: **K.4**: 95.
Mueller, S: **D.5**: 29.
Müller-Dempf, H: **F.2**: 44.
Müller-Jentsch, W: **I.5**: 47.
Mueser, P: **F.8**: 44.
Mufune, P: **B.2**: 76.
Mugford, S: **K.1**: 354, 392.
Mugny, G: **C.3**: 42. **C.4**: 31.
Mukerji, C: **D.1**: 35.
Mukherjee, R: **E.3**: 67.
Mukonoweshuro, E: **F.7**: 62. **K.1**: 221.
Mulgan, G: **H.4**: 83.
Mullen, B: **C.2**: 31. **C.4**: 23. **D.7**: 139.
Mullender, A: **C.4**: 51.
Muller, J: **F.1**: 37.
Mulligan, G: **G.1**: 36. **G.3.2**: 68.
Mullings, C: **F.3**: 288.
Mullins, L: **F.2**: 52.
Mullins, M: **D.5**: 22.
Mullins, P: **G.3.2**: 356.
Mulvey, C: **I.2**: 2.
Mulvey, L: **D.8**: 43.
Mulvie, C: **K.3**: 19.
Mulvihill, M: **F.3**: 60. **H.4**: 17.
Mulwanda, M: **G.3.2**: 362.

Mundy-Castle, A: **C.2**: 118.
Munene, J: **C.5**: 55.
Munger, F: **E.2**: 69.
Munk-Jorgensen, P: **F.3**: 169.
Munshi, S: **E.3**: 61.
Munt, I: **H.7**: 18. **J.5**: 3.
Munton, R: **G.3.1**: 19, 46, 124.
Muoghalu, L: **G.3.2**: 138.
Muramatsu, Y: **E.1**: 5.
Murata, S: **B.1**: 98.
Muratov, S: **D.7**: 378.
Murdie, R: **G.3.2**: 178.
Murdock, G: **D.7**: 296. **K.1**: 106.
Murdock, S: **F.1**: 6, 23. **F.7**: 69.
Murguialday, C: **F.5**: 107.
Murie, A: **E.3**: 10.
Murnighan, J: **B.2**: 38. **C.4**: 11–12.
Murph, W: **K.1**: 60.
Murphey, D: **F.7**: 169.
Murphy, A: **F.7**: 20. **G.3**: 8. **G.3.2**: 8, 142, 200. **H.2**: 3.
Murphy, E: **K.4**: 107.
Murphy, F: **D.9**: 20.
Murphy, J: **D.6**: 6. **K.4**: 114.
Murphy, K: **I.3**: 37.
Murphy, L: **I.5**: 175.
Murphy, M: **F.1**: 29, 51. **H.4**: 13.
Murphy, P: **C.6**: 11. **I.6**: 8. **K.1**: 404.
Murphy, W: **D.4**: 30.
Murray, C: **F.4**: 187. **H.3**: 14.
Murray, E: **C.1**: 85.
Murray, J: **G.3.1**: 55.
Murray, K: **F.4**: 158.
Murray, M: **F.2**: 146. **G.3.2**: 61.
Murthy, P: **F.3**: 139.
Muscarà, C: **G.3.2**: 344.
Musharaf, El, A: **F.5**: 241.
Musisi, N: **F.5**: 326.
Mustapha, A: **H.3**: 50.
Musterd, S: **G.3.2**: 204.
Muta, K: **F.4**: 53.
Mutambirwa, C: **G.3.2**: 113.
Mutch, P: **D.7**: 69.
Muthén, B: **B.2**: 54.
Muthny, F: **K.4**: 94.
Mutizwa-Mangiza, N: **G.3.1**: 125.
Muto, Y: **F.2**: 21.

Mutti, A: **E.3**: 68.
Myers, F: **D.8**: 57.
Myers, M: **K.1**: 424.
Myers, S: **I.2**: 145.
Myers, W: **I.2**: 194.
Myles, J: **H.4**: 17. **K.2**: 28.
Myshapud, S: **D.5**: 89.
Na, Y: **D.7**: 203.
Nachmias, D: **E.2**: 20.
Nachshon, O: **C.3**: 10.
Nacht, M: **D.9**: 198.
Nadel-Klein, J: **D.1**: 141.
Naderer, G: **D.7**: 120.
Nadin, V: **G.3.2**: 314.
Naffine, N: **J.3**: 25.
Naficy, H: **D.8**: 6.
Nafziger, J: **I.2**: 67.
Nag, D: **D.1**: 20.
Nag, M: **F.5**: 38.
Nag, P: **I.3**: 135.
Nagai, K: **H.4**: 53.
Nagao, D: **I.3**: 27.
Nagatsu, M: **F.4**: 280.
Nagel, B: **G.3.1**: 67.
Naimark, H: **F.2**: 114.
Nain, G: **F.5**: 68.
Nairn, R: **F.7**: 197.
Nakagawa, N: **K.1**: 175.
Nakajima, M: **B.1**: 106.
Nakamura, B: **B.1**: 99.
Nakamura, M: **D.2**: 4.
Nakayama, S: **D.6**: 23.
Nakhi, J: **C.2**: 70.
Nakicenovic, N: **H.4**: 84.
Nam, C: **F.2**: 1.
Namboodiri, N: **F.1**: 14.
Namboodiripad, E: **J.2**: 8.
Nanton, P: **F.7**: 39.
Naples, N: **I.2**: 78. **J.6**: 20.
Narain, S: **H.4**: 103.
Nasonova, L: **D.1**: 120.
Nasrallah, F: **E.1**: 21.
Nassehi, A: **B.1**: 25.
Nasu, H: **B.1**: 15.
Natsoulas, T: **C.2**: 13. **C.3**: 17.
Nava, M: **H.5**: 14.

Navarro, V: **F.3**: 287. **I.3**: 62. **K.4**: 176.
Nayar, K: **G.1**: 5.
Nayar, P: **D.7**: 141.
Naylor, J: **F.4**: 83.
Nazarov, I: **E.3**: 31.
Nazir, P: **G.3.1**: 114.
Ncube, W: **D.4**: 10.
Ndiaye, M: **J.4**: 11.
Ndoko, N: **F.4**: 190.
Neal, A: **C.2**: 5. **H.3**: 11.
Neale, B: **K.1**: 41.
Neale, J: **F.3**: 209.
Neale, M: **C.2**: 114.
Near, J: **C.1**: 84. **I.3**: 61.
Nebgen, M: **D.9**: 43.
Neck, C: **C.4**: 24.
Neckel, S: **J.6**: 3.
Neckerman, K: **I.2**: 209. **K.1**: 290.
Necochea, A: **G.3.2**: 253.
Nedelmann, B: **D.1**: 46.
Neenan, P: **F.2**: 100.
Negodaev, I: **H.4**: 99.
Negrete Salas, M: **F.8**: 97.
Negrine, R: **D.7**: 363.
Negrón, M: **G.3.2**: 64.
Negroponte, N: **D.7**: 65.
Neifer-Dichmann, E: **I.3**: 93.
Neil, D: **D.7**: 155.
Neirynck, J: **H.4**: 100.
Nelkin, D: **F.3**: 146, 172.
Nelsen, H: **D.5**: 109.
Nelson, G: **C.3**: 15.
Nelson, J: **F.4**: 308. **G.3.2**: 250.
Nelson, R: **C.5**: 78.
Nelson, T: **C.7**: 66.
Nelson-Le Gall, S: **D.9**: 168.
Németh, G: **D.5**: 98.
Nencel, L: **B.1**: 28.
Nervo, G: **K.2**: 86.
Nestel, G: **I.2**: 125.
Netland, H: **D.5**: 105.
Neto, F: **C.2**: 240. **F.2**: 67. **G.3.1**: 73.
Neuberger, J: **F.3**: 203. **F.5**: 240.
Neufeld, J: **D.9**: 47.
Neuman, S: **D.7**: 366. **F.4**: 80.
Neuman, W: **D.4**: 39. **D.7**: 257.
Neumann, G: **I.5**: 152.

Neumark, D: **H.3**: 15.
Neveu, C: **F.7**: 13. **F.8**: 70.
Nevile, J: **H.3**: 20.
Nevo, N: **G.3.1**: 81. **H.4**: 102.
Newburn, T: **D.3**: 79.
Newcomb, M: **C.2**: 206. **F.2**: 130.
Newell, L: **D.7**: 79.
Newell, P: **F.2**: 108, 111.
Newell, S: **I.3**: 140.
Newhagen, J: **D.7**: 369. **K.4**: 11.
Newhall, A: **F.5**: 117.
Newland, C: **D.9**: 153.
Newman, D: **H.3**: 30.
Newman, D: **C.2**: 152.
Newman, L: **C.3**: 162.
Newman, M: **B.2**: 120.
Newport, E: **D.7**: 53.
Newsome, Y: **F.7**: 174.
Newton, T: **C.5**: 28.
Neyer, F: **F.4**: 112.
Neysmith, S: **F.5**: 140.
Ng, I: **I.5**: 87.
Ng, S: **I.3**: 63.
Ng, Y: **C.7**: 60.
Ngo, H: **F.5**: 185.
Ngondo a Pitshandenge, I: **F.3**: 200.
Ngub'usim, M: **D.9**: 28.
Nice, D: **J.6**: 18.
Nice, V: **F.4**: 300.
Nicholls, P: **D.1**: 59.
Nichols, T: **I.3**: 110, 112.
Nicholson, D: **G.3.1**: 41.
Nicholson, R: **D.7**: 51.
Nicol, C: **H.5**: 5.
Niehoff, B: **D.9**: 116.
Nielsen, D: **D.1**: 85.
Nielsen, J: **G.1**: 31.
Nielsin, L: **I.2**: 95.
Niemelä, H: **K.4**: 85.
Nieminen, M: **F.4**: 123.
Nientied, P: **G.3.2**: 325.
Nies, H: **K.4**: 137.
Nieswiadomy, M: **H.3**: 76.
Nieuwenbroek, N: **B.2**: 114, 124.
Niezen, R: **D.1**: 77.
Nigal, D: **F.3**: 206.

Nigro, L: **J.4**: 2.
Nijsmans, M: **I.4**: 102.
Nikandrov, N: **C.1**: 142.
Nikiforov, A: **K.1**: 117.
Nikiforov, G: **H.4**: 37.
Nikol'skaia, T: **B.1**: 41.
Nilsson, N: **D.7**: 239.
Nimwegen, van, N: **F.1**: 52. **F.2**: 153.
Niranjana, S: **G.3.1**: 7.
Nirenstein, F: **F.7**: 202.
Nisbett, R: **C.1**: 162.
Nishida, T: **C.3**: 112.
Nichihara, K: **B.1**: 30.
Nishihira, S: **C.7**: 46.
Nishine, K: **D.9**: 144.
Nishiyama, Y: **G.3.2**: 15.
Nitta, M: **I.1**: 8. **I.3**: 130.
Nitta, N: **I.4**: 54.
Nkomo, S: **I.4**: 82.
Noam, E: **D.7**: 385.
Noble, T: **F.3**: 6.
Noblit, G: **D.9**: 62, 136.
Nobutaka, I: **D.5**: 22.
Noe, S: **G.3.2**: 299.
Nofsinger, R: **D.7**: 142.
Noguchi, Y: **K.2**: 25.
Nohrstedt, S: **D.7**: 37.
Noin, D: **F.3**: 77.
Nolder, M: **C.1**: 9.
Nolen-Hoeksema, S: **C.2**: 80.
Nollen, S: **I.4**: 18.
Noon, M: **I.5**: 171.
Noonan, B: **K.1**: 121.
Noponen, H: **G.3.2**: 183.
Norem, J: **C.2**: 59.
Norling, F: **J.4**: 10.
Norman, R: **C.4**: 42.
Norman, W: **D.3**: 22.
Norrell, R: **F.7**: 190.
Norrick, N: **D.7**: 165.
Norrie, K: **F.3**: 42.
Norris, C: **B.1**: 49.
Norris, F: **K.1**: 132.
North, J: **H.4**: 69.
Northrop, E: **F.5**: 6.
Northrup, H: **I.5**: 34, 156.
Norton, B: **H.2**: 16.

Norton, J: **F.5**: 26.
Nott, S: **F.5**: 259.
Novacek, J: **C.2**: 192, 231.
Novitz, D: **C.3**: 129.
Novoseltsev, A: **D.5**: 97.
Nowak-Sapota, K: **F.2**: 53.
Nowakowska, B: **F.2**: 53.
Nowell-Smith, G: **D.7**: 237.
Nowlan, D: **F.3**: 303.
Nowlin, W: **I.3**: 108.
Nowotny, H: **B.1**: 7.
Nudeshima, J: **K.4**: 248.
Nugent, J: **F.4**: 282.
Nuijens, J: **K.4**: 137.
Nukandrov, V: **C.1**: 108.
Nuna, S: **D.9**: 16.
Nunnelley, W: **F.7**: 147.
Nunno, M: **K.1**: 25.
Nusberg, C: **F.2**: 61.
Nussbaum, J: **D.7**: 77.
Nyanguru, A: **K.4**: 141.
Nybom, T: **D.9**: 217.
Nyden, P: **G.3.2**: 241.
Nye, D: **H.5**: 15.
Nyerges, T: **B.2**: 51.
Nygren, O: **F.1**: 39.
Nyman, K: **I.3**: 122.
Nystuen, J: **G.3.2**: 310.
O Huallacháin, B: **G.3.2**: 217.
O Shea, D: **K.4**: 111.
O'Brien, D: **F.7**: 96. **G.3.1**: 65.
O'Brien, M: **D.8**: 56. **F.5**: 27, 254.
O'Cearbhaill, D: **G.2**: 15, 19.
O'Connell, F: **I.5**: 34.
O'Connor, D: **F.4**: 210.
O'Connor, E: **I.3**: 27.
O'Connor, J: **G.1**: 45.
O'Connor, M: **I.3**: 49.
O'Connor, P: **F.4**: 262–263.
O'Connor, S: **D.4**: 42.
O'Donovan, K: **D.4**: 11.
O'Driscoll, M: **I.4**: 77.
O'Farrell, B: **I.2**: 202.
O'Gorman, H: **B.2**: 126.
O'Hare, A: **E.2**: 64.
O'Hare, P: **K.1**: 377.

O'Keefe, P: **G.3.1**: 127.
O'Mahony, P: **C.6**: 11.
O'Malley, P: **K.1**: 354, 392.
O'Muircheartaigh, C: **F.3**: 52.
O'Neill, B: **F.6**: 7.
O'Neill, D: **D.7**: 315.
O'Neill, J: **D.7**: 57.
O'Neill, P: **H.7**: 5.
O'Regan, K: **I.2**: 33.
O'Reilly, C: **C.5**: 15.
O'Sullivan, M: **C.3**: 161.
O'Toole, B: **K.4**: 112.
O'Toole, J: **F.3**: 282.
Oakes, P: **C.3**: 154.
Oakley, A: **E.2**: 77.
Oakley, P: **E.3**: 15, 18.
Oberhauser, A: **F.8**: 141.
Obraniak, W: **F.2**: 53.
Obudho, R: **G.3.2**: 362.
Oc, T: **G.3.2**: 275.
Oda, T: **K.2**: 22.
Oddone, de, N: **F.3**: 54.
Odebiyi, A: **F.3**: 177. **G.3.1**: 129.
Odem, M: **K.1**: 192.
Oesterle-Schwerin, J: **F.4**: 195.
Oey-Gardiner, M: **F.5**: 175. **I.4**: 23.
Offe, C: **J.2**: 3, 17.
Ogawa, B: **D.7**: 134.
Ogawa, N: **F.3**: 97.
Ogden, P: **F.8**: 125, 150.
Ogden, S: **I.5**: 177.
Ogley, R: **C.1**: 88.
Ogunbekun, I: **K.4**: 103.
Ogunshakin, L: **G.3.2**: 118, 139.
Ogura, M: **F.8**: 107.
Ohashi, T: **H.5**: 27.
Ohkawa, K: **B.1**: 101.
Ohler, J: **D.9**: 12.
Ohlin, L: **C.2**: 42.
Ohno, M: **D.9**: 147.
Ohsawa, Y: **B.2**: 44.
Oishi, Y: **D.7**: 238.
Ojeda, G: **F.3**: 58.
Ojofeitimi, E: **F.3**: 177.
Okafor, S: **K.4**: 18.
Okediji, O: **F.3**: 177.
Okin, S: **F.5**: 245.

Oklobdžija, M: **F.4**: 90.
Okon-Horodynska, E: **I.4**: 96.
Okowa, W: **G.3.2**: 163.
Oksa, J: **G.3.1**: 43, 116.
Okuda, K: **I.4**: 37.
Okuda, S: **G.1**: 21.
Oladejo, J: **D.7**: 49.
Olatubara, C: **G.3.2**: 163.
Olayiwola, D: **D.5**: 19.
Old, R: **D.6**: 3.
Oldenquist, A: **C.1**: 143.
Oldersma, J: **F.5**: 181.
Olenja, J: **G.3.1**: 24.
Olin-Ammentorp, J: **F.5**: 216.
Olio, K: **K.1**: 36.
Oliveira, de, M: **D.7**: 80.
Oliveira, de, O: **F.5**: 236.
Oliver, B: **F.7**: 48.
Oliver, C: **C.5**: 33.
Oliver, M: **E.2**: 62. **I.2**: 228.
Oliver, N: **H.4**: 85.
Oliver, P: **B.2**: 67.
Olivier, L: **F.4**: 166.
Oliviera-Roca, M: **F.1**: 62.
Olmo, del, R: **K.1**: 392.
Olmstead, K: **D.7**: 235.
Olmsted, N: **G.3.2**: 149.
Olowu, S: **F.3**: 177.
Olsen, F: **F.5**: 245.
Olsen, W: **G.3.1**: 1.
Olshan, M: **E.3**: 38.
Olson, C: **I.3**: 21. **I.5**: 61.
Olson, D: **D.7**: 158. **F.4**: 22, 57. **H.7**: 28.
Olson, J: **D.7**: 187. **K.1**: 358.
Olson, R: **F.4**: 162.
Omiunu, F: **G.3.2**: 184.
Omodei, M: **I.2**: 76.
Omran, A: **F.3**: 41.
Omvedt, G: **E.2**: 1.
Onda, M: **G.3.2**: 16.
Ong, A: **I.2**: 96.
Ong, P: **F.5**: 18. **F.8**: 122. **I.1**: 10. **I.4**: 40.
Ongile, G: **I.2**: 171.
Onibokun, P: **G.3.2**: 166.
Ooms, T: **F.4**: 30.
Oosthuizen, L: **I.3**: 142, 144.

Openshaw, S: **B.2**: 35.
Opitz, P: **F.8**: 163.
Opotow, S: **D.9**: 62, 106.
Opp, K: **J.5**: 8.
Oppenheim, N: **H.4**: 42.
Oppenheimer, A: **C.1**: 65.
Oppenheimer, G: **K.1**: 324.
Oppong, C: **F.3**: 127.
Ordorica Mellado, M: **F.1**: 2.
Orf, L: **C.2**: 199.
Orfield, G: **F.7**: 8.
Orlik, M: **D.2**: 27.
Orlov, V: **E.3**: 46.
Orlova, E: **D.1**: 100.
Orlova, I: **D.8**: 40.
Ormay, A: **C.4**: 32.
Ormel, J: **C.2**: 41, 215.
Orrù, M: **K.1**: 398.
Orton, C: **K.2**: 65.
Orubuloye, I: **F.6**: 9.
Orum, A: **B.1**: 90. **G.3.2**: 3.
Osada, T: **I.3**: 1.
Osasona, O: **G.3.2**: 118, 139.
Osawa, M: **I.2**: 146.
Oschlies, W: **D.7**: 97.
Osei-Hwedie, K: **F.2**: 151.
Osher, F: **K.1**: 260. **K.4**: 47.
Osipov, G: **A.1**: 23.
Osipova, E: **J.2**: 31.
Oskamp, S: **G.1**: 21.
Osofsky, H: **F.3**: 193.
Østergaard, L: **F.5**: 280.
Osteria, T: **K.1**: 264.
Osterman, P: **K.1**: 290. **K.2**: 107.
Ostrower, F: **D.8**: 42.
Oswald, I: **D.8**: 68.
Oswald, S: **B.2**: 24.
Otani, K: **F.4**: 111.
Otani, T: **I.4**: 109.
Oteiza, E: **H.4**: 87.
Otero, H: **F.7**: 167.
Otis, J: **F.3**: 246.
Otten, M: **I.3**: 11.
Otto, H: **K.3**: 37.
Oudshoorn, N: **F.5**: 157.
Ouellet, L: **F.3**: 144.
Outram, Q: **I.5**: 84.

Over, D: **C.6**: 13.
Overall, C: **F.3**: 207.
Oversloot, H: **I.3**: 77.
Owen, D: **B.1**: 86. **F.5**: 279.
Owen, U: **G.3.2**: 92.
Owen, V: **D.9**: 184.
Owens, D: **F.3**: 153. **K.4**: 229.
Owens, R: **K.1**: 87.
Oxhorn, P: **J.5**: 22.
Oxley, M: **G.3.2**: 95.
Oyama, S: **C.1**: 106.
Ozkarahan, I: **K.4**: 17.
Ozornoy, G: **H.3**: 48.
Paasch, K: **F.4**: 217.
Paasi, A: **G.3**: 2.
Pacheco, J: **J.4**: 7.
Pacheco Vasquez, P: **G.3.2**: 8, 142.
Pacione, M: **D.5**: 101.
Packman, J: **K.2**: 46.
Packwood, T: **K.4**: 49.
Pacolet, J: **K.4**: 138.
Padavic, I: **I.2**: 75.
Padieu, R: **I.4**: 13, 93.
Padilla, A: **D.7**: 19.
Padrón, G: **K.4**: 16.
Páez, D: **F.3**: 154, 219.
Page, M: **K.4**: 119.
Pahl, R: **D.1**: 39.
Paik, H: **D.7**: 381.
Paikoff, R: **F.4**: 286.
Pain, R: **F.5**: 228.
Paine, L: **F.4**: 329.
Painter, J: **J.4**: 6.
Paksoy, H: **D.1**: 30.
Palermo, G: **K.1**: 190.
Palfrey, C: **K.3**: 12.
Pałka, B: **I.2**: 214.
Palma, Di, G: **E.3**: 26–27.
Palmer, C: **C.4**: 34.
Palmer, I: **I.2**: 98.
Palmer, J: **D.8**: 51. **I.3**: 89. **K.2**: 45.
Palmer, M: **D.7**: 101, 281.
Palmonari, A: **C.3**: 29.
Palsky, G: **F.1**: 37.
Pálsson, G: **G.1**: 6.
Pampalon, R: **F.3**: 258.

Panayi, P: **F.7**: 186.
Pandey, J: **C.1**: 14. **C.7**: 72.
Pandey, S: **I.3**: 135. **J.5**: 6.
Paniagua Gil, J: **K.1**: 365.
Panitch, L: **I.2**: 199.
Pankhurst, A: **G.3.2**: 65.
Pankhurst, D: **G.3.1**: 85.
Pannell, C: **F.3**: 9.
Pant, P: **F.3**: 252.
Panter-Brick, C: **F.3**: 110.
Pantzar, M: **C.5**: 69.
Paolini, A: **D.8**: 58.
Papadakis, E: **K.1**: 333.
Papalexandris, N: **I.4**: 69.
Papataxiarchis, E: **F.5**: 266.
Papathanasis, A: **I.3**: 85.
Paponnet-Cantat, C: **K.1**: 430.
Papworth, R: **I.2**: 188.
Paquette, J: **D.9**: 71.
Parcel, T: **B.2**: 104. **F.4**: 27.
Pardeck, J: **D.6**: 6.
Pareek, U: **I.3**: 135.
Parekh, B: **E.2**: 16. **F.7**: 13.
Parenteau, R: **G.3.2**: 144.
Parfitt, G: **C.2**: 8.
Parida, M: **K.2**: 17.
Parikh, P: **D.7**: 125.
Parish, W: **F.4**: 56, 348.
Park, A: **F.7**: 158.
Park, B: **C.3**: 41. **C.4**: 1.
Park, R: **K.4**: 32.
Park, S: **B.1**: 125.
Park, Y: **D.7**: 340.
Parker, B: **C.2**: 174.
Parker, D: **C.2**: 93. **G.3.2**: 85.
Parker, H: **K.1**: 35.
Parker, I: **D.7**: 136.
Parker, J: **C.2**: 191.
Parker, R: **F.6**: 5. **K.2**: 47.
Parker, S: **F.4**: 15. **K.1**: 35.
Parker-Jenkins, M: **D.9**: 130.
Parkes, C: **F.2**: 71.
Parkes, K: **C.1**: 31.
Parkinson, M: **G.3.2**: 326.
Parks, C: **C.3**: 67.
Parmalee, P: **E.1**: 14.
Parra, F: **C.7**: 63.

Parrillo, V: **F.4**: 4, 64.
Parris, S: **F.3**: 172.
Parry-Jones, W: **F.3**: 196.
Parsloe, P: **K.3**: 48.
Parson, N: **F.7**: 238.
Parsons, C: **C.2**: 47. **I.3**: 27.
Parsons, D: **I.2**: 31.
Parsons, T: **B.1**: 96.
Partida Bush, V: **F.1**: 38.
Parton, D: **K.1**: 105.
Parton, N: **K.2**: 54.
Pascual, L: **D.9**: 47–48.
Pacmoro, W: **C.5**: 51. **E.3**: 20.
Passow, A: **D.9**: 46, 78.
Patai, D: **F.5**: 144.
Patarra, N: **F.4**: 40.
Patel, T: **F.3**: 51.
Pater, de, B: **G.3**: 7.
Patkar, V: **C.3**: 103.
Patrick, C: **D.4**: 43.
Patrushev, V: **I.6**: 20.
Patterson, D: **F.4**: 164.
Patterson, G: **F.7**: 25.
Patterson, M: **C.3**: 50.
Patterson, T: **K.4**: 10.
Pattie, C: **B.2**: 47.
Pattnayak, S: **F.7**: 251.
Patton, M: **F.4**: 157.
Patzelt, W: **D.7**: 229.
Pauchant, T: **H.4**: 46.
Paugam, S: **K.1**: 228, 286.
Paulhus, D: **C.3**: 32.
Paunonen, S: **C.3**: 152.
Pausewang, S: **G.3.1**: 92.
Pavageau, C: **G.3.2**: 134–135.
Paviani, A: **G.3.2**: 141.
Pavitt, C: **D.7**: 118.
Pavlov, E: **B.2**: 107.
Pavón, N: **F.4**: 227.
Pavot, W: **C.2**: 82, 89.
Pawl, J: **F.4**: 318.
Paxson, C: **F.2**: 58.
Payne, G: **H.4**: 56.
Payne, J: **I.2**: 157.
Payne, M: **D.7**: 386.
Payne, S: **K.1**: 295.

Paynter, R: **E.2**: 50.
Peacock, N: **F.1**: 25.
Pearce, J: **I.3**: 86.
Pearlstein, R: **C.1**: 34.
Pearson, B: **D.7**: 58.
Pearson, C: **F.4**: 171. **I.3**: 96. **K.1**: 38.
Pearson, D: **C.1**: 82.
Pearson, F: **K.1**: 89.
Pearson, G: **K.1**: 338.
Pearson, J: **F.4**: 186.
Pearson, R: **A.2**: 4. **D.9**: 210.
Pease, K: **K.1**: 65. **K.3**: 29.
Pebley, A: **F.3**: 261.
Peck, J: **I.4**: 132.
Pecora, P: **K.3**: 15.
Pecotte, B: **F.1**: 23.
Pedersen, C: **H.5**: 15.
Pedersen, F: **F.1**: 60.
Pedersen, P: **I.5**: 152.
Pedersen, W: **F.3**: 197.
Peek, C: **D.5**: 16.
Peekna, H: **C.3**: 100.
Peel, M: **I.5**: 199.
Peelo, M: **K.1**: 24.
Peer-Goldin, I: **C.2**: 212.
Peet, R: **H.2**: 11.
Peeters, G: **D.1**: 19.
Peil, M: **F.4**: 55. **G.3.2**: 345.
Peirce, J: **D.7**: 74.
Pejaranonda, C: **F.3**: 121.
Pelachaud, G: **D.7**: 17, 54.
Pelham, B: **C.2**: 198.
Pelikan, J: **C.1**: 71.
Pellegrino, E: **D.3**: 44.
Pels, P: **B.1**: 28.
Peña, M: **F.5**: 3.
Pendaries, J: **B.2**: 33. **D.1**: 18.
Pendleton, A: **I.3**: 9. **I.5**: 59.
Pendleton, L: **D.7**: 359.
Peneau, J: **G.3.2**: 73.
Peng, H: **I.5**: 53.
Penhale, B: **B.2**: 35.
Penn, D: **F.6**: 26.
Penn, R: **H.4**: 90.
Pennington, R: **F.3**: 89.
Penrod, J: **K.4**: 164.
Pepinsky, H: **K.1**: 72, 416.

Peplau, L: **C.1**: 107.
Pepper, D: **G.1**: 8.
Peräkylä, A: **D.7**: 173.
Percy, S: **G.3.2**: 56.
Pereboom, D: **D.6**: 17.
Pereira, P: **F.4**: 118.
Peres, Y: **F.4**: 65.
Peretz, H: **A.1**: 28.
Pérez, J: **C.4**: 31.
Pérez-Sanchez, M: **F.2**: 72.
Pergola, della, S: **F.7**: 159.
Peri, N: **C.3**: 46.
Pericoli, T: **D.8**: 64.
Perie, M: **C.2**: 132.
Perinbanayagam, R: **D.7**: 137.
Perkins, R: **K.4**: 212.
Perlmutter, H: **D.1**: 88.
Pernanen, K: **K.1**: 304.
Perner, J: **C.2**: 105.
Pernia, E: **G.3.2**: 353.
Peron, R: **H.4**: 5.
Péron, Y: **F.4**: 214.
Peroni, G: **I.6**: 29.
Perrin, P: **K.4**: 45.
Perron, M: **F.3**: 246.
Perrotti, E: **F.4**: 225.
Perrow, C: **C.5**: 73.
Perry, H: **F.7**: 233.
Perry, N: **D.4**: 5.
Perry, P: **J.6**: 36.
Personnaz, B: **D.1**: 43.
Persson, I: **I.2**: 38.
Pervin, L: **C.2**: 186.
Pervomajskii, V: **C.1**: 26.
Pesando, J: **H.3**: 83.
Peshkin, A: **F.7**: 59.
Pessar, P: **F.8**: 113.
Pessino, C: **F.8**: 55.
Pestieau, P: **I.4**: 51.
Petee, T: **D.5**: 137. **K.1**: 156.
Petelin, B: **K.1**: 119.
Peter, B: **A.1**: 8.
Péter, J: **F.3**: 259.
Peter, O: **C.3**: 65.
Peters, J: **D.1**: 6. **D.7**: 279.
Petersen, A: **K.4**: 165.

Petersen, B: **F.5**: 271.
Petersen, D: **K.1**: 344.
Petersen, I: **J.5**: 32.
Petersen, T: **B.2**: 48, 80. **H.4**: 10.
Petersilia, J: **K.1**: 180.
Peterson, B: **J.6**: 49.
Peterson, D: **C.1**: 89. **C.3**: 104.
Peterson, J: **F.3**: 128. **G.2**: 33.
Peterson, P: **K.1**: 292.
Peterson, R: **B.2**: 21, 40. **D.4**: 20.
Petersson, J: **F.2**: 41.
Petit, B: **I.4**: 84.
Petrie, P: **F.4**: 324. **K.2**: 65.
Petrissans, C: **F.7**: 135.
Petronio, S: **C.3**: 20.
Petrov, M: **D.1**: 50.
Petruchenia, J: **K.3**: 36.
Pettigrew, T: **C.4**: 41. **F.7**: 152.
Peyronnie, la, D: **G.3.2**: 173.
Peyronnin, K: **I.3**: 80.
Peyrot, M: **K.1**: 362.
Pfahl-Traughber, A: **F.7**: 36.
Pfeffer, J: **I.3**: 22.
Pfeffer, M: **I.2**: 97.
Pfeifer, B: **F.8**: 13.
Pfeiffer, K: **F.5**: 216.
Pffaf, C: **D.7**: 93.
Pham, M: **H.5**: 4.
Pharoah, T: **G.3.2**: 315.
Phelan, G: **I.4**: 41.
Phelps, E: **F.2**: 10.
Phenix, L: **J.5**: 4.
Philippe, V: **A.2**: 2.
Phillips, C: **K.3**: 12.
Phillips, D: **I.3**: 12. **K.2**: 40–41. **K.4**: 53.
Phillips, H: **G.3.2**: 365.
Phillips, J: **I.3**: 3.
Phillips, K: **K.4**: 81.
Phillips, L: **C.5**: 2. **G.3.1**: 60.
Phillips, M: **E.3**: 56.
Phillipson, C: **F.2**: 8.
Phoenix, A: **F.4**: 299.
Piazza, T: **F.7**: 243.
Picard, R: **D.7**: 30.
Piccone, P: **B.1**: 4.
Pickles, A: **F.1**: 4. **G.3.2**: 106.
Pickles, J: **G.3.1**: 123.

Pickowicz, P: **G.3.1**: 6.
Picon, B: **H.4**: 35.
Pierannunzi, C: **F.7**: 233.
Pierau, K: **B.2**: 108.
Pierce, G: **C.1**: 152. **C.3**: 153.
Pierce, J: **F.4**: 142.
Pierro, A: **F.3**: 181.
Pigg, K: **G.3.1**: 107.
Piguet, J: **H.4**: 100.
Pike, G: **D.9**: 210.
Pile, S: **G.3.1**: 62.
Pillemer, K: **F.4**: 287.
Piller, C: **D.6**: 10.
Pilling, S: **K.4**: 130.
Pinassi, D: **C.7**: 47.
Pinch, S: **I.2**: 207. **K.4**: 122.
Pinçon, M: **B.2**: 106.
Pinçon-Charlot, M: **B.2**: 106.
Pineau, G: **I.4**: 118.
Pineault, R: **K.4**: 6.
Pinker, S: **D.7**: 210.
Pinkerton, J: **G.3.1**: 65.
Pinnelli, A: **F.3**: 244.
Pino Artacho, del, J: **B.1**: 146.
Pinto, L: **H.5**: 11.
Pion, G: **G.3.2**: 98.
Piore, M: **I.5**: 29.
Piper, A: **D.3**: 71.
Pippin, R: **D.1**: 81.
Pirog-Good, M: **K.1**: 108.
Pirozhkov, V: **H.4**: 34.
Pisciotta, A: **K.1**: 192.
Pitamber, S: **F.5**: 241. **K.4**: 84.
Pitrat, J: **C.2**: 115.
Pittam, J: **D.7**: 55.
Pittman, D: **D.2**: 24.
Pittman, W: **K.1**: 312.
Pitts, M: **K.4**: 81.
Pivnick, A: **F.3**: 60.
Plane, D: **F.1**: 65. **F.8**: 44.
Plasseraud, Y: **F.7**: 109.
Platonov, K: **C.2**: 216.
Platonov, S: **I.6**: 44.
Plato, von, A: **J.6**: 57.
Platteau, J: **H.2**: 8.
Pleck, J: **F.4**: 265. **F.6**: 32.

Plessix Gray, du, F: **F.5**: 308.
Pligt, van der, J: **F.6**: 14.
Pliner, P: **H.5**: 9.
Plomin, R: **F.1**: 40. **F.4**: 310.
Plunkett, K: **D.7**: 73.
Plutzer, E: **F.5**: 116.
PNUD: **F.1**: 71.
Podgórecki, A: **D.4**: 26. **E.1**: 23. **E.3**: 5.
Podgorelec, S: **F.8**: 31.
Podhorzer, M: **K.4**: 77.
Podus, D: **D.5**: 138.
Poe, N: **K.4**: 82.
Poggi, D: **F.5**: 165.
Pohoski, M: **E.2**: 36.
Poindexter, M: **D.7**: 380.
Poirine, B: **D.9**: 113.
Pokhlebkin, V: **I.6**: 19.
Pol'shchikov, P: **E.3**: 37.
Polan, S: **K.1**: 192.
Polek, D: **F.4**: 156.
Polinard, J: **F.8**: 61.
Polistina, A: **G.3.2**: 250, 288.
Polivy, J: **C.2**: 224.
Pollack, G: **F.4**: 8.
Pollack, N: **H.2**: 12.
Pollak, R: **F.1**: 67.
Pollak, T: **K.4**: 77.
Pollard, C: **D.7**: 206.
Pollard, J: **F.3**: 257, 277.
Pollert, A: **H.4**: 15. **I.2**: 18.
Pollin, R: **J.3**: 34.
Pollitt, P: **F.4**: 210.
Pollner, M: **D.1**: 29.
Polsky, A: **K.3**: 33.
Polvi, N: **K.3**: 29.
Pombeni, M: **C.3**: 29.
Pong, S: **D.9**: 38.
Pongrácz, T: **F.3**: 130.
Pongratz, H: **H.4**: 1.
Ponomarchuk, V: **I.6**: 43.
Poñtinen, S: **E.2**: 36.
Pookong, K: **F.7**: 26.
Poole, M: **F.2**: 152. **I.2**: 76.
Poole, R: **B.1**: 64.
Pope, K: **D.3**: 41.
Popenoe, D: **F.4**: 47.
Popkewitz, T: **D.9**: 46.

Popkin, S: **F.7**: 208. **K.1**: 290.
Popov, V: **E.1**: 6.
Popovic, A: **F.8**: 7.
Poppe, L: **C.3**: 153.
Poresh, V: **D.5**: 111.
Porritt, J: **G.1**: 37.
Porter, A: **K.1**: 46.
Porter, C: **D.7**: 258.
Porter, D: **C.2**: 120.
Porter, M: **F.5**: 39.
Porter, P: **I.6**: 32.
Porter, R: **D.9**: 14.
Porter, V: **D.7**: 300.
Portnov, B: **G.3.2**: 191.
Portugali, J: **F.7**: 140. **I.2**: 50.
Posch, P: **D.9**: 117.
Poser, W: **D.7**: 201.
Posner, T: **K.4**: 243.
Possen, U: **I.4**: 51.
Post, D: **D.9**: 38.
Post, S: **K.4**: 149.
Postiglione, G: **D.9**: 90.
Potas, I: **K.1**: 164.
Potkin, A: **G.1**: 41.
Potrykowska, A: **F.3**: 294.
Pott-Buter, H: **K.2**: 65.
Potter, G: **K.1**: 340.
Potter, R: **G.3.2**: 339.
Potter, W: **K.1**: 1.
Pottieger, A: **K.1**: 185.
Pottier, F: **D.9**: 181.
Potts, D: **G.3.2**: 113.
Potts, M: **F.3**: 54. **K.4**: 35.
Pouch, T: **D.9**: 181.
Poulain, M: **D.9**: 216.
Poulin, R: **C.3**: 132.
Powe, L: **D.7**: 255.
Powell, D: **K.1**: 21.
Powell, J: **C.3**: 50. **K.4**: 27.
Powell, R: **K.4**: 119.
Powell, T: **C.5**: 72.
Powell, W: **C.5**: 47.
Powell-Griner, E: **F.1**: 56. **F.3**: 38.
Power, J: **F.8**: 151.
Power, M: **C.1**: 99.
Powers, M: **F.3**: 53. **K.4**: 171.

Powers, R: **B.2**: 50.
Powlick, P: **J.6**: 2.
Poyner, B: **K.1**: 64.
Pozdnyakov, E: **J.8**: 8.
Pradeilles, J: **H.4**: 30.
Pradhan, P: **C.4**: 46.
Prahl, R: **B.2**: 67.
Prais, S: **D.9**: 167.
Prakash, C: **C.2**: 106.
Prašnikar, J: **I.5**: 204.
Pratkanis, A: **C.2**: 131.
Pratt, C: **F.4**: 283.
Pratt, G: **G.3.2**: 174. **I.2**: 48, 114.
Pratt, J: **D.4**: 6.
Pratto, F: **C.3**: 148. **C.7**: 67. **F.5**: 303. **F.7**: 222.
Prazauskas, A: **F.7**: 158.
Preble, E: **F.3**: 227.
Prechel, H: **C.5**: 36.
Prehn, O: **D.7**: 297.
Preisendörfer, P: **I.4**: 64.
Press, A: **D.7**: 327.
Press, S: **K.2**: 4.
Pressburger, T: **G.3.1**: 31.
Presser, S: **E.3**: 29.
Preston, S: **F.3**: 296.
Preston, V: **G.3.2**: 171. **I.2**: 1.
Preston-Shoot, M: **K.3**: 27.
Prétot, X: **D.4**: 16.
Prévost, C: **D.8**: 11.
Price, A: **F.5**: 216. **G.3.2**: 332.
Price, D: **K.1**: 374.
Price, M: **K.4**: 79.
Price, R: **I.2**: 235.
Priebe, S: **J.6**: 38.
Pries, L: **I.4**: 4.
Pringle, D: **F.3**: 298.
Prins, H: **C.1**: 105.
Prinsky, L: **D.8**: 53.
Prior, A: **K.1**: 24.
Prior, L: **C.1**: 35.
Prioux, F: **F.3**: 94.
Pritchard, C: **F.5**: 258.
Pritlove, J: **K.4**: 53.
Probst, S: **D.7**: 188.
Proctor, R: **B.1**: 79.
Pronovost, D: **J.4**: 13.
Prosch, B: **J.5**: 27.

Pross, H: **D.1**: 87.
Prothrow-Stith, D: **K.1**: 410.
Provan, K: **K.4**: 83.
Provasi, G: **I.5**: 51.
Provenzo, E: **I.6**: 42.
Provost, M: **F.4**: 169, 304.
Prue, K: **I.3**: 37.
Prus, R: **H.5**: 34.
Pryke, M: **G.3.2**: 193.
Pryor, F: **D.5**: 82.
Prysby, C: **J.1**: 14.
Przybyłowska, I: **D.9**: 220.
Puokott, T: **K.2**: 20.
Pütz, M: **D.7**: 42.
Puffer, S: **C.5**: 4. **H.4**: 65.
Pugh, J: **D.1**: 40.
Pujadas, I: **F.3**: 274.
Pujadas Munoz, J: **F.4**: 36. **F.8**: 17.
Pujal, M: **C.3**: 42.
Pulaska-Turyna, B: **F.3**: 263.
Pulkhritudova, E: **D.7**: 303.
Pullman, C: **I.3**: 87.
Pumberger, K: **I.5**: 118.
Punchanka, A: **B.1**: 76.
Purdue, M: **G.3.2**: 290.
Puskas, D: **K.4**: 71.
Pustejovsky, J: **D.7**: 210.
Puthran, K: **K.3**: 46.
Putman, D: **F.6**: 42.
Putz, B: **C.3**: 151.
Pye, J: **D.9**: 34.
Pyrgiotis, Y: **G.3.2**: 326.
Pyskoty, C: **K.1**: 363.
Quadagno, J: **K.2**: 28.
Quah, S: **E.2**: 78.
Quan, Z: **G.3.2**: 358.
Quataert, D: **D.1**: 44.
Quaye, R: **K.4**: 227.
Queloz, N: **F.3**: 196.
Quick, A: **K.4**: 160.
Quigley, J: **I.2**: 33.
Quine, S: **F.3**: 289.
Quinlan, P: **C.1**: 90.
Quinney, R: **K.1**: 72.
Quintrand, P: **G.3.2**: 49.
Qureshi, R: **D.5**: 168.

Qvortrup, L: **G.2**: 15. **G.3.1**: 100.
Rabban, D: **I.5**: 149.
Rabbie, J: **C.4**: 43.
Rabbitt, P: **C.2**: 154. **C.7**: 38.
Rabie, J: **G.3.2**: 78.
Rabier, J: **C.7**: 26.
Rabine, M: **K.1**: 392.
Rabinovich, V: **H.4**: 89.
Rabrenovic, G: **H.4**: 23.
Rabušic, L: **F.2**: 62.
Racine, G: **K.1**: 248.
Radaelli, G: **I.2**: 237.
Radley, A: **C.1**: 146, 155. **I.3**: 142.
Radtke, F: **F.8**: 106.
Raehlmann, I: **I.5**: 43.
Rafacz-Krzyżanowska, M: **I.3**: 116.
Rageau, J: **F.7**: 49.
Raghupathi, W: **C.2**: 147.
Ragin, C: **A.2**: 8.
Ragland, S: **F.8**: 147.
Rahardjo, S: **F.2**: 1.
Rahman, M: **B.2**: 1.
Rahman, S: **J.4**: 10.
Rahmato, D: **G.3.1**: 88.
Rain, J: **I.3**: 100.
Rains, P: **K.1**: 192, 214.
Rainville, M: **F.3**: 246.
Raisian, J: **H.3**: 74.
Raison, J: **G.3.1**: 13.
Raitasalo, R: **F.3**: 226. **I.3**: 122.
Rajagopal, A: **D.7**: 367.
Rajan, A: **F.1**: 21.
Rajan, L: **E.2**: 77.
Rajulton, F: **F.3**: 69. **F.8**: 30.
Rakhimov, R: **F.7**: 179.
Rakodi, C: **G.3.2**: 104, 244.
Rakow, L: **D.7**: 394.
Ralet, O: **K.1**: 335.
Rallo, J: **F.4**: 11.
Rallu, J: **F.1**: 22.
Ralston, H: **D.5**: 54.
Rambanapasi, C: **J.6**: 34.
Rambaud, P: **H.4**: 6.
Ramesh, C: **C.3**: 26.
Ramet, S: **J.6**: 46.
Ramkanth, J: **I.5**: 14.
Ramkhalawansingh, C: **I.4**: 72.

Ramon, S: **K.4**: 108.
Ramsbey, T: **I.2**: 80.
Ramsey, S: **C.7**: 24, 75.
Ramu, G: **F.4**: 330.
Randall, D: **I.3**: 39.
Randall, M: **F.5**: 134.
Ranger-Moore, J: **C.5**: 25.
Rani, G: **I.2**: 142.
Ranis, P: **E.2**: 82. **I.4**: 9.
Rank, M: **K.4**: 21.
Rankin, B: **G.3.1**: 39. **H.3**: 88.
Rankin, J: **F.4**: 41.
Rankin, S: **G.3.2**: 341.
Rannik, E: **H.2**: 2.
Rannut, M: **D.7**: 342.
Rantakallio, P: **K.1**: 331.
Rao, P: **I.5**: 16.
Rao, R: **I.5**: 16.
Rapaport, E: **K.1**: 3.
Rapoport, A: **C.1**: 106.
Rapoport, D: **D.5**: 68. **J.5**: 37.
Rapp, R: **F.5**: 113.
Rappelli, F: **I.2**: 23.
Rasegård, S: **C.5**: 11.
Rasinski, K: **C.2**: 62. **C.7**: 8.
Raskin, R: **C.2**: 192, 231.
Rasmussen, D: **K.1**: 138.
Raspe, P: **F.4**: 94.
Rassekh, S: **A.3**: 5.
Rathbun, P: **F.8**: 36.
Ratnam, S: **F.3**: 129.
Rattansi, A: **F.7**: 252.
Rattner, A: **F.7**: 63.
Rauch, J: **F.8**: 51.
Raum, O: **D.5**: 93.
Ravallion, M: **H.3**: 55. **K.1**: 249.
Raveau, F: **F.2**: 67.
Raviv, A: **C.1**: 124. **C.3**: 155.
Ravix, J: **C.5**: 62.
Ravizza, M: **D.3**: 19, 87.
Ravlin, E: **C.3**: 91.
Ray, B: **F.8**: 1.
Ray, D: **H.7**: 7.
Ray, J: **D.4**: 16.
Ray, K: **K.1**: 34.
Raymond, P: **C.3**: 89.

Rayside, D: **G.3.2**: 70.
Raza, B: **I.2**: 86.
Raza, M: **D.5**: 165.
Razack, S: **F.5**: 69.
Re, E: **J.2**: 7.
Read, J: **F.3**: 229. **K.2**: 65.
Read, M: **F.7**: 215.
Read, S: **C.2**: 103.
Reamer, F: **D.3**: 27.
Reardon, K: **C.1**: 118.
Reason, J: **C.1**: 133.
Rebach, H: **A.3**: 3.
Redclift, M: **D.2**: 21.
Reddington, K: **K.4**: 172.
Reddy, P: **F.4**: 334. **I.3**: 16.
Reddy, T: **D.7**: 124. **I.5**: 123, 170.
Redhead, S: **I.6**: 8. **K.1**: 426.
Reed, M: **B.1**: 116. **C.5**: 70.
Reed-Danahay, D: **D.1**: 3.
Reenen, van, L: **I.3**: 19.
Rees, C: **K.3**: 42.
Rees, D: **I.5**: 83.
Rees, M: **G.3.2**: 8, 200.
Rees, Van, W: **G.2**: 15. **G.3.2**: 53.
Reeves, B: **D.7**: 369. **K.4**: 11.
Regales, M: **F.3**: 17.
Regard, F: **D.8**: 14.
Réger, Z: **D.7**: 70.
Regin, C: **K.4**: 90.
Register, C: **D.9**: 110.
Regoli, B: **F.7**: 256.
Regt, de, W: **F.8**: 32.
Regulska, J: **G.3.2**: 174. **J.4**: 26.
Rehfeldt, R: **F.8**: 13.
Rehfeldt, U: **I.5**: 139.
Rehg, W: **D.3**: 68.
Reich, J: **F.2**: 15.
Reich, M: **I.5**: 193.
Reichardt, C: **B.2**: 18.
Reichert, E: **K.1**: 421.
Reichmann, S: **C.4**: 49. **I.2**: 232.
Reid, D: **C.3**: 32.
Reid, J: **F.3**: 208. **I.5**: 34.
Reid, K: **J.6**: 26.
Reid, N: **G.3.2**: 208.
Reif, K: **C.7**: 26.
Reilly, B: **F.1**: 42. **I.4**: 36.

Reimer, M: **B.2**: 37.
Reinarman, C: **K.1**: 324.
Reiner, R: **J.3**: 2.
Reis, F: **A.1**: 22.
Reis, H: **C.1**: 165. **C.2**: 200.
Reiser, M: **B.2**: 52, 54.
Reiss, A: **K.1**: 181.
Reiter, E: **D.2**: 15. **F.5**: 31.
Reiterer, A: **G.3.2**: 197.
Remele, K: **D.3**: 10.
Remes, P: **D.7**: 67.
Remondet, J: **I.3**: 41.
Remotti, F: **D.1**: 56.
Remus, W: **B.2**: 39.
Remy, P: **I.3**: 31.
Renaut, A: **C.1**: 153.
Renn, R: **I.3**: 101.
Renne, E: **D.1**: 48.
Rennie, S: **G.3.1**: 81. **H.4**: 45.
Rennolls, K: **B.2**: 125.
Rensburg, van, H: **K.4**: 89.
Renshaw, J: **K.4**: 184.
Rentao, H: **F.1**: 37.
Renwick, S: **K.1**: 139.
Repassy, H: **G.3.1**: 3, 81.
Replogle, R: **F.6**: 43.
Requena, F: **E.2**: 38.
Rerih, E: **C.3**: 66.
Resandt, van, A: **D.9**: 187.
Reshef, Y: **I.3**: 45. **I.5**: 90.
Resnick, S: **E.2**: 55.
Resnik, J: **D.4**: 42.
Ress, C: **D.7**: 319.
Retkiewicz, H: **I.2**: 238.
Rettig, K: **F.4**: 51.
Retzinger, S: **C.3**: 119. **F.4**: 257.
Revelle, C: **K.2**: 21.
Rey, J: **G.3.2**: 173.
Reyes, H: **K.4**: 45.
Reymond, H: **F.1**: 37.
Reynolds, G: **C.1**: 147.
Reynolds, R: **C.3**: 12.
Reynolds, S: **I.3**: 121.
Rezek, P: **C.2**: 74.
Reznik, S: **F.7**: 127.
Rezza, G: **K.1**: 380.

Rhiel, G: **I.2**: 10.
Rhoads, J: **B.1**: 94.
Rhode, D: **F.5**: 108.
Rhodes, W: **K.1**: 183, 186.
Rhodewalt, F: **C.2**: 237.
Riach, P: **I.2**: 41, 64.
Ribau, P: **F.7**: 133.
Ribbens, J: **F.5**: 203.
Ribeiro, M: **G.3.2**: 202.
Ricciardi, L: **I.2**: 227.
Riccucci, N: **I.6**: 24.
Rice, D: **K.4**: 250.
Rice, R: **C.2**: 211. **I.3**: 102.
Rich, E: **K.4**: 164.
Rich, J: **I.2**: 41, 64.
Richard, M: **F.7**: 80.
Richard, R: **F.2**: 132, 138. **F.6**: 14.
Richards, A: **C.1**: 52. **F.5**: 32.
Richards, E: **D.5**: 22. **I.5**: 133.
Richards, M: **F.4**: 120.
Richardson, B: **F.4**: 346.
Richardson, D: **D.3**: 39.
Richardson, J: **D.5**: 35.
Richardson, L: **B.1**: 22. **F.5**: 170.
Richardson, M: **D.9**: 161.
Richardson, S: **K.1**: 30.
Richardson, W: **J.4**: 2.
Richman, J: **K.1**: 363.
Richmond, C: **F.7**: 97.
Rickaby, P: **D.8**: 70. **G.3.2**: 258.
Ricks, C: **D.7**: 85.
Ridgeway, C: **D.1**: 127.
Rieber, R: **J.8**: 14.
Riecher, A: **F.3**: 169.
Rieder, I: **F.5**: 81.
Riefler, R: **G.3.2**: 323.
Riera, P: **H.7**: 18.
Rieske, B: **F.3**: 162.
Riger, A: **C.1**: 91.
Riger, S: **F.5**: 13.
Rigg, C: **F.5**: 244.
Riggle, E: **J.6**: 16.
Riggs, F: **F.7**: 75–76.
Rijnierse, P: **C.1**: 5.
Rijsselt, van, R: **F.2**: 6.
Riles, A: **F.4**: 250.
Riley, G: **B.2**: 59. **F.4**: 125.

Riley, J: **F.3**: 284.
Rimashevskay a, N: **F.5**: 261.
Rimé, B: **D.7**: 147.
Rimmer, P: **E.1**: 24.
Rindfleisch, N: **K.1**: 25.
Rindfuss, R: **F.4**: 306.
Rink, D: **E.3**: 39.
Ritchey, F: **C.3**: 37.
Ritchie, L: **D.7**: 152.
Rittenhouse, C: **K.1**: 4.
Ritter, G: **E.3**: 34.
Ritter, J: **F.2**: 70. **F.3**: 12.
Ritti, R: **K.1**: 123.
Ritzer, G: **B.1**: 120, 131.
Ritzmann, R: **C.1**: 30.
Rivas, D: **K.4**: 184.
Riveline, C: **H.4**: 18, 32.
Rivera, E: **G.3.2**: 189.
Rivero, J: **F.5**: 305.
Rivero H., J: **D.9**: 5.
Rix, B: **K.4**: 255, 267.
Rizakou, E: **K.4**: 172.
Rizzo, N: **K.1**: 50.
Rizzuto, A: **C.1**: 54–55.
Roach, D: **K.4**: 52.
Robb, P: **D.5**: 169.
Robbins, A: **C.2**: 209. **F.6**: 50.
Robbins, B: **D.1**: 89. **J.6**: 48.
Robbins, T: **D.5**: 73.
Róbert, P: **D.9**: 91. **E.2**: 23. **K.1**: 149.
Roberts, A: **D.7**: 343. **K.1**: 76.
Roberts, D: **K.1**: 375.
Roberts, E: **K.1**: 151.
Roberts, H: **F.5**: 58.
Roberts, J: **D.7**: 359. **K.1**: 151.
Roberts, R: **C.2**: 109. **D.8**: 37. **F.4**: 68.
Roberts, S: **G.3.2**: 18. **H.5**: 33.
Robertson, A: **F.4**: 9. **K.2**: 80.
Robertson, E: **K.2**: 75.
Robertson, I: **I.1**: 15. **I.3**: 138.
Robertson, J: **F.5**: 11. **G.3.2**: 282.
Robertson, K: **G.3.2**: 287.
Robertson, M: **G.3.2**: 108, 132. **K.1**: 356.
Robertson, R: **B.1**: 145. **D.5**: 73.
Robertson, T: **H.5**: 23.
Robertson, W: **G.3.2**: 122.

Robins, D: **K.1**: 406.
Robins, K: **G.3.2**: 62. **J.7**: 11.
Robinson, A: **C.2**: 199.
Robinson, C: **K.4**: 115.
Robinson, D: **D.8**: 36. **K.4**: 210.
Robinson, J: **C.2**: 189. **C.7**: 5. **F.5**: 169. **H.4**: 62. **I.2**: 121.
Robinson, O: **I.2**: 34.
Robinson, P: **I.2**: 245.
Robinson, R: **F.5**: 205. **K.4**: 203.
Robinson, W: **D.9**: 135.
Robson, S: **D.3**: 42.
Roca, J: **I.5**: 79.
Rocha, da, M: **F.3**: 56.
Roche, W: **C.5**: 83.
Rochford, E: **C.7**: 22.
Rockart, J: **D.7**: 10.
Rockel, M: **I.6**: 28.
Rockoff, H: **H.1**: 4.
Rodda, A: **G.1**: 48.
Rodeghier, M: **D.9**: 120.
Rodeheaver, D: **K.1**: 130.
Rodenstein, M: **G.3.2**: 267.
Rodger, J: **F.4**: 339. **K.3**: 10.
Rodgers, J: **F.4**: 232. **F.6**: 13. **K.1**: 229, 250.
Rodgers, R: **F.4**: 332. **H.4**: 20.
Rodgers, W: **D.4**: 3, 23. **H.6**: 5.
Rodgerson, G: **F.5**: 114.
Rodin, J: **C.2**: 233. **F.3**: 71.
Rodriguez, C: **I.2**: 178.
Rodríguez, R: **H.4**: 72.
Rodríguez Pastor, H: **F.7**: 35.
Rodríguez-Bachiller, A: **G.3.2**: 236.
Roeder, H: **D.7**: 321.
Roegge, C: **C.2**: 144.
Roehner, B: **G.3.2**: 45.
Roelandt, T: **F.7**: 1, 237.
Roemer, J: **C.3**: 49.
Roemer, M: **K.4**: 224.
Roess, A: **A.2**: 20.
Rogan, R: **C.3**: 111.
Rogers, A: **F.1**: 7.
Rogers, R: **D.5**: 138. **F.7**: 190. **K.1**: 330.
Rogers, S: **F.5**: 256. **G.3.1**: 131. **I.5**: 93.
Rogers, T: **F.3**: 210.
Rogerson, C: **G.3.2**: 362.
Rogerson, P: **F.1**: 65.

Roggenbuck, J: **I.6**: 17.
Roggeveen, J: **C.2**: 176.
Rogler, L: **C.1**: 75.
Rohe, W: **K.2**: 5.
Rohner, R: **F.2**: 84.
Rohrschneider, R: **J.5**: 24.
Roio, del, J: **E.2**: 81.
Rokicka, E: **J.6**: 41.
Rolandelli, D: **F.5**: 285.
Roll, J: **K.2**: 109.
Rollinson, P: **F.2**: 64.
Rollinson, T: **I.4**: 3.
Roloff, J. **F.3**. 5.
Rolston, B: **D.8**: 44.
Romanczyk, A: **C.2**: 158.
Romann, M: **F.7**: 180.
Rombauts, J: **C.1**: 11.
Romein, A: **G.3.2**: 29.
Romelsjö, A: **K.1**: 307, 378.
Romm, N: **J.2**: 14.
Romo, I: **F.3**: 154, 219.
Rondinelli, D: **G.3.2**: 233.
Rong, M: **G.3.2**: 255.
Rønningen, M: **G.3.1**: 116–117.
Rood, S: **F.7**: 95.
Rook, K: **F.4**: 252.
Room, G: **K.2**: 96.
Room, R: **C.1**: 161.
Root, B: **F.8**: 18.
Rootes, C: **J.5**: 11.
Rooum, D: **K.4**: 225.
Ropers, R: **K.1**: 259.
Rorty, A: **D.3**: 72.
Rosa, K: **F.5**: 231.
Rose, D: **D.1**: 106. **G.3.2**: 174. **K.2**: 35.
Rose, H: **E.2**: 62. **F.3**: 112.
Rose, L: **G.3.1**: 120.
Rose, M: **D.1**: 122.
Rose, W: **K.2**: 58.
Rosén, B: **K.1**: 393.
Rosen, D: **C.1**: 98.
Rosen, H: **I.2**: 190.
Rosen, L: **B.1**: 109.
Rosen, M: **C.5**: 7. **K.1**: 393.
Rosenbaum, J: **D.8**: 53. **F.7**: 208. **K.1**: 290.
Rosenbaum, M: **F.2**: 108.

Rosenbaum, S: **D.3**: 63. **F.6**: 36.
Rosenberg, A: **K.1**: 239.
Rosenberg, D: **F.5**: 225.
Rosenberg, E: **F.2**: 73. **F.4**: 289.
Rosenberger, N: **F.5**: 11.
Rosenblatt, A: **K.4**: 31.
Rosenfeld, R: **F.5**: 70. **K.1**: 211.
Rosenhead, J: **K.4**: 172.
Rosenstein, C: **F.8**: 122.
Rosenthal, D: **C.7**: 3. **F.3**: 219. **F.6**: 1.
Rosenthal, G: **D.1**: 114. **I.1**: 10.
Rosenthal, R: **G.3.2**: 108, 160.
Rosenwaike, I: **F.3**: 278.
Rosenzweig, M: **K.4**: 104.
Roser, C: **D.7**: 270. **F.8**: 129.
Rosler, M: **G.3.2**: 40.
Rosner, M: **C.1**: 143. **I.4**: 57.
Rosnow, R: **D.7**: 153.
Ross, A: **D.6**: 28.
Ross, C: **F.4**: 221.
Ross, J: **F.3**: 43.
Ross, L: **C.1**: 162. **C.3**: 105.
Ross, M: **F.7**: 206.
Rosser, S: **F.5**: 76.
Rostocki, W: **B.2**: 122.
Rotania, A: **I.3**: 88.
Rotenberg, K: **C.3**: 14.
Roth, N: **I.2**: 38.
Roth, P: **C.1**: 62.
Roth, R: **D.7**: 111.
Rothberg, J: **J.7**: 21.
Rothenberg, J: **G.3.2**: 137.
Rotheram-Borus, M: **K.1**: 401.
Rothgeb, J: **B.2**: 125.
Rothstein, A: **C.1**: 39.
Rotschild-Souriac, M: **I.5**: 98.
Rottenburg, R: **I.3**: 81.
Rouault-Galdo, D: **I.2**: 38.
Rouban, L: **H.4**: 18.
Roumani, M: **J.7**: 9.
Rounsaville, B: **K.1**: 323.
Rouquette, M: **G.3.2**: 25.
Rouse, J: **D.6**: 20.
Rousseau, M: **G.2**: 11.
Roussillon, A: **A.1**: 33.
Roussou, M: **D.7**: 63.
Routh, D: **H.6**: 2.

Roux, J: **K.4**: 55.
Roux, M: **F.3**: 85.
Roux, P: **C.4**: 31.
Roversi, A: **I.6**: 36.
Rovine, M: **F.4**: 314.
Rowe, D: **D.7**: 324. **F.6**: 13.
Rowe, J: **K.2**: 58.
Rowe, W: **D.3**: 20, 87.
Rowland, D: **F.4**: 49. **K.4**: 139.
Rowland, N: **K.1**: 359.
Rowland-Serdar, B: **F.5**: 159.
Roxborough, I: **H.3**: 29.
Roy, C: **F.5**: 299. **I.4**: 93.
Roy, D: **D.6**: 3.
Roy, O: **D.5**: 173. **F.7**: 17, 73. **G.3.2**: 188.
Roy, P: **I.2**: 241.
Roy, R: **C.7**: 19.
Royo, E: **G.3.2**: 250.
Royster, D: **D.9**: 168.
Rozenblat, C: **G.3.2**: 21.
Rozenblatt, P: **I.5**: 23.
Ruan, D: **C.3**: 47.
Ruback, R: **C.1**: 14.
Rubellin-Devichi, J: **F.2**: 90.
Rubin, B: **I.5**: 92. **J.6**: 8.
Rubin, D: **D.5**: 13.
Rubin, J: **H.4**: 9.
Rubini, M: **C.3**: 42.
Rubinstein, R: **F.2**: 45.
Rubiostipec, M: **C.1**: 66.
Ruby, C: **K.1**: 213.
Ruccio, D: **B.1**: 61. **E.2**: 55.
Rucht, D: **E.3**: 51.
Rucker, R: **D.9**: 102.
Rudas, T: **E.2**: 23.
Rudder, De, V: **D.1**: 18. **F.7**: 201.
Rude, D: **D.4**: 24.
Rude-Antoine, E: **F.4**: 229.
Rudin, C: **D.7**: 193.
Rudley, D: **I.5**: 39.
Rudzitis, G: **F.8**: 41.
Rueschemeyer, D: **A.2**: 8. **B.2**: 4.
Ruether, R: **D.5**: 88.
Ruf, B: **I.4**: 71.
Ruggeri, F: **C.5**: 23.
Ruggiero, V: **K.1**: 187.

Rugo, L: **I.4**: 46.
Ruhm, C: **I.2**: 4.
Ruiz, L: **G.3.1**: 93.
Rukmana, N: **G.3.2**: 256, 325.
Rul-Lan Buades, G: **J.8**: 9.
Ruland, L: **I.2**: 189.
Rumberger, R: **I.4**: 25.
Rumiantsev, M: **F.7**: 187.
Rummery, S: **F.5**: 201.
Runciman, W: **C.7**: 7. **I.5**: 144.
Rusbult, C: **C.3**: 1.
Rusin, J: **F.7**: 208. **K.1**: 290.
Rusonik, A: **I.5**: 121.
Russbach, R: **K.4**: 45.
Russell, A: **I.3**: 109.
Russell, D: **K.1**: 135.
Russell, J: **C.3**: 128. **D.7**: 13. **F.7**: 195. **G.3.2**: 315.
Russell, M: **K.1**: 376.
Russell, P: **C.7**: 25.
Russo, A: **F.5**: 130.
Russo, C: **I.5**: 63.
Russon, A: **C.3**: 59.
Rustin, M: **C.1**: 21.
Rutheiser, C: **D.9**: 111.
Rutkevich, M: **F.1**: 41.
Rutledge, L: **F.4**: 156.
Rutten, P: **D.8**: 31.
Rutter, C: **F.3**: 220.
Rutter, F: **K.3**: 19.
Ryan, C: **C.4**: 1. **D.7**: 276. **I.6**: 31.
Ryan, E: **D.7**: 77.
Ryan, G: **K.1**: 100.
Ryan, J: **D.8**: 393. **F.7**: 48. **J.4**: 8.
Ryan, M: **F.4**: 192. **K.4**: 228.
Ryan, P: **I.4**: 121.
Rybczynski, W: **I.6**: 45.
Rychard, A: **E.2**: 29, 47.
Rychtarikova, J: **D.1**: 55. **F.3**: 248.
Rynes, S: **I.3**: 18.
Ryn, van, M: **I.2**: 235.
Ryu, S: **I.4**: 55.
Rzepka, D: **K.1**: 198.
Rzepnicki, T: **K.3**: 13.
Saar, E: **F.2**: 136.
Saari, D: **C.7**: 56.
Saayman, G: **G.3.2**: 365.
Saba, R: **I.3**: 78.

Sabatier, C: **F.4**: 322.
Sabbagh, D: **K.1**: 157.
Sacco, W: **C.1**: 97.
Sachdev, I: **C.4**: 44.
Sachs, C: **F.5**: 61. **G.3.1**: 81. **H.4**: 44.
Sackmann, S: **C.5**: 17.
Sacks, J: **D.5**: 30.
Sadik, N: **F.3**: 312.
Saenz, R: **F.8**: 95, 123. **G.3.1**: 39. **K.1**: 251.
Safi, L: **J.3**: 12.
Sag, I: **D.7**: 206.
Sagar, P: **D.9**: 29.
Sagaza, H: **F.2**: 56.
Saghal, G: **D.1**: 22.
Saglio, J: **H.3**: 1.
Sah, R: **F.4**: 33.
Sahner, H: **A.1**: 26.
Sahu, P: **F.3**: 256.
Sainsbury, E: **K.3**: 17.
Saint-Germain, M: **H.3**: 63. **J.5**: 35.
Sainz, J: **I.2**: 16.
Saito, M: **F.3**: 22.
Saito, Y: **F.2**: 140.
Sakamoto, A: **I.2**: 29.
Sakamoto, K: **F.4**: 69.
Sakdisubha, K: **D.7**: 123.
Sakurai, T: **E.3**: 13.
Salaman, G: **I.3**: 136.
Salami, L: **D.7**: 14.
Salamon, L: **K.1**: 235.
Salas, E: **C.4**: 25. **D.7**: 139. **I.4**: 125.
Salau, A: **G.3.2**: 163, 339.
Saldaña, E: **D.7**: 192.
Salecl, R: **J.2**: 6, 18.
Salem, D: **K.1**: 243.
Salim, Z: **F.5**: 241.
Saller, R: **F.4**: 50.
Salles, V: **J.2**: 22.
Sallez, A: **G.3.2**: 326.
Salmaso, S: **K.1**: 380.
Salmen, L: **K.1**: 246, 276.
Salo, M: **G.3.2**: 107–108.
Salole, G: **G.3.1**: 118.
Salovey, P: **C.2**: 233.
Salt, H: **F.3**: 228.
Salt, J: **F.3**: 1.

Salt, R: **F.4**: 266.
Saltman, J: **G.3.2**: 167, 198.
Saltman, M: **D.4**: 13.
Saltman, R: **K.4**: 192.
Salutskii, A: **G.3.1**: 89.
Salvatore, D: **D.3**: 37.
Salzberg, A: **F.3**: 201.
Salzberg, C: **F.3**: 201.
Salzer, M: **B.2**: 37.
Samar, V: **F.6**: 40.
Sampson, E: **C.1**: 171.
Sampson, R: **G.2**: 24. **K.1**: 425.
Samuel, T: **K.1**: 58.
San Juan, C: **F.3**: 154.
Sanches, J: **D.7**: 350.
Sánchez Tostado, L: **K.1**: 388.
Sanchez-Mazas, M: **C.4**: 31.
Sandberg, A: **I.5**: 184.
Sandelands, L: **I.3**: 15.
Sanders, A: **D.4**: 4.
Sanders, J: **K.1**: 254, 275.
Sanders, W: **K.2**: 73.
Sandidge, R: **D.9**: 70, 80.
Sandler, I: **J.8**: 20.
Sandler, J: **C.1**: 3. **D.9**: 70, 149.
Sandomirsky, S: **D.5**: 50.
Sandoval, S: **I.2**: 42.
Sandvik, E: **C.2**: 36, 89.
Sandy, R: **F.2**: 91.
Sang, D: **F.8**: 112.
Sanjian, A: **F.4**: 143.
Sankar, Y: **D.3**: 24.
Sant, M: **G.3.2**: 309.
Santalainen, T: **H.6**: 7.
Santamaria, U: **B.1**: 24. **D.1**: 18.
Santana, S: **F.3**: 183.
Santero, T: **I.2**: 108.
Santi, L: **B.2**: 64.
Santiago, A: **E.2**: 62. **H.3**: 26. **K.1**: 290.
Santo-Martino, R: **A.1**: 33.
Santoro, E: **C.2**: 72.
Santos, S: **F.7**: 172.
Santow, G: **F.3**: 99.
Sapper, S: **I.5**: 135.
Sapunov, M: **C.3**: 56.
Saraceno, C: **E.3**: 7.
Sarason, B: **C.1**: 152. **C.3**: 153.

Sarason, I: **C.1**: 152. **C.3**: 153. **J.8**: 20.
Sarcinelli, F: **A.1**: 9.
Sardon, J: **F.4**: 193.
Sargant, N: **D.9**: 128.
Saroja, K: **F.5**: 194.
Sarris, A: **G.3.1**: 108.
Sarup, M: **F.7**: 230.
Sasaki, M: **C.7**: 73.
Sasse, H: **K.1**: 380.
Sasseville, T: **F.4**: 284.
Sastry, N: **I.3**: 135.
Sathananthan, S: **G.3.1**: 128.
Sathar, Z: **F.3**: 241.
Satō, I: **C.4**: 33.
Sattler, D: **C.3**: 102.
Satzewich, V: **F.7**: 254.
Saudagaran, S: **I.4**: 80.
Saulniers, S: **G.3.1**: 74.
Saunders, B: **K.1**: 306.
Saunders, M: **D.9**: 200.
Saurman, D: **I.3**: 78.
Sautoy, Du, T: **G.3.2**: 303.
Savage, M: **G.3**: 6. **J.6**: 63.
Savatier, J: **I.2**: 21, 37.
Savchenko, V: **K.1**: 1.
Savola, K: **F.2**: 10.
Savouri, S: **F.8**: 103.
Sawicki, J: **F.5**: 74.
Sawinski, Z: **E.3**: 74.
Sawińskim, Z: **I.4**: 14.
Sax, W: **D.5**: 157.
Saxe, L: **C.1**: 159. **K.4**: 48.
Saxton, M: **I.3**: 3.
Sayad, A: **F.8**: 60.
Sayeed, O: **H.4**: 22.
Sayer, A: **G.1**: 51.
Sayer, J: **K.3**: 7.
Sayers, S: **C.3**: 144.
Scanlan, J: **B.2**: 65.
Scargill, D: **H.3**: 44.
Scarpaci, J: **K.4**: 78.
Scarr, D: **J.7**: 10.
Scase, R: **I.2**: 215.
Scattergood, H: **H.4**: 90.
Schaafstal, A: **C.2**: 165.
Schadewald, M: **C.7**: 5.

Schaefer, C: **D.5**: 33.
Schaeffer, N: **B.2**: 21. **K.2**: 50.
Schafer, W: **F.4**: 271.
Schaffer, R: **K.4**: 39.
Schaller, M: **C.3**: 132. **C.4**: 55.
Schampers, T: **F.8**: 145.
Schatzer, P: **F.8**: 162.
Schatzki, T: **G.1**: 35.
Schaubroeck, J: **C.2**: 195. **C.4**: 4.
Schaufeli, W: **C.2**: 215.
Schedler, A: **H.3**: 56.
Scheepers, P: **I.2**: 225.
Scheer, M: **D.7**: 105.
Scheid-Cook, T: **K.4**: 69.
Schein, R: **G.3.2**: 87.
Schell, L: **G.3.2**: 39.
Schellekens, J: **F.3**: 138.
Schellenbach, C: **C.3**: 40.
Scheller, G: **F.4**: 147.
Schensul, J: **K.1**: 367.
Scher, I: **F.3**: 228.
Scherer, H: **D.7**: 302.
Scherer, K: **C.2**: 99.
Scherr, A: **F.7**: 82.
Schettkat, R: **I.3**: 13.
Schienstock, G: **I.4**: 76.
Schierup, C: **F.7**: 191.
Schie, Van, E: **C.7**: 15.
Schiffer, J: **G.3.2**: 366. **H.7**: 25.
Schiffer, M: **D.7**: 304.
Schiller, B: **J.7**: 6.
Schilling, E: **C.2**: 200, 203.
Schilling, G: **K.4**: 257.
Schillinger, E: **D.7**: 258.
Schippers, J: **I.2**: 35.
Schkade, L: **C.2**: 147.
Schlaffer, E: **F.5**: 54, 148.
Schlemmer, L: **J.3**: 4.
Schlenker, B: **C.2**: 235.
Schlesinger, P: **D.7**: 285–286. **K.1**: 106.
Schlossman, S: **K.1**: 192.
Schlottmann, A: **F.8**: 44.
Schmähl, W: **K.2**: 9, 27.
Schmalhofer, F: **C.2**: 24.
Schmelz, U: **F.7**: 159.
Schmidt, B: **I.2**: 203.
Schmidt, E: **F.5**: 326.

Schmidt, H: **D.7**: 319.
Schmool, M: **F.4**: 253. **F.7**: 119.
Schnabel, C: **I.5**: 130, 183.
Schnake, M: **J.3**: 18.
Schnapper, D: **E.1**: 7. **K.1**: 228.
Schneider, B: **I.3**: 66.
Schneider, C: **J.5**: 16.
Schneider, D: **D.9**: 208.
Schneider, H: **K.1**: 67.
Schneider, M: **C.1**: 148.
Schnelderman, H: **J.3**: 11.
Schnell, R: **B.2**: 102, 131.
Schoenberg, R: **B.2**: 54.
Schoenberger, E: **B.2**: 98.
Schoenberger, R: **H.3**: 71.
Schoenfeld, E: **D.5**: 79.
Schoepfle, O: **D.9**: 131.
Schofer, S: **D.7**: 92.
Scholl, R: **I.5**: 138.
Schollaert, P: **F.3**: 87.
Scholtens, A: **D.7**: 167.
Scholz, J: **D.4**: 1.
Schönherr, U: **D.8**: 1.
Schöpflin, G: **D.1**: 84.
Schopp, R: **D.4**: 2.
Schott, R: **C.2**: 111.
Schram, A: **D.1**: 51.
Schroder, B: **A.2**: 6.
Schroeder, R: **B.1**: 66.
Schryver, de, A: **F.3**: 215.
Schubarth, W: **F.7**: 219.
Schudson, M: **D.1**: 35.
Schuessler, K: **B.2**: 19, 52.
Schuh, R: **K.4**: 26, 29.
Schuller, A: **K.4**: 38.
Schuller, R: **F.2**: 27.
Schuller, T: **D.9**: 185. **F.2**: 50. **I.2**: 135.
Schulman, M: **G.3.1**: 20. **H.3**: 38.
Schultz, C: **F.4**: 22.
Schultz, N: **F.4**: 22.
Schultz, T: **K.4**: 104.
Schultze, G: **F.8**: 66.
Schultze, Q: **D.5**: 152.
Schulz, J: **F.2**: 43.
Schulz, W: **D.7**: 302.
Schumaker, J: **C.2**: 43.

Schuman, H: **B.2**: 111, 117.
Schunicht, C: **D.7**: 319.
Schupp, J: **H.3**: 3.
Schupp, R: **I.5**: 194.
Schusterman, R: **G.2**: 2.
Schuurman, J: **G.3.2**: 29.
Schwalbe, M: **C.2**: 222.
Schwarcz, V: **F.7**: 99.
Schwartz, B: **E.3**: 58.
Schwartz, I: **K.1**: 75.
Schwartz, J: **J.7**: 13.
Schwartz, M: **K.1**: 54, 101.
Schwartz-Shea, P: **F.5**: 159.
Schwartzberg, S: **C.2**: 39.
Schwartzman, S: **A.1**: 3.
Schwarz, N: **D.7**: 119–120, 176.
Schwarze, J: **H.3**: 75.
Schweiger, A: **K.1**: 361.
Scimecca, J: **C.3**: 109.
Scognamiglio, G: **F.5**: 111.
Scott, A: **B.1**: 83. **G.3.2**: 1.
Scott, D: **H.7**: 22.
Scott, J: **B.2**: 75, 117. **D.1**: 112.
Scott, R: **C.2**: 185.
Scott, W: **C.2**: 185. **F.7**: 16.
Scott-Jones, D: **D.9**: 168. **F.3**: 73.
Scratchley, L: **C.2**: 117.
Scribner, J: **D.9**: 62.
Scutt, J: **F.3**: 108. **F.5**: 50, 272.
Searle, C: **D.9**: 85. **J.5**: 18.
Searle, J: **B.1**: 10.
Searle, S: **I.2**: 133.
Searles, P: **D.4**: 39. **F.5**: 84.
Sears, A: **K.4**: 169.
Sears, J: **F.6**: 17.
Seat, L: **D.5**: 23.
Sebba, R: **F.2**: 96.
Seccombe, K: **F.4**: 220, 270.
Seck, M: **F.3**: 177.
Sedikides, C: **C.3**: 160.
Sedlak, A: **F.4**: 1.
See, K: **K.1**: 290.
Seekings, J: **F.5**: 282.
Segal, L: **F.5**: 124.
Segal, U: **K.1**: 28.
Segall, A: **F.5**: 173.
Segar, J: **H.3**: 30.

Seger, M: **G.3.2**: 74.
Séguin, L: **C.1**: 95.
Seidler, V: **F.5**: 118, 262.
Seidman, S: **B.1**: 22.
Seifert, H: **I.3**: 30.
Seifert-Vogt, H: **F.8**: 139.
Seitchik, A: **I.4**: 53.
Sekaran, U: **I.2**: 149.
Seki, K: **F.4**: 105.
Sela-Amit, M: **K.1**: 63.
Selanio, V: **E.2**: 24.
Selby, H: **G.3.2**: 8, 54.
Selden, M: **G.3.1**: 6.
Seligman, A: **D.5**: 138.
Seligman, C: **G.2**: 16.
Seligson, M: **K.2**: 56, 65.
Sélim, M: **H.4**: 61.
Selman, P: **H.7**: 10.
Seltzer, J: **B.2**: 21. **F.4**: 75, 188, 323. **K.2**: 50.
Selvanathan, E: **H.5**: 17.
Selvini, M: **F.4**: 38.
Selz, K: **C.7**: 80.
Semi, E: **F.7**: 6.
Semprini, A: **D.7**: 72.
Semyonov, M: **I.2**: 144, 173.
Sen, A: **C.1**: 78. **F.1**: 54. **K.1**: 7.
Senauer, B: **F.2**: 86.
Senchuk, D: **C.2**: 15.
Seneca, J: **H.4**: 9.
Sephton, P: **I.5**: 132.
Sepstrup, P: **D.7**: 389.
Serbin, A: **F.7**: 214.
Sered, S: **F.5**: 4.
Seremetakis, C: **D.2**: 14.
Sergeev, V: **F.7**: 158.
Sergeyev, A: **D.1**: 21.
Seron, X: **C.2**: 25.
Serow, W: **F.3**: 15, 100. **F.8**: 102.
Servaes, J: **D.7**: 251.
Servais, J: **I.5**: 102.
Serwański, J: **D.7**: 106.
Sessa, V: **I.3**: 80.
Sessar, K: **K.1**: 78.
Sestito, P: **H.7**: 27.
Setbon, G: **K.4**: 235.
Sethi, P: **K.4**: 98.

Seubert, V: **A.1**: 36.
Sev'er, A: **C.4**: 63.
Sevenhuijsen, S: **F.5**: 161.
Sexton, T: **F.2**: 11.
Seymour-Smith, C: **F.5**: 322.
Seymour-Ure, C: **D.7**: 236.
Sgall, P: **D.7**: 205.
Shabbir, T: **D.9**: 35.
Shackleton, V: **I.3**: 140.
Shadish, W: **B.2**: 9.
Shafer, B: **D.1**: 112. **F.7**: 94.
Shaffir, W: **B.2**: 103.
Shafiqul Islam, S: **F.3**: 122.
Shah, M: **I.2**: 74.
Shah, N: **F.8**: 79. **I.2**: 74.
Shakhnazarov, G: **J.2**: 23.
Shakir, A: **D.6**: 1.
Shalaby, M: **G.3.1**: 27.
Shamai, S: **I.4**: 20.
Shamir, B: **C.5**: 43.
Shamir, R: **J.3**: 16.
Shams, H: **G.3.1**: 108.
Shamshurin, V: **B.1**: 149.
Shan, F: **F.1**: 36.
Shanahan, J: **D.7**: 270, 326, 382.
Shanahan, M: **I.4**: 55.
Shankari, U: **E.3**: 28.
Shanmugaratnam, N: **G.1**: 12.
Shannon, L: **C.2**: 164. **K.1**: 60.
Shaojie, S: **C.1**: 10.
Shapiro, D: **C.5**: 77. **D.3**: 6. **I.3**: 121.
Shapiro, E: **C.1**: 158.
Shapiro, J: **F.2**: 110.
Shapiro, P: **C.4**: 16.
Sharbatoghlie, A: **G.3.2**: 361.
Sharda, R: **J.4**: 17.
Sharma, A: **C.5**: 77.
Sharma, B: **I.4**: 79. **I.5**: 132.
Sharma, M: **G.3.1**: 81, 122.
Sharma, S: **E.3**: 63. **F.7**: 122.
Sharot, S: **D.5**: 183.
Sharp, W: **C.4**: 37.
Sharpley, D: **I.3**: 138.
Shavelson, R: **B.2**: 10.
Shaver, F: **G.3.1**: 81. **H.4**: 55.
Shaver, P: **C.2**: 189.
Shavit, Y: **F.4**: 142.

Shavitt, S: **J.6**: 16.
Shaw, D: **G.3.1**: 124.
Shaw, J: **I.5**: 56.
Shaw, R: **F.4**: 319.
Shaw, W: **D.9**: 12.
Shea, C: **C.3**: 132.
Shearin, E: **C.3**: 153.
Shearing, C: **D.1**: 15.
Shechter, M: **G.1**: 46.
Shedlin, M: **F.3**: 54.
Sheehan, J: **E.3**: 3.
Sheehan, M: **F.4**: 183.
Sheehan, P: **C.2**: 81.
Sheeran, P: **C.3**: 78.
Shehadi, N: **E.1**: 21.
Shehan, C: **F.4**: 220.
Shelden, R: **K.1**: 171.
Sheldon, K: **F.5**: 36.
Shell, R: **C.3**: 132.
Shelton, B: **I.2**: 181.
Shemmings, D: **K.3**: 5.
Shen, J: **F.1**: 5.
Shenhav, Y: **I.4**: 73.
Shepherd, J: **C.3**: 149. **K.2**: 32.
Shepherd, R: **C.7**: 28.
Sheppard, M: **K.4**: 36, 124.
Shepperd, J: **C.2**: 7. **F.2**: 143.
Sheptycki, J: **K.1**: 418.
Sher, K: **F.2**: 79.
Sherkat, D: **D.5**: 31.
Sherman, B: **F.3**: 126.
Sherman, S: **C.2**: 32.
Shermukhamedova, S: **A.1**: 21.
Sherry, D: **D.6**: 16.
Sherwin, B: **D.5**: 182.
Sherwood, D: **G.1**: 21.
Sherwood, K: **F.3**: 15. **G.3**: 1.
Sheshinski, E: **K.4**: 196.
Shewan, D: **D.9**: 163.
Shibley, M: **D.5**: 46, 150.
Shibuya, K: **F.5**: 185.
Shields, M: **F.3**: 64.
Shigehisa, T: **F.2**: 102.
Shihadeh, E: **F.4**: 87.
Shilhav, Y: **D.7**: 28.
Shilling, C: **E.2**: 8.

Shils, E: **D.1**: 47.
Shim, S: **H.5**: 35.
Shimada, H: **H.4**: 67.
Shimizu, M: **H.4**: 53.
Shimizu, S: **K.1**: 355.
Shimoda, N: **J.3**: 10.
Shinn, M: **C.3**: 79.
Shiobara, T: **E.3**: 60.
Shionoya, Y: **H.1**: 5.
Shiose, Y: **D.9**: 126. **F.2**: 132.
Shipper, F: **I.3**: 141.
Shirakura, Y: **E.1**: 10.
Shirom, A: **I.3**: 51.
Shkondin, M: **D.7**: 328.
Shlapentokh, V: **F.4**: 106.
Shmeleva, M: **G.3.2**: 93.
Shogren, J: **D.4**: 17.
Shoji, K: **E.3**: 53.
Shooter, G: **C.1**: 9.
Shore, E: **K.1**: 326.
Shore, L: **C.5**: 14. **I.3**: 25.
Shortall, S: **G.3.1**: 10.
Shover, N: **K.1**: 57.
Shriver, D: **H.4**: 63.
Shrum, W: **D.8**: 9.
Shubik, M: **H.4**: 97.
Shughart, W: **H.4**: 52.
Shukla, V: **G.3.2**: 187, 240, 349.
Shumway, J: **G.3.2**: 181.
Sibanda, P: **C.2**: 118.
Sibayan, B: **D.7**: 38, 79.
Sibeon, R: **K.3**: 45.
Sicherman, N: **I.2**: 49.
Sickles, R: **F.3**: 238.
Sidabutar, P: **G.3.2**: 256, 325.
Sidanius, J: **F.5**: 303. **F.7**: 222.
Siddharthan, K: **K.4**: 28.
Siddiqui, H: **K.2**: 99.
Siebentritt, G: **G.3.1**: 49.
Sieber, J: **A.3**: 6. **F.2**: 17.
Siedhoff, M: **F.8**: 175.
Siefert, M: **D.1**: 31.
Siegal, M: **C.7**: 79.
Siegel, F: **E.3**: 56. **J.3**: 27.
Siegelkow, E: **F.4**: 21.
Siegers, J: **F.3**: 96. **I.2**: 35, 117.
Siegler, R: **C.2**: 127.

Siever, L: **K.4**: 37.
Sigel, R: **D.9**: 52.
Sigelman, C: **C.3**: 25.
Sigelman, L: **B.2**: 3. **F.7**: 145.
Signitzer, B: **D.7**: 187.
Sigusch, V: **F.6**: 53–54.
Sihvo, J: **D.5**: 108.
Šiklová, J: **J.2**: 17.
Sikorska, J: **E.2**: 29. **H.5**: 28.
Siksiö, O: **G.3.2**: 116.
Silberman, J: **D.4**: 17.
Silberschmidt, M: **F.5**: 218.
Silva, K: **G.3.2**: 226.
Silva, P: **F.2**: 106. **G.3.1**: 38. **K.1**: 364.
Silveira, F: **C.7**: 35.
Silver, C: **H.7**: 23.
Silver, R: **F.4**: 153.
Silverberg, M: **K.2**: 42.
Silverblatt, R: **I.5**: 162.
Silverman, D: **D.7**: 173.
Silverman, J: **K.4**: 37.
Silverman, M: **F.8**: 8, 150.
Silverman, R: **K.1**: 92.
Silverstein, L: **I.2**: 147.
Silverstone, R: **H.4**: 94.
Sim, D: **D.8**: 393. **F.7**: 12.
Sime, W: **C.2**: 195.
Simmons, A: **B.1**: 60. **F.8**: 16.
Simmons, L: **J.5**: 10.
Simmons, R: **C.3**: 96.
Simon, F: **J.3**: 41.
Simon, H: **E.2**: 76.
Simon, P: **B.1**: 20. **D.1**: 18. **F.3**: 193.
Simon, R: **F.5**: 143. **K.1**: 174.
Simons, M: **F.5**: 210.
Simons, R: **F.4**: 203. **K.1**: 279.
Simonton, D: **C.2**: 27.
Simotas, L: **D.4**: 42.
Simpkins, N: **G.3.1**: 82.
Simpson, A: **F.7**: 215.
Simpson, D: **I.5**: 115.
Simpson, G: **I.5**: 78.
Simpson, J: **F.6**: 20.
Simpson, L: **F.4**: 38.
Simpson, S: **K.1**: 408.
Simpson, W: **I.2**: 68.

Šimunko, J: **F.7**: 102.
Simush, P: **G.3.1**: 91.
Sinclair, A: **J.4**: 1.
Sinclair, P: **C.2**: 40.
Sing, D: **I.2**: 47.
Singer, B: **D.7**: 242.
Singer, D: **F.7**: 259. **F.8**: 150.
Singer, E: **B.2**: 126. **F.3**: 59, 210.
Singer, J: **C.1**: 36.
Singer, M: **I.3**: 150. **K.1**: 367.
Singer-Kérel, J: **F.8**: 150.
Singh, K: **F.3**: 129.
Singh, R: **F.8**: 49.
Singh, T: **K.1**: 283.
Singh-Sengupta, S: **I.4**: 83.
Singhal, K: **H.3**: 85.
Singley, C: **F.5**: 216.
Sinha, A: **F.7**: 50.
Sinha, J: **I.4**: 83.
Sinha, Y: **C.7**: 72.
Sink, D: **K.2**: 30.
Sinopoli, R: **F.5**: 82.
Sirageldin, I: **K.4**: 20.
Sirotnik, K: **D.9**: 46, 58.
Sistrunk, F: **I.5**: 38.
Siune, K: **D.7**: 246.
Siurala, L: **F.2**: 155.
Sivan, E: **D.5**: 184. **J.5**: 37.
Sivanandan, A: **F.7**: 226.
Siverson, C: **D.2**: 13.
Sixsmith, A: **F.2**: 66.
Sixsmith, J: **F.2**: 66.
Siyal, H: **G.3.2**: 342.
Sjoberg, G: **B.1**: 90.
Sjoquist, D: **I.2**: 8. **I.4**: 42.
Skapska, G: **D.2**: 22.
Skellington, R: **F.7**: 252.
Skene, L: **K.4**: 255, 261.
Skinner, C: **B.2**: 35.
Skinner, M: **C.2**: 31. **K.2**: 75.
Skinner, S: **B.2**: 127.
Skinner, W: **F.3**: 148.
Skivington, J: **C.5**: 75.
Skjeie, H: **F.5**: 238.
Sklair, L: **E.1**: 19. **G.3.2**: 366. **H.2**: 17.
Skowronski, J: **C.2**: 164.
Skulenko, M: **D.7**: 329.

Skurski, J: **J.1**: 8.
Skutliová, J: **F.3**: 65.
Skvoretz, J: **C.4**: 58.
Slack, J: **F.3**: 147.
Sladovich, H: **H.4**: 14.
Slingsby, J: **C.3**: 100.
Slivkin, I: **H.4**: 37.
Sloane, A: **I.4**: 10.
Slonaker, W: **I.2**: 130.
Slotnik, B: **C.4**: 62.
Slottje, D: **H.3**: 34, 76.
Slovik, L: **C.3**: 1.
Slowe, P: **G.1**: 54.
Sly, D: **F.3**: 286.
Small, J: **F.7**: 68.
Small, K: **G.3.2**: 76, 240.
Small, S: **F.7**: 199.
Smandych, R: **F.2**: 125.
Smart, A: **G.3.2**: 366. **H.3**: 39.
Smart, B: **B.1**: 12.
Smart, C: **F.4**: 131.
Smart, J: **G.3.2**: 366. **H.3**: 39.
Smart, R: **K.1**: 387.
Smart, S: **C.3**: 70.
Smellie, E: **F.7**: 220.
Smelser, N: **A.1**: 41. **A.2**: 7. **D.9**: 195.
Smil, V: **F.3**: 310.
Smilanskey, S: **B.1**: 53.
Smirnov, I: **B.1**: 81.
Smith, A: **C.2**: 67. **D.1**: 83. **F.7**: 83. **K.4**: 142.
Smith, B: **B.1**: 77. **F.3**: 144. **G.3.2**: 2, 230, 240. **I.5**: 92.
Smith, C: **C.4**: 6. **C.7**: 52. **D.5**: 107. **D.7**: 359. **H.3**: 32. **K.1**: 173.
Smith, D: **A.2**: 8. **D.9**: 200. **E.2**: 18. **F.4**: 16. **G.3.2**: 47. **I.5**: 84. **J.5**: 14. **K.1**: 10, 80.
Smith, G: **C.7**: 12. **G.3.2**: 37. **K.1**: 308.
Smith, H: **D.3**: 87–88. **D.9**: 193. **K.4**: 127.
Smith, J: **B.2**: 13. **F.5**: 151. **J.5**: 7. **K.3**: 8. **K.4**: 246.
Smith, K: **F.3**: 269. **H.6**: 4.
Smith, L: **G.2**: 15. **H.3**: 90. **K.4**: 14.
Smith, M: **C.5**: 1. **D.1**: 132. **F.4**: 160. **F.7**: 9. **I.2**: 26. **K.1**: 190. **K.4**: 217.
Smith, N: **J.3**: 32.
Smith, P: **C.3**: 84. **F.2**: 82. **F.3**: 266. **I.5**: 65. **J.7**: 8.
Smith, R: **F.7**: 181.
Smith, S: **C.1**: 98. **D.7**: 108. **F.2**: 83. **I.2**: 141. **K.4**: 50.
Smith, T: **B.2**: 125. **C.7**: 48. **D.3**: 58. **K.2**: 74.
Smith, V: **D.4**: 21, 33.
Smith-Howell, D: **D.7**: 288.
Smither, J: **I.3**: 153.
Smook, A: **K.4**: 265.
Smucker, D: **D.5**: 149.
Smucker, J: **I.2**: 219.
Smythe, T: **K.4**: 225.
Snape, E: **I.3**: 152.
Sneddon, I: **F.3**: 145.
Snider, G: **K.2**: 69.
Sniderman, P: **F.7**: 243.
Snidman, N: **F.2**: 109.
Sniezek, J: **C.2**: 169.
Snippenburg, van, L: **F.2**: 6.
Snizek, W: **C.5**: 6.
Snow, N: **C.3**: 99.
Snow, R: **D.7**: 283.
Snowling, M: **D.7**: 56.
Snyder, L: **D.7**: 270. **F.8**: 129.
Snyder, N: **D.9**: 151.
Soares, G: **A.2**: 16.
Sobótka, E: **J.8**: 6.
Söderfeldt, B: **G.3**: 6.
Sohi, A: **I.6**: 4.
Soissons, M: **G.3.2**: 313.
Soja, N: **C.1**: 41.
Sokal, R: **F.1**: 12.
Sokolov, A: **E.3**: 49.
Sokołowska, M: **K.4**: 106.
Solimene, L: **I.5**: 167.
Solliday, E: **F.7**: 144, 152.
Sollis, P: **F.1**: 58.
Solomos, J: **F.7**: 13, 39, 221, 236, 246.
Solon, G: **F.4**: 73.
Solonin, Y: **D.1**: 21.
Solorzano, D: **I.4**: 33.
Solymosi, Z: **E.2**: 9.
Somers, M: **I.3**: 7.
Somers, R: **G.3.2**: 269.
Sommer, D: **F.5**: 254.
Sommer, R: **C.1**: 100.
Sonenstein, F: **F.6**: 32. **K.2**: 41, 64.
Soni, D: **G.3.1**: 16, 123.
Sonis, M: **I.2**: 50.

Sontheimer, S: **F.5**: 48.
Sooklal, L: **C.6**: 7.
Soothill, K: **K.1**: 141.
Sørensen, A: **F.5**: 35.
Sorensen, E: **I.2**: 92.
Sorensen, T: **H.3**: 45.
Sorenson, A: **B.2**: 54, 110. **E.2**: 71.
Sorkin, R: **C.5**: 34.
Sorlin, P: **D.8**: 12.
Sosna, M: **E.3**: 3.
Soudière, de, L: **D.1**: 66.
Soukup, P: **D.7**: 284.
South, N: **F.3**: 158.
South, S: **F.4**: 247. **K.2**: 36.
Souza-Lobo, E: **J.5**: 19.
Souza, d', D: **D.9**: 121.
Souza, d', R: **I.3**: 135.
Sox, C: **F.3**: 153. **K.4**: 229.
Soyinka, W: **D.8**: 2.
Soyland, A: **D.7**: 122.
Spacapan, S: **C.3**: 156.
Spangler, W: **J.6**: 31, 43.
Sparks, C: **D.1**: 2. **D.7**: 241, 307.
Sparks, P: **C.7**: 28.
Spearman, M: **G.3.1**: 52.
Spears, R: **C.3**: 78.
Spector, P: **C.1**: 37. **I.3**: 73.
Speer, A: **C.2**: 181.
Speer, J: **J.6**: 45.
Speigner, W: **F.3**: 5.
Spelke, E: **C.1**: 41.
Speller, T: **I.2**: 225.
Spellman, L: **G.3.2**: 129.
Spence, J: **C.2**: 209. **F.6**: 50.
Spence, N: **I.2**: 13–14, 165.
Spencer, J: **G.3.1**: 55.
Spergel, I: **F.2**: 157.
Sperl, S: **F.7**: 33.
Spickard, J: **D.5**: 15, 46.
Spiegel, U: **K.1**: 59.
Spielberger, C: **J.8**: 20.
Spierings, F: **K.1**: 277.
Spilerman, S: **I.4**: 62.
Spillers, H: **D.1**: 7.
Spinedi, M: **I.6**: 37.
Spinrad, W: **J.6**: 4.

Spittler, G: **G.3.1**: 2.
Spitzberg, I: **D.9**: 204.
Spitze, G: **F.4**: 349. **I.3**: 55.
Spletzer, J: **I.4**: 131.
Spoormans, H: **J.3**: 5.
Spranca, M: **C.7**: 45.
Spriano, G: **G.3.2**: 326.
Sprinzak, E: **J.5**: 37.
Sproull, L: **D.7**: 11.
Spurgeon, D: **F.3**: 155.
Spurr, S: **I.4**: 108.
Squarzon, C: **I.5**: 22.
Squires, A: **K.4**: 146.
Squires, G: **G.3.2**: 192.
Squires, P: **I.3**: 153.
Srilatha, V: **K.4**: 46.
Srivastva, S: **C.5**: 30.
Srivatsan, R: **D.7**: 107.
Srubar, I: **J.2**: 30.
St. Clair, C: **F.3**: 153, 198.
St. Leger, F: **K.4**: 123.
Staab, J: **D.7**: 319.
Staah, J: **F.5**: 271.
Staats, A: **C.1**: 139.
Staber, U: **I.2**: 6.
Stace, D: **I.3**: 124.
Stacey, B: **F.2**: 154.
Stacey, J: **D.1**: 2. **F.4**: 354. **F.5**: 80, 109.
Stacy, A: **C.2**: 206.
Staeuble, I: **C.1**: 114.
Stafford, A: **I.4**: 67.
Stafford, H: **H.7**: 13.
Stager, J: **C.1**: 119.
Stagg, C: **J.4**: 17.
Staggenborg, S: **F.3**: 57.
Stagl, J: **G.2**: 30.
Stahl, A: **F.4**: 311.
Stallard, E: **F.3**: 268.
Stallworth, L: **F.7**: 222.
Stamatakis, N: **D.7**: 63.
Stamatiou, M: **I.2**: 66.
Štambuk, M: **F.3**: 15. **G.3.1**: 97.
Stamp, P: **F.5**: 326. **F.7**: 53.
Stamps, A: **G.3.2**: 177.
Stanback, T: **G.3.2**: 347.
Stanfield, J: **F.7**: 255.
Stangor, C: **C.4**: 14. **C.7**: 4.

INTERNATIONAL BIBLIOGRAPHY OF SOCIOLOGY — 1991

Stanley, B: **F.2**: 17.
Stanley, T: **B.2**: 18.
Stanton, B: **G.3.1**: 1.
Stanton, W: **F.2**: 106.
Stapleton, D: **I.2**: 127.
Stappers, J: **D.7**: 297.
Stark, J: **D.1**: 75–76.
Stark, O: **F.8**: 165.
Stark, R: **D.5**: 99.
Starks, R: **F.7**: 233.
Starovoitova, G: **G.3.2**: 185.
Starr, R: **F.4**: 155.
Stasser, G: **D.7**: 179.
Statham, A: **F.5**: 170.
Statham, D: **C.2**: 81.
Stauth, G: **J.5**: 28.
Stavenhagen, R: **I.1**: 10.
Steadman, P: **D.8**: 70.
Stebbins, R: **B.2**: 103.
Steel, G: **C.1**: 119.
Steensma, H: **D.4**: 40.
Steffensmeier, D: **K.1**: 47, 79.
Stehr, N: **D.6**: 21.
Steier, F: **C.2**: 88.
Steifel, C: **K.1**: 47.
Stein, L: **J.6**: 67.
Stein, S: **C.1**: 23.
Steinberg, A: **C.1**: 30.
Steinberg, B: **J.8**: 12.
Steinberg, E: **D.7**: 219.
Steinberg, F: **G.3.2**: 5, 118, 256, 325.
Steinberg, J: **G.3.2**: 189, 340.
Steinberg, M: **E.2**: 72.
Steiner, D: **I.3**: 100.
Steiner, J: **C.2**: 210.
Steiner, L: **F.5**: 93.
Steinman, M: **F.4**: 175.
Steinweber, H: **F.5**: 221. **K.4**: 179.
Stempel, G: **D.7**: 280.
Stenberg, S: **K.2**: 78.
Stenger, H: **D.6**: 29.
Stengers, I: **K.1**: 335.
Stenner, K: **F.6**: 16.
Stenson, K: **K.1**: 127.
Stepan, N: **J.2**: 10.
Stepan-Norris, J: **I.5**: 163.

Stephan, C: **F.4**: 216.
Stephan, W: **F.4**: 216.
Stephens, G: **I.4**: 75.
Stephens, M: **D.9**: 115. **I.4**: 15.
Stephens, R: **K.1**: 385.
Stephenson, G: **C.1**: 56.
Stepick, A: **G.3.2**: 8.
Stepin, V: **D.1**: 95.
Stern, N: **K.1**: 271.
Stern, R: **C.1**: 44. **I.4**: 58.
Stets, J: **C.3**: 143. **F.4**: 239.
Steube, W: **D.9**: 197.
Stevens, E: **C.3**: 45.
Stevenson, R: **H.7**: 7.
Stevenson-Hinde, J: **F.2**: 71.
Stewart, A: **B.1**: 6.
Stewart, D: **F.4**: 141. **J.4**: 23.
Stewart, G: **F.3**: 303. **K.1**: 24. **K.2**: 32.
Stewart, J: **F.4**: 8. **K.1**: 24, 364. **K.2**: 32.
Stewart, K: **D.1**: 34.
Stewart, M: **K.1**: 2.
Stewart, N: **J.7**: 17.
Stewart, R: **F.4**: 99.
Stewart, W: **J.4**: 17.
Steyn, A: **F.4**: 13.
Stiehr, K: **K.1**: 386.
Stiens, G: **F.2**: 34.
Stier, H: **I.2**: 180.
Stillinger, C: **C.3**: 105.
Stillman, N: **F.7**: 178.
Stinchcombe, A: **B.1**: 93.
Stinson, L: **C.3**: 146.
Stirling, J: **I.5**: 4.
Stockwell, E: **H.3**: 11.
Stoddart, T: **D.9**: 47.
Stoecker, R: **B.2**: 7.
Stoker, G: **G.3.2**: 303.
Stokes, G: **D.9**: 179.
Stokhof, M: **D.7**: 197.
Stokke, K: **G.3.1**: 25.
Stolk, M: **I.2**: 66.
Stoller, R: **F.6**: 35.
Stolte-Heiskanen, V: **I.2**: 151.
Stölting, E: **F.8**: 128.
Stompka, P: **A.1**: 19.
Stone, A: **B.2**: 120. **C.2**: 150.
Stone, B: **J.7**: 3.

406

Stone, J: **I.5**: 188.
Stone, T: **J.6**: 5.
Stone, V: **I.3**: 98.
Stonebridge, L: **C.1**: 58.
Stones, M: **B.1**: 48. **C.2**: 60.
Stones, R: **B.1**: 141.
Stonich, S: **G.3.1**: 58.
Storck, I: **F.3**: 170.
Storer, D: **F.7**: 48.
Storey, R: **I.2**: 62.
Story, A: **C.2**: 132.
Stout, S: **C.3**: 93.
Stouthamer-Loeber, M: **K.1**: 94.
Strack, F: **D.7**: 119–120, 176.
Strang, D: **B.2**: 27, 48.
Strang, H: **K.1**: 405.
Strathern, M: **F.5**: 270.
Strathman, A: **C.1**: 96.
Stratton, J: **K.1**: 105.
Stratton, P: **H.5**: 6.
Stratton-Devine, K: **I.5**: 90.
Straub, K: **F.5**: 264.
Straubhaar, J: **D.7**: 270, 357.
Strauman, T: **C.2**: 236. **C.7**: 18.
Straus, D: **C.2**: 149.
Straus, M: **F.4**: 163. **K.1**: 81, 424.
Strauss, A: **B.1**: 119. **K.4**: 168.
Strauss, J: **K.4**: 51.
Straussfogel, D: **G.3.2**: 50.
Streatfield, K: **F.3**: 280, 292.
Strebler, M: **I.3**: 125.
Streckeisen, U: **I.2**: 122.
Streeck, W: **I.5**: 154.
Street, E: **K.3**: 9.
Street, R: **K.4**: 56.
Strien, Van, P: **C.1**: 114.
Strine, J: **D.7**: 334.
Stroebe, W: **C.4**: 47.
Strohmeier, K: **G.3.2**: 41.
Stromberg, P: **D.7**: 32.
Strömberg, T: **G.3**: 6.
Stromquist, V: **C.7**: 18.
Stroobants, M: **I.4**: 52.
Strossen, N: **D.4**: 42.
Stroup, R: **G.1**: 10.
Strus, Z: **D.9**: 159.

Struthers, N: **C.3**: 151.
Strzemińska, H: **I.3**: 131.
Studd, M: **C.5**: 26.
Stump, D: **B.1**: 35.
Styles, I: **J.8**: 1.
Suárez Hernández, G: **J.6**: 35.
Suczek, B: **K.4**: 168.
Sue, R: **I.6**: 7.
Suedfeld, P: **C.1**: 119.
Sufian, A: **F.4**: 249.
Sugarman, A: **C.1**: 15.
Suitor, J: **F.4**: 74, 287.
Suliman, T: **K.1**: 313.
Sullivan, A: **G.3.2**: 89.
Sullivan, G: **I.3**: 108.
Sullivan, J: **C.1**: 64.
Sullivan, L: **C.7**: 4. **K.4**: 190.
Sullivan, O: **B.2**: 36.
Suls, J: **C.2**: 200–201. **C.6**: 10.
Sulton, A: **K.1**: 182.
Summers, C: **F.5**: 326.
Summers, G: **G.3.1**: 39.
Summers, M: **F.7**: 233.
Sun, L: **D.1**: 10.
Sunderland, E: **F.4**: 219.
Sunderland, J: **C.4**: 52.
Sung, J: **D.9**: 13.
Sunley, P: **J.1**: 9.
Sunstein, C: **F.5**: 79.
Supple, K: **F.4**: 309.
Suri, K: **F.3**: 308.
Susskind, L: **I.5**: 66.
Sussman, G: **D.7**: 184.
Suštar: **D.5**: 91.
Susumu, S: **D.5**: 22.
Suttles, G: **C.4**: 33.
Sutton, R: **C.2**: 139. **C.3**: 130.
Suzuki, I: **D.1**: 12.
Suzuki, M: **D.5**: 52.
Suzuki, T: **F.4**: 197.
Svallfors, S: **K.2**: 87.
Sveinsson, J: **G.3.2**: 105.
Švob, M: **F.5**: 23.
Swaan, de, A: **D.7**: 52.
Swales, J: **H.5**: 26.
Swaminathan, A: **C.5**: 16.
Swan, A: **F.2**: 146.

Swanson, D: **G.1**: 21.
Swardt, de, C: **F.5**: 210.
Swartz, L: **F.7**: 37. **K.4**: 74, 182.
Swartz, M: **D.1**: 49.
Swatos, W: **B.1**: 117.
Sweeney, P: **I.5**: 37.
Sweet, J: **F.4**: 238.
Swidler, A: **B.1**: 9.
Swietochowski, T: **D.1**: 84.
Swinth, R: **G.1**: 26.
Switzer, F: **C.2**: 169.
Switzer, G: **C.2**: 181.
Syben, G: **I.3**: 4,
Syme, G: **G.2**: 16.
Symes, D: **G.3.1**: 4.
Symons, T: **F.1**: 15.
Synnott, A: **C.3**: 82.
Sypnowich, M: **D.3**: 56.
Syrovátka, A: **F.3**: 65.
Sysyn, F: **J.2**: 17.
Szabó, D: **K.1**: 56, 71.
Szabó, I: **D.1**: 136.
Szabó, L: **K.2**: 79.
Szacki, J: **J.2**: 17.
Szalai, J: **F.5**: 307.
Szalay, L: **D.7**: 185.
Szasz, T: **K.1**: 384.
Sze, J: **A.1**: 43.
Szebenyi, P: **D.9**: 82.
Székelyi, M: **E.2**: 9.
Szivos, S: **C.3**: 75.
Szorady, R: **F.2**: 16.
Szpiczakowska, M: **F.8**: 82.
Szpirulisz, I: **H.4**: 86.
Sztaudynger-Kaliszewicz, A: **F.2**: 53.
Sztompka, P: **B.1**: 139.
Tabachnick, B: **D.3**: 41.
Tabak, F: **G.3.1**: 90.
Tabatabai, H: **K.1**: 273.
Taboada-Léonetti, I: **F.8**: 83.
Taeuber, K: **G.3.2**: 192.
Taffin, C: **G.3.2**: 134. **H.3**: 16. **H.5**: 2.
Tåhlin, M: **I.1**: 14.
Tainio, R: **H.6**: 7.
Tait, J: **G.1**: 13.
Tajima, J: **F.7**: 142.

Takagi, K: **J.3**: 20.
Takahashi, H: **F.2**: 28. **G.3.2**: 13.
Takahashi, M: **D.3**: 64.
Takahashi, Y: **C.3**: 138.
Takase, T: **C.5**: 58.
Takatori, A: **I.6**: 16.
Takenaka, H: **F.3**: 21.
Takeuchi, D: **F.4**: 31.
Takeuchi, M: **D.7**: 164.
Takeyama, S: **D.1**: 72.
Talapina, S: **F.2**: 148.
Tall, I: **H.4**: 30.
Tallack, D: **D.8**: 76.
Tallis, S: **F.3**: 177.
Tamilselvi, R: **D.7**: 124. **I.5**: 170.
Tan, H: **I.4**: 133.
Tanaka, H: **F.4**: 293.
Tanche, B: **K.1**: 383.
Tang, S: **C.3**: 106.
Tang, X: **B.1**: 8.
Tang, Y: **B.1**: 72.
Tangney, J: **C.2**: 190.
Taniguchi, H: **B.1**: 147.
Tanja, V: **D.5**: 167.
Tannenbaum, S: **I.4**: 125.
Tanner, M: **G.3.1**: 124.
Tanosaki, A: **G.2**: 20.
Tanur, J: **K.2**: 4.
Taormina, R: **A.3**: 4.
Tapia, R: **F.7**: 3.
Tapinos, G: **F.3**: 301.
Taraban, C: **C.3**: 133.
Tarallo, B: **F.7**: 9.
Tarallo, F: **D.7**: 80.
Tardos, R: **D.7**: 28.
Tarimcilar, M: **K.4**: 152.
Tarjányi, J: **D.7**: 31.
Tarnow, E: **C.3**: 71.
Tarrow, S: **J.5**: 13.
Tassé, L: **F.2**: 59.
Tataryn, D: **C.2**: 1.
Tate, C: **J.3**: 28.
Tateiwa, S: **F.4**: 2.
Taubman, P: **F.3**: 238.
Tauchen, H: **F.4**: 154.
Tavuchis, N: **C.3**: 118.
Tayler, C: **D.9**: 135.

Taylor, A: **D.9**: 168.
Taylor, B: **F.5**: 179. **I.3**: 123.
Taylor, J: **D.1**: 11. **D.8**: 78. **F.1**: 55. **F.8**: 165.
Taylor, K: **I.3**: 65. **K.4**: 212.
Taylor, L: **D.7**: 179.
Taylor, M: **G.2**: 15. **H.7**: 5–6.
Taylor, P: **I.6**: 14. **J.1**: 4. **J.2**: 27. **K.3**: 3.
Taylor, R: **C.3**: 34. **E.1**: 2. **F.7**: 103. **K.1**: 88.
Taylor, S: **F.4**: 246.
Taylor-Gooby, P: **E.3**: 59.
Teachman, J: **F.3**: 87. **F.4**: 42, 92, 122, 217.
Teeffelen, T: **D.7**: 2.
Tehranian, M: **F.7**: 204.
Teichert, V: **F.4**: 342.
Teichler, U: **D.9**: 197.
Tejani, K: **F.3**: 7.
Tekiner, R: **F.7**: 116.
Teller, A: **G.1**: 19.
Temple, M: **K.1**: 366.
Templer, A: **I.2**: 168.
TenHouten, W: **C.1**: 25.
Tenhula, J: **F.8**: 84.
Tennen, H: **C.2**: 200–201.
Teram, E: **I.1**: 7. **K.1**: 214.
Terkla, D: **I.2**: 17.
Terrenoire, G: **I.4**: 93. **K.4**: 251.
Terrenoire, J: **I.4**: 93, 110.
Terry, C: **I.3**: 49.
Tesfaghiorghis, H: **F.3**: 107.
Tesler, L: **D.7**: 50.
Tesser, A: **C.2**: 232. **C.3**: 3.
Testa, M: **C.3**: 80.
Tester, S: **K.4**: 137.
Tetlock, P: **F.7**: 243.
Tetrick, L: **C.5**: 14.
Tetzlaff, D: **D.1**: 111.
Teule, R: **G.3.2**: 190. **K.1**: 220.
Tewfik, M: **G.3.2**: 118, 231.
Tham, H: **K.1**: 91.
Théberge, P: **D.7**: 290.
Theeuwes, J: **I.3**: 40.
Theisen, H: **K.4**: 271.
Thelin, J: **D.9**: 214.
Théry, H: **F.1**: 53.
Thieme, G: **F.3**: 250.
Thion, M: **D.8**: 38.

Third World Network: **G.1**: 43.
Thireau, I: **E.3**: 8.
Thoburn, W: **D.3**: 38.
Thoennes, N: **F.4**: 186.
Thomas, D: **F.5**: 174. **K.4**: 51.
Thomas, G: **G.3.2**: 32.
Thomas, J: **D.9**: 140. **F.4**: 217. **G.3.1**: 39. **K.1**: 251.
Thomas, L: **K.3**: 19.
Thomas, N: **F.1**: 33.
Thomas, P: **B.2**: 97. **K.3**: 12.
Thomas, R: **I.5**: 172.
Thomas-Slayter, B: **G.2**: 4.
Thomasma, D: **K.4**: 252.
Thompson, A: **C.1**: 19.
Thompson, B: **F.4**: 150.
Thompson, C: **C.2**: 164.
Thompson, D: **D.3**: 75.
Thompson, E: **D.5**: 1.
Thompson, G: **E.1**: 9.
Thompson, J: **B.1**: 27. **J.8**: 21.
Thompson, L: **C.3**: 44.
Thompson, P: **G.3.2**: 85.
Thompson, R: **I.5**: 5, 34.
Thompson, S: **C.3**: 156.
Thompson, T: **F.2**: 3. **K.1**: 280.
Thompson-Hoffman, S: **F.3**: 170.
Thomsen, C: **C.1**: 64.
Thomson, G: **D.3**: 80.
Thomson, J: **C.2**: 12. **D.3**: 84.
Thoraval, J: **E.3**: 14.
Thornburg, D: **G.3.2**: 111.
Thornicroft, K: **I.5**: 72.
Thornton, A: **F.4**: 75, 215.
Thornton, G: **I.3**: 37.
Thornton, M: **D.2**: 10. **F.5**: 86, 215.
Thornton, R: **K.1**: 253.
Thorpe, R: **K.3**: 36.
Thorsen, L: **G.3.1**: 44.
Thrupp, L: **I.3**: 120.
Thuderoz, C: **I.4**: 100.
Thumerelle, P: **F.3**: 262, 273.
Thumerelle-Delaney, N: **F.3**: 262.
Thumma, S: **D.5**: 53, 125.
Thurman, Q: **J.6**: 18.
Tiano, S: **I.2**: 162.
Tiborné, P: **F.3**: 36.

Tice, D: **C.2**: 227.
Tichi, C: **D.2**: 6.
Ticktin, H: **F.7**: 245.
Tiefenbacher, J: **J.4**: 26.
Tiefer, L: **F.6**: 51.
Tielman, R: **F.6**: 4.
Tien, H: **F.3**: 83.
Tienda, M: **F.8**: 39.
Tiesdell, S: **G.3.2**: 275.
Tiffany, S: **K.1**: 332.
Tiggemann, M: **C.2**: 83, 97. **I.2**: 234.
Tilak, J: **F.3**: 290.
Tillie, P: **F.2**: 90.
Tilly, C: **F.7**: 158.
Timæus, I: **F.3**: 254.
Timera, M: **F.7**: 19.
Timm, J: **C.2**: 9.
Timmermans, H: **H.5**: 36.
Ting-Toomey, S: **C.3**: 112. **D.7**: 132.
Tipper, S: **C.2**: 54, 125.
Tipple, A: **G.3.2**: 128, 161.
Tirrell, L: **D.7**: 172.
Tiryakian, E: **A.1**: 20, 25.
Tisak, J: **C.7**: 52.
Tisdall-Yamada, Y: **D.5**: 22.
Tishkov, V: **F.7**: 158.
Titma, M: **F.2**: 136.
Titterton, M: **K.4**: 221.
Tittle, C: **D.5**: 137. **K.1**: 153.
Tjaden, P: **F.4**: 186.
Tobias, B: **C.2**: 1.
Toby, J: **K.1**: 89.
Toch, H: **J.3**: 42.
Toch, T: **D.9**: 59.
Todd, R: **C.3**: 100.
Todes, D: **C.1**: 106.
Toffler, A: **E.3**: 45.
Toit, du, B: **F.7**: 90.
Tokatlian, J: **H.7**: 8.
Tollefson, J: **D.7**: 345.
Tolley, H: **F.3**: 268.
Tolley, K: **K.1**: 359. **K.4**: 210.
Tolnay, S: **F.4**: 212.
Toma, R: **F.8**: 126.
Tomaney, J: **H.7**: 2. **I.3**: 70.
Tomasevski, K: **F.3**: 159.

Tombs, S: **I.3**: 111.
Tominaga, K: **D.1**: 69.
Tomita, F: **G.2**: 32.
Tomka, M: **D.5**: 63.
Tomlinson, D: **K.4**: 131.
Tomlinson, J: **K.4**: 211.
Tomsic, J: **D.9**: 192.
Toney, M: **F.8**: 38. **G.3.1**: 39.
Tong, D: **D.9**: 50.
Tonnelier, F: **F.3**: 262.
Tonry, M: **C.2**: 42.
Tooke, W: **F.6**: 31.
Toothaker, L: **B.2**: 15.
Toporov, V: **D.1**: 97.
Torelli, C: **I.2**: 38.
Torgersen, U: **G.3.2**: 125.
Torguson, J: **F.3**: 9.
Torkel, S: **I.3**: 153.
Toro, P: **G.3.2**: 98. **K.1**: 239, 243.
Torrance, N: **D.7**: 158.
Torre, A: **C.5**: 62.
Torrelli, M: **F.3**: 218.
Torres, A: **I.2**: 185.
Torres, E: **C.2**: 175.
Torres, L: **F.5**: 130. **I.5**: 110.
Tosi, A: **G.3.2**: 90.
Tosics, I: **K.2**: 7.
Toth, J: **E.2**: 33.
Toulouse, C: **J.4**: 22.
Touraine, A: **G.3.2**: 188. **I.2**: 229.
Tourangeau, R: **C.2**: 62. **C.7**: 8.
Townsend, J: **F.1**: 64.
Townsley, R: **K.1**: 34.
Trabka, E: **A.3**: 2. **F.8**: 169.
Trabucchi, M: **K.2**: 86.
Trahan, W: **C.5**: 54.
Tran, T: **I.2**: 61.
Tranda, B: **D.5**: 144.
Traube, E: **D.8**: 75.
Travers, A: **C.3**: 36.
Travis, C: **C.1**: 106. **F.5**: 224.
Trebilcock, A: **F.5**: 230.
Trebitsch, M: **D.1**: 18.
Trees, S: **H.3**: 22.
Treffeisen, P: **G.3.2**: 222, 240.
Trejo, S: **I.3**: 24. **I.5**: 161.
Trejos S., J: **K.1**: 262.

Tremblay, C: **F.3**: 246.
Tremblay, G: **D.7**: 387.
Tremblay, R: **F.4**: 351. **G.3.1**: 102.
Tremblay, S: **F.4**: 304.
Trent, K: **F.3**: 38.
Trépanier, C: **F.7**: 54.
Trezza, G: **C.7**: 75.
Triandis, H: **C.7**: 23.
Tribalat, M: **F.8**: 114.
Trickett, E: **K.1**: 243.
Trigueiros, L: **D.2**: 17.
Trinder, E: **D.3**: 4.
Trinh, T: **F.5**: 137.
Tripathi, R: **F.7**: 152.
Triseliotis, J: **F.2**: 98.
Trochim, W: **B.2**: 18.
Troen, S: **G.3.2**: 259.
Trow, M: **D.9**: 217.
Troyer, D: **C.2**: 181.
Troyer, R: **K.4**: 128.
Trubisky, P: **C.3**: 112.
Trudeau, G: **I.3**: 139.
Truetzschler, W: **D.7**: 246.
Trzcinski, E: **I.3**: 74.
Tsang, M: **I.4**: 25.
Tschann, J: **F.4**: 132.
Tseëlon, E: **F.5**: 51.
Tsiareshchanka, V: **D.3**: 83.
Tsuboi, T: **F.2**: 121.
Tsuda, M: **B.1**: 85.
Tsukashima, R: **F.7**: 11.
Tsuru, T: **I.5**: 165.
Tsutumi-Yoshida, K: **G.3.2**: 301.
Tsuya, N: **F.4**: 295.
Tu, W: **F.7**: 99.
Tuch, S: **I.3**: 104.
Tuckel, P: **B.2**: 92.
Tucker, G: **D.7**: 19.
Tucker, S: **B.2**: 17.
Tucker, W: **K.2**: 34.
Tudor, M: **C.3**: 15.
Tufte, E: **D.7**: 140.
Tullis, L: **K.1**: 311, 360.
Tuma, N: **B.2**: 34, 48.
Tumber, H: **K.1**: 106.
Tummers, M: **I.2**: 60.

Tunnard, J: **F.4**: 192.
Tunstall, J: **D.7**: 281.
Tuohimaa, S: **F.5**: 78.
Turkheimer, E: **C.2**: 49.
Turmel, F: **C.1**: 12.
Turnbull, P: **I.5**: 182.
Turner, B: **B.1**: 145. **F.2**: 16.
Turner, J: **C.1**: 166. **C.3**: 154.
Turner, M: **G.3.1**: 77.
Turner, R: **C.7**: 78.
Turner, S: **C.2**: 5. **K.1**: 180.
Turnock, D: **G.3.1**: 51.
Turshen, M: **F.5**: 47.
Turski, G: **C.3**: 126.
Tushman, M: **C.5**: 78.
Tustin, F: **F.3**: 214.
Tyler, F: **C.1**: 163.
Tyler, T: **F.2**: 27.
Tyrant, M: **D.9**: 89.
Tzelgov, J: **B.2**: 83.
Tzeng, O: **K.1**: 44.
Udayakumar, S: **D.7**: 124. **I.5**: 170.
Udwin, O: **F.2**: 104.
Ufford, van, J: **F.7**: 85.
Ugalde, A: **K.4**: 74.
Ughanwa, D: **D.8**: 39.
Uhlaner, C: **J.6**: 1.
Ujihara, S: **I.1**: 8. **I.5**: 20.
Ulack, R: **F.3**: 148.
Ulč, O: **F.7**: 93.
Ultee, W: **I.2**: 36.
Umann, E: **J.6**: 38.
Umesh, U: **B.2**: 21, 40.
Undy, R: **I.5**: 65.
Ungar, S: **J.8**: 3.
Unger, L: **C.3**: 97.
United Nations Office. Centre for Social Development and Humani: **F.5**: 324.
United Nations. Centre for Social Development and Humanitarian Affairs: **F.5**: 325.
United Nations. Department of International Economic and Social Affairs: **F.2**: 25. **F.3**: 242, 300, 311.
Unsworth, C: **K.4**: 64.
Unterhalter, E: **D.9**: 53.
Uphoff, N: **C.4**: 18. **E.3**: 15.
Upton, G: **B.2**: 49, 124.
Urban, J: **J.2**: 17.

Urciuoli, B: **D.7**: 59.
Urevbu, A: **H.4**: 92.
Uri, N: **I.2**: 110.
Urjewicz, C: **F.7**: 87.
Ursin, H: **C.1**: 119.
Useem, B: **D.9**: 120.
Useem, M: **H.4**: 4.
Usenova, M: **F.4**: 100.
Ussel, de, J: **F.4**: 184.
Ussher, J: **C.2**: 75. **F.5**: 59.
Ustjugova, E: **D.1**: 21.
Uthoff, A: **F.1**: 46.
Utsunomiya, K: **B.1**: 136.
Uvarai, L: **D.6**: 24.
Uys, R: **I.2**: 176.
Uzukwu, E: **D.5**: 110.
Vaillancourt, F: **D.7**: 16.
Vaksberg, A: **K.1**: 151.
Valencia, J: **F.3**: 154, 219.
Valencia, R: **D.9**: 42.
Vali, D: **K.1**: 50.
Vallacher, R: **C.7**: 80.
Vallas, S: **I.5**: 58.
Valle, R: **H.4**: 81. **K.1**: 20.
Valverde, J: **D.5**: 143.
Vandenberg, B: **B.1**: 37.
Vandenberg, R: **I.3**: 101.
Vanderleeuw, J: **J.6**: 62.
Vangelisti, A: **C.3**: 140.
VanYperen, N: **C.3**: 33. **F.4**: 246.
Varacalli, J: **D.5**: 146.
Varady, D: **G.3.2**: 155.
Vargas, L: **E.3**: 15.
Vargas-Lundius, R: **K.1**: 257.
Varsányi, E: **C.4**: 35.
Vartanov, A: **D.7**: 384.
Vasil, R: **F.7**: 212.
Vasillopulos, C: **I.3**: 85.
Vasoo, F: **G.2**: 18.
Vasudeva, S: **D.7**: 124, 128.
Vatz, R: **C.7**: 13.
Vaughan, P: **D.7**: 9.
Vaus, de, D: **F.5**: 12.
Vayda, A: **B.1**: 2.
Vázquez, A: **K.1**: 48.
Veatch, R: **D.3**: 44.

Veauvy, C: **D.1**: 18.
Vecchi, G: **K.2**: 86.
Večerník, J: **H.3**: 66.
Vedder, R: **I.2**: 201.
Veena, D: **F.8**: 11.
Veenhoven, R: **C.2**: 56, 104.
Veenman, J: **F.7**: 1.
Vega, W: **K.1**: 20. **K.4**: 114.
Vega J., P: **D.7**: 289.
Veiel, H: **F.5**: 289.
Veiga, J: **C.4**: 19.
Velaskar, P: **D.9**: 133.
Velásquez, G: **K.4**: 68.
Velden, van der, R: **D.9**: 122.
Veldman, A: **I.3**: 137.
Velez, W: **G.3.2**: 192.
Velmans, M: **C.2**: 126.
Veltman, C: **D.7**: 86.
Vengroff, R: **J.4**: 11.
Ventisette, M: **F.3**: 114.
Verbunt, G: **F.8**: 10.
Vereš, P: **F.3**: 14.
Verette, J: **C.3**: 1.
Vergara, A: **F.3**: 154, 219.
Vergès, F: **F.5**: 204.
Vergnaud, G: **C.1**: 120.
Vergnaud, J: **D.7**: 68.
Verkaik, A: **I.4**: 126.
Verma, A: **I.5**: 202.
Vermeulen, S: **D.3**: 86.
Vermunt, R: **D.4**: 40.
Verney, D: **J.3**: 19.
Verona, R: **G.3.2**: 250, 288.
Verot, P: **G.3.2**: 326.
Verplanken, B: **C.7**: 53.
Verschueren, J: **F.7**: 193.
Verspoor, A: **D.9**: 157.
Vervaeke, M: **C.2**: 86.
Vestal, T: **K.1**: 18.
Vettehen, H: **J.6**: 42.
Vial, A: **H.7**: 20.
Vichich, I: **I.3**: 88.
Vickers, J: **H.3**: 57.
Victor, C: **F.3**: 168. **K.2**: 85. **K.4**: 199.
Vidich, A: **B.1**: 137. **E.2**: 11.
Vidmar, N: **I.3**: 107.
Vieillard-Baron, H: **G.3.2**: 188, 216.

Vieillette, S: **F.3**: 246.
Viktorov, V: **I.6**: 44.
Viktorova, V: **A.1**: 17.
Villacorta, W: **D.7**: 60, 79.
Villemez, W: **I.5**: 17.
Vincent, D: **K.2**: 88.
Vincent, J: **F.2**: 26.
Vincineau, M: **F.3**: 217.
Vine, P: **G.1**: 39.
Viney, R: **I.2**: 137.
Viney, X: **I.4**: 120.
Vining, A: **K.1**: 164.
Vinnik, V: **I.6**: 43.
Vinokur, A: **I.2**: 235.
Viscasillas, G: **D.7**: 270, 357.
Viscusi, W: **I.4**: 56. **K.1**: 391.
Visher, C: **K.1**: 80.
Vishwanath, T: **F.8**: 93.
Viswanath, V: **F.5**: 28.
Vitányi, I: **F.4**: 44.
Vivekananda, F: **F.3**: 177.
Vizard, E: **F.2**: 77.
Vizelberg, I: **F.2**: 129.
Vliet, van der, R: **F.6**: 24.
Vobruba, G: **I.2**: 54.
Vocci, F: **K.1**: 319.
Vodopjanova, N: **C.1**: 122.
Voelkl, K: **C.3**: 80.
Vogel, D: **D.3**: 32.
Vogel, J: **D.1**: 64.
Vogel, U: **F.5**: 297.
Vogelman, L: **K.1**: 419.
Vogt, W: **B.1**: 126.
Voland, E: **F.4**: 21.
Volkan, V: **J.8**: 13.
Volken, H: **C.1**: 153.
Volling, B: **F.4**: 302, 314.
Vollmeyer, R: **D.7**: 319.
Vollrath, D: **C.4**: 56.
Volovik, V: **D.2**: 27.
Volpato, C: **C.3**: 77.
Volpp, K: **K.4**: 38.
Volsky, V: **J.3**: 33.
Vondráček, J: **F.3**: 65.
Vonk, H: **D.9**: 82.
Vookles, J: **C.2**: 236.

Voorhis, van, P: **I.4**: 24.
Vos-Schippers, B: **K.4**: 265.
Voss, P: **F.1**: 23.
Voswinkel, S: **I.5**: 1.
Voye, L: **F.2**: 131–132.
Voytek, K: **J.4**: 15.
Vree, de, J: **J.1**: 1.
Vries, de, M: **C.6**: 18.
Vroomen, J: **D.7**: 56.
Vuchinich, S: **F.4**: 42.
Vylder, de, S: **I.1**: 10.
Waal, de, F: **D.4**: 3.
Wachter, K: **F.1**: 20.
Wachter, R: **K.4**: 229.
Waddell, M: **C.1**: 51.
Waddell, P: **G.3.2**: 187, 240.
Waddington, I: **I.6**: 8. **K.1**: 404.
Waddington, P: **K.1**: 12.
Waddock, S: **C.5**: 85.
Waddoups, J: **I.2**: 196.
Wadhwani, S: **I.3**: 60.
Wadsworth, M: **H.3**: 59.
Wagg, S: **I.6**: 5.
Waggoner, D: **D.9**: 170.
Wagner, G: **B.1**: 110. **E.1**: 12. **H.3**: 3.
Wagner, H: **C.2**: 30. **D.7**: 302.
Wagner, I: **K.4**: 101.
Wagner, K: **H.4**: 28.
Wagner, M: **K.4**: 13.
Wagner, U: **F.4**: 152.
Wagner, W: **C.1**: 56. **K.1**: 45.
Wahl, A: **A.2**: 8. **I.5**: 174.
Wahl, S: **F.3**: 10.
Waikar, S: **C.3**: 71.
Wainai, K: **H.4**: 53.
Waite, B: **C.3**: 59.
Waite, L: **F.4**: 75, 276. **I.2**: 159. **K.2**: 41, 68.
Waitzkin, H: **K.4**: 75.
Wajcman, J: **F.5**: 103. **H.4**: 88.
Wakabayashi, N: **C.5**: 37.
Wakamatsu, Y: **D.9**: 178.
Wakasa, K: **B.1**: 82.
Wakeley, P: **C.2**: 47.
Walby, S: **F.5**: 110. **K.1**: 141.
Wald, K: **F.3**: 183.
Waldinger, R: **F.7**: 224.
Waldorf, B: **F.8**: 157.

Waldron, A: **J.7**: 24.
Walford, G: **B.2**: 100.
Walford, N: **B.2**: 35.
Walicki, A: **K.2**: 19.
Walker, A: **F.4**: 283.
Walker, C: **G.3.2**: 98.
Walker, G: **F.3**: 245.
Walker, I: **C.3**: 101.
Walker, J: **D.7**: 293.
Walker, L: **F.7**: 158.
Walker, M: **C.3**: 114. **D.3**: 16.
Walker, N: **D.1**: 134.
Walker, R: **I.2**: 206. **K.4**: 1.
Walker, S: **F.5**: 293. **J.3**: 27.
Wall, D: **K.1**: 243.
Wall, E: **D.4**: 12.
Wall, J: **C.3**: 108. **D.4**: 24.
Wall, P: **I.2**: 243.
Wall, R: **F.5**: 21.
Wallace, C: **F.5**: 287.
Wallace, G: **D.1**: 45.
Wallace, J: **K.1**: 350.
Wallace, M: **B.2**: 105. **I.5**: 95.
Wallace, R: **F.3**: 234. **G.3.2**: 121, 308.
Wallace, W: **B.1**: 130.
Wallach, B: **G.1**: 2.
Wallach, M: **K.4**: 47.
Wallbott, H: **C.2**: 99. **C.3**: 134–135.
Wallendorf, M: **H.6**: 10.
Waller, P: **F.2**: 7.
Waller, W: **C.2**: 167.
Walle, van de, D: **H.3**: 55.
Wallis, A: **G.3.2**: 170.
Wallis, B: **G.3.2**: 40.
Wallis, J: **D.5**: 100.
Wallisch, G: **D.7**: 271.
Wallock, L: **G.3.2**: 281.
Wallwork, E: **C.1**: 46.
Walmsley, D: **G.3.2**: 44. **H.5**: 7.
Walsh, B: **F.2**: 113.
Walsh, C: **D.7**: 46.
Walsh, J: **G.3.1**: 56. **H.4**: 98.
Walter, F: **K.4**: 90.
Walter, T: **F.3**: 199.
Walters, S: **F.5**: 115.
Walters, V: **I.5**: 91.

Walther, U: **F.2**: 34.
Waltz, J: **C.3**: 153.
Walwei, U: **I.5**: 114.
Wan, C: **C.6**: 10.
Wang, F: **E.2**: 41.
Wang, G: **F.7**: 57, 99.
Wang, I: **H.3**: 42.
Wang, K: **G.3.2**: 129.
Wang, L: **F.7**: 99.
Waniez, P: **F.1**: 37, 53.
Waning, van, A: **C.1**: 60.
Wanmali, S: **G.3.1**: 12.
Waquet, P: **D.4**: 19.
Warburg, M: **D.5**: 186.
Ward, B: **F.5**: 32.
Ward, C: **F.7**: 152, 209.
Ward, D: **C.4**: 51.
Ward, H: **K.2**: 48.
Ward, K: **F.5**: 10, 70.
Ward, L: **K.4**: 127.
Warde, A: **G.3.2**: 112.
Wardey, Z: **C.1**: 28.
Ware, V: **F.5**: 67.
Warf, B: **G.1**: 30. **I.2**: 1.
Wark, M: **D.1**: 138.
Warner, K: **K.1**: 325.
Warner, M: **I.4**: 74.
Warner, R: **F.5**: 75.
Warr, M: **C.3**: 122.
Warren, B: **C.1**: 86. **I.4**: 111.
Warren, C: **F.3**: 81.
Warren, L: **G.1**: 9.
Warren, M: **K.1**: 239.
Warren, P: **C.3**: 101.
Warren, R: **F.8**: 146.
Warton, P: **D.3**: 14.
Warzywoda-Kruszynska, W: **E.2**: 31. **I.5**: 89.
Wasem, C: **G.3.1**: 59.
Wasil, E: **J.4**: 17.
Wasilewski, J: **C.6**: 2.
Wastl-Walter, D: **G.3.2**: 74.
Watanabe, S: **E.3**: 44.
Watanuki, J: **F.5**: 20.
Watari, A: **D.7**: 234.
Watcher, R: **F.3**: 153.
Waterbury, J: **E.2**: 43.
Waterhouse, L: **K.1**: 43.

Waters, E: **G.3.2**: 229.
Waters, M: **E.2**: 61.
Watillon, A: **C.1**: 13.
Watkeys, J: **K.1**: 33.
Watkins, C: **G.3.1**: 48.
Watson, A: **H.7**: 10. **I.6**: 17.
Watson, D: **C.3**: 137.
Watson, H: **K.1**: 305.
Watson, J: **F.6**: 34.
Watson, S: **D.1**: 73.
Watson, V: **G.3.2**: 368.
Watson, W: **C.4**: 37.
Watson-Gegeo, K: **D.7**: 35.
Watt, W: **D.5**: 170.
Wattenberg, B: **F.1**: 26.
Watts, H: **H.4**: 51. **H.7**: 13.
Watts, M: **F.5**: 269, 326. **G.1**: 58. **J.7**: 14.
Watts, R: **F.4**: 85.
Watts, T: **D.9**: 11. **K.2**: 111.
Watzlawczik, G: **F.5**: 221. **K.4**: 150.
Waugh, E: **D.5**: 168.
Wauthier, C: **D.7**: 231.
Wazaki, H: **E.1**: 8.
Wearing, A: **C.2**: 104.
Weaver, B: **C.2**: 54.
Webb, B: **K.1**: 64.
Webb, J: **G.3.2**: 129.
Webb, N: **B.2**: 10.
Webb, S: **K.3**: 41.
Webb, V: **D.7**: 3.
Webb, Y: **K.4**: 129.
Webber, F: **F.7**: 21.
Webber, M: **I.2**: 191. **K.1**: 287.
Webley, P: **F.2**: 107. **H.2**: 20.
Webster, A: **D.5**: 135.
Webster, D: **C.4**: 28.
Webster, E: **I.5**: 78.
Webster, R: **K.1**: 37.
Wedderburn, K: **I.5**: 104.
Wedel, J: **J.3**: 29.
Wedell, D: **C.3**: 158.
Wedge, P: **K.3**: 35.
Weed, F: **C.5**: 59.
Weekes, J: **C.2**: 45.
Weeks, J: **F.6**: 2.
Weeks, W: **F.5**: 125.

Weenig, M: **C.3**: 16.
Wegener, B: **E.2**: 21. **H.3**: 46.
Wegener, M: **G.3.2**: 326.
Wegner, D: **C.3**: 89.
Wei, J: **F.3**: 53.
Weigert, A: **C.1**: 160.
Weiher, A: **K.1**: 51.
Weiher, G: **G.3.2**: 110.
Weil, D: **I.5**: 143.
Weiler, P: **K.4**: 63.
Weimann, G: **C.6**: 6. **F.7**: 63.
Weinand, H: **H.3**: 45. **H.5**: 7.
Weinberg, L: **C.7**: 13.
Weinberger, J: **C.2**: 178. **F.2**: 76.
Weinberger, M: **G.1**: 50.
Weiner, B: **C.2**: 100, 170. **C.3**: 65.
Weiner, D: **G.3.1**: 123.
Weingrod, A: **F.7**: 180.
Weinreich, P: **F.7**: 70, 152.
Weinstein, J: **G.3.2**: 321.
Weinstein, M: **F.4**: 255.
Weintraub, S: **F.8**: 37, 40, 53, 120, 124.
Weintrop, J: **H.4**: 65.
Weir, J: **K.1**: 20.
Weir, R: **K.4**: 258.
Weisberg, J: **I.3**: 28.
Weisburd, D: **K.1**: 68.
Weisheit, R: **K.1**: 95.
Weiss, A: **E.2**: 63. **F.2**: 19.
Weiss, K: **F.3**: 161.
Weißbecker, H: **D.7**: 291.
Weissler, K: **C.6**: 14.
Weissman, M: **K.1**: 410.
Weitz, R: **F.3**: 188.
Weitzer, R: **J.5**: 23.
Weitzman, B: **C.3**: 79.
Weitzman, L: **F.4**: 128.
Welch, M: **D.5**: 137.
Welch, S: **F.7**: 145.
Weldon, E: **C.4**: 46.
Weldon, M: **C.5**: 34.
Weller, M: **F.3**: 206.
Welles, J: **C.1**: 33.
Wellington, A: **I.3**: 23.
Wellman, H: **C.2**: 55.
Wells, C: **F.3**: 70.
Wells, K: **K.2**: 52.

Wells, L: **F.4**: 41.
Welsh, M: **F.3**: 54.
Welte, J: **K.1**: 297, 376.
Wenden, de, C: **F.7**: 45. **F.8**: 133, 150.
Wendt, A: **I.2**: 130.
Wenfeng, M: **C.1**: 10.
Wentling, T: **C.2**: 144.
Wenzel, H: **B.1**: 124.
Werblowsky, R: **F.3**: 50.
Werle, F: **D.9**: 21.
Wernick, A: **D.7**: 113.
Werth, B: **K.1**: 218.
Wertz, D. **K.4**. 255, 263.
Wesch, D: **K.1**: 32.
Weßels, B: **J.5**: 36.
Wessels, W: **I.5**: 127, 136.
Wessen, A: **K.4**: 95.
West, C: **E.3**: 56. **F.5**: 1. **F.7**: 5.
West, P: **F.4**: 297. **G.1**: 33.
West, S: **C.7**: 24.
Westcott, H: **F.2**: 69.
Westen, D: **C.2**: 135.
Westenholtz, A: **I.5**: 196.
Westerfield, D: **K.4**: 219.
Westergård-Nielsen, N: **I.5**: 152.
Western, B: **H.4**: 64.
Western, M: **B.2**: 32.
Westman, D: **I.3**: 91.
Weston, D: **F.4**: 318.
Weston, K: **F.4**: 43.
Westphal, W: **C.2**: 68.
Westwood, R: **C.3**: 106.
Westwood, S: **D.9**: 140.
Wettersten, J: **D.6**: 11.
Wexler, P: **D.7**: 99.
Wharton, A: **F.5**: 127, 220.
Whatmore, S: **G.3.1**: 33.
Wheaton, W: **G.3.2**: 240.
Wheeler, D: **C.3**: 39.
Wheeler, L: **C.1**: 165. **C.2**: 200.
Wheeler, R: **C.2**: 101.
Whelan, C: **E.2**: 64. **I.2**: 246.
Whelan, T: **I.6**: 27.
Whicker, M: **B.2**: 3.
Whiffen, V: **F.4**: 284.
Whimster, S: **G.3.2**: 35.

Whitbeck, L: **F.4**: 203. **K.1**: 279.
White, C: **F.4**: 18.
White, E: **F.5**: 222.
White, H: **D.2**: 24.
White, J: **F.3**: 203. **F.4**: 332.
White, K: **F.3**: 221. **F.4**: 108.
White, M: **D.7**: 348.
White, P: **C.1**: 144. **K.1**: 265.
White, W: **K.1**: 176.
Whitebook, M: **I.3**: 12. **K.2**: 41.
Whiteford, M: **K.4**: 72.
Whiteford, P: **F.8**: 2.
Whitehand, J: **G.3.2**: 48.
Whitehead, C: **G.3.2**: 94.
Whitehead, J: **F.5**: 200.
Whitfield, K: **D.9**: 169.
Whitney, G: **C.3**: 1.
Whitston, C: **I.5**: 57.
Whitt, J: **D.8**: 4.
Whittington, D: **G.1**: 38.
Whitworth, S: **F.3**: 55.
Whynes, D: **F.8**: 43. **K.1**: 372.
Whyte, W: **I.3**: 79.
Wial, H: **I.2**: 22.
Wiche, R: **D.7**: 205.
Wickens, P: **I.3**: 60.
Wicker, A: **C.1**: 100. **I.4**: 6.
Wickham-Crowley, T: **A.2**: 8.
Wickremasinghe, A: **F.1**: 8. **K.4**: 177.
Widerberg, K: **F.4**: 321.
Widja, I: **D.9**: 3.
Wielers, R: **I.2**: 3.
Wiemann, J: **D.7**: 160.
Wiemeyer, J: **I.5**: 160.
Wiener, C: **K.4**: 168.
Wiener, J: **K.4**: 215.
Wierzbicka, A: **D.7**: 133.
Wiesenhütter, P: **K.4**: 38.
Wieviorka, M: **F.7**: 231.
Wiewel, W: **G.3.2**: 241.
Wigdor, A: **I.3**: 57.
Wigdor, B: **K.1**: 412.
Wigg, A: **G.3.2**: 85.
Wiggins, R: **F.3**: 52.
Wijck, van, P: **C.7**: 41. **H.3**: 77.
Wijngaard, van den, M: **F.5**: 157.
Wikler, D: **F.3**: 66. **K.4**: 242.

Wikler, N: **F.3**: 66.
Wikström, P: **K.1**: 161.
Wilcox, C: **F.5**: 87, 310.
Wildasin, D: **I.2**: 28.
Wilder, D: **C.4**: 16.
Wilder, H: **F.4**: 126.
Wilder, M: **E.2**: 62. **H.3**: 26.
Wilderom, C: **K.4**: 138.
Wilding, J: **C.2**: 75.
Wiley, C: **I.5**: 39.
Wiley, M: **F.5**: 288.
Wilhite, S: **C.2**: 157.
Wilkanowicz, S: **D.5**: 134.
Wilkes, K: **C.1**: 116.
Wilkie, J: **F.4**: 25.
Wilkin, D: **K.4**: 61.
Wilkins, L: **K.1**: 133.
Wilkinson, A: **I.3**: 152.
Wilkinson, B: **I.5**: 108.
Wilkinson, C: **I.2**: 155.
Wilkinson, K: **G.2**: 8.
Wilkinson, R: **K.4**: 160.
Wilkinson, S: **C.1**: 117.
Will, W: **F.3**: 178.
Willems, A: **I.2**: 225.
Willems, P: **F.4**: 17.
Willemyns, M: **D.7**: 55.
Willes, M: **D.7**: 16.
Willett, J: **C.1**: 36.
Willett, K: **J.4**: 17.
Williams, A: **D.7**: 77.
Williams, B: **F.7**: 97, 128.
Williams, C: **C.2**: 78. **D.7**: 341. **F.4**: 273.
Williams, D: **F.4**: 31. **I.6**: 17.
Williams, E: **D.7**: 221.
Williams, F: **H.4**: 95.
Williams, G: **C.1**: 51. **F.7**: 134.
Williams, J: **D.4**: 42. **I.6**: 5. **K.1**: 130.
Williams, K: **C.6**: 10. **D.9**: 135. **F.4**: 186.
Williams, L: **D.5**: 16.
Williams, W: **D.2**: 13.
Williamson, J: **F.2**: 7.
Willie, C: **D.9**: 45.
Willigen, van, J: **F.5**: 198.
Willis, C: **C.2**: 156.
Willis, D: **F.3**: 172.
Willis, E: **I.5**: 29.
Willis, K: **G.3.2**: 128, 161.
Willis, S: **D.2**: 20.
Willis, W: **D.7**: 317. **K.1**: 216.
Willits, F: **G.3.1**: 61.
Willower, D: **D.9**: 62, 129.
Wils, A: **F.4**: 123.
Wilsdorf, S: **J.5**: 15.
Wilson, A: **F.2**: 36.
Wilson, C: **F.3**: 101.
Wilson, D: **C.2**: 118. **C.5**: 27. **K.2**: 101.
Wilson, E: **F.5**: 114.
Wilson, F: **B.1**: 63. **H.4**: 77. **I.5**: 11.
Wilson, G: **F.1**: 58. **H.5**: 37. **K.1**: 233.
Wilson, H: **K.1**: 5.
Wilson, J: **D.5**: 50. **H.5**: 40. **I.5**: 94.
Wilson, K: **F.7**: 48.
Wilson, L: **K.1**: 96.
Wilson, M: **F.5**: 186.
Wilson, N: **F.2**: 36. **I.5**: 199.
Wilson, P: **D.9**: 70, 80. **K.1**: 164.
Wilson, R: **D.9**: 169. **F.4**: 292.
Wilson, T: **D.9**: 168, 203. **G.3.2**: 91. **K.2**: 101.
Wilson, W: **G.3.2**: 223.
Wilson-Figueroa, M: **F.8**: 38. **G.3.1**: 39.
Wilson-Sadberry, K: **D.9**: 168.
Winchester, H: **G.3.2**: 214. **H.7**: 5. **I.2**: 240. **K.1**: 265.
Windahl, S: **D.7**: 187.
Winden, van, F: **D.1**: 51.
Windhauser, J: **D.7**: 280.
Windle, M: **K.1**: 297.
Windolf, P: **I.5**: 195.
Winefield, A: **C.2**: 83, 97. **I.2**: 234.
Winefield, H: **C.2**: 83, 97. **I.2**: 234.
Winegarden, C: **F.8**: 62.
Winfield, L: **D.9**: 168.
Winick, C: **K.1**: 324.
Wink, P: **C.2**: 234.
Winkel, F: **K.1**: 14, 126.
Winkler, A: **I.2**: 111.
Winn, L: **K.2**: 89.
Winslow, A: **F.5**: 227.
Winter, D: **F.3**: 167. **J.6**: 49.
Winter, M: **G.3.2**: 8, 42, 142, 200.
Winterbottom, S: **H.7**: 10.
Winterton, J: **I.5**: 42.

Wintram, C: **F.5**: 91.
Wiseman, J: **C.1**: 161.
Wisner, B: **G.3.1**: 123. **K.4**: 200.
Wistrich, R: **F.7**: 218.
Wit, De, M: **F.3**: 69.
Witsberger, C: **K.2**: 41, 68.
Witt, C: **I.6**: 26.
Witt, S: **I.2**: 207. **I.6**: 15, 26.
Witte, A: **F.4**: 154.
Wittebols, J: **D.7**: 301.
Wittink, R: **I.3**: 137.
Wittmer, J: **C.3**: 114.
Witty, T: **F.3**: 204.
Witz, A: **I.4**: 104.
Witzig, D: **F.5**: 216.
Wizenberg, D: **D.8**: 71.
Wlodarek, J: **F.2**: 142.
Wnuk-Lipiński, E: **E.2**: 29–30.
Wohlfarth, T: **C.2**: 41.
Woittiez, I: **I.2**: 60.
Wojciechowska-Miszalska, A: **F.2**: 20. **F.4**: 76.
Wojtyniak, B: **F.3**: 125, 279.
Wolch, J: **K.1**: 238, 240, 291.
Wold, A: **D.7**: 212.
Wolf, D: **K.1**: 16. **K.2**: 41, 64.
Wolfe, A: **C.2**: 64. **E.1**: 1.
Wolfe, B: **F.2**: 7.
Wolfe, D: **F.4**: 155.
Wolfe, N: **I.4**: 24.
Wolfe, S: **K.4**: 193.
Wolfenstein, E: **A.2**: 14.
Wolff, E: **F.5**: 153. **I.3**: 90.
Wolff, K: **A.2**: 23.
Wolff, R: **E.2**: 55.
Wolff, S: **D.7**: 191.
Wolfson, M: **K.4**: 163.
Woliver, L: **F.5**: 196.
Wollitzer, P: **D.9**: 195.
Wolman, H: **H.7**: 11.
Wolpe, H: **D.9**: 53.
Wolpin, J: **I.3**: 103.
Wolter, K: **F.1**: 24.
Womack, B: **D.1**: 113.
Women Working Worldwide: **I.5**: 6.
Wonderlich, S: **F.4**: 159.
Wong, D: **C.2**: 57.

Wong, F: **D.7**: 249.
Wong, M: **C.2**: 172. **C.3**: 6.
Wong, R: **H.4**: 11.
Wong, S: **D.9**: 127.
Wood, J: **G.1**: 4.
Wood, L: **C.3**: 62. **D.7**: 77. **J.7**: 13.
Wood, P: **G.3.2**: 194. **H.4**: 74.
Wood, S: **H.4**: 29. **I.5**: 54.
Wood, W: **D.7**: 249.
Woodbury, M: **B.2**: 54.
Woodbury-Fariña, M: **C.1**: 66.
Woodcock, A: **F.6**: 16.
Wooden, M: **I.2**: 172. **I.5**: 198.
Woods, R: **F.3**: 101.
Woodward, J: **F.1**: 7.
Woodward, N: **C.5**: 42.
Wooffitt, R: **D.7**: 95.
Woolfe, S: **K.3**: 14.
Woollett, A: **F.4**: 299.
Woon, Y: **G.3.1**: 7.
Worden, R: **J.3**: 46.
World Bank: **F.5**: 9.
World Health Organization: **F.3**: 149.
Worobey, J: **F.7**: 31.
Worsham, N: **C.2**: 73.
Wortman, C: **I.2**: 139.
Wouters, C: **C.3**: 131.
Woycke, J: **J.6**: 31.
Wrabetz, A: **C.1**: 92.
Wrench, J: **I.2**: 11.
Wright, G: **F.4**: 86.
Wright, M: **K.1**: 191.
Wright, R: **C.2**: 168. **D.8**: 16. **F.3**: 282. **I.2**: 102, 223.
Wright, S: **D.5**: 34.
Wright, T: **C.7**: 31. **F.7**: 148.
Wrightsman, L: **C.2**: 189. **D.4**: 5.
Wrinkle, R: **F.8**: 61.
Wrye, H: **C.1**: 33.
Wu, D: **D.1**: 9. **F.7**: 58, 99.
Wu, L: **B.2**: 34, 48.
Wulczyn, F: **K.2**: 38.
Wundersitz, J: **J.3**: 25.
Wunnava, P: **I.2**: 46.
Wuthnow, R: **C.3**: 95. **D.3**: 3.
Wyer, R: **J.6**: 16.
Wyld, D: **I.5**: 99.

Wynne, B: **D.6**: 3.
Wynne-Harley, D: **F.2**: 51.
Xiberras, M: **K.1**: 383.
Xie, Y: **B.2**: 109. **G.3.2**: 219, 318. **I.4**: 49.
Xu, Y: **J.6**: 19.
Yablokov, A: **G.1**: 40.
Yadava, K: **F.8**: 49.
Yadov, V: **E.3**: 35.
Yalch, R: **D.7**: 109.
Yalman, N: **D.5**: 27.
Yamada, M: **D.3**: 30.
Yamada, T: **B.1**: 150.
Yamagishi, H: **G.2**: 21.
Yamamoto, M: **F.4**: 78.
Yamamoto, Y: **D.9**: 32.
Yammarino, F: **B.2**: 127.
Yamskov, A: **F.7**: 158.
Yang, P: **K.4**: 205.
Yang, Q: **F.3**: 98.
Yang, X: **E.2**: 41.
Yang, Z: **C.3**: 112. **G.3.1**: 29.
Yanitsky, O: **J.5**: 9.
Yankah, K: **D.7**: 168.
Yano, H: **H.4**: 27.
Yanovskaya, Y: **C.7**: 62.
Yanowitch, M: **E.1**: 4.
Yapa, L: **G.3.1**: 25.
Yardley, J: **C.2**: 211.
Yarnold, B: **J.5**: 29.
Yates, A: **I.5**: 125.
Yavas, U: **H.5**: 39.
Yazawa, S: **F.5**: 209.
Yazbeck, A: **F.3**: 238.
Yeager, C: **F.5**: 224.
Yeandle, S: **F.4**: 116.
Yearley, S: **G.1**: 22.
Yee, B: **F.4**: 126.
Yee, C: **C.7**: 23.
Yee, D: **C.2**: 18.
Yekel, H: **K.3**: 25.
Yeste Moyano, R: **G.3.1**: 112.
Yi, Y: **C.5**: 2.
Yiannakis, J: **F.7**: 48, 55.
Yiftachel, O: **F.7**: 129. **H.3**: 27.
Yochum, G: **I.2**: 10.
Yoder, J: **I.2**: 134.

Yogev, A: **C.3**: 28.
Yoon, I: **F.7**: 56.
Yoshihara, N: **G.2**: 17.
Yoshikane, H: **I.6**: 11.
Yoshise, Y: **G.3.2**: 57.
Yoshizumi, K: **F.4**: 242.
Young, A: **C.2**: 141. **F.7**: 8.
Young, C: **F.1**: 10. **F.2**: 10, 35.
Young, H: **F.6**: 47.
Young, J: **C.1**: 64. **K.1**: 99.
Young, M: **D.7**: 312. **F.2**: 50. **J.3**: 39.
Young, R: **D.5**: 22.
Young, V: **K.1**: 182.
Youngblade, L: **F.4**: 314.
Yrjönen, R: **J.6**: 53.
Yu, K: **C.2**: 179.
Yudelman, D: **F.8**: 109.
Yuen, B: **G.3.2**: 289.
Yuen, P: **K.4**: 214.
Yuju, H: **F.1**: 37.
Yukhneva, N: **F.7**: 83.
Yule, W: **F.2**: 104.
Yun, H: **I.4**: 113.
Yurovskaya, E: **D.1**: 21.
Yusuf, F: **F.3**: 31.
Yusuff, K: **I.6**: 4.
Yuval-Davis, N: **F.5**: 124.
Yzerbyt, V: **C.7**: 57.
Zaaijer, M: **G.3.2**: 325.
Zaffaroni, E: **J.3**: 9.
Zagórski, Z: **E.2**: 84.
Zakai, D: **C.3**: 46.
Zakar, A: **I.4**: 65.
Zakharova, O: **F.1**: 13.
Zald, M: **A.1**: 37.
Zampa, F: **C.5**: 65.
Zampelli, E: **I.2**: 24.
Zand, M: **F.7**: 83.
Zang, X: **J.6**: 44.
Zaniewski, K: **G.3.2**: 123.
Zappella, M: **C.7**: 47.
Zarychta, H: **H.3**: 87. **I.5**: 46.
Zarzycka, Z: **F.2**: 53.
Zaslow, M: **F.2**: 115.
Zasurskogo, I: **D.7**: 328.
Zatz, M: **D.4**: 9.
Zautra, A: **C.1**: 92. **F.2**: 15.

Zax, J: **H.3**: 60. **I.5**: 116.
Zdor, A: **D.1**: 21.
Zechariah, J: **I.5**: 7.
Zeckhauser, R: **C.2**: 153.
Zegeye, A: **E.2**: 12.
Zeghiche, A: **G.3.2**: 337.
Zehner, E: **D.5**: 121–122.
Zeitlin, J: **H.2**: 5.
Zeitlin, M: **I.5**: 163.
Zelazo, M: **B.2**: 89.
Zelinsky, W: **G.1**: 44.
Zelwer, B: **F.8**: 20.
Zemskov, V: **K.1**: 194.
Zeng, Y: **F.4**: 333.
Zenner, W: **F.7**: 183.
Zerilli, L: **F.5**: 279.
Zeroulou, Z: **F.8**: 14.
Zerubavel, E: **C.2**: 148.
Zetka, J: **I.4**: 2.
Zhang, S: **G.3.1**: 29.
Zheng, X: **G.3.2**: 199.
Zhikharevich, B: **G.3.1**: 124.
Zhitenev, V: **C.7**: 44.
Zhol', K: **D.5**: 26.
Zhou, M: **F.7**: 170.
Zhou, X: **C.3**: 85.
Zhu, W: **D.7**: 16.
Zhuravlev, V: **D.8**: 33.
Zick, C: **F.3**: 269.
Ziderman, A: **I.4**: 130.
Ziegler, R: **F.5**: 226. **I.4**: 64.
Zietlow, P: **F.4**: 222.
Zigler, E: **C.2**: 238. **F.2**: 116.
Zil'bert, B: **D.7**: 83.
Zilversmit, A: **F.5**: 216.
Zimmer, C: **I.3**: 115.
Zimmer, Z: **F.4**: 199.
Zimmermann, K: **F.3**: 276.
Zimring, F: **K.1**: 210, 392.
Zinberg, D: **D.9**: 175.
Zinkin, L: **C.1**: 109.
Zinkin, M: **F.8**: 76.
Zion, W: **F.3**: 207.
Zippay, A: **E.2**: 15. **I.4**: 123.
Zipprian, H: **B.1**: 110.
Zirkel, S: **C.2**: 59.

Zis', A: **D.8**: 26.
Žižek, S: **D.3**: 1. **J.2**: 18. **J.3**: 14.
Zlobin, N: **E.3**: 69.
Zmuidinas, M: **C.3**: 65.
Zollberg, A: **F.8**: 177.
Zoller, J: **G.3.2**: 49.
Zoomers, E: **E.2**: 65. **G.3.1**: 103.
Zoski, K: **B.2**: 93.
Zubok, V: **A.1**: 2.
Zuckerman, H: **F.5**: 208.
Zullow, H: **H.3**: 40.
Zumbado Jimenez, F: **G.3.2**: 117.
Zureik, E: **J.5**: 12.
Zuttermeister, P: **D.5**: 18.
Zuwerink, J: **F.7**: 247.
Zvekić, U: **K.1**: 84.
Zvezdkina, E: **C.2**: 241.
Zwarts, F: **D.7**: 205.
Zweigenhaft, R: **E.2**: 3.
Zwi, A: **K.4**: 74.
Zylberberg, J: **D.9**: 126. **F.2**: 132.

PLACENAME INDEX
INDEX DES ENDROITS

Afghanistan
F.1: 1. **F.7**: 164.

Africa
Entries also appear under:
NORTH AFRICA; SOUTHERN AFRICA; SUB-SAHARAN AFRICA; WEST AFRICA
C.5: 55. **D.1**: 101. **D.5**: 106. **D.7**: 231. **D.8**: 2, 18. **D.9**: 27–28. **E.1**: 8. **F.1**: 44. **F.3**: 151, 177. **F.4**: 190. **F.5**: 47, 241, 326. **G.3.2**: 254. **H.4**: 92. **I.2**: 112, 143. **I.5**: 151. **J.4**: 11. **J.6**: 28, 55. **J.7**: 5. **K.3**: 2.

Alabama
F.7: 147.

Alaska
D.7: 315.

Alberta
D.5: 103. **K.1**: 16.

Algeria
F.4: 352. **F.8**: 60. **G.3.2**: 164, 207, 337. **I.2**: 207. **J.3**: 22.

Amazon
H.7: 15.

Americas
Entries also appear under:
CENTRAL AMERICA; LATIN AMERICA; NORTH AMERICA; SOUTH AMERICA

Andes
A.2: 6. **K.1**: 11, 321.

Andhra Pradesh
E.3: 28. **F.3**: 139.

Antigua
G.3.2: 32.

Argentina
D.7: 382. **D.9**: 48. **E.2**: 82. **F.6**: 41. **F.7**: 85, 90, 134, 167. **F.8**: 161. **G.2**: 2. **I.2**: 9. **I.4**: 9.

Arizona
I.2: 104. **J.5**: 35.

Asia
Entries also appear under:
CENTRAL ASIA; HIMALAYAS; SOUTH ASIA; SOUTHEAST ASIA
A.1: 43. **C.7**: 31. **D.1**: 126. **D.5**: 71, 95, 122. **D.7**: 16. **D.9**: 109. **E.1**: 2. **E.3**: 42. **F.1**: 43. **F.5**: 166. **G.3.2**: 233, 343, 348, 367. **H.1**: 2–3. **H.7**: 24. **J.7**: 5. **K.1**: 255.

Australia
Entries also appear under:
AUSTRALIAN CAPITAL TERRITORY; NEW SOUTH WALES; NORTHERN TERRITORY; QUEENSLAND; SOUTH AUSTRALIA; VICTORIA; WESTERN AUSTRALIA
B.2: 32. **C.1**: 25. **C.7**: 20. **D.1**: 25, 73. **D.7**: 39, 155, 336, 358. **D.9**: 4, 137, 179. **E.1**: 2. **F.2**: 35, 43. **F.3**: 84, 289. **F.4**: 15, 22, 176, 207. **F.5**: 50, 201. **F.7**: 26, 29, 40–41, 48, 81, 228. **F.8**: 2, 23, 67, 85, 112, 116. **G.1**: 34. **G.2**: 26. **G.3.1**: 98. **G.3.2**: 348, 356. **H.3**: 20. **H.7**: 5. **I.2**: 2, 52, 131, 172, 191, 240. **I.4**: 41, 78, 133. **I.5**: 28, 131. **J.3**: 43. **J.6**: 12–13, 32. **J.8**: 1. **K.1**: 164, 370, 390, 405. **K.2**: 15, 23, 69, 105. **K.3**: 36. **K.4**: 241.

Australian Capital Territory
D.7: 42.

Austria
C.1: 71. **D.8**: 17. **D.9**: 66, 215. **F.4**: 258. **F.5**: 54. **I.2**: 220. **K.1**: 428.

Azerbaijan
F.7: 87.

Bahrain
G.1: 7. **H.5**: 39.

Bali
F.4: 236. **F.5**: 246.

Baltic States
F.7: 109.

Bangladesh
D.5: 164, 177, 179. **D.9**: 141. **F.2**: 23. **F.3**: 80, 122, 125, 141, 235, 264, 279–280. **F.5**: 38, 302. **F.8**: 80. **G.1**: 41. **H.4**: 43, 61. **I.2**: 101. **J.6**: 24. **J.7**: 7.

Barbados
C.7: 51. **D.7**: 386.

Belgium
D.7: 75. **F.3**: 297. **F.4**: 17, 343. **F.7**: 193. **G.2**: 29. **G.3.2**: 26. **K.2**: 3, 37.

Belize
D.9: 111, 119. **E.2**: 53. **F.8**: 129.

Bhutan
F.7: 50.

Bihar
E.2: 37.

Bolivia
C.7: 2. **F.8**: 149. **G.3.2**: 203. **H.7**: 15. **I.5**: 153. **K.4**: 184.

Borneo
G.1: 59.

Brazil
Entries also appear under:
RIO DE JANEIRO; RIO GRANDE DO SUL; SAO PAULO
C.1: 38. D.2: 17. D.7: 80, 250, 388. D.9: 21. E.2: 81. F.1: 53. F.2: 101. F.3: 78, 176, 231. F.5: 162. F.6: 5. G.1: 27. G.3.1: 73. G.3.2: 11, 141, 280. H.3: 29. H.7: 4, 8. I.3: 88. I.4: 1. I.5: 176. J.2: 22. J.3: 6. J.5: 19. K.1: 26, 116.

British Columbia
D.7: 41.

Bulgaria
D.7: 97, 193.

Burkina Faso
K.4: 91.

Burundi
F.3: 282.

California
D.4: 31. D.7: 5, 199. D.9: 37. F.3: 160. F.4: 126, 354. F.5: 18, 64. F.7: 9, 59, 115. G.2: 34. G.3.2: 1, 76, 150, 239. H.5: 8. I.2: 25, 205. I.3: 123. K.1: 180.

Cameroon
C.2: 10. F.5: 293. G.3.1: 96.

Canada
Entries also appear under:
ALBERTA; BRITISH COLUMBIA; NOVA SCOTIA; ONTARIO; QUEBEC
D.1: 91, 131. D.3: 26. D.5: 142, 149, 168. D.7: 242, 332. D.9: 199. F.1: 48. F.2: 30, 125. F.3: 30, 69, 88, 95, 155, 246, 258. F.4: 199. F.5: 39, 69, 75, 140. F.7: 80, 112, 131, 200, 254. F.8: 1, 23, 50, 71, 74, 121, 171. G.3.2: 30, 83, 178, 195, 237–238, 260. H.3: 63. H.4: 39, 46. H.5: 31. I.2: 34, 84, 91, 115, 219. I.3: 107. I.4: 17. I.5: 29, 72, 140. I.6: 38. J.8: 19. K.1: 58, 86, 92, 216, 287, 412. K.2: 13, 93. K.3: 29. K.4: 87, 133, 193, 204.

Caribbean
D.9: 24. F.2: 84. F.3: 33, 76. F.7: 7. F.8: 37, 40, 120, 124, 167. G.3.2: 364.

Central America
F.1: 46. F.5: 77. F.8: 6. K.1: 262.

Central Asia
D.7: 34. F.1: 18. F.7: 17, 47, 88, 179. G.1: 53.

Central Europe
D.5: 91, 134. G.3.2: 74.

Chile
D.1: 140. E.2: 4. G.3.2: 253, 295. I.5: 153. J.5: 16.

China
B.1: 8, 72. C.1: 10. C.2: 179. C.3: 47, 106, 108. D.1: 4, 9–10, 113. D.5: 20. D.7: 348, 354–355. D.9: 50, 124. E.2: 7, 41, 80. E.3: 8,

China continued
14. F.1: 5, 36, 39. F.2: 62. F.3: 9, 35, 53, 83, 91, 98, 120, 237. F.4: 16, 250, 333. F.5: 223, 312. F.7: 57–58, 99. F.8: 101. G.3.1: 6, 29, 34. G.3.2: 34, 67, 169, 219, 243, 255, 318, 323, 338, 358, 366. H.2: 17. H.3: 39. H.4: 11. I.2: 62, 173. I.4: 65, 68, 70, 74. J.2: 16. J.6: 5, 44. J.7: 24. K.4: 205.

Colombia
F.3: 58, 134. G.3.2: 329. K.1: 320.

Colorado
G.3.2: 229. H.3: 9.

Costa Rica
D.5: 143. D.7: 289. E.2: 25. F.3: 134. F.5: 324. F.8: 90. G.3.2: 29, 117, 265. I.3: 120. J.6: 10.

Croatia
G.3.1: 97.

Cuba
F.3: 85, 183, 278. F.8: 134. J.1: 7. J.6: 33, 35.

Cyprus
D.7: 43. I.4: 60.

Czechoslovakia
D.5: 151. D.7: 97. F.1: 30. F.3: 65, 140, 248, 309. F.4: 88. F.7: 93. H.3: 66. H.5: 18. I.4: 105.

Denmark
D.9: 178. F.4: 235. G.3.2: 38, 315, 350. I.2: 95, 208. K.4: 165.

Dominican Republic
D.7: 357. F.8: 113. H.4: 13. K.1: 257.

Eastern Europe
C.6: 2. D.1: 75–76, 84. D.5: 69, 91, 97, 134. E.3: 26–27. F.4: 44. F.5: 81, 318. F.7: 23. F.8: 64, 99, 126. H.5: 10. I.4: 65. I.6: 41. J.1: 18. J.2: 2–3. J.6: 46.

Ecuador
F.3: 260. F.8: 34. G.2: 14. G.3.2: 59, 251. H.7: 15. I.2: 90.

Egypt
D.5: 145. F.2: 147. F.3: 64, 173, 253. F.5: 5, 145. G.3.1: 27. G.3.2: 5. H.3: 21, 91.

El Salvador
F.3: 81. G.3.1: 49.

England
D.4: 4, 28. D.7: 7. D.8: 48, 60, 70. D.9: 72. E.2: 72. F.3: 24, 101. F.4: 245. F.6: 34. F.7: 13, 24, 97, 126, 139, 177, 199. F.8: 23, 68, 70, 108. G.1: 25. G.3: 1. G.3.2: 48, 85, 94, 96, 193, 205, 275–276, 313. H.3: 79. H.4: 24. I.2: 13–14, 40. I.4: 132. I.5: 133. J.3: 21, 40. J.4: 22. K.1: 30, 157, 418. K.2: 74. K.3: 29. K.4: 131, 134, 244.

Estonia
H.2: 2.

INTERNATIONAL BIBLIOGRAPHY OF SOCIOLOGY — 1991

Ethiopia
   D.9: 85. **F.3**: 103, 107. **G.3.1**: 88, 92. **G.3.2**: 65. **K.1**: 18. **K.4**: 213.

Europe
   Entries also appear under:
   BALTIC STATES; CENTRAL EUROPE; EASTERN EUROPE; SCANDINAVIA; WESTERN EUROPE
   C.7: 26. **D.1**: 8, 55, 81. **D.5**: 94. **D.7**: 101, 246, 251, 281, 297, 323, 372, 385, 389. **D.8**: 12. **D.9**: 82, 167, 197. **E.2**: 58. **E.3**: 73. **F.1**: 12, 21–22, 27, 50. **F.2**: 26, 153. **F.3**: 14–15, 18, 25, 86. **F.4**: 52, 183. **F.5**: 124, 186, 205. **F.6**: 7. **F.7**: 6, 21, 98, 188. **F.8**: 59, 102, 115, 128. **G.2**: 6, 15. **G.3.1**: 21, 32, 84, 121. **G.3.2**: 24, 41, 167, 326. **H.2**: 3, 18–19. **I.3**: 60. **I.4**: 117. **I.5**: 4, 60, 80, 184. **I.6**: 5. **J.2**: 27. **J.8**: 7, 9. **K.1**: 293. **K.2**: 20. **K.3**: 43. **K.4**: 13, 116, 197, 240, 267.

Fiji
   J.3: 24. **J.7**: 10.

Finland
   D.5: 44, 108, 129. **E.2**: 36. **F.2**: 155. **F.3**: 102, 165, 222, 226. **F.4**: 123. **F.6**: 38. **G.3.1**: 50. **H.2**: 2. **H.6**: 7. **I.2**: 208. **J.5**: 5. **J.6**: 53.

Florida
   I.2: 204.

France
   A.1: 28. **B.2**: 106. **C.5**: 12. **D.1**: 3, 59. **D.2**: 9, 25. **D.5**: 115. **D.7**: 6, 112, 182, 309, 350. **D.8**: 35. **D.9**: 40, 100, 181, 216. **E.1**: 7. **F.1**: 66. **F.2**: 144. **F.3**: 251, 273. **F.4**: 229. **F.5**: 120, 165, 265. **F.7**: 19, 45, 66, 155, 259, 268. **F.8**: 3, 19, 22, 26, 29, 48, 60, 68, 75, 81, 114, 131–132, 141, 143, 150. **G.3.1**: 21, 101, 131. **G.3.2**: 21, 145, 188, 201, 340. **H.3**: 44. **H.4**: 12. **H.5**: 12. **I.2**: 183. **I.3**: 140. **I.4**: 63, 66, 118. **I.5**: 1, 11, 23, 157. **J.7**: 12. **K.1**: 149, 179, 265. **K.2**: 18, 81.

Gambia
   F.5: 269.

Georgia
   J.6: 64.

Georgia U.S.A.
   G.3.2: 229.

Germany
   B.1: 73. **C.2**: 107. **C.5**: 45–46. **D.1**: 87, 96, 99, 114. **D.5**: 104, 131. **D.7**: 93, 105, 300, 302, 319. **D.9**: 40, 144. **E.2**: 35, 45. **E.3**: 1, 23, 34. **F.2**: 142. **F.3**: 5, 16, 249–250, 276–277. **F.4**: 260, 342. **F.5**: 52, 54–55, 148, 225, 251, 296. **F.7**: 85, 92, 143, 194, 219, 240, 268. **F.8**: 12, 64, 66, 132, 172, 175. **G.3.2**: 247, 315. **H.2**: 18. **H.3**: 3. **H.4**: 2, 28, 58, 76. **H.7**: 22. **I.1**: 2. **I.2**: 40, 45, 93, 164, 203, 220. **I.3**: 4, 13, 30, 93. **I.4**: 64, 127. **I.5**: 1, 30, 130, 154, 160, 183, 195. **J.3**: 17, 31. **J.5**: 8, 27, 31, 36. **J.6**: 3, 37–38, 52, 56–57. **K.1**: 67, 78, 218. **K.2**: 16, 27, 102. **K.4**: 38, 73, 90, 181.

Germany East
   A.1: 31. **D.7**: 97, 377. **E.3**: 39. **F.2**: 137. **H.3**: 75. **J.5**: 15. **K.1**: 402.

Ghana
   F.3: 132. **F.5**: 257. **F.8**: 94. **G.3.1**: 108. **G.3.2**: 213. **K.4**: 227.

Greece
   D.2: 14. **D.5**: 138. **E.1**: 11. **F.3**: 133. **F.5**: 266, 325. **G.2**: 7. **G.3.1**: 17, 70, 80. **G.3.2**: 346. **I.4**: 69.

Grenada
   D.7: 251. **F.3**: 178. **H.7**: 14. **J.6**: 14.

Guatemala
   F.5: 188, 292. **F.8**: 20. **I.2**: 16.

Guyana
   F.3: 6. **F.5**: 200. **F.7**: 128. **K.4**: 112.

Haiti
   F.3: 295. **F.8**: 69. **G.3.1**: 83.

Haryana
   F.3: 131. **G.3.2**: 101.

Hawaii
   F.4: 255. **F.7**: 204.

Himachal Pradesh
   F.3: 20.

Himalayas
   F.3: 20.

Holland
   Entries also appear under:
   NETHERLANDS

Honduras
   G.3.1: 58.

Hong Kong
   C.3: 43. **D.7**: 305. **D.9**: 38, 90. **F.2**: 19. **G.3.2**: 261–262, 366. **H.3**: 39. **H.7**: 25. **K.1**: 318. **K.4**: 214.

Hungary
   A.1: 16. **D.1**: 58, 60. **D.5**: 128. **D.7**: 70. **D.8**: 61. **D.9**: 91, 146. **E.3**: 22. **F.2**: 150. **F.3**: 259, 284, 305. **F.4**: 70, 98. **F.5**: 307, 319. **F.7**: 25. **G.3.1**: 3. **H.5**: 18. **I.4**: 32. **K.1**: 19, 289. **K.2**: 7, 79.

Iceland
   G.1: 6. **G.3.2**: 105.

Illinois
   F.5: 164. **F.7**: 56. **G.3.2**: 241, 277. **K.1**: 285.

India
   Entries also appear under:
   ANDHRA PRADESH; BIHAR; HARYANA; HIMACHAL PRADESH; KARNATAKA; KERALA; MADHYA PRADESH; MAHARASHTRA; ORISSA; PUNJAB; RAJASTHAN; TAMIL NADU; UTTAR PRADESH; WEST BENGAL
   B.1: 92. **C.1**: 14. **C.2**: 9. **C.4**: 13, 29. **D.1**: 40. **D.5**: 45, 54, 85, 154–155, 157, 169. **D.7**: 107, 186. **D.8**: 27. **D.9**: 16, 29, 55, 133. **E.1**: 18. **E.2**: 1, 22, 46, 79. **E.3**: 43, 63. **F.2**: 94–95.

India continued
F.3: 245, 256, 290, 308. **F.4**: 330. **F.5**: 9, 28, 155, 198, 223. **F.7**: 29, 122, 171, 184. **F.8**: 78, 88, 156. **G.2**: 13. **G.3.1**: 7, 37. **G.3.2**: 321, 349. **H.3**: 84. **H.4**: 47, 70, 101. **I.2**: 15, 81, 142. **I.5**: 7. **J.5**: 6. **J.7**: 7. **K.1**: 28–29, 266, 269, 271, 283. **K.2**: 99. **K.3**: 34, 46. **K.4**: 46.

Indonesia
Entries also appear under:
BALI; IRIAN JAYA; JAVA

D.5: 166–167. **D.9**: 61. **F.4**: 211. **F.5**: 175. **G.2**: 23. **G.3.2**: 256. **H.3**: 55. **I.4**: 43. **K.1**: 249. **K.4**: 97.

Iowa
G.3.1: 35.

Iran
D.5: 27, 80. **D.7**: 78. **D.8**: 6. **D.9**: 102. **F.1**: 49. **F.4**: 219. **F.5**: 217. **F.7**: 88. **F.8**: 142. **G.3.2**: 361. **J.5**: 28.

Iraq
D.1: 42. **D.8**: 34. **F.5**: 16. **F.7**: 133. **K.1**: 245.

Ireland
D.9: 213. **E.2**: 64. **F.3**: 298. **F.4**: 151. **F.5**: 37, 197. **F.8**: 56. **G.2**: 6, 19. **G.3.1**: 10, 56. **I.2**: 236, 246. **I.4**: 36. **I.5**: 108. **K.1**: 337. **K.2**: 55, 71.

Irian Jaya
G.1: 18.

Israel
Entries also appear under:
ISRAELI OCCUPIED TERRITORIES

C.3: 4, 28. **D.1**: 108. **D.2**: 1, 3. **D.5**: 186. **D.7**: 28. **D.9**: 142. **E.2**: 20. **F.3**: 291. **F.4**: 65, 80, 142. **F.5**: 4, 60. **F.7**: 63, 114, 116, 129, 140, 159–160, 174, 180. **F.8**: 13, 89, 92. **G.3.2**: 259. **H.3**: 27. **H.4**: 102. **I.2**: 50. **I.3**: 97. **I.4**: 20. **I.5**: 36. **J.3**: 16. **J.5**: 12. **J.6**: 8, 29. **J.7**: 4. **K.1**: 208. **K.2**: 100, 108. **K.3**: 25.

Israeli Occupied Territories
D.9: 206.

Italy
D.2: 12. **D.8**: 45, 64. **D.9**: 40. **E.3**: 7, 68.

Ivory Coast
D.1: 64. **F.2**: 58. **I.2**: 5, 198.

Jamaica
D.9: 161. **I.3**: 64.

Japan
A.1: 5, 13, 42. **A.2**: 5. **C.2**: 19. **C.4**: 33. **C.5**: 12, 37, 57. **C.7**: 46. **D.1**: 33, 54, 69, 97, 139. **D.2**: 4, 8, 11. **D.5**: 22–23, 25, 81, 120. **D.6**: 23. **D.7**: 26, 105, 335. **D.9**: 115. **E.1**: 6. **E.2**: 57, 67. **E.3**: 53, 60. **F.2**: 28, 32, 43, 48, 56, 63, 102, 121. **F.3**: 97, 152, 296. **F.4**: 2, 12, 14, 23, 69, 105, 111, 293, 295. **F.5**: 11, 20, 185, 209, 246, 285, 311. **F.6**: 33. **F.7**: 89, 92, 142, 195. **F.8**: 96. **G.2**: 17. **G.3.1**: 69, 84. **G.3.2**: 6, 12–13, 81, 130, 199, 274, 282. **H.2**:

Japan continued
1. **H.4**: 29, 48–49, 69, 104. **I.1**: 8, 16. **I.2**: 154, 211. **I.3**: 1, 42, 53, 60, 95, 128, 130, 132. **I.4**: 26, 54, 106. **I.5**: 7, 20, 32, 68, 173. **I.6**: 30. **K.1**: 155, 394, 396, 400. **K.4**: 248.

Java
D.2: 13. **G.3.1**: 30.

Jordan
D.9: 19, 156. **F.5**: 146. **F.7**: 141. **G.3.2**: 231. **I.4**: 97.

Kansas
G.3.2: 122.

Karnataka
C.7: 9. **F.3**: 265. **F.4**: 334.

Kentucky
H.7: 28.

Kenya
D.1: 49. **F.3**: 72. **F.4**: 67. **F.5**: 218, 253. **F.7**: 53. **G.2**: 4. **G.3.1**: 24. **G.3.2**: 10, 104, 286, 334. **I.2**: 171.

Kerala
F.5: 211. **G.3.1**: 106.

Korea
Entries also appear under:
NORTH KOREA; SOUTH KOREA

C.3: 111. **D.5**: 7. **D.7**: 58, 183, 189. **F.4**: 194. **F.7**: 64. **H.3**: 42.

Kuwait
F.8: 79. **I.2**: 74.

Latin America
A.2: 24. **C.1**: 72. **D.1**: 71. **D.7**: 270, 321. **D.9**: 138, 153. **E.3**: 19. **F.3**: 75. **F.4**: 71, 331. **F.5**: 104, 274. **F.7**: 38, 214. **F.8**: 127. **G.2**: 33. **G.3.1**: 54, 60, 93. **G.3.2**: 11, 43, 136, 179. **H.4**: 87. **I.1**: 10. **J.2**: 5, 10, 13.

Lebanon
D.5: 174. **E.1**: 21. **F.7**: 18. **I.4**: 97.

Lesotho
G.3.2: 335.

Liberia
F.3: 286.

Lithuania
D.9: 125. **F.8**: 82.

Louisiana
F.7: 54.

Madagascar
G.3.1: 13.

Madhya Pradesh
H.7: 21.

Maharashtra
H.3: 13.

Maine
C.4: 34.

Malawi
F.2: 103. **H.4**: 4. **I.4**: 128.

Malaysia
　D.8: 55. **E.1**: 24. **G.3.1**: 5. **I.5**: 2, 18.
Mali
　H.4: 30.
Massachusetts
　G.3.2: 229.
Mauritius
　F.7: 62.
Mediterranean Region
　C.2: 6. **F.3**: 293. **G.3.1**: 11. **G.3.2**: 346.
Mexico
　C.7: 63. **D.5**: 116. **D.7**: 185, 226. **F.1**: 2, 38. **F.3**: 278, 311. **F.4**: 35, 227. **F.5**: 3, 236. **F.6**: 55. **F.8**: 5, 32, 37, 53, 97, 120, 124, 165. **G.3.1**: 42, 113. **G.3.2**: 8, 19, 54, 109, 200. **H.2**: 10. **H.3**: 10, 29, 56. **H.4**: 77. **H.5**: 1. **I.2**: 162. **I.3**: 56. **J.6**: 45. **J.8**: 17. **K.4**: 72, 166.
Michigan
　F.3: 112. **I.4**: 45. **K.1**: 90.
Micronesia
　K.1: 27.
Middle East
　D.7: 254. **F.5**: 171, 239. **F.7**: 178. **F.8**: 35, 145, 148. **G.1**: 39. **G.3.1**: 90. **I.4**: 97.
Mississippi
　D.9: 108. **I.2**: 97.
Missouri
　F.7: 146.
Morocco
　D.7: 380. **I.6**: 21. **J.3**: 8.
Mozambique
　F.5: 36.
Namibia
　G.3.2: 362.
Nebraska
　G.3.1: 9. **H.7**: 26.
Nepal
　D.5: 86. **E.3**: 17. **F.3**: 110, 252, 292. **F.4**: 66, 248, 327.
Netherlands
　B.2: 128. **D.7**: 75. **D.9**: 219. **E.2**: 17, 38. **E.3**: 23. **F.1**: 30, 52. **F.3**: 272. **F.4**: 17, 32. **F.7**: 111, 173, 248. **F.8**: 173. **G.2**: 6. **G.3**: 7. **G.3.1**: 119, 127. **G.3.2**: 204, 315. **H.5**: 18. **I.2**: 36, 117–118, 225. **I.3**: 40. **J.3**: 5. **K.1**: 178, 220, 316–317, 335, 339. **K.2**: 37. **K.4**: 134, 137.
Nevada
　K.1: 244.
New Jersey
　G.3.2: 229. **H.3**: 26. **J.4**: 26.
New Mexico
　F.3: 304.
New South Wales
　G.3.2: 309. **H.5**: 7.

New York
　D.7: 59. **F.3**: 234. **F.7**: 170. **G.3.1**: 26, 105. **G.3.2**: 28, 87, 239, 281, 308, 332. **I.1**: 9. **I.2**: 1, 185. **K.1**: 263. **K.3**: 47.
New Zealand
　D.1: 90. **D.7**: 51. **F.7**: 197, 209, 212. **H.6**: 3. **I.3**: 63. **K.1**: 22, 298, 364.
Nicaragua
　D.9: 73. **E.3**: 52. **F.5**: 107, 219. **J.5**: 26. **J.6**: 36.
Nigeria
　C.7: 77. **D.5**: 40, 112, 117, 162. **D.7**: 14, 49. **D.8**: 19. **F.1**: 8. **F.3**: 113. **F.4**: 55. **F.6**: 9. **G.1**: 38. **G.3**: 4. **G.3.2**: 139, 163, 166, 184, 206, 345. **H.3**: 50. **I.3**: 6. **I.4**: 128. **I.5**: 8. **I.6**: 4. **K.4**: 18, 103, 177, 208.
North Africa
　F.7: 178. **I.2**: 186.
North America
　D.7: 270. **F.1**: 27. **I.5**: 121.
North Carolina
　D.9: 11.
North Korea
　D.7: 340.
Northern Ireland
　D.7: 30, 296. **D.8**: 44. **E.2**: 18. **F.5**: 62, 320. **F.7**: 18, 192. **F.8**: 151. **G.3.2**: 61, 291–292. **H.4**: 28, 40. **I.2**: 156. **J.5**: 20. **K.1**: 270, 299. **K.4**: 123.
Northern Territory
　F.1: 55.
Norway
　D.2: 29. **D.9**: 125. **F.5**: 53, 238. **G.3.1**: 44–45, 99, 117. **I.2**: 208. **I.3**: 11. **I.5**: 15. **K.1**: 315. **K.2**: 67.
Nova Scotia
　F.8: 73.
Ohio
　E.2: 15. **F.3**: 223. **G.2**: 12. **G.3.1**: 79. **G.3.2**: 155, 229.
Ontario
　E.2: 68. **F.3**: 303. **G.3.2**: 70, 266. **I.4**: 28, 46. **I.5**: 91. **K.1**: 387.
Orissa
　K.2: 17.
Pacific Region
　Entries also appear under:
　　MICRONESIA; POLYNESIA
　D.1: 52. **D.7**: 16. **E.1**: 2. **E.3**: 41. **F.7**: 74. **G.3.2**: 367.
Pakistan
　D.5: 161. **D.9**: 134. **E.2**: 63. **F.3**: 241. **F.4**: 268. **F.7**: 104, 148. **F.8**: 137. **G.3.1**: 18, 74, 114. **G.3.2**: 97, 342. **I.2**: 85–86. **J.7**: 7.
Panama
　F.2: 134.

Papua New Guinea
F.5: 190. F.6: 30. H.7: 1. K.1: 53.

Paraguay
E.2: 65. E.3: 75. F.3: 54. G.3.1: 67. J.6: 61.

Pennsylvania
F.7: 67, 189. G.2: 3. I.5: 101.

Peru
D.7: 244, 333. F.7: 35. F.8: 55, 86. G.3.1: 103–104. G.3.2: 4. H.3: 24, 28. I.2: 116, 160. I.3: 31. I.5: 153, 201. J.7: 18. K.1: 261.

Philippines
D.5: 8. D.7: 8, 21, 79, 87. F.3: 128. F.7: 95. F.8: 170. G.3.1: 28. I.2: 99.

Poland
D.3: 90. D.5: 41, 144. D.9: 159. E.1: 23. E.2: 29, 35–36, 84. E.3: 74. F.2: 53, 142. F.3: 3, 49, 263, 294. F.7: 113, 217, 244. F.8: 176. G.1: 49. G.3.2: 123. H.2: 7. I.2: 226, 238. I.3: 131. I.4: 14, 96, 105. I.5: 69. J.3: 29. J.5: 30.

Polynesia
D.9: 113.

Portugal
G.2: 6.

Puerto Rico
C.1: 66. F.3: 278. F.4: 230. F.8: 166. J.1: 22. K.1: 48.

Punjab
F.3: 261.

Quebec
D.7: 150, 387. E.3: 66. F.2: 138. F.3: 8. F.8: 77. G.1: 54. G.3: 9. G.3.1: 101. G.3.2: 144. K.2: 35. K.4: 6.

Queensland
D.7: 55. G.3.2: 14.

Rajasthan
F.3: 51. F.4: 204, 224.

Reunion
G.3.2: 135.

Rio de Janeiro
F.4: 19. I.4: 22.

Rio Grande do Sul
G.3.2: 202.

Romania
D.5: 135. D.7: 97. E.3: 54. F.8: 126. G.3.1: 51. K.2: 63.

Russia
A.1: 21. D.1: 97. D.5: 111. D.7: 258. E.2: 49. F.7: 83, 187. F.8: 159. G.3.2: 69, 354. K.2: 19.

Rwanda
F.4: 48.

Sao Paulo
F.4: 40. F.7: 4. G.3.2: 359.

Saudi Arabia
D.8: 65. F.4: 249. F.5: 152. G.3.2: 322, 351. I.2: 51.

Scandinavia
D.7: 223. G.3.1: 100. K.2: 76.

Scotland
D.7: 343. F.4: 237. F.7: 12. F.8: 80. G.3.2: 165. H.4: 8, 71. I.6: 33. K.1: 43, 189, 300, 302. K.2: 10, 45. K.3: 20. K.4: 221–222.

Senegal
D.7: 346. D.9: 89. F.5: 192, 269. G.3.1: 78.

Sierra Leone
F.3: 100. F.4: 102, 150.

Singapore
D.7: 318. E.2: 78. F.3: 129. G.3.2: 279, 289. I.4: 113.

Solomon Islands
D.7: 35.

South Africa
D.5: 49, 65, 67. D.9: 53–54, 84. F.3: 19. F.4: 13, 18, 166, 187. F.5: 183, 195, 213, 249, 282. F.7: 28, 37, 46, 103, 174, 192, 227, 266. F.8: 21, 109. G.1: 23. G.3.1: 8, 95, 123. G.3.2: 114, 341, 362, 365, 368. H.3: 30. I.2: 168. I.3: 16, 76. I.5: 71, 77, 128, 147, 150. J.3: 4. K.1: 221, 419–420. K.4: 79, 89, 182, 200.

South America
Entries also appear under:
AMAZON; ANDES
G.1: 23. G.3.2: 368. I.5: 150.

South Asia
F.2: 78.

South Australia
K.4: 122.

South Korea
D.9: 180. E.2: 70. G.3.1: 126. G.3.2: 328. I.4: 86.

Southeast Asia
D.5: 96. E.3: 42. F.7: 92. F.8: 143. G.3.2: 353, 363. J.1: 21.

Southern Africa
D.5: 93. D.9: 92. F.3: 89. F.5: 321.

Spain
B.2: 106. D.2: 7. D.5: 123. E.2: 38. E.3: 33. F.1: 3. F.3: 17, 274, 281. F.4: 184. F.5: 315. F.8: 158. G.2: 6. G.3.1: 112. H.4: 54. H.7: 18. I.2: 210, 239. I.5: 79, 168. K.1: 282, 388. K.2: 90. K.4: 14, 80.

Sri Lanka
D.9: 93. F.3: 134. F.5: 231. F.8: 145. G.3.1: 25, 128. G.3.2: 226.

Sub-Saharan Africa
D.7: 337. F.3: 82, 171. G.3.2: 79, 360. I.2: 98. K.4: 20.

Sudan
E.1: 20. G.3.1: 86, 127. J.4: 25. K.4: 84.

Swaziland
G.3.1: 120.

Sweden
 D.5: 28, 72. **D.7**: 37, 45. **D.8**: 69. **E.3**: 9. **F.2**: 41. **F.4**: 47, 144, 242, 321. **F.5**: 180, 233, 235, 248, 267. **F.7**: 191. **G.1**: 11. **G.3.2**: 100, 102, 140, 143, 287, 311, 331. **H.3**: 65, 69, 81. **H.5**: 13. **I.2**: 208, 219. **I.5**: 15, 28, 35. **K.1**: 161, 393. **K.2**: 12, 78, 87, 104. **K.4**: 134, 192.

Switzerland
 D.1: 117, 119. **D.7**: 391. **F.5**: 54, 212. **F.8**: 9. **I.2**: 122. **I.3**: 118.

Syria
 D.1: 44. **I.4**: 97.

Taiwan
 D.5: 20. **F.4**: 16. **F.5**: 263, 328. **H.3**: 18. **I.5**: 53, 132.

Tamil Nadu
 G.3.2: 183.

Tanzania
 G.3.2: 84, 104, 362. **H.3**: 54.

Tennessee
 I.5: 120.

Texas
 F.7: 69. **G.3.2**: 126, 187, 230. **H.5**: 29. **K.1**: 251. **K.4**: 39.

Thailand
 D.1: 11. **D.5**: 83, 121. **F.2**: 58. **F.3**: 121. **G.3.1**: 135.

Togo
 H.4: 30.

Trinidad and Tobago
 F.5: 119. **I.4**: 128. **J.5**: 18.

Tunisia
 D.1: 70. **F.3**: 134. **H.3**: 91.

Turkey
 D.5: 27. **D.7**: 252. **F.3**: 123. **F.4**: 231. **F.5**: 152. **F.7**: 16, 141. **G.3.1**: 90.

U.S.A.
 Entries also appear under:

 ALABAMA; ALASKA; ARIZONA; CALIFORNIA; COLORADO; FLORIDA; HAWAII; GEORGIA; ILLINOIS; IOWA; KANSAS; KENTUCKY; LOUISIANA; MAINE; MASSACHUSETTS; MICHIGAN; MISSISSIPPI; MISSOURI; NEBRASKA; NEVADA; NEW JERSEY; NEW MEXICO; NEW YORK; NORTH CAROLINA; OHIO; PENNSYLVANIA; TENNESSEE; TEXAS; UTAH; VIRGINIA; WASHINGTON; WISCONSIN

 A.1: 2, 11, 18. **A.3**: 2, 6. **B.1**: 131. **B.2**: 22, 126. **C.1**: 147, 154, 161. **C.2**: 5, 96, 102. **C.3**: 95, 111. **C.5**: 36, 46, 57, 73. **C.7**: 58. **D.1**: 7, 65, 67, 86, 91, 115–116, 131. **D.2**: 6, 20. **D.4**: 5, 7, 37. **D.5**: 36, 41, 46, 81, 118, 138, 149–150, 152, 168, 171, 188. **D.6**: 10. **D.7**: 18, 33, 36, 58, 106, 183, 185, 230, 232, 240, 243, 250, 255–256, 260, 262, 271–272, 277, 280, 287, 304, 317, 327, 348, 351–352, 363, 366–367, 375, 381. **D.8**: 29, 42, 51, 56, 58, 76. **D.9**: 6, 26, 36, 42, 59, 111–112, 120, 148, 164, 168, 170, 182, 186, 198, 202, 204–205, 211–212,

U.S.A. continued
 214. **E.1**: 1. **E.2**: 3, 12, 28, 35, 39, 50, 66. **E.3**: 6, 23, 50–51, 71. **F.1**: 20, 26, 34, 56, 65, 70. **F.2**: 36, 43, 45–46, 79, 140–141, 157. **F.3**: 40, 44, 57, 68, 86, 119, 124, 147, 164, 170, 178, 201, 210, 267, 287. **F.4**: 4–5, 26, 29, 61, 92, 108, 115, 118, 124–125, 148–149, 155, 158, 212, 223, 234, 264, 290, 292, 306, 341, 347. **F.5**: 30, 70, 75, 84, 106, 117, 123, 142–143, 160, 170, 177, 180, 196, 199, 205, 276, 300. **F.6**: 17, 26, 35–36, 40. **F.7**: 2–3, 12, 22, 30, 43, 66, 86, 94, 96, 98, 100, 107–108, 115, 120, 125, 135–136, 145, 169, 174, 183, 190, 205, 207, 225, 233, 238, 250, 255. **F.8**: 4–5, 15, 23, 40, 44, 52–53, 62, 65, 69, 84, 87, 91, 100, 111, 118, 120–121, 124, 126, 146–147, 155, 167, 169–170, 176. **G.1**: 2, 4, 54. **G.2**: 8, 10, 28, 30, 33. **G.3.1**: 53, 55, 59, 75, 107, 133. **G.3.2**: 3, 19, 27–28, 66, 99, 110–111, 120, 137, 149, 156, 162, 196, 217, 228–229, 263, 284, 293, 317, 333, 347–348. **H.2**: 1, 12, 16. **H.3**: 17, 51, 62. **H.4**: 26, 33, 38, 46, 49, 62. **H.5**: 15. **H.7**: 19, 23. **I.1**: 12. **I.2**: 53, 61, 92, 110, 132, 149, 155, 161, 174, 192, 201–202, 228, 233. **I.3**: 13, 53, 57, 76, 83, 90–91. **I.4**: 7, 32, 41, 114, 133. **I.5**: 29, 48, 72, 92, 107, 111, 189, 197. **I.6**: 1. **J.1**: 5, 10, 19. **J.2**: 24, 29. **J.3**: 42, 45. **J.4**: 2, 18. **J.5**: 2, 10, 23, 29, 31. **J.6**: 1–2, 31, 40, 47, 49, 54. **J.7**: 1, 3, 21, 23. **J.8**: 17, 19. **K.1**: 17, 46, 49–50, 54, 61, 79, 142, 156, 160, 172–173, 175, 182, 195, 197, 210, 217, 219, 222, 229, 235, 243, 247, 250, 259, 267, 280, 288, 290, 303, 321, 330, 336, 340–341, 360, 381, 384–385, 389, 410, 422. **K.2**: 13, 23, 33–34, 40, 52, 83–84, 95, 110. **K.3**: 16, 18, 33. **K.4**: 32, 34, 63, 82, 95, 104, 113, 149, 155, 161–162, 171, 174, 176, 191, 198, 207, 215, 219, 226, 247, 250–251, 262.

U.S.S.R.
 Entries also appear under:

 AZERBAIJAN; ESTONIA; GEORGIA; LITHUANIA; RUSSIA; UKRAINE; UZBEKISTAN

 A.1: 35. **C.2**: 38. **C.3**: 56. **C.7**: 53. **D.1**: 31, 37, 84. **D.2**: 16, 27. **D.3**: 78, 81. **D.5**: 4, 97, 132, 173. **D.6**: 2. **D.7**: 34, 259, 263, 265, 312, 342, 360, 378–379. **D.8**: 59, 68. **E.1**: 4. **E.3**: 4, 27, 36. **F.1**: 13, 18, 41. **F.3**: 240. **F.4**: 106, 143. **F.5**: 31, 252, 261, 308. **F.7**: 36, 47, 71, 77, 127, 158. **F.8**: 99, 126. **G.3.1**: 63, 89, 91, 124. **G.3.2**: 75, 185. **H.3**: 48–49. **H.7**: 24. **I.2**: 199. **I.3**: 77. **I.6**: 19, 22, 41. **J.1**: 10. **J.2**: 26. **J.3**: 30. **J.4**: 21. **K.1**: 21, 117, 150–152, 194. **K.4**: 228.

Ukraine
 K.1: 1.

United Kingdom
 Entries also appear under:

 ENGLAND; NORTHERN IRELAND; SCOTLAND; WALES

INTERNATIONAL BIBLIOGRAPHY OF SOCIOLOGY — 1991

United Kingdom continued
B.2: 106. **C.1**: 67, 70, 105. **C.4**: 12. **C.7**: 69. **D.1**: 62, 67, 141. **D.3**: 79. **D.5**: 165. **D.7**: 189, 236, 268, 274, 294, 296, 310, 313, 349, 353, 363. **D.8**: 78. **D.9**: 25, 34, 71, 93, 128, 139–140, 185, 189, 200. **E.2**: 16, 74, 76. **F.1**: 17, 51. **F.2**: 46, 74, 102, 111, 113, 146. **F.3**: 1, 4, 111, 118, 157–158, 167, 189, 229, 288. **F.4**: 79, 94, 101, 116, 139, 185, 253, 259, 293, 315. **F.5**: 21, 110, 114, 138, 240, 244, 247, 323. **F.7**: 13–14, 27, 32, 65, 68, 72, 119, 123, 149, 161, 185, 220, 236, 253, 268. **F.8**: 19, 28, 103. **G.1**: 47. **G.2**: 6, 25, 35–36. **G.3.1**: 48, 62, 71, 124. **G.3.2**: 30, 46, 52, 92, 103, 159, 236, 245, 258, 270, 290, 300, 303, 314. **H.3**: 89. **H.4**: 40, 50–51, 56, 71, 74–75. **H.7**: 19. **I.1**: 6. **I.2**: 18, 65, 102, 128, 138, 152–153, 157, 166, 188, 207, 213, 216, 222–223, 226, 237, 245. **I.3**: 6, 10, 109–110, 140. **I.4**: 38, 67, 78, 133. **I.5**: 4, 35, 42, 54, 75–76, 84, 113, 122, 126, 144, 179. **I.6**: 3, 5, 14, 39. **J.1**: 13. **J.2**: 4. **J.3**: 2, 39. **J.4**: 6. **J.5**: 11. **J.6**: 63. **K.1**: 9, 54, 64, 98, 141, 195, 205, 225, 242, 253, 267, 338, 372. **K.2**: 13–14, 23, 37, 43–44, 47, 54, 58–59, 88–89. **K.3**: 5, 12, 23, 39, 42. **K.4**: 14, 27, 30, 35, 42, 49, 107–109, 115, 118, 120, 125, 127, 130, 137, 146, 159, 167, 199, 201, 210, 216, 231.

Uruguay
G.3.2: 20.

Utah
K.3: 15.

Uttar Pradesh
C.7: 9. **I.2**: 140.

Uzbekistan
D.1: 30. **D.7**: 339.

Vatican City
D.5: 116.

Venezuela
F.7: 132. **G.3.2**: 11, 64, 327. **H.7**: 8. **J.1**: 8. **J.6**: 45.

Victoria
G.3.2: 44, 146. **I.2**: 191. **K.4**: 122.

Vietnam
D.8: 77. **G.3.1**: 14.

Virginia
G.3.2: 229.

Wales
D.9: 72. **F.1**: 4. **F.4**: 245. **F.8**: 23. **G.3.2**: 85. **I.6**: 15. **K.1**: 157.

Washington
H.4: 41. **J.6**: 18. **K.3**: 15, 21.

West Africa
F.4: 331. **F.8**: 136.

West Bengal
C.7: 9. **F.5**: 43. **G.3.2**: 63.

Western Australia
F.7: 55.

Western Europe
D.9: 187. **E.3**: 51. **F.4**: 44. **F.5**: 310. **F.8**: 10, 135, 172. **G.3.1**: 52. **H.4**: 69. **I.2**: 63. **I.6**: 29. **J.5**: 24.

Wisconsin
I.5: 61. **K.1**: 60. **K.4**: 217.

Yugoslavia
Entries also appear under:

CROATIA
D.5: 10. **F.3**: 293. **F.5**: 23. **F.7**: 137, 165. **F.8**: 7. **I.3**: 94. **J.2**: 2. **J.7**: 15, 19.

Zaire
F.1: 71. **F.3**: 200. **H.4**: 31.

Zambia
F.2: 151. **F.8**: 107. **G.3.2**: 104, 362. **K.4**: 59.

Zimbabwe
C.2: 118. **D.4**: 10. **D.9**: 104. **F.5**: 45. **G.3.1**: 12, 85, 125, 130, 132. **G.3.2**: 23, 113, 168. **I.2**: 94, 167. **K.3**: 40. **K.4**: 141.

SUBJECT INDEX

Abandoned children **F.2**: 94. **K.1**: 39.

Ability **C.2**: 116. **D.7**: 56. **I.3**: 14.

Aborigines **C.1**: 25. **D.8**: 57. **D.9**: 4. **F.1**: 55. **K.2**: 73.

Abortion **D.3**: 11. **D.5**: 6. **F.3**: 30, 34, 38, 49, 52, 54, 57, 59, 62, 67, 70. **F.4**: 178. **F.5**: 223. **F.7**: 117. **J.6**: 15. **K.3**: 30.

Absenteeism **I.3**: 21, 52, 73, 78. **I.5**: 199.

Academic achievement **C.2**: 172. **D.9**: 38, 110, 116, 122, 142, 155. **F.3**: 88. **F.4**: 16, 120, 142. **H.3**: 71. **I.3**: 150.

Academic freedom **D.7**: 308. **I.4**: 114.

Academic profession **A.1**: 15. **A.2**: 6. **D.9**: 193. **I.4**: 23, 68, 114. **J.6**: 48. **K.1**: 182.

Academic success **D.9**: 161, 166. **I.4**: 62.

Access to education **D.9**: 132, 149.

Access to employment **I.2**: 79.

Accidents
Entries also appear under:
NUCLEAR ACCIDENTS; OCCUPATIONAL ACCIDENTS; WORK ACCIDENTS
C.2: 184. **F.2**: 51.

Accountability **C.4**: 36, 43. **H.4**: 33.

Accountants **D.3**: 31. **I.4**: 86.

Accounting
Entries also appear under:
PUBLIC ACCOUNTING
D.3: 31.

Acculturation **C.1**: 75. **C.2**: 78. **D.1**: 139.

Accumulation rate **H.2**: 16.

Achievement **C.3**: 2. **F.4**: 103. **I.3**: 96. **J.6**: 58.

Achievement motivation
Entries also appear under:
ACADEMIC ACHIEVEMENT
D.9: 18, 161.

Ackerman, Bruce **J.2**: 15.

Action theory **B.1**: 129. **C.2**: 15, 63.

Activists **D.5**: 78. **J.5**: 21, 35. **J.6**: 11, 39.

Actors **I.2**: 54. **I.4**: 30.

Adaptation to change **F.8**: 73.

Addict
Entries also appear under:
DRUG ADDICTS

Addiction
Entries also appear under:
DRUG ADDICTION
C.1: 127. **C.6**: 18.

Administration
Entries also appear under:
DEVELOPMENT ADMINISTRATION; EDUCATION ADMINISTRATION; HEALTH ADMINISTRATION; PUBLIC ADMINISTRATION; SCHOOL ADMINISTRATION
C.2: 176.

Administration of justice **J.3**: 13. **K.1**: 173.

Administrative organization **C.2**: 111.

Adolescence **C.1**: 76, 115. **C.2**: 18, 58, 225. **C.3**: 29. **F.2**: 120, 130. **F.3**: 112, 197. **F.4**: 351. **F.5**: 172. **I.4**: 55. **K.1**: 217, 279.

Adolescents **C.2**: 187. **C.3**: 3, 75–76, 110. **C.7**: 3. **D.5**: 51. **D.7**: 103, 386. **D.9**: 106, 161. **F.2**: 2, 17, 106, 119, 142–143, 145. **F.3**: 73, 126, 186, 200. **F.4**: 32, 273, 320. **F.6**: 1, 13–14, 32. **F.7**: 84. **H.4**: 78. **I.2**: 145, 208. **J.6**: 59. **K.1**: 9, 12, 42, 108, 297, 331, 333, 350, 361, 369, 401, 410. **K.4**: 128.

Adorno, Theodor W. **D.8**: 1, 21.

Adult education **D.9**: 1, 5–6, 23, 28, 34, 63, 128, 140, 183. **I.4**: 126.

Adults **C.1**: 77, 92. **C.2**: 3, 58, 158, 195. **C.3**: 11. **D.5**: 12. **F.2**: 15, 69–70, 96, 105. **F.3**: 226, 254. **F.4**: 134, 159, 285, 287. **H.3**: 59. **I.2**: 122. **I.3**: 12. **K.1**: 35–36, 81, 279, 407.

Advertisements **F.5**: 306.

Advertising **C.2**: 171. **D.7**: 100–101, 103–109, 111–116, 232, 370, 391. **D.9**: 28. **H.5**: 3. **K.1**: 298, 373.

Aesthetics **D.8**: 5, 32.

Affectivity **C.1**: 37. **C.2**: 36, 82. **C.7**: 4. **F.6**: 30.

Affiliation
Entries also appear under:
POLITICAL AFFILIATION; RELIGIOUS AFFILIATION
C.3: 6, 37. **D.7**: 35. **F.4**: 246.

Affirmative action **F.5**: 277. **F.7**: 265. **I.2**: 110, 131, 134, 204. **I.3**: 123.

African languages **D.7**: 215.

African National Congress **K.1**: 221.

Africans **F.8**: 24, 111. **K.2**: 18.
Afrikaners **F.7**: 46. **F.8**: 161.
Age
Entries also appear under:
OLD AGE
Age at marriage **F.4**: 118, 208, 249, 334. **F.5**: 2.
Age difference **F.4**: 249. **I.3**: 25.
Age groups **C.3**: 155. **C.7**: 20. **E.2**: 67. **F.1**: 65. **F.2**: 1, 7, 12–14, 20, 44. **G.3.1**: 34. **I.2**: 135. **J.6**: 56. **K.1**: 47. **K.2**: 36.
Aged
Entries also appear under:
CARE OF THE AGED
C.1: 2. **D.7**: 294. **F.2**: 10, 23, 34, 36, 38–39, 45–46, 48–53, 55–56, 59–61, 64–66. **F.4**: 287. **F.5**: 55, 160. **F.7**: 15. **Г.0**: 74, 85. **G.3.2**: 37. **H.3**: 73. **K.1**: 412. **K.2**: 17, 28, 74, 85. **K.3**: 42. **K.4**: 116–117, 122, 126, 133, 138, 141–142, 147, 149, 199.
Ageing **C.2**: 154, 160. **D.7**: 44, 77. **F.1**: 68. **F.2**: 24–25, 27–33, 35, 37, 40, 43, 54, 57–58, 62–63. **F.3**: 168. **F.4**: 68, 345. **F.5**: 35. **J.6**: 23.
Aggregate analysis **D.4**: 39.
Aggregate demand **H.5**: 5.
Agrarian movements **J.5**: 17.
Agrarian reform **G.3.1**: 106.
Agrarian society **E.3**: 75. **G.3.1**: 2.
Agricultural co-operatives **G.3.1**: 96.
Agricultural economics **H.4**: 45.
Agricultural enterprises
Entries also appear under:
FAMILY FARMS; SMALL FARMS
G.3.1: 10, 19, 44, 46, 50, 52, 56, 79, 105. **I.3**: 142, 144.
Agricultural history **H.4**: 55.
Agricultural policy **G.3.1**: 56, 75. **H.4**: 6.
Agricultural population **G.3.1**: 97.
Agricultural production **G.3.1**: 24.
Agricultural productivity **H.4**: 3.
Agricultural projects **G.3.1**: 22.
Agricultural research **G.3.1**: 66.
Agricultural workers **F.7**: 254. **G.3.1**: 86.
Agriculture **F.5**: 24, 293, 301. **F.8**: 110. **G.3**: 3, 9. **G.3.1**: 1, 11, 17, 28, 57, 81, 90, 107, 110, 114, 133. **G.3.2**: 10, 343. **H.4**: 1, 4, 19, 44, 82.
Aid
Entries also appear under:
FOREIGN AID; HEALTH AID; STATE AID
AIDS **C.3**: 78. **D.3**: 27. **D.5**: 38. **D.7**: 173. **F.2**: 16. **F.3**: 144–160, 163–164, 172, 176–177, 180–182, 185–186, 188, 202, 207, 209–210, 212, 216–219, 223–224, 227–228, 231, 234. **F.5**: 25, 45. **F.6**: 4. **I.2**: 222. **I.5**: 99. **K.1**: 144, 367. **K.3**: 2, 46–47. **K.4**: 168–172, 210, 235, 245–246.
Air transport **D.7**: 256.
Airlines **I.3**: 3.
Airports **G.3.2**: 224.
Alcohol **C.2**: 206. **D.7**: 333, 359. **F.2**: 129. **F.4**: 297. **H.5**: 17. **I.6**: 19. **K.1**: 299–301, 305, 307, 326, 333, 342–343, 347, 351–352, 355, 359, 363, 366, 369, 374, 376, 378.
Alcoholic beverages
Entries also appear under:
WINE
Alcoholism **C.1**: 174. **C.2**: 173. **D.2**: 24. **F.2**: 79. **K.1**: 296, 302–304, 306, 308–310, 312, 329, 356, 361, 382.
Algorithms **B.2**: 62.
Alienation
Entries also appear under:
POLITICAL ALIENATION
C.3: 56.
Alliances **C.5**: 86.
Alternative technology **G.3.1**: 66.
Altruism **C.2**: 181, 184. **C.3**: 95–97, 99–100, 103. **C.4**: 34. **C.7**: 25. **D.4**: 23. **D.5**: 86. **G.1**: 31.
Amendments
Entries also appear under:
CONSTITUTIONAL AMENDMENTS
Amerindians
Entries also appear under:
SOUTH AMERINDIANS
A.2: 6. **F.7**: 38, 105, 169. **K.1**: 49.
Amish **D.5**: 149. **E.3**: 38.
Ancestry **F.1**: 11.
Androgyny **C.2**: 226.
Animal experimentation **D.3**: 63.
Animals **F.5**: 121–122.
Anonymity **D.3**: 57. **H.3**: 30.
Anorexia **C.2**: 74.
Ansari, M.A. **D.5**: 169.
Anthropological theory **B.1**: 28.
Anthropology
Entries also appear under:
CULTURAL ANTHROPOLOGY; ECONOMIC ANTHROPOLOGY; MEDICAL ANTHROPOLOGY; RURAL ANTHROPOLOGY
B.2: 26. **F.5**: 171. **K.1**: 404.
Anthropology of law **D.4**: 35.
Anthropometry **K.4**: 177.
Antiquity
Entries also appear under:
GREEK ANTIQUITY; ROMAN ANTIQUITY

Anti-semitism **D.5**: 88. **F.7**: 36, 216–218, 241, 244.
Anti-social behaviour **K.1**: 109, 309.
Anxiety **C.2**: 5, 8, 191, 240. **C.3**: 50, 159. **F.4**: 318. **G.3.2**: 2. **K.1**: 329.
Apartheid **D.7**: 243. **F.7**: 269. **F.8**: 109. **G.3.2**: 341, 362.
Applied research **A.2**: 17.
Apprenticeship **I.4**: 127.
Aquaculture **G.1**: 1.
Arab countries **D.7**: 254. **F.7**: 178. **F.8**: 152.
Arabic language **D.7**: 62.
Arabs **C.3**: 28. **D.7**: 2. **D.9**: 142. **F.4**: 142. **F.7**: 47, 129, 140–141, 160, 180. **H.3**: 27. **K.2**: 100. **K.4**: 55.
Arbitration
Entries also appear under:
COMPULSORY ARBITRATION
C.3: 104. **I.5**: 3, 61, 74, 82.
Archaeological methodology **F.5**: 139.
Archaeology **F.5**: 99.
Architecture **D.8**: 65, 70. **G.3.2**: 5, 285. **K.1**: 66.
Arendt, Hannah **J.2**: 15.
Armed forces **J.7**: 1, 6, 12, 14, 17–18.
Armies **I.5**: 165. **J.7**: 15.
Arms limitation **C.7**: 48. **J.7**: 20.
Arms race **J.7**: 20. **J.8**: 1, 3.
Aronowitz, Stanley **J.1**: 6.
Art
Entries also appear under:
DRAMATIC ART; PERFORMING ARTS
C.1: 80. **D.7**: 365, 393. **D.8**: 3, 7, 23–24, 26, 32–33, 44–45, 56, 71, 73, 393. **G.3.2**: 40.
Art market **D.8**: 41.
Artificial insemination **F.3**: 66.
Artificial intelligence **C.2**: 64, 115. **D.6**: 24. **D.7**: 118. **E.3**: 3. **I.5**: 51.
Artificial reproduction **K.4**: 257.
Artisans **I.4**: 37.
Artistic creation **C.2**: 27.
Arts **C.1**: 110. **D.8**: 42, 64, 76.
Asbestos **H.4**: 7.
Asians **D.9**: 109. **F.2**: 19. **F.7**: 9, 41, 84, 142. **F.8**: 112. **I.2**: 74, 180. **J.6**: 1. **K.1**: 12, 264. **K.4**: 42.
Aspirations **F.4**: 96. **F.7**: 20.
Assassination
Entries also appear under:
MURDER
Associations **C.4**: 2.
Athletes **I.6**: 4.

Attention **C.1**: 82. **C.2**: 54, 67. **C.3**: 148. **D.7**: 369.
Attitude change **C.1**: 63. **C.4**: 61. **C.7**: 24.
Attitude formation **C.7**: 80.
Attitudes
Entries also appear under:
COLLECTIVE ATTITUDES; CULTURAL ATTITUDES; POLITICAL ATTITUDES; RELIGIOUS ATTITUDES
B.2: 19–20. **C.7**: 3, 8–9, 28, 40, 57, 60, 63–64, 75. **D.3**: 90. **D.7**: 51, 344. **D.9**: 108, 120. **F.2**: 27, 96, 122. **F.3**: 30, 52, 59, 62, 160, 202–203. **F.4**: 258. **F.5**: 147. **F.8**: 61. **G.1**: 13. **H.4**: 104. **H.5**: 19, 31. **I.2**: 219. **I.4**: 5, 18, 69. **I.5**: 2, 134. **J.1**: 2, 11. **J.8**: 1. **K.1**: 206, 223. **K.2**: 29.
Attitudes to work **F.2**: 151. **I.3**: 58, 97–98, 101, 106.
Attribution **C.2**: 100, 170. **C.3**: 24. **I.5**: 3.
Audience **D.7**: 161, 170, 230, 257. **F.3**: 187.
Authoritarian leadership **J.3**: 14.
Authoritarian regimes **J.5**: 16, 22.
Authoritarianism **F.3**: 178. **F.8**: 59. **J.3**: 1. **J.6**: 49.
Authority
Entries also appear under:
RELIGIOUS AUTHORITIES
C.3: 155.
Autobiography **F.5**: 254.
Automation
Entries also appear under:
OFFICE AUTOMATION
H.4: 81. **I.4**: 21.
Automobile industry **D.7**: 114. **H.4**: 69. **I.3**: 53, 67, 87. **I.5**: 121.
Automobiles **F.7**: 234. **H.4**: 30. **I.2**: 210.
Avoidance **K.4**: 58.
Azeri **F.7**: 87.
Bacon, Francis **D.8**: 14.
Bangladeshis **F.8**: 70.
Banking **H.6**: 3. **I.4**: 10. **K.1**: 318.
Banks
Entries also appear under:
WORLD BANK
F.5: 235. **H.6**: 7, 9. **I.4**: 50. **K.1**: 120.
Baptist Churches **D.5**: 113.
Bargaining
Entries also appear under:
COLLECTIVE BARGAINING; WAGE BARGAINING
C.3: 26, 90, 106, 121, 127. **C.4**: 40. **C.5**: 77. **I.5**: 64, 71–73, 139.
Bargaining power **I.5**: 70.
Basques **F.7**: 135.
Baudrillard, Jean **B.1**: 88–89.

Bedouin **F.3**: 291.
Beer, Stafford **C.5**: 11.
Beggars **D.5**: 74. **K.1**: 233.
Behaviour **C.4**: 4.
Behaviour in groups **C.4**: 8.
Behavioural sciences **A.1**: 30. **B.1**: 104. **B.2**: 25. **C.1**: 32. **C.2**: 169, 207, 218. **C.7**: 29. **D.4**: 3, 27. **D.7**: 326. **G.1**: 62. **J.1**: 1.
Behaviourism **C.1**: 136. **C.2**: 7, 87.
Beliefs
Entries also appear under:
MEDICAL BELIEFS; RELIGIOUS BELIEFS
C.2: 11, 102, 123. **C.3**: 12. **C.7**: 7–8, 12, 74, 77, 79. **D.3**: 30, 41. **D.5**: 91. **F.3**: 160, 228. **K.1**: 132, 233, 349.
Bendix, R. **B.1**: 101.
Bengali **D.1**: 20.
Bhuiyan **K.2**: 17.
Biculturalism **D.7**: 331. **F.7**: 114.
Bilingual education **D.9**: 15, 41.
Bilingualism **D.7**: 45, 331, 333, 348–350.
Biochemistry **C.7**: 13.
Biographies
Entries also appear under:
ORAL BIOGRAPHIES
B.2: 33. **D.1**: 114.
Biology
Entries also appear under:
HUMAN BIOLOGY; SOCIAL BIOLOGY
A.1: 4. **D.4**: 27, 29. **D.6**: 3. **F.6**: 15, 51.
Biotechnology **D.3**: 46, 49. **F.3**: 115, 142. **H.4**: 80, 82. **J.4**: 13. **K.4**: 271.
Birth **F.1**: 59. **F.3**: 35, 65, 74, 88, 106, 109–110, 124, 132–133, 237, 270. **F.4**: 303, 325. **I.4**: 35. **K.1**: 19, 123.
Birth control **F.3**: 41–44, 97, 141.
Birth intervals **F.3**: 80.
Birth order **F.3**: 118. **I.6**: 4.
Birth rate **F.1**: 20. **F.3**: 84, 91.
Birth spacing **F.3**: 78, 87.
Black politics **D.5**: 31. **J.6**: 67.
Blacks **C.2**: 5. **D.1**: 94. **D.5**: 146. **D.7**: 5, 67. **D.8**: 42. **D.9**: 11, 120, 168, 176. **E.2**: 3, 12, 66. **F.1**: 34. **F.3**: 112, 164, 179, 225, 238. **F.4**: 59, 149, 205, 212, 218, 273, 341. **F.5**: 68. **F.7**: 2–5, 7–8, 10, 12, 22, 30, 35, 37, 51, 66, 86, 124, 136, 145–146, 174, 181, 195, 208, 214, 220–221, 223, 226–227, 234, 238, 261. **F.8**: 87, 109. **G.3.2**: 120, 122, 126, 149–150, 162, 306, 336. **H.3**: 17, 26, 38, 88. **I.2**: 8, 53, 55, 75, 141, 168, 185, 224, 228. **I.4**: 42. **J.5**: 3, 7. **K.1**: 10, 12, 42, 182. **K.4**: 2, 39.
Blasphemy **D.5**: 175.

Blindness **C.2**: 138.
Books **D.8**: 51–52, 67.
Borders **F.8**: 5, 45. **G.1**: 54. **H.5**: 39. **H.7**: 8. **J.8**: 17, 19.
Boundaries **C.2**: 199.
Bourgeoisie **E.2**: 43.
Boys **F.3**: 244. **F.6**: 25.
Bradley, F.H. **D.6**: 9.
Brahmanism **D.5**: 158.
Braverman, H. **I.1**: 1.
Breast-feeding **F.3**: 79–80. **F.4**: 268.
Breweries **H.4**: 51.
Brides **F.4**: 244.
Bridewealth **F.4**: 204.
Broadcasting
Entries also appear under:
POLITICAL BROADCASTING
D.7: 236–237, 246, 253, 296, 300, 323, 351, 354, 367, 378.
Broadcasts **D.7**: 311.
Buddhism **D.1**: 11. **D.5**: 81, 83–85, 87.
Buddhists **D.5**: 82.
Budgeting **K.4**: 152.
Budgets
Entries also appear under:
HOUSEHOLD BUDGETS; TIME BUDGETS
Buildings **D.8**: 65, 70.
Bulgarians **F.7**: 16.
Bunu **D.1**: 48.
Burawoy, M. **I.1**: 1.
Bureaucracy **C.5**: 29. **E.2**: 20. **I.5**: 190. **J.3**: 31. **J.4**: 13–14.
Burke, Edmund **B.1**: 149.
Burr, Donald **C.6**: 1.
Buses **F.3**: 230.
Business communities **C.1**: 125.
Business cycles **E.2**: 83. **I.2**: 44.
Business ethics **D.3**: 31–32, 52–54. **I.3**: 95.
Business information **I.5**: 33.
Business management **C.3**: 27. **C.5**: 5, 65. **D.7**: 10. **H.4**: 60. **I.3**: 131, 151. **I.4**: 82. **J.4**: 10–11. **K.4**: 180.
Business organization **C.5**: 69, 75. **F.2**: 32. **H.4**: 30, 65.
Business practices **I.3**: 29.
Butter **H.5**: 31.
Cajun **F.7**: 54.
Camps **K.1**: 166.
Cancer **F.3**: 166.
Candidates **C.7**: 56. **I.3**: 138. **J.6**: 16.

Capital **D.4**: 9. **G.3.2**: 222.
Capital punishment **K.1**: 176, 193.
Capitalism **B.1**: 150. **D.1**: 111. **D.2**: 20. **D.3**: 54. **D.5**: 78. **F.5**: 129, 148. **G.2**: 28. **G.3.1**: 86. **H.2**: 11–12. **J.2**: 3. **J.3**: 33.
Capitalist countries **I.4**: 32.
Capitalist society **B.1**: 47. **H.2**: 6, 19.
Care of the aged **F.2**: 41. **F.4**: 54–55, 95. **K.2**: 12, 17, 25, 28, 33, 71–72, 74, 86. **K.3**: 42. **K.4**: 34, 110, 116–117, 133–137, 139, 141, 144–148, 199.
Career development **I.4**: 59–61, 63–65.
Caring **F.4**: 20, 210, 339. **F.5**: 53, 140, 164. **K.2**: 3. **K.3**: 31.
Carpatho-Rusyn **F.7**: 100.
Case studies **B.2**: 7, 74, 105.
Casework **K.3**: 43.
Cash crops **H.4**: 45.
Caste **C.4**: 13. **E.2**: 1, 24, 37, 73, 79. **F.3**: 110. **I.5**: 123.
Catholic Church **D.3**: 89. **D.5**: 106, 114, 116, 130–131, 140. **D.9**: 126. **H.2**: 10.
Catholicism **D.3**: 23. **D.5**: 126, 136, 141–142.
Catholics **D.5**: 104, 137, 146. **E.2**: 18.
Causal analysis **C.1**: 144.
Causal explanation **C.2**: 51.
Causality **B.1**: 55. **C.1**: 141. **D.7**: 207. **F.3**: 276.
Causes of death **F.7**: 226. **K.4**: 178.
Celibacy **F.6**: 7.
Censorship **F.5**: 114.
Censuses
Entries also appear under:
POPULATION CENSUSES
G.3.2: 107.
Centralization **D.9**: 153. **H.4**: 4.
Centrally-planned economies **C.5**: 39.
Centre-periphery relations **F.7**: 148. **J.4**: 3.
Ceremonies **D.2**: 27. **D.5**: 15.
Certeau, de, Michel **A.2**: 11.
Chaos theory **C.1**: 8. **D.6**: 5. **H.7**: 16.
Character
Entries also appear under:
NATIONAL CHARACTER
C.2: 6. **C.3**: 129. **D.3**: 21. **F.2**: 148.
Charisma **J.6**: 4, 31.
Charitable giving **C.3**: 101.
Charitable organizations **E.3**: 42.
Chemical industry **I.3**: 111.
Cherkess **F.8**: 7.

Child abuse **C.3**: 40. **F.2**: 68, 77, 99. **F.4**: 135, 148, 150–151, 155, 157–159, 162, 164, 169–172, 174. **K.1**: 25, 27–28, 30–34, 36–37, 41–45. **K.3**: 20.
Child adoption **F.1**: 40. **F.2**: 73, 83, 98. **F.4**: 264, 272, 278, 289, 315. **F.7**: 68, 125. **K.3**: 35.
Child care **F.2**: 68, 93, 100, 115. **F.4**: 24, 177, 275, 277, 324. **I.2**: 77, 108, 147. **I.3**: 12. **K.2**: 35–37, 39–45, 47–48, 50–56, 58–62, 64–66, 68–69. **K.3**: 7. **K.4**: 51, 155.
Child costs **F.4**: 122, 270. **K.2**: 60, 68.
Child development **C.2**: 73, 105, 156. **C.7**: 79. **F.2**: 2, 72, 89, 93, 109. **F.3**: 214. **F.4**: 282.
Child fostering **K.2**: 38, 53. **K.3**: 35.
Child health **F.2**: 85. **F.4**: 335. **K.4**: 215.
Child labour **I.2**: 167, 194. **K.1**: 29.
Child mortality **F.3**: 80, 200, 237, 242, 244–245, 252–253, 270, 282, 286, 291. **F.4**: 33.
Child neglect **F.2**: 99. **K.1**: 44.
Child psychology **C.1**: 22. **C.2**: 55, 185. **C.3**: 59.
Child rearing **D.5**: 89. **F.4**: 279, 325, 328.
Childhood
Entries also appear under:
EARLY CHILDHOOD
C.1: 39. **C.2**: 182. **F.2**: 76, 96, 105–106, 116. **F.3**: 126, 295. **F.4**: 80, 91, 310. **H.3**: 59. **K.1**: 38. **K.3**: 22. **K.4**: 9.
Children
Entries also appear under:
ABANDONED CHILDREN; DISABLED CHILDREN; GIFTED CHILDREN
C.1: 41. **C.2**: 11–12, 108, 123, 130, 138, 140, 155, 158, 166. **C.3**: 11, 14, 28, 58, 87. **C.4**: 8. **C.7**: 18. **D.2**: 6. **D.3**: 14. **D.4**: 5. **D.5**: 89. **D.7**: 26, 70, 73, 89, 93, 121, 212, 218, 353, 361, 366, 381, 392. **D.8**: 66. **D.9**: 130, 151. **E.3**: 14. **F.1**: 11. **F.2**: 17, 69, 71, 74–75, 78–82, 84, 86, 89–91, 95–96, 101–102, 104, 107, 110, 117, 125. **F.3**: 33, 36, 53, 76, 182, 261, 280, 283. **F.4**: 1, 8, 11, 16, 27, 31, 81, 92–93, 99, 120, 124, 132, 152, 188, 215, 270, 274, 276, 287–288, 294, 303, 313, 319, 323, 331, 338, 347, 353. **F.5**: 75, 285. **F.7**: 31. **G.3.2**: 82, 225. **H.3**: 6. **H.5**: 9. **I.2**: 194. **I.4**: 20. **K.1**: 26, 81, 222, 235, 280, 356, 364, 373. **K.2**: 16, 36, 46, 49, 52, 54, 63, 110. **K.3**: 9, 35, 37. **K.4**: 20, 70, 90, 112, 177, 211, 233.
Children in care **K.4**: 52.
Children's rights **F.2**: 92, 97, 103, 108, 111–114. **F.4**: 15. **I.2**: 167. **K.2**: 67.
Chinese **F.7**: 26, 35, 57, 170. **F.8**: 67. **H.4**: 36.
Choice **C.2**: 24, 32, 70. **C.7**: 45.
Christian churches
Entries also appear under:
BAPTIST CHURCHES; CATHOLIC CHURCH; HUTTERITES; LUTHERAN CHURCH;

MENNONITES; MORMONISM; ORTHODOX CHURCH; PROTESTANT CHURCHES; SEVENTH-DAY ADVENTISM
D.5: 93, 100–101, 128, 134, 147, 151. **D.7**: 58. **F.4**: 183. **F.6**: 46.

Christian orders
Entries also appear under:
JESUITS

Christian theology **D.5**: 88.

Christianity
Entries also appear under:
CATHOLICISM; MORMONISM; PENTECOSTALISM
D.5: 83, 92, 95–98, 105, 112, 117, 120, 122–123, 133, 138, 148, 167, 170. **F.4**: 198. **F.6**: 17.

Christianization **D.5**: 99.

Christians **B.1**: 117. **D.5**: 94, 104. **F.5**: 15. **F.7**: 238. **H.2**: 15.

Christmas **H.6**: 2.

Church and state **D.5**: 108.

Church hierarchy **D.5**: 121.

Church history **J.3**: 29.

Churches **F.6**: 46.

Cinema **D.8**: 6, 12, 20, 27, 50, 58, 77.

Circus **D.7**: 25, 72.

Cities **C.7**: 58. **D.1**: 3. **D.9**: 154. **E.2**: 6. **F.2**: 80. **F.3**: 22, 200, 311. **F.8**: 32. **G.1**: 44. **G.3**: 11. **G.3.2**: 1, 3, 7, 9, 11–12, 16, 18–20, 24, 30, 35–36, 40–41, 46, 59, 62, 64, 67, 69, 92–93, 115, 161, 164, 179, 193, 206, 218, 222, 227, 232, 238–239, 241, 244, 246–248, 252, 275, 278, 280, 282, 284, 290–291, 298, 301, 312, 314, 339, 346, 359. **H.3**: 24. **H.4**: 8. **H.7**: 12. **I.1**: 12. **K.1**: 61, 130, 205, 230. **K.4**: 14.

Citizens **E.1**: 5. **G.2**: 18. **G.3.2**: 248.

Citizenship **C.5**: 68. **D.4**: 6. **D.7**: 241. **E.3**: 22. **F.5**: 279. **F.8**: 8, 160. **G.3.2**: 7, 176. **J.2**: 4. **J.3**: 6, 18.

City size **G.3.2**: 45.

Civil disobedience **D.3**: 10.

Civil liberties **B.2**: 111. **D.7**: 308. **J.3**: 27.

Civil proceedings **D.4**: 34. **J.6**: 21.

Civil religion **D.5**: 3. **J.8**: 3.

Civil rights
Entries also appear under:
RIGHT TO WORK
F.4: 185. **F.7**: 2, 10, 145, 147. **J.5**: 1. **J.6**: 52.

Civil servants **I.6**: 24.

Civil service **I.2**: 142. **I.3**: 123. **I.4**: 23.

Civil society **D.1**: 1, 18, 47, 68. **E.3**: 26. **J.3**: 10, 20. **K.2**: 63.

Civil war **G.3.1**: 132. **J.7**: 15. **K.1**: 11.

Civil-military relations **J.7**: 5, 7, 18.

Civilization **B.1**: 5, 12, 18. **D.1**: 7, 57, 62, 65, 81–82, 86, 88, 90, 93, 95–96, 105, 109, 116–117. **F.7**: 43, 94. **G.3.2**: 92. **H.5**: 15. **I.6**: 36. **J.8**: 8.

Class
Entries also appear under:
BOURGEOISIE; MIDDLE CLASS; RULING CLASS; UNDERCLASS; UPPER CLASS; WORKING CLASS
B.2: 32. **C.2**: 26. **C.4**: 13. **C.5**: 39. **C.7**: 15. **D.1**: 14. **D.7**: 209, 327, 357. **D.9**: 114. **E.2**: 3, 12, 51–52, 54–69, 71–72, 74–80, 82, 84. **F.2**: 49. **F.3**: 287, 289. **F.5**: 56, 258. **F.7**: 1, 3, 12, 56, 66, 149, 207. **G.2**: 3–4. **G.3.1**: 85, 132. **G.3.2**: 14, 112, 214. **H.3**: 73. **H.4**: 44, 77. **H.5**: 16. **H.6**: 9. **I.2**: 89. **I.4**: 9, 11. **I.5**: 123. **J.4**: 22. **J.6**: 25, 59. **K.1**: 86. **K.2**: 35. **K.4**: 3.

Class conflict **E.2**: 11, 69.

Class consciousness **E.1**: 22.

Class formation **E.2**: 53, 70.

Class struggle **E.2**: 28.

Classification
Entries also appear under:
JOB CLASSIFICATION
B.1: 23. **B.2**: 106. **C.1**: 132. **E.2**: 60. **G.3.2**: 12. **K.1**: 188.

Classrooms **D.9**: 116, 126, 154.

Clientelism **C.5**: 44. **E.2**: 20. **I.5**: 18.

Clinical interviews **C.1**: 66. **D.7**: 154.

Clinical psychology **K.4**: 81, 182.

Clothes **D.2**: 5.

Clothing industry **F.5**: 36. **H.4**: 50, 58. **I.2**: 183.

Cluster analysis **B.2**: 50. **G.3.2**: 217. **I.5**: 88.

Coal industry **I.5**: 42.

Coal mining **D.4**: 17. **G.3.2**: 14. **I.4**: 54.

Coalitions **C.5**: 71, 81.

Coasts **G.1**: 7.

Coca **K.1**: 320–321.

Cocaine **K.1**: 322–323, 327.

Cognition
Entries also appear under:
SOCIAL COGNITION
B.2: 96. **C.1**: 20, 85–86, 169. **C.2**: 111, 113–117, 119–134, 136–141. **C.3**: 73, 102. **C.4**: 23. **C.7**: 4, 6, 14, 39. **D.6**: 13. **D.7**: 61. **D.9**: 151. **E.3**: 64. **H.5**: 24.

Cognitive development **B.2**: 45. **C.2**: 112, 123, 127, 238.

Cognitive dissonance **C.7**: 70.

Cohabitation **F.4**: 217, 230, 238–239.

Cohort analysis **F.3**: 167.

Cohorts **F.3**: 34. **J.1**: 2. **J.6**: 56. **K.1**: 123.

Collective action **B.2**: 67. **C.7**: 16. **F.8**: 9. **G.2**: 3, 12. **G.3.2**: 53. **H.4**: 73. **I.5**: 118. **J.5**: 13, 33.

Collective attitudes **E.3**: 58.

Collective bargaining **D.9**: 110. **H.3**: 69. **I.5**: 60, 62–63, 65–66, 68, 74–75.

Collective behaviour **C.4**: 36. **C.7**: 78.

Collective economies **J.2**: 26.

Collectivism **C.7**: 23.

Collusion **C.3**: 54.

Colonial history **J.3**: 24.

Colonial policy **D.9**: 93.

Colonialism
Entries also appear under:
NEOCOLONIALISM

Colonization **D.9**: 111. **H.7**: 15.

Commerce **D.7**: 29. **F.6**: 28.

Commercial concentration **H.4**: 73.

Commercial policy **F.8**: 37.

Commodities **H.2**: 9.

Common law **D.4**: 30. **F.4**: 199.

Communalism **D.5**: 154.

Communication
Entries also appear under:
INTERCULTURAL COMMUNICATION; INTERPERSONAL COMMUNICATION; MASS COMMUNICATION; NON-VERBAL COMMUNICATION; ORAL COMMUNICATION; POLITICAL COMMUNICATION; VERBAL COMMUNICATION; VISUAL COMMUNICATION

B.1: 110. **C.2**: 17. **C.3**: 3, 28, 30, 74, 83, 107, 135, 147. **C.5**: 20. **D.1**: 28. **D.2**: 1. **D.3**: 68. **D.7**: 28, 118, 121, 123–126, 128, 131–132, 134, 138, 141–143, 145–149, 152, 156, 158–161, 163–165, 168–171, 173–179, 181, 183, 187–190, 192, 241–242, 277, 281, 284. **D.9**: 30. **E.1**: 3. **F.4**: 85. **F.5**: 93. **I.6**: 25. **J.7**: 20. **K.1**: 14. **K.4**: 11–12, 56.

Communication networks **C.3**: 16. **D.7**: 129, 139, 162.

Communication research **K.4**: 194.

Communications technology **H.4**: 94.

Communism **A.1**: 34. **B.2**: 111. **D.5**: 63. **E.3**: 22. **G.3.1**: 6. **I.5**: 157. **J.2**: 14. **J.3**: 29. **K.1**: 17.

Communist parties **I.5**: 157. **J.5**: 5.

Communists **J.5**: 5.

Community
Entries also appear under:
BUSINESS COMMUNITIES; ETHNIC COMMUNITIES; LOCAL COMMUNITIES; RELIGIOUS COMMUNITIES; RURAL COMMUNITIES; SCIENTIFIC COMMUNITIES; URBAN COMMUNITIES

C.3: 108. **C.5**: 9. **D.1**: 6, 112–113. **D.5**: 137, 179. **D.7**: 39, 190, 290. **F.4**: 61. **F.5**: 138. **F.6**: 3. **F.7**: 6, 73, 110, 151. **F.8**: 77. **G.1**: 31. **G.2**: 3–4, 8–11, 17, 21, 24–25, 31. **G.3.2**: 13, 16, 71, 285. **I.2**: 44, 78. **J.6**: 36. **K.1**: 170, 223, 306. **K.3**: 7, 12. **K.4**: 111.

Community care **K.4**: 107, 109, 112, 115–119, 122, 124, 127, 130.

Community development **D.9**: 5. **G.2**: 6–7, 14, 28, 33–34, 36. **G.3.1**: 36. **G.3.2**: 241, 283. **H.6**: 8. **J.5**: 6. **K.1**: 69. **K.4**: 184.

Community integration **D.9**: 84.

Community life **G.2**: 20.

Community organizations **G.2**: 1–2, 5, 28. **G.3.1**: 105. **G.3.2**: 6. **J.5**: 3.

Community participation **G.2**: 16, 18. **G.3.2**: 15, 249. **J.3**: 35. **K.4**: 14.

Community power **G.2**: 26, 28.

Community services **F.7**: 15, 150. **G.2**: 22. **J.6**: 20. **K.1**: 362. **K.4**: 27, 110, 119, 167, 183, 206.

Commuting **F.3**: 303. **G.3.2**: 2. **H.3**: 60. **I.2**: 68.

Company management
Entries also appear under:
BUSINESS MANAGEMENT

Comparative advantage **I.5**: 189.

Comparative analysis **B.2**: 74. **D.1**: 8, 77. **F.3**: 79. **F.7**: 20, 61. **I.4**: 79. **K.4**: 137.

Compensation **H.3**: 60. **I.2**: 243. **I.3**: 107, 114, 116. **I.4**: 80. **I.5**: 188.

Competition
Entries also appear under:
PRICE COMPETITION

C.3: 131. **F.5**: 70. **F.7**: 69. **H.5**: 41. **I.2**: 44. **I.5**: 111, 124.

Competitiveness **H.4**: 40.

Complex organization **C.5**: 6, 9.

Compulsory arbitration **I.5**: 101.

Computer science **F.5**: 242.

Computerization **D.1**: 109. **D.6**: 6.

Computers **A.3**: 7. **B.2**: 3, 115, 128. **C.2**: 64, 120, 144. **C.3**: 11. **D.7**: 10–11, 65, 129. **D.9**: 2. **G.3.2**: 250. **H.4**: 83, 104. **J.3**: 37.

Comte, Auguste **B.1**: 63.

Conceptualization **C.2**: 33.

Conciliation **C.3**: 94.

Conditioning **C.2**: 167.

Confidentiality **D.3**: 44.

Conflict
Entries also appear under:
CLASS CONFLICT; GENERATION CONFLICTS; INTERETHNIC CONFLICT; INTERPERSONAL CONFLICTS; MARITAL CONFLICT; RACIAL CONFLICT

C.1: 16, 63, 88. **C.2**: 32. **C.3**: 106, 110, 115–116, 119. **C.4**: 20, 41. **D.4**: 22. **D.5**: 60. **D.7**: 96, 319. **D.8**: 44. **D.9**: 25, 106. **F.4**: 107. **F.5**: 4. **F.7**: 152. **G.3.1**: 106. **G.3.2**: 44. **H.5**: 37. **I.5**: 35, 108. **J.7**: 8. **K.1**: 40.

Conflict resolution **C.3**: 105, 109, 111, 113, 117, 120–121. **C.5**: 13, 19. **D.4**: 31. **F.4**: 152. **I.5**: 26, 73, 77, 91, 93, 96.

Confucianism **C.2**: 21, 57. **D.1**: 101. **D.5**: 3, 7. **H.1**: 2.

Connor, Eugene **F.7**: 147.

Consensus **C.3**: 41. **C.4**: 61. **C.7**: 11. **H.7**: 26. **K.1**: 206.

Conservation
Entries also appear under:
NATURE CONSERVATION
G.1. 2, 9, 13, 33.

Conservatism **C.2**: 16. **D.1**: 6. **F.4**: 328. **J.1**: 2. **J.6**: 54. **K.2**: 91. **K.4**: 186.

Conservatives **D.9**: 44.

Constitution **D.7**: 255. **F.6**: 40. **F.7**: 74. **J.3**: 6. **J.4**: 2.

Constitutional amendments **D.5**: 177.

Constitutional law **F.5**: 131.

Constitutionalism **J.4**: 12.

Construction industry **H.4**: 38. **I.3**: 4, 122. **I.4**: 43.

Consumer behaviour **H.5**: 5–6, 23. **I.6**: 40.

Consumer credit **K.1**: 225.

Consumer expenditure **H.3**: 7, 40.

Consumer preferences **K.4**: 28.

Consumerism **H.5**: 14.

Consumers **D.7**: 290. **F.2**: 117. **G.3.2**: 252. **H.3**: 40. **H.5**: 3, 11, 15, 19, 22, 24, 35–36, 38–39. **I.5**: 9. **K.4**: 220.

Consumption
Entries also appear under:
ENERGY CONSUMPTION; FOOD CONSUMPTION; WATER CONSUMPTION
D.2: 20. **D.7**: 116. **G.3.2**: 112. **H.1**: 1. **H.3**: 24, 28. **H.5**: 4, 10, 12–13, 16–18, 21, 27–28. **J.5**: 10.

Contraception **F.3**: 37, 39, 44, 48, 61, 63–64, 81, 154. **F.6**: 1, 14, 32.

Contracts
Entries also appear under:
LABOUR CONTRACT; SOCIAL CONTRACT
I.2: 217. **I.5**: 50, 127, 136, 163.

Control theory **D.7**: 66. **I.3**: 15.

Cooperatives
Entries also appear under:
AGRICULTURAL COOPERATIVES; PRODUCTION COOPERATIVES
H.2: 15. **H.4**: 54.

Corporate culture **C.5**: 10, 15, 17, 19, 67. **H.2**: 1. **H.4**: 33, 67. **I.5**: 19, 173.

Corporate power **H.4**: 68.

Corporatism **F.5**: 267. **H.4**: 64. **I.5**: 108. **K.4**: 214.

Correctional education **K.1**: 166.

Correlation **B.1**: 48. **C.1**: 37.

Corruption **D.1**: 135.

Coser, Rose Lamb **C.6**: 12.

Cosmogony **C.5**: 30, 48.

Cosmology **F.6**: 30.

Cost of living **F.2**: 58. **H.3**: 55.

Cost-benefit analysis **F.4**: 21. **I.2**: 235. **I.3**: 38.

Costs
Entries also appear under:
CHILD COSTS; PRODUCTION COSTS; SOCIAL COSTS
D.7: 92.

Councillors **J.5**: 38.

Counselling **D.7**: 173. **F.3**: 228. **F.4**: 213, 259. **K.3**: 18, 46. **K.4**: 128.

Counsellors **C.1**: 124.

Counterculture **G.1**: 8.

Countries
Entries also appear under:
ARAB COUNTRIES; EASTERN COUNTRIES; WESTERN COUNTRIES

Countryside **D.1**: 3.

Coup d'etat **J.6**: 28, 30. **J.7**: 10.

Courts
Entries also appear under:
JUVENILE COURTS; SUPREME COURT
D.4: 5. **I.5**: 101. **K.1**: 173.

Courtship **C.3**: 143. **F.6**: 50. **K.1**: 408.

Cousin
Entries also appear under:
PARALLEL COUSINS

Craft workers **F.4**: 78. **I.3**: 56.

Creativity **C.2**: 33. **D.8**: 41.

Credit
Entries also appear under:
CONSUMER CREDIT
H.5: 9. **H.6**: 5, 11.

Credit market **H.6**: 8.

Crime
Entries also appear under:
ORGANIZED CRIME; VICTIMS OF CRIME
D.7: 273. **F.5**: 198. **J.3**: 43. **K.1**: 47, 53, 55–57, 59–61, 64–65, 67–68, 74, 79, 81, 83, 88–89, 93, 95, 98, 105–106, 111, 114, 116, 119, 124, 128, 132–134, 137–138, 140–142, 145, 147, 149, 157, 159–161, 163, 212, 302, 381, 425. **K.3**: 22.

Crime prevention **K.1**: 66, 102, 126–127, 164.

Criminal justice **D.4**: 4, 6, 43. **F.3**: 144. **F.7**: 220. **J.1**: 3. **J.3**: 2, 9. **K.1**: 106, 144, 174–175, 182, 192, 198, 200, 202, 207, 209.

Criminal law **D.4**: 22, 37. **J.3**: 2. **K.1**: 15, 40, 131, 181, 204.

Criminal sentencing **D.4**: 14, 20, 28. **K.1**: 170, 176, 183.

Criminality **K.1**: 48, 58, 85, 109, 129, 334.

Criminology **K.1**: 54, 67, 70–73, 78, 99, 101, 158, 182.

Critical theory **B.1**: 4, 29, 49, 76, 107. **E.3**: 21.

Criticism
Entries also appear under:
LITERARY CRITICISM
D.8: 9, 55.

Crops
Entries also appear under:
CASH CROPS

Cross-cultural analysis **C.1**: 66. **C.3**: 111. **D.1**: 52. **F.5**: 32, 34. **H.7**: 13.

Cross-national analysis **C.5**: 63. **H.5**: 17. **I.2**: 184. **K.1**: 77.

Cuban revolution **F.2**: 156.

Cults **D.1**: 11. **D.5**: 8, 14, 34, 61, 153, 157. **J.1**: 5.

Cultural adaptation **F.7**: 112.

Cultural anthropology **D.1**: 56. **D.4**: 36.

Cultural assimilation **F.7**: 107. **F.8**: 65, 84.

Cultural attitudes **C.7**: 73.

Cultural barriers **F.7**: 64.

Cultural behaviour **C.1**: 145.

Cultural change **D.2**: 17. **D.7**: 41. **E.3**: 26. **F.5**: 108. **F.8**: 70.

Cultural differentiation **B.1**: 109. **C.7**: 23.

Cultural diffusion **D.7**: 141.

Cultural diversity **D.8**: 36. **F.2**: 149.

Cultural factors **C.3**: 106. **I.3**: 107.

Cultural identity **D.1**: 4, 73. **F.7**: 99, 123. **K.4**: 2.

Cultural influence **C.2**: 52. **K.4**: 72.

Cultural nationalism **D.1**: 33.

Cultural pluralism **D.9**: 119.

Cultural relations **C.1**: 73. **D.1**: 22, 55, 67.

Cultural studies **A.2**: 14. **D.1**: 32. **D.2**: 18. **F.5**: 80, 109.

Cultural systems **C.4**: 3. **D.7**: 192.

Cultural tradition **C.5**: 38. **D.1**: 69. **H.4**: 1.

Culture
Entries also appear under:
CORPORATE CULTURE; INDIGENOUS CULTURE; LOCAL CULTURE; MASS CULTURE; MATERIAL CULTURE; NATIONAL CULTURE; POLITICAL CULTURE; SUBCULTURE; THEORY OF CULTURE; WORKING CLASS CULTURE

B.1: 69, 89. **C.1**: 72, 94. **C.2**: 52. **C.3**: 35, 112, 157. **D.1**: 12–15, 17, 21, 24–25, 27–28, 40, 44, 46, 61–65, 72, 78, 80, 86, 92–93, 99–100, 106, 116, 132. **D.2**: 1–2, 21, 26. **D.3**: 85. **D.4**: 37. **D.6**: 18. **D.7**: 13, 28, 100, 336. **D.8**: 2, 8, 23–24, 26, 33, 57, 71. **D.9**: 124. **E.3**: 3, 67, 69. **F.2**: 134. **F.3**: 293. **F.4**: 44. **F.5**: 206. **F.7**: 58. **H.3**: 12. **H.5**: 10. **I.3**: 53. **I.6**: 18. **J.1**: 6. **J.2**: 12. **J.5**: 7. **J.7**: 22. **K.1**: 226.

Curriculum **D.8**: 10. **D.9**: 26, 33, 37, 46–47, 78, 127, 177. **F.5**: 117.

Customary law **D.4**: 10.

Customs **C.5**: 19. **D.2**: 7, 13.

Cypriot language **D.7**: 63.

Dairy industry **G.3.1**: 62. **H.4**: 3, 101.

Dalaï Lama **D.5**: 84.

Damage **G.1**: 42.

Dance **A.2**: 12. **D.5**: 117. **D.8**: 54.

Dance music **D.7**: 67.

Data analysis **B.2**: 36, 40, 64, 74, 88. **K.1**: 61.

Data bases **F.3**: 29.

Data collection **B.2**: 108. **F.8**: 147. **G.3.2**: 80.

Data processing **B.2**: 78. **C.1**: 84. **D.6**: 6.

Data transmission **A.3**: 6.

Dating **H.5**: 32.

Daughters **F.4**: 265, 283, 291, 300, 317, 327.

Death **C.1**: 19. **F.2**: 28–29, 45, 47. **F.3**: 27, 199, 203, 235. **F.4**: 8, 311. **F.5**: 156. **K.1**: 3, 397. **K.4**: 57, 148.

Debt **C.2**: 29. **K.1**: 225.

Decentralization **D.9**: 112. **G.3**: 5. **G.3.2**: 230, 298, 303. **J.4**: 3. **K.4**: 78.

Decision
Entries also appear under:
SITING DECISIONS
C.7: 6. **D.3**: 66. **F.4**: 107. **J.6**: 26. **K.4**: 59.

Decision analysis **B.2**: 82. **C.5**: 27.

Decision making
Entries also appear under:
GROUP DECISION MAKING
C.1: 131. **C.2**: 114, 144–153. **C.3**: 5. **C.5**: 21. **D.4**: 21, 38. **E.2**: 44. **F.2**: 51. **F.5**: 324. **F.8**: 118. **H.6**: 5. **H.7**: 7, 19. **I.4**: 6. **I.5**: 38, 202. **K.1**: 358. **K.4**: 34, 83.

Decision models **K.4**: 172.

Decision theory **D.3**: 5.

Deconstruction **B.1**: 49, 148.

Deforestation **G.1**: 27.

Deindustrialization **H.4**: 8. **I.1**: 12.

Delinquency
Entries also appear under:
JUVENILE DELINQUENCY

F.4: 41. **G.2**: 9. **K.1**: 8, 51, 108, 146, 153.

Demand
Entries also appear under:
AGGREGATE DEMAND
C.4: 14. **G.3.2**: 102. **K.4**: 28.

Demilitarization **J.7**: 2.

Democracy
Entries also appear under:
INDUSTRIAL DEMOCRACY; SOCIAL DEMOCRACY
B.2: 4. **D.9**: 48. **F.5**: 104. **F.7**: 13. **G.3.1**: 92. **G.3.2**: 329. **H.2**: 12. **J.1**: 12. **J.2**: 3, 5–6, 12, 18–19, 22, 29. **J.6**: 6, 21. **K.1**: 416. **K.2**: 92. **K.4**: 271.

Democratic countries **E.2**: 10.

Democratization **D.7**: 263. **D.9**: 180. **E.2**: 70. **E.3**: 27. **F.3**: 178. **G.3.2**: 253. **J.2**: 13. **J.3**: 1, 5.

Demographers **F.1**: 69.

Demographic change **F.1**: 48–50, 66–67. **F.3**: 6, 10, 14–16, 22, 25, 82, 96, 156, 301. **F.4**: 26, 40. **G.3**: 1. **I.2**: 98. **K.1**: 79.

Demographic research **F.1**: 52. **F.3**: 12. **H.3**: 51. **K.1**: 19.

Demography
Entries also appear under:
TRIBAL DEMOGRAPHY
B.2: 129. **F.1**: 6–7, 10, 13–14, 16–18, 21, 31, 39, 43, 51, 54, 57, 71. **F.2**: 42, 85, 153. **F.3**: 1, 5, 90, 100, 127, 130. **F.4**: 123, 247. **F.8**: 114. **H.3**: 19. **I.2**: 198. **K.1**: 255, 330, 425. **K.2**: 36.

Deontology **C.6**: 13. **D.3**: 15.

Department
Entries also appear under:
GOVERNMENT DEPARTMENTS
Deprivation **K.1**: 49, 221.

Deregulation **D.7**: 297. **I.5**: 1.

Derrida, Jacques **D.3**: 50. **D.6**: 12.

Descent **F.4**: 60.

Detente **J.8**: 10.

Determinism **C.2**: 85.

Deterrence **K.1**: 91.

Developed countries **F.5**: 97. **K.1**: 224.

Developing countries **C.1**: 163. **C.7**: 71. **D.7**: 60, 184, 380. **D.9**: 1, 10, 35, 39, 68, 152, 157. **E.3**: 16, 37, 40, 47. **F.2**: 80. **F.3**: 43, 134, 183, 216, 232, 242, 300–301. **F.4**: 338. **F.5**: 14, 48, 97, 130, 243, 250, 280. **F.8**: 18, 52, 105, 168. **G.1**: 43. **G.3.1**: 1, 102. **G.3.2**: 128, 163, 206, 222, 231, 299, 324–325, 339, 355. **H.3**: 6, 14, 25, 42, 55, 57–58. **I.2**: 231. **I.3**: 88. **I.4**: 130. **I.5**: 204. **J.3**: 33. **J.4**: 10. **K.1**: 84, 246, 273, 311. **K.4**: 74, 91.

Development
Entries also appear under:
ECONOMIC DEVELOPMENT; RURAL DEVELOPMENT; SOCIO-ECONOMIC DEVELOPMENT; SUSTAINABLE DEVELOPMENT; URBAN DEVELOPMENT

Development administration **I.3**: 89.

Development planning **E.3**: 43, 48. **G.3.1**: 103. **H.7**: 14, 24.

Development policy **C.7**: 19. **D.3**: 36. **D.9**: 209. **G.3.1**: 128. **H.7**: 4, 11, 20.

Development projects **E.3**: 15. **K.1**: 246, 278.

Development strategies **G.3.2**: 334. **H.2**: 17.

Development studies **F.5**: 241.

Deviance **D.5**: 137. **D.9**: 143. **F.2**: 18, 130. **F.3**: 196. **F.4**: 162. **F.6**: 45. **K.1**: 113, 149, 407.

Diachronic analysis **D.7**: 216.

Dialectics **B.1**: 50, 122. **D.1**: 23. **D.7**: 196.

Dialects **G.1**: 58.

Diet **C.2**: 30, 229, 236.

Dietary disorders
Entries also appear under:
ANOREXIA
F.3: 175. **F.5**: 57.

Differential analysis **F.3**: 245, 295.

Disability **K.4**: 19.

Disabled children **D.9**: 19. **F.3**: 229. **F.4**: 82. **K.4**: 120.

Disabled persons **D.7**: 363. **F.3**: 170, 232. **F.4**: 8. **K.4**: 139.

Disabled rehabilitation **K.4**: 130.

Disabled workers **F.3**: 4. **I.2**: 176, 222.

Disarmament **J.7**: 20.

Disaster relief **K.1**: 2, 5.

Disasters **C.2**: 80. **C.5**: 72. **C.7**: 22. **D.7**: 315. **F.2**: 104. **K.4**: 45.

Discourse analysis **C.3**: 12. **D.5**: 13. **D.7**: 12, 119–120, 122, 130, 135–137, 154, 165, 167, 172, 191, 268, 392. **F.5**: 203. **I.2**: 145. **K.3**: 10.

Discrimination
Entries also appear under:
EMPLOYMENT DISCRIMINATION; RACIAL DISCRIMINATION; SEX DISCRIMINATION; WAGE DISCRIMINATION
C.1: 83. **C.7**: 75. **F.3**: 4. **F.5**: 170, 187. **F.7**: 14, 183. **G.3.2**: 99, 110, 167. **H.4**: 56. **I.2**: 41, 52, 70, 130, 222. **I.3**: 14, 91.

Diseases
Entries also appear under:
AIDS; ANOREXIA; HEART DISEASE; LEPROSY; MALARIA; OCCUPATIONAL DISEASES; SEXUALLY TRANSMITTED DISEASES
C.7: 6. **F.1**: 31. **F.3**: 143, 149, 161, 164, 167, 177, 179, 184, 190–191, 213, 216, 284. **K.4**: 72, 85, 94, 184.

Disintegration **C.1**: 19.

Dismissals **I.3**: 20, 42–43, 91. **I.5**: 86, 100, 107, 155.

Disobedience
Entries also appear under:
CIVIL DISOBEDIENCE

Dissent **I.4**: 14.

Distribution **H.4**: 5. **I.4**: 44.

Distributive justice **D.3**: 1. **E.2**: 44. **F.2**: 46. **H.3**: 46, 61, 64.

Diversification **I.3**: 130. **I.4**: 47.

Division of labour
Entries also appear under:
INTERNATIONAL DIVISION OF LABOUR
E.2: 33. **F.4**: 34, 74. **F.5**: 14, 164, 180, 301. **G.3.2**: 351. **I.2**: 103–104, 182. **I.3**: 88. **I.4**: 16, 104. **J.1**: 9.

Divorce **C.2**: 3. **D.5**: 34. **F.4**: 118–121, 123–124, 126–135, 137–147.

Divorced persons **F.4**: 117, 122, 136.

Dogma **B.1**: 31.

Domestic violence **D.4**: 11. **F.4**: 148–149, 153–154, 156, 160–161, 163, 165–168, 173, 175–176. **K.1**: 63, 418, 421. **K.2**: 104.

Domestic workers **I.3**: 64.

Domination **C.2**: 24. **C.3**: 59. **D.6**: 26.

Dominicans **F.8**: 166.

Donaldson, Margaret C. **C.2**: 140.

Down's syndrome **F.3**: 189.

Dowry **F.4**: 204. **F.5**: 194, 198.

Drama **D.7**: 311.

Dramatic art **D.8**: 13, 22, 28.

Drinkers **C.2**: 206. **K.1**: 374.

Drug abuse **C.3**: 76. **F.3**: 150, 158, 197–198. **F.4**: 178. **K.1**: 11, 200, 300, 310, 316, 323–325, 328, 335–336, 339–341, 345, 347–348, 354, 356–357, 360–362, 370, 372, 377, 381, 383, 388–390, 395. **K.4**: 47.

Drug addiction **K.4**: 236.

Drug addicts **K.1**: 317, 334, 368, 375, 380, 385.

Drug trafficking **K.1**: 152, 311, 318, 371.

Drugs
Entries also appear under:
COCA; COCAINE
C.2: 173. **D.9**: 163. **F.3**: 60, 202, 206. **H.3**: 67. **I.3**: 37, 58. **I.5**: 134. **K.1**: 95, 138, 301, 313–315, 319, 321, 337, 342, 344, 350, 358, 365, 367, 384, 392. **K.4**: 68.

Duke, David **F.7**: 225.

Durkheim, Emile **B.1**: 84, 105. **J.2**: 1.

Dynamic models **C.2**: 215.

Dynamics **D.3**: 70. **F.3**: 291. **G.3.2**: 364. **H.4**: 85. **I.1**: 11.

Dyslexia **D.7**: 98.

Early childhood **F.4**: 301.

Early motherhood **D.9**: 151. **F.3**: 73, 130. **F.4**: 273. **K.1**: 231. **K.2**: 42.

Early retirement **I.2**: 221. **K.2**: 28.

Earnings **F.4**: 30, 88. **F.8**: 57. **H.3**: 43, 59, 65–66, 88. **I.2**: 87–88, 105, 166. **I.3**: 22. **I.4**: 18, 40.

Earthquakes **G.3.2**: 151.

Eastern countries **D.1**: 53.

Ecologism **D.7**: 114. **J.5**: 9, 31.

Ecology
Entries also appear under:
HUMAN ECOLOGY
B.1: 81. **C.1**: 100. **C.5**: 56. **D.2**: 21. **D.5**: 14, 147. **D.9**: 117. **F.5**: 76, 94. **G.1**: 8, 14–16, 19, 22, 26, 39–42, 45, 48, 53. **G.3.2**: 22. **J.3**: 30.

Econometric models **F.8**: 139. **H.7**: 28.

Econometrics **F.8**: 62. **I.2**: 190.

Economic anthropology **G.1**: 6.

Economic change **A.1**: 16. **E.3**: 41. **H.3**: 3.

Economic choice **I.3**: 98.

Economic concentration
Entries also appear under:
COMMERCIAL CONCENTRATION

Economic conditions **D.7**: 330. **E.1**: 11. **E.2**: 4, 18, 47, 63, 66. **E.3**: 47. **F.1**: 26. **F.2**: 47. **F.3**: 141, 275, 292. **F.4**: 31, 203. **F.5**: 326. **F.7**: 2, 8, 66, 254. **F.8**: 111, 114. **G.1**: 6, 53. **G.3.1**: 54, 113, 131. **G.3.2**: 70, 75, 361. **H.1**: 4. **H.2**: 19. **H.3**: 23, 49, 57. **I.2**: 132. **J.1**: 22. **K.4**: 20.

Economic crisis **H.3**: 10, 56. **I.1**: 6.

Economic decline **D.9**: 36.

Economic development **D.3**: 43. **E.1**: 19. **E.3**: 67. **F.5**: 244. **F.7**: 171. **G.1**: 12, 45. **G.3.2**: 330, 352. **H.2**: 17. **H.3**: 1, 14, 17, 41, 78. **H.7**: 1, 19, 26, 28. **I.6**: 41. **K.1**: 84.

Economic elites **H.4**: 68.

Economic equality **H.3**: 32. **I.2**: 127. **K.1**: 137.

Economic forecasts **F.1**: 26.

Economic geography **B.2**: 98. **G.1**: 63. **G.3.2**: 302. **H.7**: 5.

Economic growth **D.9**: 152. **F.3**: 306. **F.5**: 6. **H.1**: 2. **H.3**: 18. **H.7**: 25. **I.2**: 24.

Economic inequality **H.3**: 28, 48. **K.1**: 92. **K.4**: 87.

Economic integration **G.3.1**: 32.

Economic justice **F.5**: 46.

Economic methodology **H.5**: 37.

Economic organization **H.1**: 3.

Economic performance **F.2**: 24. **H.4**: 65. **I.5**: 26, 32.

Economic planning **F.3**: 112. **G.3.1**: 14. **H.7**: 3, 7.

Economic policy

Entries also appear under:
   INDUSTRIAL POLICY
   C.7: 2. **F.8**: 167. **G.3.1**: 107. **G.3.2**: 75. **K.1**: 240.
Economic psychology **C.1**: 125. **F.2**: 107.
Economic reform **E.3**: 22. **H.7**: 5–6. **I.3**: 131.
Economic resources **F.4**: 205.
Economic sociology **H.1**: 5.
Economic status **F.3**: 90. **F.7**: 10.
Economic structure **J.2**: 30.
Economic systems **D.5**: 82. **E.2**: 47. **H.2**: 2.
Economic theory **A.1**: 10. **H.2**: 5.
Economic thought **H.3**: 4.
Economics of education **D.9**: 210.
Education
   Entries also appear under:
   ACCESS TO EDUCATION; ADULT EDUCATION; BILINGUAL EDUCATION; CORRECTIONAL EDUCATION; ECONOMICS OF EDUCATION; EDUCATIONAL SOCIOLOGY; HEALTH EDUCATION; HIGHER EDUCATION; MULTICULTURAL EDUCATION; PARENT'S EDUCATION; PRIMARY EDUCATION; PRIVATE EDUCATION; RELIGIOUS EDUCATION; SECONDARY EDUCATION; VOCATIONAL EDUCATION; WOMEN'S EDUCATION
   B.1: 126. **B.2**: 100. **C.1**: 89, 110. **D.3**: 29. **D.7**: 340, 343, 390. **D.9**: 2–3, 7–9, 14, 17, 22, 27, 30, 35, 39, 53–55, 57, 61–62, 65, 68, 71, 73, 90–91, 96, 98, 105, 107, 111, 113–115, 120, 123, 125, 138, 153, 158, 163. **E.2**: 36. **F.3**: 11, 38, 233, 245, 252, 280, 308. **F.4**: 242. **F.5**: 170, 283. **F.7**: 1, 14, 188, 230, 253. **I.2**: 49, 116, 160, 225. **I.4**: 15–16, 120, 129. **J.4**: 12. **J.5**: 5. **K.1**: 94. **K.4**: 51.
Education administration **D.9**: 83.
Education policy **D.9**: 40, 42–44, 49, 51, 53–54, 56–59, 63, 66–67, 70, 80, 104, 159, 171.
Education reform **D.9**: 43, 47–48, 50, 72, 75, 78, 136, 215.
Education systems **D.7**: 84. **D.9**: 89, 93, 97, 99, 102, 112, 146.
Educational development **D.9**: 36, 141.
Educational needs **D.9**: 130.
Educational objectives **D.9**: 18, 212, 214.
Educational planning **D.9**: 148.
Educational sociology **D.7**: 46. **D.9**: 127, 144–145, 147.
Effect **C.2**: 180.
Effects
   Entries also appear under:
   ENVIRONMENTAL EFFECTS; PSYCHOLOGICAL EFFECTS
Ego **C.2**: 3. **F.4**: 11. **F.5**: 172.
Elections

Entries also appear under:
   GENERAL ELECTIONS; LOCAL ELECTIONS; PRESIDENTIAL ELECTIONS
   D.9: 11. **I.5**: 191. **J.6**: 60, 64.
Electoral behaviour **C.2**: 70. **D.1**: 51. **J.6**: 51.
Electoral campaign financing **J.6**: 65.
Electoral campaigning **D.7**: 280.
Electoral college **J.6**: 58.
Electoral results **I.5**: 191.
Electoral sociology **I.5**: 162.
Electricity **H.7**: 7.
Electronics **D.7**: 192. **H.4**: 86. **H.5**: 35.
Electronics industry **D.9**: 40. **H.4**: 58. **I.5**: 6, 126.
Elias, Norbert **A.2**: 13, 15. **B.1**: 5, 7. **C.3**: 63. **D.1**: 96. **J.1**: 3.
Elites
   Entries also appear under:
   ECONOMIC ELITES; POLITICAL ELITES
   E.2: 10, 20, 46. **I.6**: 4. **J.4**: 21. **J.6**: 44.
Emancipation
   Entries also appear under:
   WOMEN'S EMANCIPATION
   F.4: 195.
Emigrants **F.5**: 7. **F.8**: 56, 71, 151. **G.3.1**: 7. **H.3**: 49.
Emigration **F.5**: 5. **F.8**: 22, 26, 40, 69, 111, 113, 116, 120, 124–126, 129, 131, 139–140, 145, 152, 155–156, 165, 167, 172. **H.3**: 20.
Emotions **C.1**: 85, 160. **C.2**: 4, 21–22, 28, 30–31, 53, 57, 99–100, 109, 117, 122, 129, 196. **C.3**: 73, 100, 119, 124–128, 130–138, 140. **D.3**: 67. **D.7**: 13, 295. **F.2**: 89. **F.4**: 31, 257. **I.3**: 3, 82.
Empathy **B.1**: 32. **C.3**: 101.
Empirical research **A.1**: 28, 36. **B.2**: 12, 24, 43. **F.2**: 22.
Empiricism **D.6**: 31.
Employees **C.3**: 104. **C.5**: 68. **D.4**: 34. **F.2**: 95. **F.7**: 265. **H.3**: 80, 86. **I.2**: 176. **I.3**: 26–28, 37, 41, 45, 58, 63, 73, 91, 101, 106, 139. **I.4**: 18, 64, 83, 118. **I.5**: 5, 10, 16, 33, 90, 133, 192, 202.
Employers **D.9**: 210. **I.3**: 6, 16, 29, 76. **I.4**: 8. **I.5**: 192, 194. **K.1**: 344.
Employment
   Entries also appear under:
   ACCESS TO EMPLOYMENT; FULL EMPLOYMENT; PART-TIME EMPLOYMENT; PUBLIC EMPLOYMENT; RURAL EMPLOYMENT; TEMPORARY EMPLOYMENT; URBAN EMPLOYMENT; WOMEN'S EMPLOYMENT; YOUTH EMPLOYMENT
   C.2: 83. **C.5**: 56. **D.9**: 207. **F.2**: 78, 95. **F.3**: 96, 127. **F.4**: 114, 260. **F.5**: 283. **F.8**: 37, 123. **G.3.2**: 68. **H.3**: 75. **H.4**: 40, 90, 101. **H.5**: 26.

H.7: 11. **I.2**: 4, 10–12, 14–15, 17–19, 23, 27, 32, 40, 53, 58, 65, 70, 81–82, 90, 97–98, 104–105, 116, 123, 131–132, 134–135, 147, 149–150, 152, 155–157, 159, 161, 165, 174, 178, 194, 198, 211, 213–215, 229, 234. **I.3**: 13, 23, 30, 60, 71, 131. **I.4**: 78, 103. **I.5**: 17, 20, 103, 106, 179. **K.2**: 28, 73.

Employment discrimination **F.7**: 250. **I.2**: 46, 131, 209.

Employment opportunities **I.2**: 8, 212. **I.4**: 62. **J.7**: 6.

Employment policy **I.2**: 38, 207, 219–220, 233, 235. **I.3**: 93. **I.5**: 136.

Employment stability **I.2**: 21.

Endogamy **F.4**: 206.

Energy
Entries also appear under:
NUCLEAR ENERGY
G.3.2: 258.

Energy consumption **F.8**: 36.

Energy utilization **F.1**: 47.

Engineering **D.9**: 190. **H.4**: 14, 24. **I.2**: 121. **I.4**: 132.

Engineers **H.4**: 32. **I.2**: 24, 66. **I.4**: 66, 95–97, 106, 113, 115.

English language **D.7**: 18–19, 45, 59, 64, 85, 141, 189, 198, 204, 219, 268.

Enlightenment thought **B.1**: 114. **E.2**: 11.

Enterprises
Entries also appear under:
AGRICULTURAL ENTERPRISES; FAMILY FIRMS; FOREIGN ENTERPRISES; MULTINATIONAL ENTERPRISES; SMALL AND MEDIUM SIZED ENTERPRISES; SOCIALIST ENTERPRISES
C.5: 12. **D.1**: 17. **F.7**: 34, 56. **F.8**: 46. **G.3.2**: 187. **H.7**: 2, 13. **I.1**: 2. **I.2**: 99. **I.3**: 31, 95, 151. **I.4**: 64, 100. **I.5**: 46.

Entertainment **D.5**: 161. **D.7**: 390.

Entrepreneurs **F.5**: 226. **H.4**: 78.

Entrepreneurship **E.2**: 63. **F.5**: 247. **F.7**: 51. **H.4**: 36. **I.4**: 15.

Entry to working life **D.9**: 181.

Environment
Entries also appear under:
FAMILY ENVIRONMENT; HUMAN ENVIRONMENT; OCCUPATIONAL ENVIRONMENT; RURAL ENVIRONMENT; SCHOOL ENVIRONMENT; SOCIAL ENVIRONMENT; URBAN ENVIRONMENT; WORK ENVIRONMENT
C.2: 37, 90, 157. **C.4**: 28. **C.5**: 55. **C.7**: 55, 59. **D.7**: 178. **D.8**: 65. **F.2**: 37, 96. **F.3**: 313. **F.6**: 18. **F.7**: 203. **G.1**: 5, 12, 18, 28, 52. **G.3.2**: 46, 81, 239. **I.6**: 6. **J.5**: 9. **K.4**: 7.

Environmental degradation **D.7**: 250. **H.4**: 103.

Environmental economics **G.1**: 63. **K.1**: 346.

Environmental effects **G.1**: 7. **I.6**: 27.

Environmental impact studies **G.1**: 34.

Environmental management **D.3**: 38–39.

Environmental planning **H.7**: 10, 15.

Environmental policy **F.3**: 2. **F.5**: 48. **G.1**: 16, 22. **G.3.2**: 353. **I.2**: 235.

Environmental protection **G.1**: 25, 37.

Environmental quality **G.3.2**: 138.

Epidemiology **C.1**: 66, 72. **F.2**: 11. **F.3**: 164, 173, 179, 185, 233. **K.1**: 347.

Epistemology **B.1**: 30–34, 36–37, 40–42. **D.4**: 8. **D.9**: 177.

Equal opportunities **F.4**: 324. **F.5**: 212. **H.3**: 90. **I.2**: 110, 212. **I.5**: 105–106.

Equal pay **F.5**: 64. **H.3**: 86. **I.2**: 92, 115–116.

Equality
Entries also appear under:
ECONOMIC EQUALITY; SEX EQUALITY
E.2: 18, 44. **F.5**: 161, 310. **F.7**: 221. **G.3.2**: 23. **I.4**: 20. **K.1**: 145, 173.

Equilibrium **J.5**: 32.

Equity **C.3**: 33. **D.3**: 4. **G.3.2**: 23, 257. **I.6**: 9. **K.4**: 193, 250.

Eschatology **F.2**: 45.

Ethics
Entries also appear under:
BUSINESS ETHICS; MEDICAL ETHICS; PROFESSIONAL ETHICS; PROTESTANT ETHICS; WORK ETHIC
A ↙: 3. **B.1**: 64. **B.2**: 6. **C.1**: 46, 58. **C.2**: 95, 220. **C.3**: 49. **D.3**: 2–3, 7–9, 11, 13, 15, 18, 24, 27, 29–30, 33–43, 45–50, 55–56, 61–63, 69, 73. **D.5**: 29, 182. **D.6**: 3. **D.7**: 163, 279. **D.9**: 212. **F.2**: 17. **F.3**: 32, 71, 207. **F.4**: 308, 327. **F.5**: 90. **F.6**: 5. **G.1**: 14, 16, 19, 61. **H.2**: 10, 15. **H.3**: 61. **H.4**: 36, 60. **H.5**: 41. **J.2**: 7. **J.3**: 45. **J.4**: 2, 23. **K.2**: 84. **K.4**: 193, 249–251, 255, 257, 261, 263, 267.

Ethnic assimilation **F.7**: 72, 92, 106, 135.

Ethnic communities **D.7**: 88. **F.7**: 82, 126.

Ethnic groups **C.7**: 21. **E.2**: 22. **F.4**: 207. **F.7**: 3, 11, 17, 34–35, 40, 45, 71, 81, 102, 115, 121, 137, 160. **F.8**: 48, 61, 81. **G.3.2**: 185. **H.4**: 36. **I.2**: 189, 225. **I.4**: 7. **K.1**: 350.

Ethnic minorities **D.7**: 21. **D.9**: 45. **F.7**: 1, 12–13, 15, 25, 27, 58, 61, 111, 129, 193–194, 237, 268. **F.8**: 19. **I.4**: 33. **K.1**: 232.

Ethnic pluralism **F.7**: 62, 110. **F.8**: 117.

Ethnic policy **E.2**: 1. **F.7**: 39, 65.

Ethnicity **D.1**: 41. **D.7**: 360. **D.9**: 133. **F.1**: 8. **F.4**: 37, 93. **F.7**: 46–48, 53, 56, 59, 63–64, 67–71, 73–80, 82, 84, 87–88, 90, 93, 96–98, 101, 103–104, 111, 115, 119–122, 124–125, 128,

130, 134–135, 150, 161. **F.8**: 10, 127. **G.2**: 4. **G.3.2**: 156, 197. **I.2**: 16. **I.4**: 16. **I.5**: 162. **J.6**: 36. **J.7**: 9. **K.2**: 35. **K.3**: 14. **K.4**: 2–3, 58.
Ethnocentrism **C.4**: 15. **F.7**: 21, 206.
Ethnographic research **G.3.2**: 107.
Ethnography **C.5**: 7. **D.1**: 141. **D.7**: 287. **F.5**: 141. **G.3.2**: 108. **I.2**: 96. **J.6**: 27.
Ethnolinguistics **D.7**: 55, 199.
Ethnologists **D.1**: 66.
Ethnology **B.1**: 34. **D.1**: 35. **F.7**: 159. **G.1**: 6. **G.3.1**: 131.
Ethnomethodology **D.1**: 29.
Ethology **A.1**: 15. **C.2**: 183. **D.4**: 35.
Ethos **B.1**: 52. **D.1**: 98.
Etiology **K.4**: 72.
Etiquette **D.2**: 8.
Eugenics **F.5**: 223. **J.2**: 10.
European Communities
Entries also appear under:
SINGLE EUROPEAN MARKET
D.7: 22. **D.9**: 66. **E.1**: 15. **F.7**: 162, 215. **F.8**: 130. **G.3.2**: 319. **H.4**: 6. **I.3**: 84, 118. **I.5**: 21. **J.8**: 4, 6–7, 9–10. **K.2**: 9, 27, 72, 96. **K.3**: 38.
Europeans **F.8**: 127.
Euthanasia **D.3**: 59. **K.4**: 252, 258, 265.
Evaluation
Entries also appear under:
JOB EVALUATION; PROJECT EVALUATION
B.2: 9, 123. **C.2**: 144, 152. **D.1**: 19. **D.7**: 170. **F.1**: 24. **F.3**: 114. **H.6**: 4. **I.3**: 57, 121.
Evaluation techniques **H.4**: 4.
Evangelism **D.5**: 108–109, 125, 152. **D.7**: 375.
Evangelization **D.5**: 110.
Evans, Walker **D.7**: 3.
Everyday life **C.1**: 91. **C.2**: 20, 47, 59, 66, 148, 164. **D.2**: 19, 22–23, 25, 28–29. **D.4**: 32. **D.7**: 107. **F.2**: 15. **F.3**: 194. **F.4**: 342. **H.4**: 92. **I.4**: 61. **K.4**: 88.
Evolution
Entries also appear under:
HUMAN EVOLUTION
B.1: 119. **D.1**: 8. **D.3**: 77. **F.1**: 25. **F.7**: 206.
Evolutionary psychology **C.5**: 26.
Evolutionism **B.1**: 151.
Exchange
Entries also appear under:
MARRIAGE EXCHANGE; SOCIAL EXCHANGE
C.3: 33. **G.3.2**: 42.
Executives **C.5**: 19.
Exile **F.7**: 164. **F.8**: 142. **K.1**: 194.
Exodus **I.6**: 22.
Exogamy **F.4**: 206.

Expectation **B.1**: 104. **C.2**: 35, 103. **I.2**: 166.
Expenditure
Entries also appear under:
CONSUMER EXPENDITURE; HEALTH EXPENDITURE; PUBLIC EXPENDITURE
I.2: 77.
Experimental methods **I.2**: 41.
Experimentation
Entries also appear under:
ANIMAL EXPERIMENTATION
H.4: 4.
Experiments **C.1**: 96. **C.5**: 61.
Expert systems **B.2**: 8.
Experts **I.4**: 105.
Explanation
Entries also appear under:
CAUSAL EXPLANATION
B.1: 2, 10, 69. **C.2**: 103. **D.3**: 6.
Export-oriented industry **I.2**: 162.
Exports **F.8**: 37.
Extreme right **F.7**: 219.
Facial expressions **C.2**: 31. **C.3**: 64, 81, 134–135, 147.
Factories **F.5**: 36. **I.4**: 4, 32. **I.5**: 8.
Failure **C.2**: 103. **F.8**: 157.
Faith **D.5**: 94, 111.
Falkland War **C.3**: 94. **J.7**: 17.
Family
Entries also appear under:
ONE-PARENT FAMILIES; SOCIOLOGY OF THE FAMILY
C.1: 80. **C.3**: 29. **C.7**: 56. **D.2**: 12. **D.4**: 20. **D.5**: 50, 89, 168. **D.7**: 24, 354. **D.9**: 38, 118, 122, 142. **E.2**: 56, 73. **E.3**: 24. **F.1**: 60. **F.2**: 100, 140. **F.3**: 12, 41, 84, 130. **F.4**: 1–2, 4–10, 12–13, 17–19, 22–23, 32, 34, 36, 40, 42, 44–48, 50, 53, 57, 61, 63, 66, 69–70, 72, 75, 78, 81–83, 86, 88–91, 93, 95, 97, 99–101, 103–105, 108, 110, 112–113, 115, 118, 138, 142, 163, 180, 183, 200, 203, 245, 258, 289, 296, 329, 332, 338, 347, 351. **F.5**: 4, 30, 36, 116, 234, 274, 313, 326, 328. **F.7**: 19, 81. **F.8**: 17–18, 25, 54, 81. **G.3.1**: 58, 131. **G.3.2**: 121, 169. **H.3**: 19, 22. **I.2**: 48, 56, 69, 72, 89, 133, 202. **I.4**: 60. **I.6**: 11. **K.1**: 34, 54, 268, 331, 425. **K.2**: 6, 35, 52, 75, 109. **K.3**: 15, 21, 25. **K.4**: 25, 121.
Family allowances **K.2**: 49, 79.
Family disintegration **F.4**: 41, 316. **K.1**: 425.
Family environment **F.4**: 27, 37, 340.
Family farms **F.4**: 14, 51, 114. **G.3.1**: 33, 80.
Family firms **I.4**: 6.
Family history **K.1**: 309, 374.
Family income **F.4**: 341. **I.4**: 53.

Family law **F.4**: 127, 130–131, 177, 180, 184, 186, 188–190, 192. **F.5**: 160.
Family life **D.2**: 12. **F.2**: 141. **F.4**: 16, 51, 76, 342.
Family planning **D.9**: 133. **F.1**: 51. **F.3**: 36, 40, 42–45, 47, 51, 68, 71, 109.
Family policy **F.4**: 52, 84. **K.2**: 4.
Family relations **C.2**: 185. **F.3**: 184, 225. **F.4**: 34, 43, 54, 59, 85, 114, 116. **K.4**: 34.
Family size **F.3**: 104. **F.4**: 65, 333, 353. **H.3**: 5.
Family structure **F.4**: 330–331, 334–336, 339, 341, 345, 347, 352–354.
Family therapy **C.1**: 59. **F.4**: 38.
Famine **F.1**: 43. **G.3.2**: 65. **K.1**: 18, 245, 255.
Fanaticism
Entries also appear under:
RELIGIOUS FANATICISM
Farmers **F.3**: 92. **G.1**: 13. **G.3.1**: 10–11, 62, 67, 99. **H.3**: 38. **I.2**: 143.
Farming **G.3.1**: 20. **G.3.2**: 84. **H.3**: 9. **H.4**: 12, 101. **I.2**: 97.
Fascism **D.8**: 45.
Fashion **D.1**: 20, 138. **D.2**: 4, 10. **I.2**: 183.
Fatherhood **F.4**: 285, 290.
Fathers **B.2**: 110. **C.1**: 24, 58. **F.4**: 122, 266, 269, 282, 291–292, 301–302, 313, 323. **F.6**: 27, 44.
Fear **C.2**: 30. **C.3**: 122. **F.5**: 228. **I.3**: 33. **I.5**: 118. **K.1**: 83, 88–89, 114.
Federalism **D.7**: 334.
Female labour **F.3**: 95–96. **H.3**: 76. **I.2**: 93, 108, 126, 141, 173, 181.
Female sterilization **F.3**: 69.
Femininity **C.3**: 144. **D.2**: 10. **F.5**: 263, 299.
Feminism **A.2**: 10. **B.1**: 3, 29, 42, 51, 102. **C.5**: 35. **D.5**: 17, 36, 92. **D.8**: 37, 50. **F.3**: 115. **F.4**: 20, 58. **F.5**: 62–72, 74–77, 79–88, 90–104, 106–110, 112–114, 116–118, 120–124, 127, 129–134, 136–141, 143–144, 180–181, 204, 228, 276, 287. **G.2**: 36. **I.2**: 115. **J.5**: 21. **K.1**: 52, 97, 101. **K.3**: 16.
Fenichel, Otto **C.1**: 42.
Fertility **F.1**: 33. **F.3**: 11, 40, 51, 75–76, 79, 81, 83, 86, 88, 90–91, 94–95, 97–105, 107, 111, 113, 122–123, 128–129, 131, 134–141, 276. **F.4**: 33, 208, 248, 306, 330. **F.5**: 2, 38, 236. **F.8**: 15.
Fertility decline **F.3**: 77, 121.
Field work **A.2**: 18. **B.2**: 23, 103. **D.1**: 66.
Filipino language **D.7**: 38.
Filipinos **F.8**: 122, 155.
Film industry **D.8**: 59. **I.5**: 94.
Films **D.7**: 107, 143. **D.8**: 12, 20, 50, 62, 75. **E.1**: 14. **F.4**: 3. **F.5**: 137, 276. **K.1**: 423.

Finance
Entries also appear under:
INTERNATIONAL FINANCE; PUBLIC FINANCE
H.6: 6. **K.2**: 3.
Financial management **K.1**: 167.
Financial reporting **D.7**: 208.
Finnish language **D.7**: 45.
Fire **G.3.2**: 308.
Fire services **I.1**: 9. **K.2**: 21.
Firearms **D.2**: 26. **K.1**: 90.
Fisheries **G.1**: 6. **H.4**: 47.
Fishermen **C.4**: 34.
Fleck, Ludwik **D.6**: 11.
Flexible hours of work **I.3**: 34, 131, 154.
Flexible specialization **I.1**: 16. **I.2**: 154.
Floods **C.7**: 22. **G.3.2**: 85.
Folklore **C.5**: 84.
Food **F.1**: 45. **F.3**: 256. **F.5**: 61. **G.3.1**: 44. **H.3**: 68.
Food consumption **C.2**: 74.
Food habits **D.2**: 21.
Food industry **C.5**: 16. **C.7**: 55. **D.2**: 15, 21. **H.4**: 98. **I.2**: 129. **I.5**: 10.
Food policy **E.3**: 43. **K.2**: 4.
Food security **F.5**: 321.
Forecasting techniques **B.2**: 39. **F.1**: 29–30. **F.3**: 176. **I.3**: 148. **K.4**: 102.
Forecasts
Entries also appear under:
ECONOMIC FORECASTS; POPULATION FORECASTS
B.2: 60. **C.1**: 126.
Foreign aid **G.3.1**: 127.
Foreign enterprises **G.3.2**: 21.
Foreign investment **F.8**: 37.
Foreign languages **D.7**: 335.
Foreign policy **F.3**: 178. **H.7**: 8. **J.6**: 2.
Foreign relations **K.1**: 321.
Foreign trade **F.8**: 37. **K.4**: 186.
Foreign trade policy
Entries also appear under:
PROTECTIONISM
Foreign workers **D.7**: 218. **F.8**: 79. **I.2**: 45, 200.
Foreigners **F.8**: 175.
Forensic medicine **K.4**: 178.
Forensic psychiatry **C.1**: 26.
Forestry **I.4**: 46.
Forestry development **G.3.1**: 104. **G.3.2**: 27.
Forestry industry **G.1**: 11. **H.4**: 43.

Forests **G.1**: 41.
Formalization **D.6**: 4. **K.4**: 22.
Foucault, Michel **B.1**: 52, 114. **D.6**: 12. **F.5**: 74, 277. **J.5**: 28. **K.1**: 52.
Fourier, Charles **D.1**: 79.
Fraasen, Van, Bas **D.6**: 31.
Fraternities **C.3**: 66.
Fraud **I.4**: 10. **K.1**: 163.
Freedom
Entries also appear under:
ACADEMIC FREEDOM; CIVIL LIBERTIES
D.3: 20, 22. **J.3**: 17. **K.1**: 7.
Freedom of religion **D.5**: 100.
Freedom of speech **D.7**: 253. **I.5**: 81. **J.3**: 26.
Freedom of the press **D.7**: 255, 262. **J.3**: 16.
Freemasonry **F.7**: 36.
French language **D.7**: 350.
Freud, Sigmund **C.1**: 1, 18–19, 46, 55, 112.
Friendship **C.3**: 7, 18, 35, 38, 129. **D.3**: 12, 25.
Fromm, Erich **C.1**: 29.
Full employment **I.2**: 220. **K.2**: 107.
Funerary rites **D.2**: 14.
Gaelic language **D.7**: 343.
Gambling **H.4**: 36. **I.6**: 3. **K.1**: 9, 59.
Game theory **B.2**: 37. **J.1**: 9.
Games **C.2**: 120. **C.7**: 76. **I.6**: 42. **J.3**: 37. **J.5**: 1. **J.7**: 4.
Gangs **C.4**: 33. **F.2**: 126, 157. **F.7**: 73. **G.3.2**: 196. **K.1**: 16.
Gardens **G.3.1**: 27. **I.6**: 39.
Gender **B.1**: 128. **B.2**: 23. **C.1**: 65. **C.2**: 36, 99, 171, 239. **C.3**: 31, 45, 78, 151. **C.6**: 3. **C.7**: 67. **D.1**: 20, 127. **D.4**: 9. **D.5**: 1, 13, 16–17, 79. **D.7**: 107, 150, 327. **D.8**: 66. **D.9**: 38, 121. **E.3**: 19. **F.1**: 28, 42, 64. **F.2**: 31, 49, 87, 143. **F.3**: 169, 269. **F.4**: 59, 83, 93, 270. **F.5**: 1, 3, 8, 10–14, 17, 30, 40, 75, 87, 128, 137, 139, 147, 163, 167, 169–171, 173, 178–180, 182–183, 185, 215, 217, 220, 222, 233, 264, 266–267, 279, 282, 284, 286–288, 310. **F.6**: 15, 19. **F.7**: 53, 149, 234. **F.8**: 20, 39, 90. **G.3.1**: 24, 85. **G.3.2**: 112, 183, 214, 244, 265. **H.3**: 28, 73. **H.4**: 17, 44. **I.2**: 78, 80, 95–97, 100, 103, 105, 113, 123, 129, 132, 135–136, 166. **I.3**: 18, 44, 133. **I.4**: 24, 82, 119. **I.5**: 18, 82, 96, 145. **J.2**: 10. **J.5**: 19. **J.6**: 13. **K.1**: 47, 86, 185, 198. **K.3**: 42. **K.4**: 58.
Gender differentiation **C.3**: 6. **D.9**: 89. **F.4**: 241, 284. **F.5**: 63, 167, 172, 174–177, 197, 201–202, 205, 232, 235, 253, 260. **G.3.1**: 33, 82. **H.3**: 69, 71. **H.4**: 102. **I.2**: 101, 144. **I.3**: 55. **J.7**: 1, 12. **K.1**: 352, 425.

Gender relations **C.4**: 63. **D.6**: 8. **F.4**: 354. **F.5**: 35, 42, 49, 210, 218, 269, 295, 318, 322. **G.3.2**: 174. **H.4**: 90.
Gender roles **C.3**: 144. **D.4**: 20. **F.1**: 61. **F.5**: 63, 123, 262, 271–272, 274, 276, 280–281, 283, 285, 289–290, 299, 303, 305, 312–313, 315, 317, 319. **G.3.1**: 3–4, 45. **I.2**: 133. **K.1**: 395.
Genealogy **F.4**: 60. **F.5**: 100.
General elections **J.6**: 63.
General theories **B.1**: 134.
Generation conflicts **F.2**: 4, 7.
Generation differences **F.2**: 20.
Generations **E.3**: 14, 23. **F.2**: 6, 14, 44. **I.4**: 22. **J.6**: 17.
Genetics
Entries also appear under:
HUMAN GENETICS
C.1: 20. **C.2**: 37. **F.1**: 40. **F.3**: 59, 161. **K.4**: 13, 37, 249, 255, 261, 263, 267, 270–271.
Genocide **C.2**: 107.
Geographic location **G.1**: 30. **G.3**: 6. **K.4**: 59.
Geographic mobility **F.5**: 8. **F.8**: 43, 105, 108.
Geographical information systems **G.3.2**: 268–269. **H.7**: 10.
Geography
Entries also appear under:
ECONOMIC GEOGRAPHY; HISTORICAL GEOGRAPHY; POLITICAL GEOGRAPHY; POPULATION GEOGRAPHY; URBAN GEOGRAPHY
C.2: 38. **D.7**: 92. **F.1**: 64. **G.1**: 51–52, 54–56, 58–61. **G.3.2**: 33. **H.7**: 8. **I.2**: 7. **J.3**: 44. **J.6**: 25.
German language **D.7**: 93, 99, 218.
German unification **E.2**: 45. **F.5**: 251.
Germans **F.7**: 113. **F.8**: 13.
Gerontology **F.2**: 29.
Gestures **C.3**: 30.
Ghetto **G.3.2**: 216. **K.1**: 220, 231–232.
Gift **H.6**: 2.
Gifted children **C.6**: 14. **D.9**: 156.
Girls **C.2**: 118. **F.1**: 39. **F.3**: 244, 280. **F.5**: 33, 186.
Global warming **H.4**: 103.
Goddesses **D.5**: 157.
Gods **D.5**: 14.
Goffman, Erving **B.1**: 5, 97.
Gold mines **F.8**: 109.
Golding, William **D.8**: 14.
Gompertz, Benjamin **F.3**: 257.
Gorbachev, Mikhail **H.3**: 48.
Gough, H. **C.6**: 11.

Government
Entries also appear under:
   LOCAL GOVERNMENT
D.3: 47–48. **F.3**: 210. **G.3.2**: 4. **H.3**: 74. **I.5**: 16. **I.6**: 14.

Government departments **D.9**: 65.

Government policy **F.2**: 43. **F.3**: 44. **F.8**: 52, 131. **G.3.2**: 167. **I.2**: 194, 221. **K.2**: 28, 33, 44. **K.4**: 171.

Government programmes **H.3**: 26.

Graduates **C.2**: 145. **F.8**: 14. **I.2**: 231. **I.3**: 18. **I.4**: 90.

Grammar **D.7**: 197, 215.

Greek Antiquity **D.5**: 99.

Greek languages **D.7**: 43.

Greeks **F.4**: 225.

Green, T.H. **F.5**: 88.

Group analysis **C.4**: 14, 23, 32, 42, 50, 53–54.

Group behaviour **C.2**: 239. **C.4**: 19, 21–22, 31, 43, 47, 55, 59, 61–62. **C.7**: 50.

Group composition **C.4**: 23.

Group conformity **C.4**: 28. **I.3**: 80.

Group decision making **C.4**: 24–26, 28, 36–37, 40, 45, 50, 56.

Group dynamics **C.4**: 1, 12, 27, 35, 38. **J.1**: 21.

Group identity **C.4**: 16, 60. **C.7**: 25. **D.1**: 82. **D.7**: 285. **F.8**: 17.

Group influence **C.4**: 7.

Group interaction **C.3**: 86. **C.4**: 37, 44. **C.7**: 24.

Group membership **C.3**: 154. **C.4**: 13.

Group performance **C.4**: 11, 17, 46, 56. **I.3**: 96.

Group protest **D.9**: 120.

Group theory **C.4**: 3.

Group work **C.4**: 51.

Growth poles **C.5**: 62.

Guerrillas **G.3.1**: 132. **K.1**: 11.

Guilt **C.2**: 110, 238. **J.3**: 25.

Gulf War **D.7**: 260. **F.4**: 83. **J.7**: 11. **J.8**: 10.

Gumperz, John J. **D.7**: 156.

Gurvitsch, Aron **B.1**: 99.

Gypsies **C.7**: 30. **D.7**: 70. **F.7**: 23, 65, 93, 111. **K.1**: 19.

Habermas, Jürgen **B.1**: 24, 59, 91, 107, 110, 112, 116. **D.3**: 58. **D.9**: 30. **J.2**: 15.

Habitats **G.1**: 1.

Habits
Entries also appear under:
   FOOD HABITS
C.2: 139. **K.4**: 153.

Hall, Stuart **C.7**: 68.

Handicrafts **I.2**: 140.

Happiness **C.2**: 56, 60, 62, 212. **F.4**: 220.

Hayek, Friedrich **D.1**: 74.

Haynsworth, Clement F. **D.4**: 7.

Hazardous wastes **D.7**: 188. **J.5**: 14.

Heads of state **J.3**: 14.

Health
Entries also appear under:
   CHILD HEALTH; MENTAL HEALTH; PUBLIC HEALTH; WOMEN'S HEALTH
B.1: 81. **C.1**: 122. **C.2**: 22, 209. **D.5**: 12, 18, 185. **F.2**: 54, 86–87, 143. **F.3**: 12, 56, 108, 118, 147, 162, 168, 179, 221. **F.4**: 252. **F.5**: 173. **F.7**: 24, 31. **F.8**: 31. **G.1**: 5, 14. **G.3.1**: 129. **H.4**: 22. **I.2**: 177. **I.3**: 73, 75. **K.1**: 241, 260, 268, 349. **K.4**: 9, 11, 14, 38–40, 44, 46, 50, 62, 81, 91, 93, 105–106, 133, 141, 146, 166, 181, 201, 225, 234, 238.

Health administration **K.4**: 228.

Health aid **K.4**: 45.

Health care
Entries also appear under:
   MEDICAL CARE; PRIVATE HEALTH CARE
F.2: 16, 46. **F.3**: 181, 279. **F.5**: 25. **I.3**: 122. **K.2**: 89. **K.3**: 30, 39. **K.4**: 6, 15–16, 25, 28, 43, 54, 61, 66, 68, 70, 76, 78, 80, 82, 87–89, 103, 111, 121, 157, 164, 168, 170, 172–173, 190, 196, 203, 211, 214, 216, 221, 223, 227, 239, 243–244, 250, 260.

Health care a-reform **K.4**: 202.

Health centres **K.4**: 59.

Health economics **K.4**: 138, 156, 159, 162–163, 204, 247.

Health education **K.4**: 41, 220.

Health expenditure **K.4**: 149–150, 157, 226.

Health insurance **I.2**: 111. **K.4**: 77, 179, 224.

Health planning **K.4**: 33.

Health policy **D.5**: 38. **F.3**: 209, 227. **F.5**: 221. **K.2**: 86. **K.4**: 167, 169, 183, 186–187, 191, 193, 195, 197, 199–200, 204, 209, 211, 213, 215, 218–219, 222, 226, 228–230, 232, 240, 242.

Health services **F.2**: 128. **K.2**: 21. **K.3**: 12. **K.4**: 8, 10, 42–43, 84, 95, 113, 119, 150, 165, 175, 180, 187, 192, 194–195, 206–208, 210, 228.

Heart disease **K.4**: 32, 230.

Hebrew language **D.7**: 28.

Hegel, Georg Friedrich W. **B.1**: 70, 122. **D.6**: 12.

Herero **F.3**: 89.

Hermeneutics **B.1**: 25, 54. **C.5**: 84. **D.5**: 19. **D.6**: 7.

Heuristics **C.1**: 126.

Hierarchy
Entries also appear under:
   CHURCH HIERARCHY

A.1: 32. **B.2**: 52. **C.6**: 4. **E.2**: 57. **E.3**: 74. **G.3.2**: 243. **J.4**: 17. **K.4**: 152.

High technology **C.5**: 74. **H.4**: 41. **I.2**: 25. **I.3**: 47. **I.4**: 40, 66. **K.4**: 16.

Higher education **D.3**: 75. **D.9**: 121, 145, 173, 175, 177, 179, 181–182, 184–187, 189–190, 194–195, 197–201, 203–205, 211–212, 214, 216–217, 219–220. **F.5**: 77, 242, 256.

Hindi language **D.7**: 228.

Hinduism **C.1**: 151. **D.5**: 154, 156–158.

Hindus **C.4**: 29. **C.7**: 31. **D.5**: 155. **F.5**: 155. **F.7**: 29. **J.3**: 24.

Hispanics **B.2**: 22. **C.1**: 75. **D.9**: 14. **F.3**: 278. **F.7**: 31, 69, 107, 172. **F.8**: 38, 95. **H.3**: 9, 26. **I.2**: 178. **J.6**: 1.

Historical geography **G.1**: 55, 57, 64.

Historiography **E.3**: 54. **K.1**: 116.

History

Entries also appear under:
AGRICULTURAL HISTORY; CHURCH HISTORY; COLONIAL HISTORY; FAMILY HISTORY; ORAL HISTORY; SOCIAL HISTORY

A.1: 14, 17. **B.1**: 89. **C.1**: 114, 157. **C.5**: 30. **E.3**: 76. **F.5**: 67. **F.8**: 5. **G.1**: 55. **H.1**: 4.

History of medicine **K.4**: 23.

History of music **D.8**: 25.

History of science **D.6**: 14.

History of sociology **A.1**: 8, 12, 26.

HIV **F.2**: 22, 128. **F.3**: 60, 159, 165, 182–183, 187, 193, 198, 201, 222, 228. **F.6**: 4. **F.8**: 21. **K.1**: 380. **K.3**: 46. **K.4**: 229.

Hobbes, Thomas **E.1**: 12.

Holidays **D.2**: 27.

Holocaust **C.2**: 107.

Home economics **H.5**: 20.

Home ownership **F.8**: 1. **G.3.2**: 105. **H.5**: 2.

Homeless people **F.8**: 43. **G.3.2**: 98. **K.1**: 26, 219, 223, 235–236, 260, 285, 287, 294, 301, 310, 347, 355–356.

Homelessness **C.3**: 37, 79. **F.2**: 128. **G.3.1**: 26. **G.3.2**: 40, 107–108, 121, 132, 154, 160, 224. **K.1**: 230, 237–244, 248, 253, 263, 274, 277, 279, 288, 291, 357. **K.2**: 13. **K.4**: 47–48, 119, 189.

Homicide

Entries also appear under:
MURDER

F.4: 338. **K.1**: 49, 90, 92, 130, 156, 430.

Homogamy **E.2**: 39.

Homosexuality **C.1**: 107. **C.3**: 25, 141. **C.7**: 25. **D.5**: 125. **F.3**: 202. **F.4**: 43, 181, 195, 235, 277. **F.6**: 2–4, 11, 17, 22, 30, 40, 47. **G.1**: 56. **K.1**: 429.

Horticulture **G.3.1**: 119.

Hospital management **K.4**: 17, 152.

Hospitality **G.3.1**: 70.

Hospitals

Entries also appear under:
MENTAL HOSPITALS

F.7: 37. **K.1**: 305, 359. **K.3**: 4, 11, 32. **K.4**: 18, 22, 49, 73, 83, 101, 131, 161, 182.

Hostages **C.3**: 26.

Hostility **G.3.1**: 70. **K.1**: 417.

Hotel industry **I.2**: 129.

Hours of work **I.2**: 43, 60. **I.3**: 9, 19, 30, 93.

Household budgets **H.5**: 20.

Household expenditure **H.5**: 13.

Household income **G.3.1**: 58. **H.2**: 14. **H.3**: 75.

Households **B.2**: 28, 36. **C.1**: 14. **F.1**: 29, 35, 58. **F.2**: 38, 58. **F.3**: 252–253. **F.4**: 26, 28, 74, 89. **F.5**: 14, 155, 164, 174, 195, 315. **F.8**: 36, 49, 73, 90, 113. **G.1**: 21. **G.2**: 1. **G.3.1**: 12, 27, 52. **G.3.2**: 38, 54, 115–116, 208. **H.3**: 19, 24. **H.5**: 37. **I.2**: 48. **K.1**: 272.

Housework **F.4**: 74. **F.5**: 180. **I.3**: 44.

Housing

Entries also appear under:
SOCIAL HOUSING; URBAN HOUSING

D.2: 9. **E.3**: 10. **F.1**: 4. **F.2**: 52, 64, 66. **F.4**: 141. **F.5**: 155. **F.7**: 146, 237, 246, 268. **G.2**: 20, 34. **G.3.2**: 40, 94–95, 97, 99–101, 103–104, 106, 109–110, 113–115, 117, 119–120, 122, 124, 126–127, 130, 134–136, 138–139, 142, 144–145, 150, 152, 156, 158–159, 162–163, 166–170. **H.4**: 9. **I.3**: 16. **I.4**: 43. **K.1**: 64. **K.2**: 7. **K.4**: 50, 119, 126, 142.

Housing allowances **K.2**: 10.

Housing construction **G.3.2**: 151.

Housing market **G.3.2**: 116, 133, 137, 140, 143, 155, 165. **H.3**: 60.

Housing needs **G.3.2**: 131.

Housing policy **G.3.2**: 123, 125, 128, 147, 153, 159, 164, 172, 241. **K.2**: 34.

Housing prices **G.3.2**: 96.

Housing reform **H.3**: 54.

Housing shortage **G.3.2**: 121.

Human biology **K.1**: 109.

Human body **D.7**: 234. **D.8**: 43. **E.2**: 8. **F.3**: 142.

Human ecology **F.3**: 2.

Human environment **G.1**: 62.

Human evolution **C.7**: 27.

Human genetics **D.3**: 18. **K.4**: 251.

Human nature **B.1**: 130, 140. **C.1**: 102. **C.2**: 42–43. **D.1**: 27. **D.4**: 23.

Human relations **C.3**: 63. **D.7**: 4. **F.4**: 94. **G.1**: 17.

Human resources **D.3**: 7. **E.2**: 17. **F.3**: 7. **F.4**: 63. **F.7**: 56. **H.3**: 13. **H.7**: 27. **I.2**: 51, 106, 179, 187, 210. **I.3**: 44, 47, 68, 124, 129–130, 135, 143. **I.4**: 117.

Human rights **F.3**: 159. **F.5**: 154. **F.6**: 3. **F.8**: 33. **I.5**: 80. **J.3**: 3.

Human settlements **G.3**: 11.

Humanism **D.1**: 132.

Humanities **A.1**: 35, 37. **D.9**: 179.

Humanity **D.1**: 53. **D.7**: 278.

Hume, David **B.1**: 56.

Humour **C.2**: 44. **C.3**: 51. **F.2**: 110.

Husbands **F.3**: 105. **F.4**: 87, 252. **F.5**: 5. **I.2**: 36, 106.

Hutterites **D.5**: 149.

Hygiene **F.3**: 179.

Hypnosis **C.2**: 45, 81.

Icons **D.8**: 18.

Idealism **D.1**: 23, 85.

Identification **C.3**: 29. **C.4**: 60. **C.7**: 80. **F.7**: 63, 69, 86. **K.4**: 121.

Identity
Entries also appear under:
CULTURAL IDENTITY; NATIONAL IDENTITY; PROFESSIONAL IDENTITY; REGIONAL IDENTITY
B.1: 142. **C.2**: 6, 46, 65, 70, 221. **C.4**: 60. **D.1**: 9, 41, 56, 71. **D.3**: 13. **D.5**: 39, 115, 125, 169. **D.7**: 31–32, 44, 63. **F.2**: 19, 73, 139. **F.4**: 250. **F.5**: 151. **F.6**: 49. **F.7**: 37, 85, 89, 100–101, 123–124, 159, 164. **G.1**: 58. **I.2**: 136. **I.3**: 5. **I.4**: 5, 60, 95. **J.1**: 18. **J.6**: 3, 36. **K.4**: 212.

Ideology **C.2**: 230. **C.3**: 48. **C.5**: 60. **C.7**: 35–36, 68. **D.1**: 17, 24, 103, 108. **D.6**: 15, 25. **D.7**: 28, 32, 113, 130, 268, 291. **D.9**: 75. **F.3**: 30. **F.4**: 12, 110. **F.5**: 282. **F.7**: 236. **I.1**: 5. **I.4**: 9, 57. **I.5**: 19, 58. **J.2**: 11, 23. **J.6**: 15, 29. **J.7**: 10. **K.2**: 80.

Igbo **D.8**: 19.

Ijesa **D.5**: 19.

Illegal immigrants **D.7**: 33.

Illegitimacy **F.3**: 65.

Images **C.1**: 7. **C.6**: 1. **D.1**: 43. **D.6**: 13. **D.7**: 15, 325. **D.8**: 58. **D.9**: 28. **E.1**: 6. **F.4**: 161, 292. **F.5**: 99, 271. **G.1**: 58. **H.6**: 6. **J.1**: 10. **J.6**: 16. **J.7**: 16. **K.1**: 398.

Imagination **C.2**: 167.

IMF **H.3**: 25.

Imitations **C.3**: 59, 134.

Immigrant adaptation **F.8**: 68, 75, 77.

Immigrant assimilation **D.7**: 123. **F.7**: 92. **F.8**: 22.

Immigrants
Entries also appear under:
ILLEGAL IMMIGRANTS
D.7: 93. **D.9**: 52. **F.1**: 32. **F.4**: 64. **F.5**: 18, 248. **F.7**: 7, 9, 26, 32, 56, 100, 106, 108, 143, 167, 228, 240, 254. **F.8**: 1–2, 9, 15, 19, 23, 28, 46, 50, 54, 57, 60, 64, 67–68, 72–73, 76, 111, 114, 127, 131. **H.3**: 65. **I.2**: 52, 72, 164, 180, 191, 203. **J.6**: 12, 17. **K.1**: 20, 54, 58. **K.2**: 81. **K.4**: 42.

Immigration **A.3**: 2. **E.2**: 81. **F.4**: 322. **F.7**: 27, 90, 110, 191, 258. **F.8**: 24–27, 29, 40, 61–62, 69, 74, 92, 111–113, 116–118, 120–124, 127, 130–131, 134–135, 139–140, 144–146, 152, 155, 162, 165, 167, 169, 171–172. **H.3**: 20.

Immigration policy **F.3**: 23. **F.8**: 52, 124, 132–133, 154, 173. **J.6**: 52.

Imperialism **J.7**: 24.

Incest **F.4**: 170.

Income
Entries also appear under:
FAMILY INCOME; HOUSEHOLD INCOME; LOW INCOME; PER CAPITA INCOME
D.7: 116. **E.2**: 15, 17. **F.1**: 28. **F.4**: 25. **F.5**: 189, 194. **F.7**: 7. **G.3.2**: 152. **H.3**: 28, 60, 62, 75–77. **H.4**: 88. **I.3**: 8. **K.2**: 29, 106. **K.4**: 85, 104, 160.

Income distribution **B.2**: 28. **H.3**: 56, 66, 81, 89. **I.2**: 28. **K.1**: 269–270, 284.

Income inequality **D.3**: 37. **F.8**: 54. **H.3**: 63, 73, 76, 78, 84. **I.2**: 105, 141, 144. **I.4**: 11. **K.1**: 54.

Income redistribution **I.2**: 54.

Independence **C.4**: 31. **D.9**: 153. **F.7**: 87.

Indexation **K.1**: 229.

Indians **F.5**: 195. **F.7**: 28–29. **G.3.1**: 95.

Indicators
Entries also appear under:
SOCIAL INDICATORS

Indigenous culture **D.5**: 96.

Indigenous populations
Entries also appear under:
ABORIGINES
F.7: 38, 105. **G.3.1**: 87. **K.2**: 81.

Individual and society **J.3**: 15.

Individual behaviour **C.2**: 219. **F.6**: 12.

Individualism **B.1**: 102. **C.2**: 19, 50. **C.3**: 95. **D.5**: 21. **E.1**: 13, 18. **F.5**: 30. **I.5**: 118.

Individuality **B.1**: 57.

Individuals **B.1**: 66, 84. **C.1**: 135. **C.2**: 13, 25, 34, 72, 92, 125, 136, 187. **C.3**: 23. **C.4**: 36, 38, 54. **D.1**: 46. **D.3**: 18. **D.7**: 36. **D.9**: 122. **F.4**: 103. **F.6**: 20. **I.1**: 14. **I.2**: 182. **I.3**: 22.

Indo-European languages **D.7**: 350.

Indochinese **F.8**: 77, 84. **I.2**: 61.

Indonesians **F.2**: 147.

Induction **B.1**: 58.

Industrial areas **H.7**: 12. **I.2**: 238.
Industrial democracy **I.1**: 10. **I.5**: 40.
Industrial design **D.8**: 39.
Industrial development **E.2**: 63. **G.3.2**: 272. **H.3**: 27.
Industrial investment **D.9**: 196.
Industrial labour **H.4**: 25. **I.4**: 4.
Industrial management **H.2**: 1. **H.4**: 15. **I.5**: 29.
Industrial organization **C.5**: 62.
Industrial planning **G.3.2**: 289.
Industrial policy **H.4**: 75. **I.2**: 206. **I.4**: 132. **I.5**: 176.
Industrial psychology **I.1**: 15. **I.3**: 103.
Industrial sector **H.3**: 70.
Industrial sociology **C.1**: 143. **I.1**: 6, 13. **I.2**: 174. **I.4**: 76.
Industrial technology **D.9**: 40.
Industrial workers **I.4**: 123. **I.5**: 2, 123.
Industrialization **E.3**: 57. **G.3.2**: 163. **I.5**: 150.
Industry
Entries also appear under:
AUTOMOBILE INDUSTRY; CHEMICAL INDUSTRY; CLOTHING INDUSTRY; COAL INDUSTRY; CONSTRUCTION INDUSTRY; DAIRY INDUSTRY; ELECTRONICS INDUSTRY; EXPORT-ORIENTED INDUSTRY; FILM INDUSTRY; FOOD INDUSTRY; FORESTRY INDUSTRY; HOTEL INDUSTRY; LOCATION OF INDUSTRY; MACHINERY INDUSTRY; METALWORKING INDUSTRIES; PULP AND PAPER INDUSTRY; RECORD INDUSTRY; SERVICE INDUSTRY; SMALL-SCALE INDUSTRY; SUGAR INDUSTRY; TELECOMMUNICATIONS INDUSTRY; TEXTILE INDUSTRY
C.5: 57. **D.9**: 189, 192–193. **E.2**: 28. **F.5**: 185. **G.3.2**: 272, 323. **H.4**: 28, 49. **I.1**: 6, 11. **I.2**: 207. **I.3**: 110. **I.5**: 173. **K.1**: 318.
Infancy **F.3**: 12. **F.4**: 302, 310.
Infant mortality **F.3**: 78, 237, 252, 264–266, 289–290, 292. **F.4**: 311. **K.4**: 174.
Infanticide **K.1**: 15.
Infants **C.1**: 22. **F.1**: 56, 65. **F.2**: 70, 72, 87. **F.3**: 260. **F.4**: 325. **K.1**: 368.
Infertility **F.3**: 89, 108, 119, 135. **F.4**: 303. **K.4**: 257.
Inflation **H.3**: 22, 29.
Informal sector **C.5**: 39. **F.5**: 250. **F.8**: 166. **H.2**: 4. **H.3**: 50. **I.3**: 64.
Information
Entries also appear under:
BUSINESS INFORMATION; POLITICAL INFORMATION; SOCIAL INFORMATION
B.2: 51, 60, 87. **C.2**: 152. **C.3**: 45, 61, 158. **C.4**: 14, 34. **C.5**: 34. **C.7**: 57. **D.3**: 40, 57. **D.4**: 21. **D.7**: 37, 74, 120, 134, 264. **F.5**: 163. **G.3**: 5. **I.4**: 3. **I.5**: 32, 68. **K.4**: 83.
Information acquisition **C.2**: 24, 161.
Information exchange **C.3**: 44.
Information networks **C.3**: 16.
Information processing **A.3**: 2, 4, 8. **C.2**: 105, 126. **C.6**: 8. **J.6**: 16.
Information society **K.2**: 63.
Information systems **B.2**: 69. **G.3.1**: 102. **H.5**: 27.
Information technology **C.5**: 71. **D.7**: 91, 184. **G.3.1**: 100, 119. **G.3.2**: 312. **H.4**: 94. **K.4**: 101.
Information theory **B.2**: 79. **D.7**: 152, 187.
In-group **C.4**. 1, 16, 60. **F.7**. 172.
Initiation **I.4**: 89. **K.1**: 94.
Injuries **F.3**: 208. **I.3**: 107, 110–111.
Injustice **C.3**: 116.
Innovation **C.5**: 76, 78. **G.3.2**: 131. **H.4**: 91, 93. **I.4**: 17.
Innovation policies **H.4**: 39.
Input-output analysis **I.2**: 12.
Insemination
Entries also appear under:
ARTIFICIAL INSEMINATION
Institutionalism **H.1**: 3.
Institutions
Entries also appear under:
POLITICAL INSTITUTIONS; RELIGIOUS INSTITUTIONS
C.1: 137. **C.5**: 33, 47. **C.6**: 12. **D.5**: 84, 114. **E.3**: 6. **F.7**: 30. **G.3.1**: 92. **H.4**: 72, 96. **K.1**: 362. **K.4**: 132, 141.
Insurance
Entries also appear under:
HEALTH INSURANCE; UNEMPLOYMENT INSURANCE
G.3.2: 192. **K.1**: 163. **K.4**: 63.
Insurrection **J.5**: 18.
Intellectual property **G.1**: 61.
Intellectuals **D.1**: 53. **E.2**: 22. **F.7**: 5, 244. **J.1**: 11. **J.6**: 54.
Intelligence
Entries also appear under:
ARTIFICIAL INTELLIGENCE
C.2: 37, 48–49. **D.1**: 128. **F.2**: 102.
Intelligence tests **C.1**: 102. **C.2**: 79, 93. **K.1**: 379.
Intelligentsia **D.1**: 37.
Interactionism **C.3**: 31, 91.
Intercultural communication **C.3**: 53. **C.5**: 18. **D.1**: 104. **D.7**: 132–133, 155, 185. **D.8**: 19.
Interdependence **C.4**: 31.
Interdisciplinary research **B.1**: 84.

Interest groups **D.4**: 17. **J.5**: 24, 36. **J.6**: 50. **K.1**: 96.

Interethnic conflict **F.7**: 103, 148, 158, 165, 206.

Interethnic marriages **F.4**: 207.

Interethnic relations **C.4**: 15. **D.2**: 3. **F.7**: 71–72, 128, 143, 154, 157, 159, 164, 172, 174, 178–180, 182–183, 187–188, 197, 201, 204, 263. **K.1**: 10, 12.

Intergenerational relations **D.7**: 44. **E.2**: 31. **F.2**: 8–9, 13. **F.4**: 68, 197, 211, 349. **F.5**: 197.

Intergroup relations **C.1**: 56. **C.3**: 21, 109. **C.4**: 13, 15, 20, 29, 41, 52. **F.7**: 29, 173, 209.

Intermarriage **D.5**: 129. **F.4**: 216.

Internal migration **F.8**: 92, 94–95, 101, 103, 165.

International agreements **I.2**: 67.

International cooperation **C.3**: 21. **C.5**: 18. **D.7**: 389. **F.7**: 239.

International division of labour **I.2**: 162.

International finance **G.3.2**: 35.

International migration **F.8**: 128, 136–141, 148, 152, 154, 164, 166–167, 171, 176.

International relations **D.5**: 116. **J.8**: 13.

International trade
Entries also appear under:
EXPORTS

Internationalism **J.8**: 11.

Internationalization **D.1**: 54. **D.7**: 335. **D.9**: 191, 195. **K.4**: 216.

Interpersonal attraction **C.3**: 9–10, 22, 55, 92, 146.

Interpersonal communication **C.1**: 159. **C.3**: 20, 48, 144. **D.3**: 6. **D.7**: 180. **F.4**: 85, 226.

Interpersonal conflicts **C.3**: 112. **F.4**: 136.

Interpersonal perception **C.3**: 148, 153, 160–161.

Interpersonal relations **C.1**: 152. **C.3**: 1, 5, 8, 13–15, 17, 21, 23, 32, 34, 36, 42, 47, 50, 61, 65, 69, 71, 80, 89, 118, 133, 141, 149, 155. **C.4**: 58. **C.5**: 87. **C.7**: 37. **D.7**: 159. **F.2**: 71, 120. **F.4**: 182, 254. **F.5**: 63. **I.3**: 17. **K.1**: 63, 363.

Interviewers **B.2**: 102, 107. **H.5**: 25.

Interviews
Entries also appear under:
THERAPEUTIC INTERVIEWS
B.2: 90–91, 96, 98, 112, 122–123. **F.4**: 240. **I.3**: 150.

Intifada **D.7**: 364. **F.5**: 56, 60. **J.5**: 12.

Intimacy **F.4**: 262. **H.6**: 2.

Inventories **K.1**: 42.

Investment
Entries also appear under:
FOREIGN INVESTMENT; INDUSTRIAL INVESTMENT

F.4: 21, 89. **G.3.2**: 192. **H.3**: 39. **I.2**: 106, 179.

Investment returns
Entries also appear under:
RENT
D.5: 29.

Irigaray, Luce **F.5**: 102.

Irish **F.5**: 21. **F.7**: 67.

Irrationality **C.7**: 7.

Irrigation **E.3**: 28. **G.3.1**: 28.

Islam
Entries also appear under:
SUNNISM
B.1: 140. **C.2**: 102. **D.1**: 57. **D.5**: 97, 163–167, 170, 173, 176, 178–179, 184. **D.7**: 313. **F.3**: 11, 41, 293. **F.5**: 15, 192, 229, 302. **F.8**: 7, 65.

Islam and politics **D.5**: 175. **J.3**: 12.

Islamic countries **D.1**: 57. **D.3**: 31. **D.7**: 266. **F.5**: 217.

Islamic economics **C.7**: 61.

Islamic law **F.3**: 41.

Islamization **D.5**: 161.

Italians **D.7**: 75, 218. **F.7**: 32.

Jainism **D.5**: 74.

Japanese **D.5**: 22. **D.7**: 64. **F.7**: 96. **F.8**: 96.

Japanese language **D.7**: 201, 204.

Jazz **D.8**: 1.

Jealousy **C.2**: 233.

Jehovah's witnesses **D.5**: 120.

Jesuits **D.9**: 7, 119.

Jews **C.2**: 107. **C.3**: 51. **D.7**: 265. **D.9**: 142. **F.4**: 65, 82, 142, 253, 311. **F.5**: 4. **F.7**: 36, 66, 71, 83, 97–98, 109, 114, 119, 123, 127, 139, 159–160, 174, 178, 180, 183, 216, 241. **F.8**: 156. **H.2**: 13. **H.3**: 27. **I.6**: 22.

Job analysis **I.2**: 57. **I.3**: 54.

Job change **I.4**: 21.

Job classification **I.3**: 37.

Job description **I.3**: 49.

Job evaluation **C.2**: 23. **I.3**: 7, 25, 38.

Job satisfaction **F.5**: 12. **I.3**: 96–97, 99–100, 102–105. **I.4**: 111. **I.5**: 126.

Job search **F.8**: 93. **I.2**: 23, 31, 66, 114, 231.

Job security **I.2**: 217. **I.5**: 41.

Joint ventures **G.3.2**: 317.

Journalism **D.7**: 235, 241, 259, 266, 269, 271–272, 277, 303, 317–318, 325, 328–329, 367. **D.8**: 78. **K.1**: 141.

Journalists **D.7**: 229. **I.5**: 171.

Joy **C.3**: 100.

Judaism **D.5**: 97, 183–184, 186.

Judgement
Entries also appear under:
SOCIAL JUDGEMENT
B.2: 86. **C.2**: 71, 100, 167, 169. **C.3**: 41. **C.4**: 1. **C.7**: 45. **D.3**: 66. **D.7**: 176. **F.3**: 187. **I.5**: 88.

Judges **D.4**: 24. **F.5**: 300.

Judicial process **D.4**: 13, 28.

Judicial review **J.3**: 19.

Judiciary power **D.4**: 7. **J.3**: 11.

Juries **D.4**: 21.

Jurisprudence **I.4**: 89. **J.2**: 7.

Justice
Entries also appear under:
ADMINISTRATION OF JUSTICE; CRIMINAL JUSTICE; DISTRIBUTIVE JUSTICE; ECONOMIC JUSTICE; SOCIAL JUSTICE
C.5: 68. **C.7**: 41. **D.3**: 4, 76. **D.4**: 3, 14, 23, 29. **D.5**: 79. **D.7**: 273. **G.3.1**: 31. **H.3**: 77. **H.6**: 4. **J.3**: 2, 13, 25. **J.4**: 20. **J.6**: 21. **K.1**: 177, 185, 328.

Juvenile courts **D.8**: 53. **J.3**: 25. **K.1**: 199.

Juvenile delinquency **D.4**: 28. **K.1**: 39, 60, 80, 94, 100, 113, 115, 123, 139, 154–155, 164, 177–178, 185–186, 192, 198, 208, 216, 302, 410. **K.3**: 18.

Kant, Immanuel **D.6**: 12.

Kanter, Rosabeth **F.5**: 226.

Khomeini **D.5**: 159.

Kibbutzim **I.4**: 20. **K.1**: 208.

Kikuyu **F.3**: 72.

Kinship **F.2**: 62. **F.4**: 43, 79, 98. **F.5**: 266. **G.3.2**: 115.

Kinship systems
Entries also appear under:
ENDOGAMY; EXOGAMY

Klein, Melanie **C.1**: 21, 109.

Knowledge
Entries also appear under:
SOCIOLOGY OF KNOWLEDGE
A.1: 11, 17. **A.2**: 7. **B.1**: 29, 35, 40, 79. **C.1**: 27. **C.2**: 2, 42, 88, 161. **C.3**: 155. **C.5**: 17. **C.7**: 12, 79. **D.6**: 1, 4, 15, 21, 25, 30. **D.7**: 166. **D.9**: 196. **E.2**: 22. **F.5**: 136. **F.8**: 106. **G.3.2**: 49. **H.5**: 9. **I.4**: 52. **J.6**: 47. **K.1**: 193.

Korean language **D.7**: 82, 189.

Koreans **F.7**: 56, 89. **F.8**: 170.

Kowalski, Alourdes **D.5**: 188.

Kurds **F.7**: 33, 133.

Labour
Entries also appear under:
CHILD LABOUR; DIVISION OF LABOUR; FEMALE LABOUR
C.2: 98. **D.7**: 107. **E.2**: 74. **F.3**: 299. **F.4**: 25. **F.5**: 2, 166. **F.8**: 94. **I.1**: 1, 4, 14. **I.2**: 43, 94, 101, 171, 177, 201, 217. **I.3**: 4–5, 48, 77. **I.4**: 2, 9, 43. **I.5**: 70, 145, 176. **J.5**: 10.

Labour collectives **H.4**: 30.

Labour contract **I.3**: 81. **I.4**: 84.

Labour demand **F.8**: 144. **I.2**: 190.

Labour disputes **I.5**: 78, 85–86.

Labour economics **C.5**: 40.

Labour force **F.3**: 28. **F.7**: 3. **I.2**: 165–166, 173, 181, 184, 186, 190, 198, 201. **I.4**: 72. **J.7**: 13.

Labour intensity **I.3**: 112.

Labour law **E.2**: 69. **I.2**: 138, 214. **I.3**: 42. **I.4**: 8. **I.5**: 98–100, 102, 104, 107, 109, 111–114, 116, 168.

Labour market **C.4**: 48. **F.2**: 145. **F.5**: 150, 267. **F.8**: 72. **G.3.1**: 130. **G.3.2**: 181. **H.3**: 60. **H.4**: 56. **I.2**: 2–3, 5, 7, 11, 16, 18, 25–26, 28–29, 33–36, 38, 40, 42, 45, 48–50, 52, 56, 64–65, 71–72, 83, 85, 95–96, 102, 119, 124, 137, 144–145, 164, 172, 189, 191–192, 196, 203, 215, 242. **I.3**: 83. **I.4**: 29–30, 116. **I.5**: 17.

Labour market segmentation **D.5**: 64. **I.2**: 22, 185.

Labour migration **F.5**: 18. **F.8**: 136, 141, 148, 167. **I.2**: 169.

Labour mobility **F.8**: 35. **I.2**: 22, 68, 179. **I.4**: 34.

Labour policy **I.2**: 134, 206.

Labour redundancy **I.2**: 37. **I.5**: 115.

Labour relations **F.5**: 19. **I.3**: 64, 126. **I.4**: 26, 47. **I.5**: 1, 5, 7, 12–13, 16, 20, 22, 24–31, 34–37, 40, 42–43, 45, 47, 49, 51–60, 62, 67, 69, 71, 74, 77, 81, 85, 89, 91, 93–94, 97–98, 103, 108–109, 119, 138, 153, 169, 197.

Labour shortage **I.2**: 163.

Labour structure **I.2**: 124.

Labour supply **G.3.1**: 54. **I.2**: 18, 58, 60, 93, 108, 111, 126, 180, 224.

Labour turnover **I.2**: 77. **I.3**: 28, 46, 54, 63.

Lacan, Jacques **B.1**: 114. **C.1**: 27.

Lactation **F.3**: 110.

Land claims **F.7**: 129.

Land property **G.3.1**: 31. **G.3.2**: 222.

Land reclamation **G.1**: 7. **G.3.2**: 273.

Land reform **G.3.1**: 73.

Land settlement **G.3.2**: 65.

Land tenure **G.3.1**: 8, 13, 35, 38, 89–90, 113, 120. **H.3**: 54.

Land use **D.6**: 10. **G.3.1**: 41. **G.3.2**: 60, 130, 187. **H.4**: 70. **H.7**: 10, 18.

Landscape **D.1**: 25. **G.3.1**: 19, 46. **G.3.2**: 5.

Language
Entries also appear under:

FOREIGN LANGUAGES; NATIONAL LANGUAGE; SIGN LANGUAGE; WRITTEN LANGUAGE
C.1: 41. **C.3**: 53. **D.4**: 44. **D.5**: 13. **D.7**: 4, 7, 16, 20, 22, 25, 32, 35, 39, 42, 44, 48, 52–53, 61, 69–70, 76, 87, 89, 95, 97, 106, 115, 122, 130, 172, 185, 189, 203, 206–207, 209–210, 214, 269, 271, 332, 336–337, 348, 372. **D.9**: 14, 164, 202. **F.5**: 78, 132. **F.8**: 57, 82. **G.1**: 29. **H.3**: 63.

Language acquisition **D.7**: 23, 40–41, 46, 73.

Language change **C.2**: 134. **D.7**: 75.

Language disorder
Entries also appear under:
DYSLEXIA
D.7: 24, 98.

Language planning **D.7**: 339, 341, 345.

Language policy **D.7**: 18, 334–335, 338–340, 342, 345. **D.9**: 15.

Language teaching **D.7**: 64, 212.

Laudan, Larry **D.6**: 22.

Laughter **D.5**: 48.

Law
Entries also appear under:
ANTHROPOLOGY OF LAW; COMMON LAW; CONSTITUTIONAL LAW; CRIMINAL LAW; CUSTOMARY LAW; FAMILY LAW; ISLAMIC LAW; LABOUR LAW; MARITAL LAW; MODERN LAW; NATURAL LAW; PUBLIC LAW; SOCIOLOGY OF LAW
C.7: 59. **D.3**: 45, 79. **D.4**: 13, 27, 32–33, 36, 38–39, 42, 44. **D.5**: 4, 9, 24, 182. **D.7**: 96, 273. **F.3**: 42, 111. **F.4**: 183, 250. **F.5**: 86, 259. **F.7**: 196. **I.3**: 118. **I.5**: 105. **K.2**: 46. **K.3**: 27. **K.4**: 258.

Law and order **J.1**: 2. **J.6**: 18. **K.1**: 40.

Lawyers
Entries also appear under:
SOLICITORS
I.4: 109.

Leaders
Entries also appear under:
POLITICAL LEADERS
C.3: 91. **C.6**: 3, 5–7, 18. **G.3.1**: 65. **J.3**: 14.

Leadership
Entries also appear under:
AUTHORITARIAN LEADERSHIP; POLITICAL LEADERSHIP
C.6: 1, 8–9, 14, 16. **F.5**: 230. **G.3.2**: 48. **I.5**: 14. **J.6**: 22, 31, 43.

League of Arab States **A.1**: 33.

Learning **C.2**: 163, 166. **C.7**: 1. **D.7**: 73. **D.9**: 24, 31, 117, 194. **F.5**: 167. **I.4**: 56. **K.3**: 24.

Learning difficulties **C.3**: 75. **K.4**: 118.

Left **C.1**: 42. **F.5**: 94. **J.3**: 32, 34. **J.6**: 11. **K.1**: 54, 101, 354.

Legal aspects **B.2**: 55. **F.3**: 159. **J.2**: 7.

Legal codes **D.4**: 18.

Legal profession **D.4**: 42. **I.4**: 100, 108.

Legal protection **F.7**: 196.

Legal reform **D.2**: 12. **D.4**: 39. **F.4**: 187. **F.5**: 86.

Legal science **C.7**: 5.

Legal status **F.2**: 92. **F.4**: 217. **F.5**: 50, 199–200. **F.7**: 130. **F.8**: 131.

Legal systems **D.4**: 32.

Legal theory **B.1**: 152.

Legislation
Entries also appear under:
SOCIAL LEGISLATION
D.4: 17. **F.4**: 321.

Legislative process **D.4**: 22, 25.

Legislature **D.7**: 33.

Legitimacy **H.4**: 66. **H.7**: 3. **J.4**: 9.

Legitimation **C.5**: 79. **E.3**: 26. **G.3.2**: 261–262. **I.4**: 92.

Leibniz, Gottfried **B.1**: 75.

Leisure
Entries also appear under:
SOCIOLOGY OF LEISURE
F.3: 299. **I.6**: 10–11, 16, 21, 30, 35, 39, 45.

Leisure time **I.6**: 20.

Leisure utilization **J.7**: 4.

Length of life **F.3**: 299.

Leprosy **D.1**: 142.

Lesbians **C.3**: 141. **F.4**: 181, 277. **F.6**: 3, 11, 22, 26, 40. **G.1**: 56. **K.1**: 429.

Liability **I.3**: 76. **K.1**: 319.

Liberalism **F.5**: 82. **K.4**: 256.

Liberalization **E.3**: 27.

Liberals **C.1**: 110. **F.3**: 63.

Liberation **D.5**: 110.

Liberation theology **D.5**: 107. **H.2**: 10.

Life cycles **C.2**: 58. **F.2**: 57, 119. **F.3**: 267. **F.4**: 49, 289. **G.3.2**: 18. **I.2**: 146.

Life expectancy **F.3**: 268.

Life satisfaction **C.2**: 40. **C.3**: 43. **I.3**: 100.

Life stories **E.2**: 9.

Life styles **D.2**: 9. **F.4**: 343. **G.1**: 8. **K.1**: 333, 380.

Limbu **E.3**: 17.

Linear models **B.2**: 68, 72.

Linguistic minorities **D.7**: 9, 341, 347. **F.7**: 130.

Linguistic theory **C.2**: 142. **D.7**: 68, 217, 222.

Linguistics
Entries also appear under:
SOCIOLINGUISTICS
C.3: 126. **D.6**: 4. **D.7**: 55, 121, 133, 193, 200, 208, 211–212, 216, 220–221, 227.

Literacy **A.3**: 5. **D.1**: 77. **D.7**: 46, 366. **D.9**: 16, 29, 85. **F.5**: 237. **I.2**: 188.

Literary criticism **D.8**: 11.

Literature
Entries also appear under:
NOVELS; POETRY; POPULAR LITERATURE
D.1: 7. **D.5**: 175. **D.7**: 2, 271. **D.8**: 30, 69. **G.3.1**: 10.

Liu, Chung-yüan **D.5**: 3.

Living arrangements **F.2**: 38, 66, 153. **F.4**: 309, 343, 351.

Living conditions **F.2**: 147. **F.7**: 16. **K.1**: 393. **K.4**: 9.

Loans **H.6**: 5.

Local communities **H.3**: 1. **K.4**: 6.

Local culture **D.1**: 118. **G.2**: 27.

Local elections **D.7**: 302. **J.6**: 62, 67.

Local government **D.7**: 272. **F.3**: 147. **F.5**: 249. **F.7**: 175. **G.2**: 19, 29. **G.3.2**: 254. **J.4**: 6–7, 19–20, 22, 26. **J.6**: 24.

Local government services **K.2**: 74.

Local politics **F.7**: 233. **G.3.2**: 197.

Location of industry **B.2**: 44. **G.3.2**: 187, 289. **H.4**: 24, 40. **I.2**: 206.

Locke, John **B.1**: 60.

Logic **B.1**: 34, 47. **D.6**: 16. **D.7**: 119–120, 196–197.

Loneliness **C.2**: 240. **C.3**: 60. **F.2**: 52.

Lorenz curves **I.4**: 44.

Love **C.3**: 8, 38, 123, 129.

Low income **G.3.2**: 121, 136, 158, 168, 181. **I.2**: 65, 78. **J.6**: 20.

Luhmann, Niklas **E.1**: 3.

Lutheran Church **D.5**: 108.

Machine tools **H.4**: 93. **I.3**: 50.

Machinery industry **I.4**: 37.

Macroanalysis **F.7**: 42.

Macroeconomics **I.6**: 37.

Macrosociology **A.1**: 20. **D.1**: 99.

Madness **C.1**: 35.

Magic **D.5**: 127.

Mail surveys **B.2**: 84, 113, 118, 121, 127. **G.1**: 20.

Majority rule **J.3**: 4.

Malaria **K.4**: 97.

Male-female relationships
Entries also appear under:
PARTNERS
C.3: 57. **F.4**: 22, 153, 175, 222. **F.5**: 281. **K.1**: 24. **I.3**: 65.

Management
Entries also appear under:
BUSINESS MANAGEMENT; ENVIRONMENTAL MANAGEMENT; FINANCIAL MANAGEMENT; HOSPITAL MANAGEMENT; INDUSTRIAL MANAGEMENT; PERSONNEL MANAGEMENT; PRODUCT MANAGEMENT; PRODUCTION MANAGEMENT; PUBLIC MANAGEMENT; RESOURCE MANAGEMENT; SALES MANAGEMENT; TOP MANAGEMENT; URBAN MANAGEMENT; WASTE MANAGEMENT; WATER MANAGEMENT
A.1: 30. **C.5**: 42, 54. **C.7**: 44. **D.3**: 24. **D.4**: 19. **D.8**: 26. **D.9**: 184. **F.5**: 147, 163. **G.3.1**: 29. **G.3.2**: 264. **H.4**: 16–17, 20–21, 27, 32, 34, 37, 46, 54, 91. **H.7**: 17. **I.2**: 113. **I.3**: 2, 92, 121, 140. **I.4**: 81, 106. **I.5**: 25, 31, 38–39, 44, 77, 86, 172, 193, 203. **J.4**: 9, 25. **K.2**: 92. **K.4**: 109.

Management development **I.5**: 52.

Management research **I.4**: 76.

Management techniques **G.2**: 14.

Managers **C.2**: 152. **E.2**: 17. **F.5**: 202. **I.2**: 120, 168. **I.4**: 69, 71, 73–75, 78–79, 83, 111.

Mandinka **F.5**: 269.

Mankind **D.1**: 100.

Manual work **I.3**: 67.

Manufacturing **H.4**: 26, 40, 70. **I.2**: 192, 206. **I.3**: 10, 45, 51, 72. **J.6**: 25.

Maori **F.7**: 197, 212.

Maori language **D.7**: 51.

Mapping **D.7**: 159. **F.1**: 37. **G.1**: 17.

Marginality **K.1**: 228, 261.

Marginalized people **F.2**: 133.

Marine pollution **D.7**: 315.

Marital conflict **F.4**: 121, 132, 168, 201, 213, 241, 246, 257, 259, 294.

Marital interaction **C.1**: 59. **C.3**: 140. **F.4**: 169, 197, 226, 240, 314. **I.4**: 75.

Marital law **F.4**: 181–182. **F.5**: 198.

Marital roles **F.4**: 263.

Marital satisfaction **F.4**: 74, 203, 233–234, 251.

Marital separation **F.4**: 145, 269, 276.

Marital stability **F.4**: 251.

Marital status **F.3**: 38, 92, 269. **F.4**: 220, 232, 261. **I.2**: 89.

Market
Entries also appear under:
ART MARKET; CREDIT MARKET; HOUSING MARKET; LABOUR MARKET; MARKET ACCESS; MEAT MARKET
D.3: 3. **D.8**: 72. **E.1**: 22. **G.1**: 10. **H.2**: 7. **H.3**: 37. **H.5**: 30. **I.2**: 93. **I.5**: 17.

Market access **H.5**: 1.

Market economy **F.2**: 135. **F.5**: 225. **H.2**: 6, 8, 18. **H.3**: 82. **H.7**: 20. **J.3**: 34.

Market forces **H.3**: 81.
Market research **B.2**: 129. **D.7**: 29. **H.5**: 25.
Market structure **H.4**: 52.
Marketing
Entries also appear under:
ADVERTISING
B.2: 101. **H.5**: 27, 40. **I.3**: 29, 153. **K.4**: 220.
Marriage
Entries also appear under:
AGE AT MARRIAGE; INTERETHNIC MARRIAGES; INTERMARRIAGE; RELIGIOUS MARRIAGE
C.1: 9, 59. **C.3**: 57. **D.5**: 127. **F.3**: 74, 94, 109, 119, 254. **F.4**: 29, 75, 80, 111, 138, 143, 160, 169, 181–182, 187, 193–196, 198–200, 202, 205, 209–212, 214–215, 218, 221–225, 227, 229–230, 235–238, 242–245, 248, 250–251, 253, 255–256, 258, 262, 304, 306. **F.5**: 5. **F.7**: 80, 167. **H.3**: 15, 35. **K.2**: 106.
Marriage exchange **C.3**: 142.
Married men **I.4**: 53.
Married persons **I.2**: 139. **J.7**: 13.
Married women **F.4**: 114, 130, 180, 218, 240. **F.5**: 8. **G.3.1**: 10. **I.2**: 119, 180. **J.7**: 3.
Marx, Karl **E.2**: 54.
Marxian analysis **B.1**: 128.
Marxism **B.1**: 43, 45–46, 61. **F.3**: 115. **F.5**: 104, 132. **J.1**: 9. **J.2**: 14, 21, 31. **J.6**: 5.
Marxism-Leninism **J.2**: 8.
Masculinity **C.3**: 144. **F.5**: 118, 262, 268, 294, 304.
Masochism **C.1**: 15.
Mass communication **B.2**: 11. **D.7**: 238. **D.8**: 73.
Mass culture **D.1**: 80. **D.2**: 5. **F.7**: 195.
Mass society **D.7**: 238.
Mate selection **F.3**: 113. **F.4**: 211, 247. **F.6**: 31.
Material culture **G.1**: 23.
Materialism **F.2**: 141.
Maternity leave **I.2**: 213.
Mathematical analysis **B.2**: 50, 52, 85.
Mathematical methods **B.2**: 83.
Mathematical models **G.3.2**: 137.
Mathematics **B.1**: 61. **C.2**: 166. **D.6**: 17.
Mauritians **F.8**: 68.
Mbanderu **F.3**: 89.
McCarthyism **J.6**: 48.
McLuhan, Marshall **D.7**: 47.
Mead, George Herbert **B.1**: 67, 119.
Meals **D.2**: 11.
Means of transport **G.3.2**: 2.
Measurement

Entries also appear under:
PRODUCTIVITY MEASUREMENT; UTILITY MEASUREMENT; WELFARE MEASUREMENT
B.2: 18, 20, 46–47, 68, 110. **C.2**: 62, 89. **C.7**: 40. **D.3**: 83. **E.3**: 29. **F.2**: 12. **F.8**: 146. **G.3.2**: 98.
Meat market **I.5**: 169.
Mechanization **F.5**: 269.
Media
Entries also appear under:
PRESS
B.2: 11. **D.1**: 31–32. **D.7**: 83, 126, 134, 138, 177, 230, 232–234, 237–238, 241–242, 244, 247, 249–250, 254, 257, 259, 262, 264, 269–270, 272–273, 275–280, 282–284, 286–287, 289, 293–294, 298–299, 301, 312–313, 316–317, 326, 367. **D.8**: 29. **F.2**: 124. **F.3**: 146. **F.7**: 101. **F.8**: 129. **J.3**: 16, 43. **K.1**: 106.
Media policy **D.7**: 274, 297, 385, 387.
Mediation **C.3**: 107–108, 113–114, 117. **D.4**: 24. **D.8**: 9. **F.4**: 133. **I.5**: 88, 91.
Medical anthropology **K.4**: 15.
Medical beliefs **F.7**: 24.
Medical care **K.1**: 264. **K.4**: 20, 42, 45, 99, 104, 148–149, 161, 175–176, 186, 195, 201, 204, 219, 224.
Medical ethics **D.3**: 59. **F.3**: 163. **K.4**: 148–149, 242, 245–247, 253–254, 260, 262–265.
Medical personnel **B.2**: 118. **F.3**: 181. **I.4**: 28, 104. **K.3**: 30. **K.4**: 44, 58, 259.
Medical sociology **A.2**: 3. **F.3**: 221. **K.4**: 56, 243.
Medicine
Entries also appear under:
HISTORY OF MEDICINE; SOCIAL MEDICINE; SURGERY; TRADITIONAL MEDICINE
D.1: 40. **D.3**: 62. **K.4**: 4–5, 30, 55, 81, 91, 96, 98, 105.
Medimurje **F.7**: 102.
Memory **C.1**: 56, 98. **C.2**: 154–166. **C.3**: 68, 89. **C.4**: 14. **D.1**: 114. **D.7**: 108–109, 369. **E.3**: 58. **F.2**: 96. **F.3**: 33. **F.5**: 204. **F.8**: 63. **H.5**: 32. **K.1**: 308.
Men
Entries also appear under:
MARRIED MEN
B.2: 23. **C.2**: 83, 98, 205, 226. **C.4**: 63. **D.2**: 13. **E.2**: 35, 68. **F.1**: 61. **F.3**: 68, 92. **F.4**: 25, 39, 223, 228, 260, 285. **F.5**: 3, 26, 96, 118, 150, 193, 253, 262, 271, 322. **F.6**: 25, 29, 32, 57. **F.7**: 238. **H.3**: 15, 59. **I.2**: 117–118, 120–121, 125, 148. **I.3**: 34. **K.1**: 199, 263, 307, 406, 417. **K.3**: 23.
Men's role **F.5**: 268, 294.
Mennonites **D.5**: 149.

Menopause **F.5**: 22.
Menstruation **C.2**: 75. **K.1**: 4.
Mental deficiencies **K.4**: 35, 118, 120, 127.
Mental health **C.1**: 6, 68–69, 72, 75, 91, 140. **C.2**: 20, 28. **C.3**: 34. **C.7**: 13. **D.1**: 98. **D.8**: 53. **F.2**: 59, 106. **F.3**: 196–197, 220, 225–226. **F.4**: 307. **G.3.1**: 59. **I.2**: 232, 241. **I.3**: 8. **J.7**: 21. **K.1**: 256, 260. **K.4**: 10, 27, 31, 36, 114, 124–125, 198–199, 222–223, 232–233.
Mental hospitals **K.1**: 190. **K.4**: 100, 131, 217.
Mental illness **C.1**: 70. **C.2**: 204, 228. **D.4**: 2. **F.3**: 174, 192, 194–195. **F.4**: 210. **F.5**: 59. **K.1**: 20, 107, 129, 347. **K.4**: 37, 47, 64, 69, 107–108, 119, 130, 189, 212.
Mental stress **C.1**: 30–31, 92, 148. **C.2**: 8, 41, 47, 73, 80, 99, 121, 203. **C.3**: 2, 40, 159. **C.4**: 25. **F.2**: 104, 120, 142–143. **F.3**: 204, 220, 225, 230. **F.4**: 39, 57, 82, 91, 97, 252, 284. **F.5**: 288. **F.8**: 20. **H.3**: 11. **I.3**: 3, 115, 117, 121. **I.4**: 48. **J.7**: 21. **J.8**: 20. **K.1**: 378, 417. **K.3**: 1, 44. **K.4**: 48, 93.
Mentally disabled **K.4**: 221.
Mergers **C.3**: 124. **C.5**: 77. **I.5**: 120.
Messages **A.3**: 8. **D.7**: 369.
Mestizos **F.7**: 3.
Metalworking industries **I.4**: 22.
Metaphor **D.7**: 172, 214.
Methodology
Entries also appear under:
ARCHAEOLOGICAL METHODOLOGY; ECONOMIC METHODOLOGY; SOCIOLOGICAL METHODOLOGY
B.1: 11, 40–41, 54, 76, 90, 120. **B.2**: 2, 11, 15, 42, 59, 112, 122–125. **C.4**: 18. **C.7**: 28. **E.1**: 25. **E.3**: 30–31. **F.5**: 71, 182. **G.3.2**: 98. **H.3**: 34. **J.5**: 33. **K.3**: 37.
Metropolis **G.3.2**: 19, 259, 305. **I.1**: 16.
Metropolitan areas **F.7**: 51. **F.8**: 46. **G.3**: 5, 9. **G.3.2**: 44, 58, 60, 110, 175, 184, 199, 205, 217, 299, 302, 352. **H.3**: 53. **H.7**: 28. **I.2**: 228.
Mexicans **D.9**: 42. **F.8**: 4, 61. **K.1**: 20.
Microanalysis **F.7**: 42.
Microeconomics **F.5**: 189.
Microsociology **A.1**: 24. **C.5**: 83.
Middle Ages **F.2**: 10, 13, 21, 32, 76. **F.4**: 295. **G.3.1**: 61.
Middle class **D.1**: 20. **E.2**: 4, 70, 84. **F.4**: 19. **F.7**: 208. **F.8**: 149. **G.3.2**: 139. **J.6**: 63. **K.1**: 68, 361.
Middle right **F.8**: 29.
Midwives **K.4**: 39, 65.
Migrant workers **F.7**: 16, 254. **F.8**: 21, 141, 145, 152, 170, 172. **I.2**: 67, 191. **K.2**: 18.

Migrants **D.7**: 42, 350. **F.1**: 10. **F.4**: 90. **F.5**: 260. **F.7**: 24, 41. **F.8**: 17, 33, 49, 78, 80–81, 107, 109, 150, 159. **G.3**: 10. **G.3.2**: 200, 203. **I.2**: 183.
Migrants' children **F.7**: 59.
Migration
Entries also appear under:
INTERNAL MIGRATION; INTERNATIONAL MIGRATION; LABOUR MIGRATION; RETURN MIGRATION; RURAL-URBAN MIGRATION; SEASONAL MIGRATION; URBAN-RURAL MIGRATION
F.1: 55, 65. **F.3**: 76, 159, 215, 304. **F.4**: 87. **F.5**: 8, 23. **F.7**: 1, 49, 102, 160, 237. **F.8**: 6, 10–12, 16, 18, 30–32, 34–36, 38–39, 41–42, 47, 51, 53, 55, 63, 69, 71, 85, 87, 89, 95–96, 106, 122, 138, 147, 150–151, 161, 163, 166, 168, 175–177. **G.3.1**: 37, 58, 83. **G.3.2**: 91, 201, 265. **I.2**: 7.
Migration policy **F.3**: 28.
Migration research **F.8**: 44.
Militarism **J.7**: 24.
Military **J.7**: 9–10, 19. **J.8**: 14.
Military industrial complex **J.7**: 2.
Military personnel **D.7**: 319. **J.7**: 3–4, 13–14, 21.
Military regimes **G.3.1**: 38.
Mill, John Stuart **B.1**: 58, 63, 113.
Miller, James Grier **C.5**: 11.
Mills **G.3.2**: 48.
Mills, Charles Wright **B.1**: 132.
Miners **E.2**: 69.
Mines
Entries also appear under:
GOLD MINES
Minimum wages **I.3**: 23.
Mining
Entries also appear under:
COAL MINING
I.5: 84, 153.
Minorities
Entries also appear under:
ETHNIC MINORITIES; LINGUISTIC MINORITIES; RELIGIOUS MINORITIES
C.3: 42. **C.4**: 5, 31, 44. **D.7**: 55, 212. **D.9**: 170. **F.5**: 187. **F.7**: 14, 34, 65, 75–76, 79, 113, 132, 183–184, 186, 188. **F.8**: 62, 76, 106. **G.2**: 34. **G.3.1**: 39. **I.2**: 215. **K.2**: 100. **K.4**: 114.
Minority groups **F.7**: 20.
Minority rights **J.3**: 4.
Missionaries **D.5**: 25.
Mitterrand, François **J.6**: 27.
Modelling **B.2**: 14, 51, 77, 81. **F.1**: 29. **F.3**: 29. **G.3.2**: 50.
Models

Entries also appear under:
DECISION MODELS; DYNAMIC MODELS; ECONOMETRIC MODELS; LINEAR MODELS; MATHEMATICAL MODELS; STATISTICAL MODELS; STOCHASTIC MODELS
B.1: 48. **B.2**: 19, 27, 34, 39, 50, 54, 59–61, 71, 88, 109. **C.1**: 91. **C.7**: 38, 78. **D.5**: 51. **D.7**: 118, 149. **E.2**: 13. **F.2**: 22, 85. **F.8**: 30. **G.3.2**: 68. **I.4**: 49. **J.3**: 17. **J.4**: 1. **K.4**: 229.

Modern law **F.5**: 297.

Modernism **B.1**: 13–14. **D.1**: 59, 81. **G.1**: 29. **G.3.2**: 51, 279.

Modernity **D.1**: 82. **D.6**: 20. **D.8**: 8. **E.2**: 11. **F.7**: 242. **G.1**: 57, 64. **K.3**: 41.

Modernization **A.1**: 20. **B.1**: 101. **D.1**: 69. **E.2**: 41. **E.3**: 21. **F.3**: 51. **F.5**: 24. **F.7**: 122. **G.3.2**: 255, 267, 280.

Monarchy **C.7**: 69. **D.7**: 6.

Monasteries **D.5**: 102.

Money **D.5**: 127. **F.4**: 113. **H.5**: 9. **H.6**: 2, 10–11.

Monogamy **F.4**: 228.

Monroe, Marilyn **D.8**: 7.

Moonlighting **I.4**: 34.

Moral philosophy **B.1**: 71. **D.3**: 68.

Morality **B.1**: 64. **C.2**: 14, 65, 197. **C.3**: 102. **D.3**: 64–65, 69, 75–80, 82, 85, 89–90. **D.5**: 30. **F.3**: 145. **F.4**: 101, 305, 339. **I.4**: 102. **J.7**: 11.

Morals **B.1**: 126. **C.2**: 190. **C.3**: 142. **C.5**: 61. **D.3**: 63, 66–67, 70–72, 74, 81, 83–84, 86–88. **D.5**: 137. **E.2**: 27. **H.2**: 8. **I.2**: 37. **J.3**: 40, 45. **K.3**: 26.

Morbidity **F.3**: 156, 166, 168, 171, 179, 200, 205, 226. **K.4**: 147.

Mormonism **D.5**: 103, 120, 127.

Mortality
Entries also appear under:
CHILD MORTALITY; INFANT MORTALITY
E.3: 33. **F.3**: 78, 171, 234–235, 240–241, 243, 245–246, 248–251, 254–255, 257–259, 261–264, 269, 271–279, 281–288, 292–298. **F.4**: 333. **K.1**: 307. **K.4**: 32.

Mortuary customs
Entries also appear under:
FUNERARY RITES

Moses, Robert **G.3.2**: 281.

Motherhood
Entries also appear under:
EARLY MOTHERHOOD; SURROGATE MOTHERHOOD
D.2: 2. **F.1**: 25. **F.3**: 106. **F.4**: 279, 299, 325. **F.5**: 72, 151, 196, 296.

Mothers
Entries also appear under:
EARLY MOTHERHOOD; WORKING MOTHERS

B.2: 110. **C.1**: 33. **D.7**: 121. **F.3**: 33, 36, 118, 229, 245, 280. **F.4**: 56, 141, 178, 283, 300–301, 303, 348. **F.5**: 160, 315. **K.2**: 42, 64. **K.4**: 51.

Motivation
Entries also appear under:
ACHIEVEMENT MOTIVATION
C.2: 134, 168–170, 172–176, 178–179. **C.3**: 6, 97. **C.5**: 15, 43. **D.3**: 65. **D.5**: 33. **F.4**: 103. **H.7**: 11. **I.3**: 96. **I.4**: 71, 79, 125. **K.1**: 110, 352.

Motivational analysis **C.3**: 102.

Mourning **C.2**: 39.

Mukogodo **F.4**: 67.

Multicultural education **D.9**: 4, 20, 45.

Multiculturalism **D.1**: 22, 89, 110. **D.7**: 18. **D.9**: 164. **F.7**: 131, 144, 155, 167, 191.

Multidimensional scales **I.5**: 88.

Multiethnic countries **D.9**: 52. **F.7**: 152. **K.2**: 61.

Multilingualism **D.7**: 337, 345–346.

Multinational enterprises **D.3**: 53. **H.4**: 61, 69. **I.3**: 6. **I.4**: 75.

Multiparty system **J.5**: 32. **J.6**: 64.

Multivariate analysis **B.2**: 29.

Munda **F.5**: 237.

Municipal council **C.5**: 11. **D.3**: 56.

Murder **D.4**: 11. **F.4**: 166. **F.7**: 189.

Museum collections **D.8**: 35.

Museums **D.8**: 3, 17, 66.

Music
Entries also appear under:
DANCE MUSIC; HISTORY OF MUSIC; POP MUSIC; ROCK MUSIC
D.5: 117. **D.7**: 109. **D.8**: 16, 21, 29, 37–38. **D.9**: 20. **K.4**: 86.

Musical instruments
Entries also appear under:
STRING INSTRUMENTS

Musicians **C.2**: 27. **C.4**: 12. **D.7**: 290.

Muslims **B.1**: 151. **C.2**: 102. **C.4**: 29. **C.7**: 31. **D.5**: 162, 165, 168–169, 171. **F.2**: 19. **F.3**: 293. **F.4**: 229. **F.5**: 42, 145, 152, 273. **F.7**: 29, 61, 177, 185.

Myles, Horton **J.5**: 4.

Mysticism **D.5**: 21. **I.3**: 95.

Myths **C.5**: 48. **G.3.2**: 305.

Names **C.3**: 62. **C.4**: 39. **F.7**: 22.

Naming **D.7**: 182, 195. **F.7**: 22.

Narcissism **C.1**: 16. **C.2**: 66, 192, 231.

Narratives **C.1**: 94. **D.1**: 114. **D.7**: 26, 89, 256. **F.4**: 240.

Nation **J.1**: 8. **J.2**: 9–10.

Nation state **D.1**: 39. **E.2**: 55. **F.7**: 78, 255. **F.8**: 8. **J.2**: 28.
National character **D.1**: 117, 119. **D.2**: 7. **F.7**: 94.
National consciousness **D.1**: 37, 60.
National culture **C.5**: 46. **D.7**: 237.
National identity **D.1**: 9, 33, 58, 64, 70, 83–84, 87, 90, 103. **D.7**: 286. **F.5**: 191, 302. **F.7**: 97, 99, 116. **F.8**: 82. **I.2**: 50. **J.8**: 16.
National integration **F.7**: 104.
National language **D.7**: 49.
National liberation movements **F.5**: 56.
National parks **G.1**: 33.
National stereotypes **C.7**: 42.
Nationalism
  Entries also appear under:
  CULTURAL NATIONALISM
  D.1: 83, 103. **D.5**: 98. **F.5**: 319. **F.7**: 75–76, 79, 161, 182, 187. **I.2**: 45. **J.2**: 1–2, 17, 24.
Nationalities policy **D.7**: 193. **F.7**: 83.
Nationality **D.1**: 7. **F.7**: 100. **F.8**: 133.
Natural law **D.1**: 85. **F.5**: 297.
Natural resources **G.1**: 2, 34.
Naturalism **B.1**: 35.
Nature **C.1**: 55. **G.1**: 15, 33.
Nature conservation **D.7**: 245.
Navajos **D.5**: 15.
Navy **J.7**: 6.
Needs
  Entries also appear under:
  HOUSING NEEDS
  C.3: 136.
Negotiation **C.2**: 114.
Neighbourhood associations **C.5**: 9.
Neighbourhoods **F.2**: 126. **F.7**: 140, 149. **G.2**: 12, 19, 22. **G.3.2**: 53, 177, 194, 198, 204, 303. **H.7**: 23. **J.5**: 35. **J.6**: 20. **K.1**: 88.
Neighbouring relationships **D.4**: 31. **G.3.2**: 211.
Neocolonialism **J.8**: 10.
Network analysis **B.2**: 5, 76, 79. **C.4**: 58. **C.5**: 25. **D.7**: 10–11, 50, 65. **D.9**: 2. **I.2**: 232.
Neurology **C.1**: 25.
Neuroses **C.2**: 41, 203.
New right **F.4**: 61.
New technology **D.7**: 325. **I.2**: 210.
New towns **G.3.2**: 231.
Newly industrializing countries **I.4**: 113.
News **D.7**: 243, 245, 247, 250, 268–269, 291, 330, 360, 367, 393–394. **D.8**: 393. **F.3**: 146. **H.3**: 40. **K.1**: 396.
Nietzsche, Friedrich **B.1**: 86. **D.7**: 163.
Nigerians **J.2**: 24.

Noise **C.2**: 67. **G.1**: 50.
Non-governmental organizations **F.5**: 28. **G.3.1**: 118. **K.1**: 246.
Non-linear dynamics **B.1**: 115.
Non-profit organizations **H.4**: 23.
Non-verbal communication **C.6**: 5.
Normal **C.3**: 36.
North Africans **F.7**: 45. **F.8**: 22, 48, 75, 141.
Novels **D.8**: 19.
Nuclear accidents **C.5**: 45. **C.7**: 53. **D.7**: 37, 312. **K.1**: 1.
Nuclear energy **J.5**: 31.
Nuclear weapons **C.7**: 48.
Nurses **C.2**: 152, 218. **I.2**: 108, 148, **I.3**: 63, **I.4**: 28, 48. **K.3**: 32. **K.4**: 3, 17, 58, 67, 73, 231.
Nutrition **F.2**: 86. **F.3**: 256. **H.3**: 68. **K.4**: 177, 197.
Objectivity **C.7**: 32. **D.5**: 35, 73. **D.7**: 317. **F.7**: 260.
Obligation **D.7**: 211. **F.4**: 79, 308. **I.5**: 192.
Observation **B.2**: 59. **C.2**: 23.
Occupational accidents **I.3**: 107, 111, 113.
Occupational choice **C.3**: 57. **I.2**: 75–76. **I.4**: 19, 29, 51, 67, 75.
Occupational diseases **H.4**: 7. **I.3**: 117, 119.
Occupational environment **F.4**: 27. **I.3**: 31.
Occupational groups **I.4**: 12.
Occupational life **I.3**: 115.
Occupational mobility **B.2**: 32. **E.2**: 21. **G.3.2**: 207. **I.2**: 191, 207. **I.3**: 65. **I.4**: 28.
Occupational prestige **I.2**: 79. **I.4**: 14.
Occupational promotion **I.2**: 26. **I.3**: 80. **I.4**: 68, 108.
Occupational roles **F.5**: 288.
Occupational safety **F.5**: 156. **I.3**: 108–109, 112, 114, 118, 120.
Occupational segregation **F.5**: 176. **I.2**: 114. **I.3**: 36. **I.4**: 36.
Occupational sociology **F.5**: 202. **I.3**: 14, 104. **I.4**: 7. **I.5**: 97.
Occupational status **E.2**: 38. **I.4**: 35.
Occupational stratification **I.2**: 47.
Occupational structure **I.4**: 45.
Occupations
  Entries also appear under:
  ACADEMIC PROFESSION; LEGAL PROFESSION
  B.2: 78. **C.2**: 116. **D.7**: 195. **E.2**: 73. **F.1**: 4. **F.4**: 39, 200, 252. **F.7**: 222. **I.2**: 4, 118, 166. **I.4**: 11, 20, 42, 44, 60, 86, 88. **J.6**: 50.
OECD **D.7**: 116. **K.1**: 224.

Offenders **D.4**: 2, 4. **F.6**: 47. **I.5**: 112. **K.1**: 57, 68–69, 78, 96, 100, 103, 107, 110, 136, 142, 161, 166, 169, 172, 174, 182–183, 187, 191, 204, 206, 213, 215, 328. **K.3**: 19, 29.

Office automation **I.3**: 27. **I.4**: 2.

Office workers **D.7**: 182. **I.2**: 145.

Oil **D.7**: 315.

Old age **F.2**: 21, 67. **F.3**: 240.

Old age benefits **K.2**: 9, 28.

Older workers **I.2**: 117. **I.3**: 41.

Olson, Mancur **E.2**: 54.

Ombudsman **I.5**: 88. **K.1**: 417. **K.2**: 67.

Onabasulu **F.6**: 30.

One-parent families **F.4**: 298, 320, 344, 348. **I.2**: 223. **K.2**: 14.

Ong, Walter J. **D.7**: 284.

On-the-job training **I.4**: 119, 124.

Ontogeny **C.1**: 40.

Ontology **C.2**: 9. **D.6**: 27. **G.1**: 35.

Opinion
Entries also appear under:
POLITICAL OPINIONS; PUBLIC OPINION
C.4: 28. **F.8**: 82.

Opinion formation **C.6**: 6.

Optimism **H.3**: 40.

Oral biographies **B.2**: 16.

Oral communication **D.7**: 158.

Oral history **F.5**: 144.

Oral tradition **D.7**: 67.

Organization
Entries also appear under:
ADMINISTRATIVE ORGANIZATION; BUSINESS ORGANIZATION; COMPLEX ORGANIZATION; ECONOMIC ORGANIZATION; INDUSTRIAL ORGANIZATION; SOCIOLOGY OF ORGANIZATIONS; WORK ORGANIZATION
C.1: 168. **C.3**: 116. **C.5**: 11, 18, 37, 41, 46–47, 51–53, 55, 60–61, 66, 79–80, 83, 86–87. **F.4**: 267. **F.5**: 138, 184. **G.2**: 24. **H.4**: 22, 32, 49, 97. **I.1**: 3. **I.3**: 54. **I.5**: 23, 43. **J.3**: 18. **K.3**: 28.

Organization theory **C.5**: 70, 78. **I.5**: 50.

Organizational analysis **A.3**: 4. **C.5**: 7, 24. **J.6**: 58.

Organizational behaviour **C.2**: 111. **C.3**: 130. **C.5**: 1, 14, 28, 30, 33, 35, 54, 57, 59, 64, 68, 72, 81, 84. **D.7**: 182. **I.3**: 86. **K.1**: 362.

Organizational change **C.5**: 13, 16, 32, 36, 56, 58. **I.3**: 79, 124.

Organizational effectiveness **C.5**: 50. **C.6**: 8.

Organizational goals **H.4**: 20.

Organizational research **C.5**: 2.

Organizational structure **C.5**: 9, 12, 20, 75, 82. **H.4**: 23. **J.4**: 1.

Organizations
Entries also appear under:
COMMUNITY ORGANIZATIONS; NON-GOVERNMENTAL ORGANIZATIONS; NON-PROFIT ORGANIZATIONS; PEASANT ORGANIZATIONS; PROFESSIONAL ORGANIZATIONS; REGIONAL ORGANIZATIONS; VOLUNTARY ORGANIZATIONS; WOMEN'S ORGANIZATIONS
C.4: 2. **C.5**: 3, 15, 17, 21–22, 25–26, 38, 40, 43, 48–49, 63, 73, 76. **D.8**: 4. **F.5**: 193, 267. **G.2**: 2. **G.3.1**: 15. **H.4**: 10, 49, 96. **I.3**: 27, 53, 56, 89, 117, 126. **I.4**: 31, 102. **I.5**: 146. **J.8**: 2. **K.2**: 30.

Organized crime **K.1**: 117, 150–151.

Orthodox Church **D.5**: 135.

Otieno, Wambui **F.7**: 53.

Otto, Rudolf **D.5**: 59.

Out-groups **C.4**: 1, 16. **F.7**: 172.

Overpopulation **F.1**: 44. **F.3**: 308. **K.1**: 171.

Overtime **I.3**: 24.

Pakeha **F.7**: 197.

Pakistanis **F.7**: 177.

Palestinians **D.2**: 3. **I.2**: 50. **J.5**: 12. **K.2**: 100.

Panel surveys **B.2**: 114.

Pantheism **D.5**: 159.

Paradigms **A.1**: 15. **C.7**: 40. **D.7**: 128.

Parallel cousins **F.4**: 206.

Parent-child relations **B.2**: 110. **C.3**: 110. **C.7**: 47. **F.2**: 105–106. **F.3**: 60. **F.4**: 191, 265–266, 271, 274, 283, 286, 291, 295, 297, 300–301, 304, 307, 309–310, 313–314, 318, 320, 322–323, 327. **K.1**: 85, 369.

Parenthood **F.4**: 267, 278, 284, 293, 296, 316–317. **I.3**: 74.

Parents
Entries also appear under:
STEP-PARENTS
C.3: 3, 43. **C.7**: 3. **D.7**: 343–344, 361. **D.9**: 118, 134. **F.1**: 11, 56. **F.4**: 21, 30, 32–33, 81, 118, 162, 164, 215, 270, 272, 280, 287, 308, 311–312, 321, 329. **F.5**: 224. **F.8**: 143. **I.3**: 84, 148. **K.2**: 50, 68.

Parents' education **F.3**: 282.

Parliament **J.3**: 19.

Parliamentarians **D.7**: 229.

Parsons, Talcott **B.1**: 15, 96, 105, 108, 124, 145. **D.8**: 5. **E.1**: 12.

Partisanship **J.6**: 1, 12.

Partners **C.3**: 8, 136. **F.4**: 239, 254. **F.6**: 47.

Part-time employment **I.2**: 34, 128, 222.

Party systems
Entries also appear under:
MULTIPARTY SYSTEM

Passions **C.2**: 122.
Paternalism **F.5**: 233. **K.4**: 259.
Pathology **C.5**: 41.
Patients **C.1**: 2. **F.7**: 37. **K.4**: 12, 32, 56, 61, 69, 72, 75, 247, 259, 264.
Patriarchy **D.5**: 36. **E.3**: 14. **F.5**: 129, 297. **I.2**: 129.
Pay
Peace **J.8**: 14, 22.
Peace movements **J.5**: 2.
Peaceful co-existence **F.7**: 144.
Peasant movements **E.3**: 75. **G.3.1**: 84, 87.
Peasant organizations **G.3.1**: 96.
Peasant societies **H.4**: 31.
Peasantry **G.3.1**: 83–84, 86, 88–91, 93, 113.
Peasants **E.2**: 25, 27. **F.5**: 162, 301. **F.8**: 86, 137. **G.3.1**: 92, 94. **H.2**: 9. **H.4**: 11. **K.1**: 11.
Peer groups **C.3**: 43, 137. **C.4**: 7. **F.4**: 81. **K.4**: 128.
Peirce, C.S. **B.1**: 56.
Penal policy **K.1**: 133, 181, 184, 213–214.
Pen, Le, Jean-Marie **F.7**: 259.
Pensions **H.3**: 83. **I.3**: 32.
Pentecostalism **D.5**: 143.
Per capita income **H.3**: 85.
Perception
Entries also appear under:
INTERPERSONAL PERCEPTION; SOCIAL PERCEPTION
B.1: 99. **C.2**: 12, 69, 77, 106, 160. **C.3**: 155–156. **C.5**: 68. **D.3**: 74. **D.7**: 64, 69, 348. **F.2**: 69, 147. **F.3**: 181, 187. **F.4**: 81, 301. **F.5**: 239. **H.3**: 49, 64. **I.3**: 96. **I.4**: 83. **J.1**: 10. **J.3**: 41. **J.5**: 20. **K.1**: 45.
Perception of others **C.3**: 150, 152, 154, 157–158. **F.7**: 195.
Perestroika **D.1**: 31, 37. **D.3**: 78. **D.7**: 259, 298–299. **E.1**: 4. **E.3**: 35. **F.5**: 252, 318. **G.3.2**: 75. **J.2**: 12.
Performing arts **D.8**: 4, 9–10, 37.
Periodicals **D.7**: 288, 290. **F.5**: 271. **I.6**: 12. **K.4**: 94.
Personal aggression **C.3**: 143. **C.4**: 8. **C.7**: 10. **D.3**: 76. **F.2**: 74, 110. **F.4**: 239. **F.6**: 50. **K.1**: 417, 423, 427.
Personality **C.1**: 162, 170. **C.2**: 180–181, 183–219. **C.3**: 132, 152, 159. **C.6**: 11. **D.1**: 70, 132. **D.5**: 159. **F.4**: 340. **F.6**: 50. **G.1**: 62. **J.6**: 22, 31. **K.1**: 329.
Personality disorders **C.1**: 61.
Personality traits **C.3**: 162.

Personnel management **C.2**: 151. **D.3**: 7. **D.4**: 34. **I.3**: 109, 123, 125–133, 135–136, 139, 141–149, 152, 154.
Personnel selection **I.2**: 26. **I.3**: 137–138, 140, 150, 153.
Persuasion **D.7**: 61, 108, 170.
Pessimism **C.1**: 19. **H.3**: 40.
Pesticides **I.3**: 120.
Petrochemicals **I.4**: 1.
Peul **C.2**: 10.
Pharmaceuticals **F.3**: 195.
Phenomenology **B.1**: 136. **C.4**: 23. **D.5**: 19. **F.4**: 170.
Philosophy
Entries also appear under:
MORAL PHILOSOPHY; POLITICAL PHILOSOPHY; SOCIAL PHILOSOPHY
A.1: 28. **B.1**: 40, 45, 53–54, 59, 63, 65, 67, 72–75, 78–79, 81. **C.1**: 25. **C.2**: 188. **C.3**: 38. **D.1**: 21, 27, 71, 81, 99, 134. **D.3**: 13, 84. **D.6**: 6, 18, 28. **D.9**: 26. **F.5**: 83, 137. **G.1**: 15. **H.3**: 4. **J.2**: 15.
Philosophy of science **D.6**: 9, 14, 20, 22.
Phonetics **D.7**: 205.
Phonology **C.2**: 156. **D.7**: 14.
Photography **D.7**: 325. **D.8**: 7, 43, 78.
Physical appearance **F.5**: 1.
Physically disabled **F.3**: 204.
Physicians **I.4**: 92, 101. **K.1**: 363. **K.4**: 6, 12, 30, 63, 70, 84, 95, 247, 264.
Physics **C.7**: 14. **D.7**: 69.
Piaget, Jean **A.2**: 9.
Planning methods **J.4**: 13.
Planning systems **H.7**: 17. **J.4**: 7. **J.6**: 29.
Planning theory **H.7**: 16.
Plant shutdowns **E.2**: 15. **H.7**: 13. **J.6**: 25.
Plantations **G.3.1**: 113.
Play **C.1**: 60.
Playing activities **C.3**: 58. **F.2**: 117.
Pluralism
Entries also appear under:
ETHNIC PLURALISM; RELIGIOUS PLURALISM; SOCIAL PLURALISM
B.1: 68. **D.5**: 105. **D.7**: 300. **F.7**: 70, 191. **J.1**: 12. **J.2**: 19. **J.7**: 19.
Poetry **D.7**: 26.
Poincaré, Henri **B.1**: 36.
Poles **D.7**: 106. **F.8**: 82, 158.
Police **C.1**: 70. **C.4**: 43. **C.5**: 46. **D.4**: 4. **J.3**: 35, 37–39, 41–44, 46. **K.1**: 12–14, 43, 83, 102, 124–126. **K.3**: 20.
Policing **F.6**: 34. **J.3**: 45. **K.1**: 6, 10, 98, 372, 418.

Policy analysis **G.3.2**: 333.
Policy making **D.3**: 4. **I.2**: 208. **J.4**: 19.
Policy research **K.2**: 1.
Political action **D.7**: 276.
Political activity **E.2**: 49. **F.8**: 3. **J.5**: 21, 30. **J.6**: 27.
Political affiliation **J.1**: 18. **J.6**: 12.
Political alienation **J.1**: 19.
Political attitudes **D.7**: 382. **F.7**: 219. **J.1**: 16. **J.6**: 32, 37, 39, 41. **K.2**: 82.
Political behaviour **H.4**: 68.
Political broadcasting **D.7**: 370.
Political change **A.1**: 16, 25, 34. **D.7**: 97, 377. **E.3**: 4, 19, 26. **F.4**: 184. **F.5**: 213. **F.7**: 127. **J.1**: 21. **J.3**: 4, 32. **J.6**: 38, 40, 57.
Political communication **D.7**: 112, 302. **J.3**: 3.
Political conditions **E.2**: 47. **F.3**: 91. **F.7**: 192. **J.1**: 7.
Political culture **D.1**: 91. **J.1**: 5–6, 10–11. **J.6**: 6–7, 33.
Political economy **D.7**: 264. **G.3.2**: 33. **H.2**: 19. **H.3**: 53. **H.4**: 59. **I.5**: 79. **I.6**: 30. **J.6**: 34.
Political elites **J.6**: 3.
Political generations **J.6**: 11.
Political geography **D.7**: 59. **J.3**: 23.
Political information **J.6**: 47.
Political instability **F.7**: 62. **J.6**: 28.
Political institutions **I.5**: 146.
Political integration **E.2**: 10.
Political leaders **J.6**: 4.
Political leadership **C.6**: 2. **J.6**: 35.
Political mobilization **F.7**: 221. **F.8**: 48. **J.5**: 13, 16.
Political movements
 Entries also appear under:
  NATIONAL LIBERATION MOVEMENTS
 J.5: 4, 23.
Political opinions **F.2**: 33. **J.6**: 56.
Political order **D.7**: 286.
Political participation **B.1**: 38. **F.7**: 4. **G.3.2**: 7. **J.3**: 6. **J.6**: 13, 17, 21, 23–24, 29, 33–34, 55.
Political parties
 Entries also appear under:
  COMMUNIST PARTIES; RIGHT WING PARTIES
 D.5: 109. **D.9**: 44. **F.7**: 225. **I.5**: 119. **J.5**: 11, 32, 36. **J.6**: 53. **J.8**: 5.
Political philosophy **D.4**: 29. **F.5**: 297.
Political power **E.3**: 2. **G.1**: 30. **J.6**: 9, 14.
Political protest **J.5**: 15, 27.
Political psychology **C.1**: 34, 64. **J.1**: 12, 14. **J.6**: 22, 43. **J.8**: 12.

Political recruitment **J.6**: 3.
Political regimes
 Entries also appear under:
  AUTHORITARIAN REGIMES; MILITARY REGIMES
Political representation **J.5**: 19.
Political science
 Entries also appear under:
  TEACHING OF POLITICAL SCIENCE
 A.1: 2. **D.7**: 292. **J.2**: 21.
Political socialization **D.1**: 136.
Political society **B.1**: 126.
Political sociology **J.1**: 11–12, 14–15, 22.
Political structure **G.2**: 19.
Political systems **J.3**: 1, 8, 22. **J.5**: 13, 32.
Political theory **J.1**: 17. **J.2**: 21.
Political thought **D.6**: 12. **J.2**: 15.
Political violence **D.7**: 285. **J.1**: 8. **K.4**: 74.
Politicians **D.7**: 295. **J.6**: 3.
Politicization **F.7**: 120.
Polls
 Entries also appear under:
  PUBLIC OPINION POLLS
Pollution
 Entries also appear under:
  MARINE POLLUTION
 G.1: 32. **G.3.2**: 39.
Pollution control **G.1**: 24, 63.
Pollution levels **G.1**: 46.
Polygamy **F.5**: 297.
Polygyny **F.4**: 228, 231.
Poor **C.3**: 79. **G.3.2**: 104, 128, 147, 183. **I.2**: 65, 246. **J.6**: 9. **K.1**: 173, 218, 246–247, 262–263, 265. **K.2**: 63, 84, 88.
Pop music **D.7**: 181.
Popular culture **D.1**: 31, 35, 80, 91, 111. **D.2**: 5–6, 20. **D.5**: 152. **D.7**: 230, 307, 321, 351. **D.8**: 9, 32, 46, 60. **F.5**: 115. **J.6**: 40.
Popular literature **D.7**: 303. **D.8**: 51, 68.
Popular music **D.8**: 21, 31, 47, 49, 53, 55. **H.3**: 40.
Popularity **J.6**: 10.
Population
 Entries also appear under:
  AGRICULTURAL POPULATION; INDIGENOUS POPULATIONS; RURAL POPULATION; URBAN POPULATION
 B.2: 131. **F.1**: 12, 22, 33–34, 46, 50, 52–53, 59, 68. **F.3**: 1–2, 7, 16, 20, 29, 56, 76, 85, 89, 131, 309. **F.4**: 17. **F.5**: 187. **F.8**: 61, 87, 92. **G.3.1**: 37. **G.3.2**: 12, 207. **I.2**: 207. **K.2**: 97.
Population ageing **F.2**: 26, 42. **K.2**: 97.
Population censuses **B.2**: 35. **E.2**: 64. **F.1**: 11, 18, 29, 36, 41. **F.3**: 9.

Population decline **F.3**: 28.
Population density **C.1**: 14. **F.1**: 37, 63. **F.3**: 24. **G.3.2**: 180. **K.1**: 159. **K.4**: 21.
Population distribution **F.3**: 17.
Population dynamics **F.1**: 5, 62. **F.3**: 104. **G.3.2**: 41, 209.
Population forecasts **F.1**: 3, 7, 24, 26–27, 30. **F.3**: 304.
Population geography **F.1**: 9.
Population growth **F.1**: 2, 45. **F.3**: 303–304, 306, 310–311, 313.
Population movements **F.3**: 8, 18.
Population policy **F.1**: 48. **F.3**: 3, 11, 19, 28, 72, 83, 97, 137, 300, 305, 307, 311–312.
Population projections **F.1**: 23, 38, 70. **F.8**: 47.
Population theory **F.1**: 19.
Populism **D.8**: 46. **E.2**: 28. **H.2**: 12.
Pornography **D.1**: 112. **F.5**: 33, 84, 114. **F.6**: 35–36. **K.1**: 23.
Portuguese **F.7**: 149.
Portuguese language **D.7**: 350.
Positivism **B.1**: 127. **C.1**: 139. **J.2**: 14.
Postal services **I.3**: 35.
Post-communist societies **D.1**: 58. **F.5**: 225. **H.4**: 16.
Post-Fordism **D.1**: 138. **D.9**: 9. **H.2**: 5. **H.4**: 29, 59. **J.2**: 21.
Post-industrial society **H.4**: 8, 17.
Postmodernism **B.1**: 3, 8, 12–14, 17–18, 22, 26, 49, 51, 88, 121. **C.1**: 47, 167. **D.1**: 32, 82, 92–93, 122. **D.2**: 28. **D.6**: 5. **D.7**: 287. **D.8**: 20, 47. **F.4**: 354. **F.5**: 95. **G.1**: 29, 58. **G.3.2**: 62, 232. **I.2**: 96. **I.6**: 33. **J.2**: 20. **K.3**: 41. **K.4**: 76.
Post-structuralism **F.5**: 102. **F.6**: 10.
Poverty
Entries also appear under:
RURAL POVERTY; URBAN POVERTY
C.1: 129. **D.1**: 123. **D.9**: 108. **F.1**: 44. **F.2**: 3. **F.3**: 269. **F.4**: 232, 347. **F.5**: 6, 257. **F.8**: 38, 54, 60. **G.3.1**: 20. **G.3.2**: 168, 209–210. **H.3**: 8, 36, 62, 85. **I.2**: 65, 78, 246. **K.1**: 54, 217, 220–222, 224–229, 233, 244–245, 249–252, 254, 256, 259, 266–272, 275–276, 278, 280, 283–284, 286, 289, 292–293, 295. **K.2**: 84, 103.
Power **C.3**: 115–116. **C.4**: 15, 44, 51. **C.6**: 18. **C.7**: 13. **D.6**: 21, 26. **D.7**: 61, 168–169, 316. **D.9**: 25, 137. **E.2**: 22. **E.3**: 45. **F.4**: 85, 263. **F.5**: 96, 134, 181, 253, 287. **G.1**: 64. **G.3.1**: 93. **H.4**: 17, 33. **J.1**: 3.
Power distribution **I.5**: 44.
Pragmatics **D.7**: 62, 205. **F.7**: 193.
Pragmatism **F.5**: 233.

Preaching **D.5**: 13.
Pregnancy **F.2**: 145. **F.3**: 59, 112, 125–126. **F.4**: 35, 111. **I.2**: 130, 145, 159. **K.4**: 104, 171, 215, 262.
Prejudice **C.7**: 4, 58. **F.7**: 228, 247. **I.2**: 52.
Premarital intercourse **F.4**: 137. **F.6**: 39.
Presidency **D.7**: 288. **J.4**: 5. **J.6**: 10, 31.
Presidential elections **D.7**: 280. **F.7**: 217.
Press **C.6**: 1. **D.7**: 105–106, 231, 251–252, 258, 265, 268–269, 272, 276, 289, 293, 295, 302, 305, 307–310, 315, 319. **F.3**: 195. **F.7**: 269. **F.8**: 26. **K.1**: 141.
Prestige
Entries also appear under:
OCCUPATIONAL PRESTIGE
E.3: 74.
Prevention of delinquency **K.1**: 75.
Price competition **G.1**: 36.
Prices
Entries also appear under:
HOUSING PRICES; RETAIL PRICES
D.7: 116. **H.5**: 24, 30, 32. **K.4**: 104.
Pricing **H.5**: 9. **I.6**: 2.
Primary education **C.2**: 118. **D.9**: 152–154, 156–157.
Primary schools **D.9**: 150.
Primitivism **D.1**: 94.
Prisoner's dilemma **B.2**: 38. **C.3**: 67, 93.
Prisoners **C.3**: 93. **F.4**: 191, 319. **F.7**: 226, 238. **K.1**: 24, 174, 179, 194. **K.4**: 100.
Prisons **I.4**: 24. **K.1**: 171, 177, 187–190, 195, 197, 199, 201, 209–211. **K.4**: 217.
Privacy
Entries also appear under:
RIGHT OF PRIVACY
I.5: 100. **K.4**: 263.
Private collections **D.8**: 3.
Private education **D.9**: 95, 108.
Private health care **K.4**: 79.
Private sector **D.3**: 57. **H.4**: 18. **I.5**: 92, 159. **J.4**: 4. **K.4**: 180.
Privatization **D.9**: 49. **H.7**: 20. **I.5**: 44–45, 177. **J.4**: 6, 15.
Probability **B.1**: 56. **B.2**: 82. **C.2**: 167. **C.7**: 12. **D.7**: 175.
Probation system **K.1**: 167, 180, 205. **K.3**: 48.
Product management **H.5**: 22.
Production
Entries also appear under:
AGRICULTURAL PRODUCTION
D.9: 27. **G.3.2**: 214, 261. **I.3**: 62. **J.5**: 10.
Production control **I.3**: 117.

Production co-operatives **H.4**: 31.
Production costs **I.5**: 188.
Production management **H.4**: 85.
Production policy **I.5**: 18.
Production specialization **H.2**: 5.
Production systems **D.8**: 15. **H.4**: 29, 50.
Productivity
Entries also appear under:
AGRICULTURAL PRODUCTIVITY
C.4: 17, 47. **F.5**: 233, 301. **G.3.1**: 27. **H.3**: 15. **H.4**: 20, 28, 40. **I.4**: 25. **I.5**: 182–183, 188.
Productivity measurement **H.4**: 53.
Professional ethics **D.3**: 44. **I.4**: 91, 93, 102, 110, 115.
Professional identity **I.4**: 111.
Professional organizations **K.4**: 3.
Professional workers **C.5**: 4, 82. **D.3**: 80. **F.5**: 19. **F.7**: 29. **I.4**: 63, 87–90, 95, 104–105, 107. **K.1**: 326.
Professionalism **D.1**: 89. **I.4**: 39. **I.5**: 149. **K.3**: 28.
Professionalization **K.1**: 214.
Profit **K.2**: 51.
Profit sharing **I.5**: 48, 199.
Project evaluation **E.3**: 15, 30, 48. **F.2**: 100. **G.3.1**: 22. **G.3.2**: 85.
Proletarianization **D.9**: 203.
Proletariat **H.4**: 2.
Pronatalist policy **F.3**: 23, 28. **F.5**: 214.
Propaganda **D.5**: 135. **D.7**: 329.
Property
Entries also appear under:
INTELLECTUAL PROPERTY; LAND PROPERTY
G.3.2: 129. **H.5**: 2. **K.1**: 138.
Prophecy **D.5**: 135.
Prostitution **F.3**: 193. **F.6**: 25, 34, 38, 41, 55. **J.5**: 23. **K.1**: 131, 348. **K.3**: 23.
Protectionism **D.8**: 16.
Protest movements **E.3**: 39. **J.5**: 13, 34.
Protestant churches **D.5**: 106.
Protestant ethics **C.7**: 51. **D.5**: 145.
Protestantism **B.1**: 150. **D.5**: 7, 126, 136.
Protestants **D.5**: 115, 144. **E.2**: 18.
Prototypes **D.7**: 220.
Proudhon, Pierre Joseph **D.1**: 79.
Proverbs **C.3**: 53.
Psychiatrists **K.1**: 50.
Psychiatry
Entries also appear under:
FORENSIC PSYCHIATRY

C.1: 66, 69–73. **K.1**: 36. **K.4**: 2, 58, 80, 124, 147.
Psychoanalysis **A.2**: 14. **C.1**: 1, 3–5, 8, 12–13, 15–19, 21, 23, 26–27, 29, 33, 38, 40, 42–43, 45–55, 57–58, 60–62, 65. **C.3**: 51. **C.4**: 57. **F.6**: 56.
Psycholinguistics **D.7**: 185, 213.
Psychological effects **C.2**: 41, 97. **I.2**: 234.
Psychological factors **C.3**: 106. **D.5**: 33. **D.7**: 136.
Psychologists **C.1**: 89, 137. **D.3**: 41.
Psychology
Entries also appear under:
CHILD PSYCHOLOGY; CLINICAL PSYCHOLOGY; ECONOMIC PSYCHOLOGY; EVOLUTIONARY PSYCHOLOGY; INDUSTRIAL PSYCHOLOGY; POLITICAL PSYCHOLOGY; SOCIAL PSYCHOLOGY
B.1: 70. **C.1**: 77–83, 90–93, 95–101, 104–106, 108–132, 134–135, 137–141. **C.2**: 61, 68–69, 78, 111, 142, 194, 216, 220. **C.3**: 27. **C.5**: 40. **C.7**: 36. **D.1**: 137. **D.7**: 19, 147–148, 194, 230. **F.2**: 81, 84. **F.3**: 184. **F.4**: 202. **F.6**: 52. **F.7**: 70, 124. **G.3.1**: 55, 91. **H.4**: 37. **I.3**: 65. **K.1**: 204. **K.4**: 57, 81, 86, 237, 259.
Psychometrics **C.1**: 102. **C.7**: 52. **I.3**: 149.
Psychopathology **C.1**: 141. **C.2**: 10. **C.6**: 11.
Psychoses **C.1**: 50. **J.6**: 38. **K.1**: 15, 313.
Psychosociology **K.4**: 94, 182.
Psychotherapy **B.2**: 43. **C.1**: 28, 43, 94, 107, 113, 140.
Puberty **C.2**: 187. **F.4**: 286.
Public accounting **I.4**: 31.
Public administration **D.3**: 61. **G.3.2**: 90. **J.4**: 2, 5, 8, 12, 16, 18, 21, 23–25.
Public choice **C.2**: 94. **C.7**: 61–62.
Public employment **I.2**: 53.
Public expenditure **H.4**: 38. **K.2**: 36.
Public finance **F.8**: 50.
Public goods **B.2**: 58. **D.5**: 102.
Public health **F.3**: 171, 173, 183, 235, 261. **G.3.2**: 267. **K.4**: 7, 60, 74, 90, 159–160, 166, 169, 218, 224, 235, 237.
Public interest **F.2**: 141. **F.4**: 15.
Public law **D.4**: 16.
Public management **C.5**: 45. **H.4**: 18. **J.4**: 10–11, 17.
Public opinion **C.7**: 2, 26, 44, 46, 69. **D.2**: 16. **D.7**: 36, 313. **F.3**: 160. **F.4**: 70. **F.7**: 106, 145, 194. **G.3.2**: 114. **H.3**: 37. **J.1**: 13. **J.5**: 24. **J.6**: 2, 50. **J.7**: 10.
Public opinion polls **A.2**: 19. **C.7**: 48.
Public policy **D.7**: 336. **F.1**: 55. **F.2**: 56, 126. **F.7**: 39. **G.3.2**: 308. **H.7**: 25. **I.5**: 48. **K.2**: 4.
Public relations **D.7**: 274.

Public sector **A.2**: 20. **F.5**: 146. **F.7**: 249. **I.3**: 89, 143. **I.4**: 79. **I.5**: 62–63, 92, 116, 161, 187. **J.4**: 1, 4, 9, 15. **K.4**: 180.
Public servants **F.3**: 63.
Public services **H.7**: 7, 19. **I.2**: 47. **J.4**: 4.
Publishing **F.5**: 10.
Puerto Ricans **D.7**: 59. **I.2**: 185.
Pulp and paper industry **K.1**: 342.
Punishment
Entries also appear under:
CAPITAL PUNISHMENT
B.1: 60. **C.3**: 87. **D.1**: 134. **F.2**: 84. **K.1**: 81, 124, 212, 424.
Punjabi **F.7**: 115.
Pupils **D.9**: 135.
Purdah **F.5**: 42.
Qualitative analysis **I.2**: 239.
Quality circles **I.3**: 92. **I.5**: 31.
Quality control **H.4**: 27. **I.3**: 1. **K.2**: 4. **K.4**: 82.
Quality of life **C.2**: 174. **F.4**: 51. **G.3.1**: 36, 68. **G.3.2**: 138. **H.3**: 13–14, 34, 42. **I.1**: 10. **I.3**: 48, 68. **K.4**: 62, 173.
Questionnaires **B.2**: 90, 112, 115, 118, 120, 122, 130. **C.1**: 128. **C.7**: 52. **K.1**: 332.
Race **B.1**: 128. **C.1**: 97. **D.1**: 7. **D.7**: 243. **D.9**: 108, 121. **E.2**: 3, 66. **F.1**: 56. **F.3**: 38, 287. **F.4**: 347–348. **F.7**: 3, 39, 44, 66, 68, 75–76, 86, 116–118, 125, 149, 177, 186, 195, 197–198, 234, 242, 246, 262. **F.8**: 10. **G.3.2**: 176, 336. **H.3**: 88. **H.6**: 9. **I.2**: 75, 132. **I.3**: 69, 104. **I.4**: 24, 40, 82. **I.5**: 162. **J.1**: 19. **J.2**: 10. **J.6**: 62. **K.1**: 86, 97, 350, 375. **K.2**: 80. **K.4**: 2.
Race relations **D.7**: 310, 351. **D.9**: 84, 205. **E.2**: 12. **F.7**: 4, 12, 95, 136, 145–147, 156, 162, 171, 173, 175, 177, 183, 185, 189–192, 196, 199–200, 202, 207–208, 211–212, 252, 265. **F.8**: 4, 28, 70, 87. **G.3.2**: 198.
Racial conflict **E.3**: 63. **F.7**: 18, 205. **K.1**: 206.
Racial differentiation **F.4**: 212. **G.3.2**: 211. **I.2**: 196. **J.7**: 1.
Racial discrimination **F.7**: 211, 215, 220, 223–224, 227–229, 233–234, 239, 245, 248–250, 253, 265–266, 269. **F.8**: 10. **G.3.2**: 120, 192. **I.2**: 42, 64, 189, 209, 225. **I.5**: 9.
Racial inequality **F.7**: 145, 250, 252. **K.4**: 3.
Racial segregation **F.7**: 251. **G.3.2**: 156, 194, 336.
Racial stereotypes **F.7**: 154.
Racism **D.7**: 5. **F.5**: 67–68. **F.7**: 14, 21, 73, 145, 156, 190, 200–204, 207, 211, 215, 222, 225, 230–231, 235–236, 243, 252–256, 258–260, 263–264, 266. **G.3.2**: 173. **K.1**: 200, 258.
Radicalism **C.5**: 61. **D.5**: 184.

Radio **C.1**: 124. **D.7**: 263, 291, 297, 304, 311, 365.
Radioactive waste **K.1**: 1.
Railway transport **J.5**: 34. **K.1**: 140.
Railways **I.3**: 9. **I.5**: 59.
Rajneesh **C.4**: 20.
Randall, Margaret **F.5**: 134.
Random sampling **B.2**: 68.
Rape **C.7**: 80. **D.4**: 39. **F.4**: 187. **F.6**: 12. **K.1**: 46, 52, 87, 97, 118, 125, 135, 141–142, 144, 162, 215.
Rational choice **B.1**: 71.
Rationality **B.1**: 68, 129–130, 135. **C.2**: 84, 91. **C.3**: 125. **C.7**: 53, 78. **D.1**: 107, 124–125, 128. **D.5**: 163. **D.6**: 22. **E.2**: 54. **H.7**: 20. **I.4**: 39. **K.4**: 76.
Rationalization **E.2**: 11.
Rawls, J. **B.1**: 19.
Readers **D.8**: 74.
Real estate **G.3.2**: 28, 271, 317. **K.1**: 59.
Realism **B.1**: 140.
Reason **C.2**: 57. **D.4**: 13.
Reasoning **B.2**: 74. **C.2**: 112. **C.3**: 24, 142. **C.6**: 13. **C.7**: 5. **D.7**: 196. **F.5**: 297.
Recession **F.8**: 35. **H.3**: 40, 58. **I.2**: 240.
Recidivism **K.1**: 209.
Reciprocity **C.3**: 67. **D.7**: 217, 221–222. **F.4**: 97.
Record industry **D.8**: 16.
Recording **B.2**: 90.
Recreation **F.8**: 36. **H.5**: 34. **I.6**: 1–2, 17, 25, 28, 40, 45–46.
Recruitment
Entries also appear under:
POLITICAL RECRUITMENT
B.2: 67. **I.2**: 204. **I.3**: 71, 80, 125. **I.5**: 180.
Recycling **G.1**: 21, 31. **G.3.2**: 302.
Reference works **D.7**: 9.
Reform
Entries also appear under:
AGRARIAN REFORM; ECONOMIC REFORM; EDUCATION REFORM; HOUSING REFORM; LAND REFORM; LEGAL REFORM; SOCIAL REFORM
D.9: 165. **E.3**: 22. **F.4**: 321. **G.3.2**: 323, 329. **I.3**: 62. **K.4**: 90, 190, 203, 205.
Reformism **I.2**: 53.
Refugees **C.2**: 28, 78. **D.1**: 98. **F.7**: 112. **F.8**: 20, 45, 52, 64, 69, 76–77, 84, 115, 117, 142–143, 163–164. **G.3.1**: 49. **I.2**: 61, 172. **K.4**: 10, 233.
Regime transition **D.7**: 302. **F.2**: 135.
Regional analysis **D.9**: 174. **F.1**: 64. **G.3.1**: 20. **H.3**: 88.

Regional development **F.8**: 53. **G.3**: 7. **G.3.1**: 104, 123. **G.3.2**: 11, 29, 59, 270, 272. **H.3**: 48. **H.4**: 74. **H.7**: 4, 6, 8, 21, 27. **J.4**: 8.

Regional disparities **D.9**: 29, 141. **E.1**: 11. **F.3**: 248-251, 262-263, 273, 285, 288, 298. **G.3.2**: 179, 272, 361. **H.3**: 2, 44, 84. **K.4**: 234.

Regional economics **H.3**: 45, 47, 89. **I.1**: 11. **I.2**: 17.

Regional identity **D.1**: 75-76. **F.7**: 54, 88.

Regional organizations **G.2**: 29.

Regional planning **G.3.1**: 101, 125. **G.3.2**: 163, 290, 295, 338, 343, 361. **H.7**: 9, 21-22.

Regional policy **H.7**: 2, 22. **J.2**: 27. **K.4**: 240.

Regionalization **D.7**: 357.

Regions **G.3**: 2, 8.

Regression analysis **B.2**: 85. **C.1**: 61. **F.3**: 47. **I.2**: 70.

Regulation **D.7**: 114. **H.5**: 3. **I.5**: 45. **J.4**: 18. **J.6**: 50.

Relative deprivation **H.3**: 46. **I.5**: 164.

Relativism **D.1**: 110, 133. **D.6**: 31.

Reliability **B.2**: 19-20. **C.1**: 128.

Religion
Entries also appear under:
CIVIL RELIGION; SOCIOLOGY OF RELIGION
C.1: 140. **C.4**: 13. **D.1**: 99. **D.5**: 5, 12-13, 22-24, 26, 30, 35, 38-39, 41-42, 44-45, 47-49, 55, 58, 68, 70-71, 79, 91, 96, 101, 105, 109, 111, 150, 177. **F.2**: 144. **F.3**: 30, 87. **F.4**: 100. **F.5**: 284. **F.6**: 43. **F.7**: 80, 119. **I.2**: 37. **K.1**: 70.

Religion and politics
Entries also appear under:
ISLAM AND POLITICS
D.5: 40, 95, 128, 174. **D.9**: 206. **K.2**: 15.

Religiosity **D.5**: 9, 37, 57, 185. **F.2**: 132.

Religious affiliation **D.5**: 10, 50. **D.7**: 35. **F.7**: 86.

Religious attitudes **F.2**: 5.

Religious authorities **D.5**: 141.

Religious beliefs **D.5**: 28, 33, 72, 76, 141. **F.4**: 243.

Religious change **D.5**: 31, 63, 67, 158.

Religious communities **D.5**: 185. **F.5**: 237. **G.2**: 30.

Religious consciousness **F.2**: 138.

Religious conversion **D.5**: 51, 112.

Religious education **D.5**: 52. **D.9**: 7, 159.

Religious experiences **D.5**: 11, 18.

Religious fanaticism **D.5**: 56.

Religious forces **D.5**: 69.

Religious fundamentalism **C.7**: 72. **D.5**: 16, 92. **F.5**: 44.

Religious groups **D.5**: 4, 132. **J.5**: 29.

Religious ideas **D.5**: 154.

Religious influences **F.6**: 39.

Religious institutions **D.5**: 138.

Religious life **D.5**: 168.

Religious marriage **F.2**: 131.

Religious minorities **D.5**: 122. **F.7**: 130.

Religious missions **D.5**: 22.

Religious movements **D.5**: 17, 21, 53-54. **F.3**: 50. **J.5**: 53.

Religious norms **D.5**: 6.

Religious orders **D.5**: 102.

Religious pluralism **D.5**: 139.

Religious practice **D.5**: 72.

Religious revival **D.5**: 118.

Religious syncretism **D.5**: 32.

Religious thought **D.5**: 77. **F.4**: 328.

Remittances **F.8**: 80.

Rent **G.3.2**: 129. **H.3**: 16.

Rent control **G.3.2**: 154.

Repression **G.3.1**: 132. **K.1**: 221.

Reproductive technology **D.3**: 89. **F.3**: 32, 45, 71, 115, 142. **F.4**: 303.

Research
Entries also appear under:
AGRICULTURAL RESEARCH; APPLIED RESEARCH; COMMUNICATION RESEARCH; DEMOGRAPHIC RESEARCH; EMPIRICAL RESEARCH; ETHNOGRAPHIC RESEARCH; INTERDISCIPLINARY RESEARCH; MANAGEMENT RESEARCH; MIGRATION RESEARCH; ORGANIZATIONAL RESEARCH; POLICY RESEARCH; SOCIAL RESEARCH; SOCIAL SCIENCE RESEARCH; SOCIOLOGICAL RESEARCH

A.2: 3, 12. **A.3**: 2. **B.1**: 90. **B.2**: 1, 4, 6, 11, 15, 100, 103, 107. **C.1**: 75, 89. **C.2**: 150. **D.3**: 26. **D.7**: 128, 171, 233. **D.9**: 217. **E.3**: 51. **F.2**: 10, 17. **F.4**: 72. **F.5**: 66. **K.1**: 283. **K.2**: 40. **K.3**: 37.

Research and development **I.3**: 47, 128. **I.4**: 73, 106.

Research methods
Entries also appear under:
FIELD WORK
B.2: 22, 98. **C.1**: 83. **D.7**: 282. **F.4**: 112.

Residence **D.1**: 16. **F.8**: 15. **G.3.2**: 129.

Resident satisfaction **G.3.2**: 109, 180.

Residential areas **F.3**: 24. **G.3.2**: 152, 191.

Residential differentiation **G.3.2**: 214.

Residential mobility **C.2**: 86. **F.7**: 170. **F.8**: 105. **G.3.2**: 141, 203, 208.
Residential segregation **F.7**: 146. **G.3.2**: 175. **I.2**: 55.
Resistance movements **F.5**: 231. **J.7**: 14.
Resource allocation **E.2**: 44. **F.5**: 174. **G.2**: 16. **H.5**: 33. **K.4**: 173.
Resource management **G.1**: 10.
Responsibility **C.7**: 80. **D.3**: 19–21, 33, 87. **D.4**: 2. **F.3**: 181. **F.5**: 159. **H.4**: 66. **I.5**: 39. **J.5**: 14. **K.1**: 7.
Retail prices **H.4**: 42. **H.5**: 26.
Retail trade **B.2**: 77. **G.2**: 10. **H.4**: 5, 42, 98. **H.5**: 7–8, 29, 34, 36. **I.5**: 10. **K.1**: 202.
Retirement
Entries also appear under:
EARLY RETIREMENT
F.2: 39, 47, 50, 61. **F.8**: 36. **I.2**: 125. **I.3**: 48, 75.
Return migration **F.8**: 152, 157, 160.
Revolution **D.1**: 24. **D.5**: 128. **D.7**: 97. **E.3**: 2, 49, 52, 70, 73. **F.5**: 107, 219. **F.8**: 52. **J.2**: 28. **J.5**: 8, 26–28. **J.6**: 14. **K.1**: 17.
Rhetoric **D.7**: 284. **I.2**: 69.
Rice **F.5**: 269.
Right
Entries also appear under:
EXTREME RIGHT; MIDDLE RIGHT; NEW RIGHT
J.6: 11. **K.4**: 186.
Right of privacy **K.1**: 141, 375.
Right to work **H.3**: 76.
Right wing parties **F.7**: 259, 264.
Rights
Entries also appear under:
CHILDREN'S RIGHTS; CIVIL RIGHTS; HUMAN RIGHTS; MINORITY RIGHTS; WOMEN'S RIGHTS
D.3: 57. **F.4**: 185, 191. **F.5**: 206. **I.2**: 67, 167, 247. **I.5**: 192. **J.5**: 23. **K.1**: 112. **K.2**: 32. **K.3**: 17. **K.4**: 65.
Riots **C.4**: 43. **G.3.2**: 173.
Risk **C.5**: 8. **C.7**: 30, 60. **D.1**: 36, 102. **D.9**: 208. **F.2**: 51. **F.3**: 61, 180–181, 289. **F.6**: 1. **H.4**: 97. **H.6**: 5. **I.4**: 30. **K.1**: 18, 144, 386, 391. **K.2**: 62. **K.4**: 8, 46.
Ritual
Entries also appear under:
FUNERARY RITES
D.2: 27. **D.5**: 15, 86. **J.1**: 5. **J.6**: 27. **J.7**: 8. **K.1**: 317.
Road safety **C.2**: 12. **C.5**: 59. **K.1**: 333.
Roads **G.1**: 50. **G.3.2**: 310.
Rock music **D.8**: 25, 40, 60–61.
Role **C.4**: 10.

Role change **C.6**: 10.
Role taking **C.6**: 17.
Roman Antiquity **D.5**: 99.
Romanians **F.7**: 25.
Ruling class **E.2**: 65.
Rumours **D.7**: 94, 153.
Rural anthropology **G.3.1**: 26.
Rural areas **D.1**: 3. **D.5**: 103. **D.7**: 186. **D.9**: 36. **E.1**: 20. **E.3**: 8. **F.2**: 23, 30. **F.3**: 100, 125, 139, 274, 276, 280. **F.7**: 2. **F.8**: 36, 113. **G.3.1**: 8, 12, 20, 25–27, 29, 43, 48, 54–55, 59, 71, 88, 92, 121, 130. **G.3.2**: 163. **H.3**: 42. **I.2**: 94. **I.4**: 43. **I.5**: 18. **J.3**: 13. **K.1**: 251, 266, 400. **K.2**: 45. **K.4**: 59.
Rural communities **G.1**: 49. **G.3.1**: 36, 65, 98, 136. **K.4**: 208.
Rural development **F.5**: 28. **G.2**: 8. **G.3.1**: 48, 84, 92, 101–103, 105, 107, 109–110, 113–114, 116–117, 122–123, 125–129, 132–135. **G.3.2**: 338. **H.4**: 11. **J.5**: 6.
Rural economics **G.3.1**: 14, 77. **H.3**: 68.
Rural employment **G.3.1**: 17, 52, 112. **I.2**: 173.
Rural environment **G.3.1**: 6.
Rural life **G.3.1**: 50, 61.
Rural planning **G.3.1**: 51. **H.7**: 10.
Rural policy **G.3.1**: 16, 40, 112.
Rural population **F.3**: 15. **G.3.1**: 9, 21, 49, 97, 132.
Rural poverty **G.3.1**: 18, 68, 105, 108. **H.3**: 84. **I.2**: 81. **K.1**: 257, 273, 282.
Rural society **E.2**: 13, 53. **E.3**: 16. **G.3.1**: 15, 39, 100. **H.7**: 24. **I.2**: 76.
Rural sociology **E.2**: 33. **F.3**: 107. **G.3.1**: 1, 7, 20, 42, 47, 58, 70, 72, 76, 116.
Rural women **F.3**: 110. **F.5**: 7, 24. **G.3.1**: 5, 7, 34, 53, 60. **I.2**: 81.
Rural-urban migration **F.8**: 86, 88, 91, 93, 97, 99, 101, 107. **G.3**: 10. **G.3.1**: 126. **G.3.2**: 200, 351.
Rural-urban relations **G.3**: 4.
Rushdie, Salman **D.5**: 175. **D.7**: 313. **F.7**: 185.
Russians **I.3**: 97.
Sacred **D.1**: 77. **F.2**: 131. **H.6**: 10. **J.5**: 37.
Sacrifice **D.5**: 60, 174.
Safety
Entries also appear under:
OCCUPATIONAL SAFETY; ROAD SAFETY
Saint-Simon, C. **D.1**: 79.
Sales management **F.6**: 28.
Salvadorans **C.2**: 28. **D.1**: 98.
Samples **B.2**: 35. **I.3**: 150.
Sampling

Entries also appear under:
RANDOM SAMPLING
B.2: 5, 47, 104, 119. **D.4**: 43. **I.2**: 137.

Sandel, M.J. **B.1**: 19.

Satanism **D.5**: 61.

Satisfaction
Entries also appear under:
JOB SATISFACTION; LIFE SATISFACTION; MARITAL SATISFACTION; RESIDENT SATISFACTION
C.3: 91, 140–141. **F.4**: 281, 309. **F.5**: 7, 220. **G.3.1**: 7. **H.5**: 22.

Savings **F.2**: 107.

Scale analysis **B.2**: 41, 70.

Scheler, Max **B.1**: 73.

Schizophrenia **C.2**: 125. **F.3**: 169, 206. **K.4**: 2.

Schmitt, Carl **J.2**: 19.

Schmoller, von, Gustav **H.1**: 5.

School administration **D.9**: 11.

School environment **D.9**: 126.

School leavers **I.2**: 23.

Schooling **D.9**: 89, 95, 168. **F.4**: 63, 80. **F.5**: 175. **I.4**: 25, 112.

Schools
Entries also appear under:
PRIMARY SCHOOLS; SECONDARY SCHOOLS
C.2: 144. **C.4**: 8. **C.5**: 53. **D.9**: 3, 25, 32–33, 43, 58–59, 61, 74, 78, 84, 88, 92, 100, 106, 112–113, 117–118, 124, 129, 131, 134, 139, 143, 155, 163. **F.4**: 118. **F.5**: 291. **F.7**: 121. **I.4**: 99. **K.1**: 37, 89. **K.2**: 35.

Schultz, Alfred **B.1**: 129.

Schumpter, Joseph **H.1**: 5.

Schutz, Alfred **B.1**: 15.

Science
Entries also appear under:
BEHAVIOURAL SCIENCES; COMPUTER SCIENCE; HISTORY OF SCIENCE; PHILOSOPHY OF SCIENCE
B.1: 34, 40, 55, 79. **C.1**: 80, 99, 110. **D.5**: 26, 163, 176. **D.6**: 2–3, 5, 7–8, 18, 21, 23, 28. **D.9**: 190. **F.4**: 72. **F.5**: 121–122, 182. **F.7**: 260. **F.8**: 44. **G.1**: 19. **H.4**: 92. **I.2**: 151. **K.4**: 267.

Science fiction **D.8**: 68.

Science policy **J.4**: 13.

Scientific and technical progress **C.2**: 193. **H.4**: 99.

Scientific communities **D.7**: 138.

Scientific progress **D.6**: 19.

Scientists
Entries also appear under:
SOCIAL SCIENTISTS

D.9: 175. **F.5**: 208. **I.2**: 24. **I.4**: 106.

Sea transport **I.4**: 41.

Searle, J.R. **D.7**: 211.

Seasonal migration **F.8**: 90, 100.

Seasonality **F.1**: 59.

Secondary education **D.9**: 119, 171. **F.7**: 59.

Secondary schools **C.3**: 58. **D.9**: 164–166, 170.

Sects **C.4**: 20. **J.5**: 18.

Secularism **D.5**: 27, 30.

Secularization **D.5**: 2–3, 58, 62–63, 123, 183.

Sedentarization **F.3**: 291.

Segregation
Entries also appear under:
OCCUPATIONAL SEGREGATION; RACIAL SEGREGATION; RESIDENTIAL SEGREGATION
F.5: 153, 220. **F.7**: 140, 170, 181. **G.1**: 60. **G.3.2**: 156. **H.3**: 69. **I.2**: 129. **I.3**: 133. **I.4**: 44.

Sekani **D.7**: 41.

Self **B.1**: 19. **C.1**: 53, 150. **C.2**: 61, 64–65, 70, 88, 92, 98, 131, 164, 176, 198, 221–222, 225, 228, 230, 238. **C.3**: 70, 158. **C.5**: 43. **C.7**: 19. **D.3**: 8. **D.5**: 159. **F.2**: 45. **F.4**: 28. **F.5**: 151, 159. **I.3**: 149.

Self-assessment **I.3**: 7.

Self-attention **C.2**: 223.

Self-categorization **C.3**: 74.

Self-concept **C.2**: 226, 229, 240. **C.3**: 15. **F.2**: 99.

Self-consciousness **C.2**: 235, 241.

Self-determination **K.3**: 34.

Self-employed workers **I.2**: 6. **I.4**: 45.

Self-esteem **C.1**: 124. **C.2**: 117, 192, 215, 224, 227, 231, 233–234, 236–237. **C.3**: 71–72. **C.4**: 52. **C.7**: 34. **F.6**: 1.

Self-evaluation **C.2**: 232. **C.3**: 137. **C.4**: 18. **D.9**: 135.

Self-government **F.7**: 95.

Self-help **C.4**: 51.

Self-perception **D.9**: 135. **F.2**: 152. **I.2**: 118.

Semantics **C.2**: 180. **D.1**: 40. **D.7**: 133, 205, 208, 210, 224, 226. **F.7**: 75–76. **J.1**: 8.

Semiology **D.8**: 38.

Semiotics **C.1**: 49. **D.7**: 72.

Sensation **F.2**: 130. **F.3**: 197.

Separatism **D.5**: 169.

Service industry **G.3.2**: 352. **H.4**: 2, 57. **I.2**: 105, 136. **K.4**: 134.

Sesotho language **D.7**: 311.

Seventh-Day Adventism **D.5**: 89.

Sewing **F.5**: 36.

Sex **C.1**: 65. **C.7**: 3. **D.1**: 7. **F.1**: 60. **F.2**: 67. **F.4**: 137. **F.5**: 26, 75, 153. **F.6**: 43, 48.

Sex differentiation **C.7**: 10. **F.5**: 204, 223, 301. **I.3**: 137.

Sex discrimination **F.5**: 50, 155, 161, 168, 181, 199, 215, 257, 259, 306. **I.2**: 85, 102, 104, 116, 131, 137–138, 152, 161. **I.3**: 108. **I.4**: 108. **K.1**: 174.

Sex distribution **F.3**: 13. **F.4**: 227. **K.1**: 425.

Sex equality **F.5**: 111, 158, 193, 214.

Sex inequality **F.5**: 217. **I.2**: 35. **I.5**: 96. **K.1**: 375.

Sex roles **F.5**: 172, 264, 278, 291, 314. **I.2**: 103–104, 161.

Sexism **D.5**: 16. **F.5**: 68, 95, 224.

Sexual assault **F.2**: 77. **F.4**: 135, 151, 157, 159, 171–172. **F.5**: 119, 228. **I.3**: 66. **K.1**: 33–38, 43, 45, 50, 87, 100, 122, 144.

Sexual behaviour **D.3**: 79. **F.3**: 180, 212. **F.4**: 254. **F.6**: 5, 7, 9, 12, 20, 24–25, 27–29, 37, 42, 44–45, 50–51. **K.1**: 380.

Sexual harassment **C.5**: 26. **D.4**: 12, 41. **F.5**: 13, 85, 300. **F.6**: 6, 18, 46. **I.2**: 222. **I.3**: 76.

Sexual intercourse
Entries also appear under:
PREMARITAL INTERCOURSE
F.3: 61. **F.6**: 1, 8, 13–14, 16, 33.

Sexual perversions **C.1**: 51.

Sexual reproduction **D.6**: 8. **F.3**: 56, 111, 123. **F.5**: 270. **K.4**: 65.

Sexuality **C.1**: 7. **D.5**: 37. **F.3**: 72, 108. **F.5**: 287, 319. **F.6**: 2, 10–11, 19, 48–49, 52–54, 56–57. **J.3**: 24.

Sexually transmitted diseases **F.3**: 215–216.

Sheeler, Charles **D.7**: 3.

Sherman, Cindy **D.8**: 43.

Shipbuilding **I.4**: 54.

Short time working **I.3**: 26.

Shortage
Entries also appear under:
HOUSING SHORTAGE; LABOUR SHORTAGE
Siblings **C.3**: 75. **D.9**: 142. **F.3**: 190. **F.4**: 73, 142, 310, 340, 346, 349. **K.3**: 35.

Sign language **D.7**: 186.

Signs **D.7**: 53, 90.

Simmel, Georg **D.1**: 99.

Simulation **C.3**: 36. **C.5**: 20. **I.5**: 51.

Single European market **G.2**: 31. **I.4**: 47. **K.2**: 20, 27.

Siting decisions **D.6**: 10.

Size of enterprise **H.4**: 73.

Skilled workers **I.2**: 192. **I.3**: 50. **I.4**: 37.

Skills **D.8**: 10. **F.2**: 152. **H.7**: 11. **I.3**: 87, 90. **I.4**: 18, 52, 132. **K.1**: 139. **K.3**: 8.

Skin colour **F.7**: 261.

Slums **F.5**: 316. **G.3.2**: 146, 190.

Small and medium sized enterprises **D.3**: 52. **F.5**: 169, 247. **F.8**: 40. **H.4**: 39, 48, 62, 70, 74, 76.

Small farms **G.3.1**: 67, 77, 108.

Small groups **C.4**: 6, 9, 21, 45, 56–57, 63.

Small states **D.9**: 65.

Small towns **G.3.2**: 255.

Small-scale industry **E.3**: 38. **G.3.1**: 25. **H.4**: 75. **I.3**: 122.

Smell **C.3**: 82.

Smoking **C.1**: 134. **C.7**: 49. **D.7**: 103. **F.2**: 146. **F.4**: 297. **I.3**: 78. **K.1**: 298, 330–332, 346, 373, 386, 391, 393.

Sociability **F.4**: 346.

Social action **B.1**: 133. **D.7**: 149. **F.5**: 125. **K.4**: 237.

Social adaptation **D.1**: 5. **F.3**: 194. **G.2**: 31.

Social approval **J.6**: 19.

Social behaviour **C.3**: 62, 70. **C.7**: 17–18, 75. **D.1**: 137. **H.4**: 84. **I.3**: 15. **J.3**: 46.

Social biology **D.4**: 35. **E.2**: 2. **F.4**: 77. **G.1**: 3.

Social change **A.1**: 16. **B.1**: 12, 108, 139. **C.2**: 10, 187. **C.5**: 47. **D.4**: 10. **D.5**: 26. **D.6**: 28. **D.7**: 41, 124. **D.8**: 55–56. **D.9**: 51. **E.1**: 1, 25. **E.3**: 1, 4–5, 7–13, 19–20, 24–25, 28–29, 31, 33, 41, 45, 47, 49–50, 57–61, 65, 67, 71, 74. **F.2**: 150. **F.3**: 63, 72. **F.5**: 178, 307, 314. **F.7**: 127. **F.8**: 39. **G.2**: 3. **G.3.1**: 48, 123, 131. **G.3.2**: 205, 346, 359. **H.3**: 3–4. **H.4**: 1, 99. **I.4**: 96. **J.6**: 53. **K.1**: 147, 284. **K.2**: 22. **K.3**: 36.

Social cognition **C.2**: 135. **D.1**: 19. **D.4**: 38. **D.7**: 176. **J.6**: 16.

Social conditions **D.1**: 38, 117, 139. **D.5**: 155. **D.7**: 351. **D.9**: 85. **E.1**: 1–2, 4, 7, 15, 18, 21, 24. **E.2**: 4, 12, 15, 18, 63, 66, 74, 78. **E.3**: 50, 66. **F.1**: 17. **F.2**: 78, 101, 134. **F.3**: 72, 232, 275, 292. **F.5**: 32, 37, 155, 240. **F.7**: 2, 4, 12, 59, 66–67, 98. **F.8**: 69, 84, 114, 152. **G.1**: 6, 25. **G.3.1**: 48, 113, 120, 131. **G.3.2**: 70, 75, 345. **H.3**: 6, 57. **H.4**: 86. **I.2**: 156. **J.1**: 22. **J.3**: 29. **J.6**: 46. **K.2**: 100. **K.4**: 38.

Social conflicts **E.2**: 52.

Social conscience **C.7**: 33.

Social consciousness **D.1**: 120, 135.

Social contract **H.3**: 29.

Social control **C.2**: 136. **C.4**: 20. **C.5**: 15. **D.1**: 51, 111, 123. **E.3**: 65. **F.5**: 228. **G.1**: 28. **J.3**: 9. **K.1**: 8, 119, 408. **K.4**: 36, 69.

Social co-operation **C.3**: 67. **I.5**: 8.

Social costs **K.1**: 346.

Social democracy **I.5**: 15.

Social desirability **C.3**: 84.

Social development **E.1**: 23. **E.3**: 18, 30–31, 46, 63, 69–70. **F.2**: 154. **F.5**: 165. **G.3.2**: 16. **H.2**: 11. **K.1**: 293.

Social differentiation **F.3**: 246.

Social disorganization **K.1**: 49, 92.

Social distance **C.7**: 21. **F.7**: 40.

Social doctrines **D.3**: 23.

Social dynamics **F.1**: 62. **G.2**: 3.

Social environment **D.1**: 38. **K.1**: 146.

Social exchange **C.3**: 54. **G.3.2**: 42.

Social factors **D.7**: 177. **F.3**: 32, 90. **K.1**: 307.

Social group work **F.5**: 91. **K.3**: 19.

Social history **B.1**: 11. **D.5**: 19. **E.3**: 34, 62. **F.7**: 111.

Social housing **G.3.2**: 147, 149.

Social indicators **F.1**: 16. **H.3**: 11, 14.

Social inequality **D.9**: 123, 125. **E.2**: 8, 29–31, 42, 44, 47–48, 71, 73. **F.4**: 48. **F.7**: 82. **G.3.2**: 206. **H.3**: 7. **H.4**: 2. **H.5**: 28. **K.4**: 87, 106.

Social influence **C.1**: 56. **C.3**: 76–77. **D.1**: 43.

Social information **C.3**: 46, 148. **F.3**: 210.

Social infrastructure **H.7**: 24.

Social integration **E.1**: 15. **F.1**: 32. **F.4**: 142. **F.7**: 181, 208, 240. **F.8**: 66, 83, 171. **J.7**: 9. **J.8**: 6, 9.

Social interaction **B.1**: 97. **C.1**: 135, 145. **C.3**: 39, 46, 50, 73, 88. **C.4**: 64. **D.2**: 23. **D.7**: 249. **K.1**: 139.

Social isolation **F.4**: 239.

Social judgement **C.3**: 78, 158. **C.7**: 15, 66.

Social justice **C.3**: 49. **D.3**: 67. **D.4**: 40. **D.5**: 142, 147. **F.5**: 227. **I.2**: 247.

Social legislation **D.4**: 16.

Social life **D.1**: 48. **D.2**: 7, 13. **G.3.2**: 279.

Social medicine **F.3**: 179. **K.4**: 75.

Social mobility **E.2**: 3, 5, 23, 26, 37, 58, 67, 71. **E.3**: 63. **F.5**: 185. **F.7**: 3. **F.8**: 108. **G.3.2**: 207. **H.3**: 46. **I.2**: 164, 207. **I.4**: 33. **K.4**: 9.

Social movements **D.5**: 53, 66, 107. **E.2**: 27. **E.3**: 44, 51, 64. **F.7**: 214. **F.8**: 34. **G.3.2**: 184, 202. **I.2**: 212. **J.5**: 4, 7, 10, 29, 31, 33–34, 53. **K.4**: 78.

Social networks **C.3**: 52. **C.4**: 10, 30, 48–49, 58. **C.5**: 87. **D.7**: 14. **E.1**: 17. **F.3**: 126. **F.4**: 97, 112. **F.5**: 289. **F.7**: 9. **G.2**: 1. **G.3.1**: 65, 76. **I.3**: 105. **J.3**: 29. **K.1**: 20.

Social norms **D.1**: 107, 121, 124–125.

Social order **B.1**: 87. **D.1**: 11, 113. **E.1**: 12–13. **E.3**: 53.

Social origin **E.2**: 9, 36.

Social perception **C.3**: 147, 151–152, 159, 162. **C.4**: 55. **F.7**: 241.

Social philosophy **A.1**: 39. **J.8**: 5.

Social planning **B.1**: 100. **G.3.2**: 260.

Social pluralism **D.1**: 22. **E.2**: 16.

Social policy **B.2**: 53. **D.1**: 129. **E.1**: 4. **E.2**: 1. **F.5**: 53, 177. **F.7**: 39, 191. **G.3.2**: 98. **H.2**: 18. **I.2**: 220. **I.3**: 84. **I.4**: 47. **I.5**: 46, 114. **K.1**: 55, 103, 338, 341, 354. **K.2**: 1, 11, 15, 23, 31, 38, 62, 66, 86, 91, 95–96, 101, 111. **K.3**: 38.

Social problems **D.6**: 28. **D.7**: 34. **E.1**: 1. **E.2**: 84. **F.1**: 50. **F.4**: 143. **K.1**: 4, 17, 21–22, 65, 138, 392. **K.2**: 30, 80.

Social psychology **C.1**: 142, 144–146, 149–151, 153–155, 157–174. **C.2**: 45, 70, 189. **C.3**: 98. **C.4**: 5, 29. **C.7**: 78. **D.1**: 132. **D.2**: 23. **F.7**: 29, 72, 256. **I.5**: 55. **K.1**: 379.

Social reform **D.5**: 104.

Social relations **C.3**: 19, 79, 159. **D.5**: 70. **F.6**: 47. **H.2**: 8.

Social representations **C.7**: 20, 36. **F.2**: 67. **F.3**: 154.

Social reproduction **E.1**: 20. **F.5**: 184.

Social research **A.2**: 16. **B.1**: 41. **D.1**: 26. **D.3**: 62. **E.2**: 71. **G.3.2**: 132, 160, 223.

Social roles **C.1**: 103. **C.4**: 63. **C.6**: 12, 15. **K.1**: 385. **K.4**: 5.

Social science research **B.1**: 28, 34.

Social sciences **A.1**: 3–4, 9, 11, 21–22, 27, 30, 32–35, 43. **A.2**: 2, 7, 16, 24. **A.3**: 6. **B.1**: 2, 10, 41, 59, 65, 68, 93, 115. **B.2**: 57, 75. **C.1**: 25, 71, 108. **C.2**: 88. **C.3**: 38. **D.1**: 112. **D.6**: 4. **E.3**: 20, 59. **F.3**: 148. **G.3.1**: 133. **G.3.2**: 90. **J.1**: 12.

Social scientists **A.2**: 4. **B.1**: 38. **F.2**: 114. **J.6**: 48.

Social security **F.5**: 221. **F.8**: 2. **I.4**: 38. **K.2**: 18, 20, 22–24, 26–29, 73, 75, 79, 90, 99, 108–110. **K.4**: 85.

Social services **F.4**: 92. **F.7**: 12. **F.8**: 13. **G.2**: 35. **K.1**: 33. **K.2**: 50, 76, 89, 95, 97–98, 100, 102, 105. **K.3**: 12, 16, 36, 38, 45. **K.4**: 19, 26, 29, 40, 71, 88, 123, 165, 187, 201, 232, 238.

Social status **C.3**: 85. **C.4**: 44. **D.1**: 127. **E.2**: 32, 36, 38–40, 57. **F.2**: 67, 105, 123. **F.4**: 37, 93. **F.5**: 183, 299. **F.7**: 11, 81. **H.6**: 2. **K.1**: 153.

Social stereotypes **F.5**: 271.

Social stratification **E.2**: 2, 6, 13, 19, 26, 34, 41–42, 50, 61. **F.5**: 255. **F.7**: 261. **H.3**: 82.

Social structure **B.1**: 128, 138. **B.2**: 27. **C.7**: 20. **D.1**: 42. **D.8**: 30. **E.1**: 6, 9, 11, 16, 18. **E.2**: 7, 14, 20, 42, 45, 58, 80. **E.3**: 6, 12, 49, 65, 67. **F.3**: 131–132, 220. **F.4**: 66. **F.7**: 82, 262. **G.2**: 24. **G.3.2**: 119, 266. **I.4**: 57. **J.2**: 30. **K.1**: 399.

Social success **F.2**: 76.

Social surveys **B.2**: 119, 128.

Social systems **D.2**: 22. **D.4**: 26. **E.1**: 3, 5, 10, 25. **F.2**: 44.

Social theory **B.1**: 6, 67, 92, 94, 100, 137, 152. **C.1**: 53. **C.7**: 28. **D.4**: 41. **D.6**: 5. **F.7**: 222. **G.1**: 57. **G.3.1**: 66. **G.3.2**: 119. **J.1**: 11. **K.2**: 8.

Social values **C.6**: 16. **D.1**: 116, 128–129, 132. **D.8**: 65. **E.1**: 18. **F.3**: 45.

Social welfare **E.3**: 59. **F.5**: 140. **K.1**: 227. **K.2**: 82, 92. **K.3**: 36.

Social work **D.5**: 156. **F.3**: 63. **K.2**: 52, 58. **K.3**: 2–8, 10, 12–18, 21–28, 32–35, 37–43, 45. **K.4**: 36, 109.

Social workers **F.4**: 24. **K.1**: 43. **K.3**: 20, 42, 44.

Socialism
Entries also appear under:
STATE SOCIALISM
D.1: 113. **D.9**: 98. **E.3**: 13. **F.4**: 106. **F.5**: 127, 180, 319. **F.7**: 187. **G.1**: 10. **G.3.2**: 123. **J.2**: 25, 30. **J.3**: 7. **J.6**: 5. **K.4**: 90.

Socialist countries **I.4**: 32.

Socialist economies **H.2**: 17, 19. **K.2**: 7.

Socialist enterprises **I.3**: 81.

Socialists **G.3.2**: 74.

Socialization
Entries also appear under:
POLITICAL SOCIALIZATION
C.3: 132. **D.1**: 1, 140. **F.4**: 103. **F.6**: 56. **F.8**: 81. **I.3**: 5. **I.4**: 31. **K.1**: 74. **K.4**: 240.

Society
Entries also appear under:
AGRARIAN SOCIETY; CAPITALIST SOCIETY; CIVIL SOCIETY; INDIVIDUAL AND SOCIETY; INFORMATION SOCIETY; MASS SOCIETY; PEASANT SOCIETIES; POLITICAL SOCIETY; POST-COMMUNIST SOCIETY; POST-INDUSTRIAL SOCIETY; RURAL SOCIETY; TRADITIONAL SOCIETY; URBAN SOCIETY
B.1: 9, 147. **D.8**: 23.

Sociobiology **D.1**: 78. **E.3**: 2–3. **F.1**: 8.

Socio-economic development **B.2**: 4. **D.3**: 34. **D.9**: 16. **E.3**: 68. **F.3**: 85, 291. **F.5**: 243. **G.3.2**: 298, 360. **H.3**: 31. **I.4**: 97. **K.1**: 77.

Sociolinguistics **C.3**: 78. **D.7**: 9, 27, 44–46, 55, 67, 77–81, 83, 87, 143, 154, 156, 194–195, 198, 209, 216, 218, 225, 227, 269, 341, 347, 349.

Sociological analysis **B.2**: 40, 48, 56, 63. **D.1**: 102, 120. **D.3**: 83. **F.7**: 269.

Sociological methodology **A.1**: 23. **B.1**: 98. **B.2**: 13, 33, 61. **G.3.1**: 47. **H.1**: 5.

Sociological research **A.2**: 2, 5, 22. **B.1**: 141, 144. **B.2**: 30, 57. **D.8**: 68. **E.2**: 60.

Sociological theory **A.2**: 21. **B.1**: 87, 103, 105, 107, 111, 119, 123–124, 131, 135, 140–141, 147, 151. **F.2**: 18. **I.4**: 76. **J.8**: 22. **K.1**: 212.

Sociologists **A.1**: 8, 12. **A.2**: 1, 9–10, 13, 15. **B.1**: 97, 117. **C.3**: 63.

Sociology
Entries also appear under:
ECONOMIC SOCIOLOGY; EDUCATIONAL SOCIOLOGY; ELECTORAL SOCIOLOGY; HISTORY OF SOCIOLOGY; MEDICAL SOCIOLOGY; OCCUPATIONAL SOCIOLOGY; POLITICAL SOCIOLOGY; RURAL SOCIOLOGY; URBAN SOCIOLOGY
A.1: 1–2, 5–7, 13–14, 16, 18–19, 22, 25, 28–29, 31, 36–39, 41–42. **A.2**: 17, 23. **A.3**: 3, 7. **B.1**: 20, 45, 66, 83, 88–90, 96, 118, 120, 126–127, 134, 137, 140. **B.2**: 115. **C.2**: 64. **C.3**: 82. **C.6**: 15. **D.1**: 36, 99. **D.2**: 25. **D.5**: 107. **E.1**: 9, 16. **E.3**: 5, 76. **F.3**: 221. **F.4**: 60, 204. **F.5**: 10, 92. **F.6**: 49. **F.7**: 252. **J.2**: 14. **K.1**: 404. **K.2**: 4, 26. **K.3**: 45.

Sociology of development **E.3**: 68.

Sociology of knowledge **B.1**: 28, 39. **D.6**: 29. **D.9**: 127. **F.8**: 106.

Sociology of law **D.4**: 26. **K.1**: 104.

Sociology of leisure **I.6**: 7.

Sociology of organizations **C.5**: 85. **D.9**: 129.

Sociology of religion **B.1**: 125. **D.5**: 46, 66, 73, 93.

Sociology of science **D.6**: 11.

Sociology of sport **I.6**: 34.

Sociology of the family **F.4**: 109.

Sociology of work **F.5**: 317. **I.1**: 1, 4–5, 7, 13. **I.3**: 39.

Sociometric status **H.3**: 26.

Software **B.2**: 84. **H.4**: 41.

Solicitors **I.4**: 100.

Solidarity **C.2**: 50. **F.4**: 68. **J.7**: 17.

Solvent abuse **C.3**: 76.

Somalis **F.7**: 126.

Somatology **C.2**: 47.

Soninke **F.7**: 19.

Sons **F.3**: 64, 139. **F.4**: 266, 291.

South Amerindians **G.3.1**: 87.

Sovereignty **F.5**: 246. **J.8**: 16.

Space economics **C.3**: 151. **D.1**: 115. **G.3.2**: 96, 152. **H.4**: 40–41, 75.

Spaniards **F.7**: 155.

Spanish language **D.7**: 59, 68, 86, 202, 226. **F.8**: 86. **K.4**: 12.

Spatial dimension **B.2**: 77. **D.7**: 171. **F.2**: 20. **F.3**: 213. **F.5**: 128. **F.7**: 42. **G.1**: 35–36, 57. **G.3**: 2. **G.3.2**: 29, 178–179, 181–182, 186–187, 193, 195, 199, 206, 214, 219–222. **I.2**: 1. **I.4**: 42. **J.2**: 16. **J.3**: 44.

Spatial distribution **F.3**: 9. **H.5**: 36. **K.1**: 285.

Speech **C.3**: 45. **D.7**: 42, 70, 135, 333.

Speech analysis **C.2**: 165. **D.7**: 151.

Spirits **C.1**: 43.

Spiritualism **D.1**: 27. **D.5**: 36.

INTERNATIONAL BIBLIOGRAPHY OF SOCIOLOGY — 1991

Sport
Entries also appear under:
SOCIOLOGY OF SPORT
D.7: 324. **F.2**: 40. **F.7**: 229, 251, 256, 263. **H.5**: 6. **I.5**: 9. **I.6**: 4–5, 8–9, 12–14, 18, 23, 32, 36–38, 43–44. **K.1**: 404, 406.

Squatters **G.2**: 2, 33. **G.3.2**: 213. **H.3**: 54. **K.1**: 261.

Staff **I.3**: 145. **I.4**: 38.

Stagnation **H.3**: 49.

Standard of living **F.2**: 58. **F.4**: 73. **H.3**: 20, 30, 32–33.

State
Entries also appear under:
CHURCH AND STATE; NATION STATE; SMALL STATES
D.5: 71, 177. **D.7**: 285. **D.9**: 199. **F.5**: 11, 302, 326. **F.7**: 129, 134. **G.3.2**: 53. **J.2**: 16. **J.3**: 21. **K.2**: 8.

State aid **D.9**: 39.

State and law **J.3**: 15.

State formation **J.3**: 23.

State intervention **F.8**: 94.

State socialism **E.3**: 11.

Statistical analysis **B.2**: 36, 66, 69, 80. **I.4**: 13.

Statistical data **B.2**: 49, 106. **K.4**: 163.

Statistical methods **B.2**: 10, 41, 77, 99. **C.4**: 9.

Statistical models **B.2**: 14, 53. **G.3.2**: 106. **K.4**: 102.

Statistics **B.1**: 100. **B.2**: 65. **K.1**: 160. **K.2**: 4.

Status attainment **E.2**: 21, 35.

Status congruency **I.4**: 111.

Steel industry **C.5**: 36. **I.5**: 27.

Step-parents **F.4**: 22, 281, 326.

Stereotypes
Entries also appear under:
NATIONAL STEREOTYPES; RACIAL STEREOTYPES; SOCIAL STEREOTYPES
C.2: 239. **C.3**: 92. **C.4**: 16, 55. **C.7**: 10, 21, 31, 66–67, 74. **F.4**: 83. **F.5**: 272, 286, 306. **F.7**: 209. **I.3**: 49. **I.4**: 38. **J.7**: 16.

Sterilization
Entries also appear under:
FEMALE STERILIZATION
F.3: 44. **I.3**: 120.

Stochastic models **F.1**: 14. **F.8**: 49. **G.3.2**: 308.

Stochastic processes **C.3**: 54.

Stock exchange **I.2**: 1.

Stories
Entries also appear under:
LIFE STORIES
Strategic planning **C.5**: 5, 22. **D.7**: 178. **D.9**: 184. **G.3.2**: 309. **H.7**: 26. **I.5**: 52. **J.1**: 20.

Strikes **E.2**: 69, 76. **G.1**: 47. **I.5**: 76, 79, 84–85, 87, 92, 95.

String instruments **C.4**: 12.

Structural adjustment **G.3.1**: 108. **H.3**: 50, 56. **I.2**: 98, 143, 228. **I.3**: 83. **K.1**: 249. **K.4**: 20.

Structural analysis **B.2**: 62. **C.4**: 6. **F.1**: 63. **H.3**: 46.

Structural change **G.3.1**: 52, 106.

Structuralism **B.1**: 11. **J.2**: 30.

Students **B.2**: 24. **C.1**: 96, 101. **C.2**: 4, 39. **C.3**: 28, 151. **D.5**: 37. **D.7**: 7. **D.9**: 24, 106, 109–110, 124, 139, 176, 197, 200–201, 206, 208, 210, 220. **F.2**: 121, 134, 147. **F.4**: 216. **F.5**: 263. **J.2**: 24. **J.6**: 41. **J.8**: 1. **K.1**: 45, 421. **K.4**: 57, 96.

Subcontracting **H.4**: 48.

Subculture **D.8**: 53. **F.2**: 123. **K.1**: 16, 413.

Subjectivity **C.7**: 14, 65. **D.7**: 107. **F.5**: 26.

Subsidiarity **K.2**: 102.

Subsidies **H.3**: 90.

Subsistence economy **H.4**: 45.

Substance abuse **K.1**: 297, 303, 349, 351, 379, 387, 395.

Suburban areas **D.2**: 20. **F.3**: 16. **G.3.2**: 6, 17, 25, 50, 56, 173, 188, 205, 336, 354. **H.5**: 8. **J.3**: 13.

Sugar industry **H.4**: 13.

Suicide **F.3**: 267. **F.8**: 23. **J.7**: 21. **K.1**: 394–402.

Sunnism **D.5**: 145.

Superstition **D.1**: 80.

Supervisors **I.3**: 25.

Supply
Entries also appear under:
LABOUR SUPPLY
Supply and demand **G.3.2**: 352.

Supreme Court **D.4**: 7, 34. **F.5**: 300. **J.3**: 28. **K.1**: 176.

Surgery **F.5**: 1.

Surrogate motherhood **F.4**: 305, 308.

Survey analysis **B.2**: 31, 89–90, 92, 130. **C.2**: 62. **H.5**: 25.

Surveys
Entries also appear under:
MAIL SURVEYS; PANEL SURVEYS; SOCIAL SURVEYS
B.2: 20–21, 25, 91, 94–95, 97, 101–102, 111, 116, 124–126, 131. **C.5**: 14. **D.7**: 349. **F.2**: 89. **F.8**: 63. **I.3**: 6. **I.5**: 54.

Survival strategy **C.1**: 36. **G.3.1**: 62.

Sustainable development **H.4**: 19, 44. **J.8**: 2.

Swahili **D.1**: 49.

Symbolism **C.5**: 60. **D.1**: 73, 116. **F.2**: 144. **F.6**: 51.

Symbols **B.1**: 143. **C.1**: 98. **J.1**: 5.
Sympathy **C.2**: 14.
Synagogues **F.4**: 253.
Synchronic analysis **D.7**: 216.
Syntax **D.7**: 205.
Systems analysis **A.3**: 4. **C.5**: 41, 80.
Taboo **F.3**: 199.
Tadzhiks **F.7**: 179.
Tax evasion **D.5**: 57. **H.2**: 20. **I.4**: 51.
Taxation **D.4**: 1. **G.1**: 63. **G.3.2**: 218. **H.6**: 4.
Taxpayers **D.5**: 57. **H.6**: 4.
Taylor, Charles **C.2**: 65.
Tea **F.5**: 311.
Teacher training **D.9**: 82. **K.3**: 24.
Teachers **D.3**: 90. **D.9**: 21, 47, 60, 72, 145. **E.2**: 4. **I.4**: 59, 98–99, 107, 112. **I.5**: 61, 72, 83.
Teacher-student relationship **D.9**: 19.
Teaching
 Entries also appear under:
 LANGUAGE TEACHING
 D.3: 41. **D.9**: 44, 117, 164, 202. **F.6**: 22. **K.3**: 27.
Teaching methods **C.2**: 118.
Teaching of economics **D.9**: 33.
Teaching of political science **D.9**: 24.
Technical cooperation **G.3.2**: 254. **K.4**: 97.
Technicians **I.4**: 1.
Technological change **D.7**: 257, 292. **D.9**: 55. **E.3**: 36. **G.3.2**: 246, 284. **H.3**: 52. **H.4**: 84, 93, 98, 101. **I.2**: 10. **I.3**: 27, 45, 87. **I.5**: 167, 184.
Technology
 Entries also appear under:
 ALTERNATIVE TECHNOLOGY; BIOTECHNOLOGY; COMMUNICATIONS TECHNOLOGY; HIGH TECHNOLOGY; INFORMATION TECHNOLOGY; NEW TECHNOLOGY; REPRODUCTIVE TECHNOLOGY
 B.1: 12, 40. **B.2**: 17. **C.2**: 19. **C.5**: 57, 78. **D.1**: 115. **D.6**: 10, 23, 26, 28. **D.7**: 126, 150. **D.9**: 67, 175. **F.5**: 103, 196. **G.3.2**: 232. **H.4**: 79, 85–88, 90, 92–93, 96–97, 100, 102–103. **I.2**: 12, 24, 91, 123. **I.3**: 4. **I.5**: 42, 137, 171–172. **J.3**: 37. **J.7**: 11, 22. **K.1**: 363, 427. **K.4**: 98, 271.
Technology policy **J.4**: 13.
Telecommunications **D.7**: 91–92, 184. **D.9**: 12, 31, 67. **H.4**: 95.
Telecommunications industry **H.4**: 59.
Telephone **B.2**: 92. **D.7**: 150. **F.7**: 119. **H.5**: 25.
Television **D.2**: 6. **D.5**: 152. **D.7**: 240, 287, 293, 297, 323, 327, 351–355, 357–359, 361–367, 369–370, 372, 375–382, 384–387, 389–394. **D.8**: 393. **E.1**: 14. **F.4**: 5. **F.5**: 285.

Temporary employment **I.2**: 9, 63. **I.4**: 116.
Tenants **G.3.2**: 148. **K.4**: 142.
Territory **C.2**: 86. **G.1**: 28.
Terror **F.8**: 20.
Terrorism **D.1**: 45. **D.7**: 244, 285, 301.
Terrorists **C.1**: 34.
Tests **B.2**: 93, 97. **I.6**: 24.
Textbooks **D.9**: 26.
Textile industry **D.9**: 40. **G.3.2**: 28. **H.4**: 90. **I.2**: 123, 140. **I.3**: 88, 130.
Texts **C.2**: 16.
Thai **D.1**: 5. **D.7**: 123.
Thai language **D.7**: 27.
Thatcher, Margaret **G.3.2**: 52.
Theatre **D.8**: 22, 72.
Theft **K.1**: 57, 91, 121, 202.
Theology
 Entries also appear under:
 CHRISTIAN THEOLOGY; LIBERATION THEOLOGY
 D.3: 23.
Theory of culture **D.1**: 34.
Therapeutic interviews **K.3**: 9.
Therapeutics **C.2**: 137.
Therapy
 Entries also appear under:
 FAMILY THERAPY
 C.1: 35, 44, 59, 85, 97. **C.2**: 119. **F.4**: 213. **I.4**: 102. **K.1**: 204, 215. **K.4**: 86.
Thieves **K.1**: 110, 358.
Thinking **C.2**: 139. **C.3**: 160.
Thomas, William Isaac **F.7**: 44.
Thompson, Hunter S. **D.7**: 271.
Threat **B.2**: 95. **C.4**: 15. **J.6**: 49.
Time **B.1**: 7. **C.1**: 173. **I.1**: 3.
Time budgets **B.2**: 89.
Time series **F.5**: 2. **K.1**: 77, 157.
Tobacco **D.7**: 103, 116. **F.2**: 129. **K.1**: 298.
Tocqueville, de, Alexis **D.5**: 118.
Tolerance **G.3.2**: 91.
Tools
 Entries also appear under:
 MACHINE TOOLS
Top management **I.4**: 80.
Toposa **F.2**: 44.
Totalitarianism **D.8**: 34.
Touraine, Alain **B.1**: 83.
Tourism **I.5**: 21. **I.6**: 6, 15, 21, 31, 40–41.
Tourist trade **I.6**: 26–27, 29.
Towns

Entries also appear under:
NEW TOWNS; SMALL TOWNS
E.2: 48. **G.1**: 42. **G.3**: 11. **G.3.2**: 5, 7, 14, 22, 30, 35, 40, 48, 70, 74, 92, 164, 185, 235, 238, 246, 258, 284, 312–314, 339, 346. **H.5**: 1. **I.4**: 20.

Toxicity **G.1**: 43. **K.4**: 7.

Toys **F.2**: 117. **I.6**: 42.

Trade
Entries also appear under:
FOREIGN TRADE; RETAIL TRADE; TOURIST TRADE
F.7: 11. **F.8**: 51. **H.3**: 10. **H.5**: 3.

Trade union membership **I.5**: 131–132, 156, 164, 175, 195.

Trade unionism **I.3**: 106. **I.5**: 65, 123, 144, 150, 152–153, 176, 187.

Trade unions **E.2**: 25. **F.5**: 227, 230. **H.3**: 76, 81. **I.2**: 53. **I.5**: 79, 116, 118–122, 124–130, 133, 135–141, 143, 145–149, 151, 154–155, 157–163, 165, 167–174, 177–186, 188–194. **J.4**: 6. **J.5**: 30. **K.4**: 79.

Tradition
Entries also appear under:
CULTURAL TRADITION; ORAL TRADITION
C.2: 217. **D.1**: 50. **F.3**: 35. **F.7**: 28. **G.3.1**: 88.

Traditional medicine **C.1**: 43. **F.3**: 120. **K.4**: 55.

Traditional society **D.1**: 126.

Traffic
Entries also appear under:
URBAN TRAFFIC
F.3: 230. **G.1**: 50. **G.3.2**: 316. **J.3**: 41.

Training
Entries also appear under:
ON-THE-JOB TRAINING; TEACHER TRAINING; VOCATIONAL TRAINING
C.1: 137. **D.8**: 10. **D.9**: 209. **G.3.1**: 135. **G.3.2**: 254, 256. **H.7**: 11. **I.2**: 157. **I.4**: 25, 67, 116, 125, 130. **K.3**: 30, 46.

Transaction costs **H.5**: 38.

Transactional analysis **I.3**: 85.

Transition from school to work **D.9**: 13.

Translation **D.7**: 372.

Transport
Entries also appear under:
AIR TRANSPORT; MEANS OF TRANSPORT; RAILWAY TRANSPORT; SEA TRANSPORT; URBAN TRANSPORT
D.3: 4. **G.3.2**: 317.

Transport policy **D.7**: 91.

Transportation **D.7**: 92. **G.3.2**: 33.

Travel **F.3**: 159. **H.4**: 42.

Tribal demography **F.3**: 20.

Tribalism **D.9**: 37.

Tribes **D.9**: 51. **E.3**: 17.

Turkana **F.2**: 44.

Turkish language **D.7**: 93, 193.

Turks **F.8**: 66, 172. **I.2**: 66.

Twinning **G.1**: 44.

Typology **C.5**: 85.

Ukrainians **F.8**: 171.

Uncertainty **C.1**: 126. **C.7**: 12. **D.1**: 102. **D.4**: 15. **F.8**: 110. **I.2**: 190.

Underclass **E.2**: 62. **G.3.2**: 176, 210. **I.2**: 240. **K.1**: 290, 292.

Underdevelopment **C.2**: 40. **D.3**: 60. **D.9**: 16–17, 111, 138. **F.7**: 18. **G.3.2**: 248. **J.6**: 9.

Underemployment **I.2**: 68, 215.

Understanding **C.2**: 16, 123. **D.3**: 14.

Unemployed **I.2**: 235.

Unemployment
Entries also appear under:
URBAN UNEMPLOYMENT
C.2: 83. **E.2**: 15. **F.3**: 167. **F.4**: 116, 260. **F.8**: 62. **I.2**: 208, 224–227, 229, 231, 233–234, 236–243, 245–247. **I.3**: 33. **I.4**: 53. **K.1**: 157, 257.

Unemployment insurance **I.2**: 244.

United Nations **F.2**: 103, 112–113. **F.7**: 198.

Universities **A.1**: 6. **D.7**: 5. **D.9**: 104, 144, 174, 176, 178, 180, 188, 191, 193, 196, 198–199, 202, 206–207, 209, 213, 215–217, 219–220. **F.5**: 133. **I.3**: 69. **I.4**: 23, 68, 98. **I.5**: 87, 182. **J.2**: 24.

Unmarried persons **F.3**: 140. **F.5**: 27.

Unskilled workers **F.8**: 57. **I.2**: 188.

Upper class **F.8**: 149.

Urban areas **D.5**: 101. **D.7**: 186. **D.9**: 46, 58, 78, 89. **F.3**: 196, 276. **G.3.2**: 10, 39, 49, 57, 66, 68, 73, 81, 84–85, 89, 162, 166, 169, 183, 192, 195, 202, 210, 352. **J.3**: 13. **K.1**: 86, 88. **K.4**: 209, 213.

Urban communities **D.7**: 67. **K.4**: 208.

Urban concentration **G.3.2**: 107, 230.

Urban design **G.3.2**: 318.

Urban development **G.2**: 23. **G.3.2**: 29, 139, 163, 219, 233, 241, 243, 247, 253–254, 256, 258, 264–265, 268, 270–271, 276, 278, 281, 286, 288, 290, 295, 320, 346. **H.3**: 41. **H.4**: 70. **H.7**: 23. **J.4**: 22.

Urban economics **G.3.2**: 21, 35, 52, 67, 137, 152, 289, 292, 323, 352. **H.3**: 53. **H.7**: 28. **I.2**: 68. **K.1**: 230.

Urban employment **G.3.2**: 181. **I.2**: 1, 13, 173. **I.4**: 45.

Urban environment **G.3.2**: 36, 191.

Urban geography **G.3.2**: 20, 87, 209.

INTERNATIONAL BIBLIOGRAPHY OF SOCIOLOGY — 1991

Urban growth **E.2**: 48. **G.3.2**: 165, 229, 235, 263, 299, 321–322, 342. **I.2**: 5.
Urban housing **G.2**: 34. **G.3.2**: 112–113, 157, 161.
Urban life **D.7**: 94. **G.3.2**: 34, 64, 82, 86, 138, 182, 319. **H.3**: 11.
Urban management **G.3.2**: 269, 324–325.
Urban planning **G.3.2**: 23, 236, 240, 242, 250–252, 257, 261–262, 267, 277, 288, 293–294, 304, 326, 362. **H.7**: 19.
Urban policy **G.3.2**: 190, 243, 283, 286, 295, 309, 319–320, 327, 331, 333, 335. **H.7**: 2. **K.2**: 13, 30.
Urban population **F.1**: 38. **G.3.2**: 180, 185, 342. **I.6**: 20.
Urban poverty **G.2**: 13. **G.3.2**: 4, 120, 176, 213, 226. **K.1**: 232, 258, 265, 285, 291. **K.4**: 114.
Urban renewal **D.8**: 48. **F.5**: 178. **G.3.2**: 46, 48, 234, 239, 245, 249, 266, 274–275, 292, 300, 311, 328, 330–332.
Urban services **G.2**: 13. **K.4**: 46.
Urban society **F.7**: 34. **G.3.2**: 54, 142, 178, 184. **I.2**: 76, 171. **K.1**: 292.
Urban sociology **D.5**: 99. **F.3**: 252. **G.3.2**: 4, 7, 26, 31–32, 37, 43, 47, 55, 62, 71–72, 80, 83, 88, 90–91, 144, 186, 189, 196, 211, 223, 225, 238, 260, 276, 351.
Urban space **G.3.2**: 174, 220, 224, 246. **I.4**: 42.
Urban structure **G.3.2**: 19, 38, 199, 302.
Urban traffic **G.3.2**: 310, 315.
Urban transport **G.3.2**: 33, 79.
Urban unemployment **I.2**: 228.
Urban youth **I.2**: 33. **K.1**: 231.
Urbanism **G.3.2**: 91, 306.
Urbanization **F.2**: 25. **F.3**: 17. **F.4**: 352. **F.5**: 316. **G.3**: 1. **G.3.1**: 16. **G.3.2**: 61, 163–164, 335, 337–338, 340–341, 343–350, 352–353, 355–356, 358–368. **H.5**: 31. **H.7**: 1.
Urban-rural migration **F.8**: 102, 110.
Utilitarianism **C.3**: 49.
Utility measurement **B.2**: 58.
Utopias **B.1**: 24. **D.5**: 59.
Uzbek **F.7**: 179.
Uzbek language **D.7**: 339.
Validity **C.1**: 128. **C.3**: 137. **C.5**: 2. **D.4**: 43. **F.6**: 20.
Vallabha **C.2**: 9.
Value **C.1**: 63. **D.1**: 77, 110, 127, 130. **F.2**: 91. **G.3.2**: 129. **I.1**: 14.
Value systems **F.7**: 169. **I.4**: 27.
Value theory **H.1**: 1.

Values **A.1**: 36. **B.1**: 79. **C.1**: 140. **C.3**: 91, 120. **C.5**: 10. **C.7**: 34. **D.1**: 109, 115, 131, 133, 136. **D.3**: 7, 24, 75. **D.7**: 388. **D.9**: 179. **F.2**: 141. **F.4**: 76. **G.2**: 11. **H.4**: 67. **J.6**: 56. **K.3**: 6, 17.
Vanberg, Viktor **D.1**: 74.
Vendors **G.3.2**: 63.
Verbal communication **C.3**: 22. **D.7**: 144.
Verbs **D.7**: 207.
Verification **B.2**: 89.
Veto **C.4**: 62.
Victims **B.1**: 53. **K.1**: 23, 34, 45, 86.
Victims of crime **K.1**: 14, 76, 78, 112, 126, 132, 134, 161, 184, 191.
Victims of violence **F.4**: 159, 164. **K.1**: 35.
Videos **D.5**: 161. **D.7**: 34, 361. **D.8**: 37. **F.2**: 81. **I.6**: 42.
Vietnamese **F.7**: 112. **F.8**: 3.
Viewers **D.7**: 249.
Villages **E.1**: 6. **G.1**: 4, 49. **G.3**: 11. **G.3.1**: 6–7, 30, 37, 50, 69, 76, 78, 84, 86. **G.3.2**: 328.
Violence
Entries also appear under:
DOMESTIC VIOLENCE; POLITICAL VIOLENCE
C.3: 104, 119. **D.5**: 60, 65, 68, 166, 178. **D.7**: 30, 243, 249. **F.2**: 9. **F.4**: 152. **F.5**: 119, 228, 272. **F.8**: 11. **G.3.2**: 77. **I.5**: 78, 95. **J.2**: 6. **J.5**: 20, 37. **J.7**: 11, 24. **K.1**: 226, 304, 403, 405–408, 410–416, 419–420, 422–430.
Visual communication **D.7**: 140.
Vocabulary **C.2**: 156.
Vocational education **D.9**: 167. **G.3.2**: 236. **I.4**: 130.
Vocational training **D.9**: 192. **F.7**: 265. **I.4**: 74, 117–118, 121–124, 126, 128–129, 131–133.
Voluntary organizations **C.4**: 4. **D.3**: 3. **G.2**: 31. **G.3.1**: 118. **I.4**: 129.
Voluntary work **C.5**: 4. **F.8**: 13. **G.2**: 35. **I.4**: 87. **J.5**: 6. **K.2**: 105. **K.3**: 47. **K.4**: 126.
Voodoo **D.5**: 188.
Voters **J.6**: 32, 66.
Voting **D.1**: 51. **F.5**: 87. **F.7**: 105. **I.5**: 162, 191. **J.6**: 15, 19, 42.
Voting behaviour **B.2**: 47, 73. **F.5**: 20. **I.5**: 87. **J.3**: 28. **J.6**: 26, 59, 62.
Voting turnout **J.6**: 61, 66.
Wage bargaining **H.3**: 69. **I.5**: 148.
Wage determination **H.3**: 5. **I.3**: 18.
Wage differentials **F.1**: 42. **F.5**: 153, 232. **H.3**: 61, 71, 74, 83, 90. **I.2**: 181.
Wage discrimination **F.5**: 235.
Wage earners **F.4**: 302.

Wage flexibility **I.3**: 33.
Wage incentives **I.3**: 51.
Wage levels **H.3**: 70, 87.
Wage mobility **E.2**: 15.
Wage negotiations **I.3**: 10. **I.5**: 68, 125.
Wage rates **F.5**: 176. **H.3**: 67. **I.3**: 44.
Wage theory **I.2**: 60, 205.
Wage-employment relationship **H.3**: 80. **I.3**: 6.
Wages
> *Entries also appear under:*
> MINIMUM WAGES
>
> **F.1**: 42. **F.5**: 156, 235. **F.8**: 27. **H.3**: 2, 43, 69, 82, 91. **I.1**: 14. **I.2**: 3, 47, 57, 92–93, 116. **I.3**: 32, 61, 83, 114. **I.4**: 36. **I.5**: 50, 61, 124, 165, 186.

War
> *Entries also appear under:*
> CIVIL WAR
>
> **D.1**: 114. **D.5**: 60, 154. **D.8**: 78. **F.1**: 1. **F.2**: 117. **F.7**: 186. **G.1**: 39. **J.7**: 8, 16. **J.8**: 14, 18, 20–22.

Waste
> *Entries also appear under:*
> HAZARDOUS WASTES; RADIOACTIVE WASTE

Waste management **D.7**: 188. **G.1**: 26, 43.
Water **D.1**: 48. **G.1**: 42. **G.3.2**: 363.
Water consumption **G.1**: 38.
Water management **G.2**: 16.
Water policy **I.5**: 177.
Wealth **E.3**: 45. **H.3**: 32.
Weapons
> *Entries also appear under:*
> NUCLEAR WEAPONS
>
> **J.7**: 22. **J.8**: 3. **K.1**: 411, 422.

Weavers **F.2**: 95.
Weber, Max **B.1**: 66, 86, 95, 111, 117–118, 125, 130, 133, 136, 138. **D.5**: 93. **D.9**: 144, 179. **H.1**: 5. **J.2**: 1.
Welfare
> *Entries also appear under:*
> SOCIAL WELFARE
>
> **C.7**: 60. **F.2**: 75. **F.3**: 266. **F.4**: 33, 56, 338. **F.5**: 309. **F.7**: 30. **F.8**: 138. **I.2**: 223. **K.1**: 293. **K.2**: 32, 52, 54, 64, 70, 76, 80, 84–85, 99, 111. **K.3**: 31, 33. **K.4**: 21, 241.

Welfare measurement **K.1**: 250, 272.
Welfare policy **F.4**: 15. **K.2**: 87, 103, 107.
Welfare state **D.1**: 123. **F.4**: 47. **F.5**: 184, 225. **I.3**: 62. **K.2**: 2, 77–78, 81, 83, 88, 91, 93–94, 101, 104, 108.
Well-being **B.1**: 48. **C.2**: 36, 38, 58, 76, 82, 89, 96, 101, 104, 211. **C.3**: 49, 84. **C.7**: 65. **F.2**: 40, 47. **F.4**: 59, 121, 134, 140, 265, 335. **F.5**: 14, 211. **G.3.1**: 61. **H.3**: 18, 23, 45.
Welsh **F.7**: 134.
Welsh language **D.7**: 344.
Western countries **D.1**: 53. **D.5**: 55. **D.7**: 2. **F.7**: 106. **J.2**: 31. **K.1**: 117. **K.2**: 65.
Westernization **D.5**: 7. **F.7**: 28.
White collar workers **I.4**: 90. **K.1**: 163.
Whites **D.7**: 5. **D.8**: 42. **D.9**: 176. **E.2**: 3. **F.3**: 238. **F.4**: 212, 218. **F.5**: 67. **F.7**: 3, 43, 146, 172, 197, 208, 234. **H.3**: 88. **I.2**: 8, 75, 141. **I.4**: 42. **K.1**: 12.
Who **K.4**: 68.
Widowhood **F.4**: 62.
Wildlife **I.6**: 28.
Williams, Raymond **D.7**: 376. **G.2**: 27.
Wine **C.5**: 16. **H.5**: 12.
Witchcraft **D.1**: 142. **D.5**: 187.
Wives **F.5**: 8.
Wolfe, Tom **D.7**: 271.
Women
> *Entries also appear under:*
> MARRIED WOMEN; RURAL WOMEN
>
> **C.1**: 68. **C.2**: 3, 75, 83, 98, 218, 226, 229, 234. **C.4**: 63. **D.1**: 22. **D.2**: 12–14. **D.4**: 11, 42. **D.7**: 327, 394. **D.8**: 43, 74–75. **D.9**: 68, 133. **E.2**: 46. **E.3**: 7, 24. **F.1**: 54. **F.2**: 45, 55, 60. **F.3**: 5, 30, 33, 38, 60, 68, 71–72, 96, 108–109, 127, 133, 141–142, 158, 208, 216, 232, 293. **F.4**: 39, 63, 90, 133, 145, 153, 156, 159, 161, 224, 228, 230, 260–263, 321. **F.5**: 4, 15–16, 20–23, 25, 27–28, 32–33, 36–37, 43–46, 48–52, 54–57, 65–67, 96, 107, 116, 130, 138–140, 144–145, 148, 156, 158–159, 161–162, 165, 170–171, 188, 191–192, 195, 198–199, 203, 206–208, 211–212, 214, 219, 221, 225, 228–230, 237, 240–241, 244, 246, 248, 251–255, 257, 260, 276, 280, 292–293, 307–308, 318, 322. **F.6**: 29, 37, 41. **F.8**: 20, 24, 70, 74, 170. **G.1**: 48. **G.2**: 25, 36. **G.3.1**: 44, 60, 75, 80–81, 122. **H.3**: 8, 35, 58. **I.2**: 75, 78–79, 85, 87, 92–93, 98–99, 111, 114, 116–118, 121, 132, 134, 142, 146, 150, 152, 155–157, 162, 184, 213, 215. **I.3**: 137. **I.4**: 69. **J.3**: 38. **J.4**: 25. **J.7**: 1. **J.8**: 21. **K.1**: 4, 20, 24, 50, 63, 136–137, 174, 236, 248, 294, 305, 326, 341, 356, 419, 421. **K.2**: 33, 56, 104. **K.3**: 32. **K.4**: 3, 36, 84, 105, 179, 243.

Women and politics **F.5**: 79, 112, 149, 184, 209, 227, 249, 265, 324–325. **J.4**: 26. **J.5**: 38. **J.6**: 55.
Women workers **F.3**: 95. **F.4**: 56, 114. **F.5**: 2, 18, 41, 53, 146, 150, 166, 220, 226, 231, 247, 250, 259, 278, 309, 317, 321. **F.8**: 170. **H.3**: 91. **H.4**: 62, 77. **I.2**: 36, 72, 74, 76, 82–84, 86,

88–91, 94, 106, 112, 119–120, 122, 127–128, 130, 139–140, 143, 145, 147, 149, 151–156, 160, 180. **I.3**: 34, 88, 108. **I.4**: 27, 59, 98. **I.5**: 6, 145, 170. **J.6**: 20.
Women's education **F.5**: 133, 186, 242, 256, 275.
Women's emancipation **F.5**: 31, 135, 189, 213.
Women's employment **F.4**: 87. **F.5**: 17, 19, 260, 275, 278, 323. **G.3.1**: 71. **I.2**: 77, 110, 124, 158. **I.4**: 104. **K.4**: 150.
Women's health **F.5**: 22, 47, 58–59, 190. **K.1**: 295. **K.4**: 215, 234.
Women's movements **F.5**: 60, 62, 70, 106, 119, 125, 142–143, 149, 210. **J.5**: 19, 38.
Women's organizations **F.5**: 328.
Women's promotion **F.5**: 202.
Women's rights **F.5**: 69, 154, 160, 193, 238, 245.
Women's role **F.5**: 239, 243, 273, 311. **G.3.1**: 74, 79. **H.3**: 57.
Women's status **D.5**: 54, 155. **F.5**: 5, 42, 152, 155, 169, 189, 200, 234, 236, 258, 260–261, 299, 302, 316, 320.
Women's work **F.5**: 39, 61, 236, 290, 313. **G.3.1**: 82. **H.4**: 55. **I.2**: 73.
Work accidents **I.3**: 110, 116.
Work at home **H.4**: 35.
Work environment **I.2**: 161. **I.3**: 11–12, 82.
Work ethic **C.7**: 51. **I.3**: 59. **I.4**: 61.
Work experience **I.3**: 150. **I.4**: 55, 67.
Work incentives **I.2**: 69. **I.3**: 39, 57, 61. **I.4**: 61.
Work motivation **C.2**: 98. **I.4**: 50.
Work organization **C.5**: 23, 49. **H.2**: 5. **I.3**: 67. **I.4**: 57.
Work place **F.5**: 160. **G.1**: 47. **I.2**: 240. **I.3**: 15, 17, 35, 66, 70, 90, 121–122, 126. **I.5**: 11, 96, 110, 134. **K.1**: 344.
Work study **F.4**: 34. **I.4**: 50.
Workers
Entries also appear under:
AGRICULTURAL WORKERS; DISABLED WORKERS; DOMESTIC WORKERS; FOREIGN WORKERS; INDUSTRIAL WORKERS; MIGRANT WORKERS; OFFICE WORKERS; OLDER WORKERS; PROFESSIONAL WORKERS; SELF-EMPLOYED WORKERS; SKILLED WORKERS; SOCIAL WORKERS; UNSKILLED WORKERS; WHITE COLLAR WORKERS; WOMEN WORKERS; YOUNG WORKERS
F.4: 329. **F.8**: 62. **H.3**: 2, 43. **H.7**: 11. **I.2**: 37, 55, 100, 133, 139, 162, 199, 219. **I.3**: 65, 87. **I.4**: 22, 25, 42, 56, 70, 113, 131. **I.5**: 57–58.
Workers' movements **I.4**: 43.
Workers' participation **H.4**: 54. **I.2**: 177. **I.3**: 79, 94. **I.5**: 110, 196–197, 199, 202, 204.
Workers' representation **I.4**: 58. **I.5**: 23.

Workers' self-management **I.5**: 201.
Workers' stock ownership **I.4**: 57.
Working class **E.1**: 22. **E.2**: 49, 65, 72, 74, 81–83. **E.3**: 49. **F.3**: 166. **F.4**: 194. **F.5**: 145, 195, 234. **F.8**: 27. **H.4**: 25. **I.4**: 1. **I.5**: 157. **J.5**: 30. **J.6**: 6.
Working class culture **E.2**: 68. **F.5**: 3, 294.
Working conditions
Entries also appear under:
OVERTIME
C.1: 31. **F.5**: 260. **F.7**: 16. **I.3**: 3, 9, 35–36, 44, 56, 58, 68, 72–74, 146. **I.4**: 41. **K.1**: 342.
Working groups **C.3**: 85. **C.4**: 12. **I.3**: 77.
Working life
Entries also appear under:
ENTRY TO WORKING LIFE
H.2: 2. **I.4**: 89, 119.
Working mothers **C.6**: 10. **F.2**: 89. **F.4**: 87, 280, 288. **I.2**: 89, 147, 159.
Working time arrangements **I.2**: 54, 127.
Working women **I.2**: 157.
Workshops **H.4**: 77.
World Bank **G.3.1**: 110. **G.3.2**: 158.
World economy **G.3.1**: 114.
World order **D.1**: 63. **D.5**: 24. **J.8**: 4, 10.
World religions
Entries also appear under:
CHRISTIANITY; HINDUISM; ISLAM; JUDAISM
World view **F.2**: 5.
Worship **D.5**: 86, 148.
Wright, Frank Lloyd **D.8**: 15.
Writers **D.8**: 11, 30.
Writing **D.1**: 77. **D.7**: 17, 54, 158, 190, 324.
Written language **D.7**: 135, 191.
Xenophobia **C.4**: 31. **F.7**: 219.
Yiddish language **D.7**: 88, 99.
Yoruba **C.7**: 77. **D.5**: 162. **F.6**: 9.
Young workers **F.1**: 42.
Youth
Entries also appear under:
URBAN YOUTH
C.2: 107, 204. **C.3**: 9, 43. **D.4**: 32. **D.7**: 134, 181, 263. **D.8**: 61. **D.9**: 13, 169, 183. **F.2**: 10, 118, 123, 125, 127–129, 131, 133–141, 144, 146, 148–158. **F.4**: 32, 76, 116. **F.6**: 17, 39. **F.7**: 177. **F.8**: 13, 28, 38, 62, 143. **G.3.2**: 143. **I.2**: 23, 31, 166, 174, 215, 229, 234. **I.3**: 23. **I.4**: 67, 133. **I.5**: 89. **J.3**: 13. **J.6**: 11, 39, 41. **K.1**: 172, 214, 235, 237, 253, 287, 300, 315, 387, 401. **K.2**: 16, 42. **K.3**: 23, 37. **K.4**: 118.
Youth and politics **D.1**: 136. **F.7**: 219.
Youth culture **F.2**: 121-122, 124.

Youth employment **H.3**: 67. **I.2**: 8. **I.4**: 116, 132.
Youth unrest **C.4**: 33. **K.1**: 404.
Yü, Han **D.5**: 3.
Yugoslavs **F.8**: 81.
Zen **D.5**: 81. **I.3**: 95.
Zionism **F.7**: 178. **G.3.2**: 259.
Zoning **G.3.1**: 22. **G.3.2**: 271.
Zoroastrianism **D.5**: 75, 80.
Zumbercani **F.7**: 137.

INDEX DES MATIÈRES

Abandon d'enfant **F.2**: 99. **K.1**: 44.
Aborigènes **C.1**: 25. **D.8**: 57. **D.9**: 4. **F.1**: 55. **K.2**: 73.
Absentéisme **I.3**: 21, 52, 73, 78. **I.5**: 199.
Accès à l'éducation **D.9**: 132, 149.
Accès à l'emploi **I.2**: 79.
Accès au marché **H.5**: 1.
Accidents **C.2**: 184. **F.2**: 51.
Accidents du travail **I.3**: 107, 110–111, 113, 116.
Accidents nucléaires **C.5**: 45. **C.7**: 53. **D.7**: 37, 312. **K.1**: 1.
Accomplissement **C.3**: 2. **F.4**: 103. **I.3**: 96. **J.6**: 58.
Accomplissement scolaire **C.2**: 172. **D.9**: 38, 110, 116, 122, 142, 155. **F.3**: 88. **F.4**: 16, 120, 142. **H.3**: 71. **I.3**: 150.
Accords internationaux **I.2**: 67.
Acculturation **C.1**: 75. **C.2**: 78. **D.1**: 139.
Ackerman, Bruce **J.2**: 15.
Acquisition d'information **C.2**: 24, 161.
Acquisition de connaissances **C.2**: 163, 166. **C.7**: 1. **D.7**: 73. **D.9**: 24, 31, 117, 194. **F.5**: 167. **I.4**: 56. **K.3**: 24.
Acquisition du langage **D.7**: 23, 40–41, 46, 73.
Acteurs **I.2**: 54. **I.4**: 30.
Action collective **B.2**: 67. **C.7**: 16. **F.8**: 9. **G.2**: 3, 12. **G.3.2**: 53. **H.4**: 73. **I.5**: 118. **J.5**: 13, 33.
Action politique **D.7**: 276.
Action sociale **B.1**: 133. **D.7**: 149. **F.5**: 125. **K.4**: 237.
Activistes **D.5**: 78. **J.5**: 21, 35. **J.6**: 11, 39.
Activité bancaire **H.6**: 3. **I.4**: 10. **K.1**: 318.
Activité politique **E.2**: 49. **F.8**: 3. **J.5**: 21, 30. **J.6**: 27.
Activités ludiques **C.3**: 58. **F.2**: 117.
Adaptation au changement **F.8**: 73.
Adaptation culturelle **F.7**: 112.
Adaptation des immigrants **F.8**: 68, 75, 77.
Adaptation sociale **D.1**: 5. **F.3**: 194. **G.2**: 31.

Adhésion syndicale **I.5**: 131–132, 156, 164, 175, 195.
Administration **C.2**: 176.
Administration de l'enseignement **D.9**: 83.
Administration de la justice **J.3**: 13. **K.1**: 173.
Administration de la santé **K.4**: 228.
Administration du développement **I.3**: 89.
Administration locale **D.7**: 272. **F.3**: 147. **F.5**: 249. **F.7**: 175. **G.2**: 19, 29. **G.3.2**: 254. **J.4**: 6–7, 19–20, 22, 26. **J.6**: 24.
Administration publique **D.3**: 61. **G.3.2**: 90. **J.4**: 2, 5, 8, 12, 16, 18, 21, 23–25.
Administration scolaire **D.9**: 11.
Adolescence **C.1**: 76, 115. **C.2**: 18, 58, 225. **C.3**: 29. **F.2**: 120, 130. **F.3**: 112, 197. **F.4**: 351. **F.5**: 172. **I.4**: 55. **K.1**: 217, 279.
Adolescents **C.2**: 187. **C.3**: 3, 75–76, 110. **C.7**: 3. **D.5**: 51. **D.7**: 103, 386. **D.9**: 106, 161. **F.2**: 2, 17, 106, 119, 142–143, 145. **F.3**: 73, 126, 186, 200. **F.4**: 32, 273, 320. **F.6**: 1, 13–14, 32. **F.7**: 84. **H.4**: 78. **I.2**: 145, 208. **J.6**: 59. **K.1**: 9, 12, 42, 108, 297, 331, 333, 350, 361, 369, 401, 410. **K.4**: 128.
Adoption d'enfant **F.1**: 40. **F.2**: 73, 83, 98. **F.4**: 264, 272, 278, 289, 315. **F.7**: 68, 125. **K.3**: 35.
Adorno, Theodor W. **D.8**: 1, 21.
Adultes **C.1**: 77, 92. **C.2**: 3, 58, 158, 195. **C.3**: 11. **D.5**: 12. **F.2**: 15, 69–70, 96, 105. **F.3**: 226, 254. **F.4**: 134, 159, 285, 287. **H.3**: 59. **I.2**: 122. **I.3**: 12. **K.1**: 35–36, 81, 279, 407.
Adventisme du septième jour **D.5**: 89.
Aéroports **G.3.2**: 224.
Affectation des ressources **E.2**: 44. **F.5**: 174. **G.2**: 16. **H.5**: 33. **K.4**: 173.
Affectivité **C.1**: 37. **C.2**: 36, 82. **C.7**: 4. **F.6**: 30.
Affiliation **C.3**: 6, 37. **D.7**: 35. **F.4**: 246.
Affiliation politique **J.1**: 18. **J.6**: 12.
Affiliation religieuse **D.5**: 10, 50. **D.7**: 35. **F.7**: 86.
Africains **F.8**: 24, 111. **K.2**: 18.

476

Âgé **C.1**: 2. **D.7**: 294. **F.2**: 10, 23, 36, 38–39, 45–46, 48–49, 51–52, 55–56, 59–61, 64–66. **F.4**: 287. **F.5**: 55, 168. **F.7**: 15. **F.8**: 74, 85. **G.3.2**: 37. **H.3**: 73. **K.1**: 412. **K.2**: 17, 28, 74, 85. **K.3**: 42. **K.4**: 116–117, 122, 126, 133, 138, 141–142, 147, 149, 199.

Âge au mariage **F.4**: 118, 208, 249, 334. **F.5**: 2.

Agression personnelle **C.3**: 143. **C.4**: 8. **C.7**: 10. **D.3**: 76. **F.2**: 74, 110. **F.4**: 239. **F.6**: 50. **K.1**: 417, 423, 427.

Agression sexuelle **F.2**: 77. **F.4**: 135, 151, 157, 159, 171–172. **F.5**: 119, 228. **I.3**: 66. **K.1**: 33–38, 43, 45, 50, 87, 100, 122, 144.

Agriculteurs **F.3**: 92. **G.1**: 13. **G.3.1**: 10–11, 62, 67, 99. **H.3**: 38. **I.2**: 143.

Agriculture **F.5**: 24, 293, 301. **F.8**: 110. **G.3**: 3, 9. **G.3.1**: 1, 11, 17, 28, 57, 81, 90, 107, 110, 114, 133. **G.3.2**: 10, 343. **H.4**: 1, 4, 19, 44, 82.

Agriexploitation **G.3.1**: 20. **G.3.2**: 84. **H.3**: 9. **H.4**: 12, 101. **I.2**: 97.

Aide à l'enfance **F.2**: 68, 93, 100, 115. **F.4**: 24, 177, 275, 277, 324. **I.2**: 77, 108, 147. **I.3**: 12. **K.2**: 35–37, 39–45, 47–48, 50–56, 58–62, 64–66, 68–69. **K.3**: 7. **K.4**: 51, 155.

Aide à l'étranger **G.3.1**: 127.

Aide aux gens âgés **F.2**: 41. **F.4**: 54–55, 95. **K.2**: 12, 17, 25, 28, 33, 71–72, 74, 86. **K.3**: 42. **K.4**: 34, 110, 116–117, 133–137, 139, 141, 144–148, 199.

Aide de l'État **D.9**: 39.

Aires métropolitaines **F.7**: 51. **F.8**: 46. **G.3**: 5, 9. **G.3.2**: 44, 58, 60, 110, 175, 184, 199, 205, 217, 299, 302, 352. **H.3**: 53. **H.7**: 28. **I.2**: 228.

Ajustement structurel **G.3.1**: 108. **H.3**: 50, 56. **I.2**: 98, 143, 228. **I.3**: 83. **K.1**: 249. **K.4**: 20.

Alcool **C.2**: 206. **D.7**: 333, 359. **F.2**: 129. **F.4**: 297. **H.5**: 17. **I.6**: 19. **K.1**: 299–301, 305, 307, 326, 333, 342–343, 347, 351–352, 355, 359, 363, 366, 369, 374, 376, 378.

Alcoolisme **C.1**: 174. **C.2**: 173. **D.2**: 24. **F.2**: 79. **K.1**: 296, 302–304, 306, 308–310, 312, 329, 356, 361, 382.

Algorithme **B.2**: 62.

Aliénation **C.3**: 56.

Aliénation politique **J.1**: 19.

Alimentation **C.2**: 30, 229, 236.

Aliments **F.1**: 45. **F.3**: 256. **F.5**: 61. **G.3.1**: 44. **H.3**: 68.

Allaitement **F.3**: 110.

Allaitement naturel **F.3**: 79–80. **F.4**: 268.

Alliances **C.5**: 86.

Allocations familiales **K.2**: 49, 79.

Allocations logement **K.2**: 10.

Allocations vieillesse **K.2**: 9, 28.

Alphabétisation **A.3**: 5. **D.1**: 77. **D.7**: 46, 366. **D.9**: 16, 29, 85. **F.5**: 237. **I.2**: 188.

Altruisme **C.2**: 181, 184. **C.3**: 95–97, 99–100, 103. **C.4**: 34. **C.7**: 25. **D.4**: 23. **D.5**: 86. **G.1**: 31.

Aménagement d'habitation **F.2**: 38, 66, 153. **F.4**: 309, 343, 351.

Aménagement du temps de travail **I.2**: 54, 127.

Aménagement hydraulique **G.2**: 16.

Aménagement urbain **G.3.2**: 23, 236, 240, 242, 250–252, 257, 261–262, 267, 277, 288, 293–294, 304, 326, 362. **H.7**: 19.

Amendements à la constitution **D.5**: 177.

Amérindiens **A.2**: 6. **F.7**: 38, 105, 169. **K.1**: 49.

Amérindiens du Sud **G.3.1**: 87.

Amiante **H.4**: 7.

Amish **D.5**: 149. **E.3**: 38.

Amitié **C.3**: 7, 18, 35, 38, 129. **D.3**: 12, 25.

Analyse causale **C.1**: 144.

Analyse comparative **B.2**: 74. **D.1**: 8, 77. **F.3**: 79. **F.7**: 20, 61. **I.4**: 79. **K.4**: 137.

Analyse coût-avantage **F.4**: 21. **I.2**: 235. **I.3**: 38.

Analyse d'enquête **B.2**: 31, 89–90, 92, 130. **C.2**: 62. **H.5**: 25.

Analyse de décision **B.2**: 82. **C.5**: 27.

Analyse de discours **C.3**: 12. **D.5**: 13. **D.7**: 12, 119–120, 122, 130, 135–137, 154, 165, 167, 172, 191, 268, 392. **F.5**: 203. **I.2**: 145. **K.3**: 10.

Analyse de groupe **C.4**: 14, 23, 32, 42, 50, 53–54.

Analyse de motivation **C.3**: 102.

Analyse de régression **B.2**: 85. **C.1**: 61. **F.3**: 47. **I.2**: 70.

Analyse de réseau **B.2**: 5, 76, 79. **C.4**: 58. **C.5**: 25. **D.7**: 10–11, 50, 65. **D.9**: 2. **I.2**: 232.

Analyse de systèmes **A.3**: 4. **C.5**: 41, 80.

Analyse des données **B.2**: 36, 40, 64, 74, 88. **K.1**: 61.

Analyse des politiques gouvernementales **G.3.2**: 333.

Analyse des tâches **I.2**: 57. **I.3**: 54.

Analyse diachronique **D.7**: 216.

Analyse différentielle **F.3**: 245, 295.

Analyse du discours **C.2**: 165. **D.7**: 151.

Analyse hiérarchique **B.2**: 41, 70.

Analyse input-output **I.2**: 12.

Analyse marxiste **B.1**: 128.

Analyse mathématique **B.2**: 50, 52, 85.

Analyse organisationnelle **A.3**: 4. **C.5**: 7, 24. **J.6**: 58.

Analyse par agrégats **D.4**: 39.
Analyse par cohorte **F.3**: 167.
Analyse par grappe **B.2**: 50. **G.3.2**: 217. **I.5**: 88.
Analyse qualitative **I.2**: 239.
Analyse régionale **D.9**: 174. **F.1**: 64. **G.3.1**: 20. **H.3**: 88.
Analyse sociologique **B.2**: 40, 48, 56, 63. **D.1**: 102, 120. **D.3**: 83. **F.7**: 269.
Analyse statistique **B.2**: 36, 66, 69, 80. **I.4**: 13.
Analyse structurale **B.2**: 62. **C.4**: 6. **F.1**: 63. **H.3**: 46.
Analyse synchronique **D.7**: 216.
Analyse transactionnelle **I.3**: 85.
Analyse transculturelle **C.1**: 66. **C.3**: 111. **D.1**: 52. **F.5**: 32, 34. **H.7**: 13.
Analyse transnationale **C.5**: 63. **H.5**: 17. **I.2**: 184. **K.1**: 77.
Androgynie **C.2**: 226.
Angoisse **C.2**: 5, 8, 191, 240. **C.3**: 50, 159. **F.4**: 318. **G.3.2**: 2. **K.1**: 329.
Animaux **F.5**: 121–122.
Animaux sauvages **I.6**: 28.
Anonymat **D.3**: 57. **H.3**: 30.
Anorexie **C.2**: 74.
Ansari, M.A. **D.5**: 169.
Anthropologie **B.2**: 26. **F.5**: 171. **K.1**: 404.
Anthropologie culturelle **D.1**: 56. **D.4**: 36.
Anthropologie du droit **D.4**: 35.
Anthropologie économique **G.1**: 6.
Anthropologie médicale **K.4**: 15.
Anthropologie rurale **G.3.1**: 26.
Anthropométrie **K.4**: 177.
Antiquité grecque **D.5**: 99.
Antiquité romaine **D.5**: 99.
Antisémitisme **D.5**: 88. **F.7**: 36, 216–218, 241, 244.
Apartheid **D.7**: 243. **F.7**: 269. **F.8**: 109. **G.3.2**: 341, 362.
Apparence physique **F.5**: 1.
Appartenance au groupe **C.3**: 154. **C.4**: 13.
Apprentissage **I.4**: 127.
Approbation sociale **J.6**: 19.
Aptitude **C.2**: 116. **D.7**: 56. **I.3**: 14.
Aquaculture **G.1**: 1.
Arabes **C.3**: 28. **D.7**: 2. **D.9**: 142. **F.4**: 142. **F.7**: 47, 129, 140–141, 160, 180. **H.3**: 27. **K.2**: 100. **K.4**: 55.
Arbitrage **C.3**: 104. **I.5**: 3, 61, 74, 82.
Arbitrage forcé **I.5**: 101.

Archéologie **F.5**: 99.
Architecture **D.8**: 65, 70. **G.3.2**: 5, 285. **K.1**: 66.
Arendt, Hannah **J.2**: 15.
Argent **D.5**: 127. **F.4**: 113. **H.5**: 9. **H.6**: 2, 10–11.
Armée de terre **I.5**: 165. **J.7**: 15.
Armes **J.7**: 22. **J.8**: 3. **K.1**: 411, 422.
Armes á feu **D.2**: 26. **K.1**: 90.
Armes nucléaires **C.7**: 48.
Aronowitz, Stanley **J.1**: 6.
Art dramatique **D.8**: 13, 22, 28.
Artisanat **I.2**: 140.
Artisans **F.4**: 78. **I.3**: 56. **I.4**: 37.
Arts **C.1**: 80, 110. **D.7**: 365, 393. **D.8**: 3, 7, 23–24, 26, 32–33, 42, 44–45, 56, 64, 71, 73, 76, 393. **G.3.2**: 40.
Arts du spectacle **D.8**: 4, 9–10, 37.
Ascendance **F.1**: 11.
Asiatiques **D.9**: 109. **F.2**: 19. **F.7**: 9, 41, 84, 142. **F.8**: 112. **I.2**: 74, 180. **J.6**: 1. **K.1**: 12, 264. **K.4**: 42.
Aspects juridiques **B.2**: 55. **F.3**: 159. **J.2**: 7.
Aspirations **F.4**: 96. **F.7**: 20.
Assimilation culturelle **F.7**: 107. **F.8**: 65, 84.
Assimilation des immigrants **D.7**: 123. **F.7**: 92. **F.8**: 22.
Assimilation ethnique **F.7**: 72, 92, 106, 135.
Assistance socio-psychologique **D.7**: 173. **F.3**: 228. **F.4**: 213, 259. **K.3**: 18, 46. **K.4**: 128.
Associations **C.4**: 2.
Associations de quartier **C.5**: 9.
Assurance chômage **I.2**: 244.
Assurance maladie **I.2**: 111. **K.4**: 77, 179, 224.
Assurances **G.3.2**: 192. **K.1**: 163. **K.4**: 63.
Ateliers **H.4**: 77.
Athlètes **I.6**: 4.
Attention **C.1**: 82. **C.2**: 54, 67. **C.3**: 148. **D.7**: 369.
Attention à soi **C.2**: 223.
Attitude envers le travail **I.3**: 101.
Attitude moraliste envers le travail **C.7**: 51. **I.3**: 59. **I.4**: 61.
Attitudes **B.2**: 19–20. **C.7**: 3, 8–9, 28, 40, 57, 60, 63–64, 75. **D.3**: 90. **D.7**: 51, 344. **D.9**: 108, 120. **F.2**: 27, 96, 122. **F.3**: 30, 52, 59, 62, 160, 202–203. **F.4**: 258. **F.5**: 147. **F.8**: 61. **G.1**: 13. **H.4**: 104. **H.5**: 19, 31. **I.2**: 219. **I.4**: 5, 18, 69. **I.5**: 2, 134. **J.1**: 2, 11. **J.8**: 1. **K.1**: 206, 223. **K.2**: 29.
Attitudes collectives **E.3**: 58.
Attitudes culturelles **C.7**: 73.

478

Attitudes politiques **D.7**: 382. **F.7**: 219. **J.1**: 16. **J.6**: 32, 37, 39, 41. **K.2**: 82.
Attitudes religieuses **F.2**: 5.
Attraction interpersonnelle **C.3**: 9–10, 22, 55, 92, 146.
Attribution du nom **D.7**: 182, 195. **F.7**: 22.
Autoassistance **C.4**: 51.
Autobiographies **F.5**: 254.
Autodétermination **K.3**: 34.
Automation **H.4**: 81. **I.4**: 21.
Automobile **F.7**: 234. **H.4**: 30. **I.2**: 210.
Autonomie **F.7**: 95.
Autoritarisme **F.3**: 178. **F.8**: 59. **J.3**: 1. **J.6**: 49.
Autorité **C.3**: 155.
Autorités religieuses **D.5**: 141.
Avantage comparé **I.5**: 189.
Avocat **I.4**: 100.
Avortement **D.3**: 11. **D.5**: 6. **F.3**: 30, 34, 38, 49, 52, 54, 57, 59, 62, 67, 70. **F.4**: 178. **F.5**: 223. **F.7**: 117. **J.6**: 15. **K.3**: 30.
Azeri **F.7**: 87.
Bacon, Francis
 D.8: 14.
Baisse de la fécondité **F.3**: 77, 121.
Bangladeshis **F.8**: 70.
Banque mondiale **G.3.1**: 110. **G.3.2**: 158.
Barrières culturelles **F.7**: 64.
Bases de données **F.3**: 29.
Basques **F.7**: 135.
Bataille des prix **G.1**: 36.
Bâtiment **D.8**: 65, 70.
Baudrillard, Jean
 B.1: 88–89.
Bédouin **F.3**: 291.
Beer, Stafford
 C.5: 11.
Behaviorisme **C.1**: 136. **C.2**: 7, 87.
Bendix, R.
 B.1: 101.
Bengali **D.1**: 20.
Besoins d'éducation **D.9**: 130.
Besoins de logement **G.3.2**: 131.
Beurre **H.5**: 31.
Biculturalisme **D.7**: 331. **F.7**: 114.
Bien-être **B.1**: 48. **C.2**: 36, 38, 58, 76, 82, 89, 96, 101, 104, 211. **C.3**: 49, 84. **C.7**: 60, 65. **F.2**: 40, 47, 75. **F.3**: 266. **F.4**: 33, 56, 59, 121, 134, 140, 265, 335, 338. **F.5**: 14, 211, 309. **F.7**: 30. **F.8**: 138. **G.3.1**: 61. **H.3**: 18, 23, 45. **I.2**: 223. **K.1**: 293. **K.2**: 32, 52, 54, 64, 70, 76, 80, 84–85, 99, 111. **K.3**: 31, 33. **K.4**: 21, 241.

Bien-être social **E.3**: 59. **F.5**: 140. **K.1**: 227. **K.2**: 82, 92. **K.3**: 36.
Biens publics **B.2**: 58. **D.5**: 102.
Bilinguisme **D.7**: 45, 331, 333, 348–350.
Biochimie **C.7**: 13.
Biographies **B.2**: 33. **D.1**: 114.
Biographies orales **B.2**: 16.
Biologie **A.1**: 4. **D.4**: 27, 29. **D.6**: 3. **F.6**: 15, 51.
Biologie humaine **K.1**: 109.
Biologie sociale **D.4**: 35. **E.2**: 2. **F.4**: 77. **G.1**: 3.
Biotechnologie **D.3**: 46, 49. **F.3**: 115, 142. **H.4**: 80, 82. **J.4**: 13. **K.4**: 271.
Blancs **D.7**: 5. **D.8**: 42. **D.9**: 176. **E.2**: 3. **F.3**: 238. **F.4**: 212, 218. **F.5**: 67. **F.7**: 3, 43, 146, 172, 197, 208, 234. **H.3**: 88. **I.2**: 8, 75, 141. **I.4**: 42. **K.1**: 12.
Blasphème **D.5**: 175.
Bohémiens **C.7**: 30. **D.7**: 70. **F.7**: 23, 65, 93, 111. **K.1**: 19.
Bonheur **C.2**: 56, 60, 62, 212. **F.4**: 220.
Bouddhisme **D.1**: 11. **D.5**: 81, 83–85, 87.
Bouddhistes **D.5**: 82.
Bourgeoisie **E.2**: 43.
Bourse **I.2**: 1.
Bradley, F.H.
 D.6: 9.
Brahmanisme **D.5**: 158.
Brasserie **H.4**: 51.
Braverman, H.
 I.1: 1.
Bruit **C.2**: 67. **G.1**: 50.
Budgets des ménages **H.5**: 20.
Budgets temps **B.2**: 89.
Burawoy, M.
 I.1: 1.
Bureaucratie **C.5**: 29. **E.2**: 20. **I.5**: 190. **J.3**: 31. **J.4**: 13–14.
Bureautique **I.3**: 27. **I.4**: 2.
Burke, Edmund
 B.1: 149.
Burr, Donald
 C.6: 1.
But de l'organisation **H.4**: 20.
Buveurs **C.2**: 206. **K.1**: 374.
Cadres **C.2**: 152. **C.5**: 19. **E.2**: 17. **F.5**: 202. **I.2**: 120, 168. **I.4**: 69, 71, 73–75, 78–79, 83, 111.
Cadres supérieurs **I.4**: 80.
Cajun **F.7**: 54.
Campagne **D.1**: 3.
Campagne électorale **D.7**: 280.

Cancer **F.3**: 166.
Candidats **C.7**: 56. **I.3**: 138. **J.6**: 16.
Capital **D.4**: 9. **G.3.2**: 222.
Capitalisme **B.1**: 150. **D.1**: 111. **D.2**: 20. **D.3**: 54. **D.5**: 78. **F.5**: 129, 148. **G.2**: 28. **G.3.1**: 86. **H.2**: 11–12. **J.2**: 3. **J.3**: 33.
Caractère **C.2**: 6. **C.3**: 129. **D.3**: 21. **F.2**: 148.
Caractère national **D.1**: 117, 119. **D.2**: 7. **F.7**: 94.
Carpatho-Rusyn **F.7**: 100.
Cartographie **D.7**: 159. **F.1**: 37. **G.1**: 17.
Castes **C.4**: 13. **E.2**: 1, 24, 37, 73, 79. **F.3**: 110. **I.5**: 123.
Catégorisation de soi **C.3**: 74.
Catholicisme **D.3**: 23. **D.5**: 126, 136, 141–142.
Catholiques **D.5**: 104, 137, 146. **E.2**: 18.
Causalité **B.1**: 55. **C.1**: 141. **D.7**: 207. **F.3**: 276.
Cécité **C.2**: 138.
Célibat **F.6**: 7.
Célibataires **F.3**: 140. **F.5**: 27.
Censure **F.5**: 114.
Centralisation **D.9**: 153. **H.4**: 4.
Centre droit **F.8**: 29.
Cercles de qualité **I.3**: 92. **I.5**: 31.
Cérémonies **D.2**: 27. **D.5**: 15.
Certeau, de, Michel **A.2**: 11.
Chances d'obtenir un emploi **I.2**: 8, 212. **I.4**: 62. **J.7**: 6.
Changement culturel **D.2**: 17. **D.7**: 41. **E.3**: 26. **F.5**: 108. **F.8**: 70.
Changement d'attitude **C.1**: 63. **C.4**: 61. **C.7**: 24.
Changement d'organisation **C.5**: 13, 16, 32, 36, 56, 58. **I.3**: 79, 124.
Changement de rôle **C.6**: 10.
Changement démographique **F.1**: 48–50, 66–67. **F.3**: 6, 10, 14, 16, 22, 25, 82, 96, 156, 301. **F.4**: 26, 40. **G.3**: 1. **I.2**: 98. **K.1**: 79.
Changement économique **A.1**: 16. **E.3**: 41. **H.3**: 3.
Changement linguistique **C.2**: 134. **D.7**: 75.
Changement politique **A.1**: 16, 25, 34. **D.7**: 97, 377. **E.3**: 4, 19, 26. **F.4**: 184. **F.5**: 213. **F.7**: 127. **J.1**: 21. **J.3**: 4, 32. **J.6**: 38, 40, 57.
Changement religieux **D.5**: 31, 63, 67, 158.
Changement social **A.1**: 16. **B.1**: 12, 108, 139. **C.2**: 10, 187. **C.5**: 47. **D.4**: 10. **D.5**: 26. **D.6**: 28. **D.7**: 41, 124. **D.8**: 55–56. **D.9**: 51. **E.1**: 1, 25. **E.3**: 1, 4–5, 7–13, 19–20, 24–25, 28–29, 31, 33, 41, 45, 47, 49–50, 57–61, 65, 67, 71, 74. **F.2**: 150. **F.3**: 63, 72. **F.5**: 178, 307, 314.

F.7: 127. **F.8**: 39. **G.2**: 3. **G.3.1**: 48, 123, 131. **G.3.2**: 205, 346, 359. **H.3**: 3–4. **H.4**: 1, 99. **I.4**: 96. **J.6**: 53. **K.1**: 147, 284. **K.2**: 22. **K.3**: 36.
Changement structurel **G.3.1**: 52, 106.
Changement technologique **D.7**: 257, 292. **D.9**: 55. **E.3**: 36. **G.3.2**: 246, 284. **H.3**: 52. **H.4**: 84, 93, 98, 101. **I.2**: 10. **I.3**: 27, 45, 87. **I.5**: 167, 184.
Charbonnages **D.4**: 17. **G.3.2**: 14. **I.4**: 54.
Charisme **J.6**: 4, 31.
Châtiment **B.1**: 60. **C.3**: 87. **D.1**: 134. **F.2**: 84. **K.1**: 81, 124, 212, 424.
Chauffage mondiale **H.4**: 103.
Chefs d'entreprise **F.5**: 226. **H.4**: 78.
Chemins de fer **I.3**: 9. **I.5**: 59.
Chinois **F.7**: 26, 35, 57, 170. **F.8**: 67. **H.4**: 36.
Chirurgie **F.5**: 1.
Choix collectif **C.2**: 94. **C.7**: 61–62.
Choix d'une profession **C.3**: 57. **I.2**: 75–76. **I.4**: 19, 29, 51, 67, 75.
Choix du conjoint **F.3**: 113. **F.4**: 211, 247. **F.6**: 31.
Choix économique **I.3**: 98.
Choix rationnelle **B.1**: 71.
Chômage **C.2**: 83. **E.2**: 15. **F.3**: 167. **F.4**: 116, 260. **F.8**: 62. **I.2**: 208, 224–227, 229, 231, 233–234, 236–243, 245–247. **I.3**: 33. **I.4**: 53. **K.1**: 157, 257.
Chômage partiel **I.2**: 68, 215.
Chômage urbain **I.2**: 228.
Chômeurs **I.2**: 235.
Chrétiens **B.1**: 117. **D.5**: 94, 104. **F.5**: 15. **F.7**: 238. **H.2**: 15.
Christianisation **D.5**: 99.
Christianisme **D.5**: 83, 92, 95–98, 105, 112, 117, 120, 122–123, 133, 138, 148, 167, 170. **F.4**: 198. **F.6**: 17.
Cinéma **D.8**: 6, 12, 20, 27, 50, 58, 77.
Circulation **F.3**: 230. **G.1**: 50. **G.3.2**: 316. **J.3**: 41.
Circulation urbaine **G.3.2**: 310, 315.
Cirque **D.7**: 25, 72.
Citoyenneté **C.5**: 68. **D.4**: 6. **D.7**: 241. **E.3**: 22. **F.5**: 279. **F.8**: 8, 160. **G.3.2**: 7, 176. **J.2**: 4. **J.3**: 6, 18.
Citoyens **E.1**: 5. **G.2**: 18. **G.3.2**: 248.
Civilisation **B.1**: 5, 12, 18. **D.1**: 7, 57, 62, 65, 81–82, 86, 88, 90, 93, 95–96, 105, 109, 116–117. **F.7**: 43, 94. **G.3.2**: 92. **H.5**: 15. **I.6**: 36. **J.8**: 8.
Classe **B.2**: 32. **C.2**: 26. **C.4**: 13. **C.5**: 39. **C.7**: 15. **D.1**: 14. **D.7**: 209, 327, 357. **D.9**: 114. **E.2**: 3, 12, 51–52, 54–69, 71–72, 74–80, 82, 84. **F.2**: 49. **F.3**: 287, 289. **F.5**: 56, 258. **F.7**: 1, 3, 12,

56, 66, 149, 207. **G.2**: 3–4. **G.3.1**: 85, 132. **G.3.2**: 14, 112, 214. **H.3**: 73. **H.4**: 44, 77. **H.5**: 16. **H.6**: 9. **I.2**: 89. **I.4**: 9, 11. **I.5**: 123. **J.4**: 22. **J.6**: 25, 59. **K.1**: 86. **K.2**: 35. **K.4**: 3.

Classe dirigeante **E.2**: 65.

Classe moyenne **D.1**: 20. **E.2**: 4, 70, 84. **F.4**: 19. **F.7**: 208. **F.8**: 149. **G.3.2**: 139. **J.6**: 63. **K.1**: 68, 361.

Classe ouvrière **E.1**: 22. **E.2**: 49, 65, 72, 74, 81–83. **E.3**: 49. **F.3**: 166. **F.4**: 194. **F.5**: 145, 195, 234. **F.8**: 27. **H.4**: 25. **I.4**: 1. **I.5**: 157. **J.5**: 30. **J.6**: 6.

Classe supérieure **F.8**: 149.

Classification **B.1**: 23. **B.2**: 106. **C.1**: 132. **E.2**: 60. **G.3.2**: 12. **K.1**: 188.

Classification des emplois **I.3**: 37.

Clientélisme **C.5**: 44. **E.2**: 20. **I.5**: 18.

Coalition **C.5**: 71, 81.

Coca **K.1**: 320–321.

Cocaïne **K.1**: 322–323, 327.

Code déontologique des affaires **D.3**: 31–32, 52–54. **I.3**: 95.

Code déontologique médical **D.3**: 59. **F.3**: 163. **K.4**: 148–149, 242, 245–247, 253–254, 260, 262–265.

Codes juridiques **D.4**: 18.

Coexistence pacifique **F.7**: 144.

Cognition **B.2**: 96. **C.1**: 20, 85–86, 169. **C.2**: 111, 113–117, 119–134, 136–141. **C.3**: 73, 102. **C.4**: 23. **C.7**: 4, 6, 14, 39. **D.6**: 13. **D.7**: 61. **D.9**: 151. **E.3**: 64. **H.5**: 24.

Cognition sociale **C.2**: 135. **D.1**: 19. **D.4**: 38. **J.6**: 16.

Cohabitation **F.4**: 217, 230, 238–239.

Cohortes **F.3**: 34. **J.1**: 2. **J.6**: 56. **K.1**: 123.

Collections de musées **D.8**: 35.

Collections privées **D.8**: 3.

Collectivisme **C.7**: 23.

Collectivité **C.3**: 108. **C.5**: 9. **D.1**: 6, 112–113. **D.5**: 137, 179. **D.7**: 39, 190, 290. **F.4**: 61. **F.5**: 138. **F.6**: 3. **F.7**: 6, 73, 110, 151. **F.8**: 77. **G.1**: 31. **G.2**: 3–4, 8–11, 17, 21, 24–25, 31. **G.3.2**: 13, 16, 71, 285. **I.2**: 44, 78. **J.6**: 36. **K.1**: 170, 223, 306. **K.3**: 7, 12. **K.4**: 111.

Collectivité de travail **H.4**: 30.

Collectivités locales **H.3**: 1. **K.4**: 6.

Collectivités rurales **G.1**: 49. **G.3.1**: 36, 65, 98, 136. **K.4**: 208.

Collectivités urbaines **D.7**: 67. **K.4**: 208.

Collège électoral **J.6**: 58.

Collusion **C.3**: 54.

Colonisation **D.9**: 111. **H.7**: 15.

Colonisation rurale **G.3.2**: 65.

Cols blanc **I.4**: 90. **K.1**: 163.

Commandement autoritaire **J.3**: 14.

Commerce **D.7**: 29. **F.6**: 28. **F.7**: 11. **F.8**: 51. **H.3**: 10. **H.5**: 3.

Commerce de détail **B.2**: 77. **G.2**: 10. **H.4**: 5, 42, 98. **H.5**: 7–8, 29, 34, 36. **I.5**: 10. **K.1**: 202.

Commerce extérieur **F.8**: 37. **K.4**: 186.

Commercialisation **B.2**: 101. **H.5**: 27, 40. **I.3**: 29, 153. **K.4**: 220.

Communalisme **D.5**: 154.

Communauté scientifique **D.7**: 138.

Communautés ethniques **D.7**: 88. **F.7**: 82, 126.

Communautés européennes **D.7**: 22. **D.9**: 66. **E.1**: 15. **F.7**: 162, 215. **F.8**: 130. **G.3.2**: 319. **H.4**: 6. **I.3**: 84, 118. **I.5**: 21. **J.8**: 4, 6–7, 9–10. **K.2**: 9, 27, 72, 96. **K.3**: 38.

Communautés religieuses **D.5**: 185. **F.5**: 237. **G.2**: 30.

Communication **B.1**: 110. **C.2**: 17. **C.3**: 3, 28, 30, 74, 83, 107, 135, 147. **C.5**: 20. **D.1**: 28. **D.2**: 1. **D.3**: 68. **D.7**: 28, 118, 121, 123, 125–126, 128, 131–132, 134, 138, 141–143, 145–149, 152, 156, 158–161, 163–165, 168–171, 173–179, 181, 183, 187–190, 192, 241–242, 277, 281, 284. **D.9**: 30. **E.1**: 3. **F.4**: 85. **F.5**: 93. **I.6**: 25. **J.7**: 20. **K.1**: 14. **K.4**: 11–12, 56.

Communication confidentielle **D.3**: 44.

Communication de masse **B.2**: 11. **D.7**: 238. **D.8**: 73.

Communication interculturelle **C.3**: 53. **C.5**: 18. **D.1**: 104. **D.7**: 132–133, 155, 185. **D.8**: 19.

Communication interpersonnelle **C.1**: 159. **C.3**: 20, 48, 144. **D.3**: 6. **D.7**: 180. **F.4**: 85, 226.

Communication non-verbale **C.6**: 5.

Communication orale **D.7**: 158.

Communication politique **D.7**: 112, 302. **J.3**: 3.

Communication verbale **C.3**: 22. **D.7**: 144.

Communication visuelle **D.7**: 140.

Communisme **A.1**: 34. **B.2**: 111. **D.5**: 63. **E.3**: 22. **G.3.1**: 6. **I.5**: 157. **J.2**: 14. **J.3**: 29. **K.1**: 17.

Communistes **J.5**: 5.

Compensation **H.3**: 60. **I.2**: 243. **I.3**: 107, 114, 116. **I.4**: 80. **I.5**: 188.

Compétences **D.8**: 10. **F.2**: 152. **H.7**: 11. **I.3**: 87, 90. **I.4**: 18, 52, 132. **K.1**: 139. **K.3**: 8.

Compétitivité **H.4**: 40.

Complexe militaro-industriel **J.7**: 2.

Comportement antisocial **K.1**: 109, 309.

Comportement collectif **C.4**: 36. **C.7**: 78.

Comportement culturel **C.1**: 145.

Comportement de l'organisation **C.2**: 111. **C.3**: 130. **C.5**: 1, 14, 28, 30, 33, 35, 54, 57, 59, 64, 68, 72, 81, 84. **D.7**: 182. **I.3**: 86. **K.1**: 362.

Comportement du consommateur **H.5**: 5–6, 23. **I.6**: 40.

Comportement du groupe **C.2**: 239. **C.4**: 19, 21–22, 31, 43, 47, 55, 59, 61–62. **C.7**: 50.

Comportement électoral **B.2**: 47, 73. **C.2**: 70. **D.1**: 51. **F.5**: 20. **I.5**: 87. **J.3**: 28. **J.6**: 26, 51, 59, 62.

Comportement en groupe **C.4**: 8.

Comportement individuel **C.2**: 219. **F.6**: 12.

Comportement politique **H.4**: 68.

Comportement sexuel **D.3**: 79. **F.3**: 180, 212. **F.4**: 254. **F.6**: 5, 7, 9, 12, 20, 24–25, 27–29, 37, 42, 44–45, 50–51. **K.1**: 380.

Comportement social **C.3**: 62, 70. **C.7**: 17–18, 75. **D.1**: 137. **H.4**: 84. **I.3**: 15. **J.3**: 46.

Composition du groupe **C.4**: 23.

Comptabilité **D.3**: 31.

Comptabilité publique **I.4**: 31.

Comptables **D.3**: 31. **I.4**: 86.

Comte, Auguste
B.1: 63.

Concentration commerciale **H.4**: 73.

Concentration urbaine **G.3.2**: 107, 230.

Conception de soi **C.2**: 226, 229, 240. **C.3**: 15. **F.2**: 99.

Conceptualisation **C.2**: 33.

Conciliation **C.3**: 94.

Concurrence **C.3**: 131. **F.5**: 70. **F.7**: 69. **H.5**: 41. **I.2**: 44. **I.5**: 111, 124.

Condamnation pénale **D.4**: 14, 20, 28. **K.1**: 170, 176, 183.

Conditionnement **C.2**: 167.

Conditions de travail **C.1**: 31. **F.5**: 260. **F.7**: 16. **I.3**: 3, 9, 35–36, 44, 56, 58, 69, 72–74, 146. **I.4**: 41. **K.1**: 342.

Conditions de vie **F.2**: 147. **F.7**: 16. **K.1**: 393. **K.4**: 9.

Conditions économiques **D.7**: 330. **E.1**: 11. **E.2**: 4, 18, 47, 63, 66. **E.3**: 47. **F.1**: 26. **F.2**: 47. **F.3**: 141, 275, 292. **F.4**: 31, 203. **F.5**: 326. **F.7**: 2, 8, 66, 254. **F.8**: 111, 114. **G.1**: 6, 53. **G.3.1**: 54, 113, 131. **G.3.2**: 70, 75, 361. **H.1**: 4. **H.2**: 19. **H.3**: 23, 49, 57. **I.2**: 132. **J.1**: 22. **K.4**: 20.

Conditions politiques **E.2**: 47. **F.3**: 91. **F.7**: 192. **J.1**: 7.

Conditions sociales **D.1**: 38, 117, 139. **D.5**: 155. **D.7**: 351. **D.9**: 85. **E.1**: 1–2, 4, 7, 15, 18, 21, 24. **E.2**: 4, 12, 15, 18, 63, 66, 74, 78. **E.3**: 50, 66. **F.1**: 17. **F.2**: 78, 101, 134. **F.3**: 72, 232, 275, 292. **F.5**: 32, 37, 155, 240. **F.7**: 2, 4, 12, 59, 66–67, 98. **F.8**: 69, 84, 114, 152. **G.1**: 6,

25. **G.3.1**: 48, 113, 120, 131. **G.3.2**: 70, 75, 345. **H.3**: 6, 57. **H.4**: 86. **I.2**: 156. **J.1**: 22. **J.3**: 29. **J.6**: 46. **K.2**: 100. **K.4**: 38.

Conflit **C.1**: 16, 63, 88. **C.2**: 32. **C.3**: 106, 110, 115–116, 119. **C.4**: 20, 41. **D.4**: 22. **D.5**: 60. **D.7**: 96, 319. **D.8**: 44. **D.9**: 25, 106. **F.4**: 107. **F.5**: 4. **F.7**: 152. **G.3.1**: 106. **G.3.2**: 44. **H.5**: 37. **I.5**: 35, 108. **J.7**: 8. **K.1**: 40.

Conflit conjugal **F.4**: 121, 132, 168, 201, 213, 241, 246, 257, 259, 294.

Conflits de classe **E.2**: 11, 69.

Conflits de générations **F.2**: 4, 7.

Conflits du travail **I.5**: 78, 85–86.

Conflits interethniques **F.7**: 103, 148, 158, 165, 206.

Conflits interpersonnels **C.3**: 112. **F.4**: 136.

Conflits raciaux **E.3**: 63. **F.7**: 18, 205. **K.1**: 206.

Conflits sociaux **E.2**: 52.

Conformité au groupe **C.4**: 28. **I.3**: 80.

Confucianisme **C.2**: 21, 57. **D.1**: 101. **D.5**: 3, 7. **H.1**: 2.

Congé de maternité **I.2**: 213.

Congruence du statut **I.4**: 111.

Conjoncture démographique **F.3**: 8, 18.

Connaissance **A.1**: 11, 17. **A.2**: 7. **B.1**: 29, 35, 40, 79. **C.1**: 27. **C.2**: 2, 42, 88, 161. **C.3**: 155. **C.5**: 17. **C.7**: 12, 79. **D.6**: 1, 4, 15, 21, 25, 30. **D.7**: 166. **D.9**: 196. **E.2**: 22. **F.5**: 136. **F.8**: 106. **G.3.2**: 49. **H.5**: 9. **I.4**: 52. **J.6**: 47. **K.1**: 193.

Connor, Eugene
F.7: 147.

Conscience de classe **E.1**: 22.

Conscience de soi **C.2**: 235, 241.

Conscience nationale **D.1**: 37, 60.

Conscience religieuse **F.2**: 138.

Conscience sociale **C.7**: 33. **D.1**: 120, 135.

Conseil municipal **C.5**: 11. **D.3**: 56.

Conseillers **C.1**: 124. **J.5**: 38.

Consensus **C.3**: 41. **C.4**: 61. **C.7**: 11. **H.7**: 26. **K.1**: 206.

Conservateurs **D.9**: 44.

Conservation de la nature **D.7**: 245.

Conservatisme **C.2**: 16. **D.1**: 6. **F.4**: 328. **J.1**: 2. **J.6**: 54. **K.2**: 91. **K.4**: 186.

Consommateurs **D.7**: 290. **F.2**: 117. **G.3.2**: 252. **H.3**: 40. **H.5**: 3, 11, 15, 19, 22, 24, 35–36, 38–39. **I.5**: 9. **K.4**: 220.

Consommation **D.2**: 20. **D.7**: 116. **G.3.2**: 112. **H.1**: 1. **H.3**: 24, 28. **H.5**: 4, 10, 12–13, 16–18, 21, 27–28. **J.5**: 10.

Consommation alimentaire **C.2**: 74.

Consommation d'eau **G.1**: 38.

482

Consommation d'énergie **F.8**: 36.
Constitution **D.7**: 255. **F.6**: 40. **F.7**: 74. **J.3**: 6. **J.4**: 2.
Constitutionalisme **J.4**: 12.
Construction de l'état **J.3**: 23.
Construction de logement **G.3.2**: 151.
Construction navale **I.4**: 54.
Consumérisme **H.5**: 14.
Contestation de groupe **D.9**: 120.
Contestation politique **J.5**: 15, 27.
Contraception **F.3**: 37, 39, 44, 48, 61, 63–64, 81, 154. **F.6**: 1, 14, 32.
Contrat de travail **I.3**: 81. **I.4**: 84.
Contrat social **H.3**: 29.
Contre-culture **G.1**: 8.
Contremaîtres **I.3**: 25.
Contribuables **D.5**: 57. **H.6**: 4.
Contrôle de qualité **H.4**: 27. **I.3**: 1. **K.2**: 4. **K.4**: 82.
Contrôle des loyers **G.3.2**: 154.
Conversion religieuse **D.5**: 51, 112.
Coopération internationale **C.3**: 21. **C.5**: 18. **D.7**: 389. **F.7**: 239.
Coopération sociale **C.3**: 67. **I.5**: 8.
Coopération technique **G.3.2**: 254. **K.4**: 97.
Coopératives **H.2**: 15. **H.4**: 54.
Coopératives de production **H.4**: 31.
Corporatisme **F.5**: 267. **H.4**: 64. **I.5**: 108. **K.4**: 214.
Corps humain **D.7**: 234. **D.8**: 43. **E.2**: 8. **F.3**: 142.
Corps législatif **D.7**: 33.
Corrélation **B.1**: 48. **C.1**: 37.
Corruption **D.1**: 135.
Coser, Rose Lamb **C.6**: 12.
Cosmogonie **C.5**: 30, 48.
Cosmologie **F.6**: 30.
Côtes **G.1**: 7.
Couleur de la peau **F.7**: 261.
Cour Suprême **D.4**: 7, 34. **F.5**: 300. **J.3**: 28. **K.1**: 176.
Courbes de Lorenz **I.4**: 44.
Course aux armements **J.7**: 20. **J.8**: 1, 3.
Courtisement **C.3**: 143. **F.6**: 50. **K.1**: 408.
Cousin parallèle **F.4**: 206.
Coût **D.7**: 92.
Coût de l'enfant **F.4**: 122, 270. **K.2**: 60, 68.
Coûts de la vie **F.2**: 58. **H.3**: 55.
Coûts de production **I.5**: 188.
Coûts de transaction **H.5**: 38.

Coûts sociaux **K.1**: 346.
Coutumes **C.5**: 19. **D.2**: 7, 13.
Couture **F.5**: 36.
Création artistique **C.2**: 27.
Créativité **C.2**: 33. **D.8**: 41.
Crédit **H.5**: 9. **H.6**: 5, 11.
Crédit à la consommation **K.1**: 225.
Criminalité **K.1**: 48, 58, 85, 109, 129, 334.
Criminologie **K.1**: 54, 67, 70–73, 78, 99, 101, 158, 182.
Crise du logement **G.3.2**: 121.
Crise économique **H.3**: 10, 56. **I.1**: 6.
Critique **D.8**: 9, 55.
Critique littéraire **D.8**: 11.
Croissance démographique **F.1**: 2, 45. **F.3**: 303–304, 306, 310–311, 313.
Croissance économique **D.9**: 152. **F.3**: 306. **F.5**: 6. **H.1**: 2. **H.3**: 18. **H.7**: 25. **I.2**: 24.
Croissance urbaine **E.2**: 48. **G.3.2**: 165, 229, 235, 263, 299, 321–322, 342. **I.2**: 5.
Croyance **C.2**: 11, 102, 123. **C.3**: 12. **C.7**: 7–8, 12, 74, 77, 79. **D.3**: 30, 41. **D.5**: 91. **F.3**: 160, 228. **K.1**: 132, 233, 349.
Croyances médicales **F.7**: 24.
Croyances religieuses **D.5**: 28, 33, 72, 76, 141. **F.4**: 243.
Culpabilité **C.2**: 110, 238. **J.3**: 25.
Culte **D.5**: 86, 148.
Cultes **D.1**: 11. **D.5**: 8, 14, 34, 61, 153, 157. **J.1**: 5.
Culture **B.1**: 69, 89. **C.1**: 72, 94. **C.2**: 52. **C.3**: 35, 112, 157. **D**: 1. **D.1**: 12–15, 17, 21, 24–25, 28, 40, 44, 46, 61–65, 72, 78, 80, 86, 92–93, 99–100, 106, 116, 118, 132. **D.2**: 1–2, 21, 26. **D.3**: 85. **D.4**: 37. **D.6**: 18. **D.7**: 13, 28, 100, 336. **D.8**: 2, 8, 23–24, 26, 33, 57, 71. **D.9**: 124. **E.3**: 3, 67, 69. **F.2**: 134. **F.3**: 293. **F.4**: 44. **F.5**: 206. **F.7**: 58. **H.3**: 12. **H.5**: 10. **I.3**: 53. **I.6**: 18. **J.1**: 6. **J.2**: 12. **J.5**: 7. **J.7**: 22. **K.1**: 226.
Culture commerciale **H.4**: 45.
Culture d'entreprise **C.5**: 10, 15, 17, 19, 67. **H.2**: 1. **H.4**: 33, 67. **I.5**: 19, 173.
Culture de masse **D.1**: 80. **D.2**: 5. **F.7**: 195.
Culture indigène **D.5**: 96.
Culture locale **D.1**: 118. **G.2**: 27.
Culture matérielle **G.1**: 23.
Culture nationale **C.5**: 46. **D.7**: 237.
Culture ouvrière **E.2**: 68. **F.5**: 3, 294.
Culture politique **D.1**: 91. **J.1**: 5–6, 10–11. **J.6**: 6–7, 33.

Culture populaire **D.1**: 31, 35, 80, 91, 111. **D.2**: 5–6, 20. **D.5**: 152. **D.7**: 230, 307, 321, 351. **D.8**: 9, 32, 46, 60. **F.5**: 115. **J.6**: 40.

Curriculum **D.8**: 10. **D.9**: 26, 33, 37, 47, 78, 127, 177.

Cycle de vie **C.2**: 58. **F.2**: 57, 119. **F.3**: 267. **F.4**: 49, 289. **G.3.2**: 18. **I.2**: 146.

Cycles économiques **E.2**: 83. **I.2**: 44.

Dalaï Lama **D.5**: 84.

Danse **A.2**: 12. **D.5**: 117. **D.8**: 54.

Datation **H.5**: 32.

Débilité mentale **K.4**: 35, 118, 120, 127.

Déboisement **G.1**: 27.

Décentralisation **D.9**: 112. **G.3**: 5. **G.3.2**: 230, 298, 303. **J.4**: 3. **K.4**: 78.

Déchets dangereux **D.7**: 188. **J.5**: 14.

Déchets radioactifs **K.1**: 1.

Décision **C.7**: 6. **D.3**: 66. **F.4**: 107. **J.6**: 26. **K.4**: 59.

Décisions d'implantation **D.6**: 10.

Déclin économique **D.9**: 36.

Déconstruction **B.1**: 49, 148.

Déesse **D.5**: 157.

Dégâts **G.1**: 42.

Dégradation de l'environnement **D.7**: 250. **H.4**: 103.

Délinquance **F.4**: 41. **G.2**: 9. **K.1**: 8, 51, 108, 146, 153.

Délinquance juvénile **D.4**: 28. **K.1**: 39, 60, 80, 94, 100, 113, 115, 123, 139, 154–155, 164, 177–178, 185–186, 192, 198, 208, 216, 302, 410. **K.3**: 18.

Délinquants **D.4**: 2, 4. **F.6**: 47. **I.5**: 112. **K.1**: 57, 68–69, 78, 96, 100, 103, 107, 110, 136, 142, 161, 166, 169, 172, 174, 182–183, 187, 191, 204, 206, 213, 215, 328. **K.3**: 19, 29.

Délits **D.7**: 273. **F.5**: 198. **J.3**: 43. **K.1**: 47, 53, 55–57, 59–61, 64–65, 67–68, 74, 79, 81, 83, 88–89, 93, 95, 98, 105–106, 111, 114, 116, 119, 124, 128, 132–134, 137–138, 140–142, 145, 147, 149, 157, 159–161, 163, 212, 302, 381, 425. **K.3**: 22.

Demande **C.4**: 14. **G.3.2**: 102. **K.4**: 28.

Demande de main-d'oeuvre **F.8**: 144. **I.2**: 190.

Demande globale **H.5**: 5.

Démilitarisation **J.7**: 2.

Démocratie **B.2**: 4. **D.9**: 48. **F.5**: 104. **F.7**: 13. **G.3.1**: 92. **G.3.2**: 329. **H.2**: 12. **J.1**: 12. **J.2**: 3, 5–6, 12, 18–19, 22, 29. **J.6**: 6, 21. **K.1**: 416. **K.2**: 92. **K.4**: 271.

Démocratie industrielle **I.5**: 40.

Démocratisation **D.7**: 263. **D.9**: 180. **E.2**: 70. **E.3**: 27. **F.3**: 178. **G.3.2**: 253. **J.2**: 13. **J.3**: 1, 5.

Démographes **F.1**: 69.

Démographie **B.2**: 129. **F.1**: 6–7, 10, 13–14, 16–18, 21, 31, 39, 43, 51, 54, 57, 71. **F.2**: 42, 85, 153. **F.3**: 1, 5, 90, 100, 127, 130. **F.4**: 123, 247. **F.8**: 114. **H.3**: 19. **I.2**: 198. **K.1**: 255, 330, 425. **K.2**: 36.

Démographie tribale **F.3**: 20.

Densité de main d'oeuvre **I.3**: 112.

Densité de population **C.1**: 14. **F.1**: 63. **F.3**: 24. **G.3.2**: 180. **K.1**: 159. **K.4**: 21.

Déontologie **D.3**: 44. **I.4**: 91, 93, 102, 110, 115.

Dépenses **I.2**: 77.

Dépenses de consommation **H.3**: 7, 40.

Dépenses de mènage **H.5**: 13.

Dépenses de santé **K.4**: 149–150, 157, 226.

Dépenses publiques **H.4**: 38. **K.2**: 36.

Dépeuplement **F.3**: 28.

Déréglementation **D.7**: 297. **I.5**: 1.

Déroulement de carrière **I.4**: 59–61, 63–65.

Derrida, Jacques **D.3**: 50. **D.6**: 12.

Désarmement **J.7**: 20.

Désastres **C.2**: 80. **C.5**: 72. **C.7**: 22. **D.7**: 315. **F.2**: 104. **K.4**: 45.

Description d'emploi **I.3**: 49.

Désindustrialisation **H.4**: 8. **I.1**: 12.

Désintegration **C.1**: 19.

Désintégration de la famille **F.4**: 41, 316. **K.1**: 425.

Désirabilité sociale **C.3**: 84.

Désorganisation sociale **K.1**: 49, 92.

Détente **J.8**: 10.

Déterminisme **C.2**: 85.

Dette **C.2**: 29. **K.1**: 225.

Deuil **C.2**: 39.

Développement cognitif **B.2**: 45. **C.2**: 112, 123, 127, 238.

Développement de l'éducation **D.9**: 36, 141.

Développement de l'enfant **C.2**: 73, 105, 156. **C.7**: 79. **F.2**: 2, 72, 89, 93, 109. **F.3**: 214. **F.4**: 282.

Développement des collectivités **D.9**: 5. **G.2**: 6–7, 14, 28, 33–34, 36. **G.3.1**: 36. **G.3.2**: 241, 283. **H.6**: 8. **J.5**: 6. **K.1**: 69. **K.4**: 184.

Développement économique **D.3**: 43. **E.1**: 19. **E.3**: 67. **F.5**: 244. **F.7**: 171. **G.1**: 12, 45. **G.3.2**: 330, 352. **H.2**: 17. **H.3**: 1, 14, 17, 41, 78. **H.7**: 1, 19, 26, 28. **I.6**: 41. **K.1**: 84.

Développement forestier **G.3.1**: 104. **G.3.2**: 27.

Développement industriel **E.2**: 63. **G.3.2**: 272. **H.3**: 27.

Développement régional **F.8**: 53. **G.3**: 7. **G.3.1**: 104, 123. **G.3.2**: 11, 29, 59, 270, 272. **H.3**: 48. **H.4**: 74. **H.7**: 4, 6, 8, 21, 27. **J.4**: 8.

Développement rural **F.5**: 28. **G.2**: 8. **G.3.1**: 48, 84, 92, 101–103, 105, 107, 109–110, 113–114, 116–117, 122–123, 125–129, 132–135. **G.3.2**: 338. **H.4**: 11. **J.5**: 6.

Développement social **E.1**: 23. **E.3**: 18, 30–31, 46, 63, 69–70. **F.2**: 154. **F.5**: 165. **G.3.2**: 16. **H.2**: 11. **K.1**: 293.

Développement socio-économique **B.2**: 4. **D.3**: 34. **D.9**: 16. **E.3**: 68. **F.3**: 85, 291. **F.5**: 243. **G.3.2**: 298, 360. **H.3**: 31. **I.4**: 97. **K.1**: 77.

Développement soutenable **H.4**: 19, 44. **J.8**: 2.

Développement urbain **G.2**: 23. **G.3.2**: 29, 139, 163, 219, 233, 241, 243, 247, 253–254, 256, 258, 264–265, 268, 270–271, 276, 278, 281, 286, 288, 290, 295, 320, 346. **H.3**: 41. **H.4**: 70. **H.7**: 23. **J.4**: 22.

Déviance **D.5**: 137. **D.9**: 143. **F.2**: 18, 130. **F.3**: 196. **F.4**: 162. **F.6**: 45. **K.1**: 113, 149, 407.

Dialectes **G.1**: 58.

Dialectique **B.1**: 50, 122. **D.1**: 23. **D.7**: 196.

Différence d'âge **F.4**: 249. **I.3**: 25.

Différences de generations **F.2**: 20.

Différenciation raciale **F.4**: 212. **G.3.2**: 211. **I.2**: 196. **J.7**: 1.

Différenciation résidentielle **G.3.2**: 214.

Différenciation sexuelle **C.3**: 6. **C.7**: 10. **D.9**: 89. **F.4**: 241, 284. **F.5**: 63, 167, 172, 174–177, 197, 201–202, 204–205, 223, 232, 235, 253, 260, 301. **G.3.1**: 33, 82. **H.3**: 69, 71. **H.4**: 102. **I.2**: 101, 144. **I.3**: 55, 137. **J.7**: 1, 12. **K.1**: 352, 425.

Différenciation sociale **F.3**: 246.

Différentiation culturelle **B.1**: 109. **C.7**: 23.

Difficulté de langue **D.7**: 24, 98.

Diffusion de la culture **D.7**: 141.

Diffusion politique **D.7**: 370.

Dimension de l'entreprise **H.4**: 73.

Dimension de la famille **F.3**: 104. **F.4**: 65, 333, 353. **H.3**: 5.

Dimension de la ville **G.3.2**: 45.

Dimension spatiale **B.2**: 77. **D.7**: 171. **F.2**: 20. **F.3**: 213. **F.5**: 128. **F.7**: 42. **G.1**: 35–36, 57. **G.3**: 2. **G.3.2**: 29, 178–179, 181–182, 186–187, 193, 195, 199, 206, 214, 219–222. **I.2**: 1. **I.4**: 42. **J.2**: 16. **J.3**: 44.

Diplômés d'université **C.2**: 145. **F.8**: 14. **I.2**: 231. **I.3**: 18. **I.4**: 90.

Direction de l'entreprise **E.2**: 63. **F.5**: 247. **F.7**: 51. **H.4**: 36. **I.4**: 15.

Discrimination **C.1**: 83. **C.7**: 75. **F.3**: 4. **F.5**: 170, 187. **F.7**: 14, 183. **G.3.2**: 99, 110, 167. **H.4**: 56. **I.2**: 41, 52, 70, 130, 222. **I.3**: 14, 91.

Discrimination dans l'emploi **F.7**: 250. **I.2**: 46, 131, 209.

Discrimination raciale **F.7**: 211, 215, 220, 223–224, 227–229, 233–234, 239, 245, 248–250, 253, 265–266, 269. **F.8**: 10. **G.3.2**: 120, 192. **I.2**: 42, 64, 189, 209, 225. **I.5**: 9.

Discrimination salariale **F.5**: 235.

Discrimination sexuelle **F.5**: 50, 155, 161, 168, 181, 199, 215, 257, 259, 306. **I.2**: 85, 102, 104, 116, 131, 137–138, 152, 161. **I.3**: 108. **I.4**: 108. **K.1**: 174.

Disparités régionales **D.9**: 29, 141. **E.1**: 11. **F.3**: 248–251, 262–263, 273, 285, 288, 298. **G.3.2**: 179, 272, 361. **H.3**: 2, 44, 84. **K.4**: 234.

Dispensaires **K.4**: 59.

Dissensus **I.4**: 14.

Dissonance cognitive **C.7**: 70.

Dissuasion **K.1**: 91.

Distance sociale **C.7**: 21. **F.7**: 40.

Distribution **H.4**: 5. **I.4**: 44.

Distribution d'énergie **I.5**: 44.

Diversification **I.3**: 130. **I.4**: 47.

Diversité des cultures **D.8**: 36. **F.2**: 149.

Divertissement **D.5**: 161. **D.7**: 390.

Divigeant **C.6**: 1, 8–9, 14, 16. **F.5**: 230. **G.3.2**: 48. **I.5**: 14. **J.6**: 22, 31, 43.

Divigeant politique **C.6**: 2. **J.6**: 35.

Division du travail **E.2**: 33. **F.4**: 34, 74. **F.5**: 14, 164, 180, 301. **G.3.2**: 351. **I.2**: 103–104, 182. **I.3**: 88. **I.4**: 16, 104. **J.1**: 9.

Division internationale du travail **I.2**: 162.

Divorce **C.2**: 3. **D.5**: 34. **F.4**: 118–121, 123–124, 126–135, 137–147.

Divorcés **F.4**: 117, 122, 136.

Doctrines sociales **D.3**: 23.

Dogme **B.1**: 31.

Domination **C.2**: 24. **C.3**: 59. **D.6**: 26.

Dominicains **F.8**: 166.

Don **H.6**: 2.

Don charitable **C.3**: 101.

Donaldson, Margaret C. **C.2**: 140.

Données statistiques **B.2**: 49, 106. **K.4**: 163.

Dot **F.4**: 204. **F.5**: 194, 198.

Drogue **C.2**: 173. **D.9**: 163. **F.3**: 60, 202, 206. **H.3**: 67. **I.3**: 37, 58. **I.5**: 134. **K.1**: 95, 138, 301, 313–315, 319, 321, 337, 342, 344, 350, 358, 365, 367, 384, 392. **K.4**: 68.

Droit **C.7**: 59. **D.3**: 45, 57, 79. **D.4**: 13, 27, 32–33, 36, 38–39, 42, 44. **D.5**: 4, 9, 24, 182. **D.7**: 96, 273. **F.3**: 42, 111. **F.4**: 183, 185, 191, 250. **F.5**: 86, 206, 259. **F.7**: 196. **I.2**: 67, 167, 247. **I.3**: 118. **I.5**: 105, 192. **J.5**: 23. **K.1**: 112. **K.2**: 32, 46. **K.3**: 17, 27. **K.4**: 65, 258.
Droit à la vie privée **K.1**: 141, 375.
Droit au travail **H.3**: 76.
Droit constitutionnel **F.5**: 131.
Droit coutumier **D.4**: 10, 30. **F.4**: 199.
Droit criminel **D.4**: 22, 37. **J.3**: 2. **K.1**: 15, 40, 131, 181, 204.
Droit de la famille **F.4**: 127, 130–131, 177, 180, 184, 188–190, 192. **F.5**: 160.
Droit du travail **E.2**: 69. **I.2**: 138, 214. **I.3**: 42. **I.4**: 8. **I.5**: 98 100, 102, 104, 107, 109, 111–114, 116, 168.
Droit matrimonial **F.4**: 181–182. **F.5**: 198.
Droit moderne **F.5**: 297.
Droit naturel **D.1**: 85. **F.5**: 297.
Droit public **D.4**: 16.
Droite **J.6**: 11. **K.4**: 186.
Droits de l'homme **F.3**: 159. **F.5**: 154. **F.6**: 3. **F.8**: 33. **I.5**: 80. **J.3**: 3.
Droits des minorités **J.3**: 4.
Droits du citoyen **F.4**: 185. **F.7**: 2, 10, 145, 147. **J.5**: 1. **J.6**: 52.
Duke, David **F.7**: 225.
Durée de vie **F.3**: 299.
Durkheim, Emile **B.1**: 84, 105. **J.2**: 1.
Dynamique **D.3**: 70. **F.3**: 291. **G.3.2**: 364. **H.4**: 85. **I.1**: 11.
Dynamique de groupe **C.4**: 1, 12, 27, 35, 38. **J.1**: 21.
Dynamique de la population **F.1**: 5, 62. **F.3**: 104. **G.3.2**: 41, 209.
Dynamique sociale **F.1**: 62. **G.2**: 3.
Dyslexie **D.7**: 98.
Eau **D.1**: 48. **G.1**: 42. **G.3.2**: 363.
Échange **C.3**: 33. **G.3.2**: 42.
Échange d'information **C.3**: 44.
Échange matrimonial **C.3**: 142.
Échange social **C.3**: 54. **G.3.2**: 42.
Échantillon **B.2**: 35. **I.3**: 150.
Échantillonnage **B.2**: 5, 47, 104, 119. **D.4**: 43. **I.2**: 137.
Échantillonnage au hasard **B.2**: 68.
Échec **C.2**: 103. **F.8**: 157.
Échelles multidimensionnelles **I.5**: 88.

Écoles **C.2**: 144. **C.4**: 8. **C.5**: 53. **D.9**: 3, 25, 32–33, 43, 58–59, 61, 74, 78, 84, 88, 92, 100, 106, 112–113, 117–118, 124, 129, 131, 134, 139, 143, 155, 163. **F.4**: 118. **F.5**: 291. **F.7**: 121. **I.4**: 99. **K.1**: 37, 89. **K.2**: 35.
Écoles primaires **D.9**: 150.
Écoles secondaires **C.3**: 58. **D.9**: 164–166, 170.
Écologie **B.1**: 81. **C.1**: 100. **C.5**: 56. **D.2**: 21. **D.5**: 14, 147. **D.9**: 117. **F.5**: 76, 94. **G.1**: 8, 14–16, 19, 22, 26, 39–42, 48, 53. **G.3.2**: 22. **J.3**: 30.
Écologie humaine **F.3**: 2.
Écologisme **D.7**: 114. **J.5**: 9, 31.
Économétrie **F.8**: 62. **I.2**: 190.
Économie agricole **H.4**: 45.
Économie collective **J.2**: 26.
Économie de l'éducation **D.9**: 210.
Économie de l'environnement **G.1**: 63. **K.1**: 346.
Économie de la santé **K.4**: 138, 156, 159, 162–163, 204, 247.
Économie de marché **F.2**: 135. **F.5**: 225. **H.2**: 6, 8, 18. **H.3**: 82. **H.7**: 20. **J.3**: 34.
Économie de subsistance **H.4**: 45.
Économie domestique **H.5**: 20.
Économie du travail **C.5**: 40.
Économie islamique **C.7**: 61.
Économie mondiale **G.3.1**: 114.
Économie politique **D.7**: 264. **G.3.2**: 33. **H.2**: 19. **H.3**: 53. **H.4**: 59. **I.5**: 79. **I.6**: 30. **J.6**: 34.
Économie régionale **H.3**: 45, 47, 89. **I.1**: 11. **I.2**: 17.
Économie rurale **G.3.1**: 14, 77. **H.3**: 68.
Économie socialiste **H.2**: 17, 19. **K.2**: 7.
Économie spatiale **C.3**: 151. **D.1**: 115. **G.3.2**: 96, 152. **H.4**: 40–41, 75.
Économie urbaine **G.3.2**: 21, 35, 52, 67, 137, 152, 289, 292, 323, 352. **H.3**: 53. **H.7**: 28. **I.2**: 68. **K.1**: 230.
Écriture **D.1**: 77. **D.7**: 17, 54, 158, 190, 324.
Écrivains **D.8**: 11, 30.
Édition **F.5**: 10.
Éducation **B.1**: 126. **B.2**: 100. **C.1**: 89, 110. **D.3**: 29. **D.7**: 340, 343, 390. **D.9**: 2–3, 7–9, 14, 17, 22, 27, 30, 35, 39, 53–55, 57, 61–62, 65, 68, 71, 73, 90–91, 96, 98, 105, 107, 111, 113–115, 120, 123, 125, 138, 153, 158, 163. **E.2**: 36. **F.3**: 11, 38, 233, 245, 252, 280, 308. **F.4**: 242. **F.5**: 170, 283. **F.7**: 1, 14, 188, 230, 253. **I.2**: 49, 116, 160, 225. **I.4**: 15–16, 120, 129. **J.4**: 12. **J.5**: 5. **K.1**: 94. **K.4**: 51.
Éducation des adultes **D.9**: 1, 5–6, 23, 28, 34, 63, 128, 140, 183. **I.4**: 126.
Éducation religieuse **D.5**: 52. **D.9**: 7, 159.
Éducation surveillée **K.1**: 166.

Effectifs en ouvriers **F.3**: 28. **F.7**: 3. **I.2**: 165–166, 173, 181, 184, 186, 190, 198, 201. **I.4**: 72. **J.7**: 13.
Effet **C.2**: 180.
Effets psychologiques **C.2**: 41, 97. **I.2**: 234.
Effets sur l'environnement **G.1**: 7. **I.6**: 27.
Efficacité organisationnel **C.5**: 50. **C.6**: 8.
Égalité **E.2**: 18, 44. **F.5**: 161, 310. **F.7**: 221. **G.3.2**: 23. **I.4**: 20. **K.1**: 145, 173.
Égalité de chances **F.4**: 324. **F.5**: 212. **H.3**: 90. **I.2**: 110, 212. **I.5**: 105–106.
Égalité de rémunération **F.5**: 64. **H.3**: 86. **I.2**: 92, 115–116.
Égalité des sexes **F.5**: 111, 158, 193, 214.
Égalité économique **H.3**: 32. **I.2**: 127. **K.1**: 137.
Église baptiste **D.5**: 113.
Église catholique **D.3**: 89. **D.5**: 106, 114, 116, 130–131, 140. **D.9**: 126. **H.2**: 10.
Église et État **D.5**: 108.
Église lutheran **D.5**: 108.
Église orthodoxe **D.5**: 135.
Églises **F.6**: 46.
Ego **C.2**: 3. **F.4**: 11. **F.5**: 172.
Élaboration d'une politique **D.3**: 4. **I.2**: 208. **J.4**: 19.
Électeurs **J.6**: 32, 66.
Élections **D.9**: 11. **I.5**: 191. **J.6**: 60, 64.
Élections générales **J.6**: 63.
Élections locales **D.7**: 302. **J.6**: 62, 67.
Élections présidentielles **D.7**: 280. **F.7**: 217.
Électricité **H.7**: 7.
Électronique **D.7**: 192. **H.4**: 86. **H.5**: 35.
Élèves **D.9**: 135.
Élèves sortants **I.2**: 23.
Elias, Norbert
　A.2: 13, 15. **B.1**: 5, 7. **C.3**: 63. **D.1**: 96. **J.1**: 3.
Élite **E.2**: 10, 20, 46. **I.6**: 4. **J.4**: 21. **J.6**: 44.
Élite économique **H.4**: 68.
Élite politique **J.6**: 3.
Émancipation **F.4**: 195.
Émigrants **F.5**: 7. **F.8**: 56, 71, 151. **G.3.1**: 7. **H.3**: 49.
Émigration **F.5**: 5. **F.8**: 22, 26, 40, 69, 111, 113, 116, 120, 124–126, 129, 131, 139–140, 145, 152, 155–156, 165, 167, 172. **H.3**: 20.
Émissions radiophoniques **D.7**: 311.
Émotion **C.1**: 85, 160. **C.2**: 4, 21–22, 28, 30–31, 53, 57, 99–100, 109, 117, 122, 129, 196. **C.3**: 73, 100, 119, 124–128, 130–138, 140. **D.3**: 67. **D.7**: 13, 295. **F.2**: 89. **F.4**: 31, 257. **I.3**: 3, 82.

Empathie **B.1**: 32. **C.3**: 101.
Empirisme **D.6**: 31.
Emploi **C.2**: 83. **C.5**: 56. **D.9**: 207. **F.2**: 78, 95. **F.3**: 96, 127. **F.4**: 114, 260. **F.5**: 283. **F.8**: 37, 123. **G.3.2**: 68. **H.3**: 75. **H.4**: 40, 90, 101. **H.5**: 26. **H.7**: 11. **I.2**: 4, 10–12, 14–15, 17–19, 23, 27, 32, 40, 53, 58, 65, 70, 81–82, 90, 97–98, 104–105, 116, 123, 131–132, 134–135, 147, 149–150, 152, 155–157, 159, 161, 165, 174, 178, 194, 198, 211, 213–215, 229, 234. **I.3**: 13, 23, 30, 60, 71, 131. **I.4**: 78, 103. **I.5**: 17, 20, 103, 106, 179. **K.2**: 28, 73.
Emploi à temps partiel **I.2**: 34, 128, 222.
Emploi des jeunes **H.3**: 67. **I.2**: 8. **I.4**: 116, 132.
Emploi public **I.2**: 53.
Emploi rural **G.3.1**: 17, 52, 112. **I.2**: 173.
Emploi temporaire **I.2**: 9, 63. **I.4**: 116.
Emploi urbain **G.3.2**: 181. **I.2**: 1, 13, 173. **I.4**: 45.
Employés **C.3**: 104. **C.5**: 68. **D.4**: 34. **F.2**: 95. **F.7**: 265. **H.3**: 80, 86. **I.2**: 176. **I.3**: 26–28, 37, 41, 45, 58, 63, 73, 91, 101, 106, 139. **I.4**: 18, 64, 83, 118. **I.5**: 5, 10, 16, 33, 90, 133, 192, 202.
Employés de bureau **D.7**: 182. **I.2**: 145.
Employés des services publics **F.3**: 63.
Employeurs **D.9**: 210. **I.3**: 6, 16, 29, 76. **I.4**: 8. **I.5**: 192, 194. **K.1**: 344.
En-groupe **C.4**: 1, 16, 60. **F.7**: 172.
Endogamie **F.4**: 206.
Énergie **G.3.2**: 258.
Énergie nucléaire **J.5**: 31.
Enfance **C.1**: 39. **C.2**: 182. **F.2**: 76, 96, 105–106, 116. **F.3**: 126, 295. **F.4**: 80, 91, 310. **H.3**: 59. **K.1**: 38. **K.3**: 22. **K.4**: 9.
Enfants **C.1**: 41. **C.2**: 11–12, 108, 123, 130, 138, 140, 155, 158, 166. **C.3**: 11, 14, 28, 58, 87. **C.4**: 8. **C.7**: 18. **D.2**: 6. **D.3**: 14. **D.4**: 5. **D.5**: 89. **D.7**: 26, 70, 73, 89, 93, 121, 212, 218, 353, 361, 366, 381, 392. **D.8**: 66. **D.9**: 130, 151. **E.3**: 14. **F.1**: 11. **F.2**: 17, 69, 71, 74–75, 78–82, 84, 86, 89, 91, 95–96, 101–102, 104, 107, 110, 117, 125. **F.3**: 33, 36, 53, 76, 182, 261, 280, 283. **F.4**: 1, 8, 11, 16, 27, 31, 81, 92–93, 99, 120, 124, 132, 152, 188, 215, 270, 274, 276, 287–288, 294, 303, 313, 319, 323, 331, 338, 347, 353. **F.5**: 75, 285. **F.7**: 31. **G.3.2**: 82, 225. **H.3**: 6. **H.5**: 9. **I.2**: 194. **I.4**: 20. **K.1**: 26, 81, 222, 235, 280, 356, 364, 373. **K.2**: 16, 36, 46, 49, 52, 54, 63, 110. **K.3**: 9, 35, 37. **K.4**: 20, 70, 90, 112, 177, 211, 233.
Enfants à la garde de l'État **K.4**: 52.
Enfants abandonnés **F.2**: 94. **K.1**: 39.
Enfants doués **C.6**: 14. **D.9**: 156.
Enfants handicapés **D.9**: 19. **F.3**: 229. **F.4**: 82. **K.4**: 120.

Enfants martyrs **C.3**: 40. **F.2**: 68, 77, 99. **F.4**: 135, 148, 150–151, 155, 157–159, 162, 164, 169–172, 174. **K.1**: 25, 27–28, 30–34, 36–37, 41–45. **K.3**: 20.

Enquêtes **B.2**: 20–21, 25, 91, 94–95, 97, 101–102, 111, 116, 124–126, 131. **C.5**: 14. **D.7**: 349. **F.2**: 89. **F.8**: 63. **I.3**: 6. **I.5**: 54.

Enquêtes par correspondance **B.2**: 84, 113, 118, 121, 127. **G.1**: 20.

Enquêtes par panel **B.2**: 114.

Enquêtes sociales **B.2**: 119, 128.

Enquêteurs **B.2**: 102, 107. **H.5**: 25.

Enregistrement **B.2**: 90.

Enseignants **D.3**: 90. **D.9**: 21, 47, 60, 72, 145. **E.2**: 4. **I.4**: 59, 98–99, 107, 112. **I.5**: 61, 72, 83.

Enseignement **D.3**: 41. **D.9**: 44, 117, 164, 202. **F.6**: 22. **K.3**: 27.

Enseignement bilingue **D.9**: 15, 41.

Enseignement de l'économie **D.9**: 33.

Enseignement de la science politique **D.9**: 24.

Enseignement des langues **D.7**: 64, 212.

Enseignement multiculturel **D.9**: 4, 20, 45.

Enseignement primaire **C.2**: 118. **D.9**: 152–154, 156–157.

Enseignement privé **D.9**: 95, 108.

Enseignement professionnel **D.9**: 167. **G.3.2**: 236. **I.4**: 130.

Enseignement secondaire **D.9**: 119, 171. **F.7**: 59.

Enseignement supérieur **D.3**: 75. **D.9**: 121, 145, 173, 175, 177, 179, 181–182, 184–187, 189–190, 194–195, 197–201, 203–205, 211–212, 214, 216–217, 219–220. **F.5**: 77, 242, 256.

Entreprise agricole **G.3.1**: 10, 19, 44, 46, 50, 52, 56, 79, 105. **I.3**: 142, 144.

Entreprises **C.5**: 12. **D.1**: 17. **F.7**: 34, 56. **F.8**: 46. **G.3.2**: 187. **H.7**: 2, 13. **I.1**: 2. **I.2**: 99. **I.3**: 31, 95, 151. **I.4**: 64, 100. **I.5**: 46.

Entreprises conjointes **G.3.2**: 317.

Entreprises étrangères **G.3.2**: 21.

Entreprises familiales **I.4**: 6.

Entreprises multinationales **D.3**: 53. **H.4**: 61, 69. **I.3**: 6. **I.4**: 75.

Entreprises socialistes **I.3**: 81.

Entretiens **B.2**: 90–91, 96, 98, 112, 122–123. **F.4**: 240. **I.3**: 150.

Entretiens cliniques **C.1**: 66. **D.7**: 154.

Entretiens thérapeutiques **K.3**: 9.

Environnement **C.2**: 37, 90, 157. **C.4**: 28. **C.5**: 55. **C.7**: 55, 59. **D.7**: 178. **D.8**: 65. **F.2**: 37, 96. **F.3**: 313. **F.6**: 18. **F.7**: 203. **G.1**: 5, 12, 18, 28, 52. **G.3.2**: 46, 81, 239. **I.6**: 6. **J.5**: 9. **K.4**: 7.

Environnement humain **G.1**: 62.

Envois de fonds **F.8**: 80.

Épargne **F.2**: 107.

Épidémiologie **C.1**: 66, 72. **F.2**: 11. **F.3**: 164, 173, 179, 185, 233. **K.1**: 347.

Épistémologie **B.1**: 30–34, 36–37, 40–42. **D.4**: 8. **D.9**: 177.

Épouse **F.5**: 8.

Époux **C.3**: 8, 136. **F.4**: 239, 254. **F.6**: 47.

Équilibre **J.5**: 32.

Équité **C.3**: 33. **D.3**: 4. **G.3.2**: 23, 257. **I.6**: 9. **K.4**: 193, 250.

Espace urbain **G.3.2**: 220, 224, 246. **I.4**: 42.

Espacement des naissances **F.3**: 78, 87.

Espérance de vie **F.3**: 268.

Esprit de parti **J.6**: 1, 12.

Esprits **C.1**: 43.

Esthétique **D.8**: 5, 32.

Esthétique industrielle **D.8**: 39.

Esthétique urbaine **G.3.2**: 318.

Estime de soi **C.1**: 124. **C.2**: 117, 192, 215, 224, 227, 231, 233–234, 236–237. **C.3**: 71–72. **C.4**: 52. **C.7**: 34. **F.6**: 1.

Établissement du budget **K.4**: 152.

Établissements humains **G.3**: 11.

État **D.5**: 71, 177. **D.7**: 285. **D.9**: 199. **F.5**: 11, 302, 326. **F.7**: 129, 134. **G.3.2**: 53. **J.2**: 16. **J.3**: 21. **K.2**: 8.

État de droit **J.3**: 15.

État providence **D.1**: 123. **F.4**: 47. **F.5**: 184, 225. **I.3**: 62. **K.2**: 2, 77–78, 81, 83, 88, 91, 93–94, 101, 104, 108.

État-nation **D.1**: 39. **E.2**: 55. **F.7**: 78, 255. **F.8**: 8. **J.2**: 28.

Éthique **A.2**: 3. **B.1**: 64. **B.2**: 6. **C.1**: 46, 58. **C.2**: 95, 220. **C.3**: 49. **D.3**: 2–3, 7–9, 11, 13, 15, 18, 24, 27, 29–30, 33–43, 45–50, 55–56, 61–63, 69, 73. **D.5**: 29, 182. **D.6**: 3. **D.7**: 163, 279. **D.9**: 212. **F.2**: 17. **F.3**: 32, 71, 207. **F.4**: 308, 327. **F.5**: 90. **F.6**: 5. **G.1**: 14, 16, 19, 61. **H.2**: 10, 15. **H.3**: 61. **H.4**: 36, 60. **H.5**: 41. **J.2**: 7. **J.3**: 45. **J.4**: 2, 23. **K.2**: 84. **K.4**: 193, 249–251, 255, 257, 261, 263, 267.

Éthique protestante **C.7**: 51. **D.5**: 145.

Ethnicité **D.1**: 41. **D.7**: 360. **D.9**: 133. **F.1**: 8. **F.4**: 37, 93. **F.7**: 46–48, 53, 56, 59, 63–64, 67–71, 73–80, 82, 84, 87–88, 90, 93, 96–98, 101, 103–104, 111, 115, 119–122, 124–125, 128, 130, 134–135, 150, 161. **F.8**: 10, 127. **G.2**: 4. **G.3.2**: 156, 197. **I.2**: 16. **I.4**: 16. **I.5**: 162. **J.6**: 36. **J.7**: 9. **K.2**: 35. **K.3**: 14. **K.4**: 2–3, 58.

Ethnocentrisme **C.4**: 15. **F.7**: 21, 206.

Ethnographie **C.5**: 7. **D.1**: 141. **D.7**: 287. **F.5**: 141. **G.3.2**: 108. **I.2**: 96. **J.6**: 27.
Ethnolinguistiques **D.7**: 55, 199.
Ethnologie **B.1**: 34. **D.1**: 35. **F.7**: 159. **G.1**: 6. **G.3.1**: 131.
Ethnologues **D.1**: 66.
Ethnométhodologie **D.1**: 29.
Ethologie **A.1**: 15. **C.2**: 183. **D.4**: 35.
Éthos **B.1**: 52. **D.1**: 98.
Étiologie **K.4**: 72.
Étiquette **D.2**: 8.
Étrangers **F.8**: 175.
Étude du travail **F.4**: 34. **I.4**: 50.
Études culturelles **A.2**: 14. **D.1**: 32. **D.2**: 18. **F.5**: 80, 109.
Études de marché **B.2**: 129. **D.7**: 29. **H.5**: 25.
Études littéraires **D.1**: 53. **D.7**: 278.
Études sur le développement **F.5**: 241.
Études sur les effets mésologiques **G.1**: 34.
Étudiants **B.2**: 24. **C.1**: 96, 101. **C.2**: 4, 39. **C.3**: 28, 151. **D.5**: 37. **D.7**: 7. **D.9**: 24, 106, 109–110, 124, 139, 176, 197, 200–201, 206, 208, 210, 220. **F.2**: 121, 134, 147. **F.4**: 216. **F.5**: 263. **J.2**: 24. **J.6**: 41. **J.8**: 1. **K.1**: 45, 421. **K.4**: 57, 96.
Eugénisme **F.5**: 223. **J.2**: 10.
Euthanasie **D.3**: 59. **K.4**: 252, 258, 265.
Évaluation **B.2**: 9, 123. **C.2**: 144, 152. **D.1**: 19. **D.7**: 170. **F.1**: 24. **F.3**: 114. **H.6**: 4. **I.3**: 57, 121.
Évaluation de projet **E.3**: 15, 30, 48. **F.2**: 100. **G.3.1**: 22. **G.3.2**: 85.
Évaluation de soi **C.2**: 232. **C.3**: 137. **C.4**: 18. **D.9**: 135.
Évaluation des emplois **C.2**: 23. **I.3**: 7, 25, 38.
Évangélisation **D.5**: 110.
Évangélisme **D.5**: 108–109, 125, 152. **D.7**: 375.
Evans, Walker **D.7**: 3.
Éventail des salaires **F.1**: 42. **F.5**: 153, 232. **H.3**: 61, 71, 74, 83, 90. **I.2**: 181.
Évitement **K.4**: 58.
Évolution **B.1**: 119. **D.1**: 8. **D.3**: 77. **F.1**: 25. **F.7**: 206.
Évolution des emplois **I.4**: 21.
Évolution humaine **C.7**: 27.
Évolutionnisme **B.1**: 151.
Exilé **F.7**: 164. **F.8**: 142. **K.1**: 194.
Exode **I.6**: 22.
Exogamie **F.4**: 206.
Expectation **B.1**: 104. **C.2**: 35, 103. **I.2**: 166.

Expérience du travail **I.3**: 150. **I.4**: 55, 67.
Expérience religieuse **D.5**: 11, 18.
Expériences **C.1**: 96. **C.5**: 61.
Expérimentation **H.4**: 4.
Expérimentation d'animal **D.3**: 63.
Experts **I.4**: 105.
Explication **B.1**: 2, 10, 69. **C.2**: 103. **D.3**: 6.
Explication causale **C.2**: 51.
Exportations **F.8**: 37.
Expression faciale **C.2**: 31. **C.3**: 64, 81, 134–135, 147.
Extrême droite **F.7**: 219.
Fabrication industrielle **H.4**: 26, 40, 70. **I.2**: 192, 206. **I.3**: 10, 45, 51, 72. **J.6**: 25.
Facteurs culturels **C.3**: 106. **I.3**: 107.
Facteurs psychologiques **C.3**: 106. **D.5**: 33. **D.7**: 136.
Facteurs sociaux **D.7**: 177. **F.3**: 32, 90. **K.1**: 307.
Faible revenu **G.3.2**: 121, 136, 158, 168, 181. **I.2**: 65, 78. **J.6**: 20.
Famille **C.1**: 80. **C.3**: 29. **C.7**: 56. **D.2**: 12. **D.4**: 20. **D.5**: 50, 89, 168. **D.7**: 24, 354. **D.9**: 38, 118, 122, 142. **E.2**: 56, 73. **E.3**: 24. **F.1**: 60. **F.2**: 100, 140. **F.3**: 12, 41, 84, 130. **F.4**: 1–2, 4–10, 12–13, 17–19, 22–23, 32, 34, 40, 42, 44–48, 50, 53, 57, 61, 63, 66, 69–70, 72, 75, 78, 81–83, 86, 88–91, 93, 95, 97, 99–101, 103–105, 108, 110, 112–113, 115, 118, 138, 142, 163, 180, 183, 200, 203, 245, 258, 289, 296, 329, 332, 338, 347, 351. **F.5**: 4, 30, 36, 116, 234, 274, 313, 326, 328. **F.7**: 19, 81. **F.8**: 17–18, 25, 54, 81. **G.3.1**: 58, 131. **G.3.2**: 121, 169. **H.3**: 19, 22. **I.2**: 48, 56, 69, 72, 89, 133, 202. **I.4**: 60. **I.6**: 11. **K.1**: 34, 54, 268, 331, 425. **K.2**: 6, 35, 52, 75, 109. **K.3**: 15, 21, 25. **K.4**: 25, 121.
Famine **F.1**: 43. **G.3.2**: 65. **K.1**: 18, 245, 255.
Fanatisme religieux **D.5**: 56.
Fascisme **D.8**: 45.
Fécondité **F.1**: 33. **F.3**: 11, 40, 51, 75–76, 79, 81, 83, 86, 88, 90–91, 94–95, 97–105, 107, 111, 113, 122–123, 128–129, 131, 134–141, 276. **F.4**: 33, 208, 248, 306, 330. **F.5**: 2, 38, 236. **F.8**: 15.
Fédéralisme **D.7**: 334.
Fémininité **C.3**: 144. **D.2**: 10. **F.5**: 263, 299.
Féminisme **A.2**: 10. **B.1**: 3, 29, 42, 51, 102. **C.5**: 35. **D.5**: 17, 36, 92. **D.8**: 37, 50. **F.3**: 115. **F.4**: 20, 58. **F.5**: 62–72, 74–77, 79–88, 90–104, 106–110, 112–114, 116–118, 120–124, 127, 129–134, 136–141, 143–144, 180–181, 204, 228, 276, 287. **G.2**: 36. **I.2**: 115. **J.5**: 21. **K.1**: 52, 97, 101. **K.3**: 16.

Femmes **C.1**: 68. **C.2**: 3, 75, 83, 98, 218, 226, 229, 234. **C.4**: 63. **D.1**: 22. **D.2**: 12-14. **D.4**: 11, 42. **D.7**: 327, 394. **D.8**: 43, 74-75. **D.9**: 68, 133. **E.2**: 46. **E.3**: 7, 24. **F.1**: 54. **F.2**: 45, 55, 60. **F.3**: 5, 30, 33, 38, 60, 68, 71-72, 96, 108-109, 127, 133, 141-142, 158, 208, 216, 232, 293. **F.4**: 39, 63, 90, 133, 145, 153, 156, 159, 161, 224, 228, 230, 260-263, 321. **F.5**: 4, 15-16, 20-23, 25, 27-28, 32-33, 36-37, 43-46, 48-52, 55-57, 65-67, 96, 107, 116, 130, 138-140, 144-145, 148, 156, 158-159, 161-162, 165, 170-171, 188, 191-192, 195, 198-199, 203, 206-208, 211-212, 214, 219, 221, 225, 228-230, 237, 240-241, 244, 246, 248, 251-255, 257, 260, 276, 280, 292-293, 307-308, 318, 322. **F.6**: 29, 37, 41. **F.8**: 20, 24, 70, 74, 170. **G.1**: 48. **G.2**: 25, 36. **G.3.1**: 44, 60, 75, 80-81, 122. **II.3**: 8, 35, 50. **I.2**: 75, 78-79, 85, 87, 92-93, 98-99, 111, 114, 116-118, 121, 132, 134, 142, 146, 150, 152, 155-157, 162, 184, 213, 215. **I.3**: 137. **I.4**: 69. **J.3**: 38. **J.4**: 25. **J.7**: 1. **J.8**: 21. **K.1**: 4, 20, 24, 50, 63, 136-137, 174, 236, 248, 294, 305, 326, 341, 356, 419, 421. **K.2**: 33, 56, 104. **K.3**: 32. **K.4**: 3, 36, 84, 105, 179, 243.

Femmes et politique **F.5**: 79, 112, 149, 184, 209, 227, 249, 265, 324-325. **J.4**: 26. **J.5**: 38. **J.6**: 55.

Femmes mariées **F.4**: 114, 130, 180, 218, 240. **F.5**: 8. **G.3.1**: 10. **I.2**: 119, 180. **J.7**: 3.

Femmes rurales **F.3**: 110. **F.5**: 7, 24. **G.3.1**: 5, 7, 34, 53, 60. **I.2**: 81.

Fenichel, Otto
 C.1: 42.

Fermes familiales **F.4**: 14, 51, 114. **G.3.1**: 33, 80.

Fermeture d'usine **E.2**: 15. **H.7**: 13. **J.6**: 25.

Feu **G.3.2**: 308.

Fiabilité **B.2**: 19-20. **C.1**: 128.

Fiancée **F.4**: 244.

Filiation **F.4**: 60.

Fille **F.4**: 265, 283, 291, 300, 317, 327.

Films **D.8**: 12. **E.1**: 14. **F.4**: 3.

Fils **F.3**: 64.

Finance **H.6**: 6. **K.2**: 3.

Financement des campagnes électorales **J.6**: 65.

Finances internationales **G.3.2**: 35.

Finances publiques **F.8**: 50.

Fiscalité **D.4**: 1. **G.1**: 63. **G.3.2**: 218. **H.6**: 4.

Fixation du prix **H.5**: 9. **I.6**: 2.

Fixation du salaire **H.3**: 5. **I.3**: 18.

Fleck, Ludwig
 D.6: 11.

Flexibilité des salaires **I.3**: 33.

FMI **H.3**: 25.

Foi **D.5**: 94, 111.

Folie **C.1**: 35.

Folklore **C.5**: 84.

Fonction publique **I.2**: 142. **I.3**: 123. **I.4**: 23.

Fonction publique locale **K.2**: 74.

Fonctionnaires **I.6**: 24.

Fondamentalisme religieux **C.7**: 72. **D.5**: 16, 92. **F.5**: 44.

Force armée **J.7**: 1, 6, 12, 14, 17-18.

Force du marché **H.3**: 81.

Forces religieuses **D.5**: 69.

Foresterie **I.4**: 46.

Forêts **G.1**: 41.

Formalisation **D.6**: 4. **K.4**: 22.

Formation **C.1**: 137. **D.8**: 10. **D.9**: 209. **G.3.1**: 135. **G.3.2**: 254, 256. **H.7**: 11. **I.2**: 157. **I.4**: 25, 67, 116, 125, 130. **K.3**: 30, 46.

Formation à la gestion **I.5**: 52.

Formation de classe **E.2**: 53, 70.

Formation des attitudes **C.7**: 80.

Formation des enseignants **K.3**: 24.

Formation des opinions **C.6**: 6.

Formation professionnelle **D.9**: 192. **F.7**: 265. **I.4**: 74, 117-118, 121-124, 126, 128-129, 131-133.

Formation sur le tas **I.4**: 119, 124.

Foucault, Michel
 B.1: 52, 114. **D.6**: 12. **F.5**: 74, 277. **J.5**: 28. **K.1**: 52.

Fourier, Charles
 D.1: 79.

Fraassen, Van, Bas
 D.6: 31.

Franc-maçonnerie **F.7**: 36.

Fraternité **C.3**: 66.

Fratrie **C.3**: 75. **D.9**: 142. **F.3**: 190. **F.4**: 73, 142, 310, 340, 346, 349. **K.3**: 35.

Fraude **I.4**: 10. **K.1**: 163.

Fraude fiscale **D.5**: 57. **H.2**: 20. **I.4**: 51.

Freud, Sigmund
 C.1: 1, 18-19, 46, 55, 112.

Fromm, Erich
 C.1: 29.

Frontière **F.8**: 5, 45. **G.1**: 54. **H.5**: 39. **H.7**: 8. **J.8**: 17, 19.

Fusions d'entreprises **C.3**: 124. **C.5**: 77. **I.5**: 120.

Gains **F.4**: 30, 88. **F.8**: 57. **H.3**: 43, 59, 65-66, 88. **I.2**: 87-88, 105, 166. **I.3**: 22. **I.4**: 18, 40.

Gauche **C.1**: 42. **F.5**: 94. **J.3**: 32, 34. **J.6**: 11. **K.1**: 54, 101, 354.

Gémellité **G.1**: 44.

Généalogie **F.4**: 60. **F.5**: 100.

Génération **E.3**: 14, 23. **F.2**: 6, 14, 44. **I.4**: 22. **J.6**: 17.

Générations politiques **J.6**: 11.

Génétique **C.1**: 20. **C.2**: 37. **F.1**: 40. **F.3**: 59, 161. **K.4**: 13, 37, 249, 255, 261, 263, 267, 270–271.

Génétique humaine **D.3**: 18. **K.4**: 251.

Génocide **C.2**: 107.

Genre **B.1**: 128. **B.2**: 23. **C.1**: 65. **C.2**: 36, 99, 171, 239. **C.3**: 31, 45, 78, 151. **C.6**: 3. **C.7**: 67. **D.1**: 20, 127. **D.4**: 9. **D.5**: 1, 13, 16–17, 79. **D.7**: 107, 150, 327. **D.8**: 66. **D.9**: 38, 121. **E.3**: 19. **F.1**: 28, 42, 64. **F.2**: 31, 49, 87, 143. **F.3**: 169, 269. **F.4**: 59, 83, 93, 270. **F.5**: 1, 3, 8, 10–14, 17, 30, 40, 75, 87, 128, 137, 139, 147, 163, 167, 169–171, 173, 178–180, 182–183, 185, 215, 217, 220, 222, 233, 264, 266–267, 279, 282, 284, 286–288, 310. **F.6**: 15, 19. **F.7**: 53, 149, 234. **F.8**: 20, 39, 90. **G.3.1**: 24, 85. **G.3.2**: 112, 183, 214, 244, 265. **H.3**: 28, 73. **H.4**: 17, 44. **I.2**: 78, 80, 95–97, 100, 103, 105, 113, 123, 129, 132, 135–136, 166. **I.3**: 18, 44, 133. **I.4**: 24, 82, 119. **I.5**: 18, 82, 96, 145. **J.2**: 10. **J.5**: 19. **J.6**: 13. **K.1**: 47, 86, 185, 198. **K.3**: 42. **K.4**: 58.

Genre humain **D.1**: 100.

Gens de maison **I.3**: 64.

Géographie **C.2**: 38. **D.7**: 92. **F.1**: 64. **G.1**: 51–52, 54–56, 58–61. **G.3.2**: 33. **H.7**: 8. **I.2**: 7. **J.3**: 44. **J.6**: 25.

Géographie de la population **F.1**: 9.

Géographie économique **B.2**: 98. **G.1**: 63. **G.3.2**: 302. **H.7**: 5.

Géographie historique **G.1**: 55, 57, 64.

Géographie politique **D.7**: 59. **J.3**: 23.

Géographie urbaine **G.3.2**: 20, 87, 209.

Gérontologie **F.2**: 29.

Gestes **C.3**: 30.

Gestion **A.1**: 30. **C.5**: 42, 54. **C.7**: 44. **D.3**: 24. **D.4**: 19. **D.8**: 26. **D.9**: 184. **F.5**: 147, 163. **G.3.1**: 29. **G.3.2**: 264. **H.4**: 16–17, 20–21, 27, 32, 34, 37, 46, 54, 91. **H.7**: 17. **I.2**: 113. **I.3**: 2, 92, 121, 140. **I.4**: 81, 106. **I.5**: 25, 31, 38–39, 44, 77, 86, 172, 193, 203. **J.4**: 9, 25. **K.2**: 92. **K.4**: 109.

Gestion administrative **C.5**: 45. **H.4**: 18. **J.4**: 10–11, 17.

Gestion d'entreprises **C.3**: 27. **C.5**: 5, 65. **D.7**: 10. **H.4**: 60. **I.3**: 131, 151. **I.4**: 82. **J.4**: 10–11. **K.4**: 180.

Gestion de l'environnement **D.3**: 38–39.

Gestion de la production **H.4**: 85.

Gestion de produits **H.5**: 22.

Gestion des déchets **D.7**: 188. **G.1**: 26, 43.

Gestion des ressources **G.1**: 10.

Gestion des ventes **F.6**: 28.

Gestion du personnel **C.2**: 151. **D.3**: 7. **D.4**: 34. **I.3**: 109, 123, 125–133, 135–136, 139, 141–149, 152, 154.

Gestion financière **K.1**: 167.

Gestion hospitalière **K.4**: 17, 152.

Gestion industrielle **H.2**: 1. **H.4**: 15. **I.5**: 29.

Gestion urbaine **G.3.2**: 269, 324.

Ghetto **G.3.2**: 216. **K.1**: 231–232.

Goffman, Erving **B.1**: 5, 97.

Golding, William **D.8**: 14.

Gompertz, Benjamin **F.3**: 257.

Gorbachev, Mikhail **H.3**: 48.

Gough, H. **C.6**: 11.

Gouvernement **D.3**: 47–48. **F.3**: 210. **G.3.2**: 4. **H.3**: 74. **I.5**: 16. **I.6**: 14.

Grammaire **D.7**: 197, 215.

Grande banditisme **K.1**: 117, 150–151.

Grecs **F.4**: 225.

Green, T.H. **F.5**: 88.

Grèves **E.2**: 69, 76. **G.1**: 47. **I.5**: 76, 79, 84–85, 87, 92, 95.

Grossesse **F.2**: 145. **F.3**: 59, 112, 125–126. **F.4**: 35, 111. **I.2**: 130, 145, 159. **K.4**: 104, 171, 215, 262.

Groupements professionnels **I.4**: 12.

Groupes d'égaux **C.3**: 43, 137. **C.4**: 7. **F.4**: 81. **K.4**: 128.

Groupes d'intérêt **D.4**: 17. **J.5**: 24, 36. **J.6**: 50. **K.1**: 96.

Groupes de travail **C.3**: 85. **C.4**: 12. **I.3**: 77.

Groupes ethniques **C.7**: 21. **E.2**: 22. **F.4**: 207. **F.7**: 3, 11, 17, 34–35, 40, 45, 71, 81, 102, 115, 121, 137, 160. **F.8**: 48, 61, 81. **G.3.2**: 185. **H.4**: 36. **I.2**: 189, 225. **I.4**: 7. **K.1**: 350.

Groupes minoritaires **F.7**: 20.

Groupes religieux **D.5**: 4, 132. **J.5**: 29.

Groupes restreints **C.4**: 6, 9, 21, 45, 56–57, 63.

Guérillas **G.3.1**: 132. **K.1**: 11.

Guerre **D.1**: 114. **D.5**: 60, 154. **D.8**: 78. **F.1**: 1. **F.2**: 117. **F.7**: 186. **G.1**: 39. **J.7**: 8, 16. **J.8**: 14, 18, 20–22.

Guerre civile **G.3.1**: 132. **J.7**: 15. **K.1**: 11.

Guerre dans la Golfe **D.7**: 260. **F.4**: 83. **J.7**: 11. **J.8**: 10.

Guerre des Malouines **C.3**: 94. **J.7**: 17.

Gumperz, John J.
D.7: 156.
Gurvitsch, Aron
B.1: 99.
Habermas, Jürgen
B.1: 24, 59, 91, 107, 110, 112, 116. **D.3**: 58. **D.9**: 30. **J.2**: 15.
Habitat **G.1**: 1.
Habitudes **C.2**: 139. **K.4**: 153.
Habitudes alimentaires **D.2**: 21.
Hall, Stuart
C.7: 68.
Handicapés **D.7**: 363. **F.3**: 170, 232. **F.4**: 8. **K.4**: 139.
Handicapés mentaux **K.4**: 221.
Handicapés physiques **F.3**: 204.
Harcèlement sexuel **C.5**: 26. **D.4**: 12, 41. **F.5**: 13, 85, 300. **F.6**: 6, 18, 46. **I.2**: 222. **I.3**: 76.
Hayek, Friedrich
D.1: 74.
Haynsworth, Clement F.
D.4: 7.
Hegel, Georg Friedrich W.
B.1: 70, 122. **D.6**: 12.
Herero **F.3**: 89.
Herméneutique **B.1**: 25, 54. **C.5**: 84. **D.5**: 19. **D.6**: 7.
Heures de travail **I.2**: 43, 60. **I.3**: 9, 19, 30, 93.
Heures supplémentaires **I.3**: 24.
Heuristique **C.1**: 126.
Hiérarchie **A.1**: 32. **B.2**: 52. **C.6**: 4. **E.2**: 57. **E.3**: 74. **G.3.2**: 243. **J.4**: 17. **K.4**: 152.
Hiérarchie ecclésiastique **D.5**: 121.
Hindouisme **C.1**: 151. **D.5**: 154, 156–158.
Hindous **C.4**: 29. **C.7**: 31. **D.5**: 155. **F.5**: 155. **F.7**: 29. **J.3**: 24.
Hispanique **B.2**: 22. **C.1**: 75. **D.9**: 14. **F.3**: 278. **F.7**: 31, 69, 107, 172. **F.8**: 38, 95. **H.3**: 9, 26. **I.2**: 178. **J.6**: 1.
Histoire **A.1**: 14, 17. **B.1**: 89. **C.1**: 114, 157. **C.5**: 30. **E.3**: 76. **F.5**: 67. **F.8**: 5. **G.1**: 55. **H.1**: 4.
Histoire agricole **H.4**: 55.
Histoire coloniale **J.3**: 24.
Histoire de l'Église **J.3**: 29.
Histoire de la famille **K.1**: 309, 374.
Histoire de la médicine **K.4**: 23.
Histoire de la musique **D.8**: 25.
Histoire de la sociologie **A.1**: 8, 12, 26.
Histoire des sciences **D.6**: 14.
Histoire orale **F.5**: 144.

Histoire sociale **B.1**: 11. **D.5**: 19. **E.3**: 34, 62. **F.7**: 111.
Histoires de vies **E.2**: 9.
Historiographie **E.3**: 54. **K.1**: 116.
HIV **F.2**: 22, 128. **F.3**: 60, 159, 165, 182–183, 187, 193, 198, 201, 222, 228. **F.6**: 4. **F.8**: 21. **K.1**: 380. **K.3**: 46. **K.4**: 229.
Hobbes, Thomas
E.1: 12.
Holocauste **C.2**: 107.
Homicide **F.4**: 338. **K.1**: 49, 90, 92, 130, 156, 430.
Hommes **B.2**: 23. **C.2**: 83, 98, 205, 226. **C.4**: 63. **D.2**: 13. **E.2**: 35, 68. **F.1**: 61. **F.3**: 68, 92. **F.4**: 25, 39, 223, 228, 260, 285. **F.5**: 3, 26, 96, 118, 150, 193, 253, 262, 271, 322. **F.6**: 25, 29, 32, 57. **F.7**: 238. **H.3**: 15, 59. **I.2**: 117–118, 120–121, 125, 148. **I.3**: 34. **K.1**: 199, 263, 307, 406, 417. **K.3**: 23.
Hommes de loi **I.4**: 109.
Hommes mariés **I.4**: 53.
Homogamie **E.2**: 39.
Homosexualité **C.1**: 107. **C.3**: 25, 141. **C.7**: 25. **D.5**: 125. **F.3**: 202. **F.4**: 43, 181, 195, 235, 277. **F.6**: 2–4, 11, 17, 22, 30, 40, 47. **G.1**: 56. **K.1**: 429.
Hôpitaux **F.7**: 37. **K.1**: 305, 359. **K.3**: 4, 11, 32. **K.4**: 18, 22, 49, 73, 83, 101, 131, 161, 182.
Hôpitaux psychiatriques **K.1**: 190. **K.4**: 100, 131, 217.
Horaire variable de travail **I.3**: 34, 131, 154.
Horticulture **G.3.1**: 119.
Hospitalité **G.3.1**: 70.
Hostilité **G.3.1**: 70. **K.1**: 417.
Huile **D.7**: 315.
Humanisme **D.1**: 132.
Humanités **A.1**: 35, 37. **D.9**: 179.
Hume, David
B.1: 56.
Humour **C.2**: 44. **C.3**: 51. **F.2**: 110.
Hutterite **D.5**: 149.
Hygiène **F.3**: 179. **K.4**: 41, 220.
Hypnose **C.2**: 45, 81.
Idéalisme **D.1**: 23, 85.
Idées religieuses **D.5**: 154.
Identification **C.3**: 29. **C.4**: 60. **C.7**: 80. **F.7**: 63, 69, 86. **K.4**: 121.
Identité **B.1**: 142. **C.2**: 6, 46, 65, 70, 221. **C.4**: 60. **D.1**: 9, 41, 56, 71. **D.3**: 13. **D.5**: 39, 115, 125, 169. **D.7**: 31–32, 44, 63. **F.2**: 19, 73, 139. **F.4**: 250. **F.5**: 151. **F.6**: 49. **F.7**: 37, 85, 89, 100–101, 123–124, 159, 164. **G.1**: 58. **I.2**: 136. **I.3**: 5. **I.4**: 5, 60, 95. **J.1**: 18. **J.6**: 3, 36.

K.4: 212.
Identité culturelle **D.1**: 4, 73. **F.7**: 99, 123. **K.4**: 2.
Identité de groupe **C.4**: 16, 60. **C.7**: 25. **D.1**: 82. **D.7**: 285. **F.8**: 17.
Identité nationale **D.1**: 9, 33, 58, 64, 70, 83, 87, 90, 103. **D.7**: 286. **F.5**: 191, 302. **F.7**: 97, 99, 116. **F.8**: 82. **I.2**: 50. **J.8**: 16.
Identité professionnelle **I.4**: 111.
Identité régionale **D.1**: 75–76. **F.7**: 54, 88.
Idéologie **C.2**: 230. **C.3**: 48. **C.5**: 60. **C.7**: 35–36, 68. **D.1**: 17, 24, 103, 108. **D.6**: 15, 25. **D.7**: 28, 32, 113, 130, 268, 291. **D.9**: 75. **F.3**: 30. **F.4**: 12, 110. **F.5**: 282. **F.7**: 236. **I.1**: 5. **I.4**: 9, 57. **I.5**: 19, 58. **J.2**: 11, 23. **J.6**: 15, 29. **J.7**: 10. **K.2**: 80.
Igbo **D.8**: 19.
Illégitimité **F.3**: 65.
Images **C.1**: 7. **C.6**: 1. **D.1**: 43. **D.6**: 13. **D.7**: 15, 325. **D.8**: 58. **D.9**: 28. **E.1**: 6. **F.4**: 161, 292. **F.5**: 99, 271. **G.1**: 58. **H.6**: 6. **J.1**: 10. **J.6**: 16. **J.7**: 16. **K.1**: 398.
Imagination **C.2**: 167.
Imitation **C.3**: 59, 134.
Immigrant clandestins **D.7**: 33.
Immigrants **D.7**: 93. **D.9**: 52. **F.1**: 32. **F.4**: 64. **F.5**: 18, 248. **F.7**: 7, 9, 26, 32, 56, 100, 106, 108, 143, 167, 228, 240, 254. **F.8**: 1–2, 9, 15, 19, 23, 28, 46, 50, 54, 57, 60, 64, 67–68, 72–73, 76, 111, 114, 127, 131. **H.3**: 65. **I.2**: 52, 72, 164, 180, 191, 203. **J.6**: 12, 17. **K.1**: 20, 54, 58. **K.2**: 81. **K.4**: 42.
Immigration **A.3**: 2. **E.2**: 81. **F.4**: 322. **F.7**: 27, 90, 110, 191, 258. **F.8**: 24–27, 29, 40, 61–62, 69, 74, 92, 111–113, 116–118, 120–124, 127, 130–131, 134–135, 139–140, 144–146, 152, 155, 162, 165, 167, 169, 171–172. **H.3**: 20.
Impérialisme **J.7**: 24.
Incertitude **C.1**: 126. **C.7**: 12. **D.1**: 102. **D.4**: 15. **F.8**: 110. **I.2**: 190.
Inceste **F.4**: 170.
Indépendance **C.4**: 31. **D.9**: 153. **F.7**: 87.
Indexation **K.1**: 229.
Indicateurs sociaux **F.1**: 16. **H.3**: 11, 14.
Indiens **F.5**: 195. **F.7**: 28–29. **G.3.1**: 95.
Individu et société **J.3**: 15.
Individualisme **B.1**: 102. **C.2**: 19, 50. **C.3**: 95. **D.5**: 21. **E.1**: 13, 18. **F.5**: 30. **I.5**: 118.
Individualité **B.1**: 57.
Individus **B.1**: 66, 84. **C.1**: 135. **C.2**: 13, 25, 34, 72, 92, 125, 136, 187. **C.3**: 23. **C.4**: 36, 38, 54. **D.1**: 46. **D.3**: 18. **D.7**: 36. **D.9**: 122. **F.4**: 103. **F.6**: 20. **I.1**: 14. **I.2**: 182. **I.3**: 22.
Indochinois **F.8**: 77, 84. **I.2**: 61.
Indonésiens **F.2**: 147.

Induction **B.1**: 58.
Industrialisation **E.3**: 57. **G.3.2**: 163. **I.5**: 150.
Industrie **C.5**: 57. **D.9**: 189, 192–193. **E.2**: 28. **F.5**: 185. **G.3.2**: 272, 323. **H.4**: 28, 49. **I.1**: 6, 11. **I.2**: 207. **I.3**: 110. **I.5**: 173. **K.1**: 318.
Industrie alimentaire **C.5**: 16. **C.7**: 55. **D.2**: 15, 21. **H.4**: 98. **I.2**: 129. **I.5**: 10.
Industrie automobile **D.7**: 114. **H.4**: 69. **I.3**: 53, 67, 87. **I.5**: 121.
Industrie chimique **I.3**: 111.
Industrie cinématographique **D.8**: 59. **I.5**: 94.
Industrie de l'acier **C.5**: 36. **I.5**: 27.
Industrie de la construction **H.4**: 38. **I.3**: 4, 122. **I.4**: 43.
Industrie de pâte à papier **K.1**: 342.
Industrie des télécommunications **H.4**: 59.
Industrie du charbon **I.5**: 42.
Industrie du disque **D.8**: 16.
Industrie du sucre **H.4**: 13.
Industrie du vêtement **F.5**: 36. **H.4**: 50, 58. **I.2**: 183.
Industrie électronique **D.9**: 40. **H.4**: 58. **I.5**: 6, 126.
Industrie exportatrice **I.2**: 162.
Industrie forestière **G.1**: 11. **H.4**: 43.
Industrie hôtelière **I.2**: 129.
Industrie laitière **G.3.1**: 62. **H.4**: 3, 101.
Industrie mécanique **I.4**: 37.
Industrie minière **I.5**: 84, 153.
Industrie textile **D.9**: 40. **G.3.2**: 28. **H.4**: 90. **I.2**: 123, 140. **I.3**: 88, 130.
Inégalité de revenu **D.3**: 37. **F.8**: 54. **H.3**: 63, 73, 76, 78, 84. **I.2**: 105, 141, 144. **I.4**: 11. **K.1**: 54.
Inégalité de sexes **F.5**: 217. **I.2**: 35. **I.5**: 96. **K.1**: 375.
Inégalité économique **H.3**: 28, 48. **K.1**: 92. **K.4**: 87.
Inégalité raciale **F.7**: 145, 250, 252. **K.4**: 3.
Inégalité sociale **D.9**: 123, 125. **E.2**: 8, 29–31, 42, 44, 47–48, 71, 73. **F.4**: 48. **F.7**: 82. **G.3.2**: 206. **H.3**: 7. **H.4**: 2. **H.5**: 28. **K.4**: 87, 106.
Infanticide **K.1**: 15.
Infirmières **C.2**: 152, 218. **I.2**: 108, 148. **I.3**: 63. **I.4**: 28, 48. **K.3**: 32. **K.4**: 3, 17, 58, 67, 73, 231.
Inflation **H.3**: 22, 29.
Influence culturelle **C.2**: 52. **K.4**: 72.
Influence du groupe **C.4**: 7.
Influence sociale **C.1**: 56. **C.3**: 76–77. **D.1**: 43.
Influences religieuses **F.6**: 39.

Information **B.2**: 51, 60, 87. **C.2**: 152. **C.3**: 45, 61, 158. **C.4**: 14, 34. **C.5**: 34. **C.7**: 57. **D.3**: 40, 57. **D.4**: 21. **D.7**: 37, 74, 120, 134, 264. **F.5**: 163. **G.3**: 5. **I.4**: 3. **I.5**: 32, 68. **K.4**: 83.
Information d'entreprise **I.5**: 33.
Information politique **J.6**: 47.
Information sociale **C.3**: 46, 148. **F.3**: 210.
Informatique **F.5**: 242.
Informatisation **D.1**: 109. **D.6**: 6.
Infrastructure sociale **H.7**: 24.
Ingénierie **D.9**: 190. **H.4**: 14, 24. **I.2**: 121. **I.4**: 132.
Ingénieurs **H.4**: 32. **I.2**: 24, 66. **I.4**: 66, 95–97, 106, 113, 115.
Initiation **I.4**: 89. **K.1**: 94.
Injures **F.3**: 208. **I.3**: 107, 110–111.
Injustice **C.3**: 116.
Innovations **C.5**: 76, 78. **G.3.2**: 131. **H.4**: 91, 93. **I.4**: 17.
Inondations **C.7**: 22. **G.3.2**: 85.
Insémination artificielle **F.3**: 66.
Insertion professionnelle **D.9**: 181.
Instabilité politique **F.7**: 62. **J.6**: 28.
Institutionnalisme **H.1**: 3.
Institutions **C.1**: 137. **C.5**: 33, 47. **C.6**: 12. **D.5**: 84, 114. **E.3**: 6. **F.7**: 30. **G.3.1**: 92. **H.4**: 72, 96. **K.1**: 362. **K.4**: 132, 141.
Institutions politiques **I.5**: 146.
Institutions religieuses **D.5**: 138.
Instruments à cordes **C.4**: 12.
Insurrection **J.5**: 18.
Intégration de la collectivité **D.9**: 84.
Intégration économique **G.3.1**: 32.
Intégration nationale **F.7**: 104.
Intégration politique **E.2**: 10.
Intégration sociale **E.1**: 15. **F.1**: 32. **F.4**: 142. **F.7**: 181, 208, 240. **F.8**: 66, 83, 171. **J.7**: 9. **J.8**: 6, 9.
Intellectuels **D.1**: 53. **E.2**: 22. **F.7**: 5, 244. **J.1**: 11. **J.6**: 54.
Intelligence **C.2**: 37, 48–49. **D.1**: 128. **F.2**: 102.
Intelligence artificielle **C.2**: 64, 115. **D.6**: 24. **D.7**: 118. **E.3**: 3. **I.5**: 51.
Intelligentsia **D.1**: 37.
Interaction conjugale **C.1**: 59. **C.3**: 140. **F.4**: 169, 197, 226, 240, 314. **I.4**: 75.
Interaction en groupe **C.3**: 86. **C.4**: 37, 44. **C.7**: 24.
Interaction sociale **B.1**: 97. **C.1**: 135, 145. **C.3**: 39, 46, 50, 73, 88. **C.4**: 64. **D.7**: 249. **K.1**: 139.
Interactionnisme **C.3**: 31, 91.

Interdépendance **C.4**: 31.
Intérêt public **F.2**: 141. **F.4**: 15.
Intermariage **D.5**: 129. **F.4**: 216.
Internationalisation **D.1**: 54. **D.7**: 335. **D.9**: 191. **K.4**: 216.
Internationalisme **J.8**: 11.
Intervalles génésiques **F.3**: 80.
Intervention de l'État **F.8**: 94.
Intifade **D.7**: 364. **F.5**: 56, 60. **J.5**: 12.
Intimité **F.4**: 262. **H.6**: 2.
Invalidité **K.4**: 19.
Inventaire **K.1**: 42.
Investissements **F.4**: 21, 89. **G.3.2**: 192. **H.3**: 39. **I.2**: 106, 179.
Investissements étrangers **F.8**: 37.
Investissements industriels **D.9**: 196.
Irigaray, Luce **F.5**: 102.
Irrationalité **C.7**: 7.
Irrigation **E.3**: 28. **G.3.1**: 28.
Islam **B.1**: 140. **C.2**: 102. **D.1**: 57. **D.5**: 97, 163–167, 170, 173, 176, 178–179, 184. **D.7**: 313. **F.3**: 11, 41, 293. **F.5**: 15, 192, 229, 302. **F.8**: 7, 65.
Islam et politique **D.5**: 175. **J.3**: 12.
Islamisation **D.5**: 161.
Isolement social **F.4**: 239.
Italiens **D.7**: 75, 218. **F.7**: 32.
Jaïnisme **D.5**: 74.
Jalousie **C.2**: 233.
Japonais **D.5**: 22. **D.7**: 64. **F.7**: 96. **F.8**: 96.
Jardins **G.3.1**: 27. **I.6**: 39.
Jazz **D.8**: 1.
Jésuite **D.9**: 7, 119.
Jeu **C.1**: 60.
Jeunes et politique **D.1**: 136. **F.7**: 219.
Jeunes travailleurs **F.1**: 42.
Jeunesse **C.2**: 107, 204. **C.3**: 9, 43. **D.4**: 32. **D.7**: 134, 181, 263. **D.8**: 61. **D.9**: 13, 169, 183. **F.2**: 10, 118, 123, 125, 127–129, 131, 133–141, 144, 146, 148–158. **F.4**: 32, 76, 116. **F.6**: 17, 39. **F.7**: 177. **F.8**: 13, 28, 38, 62, 143. **G.3.2**: 143. **I.2**: 23, 31, 166, 174, 215, 229, 234. **I.3**: 23. **I.4**: 67, 133. **I.5**: 89. **J.3**: 13. **J.6**: 11, 39, 41. **K.1**: 172, 214, 235, 237, 253, 287, 300, 315, 387, 401. **K.2**: 16, 42. **K.3**: 23, 37. **K.4**: 118.
Jeunesse urbaine **I.2**: 33. **K.1**: 231.
Jeux d'argent **H.4**: 36. **I.6**: 3. **K.1**: 9, 59.
Joie **C.3**: 100.

Journalisme **D.7**: 235, 241, 259, 266, 269, 271–272, 277, 303, 317–318, 325, 328–329, 367. **D.8**: 78. **K.1**: 141.

Journalistes **D.7**: 229. **I.5**: 171.

Judaïsme **D.5**: 97, 183–184, 186.

Jugement **B.2**: 86. **C.2**: 71, 100, 167, 169. **C.3**: 41. **C.4**: 1. **C.7**: 45. **D.3**: 66. **D.7**: 176. **F.3**: 187. **I.5**: 88.

Jugement social **C.3**: 78, 158. **C.7**: 15, 66.

Juges **D.4**: 24. **F.5**: 300.

Juifs **C.2**: 107. **C.3**: 51. **D.7**: 265. **D.9**: 142. **F.4**: 65, 82, 142, 253, 311. **F.5**: 4. **F.7**: 36, 66, 71, 83, 97–98, 109, 114, 119, 123, 127, 139, 159–160, 174, 178, 180, 183, 216, 241. **F.8**: 156. **H.2**: 13. **H.3**: 27. **I.6**: 22.

Jurisprudence **I.4**: 89. **J.2**: 7.

Jury **D.4**: 21.

Justice **C.5**: 68. **C.7**: 41. **D.3**: 4, 76. **D.4**: 3, 14, 23, 29. **D.5**: 79. **D.7**: 273. **G.3.1**: 31. **H.3**: 77. **H.6**: 4. **J.3**: 2, 13, 25. **J.4**: 20. **J.6**: 21. **K.1**: 177, 185, 328.

Justice criminelle **D.4**: 4, 6, 43. **F.3**: 144. **F.7**: 220. **J.1**: 3. **J.3**: 2, 9. **K.1**: 106, 144, 174–175, 182, 192, 198, 200, 202, 207, 209.

Justice distributive **D.3**: 1. **E.2**: 44. **F.2**: 46. **H.3**: 46, 61, 64.

Justice économique **F.5**: 46.

Justice sociale **C.3**: 49. **D.3**: 67. **D.4**: 40. **D.5**: 142, 147. **F.5**: 227. **I.2**: 247.

Kant, Immanuel **D.6**: 12.

Kanter, Rosabeth **F.5**: 226.

Khomeini **D.5**: 159.

Kibboutz **I.4**: 20. **K.1**: 208.

Kikuyu **F.3**: 72.

Klein, Melanie **C.1**: 21, 109.

Kowalski, Alourdes **D.5**: 188.

Kurdes **F.7**: 33, 133.

Lacan, Jacques **B.1**: 114. **C.1**: 27.

Laïcisme **D.5**: 27, 30.

Langage **C.1**: 41. **C.3**: 53. **D.4**: 44. **D.5**: 13. **D.7**: 4, 7, 20, 22, 25, 32, 35, 39, 42, 44, 48, 52–53, 61, 69–70, 76, 87, 89, 95, 97, 106, 115, 122, 130, 172, 185, 189, 203, 206–207, 209, 214, 269, 271, 332, 336–337, 348, 372. **D.9**: 14, 164, 202. **F.5**: 78, 132. **F.8**: 57, 82. **G.1**: 29. **H.3**: 63.

Langage par signes **D.7**: 186.

Langue allemande **D.7**: 93, 99, 218.

Langue anglaise **D.7**: 18–19, 45, 59, 64, 85, 141, 189, 198, 204, 219, 268.

Langue espagnole **D.7**: 59, 68, 86, 202, 226. **F.8**: 86. **K.4**: 12.

Langue française **D.7**: 350.

Langue gaélique **D.7**: 343.

Langue galloise **D.7**: 344.

Langue grecque **D.7**: 43.

Langue japonaise **D.7**: 201, 204.

Langue nationale **D.7**: 49.

Langues écrites **D.7**: 135, 191.

Langues étrangères **D.7**: 335.

Laudan, Larry **D.6**: 22.

Leaders **C.3**: 91. **C.6**: 3, 5–7, 18. **G.3.1**: 65. **J.3**: 14.

Leaders politiques **J.6**: 4.

Lecteurs **D.8**: 74.

Législation **D.4**: 17. **F.4**: 321.

Législation sociale **D.4**: 16.

Légitimation **C.5**: 79. **E.3**: 26. **G.3.2**: 261–262. **I.4**: 92.

Légitimité **H.4**: 66. **H.7**: 3. **J.4**: 9.

Leibniz, Gottfried **B.1**: 75.

Lèpre **D.1**: 142.

Lesbiennes **C.3**: 141. **F.4**: 181, 277. **F.6**: 3, 11, 22, 26, 40. **G.1**: 56. **K.1**: 429.

Libéralisation **E.3**: 27.

Libéralisme **F.5**: 82. **K.4**: 256.

Libération **D.5**: 110.

Libéraux **C.1**: 110. **F.3**: 63.

Liberté **D.3**: 20, 22. **J.3**: 17. **K.1**: 7.

Liberté d'expression **D.7**: 253. **I.5**: 81. **J.3**: 26.

Liberté de l'enseignement **D.7**: 308. **I.4**: 114.

Liberté de la presse **D.7**: 255, 262. **J.3**: 16.

Liberté religieuse **D.5**: 100.

Liberté surveillée **K.1**: 167, 180, 205. **K.3**: 48.

Libertés civiles **B.2**: 111. **D.7**: 308. **J.3**: 27.

Licenciements **I.3**: 20, 42–43, 91. **I.5**: 86, 100, 107, 155.

Lieu de travail **F.5**: 160. **G.1**: 47. **I.2**: 240. **I.3**: 15, 17, 35, 66, 70, 90, 121–122, 126. **I.5**: 11, 96, 110, 134. **K.1**: 344.

Ligne aérienne **I.3**: 3.

Ligue des États arabes **A.1**: 33.

Limbu **E.3**: 17.

Limitation des armements **C.7**: 48. **J.7**: 20.

Linguistique **C.3**: 126. **D.6**: 4. **D.7**: 55, 121, 133, 193, 200, 208, 211–212, 216, 220–221, 227.

Littérature **D.1**: 7. **D.5**: 175. **D.7**: 2, 271. **D.8**: 30, 69. **G.3.1**: 10.

Littérature populaire **D.7**: 303. **D.8**: 51, 68.

Liu, Chung-yüan **D.5**: 3.

Localisation géographique **G.1**: 30. **G.3**: 6. **K.4**: 59.

Localisation industrielle **B.2**: 44. **G.3.2**: 187, 289. **H.4**: 24, 40. **I.2**: 206.

Locataires **G.3.2**: 148. **K.4**: 142.

Locke, John **B.1**: 60.

Logement **D.2**: 9. **E.3**: 10. **F.1**: 4. **F.2**: 52, 64, 66. **F.4**: 141. **F.5**: 155. **F.7**: 146, 237, 246, 268. **G.2**: 20, 34. **G.3.2**: 40, 94–95, 97, 99–101, 103–104, 106, 109–110, 113–115, 117, 119–120, 122, 124, 126–127, 130, 134–136, 138–139, 142, 144–145, 150, 152, 156, 158–159, 162–163, 166–170. **H.4**: 9. **I.3**: 16. **I.4**: 43. **K.1**: 64. **K.2**: 7. **K.4**: 50, 119, 126, 142.

Logement urbain **G.2**: 34. **G.3.2**: 112–113, 157, 161.

Logements sociaux **G.3.2**: 147, 149.

Logiciel **B.2**: 84. **H.4**: 41.

Logique **B.1**: 34, 47. **D.6**: 16. **D.7**: 119–120, 196–197.

Loi islamique **F.3**: 41.

Loisir **F.3**: 299. **I.6**: 10–11, 16, 21, 30, 35, 39, 45.

Loyer **G.3.2**: 129. **H.3**: 16.

Luhmann, Niklas **E.1**: 3.

Lutte anti-pollution **G.1**: 24, 63.

Lutte de classes **E.2**: 28.

Machines outils **H.4**: 93. **I.3**: 50.

Macroanalyse **F.7**: 42.

Macroéconomie **I.6**: 37.

Macrosociologie **A.1**: 20. **D.1**: 99.

Magie **D.5**: 127.

Main-d'oeuvre féminine **F.3**: 95–96. **H.3**: 76. **I.2**: 93, 108, 126, 141, 173, 181.

Maintien de l'ordre **F.6**: 34. **J.3**: 45. **K.1**: 6, 10, 98, 372, 418.

Malades **C.1**: 2. **F.7**: 37. **K.4**: 12, 32, 56, 61, 69, 72, 75, 247, 259, 264.

Maladie diétaïque **F.5**: 57.

Maladie mentale **C.1**: 70. **C.2**: 204, 228. **D.4**: 2. **F.3**: 174, 192, 194–195. **F.4**: 210. **F.5**: 59. **K.1**: 20, 107, 129, 347. **K.4**: 37, 47, 64, 69, 107–108, 119, 130, 189, 212.

Maladie sexuellement transmissible **F.3**: 215–216.

Maladies **C.7**: 6. **F.1**: 31. **F.3**: 143, 149, 161, 164, 167, 177, 179, 184, 190–191, 213, 216, 284. **K.4**: 72, 85, 94, 184.

Maladies de coeur **K.4**: 32, 230.

Maladies professionnelles **H.4**: 7. **I.3**: 117, 119.

Malaise de la jeunesse **C.4**: 33. **K.1**: 404.

Malaria **K.4**: 97.

Mandinka **F.5**: 269.

Manuels **D.9**: 26.

Maori **F.7**: 197, 212.

Marché **D.3**: 3. **D.8**: 72. **E.1**: 22. **G.1**: 10. **H.2**: 7. **H.3**: 37. **H.5**: 30. **I.2**: 93. **I.5**: 17.

Marché de l'art **D.8**: 41.

Marché de la viande **I.5**: 169.

Marché du crédit **H.6**: 8.

Marché du logement **G.3.2**: 116, 133, 137, 140, 143, 155, 165. **H.3**: 60.

Marché du travail **C.4**: 48. **F.2**: 145. **F.5**: 150, 267. **F.8**: 72. **G.3.1**: 130. **G.3.2**: 181. **H.3**: 60. **H.4**: 56. **I.2**: 2–3, 5, 7, 11, 16, 18, 25–26, 28–29, 33–36, 38, 40, 42, 45, 48–50, 52, 56, 64–65, 71–72, 83, 85, 95–96, 102, 119, 124, 137, 144–145, 164, 172, 189, 191–192, 196, 203, 215, 242. **I.3**: 83. **I.4**: 29–30, 116. **I.5**: 17.

Marché unique européen **G.2**: 31. **I.4**: 47. **K.2**: 20, 27.

Marginalité **K.1**: 228, 261.

Marginaux **F.2**: 133.

Mari **F.3**: 105. **F.4**: 87, 252. **F.5**: 5. **I.2**: 36, 106.

Mariage **C.1**: 9, 59. **C.3**: 57. **D.5**: 127. **F.3**: 74, 94, 109, 119, 254. **F.4**: 29, 75, 80, 111, 138, 143, 160, 169, 181–182, 187, 193–196, 198–200, 202, 205, 209–212, 214–215, 218, 221–225, 227, 229–230, 235–238, 242–245, 248, 250–251, 253, 255–256, 258, 262, 304, 306. **F.5**: 5. **F.7**: 80, 167. **H.3**: 15, 35. **K.2**: 106.

Mariage religieux **F.2**: 131.

Mariages interethniques **F.4**: 207.

Marine de guerre **J.7**: 6.

Marx, Karl **E.2**: 54.

Marxisme **B.1**: 43, 45–46, 61. **F.3**: 115. **F.5**: 104, 132. **J.1**: 9. **J.2**: 14, 21, 31. **J.6**: 5.

Marxisme-Léninisme **J.2**: 8.

Masculinité **C.3**: 144. **F.5**: 118, 262, 268, 294, 304.

Masochisme **C.1**: 15.

Matérialisme **F.2**: 141.

Maternité **D.2**: 2. **F.1**: 25. **F.3**: 106. **F.4**: 279, 299, 325. **F.5**: 72, 151, 196, 296.

Maternité de substitution **F.4**: 305, 308.

Maternité précoce **D.9**: 151. **F.3**: 73, 130. **F.4**: 273. **K.1**: 231. **K.2**: 42.

Mathématiques **B.1**: 61. **C.2**: 166. **D.6**: 17.

Mauriciens **F.8**: 68.

Mbanderu **F.3**: 89.

McCarthyism **J.6**: 48.

McLuhan, Marshall **D.7**: 47.

Mead, George Herbert **B.1**: 67, 119.

Mécanisation **F.5**: 269.

Médecine **D.1**: 40. **D.3**: 62. **K.4**: 4–5, 30, 55, 81, 91, 96, 98, 105.

Médecine légal - **K.4**: 178.

Médecins **I.4**: 92, 101. **K.1**: 363. **K.4**: 6, 12, 30, 63, 70, 84, 95, 247, 264.

Médiateur **I.5**: 88. **K.1**: 417. **K.2**: 67.

Médiation **C.3**: 107–108, 113–114, 117. **D.4**: 24. **D.8**: 9. **F.4**: 133. **I.5**: 88, 91.

Médicament sociale **F.3**: 179. **K.4**: 75.

Médicament traditionnelle **C.1**: 43. **F.3**: 120. **K.4**: 55.

Mémoire **C.1**: 56, 98. **C.2**: 154–166. **C.3**: 68, 89. **C.4**: 14. **D.1**: 114. **D.7**: 108–109, 369. **E.3**: 58. **F.2**: 96. **F.3**: 33. **F.5**: 204. **F.8**: 63. **H.5**: 32. **K.1**: 308.

Menace **B.2**: 95. **C.4**: 15. **J.6**: 49.

Ménages **B.2**: 28, 36. **C.1**: 14. **F.1**: 29, 35, 58. **F.2**: 38, 58. **F.3**: 252–253. **F.4**: 26, 28, 74, 89. **F.5**: 14, 155, 164, 174, 195, 315. **F.8**: 36, 49, 73, 90, 113. **G.1**: 21. **G.2**: 1. **G.3.1**: 12, 27, 52. **G.3.2**: 38, 54, 115–116, 208. **H.3**: 19, 24. **H.5**: 37. **I.2**: 48. **K.1**: 272.

Mendiant **D.5**: 74. **K.1**: 233.

Mennonites **D.5**: 149.

Ménopause **F.5**: 22.

Menstruation **C.2**: 75. **K.1**: 4.

Mère **B.2**: 110. **C.1**: 33. **D.7**: 121. **F.3**: 33, 36, 118, 229, 245, 280. **F.4**: 56, 141, 178, 283, 300–301, 303, 348. **F.5**: 160, 315. **K.2**: 42, 64. **K.4**: 51.

Mères travailleuses **C.6**: 10. **F.2**: 89. **F.4**: 87, 280, 288. **I.2**: 89, 147, 159.

Messages **A.3**: 8. **D.7**: 369.

Mesure **B.2**: 18, 20, 46–47, 68, 110. **C.2**: 62, 89. **C.7**: 40. **D.3**: 83. **E.3**: 29. **F.2**: 12. **F.8**: 146. **G.3.2**: 98.

Mesure de l'utilité **B.2**: 58.

Mesure de la productivité **H.4**: 53.

Mesure du bien-être **K.1**: 250, 272.

Métallurgie de transformation **I.4**: 22.

Métaphore **D.7**: 172, 214.

Méthode expérimentale **I.2**: 41.

Méthodes de planification **J.4**: 13.

Méthodes de recherche **B.2**: 22, 98. **C.1**: 83. **D.7**: 282. **F.4**: 112.

Méthodes mathématiques **B.2**: 83.

Méthodes pédagogiques **C.2**: 118.

Méthodes statistiques **B.2**: 10, 41, 77, 99. **C.4**: 9.

Méthodologie **B.1**: 11, 40–41, 54, 76, 90, 120. **B.2**: 2, 11, 15, 42, 59, 112, 122–125. **C.4**: 18. **C.7**: 28. **E.1**: 25. **E.3**: 30–31. **F.5**: 71, 182. **G.3.2**: 98. **H.3**: 34. **J.5**: 33. **K.3**: 37.

Méthodologie archéologique **F.5**: 139.

Méthodologie économique **H.5**: 37.

Méthodologie sociologique **A.1**: 23. **B.1**: 98. **B.2**: 13, 33, 61. **G.3.1**: 47. **H.1**: 5.

Métis **F.7**: 3.

Métropole **G.3.2**: 19, 259, 305. **I.1**: 16.

Meutre **D.4**: 11. **F.4**: 166. **F.7**: 189.

Mexicains **D.9**: 42. **F.8**: 4, 61. **K.1**: 20.

Microanalyse **F.7**: 42.

Microéconomie **F.5**: 189.

Microsociologie **A.1**: 24. **C.5**: 83.

Migrateurs **D.7**: 42, 350. **F.1**: 10. **F.4**: 90. **F.5**: 260. **F.7**: 24, 41. **F.8**: 17, 33, 49, 78, 80–81, 107, 109, 150, 159. **G.3**: 10. **G.3.2**: 200, 203. **I.2**: 183.

Migration **F.1**: 55, 65. **F.3**: 76, 159, 215, 304. **F.4**: 87. **F.5**: 8, 23. **F.7**: 1, 49, 102, 160, 237. **F.8**: 6, 10–12, 16, 18, 30–32, 34–36, 38–39, 41–42, 47, 51, 53, 55, 63, 69, 71, 85, 87, 89, 95–96, 106, 122, 138, 147, 151, 161, 163, 166, 168, 175–177. **G.3.1**: 37, 58, 83. **G.3.2**: 91, 201, 265. **I.2**: 7.

Migration de retour **F.8**: 152, 157, 160.

Migration de travail **F.5**: 18. **F.8**: 136, 141, 148, 167. **I.2**: 169.

Migration internationale **F.8**: 128, 136–141, 148, 152, 154, 164, 166–167, 171, 176.

Migration interne **F.8**: 92, 94–95, 101, 103, 165.

Migration rurale-urbaine **F.8**: 86, 88, 91, 93, 97, 99, 101, 107. **G.3**: 10. **G.3.1**: 126. **G.3.2**: 200, 351.

Migration saisonnière **F.8**: 90, 100.

Migration urbaine-rurale **F.8**: 102, 110.

Migrations alternantes **F.3**: 303. **G.3.2**: 2. **H.3**: 60. **I.2**: 68.

Milieu de travail **I.2**: 161. **I.3**: 11–12, 82.

Milieu familial **F.4**: 27, 37, 340.

Milieu professionnel **F.4**: 27. **I.3**: 31.

Milieu rural **G.3.1**: 6.

Milieu scolaire **D.9**: 126.

Milieu social **D.1**: 38. **K.1**: 146.

Milieu urbain **G.3.2**: 36, 191.

Milieux d'affaires **C.1**: 125.

Militaires **D.7**: 319. **J.7**: 3–4, 9–10, 13–14, 19, 21. **J.8**: 14.

Militarisme **J.7**: 24.

Mill, John Stuart **B.1**: 58, 63, 113.

Miller, James Grier **C.5**: 11.

Mills, Charles Wright **B.1**: 132.

Mines d'or **F.8**: 109.

Mineurs **E.2**: 69.

Ministères **D.9**: 65.

Minorités **C.3**: 42. **C.4**: 5, 31, 44. **D.7**: 55, 212. **D.9**: 170. **F.5**: 187. **F.7**: 14, 34, 65, 75–76, 79, 113, 132, 183–184, 186, 188. **F.8**: 62, 76, 106. **G.2**: 34. **G.3.1**: 39. **I.2**: 215. **K.2**: 100. **K.4**: 114.

Minorités ethniques **D.7**: 21. **D.9**: 45. **F.7**: 1, 12–13, 15, 25, 27, 58, 61, 111, 129, 193–194, 237, 268. **F.8**: 19. **I.4**: 33. **K.1**: 232.

Minorités linguistiques **D.7**: 9, 341, 347. **F.7**: 130.

Minorités religieuses **D.5**: 122. **F.7**: 130.

Missionnaires **D.5**: 25.

Missions religieuses **D.5**: 22.

Mitterrand, François **J.6**: 27.

Mobilisation politique **F.7**: 221. **F.8**: 48. **J.5**: 13, 16.

Mobilité de la main d'oeuvre **F.8**: 35. **I.2**: 22, 68, 179. **I.4**: 34.

Mobilité des salaires **E.2**: 15.

Mobilité géographique **F.5**: 8. **F.8**: 43, 105, 108.

Mobilité professionnelle **B.2**: 32. **E.2**: 21. **G.3.2**: 207. **I.2**: 191, 207. **I.3**: 65. **I.4**: 28.

Mobilité résidentielle **C.2**: 86. **F.7**: 170. **F.8**: 105. **G.3.2**: 141, 203, 208.

Mobilité sociale **E.2**: 3, 5, 23, 26, 37, 58, 67, 71. **E.3**: 63. **F.5**: 185. **F.7**: 3. **F.8**: 108. **G.3.2**: 207. **H.3**: 46. **I.2**: 164, 207. **I.4**: 33. **K.4**: 9.

Mode **D.1**: 20, 138. **D.2**: 4, 10. **I.2**: 183.

Modèles **B.1**: 48. **B.2**: 19, 27, 34, 39, 50, 54, 59–61, 71, 88, 109. **C.1**: 91. **C.7**: 38, 78. **D.5**: 51. **D.7**: 118, 149. **E.2**: 13. **F.2**: 22, 85. **F.8**: 30. **G.3.2**: 68. **I.4**: 49. **J.3**: 17. **J.4**: 1. **K.4**: 229.

Modèles de décision **K.4**: 172.

Modèles dynamiques **C.2**: 215.

Modèles économétriques **F.8**: 139. **H.7**: 28.

Modèles linéaires **B.2**: 68, 72.

Modèles mathématiques **G.3.2**: 137.

Modèles statistiques **B.2**: 14, 53. **G.3.2**: 106. **K.4**: 102.

Modèles stochastiques **F.1**: 14. **F.8**: 49. **G.3.2**: 308.

Modelisation **B.2**: 14, 51, 77, 81. **F.1**: 29. **F.3**: 29. **G.3.2**: 50.

Modernisation **A.1**: 20. **B.1**: 101. **D.1**: 69. **E.2**: 41. **E.3**: 21. **F.3**: 51. **F.5**: 24. **F.7**: 122. **G.3.2**: 255, 267, 280.

Modernisme **B.1**: 13–14. **D.1**: 59, 81. **G.1**: 29. **G.3.2**: 51, 279.

Modernité **D.1**: 82. **D.6**: 20. **D.8**: 8. **E.2**: 11. **F.7**: 242. **G.1**: 57, 64. **K.3**: 41.

Modes de vie **D.2**: 9. **F.4**: 343. **G.1**: 8. **K.1**: 333, 380.

Monarchie **C.7**: 69. **D.7**: 6.

Monastères **D.5**: 102.

Monogamie **F.4**: 228.

Monroe, Marilyn **D.8**: 7.

Morale **B.1**: 71. **D.3**: 68.

Morales **B.1**: 126. **C.2**: 190. **C.3**: 142. **C.5**: 61. **D.3**: 63, 66–67, 70–72, 74, 81, 83–84, 86–88. **D.5**: 137. **E.2**: 27. **H.2**: 8. **I.2**: 37. **J.3**: 40, 45. **K.3**: 26.

Moralité **B.1**: 64. **C.2**: 14, 65, 197. **C.3**: 102. **D.3**: 64–65, 69, 75–80, 82, 85, 89–90. **D.5**: 30. **F.3**: 145. **F.4**: 101, 305, 339. **I.4**: 102. **J.7**: 11.

Morbidité **F.3**: 156, 166, 168, 171, 179, 200, 205, 226. **K.4**: 147.

Mormonisme **D.5**: 103, 120, 127.

Mort **C.1**: 19. **F.2**: 28–29, 45, 47. **F.3**: 27, 199, 203, 235. **F.4**: 8, 311. **F.5**: 156. **K.1**: 3, 397. **K.4**: 57, 148.

Mortalité **E.3**: 33. **F.3**: 78, 171, 234–235, 240–241, 243, 245–246, 248–251, 254–255, 257–259, 261–264, 269, 271–279, 281–288, 292–298. **F.4**: 333. **K.1**: 307. **K.4**: 32.

Mortalité des enfants **F.3**: 80, 200, 237, 242, 244–245, 252–253, 270, 282, 286, 291. **F.4**: 33.

Mortalité infantile **F.3**: 78, 237, 252, 264–266, 289–290, 292. **F.4**: 311. **K.4**: 174.

Moses, Robert **G.3.2**: 281.

Motivation **C.2**: 134, 168–170, 172–176, 178–179. **C.3**: 6, 97. **C.5**: 15, 43. **D.3**: 65. **D.5**: 33. **F.4**: 103. **H.7**: 11. **I.3**: 96. **I.4**: 71, 79, 125. **K.1**: 110, 352.

Motivation au travail **C.2**: 98. **I.4**: 50.

Motivation d'accomplissement **D.9**: 18, 161.

Mounda **F.5**: 237.

Mouvements agrariens **J.5**: 17.

Mouvements contestataires **E.3**: 39. **J.5**: 13, 34.

Mouvements de libération nationale **F.5**: 56.

Mouvements de résistance **F.5**: 231. **J.7**: 14.

Mouvements pacifistes **J.5**: 2.
Mouvements paysans **E.3**: 75. **G.3.1**: 84, 87.
Mouvements politiques **J.5**: 4, 23.
Mouvements religieux **D.5**: 17, 21, 53–54. **F.3**: 50. **J.5**: 53.
Mouvements sociaux **D.5**: 53, 66, 107. **E.2**: 27. **E.3**: 44, 51, 64. **F.7**: 214. **F.8**: 34. **G.3.2**: 184, 202. **I.2**: 212. **J.5**: 4, 7, 10, 29, 31, 33–34, 53. **K.4**: 78.
Moyen Âge **F.2**: 10, 13, 21, 32, 76. **F.4**: 295. **G.3.1**: 61.
Moyens de communication **B.2**: 11. **D.1**: 31–32. **D.7**: 83, 126, 134, 138, 177, 230, 232–234, 237–238, 241–242, 244, 247, 249–250, 254, 257, 259, 262, 264, 269–270, 272–273, 275–280, 282–284, 286–287, 289, 293–294, 298–299, 301, 312–313, 316–317, 326, 367. **D.8**: 29. **F.2**: 124. **F.3**: 146. **F.7**: 101. **F.8**: 129. **J.3**: 16, 43. **K.1**: 106.
Moyens de transport **G.3.2**: 2.
Multiculturalisme **D.1**: 22, 89, 110. **D.7**: 18. **D.9**: 164. **F.7**: 131, 144, 155, 167, 191.
Multilinguisme **D.7**: 337, 345–346.
Multipartisme **J.5**: 32. **J.6**: 64.
Musées **D.8**: 3, 17, 66.
Musiciens **C.2**: 27. **C.4**: 12. **D.7**: 290.
Musique **D.5**: 117. **D.7**: 109. **D.8**: 16, 21, 29, 37–38. **D.9**: 20. **K.4**: 86.
Musique de danse **D.7**: 67.
Musique pop **D.7**: 181.
Musique populaire **D.8**: 21, 31, 47, 49, 53, 55. **H.3**: 40.
Musique rock **D.8**: 25, 40, 60–61.
Musulman **B.1**: 151. **C.2**: 102. **C.4**: 29. **C.7**: 31. **D.5**: 162, 165, 168–169, 171. **F.2**: 19. **F.3**: 293. **F.4**: 229. **F.5**: 42, 145, 152, 273. **F.7**: 29, 61, 177, 185.
Myles, Horton **J.5**: 4.
Mysticisme **D.5**: 21. **I.3**: 95.
Mythes **C.5**: 48. **G.3.2**: 305.
Naissance **F.1**: 59. **F.3**: 35, 65, 74, 88, 106, 109–110, 124, 132–133, 237, 270. **F.4**: 303, 325. **I.4**: 35. **K.1**: 19, 123.
Narcissisme **C.1**: 16. **C.2**: 66, 192, 231.
Nation **J.1**: 8. **J.2**: 9–10.
Nationalisme **D.1**: 83, 103. **D.5**: 98. **F.5**: 319. **F.7**: 75–76, 79, 161, 182, 187. **I.2**: 45. **J.2**: 1–2, 17, 24.
Nationalisme culturel **D.1**: 33.
Nationalité **D.1**: 7. **F.7**: 100. **F.8**: 133.
Nations Unies **F.2**: 103, 112–113. **F.7**: 198.
Naturalisme **B.1**: 35.

Nature **C.1**: 55. **G.1**: 15, 33.
Nature humaine **B.1**: 130, 140. **C.1**: 102. **C.2**: 42–43. **D.1**: 27. **D.4**: 23.
Négociation **C.3**: 26, 90, 106, 121, 127. **C.4**: 40. **C.5**: 77. **I.5**: 64, 71–73, 139.
Négociation collective **D.9**: 110. **H.3**: 69. **I.5**: 60, 62–63, 65–66, 68, 74–75.
Négociations salariales **H.3**: 69. **I.3**: 10. **I.5**: 68, 125, 148.
Néocolonialisme **J.8**: 10.
Neurologie **C.1**: 25.
Nietzsche, Friedrich **B.1**: 86. **D.7**: 163.
Niveau de pollution **G.1**: 46.
Niveau de vie **F.2**: 58. **F.4**: 73. **H.3**: 20, 30, 32–33.
Niveau des salaires **H.3**: 70, 87.
Noël **H.6**: 2.
Noirs **C.2**: 5. **D.1**: 94. **D.5**: 146. **D.7**: 5, 67. **D.8**: 42. **D.9**: 11, 120, 168, 176. **E.2**: 3, 12, 66. **F.1**: 34. **F.3**: 112, 164, 179, 225, 238. **F.4**: 59, 149, 205, 212, 218, 273, 341. **F.5**: 68. **F.7**: 2–5, 7–8, 10, 12, 22, 30, 35, 37, 51, 66, 86, 124, 136, 145–146, 174, 181, 195, 208, 214, 220–221, 223, 226–227, 234, 238, 261. **F.8**: 87, 109. **G.3.2**: 120, 122, 126, 149–150, 162, 306, 336. **H.3**: 17, 26, 38, 88. **I.2**: 8, 53, 55, 75, 141, 168, 185, 224, 228. **I.4**: 42. **J.5**: 3, 7. **K.1**: 10, 12, 42, 182. **K.4**: 2, 39.
Normal **C.3**: 36.
Normes religieuses **D.5**: 6.
Normes sociales **D.1**: 107, 121, 124–125.
Nouvelle droite **F.4**: 61.
Nouvelles **D.7**: 243, 245, 247, 250, 268–269, 291, 330, 360, 367, 393–394. **D.8**: 393. **F.3**: 146. **H.3**: 40. **K.1**: 396.
Nutrition **F.2**: 86. **F.3**: 256. **H.3**: 68. **K.4**: 177, 197.
Objectifs de l'éducation **D.9**: 18, 212, 214.
Objectivité **C.7**: 32. **D.5**: 35, 73. **D.7**: 317. **F.7**: 260.
Obligation **D.7**: 211. **F.4**: 79, 308. **I.5**: 192.
Observation **B.2**: 59. **C.2**: 23.
Obtention du statut **E.2**: 21, 35.
Occidentalisation **D.5**: 7. **F.7**: 28.
OCDE **D.7**: 116. **K.1**: 224.
Odorat **C.3**: 82.
Oeuvre dramatique **D.7**: 311.
Offre de main d'oeuvre **G.3.1**: 54. **I.2**: 18, 58, 60, 93, 108, 111, 126, 180, 224.
Offre et demande **G.3.2**: 352.
Olson, Mancur **E.2**: 54.

Onabasulu **F.6**: 30.
Ong, Walter J.
D.7: 284.
Ontogénie **C.1**: 40.
Ontologie **C.2**: 9. **D.6**: 27. **G.1**: 35.
Opinion **C.4**: 28. **F.8**: 82.
Opinion politique **F.2**: 33. **J.6**: 56.
Opinion publique **C.7**: 2, 26, 44, 46, 69. **D.2**: 16. **D.7**: 36, 313. **F.3**: 160. **F.4**: 70. **F.7**: 106, 145, 194. **G.3.2**: 114. **H.3**: 37. **J.1**: 13. **J.5**: 24. **J.6**: 2, 50. **J.7**: 10.
Optimisme **H.3**: 40.
Ordinateurs **A.3**: 7. **B.2**: 3, 115, 128. **C.2**: 64, 120, 144. **C.3**: 11. **D.7**: 10–11, 65, 129. **D.9**: 2. **G.3.2**: 250. **H.4**: 83, 104. **J.3**: 37.
Ordre mondial **D.1**: 63. **D.5**: 24. **J.8**: 4, 10.
Ordre politique **D.7**: 286.
Ordre public **J.1**: 2. **J.6**: 18. **K.1**: 40.
Ordre social **B.1**: 87. **D.1**: 11, 113. **E.1**: 12–13. **E.3**: 53.
Ordres religieux **D.5**: 102.
Organisation administrative **C.2**: 111.
Organisation bénévole **E.3**: 42.
Organisation communautaire **G.2**: 1–2, 5, 28. **G.3.1**: 105. **G.3.2**: 6. **J.5**: 3.
Organisation de l'entreprise **C.5**: 69, 75. **F.2**: 32. **H.4**: 30, 65.
Organisation du travail **C.5**: 23, 49. **H.2**: 5. **I.3**: 67. **I.4**: 57.
Organisation économique **H.1**: 3.
Organisation industrielle **C.5**: 62.
Organisation régionale **G.2**: 29.
Organisations **C.1**: 168. **C.3**: 116. **C.4**: 2. **C.5**: 3, 11, 15, 17–18, 21–22, 25–26, 37–38, 40–41, 43, 46–49, 51–53, 55, 60–61, 63, 66, 73, 76, 79–80, 83, 86–87. **D.8**: 4. **F.4**: 267. **F.5**: 138, 184, 193, 267. **G.2**: 2, 24. **G.3.1**: 15. **H.4**: 10, 22, 32, 49, 96–97. **I.1**: 3. **I.3**: 27, 53–54, 56, 89, 117, 126. **I.4**: 31, 102. **I.5**: 23, 43, 146. **J.3**: 18. **J.8**: 2. **K.2**: 30. **K.3**: 28.
Organisations agricoles **G.3.1**: 96.
Organisations bénévoles **C.4**: 4. **D.3**: 3. **G.2**: 31. **G.3.1**: 118. **I.4**: 129.
Organisations complexes **C.5**: 6, 9.
Organisations professionnelles **K.4**: 3.
Origine sociale **E.2**: 9, 36.
Otages **C.3**: 26.
Otieno, Wambui
F.7: 53.
Otto, Rudolf
D.5: 59.
Ouvrages de référence **D.7**: 9.

Ouvriers industriels **I.4**: 123. **I.5**: 2, 123.
Ouvriers non-qualifiés **F.8**: 57. **I.2**: 188.
Ouvriers qualifiés **I.2**: 192. **I.3**: 50. **I.4**: 37.
Ouzbek **F.7**: 179.
Paiement **C.5**: 54. **H.4**: 40. **I.2**: 26. **I.3**: 6, 24, 33, 55.
Paix **J.8**: 14, 22.
Palestiniennes **D.2**: 3. **I.2**: 50. **J.5**: 12. **K.2**: 100.
Panthéisme **D.5**: 159.
Paradigmes **A.1**: 15. **C.7**: 40. **D.7**: 128.
Parcs nationaux **G.1**: 33.
Parenté **F.2**: 62. **F.4**: 43, 79, 98. **F.5**: 266. **G.3.2**: 115.
Parents **C.3**: 3, 43. **C.7**: 3. **D.7**: 343–344, 361. **D.9**: 118, 134. **F.1**: 11, 50. **F.4**: 21, 30, 32–33, 81, 118, 162, 164, 215, 270, 272, 280, 287, 308, 311–312, 321, 329. **F.5**: 224. **F.8**: 143. **I.3**: 84, 148. **K.2**: 50, 68.
Parlement **J.3**: 19.
Parlementaires **D.7**: 229.
Parole **C.3**: 45. **D.7**: 42, 70, 135, 333.
Parsons, Talcott
B.1: 15, 96, 105, 108, 124, 145. **D.8**: 5. **E.1**: 12.
Participation aux bénéfices **I.5**: 48, 199.
Participation de la collectivité **G.2**: 16, 18. **G.3.2**: 15, 249. **J.3**: 35. **K.4**: 14.
Participation électorale **J.6**: 61, 66.
Participation politique **B.1**: 38. **F.7**: 4. **G.3.2**: 7. **J.3**: 6. **J.6**: 13, 17, 21, 23–24, 29, 33–34, 55.
Partis communistes **I.5**: 157. **J.5**: 5.
Partis de droite **F.7**: 259, 264.
Partis politiques **D.5**: 109. **D.9**: 44. **F.7**: 225. **I.5**: 119. **J.5**: 11, 32, 36. **J.6**: 53. **J.8**: 5.
Passage à la vie active **D.9**: 13.
Passions **C.2**: 122.
Paternalisme **F.5**: 233. **K.4**: 259.
Paternité **F.4**: 285, 290.
Paternité-maternité **F.4**: 267, 278, 284, 293, 296, 316–317. **I.3**: 74.
Pathologie **C.5**: 41.
Patriarcat **D.5**: 36. **E.3**: 14. **F.5**: 129, 297. **I.2**: 129.
Pauvres **C.3**: 79. **G.3.2**: 104, 128, 147, 183. **I.2**: 65, 246. **J.6**: 9. **K.1**: 173, 218, 246–247, 262–263, 265. **K.2**: 63, 84, 88.
Pauvreté **C.1**: 129. **D.1**: 123. **D.9**: 108. **F.1**: 44. **F.2**: 3. **F.3**: 269. **F.4**: 232, 347. **F.5**: 6, 257. **F.8**: 38, 54, 60. **G.3.1**: 20. **G.3.2**: 168, 209–210. **H.3**: 8, 36, 62, 85. **I.2**: 65, 78, 246. **K.1**: 54, 217, 220–222, 224–229, 233, 244–245, 249–252, 254, 256, 259, 266–272, 275–276, 278, 280, 283–284, 286, 289,

292–293, 295. **K.2**: 84, 103.
Pauvreté rurale **G.3.1**: 18, 68, 105, 108. **H.3**: 84. **I.2**: 81. **K.1**: 257, 273, 282.
Pauvreté urbaine **G.2**: 13. **G.3.2**: 4, 120, 176, 213, 226. **K.1**: 232, 258, 265, 285, 291. **K.4**: 114.
Pays arabes **D.7**: 254. **F.7**: 178. **F.8**: 152.
Pays capitalistes **I.4**: 32.
Pays de l'Est **D.1**: 53.
Pays démocratiques **E.2**: 10.
Pays développés **F.5**: 97. **K.1**: 224.
Pays en développement **C.1**: 163. **C.7**: 71. **D.7**: 60, 184, 380. **D.9**: 1, 10, 35, 39, 68, 152, 157. **E.3**: 16, 37, 40, 47. **F.2**: 80. **F.3**: 43, 134, 183, 216, 232, 242, 300–301. **F.4**: 338. **F.5**: 14, 48, 97, 130, 243, 250, 280. **F.8**: 18, 52, 105, 168. **G.1**: 43. **G.3.1**: 1, 102. **G.3.2**: 128, 163, 206, 222, 231, 299, 324–325, 339, 355. **H.3**: 6, 14, 25, 42, 55, 57–58. **I.2**: 231. **I.3**: 88. **I.4**: 130. **I.5**: 204. **J.3**: 33. **J.4**: 10. **K.1**: 84, 246, 273, 311. **K.4**: 74, 91.
Pays islamiques **D.1**: 57. **D.3**: 31. **D.7**: 266. **F.5**: 217.
Pays multiethniques **D.9**: 52. **F.7**: 152. **K.2**: 61.
Pays nouvellement industrialisés **I.4**: 113.
Pays occidentaux **D.1**: 53. **D.5**: 55. **D.7**: 2. **F.7**: 106. **J.2**: 31. **K.1**: 117. **K.2**: 65.
Pays socialistes **I.4**: 32.
Paysage **D.1**: 25. **G.3.1**: 19, 46. **G.3.2**: 5.
Paysannerie **G.3.1**: 83–84, 86, 88–91, 93, 113.
Paysans **E.2**: 25, 27. **F.5**: 162, 301. **F.8**: 86, 137. **G.3.1**: 92, 94. **H.2**: 9. **H.4**: 11. **K.1**: 11.
Pêche **G.1**: 6. **H.4**: 47.
Peine de mort **K.1**: 176, 193.
Peirce, C.S. **B.1**: 56.
Penchant **C.1**: 127. **C.6**: 18.
Pen, Le, Jean-Marie **F.7**: 259.
Pensée des lumières **B.1**: 114. **E.2**: 11.
Pensée économique **H.3**: 4.
Pensée politique **D.6**: 12. **J.2**: 15.
Pensée religieuse **D.5**: 77. **F.4**: 328.
Pension **H.3**: 83. **I.3**: 32.
Pentecôtisme **D.5**: 143.
Pénurie de main d'oeuvre **I.2**: 163.
Perception **B.1**: 99. **C.2**: 12, 69, 77, 106, 160. **C.3**: 155–156. **C.5**: 68. **D.3**: 74. **D.7**: 64, 69, 348. **F.2**: 69, 147. **F.3**: 181, 187. **F.4**: 81, 301. **F.5**: 239. **H.3**: 49, 64. **I.3**: 96. **I.4**: 83. **J.1**: 10. **J.3**: 41. **J.5**: 20. **K.1**: 45.
Perception d'autrui **C.3**: 150, 152, 154, 157–158. **F.7**: 195.

Perception de soi **D.9**: 135. **F.2**: 152. **I.2**: 118.
Perception interpersonnelle **C.3**: 148, 153, 160–161.
Perception sociale **C.3**: 147, 151–152, 159, 162. **C.4**: 55. **F.7**: 241.
Père **B.2**: 110. **C.1**: 24, 58. **F.4**: 122, 266, 269, 282, 291–292, 301–302, 313, 323. **F.6**: 27, 44.
Perestroika **D.1**: 31, 37. **D.3**: 78. **D.7**: 259, 298–299. **E.1**: 4. **E.3**: 35. **F.5**: 252, 318. **G.3.2**: 75. **J.2**: 12.
Performance du groupe **C.4**: 11, 17, 46, 56. **I.3**: 96.
Performance économique **F.2**: 24. **H.4**: 65. **I.5**: 26, 32.
Périodiques **D.7**: 288, 290. **F.5**: 271. **I.6**: 12. **K.4**: 94.
Personnalité **C.1**: 162, 170. **C.2**: 180–181, 183–219. **C.3**: 132, 152, 159. **C.6**: 11. **D.1**: 70, 132. **D.5**: 159. **F.4**: 340. **F.6**: 50. **G.1**: 62. **J.6**: 22, 31. **K.1**: 329.
Personnel **I.3**: 145. **I.4**: 38.
Personnel médical **B.2**: 118. **F.3**: 181. **I.4**: 28, 104. **K.3**: 30. **K.4**: 44, 58, 259.
Personnes mariées **I.2**: 139. **J.7**: 13.
Perspective mondiale **F.2**: 5.
Persuasion **D.7**: 61, 108, 170.
Perversions sexuelles **C.1**: 51.
Pessimisme **C.1**: 19. **H.3**: 40.
Pesticides **I.3**: 120.
Petite enfance **F.3**: 12. **F.4**: 302, 310.
Petite industrie **E.3**: 38. **G.3.1**: 25. **H.4**: 75. **I.3**: 122.
Petites entreprises agricoles **G.3.1**: 67, 77, 108.
Petites et moyennes entreprises **D.3**: 52. **F.5**: 169, 247. **F.8**: 40. **H.4**: 39, 48, 62, 70, 74, 76.
Petites villes **G.3.2**: 255.
Petits États **D.9**: 65.
Peul **C.2**: 10.
Peur **C.2**: 30. **C.3**: 122. **F.5**: 228. **I.3**: 33. **I.5**: 118. **K.1**: 83, 88–89, 114.
Phénoménologie **B.1**: 136. **C.4**: 23. **D.5**: 19. **F.4**: 170.
Philippins **F.8**: 122, 155.
Philosophie **A.1**: 28. **B.1**: 40, 45, 53–54, 59, 63, 65, 67, 72–75, 78–79, 81. **C.1**: 25. **C.2**: 188. **C.3**: 38. **D.1**: 21, 27, 71, 81, 99, 134. **D.3**: 13, 84. **D.6**: 6, 18, 28. **D.9**: 26. **F.5**: 83, 137. **G.1**: 15. **H.3**: 4. **J.2**: 15.
Philosophie de la science **D.6**: 9, 14, 20, 22.
Philosophie politique **D.4**: 29. **F.5**: 297.
Philosophie sociale **A.1**: 39. **J.8**: 5.

Phonétique **D.7**: 205.
Phonologie **C.2**: 156. **D.7**: 14.
Photographie **D.7**: 325. **D.8**: 7, 43, 78.
Physique **C.7**: 14. **D.7**: 69.
Piaget, Jean
  A.2: 9.
Placement familial **K.2**: 38, 53. **K.3**: 35.
Planification de l'éducation **D.9**: 148.
Planification de l'environnement **H.7**: 10, 15.
Planification de la famille **F.1**: 51. **F.3**: 36, 40, 42–45, 47, 51, 68, 71, 109.
Planification de la santé **K.4**: 33.
Planification du développement **E.3**: 43, 48. **G.3.1**: 103. **H.7**: 14, 24.
Planification économique **F.3**: 112. **G.3.1**: 14. **H.7**: 3, 7.
Planification industrielle **G.3.2**: 289.
Planification linguistique **D.7**: 339, 341, 345.
Planification régionale **G.3.1**: 101, 125. **G.3.2**: 163, 290, 295, 338, 343, 361. **H.7**: 9, 21–22.
Planification rurale **G.3.1**: 51. **H.7**: 10.
Planification sociale **B.1**: 100. **G.3.2**: 260.
Planification stratégique **C.5**: 5, 22. **D.7**: 178. **D.9**: 184. **G.3.2**: 309. **H.7**: 26. **I.5**: 52. **J.1**: 20.
Plantation **G.3.1**: 113.
Plein emploi **I.2**: 220. **K.2**: 107.
Pluralisme **B.1**: 68. **D.5**: 105. **D.7**: 300. **F.7**: 70, 191. **J.1**: 12. **J.2**: 19. **J.7**: 19.
Pluralisme ethnique **F.7**: 62, 110. **F.8**: 117.
Pluralisme religieux **D.5**: 139.
Pluralisme social **D.1**: 22. **E.2**: 16.
Poésie **D.7**: 26.
Poincaré, Henri
  B.1: 36.
Pôles de croissance **C.5**: 62.
Police **C.1**: 70. **C.4**: 43. **C.5**: 46. **D.4**: 4. **J.3**: 35, 37–39, 41–44, 46. **K.1**: 12–14, 43, 83, 102, 124–126. **K.3**: 20.
Politiciens **D.7**: 295. **J.6**: 3.
Politique à l'égard des nationalités **D.7**: 193.
Politique agricole **G.3.1**: 56, 75. **H.4**: 6.
Politique alimentaire **E.3**: 43. **K.2**: 4.
Politique coloniale **D.9**: 93.
Politique commerciale **F.8**: 37.
Politique d'immigration **F.3**: 23. **F.8**: 52, 124, 132–133, 154, 173. **J.6**: 52.
Politique d'innovation **H.4**: 39.
Politique d'intégration active **F.5**: 277. **F.7**: 265. **I.2**: 110, 131, 134, 204. **I.3**: 123.
Politique de bien-être **F.4**: 15. **K.2**: 87, 103, 107.

Politique de développement **C.7**: 19. **D.3**: 36. **D.9**: 209. **G.3.1**: 128. **H.7**: 4, 11, 20.
Politique de l'eau **I.5**: 177.
Politique de l'éducation **D.9**: 40, 42–44, 49, 51, 53–54, 56–59, 63, 66–67, 70, 80, 104, 159, 171.
Politique de l'emploi **I.2**: 38, 207, 219–220, 233, 235. **I.3**: 93. **I.5**: 136.
Politique de l'environnement **F.3**: 2. **F.5**: 48. **G.1**: 16, 22. **G.3.2**: 353. **I.2**: 235.
Politique de production **I.5**: 18.
Politique de technologie **J.4**: 13.
Politique démographique **F.1**: 48. **F.3**: 3, 11, 19, 28, 72, 83, 97, 137, 300, 305, 307, 311–312.
Politique des media **D.7**: 274, 297, 385, 387.
Politique des transports **D.7**: 91.
Politique du logement **G.3.2**: 123, 125, 128, 147, 153, 159, 164, 172, 241. **K.2**: 34.
Politique du travail **I.2**: 134, 206.
Politique économique **C.7**: 2. **F.8**: 167. **G.3.1**: 107. **G.3.2**: 75. **K.1**: 240.
Politique ethnique **E.2**: 1. **F.7**: 39, 65.
Politique étrangère **F.3**: 178. **H.7**: 8. **J.6**: 2.
Politique familiale **F.4**: 52, 84. **K.2**: 4.
Politique gouvernementale **F.2**: 43. **F.3**: 44. **F.8**: 52, 131. **G.3.2**: 167. **I.2**: 194, 221. **K.2**: 28, 33, 44. **K.4**: 171.
Politique industrielle **H.4**: 75. **I.2**: 206. **I.4**: 132. **I.5**: 176.
Politique linguistique **D.7**: 18, 334–335, 338–340, 342, 345. **D.9**: 15.
Politique locale **F.7**: 233. **G.3.2**: 197.
Politique migratoire **F.3**: 28.
Politique nataliste **F.3**: 23, 28. **F.5**: 214.
Politique pénale **K.1**: 133, 181, 184, 213–214.
Politique publique **D.7**: 336. **F.1**: 55. **F.2**: 56, 126. **F.7**: 39. **G.3.2**: 308. **H.7**: 25. **I.5**: 48. **K.2**: 4.
Politique régionale **H.7**: 2, 22. **J.2**: 27. **K.4**: 240.
Politique rurale **G.3.1**: 16, 40, 112.
Politique sanitaire **D.5**: 38. **F.3**: 209, 227. **F.5**: 221. **K.2**: 86. **K.4**: 167, 169, 183, 186–187, 191, 193, 195, 197, 199–200, 204, 209, 211, 213, 215, 218–219, 222, 226, 228–230, 232, 240, 242.
Politique scientifique **J.4**: 13.
Politique sociale **B.2**: 53. **D.1**: 129. **E.1**: 4. **E.2**: 1. **F.5**: 53, 177. **F.7**: 39, 191. **G.3.2**: 98. **H.2**: 18. **I.2**: 220. **I.3**: 84. **I.4**: 47. **I.5**: 46, 114. **K.1**: 55, 103, 338, 341, 354. **K.2**: 1, 11, 15, 23, 31, 38, 62, 66, 86, 91, 95–96, 101, 111. **K.3**: 38.
Politique urbaine **G.3.2**: 190, 243, 283, 286, 295, 309, 319–320, 327, 331, 333, 335. **H.7**: 2. **K.2**: 13, 30.

Politisation **F.7**: 120.
Pollution **G.1**: 32. **G.3.2**: 39.
Pollution des mers **D.7**: 315.
Polygamie **F.5**: 297.
Polygynie **F.4**: 228, 231.
Popularité **J.6**: 10.
Population **B.2**: 131. **F.1**: 12, 22, 33–34, 46, 50, 52–53, 59, 68. **F.3**: 1–2, 7, 16, 20, 29, 56, 76, 85, 89, 131, 309. **F.4**: 17. **F.5**: 187. **F.8**: 61, 87, 92. **G.3.1**: 37. **G.3.2**: 12, 207. **I.2**: 207. **K.2**: 97.
Population agricole **G.3.1**: 97.
Population indigène **F.7**: 38, 105. **G.3.1**: 87. **K.2**: 81.
Population rurale **F.3**: 15. **G.3.1**: 9, 21, 49, 97, 132.
Population urbaine **F.1**: 38. **G.3.2**: 180, 185, 342. **I.6**: 20.
Populisme **D.8**: 46. **E.2**: 28. **H.2**: 12.
Pornographie **D.1**: 112. **F.5**: 33, 84, 114. **F.6**: 35–36. **K.1**: 23.
Portoricains **D.7**: 59. **I.2**: 185.
Positivisme **B.1**: 127. **C.1**: 139. **J.2**: 14.
Post-fordisme **D.1**: 138. **D.9**: 9. **H.2**: 5. **H.4**: 29, 59. **J.2**: 21.
Post-structuralisme **F.5**: 102. **F.6**: 10.
Postmodernisme **B.1**: 3, 8, 12–14, 17–18, 22, 26, 49, 51, 88, 121. **C.1**: 47, 167. **D.1**: 32, 82, 92–93, 122. **D.2**: 28. **D.6**: 5. **D.7**: 287. **D.8**: 20, 47. **F.4**: 354. **F.5**: 95. **G.1**: 29, 58. **G.3.2**: 62, 232. **I.2**: 96. **I.6**: 33. **J.2**: 20. **K.3**: 41. **K.4**: 76.
Pouvoir **C.3**: 115–116. **C.4**: 15, 44, 51. **C.6**: 18. **C.7**: 13. **D.6**: 21, 26. **D.7**: 61, 168–169, 316. **D.9**: 25, 137. **E.2**: 22. **E.3**: 45. **F.4**: 85, 263. **F.5**: 96, 134, 181, 253, 287. **G.1**: 64. **G.3.1**: 93. **H.4**: 17, 33. **J.1**: 3.
Pouvoir de l'entreprise **H.4**: 68.
Pouvoir de la collectivité **G.2**: 26, 28.
Pouvoir de négociation **I.5**: 70.
Pouvoir judiciaire **D.4**: 7. **J.3**: 11.
Pouvoir politique **E.3**: 2. **G.1**: 30. **J.6**: 9, 14.
Pragmatique **D.7**: 62, 205. **F.7**: 193.
Pragmatisme **F.5**: 233.
Pratique commerciale **I.3**: 29.
Pratique religieuse **D.5**: 72.
Prédication **D.5**: 13.
Préférences du consommateur **K.4**: 28.
Préjugé **C.7**: 4, 58. **F.7**: 228, 247. **I.2**: 52.
Préservation **G.1**: 2, 9, 13, 33.
Présidence **D.7**: 288. **J.4**: 5. **J.6**: 10, 31.

Presse **C.6**: 1. **D.7**: 105–106, 231, 251–252, 258, 265, 268–269, 272, 276, 289, 293, 295, 302, 305, 307–310, 315, 319. **F.3**: 195. **F.7**: 269. **F.8**: 26. **K.1**: 141.
Prestige **E.3**: 74.
Prestige professionnel **I.2**: 79. **I.4**: 14.
Prévention de la délinquance **K.1**: 66, 75, 102, 126–127, 164.
Prévisions **B.2**: 60. **C.1**: 126.
Prévisions démographiques **F.1**: 3, 7, 24, 26–27, 30. **F.3**: 304.
Prévisions économiques **F.1**: 26.
Prime enfance **F.4**: 301.
Primes de salaire **I.3**: 51.
Primitivisme **D.1**: 94.
Prise de décision **C.1**: 131. **C.2**: 114, 144–153. **C.3**: 5. **C.5**: 21. **D.4**: 21, 38. **E.2**: 44. **F.2**: 51. **F.5**: 324. **F.8**: 118. **H.6**: 5. **H.7**: 7, 19. **I.4**: 6. **I.5**: 38, 202. **K.1**: 358. **K.4**: 34, 83.
Prise de décision en groupe **C.4**: 24–26, 28, 36–37, 40, 45, 50, 56.
Prise de rôle **C.6**: 17.
Prisonniers **C.3**: 93. **F.4**: 191, 319. **F.7**: 226, 238. **K.1**: 24, 174, 179, 194. **K.4**: 100.
Prisons **I.4**: 24. **K.1**: 171, 177, 187–190, 195, 197, 199, 201, 209–211. **K.4**: 217.
Privation **K.1**: 49, 221.
Privation relative **H.3**: 46. **I.5**: 164.
Privatisation **D.9**: 49. **H.7**: 20. **I.5**: 44–45, 177. **J.4**: 6, 15.
Prix **D.7**: 116. **H.5**: 24, 30, 32. **K.4**: 104.
Prix de détail **H.4**: 42. **H.5**: 26.
Prix de la fiancée **F.4**: 204.
Prix du logement **G.3.2**: 96.
Probabilité **B.1**: 56. **B.2**: 82. **C.2**: 167. **C.7**: 12. **D.7**: 175.
Problèmes sociaux **D.6**: 28. **D.7**: 34. **E.1**: 1. **E.2**: 84. **F.1**: 50. **F.4**: 143. **K.1**: 4, 17, 21–22, 65, 138, 392. **K.2**: 30, 80.
Procès civil **D.4**: 34. **J.6**: 21.
Processus judiciaire **D.4**: 13, 28.
Processus législatif **D.4**: 22, 25.
Processus stochastiques **C.3**: 54.
Production **D.9**: 27. **G.3.2**: 214, 261. **I.3**: 62. **J.5**: 10.
Production agricole **G.3.1**: 24.
Productivité **C.4**: 17, 47. **F.5**: 233, 301. **G.3.1**: 27. **H.3**: 15. **H.4**: 20, 28, 40. **I.4**: 25. **I.5**: 182–183, 188.
Productivité agricole **H.4**: 3.
Produits de base **H.2**: 9.
Produits pétrochimiques **I.4**: 1.

Produits pharmaceutiques **F.3**: 195.
Profession legale **D.4**: 42. **I.4**: 100, 108.
Professionnalisation **K.1**: 214.
Professionnalisme **D.1**: 89. **I.4**: 39. **I.5**: 149. **K.3**: 28.
Professions **B.2**: 78. **C.2**: 116. **D.7**: 195. **E.2**: 73. **F.1**: 4. **F.4**: 39, 200, 252. **F.7**: 222. **I.2**: 4, 118, 166. **I.4**: 11, 20, 42, 44, 60, 86, 88. **J.6**: 50.
Professorat **A.1**: 15. **A.2**: 6. **D.9**: 193. **I.4**: 23, 68, 114. **J.6**: 48. **K.1**: 182.
Profit **K.2**: 51.
Programme de gouvernement **H.3**: 26.
Progrès scientifique **D.6**: 19.
Progrès scientifique et technique **C.2**: 193. **H.4**: 99.
Projections démographiques **F.1**: 23, 38, 70. **F.8**: 47.
Projet agricole **G.3.1**: 22.
Projets de développement **E.3**: 15. **K.1**: 246, 278.
Prolétariat **H.4**: 2.
Prolétarisation **D.9**: 203.
Promotion professionnelle **I.2**: 26. **I.3**: 80. **I.4**: 68, 108.
Propagande **D.5**: 135. **D.7**: 329.
Prophétie **D.5**: 135.
Propriété **G.3.2**: 129. **H.5**: 2. **K.1**: 138.
Propriété du domicile **F.8**: 1. **G.3.2**: 105. **H.5**: 2.
Propriété foncière **G.3.1**: 31. **G.3.2**: 28, 222, 271, 317. **K.1**: 59.
Propriété intellectuelle **G.1**: 61.
Prostitution **F.3**: 193. **F.6**: 25, 34, 38, 41, 55. **J.5**: 23. **K.1**: 131, 348. **K.3**: 23.
Protection de l'environnement **G.1**: 25, 37.
Protection légale **F.7**: 196.
Protectionnisme **D.8**: 16.
Protestantisme **B.1**: 150. **D.5**: 7, 126, 136.
Protestants **D.5**: 115, 144. **E.2**: 18.
Prototypes **D.7**: 220.
Proudhon, Pierre Joseph **D.1**: 79.
Proverbes **C.3**: 53.
Psychanalyse **A.2**: 14. **C.1**: 1, 3–5, 8, 12–13, 15–19, 21, 23, 26–27, 29, 33, 38, 40, 42–43, 45–55, 57–58, 60–62, 65. **C.3**: 51. **C.4**: 57. **F.6**: 56.
Psychiaie **C.1**: 66, 69–73. **K.1**: 36. **K.4**: 2, 58, 80, 124, 147.
Psychiatres **K.1**: 50.
Psychiatrie légal **C.1**: 26.
Psycholinguistique **D.7**: 185, 213.

Psychologie **B.1**: 70. **C.1**: 77–83, 90–93, 95–101, 104–105, 108–132, 134–135, 137–141. **C.2**: 61, 68–69, 78, 111, 142, 194, 216, 220. **C.3**: 27. **C.5**: 40. **C.7**: 36. **D.1**: 137. **D.7**: 19, 147–148, 194, 230. **F.2**: 81, 84. **F.3**: 184. **F.4**: 202. **F.6**: 52. **F.7**: 70, 124. **G.3.1**: 55, 91. **H.4**: 37. **I.3**: 65. **K.1**: 204. **K.4**: 57, 81, 86, 237, 259.
Psychologie clinique **K.4**: 81, 182.
Psychologie de l'enfant **C.1**: 22. **C.2**: 55, 185. **C.3**: 59.
Psychologie économique **C.1**: 125. **F.2**: 107.
Psychologie évolutionniste **C.5**: 26.
Psychologie industrielle **I.1**: 15. **I.3**: 103.
Psychologie politique **C.1**: 34, 64. **J.1**: 12, 14. **J.6**: 22, 43. **J.8**: 12.
Psychologie sociale **C.1**: 142, 144–146, 149–151, 153–155, 157–174. **C.2**: 45, 70, 189. **C.3**: 98. **C.4**: 5, 29. **C.7**: 78. **D.1**: 132. **D.2**: 23. **F.7**: 29, 72, 256. **I.5**: 55. **K.1**: 379.
Psychologues **C.1**: 89, 137. **D.3**: 41.
Psychométrie **C.1**: 102. **C.7**: 52. **I.3**: 149.
Psychopathologie **C.1**: 141. **C.2**: 10. **C.6**: 11.
Psychosociologie **K.4**: 94, 182.
Psychothérapie **B.2**: 43. **C.1**: 28, 43, 94, 107, 113, 140.
Puberté **C.2**: 187. **F.4**: 286.
Public **D.7**: 161, 170, 230, 257. **F.3**: 187.
Publicité **C.2**: 171. **D.7**: 100–101, 103–109, 111–116, 232, 370, 391. **D.9**: 28. **H.5**: 3. **K.1**: 298, 373.
Puériculture **D.5**: 89. **F.4**: 279, 325, 328.
Punjabi **F.7**: 115.
Purdah **F.5**: 42.
Qualité de l'environnement **G.3.2**: 138.
Qualité de la vie **C.2**: 174. **F.4**: 51. **G.3.1**: 36, 68. **G.3.2**: 138. **H.3**: 13–14, 34, 42. **I.1**: 10. **I.3**: 48, 68. **K.4**: 62, 173.
Quartier **F.2**: 126. **F.7**: 140, 149. **G.2**: 12, 19, 22. **G.3.2**: 53, 177, 194, 198, 204, 303. **H.7**: 23. **J.5**: 35. **J.6**: 20. **K.1**: 88.
Questionnaires **B.2**: 90, 112, 115, 118, 120, 122, 130. **C.1**: 128. **C.7**: 52. **K.1**: 332.
Race **B.1**: 128. **C.1**: 97. **D.1**: 7. **D.7**: 243. **D.9**: 108, 121. **E.2**: 3, 66. **F.1**: 56. **F.3**: 38, 287. **F.4**: 347–348. **F.7**: 3, 39, 44, 66, 68, 75–76, 86, 116–118, 125, 149, 177, 186, 195, 197–198, 234, 242, 246, 262. **F.8**: 10. **G.3.2**: 176, 336. **H.3**: 88. **H.6**: 9. **I.2**: 75, 132. **I.3**: 69, 104. **I.4**: 24, 40, 82. **I.5**: 162. **J.1**: 19. **J.2**: 10. **J.6**: 62. **K.1**: 86, 97, 350, 375. **K.2**: 80. **K.4**: 2.
Racisme **D.7**: 5. **F.5**: 67–68. **F.7**: 14, 21, 73, 145,

156, 190, 200–204, 207, 211, 215, 222, 225, 230–231, 235–236, 243, 252–256, 258–260, 263–264, 266. **G.3.2**: 173. **K.1**: 200, 258.
Radicalisme **C.5**: 61. **D.5**: 184.
Radio **C.1**: 124. **D.7**: 263, 291, 297, 304, 311, 365.
Radiodiffusion **D.7**: 236–237, 246, 253, 296, 300, 323, 351, 354, 367, 378.
Raisonnement **B.2**: 74. **C.2**: 112. **C.3**: 24, 142. **C.6**: 13. **C.7**: 5. **D.7**: 196. **F.5**: 297.
Rajneesh **C.4**: 20.
Randall, Margaret **F.5**: 134.
Rang de naissance **F.3**: 118. **I.6**: 4.
Rapport financier **D.7**: 208.
Rapports avant le mariage **F.4**: 137. **F.6**: 39.
Rassemblement des données **B.2**: 108. **F.8**: 147. **G.3.2**: 80.
Rationalisation **E.2**: 11.
Rationalité **B.1**: 68, 129–130, 135. **C.2**: 84, 91. **C.3**: 125. **C.7**: 53, 78. **D.1**: 107, 124–125, 128. **D.5**: 163. **D.6**: 22. **E.2**: 54. **H.7**: 20. **I.4**: 39. **K.4**: 76.
Rawls, J. **B.1**: 19.
Réadaptation des handicapés **K.4**: 130.
Réalisme **B.1**: 140.
Recensements **G.3.2**: 107.
Recensements de population **B.2**: 35. **E.2**: 64. **F.1**: 11, 18, 29, 36, 41. **F.3**: 9.
Récession **F.8**: 35. **H.3**: 40, 58. **I.2**: 240.
Recherche **A.2**: 3, 12. **A.3**: 2. **B.1**: 90. **B.2**: 1, 4, 6, 11, 15, 100, 103, 107. **C.1**: 75, 89. **C.2**: 150. **D.3**: 26. **D.7**: 128, 171, 233. **D.9**: 217. **E.3**: 51. **F.2**: 10, 17. **F.4**: 72. **F.5**: 66. **K.1**: 283. **K.2**: 40. **K.3**: 37.
Recherche agricole **G.3.1**: 66.
Recherche appliquée **A.2**: 17.
Recherche d'emploi **F.8**: 93. **I.2**: 23, 31, 66, 114, 231.
Recherche démographique **F.1**: 52. **F.3**: 12. **H.3**: 51. **K.1**: 19.
Recherche empirique **A.1**: 28, 36. **B.2**: 12, 24, 43. **F.2**: 22.
Recherche en sciences sociales **B.1**: 28, 34.
Recherche et développement **I.3**: 47, 128. **I.4**: 73, 106.
Recherche ethnographique **G.3.2**: 107.
Recherche interdisciplinaire **B.1**: 84.
Recherche organisationnelle **C.5**: 2.
Recherche sociale **A.2**: 16. **B.1**: 41. **D.1**: 26. **D.3**: 62. **E.2**: 71. **G.3.2**: 132, 160, 223.

Recherche sociologique **A.2**: 2, 5, 22. **B.1**: 141, 144. **B.2**: 30, 57. **D.8**: 68. **E.2**: 60.
Recherche sur la communication **K.4**: 194.
Recherche sur la gestion **I.4**: 76.
Recherche sur la migration **F.8**: 44.
Recherche sur les politiques gouvernementales **K.2**: 1.
Récidivisme **K.1**: 209.
Réciprocité **C.3**: 67. **D.7**: 217, 221–222. **F.4**: 97.
Récits **C.1**: 94. **D.1**: 114. **D.7**: 26, 89, 256. **F.4**: 240.
Récréation **F.8**: 36. **H.5**: 34. **I.6**: 1–2, 17, 25, 28, 40, 45–46.
Recrutement **B.2**: 67. **I.2**: 204. **I.3**: 71, 80, 125. **I.5**: 180.
Recrutement politique **J.6**: 3.
Récupération du sol **G.1**: 7. **G.3.2**: 273.
Recyclage **G.1**: 21, 31. **G.3.2**: 302.
Redistribution du revenu **I.2**: 54.
Réforme **D.9**: 165. **E.3**: 22. **F.4**: 321. **G.3.2**: 323, 329. **I.3**: 62. **K.4**: 90, 190, 203, 205.
Réforme agraire **G.3.1**: 106.
Réforme de l'enseignement **D.9**: 43, 47–48, 50, 72, 75, 78, 136, 215.
Réforme de logement **H.3**: 54.
Réforme économique **E.3**: 22. **H.7**: 5–6. **I.3**: 131.
Réforme foncière **G.3.1**: 73.
Réforme légale **D.2**: 12. **D.4**: 39. **F.4**: 187. **F.5**: 86.
Réforme sociale **D.5**: 104.
Réformisme **I.2**: 53.
Réfugiés **C.2**: 28, 78. **D.1**: 98. **F.7**: 112. **F.8**: 20, 45, 52, 64, 69, 76–77, 84, 115, 117, 142–143, 163–164. **G.3.1**: 49. **I.2**: 61, 172. **K.4**: 10, 233.
Régime autoritaire **J.5**: 16, 22.
Régimes fonciers **G.3.1**: 8, 13, 35, 38, 89–90, 113, 120. **H.3**: 54.
Régimes militaires **G.3.1**: 38.
Régionalisation **D.7**: 357.
Régions **G.3**: 2, 8.
Règlement de conflits **C.3**: 105, 109, 111, 113, 117, 120–121. **C.5**: 13, 19. **D.4**: 31. **F.4**: 152. **I.5**: 26, 73, 77, 91, 93, 96.
Réglementation **D.7**: 114. **H.5**: 3. **I.5**: 45. **J.4**: 18. **J.6**: 50.
Règles de la majorité **J.3**: 4.
Régulation de la production **I.3**: 117.
Régulation des naissances **F.3**: 41–44, 97, 141.

Régulation sociale **C.2**: 136. **C.4**: 20. **C.5**: 15. **D.1**: 51, 111, 123. **E.3**: 65. **F.5**: 228. **G.1**: 28. **J.3**: 9. **K.1**: 8, 119, 408. **K.4**: 36, 69.

Relation salaires-emploi **H.3**: 80. **I.3**: 6.

Relations centre-peripherie **F.7**: 148. **J.4**: 3.

Relations culturelles **C.1**: 73. **D.1**: 22, 55, 67.

Relations de voisinage **D.4**: 31. **G.3.2**: 211.

Relations des sexes **C.4**: 63. **D.6**: 8. **F.4**: 354. **F.5**: 35, 42, 49, 210, 218, 269, 295, 318, 322. **G.3.2**: 174. **H.4**: 90.

Relations du travail **F.5**: 19. **I.3**: 64, 126. **I.4**: 26, 47. **I.5**: 1, 5, 7, 12–13, 16, 20, 22, 24–31, 34–37, 40, 42–43, 45, 47, 49, 51–60, 62, 67, 69, 71, 74, 77, 81, 85, 89, 91, 93–94, 97–98, 103, 108–109, 119, 138, 153, 169, 197.

Relations enseignants-enseignés **D.9**: 19.

Relations entre générations **D.7**: 44. **E.2**: 31. **F.2**: 8–9, 13. **F.4**: 68, 197, 211, 349. **F.5**: 197.

Relations extérieures **K.1**: 321.

Relations familiales **C.2**: 185. **F.3**: 184, 225. **F.4**: 34, 43, 54, 59, 85, 114, 116. **K.4**: 34.

Relations hommes-femmes **I.3**: 65.

Relations humaines **C.3**: 63. **D.7**: 4. **F.4**: 94. **G.1**: 17.

Relations interethniques **C.4**: 15. **D.2**: 3. **F.7**: 71–72, 128, 143, 154, 157, 159, 164, 172, 174, 178–180, 182–183, 187–188, 197, 201, 204, 263. **K.1**: 10, 12.

Relations intergroupes **C.1**: 56. **C.3**: 21, 109. **C.4**: 13, 15, 20, 29, 41, 52. **F.7**: 29, 173, 209.

Relations internationales **D.5**: 116. **J.8**: 13.

Relations interpersonnelles **C.1**: 152. **C.3**: 1, 5, 8, 13–15, 17, 21, 23, 32, 34, 36, 42, 47, 50, 61, 65, 69, 71, 80, 89, 118, 133, 141, 149, 155. **C.4**: 58. **C.5**: 87. **C.7**: 37. **D.7**: 159. **F.2**: 71, 120. **F.4**: 182, 254. **F.5**: 63. **I.3**: 17. **K.1**: 63, 363.

Relations publique **D.7**: 274.

Relations raciales **D.7**: 310, 351. **D.9**: 84, 205. **E.2**: 12. **F.7**: 4, 12, 95, 136, 145–147, 156, 162, 171, 173, 175, 177, 183, 185, 189–192, 196, 199–200, 202, 207–208, 211–212, 252, 265. **F.8**: 4, 28, 70, 87. **G.3.2**: 198.

Relations sexuelles **F.3**: 61. **F.6**: 1, 8, 13–14, 16, 33.

Relations sociales **C.3**: 19, 79, 159. **D.5**: 70. **F.6**: 47. **H.2**: 8.

Relativisme **D.1**: 110, 133. **D.6**: 31.

Religion **C.1**: 140. **C.4**: 13. **D.1**: 99. **D.5**: 5, 12–13, 22–24, 26, 30, 35, 38–39, 41–42, 44–45, 47–49, 55, 58, 68, 70–71, 79, 91, 96, 101, 105, 109, 111, 150, 177. **F.2**: 144. **F.3**: 30, 87. **F.4**: 100. **F.5**: 284. **F.6**: 43. **F.7**: 80, 119. **I.2**: 37. **K.1**: 70.

Religion civile **D.5**: 3. **J.8**: 3.

Religion et politique **D.5**: 40, 95, 128, 174. **D.9**: 206. **K.2**: 15.

Religiosité **D.5**: 9, 37, 57, 185. **F.2**: 132.

Rénovation urbaine **D.8**: 48. **F.5**: 178. **G.3.2**: 46, 48, 234, 239, 245, 249, 266, 274–275, 292, 300, 311, 328, 330–332.

Répartition de la population **F.3**: 17.

Répartition du revenu **B.2**: 28. **H.3**: 56, 66, 81, 89. **I.2**: 28. **K.1**: 269–270, 284.

Répartition en zones **G.3.1**: 22. **G.3.2**: 271.

Répartition par sexe **F.3**: 13. **F.4**: 227. **K.1**: 425.

Répartition spatiale **F.3**: 9. **H.5**: 36. **K.1**: 285.

Représentation politique **J.5**: 19.

Représentations sociales **C.7**: 20, 36. **F.2**: 67. **F.3**: 154.

Répression **G.3.1**: 132. **K.1**: 221.

Reproduction artificielle **K.4**: 257.

Reproduction sexuelle **D.6**: 8. **F.3**: 56, 111, 123. **F.5**: 270. **K.4**: 65.

Reproduction sociale **E.1**: 20. **F.5**: 184.

Réseaux d'information **C.3**: 16.

Réseaux de communication **C.3**: 16. **D.7**: 129, 139, 162.

Réseaux sociaux **C.3**: 52. **C.4**: 10, 30, 48–49, 58. **C.5**: 87. **D.7**: 14. **E.1**: 17. **F.3**: 126. **F.4**: 97, 112. **F.5**: 289. **F.7**: 9. **G.2**: 1. **G.3.1**: 65, 76. **I.3**: 105. **J.3**: 29. **K.1**: 20.

Résidence **D.1**: 16. **F.8**: 15. **G.3.2**: 129.

Résistance passive **D.3**: 10.

Responsabilité **C.4**: 36, 43. **C.7**: 80. **D.3**: 19–21, 33, 87. **D.4**: 2. **F.3**: 181. **F.5**: 159. **H.4**: 33, 66. **I.5**: 39. **J.5**: 14. **K.1**: 7.

Responsabilité civile **I.3**: 76. **K.1**: 319.

Ressources économiques **F.4**: 205.

Ressources humaines **D.3**: 7. **E.2**: 17. **F.3**: 7. **F.4**: 63. **F.7**: 56. **H.3**: 13. **H.7**: 27. **I.2**: 51, 106, 179, 187, 210. **I.3**: 44, 47, 68, 124, 129–130, 135, 143. **I.4**: 117.

Ressources naturelles **G.1**: 2, 34.

Résultats électoraux **I.5**: 191.

Retard intellectuel **C.3**: 75. **K.4**: 118.

Retraite **F.2**: 39, 47, 50, 61. **F.8**: 36. **I.2**: 125. **I.3**: 48, 75.

Retraite anticipée **I.2**: 221. **K.2**: 28.

Réussite dans les études **D.9**: 161, 166. **I.4**: 62.

Réussite sociale **F.2**: 76.

Réveil religieux **D.5**: 118.

Revendications foncières **F.7**: 129.

Revenu **D.7**: 116. **E.2**: 15, 17. **F.1**: 28. **F.4**: 25. **F.5**: 189, 194. **F.7**: 7. **G.3.2**: 152. **H.3**: 28, 60, 62, 75–77. **H.4**: 88. **I.3**: 8. **K.2**: 29, 106. **K.4**: 85, 104, 160.

Revenu des ménages **G.3.1**: 58. **H.2**: 14. **H.3**: 75.
Revenu familial **F.4**: 341. **I.4**: 53.
Revenu par tête **H.3**: 85.
Revenus d'investissement **D.5**: 29.
Révolution **D.1**: 24. **D.5**: 128. **D.7**: 97. **E.3**: 2, 49, 52, 70, 73. **F.5**: 107, 219. **F.8**: 52. **J.2**: 28. **J.5**: 8, 26–28. **J.6**: 14. **K.1**: 17.
Rhétorique **D.7**: 284. **I.2**: 69.
Richesse **E.3**: 45. **H.3**: 32.
Rire **D.5**: 48.
Risque **C.5**: 8. **C.7**: 30, 60. **D.1**: 36, 102. **D.9**: 208. **F.2**: 51. **F.3**: 61, 180–181, 289. **F.6**: 1. **H.4**: 97. **H.6**: 5. **I.4**: 30. **K.1**: 18, 144, 386, 391. **K.2**: 62. **K.4**: 8, 46.
Rites funéraires **D.2**: 14.
Rituelle **D.2**: 27. **D.5**: 15, 86. **J.1**: 5. **J.6**: 27. **J.7**: 8. **K.1**: 317.
Riz **F.5**: 269.
Rôle **C.4**: 10.
Rôle de sexes **C.3**: 144. **D.4**: 20. **F.1**: 61. **F.5**: 63, 123, 262, 271–272, 274, 276, 280–281, 283, 285, 289–290, 299, 303, 305, 312–313, 315, 317, 319. **G.3.1**: 3–4, 45. **I.2**: 133. **K.1**: 395.
Rôles conjugaux **F.4**: 263.
Rôles professionnels **F.5**: 288.
Rôles sexuels **F.5**: 172, 264, 278, 291, 314. **I.2**: 103–104, 161.
Rôles sociaux **C.1**: 103. **C.4**: 63. **C.6**: 12, 15. **K.1**: 385. **K.4**: 5.
Romans **D.8**: 19.
Rotation de la main-d'oeuvre **I.2**: 77. **I.3**: 28, 46, 54, 63.
Rumeur **D.7**: 94, 153.
Rushdie, Salman
 D.5: 175. **D.7**: 313. **F.7**: 185.
Sacré **D.1**: 77. **F.2**: 131. **H.6**: 10. **J.5**: 37.
Sacrifice **D.5**: 60, 174.
Saint-Simon, C.
 D.1: 79.
Saissonalité **F.1**: 59.
Salaire minimum **I.3**: 23.
Salaires **I.5**: 50.
Salariés **F.4**: 302.
Salles de classe **D.9**: 116, 126, 154.
Sandel, M.J.
 B.1: 19.
Sans-abri **C.3**: 37, 79. **F.2**: 128. **F.8**: 43. **G.3.1**: 26. **G.3.2**: 40, 98, 107–108, 121, 132, 154, 160, 224. **K.1**: 26, 219, 223, 230, 235–238, 240–244, 248, 253, 260, 263, 274, 277, 279, 285, 287–288, 291, 294, 301, 310, 347, 355–357. **K.2**: 13. **K.4**: 47–48, 119, 189.

Santanisme **D.5**: 61.
Santé **B.1**: 81. **C.1**: 122. **C.2**: 22, 209. **D.5**: 12, 18, 185. **F.2**: 54, 86–87, 143. **F.3**: 12, 56, 108, 118, 147, 162, 168, 179, 221. **F.4**: 252. **F.5**: 173. **F.7**: 24, 31. **F.8**: 31. **G.1**: 5, 14. **G.3.1**: 129. **H.4**: 22. **I.2**: 177. **I.3**: 73, 75. **K.1**: 241, 260, 268, 349. **K.4**: 9, 14, 38–40, 44, 46, 50, 62, 81, 91, 93, 105–106, 133, 141, 146, 166, 181, 201, 225, 234, 238.
Santé d'enfants **F.2**: 85. **F.4**: 335. **K.4**: 215.
Santé mentale **C.1**: 6, 68–69, 72, 75, 91, 140. **C.2**: 20, 28. **C.3**: 34. **C.7**: 13. **D.1**: 98. **D.8**: 53. **F.2**: 59, 106. **F.3**: 196–197, 220, 225–226. **F.4**: 307. **G.3.1**: 59. **I.2**: 232, 241. **I.3**: 8. **J.7**: 21. **K.1**: 256, 260. **K.4**: 10, 27, 31, 36, 114, 124–125, 198–199, 222–223, 232–233.
Santé publique **F.3**: 171, 173, 183, 235, 261. **G.3.2**: 267. **K.4**: 7, 60, 74, 90, 159–160, 166, 169, 218, 224, 235, 237.
Satisfaction **C.3**: 91, 140–141. **F.4**: 281, 309. **F.5**: 7, 220. **G.3.1**: 7. **H.5**: 22.
Satisfaction au travail **F.5**: 12. **I.3**: 96–97, 99–100, 102–105. **I.4**: 111. **I.5**: 126.
Satisfaction conjugale **F.4**: 74, 203, 233–234, 251.
Satisfaction de l'existence **C.2**: 40. **C.3**: 43. **I.3**: 100.
Satisfaction résidentielle **G.3.2**: 109, 180.
Scheler, Max
 B.1: 73.
Schizophrénie **C.2**: 125. **F.3**: 169, 206. **K.4**: 2.
Schmitt, Carl
 J.2: 19.
Schmoller, von, Gustav
 H.1: 5.
Schultz, Alfred
 B.1: 129.
Schumpter, Joseph
 H.1: 5.
Schutz, Alfred
 B.1: 15.
Science **B.1**: 34, 40, 55, 79. **C.1**: 80, 99, 110. **D.5**: 26, 163, 176. **D.6**: 2–3, 5, 7–8, 18, 21, 23, 28. **D.9**: 190. **F.4**: 72. **F.5**: 121–122, 182. **F.7**: 260. **F.8**: 44. **G.1**: 19. **H.4**: 92. **I.2**: 151. **K.4**: 267.
Science politique **A.1**: 2. **D.7**: 292. **J.2**: 21.
Science-ficition **D.8**: 68.
Sciences du comportement **A.1**: 30. **B.1**: 104. **B.2**: 25. **C.1**: 32. **C.2**: 169, 207, 218. **C.7**: 29. **D.4**: 3, 27. **D.7**: 326. **G.1**: 62. **J.1**: 1.
Sciences juridiques **C.7**: 5.

Sciences sociales **A.1**: 3–4, 9, 11, 21–22, 27, 30, 32–35, 43. **A.2**: 2, 7, 16, 24. **A.3**: 6. **B.1**: 2, 10, 41, 59, 65, 68, 93, 115. **B.2**: 57, 75. **C.1**: 25, 71, 108. **C.2**: 88. **C.3**: 38. **D.1**: 112. **D.6**: 4. **E.3**: 20, 59. **F.3**: 148. **G.3.1**: 133. **G.3.2**: 90. **J.1**: 12.

Scientifiques **D.9**: 175. **F.5**: 208. **I.2**: 24. **I.4**: 106.

Scolarité **D.9**: 89, 95, 168. **F.4**: 63, 80. **F.5**: 175. **I.4**: 25, 112.

Searle, J.R. **D.7**: 211.

Secours aux sinistrés **K.1**: 2, 5.

Secteur industriel **H.3**: 79.

Secteur informel **C.5**: 39. **F.5**: 250. **F.8**: 166. **H.2**: 4. **H.3**: 50. **I.3**: 64.

Secteur privé **D.3**: 57. **H.4**: 18. **I.5**: 92, 159. **J.4**: 4. **K.4**: 180.

Secteur public **A.2**: 20. **F.5**: 146. **F.7**: 249. **I.3**: 89, 143. **I.4**: 79. **I.5**: 62–63, 92, 116, 161, 187. **J.4**: 1, 4, 9, 15. **K.4**: 180.

Secteur tertiaire **G.3.2**: 352. **H.4**: 2, 57. **I.2**: 105, 136. **K.4**: 134.

Sécularisation **D.5**: 2–3, 58, 62–63, 123, 183.

Sécurité alimentaire **F.5**: 321.

Sécurité de l'emploi **I.2**: 217. **I.5**: 41.

Sécurité du travail **F.5**: 156. **I.3**: 108–109, 112, 114, 118, 120.

Sécurité routière **C.2**: 12. **C.5**: 59. **K.1**: 333.

Sécurité sociale **F.5**: 221. **F.8**: 2. **I.4**: 38. **K.2**: 18, 20, 22–24, 26–29, 73, 75, 79, 90, 99, 108–110. **K.4**: 85.

Sédentarisation **F.3**: 291.

Segmentation du marché du travail **D.5**: 64. **I.2**: 22, 185.

Ségrégation **F.5**: 153, 220. **F.7**: 140, 170, 181. **G.1**: 60. **G.3.2**: 156. **H.3**: 69. **I.2**: 129. **I.3**: 133. **I.4**: 44.

Ségrégation professionnelle **F.5**: 176. **I.2**: 114. **I.3**: 36. **I.4**: 36.

Ségrégation raciale **F.7**: 251. **G.3.2**: 156, 194, 336.

Ségrégation résidentielle **F.7**: 146. **G.3.2**: 175. **I.2**: 55.

Sélection du personnel **I.2**: 26. **I.3**: 137–138, 140, 150, 153.

Sémantique **C.2**: 180. **D.1**: 40. **D.7**: 133, 205, 208, 210, 224, 226. **F.7**: 75–76. **J.1**: 8.

Sémiologie **D.8**: 38.

Sémiotique **C.1**: 49. **D.7**: 72.

Sensation **F.2**: 130. **F.3**: 197.

Séparation maritale **F.4**: 145, 269, 276.

Séparatisme **D.5**: 169.

Séries temporelles **F.5**: 2. **K.1**: 77, 157.

Service des pompiers **I.1**: 9. **K.2**: 21.

Service postal **I.3**: 35.

Services collectifs **F.7**: 15, 150. **G.2**: 22. **J.6**: 20. **K.1**: 362. **K.4**: 27, 110, 119, 167, 183, 206.

Services de santé **F.2**: 128. **K.2**: 21. **K.3**: 12. **K.4**: 8, 10, 42–43, 84, 95, 113, 119, 150, 165, 175, 180, 187, 192, 194–195, 206–208, 210, 228.

Services publics **H.7**: 7, 19. **I.2**: 47. **J.4**: 4.

Services sociaux **F.4**: 92. **F.7**: 12. **F.8**: 13. **G.2**: 35. **K.1**: 33. **K.2**: 50, 76, 89, 95, 97–98, 100, 102, 105. **K.3**: 12, 16, 36, 38, 45. **K.4**: 19, 26, 29, 40, 71, 88, 123, 165, 187, 201, 232, 238.

Services urbains **G.2**: 13. **K.4**: 46.

Sexe **C.1**: 65. **C.7**: 3. **D.1**: 7. **F.1**: 60. **F.2**: 67. **F.4**: 137. **F.5**. 26, 75, 153. **F.6**. 43, 48.

Sexisme **D.5**: 16. **F.5**: 68, 95, 224.

Sexualité **C.1**: 7. **D.5**: 37. **F.3**: 72, 108. **F.5**: 287, 319. **F.6**: 2, 10–11, 19, 48–49, 52–54, 56–57. **J.3**: 24.

Sheeler, Charles **D.7**: 3.

Sherman, Cindy **D.8**: 43.

SIDA **C.3**: 78. **D.3**: 27. **D.5**: 38. **D.7**: 173. **F.2**: 16. **F.3**: 144–152, 154–160, 163–164, 172, 176, 180–182, 185–186, 188, 202, 207, 209–210, 212, 216–219, 223–224, 228, 231, 234. **F.5**: 25, 45. **F.6**: 4. **I.2**: 222. **I.5**: 99. **K.1**: 144, 367. **K.3**: 2, 46–47. **K.4**: 168–172, 210, 235, 245–246.

Simmel, Georg **D.1**: 99.

Simulation **C.3**: 36. **C.5**: 20. **I.5**: 51.

Situation de famille **F.3**: 38, 92, 269. **F.4**: 220, 232, 261. **I.2**: 89.

Sociabilité **F.4**: 346.

Social-démocratie **I.5**: 15.

Socialisation **C.3**: 132. **D.1**: 1, 140. **F.4**: 103. **F.6**: 56. **F.8**: 81. **I.3**: 5. **I.4**: 31. **K.1**: 74. **K.4**: 240.

Socialisation politique **D.1**: 136.

Socialisme **D.1**: 113. **D.9**: 98. **E.3**: 13. **F.4**: 106. **F.5**: 127, 180, 319. **F.7**: 187. **G.1**: 10. **G.3.2**: 123. **J.2**: 25, 30. **J.3**: 7. **J.6**: 5. **K.4**: 90.

Socialisme d'État **E.3**: 11.

Socialistes **G.3.2**: 74.

Société **B.1**: 9, 147. **D.8**: 23.

Société agraire **E.3**: 75. **G.3.1**: 2.

Société capitaliste **B.1**: 47. **H.2**: 6, 19.

Société civile **D.1**: 1, 18, 47, 68. **E.3**: 26. **J.3**: 10, 20. **K.2**: 63.

Société de l'information **K.2**: 63.

Société de masse **D.7**: 238.

Société paysanne **H.4**: 31.
Société politique **B.1**: 126.
Société post-industrielle **H.4**: 8, 17.
Société rurale **E.2**: 13, 53. **E.3**: 16. **G.3.1**: 15, 39, 100. **H.7**: 24. **I.2**: 76.
Société traditionnelle **D.1**: 126.
Société urbaine **F.7**: 34. **G.3.2**: 54, 142, 178, 184. **I.2**: 76, 171. **K.1**: 292.
Sociobiologie **D.1**: 78. **E.3**: 2–3. **F.1**: 8.
Sociolinguistique **C.3**: 78. **D.7**: 9, 27, 44–46, 55, 67, 77–81, 83, 87, 143, 154, 156, 194–195, 198, 209, 216, 218, 225, 227, 269, 341, 347, 349.
Sociologie **A.1**: 1–2, 5–7, 13–14, 16, 18–19, 22, 25, 28–29, 31, 36–39, 41–42. **A.2**: 17, 23. **A.3**: 3, 7. **B.1**: 20, 45, 66, 83, 88–90, 96, 118, 120, 126–127, 134, 137, 140. **B.2**: 115. **C.2**: 64. **C.3**: 82. **C.6**: 15. **D.1**: 36, 99. **D.2**: 25. **D.5**: 107. **E.1**: 9, 16. **E.3**: 5, 76. **F.3**: 221. **F.4**: 60, 204. **F.5**: 10, 92. **F.6**: 49. **F.7**: 252. **J.2**: 14. **K.1**: 404. **K.2**: 4, 26. **K.3**: 45.
Sociologie de l'éducation **D.7**: 46. **D.9**: 127, 144–145, 147.
Sociologie de la connaissance **B.1**: 28, 39. **D.6**: 29. **D.9**: 127. **F.8**: 106.
Sociologie de la famille **F.4**: 109.
Sociologie de la profession **F.5**: 202. **I.3**: 14, 104. **I.4**: 7. **I.5**: 97.
Sociologie de la religion **B.1**: 125. **D.5**: 66, 73, 93.
Sociologie de la science **D.6**: 11.
Sociologie des loisirs **I.6**: 7.
Sociologie des organisations **C.5**: 85. **D.9**: 129.
Sociologie du développement **E.3**: 68.
Sociologie du droit **D.4**: 26. **K.1**: 104.
Sociologie du sport **I.6**: 34.
Sociologie du travail **F.5**: 317. **I.1**: 1, 4–5, 7, 13. **I.3**: 39.
Sociologie économique **H.1**: 5.
Sociologie électorale **I.5**: 162.
Sociologie industrielle **C.1**: 143. **I.1**: 6, 13. **I.2**: 174. **I.4**: 76.
Sociologie médicale **A.2**: 3. **F.3**: 221. **K.4**: 56, 243.
Sociologie politique **J.1**: 11–12, 14–15, 22.
Sociologie rurale **E.2**: 33. **F.3**: 107. **G.3.1**: 1, 7, 20, 42, 47, 58, 70, 72, 76.
Sociologie urbaine **D.5**: 99. **F.3**: 252. **G.3.2**: 4, 7, 26, 31–32, 37, 43, 47, 55, 62, 71–72, 80, 83, 88, 90–91, 144, 186, 189, 196, 211, 223, 225, 238, 260, 276, 351.
Sociologues **A.1**: 8, 12. **A.2**: 1, 9–10, 13, 15. **B.1**: 97, 117. **C.3**: 63.

Soi **B.1**: 19. **C.1**: 53, 150. **C.2**: 61, 64–65, 70, 88, 92, 98, 131, 164, 176, 198, 221–222, 225, 228, 230, 238. **C.3**: 70, 158. **C.5**: 43. **C.7**: 19. **D.3**: 8. **D.5**: 159. **F.2**: 45. **F.4**: 28. **F.5**: 151, 159. **I.3**: 149.
Soin dans la communauté **K.4**: 107, 109, 112, 115–119, 122, 124, 127, 130.
Soins **F.4**: 20, 210, 339. **F.5**: 53, 140, 164. **K.2**: 3. **K.3**: 31.
Soins médicaux **F.2**: 16, 46. **F.3**: 181, 279. **F.5**: 25. **I.3**: 122. **K.1**: 264. **K.2**: 89. **K.3**: 30, 39. **K.4**: 6, 15–16, 20, 25, 28, 42–43, 45, 54, 61, 66, 68, 70, 76, 78, 80, 82, 87–89, 99, 103–104, 111, 121, 148–149, 157, 161, 164, 168, 170, 172–173, 175–176, 186, 190, 195–196, 201, 203–204, 211, 214, 216, 219, 221, 223–224, 227, 239, 243–244, 250, 260.
Soins médicaux privée **K.4**: 79.
Solidarité **C.2**: 50. **F.4**: 68. **J.7**: 17.
Solitude **C.2**: 240. **C.3**: 60. **F.2**: 52.
Somatologie **C.2**: 47.
Sondages d'opinion publique **A.2**: 19. **C.7**: 48.
Soninke **F.7**: 19.
Sorcellerie **D.1**: 142. **D.5**: 187.
Sous-classe **E.2**: 62. **G.3.2**: 176, 210. **I.2**: 240. **K.1**: 290, 292.
Sous-développement **C.2**: 40. **D.3**: 60. **D.9**: 16–17, 111, 138. **F.7**: 18. **G.3.2**: 248. **J.6**: 9.
Sous-traitance **H.4**: 48.
Souveraineté **F.5**: 246. **J.8**: 16.
Spécialisation de la production **H.2**: 5.
Spécialisation flexible **I.1**: 16. **I.2**: 154.
Spécialistes en sciences sociales **A.2**: 4. **B.1**: 38. **F.2**: 114. **J.6**: 48.
Spectateurs **D.7**: 249.
Spiritisme **D.1**: 27. **D.5**: 36.
Sport **D.7**: 324. **F.2**: 40. **F.7**: 229, 251, 256, 263. **H.5**: 6. **I.5**: 9. **I.6**: 4–5, 8–9, 12–14, 18, 23, 32, 36–38, 43–44. **K.1**: 404, 406.
Squatters **G.2**: 2, 33. **G.3.2**: 213. **H.3**: 54. **K.1**: 261.
Stabilité conjugale **F.4**: 251.
Stabilité d'emploi **I.2**: 21.
Stagnation **H.3**: 49.
Statistique **B.1**: 100. **B.2**: 65. **K.1**: 160. **K.2**: 4.
Statut économique **F.3**: 90. **F.7**: 10.
Statut juridique **F.2**: 92. **F.4**: 217. **F.5**: 50, 199–200. **F.7**: 130. **F.8**: 131.
Statut professionnel **E.2**: 38. **I.4**: 35.
Statut social **C.3**: 85. **C.4**: 44. **D.1**: 127. **E.2**: 32, 36, 38–40, 57. **F.2**: 67, 105, 123. **F.4**: 37, 93. **F.5**: 183, 299. **F.7**: 11, 81. **H.6**: 2. **K.1**: 153.
Statut sociométrique **H.3**: 26.

Stéréotypes **C.2**: 239. **C.3**: 92. **C.4**: 16, 55. **C.7**: 10, 21, 31, 66–67, 74. **F.4**: 83. **F.5**: 272, 286, 306. **F.7**: 209. **I.3**: 49. **I.4**: 38. **J.7**: 16.

Stéréotypes nationaux **C.7**: 42.

Stéréotypes raciaux **F.7**: 154.

Stéréotypes sociaux **F.5**: 271.

Stérilisation **F.3**: 44. **I.3**: 120.

Stérilisation féminine **F.3**: 69.

Stérilité **F.3**: 89, 108, 119, 135. **F.4**: 303. **K.4**: 257.

Stimulants du travail **I.2**: 69. **I.3**: 39, 57, 61. **I.4**: 61.

Stratégie de développement **G.3.2**: 334. **H.2**: 17.

Stratégie de survie **C.1**: 36. **G.3.1**: 62.

Stratification professionnelle **I.2**: 47.

Stratification sociale **E.2**: 2, 6, 13, 19, 26, 34, 41–42, 50, 61. **F.5**: 255. **F.7**: 261. **H.3**: 82.

Structuralisme **B.1**: 11. **J.2**: 30.

Structure de l'organisation **C.5**: 9, 12, 20, 75, 82. **H.4**: 23. **J.4**: 1.

Structure de la famille **F.4**: 330–331, 334–336, 339, 341, 345, 347, 352–354.

Structure de la main d'oeuvre **I.2**: 124.

Structure du marché **H.4**: 52.

Structure économique **J.2**: 30.

Structure politique **G.2**: 19.

Structure professionnelle **I.4**: 45.

Structure sociale **B.1**: 128, 138. **B.2**: 27. **C.7**: 20. **D.1**: 42. **D.8**: 30. **E.1**: 6, 9, 11, 16, 18. **E.2**: 7, 14, 20, 42, 45, 58, 80. **E.3**: 6, 12, 49, 65, 67. **F.3**: 131–132, 220. **F.4**: 66. **F.7**: 82, 262. **G.2**: 24. **G.3.2**: 119, 266. **I.4**: 57. **J.2**: 30. **K.1**: 399.

Structure urbaine **G.3.2**: 19, 38, 199, 302.

Subculture **D.8**: 53. **F.2**: 123. **K.1**: 16, 413.

Subjectivité **C.7**: 14, 65. **D.7**: 107. **F.5**: 26.

Subsidiarité **K.2**: 102.

Subventions **H.3**: 90.

Suicide **F.3**: 267. **F.8**: 23. **J.7**: 21. **K.1**: 394–402.

Sunnisme **D.5**: 145.

Superstition **D.1**: 80.

Surabondance de main d'oeuvre **I.2**: 37. **I.5**: 115.

Surpeuplement **F.1**: 44. **F.3**: 308. **K.1**: 171.

Symboles **B.1**: 143. **C.1**: 98. **J.1**: 5.

Symbolisme **C.5**: 60. **D.1**: 73, 116. **F.2**: 144. **F.6**: 51.

Sympathie **C.2**: 14.

Synagogues **F.4**: 253.

Syncrétisme religieux **D.5**: 32.

Syndicalisme **I.3**: 106. **I.5**: 65, 123, 144, 150, 152–153, 176, 187.

Syndicats **E.2**: 25. **F.5**: 227, 230. **H.3**: 76, 81. **I.2**: 53. **I.5**: 79, 116, 118–122, 124–130, 133, 135–141, 143, 145–149, 151, 154–155, 157–163, 165, 167–174, 177–186, 188–194. **J.4**: 6. **J.5**: 30. **K.4**: 79.

Syntaxe **D.7**: 205.

Systèmes culturels **C.4**: 3. **D.7**: 192.

Systèmes d'enseignement **D.7**: 84. **D.9**: 89, 93, 97, 99, 102, 112, 146.

Systèmes d'expert **B.2**: 8.

Systèmes d'information **B.2**: 69. **G.3.1**: 102. **H.5**: 27.

Systèmes d'information géographique **G.3.2**: 268–269. **H.7**: 10.

Systèmes de planification **H.7**: 17. **J.4**: 7. **J.6**: 29.

Systèmes de production **D.8**: 15. **H.4**: 29, 50.

Systèmes de valeur **F.7**: 169. **I.4**: 27.

Systèmes économiques **D.5**: 82. **E.2**: 47. **H.2**: 2.

Systèmes juridiques **D.4**: 32.

Systèmes politiques **J.3**: 1, 8, 22. **J.5**: 13, 32.

Systèmes sociales **D.2**: 22. **D.4**: 26. **E.1**: 3, 5, 10, 25. **F.2**: 44.

Tabac **D.7**: 103, 116. **F.2**: 129. **K.1**: 298.

Tabou **F.3**: 199.

Taux d'accumulation **H.2**: 16.

Taux de natalité **F.1**: 20. **F.3**: 84, 91.

Taux de salaire **F.5**: 176. **H.3**: 67. **I.3**: 44.

Taylor, Charles **C.2**: 65.

Tcherkesse **F.8**: 7.

Techniciens **I.4**: 1.

Techniques d'évaluation **H.4**: 4.

Techniques de gestion **G.2**: 14.

Techniques de prévision **B.2**: 39. **F.1**: 29–30. **F.3**: 176. **I.3**: 148. **K.4**: 102.

Technologie **B.1**: 12, 40. **B.2**: 17. **C.2**: 19. **C.5**: 57. **D.1**: 115. **D.6**: 10, 23, 26, 28. **D.7**: 126, 150. **D.9**: 67, 175. **F.5**: 103, 196. **G.3.2**: 232. **H.4**: 79, 85–88, 90, 92–93, 96–97, 100, 102–103. **I.2**: 12, 24, 91, 123. **I.3**: 4. **I.5**: 42, 137, 171–172. **J.3**: 37. **J.7**: 11, 22. **K.1**: 363, 427. **K.4**: 98, 271.

Technologie alternative **G.3.1**: 66.

Technologie de l'information **C.5**: 71. **D.7**: 91, 184. **G.3.1**: 100, 119. **G.3.2**: 312. **H.4**: 94. **K.4**: 101.

Technologie de pointe **C.5**: 74. **H.4**: 41. **I.2**: 25. **I.3**: 47. **I.4**: 40, 66. **K.4**: 16.

Technologie des communications **H.4**: 94.

Technologie industrielle **D.9**: 40.

Technologie reproductive **D.3**: 89. **F.3**: 32, 45, 71, 115, 142. **F.4**: 303.

Technologies nouvelles **D.7**: 325. **I.2**: 210.

Télécommunications **D.7**: 91–92, 184. **D.9**: 12, 31, 67. **H.4**: 95.

Téléphone **B.2**: 92. **D.7**: 150. **F.7**: 119. **H.5**: 25.

Télévision **D.2**: 6. **D.5**: 152. **D.7**: 240, 287, 293, 297, 323, 327, 351–355, 357–359, 361–367, 369–370, 372, 375–382, 384–387, 389–394. **D.8**: 393. **E.1**: 14. **F.4**: 5. **F.5**: 285.

Temps de loisir **I.6**: 20.

Tension mentale **C.1**: 30–31, 92, 148. **C.2**: 8, 41, 47, 73, 80, 99, 121, 203. **C.3**: 2, 40, 159. **C.4**: 25. **F.2**: 104, 120, 142–143. **F.3**: 204, 220, 225, 230. **F.4**: 39, 57, 82, 91, 97, 252, 284. **F.5**: 288. **F.8**: 20. **H.3**: 11. **I.3**: 3, 115, 117, 121. **I.4**: 48. **J.7**: 21. **J.8**: 20. **K.1**: 378, 417. **K.3**: 1, 44. **K.4**: 48, 93.

Terreur **F.8**: 20.

Territoire **C.2**: 86. **G.1**: 28.

Terrorisme **D.1**: 45. **D.7**: 244, 285, 301.

Terroristes **C.1**: 34.

Tests d'aptitude **C.1**: 102. **C.2**: 79, 93. **K.1**: 379.

Textes **C.2**: 16.

Thai **D.1**: 5. **D.7**: 123.

Thatcher, Margaret
G.3.2: 52.

Thé **F.5**: 311.

Théâtre **D.8**: 22, 72.

Théologie **D.3**: 23.

Théologie chrétienne **D.5**: 88.

Théologie de libération **D.5**: 107. **H.2**: 10.

Théorie anthropologique **B.1**: 28.

Théorie critique **B.1**: 4, 29, 49, 76, 107. **E.3**: 21.

Théorie de chaos **C.1**: 8. **D.6**: 5. **H.7**: 16.

Théorie de contrôle **D.7**: 66. **I.2**: 217. **I.3**: 15. **I.5**: 50, 127, 136, 163.

Théorie de l'action **B.1**: 129. **C.2**: 15, 63.

Théorie de l'information **B.2**: 79. **D.7**: 152, 187.

Théorie de l'organisation **C.5**: 70, 78. **I.5**: 50.

Théorie de la culture **D.1**: 34.

Théorie de la décision **D.3**: 5.

Théorie de la planification **H.7**: 16.

Théorie de la population **F.1**: 19.

Théorie de la valeur **H.1**: 1.

Théorie de jeu **B.2**: 37. **J.1**: 9.

Théorie du groupe **C.4**: 3.

Théorie du salaire **I.2**: 60, 205.

Théorie économique **A.1**: 10. **H.2**: 5.

Théorie générale **B.1**: 134.

Théorie juridique **B.1**: 152.

Théorie linguistique **C.2**: 142. **D.7**: 68, 217, 222.

Théorie politique **J.1**: 17. **J.2**: 21.

Théorie sociale **B.1**: 6, 67, 92, 94, 100, 137, 152. **C.1**: 53. **C.7**: 28. **D.4**: 41. **D.6**: 5. **F.7**: 222. **G.1**: 57. **G.3.1**: 66. **G.3.2**: 119. **J.1**: 11. **K.2**: 8.

Théorie sociologique **A.2**: 21. **B.1**: 87, 103, 105, 107, 111, 119, 123–124, 131, 135, 140–141, 147, 151. **F.2**: 18. **I.4**: 76. **J.8**: 22. **K.1**: 212.

Thérapeutique **C.2**: 137.

Thérapie **C.1**: 35, 44, 59, 85, 97. **C.2**: 119. **F.4**: 213. **I.4**: 102. **K.1**: 204, 215.

Thérapie familiale **C.1**: 59. **F.4**: 38.

Thomas, William Isaac
F.7: 44.

Thompson, Hunter S.
D.7: 271.

Tisserands **F.2**: 95.

Tocqueville, de, Alexis
D.5: 118.

Tolérance **G.3.2**: 91.

Totalitarisme **D.8**: 34.

Touraine, Alain
B.1: 83.

Tourisme **I.5**: 21. **I.6**: 6, 15, 21, 31, 40–41.

Tourisme international **I.6**: 26–27, 29.

Toxicité **G.1**: 43. **K.4**: 7.

Toxicomanes **K.1**: 317, 334, 368, 375, 380, 385.

Toxicomanie **C.3**: 76. **F.3**: 150, 158, 197–198. **F.4**: 178. **K.1**: 11, 200, 300, 310, 316, 323–325, 328, 335–336, 339–341, 345, 347–348, 354, 356–357, 360–362, 370, 372, 377, 381, 388–390, 395. **K.4**: 47, 236.

Tradition **C.2**: 217. **D.1**: 50. **F.3**: 35. **F.7**: 28. **G.3.1**: 88.

Tradition culturelle **C.5**: 38. **D.1**: 69. **H.4**: 1.

Tradition orale **D.7**: 67.

Traduction **D.7**: 372.

Traffic de la drogue **K.1**: 152, 311, 318, 371.

Traitement de l'information **A.3**: 2, 4, 8. **C.2**: 105, 126. **C.6**: 8. **J.6**: 16.

Traitement des données **B.2**: 78. **C.1**: 84. **D.6**: 6.

Traits de personnalité **C.3**: 162.

Tranche d'âge **C.3**: 155. **C.7**: 20. **E.2**: 67. **F.1**: 65. **F.2**: 1, 7, 12–14, 20, 44. **G.3.1**: 34. **I.2**: 135. **J.6**: 56. **K.1**: 47. **K.2**: 36.

Transition de régime **D.7**: 302. **F.2**: 135.

Transmission de données **A.3**: 6.

Transport **D.3**: 4. **G.3.2**: 317.

Transport aérienne **D.7**: 256.

Transport ferroviaire **J.5**: 34. **K.1**: 140.

Transport maritime **I.4**: 41.

Transport urbain **G.3.2**: 33, 79.

Travail **C.2**: 98. **D.7**: 107. **E.2**: 74. **F.3**: 299. **F.4**: 25. **F.5**: 2, 166. **F.8**: 94. **I.1**: 1, 4, 14. **I.2**: 43, 94, 101, 171, 177, 201, 217. **I.3**: 4–5, 48, 77. **I.4**: 2, 9, 43. **I.5**: 70, 145, 176. **J.5**: 10.

Travail à domicile **H.4**: 35.

Travail à temps réduit **I.3**: 26.

Travail au noir **I.4**: 34.

Travail bénévole **C.5**: 4. **F.8**: 13. **G.2**: 35. **I.4**: 87. **J.5**: 6. **K.2**: 105. **K.3**: 47. **K.4**: 126.

Travail des cas individuels **K.3**: 43.

Travail des enfants **I.2**: 167, 194. **K.1**: 29.

Travail industriel **H.4**: 25. **I.4**: 4.

Travail manuel **I.3**: 67.

Travail ménager **F.4**: 74. **F.5**: 180. **I.3**: 44.

Travail social **D.5**: 156. **F.3**: 63. **K.2**: 52, 58. **K.3**: 2–8, 10, 12–18, 21–28, 32–35, 37–43, 45. **K.4**: 36, 109.

Travail social des groupes **F.5**: 91. **K.3**: 19.

Travail sur le terrain **A.2**: 18. **B.2**: 23, 103. **D.1**: 66.

Travailleurs **F.4**: 329. **F.8**: 62. **H.3**: 2, 43. **H.7**: 11. **I.2**: 37, 55, 100, 133, 139, 162, 199, 219. **I.3**: 65, 87. **I.4**: 22, 25, 42, 56, 70, 113, 131. **I.5**: 57–58.

Travailleurs âgés **I.2**: 117. **I.3**: 41.

Travailleurs agricoles **F.7**: 254. **G.3.1**: 86.

Travailleurs étrangers **D.7**: 218. **F.8**: 79. **I.2**: 45, 200.

Travailleurs handicapés **F.3**: 4. **I.2**: 176, 222.

Travailleurs indépendants **I.2**: 6. **I.4**: 45.

Travailleurs migrants **F.7**: 16, 254. **F.8**: 21, 141, 145, 152, 170, 172. **I.2**: 67, 191. **K.2**: 18.

Travailleurs professionnels **C.5**: 4, 82. **D.3**: 80. **F.5**: 19. **F.7**: 29. **I.4**: 63, 87–90, 95, 104–105, 107. **K.1**: 326.

Travailleurs sociaux **F.4**: 24. **K.1**: 43. **K.3**: 20, 42, 44.

Travailleuses **F.3**: 95. **F.4**: 56, 114. **F.5**: 2, 18, 41, 53, 146, 150, 166, 220, 226, 231, 247, 250, 259, 278, 309, 317, 321. **F.8**: 170. **H.3**: 91. **H.4**: 62, 77. **I.2**: 36, 72, 74, 76, 82–84, 86, 88–91, 94, 106, 112, 119–120, 122, 127–128, 130, 139–140, 143, 145, 147, 149, 151–156, 160, 180. **I.3**: 34, 88, 108. **I.4**: 27, 59, 98. **I.5**: 6, 145, 170. **J.6**: 20.

Tremblements de terre **G.3.2**: 151.

Tribalisme **D.9**: 37.

Tribunal **D.4**: 5. **I.5**: 101. **K.1**: 173.

Tribunaux pour enfants **D.8**: 53. **J.3**: 25. **K.1**: 199.

Tribus **D.9**: 51. **E.3**: 17.

Troubles de la personnalité **C.1**: 61.

Turkana **F.2**: 44.

Typologie **C.5**: 85.

Unification d'Allemagne **E.2**: 45. **F.5**: 251.

Universités **A.1**: 6. **D.7**: 5. **D.9**: 104, 144, 174, 176, 178, 180, 188, 191, 193, 196, 198–199, 202, 206–207, 209, 213, 215–217, 219–220. **F.5**: 133. **I.3**: 69. **I.4**: 23, 68, 98. **I.5**: 87, 182. **J.2**: 24.

Urbanisation **F.2**: 25. **F.3**: 17. **F.4**: 352. **F.5**: 316. **G.3**: 1. **G.3.1**: 16. **G.3.2**: 61, 163–164, 335, 337–338, 340–341, 343–350, 352–353, 355–356, 358–368. **H.5**: 31. **H.7**: 1.

Urbanisme **G.3.2**: 91, 306.

Usage de solvants **C.3**: 76.

Usage des stupéfiants **K.1**: 297, 303, 349, 351, 379, 387, 395.

Usage du tabac **C.1**: 134. **C.7**: 49. **D.7**: 103. **F.2**: 146. **F.4**: 297. **I.3**: 78. **K.1**: 298, 330–332, 346, 373, 386, 391, 393.

Usines **F.5**: 36. **I.4**: 4, 32. **I.5**: 8.

Utilisation de l'énergie **F.1**: 47.

Utilisation des loisirs **J.7**: 4.

Utilisation des terres **D.6**: 10. **G.3.1**: 41. **G.3.2**: 60, 130, 187. **H.4**: 70. **H.7**: 10, 18.

Utilitarisme **C.3**: 49.

Utopie **B.1**: 24. **D.5**: 59.

Vacances **D.2**: 27.

Valeur **C.1**: 63. **D.1**: 77, 110, 127, 130. **F.2**: 91. **G.3.2**: 129. **I.1**: 14.

Valeurs **A.1**: 36. **B.1**: 79. **C.1**: 140. **C.3**: 91, 120. **C.5**: 10. **C.7**: 34. **D.1**: 109, 115, 131, 133, 136. **D.3**: 7, 24, 75. **D.7**: 388. **D.9**: 179. **F.2**: 141. **F.4**: 76. **G.2**: 11. **H.4**: 67. **J.6**: 56. **K.3**: 6, 17.

Valeurs sociales **C.6**: 16. **D.1**: 116, 128–129, 132. **D.8**: 65. **E.1**: 18. **F.3**: 45.

Validité **C.1**: 128. **C.3**: 137. **C.5**: 2. **D.4**: 43. **F.6**: 20.

Vallabha **C.2**: 9.

Vanberg, Viktor **D.1**: 74.

Vaudou **D.5**: 188.

Vendeurs **G.3.2**: 63.

Vérification **B.2**: 89.

Vêtements **D.2**: 5.

Veto **C.4**: 62.

Veuvage **F.4**: 62.

Victimes **B.1**: 53. **K.1**: 23, 34, 45, 86.

Victimes de crime **K.1**: 14, 76, 78, 112, 126, 132, 134, 161, 184, 191.

Vidéo **D.5**: 161. **D.7**: 34, 361. **D.8**: 37. **F.2**: 81. **I.6**: 42.

Vie active **H.2**: 2. **I.4**: 89, 119.

Vie communautaire **G.2**: 20.

INTERNATIONAL BIBLIOGRAPHY OF SOCIOLOGY — 1991

Vie familiale **D.2**: 12. **F.2**: 141. **F.4**: 16, 51, 76, 342.

Vie privée **I.5**: 100. **K.4**: 263.

Vie professionnelle **I.3**: 115.

Vie quotidienne **C.1**: 91. **C.2**: 20, 47, 59, 66, 148, 164. **D.2**: 19, 22–23, 25, 28–29. **D.4**: 32. **D.7**: 107. **F.2**: 15. **F.3**: 194. **F.4**: 342. **H.4**: 92. **I.4**: 61. **K.4**: 88.

Vie religieuse **D.5**: 168.

Vie rurale **G.3.1**: 50, 61.

Vie sociale **D.1**: 48. **D.2**: 7, 13. **G.3.2**: 279.

Vie urbaine **D.7**: 94. **G.3.2**: 34, 64, 82, 86, 138, 182, 319. **H.3**: 11.

Vieillesse **F.2**: 21, 67. **F.3**: 240.

Vieillissement **C.2**: 154, 160. **D.7**: 44, 77. **F.1**: 68. **F.2**: 24–25, 27–33, 35, 37, 40, 43, 54, 57–58, 62–63. **F.3**: 168. **F.4**: 68, 345. **F.5**: 35. **J.6**: 23.

Vieillissement de la population **F.2**: 26, 42. **K.2**: 97.

Vietnamiens **F.7**: 112. **F.8**: 3.

Villages **E.1**: 6. **G.1**: 4, 49. **G.3**: 11. **G.3.1**: 6–7, 30, 37, 50, 69, 76, 78, 84, 86. **G.3.2**: 328.

Villes **C.7**: 58. **D.1**: 3. **D.9**: 154. **E.2**: 6. **F.2**: 80. **F.3**: 22, 200, 311. **F.8**: 32. **G.1**: 44. **G.3**: 11. **G.3.2**: 1, 3, 7, 9, 11–12, 16, 18–20, 24, 30, 35–36, 40–41, 46, 59, 62, 64, 67, 69, 92–93, 115, 161, 164, 179, 193, 206, 218, 222, 227, 232, 238–239, 241, 244, 246–248, 252, 275, 278, 280, 282, 284, 290–291, 298, 301, 312, 314, 339, 346, 359. **H.3**: 41. **H.4**: 8. **H.7**: 12. **I.1**: 12. **K.1**: 61, 130, 205, 230. **K.4**: 14.

Villes nouvelles **G.3.2**: 231.

Vin **C.5**: 16. **H.5**: 12.

Viol **C.7**: 80. **D.4**: 39. **F.4**: 187. **F.6**: 12. **K.1**: 46, 52, 87, 97, 118, 125, 135, 141–142, 144, 162, 215.

Violence **C.3**: 104, 119. **D.5**: 60, 65, 68, 166, 178. **D.7**: 30, 243, 249. **F.2**: 9. **F.4**: 152. **F.5**: 119, 228, 272. **F.8**: 11. **G.3.2**: 77. **I.5**: 78, 95. **J.2**: 6. **J.5**: 20, 37. **J.7**: 11, 24. **K.1**: 226, 304, 403, 405–408, 410–416, 419–420, 422–423, 425–430.

Violence domestique **D.4**: 11. **F.4**: 148–149, 153–154, 156, 160–161, 163, 165–168, 173, 175–176. **K.1**: 63, 418, 421. **K.2**: 104.

Violence politique **D.7**: 285. **J.1**: 8. **K.4**: 74.

Vocabulaire **C.2**: 156.

Vol **K.1**: 57, 91, 121, 202.

Voleurs **K.1**: 110, 358.

Vote **D.1**: 51. **F.5**: 87. **F.7**: 105. **I.5**: 162, 191. **J.6**: 15, 19, 42.

Voyages **F.3**: 159. **H.4**: 42.

Weber, Max
B.1: 66, 86, 95, 111, 117–118, 125, 130, 133, 136, 138. **D.5**: 93. **D.9**: 144, 179. **H.1**: 5. **J.2**: 1.

Williams, Raymond
D.7: 376. **G.2**: 27.

Wolfe, Tom
D.7: 271.

Wright, Frank Lloyd
D.8: 15.

Xénophobie **C.4**: 31. **F.7**: 219.

Yoruba **C.7**: 77. **D.5**: 162. **F.6**: 9.

Yougoslaves **F.8**: 81.

Yü, Han
D.5: 3.

Zen **D.5**: 81. **I.3**: 95.

Zionisme **F.7**: 178. **G.3.2**: 259.

Zones industrielles **H.7**: 12. **I.2**: 238.

Zones résidentielles **F.3**: 24. **G.3.2**: 152, 191.

Zones rurales **D.1**: 3. **D.5**: 103. **D.7**: 186. **D.9**: 36. **E.1**: 20. **E.3**: 8. **F.2**: 23, 30. **F.3**: 100, 125, 139, 274, 276, 280. **F.7**: 2. **F.8**: 36, 113. **G.3.1**: 8, 12, 20, 25–27, 29, 43, 48, 54–55, 59, 71, 88, 92, 121, 130. **G.3.2**: 163. **H.3**: 42. **I.2**: 94. **I.4**: 43. **I.5**: 18. **J.3**: 13. **K.1**: 251, 266, 400. **K.2**: 45. **K.4**: 59.

Zones suburbaines **D.2**: 20. **F.3**: 16. **G.3.2**: 6, 17, 25, 50, 56, 173, 188, 205, 336, 354. **H.5**: 8. **J.3**: 13.

Zones urbaines **D.5**: 101. **D.7**: 186. **D.9**: 46, 58, 78, 89. **F.3**: 196, 276. **G.3.2**: 10, 39, 49, 57, 66, 68, 73, 81, 84–85, 89, 162, 166, 169, 183, 192, 195, 202, 210, 352. **J.3**: 13. **K.1**: 86, 88. **K.4**: 209, 213.

Zoroastrisme **D.5**: 75, 80.